841-856

862-883

# MODERN FAMILY LAW
## Cases and Materials

# MODERN FAMILY LAW
## Cases and Materials

## Second Edition

**D. Kelly Weisberg**
Professor of Law
Hastings College of the Law,
University of California

**Susan Frelich Appleton**
Associate Dean of Faculty and
Lemma Barkeloo & Phoebe Couzins
Professor of Law
Washington University in St. Louis

**ASPEN LAW & BUSINESS**
A Division of Aspen Publishers, Inc.
New York        Gaithersburg

Permissions
Aspen Law & Business
1185 Avenue of the Americas
New York, NY 10036

Printed in the United States of America

ISBN 0-7355-2400-9

1  2  3  4  5  6  7  8  9  0

**Library of Congress Cataloging-in-Publication Data**

Weisberg, D. Kelly.
   Modern family law : cases and materials / D. Kelly Weisberg,
Susan Frelich Appleton. — 2nd ed.
      p.    cm.
   Includes index.
   ISBN 0-7355-2400-9
   1. Domestic relations — United States — Cases.  I. Appleton,
Susan Frelich, 1948– .  II. Title.
KF504.W45  2002
346.7301′5 — dc21                     2001055332

# About Aspen Law & Business Legal Education Division

With a dedication to preserving and strengthening the long-standing tradition of publishing excellence in legal education, Aspen Law & Business continues to provide the highest quality teaching and learning resources for today's law school community. Careful development, meticulous editing, and an unmatched responsiveness to the evolving needs of today's discerning educators combine in the creation of our outstanding casebooks, coursebooks, textbooks, and study aids.

**ASPEN LAW & BUSINESS**
**A Division of Aspen Publishers, Inc.**
**A Wolters Kluwer Company**
*www.aspenpublishers.com*

**Dedicated to**

**our families**

# Summary of Contents

# Contents

# Preface

The theme of *Modern Family Law* — the conflict between respect for privacy and deference to state authority — provides a lens for examining family law today. Each chapter of this book uses this lens to explore the actual and appropriate role of the state in various aspects of family life.

- Chapter One explores the constitutional underpinnings of a right to family privacy.

- Chapters Two and Three address the state's regulation of marriage before and after celebration.

- Chapter Four identifies the extent to which the legal system treats members of alternative families differently from, or similarly to, members of traditional families.

- Chapters Five and Six examine state regulation of divorce, including its financial consequences, and Chapter Seven examines the state's role in child custody matters.

- Chapter Eight explores the limits of family autonomy, emphasizing cases of child abuse and neglect.

- Chapter Nine considers the tension between privacy and state protection arising in adoption and use of new reproductive technologies.

*Modern Family Law* offers valuable interdisciplinary perspectives. Family law has been heavily influenced by work in the fields of family history, psychology, sociology, social work, medicine, and philosophy. Many of the excerpts, as well as the notes and questions, incorporate these different perspectives in an attempt to shed new light on the nature of legal regulation of the family.

*Modern Family Law* reflects an awareness of the impact that legal rules have on persons' lives. The law affects individuals in profound ways that legal abstractions cannot capture. The book attempts to reveal (through presentation of sociological and psychological research as well as narratives) the subjective experiences of family members when confronted with various socio-legal problems. The book emphasizes that family law is not just analyzed and applied — it is experienced.

### Changes in the Second Edition

While preserving the basic organization and overall length of the First Edition, this major revision incorporates new material on virtually every topic previously addressed. It updates earlier developments and includes significant new state and federal legislation and case law. Recent opinions from the United States Supreme Court in Stenberg v. Carhart and Troxel v. Granville appear as principal cases.

The Second Edition covers new provisions of the American Law Institute's Principles of the Law of Family Dissolution on premarital agreements, domestic partners, child custody, property division, child support, and separation agreements. It also discusses the Uniform Child Custody Jurisdiction and Enforcement Act, the new Uniform Parentage Act, the Restatement (Third) of the Law Governing Lawyers, new provisions of the ABA Model Rules of Professional Conduct, the federal Deadbeat Parents Punishment Act, the Child Victims' and Child Witnesses' Rights Act, and new laws opening adoption records, among many others.

The Second Edition incorporates important developments affecting same-sex partners, including recent state and international legislation that recognizes these relationships; post-dissolution property rights; inheritance rights; protection against discrimination in housing, employment, health benefits, and tort law; child custody rights; and regulation of adoption and assisted reproduction. It also includes new material on the legal treatment of transgendered persons.

Several new excerpts have been added (focusing on divorce, domestic violence, and antimiscegenation laws). Epilogues to principal cases have been added, updated, and expanded.

The Second Edition continues to emphasize empirical research with sensitivity to the influence of gender on family law issues. It incorporates data on abortion, teen pregnancy, divorce and annulment rates, domestic violence, developmental outcomes for children of gay and lesbian parents, international adoptions, infertility, and much more.

Like the earlier edition, this revision gives instructors considerable flexibility in designing family law courses of varying lengths and emphases. The editors have taught two-, three-, and four-unit courses based on these materials. The book can be adapted easily for shorter or longer courses. (The Teacher's Manual accompanying the book provides further pedagogical suggestions and sample syllabi.) For the problem-oriented instructor, the book includes many questions and problems, often derived from actual cases or current events.

## Editorial Matters

Cases and excerpts have all been edited, often quite extensively. Most deletions are indicated by ellipses, with some exceptions: Some concurring and dissenting opinions have been eliminated; citations have been modified or eliminated; some footnotes and references have been omitted; and paragraphs have been modified, and sometimes combined, to save space and to make the selections more coherent. Brackets are used at times to indicate substantial deletions. Original footnotes in cases and excerpts are reprinted nonconsecutively throughout the book. The editors' textual footnotes are numbered consecutively and appear in brackets to differentiate them from original footnotes.

We have relied on the seventeenth edition of A Uniform System of Citation (2000), except when that style conflicts with the publisher's style. Statutory citations are to the bound volume and supplement, if possible, rather than to the electronic version.

*D. Kelly Weisberg*
*Susan Frelich Appleton*

March 2002

# Introduction

Family law explores the legal regulation of the family and its members. These members include husband, wife, parent, and child, as well as unrelated "significant others" who now form alternative families with increasing regularity.

Fundamental to family law today is the tension between respect for family privacy and deference to state authority. This conflict forms the overarching theme of this book. Specifically, the book explores the issue: How does the law allocate responsibility for decisionmaking about private family matters? A respect for privacy gives consideration to individual family members' decisional autonomy on matters that intimately affect them. Conversely, deference to state authority recognizes that the state has important interests, such as child protection and dispute resolution, that may precipitate intervention in the family. Such concerns necessarily raise questions about the actual, as well as the appropriate, relationship of the state to the family.

Because the state accords legal protection to the family and family members, even basic definitions — what constitutes a "family" and who is a "family member" — are contested. Thus, a central issue explored throughout the book is: Which personal relationships qualify for legal protection and for what purposes?

Family law is a field in transition. Change is apparent in the evolving roles and responsibilities of family members, the definitions of a family, and the nature of legal regulation of the family and its members. The dynamic character of the field results, in part, from societal influences on family law. Over the past several decades, social developments have prompted significant changes in the field, including:

(1) the women's movement, which has led to changes in gender roles as well as public policy;
(2) the children's rights movement, which has recognized children's increased role in decisionmaking;
(3) changing sexual mores, which have resulted in the decreasing influence of morality;
(4) disillusionment with the traditional family, which has contributed to the growth of alternative family forms;
(5) dissatisfaction with traditional dispute resolution processes, which has given rise to alternative forms of dispute resolution; and
(6) developments in reproductive technology, which have altered traditional methods of family formation.

All of these developments are challenging traditional conceptions of the family and parenthood.

Family law also reflects several important legal trends:

(1) the federalization of family law (that is, the increasing congressional role in family policy);
(2) the constitutionalization of family law (that is, the growing recognition of the constitutional dimensions of the regulation of intimate relationships); and
(3) the movement toward uniformity of state law.

These factors partly explain the changing role of the state in the contemporary regulation of the family.

Family law formerly was the exclusive domain of the states. Each state formulated and applied applicable legal rules and procedures. In the past several decades, however, Congress has enacted legislation on many issues of family life — child support, child custody, child abuse and neglect, foster care, adoption, and parental leaves, to name a few. In addition, beginning in the 1960s, the Supreme Court handed down a number of decisions that limit state regulation of the family. One of the most significant developments is the Court's recognition and expansion of the notion of privacy.

Because family law primarily has been a matter of state regulation, considerable variation exists in the legal regulations applicable to the family. In an effort to bring uniformity to the field, the National Conference of Commissioners on Uniform State Laws has promulgated important model statutes (addressing marriage and divorce, premarital agreements, marital property, paternity establishment, child custody jurisdiction, spousal and child support, adoption, and the parentage of children born of new reproductive technologies). Another unifying influence is the American Law Institute (ALI), which now has completed a decade-long project to reconceptualize family law, clarifying the underlying principles and making policy recommendations to guide the states in regulating the dissolution of marriages and nontraditional family relationships.

Today's family law classes offer the challenge and excitement of exploring this rapidly changing legal landscape.

# Acknowledgments

The authors would like to thank the many people who contributed to this project. Colleagues at several institutions provided helpful suggestions, including: Professors Jane Aiken, Kathy Goldwasser, Dan Keating, Sylvia Law, David Levine, Jane Murphy, Nancy Polikoff, Nancy Staudt, Lois Weithorn, Mimi Wesson, and Peter Wiedenbeck. We also gratefully acknowledge the support of Deans Mary Kay Kane, Leo Martinez, and Joel Seligman, and the practical insights of Bob Appleton. Several persons skillfully helped with manuscript preparation and administrative tasks including Joanne Margherita and Stephen Lothrop, assisted by Jane Bettlach, Cecille Bruno, Marcia Denenholz, Jan Houf, and Sharon Strathman.

John Borden, Mark Kloempken, and Kathy Molyneux provided invaluable library reference assistance. Elena Cappella, Mike Greenwald, and Todd Feldman at the American Law Institute generously made possible the use of the latest version of the Principles of the Law of Family Dissolution even before their publication. Special thanks are merited by Jennifer Hoogs, Anne Hydorn, Jennifer McGruther, and Holly Stone, aided by Andrea Crumpler and Jerome Duggan, for their outstanding and indispensable research assistance.

Finally, the authors extend appreciation to Aspen editors, Carol McGeehan and Jessica Barmack, for their invaluable assistance, and to the anonymous reviewers for their many helpful criticisms and suggestions.

The authors would like to thank the following copyright holders for permission to excerpt their materials:

American Law Institute, Principles of the Law of Family Dissolution: Analysis and Recommendations (2002). Copyright © 2002 by The American Law Institute. Reprinted by permission of the American Law Institute.

Anderson, Jack, Adventures Among the Polygamists, 1 Investigative Reporter Magazine 4-42 (Jan. 1982). Reprinted by permission of the author.

Andrews, Lori B., Between Strangers: Surrogate Mothers, Expectant Fathers and Brave New Babies (Harper & Row 1989). Copyright © 1989 by Lori B. Andrews. Reprinted by permission.

Bartholet, Elizabeth, Where Do Black Children Belong? The Politics of Race Matching in Adoption, 139 University of Pennsylvania Law Review 1163 (1991). Copyright © 1991 by the University of Pennsylvania. Reprinted by permission.

Bernard, Jessie, The Future of Marriage 16-50 (1982). Reprinted by permission of Yale University Press.

Bernard, Jessie, The Good-Provider Role, 36 American Psychologist 1-12 passim (Jan. 1981). Copyright © 1981 by the American Psychological Association. Reprinted with permission.

Bohannon, Paul, The Six Stations of Divorce 29-32 (1970). From Divorce and After by Paul Bohannan (Ed.). Copyright © 1970 by Paul Bohannan. Used by permission of Doubleday, a division of Random House, Inc.

Bonavoglia, Angela, Kathy's Day in Court, Ms., April 1988, at 46. Copyright © 1988 by Angela Bonavoglia. A first-person account of Kathy's experience appears in The Choices We Made: 25 Women and Men Speak Out About Abortion by Angela Bonavoglia (4 Walls 8 Windows, 2001; Random House 1991).

Brief for the Amici Curiae Women Who Have Had Abortions and Friends of Amici Curiae in Support of Appellees, Webster v. Reproductive Health Services, 492 U.S. 490 (1989). Reprinted by permission of Sarah E. Burns, Counsel of Record.

Callahan, Sidney, Abortion and the Sexual Agenda, 113 Commonweal 232 (1986). Copyright © 1986 by Commonweal Foundation. Reprinted by permission of the publisher and author.

Caplow, Theodore et al., The Quality of Marriage, from Middletown Families: Fifty Years of Change and Continuity 116-135, University of Minnesota Press (1982).

Chambers, David L., The "Legalization" of the Family: Toward a Policy of Supportive Neutrality, 18 U. Mich. J.L. Reform 805, 822-825 (1985). Reprinted by permission of University of Michigan, Journal of Law Reform.

Chambers, David L., Rethinking the Substantive Rules for Custody Dis-
    putes in Divorce, 83 Mich. L. Rev. 477, 527-538 (1984). Reprinted
    from Michigan Law Review, December 1984, vol. 83, no. 3. Copy-
    right © 1984 by The Michigan Law Review Association. Reprinted
    by permission.
Ellman, Ira Mark, The Theory of Alimony, 77 California Law Review 1
    (1989). Copyright © 1989 by the Regents of the University of Cali-
    fornia. Reprinted from the California Law Review, Vol. 77 No. 1, pp.
    1-81, by permission of the University of California, Berkeley, and the
    author.
Eskridge, William N., Jr., The Case of Same-Sex Marriage 1-5 (1996).
    Abridged and reprinted with the permission of The Free Press, a Di-
    vision of Simon & Schuster, from The Case of Same-Sex Marriage:
    From Sexual Liberty to Civilized Commitment by William N. Esk-
    ridge, Jr. Copyright © 1996 by William N. Eskridge, Jr.
Friedman, Lawrence M., A History of American Law, 204-208, 498-504,
    (1988) (pp. 1-3). Abridged and reprinted with the permission of Simon
    & Schuster from A History of American Law by Lawrence M. Fried-
    man. Copyright © 1973, 1985, 1988 by Lawrence M. Friedman.
Garbarino, James & Gwen Gilliam, Understanding Abusive Families 41,
    42, 44-46 (1980). Jossey-Bass, Inc., Lexington Books, Simon & Schus-
    ter Trade.
Garrison, Marsha, Parents' Rights vs. Children's Interests: The Case of
    the Foster Child, 22 N.Y.U. Rev. L. & Soc. Change 371, 373-396
    (1996). Reprinted with permission from New York University, Re-
    view of Law and Social Change.
Gelles, Richard J., Contemporary Families, 176-178 (1995). Copyright ©
    1995 by Sage Publications, Inc. Reprinted by permission of Sage
    Publications, Inc.
Gelles, Richard J. & Murray A. Straus, Intimate Violence (1988).
    Reprinted by permission from Intimate Violence, by Richard J.
    Gelles and Murray A. Straus. Copyright © 1988 by Richard J. Gelles
    and Murray A. Straus.
Golden, Daniel, When Adoption Doesn't Work. . . ., The Boston Globe,
    June 11, 1989, Magazine at 16. Copyright © 1989 by Globe News-
    paper Company. Reprinted courtesy of The Boston Globe.
Goldstein, Joseph, et al., Before the Best Interests of the Child 3-13
    (1979). Reprinted with the permission of The Free Press, A Division
    of Simon & Schuster, from Before the Best Interests of the Child by
    Joseph Goldstein, Anna Freud, Albert J. Solnit. Copyright © 1979
    by The Free Press.
Grossberg, Michael, Governing the Hearth: Law and the Family in
    Nineteenth-Century America. Copyright © 1985 by the University
    of North Carolina Press. Used by permission of the publisher.

Halem, Lynne Carol, Divorce Reform 238-254, 269-277 (1980). Reprinted with permission of The Free Press, a Division of Simon & Schuster, from Divorce Reform: Changing Legal and Social Perspectives by Lynne Carol Halem. Copyright © 1980 by The Free Press.

Hochschild, Arlie, and Ann Machung, The Second Shift. From The Second Shift by Arlie Hochschild and Ann Machung. Copyright © 1989 by Arlie Hochschild. Used by permission of Viking Penguin, a division of Penguin Books USA Inc.

Horsburgh, Beverly, Lifting the Veil of Secrecy: Domestic Violence in the Jewish Community, 18 Harv. Women's L.J. 171, 172-172 (1995). Permission granted by the Harvard Women's Law Journal. Copyright © 1995 by the President and Fellows of Harvard College.

Irons, Peter H., The Courage of Their Convictions: Sixteen Americans Who Fought Their Way to the Supreme Court (1988). Copyright © 1988 by Peter Irons, Professor of Political Science and Director of Earl Warren Bill of Rights Project, University of California, San Diego. Abridged with permission of The Free Press, a Division of Simon & Schuster.

Kressel, Kenneth et al., Professional Intervention in Divorce: The View of Lawyers, Psychotherapists, and Clergy, in Divorce and Separation 246, 250-255 (George Levinger & Oliver C. Moles eds., 1979) at 69-71. Copyright © 1979 by HarperCollins, Inc. Reprinted by permission of the publisher.

Luker, Kristin, Abortion and the Politics of Motherhood (1984). Copyright © 1984 by The Regents of the University of California. Reprinted by permission.

Maccoby, Eleanor E. and Robert H. Mnookin, Dividing the Child 177-178, 212-214, 215, 216-217, 224-225 (1992). Reprinted by permission of the publisher from Dividing the Child by Eleanor E. Maccoby and Robert H. Mnookin, Cambridge, Mass.: Harvard University Press, Copyright © 1992 by the President and Fellows of Harvard College.

Malin, Martin H., Fathers and Parental Leave. Published originally in 72 Texas Law Review 1047 (1994). Copyright © 1994 by the Texas Law Review Association. Reprinted by permission.

Minow, Martha, Guardianship of Phillip Becker, 74 Tex. L. Rev. 1257, 1257-1258 (1996). Published originally in 74 Texas Law Review 1257 (1996). Copyright © 1996 by the Texas Law Review Association. Reprinted by permission of the publisher and the author.

Mnookin, Robert H., Child-Custody Adjudication: Judicial Functions in the Face of Indeterminacy, 39 Law & Contemp. Probs. 226, 289-291 (1975). Copyright © 1975, Law and Contemporary Problems, Duke University School of Law. Reprinted by permission of Law and Contemporary Problems, Duke University School of Law.

Neu, Jerome, What's Wrong with Incest?, Inquiry, Scandinavian University Press (1976). Reprinted by permission of the author.

Legal Policy Formulation, 18 U.C. Davis L. Rev. 1 (1984). Copyright © 1984 by The Regents of the University of California. Reprinted with permission.

Weisberg, D. Kelly, Professional Women and the Professionalization of Motherhood: Marcia Clark's Double Bind, 6 Hastings Women's L.J. 295, 312-319, 321-322 (1995). Copyright © 1995 by D. Kelly Weisberg. Reprinted by permission.

Whitehead, Mary Beth and Loretta Schwartz-Nobel, A Mother's Story (1989). Copyright © 1989 by Mary Beth Whitehead. Reprinted by permission of St. Martin's Press, LLC.

Williams, Joan, Is Coverture Dead? Beyond a New Theory of Alimony, 82 Georgetown Law Journal 2227 (1994). Copyright © 1994 by Joan Williams. Reprinted by permission.

Williams, Wendy W., Equality's Riddle: Pregnancy and the Equal Treatment/Special Treatment Debate, 13 N.Y.U. Rev. L. & Soc. Change 325, 333-349 (1984-1985). Reprinted with permission from NYU Review of Law & Social Change, New York University School of Law.

# MODERN FAMILY LAW
## Cases and Materials

# I

# Private Family Choices: Constitutional Protection for the Family and Its Members

## A. EVOLUTION OF THE RIGHT TO PRIVACY

The Supreme Court has written often that family life belongs in a "private realm" the state cannot enter. What is the source of this limitation on state authority? Whom does it protect — family units or individual family members? What room does it leave for laws governing the family? And what does "family" mean anyhow?

### 1. The Birth of Privacy

#### a. Meanings of Privacy

■ **GRISWOLD v. CONNECTICUT**
*381 U.S. 479 (1965)*

Mr. Justice DOUGLAS delivered the opinion of the Court.

Appellant Griswold is Executive Director of the Planned Parenthood League of Connecticut. Appellant Buxton is a licensed physician and a

1

professor at the Yale Medical School who served as Medical Director for the League at its Center in New Haven. [Appellants were arrested and charged with giving information, instruction, and medical advice to married persons on means of preventing conception.]

The [statute] whose constitutionality is involved . . . provides:

> Any person who uses any drug, medicinal article or instrument for the purpose of preventing conception shall be fined not less than fifty dollars or imprisoned not less than sixty days nor more than one year or be both fined and imprisoned. . . .

The appellants were found guilty as accessories and fined $100 each, against the claim that the accessory statute as so applied violated the Fourteenth Amendment. . . . We think that appellants have standing to raise the constitutional rights of the married people with whom they had a professional relationship. . . .

Coming to the merits, we are met with a wide range of questions that implicate the Due Process Clause of the Fourteenth Amendment. Overtones of some arguments suggest that Lochner v. New York, 198 U.S. 45 [(1905)], should be our guide. But we decline that invitation. We do not sit as a super-legislature to determine the wisdom, need, and propriety of laws that touch economic problems, business affairs, or social conditions. This law, however, operates directly on an intimate relation of husband and wife and their physician's role in one aspect of that relation.

The association of people is not mentioned in the Constitution nor in the Bill of Rights. The right to educate a child in a school of the parents' choice — whether public or private or parochial — is also not mentioned. Nor is the right to study any particular subject or any foreign language. Yet the First Amendment has been construed to include certain of those rights.

By Pierce v. Society of Sisters, [268 U.S. 510 (1925)], the right to educate one's children as one chooses is made applicable to the States by the force of the First and Fourteenth Amendments. By Meyer v. Nebraska, [262 U.S. 390 (1923)], the same dignity is given the right to study the German language in a private school. . . .

In NAACP v. Alabama, 357 U.S. 449, 462 [(1958)], we protected the "freedom to associate and privacy in one's associations," noting that freedom of association was a peripheral First Amendment right. . . . In other words, the First Amendment has a penumbra where privacy is protected from governmental intrusion. . . . Association . . . is a form of expression of opinion; and while it is not expressly included in the First Amendment its existence is necessary in making the express guarantees fully meaningful.

The foregoing cases suggest that specific guarantees in the Bill of Rights have penumbras, formed by emanations from those guarantees that help give them life and substance. See Poe v. Ullman, 367 U.S. 497, 516-522 [(1961)] (dissenting opinion). Various guarantees create zones of privacy. The right of association contained in the penumbra of the First Amendment is one, as we have seen. The Third Amendment in its prohibition against the quartering of soldiers "in any house" in time of peace without the consent of the owner is another facet of that privacy. The Fourth Amendment explicitly affirms the "right of the people to be secure in their persons, houses, papers, and effects, against unreasonable searches and seizures." The Fifth Amendment in its Self-Incrimination Clause enables the citizen to create a zone of privacy which government may not force him to surrender to his detriment. The Ninth Amendment provides: "The enumeration in the Constitution, of certain rights, shall not be construed to deny or disparage others retained by the people." . . . We have had many controversies over these penumbral rights of "privacy and repose." See, e.g., Skinner v. Oklahoma, 316 U.S. 535, 541 [(1942)]. . . .

The present case, then, concerns a relationship lying within the zone of privacy created by several fundamental constitutional guarantees. And it concerns a law which, in forbidding the use of contraceptives rather than regulating their manufacture or sale, seeks to achieve its goals by means having a maximum destructive impact upon that relationship. Such a law cannot stand in light of the familiar principle, so often applied by this Court, that a "governmental purpose to control or prevent activities constitutionally subject to state regulation may not be achieved by means which sweep unnecessarily broadly and thereby invade the area of protected freedoms." NAACP v. Alabama, 377 U.S. 288, 307 [(1964)]. Would we allow the police to search the sacred precincts of marital bedrooms for telltale signs of the use of contraceptives? The very idea is repulsive to the notions of privacy surrounding the marriage relationship.

We deal with a right of privacy older than the Bill of Rights — older than our political parties, older than our school system. Marriage is a coming together for better or for worse, hopefully enduring, and intimate to the degree of being sacred. It is an association that promotes a way of life, not causes; a harmony in living, not political faiths; a bilateral loyalty, not commercial or social projects. Yet it is an association for as noble a purpose as any involved in our prior decisions.

Reversed.

Mr. Justice GOLDBERG, whom THE CHIEF JUSTICE and Mr. Justice BRENNAN join, concurring.

I agree with the Court that Connecticut's birth-control law unconstitutionally intrudes upon the right of marital privacy. . . . I add these words to emphasize the relevance of [the Ninth] Amendment to the Court's holding. . . . The Amendment is almost entirely the work of James Madison. It was introduced in Congress by him and passed the

House and Senate with little or no debate and virtually no change in language. It was proffered to quiet expressed fears that a bill of specifically enumerated rights could not be sufficiently broad to cover all essential rights and that the specific mention of certain rights would be interpreted as a denial that others were protected. . . .

. . . To hold that a right so basic and fundamental and so deep-rooted in our society as the right of privacy in marriage may be infringed because that right is not guaranteed in so many words by the first eight amendments to the Constitution is to ignore the Ninth Amendment and to give it no effect whatsoever. [T]he Ninth Amendment simply lends strong support to the view that the "liberty" protected by the Fifth and Fourteenth Amendments from infringement by the Federal Government or the States is not restricted to rights specifically mentioned in the first eight amendments. . . .

Mr. Justice HARLAN, concurring in the judgment. . . .

In my view, the proper constitutional inquiry in this case is whether this Connecticut statute infringes the Due Process Clause of the Fourteenth Amendment because the enactment violates basic values "implicit in the concept of ordered liberty," Palko v. Connecticut, 302 U.S. 319, 325 [(1937)]. For reasons stated at length in my dissenting opinion in Poe v. Ullman, [367 U.S. 497, 522 (1961)], I believe that it does. While the relevant inquiry may be aided by resort to one or more of the provisions of the Bill of Rights, it is not dependent upon them or any of their traditions. The Due Process Clause of the Fourteenth Amendment stands, in my opinion, on its own bottom. . . .

. . . Judicial self-restraint will . . . be achieved in this area, as in other constitutional areas, only by continual insistence upon respect for the teachings of history, solid recognition of the basic values that underlie our society, and wise appreciation of the great roles that the doctrines of federalism and separation of powers have played in establishing and preserving American freedoms. . . .

[In a separate concurring opinion, Justice White agrees that the statute violates the liberty protected by the Due Process Clause of the Fourteenth Amendment, questioning how the statutory ban serves the state's asserted interest in deterring illicit sexual relationships.]

Mr. Justice BLACK, with whom Mr. Justice STEWART joins, dissenting. . . .

The Court talks about a constitutional "right of privacy" as though there is some constitutional provision or provisions forbidding any law ever to be passed which might abridge the "privacy" of individuals. But there is not. . . . I like my privacy as well as the next one, but I am nevertheless compelled to admit that government has a right to invade it unless prohibited by some specific constitutional provision. . . .

My Brother Goldberg has adopted the recent discovery[12] that the Ninth Amendment as well as the Due Process Clause can be used by this Court as authority to strike down all state legislation which this Court thinks violates "fundamental principles of liberty and justice," or is contrary to the "traditions and [collective] conscience of our people." He also states, without proof satisfactory to me, that in making decisions on this basis judges will not consider "their personal and private notions." One may ask how they can avoid considering them. Our Court certainly has no machinery with which to take a Gallup Poll. And the scientific miracles of this age have not yet produced a gadget which the Court can use to determine what traditions are rooted in the "[collective] conscience of our people." . . .

Mr. Justice STEWART, whom Mr. Justice BLACK joins, dissenting.

. . . I think this is an uncommonly silly law. As a practical matter, the law is obviously unenforceable, except in the oblique context of the present case. As a philosophical matter, I believe the use of contraceptives in the relationship of marriage should be left to personal and private choice, based upon each individual's moral, ethical, and religious beliefs. As a matter of social policy, I think professional counsel about methods of birth control should be available to all, so that each individual's choice can be meaningfully made. But we are not asked in this case to say whether we think this law is unwise, or even asinine. We are asked to hold that it violates the United States Constitution. And that I cannot do. . . . With all deference, I can find no such general right of privacy in the Bill of Rights, in any other part of the Constitution, or in any case ever before decided by this Court.

At the oral argument in this case we were told that the Connecticut law does not "conform to current community standards." But it is not the function of this Court to decide cases on the basis of community standards. . . . If, as I should surely hope, the law before us does not reflect the standards of the people of Connecticut, the people of Connecticut can freely exercise their true Ninth and Tenth Amendment rights to

12. See Patterson, The Forgotten Ninth Amendment (1955). . . . In Redlich, Are There "Certain Rights . . . Retained by the People"?, 37 N.Y.U. L. Rev. 787 [(1962)], Professor Redlich, in advocating reliance on the Ninth and Tenth Amendments to invalidate the Connecticut law before us, frankly states:

> But for one who feels that the marriage relationship should be beyond the reach of a state law forbidding the use of contraceptives, the birth control case poses a troublesome and challenging problem of constitutional interpretation. He may find himself saying, "The law is unconstitutional — but why?" There are two possible paths to travel in finding the answer. One is to revert to a frankly flexible due process concept even on matters that do not involve specific constitutional prohibitions. The other is to attempt to evolve a new constitutional framework within which to meet this and similar problems which are likely to arise.

Id., at 798.

persuade their elected representatives to repeal it. That is the constitutional way to take this law off the books.

## ■ MICHAEL GROSSBERG, GOVERNING THE HEARTH: LAW AND THE FAMILY IN NINETEENTH-CENTURY AMERICA
### 156-157, 175-177, 189-193 (1985)

At the heart of the nineteenth-century controversy over family limitation lay the quiet determination of American mothers and fathers to reduce the number of children they reared. They initiated what historical demographers now designate the "demographic transition": a reduction in family size that characterized most Western nations. In America, white female fertility, the critical measure of family size, declined in each decade of the century, falling from 7.04 in 1800 to 3.56 a hundred years later. . . .

Although the exact sources [of this transition] remain uncertain, some characteristics of the republican household offer clues. . . . These include the child-centered nature of the republican home in which numerous offspring seemed to inhibit proper child care; the rise of what historian Daniel Scott Smith terms "domestic feminism," or the determination of women to assert their individuality and household authority by regulating pregnancy and marital sexuality; the economic incentives of market capitalism in which large families seemed a burden and in which moderation and self-control became prized virtues; the companionate nature of republican matrimony, which fostered the separation of sexual pleasure from protection; and the emerging American insistence on overcoming what had previously been considered natural forces beyond human control. . . .

Though it is difficult to pierce the privacy surrounding family limitation, at the beginning of the nineteenth century, husbands and wives apparently still relied on age-old methods of birth control such as delayed marriage, breast feeding, and abstinence (as well as *coitus interruptus* and other active contraceptive practices). . . .

Although statutes prohibiting various forms of abortion had been on the books since the 1820s, there were few explicit restrictions on contraception until the 1870s. But federal and state acts labeling both abortion and contraception obscene capped the growing determination of family savers to ban all forms of family limitation. [For example, though] he sympathized with women's fears about childbirth and rearing large families, [Augustus] Gardner confidently insisted that efforts made "to avoid propagation, are ten thousand-fold more disastrous to the health and constitution, to say nothing of the demoralization of mind and heart. . . ." Gardner [and his followers] looked to the criminal law for relief.

Self-appointed purity campaigners led the drive against contraception. New Yorkers created the first purity society in 1872, the New York Society for the Suppression of Vice. [T]he society's point man for purity reform was a little known ex-dry goods salesman, Anthony Comstock. The son of devout Connecticut parents, he tried unsuccessfully to make his fortune as a businessman in New York City. The flagrant vices he encountered in the city shocked him into a highly publicized vigilante campaign. It culminated in his appointment as the antivice society's chief agent, thus launching his career as late nineteenth-century America's self-avowed savior of public morals.

Comstock regarded the feeble statutes then on the books as the weakest link in his war on vice. . . . In 1872 he convinced the antivice society to send him to Washington to press for a rigorous national statute. [There] the vice crusader succeeded beyond his wildest expectations. Armed with a display case of vice paraphernalia and vivid tales of his fights with the panderers of obscenity, Comstock enlisted the aid of Vice President Henry Wilson and Supreme Court Justice William Strong to draft a new obscenity law. The bill passed with little debate and became law on 1 March 1873. [It became known as the "Comstock law."]

The act's primary purpose was to ban the circulation and importation of obscene materials through the national mails. Specifically included on the list of banned goods was every article designed, adapted, or intended "for preventing conception or producing abortion, or for indecent or immoral use; and every article, instrument, substance, drug, medicine, or thing which is advertised or described in a manner calculated to lead another to use or apply it for preventing conception or producing abortion, or for any indecent or immoral purpose. . . ." The act set punishment at $5,000 fine, one to ten years at hard labor, or both. . . .

[P]urity crusaders also prodded state legislators into action. Antivice societies, and after 1885 the Social Purity Alliance, succeeded in persuading twenty-two legislatures to enact general obscenity laws and another twenty-four to specifically ban birth control and abortion. [Courts upheld convictions under these laws.]

Let loose by Congress, state legislatures, and the courts, vice hunters prowled the nation sniffing out their prey. Posing as customers or using decoy letters, federal agents and local societies purchased proscribed items and then arrested sellers. . . . Comstock in fact caught his most famous victim with a birth-control ploy. Having been warned not to tangle with the infamous Madame Restell, he took her capture as a personal challenge. In the guise of an impoverished father, Comstock pleaded for contraceptive information because his meager finances could support no more children. When she obliged, he arrested her. Faced with the almost certain prospect of jail at the age of 67, Restell slit her throat with a carving knife. Comstock experienced no remorse: "a bloody end to a bloody life."

. . . Congress strengthened the federal ban in 1908. By the 1930s eight states specifically prohibited the flow of contraceptive information while the rest acted through broadened obscenity laws. Contraception remained a taboo subject, even though, much like prohibition, the statutes expressed a moral standard clearly at odds with actual practices. . . . Birth control, no matter how essential family limitation had become to the republican family, still violated the nation's code of proper domestic behavior. Fears aroused by the immigration of seemingly fecund non-Protestant women, charges of race suicide leveled against non-immigrant mothers who regulated their child bearing, and the ever-present concern over changes in gender responsibilities reinvigorated the stigma attached to the practice.

The constitutionality of the ban was also impenetrable. In Commonwealth v. Allison (1917) the 1879 Little Comstock law of Massachusetts won judicial vindication. . . . Such judicial [cases] demonstrated the formidable opposition facing birth-control advocates. . . . Birth control continued to be an obscene subject banished from polite society. . . .

■ **CATHERINE G. RORABACK, GRISWOLD v. CONNECTICUT: A BRIEF CASE HISTORY**
*16 Ohio N.U. L. Rev. 395, 395-401 (1989)*

The [Connecticut] ban on the use of contraceptives had been on the statute books of this state for some eighty-six years. Many other jurisdictions had similar laws, but by the late 1950's these laws had been either repealed or their impact minimized by judicial interpretation. In 1958 only Connecticut had an absolute ban on contraceptive devices, one without an exception even for situations where the life of the mother might be endangered by a pregnancy. [T]here were regular attempts to obtain legislative repeal of the statute. In each biennial session of the General Assembly a repealer bill was introduced, vociferous and vituperative hearings were held, and the bill was eventually voted down. . . .

[I]t is hard to remember the attitudes toward birth control in the 1950's. The statutory prohibition on the use of contraceptives even by married persons was accepted by many as a legitimate exercise of the police powers of the state. That is not to say that private doctors did not provide such advice and services to their private patients, nor that patients able to afford private medical care did not obtain contraceptive advice. However, even that private care was often circumspect and clandestine, and some private physicians refused to provide these services at all. Certainly these services were not available to unmarried persons.

Although contraceptives were available for purchase in drugstores throughout the state, that availability was usually "under-the-counter." Druggists also sold such items on prescription of a private physician.

The activities of the state Planned Parenthood League were limited to educational and legislative programs and a referral service to clinics in neighboring New York and Rhode Island, with transportation furnished by volunteers to enable the women to take advantage of the out-of-state services.

But no medical source of contraceptive advice or services was available in this state to those dependent on publicly provided health care. It was the physicians and medical personnel operating in public clinics who were subjected to public scrutiny and threat of prosecution. And because it was here that these statutes impacted, it was the poor people of this state who were deprived of medically supervised contraceptive advice and services. [After 1940, when nine Planned Parenthood clinics were closed, no public or private facility provided free birth control.]

In 1957, Estelle Griswold, a dynamic, vivacious woman, had only recently become the executive director of the Planned Parenthood League of Connecticut. She found herself frustrated by the legal situation in Connecticut and her inability to organize Planned Parenthood clinics in the state.

In the course of preparations that year for the biennial legislative hearing on repeal of the anti-birth-control statute, she arranged for C. Lee Buxton to testify. Buxton had only recently come to New Haven as professor and chairman of the Department of Obstetrics and Gynecology at the Yale University School of Medicine. . . . He felt deeply that the statute banning the use of contraceptive devices and the accessory statute preventing him from giving what he felt to be the advice and care his patients deserved were gross invasions of his patients' rights, and highly improper impediments on his ability to practice his profession.

It was at this point, as legend has it, that Estelle invited both Lee Buxton and Fowler Harper to her home one day in the fall of 1957 and introduced them over cocktails. Fowler, then a professor at the Yale Law School, taught — among other subjects — family law. He was a social activist, involved in the community, always ready to take on a cause and to use his full energies and legal skills to cure an inequity. Yet always he maintained his humor and his feeling for his fellow human beings. He most certainly reacted with verve and gusto as Lee spoke of his frustrations about the Connecticut law banning the use of contraceptives and his inability to properly serve his patients. And, the legend holds, it was from this conversation that the litigation which culminated in *Griswold* originated. . . .

[The chosen strategy was to seek in state court a declaratory judgment that the anti-birth control statute was unconstitutional or the statute should not apply when a woman's health or life might be threatened by a pregnancy, that suits should be brought by Dr. Buxton and his patients, and that only married patients should bring these suits.]

One of the patients bringing suit was Jane Doe, a young twenty-five year old housewife. Only a short time before, she had come under Dr. Buxton's care when admitted to the emergency room of Yale New Haven Hospital for complications of pregnancy. While hospitalized she had suffered a stroke, her pregnancy could not be aborted, and she had had to continue the pregnancy until at term she had a stillbirth. As a result she was permanently paralyzed on her right side, her speech was impaired and she had residual kidney damage. It was Dr. Buxton's opinion that she would not survive another pregnancy.

The other plaintiff-patients were two married couples. One, the Poes, had had three abnormal children, none of whom had survived more than ten weeks. They sought contraceptive advice because they did not feel they could emotionally survive the birth of another such child. The other couple, the Hoes, had conflicting blood groupings and were considered unlikely to have a normal child born to them.

When these suits were begun in May of 1958, there was . . . no discussion of rights of privacy. . . . The due process arguments in the briefs filed in the Connecticut courts stressed rights to life and liberty, to health, to happy marital relationships, free of governmental intrusion. But the obverse of that phrase — privacy — was not used. This is not surprising if one thinks back to the status of privacy law at that time. [The Connecticut Supreme Court of Errors rejected the broad constitutional challenge to the statute and refused to read any exception into it.]

It was in the due process arguments presented on the appeal to the United States Supreme Court in this case that the first specific mention of "privacy" occurred in this litigation. However, the Supreme Court never reached this or any of the other substantive arguments raised on this appeal. Rather, it held [in Poe v. Ullman, 367 U.S. 497 (1961)] that there was no controversy before the Court, that there had been an absence of any prosecutions under the statutes, and that therefore Dr. Buxton and his patients faced no realistic threat of prosecution.

In Connecticut the implications of this disconcerting outcome were pondered. . . . After much consultation and discussion it was finally decided that the Planned Parenthood League of Connecticut would open one facility in New Haven, and that if no prosecution ensued it would expand such services to other cities. Thus on November 1, 1961, the Planned Parenthood League of Connecticut opened the first birth control clinic in [Connecticut] since 1940, with Estelle T. Griswold as its director and C. Lee Buxton was its medical director.

. . . The clinic was in operation only a brief ten days before Mrs. Griswold and Dr. Buxton were arrested on November 10, 1961. Informations charged them with counseling, aiding and abetting certain married women to "use a drug, medicinal article and instrument, for the purpose of preventing contraception." The clinic closed its doors, and the prosecutions proceeded.

From the beginning of this prosecution the defense attacked the statutory contraceptive ban, repeating in depth all of the prior arguments as to the unconstitutionality of the statute but adding now, specifically the infringement which it imposed on the patient's right to privacy. In doing so we drew on the development of that right as it had been expounded at length in the two dissenting opinions in *Poe*. Mr. Justice Douglas's dissent found such a right in "the totality of the constitutional scheme under which we live," [367 U.S. at 521,] while Mr. Justice Harlan found its protection in the due process protections of the fourteenth amendment [id. at 540].

## Notes and Questions

1. What are the constitutional sources of the right to privacy, according to *Griswold*? To what alternative sources do the concurring opinions point? Explain the majority's difficulty in identifying the source of this right. On what basis do the dissenters disagree?

2. What aspect of the statute disturbs the majority? If Connecticut had sought to prevent use of contraceptives by, say, banning the manufacture or sale of such materials, what result? See Andrew B. Schroeder, Note, Keeping Police Out of the Bedroom: Justice John Marshall Harlan, *Poe v. Ullman*, and the Limits of Conservative Privacy, 86 Va. L. Rev. 1045, 1081-1083, 1085 (2000); The Supreme Court, 1964 Term, 79 Harv. L. Rev. 103, 162 (1965). How significant is the fact that Connecticut prohibited couples' behavior with regard to contraceptive use, as distinguished from some other intimate activity? Compare Stanley v. Georgia, 394 U.S. 557 (1969), with Osborne v. Ohio, 495 U.S. 103 (1990) (both dealing with possession of pornography).

3. How critical is the marital status of the contraceptive users? To whom does the right to privacy belong, according to *Griswold*? Each spouse? The marital unit? See Martha Albertson Fineman, What Place for Family Privacy?, 67 Geo. Wash. L. Rev. 1207, 1212 (1999) (*Griswold* shows that the "idea of the entity of the family as something 'private' predates, and is analytically separate from, the constitutional idea of individual privacy."). Suppose the spouses disagree. Given *Griswold*, can the state resolve the disagreement in favor of one?

4. Why did Connecticut enact this legislation? What do the excerpts by historian Michael Grossberg and attorney Catherine Roraback (counsel to Planned Parenthood League of Connecticut during *Griswold*) suggest? See also Nicola Beisel, Imperiled Innocents: Anthony Comstock and Family Reproduction in Victorian America 10, 38-42 (1997) (theorizing that Comstock Laws were designed to protect children's morals and families' social positions, not to control women, as other historians have argued); Andrea Tone, Devices and Desires: A History of Contraceptives in America 40 (2001) (popular support for birth control shown by lenient

enforcement of Comstock Laws). What role do the state's reasons play in *Griswold*?

5. In an omitted footnote, Justice Black's dissent claims that the concept of a "right to privacy" originated in an 1890 article by Samuel Warren and his then law partner Louis Brandeis, The Right to Privacy, 4 Harv. L. Rev. 193 (1890). Reportedly written in response to press coverage of the wedding of Warren's socialite daughter, the article sought a legal basis for the protection of privacy. The authors settled on the common law of copyright as a shield against threats posed by new technology, such as "instantaneous photographs" and "mechanical [eavesdropping or broadcasting] devices." Id. at 195. They recommended tort damages for breaches and injunctions in limited cases. As Supreme Court Justice, Brandeis later cited the Constitution for "the right to be let alone." See, e.g., Olmstead v. United States, 277 U.S. 438, 478 (1928) (dissenting opinion) (recognizing Fourth Amendment protection against governmental wiretapping). See also Katz v. United States, 389 U.S. 347, 353 (1967) (adopting Brandeis's reasoning). Goldberg's concurrence in *Griswold* invokes Brandeis's understanding.

How closely does the *Griswold* majority's concept of privacy resemble that of Warren and Brandeis? Does *Griswold*'s notion of privacy protect the right not to have information made public? The right to be let alone? The right to self-determination? Can it cover more than one of these understandings of privacy?

Scholars have continued to examine the source and content of the right to privacy. Professor William Prosser, theorizing that privacy encompasses four distinct rights, concluded that only one, "public disclosure of private facts," concerned Warren and Brandeis. William L. Prosser, Privacy, 48 Cal. L. Rev. 383, 389, 392, 398, 401 (1960). See generally Anita Allen, Coercing Privacy, 40 Wm. & Mary L. Rev. 723 (1999); Ruth Gavison, Privacy and the Limits of Law, 89 Yale L.J. 421, 423, 436-437 (1980); Linda C. McClain, Reconstructive Tasks for a Liberal Feminist Conception of Privacy, 40 Wm. & Mary L. Rev. 759 (1999); Richard B. Parker, A Definition of Privacy, 27 Rutgers L. Rev. 275, 281 (1974); Diane L. Zimmerman, Requiem for a Heavyweight: A Farewell to Warren and Brandeis's Privacy Tort, 68 Cornell L. Rev. 291 (1983).

6. Given Warren's and Brandeis's fears about new technologies, how should their proposed right to privacy evolve now that sense-enhancing devices can gather information without physical intrusion into constitutionally protected spaces like the home? See Kyllo v. United States, 533 U.S. 27 (2001) (use of thermal imaging technology to detect heat emanating from home constitutes search under Fourth Amendment). What new challenges for privacy are posed by the Internet? See, e.g., Anita L. Allen, Gender and Privacy in Cyberspace, 52 Stan. L. Rev. 1175 (2000) (part of symposium on Cyberspace and Privacy: A New Legal Paradigm). By the genomics revolution, initiated by the Human Genome Project? See

generally, e.g., Lori B. Andrews, A Conceptual Framework for Genetic Policy: Comparing the Medical, Public Health, and Fundamental Rights Models, 79 Wash. U. L.Q. 221 (2001) (exploring three approaches to overseeing genetic tests and information); Hugh Miller III, DNA Blueprints, Personhood, and Genetic Privacy, 8 Health Matrix 179 (1998).

7. The radical birth control movement in the United States emerged as part of the Socialist Party's agenda in the early 1900s. Activist Margaret Sanger's role in the movement grew out of her encounter as a visiting nurse with a poor woman who died because she could not avoid another pregnancy. Linda Gordon, Woman's Body, Woman's Right 215 (2d ed. 1990). But an appreciation of larger issues also motivated Sanger:

> [Sanger recognized] the potential historical and political meaning of birth control. Most American socialists at this time, primarily oriented to class relations, saw birth control . . . in terms of economics. They were concerned to help raise the standard of living of workers and thus increase their freedom to take political control over their own lives. Measured against this goal, birth control was at most an ameliorative reform. Seen in terms of sexual politics, however, birth control was revolutionary because it could free women entirely from the major burden that differentiated them from men, and made them dependent on men. [Sanger] gained this perspective in Europe from the sexual liberation theorists like Havelock Ellis. . . . His idealism about the potential beauty and expressiveness of human sexuality and his rage at the damage caused by sexual repression fired Sanger with a sense of the overwhelming importance, urgency, and profundity of the issue of birth control. . . .

Id. at 216. See also Ellen Chesler, Woman of Valor: Margaret Sanger and the Birth Control Movement in America (1992).

8. African-American women experienced ambivalence about the birth control movement. According to Gordon, African-Americans "learned hostility to birth control from the way in which it was proffered to them: coercively, singling them out as a problem, rather than as a people with problems, and using it as an alternative to and buffer against structural social change and economic redistribution." Gordon, supra, at 398. Despite "fears of racial genocide," id. at 399, African-Americans saw the promise of the movement:

> Birth control also emerged as part of a growing race consciousness, as blacks saw birth control as one means of freeing themselves from the oppression and exploitation of white society through the improvement of their health and their economic and social status. [Blacks] took an active and often independent role in supporting their clinics, educating their communities, and tailoring programs to fit their own needs. . . .

Jessie M. Rodrique, The Black Community and the Birth-Control Movement, in Unequal Sisters: A Multicultural Reader in U.S. Women's

History 333, 341-342 (Ellen Carol Du Bois & Vicki L. Ruiz eds., 1990). See Dorothy Roberts, Killing the Black Body: Race, Reproduction, and the Meaning of Liberty 56, 82 (1997) (despite racist view of birth control as way to solve social problems, Black women and Black leaders understood its benefits). Such views might also reflect that, unlike their white counterparts, African-American women have long served as breadwinners for their families. See Linda Gordon, Pitied But Not Entitled: Single Mothers and the History of Welfare 1890-1935, at 136 (1994).

## ■ EISENSTADT v. BAIRD
### 405 U.S. 438 (1972)

Mr. Justice BRENNAN delivered the opinion of the Court.

Appellee William Baird was convicted at a bench trial in the Massachusetts Superior Court under Massachusetts General Laws Ann., c. 272, §21, first, for exhibiting contraceptive articles in the course of delivering a lecture on contraception to a group of students at Boston University and, second, for giving a young woman a package of Emko vaginal foam at the close of his address. The Massachusetts Supreme Judicial Court unanimously set aside the conviction for exhibiting contraceptives on the ground that it violated Baird's First Amendment rights, but by a four-to-three vote sustained the conviction for giving away the foam. Commonwealth v. Baird, 355 Mass. 746, 247 N.E.2d 574 (1969). . . .

Massachusetts General Laws Ann., c. 272, §21 [provides] a maximum five-year term of imprisonment for "whoever . . . gives away . . . any drug, medicine, instrument or article whatever for the prevention of conception," except as authorized in §21A. . . . As interpreted by the State Supreme Judicial Court, these provisions make it a felony for anyone, other than a registered physician or pharmacist acting in accordance with the terms of §21A, to dispense any article with the intention that it be used for the prevention of conception. [M]arried persons may obtain contraceptives to prevent pregnancy, but only from doctors or druggists on prescription; . . . single persons may not obtain contraceptives from anyone to prevent pregnancy. . . .

The question for our determination in this case is whether there is some ground of difference that rationally explains the different treatment accorded married and unmarried persons under Massachusetts General Laws Ann., c. 272, §§21 and 21A.[7] . . .

---

7. Of course, if we were to conclude that the Massachusetts statute impinges upon fundamental freedoms under *Griswold*, the statutory classification would have to be not merely *rationally* related to a valid public purpose but *necessary* to the achievement of a *compelling* state interest. E.g., Loving v. Virginia, 388 U.S. 1 (1967). But . . . we do not have to address the statute's validity under that test because the law fails to satisfy even the more lenient equal protection standard.

*First.* [W]e cannot agree that the deterrence of premarital sex may reasonably be regarded as the purpose of the Massachusetts law.

It would be plainly unreasonable to assume that Massachusetts has prescribed pregnancy and the birth of an unwanted child as punishment for fornication, which is a misdemeanor under Massachusetts General Laws Ann., c. 272, §18. Aside from the scheme of values that assumption would attribute to the State, it is abundantly clear that the effect of the ban on distribution of contraceptives to unmarried persons has at best a marginal relation to the proffered objective. . . . Like Connecticut's laws [in *Griswold*], §§21 and 21A do not at all regulate the distribution of contraceptives when they are to be used to prevent, not pregnancy, but the spread of disease. Nor, in making contraceptives available to married persons without regard to their intended use, does Massachusetts attempt to deter married persons from engaging in illicit sexual relations with unmarried persons. Even on the assumption that the fear of pregnancy operates as a deterrent to fornication, the Massachusetts statute is thus so riddled with exceptions that deterrence of premarital sex cannot reasonably be regarded as its aim. . . .

*Second.* . . . If health were the rationale of §21A, the statute would be both discriminatory and overbroad. . . . The Court of Appeals [stated]: "If the prohibition [on distribution to unmarried persons] . . . is to be taken to mean that the same physician who can prescribe for married patients does not have sufficient skill to protect the health of patients who lack a marriage certificate, or who may be currently divorced, it is illogical to the point of irrationality." 429 F.2d, at 1401. Furthermore, we must join the Court of Appeals in noting that not all contraceptives are potentially dangerous. . . . "If [health] was the Legislature's goal, §21 is not required" in view of the federal and state laws *already* regulating the distribution of harmful drugs. . . .

*Third.* If the Massachusetts statute cannot be upheld as a deterrent to fornication or as a health measure, may it, nevertheless, be sustained simply as a prohibition on contraception? . . . We need not and do not, however, decide that important question in this case because, whatever the rights of the individual to access to contraceptives may be, the rights must be the same for the unmarried and the married alike.

If under *Griswold* the distribution of contraceptives to married persons cannot be prohibited, a ban on distribution to unmarried persons would be equally impermissible. It is true that in *Griswold* the right of privacy in question inhered in the marital relationship. Yet the marital couple is not an independent entity with a mind and heart of its own, but an association of two individuals each with a separate intellectual and emotional makeup. If the right of privacy means anything, it is the right of the *individual*, married or single, to be free from unwarranted governmental intrusion into matters so fundamentally affecting a person as the decision whether to bear or beget a child. See Stanley v. Georgia, 394

U.S. 557 (1969). See also Skinner v. Oklahoma ex rel. Williamson, 316 U.S. 535 (1942); Jacobson v. Massachusetts, 197 U.S. 11, 29 (1905).

On the other hand, if *Griswold* is no bar to a prohibition on the distribution of contraceptives, the State could not, consistently with the Equal Protection Clause, outlaw distribution to unmarried but not married persons. In each case the evil, as perceived by the State, would be identical, and the underinclusion would be invidious.

. . . We hold that by providing dissimilar treatment for married and unmarried persons who are similarly situated, Massachusetts General Laws Ann., c. 272, §§21 and 21A, violate the Equal Protection Clause. The judgment of the Court of Appeals is affirmed.

Mr. Chief Justice BURGER, dissenting.

The judgment of the Supreme Judicial Court of Massachusetts in sustaining appellee's conviction for dispensing medicinal material without a license seems eminently correct to me. . . . The actual hazards of introducing a particular foreign substance into the human body are frequently controverted, and I cannot believe that unanimity of expert opinion is a prerequisite to a State's exercise of its police power. . . .

. . . I simply cannot believe that the limitation on the class of lawful distributors has significantly impaired the right to use contraceptives in Massachusetts. By relying in *Griswold* in the present context, the Court has passed beyond the penumbras of the specific guarantees into the uncircumscribed area of personal predilections. . . .

## Notes and Questions

1. How does *Eisenstadt* resolve the issues left open in *Griswold:* the *distribution* of contraceptives to *unmarried* individuals?

2. How does *Eisenstadt* define "privacy"? How does the meaning of "privacy" articulated in *Eisenstadt* differ from that in *Griswold*?

3. Does *Eisenstadt* answer the question whether the right to privacy belongs to the family unit or each member of the family? Does it indicate how to resolve conflicts between family members over intimate matters?

4. Why does the Court rely on the Equal Protection Clause instead of the parts of the Constitution invoked in *Griswold*? Does *Eisenstadt*'s approach provide a firmer basis for the right to privacy?

5. Why did Massachusetts enact the law challenged here? How does the Court address these state interests?

6. States routinely create legal distinctions based on marriage. See Baker v. State, 744 A.2d 864 (Vt. 1999) (noting numerous legal benefits state provides only to married couples, in challenge to ineligibility of same-sex couples to marry) (reprinted on pages 171-180). How far does *Eisenstadt* go in barring discrimination based on marital status?

7. The Court subsequently addressed the substantive issue avoided in *Eisenstadt*. Carey v. Population Services International, 431 U.S. 678 (1977), struck down a statute barring distribution of all contraceptives except by licensed pharmacists. The majority explained that limitations on access to contraceptives impose burdens similar to limitations on use; hence, both must satisfy the compelling state interest test.

8. Historian David Garrow traces efforts to decriminalize contraception (and later abortion) through both legislative reform and judicial challenges. William Baird, the defendant-appellee in *Eisenstadt*, pursued the latter course, purposefully seeking to be prosecuted for his distribution of Emko vaginal foam at a student gathering at Boston University in 1967. This approach placed Baird in direct conflict with reformers pursuing legislative change:

> [T]he Planned Parenthood League of Massachusetts (PPLM), in its May newsletter to supporters, went out of its way to disassociate itself from both Baird and his court challenge to the existing Massachusetts statute. Baird "is in no way connected with Planned Parenthood. . . . The only way to remove the limitations remaining in the law is through the legislative process."
>
> Baird told two sympathetic journalists who nonetheless characterized him as "a little too intense, a little too filled with the vision of himself as a martyr" that "Planned Parenthood is a middle class monopoly." [He even picketed its annual dinner once.] Some years later former PPFA [Planned Parenthood Federation of America] president Loraine Campbell . . . acerbicly called Baird "a thorn in our flesh for years." . . . On balance, Campbell said, "Baird did more good than harm," but then, as she memorably declared, "every social change and every forward step in history requires its nuts."

David J. Garrow, Liberty and Sexuality: The Right to Privacy and the Making of *Roe v. Wade* 322-323 (updated ed. 1998). What insights about the two avenues for law reform can be gleaned from Baird's story?

## Problems

1. Japan long banned the use of birth control pills on the ground that the pill would discourage use of condoms, in turn precipitating the spread of HIV/AIDS. See Steven R. Weisman, Japan Keeps Ban on Birth Control Pill, N.Y. Times, Mar. 19, 1992, at A3; Evy F. McElmeel, Comment, Legalization of the Birth Control Pill in Japan Will Reduce Reliance on Abortion as the Primary Method of Birth Control, 8 Pac. Rim. L. & Pol'y J. 681 (1999). Suppose a similar law were adopted in this country for similar reasons. On what bases would you challenge it? What result and why?

2. Suppose an employer provides employees with a comprehensive prescription drug plan that includes Viagra, which allows sexual intercourse for some men, but not contraceptives, which accomplish a similar objective for some women. Has the employer violated laws that prohibit sex-based discrimination in the workplace (Title VII and the Pregnancy Discrimination Act)? See Lisa A. Hayden, Gender Discrimination within the Reproductive Health Care System: Viagra v. Birth Control, 13 J.L. & Health 171 (1999). If the plan excludes both Viagra and contraceptives, has the employer eliminated any discrimination? See Erickson v. Bartell Drug Co., 141 F. Supp. 2d 1266 (W.D. Wash. 2001); Sylvia A. Law, Sex Discrimination and Insurance for Contraception, 73 Wash. L. Rev. 363 (1998).

### b. Roots of Privacy

*Griswold* and *Eisenstadt* break new ground in explicitly recognizing a constitutional right to privacy. Yet some 40 years earlier the Supreme Court expressed an understanding of the family that established a foothold for this right.

## ■ MEYER v. NEBRASKA
### *262 U.S. 390 (1923)*

Mr. Justice McReynolds delivered the opinion of the Court.

Plaintiff in error was tried and convicted . . . under an information which charged that on May 25, 1920, while an instructor in Zion Parochial School he unlawfully taught the subject of reading in the German language to Raymond Parpart, a child of 10 years, who had not attained and successfully passed the eighth grade. [A Nebraska statute prohibited any person from teaching languages other than English, except to pupils who had successfully completed the eighth grade, and classified a violation as a misdemeanor, punishable by a fine and/or imprisonment. The state supreme court affirmed the conviction.]

The problem for our determination is whether the statute as construed and applied unreasonably infringes the liberty guaranteed to the plaintiff in error by the Fourteenth Amendment: "No state . . . shall deprive any person of life, liberty or property without due process of law."

While this court has not attempted to define with exactness the liberty thus guaranteed, [w]ithout doubt, it denotes not merely freedom from bodily restraint but also the right of the individual to contract, to engage in any of the common occupations of life, to acquire useful knowledge, to marry, establish a home and bring up children, to worship God according to the dictates of his own conscience, and generally to enjoy those privileges long recognized at common law as essential to the orderly pursuit of happiness by free men. The established doctrine is that this liberty may not be interfered with, under the guise of protecting the public interest, by legislative action which is arbitrary or without reasonable relation to some purpose within the competency of the state to effect. Determination by the Legislature of what constitutes proper exercise of police power is not final or conclusive but is subject to supervision by the courts.

The American people have always regarded education and acquisition of knowledge as matters of supreme importance which should be diligently promoted. . . . Corresponding to the right of control, it is the natural duty of the parent to give his children education suitable to their station in life; and nearly all the states, including Nebraska, enforce this obligation by compulsory laws.

Practically, education of the young is only possible in schools conducted by especially qualified persons who devote themselves thereto. The calling always has been regarded as useful and honorable, essential, indeed, to the public welfare. Mere knowledge of the German language cannot reasonably be regarded as harmful. . . . Plaintiff in error taught this language in school as part of his occupation. His right thus to teach and the right of parents to engage him so to instruct their children, we think, are within the liberty of the Amendment. . . . Evidently the Legislature has attempted materially to interfere with the calling of modern language teachers, with the opportunities of pupils to acquire knowledge, and with the power of parents to control the education of their own.

It is said the purpose of the legislation was to promote civic development by inhibiting training and education of the immature in foreign tongues and ideals before they could learn English and acquire American ideals, and "that the English language should be and become the mother tongue of all children reared in this state." It is also affirmed that the foreign born population is very large, that certain communities commonly use foreign words, follow foreign leaders, move in a foreign atmosphere, and that the children are thereby hindered from becoming citizens of the most useful type and the public safety is imperiled.

That the state may do much, go very far, indeed, in order to improve the quality of its citizens, physically, mentally and morally, is clear; but the individual has certain fundamental rights which must be respected. The protection of the Constitution extends to all, to those who speak other languages as well as to those born with English on the tongue. Perhaps it would be highly advantageous if all had ready understanding of our ordinary speech, but this cannot be coerced by methods which conflict with the Constitution — a desirable end cannot be promoted by prohibited means. . . . No emergency has arisen which renders knowledge by a child of some language other than English so clearly harmful as to justify its inhibition with the consequent infringement of rights long freely enjoyed. We are constrained to conclude that the statute as applied is arbitrary and without reasonable relation to any end within the competency of the state.

As the statute undertakes to interfere only with teaching which involves a modern language, leaving complete freedom as to other matters, there seems no adequate foundation for the suggestion that the purpose was to protect the child's health by limiting his mental activities. It is well known that proficiency in a foreign language seldom comes to one not instructed at an early age, and experience shows that this is not injurious to the health, morals or understanding of the ordinary child. [Reversed.]

## ■ PIERCE v. SOCIETY OF SISTERS
### 268 U.S. 510 (1925)

Mr. Justice McREYNOLDS delivered the opinion of the Court.

These appeals are from decrees, based upon undenied allegations, which granted preliminary orders restraining appellants from threatening or attempting to enforce the Compulsory Education Act adopted November 7, 1922. . . .

The challenged act, effective September 1, 1926, requires every parent, guardian, or other person having control or charge or custody of a child between 8 and 16 years to send him "to a public school for the period of time a public school shall be held during the current year" in the district where the child resides; and failure so to do is declared a misdemeanor. . . . The manifest purpose is to compel general attendance at public schools by normal children, between 8 and 16, who have not completed the eighth grade. And without doubt enforcement of the statute would seriously impair, perhaps destroy, the profitable features of appellees' business and greatly diminish the value of their property.

Appellee, the Society of Sisters, is an Oregon corporation, organized in 1880, with power to care for orphans, educate and instruct the youth, establish and maintain academies or schools, and acquire necessary real and personal property. . . . The Compulsory Education Act of 1922 has already caused the withdrawal from its schools of children who would otherwise continue, and their income has steadily declined. The appellants, public officers, have proclaimed their purpose strictly to enforce the statute.

After setting out the above facts, the Society's bill alleges that the enactment conflicts with the right of parents to choose schools where their children will receive appropriate mental and religious training, the right of the child to influence the parents' choice of a school, the right of schools and teachers therein to engage in a useful business or profession, and is accordingly repugnant to the Constitution and void. And, further, that unless enforcement of the measure is enjoined the corporation's business and property will suffer irreparable injury.

Appellee Hill Military Academy is a private corporation organized in 1908 under the laws of Oregon, engaged in owning, operating, and conducting for profit an elementary, college preparatory, and military training school for boys between the ages of 5 and 21 years. . . . By reason of the statute and threat of enforcement appellee's business is being destroyed and its property depreciated; parents and guardians are refusing to make contracts for the future instruction of their sons, and some are being withdrawn. [The Academy alleges a violation of its Fourteenth Amendment rights and seeks an injunction.]

[The matter was heard] by three judges on motions for preliminary injunctions upon the specifically alleged facts. The court ruled that the Fourteenth Amendment guaranteed appellees against the deprivation of their property without due process of law consequent upon the unlawful interference by appellants with the free choice of patrons, present and prospective. It declared the right to conduct schools was property and that parents and guardians, as a part of their liberty, might direct the education of children by selecting reputable teachers and places. Also, that appellees' schools were not unfit or harmful to the public, and that enforcement of the challenged statute would unlawfully deprive them of patronage and thereby destroy appellees' business and property. . . .

No question is raised concerning the power of the state reasonably to regulate all schools, to inspect, supervise and examine them, their teachers and pupils; to require that all children of proper age attend some school, that teachers shall be of good moral character and patriotic disposition, that certain studies plainly essential to good citizenship must be taught, and that nothing be taught which is manifestly inimical to the public welfare.

The inevitable practical result of enforcing the act under consideration would be destruction of appellees' primary schools, and perhaps all other private primary schools for normal children within the state of Oregon. Appellees are engaged in a kind of undertaking not inherently harmful, but long regarded as useful and meritorious. Certainly there is nothing in the present records to indicate that they have failed to discharge their obligations to patrons, students, or the state. And there are no peculiar circumstances or present emergencies which demand extraordinary measures relative to primary education.

Under the doctrine of Meyer v. Nebraska, 262 U.S. 390 [(1923)], we think it entirely plain that the Act of 1922 unreasonably interferes with the liberty of parents and guardians to direct the upbringing and education of children under their control. As often heretofore pointed out, rights guaranteed by the Constitution may not be abridged by legislation which has no reasonable relation to some purpose within the competency of the state. The fundamental theory of liberty upon which all governments in this Union repose excludes any general power of the state to standardize its children by forcing them to accept instruction from public teachers only. The child is not the mere creature of the state; those who nurture him and direct his destiny have the right, coupled with the high duty, to recognize and prepare him for additional obligations. . . .

The decrees below are affirmed.

## Notes and Questions

1. *Meyer* and *Pierce* establish the foundation for the right to privacy. Why? Whose interests does each case vindicate? What is the connection between privacy and the professional and proprietary interests (of teachers and schools) protected by the Court? Note that neither *Meyer* nor *Pierce* mentions "privacy." Nonetheless, *Griswold*, the first case to articulate a constitutional right to privacy, relies on both these precedents.

Despite holdings addressing the economic claims raised by a school teacher and private schools, respectively, *Meyer* and *Pierce* include dicta establishing parental autonomy — the freedom of parents to control the upbringing of their children. Through such dicta, these cases extend substantive due process, found in the constitutional protection of personal "liberty," to limit the authority of government to interfere in certain family matters.

The broad liberal principles of family autonomy in the face of government intervention, found in *Meyer* and *Pierce*, survived the Court's subsequent repudiation of economic substantive due process. See Ferguson v. Skrupa, 372 U.S. 726, 729-730 (1963). Indeed, these cases support the "revival of substantive due process" illustrated by cases like *Griswold*, which recognize personal liberties not explicitly listed in the Constitution. See, e.g., Samuel M. Davis & Mortimer D. Schwartz, Children's Rights and the Law 52-54 (1987); Eva R. Rubin, The Supreme Court and the American Family: Ideology and Issues 195 (1986).

2. Does the nascent interest in privacy recognized in *Meyer* and *Pierce* belong to the family unit or individual family members? Do these precedents help answer similar questions posed about *Griswold* and *Eisenstadt*? What similarities are shared by the two contexts, birth control and childrearing? What distinguishes them?

3. Professor Peggy Davis emphasizes how *Meyer* and *Pierce*, rooted in antislavery traditions that originally produced the Fourteenth Amendment, promote pluralism. Slavery imposed natal alienation on slaves, prohibiting slave parents from teaching chosen moral values to their children. Peggy Cooper Davis, Contested Images of Family Values: The Role of the State, 107 Harv. L. Rev. 1348, 1363 (1994). By contrast, the

autonomy recognized by *Meyer* and *Pierce* allows families room to make their own choices and embrace their own values:

> To think of family liberty as a guarantee offered in response to slavery's denials of natal connection is to understand it, not as an end in itself, but as a means to full personhood. People are not meant to be socialized to uniform, externally imposed values. People are to be able to form families and other intimate communities within which children might be differently socialized and from which adults would bring different values to the democratic process. This reconstructed Constitution gives coherence and legitimacy to the themes of autonomy and social function sounded in *Meyer, Pierce* [and later cases]. The idea of civil freedom that grows out of the history of slavery, antislavery, and Reconstruction entails more than the right to continue one's genetic kind in private. It also entails a right of family that derives from a human right of intellectual and moral autonomy. It entails the right of every individual to affect the culture and embrace, act upon, and advocate privately chosen values. For parents and other guardians, civil freedom brings a right to choose and propagate *values*. For children, civil freedom brings nothing less than the right to grow to moral autonomy, because the child-citizen, like the child-slave, flowers to moral independence only under authority that is flexible in ways that states and masters cannot manage, and temporary in ways that states and masters cannot tolerate.

*Id.* at 1371-1372. See also William A. Galston, The Legal and Political Implications of Moral Pluralism, 57 Md. L. Rev. 236, 236-243 (1998) (defending protection of diversity in *Meyer* and *Pierce*).

4. What reasons prompted enactment of the laws struck down in *Meyer* and *Pierce*? What standard of review does the Court use to assess the state interests? Why does the Court find no "emergency" in either case?

Professor Barbara Woodhouse identifies the social and political context in which the cases arose. She explains that the Nebraska law in *Meyer* stemmed from post-World War I anti-German bias. At the time, 16 states had similar English-only laws.

> [These language laws were rooted in] the struggle between cultural pluralism and the felt need to articulate a national identity, evident in the long-standing tensions between English-speaking settlers of the Midwest and the large German, Polish, and Scandinavian communities in these states. These immigrant groups often formed isolated cultural enclaves with clubs, parochial schools, ethnic parishes, banks, stores, and insurance companies in which all business was conducted in the language of the home country. To their American-born neighbors, coming from a tradition that mixed the meliorative, unifying strains of populism and progressivism with a nativist distrust for anything foreign, this failure to assimilate seemed at once a threat and a challenge for progressive reform.

Barbara Bennett Woodhouse, "Who Owns the Child?": *Meyer* and *Pierce* and the Child as Property, 33 Wm. & Mary L. Rev. 995, 1004 (1992).

The Oregon law challenged in *Pierce* reflected a different school reform movement for universal, free public education. The law, sponsored by the American Legion and the Federation of Patriotic Societies (and backed by the Ku Klux Klan), was influenced by egalitarian Populist notions common in the 1890s.

> The guiding sentiment behind the Oregon law . . . seems to have been an odd commingling of patriotic fervor, blind faith in the cure-all powers of common schooling, anti-Catholic and anti-foreign prejudice, and the conviction that private and parochial schools were breeding grounds of Bolshevism.

Id. at 1017-1018. See also Stephen L. Carter, Parents, Religion, and Schools: Reflections on *Pierce* 70 Years Later, 27 Seton Hall L. Rev. 1194, 1196-1201 (1997); David B. Tyack, The Perils of Pluralism: The Background of the *Pierce* Case, 74 Am. His. Rev. 74 (1968). Contemporary efforts to make English the "official language" of the United States have sparked renewed examination of *Meyer.* See, e.g., Cal. Educ. Code §305 (West Supp. 2001) (eliminating bilingual education in public schools); Leila Sadat Wexler, Official English, Nationalism and Linguistic Terror: A French Lesson, 71 Wash. L. Rev. 285 (1996). For further examination of *Meyer* and *Pierce,* see Chapter VIII, section A.

   5. Additional roots of privacy can be found in Skinner v. Oklahoma, 316 U.S. 535 (1942), which invalidated as a denial of equal protection a statute punishing some criminals with sterilization. The Court applied "strict scrutiny" because the statute "involves one of the basic civil rights of man" and inflicts permanent deprivation of "a basic liberty." Id. at 541. This respect for procreative freedom contrasts with the Court's earlier approach in Buck v. Bell, 274 U.S. 200 (1927). *Buck* upheld Virginia's compulsory sterilization law as applied to an inmate of the State Colony for Epileptics and Feeble Minded, citing protection of the public welfare and saying "[t]hree generations of imbeciles are enough." Id. at 207.

   Does *Buck*'s approach survive *Griswold* and *Eisenstadt*? Does state interference with the ability to procreate implicate the same values and evoke the same analysis as interference with the ability to avoid procreation? In an omitted portion of Justice Goldberg's concurrence in *Griswold,* he observes that the dissenters' refusal to invalidate the birth control prohibition would compel them to uphold "a law requiring compulsory birth control." 381 U.S. at 497. Would it? See Robert D. Goldstein, Mother-Love and Abortion: A Legal Interpretation 52-57 (1988); Donald H. Regan, Rewriting *Roe v. Wade,* 77 Mich. L. Rev. 1569, 1645 (1979) (arguments for a right to avoid childbearing do not support right to bear children).

   *Buck,* which many regard as the culmination of this country's attraction to the eugenics movement,[1] continues to generate criticism

---

[1]. Eugenicists sought to improve the human race by curbing reproduction by criminals, the insane, and other "degenerates." See, e.g., Linda Gordon, Woman's Body, Woman's Right, 276-277 (2d ed. 1990).

decades later. See, e.g., Dorothy Roberts, Killing the Black Body: Race, Reproduction, and the Meaning of Liberty 69-72 (1997); Robert J. Cynkar, *Buck v. Bell:* "Felt Necessities" v. Fundamental Values, 81 Colum. L. Rev. 1418 (1981); Paul A. Lombardo, Three Generations, No Imbeciles: New Light on *Buck v. Bell,* 60 N.Y.U. L. Rev. 30 (1985).

6. The Court also provided an underpinning for the right to privacy in Union Pacific Railway Co. v. Botsford, 141 U.S. 250 (1891). In this personal injury suit, defendant sought to compel plaintiff to submit to a "surgical examination as to the extent of the injury sued for." The Court upheld the refusal below to issue the order, explaining "The right to one's person may be said to be a right of complete immunity: to be let alone." Id. at 251 (quoting Cooley on Torts, 29).

Which approach provides stronger support for the privacy articulated in *Griswold* and *Eisenstadt:* the special concern for control over one's body in *Botsford?* Or the protection for parental autonomy in *Meyer* and *Pierce?*

7. *Meyer* and *Pierce* proved pivotal precedents when the Supreme Court struck down the application of a broad third-party visitation statute in Troxel v. Granville, 530 U.S. 57 (2000) (reprinted on pages 863-870. Although the case sharply divided the Court, several of the Justices took the opportunity both to reaffirm parents' fundamental liberty interest in childrearing and also to note the changing nature of the American family. 530 U.S. at 63-64, 85, 90, 98 (opinions of O'Connor, Stevens, and Kennedy, JJ.). What is a "family" for purposes of understanding the rights articulated in *Meyer* and *Pierce?* Cf. infra Chapter IV. See generally, e.g., Linda D. Elrod, Epilogue: Of Families, Federalization, and a Quest for Policy, 33 Fam. L.Q. 843, 844-846 (1999) (summarizing "changing definitions of family"); David D. Meyer, The Paradox of Family Privacy, 53 Vand. L. Rev. 527, 568 (2000) (critiquing Court's "constitutional sorting" of families).

## 2. The Growth of Privacy

### a. Abortion as a Private Choice

### ■ ROE v. WADE
*410 U.S. 113 (1973)*

Mr. Justice BLACKMUN delivered the opinion of the Court. . . .

### I

The Texas statutes that concern us here . . . make it a crime to "procure an abortion," as therein defined, or to attempt one, except with respect to "an abortion procured or attempted by medical advice for the purpose of saving the life of the mother." Similar statutes are in existence in a majority of the States. . . .

## II

Jane Roe, a single woman who was residing in Dallas County, Texas, instituted this federal action in March 1970 against the District Attorney of the county. She sought a declaratory judgment that the Texas criminal abortion statutes were unconstitutional on their face, and an injunction restraining the defendant from enforcing the statutes.

Roe alleged that she was unmarried and pregnant; that she wished to terminate her pregnancy by an abortion "performed by a competent, licensed physician, under safe, clinical conditions"; that she was unable to get a "legal" abortion in Texas because her life did not appear to be threatened by the continuation of her pregnancy; and that she could not afford to travel to another jurisdiction in order to secure a legal abortion under safe conditions. She claimed that the Texas statutes were unconstitutionally vague and that they abridged her right of personal privacy, protected by the First, Fourth, Fifth, Ninth, and Fourteenth Amendments. By an amendment to her complaint Roe purported to sue "on behalf of herself and all other women" similarly situated. [The district court held that the Ninth and Fourteenth Amendments protected the fundamental right to choose to have children and that the Texas statutes were unconstitutionally vague.]

## V

The principal thrust of appellant's attack on the Texas statutes is that they improperly invade a right, said to be possessed by the pregnant woman, to choose to terminate her pregnancy. Appellant would discover this right in the concept of personal "liberty" embodied in the Fourteenth Amendment's Due Process Clause; or in personal marital, familial, and sexual privacy said to be protected by the Bill of Rights or its penumbras, see Griswold v. Connecticut, 381 U.S. 479 (1965); Eisenstadt v. Baird, 405 U.S. 438 (1972); id., at 460 (White, J., concurring in result); or among those rights reserved to the people by the Ninth Amendment, Griswold v. Connecticut, 381 U.S., at 486 (Goldberg J., concurring). Before addressing this claim, we feel it desirable briefly to survey, in several aspects, the history of abortion, for such insight as that history may afford us, and then to examine the state purposes and interests behind the criminal abortion laws.

## VI

It perhaps is not generally appreciated that the restrictive criminal abortion laws in effect in a majority of States today are of relatively recent vintage. Those laws, generally proscribing abortion or its attempt at any time during pregnancy except when necessary to preserve the pregnant woman's life, are not of ancient or even of common-law origin. Instead, they derive from statutory changes effected, for the most part, in the latter half of the 19th century. . . .

[A]t common law, abortion performed before "quickening" — the first recognizable movement of the fetus in utero, appearing usually from the 16th to the 18th week of pregnancy — was not an indictable offense. The absence of a common-law crime for pre-quickening abortion appears to have developed from a confluence of earlier philosophical, theological, and civil and canon law concepts of when life begins. . . .

. . . In a frequently cited passage, Coke took the position that abortion of a woman "quick with childe" is "a great misprision, and no murder." . . . A recent review of the common-law precedents argues, however, that those precedents contradict Coke and that even post-quickening abortion was never established as a common-law crime. This is of some importance because while most American courts ruled, in holding or dictum, that abortion of an unquickened fetus was not criminal under their received common law, others followed Coke in stating that abortion of a quick fetus was a "misprision," a term they translated to mean "misdemeanor." That their reliance on Coke on this aspect of the law was uncritical and, apparently in all the reported cases, dictum (due probably to the paucity of common-law prosecutions for post-quickening abortion), makes it now appear doubtful that abortion was ever firmly established as a common-law crime even with respect to the destruction of a quick fetus.

. . . England's first criminal abortion statute, Lord Ellenborough's Act, 43 Geo. 3, c. 58, came in 1803. It made abortion of a quick fetus, §1, a capital crime, but in §2 it provided lesser penalties for the felony of abortion before quickening, and thus preserved the "quickening" distinction. . . .

. . . In this country, the law in effect in all but a few States until mid-19th century was the pre-existing English common law. Connecticut, the first State to enact abortion legislation, adopted in 1821 that part of Lord Ellenborough's Act that related to a woman "quick with child." The death penalty was not imposed. Abortion before quickening was made a crime in that State only in 1860. In 1828, New York enacted legislation that, in two respects, was to serve as a model for early anti-abortion statutes. First, while barring destruction of an unquickened fetus as well as a quick fetus, it made the former only a misdemeanor, but the latter second-degree manslaughter. Second, it incorporated a concept of therapeutic abortion [necessary to save the life of the woman]. By 1840, when Texas had received the common law, only eight American States had statutes dealing with abortion. . . .

Gradually, in the middle and late 19th century the quickening distinction disappeared from the statutory law of most States and the degree of the offense and the penalties were increased. By the end of the 1950's a large majority of the jurisdictions banned abortion, however and whenever performed, unless done to save or preserve the life of the mother. The exceptions, Alabama and the District of Columbia, permitted abortion to preserve the mother's health. . . . In the past several years, however, a trend toward liberalization of abortion statutes has resulted in adoption, by about one-third of the States, of less stringent laws, most of them patterned after the ALI Model Penal Code, §230.3. . . .

It is thus apparent that at common law, at the time of the adoption of our Constitution, and throughout the major portion of the 19th century, abortion was viewed with less disfavor than under most American statutes currently in effect. Phrasing it another way, a woman enjoyed a substantially broader right to terminate a pregnancy than she does in most States today. [The opinion then noted that the American Medical Association, American Public Health Association, and American Bar Association all supported liberalizing abortion laws.]

### VII

Three reasons have been advanced to explain historically the enactment of criminal abortion laws in the 19th century and to justify their continued existence.

It has been argued occasionally that these laws were the product of a Victorian social concern to discourage illicit sexual conduct. Texas, however, does not advance this justification in the present case, and it appears that no court or commentator has taken the argument seriously. . . .

A second reason is concerned with abortion as a medical procedure. When most criminal abortion laws were first enacted, the procedure was a hazardous one for the woman. . . . Thus, it has been argued that a State's real concern in enacting a criminal abortion law was to protect the pregnant woman, that is, to restrain her from submitting to a procedure that placed her life in serious jeopardy.

Modern medical techniques have altered this situation. Appellants and various amici refer to medical data indicating that abortion in early pregnancy, that is, prior to the end of the first trimester, although not without its risk, is now relatively safe. Mortality rates for women undergoing early abortions, where the procedure is legal, appear to be as low as or lower than the rates for normal childbirth. Consequently, any interest of the State in protecting the woman from an inherently hazardous procedure, except when it would be equally dangerous for her to forgo it, has largely disappeared. Of course, important state interests in the areas of health and medical standards do remain. The State has a legitimate interest in seeing to it that abortion, like any other medical procedure, is performed under circumstances that insure maximum safety for the patient. This interest obviously extends at least to the performing physician and his staff, to the facilities involved, to the availability of after-care, and to adequate provision for any complication or emergency that might arise. The prevalence of high mortality rates at illegal "abortion mills" strengthens, rather than weakens, the State's interest in regulating the conditions under which abortions are performed. Moreover, the risk to the woman increases as her pregnancy continues. Thus, the State retains a definite interest in protecting the woman's own health and safety when an abortion is proposed at a late stage of pregnancy.

The third reason is the State's interest — some phrase it in terms of duty — in protecting prenatal life. Some of the argument for this justification rests on the theory that a new human life is present from the moment of conception. The State's interest and general obligation to protect life then extends, it is argued, to prenatal life. Only when the life of the pregnant mother herself is at stake, balanced against the life she carries within her, should the interest of the embryo or fetus not prevail. ... In assessing the State's interest, recognition may be given to the ... claim that as long as at least *potential* life is involved, the State may assert interests beyond the protection of the pregnant woman alone.

Parties challenging state abortion laws have sharply disputed in some courts the contention that a purpose of these laws, when enacted, was to protect prenatal life. Pointing to the absence of legislative history to support the contention, they claim that most state laws were designed solely to protect the woman. Proponents of this view point out that in many States, including Texas, by statute or judicial interpretation, the pregnant woman herself could not be prosecuted for self-abortion or for cooperating in an abortion performed upon her by another. They claim that adoption of the "quickening" distinction through received common law and state statutes tacitly recognizes the greater health hazards inherent in late abortion and impliedly repudiates the theory that life begins at conception.

It is with these interests, and the weight to be attached to them, that this case is concerned.

### VIII

The Constitution does not explicitly mention any right of privacy. In a line of decisions, however, going back perhaps as far as Union Pacific R. Co. v. Botsford, 141 U.S. 250, 251 (1891), the Court has recognized that a right of personal privacy, or a guarantee of certain areas or zones of privacy, does exist under the Constitution. In varying contexts, the Court or individual Justices have, indeed, found at least the roots of that right in the First Amendment, Stanley v. Georgia, 394 U.S. 557, 564 (1969); in the Fourth and Fifth Amendments; in the penumbras of the Bill of Rights, Griswold v. Connecticut, 381 U.S., at 484-485; in the

Ninth Amendment, id., at 486 (Goldberg, J., concurring); or in the concept of liberty guaranteed by the first section of the Fourteenth Amendment, see Meyer v. Nebraska, 262 U.S. 390, 399 (1923). These decisions make it clear that only personal rights that can be deemed "fundamental" or "implicit in the concept of ordered liberty," are included in this guarantee of personal privacy. They also make it clear that the right has some extension to activities relating to marriage, Loving v. Virginia, 388 U.S. 1, 12 (1967); procreation, Skinner v. Oklahoma, 316 U.S. 535, 541-542 (1942); contraception, Eisenstadt v. Baird, 405 U.S., at 453-454; id., at 460, 463-465 (White, J., concurring in result); family relationships, Prince v. Massachusetts, 321 U.S. 158, 166 (1944); and child rearing and education, Pierce v. Society of Sisters, 268 U.S. 510, 535 (1925); Meyer v. Nebraska, supra.

This right of privacy, whether it be founded in the Fourteenth Amendment's concept of personal liberty and restrictions upon state action, as we feel it is, or, as the District Court determined, in the Ninth Amendment's reservation of rights to the people, is broad enough to encompass a woman's decision whether or not to terminate her pregnancy. The detriment that the State would impose upon the pregnant woman by denying this choice altogether is apparent. Specific and direct harm medically diagnosable even in early pregnancy may be involved. Maternity, or additional offspring, may force upon the woman a distressful life and future. Psychological harm may be imminent. Mental and physical health may be taxed by child care. There is also the distress, for all concerned, associated with the unwanted child, and there is the problem of bringing a child into a family already unable, psychologically and otherwise, to care for it. In other cases, as in this one, the additional difficulties and continuing stigma of unwed motherhood may be involved. All these are factors the woman and her responsible physician necessarily will consider in consultation.

On the basis of elements such as these, appellant and some amici argue that the woman's right is absolute and that she is entitled to terminate her pregnancy at whatever time, in whatever way, and for whatever reason she alone chooses. With this we do not agree. Appellant's arguments that Texas either has no valid interest at all in regulating the abortion decision, or no interest strong enough to support any limitation upon the woman's sole determination, are unpersuasive. The Court's decisions recognizing a right of privacy also acknowledge that some state regulation in areas protected by that right is appropriate. As noted above, a State may properly assert important interests in safeguarding health, in maintaining medical standards, and in protecting potential life. At some point in pregnancy, these respective interests become sufficiently compelling to sustain regulation of the factors that govern the abortion decision. The privacy right involved, therefore, cannot be said to be absolute. In fact, it is not clear to us that the claim asserted by some amici that one has an unlimited right to do with one's body as one pleases bears a close relationship to the right of privacy previously articulated in the Court's decisions. The Court has refused to recognize an unlimited right of this kind in the past. Jacobson v. Massachusetts, 197 U.S. 11 (1905) (vaccination); Buck v. Bell, 274 U.S. 200 (1927) (sterilization).

We therefore conclude that the right of personal privacy includes the abortion decision, but that this right is not unqualified and must be considered against important state interests in regulation. . . . Where certain "fundamental rights" are involved, the Court has held that regulation limiting these rights may be justified only by a "compelling state interest," and that legislative enactments must be narrowly drawn to express only the legitimate state interests at stake. . . .

## IX . . .

### A

The appellee and certain amici argue that the fetus is a "person" within the language and meaning of the Fourteenth Amendment. In support of this, they outline at length and in detail the well-known facts of fetal development. If this suggestion of personhood is established, the appellant's case, of course, collapses, for the fetus' right to life would then be guaranteed specifically by the Amendment. . . .

The Constitution does not define "person" in so many words. Section 1 of the Fourteenth Amendment contains three references to "person." The first, in defining "citizens," speaks of "persons born or naturalized in the United States." The word also appears both in the Due Process Clause and in the Equal Protection Clause. "Person" is used in other places in the Constitution. . . . But in nearly all these instances, the use of the word is such that it has application only postnatally. None indicates, with any assurance, that it has any possible prenatal application.[54]

All this, together with our observation, supra, that throughout the major portion of the 19th century prevailing legal abortion practices were

54. When Texas urges that a fetus is entitled to Fourteenth Amendment protection as a person, it faces a dilemma. Neither in Texas nor in any other State are all abortions prohibited. Despite broad proscription, [a therapeutic] exception always exists. . . . But if the fetus is a person who is not to be deprived of life without due process of law, and if the mother's condition is the sole determinant, does not the Texas exception appear to be out of line with the Amendment's command? There are other inconsistencies between Fourteenth Amendment status and the typical abortion statute. It has already been pointed out that in Texas the woman is not a principal or an accomplice with respect to an abortion upon her. If the fetus is a person, why is the woman not a principal or an accomplice? Further, the penalty for criminal abortion . . . is significantly less than the maximum penalty for murder. . . . If the fetus is a person, may the penalties be different?

far freer than they are today, persuades us that the word "person," as used in the Fourteenth Amendment, does not include the unborn. . . .

**B**

The pregnant woman cannot be isolated in her privacy. She carries an embryo and, later, a fetus. . . . The situation therefore is inherently different from marital intimacy, or bedroom possession of obscene material, or marriage, or procreation, or education, with which *Eisenstadt* and *Griswold, Stanley, Loving, Skinner* and *Pierce* and *Meyer* were respectively concerned. As we have intimated above, it is reasonable and appropriate for a State to decide that at some point in time another interest, that of health of the mother or that of potential human life, becomes significantly involved. The woman's privacy is no longer sole and any right of privacy she possesses must be measured accordingly.

Texas urges that, apart from the Fourteenth Amendment, life begins at conception and is present throughout pregnancy, and that, therefore, the State has a compelling interest in protecting that life from and after conception. We need not resolve the difficult question of when life begins. When those trained in the respective disciplines of medicine, philosophy, and theology are unable to arrive at any consensus, the judiciary, at this point in the development of man's knowledge, is not in a position to speculate as to the answer.

It should be sufficient to note briefly the wide divergence of thinking on this most sensitive and difficult question. There has always been strong support for the view that life does not begin until live birth [citing Stoics and Jewish and Protestant communities]. As we have noted, the common law found greater significance in quickening. Physicians and their scientific colleagues have regarded that event with less interest and have tended to focus either upon conception, upon live birth, or upon the interim point at which the fetus becomes "viable," that is, potentially able to live outside the mother's womb, albeit with artificial aid. Viability is usually placed at about seven months (28 weeks) but may occur earlier, even at 24 weeks. [T]he existence of life from the moment of conception [is] the official belief of the Catholic Church. [T]his is a view strongly held by many non-Catholics as well, and by many physicians. Substantial problems for precise definition of this view are posed, however, by new embryological data that purport to indicate that conception is a "process" over time, rather than an event, and by new medical techniques such as menstrual extraction, the "morning-after" pill, implantation of embryos, artificial insemination, and even artificial wombs.

In areas other than criminal abortion, the law has been reluctant to endorse any theory that life, as we recognize it, begins before live birth or to accord legal rights to the unborn except in narrowly defined situations and except when the rights are contingent upon live birth [citing tort and property law]. In short, the unborn have never been recognized in the law as persons in the whole sense.

**X**

In view of all this, we do not agree that, by adopting one theory of life, Texas may override the rights of the pregnant woman that are at stake. We repeat, however, that the State does have an important and legitimate interest in preserving and protecting the health of the pregnant woman, whether she be a resident of the State or a non-resident who seeks medical consultation and treatment there, and that it has still another important and legitimate interest in protecting the potentiality of human life. These interests are separate and distinct. Each grows in substantiality as the woman approaches term and, at a point during pregnancy, each becomes "compelling."

With respect to the State's important and legitimate interest in the health of the mother, the "compelling" point, in the light of present medical knowledge, is at approximately the end of the first trimester. This is so because of the now-established medical fact . . . that until the end of the first trimester mortality in abortion may be less than mortality in normal childbirth. It follows that, from and after this point, a State may regulate the abortion procedure to the extent that the regulation reasonably relates to the preservation and protection of maternal health. Examples of permissible state regulation in this area are requirements as to the qualifications of the person who is to perform the abortion; as to the licensure of that person; as to the facility in which the procedure is to be performed, that is, whether it must be a hospital or may be a clinic or some other place of less-than-hospital status; as to the licensing of the facility; and the like.

This means, on the other hand, that, for the period of pregnancy prior to this "compelling" point, the attending physician, in consultation with his patient, is free to determine, without regulation by the State, that, in his medical judgment, the patient's pregnancy should be terminated. If that decision is reached, the judgment may be effectuated by an abortion free of interference by the State.

With respect to the State's important and legitimate interest in potential life, the "compelling" point is at viability. This is so because the fetus then presumably has the capability of meaningful life outside the mother's womb. State regulation protective of fetal life after viability thus has both logical and biological justifications. If the State is interested in protecting fetal life after viability, it may go so far as to proscribe abortion during that period, except when it is necessary to preserve the life or health of the mother. . . .

**XI**

To summarize and to repeat:

1. A state criminal abortion statute of the current Texas type, that excepts from criminality only a *life-saving* procedure on behalf of the mother, without regard to pregnancy stage and without recognition of

the other interests involved, is violative of the Due Process Clause of the Fourteenth Amendment.

(a) For the stage prior to approximately the end of the first trimester, the abortion decision and its effectuation must be left to the medical judgment of the pregnant woman's attending physician.

(b) For the stage subsequent to approximately the end of the first trimester, the State, in promoting its interest in the health of the mother, may, if it chooses, regulate the abortion procedure in ways that are reasonably related to maternal health.

(c) For the stage subsequent to viability, the State in promoting its interest in the potentiality of human life may, if it chooses, regulate, and even proscribe, abortion except where it is necessary, in appropriate medical judgment, for the preservation of the life or health of the mother. . . .

This holding, we feel, is consistent with the relative weights of the respective interests involved, with the lessons and examples of medical and legal history, with the lenity of the common law, and with the demands of the profound problems of the present day. The decision leaves the State free to place increasing restrictions on abortion as the period of pregnancy lengthens, so long as those restrictions are tailored to the recognized state interests. The decision vindicates the right of the physician to administer medical treatment according to his professional judgment up to the points where important state interests provide compelling justifications for intervention. Up to those points, the abortion decision in all its aspects is inherently, and primarily, a medical decision, and basic responsibility for it must rest with the physician. . . .

Mr. Justice REHNQUIST, dissenting. . . .

. . . I have difficulty in concluding, as the Court does, that the right of "privacy" is involved in this case. Texas, by the statute here challenged, bars the performance of a medical abortion by a licensed physician on a plaintiff such as Roe. A transaction resulting in an operation such as this is not "private" in the ordinary usage of that word. Nor is the "privacy" that the Court finds here even a distant relative of the freedom from searches and seizures protected by the Fourth Amendment to the Constitution, which the Court has referred to as embodying a right to privacy. Katz v. United States, 389 U.S. 347 (1967).

The fact that a majority of the States reflecting, after all, the majority sentiment in those States, have had restrictions on abortions for at least a century is a strong indication, it seems to me, that the asserted right to an abortion is not "so rooted in the traditions and conscience of our people as to be ranked as fundamental," Snyder v. Massachusetts, 291 U.S. 97, 105 (1934). Even today, when society's views on abortion are changing, the very existence of the debate is evidence that the "right" to an abortion is not so universally accepted as the appellant would have us believe.

To reach its result, the Court necessarily has had to find within the scope of the Fourteenth Amendment a right that was apparently completely unknown to the drafters of the Amendment. . . . There apparently was no question concerning the validity of this provision or of any of the other state statutes when the Fourteenth Amendment was adopted. The only conclusion possible from this history is that the drafters did not intend to have the Fourteenth Amendment withdraw from the States the power to legislate with respect to this matter. . . .

■ **SARAH WEDDINGTON,[2] A QUESTION OF CHOICE**
*12-14, 35-38, 44-57 (1992)*

My mouth goes dry as I put myself back in those days in Austin [Texas in 1967] when my period was late. I was in my third year of law school, going to school full-time and supporting myself by working several jobs. I was seriously dating Ron Weddington, who was finishing his undergraduate degree after returning from the army; he was planning to start law school the following summer. I had been celibate until our relationship progressed to the point that we were talking about getting married.

Each day I kept hurrying to the women's lounge in the law school between classes, hoping to find that something had happened; each day I was disappointed. I had to fight to maintain my routine, to work on my class assignments and complete the demands of my jobs. I had to fight to keep my mind from being incapacitated by the questions that haunted me: What if I were pregnant? What would I do if I were? . . .

Ron went through those anxious days with me. . . . We began to go over the possibilities. Abortion was one, but we were worried about the risks of an illegal procedure. . . . If we decided on abortion, the next problem was: Where to go? There were no ads in the phone books or newspapers; this was all undercover. You had to find someone who knew a name, a place — and I refused to tell anyone my situation. . . . Ron heard about a doctor in Piedras Negras, across from Eagle Pass, Texas, who had some medical experience in the United States and who did abortions. Abortion was illegal in Mexico, but the woman Ron spoke to told him [that] several women she knew had been to this doctor, and everything had turned out fine. He charged $400 — cash only. [Ron made the necessary arrangements, obtained a powerful painkiller, and got the name of someone who might help in case of medical trouble.]

[2]. Sarah Weddington is the attorney who represented plaintiff Jane Roe in Roe v. Wade.

I was grateful that at least the inside of the building was clean. I could not read what appeared to be a medical diploma on the wall, but it made me feel better. . . . I was one of the lucky ones. [W]hen I felt the anesthesia taking effect, my last thoughts were: I hope I don't die, and I pray that no one ever finds out about this. . . .

Roe v. Wade started at a garage sale, amid paltry castoffs. [Weddington and her friends were raising money for an abortion referral project.] The referral project volunteers were worried about being involved in covert activity. . . . While we sorted our prized junk at the garage sale, Judy [Smith] posed the primary questions that the volunteers wanted answered: Could they be prosecuted and/or convicted as accomplices to the crime of abortion simply for referring women? Would it make any legal difference if they sent women only to places where abortion was legal? . . . The [Texas] statute made it a crime to "furnish the means for procuring an abortion," but I didn't know whether that applied only to drugs and instruments, not information. I knew Texas also had a general accomplice statute that applied to a variety of crimes.

. . . I began spending time in the [University of Texas] law library, meeting with project volunteers, spending more time in the library, and talking to law professors, law students, and other lawyers. [One day] Judy announced that she wanted a lawsuit filed to challenge the constitutionality of the Texas anti-abortion statute. . . . Around the nation, the big advances seemed to be coming from courtrooms, not legislative halls. . . .

[I] had not focused on the possibility of *our* filing a lawsuit. After all, my total legal experience consisted of a few uncontested divorces for friends, ten or twelve uncomplicated wills for people with little property, one adoption for relatives, and a few miscellaneous matters. . . . The idea of challenging the Texas abortion law in federal court was overwhelming [but] I was the best free legal help available [and Ron and Weddington wanted to help others avoid what they had gone through]. [P]erhaps my inexperience was a plus. I did not fully appreciate that the odds were stacked against our endeavor. . . . As it was, none of us had any inkling of the long-term impact of what we were starting. . . .

[Weddington asked former classmate Linda Coffee, who was familiar with federal litigation, to help.] [O]ur constant worry was about the right plaintiffs. After Linda did some research, we decided neither the Austin volunteers nor the referral project would be certain to have standing. . . . Then a woman went to Dallas lawyer Henry McCluskey, a friend of Linda's who knew of the proposed lawsuit. [Weddington flew to Dallas to meet her at a pizza parlor.] She had had a rough life: She already had one child and did not want another. Her mother had taken her daughter away from her and she seldom got to see her. She had never finished the tenth grade, was working as a waitress, and knew she would lose her job if the pregnancy continued. She could barely support herself, much less a child. . . .

Linda and I explained the Texas anti-abortion law and told her why we felt it was wrong. She had found an illegal place in Dallas, she admitted, but she didn't like the looks of it. She had no money to travel to another state. As the conversation continued, Jane Roe asked if it would help if she had been raped. We said no; the Texas law had no exception for rape. It was just as illegal for a doctor to do an abortion for someone who had been raped as it was in any other situation. I did ask, "Were there any witnesses? Was there a police report? Is there any way that we could prove a rape occurred?" Her answer in each instance was no.

Neither Linda nor I questioned her further about how she had gotten pregnant. I was not going to allege something in the complaint that I could not back up with proof. Also, we did not want the Texas law changed only to allow abortion in cases of rape. We wanted a decision that abortion was covered by the right of privacy. After all, the women coming to the referral project were there as a result of a wide variety of circumstances. . . .

. . . We still had to name our plaintiffs [who would use pseudonyms to protect their privacy]. We picked names that rhymed. I liked "Jane Roe."[3] To me the name represented all women, not just one. . . . We were filing . . . against Henry Wade, the elected district attorney of Dallas County, the official responsible for law enforcement in that county. We wanted the court to tell Wade's office to leave doctors alone. [The case] became known as Roe v. Wade. . . .

■ **BRIEF FOR THE AMICI CURIAE WOMEN WHO HAVE HAD ABORTIONS AND FRIENDS OF AMICI CURIAE IN SUPPORT OF APPELLEES, WEBSTER v. REPRODUCTIVE HEALTH SERVICES**
*492 U.S. 490 (1989) (No. 88-605)*

FRIENDS LETTER — 172, AT C29-30

When I was six years old, I was forced to endure a 40 mile trip to what was referred to as "Feather Annie's." I stayed in the car with my father and two brothers while my 41 year old mother went inside the private residence. My father's serious attitude instilled fear and insecurity in my older brother and I. When my mother returned to the car she was

[3]. "Jane Roe" later published her autobiography, Norma McCorvey with Andy Meister, I am Roe: My Life, *Roe v. Wade* and Freedom of Choice (1994). McCorvey subsequently announced that she had joined opponents of legalized abortion. See "Jane Roe" Joins Anti-Abortion Group, N.Y. Times, Aug. 11, 1995, at A12. When interviewed, McCorvey explained that she had "always been pro-life [but] just didn't know it," still believed in first-trimester abortions, and had felt exploited by abortion-rights groups.

crying. She repeated the words "I'm afraid I'll die — I'm afraid some-one will find out I came here and I'll get her (referring to the woman who performed the abortion) in trouble with the law. I'm glad it's over, but I'm afraid — if I die, what will happen to the children?" It was an awful experience for a child who was too young to understand. All the way home she cried and repeated over and over her fear of dying. I do not remember . . . her expressing any regret, she expressed her relief that it was over. Her fears became contagious and needless to say it was traumatic for me and my older brother (one brother was less than 2 years old). Many years later when my brother and I recalled that day, we agreed that the only crime committed was by a society that forced a woman to have to submit herself to fear and agony of that magnitude. Our mother survived and imbued in us forever was our sympathy for her on that day. After all, she had already born six children, she was in poor health, and my father was unemployed in that year of 1936.

My mother told me that it was a terrible tragedy that the little 2-year old neighbor girl's mother died suddenly. When I became old enough to understand I found out that it was no secret, in the small town we lived in, that the young mother had died from a self induced abortion. As a very young child I was terribly disturbed over the fact that this dear cute little girl had no mother for the reason that her mother had died because she didn't want to have another baby. I felt sad that such a thing could happen, it was hard for me to accept that "Jane's" pretty young mother had to die. I saw sadness in Jane's face and unhappiness was ap-parent in her father's behavior. I cannot justify a law that allowed such unfortunate circumstances to happen.

In the 1950's my sister lost a good friend who had an illegal abor-tion. The 28-year old woman who died had five small children. Her un-planned and unwanted pregnancy was more than she was able to handle and her untimely death was the result of not having a choice of a safe and legal abortion. A law with the potential effect of depriving a loving husband and five small children of the presence of a young wife and mother is a disgrace in a compassionate society.

---

As these excerpts reveal, abortion was a dangerous procedure before legalization. In fact, abortion was the leading cause of maternal deaths in some locales. See generally Ellen Messer & Kathryn E. May, Back Rooms: Voices from the Illegal Abortion Era (1988). See also Laura Kaplan, The Story of Jane: The Legendary Underground Feminist Abor-tion Service (1995) (account of famous abortion referral-provider service that, in its four-year history, performed 11,000 illegal abortions); Leslie J. Reagan, When Abortion Was a Crime: Women, Medicine, and Law in the United States, 1867-1973 (1997).

## Notes and Questions

1. What is the nature of the right recognized by Roe v. Wade? Its parameters? Where in the Constitution does *Roe* situate this right? How does this approach compare with that of *Griswold*? Why is the right to terminate a pregnancy not absolute? Why is it "fundamental" (thereby evoking the compelling state interest test)?

2. The underpinnings of *Roe*'s privacy-based theory, as derived from *Griswold*, were developed by law professor-activist Roy Lucas in a pioneering article. Roy Lucas, Federal Constitutional Limitations on the Enforcement and Administration of State Abortion Statutes, 46 N.C. L. Rev. 730, 761-764 (1968).

3. Does the protection of childrearing and education in *Meyer* and *Pierce* support *Roe*'s holding? Does the definition of the right to privacy in *Eisenstadt* necessarily include abortion freedom? Constitutional historian David Garrow has documented that Justice Brennan's choice of the "*bear* or beget" language in *Eisenstadt* resulted from Brennan's anticipation of the abortion decision. David J. Garrow, Liberty and Sexuality: The Right to Privacy and the Making of *Roe v. Wade* 541-544 (updated ed. 1998).

4. Two types of statutory restrictions were common in the *Roe* era. One type, like the Texas statute, prohibited abortion except to save the life of the mother. A newer type, modeled on the American Law Institute's (ALI) Model Penal Code, permitted abortion if pregnancy would seriously and permanently injure the woman's health; if the fetus suffered from a grave, permanent, and irremediable mental or physical defect; or if the pregnancy resulted from rape. In a companion case to *Roe*, Doe v. Bolton, 410 U.S. 179 (1973), the Court invalidated Georgia's ALI-inspired statute, including its procedural requirements of hospitalization, accreditation, committee approval, two-doctor concurrence, and residency. On the operation of abortion committees, which often mandated simultaneous sterilization for abortion patients, see Rickie Solinger, "A Complete Disaster": Abortion and the Politics of Hospital Abortion Committees, 1950-1970, in Women and Health in America: Historical Readings 659 (Judith Walzer Leavitt ed., 2d ed. 1999).

5. After *Roe*, the Court elaborated on the meaning of "privacy" in Whalen v. Roe, 429 U.S. 589 (1977). Upholding a statute that required recording the identity of those who had obtained certain drugs pursuant to prescription, the Court stated:

> The cases sometimes characterized as protecting "privacy" have in fact involved at least two different kinds of interests. One is the individual interest in avoiding disclosure of personal matters, and another is the interest in independence in making certain kinds of important decisions.

Id. at 598-599. The Court cited *Griswold* twice, for each meaning. Does *Griswold* support both definitions? See also Richard A. Posner, The

Uncertain Protection of Privacy by the Supreme Court, 1979 Sup. Ct. Rev. 173, 192-193.

6. Why does the state's interest in protecting "potential life" become compelling only after viability? In the balance of competing individual and state interests, why should the fetus's ability to survive outside the womb determine the mother's rights? Compare Nancy Rhoden, Trimesters and Technology: Revamping *Roe v. Wade,* 95 Yale L.J. 639 (1986) (viability distinguishes early from late gestation), with Bob Woodward & Scott Armstrong, The Brethen: Inside the Supreme Court 232-233 (1979) ("insiders' " view about choice of viability as compelling point).

As *Roe* suggests, viability played an important role in prenatal torts. Early cases permitted recovery for prenatal injuries by children subsequently born alive only if the injuries occurred after viability. See, e.g., Bonbrest v. Kotz, 65 F. Supp. 138 (D.D.C. 1946). Yet many cases abandoned the requirement before *Roe.* See, e.g., Hornbuckle v. Plantation Pipe Line Co., 93 S.E.2d 727 (Ga. 1956). See also David A. Gordon, The Unborn Plaintiff, 63 Mich. L. Rev. 579 (1965). Nor is viability currently required in a number of states for the crime of fetal murder. See People v. Davis, 872 P.2d 591 (Cal. 1994) (citing *Roe* to support protection of previable fetus when no conflict with mother's privacy interests).

Many early abortion restrictions disallowed abortions only after quickening (the perception of fetal movement, usually between 16 and 18 weeks of gestation). Though quickening had no biological significance, it may have become important, in the absence of modern pregnancy tests, as the first indication of pregnancy. Without such evidence, prosecutors could not establish the elements of criminal abortion. See James C. Mohr, Abortion in America: The Origins and Evolution of National Policy, 1800-1900, at 4 (1978). Is quickening superior to viability as a benchmark? See also Reva Siegel, Reasoning from the Body: A Historical Perspective on Abortion Regulation and Questions of Equal Protection, 44 Stan. L. Rev. 261, 380 (1992) (arguing affirmatively).

What alternatives to viability or quickening might exist? See, e.g., L. W. Sumner, Abortion and Moral Theory (1981) (sentience).

7. Suppose medical technology can advance viability. See, e.g., Akron v. Akron Ctr. for Reprod. Health, 462 U.S. 416, 458 (1983) (O'Connor, J., dissenting) (suggesting this prospect puts *Roe* on a "collision course" with itself). Will the state have the authority to outlaw abortions earlier in pregnancy? Alternatively, might "artificial wombs" or abortion methods compatible with fetal survival give pregnant women *more* freedom to terminate their pregnancies by allowing the state to protect potential life without continued physical imposition on women? See Robert D. Goldstein, Mother-Love and Abortion 30 (1988); Bruce Ching, Inverting the Viability Test for Abortion Law, 22 Women's Rts. L. Rep. 37 (2000); Mark A. Goldstein, Note, Choice Rights and Abortion: The Begetting Choice Right and State Obstacles to Choice in Light of Artificial Womb

Technology, 51 S. Cal. L. Rev. 877 (1978). In answering this question, consider what interest of the pregnant woman *Roe* sought to protect: The freedom to terminate the physical burdens of pregnancy? The freedom to escape reproduction? See Rosemarie Tong, Feminist Approaches to Bioethics: Theoretical Reflections and Practical Applications 131-133 (1997) (exploring feminist arguments for a right to "fetal extinction").

8. According to *Roe*, to whom does the privacy right belong — the woman or the physician? See Siegel, supra, at 296. Why did the Court choose this approach? See Woodward & Armstrong, supra, at 174-175, 229-231. This emphasis on the physician receives reinforcement from Doe v. Bolton's broad interpretation of "health," which allows the physician to consider "all factors — physical, emotional, psychological, familial, and the woman's age — relevant to the well-being of the patient." 410 U.S. at 192. On the physician's role in abortion, see generally Susan Frelich Appleton, Doctors, Patients and the Constitution: A Theoretical Analysis of the Physician's Role in "Private" Reproductive Decisions, 63 Wash. U. L.Q. 183 (1985); Susan Frelich Appleton, More Thoughts on the Physician's Constitutional Role in Abortion and Related Choices, 66 Wash. U. L.Q. 499 (1988).

What role *should* a physician play in the decision to terminate a pregnancy? In matters of "privacy" generally? *Doe* describes the physician as follows:

> The appellants' suggestion [that involvement of a hospital committee would subject the woman to disapproval] is necessarily somewhat degrading to the conscientious physician, particularly the obstetrician, whose professional activity is concerned with the physical and mental welfare, the woes, the emotions, and the concern of his female patients. He, perhaps more than anyone else, is knowledgeable in this area of patient care, and he is aware of human frailty, so-called "error," and needs. . . .

410 U.S. at 196-197.

9. What alternative approaches might the Supreme Court have used? Many feminist commentators prefer an equal protection, over a privacy-based, approach on the theory that abortion freedom is essential for gender equality. For example, Professor Sylvia Law has argued:

> [T]he Court held in Roe v. Wade that the constitutional right to privacy protects the right of women and their physicians to determine whether or not to terminate pregnancy. Nothing the Supreme Court has ever done has been more concretely important for women. Laws denying access to abortion have a sex-specific impact. Although both men and women seek to control reproduction, only women become pregnant. Only women have abortions. Laws restricting access to abortion have a devastating sex-specific impact. Despite the decision's overwhelming importance to women, it was not grounded on the principle of sex equality. . . .

> . . . An equality doctrine that ignores the unique quality of [women's reproductive] experiences implicitly says that women can claim equality only insofar as they are like men. Such a doctrine demands that women deny an important aspect of who they are. . . .

Sylvia A. Law, Rethinking Sex and the Constitution, 132 U. Pa. L. Rev. 955, 980-981, 1007 (1984). Proponents of this approach include Justice Ginsburg, who as a litigator persuaded the Supreme Court to apply the Equal Protection Clause to gender discrimination. See, e.g., Ruth Bader Ginsburg, Some Thoughts on Autonomy and Equality in Relation to *Roe v. Wade*, 63 N.C. L. Rev. 375, 386 (1985). What are the advantages and disadvantages of an equal protection rationale for the right to abortion?

See generally, e.g., Catharine A. MacKinnon, Privacy v. Equality: Beyond *Roe v. Wade*, in Feminism Unmodified: Discourses on Life and Law 93 (1987); Laura W. Stein, Living with the Risk of Backfire: A Response to the Feminist Critiques of Privacy and Equality, 77 Minn. L. Rev. 1153 (1993); Cass R. Sunstein, Neutrality in Constitutional Law (with Special Reference to Pornography, Abortion and Surrogacy), 92 Colum. L. Rev. 1, 36 (1992). See also Joan Williams, Unbending Gender: Why Family and Work Conflict and What to Do About It 202 (2000) (feminist argument defending abortion rights "in the name of responsible motherhood") .

10. How far should the state go in protecting *potential* life? Professor Frances Olsen ponders this question:

> . . . How would men react to a law that forbad them to ejaculate outside a fertile woman's vagina? While most heterosexual men would probably prefer to ejaculate into a vagina, the idea that they could not ejaculate anywhere else would probably come to seem oppressive and absurd to them. Yet such a law would seem to promote a state interest in *potential life*, as well as a state interest in the life of sperm. To avoid overbreadth, the law could provide that if a man does ejaculate where he is not allowed to, he could avoid criminal liability by collecting as many of the sperm as possible and rushing them to a sperm bank. . . .
>
> Of course, the burden such a law would place upon men is nothing like the burden that antiabortion laws place upon women. Many men would not be affected at all; other men would simply have to make periodic trips to sperm banks. Such periodic trips would impose a minimal burden. . . . They would disrupt no one's life, disturb no long range plans. The trips would be even less disruptive than a woman's menstrual period, so really no one could properly complain. Perhaps some disgruntled men, whose real complaint might be that they were born male, might object. Their objection, however, should be lodged against mother nature, not against the law — a law reasonably drafted to maximize a man's freedom, consistent with the state's obligation to preserve life.
>
> Many people would consider this example silly, but this putative silliness reflects the value that society places upon men's lives and their free-

dom. Only convenience prevents us from valuing sperm. In fact, if men rather than women needed sperm to reproduce, some would argue that the state could not constitutionally deny men access to women's sperm.

Frances Olsen, Comment: Unraveling Compromise, 103 Harv. L. Rev. 105, 129-130 (1989). See also Walter Dellinger & Gene B. Sperling, Abortion and the Supreme Court: The Retreat from *Roe v. Wade*, 138 U. Pa. L. Rev. 83, 106 (1989) (pointing out that, if the state had a sufficiently weighty interest in fetal life, one would expect it to treat the 62 percent of fertilized ova that spontaneously abort as "nothing short of an epidemic or national health crisis").

11. What other approaches might the state adopt to further the goal of reducing abortion? Olsen suggests social support for pregnant women and children and improved access to contraceptives. She adds that states could "outlaw" the act of impregnating women who do not wish to become pregnant by both requiring a woman's informed consent and imposing a waiting period, before a man could risk impregnating her. Olsen, supra, at 130.

12. Professor Mary Ann Glendon reads *Roe* to put the "United States in a class by itself" among developed nations in the legal treatment of abortion. The United States alone recognizes a "right to abortion." In addition, U.S. abortion policy is unique because it was not formulated legislatively. Other countries require counseling and the demonstration of substantial reasons for abortion. Even among countries that make abortion freely available, the United States stands out because of its failure to provide significant support for pregnant women and social benefits for mothers. Mary Ann Glendon, Abortion and Divorce in Western Law 22-25 (1987).

Canada's abortion restrictions were invalidated in R. v. Morgantaler, [1988] 1 S.C.R. 30 (Can.). In Germany in 1975 the Constitutional Court struck down a statute guaranteeing abortion freedom, based on the government's duty to protect the fetus. See, e.g., Gerald L. Neuman, *Casey* in the Mirror: Abortion, Abuse and the Right to Protection in the United States and Germany, 43 Am. J. Comp. L. 273 (1995). German unification in 1990 required establishing one law in place of the restrictive West German regime and the permissive East German regime. Compromise legislation passed in 1995 criminalized abortion with exceptions for first-trimester abortions preceded by counseling to encourage continued pregnancy, medical grounds, and sexual abuse or rape. See D. A. Jeremy Telman, Abortion and Women's Legal Personhood in Germany: A Contribution to the Feminist Theory of the State, 24 N.Y.U. Rev. L. & Soc. Change 91 (1998); Rosemarie Will, German Unification and the Reform of Abortion Law, 3 Cardozo Women's L.J. 399 (1996). On other countries' laws and policies, see generally, e.g., Negotiating Reproductive Rights: Women's Perspectives Across Countries and Cultures (Rosalind

P. Petchesky & Karen Judd eds., 1998); Amy M. Buckley, Note, The Primacy of Democracy over Natural Law in Irish Abortion Law: An Examination of the *C* Case, 9 Duke J. Comp. & Int'l L. 275 (1998).

13. *Roe* generated considerable controversy, including efforts to overturn it via the Human Life Statute, S. 158, 97th Cong., 1st Sess. (1981), as well to codify it via the Freedom of Choice Act, S. 25, 103d Cong., 1st Sess. (1993).

See generally Ronald Dworkin, Life's Dominion: An Argument About Abortion, Euthanasia and Individual Freedom (1993); John Hart Ely, The Wages of Crying Wolf: A Comment on *Roe v. Wade*, 82 Yale L.J. 920 (1973); Richard A. Epstein, Substantive Due Process By Any Other Name: The Abortion Cases, 1973 Sup. Ct. Rev. 159; Cass R. Sunstein, One Case at a Time: Judicial Minimalism on the Supreme Court 54, 114 (1999); Laurence H. Tribe, The Supreme Court, 1972 Term, Foreword: Toward a Model of Roles in the Due Process of Life and Law, 87 Harv. L. Rev. 1 (1973).

14. *Roe* sparked new controversy with the publication of empirical evidence suggesting that the legalization of abortion provides a "primary explanation" for large decreases in crime over the last decade. John J. Donahue III & Steven D. Levitt, The Impact of Legalized Abortion on Crime, 116 Q.J. Econ. 379, 414 (2001). The authors theorize that abortion prevented the birth of unwanted children who would have grown up to commit crimes.

### b. Anti-Abortion Laws: Historical and Philosophical Perspectives

### ■ KRISTIN LUKER, ABORTION AND THE POLITICS OF MOTHERHOOD
*20-29 (1984)*

In the second half of the nineteenth century abortion began to emerge as a social problem: newspapers began to run accounts of women who had died from "criminal abortions," although whether this fact reflects more abortions, more lethal abortions, or simply more awareness is not clear. Most prominently, physicians became involved, arguing that abortion was both morally wrong and medically dangerous.

The membership of the American Medical Association (AMA), founded in 1847 to upgrade and protect the interests of the profession, was deeply divided on many issues. But by 1859 it was able to pass a resolution condemning induced abortion and urging state legislatures to pass laws forbidding it; in 1860, Henry Miller, the president-elect of the association, devoted much of his presidential address to attacking abortion; and in 1864 the AMA established a prize to be awarded to the best anti-abortion book written for the lay public. Slowly, physicians responded to the AMA's call and began to lobby in state legislatures for laws forbidding abortion. . . .

Why should nineteenth-century physicians have become so involved with the question of abortion? The physicians themselves gave two related explanations for their activities, and these explanations have been taken at face value ever since. First, they argued, they were compelled to address the abortion question because American women were committing a moral crime based on ignorance about the proper value of embryonic life. According to these physicians, women sought abortions because the doctrine of quickening led them to believe that the embryo was not alive, and therefore aborting it was perfectly proper. Second, they argued, they were obliged to act in order to save women from their own ignorance because only physicians were in possession of new scientific evidence which demonstrated beyond a shadow of a doubt that the embryo was a child from conception onward. . . .

This stand had an important advantage for physicians. It meant that the American women who practiced abortion (and who were generally thought to be members of the "better classes") could be defined as *inadvertent* murderesses. . . . Thus, a physician could condemn the "sin" without the necessity of condemning the "sinner." . . .

When examined closely . . . neither part of the physicians' claim was, strictly speaking, true. Women (and the general public) knew that pregnancy was a *biologically* continuous process from beginning to end, and physicians were not in possession of remarkable new scientific discoveries to use to prove the case. . . . What the anti-abortion physicians achieved, therefore, was a subtle transformation of the grounds of the debate. . . .

[W]hy in the middle of the nineteenth century, did some physicians become anti-abortionists? James Mohr, in a pioneering work on this topic, argues that the proliferation of healers in the nineteenth century created a competition for status and clients. The "regular" physicians, who tended to be both wealthier and better educated than members of other medical sects, therefore sought to distinguish themselves both scientifically and socially from competing practitioners. . . . By taking an anti-abortion stand, regular physicians could lay claim to superior scientific knowledge, based on the latest research developments and theories (usually from abroad) to buttress their claim that pregnancy was continuous and that any intervention in it was immoral. At the same time, they could claim to be following the Hippocratic Oath, which contains a clause proscribing at least one form of abortion practice. The abortion issue thus gave them a way of demonstrating that they were both more scientifically knowledgeable and more morally rigorous than their competitors.

Mohr suggests that there were several more practical reasons why regular physicians should have opposed abortion. On the one hand, outlawing abortion would remove a lucrative source of income from competitors they called "quacks" and perhaps remove that temptation from the path of the "regulars" as well. In addition, the "regulars" were predominantly white, upper-income, and native-born; as such, they belonged to precisely the same group that was thought to harbor the primary users of abortion. As a result, they were likely to be concerned about the depopulation of their group in the face of mounting immigration (and the higher fertility of immigrants) and about "betrayal" by their own women (because abortion required less male control and approval than the other available forms of birth control). More broadly, Mohr argues that nineteenth-century physicians had a firm ideological belief that abortion was in fact murder. . . . The historian Carl Degler has made much the same argument. . . .

It is certainly true, as Mohr claims, that the mobilization of American physicians against abortion took place in the context of a profound dilemma within the medical profession, a dilemma produced by the lack of a traditional guild structure, the proliferation of competing medical sects and dissension within the ranks of the regulars themselves. Physicians wanted to upgrade their profession by obtaining licensing laws that would restrict medical practice to only the best and the best-trained among them.

As we know, regular physicians succeeded in their campaign for licensing laws. More than almost any other profession, medicine now rigorously exercises the right to control who shall enter the profession, how they shall practice, and how competitors will be treated; its nineteenth-century stand against abortion contributed substantially to this ultimate success. It is in the context of this drive of professionalization that the political activity of American physicians against abortion must be understood. When examined closely in this context, their actual behavior raises serious doubts about whether they had, as Mohr and Degler claim, an unparalleled commitment to the "sanctity of life" of the embryo. . . .

---

For additional historical accounts, see James C. Mohr, Abortion in America: The Origins and Evolution of National Policy, 1800-1900 (1978); Carroll Smith-Rosenberg, The Abortion Movement and the AMA, 1850-1880, in Carroll Smith-Rosenberg, Disorderly Conduct: Visions of Gender in Victorian America 217 (1985).

## ■ JUDITH JARVIS THOMSON, A DEFENSE OF ABORTION
*1 Phil. & Pub. Aff. 47-63 (1971)*

[Assuming we grant that the fetus is a person from the moment of conception, how,] precisely, are we supposed to get from there to the conclusion that abortion is morally impermissible? . . .

[L]et me ask you to imagine this. You wake up in the morning and find yourself back to back in bed with an unconscious violinist. A famous unconscious violinist. He has been found to have a fatal kidney ailment, and the Society of Music Lovers has canvassed all the available medical records and found that you alone have the right blood type to help. They have therefore kidnapped you, and last night the violinist's circulatory system was plugged into yours, so that your kidneys can be used to extract poisons from his blood as well as your own. The director of the hospital now tells you, "Look, we're sorry the Society of Music Lovers did this to you — we would never have permitted it if we had known. But still, they did it and the violinist now is plugged into you. To unplug you would be to kill him. But never mind, it's only for nine months. By then he will have recovered from his ailment, and can safely be unplugged from you." Is it morally incumbent on you to accede to this situation? No doubt it would be very nice of you if you did, a great kindness. But do you *have* to accede to it? . . .

In this case, of course, you were kidnapped; you didn't volunteer for the operation that plugged the violinist into your kidneys. Can those who oppose abortion on the ground I mentioned make an exception for a pregnancy due to rape? Certainly . . .

[I]t cannot seriously be thought to be murder if the mother performs an abortion on herself to save her life. It cannot seriously be said that she *must* refrain, that she *must* sit passively by and wait for her death. . . . If anything in the world is true, it is that you do not commit murder, you do not do what is impermissible, if you reach around to your back and unplug yourself from that violinist to save your life. . . .

. . . Where the mother's life is not at stake, the argument [based on the fetus's right to life] seems to have a much stronger pull[:] "Everyone has a right to life, so the unborn person has a right to life." And isn't the child's right to life weightier than anything other than the mother's own right to life, which she might put forward as ground for an abortion?

This argument treats the right to life as if it were unproblematic. It is not, and this seems to me to be precisely the source of the mistake.

For we should now, at long last, ask what it comes to, to have a right to life. In some views having a right to life includes having a right to be given at least the bare minimum one needs for continued life. But suppose that what in fact *is* the bare minimum a man needs for continued life is something he has no right at all to be given? [T]o return to the story I told earlier, the fact that for continued life that violinist needs the continued use of your kidneys does not establish that he has a right to be given the continued use of your kidneys. He certainly has no right against you that *you* should give him continued use of your kidneys. For nobody has any right to use your kidneys unless you give him such a right; and nobody has the right against you that you shall give him this right — if you do allow him to go on using your kidneys, this is a kindness on your part, and not something he can claim from you as his due. Nor has he any right against anybody else that *they* should give him continued use of your kidneys. Certainly he had no right against the Society of Music Lovers that they should plug him into you in the first place. And if you now start to unplug yourself, having learned that you will otherwise have to spend nine years in bed with him, there is nobody in the world who must try to prevent you, in order to see to it that he is given something he has a right to be given. . . .

The emendation which may be made at this point is this: the right to life consists not in the right not to be killed, but rather in the right not to be killed unjustly. . . .

But it might be argued that there are other ways one can have acquired a right to the use of another person's body than by having been invited to use it by that person. Suppose a woman voluntarily indulges in intercourse, knowing of the chance it will issue in pregnancy, and then she does become pregnant; is she not in part responsible for the presence, in fact the very existence, of the unborn person inside her?

[D]etails make a difference. If the room is stuffy, and I therefore open a window to air it, and a burglar climbs in, it would be absurd to say, "Ah, now he can stay, she's given him a right to the use of her house — for she is partially responsible for his presence there, having voluntarily done what enabled him to get in, in full knowledge that there are such things are burglars, and that burglars burgle." It would be still more absurd to say this if I had had bars installed outside my windows, precisely to prevent burglars from getting in, and a burglar got in only because of a defect in the bars. It remains equally absurd if we imagine it is not a burglar who climbs in, but an innocent person who blunders or falls in. Again, suppose it were like this: people-seeds drift about in the air like pollen, and if you open your windows, one may drift in and take root in your carpets or upholstery. You don't want children, so you fix up your windows with fine mesh screens, the very best you can buy. As can happen, however, and on very, very rare occasions does happen, one of the screens is defective. . . . Someone may argue that you are responsible for its rooting, that it does have a right to your house, because after all you *could* have lived out your life with bare floors and furniture, or with sealed windows and doors. But this won't do — for by the same token anyone can avoid a pregnancy due to rape by having a hysterectomy, or anyway by never leaving home without a (reliable!) army. . . .

[I]t is worth drawing attention to the fact that in no state in this country is any man compelled by law to be even a Minimally Decent Samaritan to any person. . . . By contrast, in most states in this country women are compelled by law to be not merely Minimally Decent Samaritans, but Good Samaritans to unborn persons inside them. This [at least shows] that there is a gross injustice in the existing state of the law.

---

See Donald H. Regan, Rewriting *Roe v. Wade*, 77 Mich. L. Rev. 1569 (1979) (amplifying Thomson's argument to implicate equal protection); Alec Walen, Consensual Sex Without Assuming the Risk of Carrying an Unwanted Fetus: Another Foundation for the Right to Abortion, 63 Brook. L. Rev. 1051 (1997) (building on and expanding Thomson's argument). But see Richard A. Posner, The Problems of Jurisprudence 349-352 (1990) (rejecting Thomson's analysis). For an analysis contending that Thomson's argument compels the state to subsidize abortions, see Eileen L. McDonagh, Breaking the Abortion Deadlock: From Choice to Consent (1996).

## ■ SIDNEY CALLAHAN, ABORTION AND THE SEXUAL AGENDA
*113 Commonweal 232, 232-236 (1986)*

. . . Pro-life feminists, like myself, argue on good feminist principles that women can never achieve the fulfillment of feminist goals in a society permissive toward abortion. . . . Feminist theorists of the pro-choice position now put forth the demand for unrestricted abortion rights as a *moral imperative* and insist upon women's right to complete reproductive freedom. They morally justify the present situation and current abortion practices. Thus it is all the more important that pro-life feminists articulate their different feminist perspectives. . . .

. . . The moral right to control one's own body does apply to cases of organ transplants, mastectomies, contraception, and sterilization; but it is not a conceptualization adequate for abortion. The abortion dilemma is caused by the fact that 266 days following a conception in one body, another body will emerge. One's own body no longer exists as a single unit but is engendering another organism's life. . . . Strained philosophical analogies fail to apply: having a baby is not like rescuing a drowning person, being hooked up to a famous violinist's artificial life-support system, donating organs for transplant — or anything else. . . . It does not matter (*The Silent Scream* notwithstanding) whether the fetus being killed is fully conscious or feels pain. . . . Pro-life feminists who defend the fetus empathetically identify with an immature state of growth passed through by themselves, their children, and everyone now alive.

It also seems a travesty of just procedures that a pregnant woman now, in effect, acts as sole judge of her own case, under the most stressful conditions. Yes, one can acknowledge that the pregnant woman will be subject to the potential burdens arising from a pregnancy, but it has never been thought right to have an interested party, especially the more powerful party, decide his or her own case when there may be a conflict of interest. If one considers the matter as a case of a powerful versus a powerless, silenced claimant, the pro-choice feminist argument can rightly be inverted; since hers is the body, hers the risk, and hers the greater burden, then how in fairness can a woman be the sole judge of the fetal right to life? . . .

As the most recent immigrants from non-personhood, feminists have traditionally fought for justice. . . . A woman, involuntarily pregnant, has a moral obligation to the now-existing dependent fetus whether she explicitly consented to its existence or not. . . . The woman's moral obligation arises both from her status as a human being embedded in the interdependent human community and her unique lifegiving female reproductive power. . . .

. . . Pitting women against their own offspring is not only morally offensive, it is psychologically and politically destructive. Women will never climb to equality and social empowerment over mounds of dead fetuses. [Women] stand to gain from the same constellation of attitudes and institutions that will also protect the fetus in the woman's womb — and they stand to lose from the cultural assumptions that support permissive abortion. . . . By pro-choice reasoning, a man who does not want to have a child, or whose contraceptive fails, can be exempted from the responsibilities of fatherhood and child support. . . .

For that matter, why should the state provide a system of day-care or child support, or require workplaces to accommodate women's maternity and the needs of childrearing? Permissive abortion, granted in the name of women's privacy and reproductive freedom, ratifies the view that pregnancies and children are a woman's private individual responsibility. . . . The larger community is relieved of moral responsibility. . . .

## B. THE LIMITS OF PRIVACY

### 1. Privacy versus Morality

### ■ BOWERS v. HARDWICK
*478 U.S. 186 (1986)*

Justice WHITE delivered the opinion of the Court.

In August 1982, respondent Hardwick (hereafter respondent) was charged with violating the Georgia statute criminalizing sodomy [defined to include oral or anal sex] by committing that act with another adult male in the bedroom of respondent's home. After a preliminary hearing, the District Attorney decided not to present the matter to the grand jury unless further evidence developed.

Respondent then brought suit in the Federal District Court, challenging the constitutionality of the statute insofar as it criminalized consensual sodomy.[2] He asserted that he was a practicing homosexual, that the Georgia sodomy statute, as administered by the defendants, placed him in imminent danger of arrest, and that the statute for several reasons violates the Federal Constitution. The District Court granted the defendants' motion to dismiss for failure to state a claim. [A divided panel of the Court of Appeals reversed.]

This case does not require a judgment on whether laws against sodomy between consenting adults in general, or between homosexuals in particular, are wise or desirable. It raises no question about the right or propriety of state legislative decisions to repeal their laws that criminalize homosexual sodomy, or of state-court decisions invalidating those laws on state constitutional grounds. The issue presented is whether the Federal Constitution confers a fundamental right upon homosexuals to engage in sodomy and hence invalidates the laws of the many States that still make such conduct illegal and have done so for a very long time. . . .

We first register our disagreement with the Court of Appeals and with respondent that the Court's prior cases have construed the Constitution to confer a right of privacy that extends to homosexual sodomy and for all intents and purposes have decided this case. The reach of this line of cases was sketched in Carey v. Population Services International, 431 U.S. 678, 685 (1977). Pierce v. Society of Sisters, 268 U.S. 510 (1925), and Meyer v. Nebraska, 262 U.S. 390 (1923), were described as dealing with child rearing and education; Prince v. Massachusetts, 321 U.S. 158 (1944), with family relationships; Skinner v. Oklahoma ex rel. Williamson, 316 U.S. 535 (1942), with procreation; Loving v. Virginia, 388 U.S. 1 (1967), with marriage; Griswold v. Connecticut, [381 U.S. 479 (1965)], and Eisenstadt v. Baird, [405 U.S. 438 (1972)], with contraception; and Roe v. Wade, 410 U.S. 113 (1973), with abortion. . . .

Accepting the decisions in these cases and the above description of them, we think it evident that none of the rights announced in those cases bears any resemblance to the claimed constitutional right of homosexuals to engage in acts of sodomy that is asserted in this case. No

---

2. John and Mary Doe were also plaintiffs in the action. They alleged that they wished to engage in [proscribed] sexual activity . . . in the privacy of their home. . . . The District Court held, however, that because they had neither sustained, nor were in immediate danger of sustaining, any direct injury from the enforcement of the statute, they did not have proper standing to maintain the action. The Court of Appeals affirmed . . . and the Does do not challenge that holding in this Court.

The only claim properly before the Court, therefore, is Hardwick's challenge to the Georgia statute as applied to consensual homosexual sodomy. We express no opinion on the constitutionality of the Georgia statute as applied to other acts of sodomy.

connection between family, marriage, or procreation on the one hand and homosexual activity on the other has been demonstrated, either by the Court of Appeals or by respondent. Moreover, any claim that these cases nevertheless stand for the proposition that any kind of private sexual conduct between consenting adults is constitutionally insulated from state proscription is unsupportable. . . .

Precedent aside, however, respondent would have us announce, as the Court of Appeals did, a fundamental right to engage in homosexual sodomy. This we are quite unwilling to do. It is true that despite the language of the Due Process Clauses of the Fifth and Fourteenth Amendments, which appears to focus only on the processes by which life, liberty, or property is taken, the cases are legion in which those Clauses have been interpreted to have substantive content, subsuming rights that to a great extent are immune from federal or state regulation or proscription. Among such cases are those recognizing rights that have little or no textual support in the constitutional language. *Meyer, Prince,* and *Pierce* fall in this category, as do the privacy cases from *Griswold* to *Carey.*

Striving to assure itself and the public that announcing rights not readily identifiable in the Constitution's text involves much more than the imposition of the Justices' own choice of values on the States and the Federal Government, the Court has sought to identify the nature of the rights qualifying for heightened judicial protection. In Palko v. Connecticut, 302 U.S. 319, 325, 326 (1937), it was said that this category includes those fundamental liberties that are "implicit in the concept of ordered liberty," such that "neither liberty nor justice would exist if [they] were sacrificed." A different description of fundamental liberties appeared in Moore v. East Cleveland, 431 U.S. 494, 503 (1977) (opinion of Powell, J.), where they are characterized as those liberties that are "deeply rooted in this Nation's history and tradition." Id., at 503 (Powell, J.). See also Griswold v. Connecticut, 381 U.S., at 506.

It is obvious to us that neither of these formulations would extend a fundamental right to homosexuals to engage in acts of consensual sodomy. Proscriptions against that conduct have ancient roots. Sodomy was a criminal offense at common law and was forbidden by the laws of the original 13 States when they ratified the Bill of Rights. In 1868, when the Fourteenth Amendment was ratified, all but 5 of the 37 States in the Union had criminal sodomy laws. In fact, until 1961, all 50 States outlawed sodomy, and today, 24 States and the District of Columbia continue to provide criminal penalties for sodomy performed in private and between consenting adults. Against this background, to claim that a right to engage in such conduct is "deeply rooted in this Nation's history and tradition" or "implicit in the concept of ordered liberty" is, at best, facetious.

Nor are we inclined to take a more expansive view of our authority to discover new fundamental rights imbedded in the Due Process Clause.

The Court is most vulnerable and comes nearest to illegitimacy when it deals with judge-made constitutional law having little or no cognizable roots in the language or design of the Constitution. . . .

Respondent, however, asserts that the result should be different where the homosexual conduct occurs in the privacy of the home. He relies on Stanley v. Georgia, 394 U.S. 557 (1969), where the Court held that the First Amendment prevents conviction for possessing and reading obscene material in the privacy of one's home: "If the First Amendment means anything, it means that a State has no business telling a man, sitting alone in his house, what books he may read or what films he may watch." Id., at 565.

*Stanley* did protect conduct that would not have been protected outside the home, and it partially prevented the enforcement of state obscenity laws; but the decision was firmly grounded in the First Amendment. The right pressed upon us here has no similar support in the text of the Constitution, and it does not qualify for recognition under the prevailing principles for construing the Fourteenth Amendment. Its limits are also difficult to discern. Plainly enough, otherwise illegal conduct is not always immunized whenever it occurs in the home. Victimless crimes, such as the possession and use of illegal drugs, do not escape the law where they are committed at home. *Stanley* itself recognized that its holding offered no protection for the possession in the home of drugs, firearms, or stolen goods. Id., at 568, n.11. And if respondent's submission is limited to the voluntary sexual conduct between consenting adults, it would be difficult, except by fiat, to limit the claimed right to homosexual conduct while leaving exposed to prosecution adultery, incest, and other sexual crimes even though they are committed in the home. We are unwilling to start down that road.

Even if the conduct at issue here is not a fundamental right, respondent asserts that there must be a rational basis for the law and that there is none in this case other than the presumed belief of a majority of the electorate in Georgia that homosexual sodomy is immoral and unacceptable. This is said to be an inadequate rationale to support the law. The law, however, is constantly based on notions of morality, and if all laws representing essentially moral choices are to be invalidated under the Due Process Clause, the courts will be very busy indeed. Even respondent makes no such claim, but insists that majority sentiments about the morality of homosexuality should be declared inadequate. We do not agree, and are unpersuaded that the sodomy laws of some 25 States should be invalidated on this basis. . . .

[In concurring opinions, Chief Justice Burger notes, *inter alia,* that condemnation of homosexual practices is firmly rooted in Judeo-Christian and ethical standards; Justice Powell suggests the Eighth Amendment ban on cruel and unusual punishment would raise serious constitutional questions about a prison sentence for consensual sodomy.]

Justice BLACKMUN, with whom Justice BRENNAN, Justice MARSHALL, and Justice STEVENS join, dissenting.

This case is no more about "a fundamental right to engage in homosexual sodomy," as the Court purports to declare, than Stanley v. Georgia, 394 U.S. 557 (1969), was about a fundamental right to watch obscene movies, or Katz v. United States, 389 U.S. 347 (1967), was about a fundamental right to place interstate bets from a telephone booth. Rather, this case is about "the most comprehensive of rights and the right most valued by civilized men," namely, "the right to be let alone." Olmstead v. United States, 277 U.S. 438, 478 (1928) (Brandeis, J., dissenting). . . .

. . . In construing the right to privacy, the Court has proceeded along two somewhat distinct, albeit complementary, lines. First, it has recognized a privacy interest with reference to certain decisions that are properly for the individual to make. Second, it has recognized a privacy interest with reference to certain places without regard for the particular activities in which the individuals who occupy them are engaged. The case before us implicates both the decisional and the spatial aspects of the right to privacy. . . .

Only the most willful blindness could obscure the fact that sexual intimacy is "a sensitive, key relationship of human existence, central to family life, community welfare, and the development of human personality," Paris Adult Theatre I v. Slaton, 413 U.S. 49, 63 (1973); see also Carey v. Population Services International, 431 U.S. 678, 685 (1977). The fact that individuals define themselves in a significant way through their intimate sexual relationships with others suggests, in a Nation as diverse as ours, that there may be many "right" ways of conducting those relationships, and that much of the richness of a relationship will come from the freedom an individual has to choose the form and nature of these intensely personal bonds. . . .

The behavior for which Hardwick faces prosecution occurred in his own home, a place to which the Fourth Amendment attaches special significance. The Court's treatment of this aspect of the case is symptomatic of its overall refusal to consider the broad principles that have informed our treatment of privacy in specific cases. Just as the right to privacy is more than the mere aggregation of a number of entitlements to engage in specific behavior, so too, protecting the physical integrity of the home is more than merely a means of protecting specific activities that often take place there. . . . Indeed, the right of an individual to conduct intimate relationships in the intimacy of his or her own home seems to me to be the heart of the Constitution's protection of privacy. . . .

The Court's failure to comprehend the magnitude of the liberty interests at stake in this case leads it to slight the question whether petitioner, on behalf of the State, has justified Georgia's infringement on these interests. . . . First, [n]othing in the record before the Court provides any justification for finding the activity forbidden by §16-6-2 to be physically dangerous, either to the persons engaged in it or to others.[4] . . .

The assertion that "traditional Judeo-Christian values proscribe" the conduct involved cannot provide an adequate justification for §16-6-2. That certain, but by no means all, religious groups condemn the behavior at issue gives the State no license to impose their judgments on the entire citizenry. The legitimacy of secular legislation depends instead on whether the State can advance some justification for its law beyond its conformity to religious doctrine. Thus, far from buttressing his case, petitioner's invocation of Leviticus, Romans, St. Thomas Aquinas, and sodomy's heretical status during the Middle Ages undermines his suggestion that §16-6-2 represents a legitimate use of secular coercive power. A State can no more punish private behavior because of religious intolerance than it can punish such behavior because of racial animus. . . .

This case involves no real interference with the rights of others, for the mere knowledge that other individuals do not adhere to one's value system cannot be a legally cognizable interest, let alone an interest that can justify invading the houses, hearts, and minds of citizens who choose to live their lives differently. . . .

## ■ MICHAEL HARDWICK, WHAT ARE YOU DOING IN MY BEDROOM?

*in Peter H. Irons, The Courage of Their Convictions: Sixteen Americans Who Fought Their Way to the Supreme Court 393-396 (1988)*

[T]his whole case started [when] I had been working for about a year, in a gay bar that was getting ready to open up a discotheque. I was there one night until seven o'clock in the morning, helping them put in insulation. When I left, I went up to the bar and they gave me a beer. I was kind of debating whether I wanted to leave, because I was pretty exhausted, or stay and finish the beer. I decided to leave, and I opened

---

4. Although I do not think it necessary to decide today issues that are not even remotely before us, it does seem to me that a court could find simple, analytically sound distinctions between certain private, consensual sexual conduct, on the one hand, and adultery and incest (the only two vaguely specific "sexual crimes" to which the majority points), on the other. [A] State might conclude that adultery is likely to injure third persons, in particular, spouses and children of persons who engage in extramarital affairs. With respect to incest, a court might well agree with respondent that the nature of familial relationships renders true consent to incestuous activity sufficiently problematical that a blanket prohibition of such activity is warranted. Notably, the Court makes no effort to explain why it has chosen to group private, consensual homosexual activity with adultery and incest rather than with private, consensual heterosexual activity by unmarried persons or, indeed, with oral or anal sex within marriage.

the door and threw the beer bottle into this trash can by the front door of the bar. I wasn't really in the mood for the beer.

Just as I did that I saw a cop drive by. I walked about a block, and he turned around and came back and asked me where the beer was. I told him I had thrown it in the trash can in front of the bar. He insisted I had thrown the beer bottle right as he pulled up. He made me get in the car and asked me what I was doing. I told him that I worked there, which immediately identified me as a homosexual, because he knew it was a homosexual bar. He was enjoying *his* position as opposed to *my* position.

After about twenty minutes of bickering he drove me back so I could show him where the beer bottle was. . . . I told him it was in the trash can and he said he couldn't see it from the car. I said fine, just give me a ticket for drinking in public. He was just busting my chops because he knew I was gay.

Anyway, the ticket had a court date on the top and a date in the center and they didn't coincide; they were one day apart. Tuesday was the court date, and the officer had written Wednesday on top of the ticket. So Tuesday, two hours after my court date, he was at my house with a warrant for my arrest. This was Officer Torick. . . . What I didn't realize, and didn't find out until later, was that he had personally processed a warrant for the first time in ten years. . . .

I had a friend come [several weeks] later who was from out of town, in Atlanta to apply for a government job. He waited for me to get off work. . . . That night at work, another friend of mine had gotten really drunk, and I took his car keys, put him in a cab, and sent him to my house, so he was passed out on the couch in the living room. He did not hear me and my friend come in. I retired with my friend. He had left the front door open, and Officer Torick came into my house about 8:30 in the morning. He had a warrant that had not been valid for three weeks and that he didn't bother to call in and check on. Officer Torick came in and woke up the guy who was passed out on the couch, who didn't know I was there and had a friend with me.

Officer Torick then came to my bedroom. The door was cracked, and the door opened up and I looked up and there was nobody there. I just blew it off as the wind and went back to what I was involved in, which was mutual oral sex. About thirty-five seconds went by and I heard another noise and I looked up, and this officer is standing in my bedroom. He identified himself when he realized I had seen him. He said, My name is Officer Torick. Michael Hardwick, you are under arrest. I said, For what? What are you doing in my bedroom? He said, I have a warrant for your arrest. I told him the warrant isn't any good. He said, It doesn't matter, because I was acting under good faith.

I asked Torick if he would leave the room so we could get dressed and he said, There's no reason for that, because I have already seen you in your most intimate aspect. He stood there and watched us get dressed, and then he brought us over to the substation. We waited in the car for about twenty-five minutes, handcuffed to the back floor. Then he brought us downtown; brought us in and made sure everyone in the holding cells and guards and people who were processing us knew [why we were there].

## Notes and Questions

1. Why did the Court conclude that the statute does not infringe the right to privacy? Is the reasoning of the majority or dissent more persuasive? In part, the majority relies on history and tradition in determining the scope of the privacy right. What are the limitations of this approach? See Sylvia A. Law, Homosexuality and the Social Meaning of Gender, 1988 Wis. L. Rev. 187, 229-230; Thomas B. Stoddard, *Bowers v. Hardwick:* Precedent by Personal Predilection, 54 U. Chi. L. Rev. 648 (1987). Cf. Richard D. Mohr, Gays/Justice: A Study of Ethics, Society and Law 95-98 (1988).

2. In contrast to *Hardwick's* reading of the federal Constitution, some state constitutions have been interpreted to protect certain homosexual activity. E.g., Powell v. State, 510 S.E.2d 18 (Ga. 1998) (state right to privacy invalidates Georgia sodomy statute unsuccessfully challenged in *Hardwick*). See Melanie D. Price, The Privacy Paradox: The Divergent Paths of the United States Supreme Court and State Courts on Issues of Sexuality, 33 Ind. L. Rev. 863, 885-889 (2000). See also Chapter IV, page 422.

3. Can you reconcile the holding with the notion of "spatial privacy" recognized in *Griswold?* Does *Hardwick* raise the possibility of enforcement by police in the bedroom (which *Griswold* condemned)? Omitted footnote 7 of Justice Blackmun's dissent observes that, if the Georgia law "is not invalid, then the police can invade the home to enforce it."

4. Can you reconcile *Hardwick* with Roe v. Wade? Which presents the easier case for recognition of the privacy right? How could Justice Powell vote with the majority on both? After retiring, Powell conceded that the *Hardwick* dissent was more consistent with *Roe.* See Anand Agneshwar, Ex-Justice Says He May Have Been Wrong; Powell on Sodomy, Nat'l. L.J., Nov. 5, 1990, at 3.

5. A married couple also sued in *Hardwick.* They alleged they were chilled from engaging in prohibited sexual activity by the statute and Hardwick's arrest. Their claim was dismissed for lack of standing. What impact does *Hardwick* have on the freedom of sexual expression for heterosexuals? See Richard A. Posner, Sex and Reason 345 (1992). What impact does it have for homosexuals' expression of affection falling short of "sodomy"? See David Cole & William N. Eskridge, From Hand-Holding

to Sodomy: First Amendment Protection of Homosexual (Expressive) Conduct, 29 Harv. C.R.-C.L. L. Rev. 319 (1994).

6. What role does morality play in *Hardwick*? What is the proper role of morality in constitutional adjudication pitting individual rights against decisions of the community? Consider John Stuart Mill's tenet that "the only purpose for which power can be rightfully exercised over any member of a civilised community, against his will, is to prevent harm to others." John Stuart Mill, On Liberty 13 (Gateway ed. 1955) (originally published in 1859). To what extent does Mill satisfactorily resolve the issue? See Anne B. Goldstein, History, Homosexuality, and Political Values: Searching for the Hidden Determinants of *Bowers v. Hardwick*, 97 Yale L.J. 1073 (1988); David A. J. Richards, Constitutional Legitimacy and Constitutional Privacy, 61 N.Y.U. L. Rev. 800 (1986). See also Barnes v. Glen Theatre, 501 U.S. 560, 569 (1991) (citing *Hardwick*'s reliance on morality to uphold ban on nude dancing); id. at 575 (Scalia, J., concurring). Does the Court satisfactorily distinguish morality from religion? See also Boy Scouts of Am. v. Dale, 530 U.S. 640, 651 (2000) (First Amendment protects expressive activity of private organization teaching that homosexual conduct is not "morally straight").

7. In its brief, Georgia claimed that the criminal acts spread communicable diseases. To what extent does the emergence of HIV/AIDS influence the outcome? Could halting the spread of AIDS serve as a compelling state interest to justify infringing a right to privacy that encompasses consensual homosexual activity? See Thomas R. Mendicino, Note, Characterization and Disease: Homosexuals and the Threat of AIDS, 66 N.C. L. Rev. 226 (1987). Could a law designed to protect health target only homosexual conduct?

8. *Epilogue.* Although Justice Powell publicly questioned his own *Hardwick* vote as early as 1990, additional evidence about the decision-making process in the case has continued to surface. Powell's vote to uphold the law, to avoid expanding due process rights, came after he had initially decided the Court should invalidate the law. The Justice's law clerks found the change particularly troublesome:

> Especially after Powell declared that he'd made a mistake in *Hardwick*, his long line of gay clerks was plagued by questions about whether one or more of them should have come out to him before his 1986 vote. Could they have made him better prepared to wrestle with *Hardwick*? Could they have helped him see [the] human toll of sodomy laws?
>
> Not surprisingly, Cabell Chinnis [who clerked during the *Hardwick* term] is the ex-clerk most bedeviled by unanswerable questions. "I wish I knew why he changed his vote because then maybe I would be able to say to myself, 'Cabell, anything else you could have done wouldn't have made a difference.'... It's the not knowing that really kills you," Chinnis said ... in 1998. What if he had invited Powell to lunch and had come out to him? What if he had hosted a dinner in which, one by one, gay Powell

clerks had risen and said, "Justice Powell, I am a homosexual. This is my partner. We've been together four years." . . . Other ex-clerks also wonder what would have happened if they'd told the grandfatherly Powell they were gay.

Joyce Murdoch & Deb Price, Courting Justice: Gay Men and Lesbians v. the Supreme Court 342 (2001). See also id. at 344 (reporting Michael Hardwick's death from AIDS at age 37 in 1991).

9. *Equal protection.* Could Hardwick have successfully challenged enforcement of the statute as unconstitutional discrimination against homosexuals? Does the Court's rejection of privacy-due process claims foreclose equal protection attacks on similar laws? See Janet E. Halley, The Politics of the Closet: Towards Equal Protection for Gay, Lesbian, and Bisexual Identity, 36 UCLA L. Rev. 915 (1989); Cass R. Sunstein, Sexual Orientation and the Constitution: A Note on the Relationship between Due Process and Equal Protection, 55 U. Chi. L. Rev. 1161 (1988). Can the Constitution prohibit discrimination against those with a particular sexual preference or orientation without prohibiting criminalization of conduct prompted by the preference or orientation?

In the wake of *Hardwick,* 9 states and approximately 100 municipalities enacted measures prohibiting discrimination based on sexual orientation. In response, Coloradans approved state constitutional amendment 2. It banned the enactment of laws protecting homosexual orientation, conduct, practices, or relationships. Romer v. Evans, 517 U.S. 620 (1996), held the amendment unconstitutional. The Supreme Court found two equal protection flaws: The amendment made it more difficult for one group of citizens than for all others to seek aid from the government. It also "rais[ed] the inevitable inference that the disadvantage imposed is born of animosity." Id. at 634. Justice Scalia's dissent cited *Hardwick* and reasoned that "[i]f it is constitutionally permissible . . . to make homosexual conduct criminal, surely it is constitutionally permissible . . . to enact other laws merely *disfavoring* homosexual conduct." Id. at 641. Is it? See William N. Eskridge, Jr., *Hardwick* and Historiography, 1999 U. Ill. L. Rev. 631. How does the animosity condemned by the *Romer* majority differ from the moral disapproval accepted by the *Hardwick* majority? See Barbara J. Flagg, "Animus" and Moral Disapproval: A Comment on *Romer v. Evans,* 82 Minn. L. Rev. 833 (1998).

10. One commentator discerns five different conceptions of homosexuality in *Hardwick:* (1) immoral, (2) criminally harmful, (3) illness, (4) identity, and (5) normal variation of human sexuality. Goldstein, supra, at 1079-1080. Should the outcome turn on whether homosexuality amounts to chosen conduct or a genetic predeposition?

In an omitted footnote, Justice Blackmun's dissent quotes Robinson v. California, 370 U.S. 660, 667 (1962), holding that the Eighth Amendment's bar on cruel and unusual punishment prohibits conviction for the status of narcotics addiction, an illness one can contract involuntarily. Blackmun goes on to note that mental health professionals no longer view homosexuality as a disease, although "neither is it simply a matter of deliberate personal election. Homosexual orientation may well form part of the very fiber of an individual's personality." Cf. Janet E. Halley, Sexual Orientation and the Politics of Biology: A Critique of the Argument from Immutability, 46 Stan. L. Rev. 503 (1994); Symposium, Queer Law 1999: Current Issues in Lesbian, Gay, Bisexual and Transgendered Law, 27 Fordham Urb. L.J. 279, 348-364 (1999) ("Is Sexual Orientation Immutable?: Presenting Scientific Evidence in Litigation to Gain Strict Scrutiny").

Should courts be concerned about the "cause" of homosexual behavior when they do not seek such explanations for heterosexual behavior? What implications does the "unstated norm" of heterosexuality have for legal protection of privacy? See Adrienne Rich, Compulsory Heterosexuality and Lesbian Existence, 5 Signs 631 (1980).

11. *Homosexuality, family life, and procreation.* The *Hardwick* majority writes that "[n]o connection between family, marriage, or procreation on the one hand and homosexual activity on the other has been demonstrated, either by the Court of Appeals or by respondent." 478 U.S. at 191. Would evidence of such a connection have produced a different outcome? See Alissa Friedman, The Necessity for State Recognition of Same-Sex Marriage: Constitutional Requirements and Evolving Notions of Family, 3 Berkeley Women's L.J. 134 (1987-1988); Jed Rubenfeld, The Right of Privacy, 102 Harv. L. Rev. 737 (1989). What evidence would respondent need to present? To what extent would changes in American culture and society require the Court to use a more inclusive understanding of "family" today? See Jay Michaelson, On Listening to the *Kulturekampf*, or, How America Overruled *Bowers v. Hardwick*, Even Though *Romer v. Evans* Didn't, 49 Duke L.J. 1559 (2000). See also Households Headed by Gays Rose in the 90's, Data Shows, N.Y. Times, Aug. 22, 2001, at A17 (600,000 in United States, derived from census figures).

Commenting on the relationship between homosexuality and procreation, Professor Sylvia Law writes:

> Why is it important to individuals whether they can obtain access to contraceptives or abortion services? If one considers this question in ordinary language, common sense terms, or in the terms of any intellectual discipline except constitutional law, two factors are key: the capability to engage in sexual relations, and the ability to control whether to bear or beget a child. . . .
>
> . . . People have a strong affirmative interest in sexual expression and relationships. Through sexual relationships, we experience deep connection with another, vulnerability, playfulness, surcease, connection with birth and with death, and transcendence. The power of sexual experience

is such that, in every culture, the basic units of human community, nurturing, acculturation, economic sharing, companionship and daily life are built around relationships of sexual expression and taboo. . . .

[The state] grievously injures gay and lesbian people when it punishes them for the core intimate and loving relationships of their lives. Those harms include the devastating effect of criminal condemnation, as well as the rippling material disabilities that the criminal condemnation justifies. Further, because sexual expression and control of one's body are so central to both material reality and sense of self, state condemnation matters, even when it has no concrete consequences. The *Hardwick* decision is perhaps most egregious in its utter lack of empathy with the humanity and pain of those subject to the condemnation of the sodomy laws. . . .

Historically, laws regulating procreation [such as those struck down in *Griswold* and *Roe*] were not designed primarily to promote physical health, or to protect the fetus, but rather to enforce a vision of sex and procreation as ineluctably connected, and to privilege male-dominated, sexually repressed, heterosexual families. In politics and culture, these traditional moral views continue to animate opposition to abortion and homosexuality.

Law, supra, at 225-229.

Sociological studies of homosexual couples reveal how their lives parallel those of their heterosexual counterparts. See, e.g., Philip Blumstein & Pepper Schwartz, American Couples: Money, Work, Sex 494-501 (1983) (story of Marnie and Janet who live together in a suburban neighborhood, share childrearing responsibilities, and strike an observer as "married and settled"). See also Mary Mendola, The Mendola Report: A New Look at Gay Couples (1980). How might such studies have figured in the majority's analysis? See Toni M. Massaro, Gay Rights, Thick and Thin, 49 Stan. L. Rev. 45, 104 (1996) ("narratives [about real human beings and their lives] may be the only means of undermining arguments that characterize homosexuality as more like masturbation than like intimacy in heterosexual marriages").

12. Some homosexual couples choose to keep their relationships and sexuality "in the closet." See, e.g., Blumstein & Schwartz, supra. How relevant should this secrecy be in determining whether the law recognizes such couples? Is "the closet" an aspect of privacy? Does *Hardwick* encourage seclusion by gays and lesbians?

On *Hardwick*, see generally Thomas C. Grey, *Bowers v. Hardwick* Diminished, 68 U. Colo. L. Rev. 373 (1997); Janet E. Halley, *Romer v. Hardwick*, 68 U. Colo. L. Rev. 429 (1997); Marc S. Spindelman, Reorienting *Bowers v. Hardwick*, 79 N.C. L. Rev. 359 (2001); Norman Vieira, *Hardwick* and the Right of Privacy, 55 U. Chi. L. Rev. 1181 (1988); Robin L. West, Taking Preferences Seriously, 64 Tul. L. Rev. 659 (1990); Law, Community and Moral Reasoning, 77 Cal. L. Rev. 475-594 (1989) (symposium). Legal regulation of nontraditional families is explored in Chapter IV.

## 2. Burdens on Privacy

■ **STENBERG v. CARHART**
*530 U.S. 914 (2000)*

Justice BREYER delivered the opinion of the Court.

We again consider the right to an abortion. We understand the controversial nature of the problem. Millions of Americans believe that life begins at conception and consequently that an abortion is akin to causing the death of an innocent child; they recoil at the thought of a law that would permit it. Other millions fear that a law that forbids abortion would condemn many American women to lives that lack dignity, depriving them of equal liberty and leading those with least resources to undergo illegal abortions with the attendant risks of death and suffering. Taking account of these virtually irreconcilable points of view, aware that constitutional law must govern a society whose different members sincerely hold directly opposing views, and considering the matter in light of the Constitution's guarantees of fundamental individual liberty, this Court, in the course of a generation, has determined and then redetermined that the Constitution offers basic protection to the woman's right to choose. Roe v. Wade, 410 U.S. 113 (1973); Planned Parenthood of Southeastern Pa. v. Casey, 505 U.S. 833 (1992). We shall not revisit those legal principles. Rather, we apply them to the circumstances of this case [, a constitutional challenge to a law criminalizing "partial birth abortion."]

. . . We shall set [forth the three controlling principles] in the language of the joint opinion in *Casey*. First, before "viability . . . the woman has a right to choose to terminate her pregnancy." 505 U.S. at 870 (joint opinion of O'Connor, Kennedy, and Souter, JJ.).

Second, "a law designed to further the State's interest in fetal life which imposes an undue burden on the woman's decision before fetal viability" is unconstitutional. 505 U.S. at 877. An "undue burden is . . . shorthand for the conclusion that a state regulation has the purpose or effect of placing a substantial obstacle in the path of a woman seeking an abortion of a nonviable fetus."

Third, " 'subsequent to viability, the State in promoting its interest in the potentiality of human life may, if it chooses, regulate, and even proscribe, abortion except where it is necessary, in appropriate medical judgment, for the preservation of the life or health of the mother.' " 505 U.S. at 879 (quoting Roe v. Wade, 410 U.S. at 164-165).

We apply these principles to a Nebraska law banning "partial birth abortion." The statute reads as follows:

No partial birth abortion shall be performed in this state, unless such procedure is necessary to save the life of the mother whose life is endangered by a physical disorder, physical illness, or physical injury, including a life-endangering physical condition caused by or arising from the pregnancy itself.

The statute defines "partial birth abortion" as:

an abortion procedure in which the person performing the abortion partially delivers vaginally a living unborn child before killing the unborn child and completing the delivery.

It further defines "partially delivers vaginally a living unborn child before killing the unborn child" to mean:

deliberately and intentionally delivering into the vagina a living unborn child, or a substantial portion thereof, for the purpose of performing a procedure that the person performing such procedure knows will kill the unborn child and does kill the unborn child.

The law classifies violation [as a felony carrying a prison term of up to 20 years, a fine of up to $ 25,000, and automatic revocation of a doctor's license to practice medicine in Nebraska].

## I

Dr. Leroy Carhart is a Nebraska physician who performs abortions in a clinical setting. He brought this lawsuit in Federal District Court seeking a declaration that the Nebraska statute violates the Federal Constitution, and asking for an injunction forbidding its enforcement. [After a trial, the District Court held the law unconstitutional, and the Court of Appeals affirmed.]

Because Nebraska law seeks to ban one method of aborting a pregnancy, we must describe and then discuss several different abortion procedures. Considering the fact that those procedures seek to terminate a potential human life, our discussion may seem clinically cold or callous to some, perhaps horrifying to others. There is no alternative way, however, to acquaint the reader with the technical distinctions among different abortion methods and related factual matters, upon which the outcome of this case depends. . . .

1. About 90% of all abortions performed in the United States take place during the first trimester of pregnancy, before 12 weeks of gestational age. During the first trimester, the predominant abortion method is "vacuum aspiration," which involves insertion of a vacuum tube (cannula) into the uterus to evacuate the contents. Such an abortion is typically performed on an outpatient basis under local anesthesia. Vacuum aspiration is considered particularly safe. . . .

2. Approximately 10% of all abortions are performed during the second trimester of pregnancy (12 to 24 weeks). [At this stage, the] most commonly used procedure is called "dilation and evacuation" (D&E). That procedure (together with a modified form of vacuum aspiration used in the early second trimester) accounts for about 95% of all abortions performed from 12 to 20 weeks of gestational age.

3. [Despite variations, D&E usually] involves (1) dilation of the cervix; (2) removal of at least some fetal tissue using nonvacuum instruments; and (3) (after the 15th week) the potential need for instrumental disarticulation or dismemberment of the fetus or the collapse of fetal parts to facilitate evacuation from the uterus.

4. When instrumental disarticulation incident to D&E is necessary, it typically occurs as the doctor pulls a portion of the fetus through the cervix into the birth canal. . . .

5. The D&E procedure carries certain risks [including perforation and organ damage from sharp instruments and bone fragments and infection from fetal tissue accidentally left behind.] Nonetheless studies show that the risks of mortality and complication that accompany the D&E procedure between the 12th and 20th weeks of gestation are significantly lower than those accompanying induced labor procedures (the next safest midsecond trimester procedure).

6. [Dr. Carhart and Dr. Stubblefield described a variation of the D&E procedure, "intact D&E," which involves removing the fetus from the uterus through the cervix "intact," *i.e.,* in one pass.] It is used after 16 weeks at the earliest, as vacuum aspiration becomes ineffective and the fetal skull becomes too large to pass through the cervix. [If the fetus presents head first, the doctor collapses the skull and then extracts the entire fetus through the cervix. If the fetus presents feet first, the doctor pulls the fetal body through the cervix, collapses the skull, and extracts the fetus through the cervix — a procedure called "dilation and extraction" (D&X).]

8. . . . Despite the technical differences we have just described, intact D&E and D&X are sufficiently similar for us to use the terms interchangeably.

9. Dr. Carhart testified he attempts to use the intact D&E procedure during weeks 16 to 20 because [it reduces various risks, including injury from bone fragments, uterine perforations from instruments, and infection. The District Court concluded] that "the evidence is both clear and convincing that Carhart's D&X procedure is superior to, and safer than, the . . . other abortion procedures used during the relevant gestational period in the 10 to 20 cases a year that present to Dr. Carhart."

10. The materials presented at trial referred to the potential benefits of the D&X procedure in circumstances involving nonviable fetuses, such as fetuses with abnormal fluid accumulation in the brain (hydrocephaly). Others have emphasized its potential for women with prior

uterine scars, or for women for whom induction of labor would be particularly dangerous.

11. There are no reliable data on the number of D&X abortions performed annually. Estimates have ranged between 640 and 5,000 per year.

## II

[The statute violates the Constitution, as interpreted in *Roe* and *Casey*,] for at least two independent reasons. First, the law lacks any exception " 'for the preservation of the . . . health of the mother.' " *Casey*, 505 U.S. at 879 (joint opinion of O'Connor, Kennedy, and Souter, JJ.). Second, it "imposes an undue burden on a woman's ability" to choose a D&E abortion, thereby unduly burdening the right to choose abortion itself. 505 U.S. at 874. . . .

### A . . .

The fact that Nebraska's law applies both pre- and postviability aggravates the [first] constitutional problem presented. The State's interest in regulating abortion previability is considerably weaker than postviability. Since the law requires a health exception in order to validate even a postviability abortion regulation, it at a minimum requires the same in respect to previability regulation.

The quoted standard also depends on the state regulations "promoting [the State's] interest in the potentiality of human life." The Nebraska law, of course, does not directly further an interest "in the potentiality of human life" by saving the fetus in question from destruction, as it regulates only a *method* of performing abortion. Nebraska describes its interests differently. It says the law " 'shows concern for the life of the unborn,' " "prevents cruelty to partially born children," and "preserves the integrity of the medical profession." But we cannot see how the interest-related differences could make any difference to the question at hand, namely, the application of the "health" requirement.

Consequently, the governing standard requires an exception "where it is necessary, in appropriate medical judgment for the preservation of the life or health of the mother," *Casey*, supra, at 879, for this Court has made clear that a State may promote but not endanger a woman's health when it regulates the methods of abortion. [The evidence below shows that D&X abortions are safer than other procedures in some cases.]

We find [the state's various] arguments insufficient to demonstrate that Nebraska's law needs no health exception. . . . The D&X is an infrequently used abortion procedure; but the health exception question is whether protecting women's health requires an exception for those infrequent occasions. [T]he State cannot prohibit a person from obtaining treatment simply by pointing out that most people do not need it. . . .

The word "necessary" in *Casey*'s phrase "necessary, in appropriate medical judgment, for the preservation of the life or health of the mother," . . . cannot refer to an absolute necessity or to absolute proof. Medical treatments and procedures are often considered appropriate (or inappropriate) in light of estimated comparative health risks (and health benefits) in particular cases. Neither can that phrase require unanimity of medical opinion. [T]he division of medical opinion about the matter at most means uncertainty, a factor that signals the presence of risk, not its absence. . . .

**B**

The Eighth Circuit found the Nebraska statute unconstitutional because, in *Casey*'s words, it has the "effect of placing a substantial obstacle in the path of a woman seeking an abortion of a nonviable fetus." 505 U.S. at 877. It thereby places an "undue burden" upon a woman's right to terminate her pregnancy before viability. Nebraska does not deny that the statute imposes an "undue burden" *if* it applies to the more commonly used D&E procedure as well as to D&X. . . .

. . . We do not understand how one could distinguish, using [the statute's language], between D&E (where a foot or arm is drawn through the cervix) and D&X (where the body up to the head is drawn through the cervix). Evidence before the trial court makes clear that D&E will often involve a physician pulling a "substantial portion" of a still living fetus, say, an arm or leg, into the vagina prior to the death of the fetus. Indeed D&E involves dismemberment that commonly occurs only when the fetus meets resistance that restricts the motion of the fetus. . . . And these events often do not occur until after a portion of a living fetus has been pulled into the vagina. . . .

The Attorney General also points to the Nebraska Legislature's debates, where the term "partial birth abortion" appeared frequently. But those debates hurt his argument more than they help it. . . . The legislature seems to have wanted to avoid more limiting language lest it become too easy to evade the statute's strictures. . . .

In sum, using this law some present prosecutors and future Attorneys General may choose to pursue physicians who use D&E procedures, the most commonly used method for performing previability second trimester abortions. All those who perform abortion procedures using that method must fear prosecution, conviction, and imprisonment. The result is an undue burden upon a woman's right to make an abortion decision. . . .

Justice GINSBURG, with whom Justice STEVENS joins, concurring.

I write separately only to stress that amidst all the emotional uproar caused by an abortion case, we should not lose sight of the character of Nebraska's "partial birth abortion" law. As the Court observes, this law does not save any fetus from destruction, for it targets only "a *method* of performing abortion." . . . Seventh Circuit Chief Judge Posner correspondingly observed, regarding similar bans in Wisconsin and Illinois, that the law . . . prohibits the procedure because the State legislators seek to chip away at the private choice shielded by Roe v. Wade, even as modified by *Casey*. [Hope Clinic v. Ryan, 195 F.3d 857, 880-882 (7th Cir. 1999) (dissenting opinion).] Again as stated by Chief Judge Posner, "if a statute burdens constitutional rights and all that can be said on its behalf is that it is the vehicle that legislators have chosen for expressing their hostility to those rights, the burden is undue."

Justice SCALIA, dissenting.

I am optimistic enough to believe that, one day, Stenberg v. Carhart will be assigned its rightful place in the history of this Court's jurisprudence beside *Korematsu* and *Dred Scott*. The method of killing a human child — one cannot even accurately say an entirely unborn human child — proscribed by this statute is so horrible that the most clinical description of it evokes a shudder of revulsion. And the Court must know (as most state legislatures banning this procedure have concluded) that demanding a "health exception" . . . is to give live-birth abortion free rein. . . .

In my dissent in *Casey*, I wrote that the "undue burden" test made law by the joint opinion created a standard that was "as doubtful in application as it is unprincipled in origin," *Casey*, 505 U.S. at 985; "hopelessly unworkable in practice," 505 U.S. at 986; "ultimately standardless," 505 U.S. at 987. Today's decision is the proof. As long as we are debating this issue of necessity for a health-of-the-mother exception on the basis of *Casey*, it is really quite impossible for us dissenters to contend that the majority is *wrong* on the law — any more than it could be said that one is *wrong in law* to support or oppose the death penalty, or to support or oppose mandatory minimum sentences. The most that we can honestly say is that we disagree with the majority on their policy-judgment-couched-as-law. And those who believe that a 5-to-4 vote on a policy matter by unelected lawyers should not overcome the judgment of 30 state legislatures have a problem, not with the *application* of *Casey*, but with its *existence*. *Casey* must be overruled. . . .

Justice KENNEDY, with whom The Chief Justice joins, dissenting. . . .

The Court's failure to accord any weight to Nebraska's interest in prohibiting partial-birth abortion is erroneous and undermines its discussion and holding. . . . The [medical terminology of the majority shows that it] views the procedures from the perspective of the abortionist, rather than from the perspective of a society shocked when confronted with a new method of ending human life. . . .

*Casey* is premised on the States having an important constitutional role in defining their interests in the abortion debate. . . . States may take sides in the abortion debate and come down on the side of life, even life in the unborn:

> Even in the earliest stages of pregnancy, the State may enact rules and regulations designed to encourage [a woman] to know that there are philosophic and social arguments of great weight that can be brought to bear in favor of continuing the pregnancy to full term and that there are procedures and institutions to allow adoption of unwanted children as well as a certain degree of state assistance if the mother chooses to raise the child herself. [*Casey,*] 505 U.S. at 872 (joint opinion of O'Connor, Kennedy, and Souter, JJ.). . . .

Nebraska was entitled to find the existence of a consequential moral difference between [abortion procedures.] The D&X differs from the D&E because in the D&X the fetus is "killed *outside* of the womb" where the fetus has "an autonomy which separates it from the right of the woman to choose treatments for her own body." Witnesses to the procedure relate that the fingers and feet of the fetus are moving prior to the piercing of the skull; when the scissors are inserted in the back of the head, the fetus' body, wholly outside the woman's body and alive, reacts as though startled and goes limp. D&X's stronger resemblance to infanticide means Nebraska could conclude the procedure presents a greater risk of disrespect for life and a consequent greater risk to the profession and society, which depend for their sustenance upon reciprocal recognition of dignity and respect. The Court is without authority to second-guess this conclusion [so long as the state does not] impose an undue burden on the woman's right. . . .

In deferring to the physician's judgment [in requiring a health exception], the Court turns back to cases decided in the wake of *Roe*, cases which gave a physician's treatment decisions controlling weight. . . . Rather than exalting the right of a physician to practice medicine with unfettered discretion, *Casey* recognized: "Whatever constitutional status the doctor-patient relation may have as a general matter, in the present context it is derivative of the woman's position." 505 U.S. at 884 (joint opinion of O'Connor, Kennedy, and Souter, JJ.). . . .

Justice O'CONNOR [in an omitted concurring opinion] assures the people of Nebraska they are free to redraft the law to include an exception permitting the D&X to be performed when "the procedure, in appropriate medical judgment, is necessary to preserve the health of the mother." The assurance is meaningless. . . . A ban which depends on the "appropriate medical judgment" of Dr. Carhart is no ban at all. . . . This, of course, is the vice of a health exception resting in the physician's discretion. . . .

[Omitted are the separate concurring opinions of Justices Stevens and O'Connor and the separate dissenting opinions of Chief Justice Rehnquist and Justice Thomas.]

## Notes and Questions

1. To what extent does *Carhart* show that the Supreme Court's abortion jurisprudence has followed the landmark ruling in *Roe*, 27 years earlier? To what extent does it reveal a departure from *Roe*? Does abortion remain a "fundamental right"? Does it continue to rest on the right of privacy? See Linda C. McClain, The Poverty of Privacy?, 3 Colum. J. Gender & L. 119 (1992). How does the undue burden test, used by a majority in *Carhart*, differ from *Roe*'s strict scrutiny? Does the undue burden test reach a better accommodation of conflicting individual and state interests than strict scrutiny? See Michael C. Dorf, Incidental Burdens on Fundamental Rights, 109 Harv. L. Rev. 1175, 1219-1232 (1996); Kathleen M. Sullivan, The Supreme Court 1991 Term, Foreword: The Justices of Rules and Standards, 106 Harv. L. Rev. 22, 32-34 (1992). Why has the Court retained the controversial point of viability?

2. *The standard of review.* Carhart relies on Planned Parenthood of Southeastern Pennsylvania v. Casey, 505 U.S. 833 (1992), a challenge to several provisions of Pennsylvania's Abortion Control Act. The sharply divided Court could not agree on the governing standard of review. The "joint opinion" in *Casey* (presented by Justices O'Connor, Kennedy, and Souter) embraced *Roe*'s protection for abortion freedom but rejected *Roe*'s trimester framework, announcing the *undue burden standard* in place of *Roe*'s strict scrutiny. Under this approach, these Justices voted to uphold several provisions of Pennsylvania law, including the requirement that at least 24 hours before the abortion the physician must provide the woman detailed information about the procedure, its risks, and its alternatives as well as about the "probable gestational age of the unborn child" and the availability of printed materials on child support, adoption, and other services.

Four Justices (Chief Justice Rehnquist and Justices White, Scalia, and Thomas), who would have overruled *Roe* altogether, voted with the joint opinion authors to uphold these statutory sections under the *rational basis standard*. Two others (Justices Blackmun and Stevens), following *Roe*, would have applied *strict scrutiny*, which Justice Blackmun said would invalidate all the challenged provisions.

Although the authors of the joint opinion invoked stare decisis to proclaim that "[l]iberty finds no refuge in a jurisprudence of doubt," 505 U.S. at 844, Justice Scalia's acerbic critique of the undue burden standard replied that "[r]eason finds no refuge in this jurisprudence of confusion." Id. at 993 (Scalia, J., concurring in the judgment in part and dissenting in part). See Jane Maslow Cohen, A Jurisprudence of Doubt: Deliberative Autonomy and Abortion, 3 Colum. J. Gender & L. 175 (1992).

How does *Carhart* resolve the uncertainty about the standard of review applicable to abortion laws? In *Carhart* why does Justice Kennedy, one of the joint opinion authors in *Casey*, refuse to vote with the other two, Justices O'Connor and Souter?

3. How has the Court's understanding of reproductive autonomy evolved since *Roe*? *Roe*'s emphasis on the physician's role gave way in later cases to more explicit recognition of the woman's freedom. To what extent does *Carhart* return to the focus on the physician? Justice Kennedy accuses the majority of using "the perspective of the abortionist." Whose perspective should the Court use in analyzing abortion restrictions? Other restrictions on private family matters? To what extent does the required health exception give the physician unlimited authority? See, e.g., Gail Glidewell, Note, "Partial Birth" Abortion and the Health Exception: Protecting Maternal Health or Risking Abortion on Demand?, 28 Fordham Urb. L.J. 1089 (2001).

4. *The road to* Casey *and* Carhart. After Roe v. Wade and Doe v. Bolton invalidated then-existing abortion laws, state legislatures sought to fill the gap. These "second-generation challenges" tested the limits of the Court's holdings:

a. *Abortion funding.* In 1977 the Court decided three cases permitting states to refuse Medicaid coverage for nontherapeutic abortions. Beal v. Doe, 432 U.S. 438 (1977); Maher v. Roe, 432 U.S. 464 (1977); Poelker v. Doe, 432 U.S. 519 (1977). Although the government subsidized continued pregnancy and childbirth but not abortion for the indigent, the majority in *Maher* found no "unduly burdensome interference" with the abortion decision, distinguishing the "obstacle" invalidated in *Roe*. The Court treated the refusal to fund abortion as state inaction calling for the rational basis test rather than the strict scrutiny applied in *Roe*. State encouragement of childbirth over abortion, a "value judgment," satisfied this less demanding standard of review.[4]

The Court used a similar analysis to reject challenges to governmental refusals to fund abortions necessary to preserve the woman's health. In Harris v. McRae, 448 U.S. 297 (1980), the Court held that

[4]. Some challenges brought under state constitutions yielded different results. For example, in Committee to Defend Reproductive Rights v. Myers, 625 P.2d 779 (Cal. 1981), the California Supreme Court held that restrictions on public funding of elective abortions violate the state constitution's explicit privacy guarantee.

*Roe*'s protection of the right to abortion does not confer an entitlement to funds to realize that right. See also Webster v. Reproductive Health Servs., 492 U.S. 490, 507-513 (1989). How meaningful is the right to abortion without the means to effectuate that right? Does the holding in *McRae* conflict with the importance ascribed to maternal health in *Roe* and *Carhart*? For a poor woman, is the state's offer of subsidized medical care for childbirth accompanied by its refusal to pay for an abortion an "undue burden"?

See generally Susan Frelich Appleton, Beyond the Limits of Reproductive Choice: The Contributions of the Abortion-Funding Cases to Fundamental-Rights Analysis and to the Welfare-Rights Thesis, 81 Colum. L. Rev. 721 (1981); Michael J. Perry, Why the Supreme Court Was Plainly Wrong in the Hyde Amendment Case: A Brief Comment on *Harris v. McRae*, 32 Stan. L. Rev. 1113 (1980); Laurence H. Tribe, The Abortion Funding Conundrum: Inalienable Rights, Affirmative Duties, and the Dilemma of Dependence, 99 Harv. L. Rev. 330 (1985). See also David Robert Baron, The Racially Disparate Impact of Restrictions on Public-Funding of Abortion: An Analysis of Current Equal Protection Doctrine, 13 B.C. Third World L.J. 1 (1993).

b. *The undue burden standard.* Justice O'Connor expressed dissatisfaction with *Roe* long before she co-authored the joint opinion in *Casey*. In her dissent in Akron v. Akron Center for Reproductive Health, Inc., 462 U.S. 416, 452-475 (1983), she repudiated the trimester framework. There, she also announced a preference for strict scrutiny review only for "unduly burdensome" abortion restrictions, id. at 461, such as bans or third-party consent, asserting that the state has compelling interests in maternal health and potential life throughout pregnancy. See also Thornburgh v. American College of Obstetricians & Gynecologists, 476 U.S. 747, 814-833 (1986) (O'Connor, J., dissenting). Later, however, she simply labeled the trimester framework "problematic," Webster v. Reproductive Health Servs., 492 U.S. 490, 529 (1989) (O'Connor, J., concurring).

Is the undue burden standard that *Carhart* takes from *Casey* the same test used in the abortion-funding cases? In Justice O'Connor's earlier opinions? Given her previous position, why in *Casey* did Justice O'Connor adopt viability as the "compelling point"? See David Johnston, Marshall Papers Reveal Court Behind the Scenes, N.Y. Times, May 24, 1993, at A10 (reporting that first female Justice struggled with early abortion cases to the dismay of her colleagues; her last-minute vote in *Webster* prevented the overruling of *Roe*).

*Casey*'s joint opinion expressly permits under the undue burden standard some measures "designed to persuade [the woman] to choose childbirth over abortion." 505 U.S. at 878. What measures does this language allow states to enact? Can you name other protected rights whose exercise the states can try to discourage, with the Supreme Court's blessing?

c. *Facial challenges under the undue burden standard.* *Casey* triggered a division of authority about what challengers must show to meet the undue burden test. Must they satisfy the requirement of United States v. Salerno, 481 U.S. 739 (1987), showing no set of facts under which the statute can operate constitutionally? E.g., Barnes v. Moore, 970 F.2d 12 (5th Cir.), *cert. denied,* 506 U.S. 1021 (1992). Or merely a "substantial obstacle" in some fraction of the cases to which the law applies? E.g., Fargo Women's Health Org. v. Schafer, 507 U.S. 1013, 1013-1014 (1993) (O'Connor, J., concurring in denial of application for stay and injunction). See generally Ruth Burdick, Note, The *Casey* Undue Burden Standard: Problems Predicted and Encountered, and the Split Over the *Salerno* Test, 23 Hastings Const. L.Q. 825 (1996); Kevin Martin, Note, Stranger in a Strange Land: The Use of Overbreadth in Abortion Jurisprudence, 99 Colum. L. Rev. 173 (1999). How does *Carhart* answer these questions, given the rarity of the D&X procedure? In his dissent in *Carhart,* Justice Thomas writes that, under *Casey*'s undue burden standard, "Courts may not invalidate on its face a state statute regulating abortion 'based on a worst-case analysis that may never occur.' " 530 U.S. at 1019. What are the consequences of each view for other family privacy cases? See generally Dorf, supra, 109 Harv. L. Rev. at 1240-1243. For example, how would the Justices on the Court today have decided *Roe*'s companion case, Doe v. Bolton, 410 U.S. 179 (1973), challenging requirements of hospitalization, accreditation, approval by hospital committee, two-physician concurrence, and residency? See supra page 39.

d. *Informed consent.* Soon after *Roe,* the Court upheld state regulations mandating that the physician obtain the patient's prior written consent, regardless of the stage of pregnancy. Planned Parenthood v. Danforth, 428 U.S. 52 (1976). When states mandated a detailed list of abortion warnings, however, the Court invalidated these measures because of both their interference with the doctor-patient relationship and their underlying anti-abortion motivation. City of Akron v. Akron Ctr. for Reprod. Health, 462 U.S. 416, 442-449 (1983); Thornburgh v. American College of Obstetricians & Gynecologists, 476 U.S. 747, 759-765 (1986). Why did *Casey* change this result, allowing mandated pre-abortion information and waiting periods?

What is the appropriate role of the state in the physician-patient relationship? Beyond providing a forum for malpractice suits, how far can a state go to insure the patient's receipt of information? Does the right to privacy provide an answer? See Susan Frelich Appleton, Doctors, Patients and the Constitution: A Theoretical Analysis of the Physician's Role in "Private" Reproductive Decisions, 63 Wash. U. L.Q. 183, 219-235 (1985). Are detailed informed consent requirements that apply only to abortion paternalistic? Do they discriminate on the basis of sex? Do states enacting such requirements treat abortion patients as "inadvertent murderesses"? Recall Luker, supra, page 45.

Issues of informed consent and abortion funding coalesced in Rust v. Sullivan, 500 U.S. 173 (1991), in which the Court upheld regulations disallowing physicians in federally funded clinics from discussing abortion, despite the patient's request for information, the physician's judgment that patient should consider abortion, the health risks of pregnancy, or state malpractice laws requiring disclosure. To what extent does a physician's state-compelled silence on abortion create an "undue burden"?

e. *Politics and the changing Court.* To what extent is the road from *Roe* to *Casey* and then to *Carhart* best understood as a reflection of changes in the Supreme Court's composition, in an era when presidential candidates often make explicit campaign promises about how their judicial nominees will address abortion cases? Where should matters of "family values" and morality be decided: in the home, the legislature, or the courts? Or do such labels beg the question? Cf. Ruth Bader Ginsburg, Speaking in a Judicial Voice, 67 N.Y.U. L. Rev. 1185, 1208 (1992) (*Roe* halted political reform process that *Casey* might revitalize). Note Justice Ginsburg's concurrence in *Carhart,* alleging that the Nebraska statute was enacted "to chip away at the private choice shielded by Roe v. Wade."

5. *Morality.* In Bowers v. Hardwick (page 50), the majority determined that, with no fundamental right at stake, the state's interest in morality provided a rational basis for Georgia's sodomy law. Can morality justify infringement of a protected right, like abortion or "family privacy," when a more demanding standard of review (strict scrutiny or the undue burden test) applies? See, e.g., John A. Robertson, Children of Choice: Freedom and the New Reproductive Technologies 58 (1994). Compare Justice Kennedy's opinion with the majority's. Would Justice Kennedy's approach require overturning *Roe* altogether — on the ground that some state legislatures will find all abortions immoral? See also Hill v. Colorado, 530 U.S. 703, 791 (2000) (Kennedy, J., dissenting) (majority's rejection of First Amendment challenge to restrictions on protests "strikes at the heart of the reasoned, careful balance [in the *Casey* joint opinion, which recognized] that in defined instances the woman's decision whether to abort her child was in its essence a moral one, a choice the State could not dictate"). Or have Justice Kennedy and the other *Carhart* dissenters persuasively distinguished D&X from other abortions? See Akhil Reed Amar, The Supreme Court, 1999 Term, Foreword: The Document and the Doctrine, 114 Harv. L. Rev. 26, 110 (2000) ("Even if the moral nothingness of the fetus were obvious to most right-thinking folk when the fetus is a near-microscopic clump of cells, the issue in *Stenberg* is very different — late second-trimester abortions of recognizable humans, with hands, organs, dimensions, senses, brains.").

6. The abortion-funding cases dramatize that access to abortion is a component of abortion freedom. Problems of access appear to be

increasing.[5] First, violence dissuades both patients and health care providers.[6] Second, medical schools fail to provide training in abortion procedures. Studies reveal a continuing trend of decreased training. A study of obstetrics-gynecology programs nationwide revealed that only 12 percent of such residencies required training in first trimester abortion techniques.[7] Third, physician-abortion rights activists, many of whom were motivated by concern for victims of illegal abortion, now are approaching retirement age. Has *Casey's* "green light" for increased regulation had an impact? The four years following *Casey* saw a significant decline in the number of abortion providers (a decrease of about 85 per year) compared with the four years before *Casey* (about 51 per year).[8] What other pressures do abortion providers experience, apart from violence? After the Supreme Court ruling, Dr. Carhart faced loss of his clinic and his position at the University of Nebraska as the result of efforts by abortion opponents, including the governor and some state legislators.[9]

Courts and legislators address the problem of clinic violence through a variety of mechanisms. See, e.g., Hill v. Colorado, 530 U.S. 703 (2000) (100-foot buffer zone); Madsen v. Women's Health Ctr., 512 U.S. 753 (1994) (injunction); NOW, Inc. v. Scheidler, 510 U.S. 249 (1994) (damage claims under RICO); Schenk v. Pro-Choice Network, 519 U.S. 357 (1997) (injunctions). But cf. Bray v. Alexandria Women's Health Clinic, 506 U.S. 263 (1993) (Ku Klux Klan Act fails to provide federal cause of action). In addition, the Freedom of Access to Clinic Entrances Act, 18 U.S.C. §248 (1994), establishes penalties and civil remedies for the use of force, threatened force, or physical obstruction against service providers.

[5]. The extent of this problem is reflected in the decrease in the abortion rate. Approximately 1,529,000 abortions were performed in 1992, representing the lowest number since 1979. Carole Joffe, Doctors of Conscience: The Struggle to Provide Abortion Before and After *Roe v. Wade* 212 n.3 (1995) (citing Stanley Henshaw & Jennifer Van Vort, Abortion Services in the United States, 1991 and 1992, 26 Fam. Planning Persp. 100 (1994)).

[6]. Many health care providers stopped offering abortion services in response to clinic violence. Currently, the majority of American counties and hospitals do not have abortion facilities or abortion services. "Some 84 percent of all U.S. counties are without abortion facilities. The number of U.S. hospitals where abortions are performed decreased by 18 percent between 1988 and 1992, and less than one-third of the nation's hospitals with the capability to perform abortions (defined as hospitals that offer obstetrical services) do so." Joffe, supra note [5], at 3.

[7]. Id. at 3-4. Joffe argues that clinic violence, by itself, is not an adequate explanation for the decline in abortion rates. She contends that the medical community "bears chief responsibility for the present marginalization of abortion provision." Id. at 6.

[8]. See Stanley K. Henshaw, Abortion Incidence and Services in the United States, 1995-1996, 30 Fam. Plan. Persp. 263, 267-268 (1998).

[9]. See Pam Belluck, After Abortion Victory, Doctor's Troubles Persist, N.Y. Times, Nov. 7, 2000, at A18; Abortion Provider Fights University Dismissal, N.Y. Times, Mar. 13, 2001, at A13.

What do such data reveal about the limits of the law? About the application of the undue burden test?

7. To what extent does use of the undue burden test signal not just a retreat from Roe v. Wade, but also a retreat from *Griswold*? What consequences follow for the use of modern methods of birth control? For example, the IUD prevents implantation of fertilized ova, as does the morning-after pill or "emergency contraception" (ordinary birth control pills taken in appropriate doses within 72 hours of intercourse).

8. What does the undue burden test mean for modern medical advances? Consider RU-486 or mifepristone, the "abortion pill" developed by French scientists for terminations of early pregnancies and approved in 2000 by the FDA as safe and effective. Anti-abortion activists long had prevented the introduction of RU-486 in the United States by threats to boycott pharmaceutical firms attempting to market the drug. See Leonard A. Cole, The End of the Abortion Debate, 138 U. Pa. L. Rev. 217, 220 (1989). Under *Carhart*, can the government ban so-called medical abortions (abortions accomplished through medication, like RU-486) so long as surgical abortions remain available? Must there be a health exception? What must states show to justify applying to medical abortions their restrictions on surgical abortions (e.g., clinic regulations, specified procedures for disposal of fetal remains, and reporting requirements)?

What difference does the availability of an abortion pill make? By making access to abortion more "private," might it eliminate the "public" problems of clinic violence? See, e.g., Lawrence Lader, A Private Matter: RU 486 and the Abortion Crisis (1995); David J. Garrow, Abortion Before and After *Roe v. Wade:* An Historical Perspective, 62 Alb. L. Rev. 833, 852 (1999). Does the answer depend upon how states regulate use of RU-486?

9. Before *Roe*, abortion restrictions primarily affected poor women because women with means could travel to more permissive jurisdictions. See Sherri Finkbine, The Lesser of Two Evils, in The Case for Legalized Abortion Now 15 (Alan F. Guttmacher ed., 1967) (woman went to Sweden to terminate a pregnancy following use of Thalidomide). After *Roe*, those seeking postviability abortions traveled to Colorado and Kansas, which permit them in some conditions. See Gina Kolata, In Late Abortions, Decisions Are Painful and Options Few, N.Y. Times, Jan. 5, 1992, at A1. This pattern exemplifies a common phenomenon in family law: crossing state lines to find a more hospitable legal regime. Will the undue burden test exacerbate this phenomenon by providing increased opportunities for state restrictions (for example, waiting periods)? Cf. Saenz v. Roe, 526 U.S. 489 (1999) (reviewing aspects of constitutional right to travel, including protection of new residents from discrimination in provision of services). To what extent do such consequences

provide support for federal legislation? See generally Seth F. Kreimer, The Law of Choice and Choice of Law: Abortion, the Right to Travel, and Extraterritorial Regulation in American Federalism, 67 N.Y.U. L. Rev. 451 (1992).

10. Twice Congress passed federal bans on "partial birth abortions" that President Clinton vetoed. See, e.g., H.R. Doc. 105-158, 143 Conf. Rec. H8891 (daily ed. Oct. 21, 1997). President George W. Bush has said he would sign such legislation. See Robin Toner, The 2000 Campaign: Abortion; From Social Security to Environment, the Candidates' Positions, N.Y. Times, Nov. 5, 2000, §1, at 44. On what basis does Congress have the authority to enact such legislation? Is abortion interstate commerce? See, e.g., United States v. Dinwiddie, 76 F.3d 913, 919-920 (8th Cir.) (upholding Freedom of Access to Clinics Entrances Act against challenge to Congress's authority because abortion patients travel "in interstate commerce"), cert. denied, 519 U.S. 1043 (1996).

11. *Federalism in family law.* The prospect of federal abortion legislation raises questions of federalism. Traditionally, the "whole subject of the domestic relations of husband and wife, parent and child, belong[ed] to the laws of the States and not to the laws of the United States." In re Burrus, 136 U.S. 586, 593-594 (1890). State control of family law issues was so exclusive that even diversity of citizenship did not give federal courts authority to hear domestic relations cases — a principle known as the "domestic-relations exception" to federal diversity jurisdiction. See Chapter V, section G3.

*Griswold* changed the traditional approach, signaling that the Constitution limits the states' authority over family law. Also, today the Supreme Court narrowly construes the domestic-relations exception to federal diversity jurisdiction, confining it to divorce, alimony, and custody questions. See Ankenbrandt v. Richards, 504 U.S. 689, 703-704 (1992) (exception inapplicable to tort action, so Missouri mother can sue Louisiana father in federal court on behalf of daughters for damages for alleged abuse).

In recent years, Congress repeatedly has invoked — not always with success — the Commerce Clause and the Fourteenth Amendment to legislate on many family law subjects. E.g., Violence Against Women Act of 1994, 42 U.S.C. §13981 (1994). But see United States v. Morrison, 529 U.S. 598 (2000) (§13981 exceeds Congress's power). Congress has also conditioned the states' use of federal funds on compliance with federal requirements for laws governing the family. E.g., Personal Responsibility and Work Opportunity Reconciliation Act of 1996, Pub. L. 104-193, 110 Stat. 2105 (1996) (codified in scattered sections of, inter alia, 42 U.S.C.).

Should family law reflect national policy or should it vary from state to state? What explains the traditional allocation of authority over questions of family law? The increasing federalization? What impact will the Supreme Court's recent limitations on federal power have on family law? See *Morrison;* United States v. Lopez, 514 U.S. 549 (1995) (Congress lacked authority to enact Gun-Free School Zones Act). Will these limitations also prevent Congress from imposing national standards on family law through its provision of federal funds?

See generally Lynn A. Baker, Conditional Federal Spending After *Lopez*, 95 Colum. L. Rev. 1911 (1995); Naomi R. Cahn, Family Law, Federalism and the Federal Courts, 79 Iowa L. Rev. 1073 (1994); Anne C. Dailey, Federalism and Families, 143 U. Pa. L. Rev. 1787 (1995); Jill Elaine Hasday, Federalism and the Family Reconstructed, 45 UCLA L. Rev. 1297 (1998); Sylvia Law, Families and Federalism, 4 Wash. U. J.L. & Pol'y 175 (2000).

## Problem

In an effort to encourage work and "personal responsibility" and to discourage out-of-wedlock births and welfare dependency, New Jersey has adopted a "family cap." Previously, a welfare recipient received an increased allotment of public assistance on the birth of each child. On enactment of the family cap, a welfare recipient gets no such increase regardless of how large her family thereafter becomes. For those newly joining the welfare rolls even after the family cap, however, the allotment is calculated on the basis of actual family size. Hence, for example, the assistance for a family of three children varies, depending on when the children are born (before or after enactment of the family cap) and whether the parent is receiving welfare at the time of the births.

What constitutional challenges might be brought on behalf of those adversely affected by the family cap? Does the law encourage abortion? Given the state's justifications, what result and why? See C.K. v. Shalala, 883 F. Supp. 991 (D.N.J. 1995), *aff'd sub nom.* C.K. v. New Jersey Dept. of Health & Human Servs., 92 F.3d 171 (3d Cir. 1996). See generally, e.g., Susan Frelich Appleton, When Welfare Reforms Promote Abortion: "Personal Responsibility," "Family Values," and the Right to Choose, 85 Geo. L.J. 155 (1996); Yvette M. Barksdale, And the Poor Have Children: A Harm-Based Analysis of Family Caps and the Hollow Procreative Rights of Welfare Beneficiaries, 14 Law & Ineq. J. 1 (1995); Linda C. McClain, "Irresponsible" Reproduction, 47 Hastings L.J. 339 (1996). See also Mark A. Graber, The Clintonification of American Law: Abortion, Welfare, and Liberal Constitutional Theory, 58 Ohio St. L.J. 731 (1997).

## C. WHEN PRIVACY RIGHTS CONFLICT

### 1. Wives and Husbands, Children and Parents

## ■ PLANNED PARENTHOOD OF SOUTHEASTERN PENNSYLVANIA v. CASEY
*505 U.S. 833 (1992)*

Justice O'CONNOR, Justice KENNEDY, and Justice SOUTER announced the judgment of the Court and delivered the opinion of the Court [for Part V-C.]

### C

Section 3209 of Pennsylvania's abortion law provides, except in cases of medical emergency, that no physician shall perform an abortion on a married woman without receiving a signed statement from the woman that she has notified her spouse that she is about to undergo an abortion. The woman has the option of providing an alternative signed statement certifying that her husband is not the man who impregnated her; that her husband could not be located; that the pregnancy is the result of spousal sexual assault which she has reported; or that the woman believes that notifying her husband will cause him or someone else to inflict bodily injury upon her. A physician who performs an abortion on a married woman without receiving the appropriate signed statement will have his or her license revoked, and is liable to the husband for damages.

The District Court heard the testimony of numerous expert witnesses, and made detailed findings of fact regarding the effect of this statute. These included:

"273. The vast majority of women consult their husbands prior to deciding to terminate their pregnancy. . . . [. . .]

"281. Studies reveal that family violence occurs in two million families in the United States. This figure, however, is a conservative one that substantially understates (because battering is usually not reported until it reaches life-threatening proportions) the actual number of families affected by domestic violence. In fact, researchers estimate that one of every two women will be battered at some time in their life. . . .

"282. A wife may not elect to notify her husband of her intention to have an abortion for a variety of reasons, including the husband's illness, concern about her own health, the imminent failure of the marriage, or the husband's absolute opposition to the abortion. . . .

"283. The required filing of the spousal consent form would require plaintiff-clinics to change their counseling procedures and force women to reveal their most intimate decision-making on pain of criminal sanctions. The confidentiality of these revelations could not be guaranteed, since the woman's records are not immune from subpoena. . . .

"284. Women of all class levels, educational backgrounds, and racial, ethnic and religious groups are battered. . . .

"285. Wife-battering or abuse can take on many physical and psychological forms. The nature and scope of the battering can cover a broad range of actions and be gruesome and torturous [including murder, rape, child abuse, psychological intimidation, and emotional harm.]

"289. Mere notification of pregnancy is frequently a flashpoint for battering and violence within the family. The number of battering incidents is high during the pregnancy and often the worst abuse can be associated with pregnancy. . . . The battering husband may deny parentage and use the pregnancy as an excuse for abuse. . . .

"290. Secrecy typically shrouds abusive families. . . . Battering husbands often threaten [the wife] or her children with further abuse if she tells an outsider of the violence and tells her that nobody will believe her. A battered woman, therefore, is highly unlikely to disclose the violence against her for fear of retaliation by the abuser. . . . [. . .]"

These findings are supported by studies of domestic violence. . . . In well-functioning marriages, spouses discuss important intimate decisions such as whether to bear a child. But there are millions of women in this country who are the victims of regular physical and psychological abuse at the hands of their husbands. . . . Many may fear devastating forms of psychological abuse from their husbands, including [abuse of their children,] verbal harassment, threats of future violence, the destruction of possessions, physical confinement to the home, the withdrawal of financial support, or the disclosure of the abortion to family and friends. These methods of psychological abuse may act as even more of a deterrent to notification than the possibility of physical violence, but women who are the victims of the abuse are not exempt from §3209's notification requirement. And many women who are pregnant as a result of sexual assaults by their husbands will be unable to avail themselves of the exception for spousal sexual assault, §3209(b)(3), because the exception requires that the woman have notified law enforcement authorities within 90 days of the assault, and her husband will be notified of her report once an investigation begins, §3128(c). If anything in this field is certain, it is that victims of spousal sexual assault are extremely reluctant to report the abuse to the government. . . . We must not blind ourselves to the fact that the significant number of women who fear for their safety and the safety of their children are likely to be deterred from procuring an abortion as surely as if the Commonwealth had outlawed abortion in all cases.

Respondents attempt to avoid the conclusion that §3209 is invalid by pointing out that it imposes almost no burden at all for the vast majority of women seeking abortions. . . . Legislation is measured for consistency with the Constitution by its impact on those whose conduct it affects [, however.] The unfortunate yet persisting conditions we document above will mean that in a large fraction of the cases in which §3209 is relevant, it will operate as a substantial obstacle to a woman's choice to undergo an abortion. It is an undue burden, and therefore invalid. . . .

We recognize that a husband has a "deep and proper concern and interest . . . in his wife's pregnancy and in the growth and development of the fetus she is carrying." [Planned Parenthood of Central Mo. v. Danforth, 428 U.S. 52, 69 (1976).] With regard to the children he has fathered and raised, the Court has recognized his "cognizable and substantial" interest in their custody. Stanley v. Illinois, 405 U.S. 645, 651-652 (1972). . . .

Before birth, however, the issue takes on a very different cast. It is an inescapable biological fact that state regulation with respect to the child a woman is carrying will have a far greater impact on the mother's liberty than on the father's. The effect of state regulation on a woman's protected liberty is doubly deserving of scrutiny in such a case, as the State has touched not only upon the private sphere of the family but upon the very bodily integrity of the pregnant woman. The Court has held that "when the wife and the husband disagree on this decision, the view of only one of the two marriage partners can prevail. Inasmuch as it is the woman who physically bears the child and who is the more directly and immediately affected by the pregnancy, as between the two, the balance weighs in her favor." *Danforth,* supra, at 71. This conclusion rests upon the basic nature of marriage and the nature of our Constitution: "The marital couple is not an independent entity with a mind and heart of its own, but an association of two individuals each with a separate intellectual and emotional makeup. If the right of privacy means anything, it is the right of the *individual,* married or single, to be free from unwarranted governmental intrusion into matters so fundamentally affecting a person as the decision whether to bear or beget a child." Eisenstadt v. Baird, 405 U.S. at 453 (emphasis in original). . . .

There was a time, not so long ago, when a different understanding of the family and of the Constitution prevailed. In Bradwell v. State, 83 U.S. (16 Wall.) 130 (1872), three Members of this Court reaffirmed the common-law principle that "a woman had no legal existence separate from her husband, who was regarded as her head and representative in the social state; and, notwithstanding some recent modifications of this civil status, many of the special rules of law flowing from and dependent upon this cardinal principle still exist in full force in most States." Id., at 141 (Bradley, J., joined by Swayne and Field, JJ., concurring in judgment). Only one generation has passed since this Court observed that "woman is still regarded as the center of home and family life," with attendant "special responsibilities" that precluded full and independent legal status under the Constitution. Hoyt v. Florida, 368 U.S. 57, 62 (1961).

These views, of course, are no longer consistent with our understanding of the family, the individual, or the Constitution.

In keeping with our rejection of the common-law understanding of a woman's role within the family, the Court held in *Danforth* that the Constitution does not permit a State to require a married woman to obtain her husband's consent before undergoing an abortion. . . . For the great many women who are victims of abuse inflicted by their husbands, or whose children are the victims of such abuse, a spousal notice requirement enables the husband to wield an effective veto over his wife's decision [contrary to *Danforth*.]

The husband's interest in the life of the child his wife is carrying does not permit the State to empower him with this troubling degree of authority over his wife. . . . A husband has no enforceable right to require a wife to advise him before she exercises her personal choices. If a husband's interest in the potential life of the child outweighs a wife's liberty, the State could require a married woman to notify her husband before she uses a postfertilization contraceptive. Perhaps next in line would be a statute requiring pregnant married women to notify their husbands before engaging in conduct causing risks to the fetus. After all, if the husband's interest in the fetus' safety is a sufficient predicate for state regulation, the State could reasonably conclude that pregnant wives should notify their husbands before drinking alcohol or smoking. Perhaps married women should notify their husbands before using contraceptives or before undergoing any type of surgery that may have complications affecting the husband's interest in his wife's reproductive organs. And if a husband's interest justifies notice in any of these cases, one might reasonably argue that it justifies exactly what the *Danforth* Court held it did not justify — a requirement of the husband's consent as well. A State may not give to a man the kind of dominion over his wife that parents exercise over their children. . . .

### D

[Opinion of O'Connor, Kennedy, and Souter, JJ.]

. . . Except in a medical emergency, an unemancipated young woman under 18 may not obtain an abortion unless she and one of her state parents (or guardian) provides informed consent [which requires specific information from the physician and a 24-hour waiting period]. If neither a parent nor a guardian provides consent, a court may authorize the performance of an abortion upon a determination that the young woman is mature and capable of giving informed consent and has in fact given her informed consent, or that an abortion would be in her best interests.

. . . Our cases establish, and we reaffirm today, that a State may require a minor seeking an abortion to obtain the consent of a parent or guardian, provided that there is an adequate judicial bypass procedure. See, e.g., [Ohio v. Akron Ctr. for Reprod. Health, Inc., 497 U.S. 502, 510-519 (1990); Hodgson v. Minnesota, 497 U.S. 417, 461 (O'Connor, J., concurring in part and concurring in judgment in part); *id.*, at 497-501 (Kennedy, J., concurring in judgment in part and dissenting in part); City of Akron v. Akron Ctr. for Reprod. Health, 462 U.S. 416, 440 (1983); Bellotti v. Baird, 443 U.S. 622, 643-644 (1979) (plurality opinion)]. Under these precedents, in our view, the one-parent consent requirement and judicial bypass procedure are constitutional.[10]

The only argument made by petitioners respecting this provision and to which our prior decisions do not speak is the contention that the parental consent requirement is invalid because it requires informed parental consent. [Yet] some of the provisions regarding informed consent have particular force with respect to minors: the waiting period, for example, may provide the parent or parents of a pregnant young woman the opportunity to consult with her in private, and to discuss the consequences of her decision in the context of the values and moral or religious principles of their family. . . .

Chief Justice REHNQUIST, with whom Justice WHITE, Justice SCALIA, and Justice THOMAS join, . . . dissenting in part . . .

[T]he provision here involves a much less intrusive requirement of spousal notification, not consent. Such a law requiring only notice to the husband "does not give any third party the legal right to make the [woman's] decision for her, or to prevent her from obtaining an abortion should she choose to have one performed." Hodgson v. Minnesota, 497 U.S., supra, at 496 (Kennedy, J., concurring in judgment in part and dissenting in part). *Danforth* thus does not control our analysis. . . .

The question before us is therefore whether the spousal notification requirement rationally furthers any legitimate state interests. We con-

---

[10]. The Court said, for example, in *Akron*, 462 U.S. at 439-440:

The relevant legal standards are not in dispute. The Court has held that "the State may not impose a blanket provision . . . requiring the consent of a parent or person *in loco parentis* as a condition for abortion of an unmarried minor." *Danforth*, supra, at 74. In Bellotti v. Baird, 443 U.S. 622 (1979) (*Bellotti II*), a majority of the Court indicated that a State's interest in protecting immature minors will sustain a requirement of a consent substitute, either parental or judicial. See id., at 640-642 (plurality opinion for four Justices); id., at 656-657 (White, J., dissenting) (expressing approval of absolute parental or judicial consent requirement). See also *Danforth*, supra, at 102-105 (Stevens, J., concurring in part and dissenting in part). The *Bellotti II* plurality cautioned, however, that the State must provide an alternative procedure whereby a pregnant minor may demonstrate that she is sufficiently mature to make the abortion decision herself or that, despite her immaturity, an abortion would be in her best interests. 443 U.S., at 643-644. Under these decisions, it is clear that Akron may not make a blanket determination that *all* minors under the age of 15 are too immature to make this decision or that an abortion never may be in the minor's best interests without parental approval. — EDS.

clude that it does. First, a husband's interests in procreation within marriage and in the potential life of his unborn child are certainly substantial ones. The State itself has legitimate interests both in protecting these interests of the father and in protecting the potential life of the fetus, and the spousal notification requirement is reasonably related to advancing those state interests. By providing that a husband will usually know of his spouse's intent to have an abortion, the provision makes it more likely that the husband will participate in deciding the fate of his unborn child, a possibility that might otherwise have been denied him. This participation might in some cases result in a decision to proceed with the pregnancy. As Judge Alito observed in his dissent below, "the Pennsylvania legislature could have rationally believed that some married women are initially inclined to obtain an abortion without their husbands' knowledge because of perceived problems — such as economic constraints, future plans, or the husbands' previously expressed opposition — that may be obviated by discussion prior to the abortion." 947 F.2d at 726 (opinion concurring in part and dissenting in part).

The State also has a legitimate interest in promoting "the integrity of the marital relationship." 18 Pa. Cons. Stat. §3209(a) (1990). [T]he spousal notice requirement is a rational attempt by the State to improve truthful communication between spouses and encourage collaborative decisionmaking, and thereby fosters marital integrity. . . . The Pennsylvania Legislature was in a position to weigh the likely benefits of the provision against its likely adverse effects, and presumably concluded, on balance, that the provision would be beneficial. Whether this was a wise decision or not, we cannot say that it was irrational. We therefore conclude that the spousal notice provision comports with the Constitution.

[Although dissenting on the spousal notice provision, these four Justices agreed with the three authors of the joint opinion that Pennsylvania's parental consent requirement is constitutional. Justices Stevens and Blackmun concluded this requirement is unconstitutional because of the unjustified risks from delay imposed by the waiting period.]

■ **ANGELA BONAVOGLIA, KATHY'S DAY IN COURT**
*Ms., Apr. 1988, at 46-49*

On Wednesday, September 23, 1987, at 7:30 A.M., a pregnant 17-year-old we will call "Kathy" — her court-designated name — left her home in a working-class neighborhood of Birmingham, Alabama, and drove alone to the Jefferson County Family Courthouse. Kathy wanted an abortion. But in Alabama, as in 20 other states in the nation, a law exists that forbids a minor (anyone under the age of 18) to give her own consent for an abortion. Alabama's minors must ask one parent for permission, and if they can't do that, they must get a judge's approval before they can have an abortion.

Kathy is a friendly young woman with a big hearty laugh. Her face is round with residues of baby fat, and framed in a mane of blond hair. People tend to describe her as "sensible," which she is, but her sense of competence comes from having had to take care of herself much too early in life. Six years ago her mother remarried, to a man who is an alcoholic. For the last year and a half Kathy has lived mainly on her own, since she doesn't get along with her stepfather. . . .

Waiting for her at the courthouse that September day was the abortion provider Kathy had contacted when she realized she was pregnant [Diane Derzis, the director of Summit Medical Center]. Diane Derzis wanted to find a teenager willing to go to court and take her chances with the ambiguous law. If a judge turned this test case down, she would help the girl appeal, going as far as necessary in the court system to show how punitive the statute is. [Kathy had previously called the Medical Center to arrange an abortion. Her maturity led Derzis to ask her if she would wait five days until the consent law became effective and then go to court to test the new law. In exchange Derzis would arrange for Kathy to have a free abortion.]

"The money was a little bit of why I did it," said Kathy, "but I could have paid." More to the point for Kathy was that "Diane told me it would be a big help to the people who came after me. Everyone thought I was the perfect person to try this out: seventeen, living on my own. And, I thought, with all I've been through, I'm still here, I *know* I can handle this."

Following the instructions set forth in the Alabama law, Derzis had submitted Kathy's request for a judicial hearing to the Jefferson County Family Court. By law, the court had to provide Kathy with free legal representation for her hearing. Her papers were brought by a court officer to a Legal Aid lawyer, J. Wynell (Wendy) Brooks Crew, on September 21. [Judge Charles Nice would be hearing the case two days later.]

But on the day after Crew believed herself to have been appointed as Kathy's attorney, Judge Nice's bailiff approached her and a private attorney, Marcus Jones. According to Crew, the bailiff told Jones *he* had been appointed to represent the minor, and she was to represent the fetus. Wendy Crew said no. She pointed out that she had already talked to Kathy. She also noted that appointing a lawyer for the fetus would be unconstitutional, since, under Roe v. Wade, the fetus cannot be considered a person and does not have a right to representation. . . .

Crew and Jones went into the judge's office. Nice, 68, a slightly built, benevolent-looking man, had in his office pamphlets for Lifeline, an adoption agency run by the virulently anti-choice Sav-A-Life Christian ministry. Hanging on his wall was a photo of some of Lifeline's adoptive parents at their last reunion. Crew told him she wanted to stay on the case. She asked to be appointed Kathy's guardian or to be co-counsel. Judge Nice refused both requests and dismissed Crew.

Now Marcus Jones went into the conference room to meet Kathy. "I was mad," said Kathy. "I felt like I could pull this through with Wendy. Then they bring some man in fifteen minutes before the trial. Men don't really know about this. How is some man gonna stand up there and fight for me when he doesn't even know what's going on? I thought to myself, 'I'm gonna lose.' "

At approximately 9:45 A.M., Kathy and Diane Derzis walked down the hall from the conference room to Judge Nice's courtroom. . . . "I was having heart failure," [Kathy] said. She wanted Derzis to stay, but only court personnel were allowed in the room. That left Kathy in a room with four men — Nice, Jones, the bailiff, and the court officer. . . .

Jones began his questioning. . . . Kathy testified that she would not be 18 until the end of the year, and was therefore still affected by the parental consent law. To establish her maturity, Jones asked her about school. She told him that since she had not graduated, she planned to take the high school equivalency test. She also testified that she had been working full-time and part-time for the last two years and contributed to her own support.

Marcus Jones asked about her family. Kathy testified that her alcoholic stepfather abused her mother and herself. According to Kathy, he beat her so badly one night, she left and moved in with friends. . . . Kathy said she was 10 weeks pregnant. She didn't want to tell her mother about the pregnancy because her mother told her stepfather everything and if he found out about this he might get mad and end by beating her mother.

Kathy testified that she had considered adoption as well as abortion and remembers being surprised when Judge Nice continued to question her about this. . . . After 45 minutes of testimony, Judge Nice left the courtroom to make his decision. . . . Judge Nice returned and read his decision: he would not grant Kathy's request for an abortion; she was not mature enough, it was not in her best interest. The judge told Kathy she should talk to her mother about this decision.

Kathy was stunned. "I was about in tears. How can he say this about me? He didn't feel I was mature enough to make this decision myself? I could feel my eyes start pooling up, and I was going, 'Don't cry, don't cry.' "

"Everyone here at the clinic thinks I'm such a hard bitch," said Diane Derzis, "but I came back the day of that hearing and cried to think of what Kathy went through. I called Wendy and said 'I can't believe we put her through that. Why didn't we just take her to Georgia?' "

But they persevered, filing an appeal of Judge Nice's decision. [Kathy] has never said that she regrets her decision to go to court, but admits that the waiting was terrible: "I kept wishing I had already gotten it over with."

Fourteen days after the hearing, the Alabama Court of Civil Appeals overturned the judge's opinion . . . : "The trial judge in this case abused his discretion by denying the minor's request. . . . More importantly, we can neither discern from the trial court's judgment nor from the record any ground upon which the trial court's conclusion could rest. We can safely say, having considered the record, that, should this minor not meet the criteria for 'maturity' under the statute, it is difficult to imagine one who would." . . .

## Notes and Questions

1. Why did the Court strike down the spousal notification provision? How does a requirement of spousal notification differ from one of spousal consent, which the Court struck down in Planned Parenthood v. Danforth, 428 U.S. 52, 67-72 (1976)? Should one trigger a higher level of scrutiny? Which one? Does the answer depend on the meaning of "privacy"?

In part C of *Casey*, Justices Blackmun and Stevens joined with Justices O'Connor, Kennedy, and Souter to constitute a majority. Although Blackmun and Stevens would have applied a more demanding standard of review than the undue burden test, all five agreed that the spousal notification requirement is invalid, despite its exceptions.

Why do Justices O'Connor, Kennedy, and Souter conclude that spousal notification constitutes an undue burden but the 24-hour waiting period does not? See *Casey*, 505 U.S. at 881-887. Realistically, couldn't a woman more easily surmount the former simply by forging her husband's signature? Compare the Court's treatment of the two requirements, considering both the number of women apparently affected and the difficulty of the obstacle created. See Kathleen M. Sullivan, The Supreme Court 1991 Term, Foreword: The Justices of Rules and Standards, 106 Harv. L. Rev. 22, 32-34 (1992).

2. Why can the state limit a minor's decisionmaking about abortion? In Bellotti v. Baird, 443 U.S. 622 (1979), Justice Powell's plurality opinion listed three reasons: "the peculiar vulnerability of children; their inability to make critical decisions in an informed, mature manner; and the importance of the parental role in childrearing." Id. at 634. While these reasons support parental involvement requirements for minors' abortions, the *Bellotti* plurality went on to say that states with such laws must also provide an alternative that allows the minor to show that she can decide independently or that abortion would serve her best interests. A number of states with abortion restrictions responded, creating procedures for a minor to appear before a judge to "bypass" the parental consent or notification otherwise required.

As *Casey* indicates, the Supreme Court has focused on the judicial bypass in several subsequent cases. See, e.g., Hodgson v. Minnesota, 497

U.S. 417 (1990) (judicial bypass procedure makes two-parent notification requirement constitutional); Lambert v. Wiklund, 520 U.S. 292 (1997) (upholding statute requiring notification of one parent 48 hours before abortion with judicial bypass allowing waiver of notification when notification is not in minor's best interests). See generally Katheryn D. Katz, The Pregnant Child's Right to Self-Determination, 62 Alb. L. Rev. 1119 (1999).

Do parental consent requirements impose more onerous burdens than notification requirements? See Planned Parenthood of Cent. N.J. v. Farmer, 762 A.2d 620, 629 (N.J. 2000). Does the alternative of going to court make sense as a means of operationalizing a minor's right to privacy? Is this alternative itself "unduly burdensome"? See id. at 634-638. What does *Kathy's Day in Court* reveal?

3. Does privacy emerge from *Casey* as protection for the individual? The family unit? One approach advocates a constitutional doctrine that favors the "objectively weaker" party in family conflicts. See Jane Rutherford, Beyond Individual Privacy: A New Theory of Family Rights, 39 U. Fla. L. Rev. 627, 652 (1987). Who is "objectively weaker" in reproductive decisionmaking — the woman or the man? The pregnant minor or her parents?

What role does privacy doctrine play when the family unit is divided? See David D. Meyer, The Paradox of Family Privacy, 53 Vand. L. Rev. 527, 554-558 (2000) (in "splintered" families, privacy does not keep the state out but locates in the Constitution "a substantive rule for resolving a family's internal conflict").

4. Who should make the determination when women's and men's rights conflict? Should the state provide pre-abortion hearings at which an impartial arbiter decides — analogous to the judicial bypass for minors? See generally Molly Diggins, Comment, Paternal Interests in the Abortion Decision: Does the Father Have a Say?, 1989 U. Chi. Legal F. 377; Maria F. Walters, Note, Who Decides?, The Next Abortion Issue: A Discussion of Father's Rights, 91 W. Va. L. Rev. 165 (1988). See also Doe v. Smith, 486 U.S. 1308 (1988); Conn v. Conn, 525 N.E.2d 612 (Ind. Ct. App.), *aff'd,* 526 N.E.2d 958 (Ind.), *cert. denied,* 488 U.S. 955 (1988). Can you imagine circumstances in which the male should prevail?

5. To what extent did the Court rely on empirical data in invalidating the spousal notification requirement? What use does the dissent make of empirical data? Domestic violence in marriage is explored further in Chapter III, section C.3.

In contrast, in Hodgson v. Minnesota, extensive empirical evidence on family violence and the effects of bypass proceedings in practice failed to persuade a majority of the Court to strike down the law, a two-parent notification requirement with a bypass. In their testimony before the trial court, bypass judges could not identify "any positive effects of the law"; other evidence showed that the "court experience produced fear, tension, anxiety, and shame among minors, causing some who were mature, and some whose best interests would have been served by an abortion, to 'forego the bypass option and either notify their parents or carry to term.' " 497 U.S. at 441-442. See Planned Parenthood League of Mass. v. Attorney Gen., 677 N.E.2d 101 (Mass. 1997); J. Shoshanna Ehrlich, Journey Through the Courts: Minors, Abortion and the Quest for Reproductive Fairness, 10 Yale J.L. & Feminism 1, 15-16 (1998); Rachael N. Pine, Speculation and Reality: The Role of Facts in Judicial Protection of Fundamental Rights, 136 U. Pa. L. Rev. 655 (1988).

What accounts for the different weight given to "facts" in each context? Do visions of the ideal family explain *Casey*'s varying approaches to spousal notice and parental consent?

6. What is the vision of marriage reflected in the majority opinion in part C? Does the rejection of traditional gender-based roles provide a better explanation for the outcome than the empirical data? How persuasive is the majority's "parade of horribles" that might follow if the notification requirement were upheld? Do the joint opinion authors have a consistent view of women and their decisionmaking capacity, considering the approach to spousal notification, on the one hand, and the 24-hour waiting period (which they upheld), on the other?

Contrast the majority's reasoning with the assertion that by "isolating" the woman the Court has "endorsed the debasing, sexist notion that reproductive matters are really only women's 'private' concerns" and that "*real* men do not care about procreation, posterity, and mutuality in procreative and childbearing/rearing responsibilities." Lynn D. Wardle, The Quandary of Pro-Life Free Speech: A Lesson from the Abolitionists, 62 Alb. L. Rev. 853, 948 (1999).

7. The *Casey* dissent invokes an interest in fostering marital communication. How likely is state intervention to strengthen the marital unit?

Social scientists have reported that self-disclosure can result in less marital satisfaction and that secrecy (regarding infidelity and perhaps abortion) actually can foster marital stability. Thus, researchers have questioned whether spousal notification requirements would achieve their goal, especially because of the small number of cases they would affect, approximately 1% to 3% of all married women seeking abortions. Barbara Ryan & Eric Plutzer, When Married Women Have Abortions: Spousal Notification and Marital Interaction, 51 J. Marriage & Fam. 41, 47 (1989). For male narratives on the abortion decision, see Arthur B. Shostak & Gary McLouth, Men and Abortion: Lessons, Losses, and Love (1984).

8. What vision of the family emerges from the minors' abortion cases? See Anne C. Dailey, Constitutional Privacy and the Just Family, 67 Tul. L. Rev. 955 (1993); Bruce C. Hafen, Children's Liberation and the New Egalitarianism: Some Reservations About Abandoning Youth to

Their "Rights," 1976 B.Y.U. L. Rev. 605; Robert B. Keiter, Privacy, Children and Their Parents: Reflections On and Beyond the Supreme Court's Approach, 66 Minn. L. Rev. 459 (1982).

9. Can you square the judicial bypass procedure with the principle of parental autonomy articulated in *Meyer* and *Pierce*? If the Constitution protects a parent's right to control the upbringing of children, why don't parents have absolute authority to prevent a daughter's abortion if they see fit?

Suppose a minor forges a note of parental permission for abortion? Do parents have a cause of action against the physician who relies on the note? See Pammela S. Quinn, Note, Preserving Minors' Rights After *Casey:* The "New Battlefield" of Negligence and Strict Liability Statutes, 49 Duke L.J. 297 (1999).

10. Why might the Constitution allow state age-based lines for some constitutionally protected activities (for example, the right to marry), but require case-by-case assessments of maturity and best interests when the minor seeks an abortion? See John H. Garvey, Freedom and Choice in Constitutional Law, 94 Harv. L. Rev. 1756 (1981); Elizabeth S. Scott, The Legal Construction of Adolescence, 29 Hofstra L. Rev. 547, 569-576 (2000).

Note that some state constitutions provide greater protection for minors' abortion rights than the federal Constitution does. See American Academy of Pediatrics v. Lungren, 940 P.2d 797 (Cal. 1997); Planned Parenthood of Cent. N.J. v. Farmer, 762 A.2d 620 (N.J. 2000); Rachel Weissmann, What "Choice" Do They Have?: Protecting Pregnant Minors' Reproductive Rights Using State Constitutions, 1999 Ann. Surv. Am. L. 129.

11. The experience of Kathy in Alabama indicates the reluctance of some trial judges to grant bypass petitions. Cases from Texas also show the difficulty that minors have in prevailing in these proceedings. See, e.g., In re Doe, 19 S.W.3d 249 (Tex. 2000); In re Doe 4, 19 S.W.3d 337 (Tex. 2000). Data from other states, however, support a contrary conclusion. In Hodgson v. Minnesota, 497 U.S. 417 (1990), the Court noted that between 1981 and 1986 Minnesota courts considered 3,573 bypass petitions and granted all but 15. Id. at 441. See Stephanie A. Zavala, Note, Defending Parental Involvement and the Presumption of Immaturity in Minors' Decisions to Abort, 72 S. Cal. L. Rev. 1725, 1728-1729 (1999). A study of the effects of one of the early laws, Massachusetts's bypass provision, found judicial authorization is a "rubber stamp" operation. See Robert H. Mnookin, *Bellotti v. Baird:* A Hard Case, in In the Interest of Children 149, 242 (1985).

Studies have also associated parental involvement/bypass laws with a decrease in the number of abortions performed in the state. One explanation may be that minors travel to other states to avoid the requirements. See id. Other explanations include the possibilities that the laws prompt pregnancy avoidance and that concern about HIV or availability of birth control may be responsible. James L. Rogers et al., Impact of the Minnesota Parental Notification Law on Abortion and Birth, 81 Am. J. Pub. Health 294 (1991) (data show decline in both births and abortions in Minnesota, where geography prevents easy access to out-of-state abortions).

Should Congress prohibit taking minors across state lines to avoid parental involvement requirements at home? See H.R. 476, 107th Cong. (2001) (proposed "Child Custody Protection Act"). Should states without parental involvement requirements apply the requirements of the minor's home state or prohibit abortions for minors from such states? See, e.g., H.B. 690, 92nd Gen. Assem. (Ill. 2001); H.B. 1862, 91st Gen. Assem. (Ill. 1999).

12. Psychological data support the view that adolescents are as capable of informed and mature abortion decisionmaking as adults. See Gary B. Melton & Anita J. Pliner, Adolescent Abortion: A Psycholegal Analysis, in Adolescent Abortion: Psychological and Legal Issues 1 (Gary B. Melton ed., 1986); Bruce Ambuel & Julian Rappaport, Developmental Trends in Adolescents' Psychological and Legal Competence to Consent to Abortion, 16 Law & Hum. Behav. 129 (1992). Evidence shows that minors 14 years and older can reason in a relatively sophisticated way about medical treatment decisions. Lois Weithorn, Developmental Factors and Competence to Make Informed Treatment Decisions, in Legal Reforms Affecting Child and Youth Services 85, 90-94 (Gary B. Melton ed., 1982). See also Preston A. Britner et al., Evaluating Juveniles' Competence to Make Abortion Decisions: How Social Science Can Inform the Law, 5 U. Chi. L. Sch. Roundtable 35, 62 (1998) (research shows "adolescents are more similar than dissimilar to adults in their decision-making, although some differences may exist").

13. *Teenage pregnancy.* How should the current "epidemic" of teenage pregnancy influence constitutional analysis? Although the teen birth rate has been declining (20 percent between 1991 and 1999), the United States still has the highest rates of teen pregnancy and births in the Western industrialized world, with four in ten women becoming pregnant at least once before turning 20. The National Campaign to Prevent Teen Pregnancy, Facts and Stats (2001). Although many portray the devastating consequences of teenage pregnancy (educational, economic, psychological), others contend that teenage pregnancy may have positive effects for African-American females. Dr. Arline Geronimus bases this conclusion on rates of hypertension and infant mortality that rise with maternal age, increased accessibility to medical insurance for teens (through parents), and the strong tradition in the African-American community of assistance from an adolescent's relatives. Chris Raymond, Researchers: Teenage Pregnancy Is a Symptom of Societal Ills with No Simple Solu-

tion, Chron. Higher Ed., Feb. 28, 1990, at A11. See Kristin Luker, Dubious Conceptions: The Politics of Teenage Pregnancy 171 (1996) (making a similar argument for poor teens, both black and white). See also Ellen W. Freeman & Karl Rickels, Early Childbearing: Perspectives of Black Adolescents on Pregnancy, Abortion, and Contraception 158 (1993) (disadvantaged teens did not have strong feelings about wanting or avoiding pregnancy); Judith S. Musick, Young Poor, and Pregnant: The Psychology of Teenage Motherhood (1993).

Teenage pregnancy has long been a focus of federal welfare reform. Under the Personal Responsibility and Work Opportunity Act, states can provide assistance only to minor parents who meet specific educational and residential requirements, states must provide training for including men in teenage pregnancy prevention programs, and states should aggressively enforce statutory rape laws. 42 U.S.C. §§602(a)(1)(A)(v), 608(a)(4) & (5), 710 (note), 14016 (Supp. V 1999). These directives stem from empirical evidence showing that adult males father a high proportion of the children born to teenage mothers. See Jacqueline E. Darroch et al., Age Difference Between Sexual Partners in the United States, 31 Fam. Plan. Persp. 160 (1999).

See generally The Politics of Pregnancy: Adolescent Sexuality and Public Policy (Annette Lawson & Deborah L. Rhode eds., 1993); Ruth Colker, An Equal Protection Analysis of United States Reproductive Health Policy: Gender, Race, Age, and Class, 1991 Duke L.J. 324; Deborah Jones Merritt, Ending Poverty by Cutting Teenaged Births: Promise, Failure, and Paths to the Future, 57 Ohio St. L.J. 441 (1996).

14. Given the reasons for upholding parental involvement in abortion decisions, should states *require* parental involvement in decision-making for minors who carry pregnancies to term? See Elizabeth Buchanan, The Constitution and the Anomaly of the Pregnant Teenager, 24 Ariz. L. Rev. 553, 594 (1982). In Hodgson v. Minnesota, Justice Marshall condemned the Minnesota law as underinclusive for failing to require parental notice for pregnancy and childbirth, "which pose far greater risks to the minor's health than abortion." 497 U.S. at 470 n.7 (Marshall, concurring in part and dissenting in part). Cf. H.L. v. Matheson, 450 U.S. 398, 412-413 (1981) ("[i]f the pregnant girl elects to carry her child to term, the *medical* decisions to be made entail few — perhaps none — of the potentially grave emotional and psychological consequences of the decision to abort").

The New Jersey Supreme Court recently used the state constitution to reach the same conclusion as Justice Marshall. Planned Parenthood of Cent. N.J. v. Farmer, 762 A.2d 620 (N.J. 2000) (statute requiring parental notice or judicial bypass for minor's abortion but not for prenatal care and childbirth creates unjustified classification burdening fundamental right of woman to control her body and her future). See Emily Buss, The Parental Rights of Minors, 48 Buff. L. Rev. 785 (2000).

15. How would the Supreme Court decide the case in which parents acting in good faith direct their minor daughter to have an abortion, despite her expressed wish to carry to term? See In the Matter of Mary P., 444 N.Y.S.2d 545 (Fam. Ct. 1981).

## Problem

You are a judge presiding over a judicial bypass proceeding for a 14-year-old petitioner seeking an abortion without parental involvement. The attorney representing the minor elicits the following responses:

Q. At the time that the Complaint in this matter was signed, you were pregnant?

A. Yes.

Q. You had consulted with a counselor about that pregnancy?

A. Yeah.

Q. You had determined after talking to the counselor that you felt you should get an abortion?

A. Yes.

Q. You felt that you did not want to notify your parents —

A. Right.

Q. — of that decision? You did not feel for your own reasons that you could discuss it with them?

A. Right.

Q. After discussing the matter with a counselor, you still believed that you should not discuss it with your parents?

A. Right.

Q. And they shouldn't be notified?

A. Right.

Q. After talking the matter over with a counselor, the counselor concurred in your decision that your parents should not be notified?

A. Right.

Q. You were advised that an abortion couldn't be performed without notifying them?

A. Yes.

Q. You then came to me to see about filing a suit?

A. Right.

Q. You and I discussed it as to whether or not you had a right to do what you wanted to do?

A. Yes.

Q. You decided that, after our discussion, you should still proceed with the action to try to obtain an abortion without notifying your parents?

A. Right.

Q. Now, at the time that you signed the Complaint and spoke with the counselor and spoke with me, you were in the first trimester of pregnancy, within your first twelve weeks of pregnancy?

A. Yes.

Q. You feel that, from talking to the counselor and thinking the situation over and discussing it with me, that you could make the decision on your own that you wished to abort the pregnancy?

A. Yes.

Q. You are living at home?

A. Yes.

Q. You still felt, even though you were living at home with your parents that you couldn't discuss the matter with them?

A. Right.

H.L. v. Matheson, 450 U.S. 398, 402-403 n.6 (1981) (quoting transcript). On this evidence, would you grant the petition? If not, as judge, what questions would you pose to obtain the information that you need to decide whether to grant the petition? In particular, what questions would help you determine whether this minor is well informed? Mature? What resolution would serve her best interests?

Do you agree with Family Court Judge Nanette Dembitz that forcing an unwilling minor to carry a pregnancy to term can never serve her best interests? See Nanette Dembitz, The Supreme Court and a Minor's Abortion Decision, 80 Colum. L. Rev. 1251, 1255-1256 (1980).

## 2. Life and Death

■ **CRUZAN v. DIRECTOR, MISSOURI
DEPARTMENT OF HEALTH**
*497 U.S. 261 (1990)*

Chief Justice REHNQUIST delivered the opinion of the Court.

. . . On the night of January 11, 1983, Nancy Cruzan lost control of her car as she traveled down Elm Road in Jasper County, Missouri. The vehicle overturned, and Cruzan was discovered lying face down in a ditch without detectable respiratory or cardiac function. Paramedics were able to restore her breathing and heartbeat at the accident site, and she was transported to a hospital in an unconscious state. [P]ermanent brain damage usually results after 6 minutes in an anoxic state; it was estimated that Cruzan was deprived of oxygen from 12 to 14 minutes. She remained in a coma for approximately three weeks and then progressed to an unconscious state in which she was able to orally ingest some nutrition. In order to ease feeding and further the recovery, surgeons implanted a gastrostomy feeding and hydration tube in Cruzan with the consent of her then husband. Subsequent rehabilitative efforts proved unavailing. She now lies in a Missouri state hospital in what is commonly referred to as a persistent vegetative state: generally, a condition in which a person exhibits motor reflexes but evinces no indications of significant cognitive function. The State of Missouri is bearing the cost of her care.

After it had become apparent that Nancy Cruzan had virtually no chance of regaining her mental faculties, her parents asked hospital employees to terminate the artificial nutrition and hydration procedures. All agree that such a removal would cause her death. The employees refused to honor the request without court approval. . . .

We granted certiorari to consider the question of whether Cruzan has a right under the United States Constitution which would require the hospital to withdraw life-sustaining treatment from her under these circumstances.

At common law, even the touching of one person by another without consent and without legal justification was a battery. . . . This notion of bodily integrity has been embodied in the requirement that informed consent is generally required for medical treatment. . . .

The logical corollary of the doctrine of informed consent is that the patient generally possesses the right not to consent, that is, to refuse treatment. Until about 15 years ago and the seminal decision in In re Quinlan, 70 N.J. 10, 355 A.2d 647, *cert. denied sub nom.* Garger v. New Jersey, 429 U.S. 922 (1976), the number of right-to-refuse-treatment decisions were relatively few. Most of the earlier cases involved patients who refused medical treatment forbidden by their religious beliefs, thus implicating First Amendment rights as well as common law rights of self-determination. More recently, however, with the advance of medical technology capable of sustaining life well past the point where natural forces would have brought certain death in earlier times, cases involving the right to refuse life-sustaining treatment have burgeoned.

In the *Quinlan* case, young Karen Quinlan suffered severe brain damage as the result of anoxia, and entered a persistent vegetative state. Karen's father sought judicial approval to disconnect his daughter's respirator. The New Jersey Supreme Court granted the relief, holding that Karen had a right of privacy grounded in the Federal Constitution to terminate treatment. In re Quinlan, 70 N.J., at 38-42, 355 A.2d, at 662-664. Recognizing that this right was not absolute, however, the court balanced it against asserted state interests. Noting that the State's interest "weakens and the individual's right to privacy grows as the degree of bodily invasion increases and the prognosis dims," the court concluded that the state interests had to give way in that case. Id., at 41, 355 A.2d, at 664. The court also concluded that the "only practical way" to prevent the loss of Karen's privacy right due to her incompetence was to allow her guardian and family to decide "whether she would exercise it in these circumstances." Ibid.

After *Quinlan,* however, most courts have based a right to refuse [common law] treatment either solely on the common law right to informed consent or on both the common law right and a constitutional privacy right. . . . [constitution] This is the first case in which we have been squarely presented with the issue of whether the United States Constitution grants what is in com- [solely] mon parlance referred to as a "right to die." . . . [constitution]

. . . The principle that a competent person has a constitutionally protected liberty interest in refusing unwanted medical treatment may be inferred from our prior decisions. In Jacobson v. Massachusetts, 197 U.S. 11, 24-30 (1905), for instance, the Court balanced an individual's liberty interest in declining an unwanted smallpox vaccine against the State's interest in preventing disease. . . . But determining that a person has a "liberty interest" under the Due Process Clause does not end the inquiry;[7] "whether respondent's constitutional rights have been violated must be determined by balancing his liberty interests against the relevant state interests." Youngberg v. Romeo, 457 U.S. 307, 321 (1982).

Petitioners insist that under the general holdings of our cases, the forced administration of life-sustaining medical treatment, and even of artificially-delivered food and water essential to life, would implicate a competent person's liberty interest. Although we think the logic of the cases discussed above would embrace such a liberty interest, the dramatic consequences involved in refusal of such treatment would inform the inquiry as to whether the deprivation of that interest is constitutionally permissible. But for purposes of this case, we assume that the United States Constitution would grant a competent person a constitutionally protected right to refuse lifesaving hydration and nutrition.

Petitioners go on to assert that an incompetent person should possess the same right in this respect as is possessed by a competent person. . . . The difficulty with petitioners' claim is that in a sense it begs the question: an incompetent person is not able to make an informed and voluntary choice to exercise a hypothetical right to refuse treatment or any other right. Such a "right" must be exercised for her, if at all, by some sort of surrogate. Here, Missouri has in effect recognized that under certain circumstances a surrogate may act for the patient in electing to have hydration and nutrition withdrawn in such a way as to cause death, but it has established a procedural safeguard to assure that the action of the surrogate conforms as best it may to the wishes expressed by the patient while competent. Missouri requires that evidence of the incompetent's wishes as to the withdrawal of treatment be proved by clear and convincing evidence. The question, then, is whether the United

---

7. Although many state courts have held that a right to refuse treatment is encompassed by a generalized constitutional right of privacy, we have never so held. We believe this issue is more properly analyzed in terms of a Fourteenth Amendment liberty interest. See Bowers v. Hardwick, 478 U.S. 186, 194-195 (1986).

States Constitution forbids the establishment of this procedural requirement by the State. We hold that it does not.

*State interests*

Whether or not Missouri's clear and convincing evidence requirement comports with the United States Constitution depends in part on what interests the State may properly seek to protect in this situation. Missouri relies on its interest in the protection and preservation of human life, and there can be no gainsaying this interest. [T]he majority of States in this country have laws imposing criminal penalties on one who assists another to commit suicide. We do not think a State is required to remain neutral in the face of an informed and voluntary decision by a physically-able adult to starve to death.

But in the context presented here, a State has more particular interests at stake. The choice between life and death is a deeply personal decision of obvious and overwhelming finality. We believe Missouri may legitimately seek to safeguard the personal element of this choice through the imposition of heightened evidentiary requirements. It cannot be disputed that the Due Process Clause protects an interest in life as well as an interest in refusing life-sustaining medical treatment. Not all incompetent patients will have loved ones available to serve as surrogate decisionmakers. And even where family members are present, "[t]here will, of course, be some unfortunate situations in which family members will not act to protect a patient." In re Jobes, 108 N.J. 394, 419, 529 A.2d 434, 477 (1987). A State is entitled to guard against potential abuses in such situations. . . .

In our view, Missouri has permissibly sought to advance these interests through the adoption of a "clear and convincing" standard of proof to govern such proceedings. [N]ot only does the standard of proof reflect the importance of a particular adjudication, it also serves as "a societal judgment about how the risk of error should be distributed between the litigants." [Santosky v. Kramer, 455 U.S. 745, 755 (1982).] We believe that Missouri may permissibly place an increased risk of an erroneous decision on those seeking to terminate an incompetent individual's life-sustaining treatment. An erroneous decision not to terminate results in a maintenance of the status quo; the possibility of subsequent developments such as advancements in medical science, the discovery of new evidence regarding the patient's intent, changes in the law, or simply the unexpected death of the patient despite the administration of life-sustaining treatment, at least create the potential that a wrong decision will eventually be corrected or its impact mitigated. An erroneous decision to withdraw life-sustaining treatment, however, is not susceptible of correction. . . .

*evidence was not clear & convincing*

The Supreme Court of Missouri held that in this case the testimony adduced at trial did not amount to clear and convincing proof of the patient's desire to have hydration and nutrition withdrawn. . . . The testimony adduced at trial consisted primarily of Nancy Cruzan's statements made to a housemate about a year before her accident that she would not want to live should she face life as a "vegetable," and other observations to the same effect. The observations did not deal in terms with withdrawal of medical treatment or of hydration and nutrition. We cannot say that the Supreme Court of Missouri committed constitutional error in reaching the conclusion that it did.

Petitioners alternatively contend that Missouri must accept the "substituted judgment" of close family members even in the absence of substantial proof that their views reflect the views of the patient. They rely primarily upon our decisions in Michael H. v. Gerald D., 491 U.S. 110 (1989), and Parham v. J.R., 442 U.S. 584 (1979). But we do not think these cases support their claim. In *Michael H.,* we *upheld* the constitutionality of California's favored treatment of traditional family relationships; such a holding may not be turned around into a constitutional requirement that a State *must* recognize the primacy of those relationships in a situation like this. And in *Parham,* where the patient was a minor, we also *upheld* the constitutionality of a state scheme in which parents made certain decisions for mentally ill minors. Here again petitioners would seek to turn a decision which allowed a State to rely on family decisionmaking into a constitutional requirement that the State recognize such decisionmaking. But constitutional law does not work that way.

No doubt is engendered by anything in this record but that Nancy Cruzan's mother and father are loving and caring parents. If the State were required by the United States Constitution to repose a right of "substituted judgment" with anyone, the Cruzans would surely qualify. But we do not think the Due Process Clause requires the State to repose judgment on these matters with anyone but the patient herself. Close family members may have a strong feeling — a feeling not at all ignoble or unworthy, but not entirely disinterested, either — that they do not wish to witness the continuation of the life of a loved one which they regard as hopeless, meaningless, and even degrading. But there is no automatic assurance that the view of close family members will necessarily be the same as the patient's would have been had she been confronted with the prospect of her situation while competent. All of the reasons previously discussed for allowing Missouri to require clear and convincing evidence of the patient's wishes lead us to conclude that the State may choose to defer only to those wishes, rather than confide the decision to close family members. . . .

Justice O'CONNOR, concurring. . . .

I . . . write separately to emphasize that the Court does not today decide the issue whether a State must also give effect to the decisions of a surrogate decisionmaker. . . . In my view, such a duty may well be constitutionally required to protect the patient's liberty interest in refusing medical treatment. Few individuals provide explicit oral or written instructions regarding their intent to refuse medical treatment should they become incompetent. States which decline to consider any evidence other than such instructions may frequently fail to honor a patient's intent. Such failures might be avoided if the State considered an equally probative source of evidence: the patient's appointment of a proxy to make health care decisions on her behalf. Delegating the authority to make medical decisions to a family member or friend is becoming a common method of planning for the future. Several States have recognized the practical wisdom of such a procedure [by living wills and durable power of attorney statutes for health care decisionmaking]. Moreover, as patients are likely to select a family member as a surrogate, giving effect to a proxy's decisions may also protect the "freedom of personal choice in matters of . . . family life." Cleveland Board of Education v. LaFleur, 414 U.S. 632, 639 (1974).

[N]o national consensus has yet emerged on the best solution for this difficult and sensitive problem. Today we decide only that one State's practice does not violate the Constitution; the more challenging task of crafting appropriate procedures for safeguarding incompetents' liberty interests is entrusted to the "laboratory" of the States. . . .

Justice Scalia, concurring. . . .

. . . I would have preferred that we announce, clearly and promptly, that the federal courts have no business in this field; that American law has always accorded the State the power to prevent, by force if necessary, suicide — including suicide by refusing to take appropriate measures necessary to preserve one's life; that the point at which life becomes "worthless," and the point at which the means necessary to preserve it become "extraordinary" or "inappropriate," are neither set forth in the Constitution nor known to the nine Justices of this Court any better than they are known to nine people picked at random from the Kansas City telephone directory; and hence, that even when it *is* demonstrated by clear and convincing evidence that a patient no longer wishes certain measures to be taken to preserve her life, it is up to the citizens of Missouri to decide, through their elected representatives, whether that wish will be honored. . . .

The text of the Due Process Clause [protects individuals] against deprivations of liberty "without due process of law." [N]o "substantive due process" claim can be maintained unless the claimant demonstrates that the State has deprived him of a right historically and traditionally protected against state interference. That cannot possibly be established here.

At common law in England, a suicide — defined as one who "deliberately puts an end to his own existence, or commits any unlawful malicious act, the consequence of which is his own death," 4 W. Blackstone, Commentaries *189 — was criminally liable. Although the States abol-

ished the penalties imposed by the common law (i.e., forfeiture and ig-
nominious burial), they did so to spare the innocent family, and not to
legitimize the act. Case law at the time of the Fourteenth Amendment
generally held that assisting suicide was a criminal offense. . . . Thus,
"there is no significant support for the claim that a right to suicide is so
rooted in our tradition that it may be deemed 'fundamental' or 'implicit
in the concept of ordered liberty.' " Id., at 100 (quoting Palko v. Connecticut, 302 U.S. 319, 325 (1937)). . . .

. . . Are there, then, no reasonable and humane limits that ought not
to be exceeded in requiring an individual to preserve his own life? There
obviously are, but they are not set forth in the Due Process Clause. . . .
Our salvation is the Equal Protection Clause, which requires the democratic majority to accept for themselves and their loved ones what they
impose on you and me. This Court need not, and has no authority to,
inject itself into every field of human activity where irrationality and
oppression may theoretically occur, and if it tries to do so it will destroy
itself.

Justice BRENNAN, with whom Justice MARSHALL and Justice BLACK-
MUN join, dissenting. . . .

[I]f a competent person has a liberty interest to be free of unwanted
medical treatment, as both the majority and Justice O'Connor concede,
it must be fundamental. Whatever other liberties protected by the Due
Process Clause are fundamental, "those liberties that are 'deeply rooted
in this Nation's history and tradition' " are among them. . . .

Although the right to be free of unwanted medical intervention, like
other constitutionally protected interests, may not be absolute, no State
interest could outweigh the rights of an individual in Nancy Cruzan's
position. [T]he State has no legitimate general interest in someone's life,
completely abstracted from the interest of the person living that life, that
could outweigh the person's choice to avoid medical treatment. . . .

Moreover, there may be considerable danger that Missouri's rule of
decision would impair rather than serve any interest the State does have
in sustaining life. Current medical practice recommends use of heroic
measures if there is a scintilla of a chance that the patient will recover,
on the assumption that the measures will be discontinued should the patient improve. When the President's Commission in 1982 approved the
withdrawal of life support equipment from irreversibly vegetative patients, it explained that "[a]n even more troubling wrong occurs when a
treatment that might save life or improve health is not started because
the health care personnel are afraid that they will find it very difficult to
stop the treatment if, as is fairly likely, it proves to be of little benefit and
greatly burdens the patient." . . .

This is not to say that the State has no legitimate interests to assert
here. . . . Missouri has a parens patriae interest in providing Nancy

Cruzan, now incompetent, with as accurate as possible a determination of how she would exercise her rights under these circumstances. . . .

Missouri may constitutionally impose only those procedural requirements that serve to enhance the accuracy of a determination of Nancy Cruzan's wishes or are at least consistent with an accurate determination. The Missouri "safeguard" that the Court upholds today does not meet that standard. . . . Missouri's rule of decision imposes a markedly asymmetrical evidentiary burden. Only evidence of specific statements of treatment choice made by the patient when competent is admissible to support a finding that the patient, now in a persistent vegetative state, would wish to avoid further medical treatment. Moreover, this evidence must be clear and convincing. No proof is required to support a finding that the incompetent person would wish to continue treatment. [Yet,] from the point of view of the patient, an erroneous decision in either direction is irrevocable. . . .

Even more than its heightened evidentiary standard, the Missouri court's categorical exclusion of relevant evidence dispenses with any semblance of accurate factfinding. . . . The court did not specifically define what kind of evidence it would consider clear and convincing, but its general discussion suggests that only a living will or equivalently formal directive from the patient when competent would meet this standard. . . . While it might be a wise social policy to encourage people to furnish such instructions, no general conclusion about a patient's choice can be drawn from the absence of formalities. . . .

Finally, I cannot agree with the majority that where it is not possible to determine what choice an incompetent patient would make, a State's role as parens patriae permits the State automatically to make that choice itself. [Even if family members and the patient might have different views, is] there any reason to suppose that a State is *more* likely to make the choice that the patient would have made than someone who knew the patient intimately? To ask this is to answer it. . . .

[ Justice Stevens, dissenting, writes that the Constitution requires respect for Nancy Cruzan's "own best interests."]

## Notes and Questions

1. *Epilogue.* The Cruzans subsequently sought to introduce additional evidence of Nancy's wish to die. At a hearing, a probate court determined that the Cruzans had presented sufficient evidence to halt artificial nutrition and hydration. Nancy died 12 days after removal of the feeding tube. The outcome deeply troubled the hospital staff who had cared for her for seven years; they felt "violated and betrayed," observing that "it would be easier for them to cope with the process if Miss Cruzan were allowed to die quickly by lethal injection." Anger in Hos-

pital at Death Order, N.Y. Times, Dec. 16, 1990, §1, at 29. The case took its toll on the Cruzans as well, and Nancy's father committed suicide in 1996.

2. Does the majority recognize a right on the part of *competent* patients to refuse life-sustaining treatment? To the extent that the majority finds such right, what is its constitutional source? Is it "fundamental"? Does it extend to incompetent patients?

3. How does the rationale of *Cruzan* compare to the privacy-based rationale of In re Quinlan? Which rationale is more persuasive? What are the implications of each approach?

4. If the Court must look to history and tradition to determine whether an interest merits constitutional protection (recall *Roe* and *Hardwick*), then how should the Court resolve evidence of conflicting traditions, for example, the traditional prohibition against suicide (per Justice Scalia) or the tradition of patient self-determination (per Justice Brennan)?

5. The right to die, like the abortion decision, entails making a personal choice. How can such choices be made by incompetent individuals such as Nancy Cruzan? Why wasn't Nancy Cruzan's past expression of her preferences adequate? How can *prior* directives ever express what the patient wants *now*? See Nancy K. Rhoden, Litigating Life and Death, 102 Harv. L. Rev. 375, 410-419 (1988). Should a court simply impute to an incompetent patient, who had not made her wishes known, what most people would prefer? See Norman L. Cantor, *Conroy,* Best Interests and the Handling of Dying Patients, 37 Rutgers L. Rev. 543, 570-577 (1985). See also Rebecca Dresser, Relitigating Life and Death, 51 Ohio St. L.J. 425 (1990); Nancy K. Rhoden, The Limits of Legal Objectivity, 68 N.C. L. Rev. 845 (1990) (critiques of different standards).

6. What vision of the family emerges from the *Cruzan* opinions? Is this vision consistent with the portrayal of the family in the minors' abortion cases, including *Casey*? Suppose the family is divided? Compare the "asymmetrical evidentiary burden" approved in *Cruzan* (as characterized by dissenting Justice Brennan) with the asymmetry of requiring bypass proceedings for minors seeking abortions without parental involvement (but not for those carrying a pregnancy to term).

Questions about a divided family and the standard of proof came before the California Supreme Court in Conservatorship of Wendland, 28 P.3d 151 (Cal. 2001). The wife of a conscious but severely disabled patient requested withdrawal of artificial nutrition and hydration, but his mother and sister objected. The court held that withdrawal requires clear and convincing evidence of the patient's own wishes or his best interests, missing here. After the patient died of natural causes (pneumonia), his widow unsuccessfully sought clarification of what evidence will suffice for patients who have left an advance directive or designated a health care surrogate. Petition for rehearing at 2-3, Wendland v. Wendland (S087265); 2001 Cal. LEXIS 6484 (Sept. 26, 2001) (denying petition).

7. Should courts be involved routinely in right-to-die cases? In situations of doubt, who should have the burden of proof? See Rhoden, Litigating Life and Death, supra (urging presumption in favor of family decisionmaking). On the other hand, *why* would the Constitution prohibit a state from "playing it safe" in response to a given request to withdraw nutrition and hydration from an incompetent patient? What practical effects might follow from *Cruzan*?

8. Justice O'Connor urges the use of patient-executed documents to avoid the dilemma in *Cruzan*. If Nancy Cruzan had executed a "living will" directing termination of treatment, would that have changed the result? Missouri law imposes two limitations on such advance directives that would have posed problems in Nancy's case. The statute excludes nutrition and hydration from "death prolonging procedures" that one may refuse, and it makes such declaration operative only for patients in a "terminal condition." Mo. Rev. Stat. §§459.010-459.025 (2000). Missouri (like many states), however, authorizes nomination of a surrogate decisionmaker for health care with specific authority to withhold or withdraw artificially supplied nutrition and hydration. Mo. Rev. Stat. §404.820 (2000).

9. Justice Scalia recommends resort to the Equal Protection Clause. How would this approach work? Will it guard against unreasonable impositions of forced medical treatment? Unreasonable abortion restrictions? Do men and women have equal opportunities to exercise the right to die? Consider the following evidence of gender bias:

> Appellate court rulings show four major differences in how courts speak of previously competent women's or men's moral preferences. The first difference is the courts' view that a man's opinions are rational and a woman's remarks are unreflective, emotional, or immature. Second, women's moral agency in relation to medical decisions is often not recognized. Third, courts apply evidentiary standards differently to evidence about men's and women's preferences. Fourth, life-support dependent men are seen as subjected to medical assault; women are seen as vulnerable to medical neglect. Not all of these differences are present in any one case. Each difference (e.g., language describing a woman's reasoning as immature) is present in at least three cases of the gender to which it is attributed and none of the cases of the opposite gender.

Steven H. Miles & Allison August, Courts, Gender and "The Right to Die," 18 Law, Med. & Health Care 85, 87 (1990). But see Susan M. Wolf, Gender, Feminism, and Death: Physician-Assisted Suicide and Euthanasia, in Feminism and Bioethics: Beyond Reproduction 282 (Susan M. Wolf ed., 1996).

10. The 1989 Uniform Rights of the Terminally Ill Act allows a competent individual to declare in advance the wish to withhold or withdraw life-sustaining treatment in the event of a terminal condition (§2). 9C

U.L.A. 318-319 (2001). The act also allows certain third parties to consent to the withdrawal or withholding of such treatment for incompetent patients who have made no effective declaration — in order of priority: a spouse; an adult child or a majority of the children, if more than one; parents; an adult sibling; or the nearest adult relative by blood or adoption (§7). Id. at 328-329.

The Omnibus Budget Reconciliation Act, 42 U.S.C. §1395cc(f) (1994 & Supp. V 1999), requires Medicare providers (hospitals, skilled nursing facilities, home health agencies, and hospice programs) to inform adult recipients of the right to refuse treatment.

11. Justice O'Connor stresses that these problems belong in the " 'laboratory' of the States." What are the likely consequences of this approach? Can a state prevent its domiciliaries from crossing state lines to evade restrictive laws? See In re Christine Busalacchi, 1991 WL 10048 (Mo. Ct. App. 1991) (enjoining father, who desires to remove daughter's feeding-tube, from moving her to a more permissive state).

12. *Assisted suicide.* Do *Cruzan* and the abortion cases together establish a foundation for a constitutionally protected right to assisted suicide? Advocates of an expanded right to die that includes physician-assisted suicide claimed to find support in *Casey*'s language for a majority of the Supreme Court: "At the heart of liberty is the right to define one's own concept of existence, of meaning, of the universe, and of the mystery of human life. Beliefs about these matters could not define the attributes of personhood were they formed under compulsion of the State." 505 U.S. at 851. See also Ronald Dworkin, Life's Dominion: An Argument About Abortion, Euthanasia, and Individual Freedom (1993). But see, e.g., Susan J. Wolf, Physician-Assisted Suicide, Abortion, and Treatment Refusal: Using Gender to Analyze the Difference, in Physician-Assisted Suicide 167 (Robert F. Weir ed., 1997) (argument ignores role of gender in abortion cases).

Unpersuaded by the proponents' argument, the Supreme Court rejected a substantive due-process challenge to Washington's ban on physician-assisted suicide, as applied to the terminally ill. The Court concluded that the asserted "right to die" fails two tests for constitutional protection: (a) the "Due Process Clause specially protects [only] those fundamental rights and liberties which are, objectively, 'deeply rooted in this Nation's history and tradition,' " and (b) "substantive-due-process cases [require] a 'careful description' of the asserted fundamental liberty interest." Washington v. Glucksberg, 521 U.S. 702, 720-721 (1997). The majority emphasized that the assumed right in *Cruzan* was one in avoiding forced treatment, a battery. Id. at 724-725. And, *Casey*'s language was said not to "warrant the sweeping conclusion that any and all important, intimate, and personal decisions are so protected." Id. at 727. The Court held that the state's interests (for example, preserving human life, protecting vulnerable groups, and avoiding the slippery slope to euthanasia) provide a sufficient rational basis for the law. A companion case used similar reasoning to uphold New York's ban against an equal protection challenge based on the different legal consequences of physicians' termination of life-sustaining treatment (as in *Cruzan*) versus their affirmative assistance in hastening death. Vacco v. Quill, 521 U.S. 793 (1997). See generally Symposium, Physician-Assisted Suicide: Facing Death after *Glucksberg* and *Quill*, 82 Minn. L. Rev. 885 (1998) (including contributions by Professors Yale Kamisar, Sylvia Law, Robert Burt, and Susan Wolf).

What do these holdings portend for future of privacy- and autonomy-based claims? See, e.g., Susan Frelich Appleton, Assisted Suicide and Reproductive Freedom: Exploring Some Connections, 76 Wash. U. L.Q. 15 (1998); Ezekiel J. Emanuel, The Future of Euthanasia and Physician-Assisted Suicide: Beyond Rights Talk to Informed Public Policy, 82 Minn. L. Rev. 983, 989-93 (1998); Penney Lewis, Rights Discourse and Assisted Suicide, 27 Am. J.L. & Med. 45 (2001); Lois Shepherd, Looking Forward with the Right of Privacy, 49 U. Kan. L. Rev. 251 (2001). Specifically, do the Court's tests for constitutional protection provide renewed support for *Hardwick*, supra, notwithstanding the questions raised by *Romer*, supra page 59.

13. *"Death with Dignity" in Oregon.* Declining to recognize a constitutional right to assisted suicide, the Court expressly left the issue for democratic resolution. *Glucksberg*, 521 U.S. at 735. Just months after the Supreme Court decisions in 1997, Oregon's Death with Dignity Act, which voters had approved in 1994, became effective. Or. Rev. Stat. §§127.800-127.895 (1999). This legislation allows a competent adult who resides in Oregon, suffers from a terminal disease according to physicians, and voluntarily expresses a wish to die to request and then obtain, after a waiting period, medication "for the purpose of ending his or her life in a humane and dignified manner." Id. at §127.805. During the first two years, 56 individuals received prescriptions under the law, and 42 took the medication and died. See Susan R. Martyn & Henry J. Bourguignon, Now Is the Moment to Reflect: Two Years of Experience with Oregon's Physician-Assisted Suicide Law, 8 Elder L.J. 1, 6-7 (2000).

Does Oregon's law advance autonomy, expanding the "private realm of family life"? Are the restrictions sufficient to protect against involuntary euthanasia? See id. at 53-56 ( law "has no teeth" and gives too much authority to physicians). Do such measures pose special risks to undervalued persons, including women and minorities? See Patricia King & Leslie Wolf, Empowering and Protecting Patients: Lessons for Physician-Assisted Suicide from the African-American Experience, 82 Minn. L. Rev. 1015 (1998) (commenting on Supreme Court cases).

14. *The federal response.* Congress responded to Oregon's legislation by prohibiting the use of federal funds for assisted suicide. 42 U.S.C. §§14401-14408 (Supp. V 1999); 42 U.S.C. §238o (Supp. V 1999); 25

U.S.C. §1621x (Supp. V 1999); 38 U.S.C. §1707 (Supp. V 1999). The Drug Enforcement Administration determined that physicians who prescribed medications for suicide assistance violate the federal Controlled Substances Act, but a district court enjoined Attorney General Ashcroft's enforcement directive. A number of congressional bills, including the proposed Pain Relief Promotion Act, also have attempted to halt the practice of "death with dignity" in Oregon. See, e.g., Beth A. Diebold, Recent Legislative Activity, The Pain Relief Promotion Act of 1999: Whose Pain Does It Relieve?, 12 Loy. Consumer L. Rev. 356 (2000); Robert A. Klinck, Recent Development, Pain Relief Promotion Act, 38 Harv. J. on Legis. 249 (2001).

When the Supreme Court called for the debate about assisted suicide to continue, "as it should in a democratic society," 521 U.S. at 735, did the Justices mean to invite federal action that would trump "experimentation" within the " 'laboratory' of the states"? See id. at 788 (Souter, J., concurring); id. at 737 (O'Connor, J., concurring).

■ **IN RE A.C.**
*573 A.2d 1235 (D.C. App. 1990) (en banc)*

TERRY, Associate Judge. . . .

We are confronted here with two profoundly difficult and complex issues. First, we must determine who has the right to decide the course of medical treatment for a patient who, although near death, is pregnant with a viable fetus. Second, we must establish how that decision should be made if the patient cannot make it for herself. . . . We hold that in virtually all cases the question of what is to be done is to be decided by the patient — the pregnant woman — on behalf of herself and the fetus. If the patient is incompetent or otherwise unable to give an informed consent to a proposed course of medical treatment, then her decision must be ascertained through the procedure known as substituted judgment. . . .

This case came before the trial court when George Washington University Hospital petitioned the emergency judge in chambers for declaratory relief as to how it should treat its patient. . . . A.C. was first diagnosed as suffering from cancer at the age of thirteen. In the ensuing years she underwent major surgery several times, together with multiple radiation treatments and chemotherapy. A.C. married when she was twenty-seven, during a period of remission, and soon thereafter she became pregnant. She was excited about her pregnancy and very much wanted the child. . . .

On Tuesday, June 9, 1987, when A.C. was approximately twenty-five weeks pregnant, [doctors diagnosed] an apparently inoperable tumor which nearly filled her right lung. On Thursday, June 11, A.C. was admitted to the hospital as a patient. By Friday her condition had temporarily improved, and when asked if she really wanted to have her baby, she replied that she did.

Over the weekend A.C.'s condition worsened considerably. Accordingly, on Monday, June 15, members of the medical staff treating A.C. assembled, along with her family, in A.C.'s room. The doctors then informed her that her illness was terminal, and A.C. agreed to palliative treatment designed to extend her life until at least her twenty-eighth week of pregnancy. The "potential outcome [for] the fetus," according to the doctors, would be much better at twenty-eight weeks than at twenty-six weeks if it were necessary to "intervene." A.C. knew that the palliative treatment she had chosen presented some increased risk to the fetus, but she opted for this course both to prolong her life for at least another two weeks and to maintain her own comfort. When asked if she still wanted to have the baby, A.C. was somewhat equivocal, saying "something to the effect of 'I don't know, I think so.' " As the day moved toward evening, A.C.'s condition grew still worse, and at about 7:00 or 8:00 P.M. she consented to intubation to facilitate her breathing.

The next morning, June 16, the trial court convened a hearing at the hospital in response to the hospital's request for a declaratory judgment [as to whether it should deliver the fetus via caesarean section]. The court appointed counsel for both A.C. and the fetus, and the District of Columbia was permitted to intervene for the fetus as parens patriae. . . . A neonatologist, Dr. Maureen Edwards, testified that the chances of survival for a twenty-six-week fetus delivered at the hospital might be as high as eighty percent, but that this particular fetus, because of the mother's medical history, had only a fifty to sixty percent chance of survival. Dr. Edwards estimated that the risk of substantial impairment for the fetus, if it were delivered promptly, would be less than twenty percent. However, she noted that the fetus' condition was worsening appreciably at a rapid rate, and another doctor — Dr. Alan Weingold, an obstetrician who was one of A.C.'s treating physicians — stated that any delay in delivering the child by caesarean section lessened its chances of survival.

Regarding A.C.'s ability to respond to questioning and her prognosis, Dr. Louis Hamner, another treating obstetrician, testified that A.C. would probably die within twenty-four hours "if absolutely nothing else is done. . . . As far as her ability to interact, she has been heavily sedated in order to maintain her ventilatory function. She will open her eyes sometimes when you are in the room, but as far as her being able to . . . carry on a meaningful-type conversation . . . at this point, I don't think that is reasonable." . . .

There was no evidence before the court showing that A.C. consented to, or even contemplated, a caesarean section before her twenty-eighth week of pregnancy. There was, in fact, considerable dispute as to whether she would have consented to an immediate caesarean delivery at the time the hearing was held. A.C.'s mother opposed surgical intervention, testifying that A.C. wanted "to live long enough to hold that baby" and that she expected to do so, "even though she knew she was terminal." Dr. Hamner testified that, given A.C.'s medical problems, he did not think she would have chosen to deliver a child with a substantial degree of impairment. Asked whether A.C. had been "confronted with the question of what to do if there were a choice that ultimately had to be made between her own life expectancy and that of her fetus," he replied that the question "was addressed [but] at a later gestational age. We had talked about the possibility at twenty-eight weeks. . . ."

After hearing this testimony and the arguments of counsel, the trial court made oral findings of fact. It found . . . that A.C. would probably die [within a day or two; that the fetus had a 50-60 percent chance of survival]; that because the fetus was viable, "the state has [an] important and legitimate interest in protecting the potentiality of human life"; and . . . that there had been some testimony that the operation "may very well hasten the death of [A.C.]," but that there had also been testimony that delay would greatly increase the risk to the fetus and that "the prognosis is not great for the fetus to be delivered post-mortem. . . ." Most significantly, the court found [that it did not clearly know A.C.'s present views. Relying] on In re Madyun, 114 Daily Wash. L. Rptr. 2233 (D.C. Super. Ct. July 26, 1986), the court ordered that a caesarean section be performed. . . . The operation took place, but the baby lived for only a few hours, and A.C. succumbed to cancer two days later. . . .

### A. INFORMED CONSENT AND BODILY INTEGRITY

[O]ur analysis of this case begins with the tenet common to all medical treatment cases: that any person has the right to make an informed choice, if competent to do so, to accept or forego medical treatment. . . . In the same vein, courts do not compel one person to permit a significant intrusion upon his or her bodily integrity for the benefit of another person's health. In [McFall v. Shimp, 10 Pa. D.&C.3d 90 (Allegheny County Ct. 1978)], the court refused to order Shimp to donate bone marrow which was necessary to save the life of his cousin. . . . Even though Shimp's refusal would mean death for McFall, the court would not order Shimp to allow his body to be invaded. [McFall also cited the common law, which imposes no duty to rescue another.] It has been suggested that fetal cases are different because a woman who "has chosen to lend her body to bring [a] child into the world" has an enhanced duty to assure the welfare of the fetus, sufficient even to require her to undergo caesarean surgery. Robertson, [Procreative Liberty and the Control of Conception, Pregnancy and Childbirth, 69 Va. L. Rev. 403, 456 (1983)]. Surely, however, a fetus cannot have rights in this respect superior to those of a person who has already been born.[8] . . .

Decisions of the Supreme Court, while not explicitly recognizing a right to bodily integrity, seem to assume that individuals have the right, depending on the circumstances, to accept or refuse medical treatment or other bodily invasion.[9] . . .

This court and others, while recognizing the right to accept or reject medical treatment, have consistently held that the right is not absolute. . . . In those rare cases in which a patient's right to decide her own course of treatment has been judicially overridden, courts have usually acted to vindicate the state's interest in protecting third parties, even if in fetal state. See Jefferson v. Griffin Spalding County Hospital Authority, [274 S.E.2d 457 (Ga. 1981)] (ordering that caesarean section be performed on a woman in her thirty-ninth week of pregnancy to save both the mother and the fetus); Raleigh Fitkin-Paul Morgan Memorial Hospital v. Anderson, 42 N.J. 421, 201 A.2d 537 (ordering blood transfusions over the objection of a Jehovah's Witness, in her thirty-second week of pregnancy, to save her life and that of the fetus), *cert. denied,* 377 U.S. 985 (1964). . . .

What we distill from the cases discussed in this section is that every person has the right, under the common law and the Constitution, to accept or refuse medical treatment. This right of bodily integrity belongs equally to persons who are competent and persons who are not. Further, it matters not what the quality of a patient's life may be; the right of bodily integrity is not extinguished simply because someone is ill, or even at death's door. To protect that right against intrusion by others — family members, doctors, hospitals, or anyone else, however well-intentioned — we hold that a court must determine the patient's wishes by any means available, and must abide by those wishes unless there are truly extraordinary or compelling reasons to override them. When the patient is incompetent, or when the court is unable to determine competency, the substituted judgment procedure must be followed.

8. There are also practical consequences to consider. What if A.C. had refused to comply with a court order that she submit to a caesarean? Under the circumstances, she obviously could not have been held in civil contempt and imprisoned or required to pay a daily fine until compliance. . . . Enforcement could be accomplished only through physical force or its equivalent. A.C. would have to be fastened with restraints to the operating table, or perhaps involuntarily rendered unconscious by forcibly injecting her with an anesthetic, and then subjected to unwanted major surgery. Such actions would surely give one pause in a civilized society. . . .

9. We think it appropriate here to reiterate and emphasize [that this case is not about abortion. The decisional right whether to bear or beget a child] is not at issue here, for the record makes clear that A.C. sought to become pregnant, that she wanted to bear her child as close to term as possible, and that neither she nor anyone associated with her at any time sought to terminate her pregnancy. The issue presented in this case is . . . who should decide how that child should be delivered. That decision involves the right of A.C. (or any woman) to accept or forego medical treatment. The Supreme Court has not yet focused on this question in the context of a pregnancy. . . .

From the record before us, we simply cannot tell whether A.C. was ever competent, after being sedated, to make an informed decision one way or the other regarding the proposed caesarean section. . . . We think it is incumbent on any trial judge in a case like this, unless it is impossible to do so, to ascertain whether a patient is competent to make her own medical decisions. Whenever possible, the judge should personally attempt to speak with the patient and ascertain her wishes directly, rather than relying exclusively on hearsay evidence, even from doctors. [W]ithout a competent refusal from A.C. to go forward with the surgery, and without a finding through substituted judgment that A.C. would not have consented to the surgery, it was error for the trial court to proceed to a balancing analysis, weighing the rights of A.C. against the interests of the state. . . .

## B. SUBSTITUTED JUDGMENT . . .

Under the substituted judgment procedure, the court as decision-maker must "substitute itself as nearly as may be for the incompetent, and . . . act upon the same motives and considerations as would have moved her. . . ." The concept of substituted judgment, which has its roots in English law, was intended to allow courts to make dispositions from the estates of incompetents akin to those that the incompetents would have made if competent. In recent times the procedure has been used to authorize organ "donations" by incompetents, . . . and to prohibit the forced administration of medical treatment to incompetents, over religious objections, where life itself was not at stake. . . . Most cases involving substituted judgment, however, have arisen in the "right to die" context, and the courts have generally concluded that giving effect to the perceived decision of the incompetent is the proper course, even though doing so will result in the incompetent's death. . . .

We begin with the proposition that the substituted judgment inquiry is primarily a subjective one: as nearly as possible, the court must ascertain what the patient would do if competent. Due process strongly suggests (and may even require) that counsel or a guardian ad litem should be appointed for the patient unless the situation is so urgent that there is no time to do so.

[T]he greatest weight should be given to the previously expressed wishes of the patient. . . . Courts in substituted judgment cases have also acknowledged the importance of probing the patient's value system as an aid in discerning what the patient would choose. . . . Although treating physicians may be an invaluable source of such information about a patient, the family will often be the best source. . . . The court should be mindful, however, that while in the majority of cases family members will have the best interests of the patient in mind, sometimes family members will rely on their own judgments or predilections rather than serving as conduits for expressing the patient's wishes. This is why the court should endeavor, whenever possible, to make an in-person appraisal "of the patient's personal desires and ability for rational choice...."

[If the court remains uncertain, it] may supplement its knowledge about the patient by determining what most persons would likely do in a similar situation. When the patient is pregnant, however, she may not be concerned exclusively with her own welfare. Thus it is proper for the court, in a case such as this, to weigh (along with all the other factors) the mother's prognosis, the viability of the fetus, the probable result of treatment or non-treatment for both mother and fetus, and the mother's likely interest in avoiding impairment for her child together with her own instincts for survival....

[The court set aside the trial court's order because of failure to determine the patient's competence and to follow the substituted judgment procedure.] Having said that, we go no further. We need not decide whether, or in what circumstances, the state's interests can ever prevail over the interests of a pregnant patient.... Indeed, some may doubt that there could ever be a situation extraordinary or compelling enough to justify a massive intrusion into a person's body, such as a caesarean section, against that person's will. Whether such a situation may someday present itself is a question that we need not strive to answer here....[23]

BELSON, Associate Judge, concurring in part and dissenting in part....

[T]he already recognized rights and interests [referring to Roe v. Wade and tort protection for postviability injuries] are sufficient to indicate the need for a balancing process in which the rights of the viable unborn child are assigned substantial weight.... The balancing test should be applied in instances in which women become pregnant and carry an unborn child to the point of viability. This is not an unreasonable classification because, I submit, a woman who carries a child to viability is in fact a member of a unique category of persons.... This is so because she has undertaken to bear another human being, and has

---

23. In particular, we stress that nothing in this opinion should be read as either approving or disapproving the holding in In re Madyun, supra. There are substantial factual differences between *Madyun* and the present case. In this case for instance, the medical interests of the mother and the fetus were in sharp conflict; what was good for one would have been harmful to the other. In *Madyun*, however, there was no real conflict between the interests of mother and fetus; on the contrary, there was strong evidence that the proposed caesarean would be beneficial to both. Moreover, in *Madyun* the pregnancy was at full term, and Mrs. Madyun had been in labor for two and a half days; in this case, however, A.C. was barely two-thirds of the way through her pregnancy, and there were no signs of labor. If another *Madyun*-type case ever comes before this court, its result may well depend on facts that we cannot now foresee. For that reason (among others), we defer until another day any discussion of whether *Madyun* was rightly or wrongly decided.

carried an unborn child to viability. . . . Also, uniquely, the viable unborn child is literally captive within the mother's body. . . .

. . . The indisputable view that a woman carrying a viable child has an extremely strong interest in her own life, health, bodily integrity, privacy, and religious beliefs necessarily requires that her election be given correspondingly great weight in the balancing process. In a case, however, where the court in an exercise of a substituted judgment has concluded that the patient would probably opt against a caesarean section, the court should vary the weight to be given this factor in proportion to the confidence the court has in the accuracy of its conclusion. . . .

On the other side of the analysis, it is appropriate to look to the relative likelihood of the unborn child's survival. This could range from the situation in *Madyun* where the full-term child's chances for survival were apparently excellent, through a case like the one before us where the unborn child's chances for survival were from fifty to sixty percent, and on to cases where the child's chances for survival are less than even. The child's interest in being born with as little impairment as possible should also be considered. This may weigh in favor of a delivery sooner rather than later. The most important factor on this side of the scale, however, is life itself, because the viable unborn child that dies because of the mother's refusal to have a caesarean delivery is deprived, entirely and irrevocably, of the life on which the child was about to embark. [Applying this balancing test to these facts, Judge Belson would affirm the trial court's order for the caesarean.]

■ **CAROL O'BRIEN, PATIENT'S LAWYER
CALLS A.C. CASE HUMAN SACRIFICE**
*Am. Med. News, Mar. 11, 1988, at 18*

[On June 16, 1987, lawyer Robert E. Sylvester] got a call seeking legal help for a medical emergency at George Washington U. Hospital. [When] Sylvester learned he would be representing Angela Carder, a 28-year-old office worker who was dying of long-term cancer and who was also carrying a 26-week-old fetus, he came to the hospital, armed with his usual gentle approach and his medical emergency packet — "cases I've collected that lay out common issues."

At the hearing in an administrative room at the hospital, Sylvester for the first time met Carder's parents and her husband. Carder, heavily sedated in her hospital room, was not present. But at the hearing presided over by Judge Emmett G. Sullivan of D.C. Superior Court, "were five or six doctors, a court stenographer, and lawyers hired from a high-powered law firm to represent the fetus and hospital." Sylvester and the ACLU were called to represent Angela.

After talking to her parents, Sylvester learned they had been told the night before their daughter was going to die. [A]fter talking to Carder's parents, her husband, and her physicians, Sylvester, who was unable to interview Angela at the time due to her sedation, believed Angela would not have wanted to submit to caesarian delivery, given the slim chance the baby would survive and be healthy, and the definite possibility the surgery would hasten Carder's imminent death. . . .

". . . The entire obstetrics department was opposed to it," recalled Sylvester. . . . Later that evening, a baby girl was delivered. The baby lived two hours. No one ever argued that the baby was or could have been viable, Sylvester said. "Strangely, once the baby was born, very little was done to save her . . . because, clearly, this was not a viable fetus."

Sadly, Angela came out of her sedated state briefly, only to learn her baby had died. She cried before slipping back into unconsciousness, and died two days later. "The secondary cause of death was the operation," Sylvester said. . . .

Sylvester gets intensely involved in all his family welfare cases, but the Carder case has had an overwhelming personal impact. A decade ago, Sylvester's first wife died of cancer at age 29 in the same hospital where Carder ultimately succumbed to it at about the same age.

Sylvester spent much of his wife's last eight months with her at George Washington hospital, and he remembers those final days "as the most important in our lives, not the least important. Those days were precious and loving and profound. . . . To say a dying person's last few hours or days doesn't matter is like saying that person's whole life didn't matter." Sylvester's personal tragedy led him to re-evaluate his life, and subsequently nudged him out of a lucrative law practice specializing in international trade law to his current specialty of family welfare and medical emergency law. . . .

Ironically, Sylvester said, the hospital, which sought the court hearing to determine whether a C-section should be done because of liability concerns, could be faced with a potential malpractice or wrongful death suit from Carder's family because of the way the case was handled.

"I think a lawsuit is a distinct possibility," said Sylvester. "This was a human sacrifice case. Can you kill a person for the benefit of a fetus, which under the law is one level away from what we consider a person? There is no Good Samaritan requirement under the law that forces a woman to sacrifice her life for that of her fetus. The irony is Angela all along had a constitutional right to an abortion, but at the end, she had no constitutional right to avoid a life-threatening operation.

"I think gender bias was present in our case, definitely. In a powerful and subliminal way, it's true that many perceive women, especially pregnant women, as second-class citizens, as carriers. What is also compelling about this case is the court was not able to think of this competent individual — and sedation should not be confused with competence — as having vested rights and being capable of exercising them. This case ultimately is about a lack of respect for the individual, and her right to make the medical care decision that is best for herself."

## Notes and Questions

1. The *A.C.* majority stresses that this case does not concern abortion. If so, why is the stage of gestational development relevant? Does this case merely highlight the conflict between the interests of two family members? If so, how and by whom should this conflict be resolved? What light does privacy doctrine or that of liberty interests (under *Cruzan*) shed?

2. What vision of the family emerges from *A.C.*? How does it compare to those in *Casey* and *Cruzan*? To what extent does *A.C.* recall the balance among maternal, fetal, and state interests examined in *Roe* (despite the court's disclaimers)?

3. How do you explain the outcome reached by the trial court and supported by the *A.C.* dissent? A preference for the interests of the fetus over the mother's? Thinly disguised paternalism? Failure to understand such cases as power struggles over reproduction? See Nancy Ehrenreich, The Colonization of the Womb, 43 Duke L.J. 492 (1993).

4. What does *A.C.* mean when it holds that the woman's decision must control "in virtually all cases"? How would the majority decide a case like In re Madyun, described in the court's footnote 23?

5. Do all women face an equal risk of court-ordered intervention? One empirical study of 21 court-ordered obstetrical procedures reveals that a disproportionate number involve minorities and nonnative English speakers. Veronika E. B. Kolder, Janet Gallagher & Michael Parsons, Court-Ordered Obstetrical Interventions, 316 N. Eng. J. Med. 1192, 1195 (1987).

6. Even when the woman had religious objections to surgery, courts usually ordered a caesarean section before *A.C.* For example, in Jefferson v. Griffin Spalding County Hosp. Auth., 274 S.E.2d 457 (Ga. 1981), the court refused to stay an order giving custody of an almost full-term fetus to the state and requiring the pregnant woman with complete placenta previa to submit to a sonogram and caesarean section, despite her religious objections.

More recent controversies reflect judicial reconsideration. After *A.C.*, George Washington University Medical Center announced a settlement agreeing to accede to the patient's decisions "whenever possible," with judicial intervention "virtually never" appropriate. See Linda Greenhouse, Hospital Policy Sets Out Pregnant Patient Rights, N.Y. Times,

Nov. 29, 1990, at A15. Also, in In re Baby Boy Doe, 632 N.E.2d 326 (Ill. App. Ct. 1994), the court rejected a balancing of rights, holding that a competent woman's refusal of treatment (for religious reasons) must be honored despite predicted harm to the fetus.

7. When the court-ordered caesarean yields a healthy baby and the mother's complete recovery, does it necessarily mean a "happy ending"? Compare Janet Gallagher, Prenatal Invasions and Interventions: What's Wrong with Fetal Rights, 10 Harv. Women's L.J. 9, 9-10 (1987) (reporting hospital's perception of "happy ending" after forced caesarean over religious objections), with Kolder et al., supra, at 1193 (reporting father's subsequent suicide in same case).

8. In cases of court-ordered caesareans, what weight should attach to medical fallibility? See Nancy K. Rhoden, The Judge in the Delivery Room: The Emergence of Court-Ordered Cesareans, 74 Cal. L. Rev. 1951 (1986). Note that the baby died *despite* the caesarean in *A.C.*; the placenta blocking the birth canal moved without medical intervention in *Jefferson*, supra; and the mother vaginally delivered an apparently healthy child in *Baby Boy Doe*, supra.

9. Beyond blood transfusions and caesareans, so-called maternal-fetal conflicts can arise in a number of additional contexts. For example, many states do not honor advance directives (provisions for living wills and the appointment of proxy health care decisionmakers) for incompetent pregnant patients. As a result, the woman can be kept alive until the fetus can mature, despite her expressed wishes to the contrary. See Bretton J. Horttor, A Survey of Living Will and Advanced Health Care Directives, 74 N.D. L. Rev. 233 (1998) (reporting, based on survey, that 36 states prohibit the withdrawal of life support from pregnant women). Similarly, the promise of prenatal treatment to prevent transmission of HIV has raised the question of mandatory testing and the administration of AZT even to pregnant women who have not consented. See Jennifer Brown, A Troublesome Maternal-Fetal Conflict: Legal, Ethical, and Social Issues Surrounding Mandatory AZT Treatment of HIV Positive Pregnant Women, 18 Buff. Pub. Int. L.J. 67 (2000). And nonconsensual drug testing of pregnant women has been rationalized as a means of protecting fetuses from exposure to cocaine. See Ferguson v. City of Charleston, 532 U.S. 67 (2001) (state hospital's action constitutes unreasonable search in violation of Fourth Amendment).

Would a more helpful analysis present all such situations as "maternal-doctor conflicts," rather than maternal-fetal conflicts, given physicians' "central role in generating and escalating these conflicts"? See Michelle Oberman, Mothers and Doctors' Orders: Unmasking the Doctor's Fiduciary Role in Maternal-Fetal Conflicts, 94 Nw. U. L. Rev. 451, 454, 500 (2000). As larger questions of parental responsibility that include consideration of postnatal obligations? See John A. Robertson, Children of Choice: Freedom and the New Reproductive Technologies

193 (1994) (law does not require parents to donate marrow or organs to children after they are born).

## Problems

1. Nancy Klein, age 32, is 16 weeks pregnant when her husband, Martin Klein, seeks appointment as her guardian so that he can authorize an abortion. Nancy had been comatose for seven weeks following a car accident; physicians had advised Martin that terminating the pregnancy would improve Nancy's chances of recovery. The Kleins have a three-year-old daughter. Nancy's parents support Martin's petition. Abortion at this stage of pregnancy presents some risks (equal to or greater than the risks posed by continued pregnancy, according to some but not all physicians). Abortion will increase the safety of administering medication and permit aggressive rehabilitation should Nancy emerge from her coma, and physicians have little hope that Nancy will recover from her brain damage. Abortion opponents, not related to the family, seek to intervene to prevent the procedure.

Suppose you are the judge on the petition for guardianship. What additional evidence, if any, would you need to decide the case? How would you obtain it? How would you decide the case? See In the Matter of Klein, 538 N.Y.S.2d 274 (App. Div.), *appeal denied,* 536 N.E.2d 627 (N.Y.), *stay denied sub nom.* Short v. Klein, 489 U.S. 1003 (1989).

2. Wife becomes pregnant for the purpose of aborting and donating the fetal tissue to Husband, who suffers from Parkinson's disease, a condition that has been shown to respond favorably to fetal tissue transplantation. See, e.g., Susan Lee, Recent Developments in Health Law, Human Stem Cell Research: NIH Releases Draft Guidelines for Comment, 28 J.L. Med. & Ethics 81 (2000). All physicians refuse to participate in the plan, however, because of the following state criminal statute:

> 1. No physician shall perform an abortion on a woman if the physician knows that the woman conceived the unborn child for the purpose of providing fetal organs or tissue for medical transplantation to herself or another, and the physician knows that the woman intends to procure the abortion to utilize those organs or tissue for such use for herself or another.
> 2. No person shall utilize the fetal organs or tissue resulting from an abortion for medical transplantation, if the person knows that the abortion was procured for the purpose of utilizing those organs or tissue for such use.

Wife and Husband consult you, an attorney, about filing suit to challenge the constitutionality of the statute. How would you proceed? What additional information would you need? If you file suit, assess the chances of success. To what extent would your arguments change if the proposed procedure were sought to benefit the ten-year-old son of Wife and Husband rather than Husband himself? See Mo. Rev. Stat. §188.036 (2000). See also, e.g., S.D. Codified Laws §§34-14-16 to 34-14-19 (West, WESTLAW through end of 2000 Reg. Sess.) (prohibiting research that destroys human embryo when research not intended to help preserve life and health of particular embryo); Robin Toner, The Abortion Debate, Stuck in Time, N.Y. Times, Jan. 21, 2001, §4, at 1 (how abortion politics have colored debate on stem cell research).

# II

# *Getting Married*

## A. INTRODUCTION:
## PUBLIC VERSUS PRIVATE DIMENSIONS
## OF COURTSHIP AND MARRIAGE

### 1. Courtship Patterns

The premarital relationship has become increasingly private. The excerpts below explore the public and private dimensions of courtship over time.

### ■ JOHN DEMOS, A LITTLE COMMONWEALTH: FAMILY LIFE IN PLYMOUTH COLONY
*152, 154-155, 157-162 (2000)*

[T]he initial phases of courtship [in colonial Plymouth colony] lacked much formal ceremony (no dating, dances, and so forth). [W]hen a courtship had developed to a certain point of intensity, the parents became directly involved. An early order of the General Court directed

117

that "none be allowed to marry that are under the covert of parents but by their consent and approbacon." Later on, the Court came to feel that a stronger statement was necessary and amended the law [to provide for fine or corporal punishment for anyone who proposed marriage to a "daughter or mayde servant" without first securing parental consent].

[The law placed limits on the power of parents and masters to refuse consent and permitted an appeal in some cases to local magistrates.] [A]ctions of this type were rarely, if ever, initiated. Indeed, the reverse situation is what shows up in the Colony records — the situation in which a father sought to forestall an attempt to woo his daughter contrary to his own wishes. . . .

[Following the securing of parental approval, a series of steps still remained.] [T]he "betrothal" or "contract" [was] a simple ceremony which bears comparison to our own custom of "engagement." [This] was a very serious undertaking [as] failure to fulfill such a contract would create the likelihood of legal action. [S]exual intimacies *between* the contracted parties fell into a category all their own. They could not be officially condoned, but the usual penalty was relatively light. . . .

[A]nother formal step became necessary: the "publishing" of the banns [that is, posting notice of the parties' intent to marry for 14 days or making an announcement to this effect three times in a public meeting]. [Still another important matter] was a set of transactions designed to underwrite the economic welfare of the contracted couple. [A] young man would receive the bulk of his portion in the form of land and housing, a woman would be given a variety of domestic furnishings, cattle, and/or money. . . .

[F]ourteen days was the minimum interval allowable between the betrothal ceremony and the wedding itself — between "contract and covenant," in the language of the time. [M]ost couples waited considerably longer: two or three months seems to have been quite customary. [T]radition has it that this was an occasion for sober reflection, and, if need be, for reconsideration — before the final step was taken. . . .


## ■ JOHN C. MILLER, THE FIRST FRONTIER: LIFE IN COLONIAL AMERICA
### 192-194 (1972)

The long winters and small and inadequately heated houses of New England and New York created a serious problem for unmarried young men and women. Where could the rites of courtship be performed? The family fireside, around which the entire family usually congregated, was too public for the kind of intimacy the circumstances demanded, yet to remove any distance from its benign glow was apt to chill the ardor of even the most hot-blooded lover. A solution was found in the ancient and parentally approved custom of bundling. A young man and woman, fully clothed, lay down together in bed, crawled under the blankets and exchanged confidences and, insofar as possible, endearments. Bundling was governed by a rigorous code that even the most amorous were expected to observe: "Thus far and no farther" was a motto that might appropriately have been hung at the head of a bed reserved for bundling. . . .

Bundling began to go out of fashion about the time of the French and Indian War — perhaps because the British soldiers quartered in the colonies did not abide by the rules of the game. Clergyman began to take disapproving note of the practice in their sermons; what had once been regarded as a harmless and comfortable way of courting was stigmatized as a sin. Moreover, the construction of larger and better-heated houses in New England weakened the case for bundling. And so, after over a century of popularity, the custom was loaded with obloquy and banished from the land. Not until the advent of the automobile did young Americans recover one of the freedoms they had lost in the colonial period. . . .

## ■ BETH L. BAILEY, FROM FRONT PORCH TO BACK SEAT: COURTSHIP IN TWENTIETH-CENTURY AMERICA
### 19-22 (1988)

Between 1890 and 1925, dating — in practice and in name — had gradually, almost imperceptibly, become a universal custom in America. By the 1930s it had transcended its origins. [Dating had its origins in the urban lower classes who lacked the family space (such as the parlor) in which to conduct courtship activities and who took advantage of the excitement and opportunities presented by the urban environment.] The rise of dating was usually explained, quite simply, by the invention of the automobile [but, the automobile] simply accelerat[ed] and extend[ed] a process already well under way. . . .

Dating not only transformed the outward modes and conventions of American courtship, it also changed the distribution of control and power in courtship. One change was generational: the dating system lessened parental control and gave young men and women more freedom. The dating system also shifted power from women to men. [The former courtship practice of "calling" on a woman] gave women a large portion of control. First of all, courtship took place within the girl's home — in women's "sphere," as it was called in the nineteenth century — or at entertainments largely devised and presided over by women. Dating moved courtship out of the home and into man's sphere — the world outside the home. . . .

Second, in the calling system, the woman took the initiative. . . . Contrast these strictures with advice on dating etiquette from the 1940s and 1950s: An advice book for men and women warns that "girls who [try] to usurp the right of boys to choose their own dates" will "ruin a good dating career. . . ." An invitation to go out on a date . . . was an invitation into man's world — not simply because dating took place in the public sphere (commonly defined as belonging to men) [but also] because dating moved courtship into the world of the economy. Money — men's money — was at the center of the dating system. [M]oney shift[ed] control and initiative to men by making them the "hosts," [and] led contemporaries to see dating as a system of exchange. . . .

---

On the history of courtship, see generally Richard Adair, Courtship, Illegitimacy, and Marriage in Early Modern England (1996); Howard P. Chudacoff, The Age of the Bachelor: Creating an American Subculture (1999); Diana O'Hara, Courtship and Constraint: Rethinking the Meaning of Marriage in Tudor England (2000); Cathy Luchetti, "I Do": Courtship, Love and Marriage on the American Frontier (1996); Ellen Rothman, Hands and Hearts: A History of Courtship in America (1987).

Courtship today often includes a stage of cohabitation. A widespread belief is that premarital cohabitation leads to more stable marriages. In fact, research reveals that marriages that follow a period of cohabitation are not more stable, and, perhaps, even at higher risk of dissolution.[1] This finding may be due to cohabitants' attraction to nontraditional lifestyles. (Legal regulation of cohabitation, as an alternative family form, is discussed in Chapter 4, section C.)

In addition, the modern family reflects a new development. Many young adults now live with parents for extended periods.[2] Reasons include a desire to delay marriage, or a wish to obtain higher education, and the difficulty of becoming self-supporting (experienced especially by affluent youth who cannot replicate their parents' living standard).[3] Does this development entail a return to more "public" courtship? AIDS also has changed courtship attitudes and behavior (for example, by decreasing sexual experimentation).[4]

[1]. Edward O. Laumann et al., The Social Organization of Sexuality: Sexual Practices in the United States 501 (1994); Alfred DeMaris & K. Vaninadha Rao, Premarital Cohabitation and Subsequent Marital Stability in the United States: A Reassessment, 54 J. Marriage & Fam. 178 (1992); Elizabeth Thomson & Ugo Colella, Cohabitation and Marital Stability: Quality or Commitment?, 54 J. Marriage & Fam. 259 (1992).

[2]. See U.S. Census Bureau, Current Population Reports, Household and Family Characteristics: March 1998 (Update) (noting that 14.4 percent of family households still have children 18 and older living at home).

[3]. Martha Farnsworth Riche, Mysterious Young Adults, in Family in Transition 123, 123 (Arlene S. Skolnick & Jerome H. Skolnick eds., 1989).

[4]. See Peter Davis, Exploring the Kingdom of AIDS, in Family in Transition, supra note [3], at 245, 246-250 (anecdotal evidence that AIDS is decreasing sexual experimentation).

## 2. The Marriage Contract

A classic question asks: Is marriage a contract (a private agreement between two parties) or a status (a public institution regulated by the state)? Or does marriage retain features of both?

■ **MAYNARD v. HILL**
*125 U.S. 190 (1887)*

Mr. Justice FIELD.

[While] marriage is often termed by text writers and in decisions of courts as a civil contract — generally to indicate that it must be founded upon the agreement of the parties, and does not require any religious ceremony for its solemnization — it is something more than a mere contract. The consent of the parties is of course essential to its existence, but when the contract to marry is executed by the marriage, a relation between the parties is created which they cannot change. Other contracts may be modified, restricted, or enlarged, or entirely released upon the consent of the parties. Not so with marriage. The relation once formed, the law steps in and holds the parties to various obligations and liabilities. It is an institution, in the maintenance of which in its purity the public is deeply interested, for it is the foundation of the family and of society, without which there would be neither civilization nor progress. This view is well expressed by the supreme court of Maine in Adams v. Palmer, 51 Me. 481, 483 . . . :

> When the contracting parties have entered into the married state, they have not so much entered into a contract as into a new relation, the rights, duties, and obligations of which rest not upon their agreement, but upon the general law of the State, statutory or common, which defines and prescribes those rights, duties, and obligations. They are of law, not of contract. It was of contract that the relation should be established, but, being established, the power of the parties as to its extent or duration is at an end. Their rights under it are determined by the will of the sovereign, as evidenced by law. They can neither be modified nor changed by any agreement of parties. It is a relation for life, and the parties cannot terminate it at any shorter period by virtue of any contract they may make. The reciprocal rights arising from this relation, so long as it continues, are such as the law determines from time to time, and none other.

And again:

> It is not then a contract within the meaning of the clause of the constitution which prohibits the impairing the obligation of contracts. It is rather a social relation like that of parent and child, the obligations of which arise

not from the consent of concurring minds, but are the creation of the law itself, a relation the most important, as affecting the happiness of individuals, the first step from barbarism to incipient civilization, the purest tie of social life, and the true basis of human progress.

Pp. 484, 485. . . .

## ■ HENRY MAINE, ANCIENT LAW
### 163-165 (1963)

The movement of the progressive societies has been uniform in one respect. [I]t has been distinguished by the gradual dissolution of family dependency and the growth of individual obligation in its place. The Individual is steadily substituted for the Family, as the unit of which civil laws take account. The advance has been accomplished at varying rates of celerity, and there are societies not absolutely stationary in which the collapse of the ancient organization can only be perceived by careful study. . . . But, whatever its pace, the change has not been subject to reaction or recoil, and apparent retardations will be found to have been occasioned through the absorption of archaic ideas and customs from some entirely foreign source. Nor is it difficult to see what is the tie between man and man which replaces by degrees those forms of reciprocity in rights and duties which have their origin in the Family. It is Contract. Starting, as from one terminus of history, from a condition of society in which all the relations of Persons are summed up in the relations of Family, we seem to have steadily moved towards a phase of social order in which all these relations arise from the free agreement of individuals. In Western Europe the progress achieved in this direction has been considerable. Thus the status of the Slave has disappeared — it has been superseded by the contractual relation of the servant to his master. The status of the Female under Tutelage, if the tutelage be understood of persons other than her husband, has also ceased to exist; from her coming of age to her marriage all the relations she may form are relations of contract. [W]e may say that the movement of the progressive societies has hitherto been a movement *from Status to Contract.*

## ■ SUSAN MOLLER OKIN, JUSTICE, GENDER, AND THE FAMILY
### 122-123 (1989)

[M]arriage itself has long been regarded as a contract, though it is a very peculiar one: it is a contract that does not conform with the *principles* (let alone the counterprinciples) of liberal contract doctrine. It is a preformed status contract, which restricts the parties' freedom to choose their partners (for example, there must be only one partner, and of the opposite sex) and of which they are not free to choose the terms.

The courts' refusal to enforce explicit contracts between husband and wife has been by no means completely attributable to reluctance to intrude into a private community supposedly built upon trust. It has been due at least as much to the fact that the courts have regarded the terms of marriage as already established. When, for example, they have refused to enforce intramarital agreements in which wives have agreed to forgo support for other consideration, and in which husbands have agreed to pay their wives for work done in a family business, they have done so on the grounds that the wife's right to support, in the former case, and her obligation to provide services for her husband, in the latter, are fixed by the marriage contract itself. Likewise, when courts have showed a reluctance to enforce the terms of the preformed contracted itself — for example, refusing to establish a level of adequate support that a wife must receive — it has been on the grounds that, so long as husband and wife cohabit, it is up to him as the family head to determine such matters. Another respect in which marriage is an anomalous contract is that the parties to it are not required to be familiar with the terms of the relationship into which they are entering. . . .

## B. PREPARING TO MARRY: PREMARITAL CONTROVERSIES

### 1. Breach of Promise to Marry

■ **GILBERT v. BARKES**
*987 S.W.2d 772 (Ky. 1999)*

STEPHENS, Justice.

The issue we decide on this appeal is whether the claim of breach of promise to marry is still a viable legal cause of action in Kentucky. . . .

The facts which give rise to this action are as follows. Ms. Suzanne Barkes, appellee, and Dr. Alvin Gilbert, appellant, entered into a relationship beginning in January of 1989 which continued until June of 1994. Ms. Barkes claims that in September of 1990, Dr. Gilbert proposed marriage to her and that in December of 1990, she accepted. Ms. Barkes submits that she received an engagement ring from Dr. Gilbert. In reliance upon her impending marriage and at Dr. Gilbert's insistence, Ms. Barkes claims that she took early retirement in 1992. Subsequently, Ms. Barkes sold her home in January of 1993 and moved into Dr. Gilbert's home. Sometime in 1994, the parties' relationship began to deteriorate and Ms. Barkes left Dr. Gilbert's home.

In June of 1994 Ms. Barkes filed an action for Breach of Promise to Marry (BPM). [The trial court granted defendant's motion for summary judgment. The court of appeals reversed.]

## I. HISTORY OF ACTION FOR BREACH OF PROMISE TO MARRY

The right of an individual to sue for Breach of Promise to Marry is a common law hybrid of tort and contract. Its origin, however, goes back to canon law, which only enforced such a breach through specific performance of the promise. Through time such harsh measures were no longer enforced. The common law has since adopted the action.

In the fifteenth century, English courts embraced the action, primarily because the basis of marriage was largely viewed as a property transaction. However, in those early times, the aggrieved party was only able to recover monies expended on a deceitful promise to marry. In the seventeenth century, the need to prove deceit was eliminated from the cause of action.

Following the lead of England, the American colonies adopted the action. The action found a receptive audience in this country eventually becoming more popular in America than in England. Michael Grossberg, *Governing the Hearth: Law and Family in Nineteenth-Century America,* 37 (1985). . . .

The elements of the BPM action are predicated upon contract principles with the exception of damages, which has its roots in tort. . . . Because the issue of damages stems from tort principles, the amount is not limited to what is recoverable in the typical contract action for a breach of promise. Three general classes of damages have emerged from this action: compensatory damages relating to the loss of the marriage, aggravated damages for seduction under promise of marriage, and punitive damages for malicious conduct. In Kentucky, this Court laid down an exhaustive list of factors to consider when estimating damages:

> [I]t is proper to consider anxiety of mind produced by the breach; loss of time and expenses incurred in preparation for the marriage; advantages which might have accrued to plaintiff from the marriage; the loss of a permanent home and advantageous establishment; plaintiff's loss of employment in consequence of the engagement or loss of health in consequence of the breach; the length of the engagement; the depth of plaintiff's devotion to defendant; defendant's conduct and treatment of plaintiff in his whole intercourse with her; injury to plaintiff's reputation or future prospects of marriage; plaintiff's loss of other opportunities of marriage by reason of her engagement to defendant; plaintiff's lack of independent means; her altered social condition in relation to her home and family, due to defendant's conduct; and the fact that she was living unhappily at the time of the alleged promise.

[Scharringhaus v. Hazen, 107 S.W.2d 329, 336 (1937) *citing,* 9 C.J. 372.] . . .

## II. Should the Cause of Action for Breach of Promise to Marry Be Abolished from Kentucky Common Law?

In deciding whether to modify the common law, this Court must weigh the benefits versus the burdens of the proposed change. We shall examine the rationale for removing the BPM action from the common law and then we shall discuss the reasons why it should be retained.

The primary argument in favor of abolition of the BPM action is that society's views of marriage and women have changed dramatically since this cause of action was adopted. While technically either a man or a woman could bring the cause of action in question, this Court is unaware of a man ever asserting such claim before the courts of the Commonwealth. The cases which interpret this cause of action make clear the party who is sought to be protected:

> A promise to marry is not infrequently one of the base and wicked tricks of the wily seducer to accomplish his purposes by overcoming that resistance which female virtue makes to his unholy designs.

Scharringhaus v. Hazen, 269 Ky. 425, 107 S.W.2d 329, 336 (1937) (*citing* Goodall v. Thurman, 38 Tenn. 209, 1 Head 209 (Tenn. Dec. Term 1858)). This language reflects the sexism and paternalism that pervade this cause of action. While one could certainly debate whether equality has been achieved between women and men in our society, it is certainly beyond issue that women today possess far more economic, legal and political rights than did their predecessors. Accordingly, we must examine the utility of the BPM action in the context of the present day, not in the era in which it was created.

Our review of the actions taken by other jurisdictions indicates that twenty-eight states have legislatively or judicially abolished the Breach of Promise to Marry action [citations omitted]. The work of various commentators on this issue demonstrates criticism starting late in the last century and continuing up to the present [citations omitted].

[W]e now turn to the arguments in favor of its retention. There are two primary arguments in favor of retaining the BPM action. The first is that the General Assembly has implicitly adopted it by placing a statute of limitations upon the period in which such an action can be brought. KRS 413.140(1)(c). The second is that the doctrine of stare decisis compels this Court to retain the action since it is a long-standing remedy and there is no sound reason to eliminate it because it still serves the useful purpose of remedying injury to those who are left standing at the altar.

We find no merit in the first argument. . . . No legislative approval or disapproval of this court-created claim is indicated by [the statute of limitations]. The second argument is equally as unpersuasive. Stare decisis is a doctrine which has real meaning to this Court. . . . However, when this Court finds a common law cause of action to be anomalous, unworkable or contrary to public policy, it will abolish the action.

We believe the cause of action for breach of promise to marry has become an anachronism that has out-lived its usefulness and should be removed from the common law of the Commonwealth. "It is a barbarous remedy, outgrown by advancing civilization and, like other outgrown relics of a barbarous age, it must go." [Harter F. Wright, *The Action for Breach of the Marriage Promise*, 10 Va. L. Rev. 361, 382 (1924).] . . . Accordingly, the action for Breach of Promise to Marry is no longer a valid cause of action before the courts of the Commonwealth.

This Court wishes to make clear that it in no way prohibits other remedies, such as claims for breach of contract and intentional infliction of emotional distress, should a party be able to make such a case. . . . While we are removing a cause of action from the common law, we are not eradicating the ability of a party to seek a remedy for such a wrong, but rather we are modifying the form that remedy may take. . . .

### III. APPLICATION OF LAW TO THE FACTS OF THIS CASE

For several reasons, Ms. Barkes is precluded from recovery from Dr. Gilbert under any contractual theory. First, there were none of the "normal expenses attendant to a wedding" such as a bridal dress, down payment on a reception hall or the like. Ms. Barkes' economic claims were only for the sale of her house and taking early retirement. Neither of these damages are the type of direct wedding-related economic out-of-pocket expenses that are recoverable. Since only direct economic losses of this type can be recovered and there is no proof of any such losses in this case, no recovery is possible. Second, since no wedding date was ever actually set, there is no way Ms. Barkes could recover under any contractual theory because she cannot otherwise affirmatively demonstrate the parties' final and serious intent to enter into marriage. Accordingly, since both of these conditions would have to be met before Ms. Barkes could state a viable contract claim, there is no way that she could maintain any sort of contract action against Dr. Gilbert.

Under the principles of Intentional Infliction of Emotional Distress (IIED), Ms. Barkes is similarly precluded because the record demonstrates that she falls short of proving the elements of this claim. . . . To make out a claim of IIED, the following elements must be proved: (1) the wrongdoer's conduct must be intentional or reckless; (2) the conduct must be outrageous and intolerable in that it offends against generally accepted standards of decency and morality; (3) there must be a causal connection between the wrongdoer's conduct and the emotional distress; and (4) the emotional distress must be severe. . . .

[T]he first and fourth elements require a more detailed discussion. . . . Recklessness in this context requires that the wrongdoer's actions reflect a lack of consideration well in excess of the thoughtlessness that would be evident in most engagements which are broken off. To meet the necessary recklessness threshold, the wrongdoer must engage in conduct which demonstrates total disregard for the other party. The plaintiff must prove conduct that is so insensitive and irresponsible as to rise to the level of being deemed virtually intentional. It must be the conduct which any normal and prudent person would know was likely to cause extreme emotional distress.

With respect to the fourth element, there is a fairly high level of emotional distress any time any engagement is broken off. To meet the element of severe emotional distress, however, substantially more than mere sorrow is required. From the record, it is clear that Ms. Barkes has not alleged facts which could even begin to support a claim for IIED.

### CONCLUSION

The ideas which predominated in the era that begat the cause of action for Breach of Promise to Marry no longer command the allegiance of the Citizens of the Commonwealth. Accordingly, this Court must act to keep the Common Law of Kentucky in step with its citizens. For the reasons stated above we no longer believe that this cause of action should be a part of our common law. . . . We reverse the Kentucky Court of Appeals and reinstate the trial court's order dismissing this claim.

## Notes and Questions

1. *Trend.* The trend is toward abolition of the action for breach of promise to marry, as *Gilbert* explains. Illinois is among the few jurisdictions that still recognize the claim, although with limitations. In Wildey v. Springs, 840 F. Supp. 1259 (N.D. Ill. 1994), a Chicago attorney sued wealthy Oregon rancher Richard A. Springs for breach of promise to marry. The engagement allegedly occurred at the Orlando airport after the couple returned from a Florida vacation and was reaffirmed in Chicago when Springs formally proposed on one knee. Based on an Illinois statute that permits recovery for actual damages but disallows punitive damages, a jury awarded the plaintiff $60,000 for lost business profits, $25,000 for medical expenses, and $93,000 for pain and suffering. The Seventh Circuit Court of Appeals reversed based on the plaintiff's failure to comply with statutory notice requirements (i.e., she omitted to include in her written notice of suit the date when the promise to marry was made). 47 F.3d 1475 (7th Cir. 1995). Why might the plaintiff have omitted the date?

See also Schwalb v. Wood, 680 N.E.2d 773 (Ill. App. Ct. 1997) (holding that plaintiff, who sued for $25,000 in damages suffered when defendant broke engagement seven days before the wedding, substantially complied with notice requirements of Breach of Promise Act); Marcia Froelke Coburn, The End of the Affair, Chicago Mag., June 1, 2001, at 36 (describing $5 million breach of promise suit by a female personal injury lawyer against a prominent Chicago real estate developer).

2. *Historical background.* The modern action of breach of promise reflects Roman, Germanic, and canon law influences. In early Roman law, the consequences of a broken promise to marry were mild, reflecting a belief in contractual freedom.[5] In contrast, Germanic custom (adopting a moral stance) awarded damages to "punish" the breach.[6] In both traditions, the consequences were more severe if the woman broke the engagement.[7]

The Germanic view of marriage influenced the English and French ecclesiastical courts that enforced the action in the Middle Ages.[8] By 1576, English common law courts also entertained actions for breach of promise.[9] The common law action, based in assumpsit, allowed damages for mental suffering as well as expenses incurred in anticipation of marriage.

Criticisms of the action emerged in the nineteenth century. The House of Commons tried unsuccessfully to limit the action in 1879.[10] Parliament abolished the action in 1970.[11] In America, the controversy culminated in a movement in the 1930s when many states enacted statutes (termed "heart balm" or "anti-heart balm" legislation) to eliminate the action.[12]

---

[5]. Patrick Mac Chombaich de Coloquhoun, 1 A Summary of the Roman Civil Law 455 (1988). See also H. F. Jolowicz & Barry Nicholas, Historical Introduction to the Study of Roman Law 233 (3d ed. 1972) ("The contract . . . was certainly not enforceable in classical times, when all restrictions on the freedom of the parties were regarded as improper. . . .").

[6]. Rudolf Huebner, A History of Germanic Private Law 601 (1918); Paul Weidenbaum, Breach of Promise in Private International Law, 14 N.Y.U. L.Q. Rev. 451, 452 (1937).

[7]. According to Roman custom, if the groom broke the engagement without cause, the earnest money he pledged to the bride's family would be forfeited. If the bride terminated the engagement, she was forced to give double the pledged earnest money. Mac Chombaich de Coloquhoun, supra note [5], at 455. In Germanic law, if the man broke the engagement, he lost the payment he made to purchase the woman's guardianship. If the woman broke the contract, she returned the payment in addition to an equal amount in damages. Huebner, supra note [6], at 601.

[8]. Jean Brissaud, A History of French Private Law 99 (1912); 3 William Blackstone, Commentaries *92-94.

[9]. The Law Commission, Breach of Promise to Marry 2 n.4 (1969).

[10]. Edwin Hadley, Breach of Promise to Marry, 2 Notre Dame L. Rev. 190, 193 (1927).

[11]. Law Reform (Miscellaneous Provisions) Act, 1970, ch. 33, §1 (Eng.).

[12]. On the abolition movement, see generally James P. Byrnes, The Illinois Anti-Heart Balm Law, 38 Ill. L. Rev. 94 (1943-1944); Nathan P. Feinsinger, Legislative Attack on "Heart Balm," 33 Mich. L. Rev. 980 (1935).

3. *Damages.* Breach of contract is a hybrid action, reflecting roots in contract and tort law. A plaintiff can recover the monetary and social value of the marriage (expectation damages), as well as expenses incurred in preparation for the marriage (reliance damages). Damages for mental anguish and humiliation, not normally compensable in contract, may also be recoverable. Punitive damages are sometimes permitted. Some jurisdictions enhance damages for seduction.

Given that marriage has become an emotional commitment rather than a property transaction, should breach-of-promise-to-marry claims provide a cause of action? If so, what damages should be recoverable? Loss of anticipated social and financial position? Compare Stanard v. Bolin, 565 P.2d 94, 97 (Wash. 1977) (such damages "not justified in light of modern society's concept of marriage"), with Bradley v. Somers, 322 S.E.2d 665, 666 (S.C. 1984) (permitting damages for "pecuniary and social advantages").

Should emotional distress, such as the harm suffered by plaintiff Suzanne Barkes be compensated? Should measurement difficulties justify limiting damages to economic loss? Should recovery be limited to reliance damages? See Neil G. Williams, What to Do When There's No "I Do": A Model for Awarding Damages Under Promissory Estoppel, 70 Wash. L. Rev. 1019 (1995) (recommending recovery only for incurred expenditures and forgone economic opportunities). How significant are reliance damages stemming from a broken engagement? Commentators point out that the typical wedding costs $19,000.[13] As the wedding approaches, fewer costs are recoverable in the event of cancellation.

> Engagement rings can usually be returned for a full refund for 60 to 100 days after purchase. But some cities, including New York, allow caterers and hotels to charge for services and rooms that cannot be rebooked when canceled with less than six months notice. Wedding gown makers typically require an initial nonrefundable deposit of half the price of the dress, with the balance on delivery. The week before the wedding, the cake and flowers are delivered. When an engagement is broken the day of the wedding, almost none of the cost can be recovered.[14]

4. *Defenses.* Traditional defenses to breach-of-promise claims include physical and mental defects, unchastity of the plaintiff, plaintiff's lack of love for the defendant, and mutuality of the decision to terminate the

---

[13]. Belle Elving, Weddings; Ringing It Up, Wash. Post, Jan. 15, 1998, at T04; Cost of "I Do," USA Today, Apr. 17, 2000, at 1D. See also Keith Bradsher, Ditching Your Betrothed May Cost You: Wedding Rings, Gowns, Cakes and Deposits Add Up, S.F. Chron., Mar. 20, 1990, at B5 (noting that costs vary by geography and that a wedding in New York City may cost as much as $50,000 to $100,000).

[14]. Bradsher, supra note [13]. He estimates, based on a comparison of the number of marriage license applications with actual marriages, that approximately 5 percent of engagements in New York City are broken annually.

engagement. Should a plaintiff's obsessive-compulsive disorder excuse a defendant's performance? See Wildey v. Springs, 840 F. Supp. 1259 (N.D. Ill. 1994). A defendant's subsequent good faith offer to marry the plaintiff, while not a defense, may mitigate damages. What does this mitigating factor reflect about the nature of the injury?

5. At common law, and in a few states today, a false promise to marry may trigger tort liability for the separate act of seduction. See, e.g., Parker v. Bruner, 683 S.W.2d 265 (Mo. 1984) (upholding verdict for $25,000 actual and $50,000 punitive damages), cert. denied, 474 U.S. 827 (1985). This tort occurs when an unmarried and previously chaste woman consents to unlawful intercourse in reliance on a false promise to marry. At common law, the action was maintainable not by the woman, but by one entitled to her services (that is, her father or someone in loco parentis). On the history of the tort, see Lea Vandervelde, The Legal Ways of Seduction, 48 Stan. L. Rev. 817 (1996).

Seduction also constitutes a crime in some states. See, e.g., Okla. Stat. Ann. tit. 21, §1120 (West 1983 & Supp. 2001). Should legislatures abolish criminal and/or tort liability for seduction, given the fact that a woman's loss of virginity no longer has such a deleterious effect on her marital prospects? See Linda J. Lacey, Introducing Feminist Jurisprudence: An Analysis of Oklahoma's Seduction Statute, 25 Tulsa L.J. 775, 776 (1990) (arguing that penal statutes are "antiquated and unconstitutional"). Or, as one commentator suggests, should legislatures adopt the tort of "sexual fraud" based on a fraudulent misrepresentation of fact, opinion, intention, or law for the purpose of inducing sexual relations that results in serious physical, pecuniary, and emotional loss? See Jane E. Larson, "Women Understand So Little, They Call My Good Nature 'Deceit' ": A Feminist Rethinking of Seduction, 93 Colum. L. Rev. 374, 453 (1993).

6. *Victimization paradigm.* Professor Coombs points out that the criticisms prompting the abolition of breach-of-promise-to-marry suits were "extraordinarily virulent" and "embodied [negative] views of women." Mary Coombs, Agency and Partnership: A Study of Breach of Promise Plaintiffs, 2 Yale J.L. & Feminism 1, 6 (1989). Based on her study of breach-of-promise plaintiffs, Coombs notes the following paradox with policy implications:

> Early feminists believed that women were to achieve economic independence through careers bringing respect and fair wages. Marriage was to be an emotional partnership rooted in continuing mutual affection. Women were to rediscover their sexual natures. The rules of sexual behavior were to be the same for men and women.
>
> The presumption that women were seduced into sexual activity and the claim that the loss of virginity was a devastating harm to women contradicted the progressive view of women's sexuality. . . . Yet at least some of the women who brought such suits suffered real harms, for reality had

not — indeed, has not entirely — caught up to the feminist ideal. Furthermore, bringing such a suit is itself an unorthodox action for women. The plaintiffs did not simply accept the harm that had been done to them, but took action to improve their situations. . . . The paradox is that the most effective action available to these women — a breach of promise suit — required them to present themselves as passive victims, a picture contradicted by the very action of bringing suit.

Coombs, supra, at 3. Despite this victimization characterization, Coombs argues that the principle of monetary redress for relationship harms should not be abandoned, for that would constitute "an attempt to build ideological purity at the expense of the oppressed." Id. at 2-3.[15] See also Ginger S. Frost, Promises Broken: Courtship, Class, and Gender in Victorian England (1995) (historical study of nineteenth-century breach-of-promise cases, finding that fictional negative accounts influenced popular opinion more than actual case law).

## Problems

1. Marilyn is dating Donald, a married man, when she discovers that she is pregnant with his child. He promises her that if she has the abortion, he will pay her $75,000 plus medical and legal expenses. He also tells her that he will marry her when his divorce is final and that they will later have a baby together. Marilyn agrees, has the abortion, and accepts the payment. When they break up, she sues him for intentional and negligent infliction of emotional distress, battery, fraud, and misrepresentation. She alleges that the settlement agreement is unconscionable, against public policy, and was extracted under duress and coercion. Donald moves for summary judgment on the ground that the jurisdiction abrogated claims for breach of promise to marry. What result? See M.N. v. D.S., 616 N.W.2d 284 (Minn. Ct. App. 2000).

2. Karen and Harold meet through a dating service. Two months later Harold proposes marriage, and they choose a wedding date. Before the wedding, Karen moves into Harold's home, and they begin commingling their assets. After Karen moves in, she borrows $20,000 on her rental property to make improvements on Harold's home. Four years later, Karen learns Harold is having an affair and moves out. In a suit against Harold, Karen claims she allowed Harold to use her money because Harold promised to marry her. Harold testifies that he never intended to marry Karen in the first place. The couple lives in a

[15]. For feminist theorists' critique of the victimization paradigm, see Linda Gordon, Heroes of Their Own Lives: The Politics and History of Family Violence, Boston, 1880-1960 (1988); Elizabeth Schneider, Describing and Changing: Women's Self-Defense Work and the Problem of Expert Testimony on Battering, 9 Women's Rts. L. Rep. 195 (1986).

jurisdiction where the action for breach of promise to marry has been abolished. What result? See Dixon v. Smith, 695 N.E.2d 284 (Ohio Ct. App. 1997).

## 2. Gifts in Contemplation of Marriage

■  **MEYER v. MITNICK**
   *625 N.W.2d 136 (Mich. Ct. App. 2001)*

FITZGERALD, Presiding Judge.
    . . . Plaintiff Barry Meyer, D.O., and defendant Robyn Mitnick became engaged on August 9, 1996, at which time Barry gave Robyn a custom-designed engagement ring that he purchased for $19,500. On November 8, 1996, Barry asked Robyn to sign a prenuptial agreement and Robyn refused. The parties agree that the engagement was broken during that meeting, but both Barry and Robyn contend that the other party caused the breakup.
    Robyn did not return the engagement ring after the engagement ended and Barry filed the present action on December 2, 1996. Barry alleged that the engagement ring was a conditional gift given in contemplation of marriage and that, because the condition of marriage did not occur, the ring should be returned to him. Robyn filed a counter-complaint, alleging that the ring was an unconditional gift and that, because Barry broke the engagement, she was entitled to keep the ring. [The trial court granted Barry's motion for a summary judgment.]
    The issue presented is whether fault must be considered in determining ownership of an engagement ring following termination of the engagement. [A]n analysis of the conditional nature of the gift is essential to a complete analysis of the issue presented.
    One of the few cases in Michigan involving gifts in contemplation of marriage is In re Lowe Estate, 146 Mich. App. 325, 379 N.W.2d 485 (1985). In *Lowe*, the donor gave an engagement ring to the donee in 1974, but because of extenuating circumstances the couple never married. The donee held the ring until her death and, thereafter, the donor attempted to regain possession of the ring from the donee's estate. In its analysis, the Court noted the lack of case law on this issue and looked to cases from other states. The Court stated that an engagement ring is a conditional gift made in contemplation of marriage. The Court further cited the general rule that, if the engagement is broken by the donee, the donor is entitled to recover the ring. Additionally, the Court cited the general principle that, if the engagement is unjustifiably broken by the donor, he may not recover the ring. The Court specifically stated that "[t]hese results can be justified on the finding of fault in the conduct of one of the parties." Id.

However, the Court noted that "where the engagement is expressly terminated by the mutual consent of the parties, the general view is that the donor may obtain recovery since 'the principle applies that the ring was given and received upon the condition subsequent that it would be returned if the parties did not wed without the fault of either.' " Id., quoting Anno: Rights in respect of engagement and courtship presents when marriage does not ensue, 46 A.L.R.3d 578, 601. After this discussion, the Court concluded that the general rules were not applicable to the case because there was no termination of the engagement. *Lowe,* supra at 328, 379 N.W.2d 485. Rather, the possibility of marriage ended only upon the donee's death and, because she had the right to possession of the ring against all others, including the donor, at the time of her death, the ring passed to her estate and could not be recovered by the donor. Id. at 328-329, 379 N.W.2d 485.

Both parties cite *Lowe* to support their respective positions. Robyn contends that *Lowe* requires an analysis of which party was at fault for ending the engagement. Barry argues that because *Lowe* states that an engagement ring is a conditional gift, he is entitled to the ring because the condition of marriage did not occur, regardless of fault. Barry also contends, however, that if an analysis of fault is proper, he is still entitled to return of the ring because he did not unjustifiably end the engagement. . . .

While there is no Michigan law regarding ownership of engagement rings given in contemplation of marriage where the engagement is broken, the jurisdictions that have considered cases dealing with the gift of an engagement ring uniformly hold that marriage is an implied condition of the transfer of title and that the gift does not become absolute until the marriage occurs. Most courts recognize that engagement rings occupy a rather unique niche in our society. One court explained:

> Where a gift of personal property is made with the intent to take effect irrevocably, and is fully executed by unconditional delivery, it is a valid gift inter vivos. . . . Such a gift is absolute and, once made, cannot be revoked. . . . A gift, however, may be conditioned on the performance of some act by the donee, and if the condition is not fulfilled the donee may recover the gift. . . . We find the conditional gift theory particularly appropriate when the contested property is an engagement ring. The inherent symbolism of this gift forecloses the need to establish an express condition that marriage will ensue. Rather, the condition may be implied in fact or imposed by law in order to prevent unjust enrichment. [Brown v. Thomas, 379 N.W.2d 868 (Wis. Ct. App. 1985).]

. . . Like the courts in other states and the dicta in *Lowe,* we find that engagement rings should be considered, by their very nature, conditional gifts given in contemplation of marriage.

Once we recognize an engagement ring is a conditional gift, the question still remains: who gets the gift when the condition is not fulfilled? . . . Generally, courts have taken two divergent paths. The older one rules that when an engagement has been unjustifiably broken by the donor, the donor shall not recover the ring. However, if the engagement is broken by mutual agreement, or unjustifiably by the donee, the ring should be returned to the donor. The critical inquiry in this fault-based line of cases is who was at "fault" for the termination of the relationship. The other rule, the so-called, "modern trend," holds that because an engagement ring is an inherently conditional gift, once the engagement has been broken the ring should be returned to the donor. Thus, the question of who broke the engagement and why, or who was "at fault," is irrelevant. This is the no-fault line of cases.

We find the reasoning of the no-fault cases persuasive. Because the engagement ring is a conditional gift, when the condition is not fulfilled the ring or its value should be returned to the donor no matter who broke the engagement or caused it to be broken. As stated by the court in [Aronow v. Silver, 538 A.2d 851 (N.J. Super. Ct. Ch. Div. 1987)], in concluding that fault is irrelevant in an engagement setting:

> What fact justifies the breaking of an engagement? The absence of a sense of humor? Differing musical tastes? Differing political views? The painfully-learned fact is that marriages are made on earth, not in heaven. They must be approached with intelligent care and should not happen without a decent assurance of success. When either party lacks that assurance, for whatever reason, the engagement should be broken. No justification is needed. Either party may act. Fault, impossible to fix, does not count.

In sum, we hold that an engagement ring given in contemplation of marriage is an impliedly conditional gift that is a completed gift only upon marriage. If the engagement is called off, for whatever reason, the gift is not capable of becoming a completed gift and must be returned to the donor. Affirmed.

## Notes and Questions

1. *Historical background.* Before the Depression, etiquette did not dictate the gift of a diamond engagement ring. By 1945, however, "the diamond ring rapidly changed from a relatively obscure token of affection to what amounted to an American tradition." Margaret F. Brinig, Rings and Promises, 6 J.L. Econ. & Org. 203, 204 (1990). Professor Brinig attributes the change to the influence of the diamond industry (through an extensive advertising campaign) and also to the abolition of breach-of-promise-to-marry suits (which resulted, she argues, in the need to give some item as bond or pledge).

2. The common law treated actions for recovery of gifts given in contemplation of marriage distinctly from breach of promise. Recovery of such gifts rests on theories of conditional gift, fraud, or unjust enrichment. Under the gift theory, property obtained in consideration of marriage is conditioned on the performance of the marriage. If the condition is not met, the transfer has not been completed and the gift is recoverable. The central question, as *Meyer* reveals, is whether the gift was conditioned on the subsequent marriage or was absolute. Courts consider the nature of the gift, surrounding circumstances, and cause of the broken engagement. Under a fraud theory, to sustain recovery the donee must misrepresent an intent to marry and the donor must rely on that misrepresentation. The quasi-contractual remedy of unjust enrichment forces a donee to disgorge the benefit conferred.

3. Occasionally, suits involve recovery of other objects. Are other items of jewelry sufficiently distinguishable from an engagement ring to preclude recovery? Suppose a ring is given as a Christmas or birthday gift. Should it matter if the gift was given before or after the couple is engaged? How does one determine what gifts are "in contemplation of marriage"?

4. Given that etiquette and custom dictate that the bride pays for the wedding and the groom for the engagement ring, do women bear a disproportionate burden for a broken engagement under the rules reflected in *Meyer*? Should only one party be responsible for pre-wedding reliance damages? See Rebecca Tushnet, Rules of Engagement, 107 Yale L.J. 2583 (1998) (advocating a no-fault rule making both parties equally liable for money expended in reliance on broken engagements).

5. *Relevance of fault.* At common law, fault barred recovery or retention of the engagement ring. Thus, the man could recover the ring if the woman unjustifiably ended the engagement or if the couple mutually dissolved it, but not if he unjustifiably terminated the engagement. Under the modern trend, as *Meyer* explains, fault is irrelevant. See also Benassi v. Back and Neck Pain Clinic, 629 N.W.2d 475 (Minn. Ct. App. 2001) (holding that employer-ring donor is entitled to return of ring regardless of fault in terminating engagement). Does retention of fault make sense? What reasons does *Meyer* give for holding fault irrelevant? Are they persuasive? See generally Tushnet, supra; Joanne Ross Wider, Fault or No-Fault: If the Engagement Is Broken, Who Gets the Ring? 13 Matrimonial Strategist 1 (2000).

6. With the abolition of actions for breach of promise, should the law abolish actions for recovery of gifts given in contemplation of marriage (and let the loss fall where it lies)? Are remedies of the marketplace appropriate for courtship controversies? Should courts refuse to intrude on this private matter?

## Problems

1. Maria Dillon, a 20-year-old restaurant hostess meets Frank D. Zaffere III, a 44-year-old corporate lawyer, in Chicago. They begin a whirlwind romance. Shortly after they meet, Frank invites Maria to New York City for dinner and the theater. The couple becomes engaged. After a tempestuous relationship, Maria breaks the engagement. The parties reconcile. Maria again breaks up. Frank then institutes suit, demanding repayment of $40,310.48 for a fur coat, car, typewriter, engagement ring, a red pullover, a cassette, and a University of Notre Dame umbrella. Three days before filing suit, Frank writes to Maria that he still is willing to marry her on the following conditions: faithfulness, truthfulness, and a commitment to marry him within 45 days. Maria consults several attorneys. The first suggests she marry and subsequently procure a generous divorce. A second attorney suggests that she keep the $5,000 engagement ring for the time being. David Margolick, Lawyer, Hereafter Broken Heart, Sues to Mend It, N.Y. Times, Sept. 11, 1992, at B8. What do you advise?

2. At an engagement party, Gina Bruno's father gives his daughter and her fiance $28,000 for the reception and other wedding expenses. The couple receives additional gifts totaling $5,000, which they deposit in a joint savings account. When the fiance cancels the wedding the night before, Gina and her father (in a class action suit with all other donors at the engagement party) sue to recover the gifts. New York has anti-heart balm legislation. What result? See Bruno v. Guerra, 549 N.Y.S.2d 925 (Sup. Ct. 1990).

3. A woman is killed in a plane crash caused by her fiance's negligence. The fiance removes her engagement ring at the scene of the accident. The executor of her estate sues to recover the ring or its value. Should the executor prevail? See In re Hahn v. United States, 535 F. Supp. 132 (D.S.D. 1982). See also Matter of Estate of Lowe, 379 N.W.2d 485 (Mich. Ct. App. 1985).

## C. PREMARITAL CONTRACTS

### ■  SIMEONE v. SIMEONE
581 A.2d 162 (Pa. 1990)

FLAHERTY, Justice.

At issue in this appeal is the validity of a prenuptial agreement executed between the appellant, Catherine E. Walsh Simeone, and the appellee, Frederick A. Simeone. At the time of their marriage, in 1975, appellant was a twenty-three-year-old nurse and appellee was a thirty-nine-year-old neurosurgeon. Appellee had an income of approximately $90,000 per year, and appellant was unemployed. Appellee also had assets worth approximately $300,000. On the eve of the parties' wedding, appellee's attorney presented appellant with a prenuptial agreement to be signed. Appellant, without the benefit of counsel, signed the agreement. Appellee's attorney had not advised appellant regarding any legal rights that the agreement surrendered. The parties are in disagreement as to whether appellant knew in advance of that date that such an agreement would be presented for signature. . . .

The agreement limited appellant to support payments of $200 per week in the event of separation or divorce, subject to a maximum total payment of $25,000. The parties separated in 1982, and, in 1984, divorce proceedings were commenced. Between 1982 and 1984 appellee made payments which satisfied the $25,000 limit. In 1985, appellant filed a claim for alimony pendente lite [during the litigation]. [The Superior Court affirmed a special master's denial of her claim, 551 A.2d 219 (Pa. 1988)].

We granted allowance of appeal because uncertainty was expressed by the Superior Court regarding the meaning of our plurality decision in Estate of Geyer, 516 Pa. 492, 533 A.2d 423 (1987). The Superior Court viewed *Geyer* as permitting a prenuptial agreement to be upheld if it either made a reasonable provision for the spouse or was entered after a full and fair disclosure of the general financial positions of the parties and the statutory rights being relinquished. Appellant contends that this interpretation of *Geyer* is in error insofar as it requires disclosure of statutory rights only in cases where there has not been made a reasonable provision for the spouse. Inasmuch as the courts below held that the provision made for appellant was a reasonable one, appellant's efforts to overturn the agreement have focused upon an assertion that there was an inadequate disclosure of statutory rights. Appellant continues to assert, however, that the payments provided in the agreement were less than reasonable.

The statutory rights in question are those relating to alimony pendente lite. . . . The present agreement [expressly stated] that alimony pendente lite was being relinquished. It also recited that appellant "has been informed and understands" that, were it not for the agreement, appellant's obligation to pay alimony pendente lite "might, as a matter of law, exceed the amount provided." Hence, appellant's claim is not that the agreement failed to disclose the particular right affected, but rather that she was not adequately informed with respect to the nature of alimony pendente lite. . . .

There is no longer validity in the implicit presumption that supplied the basis for *Geyer* and similar earlier decisions. Such decisions rested upon a belief that spouses are of unequal status and that women are not knowledgeable enough to understand the nature of contracts that they enter. Society has advanced, however, to the point where women are no longer regarded as the "weaker" party in marriage, or in society generally. Indeed, the stereotype that women serve as homemakers while men work as breadwinners is no longer viable. Quite often today both spouses are income earners. Nor is there viability in the presumption that women are uninformed, uneducated, and readily subjected to unfair advantage in marital agreements. Indeed, women nowadays quite often have substantial education, financial awareness, income, and assets.

Accordingly, the law has advanced to recognize the equal status of men and women in our society. See, e.g., Pa. Const. art. 1, §28 (constitutional prohibition of sex discrimination in laws of the Commonwealth). Paternalistic presumptions and protections that arose to shelter women from the inferiorities and incapacities which they were perceived as having in earlier times have, appropriately, been discarded. It would be inconsistent, therefore, to perpetuate the standards governing prenuptial agreements that were described in *Geyer* and similar decisions, as these reflected a paternalistic approach that is now insupportable.

Further, *Geyer* and its predecessors embodied substantial departures from traditional rules of contract law, to the extent that they allowed consideration of the knowledge of the contracting parties and reasonableness of their bargain as factors governing whether to uphold an agreement. Traditional principles of contract law provide perfectly adequate remedies where contracts are procured through fraud, misrepresentation, or duress. Consideration of other factors, such as the knowledge of the parties and the reasonableness of their bargain, is inappropriate. Prenuptial agreements are contracts, and, as such, should be evaluated under the same criteria as are applicable to other types of contracts. Absent fraud, misrepresentation, or duress, spouses should be bound by the terms of their agreements.

Contracting parties are normally bound by their agreements, without regard to whether the terms thereof were read and fully understood and irrespective of whether the agreements embodied reasonable or good bargains. Based upon these principles, the terms of the present prenuptial agreement must be regarded as binding, without regard to whether the terms were fully understood by appellant. *Ignorantia non excusat.*

Accordingly, we find no merit in a contention raised by appellant that the agreement should be declared void on the ground that she did not consult with independent legal counsel. To impose a per se requirement that parties entering a prenuptial agreement must obtain independent legal counsel would be contrary to traditional principles of contract law, and would constitute a paternalistic and unwarranted interference with the parties' freedom to enter contracts.

Further, the reasonableness of a prenuptial bargain is not a proper subject for judicial review. . . . By invoking inquiries into reasonableness, . . . the functioning and reliability of prenuptial agreements is severely undermined. Parties would not have entered such agreements, and, indeed, might not have entered their marriages, if they did not expect their agreements to be strictly enforced. If parties viewed an agreement as reasonable at the time of its inception, as evidenced by their having signed the agreement, they should be foreclosed from later trying to evade its terms by asserting that it was not in fact reasonable. Pertinently, the present agreement contained a clause reciting that "each of the parties considers this agreement fair, just and reasonable. . . ."

Further, everyone who enters a long-term agreement knows that circumstances can change during its term, so that what initially appeared desirable might prove to be an unfavorable bargain. Such are the risks that contracting parties routinely assume. Certainly, the possibilities of illness, birth of children, reliance upon a spouse, career change, financial gain or loss, and numerous other events that can occur in the course of a marriage cannot be regarded as unforeseeable. If parties choose not to address such matters in their prenuptial agreements, they must be regarded as having contracted to bear the risk of events that alter the value of their bargains.

We are reluctant to interfere with the power of persons contemplating marriage to agree upon, and to act in reliance upon, what they regard as an acceptable distribution scheme for their property. A court should not ignore the parties' expressed intent by proceeding to determine whether a prenuptial agreement was, in the court's view, reasonable at the time of its inception or the time of divorce. These are exactly the sorts of judicial determinations that such agreements are designed to avoid. Rare indeed is the agreement that is beyond possible challenge when reasonableness is placed at issue. Parties can routinely assert some lack of fairness relating to the inception of the agreement, thereby placing the validity of the agreement at risk. And if reasonableness at the time of divorce were to be taken into account an additional problem would arise. Virtually nonexistent is the marriage in which there has been absolutely no change in the circumstances of either spouse during the course of the marriage. Every change in circumstance, foreseeable or not, and substantial or not, might be asserted as a basis for finding that an agreement is no longer reasonable.

In discarding the approach of *Geyer* that permitted examination of the reasonableness of prenuptial agreements and allowed inquiries into whether parties had attained informed understandings of the rights they were surrendering, we do not depart from the longstanding principle that a full and fair disclosure of the financial positions of the parties is required. . . . Parties to these agreements do not quite deal at arm's length, but rather at the time the contract is entered into stand in a relation of mutual confidence and trust that calls for disclosure of their financial resources. It is well settled that this disclosure need not be exact, so long as it is "full and fair." Kaufmann Estate, 404 Pa. 131, 136 n.8, 171 A.2d 48, 51 n.8 (1961). In essence therefore, the duty of disclosure under these circumstances is consistent with traditional principles of contract law.

If an agreement provides that full disclosure has been made, a presumption of full disclosure arises. . . . The present agreement recited that full disclosure had been made, and included a list of appellee's assets totalling approximately $300,000. Appellant contends that this list understated by roughly $183,000, the value of a classic car collection which appellee had included at a value of $200,000. The master, reviewing the parties' conflicting testimony regarding the value of the car collection, found that appellant failed to prove by clear and convincing evidence that the value of the collection had been understated. . . . Appellant's contention is plainly without merit.

Appellant's final contention is that the agreement was executed under conditions of duress in that it was presented to her at 5 P.M. on the eve of her wedding, a time when she could not seek counsel without the trauma, expense, and embarrassment of postponing the wedding. . . . Although appellant testified that she did not discover until the eve of her wedding that there was going to be a prenuptial agreement, testimony from a number of other witnesses was to the contrary. Appellee testified that, although the final version of the agreement was indeed presented to appellant on the eve of the wedding, he had engaged in several discussions with appellant regarding the contents of the agreement during the six month period preceding that date. Another witness testified that appellant mentioned, approximately two or three weeks before the wedding, that she was going to enter a prenuptial agreement. Yet another witness confirmed that, during the months preceding the wedding, appellant participated in several discussions of prenuptial agreements. And the legal counsel who prepared the agreement for appellee testified that, prior to the eve of the wedding, changes were made in the agreement to increase the sums payable to appellant in the event of separation or divorce. . . . It should be noted, too, that during the months when the agreement was being discussed appellant had more than sufficient time to consult with independent legal counsel if she had so desired. Under these circumstances, there was plainly no error in finding that appellant failed to prove duress.

Hence, the courts below properly held that the present agreement is valid and enforceable. Appellant is barred, therefore, from receiving alimony pendente lite. . . .

McDermott, Justice, dissenting. . . .

I am not willing to believe that our society views marriage as a mere contract for hire. . . . Our courts must seek to protect, and not to undermine, those institutions and interests which are vital to our society. [W]hile I acknowledge the longstanding rule of law that pre-nuptial agreements are presumptively valid and binding upon the parties, I am unwilling to go as far as the majority to protect the right to contract at the expense of the institution of marriage. Were a contract of marriage, the most intimate relationship between two people, not the surrender of freedom, an offering of self in love, sacrifice, hope for better or for worse, the begetting of children and the offer of effort, labor, precious time and care for the safety and prosperity of their union, then the majority would find me among them. . . .

At the time of dissolution of the marriage, a spouse should be able to avoid the operation of a pre-nuptial agreement upon clear and convincing proof that, despite the existence of full and fair disclosure at the time of the execution of the agreement, the agreement is nevertheless so inequitable and unfair that it should not be enforced in a court of this state. . . .

[T]he passage of time accompanied by the intervening events of a marriage, may render the terms of the agreement completely unfair and inequitable. While parties to a pre-nuptial agreement may indeed foresee, generally, the events which may come to pass during their marriage, one spouse should not be made to suffer for failing to foresee all of the surrounding circumstances which may attend the dissolution of the marriage. Although it should not be the role of the courts to void pre-nuptial agreements merely because one spouse may receive a better result in an action under the Divorce Code to recover alimony or equitable distribution, it should be the role of the courts to guard against the enforcement of pre-nuptial agreements where such enforcement will bring about only inequity and hardship. It borders on cruelty to accept that after years of living together, yielding their separate opportunities in life to each other, that two individuals emerge the same as the day they began their marriage. . . .

## ■ IN RE MARRIAGE OF GREENWALD
### 454 N.W.2d 34 (Wis. Ct. App. 1990)

NETTESHEIM, Judge. . . .

In 1973, Darwin, a retired widower in his early 70's, placed an ad in a local newspaper seeking a housekeeper. Josephine, twice divorced and in her late 50's, responded. She accepted the housekeeping job on a part-time basis, continued her full-time employment at Southern Colony and moved into Darwin's home. She served in this capacity for ten years, receiving free room and board but no salary. In 1981, Josephine retired from Southern Colony.

Josephine testified that this living and employment arrangement soon developed into a full marriage-like relationship. Darwin acknowledged the parties' close relationship but denied any sexual intimacies.

While living together under this arrangement, Josephine oftentimes proposed marriage. Darwin repeatedly declined these offers because of his age and his wish to preserve his estate for his children from his prior marriage.

Eventually, however, Darwin softened his stance, stating that he would consider marriage but only "under a marriage agreement." [The ensuing agreement] provided that: (1) it was made in contemplation of marriage; (2) both parties had separate estates and separate lineal heirs for whom the parties wished to provide; (3) all property owned by each party would remain titled in such party; (4) in the event of a divorce the agreement would govern the property division and neither party would claim an interest in the property owned by the other; and (5) in the event of death, the survivor would not elect against the deceased's will. In addition, the agreement provided for an annual equal sharing between Darwin and Josephine of all net income earned by both. [The duration of the agreement was 25 years.]

The parties met at Attorney Kingston's office on March 8, 1983. Attorney Kingston advised Josephine that she was entitled to a list of Darwin's separate assets and that she was entitled to consult with separate counsel. She declined both offers. After Attorney Kingston reviewed and explained the document to the parties, they signed it. Eleven days later, the parties married. Josephine was then sixty-seven years old; Darwin was eighty-one. At this time, Darwin owned property, primarily real estate, worth in excess of $670,000. Josephine owned an automobile and a minimal amount of savings and personal property.

Less than three years later, Josephine filed this action for divorce. Prior thereto, Darwin had paid Josephine $26,232.30 pursuant to the income sharing provisions of the agreement. Josephine asked the trial court to invalidate the premarital agreement, asserting that she did not enter into the agreement freely and voluntarily, that Darwin had failed to make a fair and reasonable financial disclosure prior to the agreement, and that the agreement was inherently inequitable. Darwin defended the agreement and asked the trial court to enforce it. [The trial court invalidated the agreement on the ground of lack of substantive fairness.]

We begin with the statute [Wis. Stat. §767.255, providing for a presumption of an equal property division upon dissolution absent written agreement] and the landmark case in Wisconsin concerning marital agreements [Button v. Button, 388 N.W.2d 546 (Wis. 1986)]. *Button* holds that an agreement is inequitable if it fails to satisfy any one of the following requirements: each spouse has made fair and reasonable disclosure to the other of his or her financial status; each spouse has entered into the agreement voluntarily and freely; and the substantive provisions of the agreement dividing the property upon divorce are fair to each spouse. The first two of these requirements relate to the procurement of the agreement; the latter relates to the substance of the agreement. . . .

We turn first to Josephine's cross-appeal challenging the trial court's determination that the agreement met the *Button* requirements of procedural fairness. [Procedural fairness] depends upon whether at the time the agreement was executed each spouse made fair and reasonable financial disclosure to the other spouse and whether each spouse entered into the agreement freely and voluntarily. These two factors are examined as of the date the agreement is executed.

Josephine complains that Darwin did not make a fair and reasonable disclosure of his financial status. In support she points to the absence of a formal exchange of financial records, and her claimed ignorance of Darwin's true worth. The trial court, however, determined that Josephine knew of Darwin's considerable assets.

The evidence supports this determination. Prior to and during the marriage, Josephine assisted Darwin in keeping his financial records. She made entries in Darwin's income and ledger books, including mortgage, rental and interest income payments received by Darwin. This process required Josephine to refer to the mortgage amortization schedules and bank statements reflecting Darwin's holdings. Josephine and Darwin discussed the value of certain of Darwin's duplexes when Darwin objected to tax assessments on the properties. When Josephine signed the agreement on March 8, 1983, Attorney Kingston told her that she was entitled to a list of Darwin's assets. Josephine responded that the list was not necessary because she already knew about Darwin's property from her work on his books. . . .

Moreover, a separate ground exists for affirming the trial court's determination even if a full and reasonable disclosure had not been made. . . . The trial court, in effect, determined that Josephine wanted a marriage to Darwin regardless of any agreement or its terms. The purpose of a fair and reasonable disclosure is to guard against the possibility that "[a] party might not have entered into the agreement had she or he known the facts." If a party's conduct demonstrates that specific knowledge of the other's property and finances is not important to the marital decision, and if the agreement is otherwise freely and voluntarily made, we see no sound reason why the law should later intervene and undo the parties' contract. The trial court's finding reveals that such was the case here.

Josephine, however, contends that her execution of the agreement was not free and voluntary. This requires the court to determine whether each spouse has a "meaningful choice." Factors bearing upon this question include whether each party was represented by independent counsel, whether each party had adequate time to review the agreement, whether the parties understood the terms of the agreement and their effect, and whether the parties understood their financial rights in the absence of an agreement. [*Button*, 388 N.W.2d at 550-551.]

The parties were not represented by separate counsel in this pre-*Button* situation. However, Attorney Kingston did advise Josephine of her right to separate counsel — an overture she declined. In addition, Attorney Kingston conducted a thorough reading and explanation of the proposed agreement with Josephine before she signed it. Josephine also had received Darwin's handwritten copy and Attorney Kingston's typewritten copy of the proposed agreement prior to the execution of the agreement. Most importantly, Josephine admitted that she knew the contents and thrust of the agreement when she signed it, but silently hoped that Darwin would "overlook" it. . . . In light of all the evidence on this question and, in particular, Josephine's pursuit of Darwin in the face of his refusals and conditions, Josephine's claim that she had no "meaningful choice" under *Button* rings hollow. . . .

We now address Darwin's claim on appeal that the trial court erred in its determination that the agreement did not satisfy the substantive fairness requirements of *Button*. Substantive fairness is an amorphous concept which must be determined on a case-by-case basis. In determining substantive fairness, a court must be mindful of the two principal legislative concerns reflected in sec. 767.255(11), Stats.: the protection of the parties' freedom to contract and the protection of the parties' financial interests at divorce.

In support of its determination that the agreement was substantively unfair the trial court noted the unequal bargaining position of the parties and the agreement's twenty-five year duration which effectively precluded Josephine from ever sharing in Darwin's estate. Although the trial court did not so indicate, we construe these observations as determinations, respectively, that the agreement was substantively unfair at the time of its making and at the time of the divorce. . . .

[W]e turn first to the trial court's determination that the parties bargained from an unequal position — a determination which we construe to mean that the agreement was substantively unfair at the time of its execution. *Button* recites numerous factors which the parties should consider when making their agreement. These include the objectives of the parties in executing the agreement, the economic circumstances of the parties, the property brought to the marriage by each party, each spouse's family relationships and obligations to persons other than the spouse, the earning capacity of each person, the anticipated contribution by one party to the education, training or increased earning power of the other, the future needs of the respective spouses, the age and physical and emotional health of the parties, and the expected contribution of each party to the marriage, giving appropriate economic value to each party's contribution in homemaking and child care services. [*Button*, 388 N.W.2d at 551.]

Some of the above factors support enforcement of the agreement; others support non-enforcement. Rarely, we suspect, will application of these factors lead to a clearly indicated resolution. *Button,* however, also instructs that the trial court should consider these factors and evaluate the terms of the agreement from the perspective of the parties at the execution of the agreement with a view to giving effect to the parties' freedom to contract. While the trial court recognized this principle, we conclude that the court failed to meaningfully apply it in this case.

Other than the observation that Josephine wanted to marry and Darwin did not, the trial court did not further elaborate as to why the parties' bargaining positions were unequal. We assume the trial court meant that Josephine therefore had to accept marriage upon Darwin's terms. But this is not unusual in a prospective marriage situation where one party holds substantial property intended for his or her heirs and the other does not. This fact, standing alone, should not deprive the parties of the ability to negotiate an enforceable marital agreement which preserves the estate of the more propertied party to his or her heirs. To hold that such a situation renders a marital agreement unenforceable would unreasonably impede the abilities and rights of parties to both contract and marry. . . .

In further support of its conclusion that the agreement was substantively unfair at the time of the divorce, the court noted that the agreement's twenty-five year duration effectively precluded Josephine from becoming a "full economic equal in the marriage." This reasoning, however, overlooks that this is precisely what the parties intended. *[25 yr duration]*

An agreement is not unfair at divorce just because the application of the agreement results in a property division which is not equal between the parties or which a court might not order under sec. 767.255, Stats. If, however, there are significantly changed circumstances after the execution of an agreement and the agreement as applied at divorce no longer comports with the reasonable expectations of the parties, an agreement which is fair at execution may be unfair to the parties at divorce. [*Button,* 388 N.W.2d at 552.] . . . Here, less than three years elapsed between the marriage and the divorce. Our review of the record reveals no significant change in the parties' circumstances during this time. . . . Absent such a condition, a determination of substantive unfairness is not warranted. . . . We remand with instructions to divide the parties' property in accord with the marital agreement. . . .

## Notes and Questions

1. Premarital (also "antenuptial" or "prenuptial") agreements generally limit spousal property rights in the event of dissolution and death. The use of such agreements has risen dramatically. See Lisa W. Foderaro, Prenuptial Contracts Find New Popularity, N.Y. Times, Aug. 21, 1997, at B5. Their increasing popularity stems, in part, from the high

rate of divorce, delayed marriage age, and a concern with protecting children of a prior marriage. Florence Kaslow, Enter the Prenuptial: A Prelude to Marriage or Remarriage, 9 Behav. Sci. & L. 375, 375-376 (1991).

2. The law's treatment of premarital agreements, as *Greenwald* reveals, represents the interplay of traditional contract principles respecting private ordering and family law principles of equitable distribution. Prior to the 1970s, courts held these agreements violative of public policy as an inducement to divorce. Courts also feared that a dependent spouse might become a public charge. Contemporary courts regard such agreements more favorably.

3. How do premarital agreements differ from ordinary contracts? Professor Judith Younger responds:

> The first difference is the subject matter. These agreements typically deal with one of, or a combination of, three things: property and support rights during and after marriage; the personal rights and obligations of the spouses during marriage; or the education, care, and rearing of children who may later be born to the marrying couple. These subjects are of greater interest to the state than the subjects of ordinary commercial contract; the state wishes to protect the welfare of the couple and their children during and after marriage, and to preserve the privacy of the family relationship. . . .
>
> The second difference is the relationship of the parties to each other. It is a confidential relationship involving parties who are usually not evenly matched in bargaining power. The possibility, therefore, that one party may overreach the other is greater than in the case of ordinary contracts.
>
> The third difference is the fact that antenuptial agreements are to be performed in the future, in the context of a relationship which the parties have not yet begun and which may continue for many years after the agreement is executed and before it is enforced. The possibility that later events may make it unwise, unfair, or otherwise undesirable to enforce such agreements is also greater than in the case of ordinary contracts.

Judith T. Younger, Perspectives on Antenuptial Agreements: An Update, 8 Am. Acad. Matrim. Law. 1, 3-4 (1992). See also Judith T. Younger, Perspectives on Antenuptial Agreements, 40 Rutgers L. Rev. 1059 (1988).

4. *Simeone* and *Greenwald* reflect different approaches. *Simeone,* out of deference to private ordering, treats such agreements as ordinary contracts. *Greenwald* underscores the need for special protection. Further, *Simeone* rejects an examination of substantive fairness whereas *Greenwald* requires both substantive fairness (at execution of the agreement and dissolution) and procedural fairness (that is, the agreement be entered into voluntarily and with full disclosure). See also Pollack-Halvarson v. McGuire, 576 N.W.2d 451 (Minn. Ct. App. 1998) (requiring both substantive and procedural fairness).

Some courts adopt yet a third approach. They consider substantive and procedural fairness as alternative requirements, requiring that substantive fairness be present before a court will examine the agreement for procedural fairness. See, e.g., Norris v. Norris, 419 A.2d 982 (D.C. App. 1980); In re Marriage of Spiegel, 553 N.W.2d 309, 315 (Iowa 1996).

The Uniform Premarital Agreement Act (UPAA), 9C U.L.A. 35 (2001), although requiring both procedural and substantive fairness, sets a higher standard than *Greenwald* for substantive unfairness. UPAA requires "unconscionability" to invalidate a premarital agreement.

§6. (a) A premarital agreement is not enforceable if the party against whom enforcement is sought proves that:

(1) that party did not execute the agreement voluntarily; or

(2) the agreement was unconscionable when it was executed and, before execution of the agreement, that party:

(i) was not provided a fair and reasonable disclosure of the property or financial obligations of the other party;

(ii) did not voluntarily and expressly waive, in writing, any right to disclosure of the property or financial obligations of the other party beyond the disclosure provided; and

(iii) did not have, or reasonably could not have had, an adequate knowledge of the property or financial obligations of the other party.

Under rules recently approved by the American Law Institute, premarital agreements also must meet standards of procedural fairness (i.e., informed consent and disclosure) and substantive fairness. A rebuttable presumption arises that the agreement satisfies the informed consent requirement if (1) it was executed at least 30 days prior to the marriage; (2) both parties had, or were advised to obtain, counsel and had the opportunity to do so; and (3) if one of the parties did not have counsel, the agreement contained understandable information about the parties' rights and the adverse nature of their interests. ALI, Principles of the Law of Family Dissolution: Analysis and Recomendations §7.04 (3)(a)(b) & (c) (2002). Finally, the court must undertake a review of substantive fairness at the time of enforcement, specifically regarding whether enforcement would work a "substantial injustice" based on the passage of time, the presence of children, or changed circumstances that were unanticipated and would have a significant impact on the parties or their children. Id. at §7.05. Which approach do you favor?

5. Why does *Simeone* reject judicial review of reasonableness? Should intent control? Should a recitation of reasonableness in the agreement serve as a presumption of fairness? Or are premarital agreements "in the nature of contracts of adhesion" (as an omitted concurrence in *Simeone* states)?

6. If substantive fairness should be considered, should it be determined as of execution or enforcement? Or both? What do *Simeone* and *Greenwald* respond? What is the view of UPAA and the ALI Principles, supra?

The dissent in *Simeone* suggests (in an omitted section) that the following circumstances on dissolution might lead to invalidation of a premarital agreement: (1) a spouse's diminished employment prospects if that spouse remained home due to family responsibilities, such that the spouse would become a public charge or suffer a significantly reduced standard of living; (2) a dependent spouse in a long-term marriage who helped increase the value of the other's property; (3) an unanticipated serious illness rendering the spouse unable to provide self-support. Do you agree? Some courts (and UPAA) provide that a premarital agreement will not be enforced at divorce if it would render one spouse a public charge. See, e.g., Bassler v. Bassler, 593 A.2d 82 (Vt. 1991). See also Rider v. Rider, 669 N.E.2d 160, 163 (Ind. 1996) (noting that fairness review at time of enforcement is "growing trend"); Melvin A. Eisenberg, The Limits of Cognition and the Limits of Contract, 47 Stan. L. Rev. 211, 254 (1995) (arguing that the limits of foreseeability provide a strong justification for a fairness review at divorce).

7. *Simeone* rests, in part, on the rationale that prospective spouses are on equal footing. Did the parties in *Simeone* have equal bargaining power? What relevance should a court attach to such factors as age, financial position, business acumen, obtaining (or rejecting) legal advice, the selection of counsel by the defendant, or previous divorce? Should parties be required to consult independent counsel? Do such inquiries improperly presume that women need special protection? See generally Brian Bix, Bargaining in the Shadow of Love: Premarital Agreements and How We Think About Marriage, 40 Wm. & Mary L. Rev. 145, 201-204 (1998); Gail Fommer Brod, Premarital Agreements and Gender Justice, 6 Yale L.J. & Feminism 229 (1994).

One commentator proposes a radical solution to the gendered aspects of premarital contracting. Noting that premarital agreements invariably benefit the party who has more cash, Katharine Silbaugh urges that monetary premarital agreements should not be enforced or, at least, treated with extreme skepticism in order to "properly value unpaid family labor" (i.e., protect the more vulnerable party). Katharine B. Silbaugh, Marriage Contracts and the Family Economy, 93 Nw. U. L. Rev. 65, 142 (1998). What do you think of her suggestion? Compare Leah Guggenheimer, A Modest Proposal: The Feminomics of Drafting Premarital Agreements, 17 Women's Rts. L. Rep. 147, 204 (1996) (conceding that the goal of feminist policy should be to eliminate or severely restrict private ordering but arguing that such a tactic undermines female autonomy and raises issues of special treatment).

8. The plaintiff in *Simeone* claims duress based on the proximity of the execution of the agreement to the wedding. Should the time period

in which a party has to reflect before signing the agreement be relevant? Should statutes require execution of premarital agreements a minimum amount of time before marriage? See, e.g., Minn. Stat. Ann. §519.11 (West 1990 & Supp. 1997) (prior to day of marriage). Is this sound policy? For succession purposes, some jurisdictions hold that those inter vivos conveyances of one spouse that defeat the share of the survivor spouse, if made within a short period before death, are "illusory" and presumptively void. See, e.g., Newman v. Dore, 9 N.E.2d 966 (N.Y. 1937). Should the same presumption apply to set aside premarital agreements executed a short time before marriage?

9. What do *Simeone* and *Greenwald* require in terms of disclosure? Is this synonymous with "detailed disclosure"? Should courts require a list of assets attached to the premarital agreement? See In re Thies, 903 P.2d 186 (Mont. 1995); Hengel v. Hengel, 365 N.W.2d 16 (Wis. Ct. App. 1985) (both rejecting the idea). Or, is a "general idea" good enough? See Harbom v. Harbom, 760 A.2d 272 (Md. Ct. Spec. App. 2000). Some courts take the view that the prospective spouses have a confidential relationship. Compare Wilson v. Moore, 929 S.W.2d 367 (Tenn. Ct. App. 1996) (engagement establishes confidential relationship), with DeLorean v. DeLorean, 511 A.2d 1257 (N.J. Super. Ct. Ch. Div. 1986) (no confidential relationship based on California law).

10. In *Greenwald,* the Court of Appeals reasoned that a full and reasonable disclosure was unnecessary because Josephine was determined to marry Darwin regardless. In effect, the court was saying that disclosure was irrelevant because it was unimportant to her. What bearing does Josephine's desire to marry have on the validity of the agreement? See Faun M. Phillipson, Note, Fairness of Contract vs. Freedom of Contract: The Problematic Contractual Obligation in Premarital Agreements, 5 Cardozo Women's L.J. 79 (1998) (criticizing *Greenwald* by saying that "a decision holding disclosure to be irrelevant due to the court's finding that one of the parties was strongly determined to marry the other thwarts the goal to be achieved by meaningful choice").

11. UPAA supports a wide latitude regarding prospective spouses' contractual freedom. Among the permissible areas for premarital agreements, UPAA specifies "any other matter, including personal rights and obligations, not in violation of public policy or a statute imposing a criminal penalty." Unif. Premarital Agreement Act §3(a)(8), 9C U.L.A. 43 (2001). The Comment enumerates such examples as choice of abode, the freedom to pursue career opportunities, and the upbringing of children. Id. at 374. Does this provision interfere with the doctrine of family privacy? One commentator goes so far as to suggest that premarital contracts should be mandatory. See Jeffrey Evans Stake, Mandatory Planning for Divorce, 45 Vand. L. Rev. 397 (1992). Do you agree?

12. Suppose you are about to marry (or to begin a committed relationship). What roles, responsibilities, and other decisions might you want to allocate? Support? Property rights? Names? Employment and its

consequences? Domicile? Responsibility for birth control? Number of children? Parenting responsibilities? Draft an agreement to govern your relationship. Assuming you and your partner reach a satisfactory agreement, should the courts enforce it? For illustrations, see Marjorie Maguire Shultz, Contractual Ordering of Marriage: A New Model for State Policy, 70 Cal. L. Rev. 207, 219-223 (1982); Lenore J. Weitzman, Legal Regulation of Marriage: Tradition and Change, 62 Cal. L. Rev. 1169 (1974).

Should the law enforce the following provisions in antenuptial agreements?

a. a parent shall not interfere, in the presence of the children, in punishments of the children by the other parent (e.g., Ball v. Ball, 36 So. 2d 172, 174 (Fla. 1948));

b. children born of the marriage shall attend public school (id.);

c. sexual intercourse shall be limited to only once per week (e.g., Favrot v. Barnes, 332 So. 2d 873, 875 (La. App.), *rev'd on other grounds,* 339 So. 2d 843, *cert. denied,* 429 U.S. 961 (1976));

d. the husband shall reside in a certain locale after the marriage (e.g., Isaacs v. Isaacs, 99 N.W. 268 (Neb. 1904));

e. the husband's mother shall live with the parties (e.g., Koch v. Koch, 232 A.2d 157 (N.J. Super. Ct. App. Div. 1967));

f. the children of the wife's prior marriage shall not live in the household (e.g., Mengal v. Mengal, 103 N.Y.S.2d 992 (Fam. Ct. 1951)).

g. each spouse must undergo counseling before seeking a divorce and, in addition, is precluded from divorce unless fault grounds are present or a two-year separation has occurred (see Chapter V, section D3b, Covenant Marriage);

h. if the husband obtains a no-fault divorce from the wife, he must pay her $15,000/month for five years, but if the husband divorces the wife on fault grounds, she pays him $5,000/month for two years (see Kathleen B. Vetrano, Controlling Behavior Through Divorce Penalties in a Prenuptial?, 15 Fair Share (No. 4) 21 (April 1995));

i. upon divorce, any child(ren) shall spend equal residential time with both parents (e.g., In re Marriage of Littlefield, 940 P.2d 1362 (Wash. 1997) (en banc)).

## Problem

Major league baseball player Barry Bonds meets Susann ("Sun") in Montreal in the summer of 1987 after she emigrates from Sweden. Both are 23 years of age. At the time, Sun is working as a waitress and bartender, training as a beautician and planning a career as a makeup artist for the rich and famous. By January 1988, the two take up residence at Barry's home in Phoenix, Arizona, and decide to marry. Barry is earning $106,000. The day before the wedding, at the offices of Barry's lawyers, the couple signs a premarital contract by which each waives any interest in the earnings and acquisitions obtained by the other during the marriage. Barry's attorneys advise Sun to retain counsel, but she declines. The attorneys read the agreement to her paragraph by paragraph, explaining that she will be waiving her community property rights. After a six-year marriage, Barry petitions for dissolution in California where he now resides. At the time, Barry is earning $8 million annually. Sun, who has custody of the couple's two children, is awarded child support of $10,000 per month per child, and spousal support of $10,000 per month for a four-year period.

Sun argues that the premarital agreement was not executed voluntarily. She claims that she did not understand the terms of the agreement because of her limited English skills. She also asserts that she believed the agreement pertained only to property that was owned prior to the marriage. Barry's attorneys later testify that she understood the agreement and did not appear pressured or confused but rather seemed confident and happy. What result? Is legal counsel essential to the enforceability of premarital contracts? How relevant is a party's waiver of legal counsel? See In re Marriage of Bonds, 5 P.3d 815 (Cal. 2000). Suppose Sun argues that the agreement is unconscionable because of drastically changed circumstances (i.e., Barry's increased wealth). What result? See Blue v. Blue, 2001 WL 468488 (Ky. Ct. App. 2001) (husband's wealth increased from $5 million to $77 million during 11-year marriage).

In response to *Bonds,* supra, the California legislature enacts a statute providing: "Any provision in a premarital agreement regarding spousal support, including, but not limited to, a waiver of it, is not enforceable if the party against whom enforcement of the spousal support provision is sought was not represented by independent counsel at the time the agreement containing the provision was signed, or if the provision regarding spousal support is unconscionable at the time of enforcement." Cal. Fam. Code §1612(c), 2001 Ca. Legis. Serv. 286 (S.B. 78)(West 2001). If this statute had been in effect prior to the *Bonds* case, how would the case have been decided?

## D. GETTING MARRIED: SUBSTANTIVE AND PROCEDURAL REGULATIONS

### 1. Constitutional Limits on State Regulation of Entry into Marriage

■ **LOVING v. VIRGINIA**
*388 U.S. 1 (1967)*

Mr. Chief Justice WARREN delivered the opinion of the Court.

This case presents a constitutional question never addressed by this Court: whether a statutory scheme adopted by the State of Virginia to prevent marriages between persons solely on the basis of racial classifications violates the Equal Protection and Due Process Clauses of the Fourteenth Amendment. . . .

In June 1958, two residents of Virginia, Mildred Jeter, a Negro woman, and Richard Loving, a white man, were married in the District of Columbia pursuant to its laws. Shortly after their marriage, the Lovings returned to Virginia and established their marital abode in Caroline County. [A] grand jury issued an indictment charging the Lovings with violating Virginia's ban on interracial marriages. [T]he Lovings pleaded guilty to the charge and were sentenced to one year in jail; however, the trial judge suspended the sentence for a period of 25 years on the condition that the Lovings leave the State and not return to Virginia together for 25 years. He stated in an opinion that:

> Almighty God created the races white, black, yellow, malay and red, and he placed them on separate continents. And but for the interference with his arrangement there would be no cause for such marriages. The fact that he separated the races shows that he did not intend for the races to mix. . . .

Virginia is now one of 16 States which prohibit and punish marriages on the basis of racial classifications. Penalties for miscegenation arose as an incident to slavery and have been common in Virginia since the colonial period. The present statutory scheme dates from the adoption of the Racial Integrity Act of 1924, passed during the period of extreme nativism which followed the end of the First World War. The central features of this Act, and current Virginia law, are the absolute prohibition of a "white person" marrying other than another "white person," a prohibition against issuing marriage licenses until the issuing official is satisfied that the applicants' statements as to their race are correct, certificates of "racial composition" to be kept by both local and state registrars [and a penalty of one to five years imprisonment].

In upholding the constitutionality of these provisions in the decision below, the Supreme Court of Appeals of Virginia referred to its 1955 decision in Naim v. Naim, 197 Va. 80, 87 S.E.2d 749, as stating the reasons supporting the validity of these laws. In *Naim,* the state court concluded that the State's legitimate purposes were "to preserve the racial integrity of its citizens," and to prevent "the corruption of blood," "a mongrel breed of citizens," and "the obliteration of racial pride," obviously an endorsement of the doctrine of White Supremacy. The court also reasoned that marriage has traditionally been subject to state regulation without federal intervention, and, consequently, the regulation of marriage should be left to exclusive state control by the Tenth Amendment.

[T]he State contends that, because its miscegenation statutes punish equally both the white and the Negro participants in an interracial marriage, these statutes, despite their reliance on racial classifications do not constitute an invidious discrimination based upon race. The second argument . . . is that if the Equal Protection Clause does not outlaw miscegenation statutes because of their reliance on racial classifications, the question of constitutionality would thus become whether there was any rational basis for a State to treat interracial marriages differently from other marriages. On this question, the State argues, the scientific evidence is substantially in doubt and, consequently, this Court should defer to the wisdom of the state legislature in adopting its policy of discouraging interracial marriages.

Because we reject the notion that the mere "equal application" of a statute containing racial classifications is enough to remove the classifications from the Fourteenth Amendment's proscription of all invidious racial discriminations, we do not accept the State's contention that these statutes should be upheld if there is any possible basis for concluding that they serve a rational purpose. . . . The clear and central purpose of the Fourteenth Amendment was to eliminate all official state sources of invidious racial discrimination in the States.

There can be no question but that Virginia's miscegenation statutes rest solely upon distinctions drawn according to race. The statutes proscribe generally accepted conduct if engaged in by members of different races. Over the years, this Court has consistently repudiated "(d)istinctions between citizens solely because of their ancestry" as being "odious to a free people whose institutions are founded upon the doctrine of equality." Hirabayashi v. United States, 320 U.S. 81, 100 (1943). At the very least, the Equal Protection Clause demands that racial classifications, especially suspect in criminal statutes, be subjected to the "most rigid scrutiny," Korematsu v. United States, 323 U.S. 214, 216 (1944), and, if they are ever to be upheld, they must be shown to be necessary to the accomplishment of some permissible state objective, independent of the racial discrimination which it was the object of the Fourteenth Amendment to eliminate. . . .

There is patently no legitimate overriding purpose independent of invidious racial discrimination which justifies the classification. The fact that Virginia prohibits only interracial marriages involving white persons demonstrates that the racial classifications must stand on their own justification, as measures designed to maintain White Supremacy. We have consistently denied the constitutionality of measures which restrict the rights of citizens on account of race. There can be no doubt that restricting the freedom to marry solely because of racial classifications violates the central meaning of the Equal Protection Clause.

These statutes also deprive the Lovings of liberty without due process of law in violation of the Due Process Clause of the Fourteenth Amendment. The freedom to marry has long been recognized as one of the vital personal rights essential to the orderly pursuit of happiness by free men.

Marriage is one of the "basic civil rights of man," fundamental to our very existence and survival. Skinner v. State of Oklahoma, 316 U.S. 535, 541 (1942). See also Maynard v. Hill, 125 U.S. 190 (1888). To deny this fundamental freedom on so unsupportable a basis as the racial classifications embodied in these statutes, classifications so directly subversive of the principle of equality at the heart of the Fourteenth Amendment, is surely to deprive all the State's citizens of liberty without due process of law. The Fourteenth Amendment requires that the freedom of choice to marry not be restricted by invidious racial discriminations. Under our Constitution, the freedom to marry or not marry, a person of another race resides with the individual and cannot be infringed by the State.

These convictions must be reversed. . . .

## ■ ROBERT A. PRATT, CROSSING THE COLOR LINE: A HISTORICAL ASSESSMENT AND PERSONAL NARRATIVE OF LOVING v. VIRGINIA
*41 How. L.J. 229, 234-244 (1998)*

. . . Richard Perry Loving and Mildred Delores Jeter had known each other practically all of their lives, as their families lived just up the road from each other in the rural community of Central Point, Virginia, located in Caroline County. . . . For twenty-three years, Richard's father had defied the racial mores of southern white society by working for Boyd Byrd, one of the wealthiest black farmers in the community. [T]he close-knit nature of their community [led] to an acceptance of personal relationships in a particular setting that would have been anathema elsewhere. So when white Richard Loving, age seventeen, began courting "colored" Mildred Jeter, age eleven, their budding romance drew little attention from either the white or the black communities.

Mildred (part-black and part-Cherokee) had a pretty light-brown complexion accentuated by her slim figure, which was why practically everyone who knew her called her "Stringbean" or "Bean" for short. Richard (part-English and part-Irish) was a bricklayer by trade, but spent much of his spare time drag racing a car that he co-owned with two black friends, Raymond Green (a mechanic) and Percy Fortune (a local merchant). Despite their natural shyness, both Richard and Mildred were well-liked in the community, and the fact that they attended different churches and different schools did not hinder their courtship. When he was twenty-four and she was eighteen, Richard and Mildred decided to legalize their relationship by getting married.

Mildred did not know that interracial marriage was illegal in Virginia, but Richard did. This explains why, on June 2, 1958, he drove them across the Virginia state line to Washington, D.C., to be married. . . . Mr. and Mrs. Loving returned to Central Point to live with Mildred's parents; however, their marital bliss was short-lived. Five weeks later, on July 11, their quiet life was shattered when they were awakened early in the morning as three law officers "acting on an anonymous tip" opened the unlocked door of their home, walked into their bedroom, and shined a flashlight in their faces. Caroline County Sheriff R. Garnett Brooks demanded to know what the two of them were doing in bed together. Mildred answered, "I'm his wife," while Richard pointed to the District of Columbia marriage certificate that hung on their bedroom wall. "That's no good here," Sheriff Brooks replied. He charged the couple with unlawful cohabitation, and then he and his two deputies hauled the Lovings off to a nearby jail in Bowling Green.

[After their conviction and suspended sentences, the Lovings moved to Washington, D.C., where they had three children: Sidney in 1958, Donald in 1959, and Peggy in 1960.] The years in Washington were not happy ones for the couple. Richard struggled to maintain permanent employment while Mildred busied herself tending to the needs of their three children. "I missed being with my family and friends, especially Garnet [her sister]. I wanted my children to grow up in the country, where they could run and play, and where I wouldn't worry about them so much. I never liked much about the city."

Virginia law would not allow Richard and Mildred Loving [to be] in the state at the same time; however, that did not stop them from trying or from succeeding on various occasions. Mildred and the children made frequent visits to Battery, Virginia, the rural black community where her sister and brother-in-law lived. When Mildred would arrive in Battery, some of the neighbors would begin to look at their watches to see how long it would be before Richard's car came cruising through the neighborhood. During those early years, Richard's visits . . . occurred almost exclusively after dark. . . .

The Lovings had not really been that interested in the civil rights movement, nor had they ever given much thought to challenging Virginia's law. But with a major civil rights bill being debated in Congress in 1963, Mildred decided to write to Robert Kennedy, the Attorney General of the United States. The Department of Justice referred the letter to the American Civil Liberties Union. Bernard S. Cohen, a young lawyer doing pro bono work for the ACLU in Alexandria, Virginia, agreed to take the case. He would later be joined by another young attorney, Philip J. Hirschkop. . . .

On December 12, 1966, the U.S. Supreme Court agreed to hear the case. . . . In concluding his oral argument on April 10, 1967, Cohen relayed a message to the Justices from Richard Loving: "Tell the Court I love my wife, and it is just unfair that I can't live with her in Virginia.". . .

Richard and Mildred Loving, along with their children, took up legal residence in Virginia almost immediately after the Court's ruling. Richard was finally able to build the white cinderblock house he had always wanted for his family. . . . The marriage that earned them a place in the law books ended tragically on June 29, 1975. . . . [T]heir car was broadsided by a drunk driver who ran a stop sign in Caroline County. Richard, age 42, was killed instantly. . . .

Thirty years have passed since the Supreme Court decided to validate Richard Loving's marriage to Mildred Jeter, and social attitudes regarding interracial marriage have undergone a major transformation. . . . But that sentiment is still far from universal. When he was interviewed in 1992 on the twenty-fifth anniversary of the decision, Sheriff Brooks made no apologies for having arrested the Lovings in 1958: "I was acting according to the law at the time, and I still think it should be on the books. I don't think a white person should marry a black person. I'm from the old school. The Lord made sparrows and robins, not to mix with one another.". . .

Mildred Loving, at age 58, remains the same intensely shy woman she has always been. [S]he still sees herself as an ordinary black woman who fell in love with an ordinary white man. . . . Mildred puts it this way:

> We weren't bothering anyone. And if we hurt some people's feelings, that was just too bad. All we ever wanted was to get married, because we loved each other. Some people will never change, but that's their problem, not mine. I married the only man I had ever loved, and I'm happy for the time we had together. For me, that was enough.

## ■ ZABLOCKI v. REDHAIL
### 434 U.S. 374 (1978)

Justice MARSHALL delivered the opinion of the Court.

At issue in this case is the constitutionality of a Wisconsin statute, Wis. Stat. §245.10(1), (4), (5)(1973), which provides that members of a certain class of Wisconsin residents may not marry, within the State or elsewhere, without first obtaining a court order granting permission to marry. The class is defined by the statute to include any "Wisconsin resident having minor issue not in his custody and which he is under obligation to support by any court order or judgment." The statute specifies that court permission cannot be granted unless the marriage applicant submits proof of compliance with the support obligation and, in addition, demonstrates that the children covered by the support order "are not then and are not likely thereafter to become public charges." No marriage license may lawfully be issued in Wisconsin to a person covered by the statute, except upon court order; any marriage entered into without compliance with §245.10 is declared void; and persons acquiring marriage licenses in violation of the section are subject to criminal penalties. . . .

## I

Appellee Redhail is a Wisconsin resident who, under the terms of §245.10, is unable to enter into a lawful marriage in Wisconsin or elsewhere so long as he maintains his Wisconsin residency. . . . In January 1972, when appellee was a minor and a high school student, a paternity action was instituted against him in Milwaukee County Court, alleging that he was the father of a baby girl born out of wedlock on July 5, 1971. After he appeared and admitted that he was the child's father, the court [adjudged] appellee the father and ordered him to pay $109 per month as support for the child until she reached 18 years of age. From May 1972 until August 1974, appellee was unemployed and indigent, and consequently was unable to make any support payments.

On September 27, 1974, appellee filed an application for a marriage license with appellant Zablocki, the County Clerk of Milwaukee County, and a few days later the application was denied on the sole ground that appellee had not obtained a court order granting him permission to marry, as required by §245.10. [I]t is stipulated that he would not have been able to satisfy either of the statutory prerequisites for an order granting permission to marry. First, he had not satisfied his support obligations to his illegitimate child, and as of December 1974 there was an arrearage in excess of $3,700. Second, the child had been a public charge since her birth, receiving benefits under the Aid to Families with Dependent Children program. [T]he child's benefit payments were such that she would have been a public charge even if appellee had been current in his support payments.

On December 24, 1974, appellee filed his complaint in the District Court, on behalf of himself and the class of all Wisconsin residents who had been refused a marriage license pursuant to §245.10(1) [claiming violations of equal protection and due process].

## II

[The Court turns to the issue of the appropriate level of scrutiny.] Since our past decisions make clear that the right to marry is of fundamental importance, and since the classification at issue here significantly interferes with the exercise of that right, we believe that "critical examination" of the state interests advanced in support of the classification is required.

*Critical exam = what kind of scrutiny?*

The leading case of this Court on the right to marry is Loving v. Virginia, 388 U.S. 1 (1967). [*Loving*] could have rested solely on the ground that the statutes discriminated on the basis of race in violation of the Equal Protection Clause. But the Court went on to hold that the laws arbitrarily deprived the couple of a fundamental liberty protected by the Due Process Clause, the freedom to marry. . . . Although *Loving* arose in the context of racial discrimination, prior and subsequent decisions of this Court confirm that the right to marry is of fundamental importance for all individuals. . . .

More recent decisions have established that the right to marry is part of the fundamental "right of privacy" implicit in the Fourteenth Amendment's Due Process Clause. . . . Cases subsequent to *Griswold* and *Loving* have routinely categorized the decision to marry as among the personal decisions protected by the right of privacy. . . .

It is not surprising that the decision to marry has been placed on the same level of importance as decisions relating to procreation, childbirth, child rearing, and family relationships. [I]t would make little sense to recognize a right of privacy with respect to other matters of family life and not with respect to the decision to enter the relationship that is the foundation of the family in our society. The woman whom appellee desired to marry had a fundamental right to seek an abortion of their expected child. . . . Surely, a decision to marry and raise the child in a traditional family setting must receive equivalent protection. And, if appellee's right to procreate means anything at all, it must imply some right to enter the only relationship in which the State of Wisconsin allows sexual relations legally to take place.

By reaffirming the fundamental character of the right to marry, we do not mean to suggest that every state regulation which relates in any way to the incidents of or prerequisites for marriage must be subjected to rigorous scrutiny. To the contrary, reasonable regulations that do not significantly interfere with decisions to enter into the marital relationship may legitimately be imposed. See Califano v. Jobst, 434 U.S. 47 (1977). The statutory classification at issue here, however, clearly does interfere directly and substantially with the right to marry.

Under the challenged statute, no Wisconsin resident in the affected class may marry in Wisconsin or elsewhere without a court order, and marriages contracted in violation of the statute are both void and punishable as criminal offenses. Some of those in the affected class, like appellee, will never be able to obtain the necessary court order, because they either lack the financial means to meet their support obligations or cannot prove that their children will not become public charges. These persons are absolutely prevented from getting married. Many others, able in theory to satisfy the statute's requirements, will be sufficiently burdened by having to do so that they will in effect be coerced into forgoing their right to marry. And even those who can be persuaded to meet the statute's requirements suffer a serious intrusion into their freedom of choice in an area in which we have held such freedom to be fundamental.[12]

## III

When a statutory classification significantly interferes with the exercise of a fundamental right, it cannot be upheld unless it is supported by sufficiently important state interests and is closely tailored to effectuate only those interests. Appellant asserts that two interests are served by the challenged statute: the permission-to-marry proceeding furnishes an opportunity to counsel the applicant as to the necessity of fulfilling his prior support obligations; and the welfare of the out-of-custody children is protected. We may accept for present purposes that these are legitimate and substantial interests, but, since the means selected by the State for achieving these interests unnecessarily impinge on the right to marry, the statute cannot be sustained.

There is evidence that the challenged statute, as originally introduced in the Wisconsin Legislature, was intended merely to establish a mechanism whereby persons with support obligations to children from prior marriages could be counseled before they entered into new marital relationships and incurred further support obligations. Court permission to marry was to be required, but apparently permission was automatically to be granted after counseling was completed. The statute actually enacted, however, does not expressly require or provide for any counseling whatsoever, nor for any automatic granting of permission to marry by the court, and thus it can hardly be justified as a means for ensuring counseling of the persons within its coverage. Even assuming that counseling does take place — a fact as to which there is no evidence in the record — this interest obviously cannot support the withholding of court permission to marry once counseling is completed.

With regard to safeguarding the welfare of the out-of-custody children, appellant's brief does not make clear the connection between the State's interest and the statute's requirements. At argument, appellant's

___

12. The directness and substantiality of the interference with the freedom to marry distinguish the instant case from Califano v. Jobst, 434 U.S. 47 [(1977)]. In *Jobst*, we upheld sections of the Social Security Act providing, inter alia, for termination of a dependent child's benefits upon marriage to an individual not entitled to benefits under the Act. As the opinion for the Court expressly noted, the rule terminating benefits upon marriage was not "an attempt to interfere with the individual's freedom to make a decision as important as marriage." The Social Security provisions placed no direct legal obstacle in the path of persons desiring to get married, and . . . there was no evidence that the laws significantly discouraged, let alone made "practically impossible," any marriages. Indeed, the provisions had not deterred the individual who challenged the statute from getting married, even though he and his wife were both disabled. See Califano v. Jobst. See also id. at 58 n.17 (because of availability of other federal benefits, total payments to the Jobsts after marriage were only $20 per month less than they would have been had Mr. Jobst's child benefits not been terminated).

counsel suggested that, since permission to marry cannot be granted unless the applicant shows that he has satisfied his court-determined support obligations to the prior children and that those children will not become public charges, the statute provides incentive for the applicant to make support payments to his children. This "collection device" rationale cannot justify the statute's broad infringement on the right to marry.

First, with respect to individuals who are unable to meet the statutory requirements, the statute merely prevents the applicant from getting married, without delivering any money at all into the hands of the applicant's prior children. More importantly, regardless of the applicant's ability or willingness to meet the statutory requirements, the State already has numerous other means for exacting compliance with support obligations, means that are at least as effective as the instant statute's and yet do not impinge upon the right to marry. . . .

There is also some suggestion that §245.10 protects the ability of marriage applicants to meet support obligations to prior children by preventing the applicants from incurring new support obligations. But the challenged provisions of §245.10 are grossly underinclusive with respect to this purpose, since they do not limit in any way new financial commitments by the applicant other than those arising out of the contemplated marriage. The statutory classification is substantially overinclusive as well: given the possibility that the new spouse will actually better the applicant's financial situation, by contributing income from a job or otherwise, the statute in many cases may prevent affected individuals from improving their ability to satisfy their prior support obligations. And, although it is true that the applicant will incur support obligations to any children born during the contemplated marriage, preventing the marriage may only result in the children being born out of wedlock, as in fact occurred in appellee's case. Since the support obligation is the same whether the child is born in or out of wedlock, the net result of preventing the marriage is simply more illegitimate children.

The statutory classification created by §245.10(1), (4), (5) thus cannot be justified by the interests advanced in support of it. The judgment of the District Court is, accordingly, [a]ffirmed.

Justice STEWART, concurring in the judgment.

I cannot join the opinion of the Court. To hold, as the Court does, that the Wisconsin statute violates the Equal Protection Clause seems to me to misconceive the meaning of that constitutional guarantee. The Equal Protection Clause deals not with substantive rights or freedoms but with invidiously discriminatory classifications. . . . The problem in this case is not one of discriminatory classifications, but of unwarranted encroachment upon a constitutionally protected freedom. I think that the Wisconsin statute is unconstitutional because it exceeds the bounds of permissible state regulation of marriage, and invades the sphere of liberty protected by the Due Process Clause of the Fourteenth Amendment. . . .

The Constitution does not specifically mention freedom to marry, but it is settled that the "liberty" protected by the Due Process Clause of the Fourteenth Amendment embraces more than those freedoms expressly enumerated in the Bill of Rights. And the decisions of this Court have made clear that freedom of personal choice in matters of marriage and family life is one of the liberties so protected. . . . It is evident that the Wisconsin law now before us directly abridges that freedom. The question is whether the state interests that support the abridgement can overcome the substantive protections of the Constitution. . . .

As directed against either the indigent or the delinquent parent, the law is substantially more rational if viewed as a means of assuring the financial viability of future marriages. In this context, it reflects a plausible judgment that those who have not fulfilled their financial obligations and have not kept their children off the welfare rolls in the past are likely to encounter similar difficulties in the future. But the State's legitimate concern with the financial soundness of prospective marriages must stop short of telling people they may not marry because they are too poor or because they might persist in their financial irresponsibility. . . . A legislative judgment so alien to our traditions and so offensive to our shared notions of fairness offends the Due Process Clause of the Fourteenth Amendment. . . .

Justice STEVENS, concurring in the judgment. . . .

A classification based on marital status is fundamentally different from a classification which determines who may lawfully enter into the marriage relationship.[2] The individual's interest in making the marriage decision independently is sufficiently important to merit special constitutional protection. . . .

Under this statute, a person's economic status may determine his eligibility to enter into a lawful marriage. A noncustodial parent whose children are "public charges" may not marry even if he has met his court-ordered obligations. Thus, within the class of parents who have fulfilled their court-ordered obligations, the rich may marry and the poor may not. This type of statutory discrimination is, I believe, totally unprecedented,[3] as well as inconsistent with our tradition of administering justice equally to the rich and to the poor.

2. *Jobst* is in the former category; Loving v. Virginia, 388 U.S. 1 [(1967)], is in the latter.

3. The economic aspects of a prospective marriage are unquestionably relevant to almost every individual's marriage decision. But I know of no other state statute that denies the individual marriage partners the right to assess the financial consequences of their decision independently. I seriously question whether any limitation on the right to marry may be predicated on economic status, but that question need not be answered in this case.

The statute appears to reflect a legislative judgment that persons who have demonstrated an inability to support their offspring should not be permitted to marry and thereafter to bring additional children into the world. Even putting to one side the growing number of childless marriages and the burgeoning number of children born out of wedlock, that sort of reasoning cannot justify this deliberate discrimination against the poor.

The statute prevents impoverished parents from marrying even though their intended spouses are economically independent. Presumably, the Wisconsin Legislature assumed (a) that only fathers would be affected by the legislation, and (b) that they would never marry employed women. The first assumption ignores the fact that fathers are sometimes awarded custody, and the second ignores the composition of today's work force. To the extent that the statute denies a hard-pressed parent any opportunity to prove that an intended marriage will ease rather than aggravate his financial straits, it not only rests on unreliable premises, but also defeats its own objectives.

These questionable assumptions also explain why this statutory blunderbuss is wide of the target in another respect. The prohibition on marriage applies to the noncustodial parent but allows the parent who has custody to marry without the State's leave. Yet the danger that new children will further strain an inadequate budget is equally great for custodial and non-custodial parents. . . .

. . . Even assuming that the right to marry may sometimes be denied on economic grounds, this clumsy and deliberate legislative discrimination between the rich and the poor is irrational in so many ways that it cannot withstand scrutiny under the Equal Protection Clause of the Fourteenth Amendment.

[Justice Rehnquist, dissenting, would have upheld the statute under the rational basis test as a permissible exercise of the state's power to regulate family life and to assure child support.]

## Notes and Questions on *Loving* and *Zablocki*

1. *Historical background.* The statute under which the Lovings were convicted was part of a widespread policy. Antimiscegenation laws (prohibitions on interracial sexual relations and intermarriage) stemmed from beliefs regarding the superiority of whites and the racial basis of behavior and temperament. At one time, 38 states prohibited relationships between Blacks and whites, 14 states banned those between Asians and whites, and 7 states banned those between Native Americans and whites. Rachel F. Moran, Interracial Intimacy: The Regulation of Race and Romance 17 (2001). Even before Virginia enacted its first prohibition in 1662, state officials whipped and publicly humiliated persons who entered into Black-white sexual relationships. Id. at 19. Authorities were

concerned, in part, about the status of mulatto offspring in an economy based on slavery. Id. at 20.

Concern over miscegenation increased after the Civil War when the emancipation of slaves heightened racial tension. Bolstering this climate was the eugenics movement, which originated in nineteenth-century Britain and reached its apex during the Progressive Era in America. Eugenicists believed that most maladies were hereditary and that social engineering would improve the human race. This theory led to many state restrictions on marriage, including the strengthening of antimiscegenation laws. From 1880 to 1920, 20 states and territories revised or added antimiscegenation laws, with interracial marriage singled out for the most stringent restrictions.[16]

2. Despite *Loving*, acceptance of interracial marriages lags. South Carolina removed its ban in 1998. In 2000, Alabama became the last state to invalidate the prohibition in its state constitution. The closeness of the vote in both Alabama and South Carolina reflects the prevalence of negative attitudes: 40 percent of Alabamians voted to retain their antimiscegenation law, and 39 percent of South Carolinians favored their ban. See Mike Gadd, Views on Mixed Marriage are Stuck in the Past, S.F. Chron., Jan. 7, 2001, at 6; Editorial, Voting for Change, Lancaster (PA) Intelligencer J., Nov. 15, 2000, at A18. More generally, a recent survey reports that a significant number of whites (20 percent of those aged 55-64 in a sample of 3,230 adults) still believe that Black-white marriages should be illegal. Tom W. Smith, Changes in the Generation Gap, 1972-1998, National Opinion Research Center, University of Chicago, October 2000. Black-white couples continue to face considerable prejudice and discrimination.[17]

3. *Empirical Data. Loving* marked the beginning of a steady increase in multiracial marriages in general. Such marriages have increased tenfold since 1960. Tony Pugh, Mixed Marriages on the Rise in U.S., Houston Chron., Mar. 25, 2001, at 12. In the last two decades, the number of Black-white marriages has doubled.[18] Marriages between African-Americans and whites now constitute 2% of all marriages.[19]

---

[16]. Michael Grossberg, Governing the Hearth: Law and the Family in Nineteenth Century America 136, 138-139 (1985). On the history of the Virginia statute, see Barbara K. Kopytoff & A. Leon Higginbotham, Jr., Racial Purity and Interracial Sex in the Law of Colonial and Antebellum Virginia, 77 Geo. L.J. 1967 (1980); Paul A. Lombardo, Miscegenation, Eugenics, and Racism: Historical Footnotes to *Loving v. Virginia*, 21 U.C. Davis L. Rev. 421 (1988).

[17]. For example, a study of 21 couples in the Minneapolis-St. Paul area reports that the couples experience poor service at restaurants; denials of hotel rooms; hostile words, gestures, and stares; hate phone calls, literature, and mail; unpleasant encounters with the police; and discrimination in housing and employment. Paul C. Rosenblatt et al., Multiracial Couples: Black and White Voices 118 (1995).

[18]. Bureau of the Census, U.S. Dept. of Commerce, Statistical Abstract of the United States 51 (2000) (table 54).

[19]. Id. (extrapolating from table 54).

Interestingly, intermarriage rates vary by race, sex, and ethnicity. Marriages between Blacks and whites have not kept pace with those involving other persons of color. For example, Hispanics and Asians marry partners of different races at about three times the rate of Blacks and five times the rate of whites. Pugh, supra. Rates also vary by gender. For example, Black men intermarry more frequently than Black women: 8.1 percent of Black men intermarry compared to 3.2 percent of Black women. Id. Conversely, Asian women are more likely than Asian men to intermarry: 21 percent of Asian women marry someone of a different race compared to 11 percent of Asian men. See also Moran, supra, at 103-104.

Several commentators point to the comparatively lower Black-white intermarriage rate as evidence that other races are more quickly becoming integrated into American society. See Randall Kennedy, How Are We Doing with *Loving*?: Race, Law, and Intermarriage, 77 B.U. L. Rev. 815 (1997); Moran, supra, at 105, 174-175; V. Dion Haynes & Vincent J. Schodolski, Interracial Marriages Increase But Black-White Unions Still Face Most Resistance, Chi. Trib., Sept. 8, 1998, at 1; Michael A. Fletcher, Interracial Marriages, New Orleans Times, Jan. 10, 1999, at A20. As an official recognition of multiracialism in America, the 2000 census permitted individuals to identify themselves by multiple racial and ethnic affiliations.

On interracial marriage, see Heather M. Dalmage, Tripping on the Color Line: Black-White Multiracial Families in a Racially Divided World (2000); Moran, supra; Maria P. P. Root, Love's Revolution: Interracial Marriage (2001); Werner Sollors, ed., Interracialism: Black White Intermarriage in American History, Literature, and Law (2000).

4. The rule of lex loci provides that a marriage valid where performed is valid everywhere. Why did that rule not operate in *Loving*?

5. *Loving* was a landmark discrimination decision. However, antimiscegenation statutes had come before the Court previously. See McLaughlin v. Florida, 379 U.S. 184 (1964) (invalidating a Florida miscegenation law without expressing any views about interracial marriage); Naim v. Naim, 87 S.E.2d 749 (Va.), *vacated and remanded,* 350 U.S. 891 (1955), *aff'd,* 90 S.E.2d 849 (Va.), *appeal dismissed,* 350 U.S. 985 (1956) (remanded on procedural grounds).

A lesser-known case decided two decades before *Loving*, Perez v. Lippold, 198 P.2d 17 (Cal. 1948), declared the California antimiscegenation statute unconstitutional. The opinion by Justice Traynor proclaims that the Fourteenth Amendment protects the right to marry and holds that the statute neither serves a legitimate social purpose nor employs a reasonable means of accomplishing its intended goals. Why might it have taken the Supreme Court so long to reach the same result?

6. *Loving* cites precedents concerning divorce (Maynard v. Hill), compulsory sterilization (Skinner v. Oklahoma), and, in a deleted sec-

tion, parental rights (Meyer v. Nebraska). Are the cases apt? Curiously, *Loving* does not cite Griswold v. Connecticut, decided two years earlier. What explains this omission? What contribution might *Griswold* and subsequent privacy cases make to the analysis in *Loving*?

7. Is *Loving* a case about race or about freedom of choice in marriage? What standard of review does the Court apply? What triggers such review? *Loving* establishes that the right to marry is constitutionally protected. Why should the Constitution protect the right to marry? Where in the Constitution is this right? Does it rest on substantive due process or equal protection? This question plagued commentators until *Zablocki*.

> *Loving* [failed to provide] clear authority for a right to marry that could be characterized as fundamental for purposes of substantive due process or equal protection analysis. . . . [T]he *Loving* opinion stopped short of a clear statement of a right to marry, for the reasoning depended largely on the racial character of the classification. The Court stated two alternative grounds for the decision. The first [was] that the statute was invalid solely because of the racial classification. The second . . . relied on the right to marry, but again the Court referred to the racial nature of the classification, stating, "To deny this fundamental freedom on so insupportable a basis as the racial classifications embodied in these statutes, classifications so directly subversive of the principle of equality at the heart of the Fourteenth Amendment, is surely to deprive all the State's citizens of liberty without due process of law." . . .

Note, The Constitution and the Family, 93 Harv. L. Rev. 1156, 1249 (1980). As a result, some courts restricted *Loving*'s precedential value to the racial discrimination holding. See, e.g., In re Goalen, 512 P.2d 1028 (Utah 1973), *appeal dismissed and cert. denied*, 414 U.S. 1148 (1974). What difference does it make if the right derives from the Due Process Clause or the Equal Protection Clause? On which approach did the Court decide *Zablocki*?

8. *Zablocki* establishes different degrees of scrutiny for regulations infringing the right to marry, that is, rigorous scrutiny for significant interference but minimal scrutiny for "reasonable regulations that do not significantly interfere with decisions to enter into the marital relationship." Justice Powell (in an omitted concurrence) suggests that the Court does not present any means to distinguish between the two types of regulations. Do you agree? What distinguishes the regulation in *Zablocki* from that in Califano v. Jobst, cited in *Zablocki*?

According to *Zablocki*, a significant interference calling for rigorous scrutiny must be "direct" and "substantial." Are these distinct requirements?

> The most common problem in the analysis has been the tendency of the courts to blur the distinction between directness and substantiality. Since

recognition of directness requires only an examination of the face of the statute, courts sometimes perform this simple mechanical test and then infer substantiality from directness or insubstantiality from indirectness. The result, of course, is to reduce the test to one of directness. But emphasizing directness to the exclusion of significance creates a danger that the protection of the right to marry will become illusory; only direct interferences will be scrutinized, even though in most cases, the state can achieve a similar interference by indirect means. . . .

Note, The Constitution and the Family, supra, at 1252-1253. What guidelines does *Zablocki* give for identifying a "direct" interference?

For symposia on the legacy of *Loving*, see 12 B.Y.U. J. Pub. L. 201 (1998) (articles by David Orgon Coolidge, Richard F. Duncan, Lynne Marie Kohm, and Katherine Shaw Spaht); 47 Catholic Univ. L. Rev. 1207 (1998) (articles by Anita K. Blair, Teresa Stanton Collett, and Peter Lubin and Dwight Duncan); 41 Howard L.J. 215 (1998) (articles by Margaret F. Brinig, Lawrence C. Nolan, Robert A. Pratt, and Lynn D. Wardle).

## Problems

1. A state or state agency enacts the following statutes or regulations. Which, if any, infringe on the constitutional right to marry?
   a. a statute preventing any resident who cannot provide a social security number from obtaining a marriage license (Ohio ex rel. Ten Residents of Franklin County v. Belskis, 755 N.E.2d 443 (Ohio Ct. App. 2001);
   b. a statute preventing a married woman from adopting her grandson by requiring that her spouse join in the adoption petition (Browder v. Harmeyer, 453 N.E.2d 301 (Ind. Ct. App. 1983));
   c. a prohibition on an owner of a horse from having a license because of a spouse's past conviction for possession-sale of a controlled substance (Levinson v. Washington Horse Racing Commn., 740 P.2d 898 (Wash. Ct. App. 1987));
   d. a prohibition on married students' participation in athletic programs (Indiana High Sch. Athletic Assn. v. Raike, 329 N.E.2d 66 (Ind. Ct. App. 1975)).

2. The Texas legislature amends the Texas Family Code to deny a marriage license to an applicant who is delinquent in payment of court-ordered child support. Worried about the constitutionality of the Texas legislation in light of *Zablocki*, the Dallas County District Attorney asks the Texas Attorney General for a legal opinion. Texas, unlike Wisconsin, recognizes common law marriage (discussed infra this chapter) — a practice that permits a valid marriage without a formal ceremony. The state Attorney General must consider: (1) does the existence of common

law marriage as an alternative to ceremonially initiated marriage insulate the Texas legislation from constitutional challenge, and (2) does the challenged legislation directly and substantially interfere with the right to marry?

■ **TURNER v. SAFLEY** *inmate marriages*
*482 U.S. 78 (1987)*

Justice O'CONNOR delivered the opinion of the Court.

This case requires us to determine the constitutionality of regulations promulgated by the Missouri Division of Corrections relating to inmate marriages. . . . The challenged marriage regulation . . . permits an inmate to marry only with the permission of the superintendent of the prison, and provides that such approval should be given only "when there are compelling reasons to do so." The term "compelling" is not defined, but prison officials testified at trial that generally only a pregnancy or the birth of an illegitimate child would be considered a compelling reason. Prior to the promulgation of this rule, the applicable regulation did not obligate Missouri Division of Corrections officials to assist an inmate who wanted to get married. [Plaintiff inmates brought a class action for injunctive relief and damages.]

In support of the marriage regulation, petitioners first suggest that the rule does not deprive prisoners of a constitutionally protected right. They concede that the decision to marry is a fundamental right under Zablocki v. Redhail, 434 U.S. 374 (1978), and Loving v. Virginia, 388 U.S. 1 (1967), but they imply that a different rule should obtain "in . . . a prison forum." Petitioners then argue that even if the regulation burdens inmates' constitutional rights, the restriction should be tested under a reasonableness standard. They urge that the restriction is reasonably related to legitimate security and rehabilitation concerns.

We disagree with petitioners that *Zablocki* does not apply to prison inmates. It is settled that a prison inmate "retains those [constitutional] rights that are not inconsistent with his status as a prisoner or with the legitimate penological objectives of the corrections system." Pell v. Procunier, 417 U.S. 817, 822 (1974). The right to marry, like many other rights, is subject to substantial restrictions as a result of incarceration. Many important attributes of marriage remain, however, after taking into account the limitations imposed by prison life. First, inmate marriages, like others, are expressions of emotional support and public commitment. These elements are an important and significant aspect of the marital relationship. In addition, many religions recognize marriage as having spiritual significance; for some inmates and their spouses, therefore, the commitment of marriage may be an exercise of religious faith as well as an expression of personal dedication. Third, most inmates eventually will be released by parole or commutation, and therefore most inmate marriages are formed in the expectation that they ultimately will be fully consummated. Finally, marital status often is a precondition to the receipt of government benefits (e.g., Social Security benefits), property rights (e.g., tenancy by the entirety, inheritance rights), and other, less tangible benefits (e.g., legitimation of children born out of wedlock). These incidents of marriage, like the religious and personal aspects of the marriage commitment, are unaffected by the fact of confinement or the pursuit of legitimate corrections goals.

Taken together, we conclude that these remaining elements are sufficient to form a constitutionally protected marital relationship in the prison context. Our decision in Butler v. Wilson, 415 U.S. 953 (1974), is not to the contrary. That case involved a prohibition on marriage only for inmates sentenced to life imprisonment; and, importantly, denial of the right was part of the punishment for crime.

The Missouri marriage regulation prohibits inmates from marrying unless the prison superintendent has approved the marriage after finding that there are compelling reasons for doing so. . . . In determining whether this regulation impermissibly burdens the right to marry, we note initially that the regulation prohibits marriages between inmates and civilians, as well as marriages between inmates. Although not urged by respondents, this implication of the interests of nonprisoners . . . may entail a "consequential restriction on the [constitutional] rights of those who are not prisoners." See Procunier v. Martinez, [416 U.S. 396, 409 (1974)]. We need not reach this question, however, because even under the reasonable relationship test, the marriage regulation does not withstand scrutiny.

Petitioners have identified both security and rehabilitation concerns in support of the marriage prohibition. The security concern emphasized by petitioners is that "love triangles" might lead to violent confrontations between inmates. With respect to rehabilitation, prison officials testified that female prisoners often were subject to abuse at home or were overly dependent on male figures, and that this dependence or abuse was connected to the crimes they had committed. The [prison] superintendent, petitioner William Turner, testified that in his view, these women prisoners needed to concentrate on developing skills of self-reliance, and that the prohibition on marriage furthered this rehabilitative goal. Petitioners emphasize that the prohibition on marriage should be understood in light of Superintendent Turner's experience with several ill-advised marriage requests from female inmates.

We conclude that on this record, the Missouri prison regulation, as written, is not reasonably related to these penological interests. No doubt legitimate security concerns may require placing reasonable restrictions upon an inmate's right to marry, and may justify requiring approval of the superintendent. The Missouri regulation, however, represents an exaggerated response to such security objectives. . . . Moreover, with respect to the security concern emphasized in petitioners' brief — the creation of "love triangles" — petitioners have pointed to nothing in the record suggesting that the marriage regulation was viewed as preventing such entanglements. Common sense likewise suggests that there is no logical connection between the marriage restriction and the formation of love triangles: surely in prisons housing both male and female prisoners, inmate rivalries are as likely to develop without a formal marriage ceremony as with one. Finally, this is not an instance where the "ripple effect" on the security of fellow inmates and prison staff justifies a broad restriction on inmates' rights. . . .

Nor, on this record, is the marriage restriction reasonably related to the articulated rehabilitation goal. First, in requiring refusal of permission absent a finding of a compelling reason to allow the marriage, the rule sweeps much more broadly than can be explained by petitioners' penological objectives. Missouri prison officials testified that generally they had experienced no problem with the marriage of male inmates, and the District Court found that such marriages had routinely been allowed as a matter of practice at Missouri correctional institutions prior to adoption of the rule. The proffered justification thus does not explain the adoption of a rule banning marriages by these inmates. Nor does it account for the prohibition on inmate marriages to civilians. Missouri prison officials testified that generally they had no objection to inmate-civilian marriages, and Superintendent Turner testified that he usually did not object to the marriage of either male or female prisoners to civilians. The rehabilitation concern appears from the record to have been centered almost exclusively on female inmates marrying other inmates or ex-felons. . . .

Moreover, although not necessary to the disposition of this case, we note that on this record the rehabilitative objective asserted to support the regulation itself is suspect. Of the several female inmates whose marriage requests were discussed by prison officials at trial, only one was refused on the basis of fostering excessive dependency. The District Court found that the Missouri prison system operated on the basis of excessive paternalism in that the proposed marriages of *all* female inmates were scrutinized carefully even before adoption of the current regulation . . . whereas the marriages of male inmates during the same period were routinely approved. That kind of lopsided rehabilitation concern cannot provide a justification for the broad Missouri marriage rule.

. . . On this record . . . the almost complete ban on the decision to marry is not reasonably related to legitimate penological objectives. We conclude, therefore, that the Missouri marriage regulation is facially invalid.

## Notes and Questions

1. Does *Turner*'s holding follow automatically from *Loving* and *Zablocki*?

2. What rationale supports depriving life sentence inmates of the right to marry, as the Court previously held in Butler v. Wilson, cited in *Turner*? Does this rationale dictate the automatic dissolution of marriages entered into by life sentence inmates prior to incarceration? Cf. Langone v. Coughlin, 712 F. Supp. 1061 (N.D.N.Y. 1989) (holding unconstitutional a state prohibition on marriage by inmates serving life sentences as not reasonably related to legitimate penological objectives).

3. Does it follow from *Turner* that a prisoner who marries must be permitted conjugal visits? Ferrin v. Department of Corrections Servs., 517 N.E.2d 1370 (N.Y. 1987), upheld the denial of a life sentence inmate's application to participate in a family reunion program with a woman he married while in prison, on the ground that the marriage was void from inception. Assuming the validity of such restrictions for life sentence inmates, what constitutional arguments would you advance on behalf of Safley (not a life sentence inmate) if she were denied conjugal visits? How meaningful is recognition of the right to marry without conjugal visits?

4. Should an inmate's right to marry or to have conjugal visitation depend on whether the prisoner has AIDS? In Doe v. Coughlin, 518 N.E.2d 536 (N.Y. 1987), an inmate and his wife challenged prison officials' refusal to allow him to participate in conjugal visits because he had AIDS. The court held that the inmate's condition provided a rational basis for preventing his participation. Did the court use the appropriate level of scrutiny? If the restriction is designed to prevent transmission of disease to the inmate's spouse, does that intrude on the right of marital sexual privacy established by *Griswold*? Does it intrude on the rights of the inmate's spouse? To what extent should review of inmate restrictions include consideration of the rights of the affected nonprisoners? See generally Ronald G. Turner, Sex in Prison, 36 Tenn. B.J. 12 (2000).

Does the purpose of protecting the noninmate spouse reflect a paternalism condemned by *Turner*? See Gerald Dworkin, Paternalism in Morality and the Law (Richard Wasserstrom ed., 1971); David L. Shapiro, Courts, Legislatures, and Paternalism, 74 Va. L. Rev. 519 (1988). See generally Irene Lambrou, Comment, AIDS Behind Bars: Prison Responses and Judicial Deference, 62 Temp. L. Rev. 327 (1989); Carol J. Miller, Annotation, State Regulation of Conjugal or Overnight Familial Visits in Penal or Correctional Institutions, 29 A.L.R.4th 1216 (1984).

## Problems

1. Husband, a 41-year-old inmate who is serving a life sentence in state prison, wishes to have a child with Wife, who is 44 years old. Hus-

band learns that the California Department of Corrections (CDC) prohibits family visits for inmates serving life sentences. Given his sentence and Wife's age, Husband requests that (1) a laboratory be permitted to mail him a plastic semen collection container with a prepaid return mailer, (2) he be permitted to ejaculate into the container, and (3) the filled container be returned to the laboratory via overnight mail. Alternatively, he requests that his attorney be permitted to transport the specimen to the laboratory. He and Wife are willing to bear all costs. When the CDC refuses to accommodate Husband's request, he brings an action alleging a violation of his constitutional right to procreate pursuant to 42 U.S.C. §1983 and the Due Process Clause. What result? If the court were to agree that Husband has a constitutional right to procreate noncoitally in this manner, does a female inmate have a corresponding right to be artificially inseminated? See Gerber v. Hickman, 264 F.3d 882 (9th Cir. 2001). See also Goodwin v. Turner, 908 F.2d 1395 (8th Cir. 1990).

2. Nancy Summers, a county jail guard, becomes acquainted with Mitch Keeney, an inmate serving a sentence for a property offense. When the jail director becomes aware that the couple may be romantically involved, he transfers Mitch to another facility. Nancy and Mitch correspond. Nancy continues to visit Mitch frequently. Four months after Mitch's transfer, Nancy admits to her boss that she plans to marry Mitch. The director then cites a jail regulation prohibiting employees from "becom[ing] involved socially with inmates in or out of the [jail]." He tells Nancy that she must choose between Mitch or her job. Nancy resigns and later marries Mitch. They divorce about three years later. Nancy files suit against the jail director and county sheriff claiming that, in forcing her to choose between her job or marriage, the defendants infringed her constitutional right to marry. What result? Keeney v. Heath, 57 F.3d 579 (7th Cir. 1995).

## 2. State Regulation of Entry into the Marital Relationship

### a. Substantive Restrictions

#### (i) Capacity to Marry

#### (1) Same Sex

### ■ BAKER v. STATE
*744 A.2d 864 (Vt. 1999)*

AMESTOY, C.J.

May the State of Vermont exclude same-sex couples from the benefits and protections that its laws provide to opposite-sex married couples? That is the fundamental question we address in this appeal, a question that the Court well knows arouses deeply-felt religious, moral, and political beliefs. . . . The issue before the Court [however] does not turn on the religious or moral debate over intimate same-sex relationships, but rather on the statutory and constitutional basis for the exclusion of same-sex couples from the secular benefits and protections offered married couples. . . .

Plaintiffs are three same-sex couples who have lived together in committed relationships for periods ranging from four to twenty-five years. Two of the couples have raised children together. Each couple applied for a marriage license from their respective town clerk, and each was refused a license as ineligible under the applicable state marriage laws. [Plaintiffs then sought a declaratory judgment that the refusal to issue them a license violated state law and the state constitution.]

## I. THE STATUTORY CLAIM

[T]he principal objective of statutory construction is to discern the legislative intent. . . . Vermont's marriage statutes are set forth in Chapter 1 of Title 15, entitled "Marriage," which defines the requirements and eligibility for entering into a marriage, and Chapter 105 of Title 18, entitled "Marriage Records and Licenses," which prescribes the forms and procedures for obtaining a license and solemnizing a marriage. [T]here is no doubt that the plain and ordinary meaning of "marriage" is the union of one man and one woman as husband and wife. See Webster's New International Dictionary 1506 (2d ed. 1955) (marriage consists of state of "being united to a person . . . of the opposite sex as husband or wife"); Black's Law Dictionary 986 (7th ed. 1999) (marriage is "[t]he legal union of a man and woman as husband and wife"). This understanding of the term is well rooted in Vermont common law [and] in the enabling statute governing the issuance of marriage licenses, which provides, in part, that the license "shall be issued by the clerk of the town where either the bride or groom resides." 18 V.S.A. §5131(a). "Bride" and "groom" are gender-specific terms.

Further evidence of the legislative assumption that marriage consists of a union of opposite genders may be found in the consanguinity statutes, which expressly prohibit a man from marrying certain female relatives, and a woman from marrying certain male relatives. In addition, the annulment statutes explicitly refer to "husband and wife," as do other statutes relating to married couples [referring to laws regarding testimonial privileges, inheritance, and desertion].

These statutes, read as a whole, reflect the common understanding that marriage under Vermont law consists of a union between a man and a woman. Plaintiffs essentially concede this fact. They argue, nevertheless, that the underlying purpose of marriage is to protect and encourage the union of committed couples and that, absent an explicit legislative prohibition, the statutes should be interpreted broadly to include committed same-sex couples. Plaintiffs rely principally on our decision in In re B.L.V.B., 628 A.2d 1271, 1272 (Vt. 1993) [holding that an adoption by a same-sex partner does not terminate the natural mother's rights, based on the legislative intent to safeguard the child]. Contrary to plaintiffs' claim, *B.L.V.B.* does not control our conclusion here. . . . Unlike *B.L.V.B.*, it is far from clear that limiting marriage to opposite-sex couples violates the Legislature's "intent and spirit.". . .

## II. THE CONSTITUTIONAL CLAIM

Assuming that the marriage statutes preclude their eligibility for a marriage license, plaintiffs contend that the exclusion violates their right to the common benefit and protection of the law guaranteed by Chapter I, Article 7 of the Vermont Constitution.[2] [That Article provides, in part: "That government is, or ought to be, instituted for the common benefit, protection, and security of the people, nation, or community, and not for the particular emolument or advantage of any single person, family, or set of persons, who are a part only of that community."] In considering this issue, it is important to emphasize at the outset that it is the Common Benefits Clause of the Vermont Constitution we are construing, rather than its counterpart, the Equal Protection Clause of the Fourteenth Amendment to the United States Constitution. . . . Unlike the Fourteenth Amendment, whose origin and language reflect the solicitude of a dominant white society for an historically-oppressed African-American minority (no state shall "deny" the equal protection of the laws), the Common Benefits Clause mirrors the confidence of a homogeneous, eighteenth-century group of men aggressively laying claim to the same rights as their peers in Great Britain or, for that matter, New York, New Hampshire, or the Upper Connecticut River Valley. [A]t its core the Common Benefits Clause expressed a vision of government that afforded every Vermonter its benefit and protection and provided no Vermonter particular advantage. . . .

[W]e turn to the question of whether the exclusion of same-sex couples from the benefits and protections incident to marriage under Vermont law contravenes [the Common Benefits Clause]. The first step in our analysis is to identify the nature of the statutory classification. [T]he marriage statutes apply expressly to opposite-sex couples. Thus,

2. Although plaintiffs raise a number of additional arguments based on both the United States and the Vermont Constitutions, our resolution of the Common Benefits claim obviates the necessity to address them.

the statutes exclude anyone who wishes to marry someone of the same
sex.[13]

Next, we must identify the governmental purpose or purposes to be
served by the statutory classification. The principal purpose the State advances in support of the excluding same-sex couples from the legal benefits of marriage is the government's interest in "furthering the link
between procreation and child rearing." The State has a strong interest,
it argues, in promoting a permanent commitment between couples who
have children to ensure that their offspring are considered legitimate
and receive ongoing parental support. The State contends, further, that
the Legislature could reasonably believe that sanctioning same-sex
unions "would diminish society's perception of the link between procreation and child rearing [and] advance the notion that fathers or mothers . . . are mere surplusage to the functions of procreation and child
rearing." The State argues that since same-sex couples cannot conceive
a child on their own, state-sanctioned same-sex unions "could be seen
by the Legislature to separate further the connection between procreation and parental responsibilities for raising children." Hence, the Legislature is justified, the State concludes, "in using the marriage statutes
to send a public message that procreation and child rearing are
intertwined."

    13. Relying largely on federal precedents, our colleague in her concurring and dis-
senting opinion suggests that the statutory exclusion of same-sex couples from the benefits and protections of marriage should be subject to heightened scrutiny as a "suspect" or
"quasi-suspect" classification based on sex. . . . The difficulty here is that . . . there is no
discrete class subject to differential treatment solely on the basis of sex; each sex is equally
prohibited from precisely the same conduct. Indeed, most appellate courts that have addressed the issue have rejected the claim that defining marriage as the union of one man
and one woman discriminates on the basis of sex. See, e.g., Baker v. Nelson, 191 N.W.2d
185, 186-87 (Minn. 1971); Singer v. Hara, 11 Wash. App. 247, 522 P.2d 1187, 1191-92
(Wash. Ct. App. 1974). . . . But see Baehr v. Lewin, 74 Haw. 530, 852 P.2d 44, 64 (Haw.
1993) (plurality opinion holding that state's marriage laws discriminated on basis of sex).
Although the concurring and dissenting opinion invokes the United States Supreme Court
decision in Loving v. Virginia, 388 U.S. (1967), the reliance is misplaced. There the high
court had little difficulty in looking behind the superficial neutrality of Virginia's antimiscegenation statute to hold that its real purpose was to maintain the pernicious doctrine
of white supremacy. Our colleague argues, by analogy, that the effect, if not the purpose,
of the exclusion of same-sex partners from the marriage laws is to maintain certain male
and female stereotypes to the detriment of both. To support the claim, she cites a number
of antiquated statutes that denied married women a variety of freedoms, including the
right to enter into contracts and hold property. The test to evaluate whether a facially
gender-neutral statute discriminates on the basis of sex is whether the law "can be traced
to a discriminatory purpose." Personnel Administrator v. Feeney, 442 U.S. 256, 272 (1979).
The evidence does not demonstrate such a purpose. It is one thing to show that long-
repealed marriage statutes subordinated women to men within the marital relation. It is
quite another to demonstrate that the authors of the marriage laws excluded same-sex
couples because of incorrect and discriminatory assumptions about gender roles or anxiety about gender-role confusion. That evidence is not before us. Accordingly, we are not
persuaded that sex discrimination offers a useful analytic framework for determining
plaintiffs' rights under the Common Benefits Clause.

*[handwritten margin notes: relation; = RBT; state interests; under-inclusive; child bearing; empirical evidence]*

Do these concerns represent valid public interests that are reasonably furthered by the exclusion of same-sex couples from the benefits and protections that flow from the marital relation? It is beyond dispute that the State has a legitimate and longstanding interest in promoting a permanent commitment between couples for the security of their children. It is equally undeniable that the State's interest has been advanced by extending formal public sanction and protection to the union, or marriage, of those couples considered capable of having children, i.e., men and women. And there is no doubt that the overwhelming majority of births today continue to result from natural conception between one man and one woman.

It is equally undisputed that many opposite-sex couples marry for reasons unrelated to procreation, that some of these couples never intend to have children, and that others are incapable of having children. Therefore, if the purpose of the statutory exclusion of same-sex couples is to "further[ ] the link between procreation and child rearing," it is significantly under-inclusive. The law extends the benefits and protections of marriage to many persons with no logical connection to the stated governmental goal.

Furthermore, while accurate statistics are difficult to obtain, there is no dispute that a significant number of children today are actually being raised by same-sex parents, and that increasing numbers of children are being conceived by such parents through a variety of assisted-reproductive techniques. [See] G. Green and F. Bozett, Lesbian Mothers and Gay Fathers, in Homosexuality: Research Implications for Public Policy 197, 198 (J. Gonsiorek et al. eds., 1991) (estimating that numbers of children of either gay fathers or lesbian mothers range between six and fourteen million). . . . The Vermont Legislature has not only recognized this reality, but has acted affirmatively to remove legal barriers so that same-sex couples may legally adopt and rear the children conceived through such efforts. See 15A V.S.A. §1-102(b) (allowing partner of biological parent to adopt if in child's best interest without reference to sex). The State has also acted to expand the domestic relations laws to safeguard the interests of same-sex parents and their children when such couples terminate their domestic relationship. See 15A V.S.A. §1-112 (vesting family court with jurisdiction over parental rights and responsibilities, parent-child contact, and child support when unmarried persons who have adopted minor child "terminate their domestic relationship").

Therefore, to the extent that the State's purpose in licensing civil marriage was, and is, to legitimize children and provide for their security, the statutes plainly exclude many same-sex couples who are no different from opposite-sex couples with respect to these objectives. If anything, the exclusion of same-sex couples from the legal protections incident to marriage exposes their children to the precise risks that the State argues the marriage laws are designed to secure against. In short, the marital exclusion treats persons who are similarly situated for purposes of the law differently.

The State also argues that because same-sex couples cannot conceive a child on their own, their exclusion promotes a "perception of the link between procreation and child rearing," and that to discard it would "advance the notion that mothers and fathers . . . are mere surplusage to the functions of procreation and child rearing." Apart from the bare assertion, the State offers no persuasive reasoning to support these claims. Indeed, it is undisputed that most of those who utilize nontraditional means of conception are infertile married couples, and that many assisted-reproductive techniques involve only one of the married partner's genetic material, the other being supplied by a third party through sperm, egg, or embryo donation. The State does not suggest that the use of these technologies undermines a married couple's sense of parental responsibility, or fosters the perception that they are "mere surplusage" to the conception and parenting of the child so conceived. Nor does it even remotely suggest that access to such techniques ought to be restricted as a matter of public policy to "send a public message that procreation and child rearing are intertwined." Accordingly, there is no reasonable basis to conclude that a same-sex couple's use of the same technologies would undermine the bonds of parenthood, or society's perception of parenthood.

[I]n determining whether a statutory exclusion reasonably relates to the governmental purpose it is appropriate to consider the history and significance of the benefits denied. What do these considerations reveal about the benefits and protections at issue here? In Loving v. Virginia, 388 U.S. 1, 12 (1967), the United States Supreme Court, striking down Virginia's antimiscegenation law, observed that "[t]he freedom to marry has long been recognized as one of the vital personal rights." The Court's point was clear; access to a civil marriage license and the multitude of legal benefits, protections, and obligations that flow from it significantly enhance the quality of life in our society. They do?

While the laws relating to marriage have undergone many changes during the last century, largely toward the goal of equalizing the status of husbands and wives, the benefits of marriage have not diminished in value. On the contrary, the benefits and protections incident to a marriage license under Vermont law have never been greater. They include, for example, the right to receive a portion of the estate of a spouse who dies intestate and protection against disinheritance through elective share provisions; preference in being appointed as the personal representative of a spouse who dies intestate; the right to bring a lawsuit for the wrongful death of a spouse; the right to bring an action for loss of consortium; the right to workers' compensation survivor benefits; the right to spousal benefits statutorily guaranteed to public employees, including health, life, disability, and accident insurance; the opportunity to be covered as a spouse under group life insurance policies issued to an employee; the opportunity to be covered as the insured's spouse under an individual health insurance policy; the right to claim an evidentiary privilege for marital communications; homestead rights and protections; the presumption of joint ownership of property and the concomitant right of survivorship; hospital visitation and other rights incident to the medical treatment of a family member; and the right to receive, and the obligation to provide, spousal support, maintenance, and property division in the event of separation or divorce. . . .

[L]egal benefits and protections flowing from a marriage license are of such significance that any statutory exclusion must necessarily be grounded on public concerns of sufficient weight, cogency, and authority that the justice of the deprivation cannot seriously be questioned. Considered in light of the extreme logical disjunction between the classification and the stated purposes of the law — protecting children and "furthering the link between procreation and child rearing" — the exclusion falls substantially short of this standard. . . .

The State asserts that a number of additional rationales could support a legislative decision to exclude same-sex partners from the statutory benefits and protections of marriage. . . . The most substantive of the State's remaining claims relates to the issue of childrearing. It is conceivable that the Legislature could conclude that opposite-sex partners offer advantages in this area, although we note that child-development experts disagree and the answer is decidedly uncertain. The argument, however, contains a more fundamental flaw, and that is the Legislature's endorsement of a policy diametrically at odds with the State's claim. In 1996, the Vermont General Assembly enacted, and the Governor signed, a law removing all prior legal barriers to the adoption of children by same-sex couples. At the same time, the Legislature provided additional legal protections in the form of court-ordered child support and parent-child contact in the event that same-sex parents dissolved their "domestic relationship." In light of these express policy choices, the State's arguments that Vermont public policy favors opposite-sex over same-sex parents or disfavors the use of artificial reproductive technologies, are patently without substance.

Similarly, the State's argument that Vermont's marriage laws serve a substantial governmental interest in maintaining uniformity with other jurisdictions cannot be reconciled with Vermont's recognition of unions, such as first-cousin marriages, not uniformly sanctioned in other states. See 15 V.S.A. §§1-2 (consanguinity statutes do not exclude first cousins). In an analogous context, Vermont has sanctioned adoptions by same-sex partners, see 15A V.S.A. §1-102, notwithstanding the fact that many states have not. [These] two relevant legislative choices [ ] demonstrate that uniformity with other jurisdictions has not been a governmental purpose.

The State's remaining claims (e.g., recognition of same-sex unions might foster marriages of convenience or otherwise affect the institution in "unpredictable" ways) may be plausible forecasts as to what the future may hold, but cannot reasonably be construed to provide a reasonable and just basis for the statutory exclusion. The State's conjectures are not, in any event, susceptible to empirical proof before they occur.

Finally, it is suggested that the long history of official intolerance of intimate same-sex relationships cannot be reconciled with an interpretation of Article 7 that would give state-sanctioned benefits and protection to individuals of the same sex who commit to a permanent domestic relationship. We find the argument to be unpersuasive for several reasons. First, to the extent that state action historically has been motivated by an animus against a class, that history cannot provide a legitimate basis for continued unequal application of the law. Second, whatever claim may be made in light of the undeniable fact that federal and state statutes — including those in Vermont — have historically disfavored same-sex relationships, more recent legislation plainly undermines the contention. See, e.g., Laws of Vermont, 1977, No. 51, §2, 3 (repealing former §2603 of Title 13, which criminalized fellatio). In 1991, Vermont was one of the first states to enact statewide legislation prohibiting discrimination in employment, housing, and other services based on sexual orientation. Sexual orientation is among the categories specifically protected against hate-motivated crimes in Vermont. Furthermore, as noted earlier, recent enactments of the General Assembly have removed barriers to adoption by same-sex couples, and have extended legal rights and protections to such couples who dissolve their "domestic relationship."

Thus, viewed in the light of history, logic, and experience, we conclude that none of the interests asserted by the State provides a reasonable and just basis for the continued exclusion of same-sex couples from the benefits incident to a civil marriage license under Vermont law. Accordingly, in the faith that a case beyond the imagining of the framers of our Constitution may, nevertheless, be safely anchored in the values that infused it, we find a constitutional obligation to extend to plaintiffs the common benefit, protection, and security that Vermont law provides opposite-sex married couples. It remains only to determine the appropriate means and scope of relief compelled by this constitutional mandate.... We do not purport to infringe upon the prerogatives of the Legislature to craft an appropriate means of addressing this constitutional mandate, other than to note that the record here refers to a number of potentially constitutional statutory schemes from other jurisdictions [referring to various domestic and foreign domestic partnership acts]. We do not intend specifically to endorse any one or all of the referenced acts, particularly in view of the significant benefits omitted from several of the laws.

Further, while the State's prediction of "destabilization" cannot be a ground for denying relief, it is not altogether irrelevant. A sudden change in the marriage laws or the statutory benefits traditionally incidental to marriage may have disruptive and unforeseen consequences. Absent legislative guidelines defining the status and rights of same-sex couples, consistent with constitutional requirements, uncertainty and confusion could result. Therefore, we hold that the current statutory scheme shall remain in effect for a reasonable period of time to enable the Legislature to consider and enact implementing legislation in an orderly and expeditious fashion. In the event that the benefits and protections in question are not statutorily granted, plaintiffs may petition this Court to order the remedy they originally sought.

Our colleague asserts that granting the relief requested by plaintiffs — an injunction prohibiting defendants from withholding a marriage license — is our "constitutional duty." Post, at 3. (Johnson, J., concurring in part and dissenting in part). We believe the argument is predicated upon a fundamental misinterpretation of our opinion. It appears to assume that we hold plaintiffs are entitled to a marriage license. We do not. We hold that the State is constitutionally required to extend to same-sex couples the common benefits and protections that flow from marriage under Vermont law. That the State could do so through a marriage license is obvious. But it is not required to do so, and the mandate proposed by our colleague is inconsistent with the Court's holding. . . .

. . . The State's interest in extending official recognition and legal protection to the professed commitment of two individuals to a lasting relationship of mutual affection is predicated on the belief that legal support of a couple's commitment provides stability for the individuals, their family, and the broader community. Although plaintiffs' interest in seeking state recognition and protection of their mutual commitment may — in view of divorce statistics — represent "the triumph of hope over experience," the essential aspect of their claim is simply and fundamentally for inclusion in the family of State-sanctioned human relations.

The past provides many instances where the law refused to see a human being when it should have. See, e.g., Dred Scott, 60 U.S. at 407 (concluding that African slaves and their descendants had "no rights which the white man was bound to respect"). The future may provide instances where the law will be asked to see a human when it should not. See, e.g., G. Smith, Judicial Decisionmaking in the Age of Biotechnology, 13 Notre Dame J. Ethics & Pub. Policy 93, 114 (1999) (noting concerns that genetically engineering humans may threaten very nature of human individuality and identity). The challenge for future generations will be to define what is most essentially human. The extension of the Common Benefits Clause to acknowledge plaintiffs as Vermonters who seek nothing more, nor less, than legal protection and security for their avowed commitment to an intimate and lasting human relationship is simply, when all is said and done, a recognition of our common humanity. . . .

---

The following excerpt provides background on the plaintiffs in the famous case of Baehr v. Lewin, 852 P.2d 44 (Haw. 1993) (discussed below).

## ■ WILLIAM N. ESKRIDGE, JR., THE CASE FOR SAME-SEX MARRIAGE: FROM SEXUAL LIBERTY TO CIVILIZED COMMITMENT
*1-5 (1996)*

Americans are romantics. We fantasize about finding our "one true love." . . . Ninia Baehr shares that American dream. . . . Although Ninia had dated ardently in her twenties, she never found the right person. Then her mother introduced her to Genora Dancel. . . .

Genora has happy, dancing brown eyes. Her broad, dimpled smile and friendly, easygoing disposition belie her serious work ethic. . . . In 1990 one of her jobs was as a technical engineer for KHET, the PBS television station in Honolulu. There she met C.J. Baehr (Ninia's mother), who worked in another department. They liked one another, and C.J. told Genora about her wonderful daughter Ninia, a lesbian (Genora made a mental note of that). One day Genora was waiting outside the station when Ninia came to pick her mother up. Upon seeing Ninia in the car, Genora was impressed with her beauty. When Ninia saw Genora, she thought, "Oh my God, this woman is perfect!". . .

Several days later Ninia came calling at KHET. Both she and Genora were exceedingly nervous, but mutual friends say that sparks were flying from both sides. The two women went out for drinks. That night Genora called C.J. for advice about how to proceed, but Ninia herself happened to answer the phone. They spoke for hours, indicating to each other that this was a relationship that needed to be explored. In the course of dating for several months Ninia and Genora developed a warm friendship and found they had many interests in common. Mainly they were delighted just to be with one another. Each thought of the other when they were apart, looked forward to their time together, and realized that it was becoming increasingly hard to imagine life without the other.

When Genora traveled to San Diego for a technical training course in September, the pain of separation for each was intense. Ninia called every day. During one call Genora said, "When I get back, you'll know that I love you." She was referring to an engagement ring she had purchased, a stunning arrangement of three rubies and two diamonds set in gold. Genora paused and then popped the question, "Will you marry me?" A microsecond later Ninia answered, "Yes!"

At this point most couples would announce their engagement to their families, friends and coworkers. Most couples would set a date for the ceremony and obtain a marriage license. These steps were not possible for Ninia and Genora. Lesbian and gay couples are not allowed to marry in the United States.

Still, Genora Dancel and Ninia Baehr were prepared to consider themselves committed to each other. They began to plan their life together. [T]hey decided to change their life insurance policies to name one another as beneficiaries. To their surprise, the insurance companies refused to make the change, allowing only legal spouses, not unmarried partners, to be named as beneficiaries. The couple sought advice about this policy from Bill Woods, a lawyer and longtime gay activist in Honolulu. Woods mentioned that Hawaii's discrimination against same-sex couples might be vulnerable to constitutional challenge and asked if Baehr and Dancel were interested in such a challenge. He suggested that other couples might be interested, too.

This was a tough decision. [S]hould they work for [Hawaii] to adopt a domestic partnership law, or should they leapfrog domestic partnership and seek full marriage rights[?]. As a feminist scholar and historian, Baehr was aware that many women consider marriage to be an oppressive institution that has traditionally bound women to subordinate roles. . . . Baehr had no illusions about marriage, but it galled her that so much fuss is made over the most ill-fated different-sex marriage while the most committed same-sex couple is typically ignored. . . .

For Dancel [publicity from the lawsuit] presented a problem. In the closet to her family and most of her coworkers, Dancel was apprehensive about coming out. Would her parents still love her? Would her coworkers treat her differently, even shun her? Would she lose her job? Would she suffer public harassment? These were not hypothetical concerns. Dancel had occasionally heard vicious antihomosexual remarks from her coworkers. . . . After much soul searching, the couple notified Woods that they would be interested in participating in a constitutional challenge to Hawaii's discrimination against same-sex couples. . . . Whatever the ultimate resolution of Ninia Baehr and Genora Dancel's lawsuit, it has had the effect of putting same-sex marriage on the front burner of American public life. . . .

## Notes and Questions

1. *Epilogue.* Subsequent to *Baker*, the Vermont legislature enacted a statute recognizing "civil unions." Va. Stat. Ann. tit. 15, §§1201-1207

(Supp. 2000). Same-sex couples in Vermont can now enter into a civil union with all the rights and benefits of a traditional marriage. In the first year, 2,258 civil unions were registered. Fred Bayles, Civil Unions Blur at Vt.'s State Line, USA Today, July 11, 2001, at 3A. Vermont's Supreme Court rejected a challenge by town clerks claiming that issuing the licenses violated their religious beliefs. Julie Flaherty, Vermont Civil Unions Withstand Challenges, N.Y. Times, Jan. 4, 2001, A19.

2. *Historical background.* The gay liberation movement was triggered by a police raid of the Greenwich Village Stonewall Bar in 1969. See Barry D. Adam, The Rise of a Gay and Lesbian Movement 81-82 (rev. ed. 1995). The first wave of litigation seeking recognition of same-sex marriage occurred in the 1970s. Why did the battle reoccur in the 1990s? Professor William Eskridge attributes the timing to a reduction in employment discrimination against gays and lesbians that freed up activism for other issues; an aging, wealthy gay populace who were desirous of finding long-term partners; and the AIDS epidemic, which led to a desire for more serious commitments. William N. Eskridge, Jr., The Case for Same-Sex Marriage: From Sexual Liberty to Civilized Commitment 58 (1996). See also William N. Eskridge, Jr., Gaylaw: Challenging the Apartheid of the Closet (1999).

3. *Same-sex marriage, equal protection, and Hawaii.* In the first judicial ruling favorable to same-sex unions, the Hawaii Supreme Court held that the denial of marriage licenses to three same-sex couples implicates the state constitution's equal protection clause, which explicitly bars sex-based discrimination (unlike its federal counterpart). The court reasoned that the decision whether to issue a license to marry a particular person depends on the applicant's sex. Baehr v. Lewin, 852 P.2d 44 (Haw. 1993). However, the court refused to find violations of the right to privacy or due process. On remand, the state attempted to meet the requisite burden (under a strict scrutiny standard) by trying to establish the following interests as compelling: protecting the health and welfare of children, fostering procreation within a marital setting, securing or assuring recognition of Hawaiian marriages in other jurisdictions, and protecting the public fisc and the civil liberties of its citizens from the effects of state approval of same-sex marriage. Determining that the state had failed to meet its burden, the trial court ordered the state to issue the licenses. The state supreme court affirmed. Baehr v. Miike, 910 P.2d 112 (Haw. 1996).

In the meantime, the Hawaii legislature proposed (and voters passed) a state constitutional amendment restricting marriage to heterosexual couples. Haw. Const. Art. 1, §23. As a political compromise, the legislature enacted the Reciprocal Beneficiaries Act (Haw. Rev. Stat. Ann. §§572C-1 to -7 (Michie Supp. 1998)) entitling members of same-sex relationships to survivorship rights; health-related benefits; benefits relating to jointly held property; legal status relating to wrongful death, victims' rights, and protection from domestic violence; and such miscellaneous benefits as use of university facilities. See generally Dee Ann Habegger, Living in Sin and the Law: Benefits for Unmarried Couples Dependent Upon Sexual Orientation?, 33 Ind. L. Rev. 991, 1001-1004 (2000).

4. *Same-sex marriage, privacy, and Alaska.* Alaska also played a role in the same-sex marriage controversy. In Brause v. Bureau of Vital Statistics, 1998 WL 88743 (Alaska Super. Ct. 1998), the Alaska Bureau of Vital Statistics denied the application of two gay men, Jay Brause and Gene Dugan, for a marriage license under the state's gender-neutral marriage statute. When the legislature subsequently restricted marriage to a man and woman, the plaintiffs charged that the new statute, similarly, was unconstitutional. In *Brause,* the Superior Court declared that the statute violated the plaintiffs' right to privacy. The court held that, under the state constitution, every person has a "fundamental" right to choose a life partner, regardless of sex. The court ordered a new trial and required the state to show a compelling interest for its ban. The next day, the legislature proposed a constitutional amendment (in order to "clarify" the meaning of the state constitution) to recognize only marriages between a man and a woman. The voters passed the proposed amendment by a 70 percent margin in November 1998. See generally Kevin G. Clarkson et al., The Alaska Marriage Amendment: The People's Choice on the Last Frontier, 16 Alaska L. Rev. 213 (1999).

5. How do civil unions differ from marriage? Is recognition of civil unions a step forward or backward for same-sex couples? Compare Greg Johnson, Vermont Civil Unions: The New Language of Marriage, 25 Vt. L. Rev. 15, 41-43 (2000) (noting the positive implications) with Barbara J. Cox, But Why Not Marriage: An Essay on Vermont's Civil Union Law, Same-Sex Marriage, and Separate But (Un)Equal, 25 Vt. L. Rev. 113 (2000); Mark Strasser, Mission Impossible: On *Baker,* Equal Benefits, and the Imposition of Stigma, 9 Wm. & Mary Bill Rts. J. 1 (2000) (both suggesting that *Baker* creates a "separate but equal" regime).

How do civil unions differ from other state benefits schemes for same-sex couples, such as Hawaii's reciprocal beneficiaries law and domestic partnerships laws that have been enacted by various municipalities and California? See Johnson, supra, at 41-44. Must (may) other states recognize a Vermont civil union for any purpose(s)? Why do you suppose that of 2,258 civil unions conducted in the first year after the civil union law, only 463 unions involved Vermont couples? See Bayles, supra. (Domestic partnership laws are explored in more detail infra, Chapter IV, section C4f.)

6. A valid marriage requires that the parties have the capacity to marry. Several early cases held that same-sex marriages were invalid for lack of capacity. See Kay Tobin & Randy Wicker, The Gay Crusaders 135-155 (1972) (providing background on one prominent early case).

Before *Baker*, many courts failed to analyze the underlying constitutional issues, often relying on the dictionary definition of marriage to avoid challenges claiming a right to marry. E.g., Jones v. Hallahan, 501 S.W.2d 588, 589 (Ky. Ct. App. 1973). How does *Baker* resolve this definitional issue?

The Supreme Court has adopted different levels of scrutiny to evaluate potentially discriminatory classifications under the Equal Protection Clause. To survive constitutional attack, the classification must be (1) necessary to a compelling state interest (strict scrutiny), or (2) substantially related to an important governmental objective (intermediate scrutiny), or (3) rationally related to a legitimate governmental purpose (lowest level of scrutiny). The Court evaluates racial classifications under the first test; sex-based classifications are scrutinized under the middle-tier test.

How does *Baker* resolve the claim that same-sex marriage prohibitions constitute sex-based discrimination? See generally Eskridge, Gaylaw, supra, at 207-231; Andrew Koppelman, Why Discrimination Against Lesbians and Gay Men Is Sex Discrimination, 69 N.Y.U. L. Rev. 197 (1994).

7. What state interests, according to *Baker*, might justify restrictions on same-sex marriage? Are any of the asserted state interests compelling? How does the availability of reproductive technology, such as artificial insemination and surrogacy, weaken the case against legal recognition of same-sex marriage? What other state interests might justify a ban on same-sex marriage? Are they compelling? Is a ban necessary to the achievement of these objectives? See generally Eskridge, Case for Same-Sex Marriage, supra, at 127-152.

8. *The* Loving *analogy*. How does *Loving* affect the *Baker* court's analysis? Are antimiscegenation laws analogous to restrictions against same-sex marriage? Does *Hardwick* help resolve the questions posed by same-sex marriage? See Mark S. Spindelman, Reorienting *Bowers v. Hardwick*, 79 N.C. L. Rev. 359, 430-446 (2001) (discussing and criticizing the analogy). Andrew Koppelman, who has written extensively on the similarities regarding interracial marriage prohibitions, sodomy laws, and same-sex marriage restrictions, comments:

> Beyond the immediate harm [sodomy and miscegenation bans] inflict upon their victims, their purpose is to support a regime of caste that locks some people into inferior social positions at birth. Miscegenation laws discriminated on the basis of race, and they did so in order to maintain white supremacy. Similarly, sodomy laws discriminate on the basis of sex — for example, permitting men, but not women, to have sex with women — in order to impose traditional sex roles. The Court has deemed this purpose impermissible in other contexts because it perpetuates the subordination of women. . . .

Andrew Koppelman, Note, The Miscegenation Analogy: Sodomy Law as Sex Discrimination, 98 Yale L.J. 145, 147 (1988). See also Koppelman, Why Discrimination, supra, at 220-234 (1994); Andrew Koppelman, Same-Sex Marriage and Public Policy: The Miscegenation Precedents, 16 Quinnipiac L. Rev. 105 (1996).

For other discussions of the application of *Loving* to same-sex marriage restrictions, compare Mark Strasser, Living the New Millenium: On Equal Protection and the Right to Marry, 7 U. Chi. L. Sch. Roundtable 61, 82 (2000) (arguing that antimiscegenation and same-sex marriage restrictions both impinge on individual's choice of marriage partner) with David Orgon Coolidge, Playing the *Loving* Card: Same Sex Marriage and the Politics of Analogy, 12 B.Y.U. J. Pub. L. 201, 235-236 (1998) (criticizing that the same-sex marriage debate misplaces the holding of *Loving* and the meaning of marriage itself); Richard F. Duncan, From *Loving* to *Romer:* Homosexual Marriage and Moral Discernment, 12 B.Y.U. J. Pub. L. 239, 251 (1998) (arguing that the analogy fails because both genders are indispensable to marriage).

9. Why do some gays and lesbians desire to marry? *Baker* mentions the statutory benefits for which same-sex partners are ineligible. Why else?

10. Not all gay and lesbian rights activists advocate same-sex marriage. Two prominent lesbian lawyers, Paula Ettelbrick of Lambda's Legal Defense Fund and Professor Nancy Polikoff, contend that validation of same-sex marriage will have many negative consequences, including forced assimilation, undermining the gay liberation movement, and abandonment of efforts at societal transformation. See Paula L. Ettelbrick, Wedlock Alert: A Comment on Lesbian and Gay Family Recognition, 5 J.L. & Poly. 107 (1996); Nancy D. Polikoff, Symposium, We Will Get What We Ask For: Why Legalizing Gay and Lesbian Marriage Will Not "Dismantle the Legal Structure of Gender in Every Marriage," 79 Va. L. Rev. 1535 (1993).

Both Ettelbrick and Polikoff share a distrust of marriage based on its adoption of gender-based roles. Ettelbrick argues that the traditional definition of marriage (with its ideals of sexual fidelity and procreation) should not be the determinant for whether a family receives legal benefits. Ettelbrick, supra, at 121. She points to another objection: the belief that employment and ending antigay violence are more important priorities than same-sex marriage. Id. She concludes:

> Marriage will not liberate us as lesbians and gay men. In fact, it will constrain us, make us more invisible, force our assimilation into the mainstream and undermine the goals of gay liberation. . . . Marriage runs contrary to two of the primary goals of the lesbian and gay movement: the affirmation of gay identity and culture; and the validation of many forms of relationships. . . . The moment we argue, as some among us insist on

doing, that we should be treated as equals because we are really just like married couples and hold the same values to be true, we undermine the very purpose of our movement and begin the dangerous process of silencing our different voices. . . .

We will be liberated only when we are respected and accepted for our differences and the diversity we provide to this society. Marriage is not a path to that liberation.

William B. Rubenstein, Divided We Litigate: Addressing Disputes Among Group Members and Lawyers in Civil Rights Campaigns, 106 Yale L.J. 1623, 1635 (1997) (citing Paula Ettelbrick, Since When Is Marriage a Path to Liberation?, Out/Look, Fall 1989, at 9).

11. What consequences (legal and social) follow from the recognition of same-sex marriage? See generally David L. Chambers, What If? The Legal Consequences of Marriage and the Legal Needs of Lesbian and Gay Male Couples, 95 Mich. L. Rev. 447 (1996). What would be the impact on our ideas of marriage, relationships, and homosexuality? Can you envision a society that permits same-sex marriage? How would it differ from society today? Compare G. Sidney Buchanan, Same-Sex Marriage: The Linchpin Issue, 10 U. Dayton L. Rev. 541, 560 (1985) (such fundamental change "has a significant capacity to threaten the standards . . . that the majority wishes to preserve in relation to that institution"), with William M. Eskridge, Jr., A History of Same-Sex Marriage, 79 Va. L. Rev. 1419 (1993) (reporting historical instances of same-sex unions).

Would validation of same-sex marriage lead to a society that does not recognize marriage? For radical proposals to abolish marriage, see Patricia A. Cain, Imagine There's No Marriage, 16 Quinnipiac L. Rev. 27 (1996); Martha Albertson Fineman, The Neutered Mother, the Sexual Family, and Other Twentieth Century Tragedies (1995).

One commentator writes that "[t]he same-sex marriage cases are better viewed as political efforts to raise the consciousness of the American public than as realistic efforts to effect social change through litigation." Alissa Friedman, The Necessity for State Recognition of Same-Sex Marriage: Constitutional Requirements and Evolving Notions of Family, 3 Berkeley Women's L.J. 134, 137-138 (1987-1988). Do you agree? Why might the *Baker* plaintiffs have chosen this route to social change? See Rubenstein, supra, at 1636-1638 (same-sex marriage debate exposes a "fissure" in the gay community about goals and reform strategies).

12. *Conflict of laws and Full faith and credit.* If one state were to allow same-sex marriage, an important question is the consequences for the status of same-sex marriage in other jurisdictions. That is, suppose Jane and Carol, a same-sex couple from Montana, go to State X, which recognizes same-sex marriage, get married, and then return to their home state. They seek recognition of their marriage in Montana to obtain ben-

efits available to spouses (employment, medical, and so forth). Is Montana required to give effect to their marriage contracted in State X?

The answer to this question rests on: (a) conflict-of-laws principles, and (b) the Full Faith and Credit Clause of the Constitution.

(a) *Conflict of laws.* Under traditional choice-of-laws principles, marriage validity is determined by the law of the state where the marriage was celebrated (the rule of lex loci). However, this rule only applies if recognition of the marriage would not offend the forum state's public policy. (Recall *Loving,* in which the couple married in the District of Columbia.) In contrast, the Restatement (Second) of Conflict of Laws §283(1) (1971) has modified the traditional rule as follows:

### §283. Validity of Marriage

(1) The validity of a marriage will be determined by the local law of the state which, with respect to the particular issue, has the most significant relationship to the spouses and the marriage. . . .

(2) A marriage which satisfies the requirements of the state where the marriage was contracted will everywhere be recognized as valid unless it violates the strong public policy of another state which had the most significant relationship to the spouses and the marriage at the time of the marriage.

### §284. Incidents of Foreign Marriage

A state usually gives the same incidents to a foreign marriage, which is valid under the principles stated in §283, that it gives to a marriage contracted within its territory.

How would Montana resolve the issue of the validity of Jane and Carol's marriage based on the Restatement?

Further, a few states have marriage evasion statutes that might preclude recognition of same-sex marriage. The Uniform Marriage Evasion Act (promulgated in 1912 but subsequently withdrawn because few states had adopted it) declared void all marriages entered into by parties who married in another state for the purpose of evading their home state restrictions on marriage. See Homer H. Clark, Jr., The Law of Domestic Relations in the United States 87 n.52 (2d ed. 1988) (14 jurisdictions have statutes resembling the act).

(b) *Full faith and credit.* The Full Faith and Credit Clause (art. IV, §1) of the Constitution requires that a state confer full faith and credit on "the public acts, records and judicial proceedings" of sister states. Same-sex marriage poses several issues. First, is marriage a "public act" (for example, similar to legislation), "record," or "judicial proceeding"? "Judicial proceedings" from sister states require the most complete recognition under the Full Faith and Credit Clause, which has been interpreted to foreclose choice-of-law analysis once a court has rendered a final judgment or decree. "Records" have sometimes evoked the same treatment.

By contrast, the Full Faith and Credit Clause has not been read to mandate recognition of the acts of sister states. Rather, the second state can use choice-of-law analysis, including reliance on its own public policy. Thus, Montana might refuse to give full faith and credit to Jane and Carol's marriage because Montana determines that same-sex marriage violates Montana public policy. Of course, a couple might surmount this problem by obtaining a declaratory judgment in State X as to their marriage validity.

See generally Scott Fruehwald, Choice of Law and Same-Sex Marriage, 51 Fla. L. Rev. 799 (1999); L. Lynn Hogue, State Common-Law Choice-of-Law Doctrine and Same-Sex "Marriage": How Will States Enforce the Public Policy Exception?, 32 Creighton L. Rev. 29 (1998); Larry Kramer, Same-Sex Marriage, Conflict of Laws, and the Unconstitutional Public Policy Exception, 106 Yale L.J. 1965 (1977); Andrew Koppelman, Same-Sex Marriage, Choice of Law, and Public Policy, 76 Tex. L. Rev. 921 (1998).

13. *State and federal responses to the same-sex marriage debate.* Congress and a significant number of states acted to undermine the impact of Baehr v. Lewin (the first judicial ruling favorable to same-sex marriage). In October 1996, by a vote of 85-14, Congress passed the Defense of Marriage Act (DOMA), 28 U.S.C. §1738(c) (Supp. 1998). DOMA has two parts. First, the act provides a federal definition for the terms "marriage" and "spouse" (for purposes of federal benefits) by specifying that marriage is a union of a man and a woman; the term "spouse" refers only to a person of the opposite sex. Second, DOMA specifies that states are not required to give effect to same-sex marriages under the Full Faith and Credit Clause. DOMA purportedly rests on Congress's power (in art. IV, §1) to implement the Full Faith and Credit Clause. Yet, it represents the first time Congress has exercised this authority to foster variation rather than uniformity among the states. If valid, DOMA leaves a state free to determine whether to recognize same-sex marriages celebrated elsewhere.

States also responded quickly to *Baehr.* Some inserted in their statutes a definition of marriage as a union of a man and a woman. Other states enacted legislation to prevent their courts from conferring full faith and credit to same-sex unions recognized in another state. For authorities, see Defense of Marriage Act: Hearings on S. 1740 Before the Senate Judiciary Comm., 104th Cong., 2nd Sess. 32 n.33 (1996) (statement of Professor Lynn D. Wardle citing 15 states).

Is DOMA unconstitutional under Romer v. Evans, 517 U.S. 620 (1996)? In *Romer,* the Supreme Court invalidated a Colorado constitutional amendment that prohibited a state from singling out gays and lesbians for special civil rights protections. The Court held that discrimination on the basis of sexual orientation violates equal protection. Does DOMA, by singling out same-sex marriage for denial of full faith and credit, violate *Romer?* Does it show animosity toward gays, condemned in *Romer?* See Wardle, supra, at 40-41 (arguing for DOMA's constitutionality because DOMA addresses conduct, rather than orientation, which is a permissible basis for distinguishing heterosexual marriage from same-sex unions, and also distinguishing *Romer* because the Colorado amendment swept too broadly by denying *all* civil protection to gays and lesbians). For a rebuttal, see Barbara A. Robb, Note, The Constitutionality of the Defense of Marriage Act in the Wake of Romer v. Evans, 32 N. Eng. L. Rev. 263 (1997).

14. *Cross-cultural perspective.* The Scandinavian countries have been in the forefront of recognition of same-sex unions. The Danish Registered Partnership Act, enacted in 1989, provides same-sex unions with the same benefits as marital partners with some exceptions. Same-sex couples do not have the right to adopt children nor to be married in a state church ceremony. To qualify, at least one partner must be a Danish citizen and a resident in Denmark, and the partners must publicly register. Norway adopted a similar law in 1993, Sweden in 1995, and Iceland in 1996.

In September 2000, the Netherlands became the first country to allow same-sex couples to marry. Under the new law, which took effect on April 1, 2001, at least one partner must be a Dutch citizen or domiciled in the Netherlands. Gay and lesbian couples may adopt (but only Dutch children, not children from abroad) and face a lack of international recognition of their marriages. See generally Nicholas J. Patterson, The Repercussions in the European Union of the Netherlands' Same-Sex Marriage Law, 2 Chi. J. Int'l L. 301 (2001). In August 2001, Germany joined the Scandinavian countries in recognizing same-sex couples who register as "life partners." The new law provides for health insurance, inheritance rights, the right to choose the same last name, and citizenship for non-German members of the registered couple. However, the German law does not confer full legal status (as does the Netherlands) or permit adoption. France now also recognizes same-sex couples who register. Steve Kettman, In Germany, Partners for Life, San Francisco Chron., Aug. 2, 2001, at A9. Legal regulation of nontraditional families is discussed in Chapter IV.

15. Do prohibitions on same-sex marriage have any effect on the marriage of a transsexual (also termed "transgender")? Some courts determine marriage validity based on the transsexual's genetic makeup and childbearing capacity (aspects not altered by sexual surgery). Compare Littleton v. Prange, 9 S.W.3d 223 (Tex. Ct. App. 1999) (denying standing in a wrongful death suit to a surviving transsexual spouse on the basis of chromosomes) with M.T. v. J.T., 355 A.2d 204 (N.J. Super. Ct. App. Div. 1976) (stating that the validity depends on ability to

engage in sexual activity consistent with reconciled anatomy). Why should *sexual* capacity be the test for marriage validity?

The California state legislature is currently considering protections for transsexuals against employment and housing discrimination. San Francisco is also the first public employer to approve health benefits for city employees to have sex reassignment surgery. Currently, about two dozen cities and states (including Minnesota and Washington, D.C.) protect the civil liberties of transsexuals. See Robert Salladay, State Panel Oks Gender Protections, S.F. Chron., July 4, 2001, at A1. On legal issues affecting transsexuals generally, see Taylor Flynn, Transforming the Debate: Why We Need to Include Transgender Rights in the Struggles for Sex and Sexual Orientation Equality, 101 Colum. L. Rev. 392 (2001); Phyllis Randolph Frye & Alyson Dodi Meiselman, Same-Sex Marriages Have Existed Legally in the United States for a Long Time Now, 64 Alb. L. Rev. 1031 (2001).

## Problem

J'Noel was born male, but later has sex reassignment surgery. She amends her birth certificate to show that she is now female. She has a Ph.D. in finance and is employed as an assistant professor. At her college, she meets Marshall, a businessman with one grown son, Joe, from whom he is estranged. After they begin to date, J'Noel informs Marshall of her prior history as a male. They decide to marry. Eleven years later, Marshall dies intestate. His son, Joe, petitions for letters of administration and claims to be the sole beneficiary of his father's estate. Joe alleges that his father's marriage was invalid because J'Noel was born male. What result? In re Estate of Gardiner, 22 P.3d 1086 (Kan. Ct. App. 2001).

(2) Incest

## ■ IN RE ADOPTION OF M.
*722 A.2d 615 (N.J. Super. Ct. Ch. Div. 1998)*

Batten, J.S.C.
. . . The undisputed facts are troubling beyond description. [On] January 5, 1991, adoptive parents sought to adopt child M (hereinafter "petitioner"), born November 24, 1975, and voluntarily surrendered by her natural parents to the Division of Youth and Family Services, in May 1989. The adoption was uncontested. Final judgment of adoption entered January 25, 1991 [when] [p]etitioner was then fifteen years old. Two years and ten months later, on November 21, 1993, petitioner attained age eighteen.

At some point in time subsequent to the final judgment of adoption yet prior to September 8, 1997, the marital relationship between the adoptive parents failed. Adoptive mother, on this latter date, filed her complaint for divorce against adoptive father, alleging acts of extreme cruelty. [The adoptive parents actually separated several years prior to the time they filed for divorce.] On November 18, 1997, final judgment of divorce dissolved the marriage of the adoptive parents. On July 29, 1998, petitioner, then twenty-two years of age, gave birth to an infant son. The parties acknowledge that adoptive father is the natural father of the infant.

Poignant realities emerge. First, petitioner and the adoptive father conceived the infant child in or about October 1997, at which time petitioner was twenty-one years of age. Second, conception between petitioner and adoptive father therefore likely occurred *prior* to the November 18, 1997, dissolution of his marriage to adoptive mother. Third, *a fortiori*, adoptive father engaged in a carnal relationship with his adult adoptive daughter while he was yet married to her adoptive mother. Fourth, the foregoing circumstances suggest — and the record stipulated before the court specifically confirms — that the relationship between petitioner and adoptive father had transgressed the parameters of a parent-child relationship well prior to the act of conception. Now the natural parents of the minor child, they desire to marry. Their present legal relationship as adoptive father and adoptive daughter, however, clearly renders the former an "ancestor" of, and the latter a "descendant" to, the other, thereby precluding lawful marriage between them.[6] N.J.S.A. 37:1-1. Hence, petitioner brings this application.

[Although petitioner originally moved to vacate the adoption as to both her adoptive parents, she and her adoptive mother subsequently decided to leave their relationship undisturbed. Petitioner thus sought to vacate the adoption as to her adoptive father only.]

Final judgment of adoption marks a turning point in the status of the natural and adoptive parents. Entry of such a judgment terminates all relationships between the adopted child and his/her natural parents and all of the rights, duties, and obligations of any persons that are founded on such relationships. . . . Subsequent to judgment, the adoptive parents are, as a matter of law, the parents of that child as if the child had been born to the adoptive parents in lawful wedlock.

Under New Jersey law [a] final judgment of adoption "should not be set aside unless it is in the best interest of the child and adoptive parents," and upon the showing of "truly exceptional circumstances" as de-

---

6. N.J.S.A. 37:1-1 states, in pertinent part, that:

A man shall not marry any of his ancestors or descendants, or his sister, or the daughter of his brother or sister, or the sister of his father or mother, whether such collateral kindred be of the whole or half blood. *A woman shall not marry any of her ancestors or descendants,* or her brother, or the son of her brother or sister, or the brother of her father or mother, whether such collateral kindred be of the whole or half blood. *A marriage in violation of any of the foregoing provisions shall be absolutely void.* [Emphasis added].

termined by the particular facts of each case. . . . Indeed, the Legislature has mandated that the Adoption Act of New Jersey "shall be liberally construed to the end that the *best interests of children* be promoted," and *"due regard shall be given to the rights of all persons affected by an adoption."* N.J.S.A. 9:3-37. [Emphasis added]. . . .

Certainly, the interests of "all persons affected" by this adoption have changed measurably. First, the adoptive child, in whose best interests the adoption occurred, is now, seven years later, (A) twenty-two years of age, (B) a natural mother of a two month old infant son, and (C) intent upon marriage to her son's natural father. The absence of any facts of record which might support a finding of abuse, neglect, domestic violence or other unlawful act suggests a petitioner's conscious decision that her legal relationship with her adoptive father had achieved its purpose and, parent-child status notwithstanding, the complexities and realities of human emotions and relationships warrant transposition of that status from father-daughter co-parents to husband and wife. Through marriage, petitioner legitimizes not only her relationship with her son's father but the status of her infant son as well. . . .

Clearly, the facts here . . . constitute "truly exceptional circumstances" for several reasons. First, all reported cases contemplate an application to vacate a final judgment of adoption at a time during the minority of the adoptive child; here, the petitioner, as adopted child, moves post-emancipation to vacate the judgment of adoption. In this sense, the "best interests" standard of N.J.S.A. 9:2-4 no longer pertains to the adoptive child. Second, the stated purpose of the petition to vacate is eradication of a legal impediment to petitioner's marriage to her adoptive father, a relationship to which petitioner and adoptive father would be entitled absent their present legal status as father-daughter. Third, vacation of the final judgment of adoption would also shed adoptive father of his simultaneous status as natural father and legal grandfather of the minor infant, leaving him the natural father only. Fourth, vacation of the adoption judgment, through its cure of the statutory impediment to marriage, would further legitimize the infant, thereby advancing long-standing policy of this state to protect the status of children. More "truly exceptional circumstances" are difficult to imagine. . . . Petitioner's application to vacate the final judgment of adoption as pertains to her adoptive father is — as it must be — granted. . . .

## ■ JEROME NEU, "WHAT'S WRONG WITH INCEST?"
*in Inquiry*
*(1976)*

A friend wanted to have an affair with her cousin. She asked me if I could think of any reason why she should not. I could not. . . . [W]hat reasons might there be for prohibiting [a particular type of incestuous relationship] in our society if a prohibition did not already exist?

1. An easy, but inadequate, answer is that it leads to genetic disaster. That discovery (if the claim is true) may well have come long after the prohibitions it is meant to explain, and in relation to the present, modern contraceptive technology makes it irrelevant. And the truth is that under certain conditions, as animal breeders can tell us, inbreeding can actually help maintain desirable traits. . . .

2. The next answer is far more significant: mother will not like it. This difficulty is real and serious. A person who has a right to consideration and affection is sure to be hurt. The Oedipal triangle exists (and conceived broadly enough may exist in every society), and so the suffering comes inevitably. . . . Mothers are bound to their daughters as well as to their husbands. Societal structure ensures that they are significant figures to both, and entitled to the concern of both. And the impact may be reciprocal: from harm to the mother's feelings there may follow danger to the daughter's developmental needs. . . .

3. A third answer is one that attracted Freud's interest in *Civilization and Its Discontents:* it is difficult enough to break out of the family as it is, with the addition of sexual relations and dependence it becomes virtually impossible. Incest is (literally) anti-social. Dependence comes with the relations. Sexual urges (in the context of incest prohibitions) are among the leading forces for breaking out of the family and forming complex social structures and relationships; necessary conditions for civilization. . . .

4. This relation of dependence brings us to a fourth objectionable feature of incestuous relations. [I]t is perhaps the feature that contributes most to making incest seem worse than merely odd or disagreeable. The power structure, the structure of dependency, is such that the propositioned daughter is put in an unfair position. . . .

Now, where do these points take us? [These reasons] do not explain why the prohibition should take the form of a taboo (we have only "rationalized" the taboo). Taboos allow no questioning. Reasons, precisely because they are reasons, leave room for questioning. The reasons we have brought forward depend on features (admittedly, broad structural features) of our society; and so, in a given case, may not apply. What if (looking to our second point) mother does not mind, or, what if she is dead? The inevitable suffering of a significant third party may no longer seem so inevitable. And who would be the aggrieved third party in brother-sister incest? . . . Clearly, not all of the four factors we have brought out underlie all incest taboos in all cultures, nor are they the only factors even in our own. . . .

[P]erhaps I can at least suggest that the (or a) key [reason for a taboo] may be in the notions of identity and identification. Each generation must win its identity. . . . Incest destroys difference: categories collapse, people cease to have clear and distinct sexual and social places . . . ; and with the destruction of difference people cease to have the possibility of shifting from one place to another as they develop. . . . Violation of incest taboos or their abolition would not, I think, allow the establishment of a stable, mature, independent identity. . . .

. . . The key to understanding taboos, as opposed to other sorts of social prohibitions (legal, utilitarian, etc.), may lie in those very features of taboos that are most puzzling to modern moral consciousness: taboos are universal (every society has some, including, in particular, taboos on murder and incest), and absolute (are unconditional and allow no questioning), and impose strict liability. [Such taboos] may not be irrational: they may mark the boundaries that shape a way of life.

## Note: Void versus Voidable Distinction

Statutes and the common law classify invalid marriages as either void or voidable. A void marriage is one that is invalid from inception (void ab initio), that is, it never had legal existence. On the other hand, a voidable marriage is valid until subsequently declared invalid. The distinction becomes important in terms of who may assert the invalidity of a marriage and whether the validity of the marriage may be collaterally attacked.

If a marriage is void, then either party or a third party may challenge the validity of the marriage at any time and in any proceeding. Homer H. Clark, Jr., The Law of Domestic Relations in the United States 93 (2d ed. 1988). On the other hand, if a marriage is voidable, its invalidity can only be asserted by one of the parties and only during the marriage (that is, not after death of one of the parties). Further, it cannot be collaterally attacked (that is, in a related proceeding). Id.

The consequences of a particular defect stem from history (ecclesiastical law) as well as public policy (the degree to which the defect offends public policy). Substantive defects (same-sex, bigamous, and incestuous unions) render the marriage void. Less serious substantive defects, such as age, may render the marriage voidable. See infra pages 208-210.

## Notes and Questions

1. *Historical background.* Virtually all societies have some form of incest taboos. Classic formulations exist in the psychoanalytic, sociological, and anthropological literature. See, e.g., Sigmund Freud, Totem and Taboo (1917); Claude Levi-Strauss, Elementary Structures of Kinship (1967); George Peter Murdock, Social Structure (1949); Talcott Parsons,

The Incest Taboo in Relation to Social Structure and the Socialization of the Child, 5 Brit. J. Soc. 101 (1954).

Incest proscriptions can be traced to Leviticus.[20] The Catholic Church also had early proscriptions against incest. Prior to 1215, kinship within the six and seventh degrees (using the canon law method of calculation) rendered a marriage sinful — not null as did impediments within the first five degrees. The Lateran Council of 1215 strengthened the proscriptions: marriages within the fourth degree of consanguinity became null, as did certain affinal (that is, in-law) relationships.[21]

William the Conqueror separated the lay jurisdiction from the ecclesiastical. Ecclesiastical jurisdiction prevailed over marriage. Thus, incest (similar to adultery and bigamy) became ecclesiastic offenses.[22] Between the thirteenth and the sixteenth centuries prohibitions on incestuous marriages were extensive, but mitigated by dispensations to the wealthy. Incest became a crime in 1650, punishable by death.[23] In 1908, the Punishment of Incest Act, 8 Edw. 7, ch. 45, proscribed three to seven years imprisonment.

2. *Civil and criminal consequences.* Every state proscribes the degrees of relationship of consanguinity and affinity within which persons may marry. ("Consanguinity" refers to blood relations, while "affinity" refers to relations by marriage.) Marriage to one's parent, grandparent, brother, or sister is universally prohibited, as is marriage between an aunt and nephew and an uncle and niece.[24] Rhode Island, however, exempts "any marriage which shall be solemnized among the Jews, within the degrees of affinity or consanguinity allowed by their religion." R.I. Gen. Laws §15-1-4 (1996). England allows first cousin marriages today, as do many states. See Martin Ottenheimer, Forbidden Relatives: The American Myth of Cousin Marriage 41 (1996) (19 states permit the practice). The number of states with prohibitions against marriage between affinal relatives has been decreasing: only approximately 12 states have such prohibitions.

[20]. Leviticus 18:6. "None of you shall approach to any that is near of kin to him, to uncover their nakedness."
[21]. 2 Frederick Pollock & Frederic William Maitland, The History of English Law Before the Time of Edward I 387-388 (S. F. C. Milsom ed., 1968) (1898).
[22]. Id. at 374.
[23]. 4 William Blackstone, Commentaries *64.
[24]. "A [45-year-old] mother and [26-year-old] son who married each other today pleaded no contest to incest, conceding that they knew of their relationship when they married and agreeing to seek counseling in return for staying out of jail. . . . Both defendants received suspended five-year sentences. [The son] pleaded guilty to perjury, admitting that he lied to a grand jury when he said he did not know at the time of the marriage that his bride was also his mother. . . ." Mother and Son to Seek Counseling for Incest, N.Y. Times, Dec. 14, 1984, at A20. The son brought the case to the authorities, claiming his mother refused to grant him a divorce. Mother-and-Son Couple Enter into Plea Bargain, Philadelphia Inquirer, Dec. 14, 1984, at A8.

Most jurisdictions regard incestuous marriages as void ab initio. Incest is also a crime. However, the degrees of relation for marriage restrictions are not necessarily the same as the degrees for criminal liability.

3. According to *Zablocki* (supra page 156), regulations that substantially and directly interfere with the freedom to marry must receive elevated scrutiny. Do incest laws qualify? What state interests are at stake? Several have been suggested, including the protection of the gene pool from deleterious consequences of inbreeding; protection of persons from exploitation (for example, absence of meaningful consent to marry such as by an older family member compelling a younger); protection of the family from the assumption of incompatible roles by some family members; and protection of societal concepts of decency. Are these state interests "sufficiently important" to justify the restrictions? Note that experts disagree about the harmful consequences of inbreeding.[25] If these state interests are sufficiently important, are the proscriptions sufficiently closely tailored to achieve these goals?

If the goal is prevention of the harmful consequences of procreation, should the state exempt those too old to reproduce? Require genetic testing for marriage licenses? Prohibit marriages involving a partner who carries harmful genetic traits? See, e.g., Ariz. Rev. Stat. Ann. §36-797.42 (West 1993); Ky. Rev. Stat. Ann. §402.310-.340 (Michie 1999) (genetic screening provisions). Require sterilization of such a partner? One commentator suggests more effective and less intrusive means:

> Any legitimate social interest in the production of offspring who are emotionally, physically, socially, and economically healthy is better served through other exercises of state power than through incest statutes. For example, noncompulsory genetic screening programs alerting potential marriage partners of associated genetic risks to their offspring would reach more of the at-risk couples than do incest statutes. Programs aimed at regulating known environmental factors (mutagens) which cause congenital birth defects would protect more offspring than do incest statutes. Nutritional programs for pregnant women and infant children as well as pre- and postnatal medical care would have a far greater positive impact on the physical and mental health of offspring than do incest statutes.

Carolyn S. Bratt, Incest Statutes and the Fundamental Right of Marriage: Is Oedipus Free to Marry?, 18 Fam. L.Q. 257, 281 (1984). Is protection of the gene pool a justifiable function of government? In the interests of privacy, should the decision to perpetuate possibly harmful genetic traits be left to the individual? See also Christine McNiece Metteer, Some "Incest" Is Harmless Incest: Determining the Fundamental Right to Marry of Adults Related by Affinity Without Resorting to State Incest Statutes, 10 Kan. J.L. & Pub. Pol'y 262 (2000).

[25]. See, e.g., Herbert Maisch, Incest 78-81 (Colin Bearne trans., 1973).

4. Do criminal incest laws violate the constitutional right to privacy? In Smith v. State, 6 S.W.3d 512 (Tenn. Crim. App. 1999), the appellant was convicted of engaging in an incestuous relationship with her paternal uncle, which began when she was a minor. On appeal, she argued that the incest statute violated her right to privacy under the state constitution, i.e., her right to engage in consensual sexual activities in the privacy of her home. Rejecting her argument, the court found that no fundamental right was involved and reasoned, therefore, that the statute was rationally related to the objective of promoting morality and the stability of the family.

5. *Relatives by adoption.* In re Adoption of M. addresses prohibitions on marriage of persons related by adoption. What state interest supports such restrictions? How can that interest be served by prohibiting marriage by adoptive siblings who have grown up in separate households? Compare Israel v. Allen, 577 P.2d 762 (Colo. 1978), with In re MEW, 4 Pa. D.&C.3d 51 (1977). See generally Walter Wadlington, The Adopted Child and Intra-Family Marriage Prohibitions, 49 Va. L. Rev. 478 (1963).

6. Many state statutes not only classify certain marriages as presumptively void but also subject to criminal liability officials who knowingly issue marriage licenses to such couples. The parties themselves, of course, are also subject to criminal penalties — in some jurisdictions rather draconian ones. See, e.g., Cal. Penal Code §285 (West 1999) (previous version of statute authorized up to 50 years imprisonment). Are criminal sanctions appropriate to enforce civil limitations on marriage? Recall the analogous relationship between criminal laws on sodomy and same-sex marriage bans.

## Problems

1. Movie director Woody Allen, age 56, has an affair with Soon-Yi Previn, age 22, the adopted daughter of Allen's long-term lover, actress Mia Farrow. (Soon-Yi Previn's adoptive father is Andre Previn, Farrow's former husband.) Although Allen and Farrow had had a biological child together and are the adoptive parents of two other young children, Allen and Farrow never married; in fact, they maintained separate residences.

Should a state legislature criminalize sexual relationships such as Allen's and Soon-Yi Previn's? Preclude the issuance of marriage licenses to such couples? Declare any ensuing marriages void? Consider the following commentary:

> Defining the ancient taboo becomes hard in an era of recombinant families created by divorce, remarriage and adoption. The traditional stricture — no carnal relations between parent and child or brother and

sister — still holds, but how does it apply in today's blended and extended families, where blood ties are often thin or absent? . . .

[Despite the scientific and cultural reasons for the taboo, today] the most significant damage from incest is psychological. The heart of a family, say experts, is not the bloodline but the emotional connection. "Proper human growth involves gradually separating emotionally from your family so that you can go off and start one of your own," stresses child therapist Carole West of Beverly Hills, California. "Incest disrupts that process." . . .

Anastasia Toufexis, What Is Incest?, Time, Aug. 31, 1992, at 57.[26]

2. Alice May Greenberg petitions for letters of administration to administer the estate of her deceased mother Fannie May. Alice is one of six children of Fannie and Sam May. Thereafter, Sam files an objection to the issuance to such letters of administration upon the ground that he has a paramount right, by statute, to administer Fannie's estate as the "surviving spouse of the decedent." Alice responds, joined by two sisters, that her father is not her mother's surviving spouse because, although their parents' marriage was valid in Rhode Island, it was never valid in New York. Sam and Fannie were uncle and niece. Sam moved to New York from Wisconsin. Shortly afterwards, he and Fannie (both adherents of Judaism) went to Providence, Rhode Island, where they were married by a rabbi. Two weeks later, they returned to New York and resided there for 32 years until Fannie's death. At the time, New York declared uncle-niece marriages incestuous and void and imposed penal sanctions. A Rhode Island statute also prohibited uncle-niece marriages, except those between persons of the Jewish faith within the degrees of affinity and consanguinity allowed by their religion — a requirement satisfied in this case. To whom should the court issue the letters of administration? See In re May's Estate, 114 N.E.2d 4 (N.Y. 1953).

(3) Bigamy

■ **POTTER v. MURRAY CITY**
*760 F.2d 1065 (10th Cir. 1985), cert. denied, 474 U.S. 849 (1988)*

HOLLOWAY, Chief Judge.
. . . Plaintiff is a former police officer of Murray City, Utah. The City terminated plaintiff's employment after it was learned that he practiced plural marriage. [Plaintiff] sought monetary damages against the City, its Chief of Police, and the Murray City Civil Service Commission. He also sought declaratory and injunctive relief against the State of Utah and its

[26]. Technically, incest statutes prohibit sexual conduct between related, consenting adults as well as such conduct between related adults and children. We now more commonly refer to the latter as "sexual abuse of children."

Governor and Attorney General to determine that Utah's laws prohibiting plural marriage are invalid and to enjoin their enforcement. [Article III of the Utah Constitution prohibits plural marriage. Utah Code Ann. §76-7-101 (1978) makes bigamy a felony.]

## B. THE FREE EXERCISE CLAUSE

In Reynolds v. United States, 98 U.S. (8 Otto) 145 (1878), the Supreme Court affirmed a criminal conviction of a Mormon for practicing polygamy and rejected the argument that Congress' prohibition of polygamy violated the defendant's right to the free exercise of religion. Plaintiff argues that *Reynolds* is no longer controlling because later cases have "in effect" overturned the decision. We disagree.

Plaintiff principally relies on Wisconsin v. Yoder, 406 U.S. 205 (1972). There the Supreme Court held that the religious belief of the Amish that their salvation requires life in a church community apart from the world necessitated that they be exempted from a state law requirement that children attend public school beyond the eighth grade. . . .

The parties have stipulated here . . . that plaintiff's practice of plural marriage is the result of a good faith religious belief. The plaintiff has made an undisputed showing that his two wives consented to the plural marriage, and that the wives and five children of the marriages receive love and adequate care and attention and do not want for any necessity of life. Plaintiff points out that the State defendants have not presented any empirical evidence that monogamy is superior to polygamy, nor has the Utah legislature ever considered whether its anti-polygamy laws are wise. Hence plaintiff argues that under *Yoder,* summary judgment should have been entered in his favor rather than for the defendants.

We cannot disregard *Reynolds,* however, because in *Yoder* and afterwards the Supreme Court has recognized the continued validity of *Reynolds.* In *Yoder, Reynolds* was one of four cases that the Court cited in support of the proposition that "[i]t is true that activities of individuals, even when religiously based, are often subject to regulation by the States in the exercise of their undoubted power to promote the health, safety, and general welfare, or the Federal Government in the exercise of its delegated powers." 406 U.S. at 220. Since *Yoder,* the Court has said that "[s]tatutes making bigamy a crime surely cut into an individual's freedom to associate, but few today seriously claim such statutes violate the First Amendment or any other constitutional provision." Paris Adult Theatre I v. Slaton, 413 U.S. 49, 68 n.15 (1973); see also Zablocki v. Redhail, [434 U.S. 374, 399 (1978)] (Powell, J., concurring in the judgment) (state has undeniable interest in insuring that its rules of domestic relations reflect widely held values of its people, and state regulation has included bans on incest, bigamy and homosexuality as well as various preconditions to marriage). Moreover, *Reynolds* has been cited with approval since *Yoder.* . . .

. . . Monogamy is inextricably woven into the fabric of our society. It is the bedrock upon which our culture is built. In light of these fundamental values, the State is justified, by a compelling interest, in upholding and enforcing its ban on plural marriage to protect the monogamous marriage relationship.

### C. The Right to Privacy

Plaintiff argues that his constitutional right to privacy prohibits the State of Utah from sanctioning him for entering into a polygamous marriage. . . . We find no authority for extending the constitutional right of privacy so far that it would protect polygamous marriages. . . .

### D. Laws in Desuetude

Plaintiff further argues that Utah's laws prohibiting polygamy have fallen into desuetude. He says that there have been fewer than 25 prosecutions in Utah since 1952 for such offenses, that there are at least 5,000 to 10,000 polygamist family members in the State, and that during (the city police chief's) thirty year tenure he had never arrested anyone nor seen anyone arrested or prosecuted for violating Utah's anti-bigamy statute. Thus he says that invoking laws which have long been in disuse to sanction him is a violation of the constitutional guarantees of due process and equal protection. . . . We disagree.

Polygamy has been prohibited in our society since its inception. The prohibitions continue in full force today. We cannot agree that the discharge of plaintiff for engaging in bigamy violated any constitutional guarantee. The showing made did not establish the enforcement of a "basically obsolete or an empty law whose function has long since passed." United States v. Elliott, 266 F. Supp. at 326. The showing of minimal numbers of prosecutions does not establish an abandonment of the State's laws and an irrational revival of them here. "[M]ere failure to prosecute other offenders is no basis for a finding of denial of equal protection." United States v. Blitstein, 626 F.2d 774, 782 (10th Cir. 1980), *cert. denied*, 449 U.S. 1102 (1981). . . .

### ■ JACK ANDERSON,[27] ADVENTURES AMONG THE POLYGAMISTS
*1 Investigative Rep. Mag. 4-42 (Jan. 1982)*

. . . Growing up in a devout Mormon home, I was duly drilled in the subjugation of the flesh and shielded from the lustier chapters of my her-

---

[27]. Jack Anderson is a nationally syndicated columnist.

itage. But now and again, I picked up a mournful whisper among the adults about some fallen soul who had sunk back into the old ways. I was 18 and a fledgling reporter for The Salt Lake Tribune when whispers of another relapse made the family rounds and reached my ears. I gleaned that the backslider was a second cousin of mine, once removed. . . . My curiosity was reinforced by the reporter's license to snoop into the hidden and the illegal. In due course, I located my second cousin. . . .

[He led me to the home of an elderly man with a saintly visage, Joseph Musser.] It was apparently my youth that disarmed him. At 18, I bore none of the earmarks of disreputability of the mature newsman or lawman. Gradually, Musser warmed up and began to slide into a discussion of his religious precepts. He outlined a "fundamentalist" faith which stressed the traditional doctrines and the old-fashioned virtues. . . .

He began to inch toward his main theme with a review of the moral shambles of modern life. He traced its disintegration to one untenable concept — monogamy, with its inevitable spawn of divorces and mistresses, unmarried mothers and bachelor fathers, cast-off wives and abandoned children. Did not the rise of abortion and contraception clearly foreshadow its ultimate ends: the destruction of the family? . . . Opposed to this tissue of abominations, he said, was the sacred institution of plural marriage, practiced by the Old Testament prophets and rooted in God's great commandment to the human race: "Be fruitful and multiply and replenish the earth."

We should be as the prophets, Musser said. . . . [W] must restore the patriarchal order. . . . Like Abraham, we should aspire to stand at the head of a family as numerous as the sands on the seashore. And like Abraham, we would require a great number of wives to achieve this. . . . God would provide women in abundance who were prepared to do their duty; we bearers of the seed must extend ourselves to the uttermost. . . .

Mormonism is a native American religion, a product of the frontier. Its founder was Joseph Smith, an obscure, unlettered backwoodsman who in the 1820s caused a great stir in the hinterlands of western New York by announcing himself as a prophet and describing his contacts with divine personages. [Smith published the Book of Mormon.] It was accepted as true scripture by thousands of converts who followed Smith to a new settlement in Missouri. They paid the price of being different in the coin of persecution by armed mobs, who drove them from Missouri into Illinois and, after Smith's murder, from Illinois into self-sought isolation in the barren reaches of the far West.

Most of the converts to Mormonism came out of New England. They were a puritanical people, reserved in conduct and strict about sex — attitudes further stiffened by their new faith. Among the revelations of Divine Will made by Joseph Smith to his austere following was [the religious basis for polygamy]. Only the leaders were told about the new revelation and, as Smith had anticipated, they quickly divided over the issue. The passions that flowed were mirrored in the tempestuous reactions of Smith's own wife, Emma. A prim and proper person, already well settled into monogamy when her vision-seeing husband shattered their domestic mold with his fateful revelation, she resisted at first in a fury, then came to terms with it, then broke the traces, spied on her husband and turned out the other wives. After his death, she renounced the doctrine.

Even Smith's great disciple, Brigham Young, teetered for a time on the brink of rejection, later saying of his initial reaction: "It was the first time in my life that I desired the grave." But in time, Young not only accepted polygamy but warmed to it and acquired 27 wives. . . .

[T]he Mormons had settled a thousand miles from their nearest neighbors in a land so inhospitable they thought no one else would ever want it, in order to pursue their faith without friction. At last, they felt safe, far from vigilantes, in a territory they controlled. But they underestimated the righteous enmity of the fellow who hears that someone else is savoring a fruit forbidden to him. The national press reveled in lascivious tales of Mormon wickedness, while the politicians of the dominant East were, as always, eager to please the vocal voters at the expense of the non-constituents. They could not resist the agitation and the persecution began again.

In 1869, the geographical isolation of the Mormons was broken by the completion of the transcontinental railroad, and they found themselves invaded by miners, railroaders and entrepreneurs, a rowdy bunch not previously noted for their sexual scruples, who set up a great lamentation over Mormon heresies and inequities. It was aimed more at Washington than at heaven, however, for the enterprising Mormons controlled not only the women of Utah, but the land, the commerce and the public offices. . . .

In 1882, the Edmunds Law was passed which made anyone convicted of practicing polygamy subject to a five year prison sentence. [Among the Mormons, too, polygamy] was energetically stamped out; anyone dallying with it was excommunicated. . . . So thorough going was the Mormon effort to obliterate all traces of plural marriage that by the time I came along in the third generation, only whispers remained of it. . . .

These families were generally hardworking and frugal. Although the upwardly mobile polygamist aspired to a separate home for each of his wives and broods, thus to perambulate from one to the other, most had to house their multiple families under one roof. . . . As a rule, each of the sister wives, as they are called, had her own section of the house where she received her husband and raised her own offspring. . . . The polygamous households were scattered throughout Salt Lake Valley, existing side by side with monogamous families which apparently did not suspect anything amiss. . . . To neighbors, the proliferation of brassieres on clotheslines, or new female faces at the windows or a platoon of strange tots romping in the yard, were explained away as visiting aunts and cousins. . . .

The polygamists also appeared to be a sober people of earnest disposition, who would have been enraged to hear themselves called immoral. . . . Among the men, there was no locker-room hee-hawing and lip-smacking about things sexual. Procreation was seen as the central duty of their lives. They were overshadowed by another world where souls waited to become flesh and thus gain eligibility for eternal life. Such gratifications, as attended this duty, were to be accepted as the unmentioned rewards of a job well done. . . .

But I sensed, or rather could not dispel the sense I had brought with me, that polygamy produced emotional problems for the women. I struck up conversations with wives who, once their hair was down, acknowledged it was a problem being forever a regimented and scheduled shareholder in love and home when it is the nature of love and home to demand full possession and proprietorship. . . .

[T]he most critical operation in a polygamous society is the selection process by which spouses are distributed. . . . I came quickly to suspect that the prophet Musser was making very liberal interpretations of the Lord's messages. Either that or the Lord has an unerring partiality for old codgers. The choicest girls were going to the leaders themselves or to the wealthier laymen who were the biggest contributors to the cause. . . . While the choice specimens were thus culled out, the young bulls were being diverted. Before they could claim their first wives, they were required to fulfill a "work mission." . . .

My notebooks were filling up with quotes and incidents. The ranks of my informants were growing. . . . But a gentle net was preparing to fall. Unknown to me, I was not the only investigator on the beat. . . . The task of containing the heresy and of keeping the church's skirts properly clear of it without precipitating a public scandal was a delicate one, but not beyond the subtlety of Church elders. They hired trusted private investigators to keep eye on the polygamists. The purpose was to identify any Mormons who might be attracted to the sect and to exert upon them, in quiet confrontation, the Church's powers of persuasion. Those who could not be reclaimed would be excommunicated.

Over the years, the investigators had located the key homes of the polygamists and had been able to keep up with the rotating meetings. During the meetings, investigators would slip among the parked cars outside and copy the license numbers. . . . Thus, it was that the license number of my father's old Plymouth, the only wheels available to me, kept appearing in the investigators' reports. In due course, my father was called in by his spiritual superiors for a confrontation that utterly confounded him.

The reader cannot appreciate the depths and nuances of this miscarriage of justice, or the peril of my situation, without knowing something about my father. . . . To say that his Mormon faith was orthodox and unquestioning is to understate its unyielding character. He was a granite block of integrity. . . . One day I came home to find my father in a towering rage. The unspeakable had been spoken: He had been accused of an undercover flirtation with the polygamists. His denial, fearsome though it assuredly was, had been questioned. . . . I was a long time in the doghouse. Though I was able to clear my father's name, I could scarcely repair the affront to his dignity nor soon rehabilitate my own credibility. . . . So ended my first adventures with the polygamists. . . .

---

For an empirical study of Mormon polygamous households that explores family structure and relationships (including management of everyday life), see Irwin Altman & Joseph Ginat, Polygamous Families in Contemporary Society (1996).

## Notes and Questions

1. *Epilogue.* Roy Potter was an exemplary police officer before his discharge, receiving the city's first employee-of-the-month award. Following his termination and the revelation of his plural marriage, he was excommunicated. While his case was pending trial, Potter was interviewed by the press.

> Potter insist[s], "All my wives are happy." He said he will sire as many children as he can take care of. Although Potter told a reporter he has three wives, his first wife, Denise, has apparently left him. Promiscuity is not involved, he added. "I married them for spiritual reasons. They voluntarily entered it." He maintains two separate households 20 miles apart, and his two current wives often share household items, including a vacuum cleaner. Potter now works as an electrician. His wife, Vera, 31, is an inventory control clerk and his wife, Mary, 27, is a secretary. He has three children by two wives and four children by his former wife, Denise.

Two Wives, Separate Households, S.F. Examiner, Apr. 7, 1985, at A13. See also Barlow v. Blackburn, 798 P.2d 1360 (Ariz. Ct. App. 1990) (rejecting constitutional challenge by police officer who lost job because of polygamous relationships.)

2. *Historical background.* Bigamy has a long history. Solomon reportedly had 700 wives and 300 concubines.[28] In medieval England, bigamy was an ecclesiastical offense.[29] Ecclesiastical law also made bigamous marriages void. However, a statute of 1604[30] made bigamy a felony. Bigamy was punishable by death until the reign of William III when the punishment became life imprisonment accompanied by branding of the right hand.[31] An act of George I reduced the punishment to deportation for seven years or imprisonment for two.[32]

In the United States, polygamy has been associated primarily with the Mormon religion. Law enforcement efforts frequently took the form of prosecutions of polygamists. Short Creek, an isolated community straddling the Arizona-Utah border (now called Colorado City), witnessed the most famous raids. Arizona first raided the community in 1935. In 1944 the Federal Bureau of Investigation raided the community again (as well as several others in Utah, Idaho, and Arizona). Yet another raid, in 1953, resulted in law enforcement officials taking into custody children and mothers and prosecuting the fathers. In In re State ex rel. Black, 283 P.2d 887 (Utah 1955), the Utah Supreme Court upheld a juvenile court ruling declaring children taken in the Short Creek raid wards of the state despite the parents' claim of freedom of religion. See generally Orma Linford, The Mormons and the Law: The Polygamy Cases, 9 Utah L. Rev. 308, 543 (1964); Ralph Nader, The Law v. Plural Marriages, 31 Harv. L. Rec. 10 (1960).

3. *Civil and criminal consequences.* Bigamy, like incest, has both criminal and civil consequences. Bigamy occurs when an individual attempts to contract a second marriage while a valid first marriage exists. Some jurisdictions find a defendant guilty despite a lack of criminal intent. See, e.g., Nev. Rev. Stat. Ann. §201.160 (Michie 1997); Okla. Stat. Ann. tit. 21, §881 (West 1983). Reynolds v. United States, 98 U.S. (8 Otto) 145 (1878) (cited in *Potter*), held the offense punishable even when committed under the claim of freedom of religion. The Court characterized polygamy as a religious practice, rather than a religious belief, and therefore not protected by the Constitution.

Although the First Amendment does not constitute a defense to bigamy, the law does provide a possible defense in the form of "Enoch Arden" statutes. The statutes are named after a sailor in a Tennyson poem who returns home ten years after a shipwreck to find his wife remarried after suffering years of hardship and loneliness. Under these statutes a person who remarries after the disappearance of a first spouse,

[28]. 1 Kings 11:3.
[29]. 2 Pollock & Maitland, supra note [21], at 543.
[30]. 1 Jac. 1, ch. 11.
[31]. Bartholomew, The Origin and Development of the Law of Bigamy, 74 Law Q. Rev. 259, 261 (1958).
[32]. Id.

without knowledge that the first spouse is alive, is not guilty of bigamy. The requisite period under English law was seven years; many American jurisdictions reduced this period. See, e.g., Ariz. Rev. Stat. Ann. §13-3606 (West 2001) (five years); Fla. Stat. Ann. §826.02 (West 2000) (three years).

4. A marriage is null and void if contracted when either party has a prior spouse living and is undivorced. Such a void marriage needs no decree to establish its invalidity. For some situations in which the prior spouse may be protected, see infra pages 242-244, "The Putative Spouse Doctrine and Other Curative Devices."

5. Should polygamy be legalized, as *Potter* suggests? Legal philosopher H. L. A. Hart suggests several reasons for the punishment of plural marriage: (1) to protect public records from confusion; (2) to frustrate schemes to misrepresent illegitimate children as legitimate; (3) to punish the public affront and provocation of the first spouse; and (4) to limit the likelihood of desertion, nonsupport and divorce. H. L. A. Hart, Law, Liberty and Morality 40 (1963) (noting suggestions from the commentary, American Law Institute Model Penal Code, Tent. Draft No. 4 (1955)). Do these rationales justify criminal sanctions? Do they, similarly, justify civil restrictions on the right to marry? To what extent are such prohibitions "direct" and "substantial" interferences with the right to marry? To what extent are these state interests "sufficiently important" and the means closely tailored to their accomplishment?

*Potter* states that marriage is the "bedrock" on which our culture rests, implying that legislation that restricts polygamy is essential to the protection and preservation of marriage. Should the state legislate morality? To what extent does the development of constitutional privacy doctrine support decriminalization of polygamy (and the concomitant acceptance of plural marriage)? See generally Daniel W. Shubik, Positivism and Polygamy: A Hart/Devlin Redivivus, 33 Am. J. Juris. 167 (1988).

6. A note writer, commenting on *Zablocki*, pointed out that the case "heralds a new era in constitutional law." "Conventional restrictions on the right to marry may no longer be as easily justified by reference to the traditional state interest in morality as they were in the past. Secondary state interests supporting bigamy statutes, and denying homosexuals and retarded persons the right to marry may now be open to attack." John Zawadsky, Note, Constitutional Law — Family Law — Right to Marry Deemed Fundamental, 1979 Wis. L. Rev. 682, 704. Does *Zablocki* signify that such restrictions, as well as those for incest and parental consent for minors, require a heightened standard of review? Or are these "reasonable regulations that do not significantly interfere with decisions to enter into the marital relationship," which evoke only deferential review? See generally David Chambers, Polygamy and Same-Sex Marriage, 26 Hofstra L. Rev. 53 (1997); Katha Pollitt, Polymaritally

Perverse: Polygamy and Its Relation to Same-Sex Marriage, The Nation, Oct. 4, 1999, at 10.

7. *Polygamy and child welfare.* Should any weight be given to the practice of polygamy in custody decisionmaking and adoption? In Sanderson v. Tryon, 739 P.2d 623 (Utah 1987), Jennifer Sanderson bore three children during a polygamous relationship with Robert Tryon. When the couple separated, she entered into a polygamous union with another man. Tryon, who had abandoned the practice of polygamy, sought custody. The trial court awarded custody to Tryon, presuming that, because of the mother's practice of polygamy, she neglected to provide proper care, moral training, and education. The Utah Supreme Court vacated the order and remanded, holding that "[m]oral character is only one of a myriad of factors the court may properly consider in determining a child's best interests." Id. at 627. See also Matter of Adoption of W.A.T., 808 P.2d 1083 (Utah 1991) (prospective adoptive parents' practice of polygamy should be only one factor to be considered, not threshhold disqualification). Custody decisionmaking is discussed in Chapter 7.

8. What explains the repugnance and hostility toward polygamy? Is polygamy immoral? Exploitative of women? Harmful to children? Analogous to prostitution? See Caminetti v. United States, 242 U.S. 470 (1917) (analogizing polygamy to prostitution and finding that the interstate transportation of a woman for the purpose of making her a plural wife violated the Mann Act).

9. *Conflict of laws.* Suppose a couple marries in Haiti, which allows a man to have up to four wives. The couple then moves to a jurisdiction that prohibits such marriages. Should the second jurisdiction recognize the marriages? (Note that the Full Faith and Credit Clause does not apply to the laws of a foreign country.) Should it matter for what purpose the validity is at issue? Compare In re Dalip Singh Bir's Estate, 188 P.2d 499 (Cal. Dist. Ct. App. 1948) (deceased Hindu's two wives could share his estate), with Hyde v. Hyde and Woodmansee, L. Rep. 1 P.&D. 130 (1866) (refusing to recognize a polygamous marriage for divorce purposes).

10. Bigamy and polygamy, both historically and today, occasionally come to light in collateral proceedings — especially divorce and probate hearings — in which the spouses (usually wives) are unwitting participants in plural marriage. Bigamy presented a particularly troublesome problem in colonial America.

[H]usbands occasionally traveled to the New World alone with the intention of later sending for their wives in England. However, . . . it took time for a man to get settled (to build a house, clear land, and plant crops) and provide for the necessary funds. [Some men] courted women in the new continent and in order to do so without public censure, masqueraded as single and eventually remarried. . . . Given the state of colonial society (a

wilderness where it took time for news to travel) and the vast distances between England and the colonies, bigamy was easily concealed. When it was
discovered, however, it provided immediate grounds for terminating a
marriage.

D. Kelly Weisberg, "Under Greet Temptations Heer": Women and Divorce in Puritan Massachusetts, 2 Feminist Stud. 183, 188 (1975).

11. *Polygamy today.* Polygamy continues to exist. One estimate places
the number of polygamous households in the United States between
20,000 and 50,000, over half of which are in Utah. Andrew Murr, Underground in Utah, Newsweek Int'l, June 4, 2001, at 49.

Some Mormons have been increasingly open about plural marriage
in the face of tacit acceptance by law enforcement. Recently, Utah law
enforcement responded by arresting Tom Green, husband of 5 wives
and father of 29 children, after he appeared on national television vaunt-
ing his polygamous lifestyle. In May 2001, a jury found him guilty of
four counts of bigamy and one count of failure to pay child support. He
was sentenced to five years in prison. See Julie Cart, Polygamy Verdict
Set Precedent Law: Utah Is Likely to Go After Others, L.A. Times, May
20, 2001, at A18; Michael Janofsky, Polygamist Gets 5 Years, Utah Judge
Is Lenient as Wives Plead for Husband's Freedom, Denver Post, Aug.
26, 2001, at A1.

See generally Todd M. Gillett, The Absolution of *Reynolds:* The Constitutionality of Religious Polygamy, 8 Wm. & Mary Bill Rts. J. 497
(2000); Keith E. Sealing, Polygamists Out of the Closet: Statutory and
State Constitutional Prohibitions Against Polygamy Are Unconstitutional
Under the Free Exercise Clause, 17 Ga. St. U. L. Rev. 691 (2001) (both
arguing that the Free Exercise Clause protects religiously motivated
polygamy).

12. *Polygamy and feminism.* The relationship of polygamy to feminism
remains controversial. In the account below, one Morman wife gives her
views. The author, a lawyer, is one of the wives of Alex Joseph (the
Mayor of Big Water, Utah), and mother of one of his 20 children.

■  **ELIZABETH JOSEPH, MY HUSBAND'S
    NINE WIVES**
    *N.Y. Times, May 23, 1991, at A15*

I married a married man. In fact, he had six wives when I married
him 17 years ago. Today, he has nine. . . .

. . . At first blush, [polygamy] sounds like the ideal situation for the
man and an oppressive one for the women. For me, the opposite is true.
[C]ompelling social reasons make the life style attractive to the modern
career woman.

Pick up any women's magazine and you will find article after article about the problems of successfully juggling career, motherhood and marriage. It is a complex act that many women struggle to manage daily. . . .

When I leave for the 60-mile commute to court at 7 A.M., my 2-year-old daughter, London, is happily asleep in the bed of my husband's wife, Diane. London adores Diane. When London awakes, about the time I'm arriving at the courthouse, she is surrounded by family members who are as familiar to her as the toys in her nursery. . . .

I share a home with Delinda, another wife, who works in town government. [Alex Joseph shares another house with seven other wives and their children.] Most nights, we agree we'll just have a simple dinner with our three kids. . . . Mondays, however, are different. That's the night Alex eats with us. . . . The same system with some variation governs our private time with him. While spontaneity is by no means ruled out, we basically use an appointment system. . . .

Plural marriage is not for everyone. But it is the life style for me. It offers men the chance to escape from the traditional, confining roles that often isolate them from the surrounding world. More important, it enables women, who live in a society full of obstacles, to fully meet their career, mothering and marriage obligations. Polygamy provides a whole solution. I believe American women would have invented it if it didn't already exist.

---

For another view that polygamy is beneficial to women, see Peggy Fletcher Stack, Mormonism and Feminism?, 15 Wilson Q. 30-31 (Spring 1991). But see Ann-Eliza Young, Wife No. 19, or the Story of a Life in Bondage, Being a Complete Expose of Mormonism (1877) (autobiographical account by a wife of Brigham Young).

(4) Age

■ **MOE v. DINKINS**
*533 F. Supp. 623 (S.D.N.Y. 1981), aff'd, 669 F.2d 67 (2d Cir.), cert. denied, 459 U.S. 827 (1982)*

MOTLEY, District Judge.

Plaintiffs Maria Moe, Raoul Roe and Ricardo Roe seek a judgment declaring unconstitutional, and enjoining the enforcement of, the parental consent requirement of New York Domestic Relations Law §§15.2 and 15.3 (Section 15). Section 15.2 provides that all male applicants for a marriage license between ages 16 and 18 and all female applicants between ages 14 and 18 must obtain "written consent to the marriage from both parents of the minor or minors or such as shall then be living. . . ." Section 15.3 requires that a woman between ages 14 and 16 obtain judicial approval of the marriage, as well as the parental consent required by Section 15.2. [The defendant class is represented by David Dinkins, City Clerk of New York City.]

Plaintiff Raoul Roe was eighteen years old when this action was commenced. Plaintiff Maria Moe was fifteen years old. Plaintiff Ricardo Roe is their one year old son who was born out of wedlock. Plaintiffs live together as an independent family unit. . . . Maria requested consent from her mother, a widow, to marry Raoul, but Mrs. Moe refused, allegedly because she wishes to continue receiving welfare benefits for Maria. . . . Maria and Raoul allege that they wish to marry in order to cement their family unit and to remove the stigma of illegitimacy from their son, Ricardo.

[Cristina Coe and Pedro Doe moved to intervene as plaintiffs.] Proposed plaintiff-intervenor Cristina Coe is fifteen years old. Proposed plaintiff-intervenor Pedro Doe is seventeen years old. Cristina is eight months pregnant with Pedro's child. Cristina and Pedro reside in the home of Pedro's father and step-mother. [W]hen Cristina discovered she was pregnant, she and Pedro informed Cristina's mother of their desire to have their child and to marry. Mrs. Coe refused to give Cristina her consent to marry and arranged for Cristina to have an abortion. Cristina refused to keep the appointments her mother made for her at the abortion clinic. Consequently, Mrs. Coe told Cristina she wanted to have nothing more to do with her and that she was leaving the country to live in the Dominican Republic. . . .

The claims of Cristina and Pedro present the same legal issue presented by the present plaintiffs — whether the parental consent requirement of Section 15 is constitutional. . . . [P]laintiffs argue that the intervention of Pedro and Cristina will present the court with a more complete picture of the impact of Section 15's parental consent requirement and will add to the representativeness of the named class members. Section 15 requires that Maria, who is now sixteen, must have parental consent to obtain a marriage license. Section 15 requires that Cristina must obtain judicial approval to marry, but precludes her from petitioning for judicial approval unless her parent has consented. While Maria has already borne a child, Cristina is now expecting a baby and is thus in a position to totally avoid the stigma of illegitimacy for her child. [The court held that Cristina Coe and Pedro Doe may intervene and then proceeds to consider the merits.]

Plaintiffs contend that Section 15 of the New York Domestic Relations Law, requiring parental consent for the marriage of minors between the ages of fourteen and eighteen, deprives them of the liberty which is guaranteed to them by the Due Process Clause of the Fourteenth Amendment to the Federal Constitution. A review of Supreme Court decisions defining liberties guaranteed by the Fourteenth Amendment reveals that activities relating to child-rearing and education of children, procreation, abortion, family relations, contraception, and, most recently, marriage, are constitutionally protected rights of individual privacy embodied within the concept of liberty which the Due Process Clause of the Fourteenth Amendment was designed to protect.

However, neither Zablocki [v. Redhail, 434 U.S. 374 (1978),] nor its predecessors, Loving v. Virginia, 388 U.S. 1 (1967), Griswold v. Connecticut, 381 U.S. 479 (1965), arose in the context of state regulation of marriages of minors. In that respect, this is a case of first impression.

[T]he Court has recognized the State's power to make adjustments in the constitutional rights of minors. . . . This power to adjust minors' constitutional rights flows from the State's concern with the unique position of minors. In Bellotti v. Baird, 443 U.S. 622 (1979), the Court noted "three reasons justifying the conclusion that the constitutional rights of children cannot be equated with those of adults: the peculiar vulnerability of children; their inability to make critical decisions in an informed and mature manner; and the importance of the parental role in child-rearing." Id. at 634.

Likewise, marriage occupies a unique position under the law. It has been the subject of extensive regulation and control, within constitutional limits, in its inception and termination and has "long been regarded as a virtually exclusive province of the State." Sosna v. Iowa, 419 U.S. 393, 404 (1975).

While it is evident that the New York law before this court directly abridges the right of minors to marry, in the absence of parental consent, the question is whether the State interests that support the abridgement can overcome the substantive protection of the Constitution. The unique position of minors and marriage under the law leads this court to conclude that Section 15 should not be subjected to strict scrutiny, the test which the Supreme Court has ruled must be applied whenever a state statute burdens the exercise of a fundamental liberty protected by the Constitution. . . . It is this court's view that Section 15 should be looked at solely to determine whether there exists a rational relation between the means chosen by the New York legislature and the legitimate state interests advanced by the State. Section 15 clearly meets this test.

The State interests advanced to justify the parental consent requirement of Section 15 include the protection of minors from immature decision-making and preventing unstable marriages. The State possesses paternalistic power to protect and promote the welfare of children who lack the capacity to act in their own best interest. The State interests in mature decision-making and in preventing unstable marriages are legitimate under its parens patriae power.

An age attainment requirement for marriage is established in every American jurisdiction. The requirement of parental consent ensures that at least one mature person will participate in the decision of a minor to marry. That the State has provided for such consent in Section 15 is rationally related to the State's legitimate interest in light of the fact that minors often lack the "experience, perspective and judgment" necessary to make "important, affirmative choices with potentially serious consequences." Bellotti v. Baird, 443 U.S. at 635-36.

Yet, plaintiffs fault the parental consent requirement of Section 15 as possibly arbitrary, suggesting that courts, as non-interested third parties, are in a better position to judge whether a minor is prepared for the responsibilities that attach to marriage. Although the possibility for parents to act in other than the best interest of their child exists, the law presumes that the parents "possess what the child lacks in maturity" and that "the natural bonds of affection lead parents to act in the best interest of their children." Parham v. J.R., 442 U.S. 584, 610 (1979). . . .

Plaintiffs also contend that Section 15 denied them the opportunity to make an individualized showing of maturity and denies them the only means by which they can legitimize their children and live in the traditional family unit sanctioned by law. . . . The fact that the State has elected to use a simple criterion, age, to determine probable maturity in the absence of parental consent, instead of requiring proof of maturity on a case by case basis, is reasonable, even if the rule produces seemingly arbitrary results in individual cases. "Simply because the decision of a parent is not agreeable to a child or because there is a (possible stigmatization of the child) does not automatically transfer power to make the decision from parents to some other agency or officer of the state." Parham v. J.R., 442 U.S. at 603.

Plaintiffs' reliance on the abortion and contraception cases is misplaced [citing Bellotti v. Baird; Carey v. Population Services International; Planned Parenthood v. Danforth]. These cases can be distinguished from the instant case in that

> a pregnant minor's options are much different than those facing a minor in other situations, *such as deciding whether to marry*. A minor not permitted to marry before the age of maturity is required simply to postpone her decision. She and her intended spouse may preserve the opportunity for a later marriage should they continue to desire it.

Bellotti v. Baird, 443 U.S. at 642 (emphasis added). Giving birth to an unwanted child involves an irretrievable change in position for a minor as well as for an adult, whereas the temporary denial of the right to marry does not. Plaintiffs are not irretrievably foreclosed from marrying. The gravamen of the complaint, in the instant case, is not total deprivation but only delay. . . . Accordingly, plaintiffs' motion for summary judgment in their favor is denied and summary judgment is entered in favor of defendants.

## Notes and Questions

1. All states establish certain minimum ages for marriage. Most states set that age at 18. Minors below the statutory minimum age must secure parental and/or, in some jurisdictions, judicial consent. See, e.g., Ariz. Rev. Stat. §25-102 (2000) (persons under 18 require parental consent; those under 16 must also have judicial consent). Some states permit pregnant minors to marry at younger ages. See, e.g., 2001 N.C. Sess. Laws §51-2A (West 2001) (raising minimum age for pregnant minors to marry with judicial consent from 12 to 14, whereas minors from 16-18 require parental consent). Are minors capable of informed consent on "private" matters such as marriage and abortion? Should the law treat these issues similarly?

2. *Historical background.* The age of consent for marriage at early common law was 7. Such marriages, however, were voidable as long as either party was too young to consummate the marriage. Several reasons supported the betrothal of children. Children were regarded as property whose marriage assured the passage of estates and settlement of disputes. Also, fathers took the earliest opportunity of marrying a child so that the right of marriage might not fall to the sovereign.[33] Ultimately, the Church proscribed such betrothals.[34] Parliament passed legislation in 1653 that raised the age of consent to 16 for boys and 14 for girls. For the first time, parental consent was required for the marriage of children below 21.[35] Subsequent legislation declared a marriage void if one party was under 16.[36]

In America, the development of restrictions on youthful marriages reflects an ambivalence concerning respect for family privacy versus deference to state intervention. Historian Michael Grossberg writes:

> Early in the nineteenth century most states resolved [uncertainty about the state's treatment of underage marriage] in favor of a youthful freedom to wed free of public restraints. Legislation and judicial decisions adopted this non-regulatory policy by borrowing traditional English common law age designations [14 for boys, 12 for girls]. . . .
>
> After the nation passed mid-century, however, these lax nuptial policies came under attack. Critics of nuptial mores from the professions, the press, and new reform organizations . . . singled out young brides and

[33]. 2 Pollock & Maitland, supra note [21], at 390-391.
[34]. Id. at 391.
[35]. Id. at 389.
[36]. Id. at 390.

grooms as prime sources of marital instability. [M]any lawmakers reacted
to the appeals of reformers [by] imposing limits on youthful nuptial rights.
A series of acts in the late nineteenth century and early twentieth succeeded in raising the average national statutory age of marriage to sixteen
for women and eighteen for men. By 1906 the legal trend had become so
commonplace that only seventeen states and territories clung to the old
common law standard of twelve and fourteen.

These nuptial law revisions occurred amidst a broader reassessment
of the social and economic place of the youth in American life. Persuaded
by educators, physicians, and reformers . . . , legislators began legally to
segregate youths through compulsory school laws, to provide special courts
for them with vast discretionary power over status offenses, as well as to
limit nuptial freedom. These statutes used the law to protect a Victorian
conception of youth development and marital conduct by prolonging
childhood and by saving children from themselves and their misguided
parents. . . .

Michael Grossberg, Guarding the Altar: Physiological Restrictions and
the Rise of State Intervention in Matrimony, 26 Am. J. Legal Hist. 197,
206-209 (1982). See also Michael Grossberg, Governing the Hearth: Law
and Family in Nineteenth-Century America 105-108, 142 (1985); Daniel
Scott Smith, Parental Power and Marriage Patterns: An Analysis of Historical Trends in Hingham, Massachusetts, 35 J. Marriage & Fam. 426
(1973).

3. *Empirical data.* Both men and women are marrying later, although
men marry even later than women. For example, in 1970, the median
age for women's first marriage was 20.8 but 23.2 for men. By 2000, that
age had risen to 25.1 for women and 26.8 for men.[37] What factors contribute to this gender-based difference? To delayed marriage? What are
the consequences for society of a later first-marriage age?

Early marriage correlates with several factors, including low educational level of a person's parents, a high number of siblings, and a non-
intact family during early adolescence. Racial and religious factors also
play a role: Catholics and African-Americans tend to marry later. Edward
O. Laumann et al., The Social Organization of Sexuality: Sexual Practices in the United States 478-479 (1994).

Some states require premarital counseling prior to teen marriages.
See, e.g., Cal. Fam. Code §304 (West 1994); Utah Code Ann. §30-1-
9(3)(b) (Supp. 2000). Available research on premarital counseling requirements for minors suggests its ineffectiveness. See Wesley Adams,
Marriage of Minors: Unsuccessful Attempt to Help Them, 3 Fam. L.Q.
13 (1969). See also Robert Schoen, California Divorce Rates by Age at
First Marriage and Duration of First Marriage, 37 J. Marriage & Fam.
548 (1975) (youthful marriages are less stable).

[37]. Bureau of the Census, U.S. Dept. of Commerce, Current Population Reports,
America's Families and Living Arrangements: Population Characteristics 2000 9 (2001).

4. *Cross-cultural comparison.* More than 30 countries allow marriages involving children below the age of 15. Ladan Askari, The Convention on the Rights of the Child: The Necessity of Adding a Provision to Ban Child Marriages, 5 ILSA J. Int'l & Comp. L. 123, 124 (1998). Among the causes of child marriage are poverty (i.e., early marriage relieves parents of the economic burden of raising a girl) and the belief that early marriage prevents sexual promiscuity. Some cultures subscribe to the myth that marriage to a virgin prevents or cures HIV/AIDS. United Nations Children's Fund, Early Marriage: Child Spouses, Innocenti Digest 1, 5-7 (March 2001). According to Askari, supra, international treaties fail to address the problem adequately.

5. Statutes reveal some inconsistency regarding the effect of a substantive defect of age: Some classify such marriages as void, others voidable. Historically, nonage was classified as a civil, rather than canonical, disability. Civil disabilities rendered marriages void; canonical disabilities made them voidable. Homer H. Clark, Jr., The Law of Domestic Relations in the United States 88 (2d ed. 1988).

The problem is illustrated by the following: Suppose Tom marries Jenna when he is 17. The marriage is rocky from inception. Tom, discovering that the statutory minimum age is 18, decides to leave Jenna. Later, he meets and marries Polly, but without securing an annulment of his marriage with Jenna. Tom is prosecuted for bigamy. May he raise the invalidity of his prior marriage in the criminal proceeding? If a statute holds the marriage void, then he may. But, if the statute classifies the marriage as voidable, the marriage remains valid until annulled, thereby precluding collateral attack.

6. Do statutes creating gender-based age differentials for marriage violate equal protection? Although *Moe* presented merely a substantive due process challenge, other cases have raised equal protection arguments. See, e.g., Friedrich v. Katz, 341 N.Y.S.2d 932 (Sup. Ct. 1973), *rev'd as moot,* 318 N.E.2d 606 (N.Y. 1974) (upholding statute requiring male under 21 and female under 18 to obtain written parental consent). For what reasons might states impose different age requirements? Cf. Stanton v. Stanton, 429 U.S. 501 (1977) (differential treatment for child support denies equal protection).

7. *Moe* characterizes one of the state interests as the parent's fundamental right to privacy to act in the child's best interest without state scrutiny. Does the state afford any assurance that the parents will exercise their responsibility wisely? For a case holding a nonage statute unconstitutional on this ground, see Berger v. Adornato, 350 N.Y.S.2d 520 (Sup. Ct. 1973).

Parental consent proves important if underage marriages are void and thus vulnerable to third-party attack. Requiring parental consent lessens the likelihood of (or even estops) subsequent parental efforts to invalidate the marriage.

Although *Moe* addresses withheld parental consent, some commentators believe that parents grant consent too readily. See David A. Gover & Dorothy G. Jones, Requirement of Parental Consent: A Deterrent to Marriage?, 26 J. Marriage & Fam. 205 (1964). How should the law respond to this problem? Is parental consent to marriage different than parental consent to abortion? If so, how?

8. Does an underage minor whose parents refuse consent have recourse? Case law sometimes requires that the refusal not be unreasonable. However, many statutes do not provide for override procedures. See, e.g., Application of Powers, 408 N.Y.S.2d 761 (Fam. Ct. 1978) (even were parental consent unreasonably withheld, court lacked jurisdiction because the statute neither required nor authorized judicial approval). Compare Uniform Marriage and Divorce Act (UMDA) §§203-204, 9A U.L.A. (pt. 1) 179-180 (1998) (minor may marry on either parent's consent or after a finding that the minor is capable of assuming the responsibilities of marriage and that the marriage would be in his best interests), with Cal. Fam. Code §302 (West 1994 & Supp. 1997) (requiring both parental consent and judicial authorization). Which approach best accomplishes the state interests at stake?

## Problems

1. Seventeen-year-old Jane Smith requests a license to marry Sam Jones. Her parents refuse to give their consent. Jane has previously been married to Tim Brown. That marriage, unlike this one, had her parents' approval. (The prior marriage was subsequently annulled.) The jurisdiction has a statute specifying that the county clerk shall not issue a marriage license if either applicant is under 18 years of age in the absence of parental consent or court order. Should the county clerk issue the marriage license? See Op. Tex. Atty. Gen., No. JM-359 (Oct. 18, 1985); 12 Fam. L. Rep. (BNA) 1022 (Nov. 12, 1985).

2. Tina, age 13, and Wayne, age 29, develop a sexual relationship, unbenownst to those around them. Under Maryland law, a person who is younger than age 16 may marry if he or she has parental consent and proof of pregnancy. When Tina becomes pregnant, her parents (who like and trust Wayne) give their blessing for Tina to marry. Maryland law also provides criminal liability for statutory rape for impregnating a female who is younger than 16. Should the county clerk grant the marriage license? Should Wayne be charged with statutory rape? How should the state reconcile these two laws? Should the state take any action against Tina's parents? See Amy Argetsinger, Girl, 13, Marries into Controversy, Wash. Post, Sept. 29, 1998, at A01 (reporting the story).

*(ii) State of Mind Restrictions: Fraud and Duress*

## ■ RADOCHONSKI v. RADOCHONSKI
### 91 Wash. App. 1001 (Wash. Ct. App. 1998)

ARMSTRONG, J.

. . . Barbara and Anthony Radochonski met in September 1991 and were married on March 18, 1992. They separated in November 1994. Barbara Radochonski filed a petition for dissolution on December 6, 1994, and Anthony Radochonski filed a counter-petition for invalidity of marriage [annulment] on January 9, 1995.

The trial court declared the marriage invalid on the basis of fraud in the essentials of marriage and awarded Anthony a judgment against Barbara for the amount he claimed to have spent on his wife before and during the marriage: $17,607.00. The trial court also awarded Anthony attorney fees and costs in the amount of $10,028.07.

The trial court's findings in support of fraud are as follows. Barbara lived with David Johnson, her lover, before she married Anthony. After the marriage, Barbara continued her relationship with Johnson, staying at his home on several occasions and meeting him in Poland. Barbara told Anthony that Johnson was married to another woman, and Johnson and the other woman posed as husband and wife during a visit to the Radochonskis' home. Barbara lied to Anthony about her relationship with Johnson so Anthony would marry her and she could get permanent residency status. Anthony would not have married Barbara if he had known she was marrying him to get permanent residency status.

To serve as grounds for an annulment, fraud must go to the "essentials" of marriage. RCW 26.09.040. Only one Washington case has addressed what are "essentials" of marriage: where one of the parties to a marriage ceremony determines before the ceremony that he or she will not engage in sexual intercourse with the other after marriage, not disclosing such intention to the other, and carries out such determination, the offending spouse commits a fraud in the contract of marriage affecting an essential of the marital relation, against which the injured party may be relieved by annulment of the marriage. Harding v. Harding, 11 Wash. 2d 138, 145, 118 P.2d 789 (1941). Here, although there was a conflict in the testimony, the trial court found that "it's clear that [Barbara and Anthony] had sexual intercourse."[2]

Courts have found fraud in an "essential" of marriage where one spouse has misled another on an attribute that prevents sexual relations between the parties, such as impotence, venereal disease, and drug

---

2. Anthony testified at trial that the parties only had oral sex, and that the parties never had "normal" sexual intercourse. Barbara testified that the parties had sex.

abuse, the latter on the theory that narcotics cause impotence. These attributes have gone to the essentials of marriage because they affected the sexual relations that are at the heart of the marriage.

But premarital chastity, false representations as to love and affection, misrepresentation of affection, failure to disclose out-of-wedlock children, fraudulent representation of pregnancy, and failure to end a previous relationship have all been held not to go to the essentials of marriage. Anthony has cited no authority that Barbara's wrongdoing goes to the essentials of marriage. Rather, Barbara's conduct more closely fits the pattern of those cases where the courts have found no fraud in the essentials. And we decline to extend the boundaries of essentials to include conduct such as Barbara's.

Finally, we consider whether Barbara committed fraud by marrying Anthony so she could stay in the United States as a permanent resident. Although the trial court found that Anthony would not have married Barbara "if he knew that she was marrying him for permanent residency status," the finding is not supported by the record and, in fact, is directly contradicted by Anthony's testimony that he knew before the marriage that Barbara was looking for a husband so that she could remain in the United States. Thus, Anthony cannot show reliance or the right to rely on any implied representations to the contrary.[14] . . .

We reverse and remand with instructions to vacate the decree of invalidity and judgment and attorney fee award in favor of Anthony, enter a decree of divorce, and resolve any further issues between the parties.

## Notes and Questions

1. A marriage may be set aside for lack of consent. Fraud (like duress) vitiates consent and serves as a ground for annulment. Because of the public policy in favor of preserving a marriage whenever possible, many courts apply a strict test for fraud, requiring that the misrepresentation go to the "essentials" to render the marriage voidable. "Essentials" generally includes ability and willingness to engage in sexual relations and childbearing. Given the current ease in obtaining a divorce, does this strict test make sense? Some states (for example, New York) require only that the fraud be material, that is, the plaintiff would not have married defendant but for the fraud.

---

14. The elements necessary to establish fraud — all of which must be shown by clear, cogent, and convincing evidence — are a representation of an existing fact; its materiality; its falsity; the speaker's knowledge of its falsity; his intent that it shall be acted upon by the person to whom it is made; ignorance of its falsity on the part of the person to whom it is addressed; the latter's reliance on the truth of the representation; his right to rely upon it; and his consequent damage.

2. *Annulment.* An annulment declares that no marriage occurred because some impediment existed at the time of the ceremony. In contrast, divorce terminates a valid marriage, enabling the parties to remarry. Annulments were significant when divorce was difficult to obtain. In England until the Matrimonial Causes Act of 1857, a divorce that enabled the parties to remarry was almost impossible to obtain. Discontented marital partners might, however, secure an annulment for fraud, duress, or nonage. Following divorce reform, however, the importance of annulments decreased.

Different procedural rules govern annulment and divorce. First, annulment jurisdiction exists at either party's domicile, the state where the marriage was celebrated, or any state with personal jurisdiction over the spouses. In contrast, divorce jurisdiction rests on domicile. Second, spousal and child support and division of property did not follow typically from an invalid marriage. Today, many states, by equitable remedies or statute, assimilate the financial consequences of annulment to those of divorce. Third, the "relation back" doctrine is applicable only to annulments. Because a decree of annulment establishes that a marriage never existed, benefits lost by virtue of the marriage may be reinstated. See Haacke v. Glenn, 814 P.2d 1157 (Utah Ct. App. 1991) (granting wife an annulment stemming from husband's concealment of his status as a convicted felon and thereby eliminating wife-attorney's conflict of interest with her employer, Department of Corrections).

3. Why might the plaintiff in *Radochonski* have sought an annulment rather than a divorce? (Annulments are explored in Chapter 5.)

4. When considering fraud to annul marriage, courts often distinguish between consummated and unconsummated marriages, sometimes requiring a higher standard for the former. Why? Given current sexual mores, should consummation continue to influence the law of annulment?

5. Does judicial examination of marriage for purposes of fraud constitute an invasion of privacy?

6. Some jurisdictions recognize the tort of fraudulent inducement to marry. See, e.g., Morgan v. Morgan, 388 S.E.2d 2 (Ga. Ct. App. 1989) (permitting recovery to wife for husband's false assertions that he was divorced). However, the quantum of fraud for annulment purposes is considerably less than that required for tort liability. Should a plaintiff be able to secure an annulment as well as tort damages for the same conduct? To recover in tort, must a plaintiff have suffered economic loss to recover for fraudulent inducement to marry? See Miller v. Miller, 956 P.2d 887 (Okla. 1998) (permitting recovery, even without economic loss, to husband for false representations that he fathered wife's child). See generally Robert G. Spector, Marital Torts: The Current Legal Landscape, 33 Fam. L.Q. 745, 754-757 (1999) (discussing recent case law).

7. *Duress.* Agreements to marry that are procured by force, fear, or coercion are unenforceable. Although duress generally requires physical

force or threat of force, lesser forms of duress may suffice if sufficient to overcome plaintiff's free will. Homer H. Clark, Jr., The Law of Domestic Relations in the United States 103 (2d ed. 1988). English cases disagree about whether the test should be subjective or objective. Id. at 104.

8. *Limited purpose marriages.* Prior to the legalization of abortion, couples who conceived a child would agree, sometimes, to marry "in name only" to legitimate the child, and then, after the birth, obtain a divorce. However, the parties agreed that no other marital rights and responsibilities would attach. Many American cases have recognized such "limited purpose" or "sham" marriages, probably to avoid the stigma of illegitimacy. See, e.g., Schibi v. Schibi, 69 A.2d 831 (Conn. 1949); Campbell v. Moore, 1 S.E.2d 784 (S.C. 1939). What purposes are served by failing to recognize such marriages? Are marriages to legitimate a child distinguishable from limited purpose marriages that facilitate an alien's entry into the United States (discussed infra)?

## Problems

1. Mr. Patel, an Indian engineer who resides in New Jersey, travels to India to seek a wife of the same caste. A marriage broker arranges a match with Ms. Navitlal. They meet twice to discuss marriage and their respective backgrounds. Ms. Navitlal informs him that her parents are separated and living in different locations. She does not tell him, however, that her mother presently is living with a person of a different caste. The couple is married in a civil ceremony, and the marriage is consummated. Mr. Patel returns to the United States to arrange for his wife to join him. He later returns to India where he undergoes a religious ceremony. He later testifies that he underwent the Hindu ceremony only because of threats by his wife's brothers. After Ms. Navitlal tires of waiting for her husband to send for her, she travels to the United States. There, she discovers that her husband has no desire to live with her. He asserts that she married him for the sole purpose of gaining entry into the United States. He files for annulment. She counterclaims for divorce. What result? Patel v. Navitlal, 627 A.2d 683 (N.J. Super. Ct. Ch. Div. 1992).

2. Prior to their marriage, Jim and Sandy discuss having children. Sometime after the marriage is consummated, Jim tells Sandy that he has two nonmarital children who were born during a sexual relationship that occurred prior to his marriage to Sandy. Jim also tells Sandy that he has decided that he no longer wishes to have any more children. Sandy petitions for annulment of the marriage. The jurisdiction has a statute that requires proof by clear and convincing evidence that there was "fraud as to the essentials of the marriage." What result? See Tobon v. Sanchez, 517 A.2d 885 (N.J. Super. Ct. Ch. Div. 1986).

## Note: Marriage Fraud in Immigration

Marriage to a U.S. citizen exempts an alien from the quota restrictions of the Immigration and Nationality Act (INA), 8 U.S.C. §1151(a),(b) (1994 & Supp. 1999), thereby avoiding lengthy delays in entering the country. This rule contributes to a strong incentive for aliens to marry citizens. Before 1986, when a citizen petitioned for an adjustment of status for an alien spouse, the Immigration and Naturalization Service (INS) would investigate the marriage to determine whether the marriage was genuine. If so, the INS granted the alien spouse permanent resident status.

In 1986, the Immigration Marriage Fraud Amendments (IMFA), 8 U.S.C. §§1154(b) (1994), required that if the INS finds the marriage genuine, it grants a conditional adjustment of status. The spouse obtains permanent resident status after two years, if the marriage is determined again to be genuine. However, if deportation proceedings have been initiated at any time during the marriage, then §5 requires that the alien spouse leave the United States for two years before any adjustment of status. Justification for this provision rests on the belief that marriage fraud is greater among aliens facing deportation. Although a number of federal courts upheld the constitutionality of §5, the tide turned with Escobar v. INS, 896 F.2d 564 (D.C. Cir. 1990), *withdrawn when reh'g en banc granted*, April 25, 1990, *appeal dismissed*, 925 F.2d 488 (D.C. Cir. 1991), in which the U.S. Court of Appeals held that §5 implicates the *citizen-wife's* right to privacy and due process by forcing her to choose between living without her husband or living outside the United States for two years. The Immigration Act of 1990, 8 U.S.C. §1255(e)(3) (1994 & Supp. 1999) finally changed the law by providing that §5 shall not apply if the alien establishes by clear and convincing evidence that the marriage was entered into in good faith, not for the purpose of procuring the alien's entry, and no consideration was given.

To determine the validity of a marriage between a citizen and an alien, federal investigators often explore such factors as whether the couple is cohabiting, commingling resources, holding property jointly, and has children. Are such investigations violative of the right to privacy and based on stereotypical views of married life? See Maria Isabel Medina, The Criminalization of Immigration Law: Employer Sanctions and Marriage Fraud, 5 Geo. Mason L. Rev. 669, 697, 700 (1997) (so arguing). See also Carol Sanger, Immigration Reform and Control of the Undocumented Family, 2 Geo. Immigr. L.J. 295 (1987) (criticizing immigration fraud policy for placing a strain on families, particularly those of undocumented aliens, by forcing separations within the nuclear family).

### b. Procedural Restrictions

*(i) Licensure and Solemnization*

■ **CARABETTA v. CARABETTA**
*438 A.2d 109 (Conn. 1980)*

PETERS, Associate Justice. . . .

The plaintiff and the defendant exchanged marital vows before a priest in the rectory of Our Lady of Mt. Carmel Church of Meriden, on August 25, 1955, according to the rite of the Roman Catholic Church, although they had failed to obtain a marriage license. Thereafter they lived together as husband and wife, raising a family of four children, all of whose birth certificates listed the defendant as their father. Until the present action, the defendant had no memory or recollection of ever having denied that the plaintiff and the defendant were married.

The issue before us is whether, under Connecticut law, despite solemnization according to an appropriate religious ceremony, a marriage is void where there has been noncompliance with the statutory requirement of a marriage. This is a question of first impression in this state. The trial court held that failure to obtain a marriage license was a flaw fatal to the creation of a legally valid marriage and that the court therefore lacked subject matter jurisdiction over an action for dissolution. We disagree with the court's premise and hence with its conclusion.

The determinants for a legally valid marriage are to be found in the provisions of our statutes. . . . The governing statutes at the time of the purported marriage between these parties contained two kinds of regulations concerning the requirements for a legally valid marriage. One kind of regulation concerned substantive requirements determining those eligible to be married. Thus General Statutes (Rev. 1949) §7301 declared the statutorily defined degrees of consanguinity within which a "marriage shall be void." . . . For present purposes, it is enough to observe that, on this appeal, no such substantive defect has been alleged or proven.

The other kind of regulation concerns the formalities prescribed by the state for the effectuation of a legally valid marriage. These required formalities, in turn, are of two sorts: a marriage license and a solemnization. In Hames v. Hames, [316 A.2d 379 (1972)], we interpreted our statutes not to make void a marriage consummated after the issuance of a license but deficient for want of due solemnization. Today we examine the statutes in the reverse case, a marriage duly solemnized but deficient for want of a marriage license.

As to licensing, the governing statute in 1955 was a section entitled "Marriage licenses." It provided, in subsection (a): "No persons shall be joined in marriage until both have joined in an application . . . for a license for such marriage." Its only provision for the consequence of noncompliance with the license requirement was contained in subsection (e):

". . . any person who shall join any persons in marriage without having received such (license) shall be fined not more than one hundred dollars." General Statutes (Rev. 1949) §7302, as amended by §1280b (1951 Supp.) and by §2250c (1953 Supp.). Neither this section, nor any other, described as void a marriage celebrated without license.

As to solemnization, the governing section, entitled "Who may join persons in marriage," [provides that] the celebration of a marriage by a person not authorized by this section to do so, renders a marriage void. We have enforced the plain mandate of this injunction. State ex rel. Felson v. Allen, 129 Conn. 427, 431, 29 A.2d 306 (1942).

In the absence of express language in the governing statute declaring a marriage void for failure to observe a statutory requirement, this court has held in an unbroken line of cases since Gould v. Gould, 78 Conn. 242, 247, 61 A. 604 (1905), that such a marriage, though imperfect, is dissoluble rather than void. . . . Then as now, the legislature had chosen to use the language of voidness selectively, applying it to some but not to all of the statutory requirements for the creation of a legal marriage. Now as then, the legislature has the competence to choose to sanction those who solemnize a marriage without a marriage license rather than those who marry without a marriage license. In sum, we conclude that the legislature's failure expressly to characterize as void a marriage properly celebrated without a license means that such a marriage is not invalid.

The plaintiff argues strenuously that our statutes, far from declaring void a marriage solemnized without a license, in fact validate such a marriage whenever it has been solemnized by a religious ceremony. The plaintiff calls our attention to the language of §7306, as amended, that "all marriages . . . solemnized according to the forms and usages of any religious denomination in this state shall be valid." To the extent that this language suggests greater validity for a marriage solemnized by a religious ceremony than for one solemnized by a civil ceremony, it is inconsistent with other provisions of the statutes with regard to solemnization and licensing. It has long been clear that, under our laws, all authority to join parties in matrimony is basically secular. . . . Whatever may be its antecedents, for present purposes it is sufficient to note that §7306 at the very least reenforces our conclusion that the marriage in the case before us is not void.

The conclusion that a ceremonial marriage contracted without a marriage license is not null and void finds support, furthermore, in the decisions in other jurisdictions. In the majority of states, unless the licensing statute plainly makes an unlicensed marriage invalid, "the cases find the policy favoring valid marriages sufficiently strong to justify upholding the unlicensed ceremony. This seems the correct result. Most such cases arise long after the parties have acted upon the assumption that they are married, and no useful purpose is served by avoiding the long-standing relationship. . . .

Since the marriage that the trial court was asked to dissolve was not void, the trial court erred in granting the motion to dismiss. . . .

---

The practice of "jumping the broom," described below, is a common wedding ritual in the African-American community.

## ■ HARRIETTE COLE, JUMPING THE BROOM: THE AFRICAN-AMERICAN WEDDING PLANNER
*16-18 (1993)*

When West Africans were brought forcibly to these shores some four hundred years ago, they were stripped of much of what was theirs. [A]fter the beginning of slavery, Africans were also denied the right to marry in the eyes of the law. Slaveholders apparently thought that their captives were not real people but were, instead, property to be bought and sold. As such, they had no rights. Further, if allowed formally to marry and live together, slaves might find strength in numbers that could lead to revolt. . . .

Yet the enslaved were spiritual people who had been taught rituals that began as early as childhood to prepare them for that big step into family life. . . . Out of their creativity came the tradition of jumping the broom. The broom itself held spiritual significance for many African peoples, representing the beginning of homemaking for a couple. For the Kgatla people of southern Africa, it was customary, for example, on the day after the wedding for the bride to help the other women in the family to sweep the courtyard clean, thereby symbolizing her willingness and obligation to assist in housework at her in-laws' residence until the couple moved to their own home. During slavery . . . a couple would literally jump over a broom into the seat of matrimony. Today, this tradition and many others are finding their way back into the wedding ceremony.

---

See also Katherine M. Franke, Becoming a Citizen: Reconstruction Era Regulation of African-American Marriages, 11 Yale J.L. & Human. 251 (1999). For other customs involving quasi-marriage ceremonies, see Irwin Altman & Joseph Ginat, Polygamous Families in Contemporary Society 126-142 (1996); Ceremonies of the Heart: Celebrating Lesbian Unions (Becky Butler ed., 1997); Eric Marcus, Together Forever: Gay and Lesbian Marriage 143-159 (1998).

## Notes and Questions

1. Statutes in every jurisdiction provide for the issuance of marriage licenses. Noncompliance may result in criminal consequences (in the form of sanctions for officials who violate licensing requirements) as well as civil consequences (that is, invalidity of the marriage). *Carabetta* announces the general rule that, absent statutory language to the contrary, failure to comply with a licensing requirement will not render the marriage invalid.

Sometimes courts state that this result depends on the belief of one or both of the parties. The policy of the law strongly opposes voiding a marriage entered into in good faith, believed by one or both of the parties to be legal, and followed by cohabitation.

Three justifications for licensure statutes exist: (1) they aid in enforcing marriage laws by requiring persons not qualified to marry for reasons of age, health, or existing marital status to disclose such information; (2) they serve as public health measures by preventing marriages that would be damaging to the health of one spouse or would produce unhealthy children; and (3) licensure serves as proof that the marriage has occurred. Homer H. Clark, Jr., Law of Domestic Relations in the United States 36-45 (1968). Do the statutes accomplish these purposes? For example, are the statutes effective in protecting couples from sexually transmitted disease? A person is guilty of perjury if he or she knowingly makes a false statement to obtain the license. Does this sanction deter violations? If the licensing statutes are effective in furthering their ostensible purposes, how can we enforce them if a marriage is held to be valid in the absence of a license?

2. *Formalities*. (a) *Officials*. Most states provide that marriage licenses will be issued by the county clerk or, in some states, a judge. On the validity of marriages at sea, see generally Samuel Pyeatt Menefee, "Getting Spliced": A Re-evaluation of Marriage at Sea, 10 Okla. City U. L. Rev. 267 (1985). See also 46 U.S.C. §11301(b)(8) (1994 logbook rules).

(b) *Where, how long, how much does it cost?* Statutes in approximately half the states require that licenses be procured in the county where one party resides or where the marriage is to be performed. Many statutes provide that the license expires within a short period of time (typically 30 to 60 days). Marriage license fees range from a low of $10 (see, e.g., Ind. Code Ann. §33-17-14-2 (Michie 1996 & Supp. 2000)) to a high of $70 (see, e.g., Minn. Stat. Ann. §517.08 (West 1990 & Supp. 2001)). In many states, license fees include a statutorily designated amount for funding domestic violence shelters. See, e.g., Cal. Welf. & Inst. Code §18305 (West 1991 & Supp. 2001). Are such fees, in general, constitutional? See Walter E. Harding & Martin R. Levy, Marriage License Fees: Are They Constitutional?, 17 J. Fam. L. 703 (1978).

(c) *Waiting periods*. Most states have waiting periods, with some exception for exigent circumstances (such as pregnancy). A majority of jurisdictions require a waiting period (usually 3 days) between the application and issuance of the marriage license; a few states require a waiting period after the issuance of the license but before the ceremony. Homer H. Clark, Jr., The Law of Domestic Relations in the United States 36 (2d ed. 1988). What is the function of waiting periods? Do they represent unnecessary state paternalism? Are waiting periods constitutional? Do they meet the *Zablocki* standard? See Harding & Levy, supra, at 703-707.

(d) *Solemnization.* What is the effect of a marriage, following proper licensure, solemnized by an individual not authorized by law to do so? In Ranieri v. Ranieri, 539 N.Y.S.2d 382 (App. Div.), *appeal dismissed,* 74 N.Y.2d 792 (1989) (invalidating a marriage performed by a "minister" of the Universal Life Church, a religious corporation not covered by the authorizing statute)[38] with Matter of Blackwell, 531 So. 2d 1193 (Miss. 1988) (contra).

What purpose underlies the solemnization requirement applied in *Ranieri?* So long as the parties comply with the state's licensing requirement, why would a court require such strict compliance? That is, why should the state intervene *twice* in order for the parties to enter a valid marriage?

## Problems

1. Anna and Dickie are involved in a sexual relationship. Dickie tells Anna that his family believes that he will go to hell if they do not marry. He proposes a "fake" ceremony and she agrees. They have a ceremony, solemnized by a minister, but fail to file the marriage license with the county clerk within 60 days of issuance as required by statute. Instead, Anna burns the license with Dickie's knowledge and consent. They live together for almost two months. Later, Dickie files for divorce and requests a division of property. Anna responds by denying the existence of the marriage or, in the alternative, for an order annuling the marriage on the basis of fraudulent inducement. What result? See Fryar v. Roberts, 57 S.W.2d 727 (Ark. 2001).

2. Husband and Wife participate in a Hindu marriage ceremony in which they exchange rings and vows. They plan to have a subsequent civil ceremony, which never takes place. Presiding over the religious ceremony is an ordained Hindu priest who is not licensed by the city or state of New York to perform marriage ceremonies. Following the ceremony, the parties begin proceedings three times to obtain a marriage license but none is ever secured. Each blames the other for the failure to secure the license. After the ceremony, both parties list themselves as

[38]. Any individual can become a minister in the ULC through a simple registry-by-mail procedure. See Ravenel v. Ravenel, 338 N.Y.S.2d 324, 327-328 (Sup. Ct. 1972).

"single" on their tax returns. After seven years' cohabitation (and the birth of a child), Husband brings suit seeking a declaration that the parties were never lawfully married or, in the alternative, a divorce. What result? Persad v. Balram, 724 N.Y.S.2d 560 (N.Y. Sup. Ct. 2001).

*(ii) Blood Tests*

### ■ DOE v. DYER-GOODE
*566 A.2d 889 (Pa. Super. Ct. 1989)*

DEL SOLE, Judge:

. . . The Complaint at issue alleges that Appellants sought the services of Appellee-doctor in regard to a pre-marital blood test. Although Appellant, John Doe, did consent to have his blood withdrawn, he did not consent to an "AIDS test." Nevertheless, he was informed by the doctor that he had tested positive for AIDS. John Doe subsequently retested negative for exposure to the AIDS virus. Based upon this set of submitted facts the Appellants sought to recover by setting forth six separate causes of action.

In Count 1 a claim is made by John Doe for invasion of privacy. Appellants contend that John Doe's privacy was violated in two instances. The first occurred when the Appellee doctor "interfered with and violated" the plaintiff's bodily integrity by undertaking an examination of plaintiff's HIV status without plaintiff's knowledge or consent. It is also alleged that the doctor's creation and maintenance of records which contained these results constituted a further violation of the right to privacy.

"An action for invasion of privacy is comprised of four distinct torts: (1) intrusion upon seclusion, (2) appropriation of name or likeness, (3) publicity given to private life and (4) publicity placing the person in a false light." Harris by Harris v. Easton Pub. Co., 335 Pa. Super. 141, 483 A.2d 1377, 1383 (1984). [The court notes that only the first prong applies.] Section 652B of the Restatement (Second) of Torts [states]: One who intentionally intrudes, physically or otherwise, upon the solitude or seclusion of another or his private affairs or concerns, is subject to liability to the other for invasion of his privacy, if the intrusion would be highly offensive to a reasonable person.

The "invasion of bodily integrity" cited by Appellants does not come within the ambit of this tort. Appellant, John Doe, consented to the extraction of his blood for testing. . . . Because John Doe relinquished his blood sample to the doctor, this sample was no longer held in "private seclusion" by Mr. Doe. Thus the fact that an unauthorized test was performed on this sample cannot establish a claim for invasion of privacy.

Appellants next contend that the facts of this case are sufficient, if proven, to constitute a battery based upon lack of informed consent.

[I]ndividuals who are mentally and physically able to discuss their medical condition and who are not in an emergency situation, must give their informed consent as a prerequisite to a surgical operation by a physician. . . .

In dismissing this count of the complaint the trial court held that a cause of action based upon lack of informed consent could not stand in this case because prior caselaw has only extended this doctrine to surgical or operative procedures. However, even if we were to conclude that the insertion of a needle under the skin falls into the category of a surgical or operative procedure, Appellants' claim cannot stand. There is no allegation in this case that John Doe was not informed of the risks associated with the procedure he was about to undergo — the withdrawal of a blood sample by extraction through a needle. . . . The blood sample which was withdrawn and later tested is simply a by-product of the medical procedure, much like a tissue sample taken from a patient in a biopsy procedure. Appellant gave his consent to have his blood withdrawn for a testing purpose. The fact that an additional test was performed on this blood sample cannot constitute grounds for an action in battery.

[The court also rejects appellants' claims for breach of contract (countering that no agreement was reached to perform certain tests to the exclusion of others) and breach of the duty to deal in good faith (reasoning that no facts were alleged showing that the testing violated the physician's obligation to act in the patient's best interest).]

The fifth cause of action set forth in the Complaint is based in negligence. . . . Allegations in a negligence action must aver that a given standard of care was called for and that such standard was breached or that defendant acted less reasonably than a reasonable person would act. . . . Appellants have not included in their Complaint any duty which was violated. The Complaint does not identify any duty to restrain from having an HIV blood test performed on a blood sample when consent has not been obtained, nor will we impose such a duty. Appellants' complaint also refers to the doctor's actions in which the test results were communicated to John Doe without advice about counseling, yet Appellants are unable to establish any duty requiring a physician to notify a patient of counseling options when the physician is reporting test results. Further, although the Complaint does allege that Appellants were wrongly informed that John Doe tested positive for AIDS, the Complaint does not allege that the Appellee herself performed the test. Although the test results were ultimately found to be inaccurate, the doctor cannot be faulted for reporting to her patient the results which she obtained. In fact, failure to promptly report this result which suggested a serious illness may have become the basis of a negligence claim.

The final cause of action asserted by Appellants is for intentional infliction of emotional distress. Appellants base this cause of action on the doctor's conduct in conveying to John Doe the information that he tested positive for AIDS. In considering and dismissing the cause of action from Appellants' Complaint the trial court found that Appellants failed to plead conduct which is extreme and outrageous and beyond all bounds of decency such that the action would be characterized as atrocious and utterly intolerable in a civilized society.

Order affirmed.

## Notes and Questions

1. Statutes in many states require that, to obtain a marriage license, an applicant must file a health certificate with the licensing authority (often a county clerk). This certificate states that the applicant has submitted to a medical test by a licensed physician for venereal disease. A physician must certify that the applicant either does not have such disease or, if infected, is not in a communicable stage. See, e.g., D.C. Code Ann. §30-117 (1998).

If an applicant has a positive test and has a disease that is or may become communicable, the physician cannot sign the certificate; the applicant will be unable to obtain a marriage license. Typically, all certificates connected with a premarital examination are confidential; disclosure without authority to persons not entitled by law to have access to such information may result in criminal liability.

2. Some states also require tests for rubella (German measles) for female applicants. Such tests may be waived if the applicant is over 50 years old or sterilized. Unlike tests for venereal disease, lack of immunity to rubella does not bar issuance of the marriage license. The purpose is merely informative.

3. *Historical background.* Premarital blood tests for venereal disease arose out of a concern with eugenics:

> Fears about the impact of venereal diseases on the future of the family led physicians to ally with the nascent eugenics movement in the first decades of the twentieth century. The initial impetus behind eugenics was the differential in birth rates between native-born Americans and newly arriving immigrants. . . .
>
> Some physicians, influenced by nativist views, singled out immigrant populations as particularly prone to venereal infection. A widely circulated theory held that some immigrants, following a common folk remedy of intercourse with a virgin, raped their own children as a means of attempting to rid themselves of infection. . . . Other doctors suggested that poor conditions in American cities contributed to immorality and the spread of venereal diseases. . . . Fear of sexually transmitted diseases became closely tied to growing anxieties about the city and urban masses. . . .
>
> . . . By the end of 1938, twenty-six states had enacted provisions prohibiting the marriage of infected individuals. Although by the end of

World War I almost half the states had statutes whose ostensible purpose was the prevention of venereal disease in marriage, these laws typically had little impact. Most merely required a note from a physician or, remarkably, for the groom to sign an affidavit assuring that he was free of infection. As a physician, let alone a layperson, cannot identify a syphilitic infection without laboratory exams, such oaths really constituted character references. . . .

Allan M. Brandt, No Magic Bullet: A Social History of Venereal Disease in the United States Since 1880, 19-21, 147 (1987).

4. *Double standard.* Early statutes treated men and women differently:

[A] view of sexual conduct . . . motivated and justified the earlier venereal disease testing statutes. One of the most powerful images in the crusade against venereal disease was that of the young man who, having engaged in sex with prostitutes or other "unchaste" women before marriage, would then marry — and infect — an innocent woman. In fact, a major decision concerning the constitutionality of VD testing, Peterson v. Widule, [147 N.W. 966 (Wis. 1914)], upheld the statute's requirement that men — but not women — submit to testing. The Court cited both "medical evidence" and "what we suppose to be common knowledge" that "the great majority of women who marry are pure, while a considerable percentage of men have had illicit sexual relations before marriage." Therefore, the Court reasoned that "the number of cases where newly married men transmit a venereal disease to their wives is vastly greater than the number of cases where women transmit the disease to their new husbands."

The view that venereal disease was transmitted from husbands to wives (and not from wives to husbands) was connected to two powerful social conceptions: 1) the sexual "double standard" in which premarital sexuality was vehemently condemned for women but tacitly accepted for men; and 2) the rigidly enforced division of women into the "virtuous," who did not engage in sex before marriage, and the "debased," whose sexual activity outside of marriage made them unmarriageable. . . .

Robert D. Goodman, In Sickness or in Health: The Right to Marry and the Case of HIV Antibody Testing, 38 DePaul L. Rev. 87, 113-114 (1989).

5. As *Dyer-Goode* reveals, some physicians perform blood tests for HIV as part of premarital screening without first obtaining consent. A study of 500 hospitals by Dr. Charles E. Lewis, professor of medicine at UCLA, revealed that many hospital personnel, similarly, test patients for AIDS without their knowledge or consent, in some cases in violation of hospital policy and state law. Many AIDS Tests Without Consent, S.F. Chron., Feb. 16, 1990, at A19. What interests support nonconsensual HIV testing? Are they sufficient to overcome privacy rights in this context? In any context? See Steven Eisenstat, An Analysis of the Rationality of Mandatory Testing for the HIV Antibody: Balancing the Governmental Public Health Interests with the Individual's Privacy Interest, 52 U. Pitt. L. Rev. 327 (1991).

6. Should nonconsensual HIV testing be actionable whether the couple is incorrectly or correctly informed of a positive test result? In Molien v. Kaiser, 616 P.2d 813 (Cal. 1980), defendant negligently diagnosed plaintiff's wife as having syphilis. As a result, plaintiff suffered extreme emotional distress and the destruction of his marriage. Stating that an erroneous diagnosis of syphilis foreseeably would lead to emotional distress of a spouse, the court found that the defendants owed plaintiff a duty to care, despite lack of physical harm.

Instead of premarital testing for HIV, should physicians ask each person about risk factors for AIDS and then share that information with the prospective spouse? Does it alter your view to learn that sexual partners frequently lie? In a survey conducted of 422 sexually active college students, psychologists revealed that 33 1/3 percent of the men and 10 percent of the women admitting lying to obtain sex. When asked, hypothetically, whether they would lie about testing positive for the AIDS virus, 20 percent of the men and 4 percent of the women said they would. Both Men and Women Lie About Past to Have Sex, S.F. Chron., Mar. 15, 1990, at B4. On the issue of partner notification in cases of sexually transmitted diseases, see Lawrence O. Gostin & James G. Hodge, Jr., Piercing the Veil of Secrecy in HIV/AIDS and Other Sexually Transmitted Diseases: Theories of Privacy and Disclosure in Partner Notification, 5 Duke J. Gender L. & Pol'y (1998). On the more general issue of deception in intimate relationships, see Dan Subotnik, "Sue Me, Sue Me, What Can You Do Me? I Love You": A Disquisition on Law, Sex, and Talk, 47 Fla. L. Rev. 311 (1995). See also Chapter IV, section D.

7. *Constitutionality.* Would mandatory premarital HIV testing survive constitutional challenge? Some states have even prohibited marriage with a person afflicted with AIDS. See, e.g., Utah Code Ann. §30-1-2(1) (1989). But see T.E.P. v. Leavitt, 840 F. Supp. 110 (D. Utah 1993) (statute violates Americans with Disabilities Act and Rehabilitation Act). Does either restriction violate the constitutional right to marry? Do such restrictions "directly and substantially interfere" with that right according to *Zablocki*? Does it alter your view to learn that the cost of HIV antibody testing may be as high as $300? See Goodman, supra, at 99-126.

In contrast, some states have repealed their blood-test requirements on the theory that the cost did not justify the small number of cases detected. See C. Dirk Peterson, Note, For Better or For Worse? Mandatory AIDS Testing for Marriage License Applicants, 38 J. Urb. & Contemp. L. 159 (1990) (discussing Illinois requirement and its repeal).

8. Premarital testing for HIV exposure is part of a movement of increased reporting requirements in response to AIDS. As of 1989, 28 states required the names of those testing positive on the HIV antibody test to be reported to the state. Randy Shilts, AIDS/The Inside Story, S.F. Chron., Aug. 14, 1989, at A7. Such reporting is highly controversial. Although the Center for Disease Control claims that reporting requirements can sometimes be useful for patient counseling, partner

notification, and referral of HIV-infected persons to appropriate medical care, mandatory reporting raises privacy concerns and the fear that people at high risk for AIDS may not take the test.[39] Id. See LuAnn Polito, Containing the AIDS Virus . . . Testing . . . Reporting . . . Confidentiality . . . Quarantine . . . Constitutional Considerations, 37 Clev. St. L. Rev. 369, 371-383 (1989).

## Problem

A couple challenges, under the Free Exercise Clause, a statute requiring a premarital serological test for syphilis. They claim that the blood test would require them to violate a precept of their church. What result? See In re Kilpatrick, 375 S.E.2d 794 (W. Va. 1988).

### (iii) Note: Procedural Variations

### (1) Proxy Marriages

A proxy marriage is one in which at least one party is represented at the ceremony by an agent or proxy. Marriage by proxy was once the exclusive province of European royalty. The practice was valid in England until the mid-nineteenth century, when Parliament enacted legislation that required the presence of both parties at the ceremony.[40]

Marriage by proxy has been most visible during this century in times of war, frequently to legitimize children. During World War I, Belgium, France, Italy, and the United States permitted proxy marriages by military personnel.[41] World War II witnessed renewed interest in the practice. France even permitted posthumous marriage if the soldier had expressed an intention to marry before his death.[42] After 1942, Italian soldiers in the front lines could marry via radio broadcast.[43] During that time, proxy marriages were available in Kansas, Oklahoma, and

---

[39]. Privacy concerns are illustrated by the following account: "In Denver, the state health department has received reports that scores of men named Nancy Reagan are infected with the human immunodeficiency virus. Colorado . . . is discovering that many gay men are edgy about their names being on a master list of the HIV infected. To avoid ending up on the list, they simply write down Nancy Reagan when they are tested, and that's how it gets reported to the state." Randy Shilts, AIDS/The Inside Story, S.F. Chron., Aug. 14, 1989, at A7.

[40]. Comment, Persons — Marriage — Validity of Proxy Marriages, 25 S. Cal. L. Rev. 181, 182 (1952).

[41]. Ernest G. Lorenzen, Marriage by Proxy and the Conflict of Laws, 32 Harv. L. Rev. 473, 479 (1919).

[42]. W. H. Howery, Marriage by Proxy and Other Informal Marriages, 13 U. K.C. L. Rev. 48, 54 (1944).

[43]. Id.

New Jersey for servicemen.[44] Marriages by mail, telephone, cable, and radio have occurred.

Another use of proxy marriages is to circumvent immigration laws. Prior to 1924, proxy marriages were valid for immigration purposes so long as the marriage was valid in the country where performed. However, in 1924, Congress prohibited the practice.[45] Proxy marriage has also been used to assist political refugees. In the leading British case, Apt v. Apt, 1 All. E.R. 620 (1947), Jewish refugees from Nazi Germany were married by proxy in Argentina where the husband resided. More recently, proxy marriages have facilitated emigration from behind the former Iron Curtain. Yet another group resorting to proxy marriages is prisoners.

### (2) Confidential Marriages

Some states permit "confidential" or "secret" marriages. See, e.g., Cal. Fam. Code §§500-536 (West 1994 & Supp. 2001); Mich. Comp. Laws Ann. §551.201 (West 1988). These provisions enable a couple to dispense with some procedural requirements. For example, the California Confidential Marriage Act permits an unmarried man and woman, already living together, to marry without procuring a marriage license or filing a health certificate. However, the couple must participate in a ceremony of solemnization by a person duly authorized and must file a certificate of marriage that is maintained as a permanent, but confidential, record not open to public inspection except by a superior court order upon a showing of good cause.

Statutes authorizing confidential marriages encourage cohabitants to legalize their relationship but to avoid embarassment from public disclosure of their petition for a marriage license or of the date of their marriage. Originally enacted in 1878, the California statute was publicized in 1972 when the state legislature enacted an amendment governing reporting of such marriages. Only 1,075 marriages under the renewed statute occurred in 1972. Following the publicity, in 1976 more than 30,000 confidential marriages took place in Los Angeles County alone.[46]

### (3) Other Variations

Some states provide for other variations that dispense with traditional licensure or solemnization requirements. A few states permit

---

[44]. Id. at 55, 100.

[45]. 8 U.S.C. §224(m) (1924) (superceded by 8 U.S.C. §1101(a)(35) (1994)).

[46]. Laurel Leff, "Instant" Marriages, Popular in California, May Spread in U.S., Wall St. J., Sept. 14, 1977, at 1.

marriage by declaration (e.g., Mont. Code Ann. §40-1-311 (1999); Tex. Fam. Code Ann. §§2.401-2.402 (West 1998)), or marriage by contract in which the parties subscribe to a witnessed contract, which is acknowledged before a judge (e.g., N.Y. Dom. Rel. Law §11(3) (McKinney 1999)). Unlike a marriage by declaration, however, the parties to a marriage by contract first must obtain a license.

Finally, tribal marriages, contracted according to Native American laws or customs, are also recognized in some jurisdictions. See, e.g., Nev. Rev. Stat. Ann. §122.170 (Michie 1998). Unif. Marriage and Divorce Act §206, 9A U.L.A. (pt. 1) 1998, also recognizes marriages if solemnized "in accordance with any mode of solemnization recognized by any . . . Indian Nation or Tribe, or Native Group."

### c. Informal Marriages

#### (i) Common Law Marriage

### ■ JENNINGS v. HURT
*N.Y.L.J., Oct. 4, 1989, at 24 (Sup. Ct. N.Y. County)*, **aff'd**, *554 N.Y.S.2d 220 (App. Div. 1990)*, **appeal denied**, *568 N.Y.S.2d 347 (N.Y. 1991)*

Justice SILBERMANN.
[Plaintiff Sandra Jennings alleged the existence of a common law marriage. Actor-defendant William Hurt moved to dismiss.]

South Carolina is one of thirteen states (including the District of Columbia) that recognize common-law marriages. South Carolina became a common law state early in the eighteenth century when it adopted the law of common-law marriage which was recognized in the Ecclesiastic Courts in England. . . .

South Carolina law is aptly stated in the case of Fryer v. Fryer, S.C. Eq. 85 (S.C. App. 1832):

> Marriage, with us, so far as the law is concerned has ever been regarded as a mere civil contract. Our law prescribes no ceremony. It required nothing but the agreement of the parties, with an intention that the agreement shall, per se, constitute the marriage. They may express the agreement by parol, they may signify it by whatever ceremony their whim, or their taste, or their religious belief, may select: it is the agreement itself, and not the form in which it is couched, which constitutes the contract. The words used, or the ceremony performed, are mere evidence of a present intention and agreement of the parties. . . .

Although common-law marriages were abolished in New York as of April 29, 1933, New York does give effect to common-law marriages if they are recognized as valid under the law of the state in which it was supposedly contracted.

The sole question to be decided by this court is whether Sandra Jennings is the common-law wife of William Hurt?

Since it is conceded that the parties never had a ceremonial marriage, the answer to that question rests upon certain events that allegedly transpired during the parties' stay in South Carolina and the law of South Carolina. . . .

Jennings and Hurt met in Saratoga, New York in the summer of 1981 while each of them was working there. Shortly thereafter, upon their return to New York City, the parties began living together. [They ceased living together in 1984.] At the time their relationship began, Jennings knew Hurt was still married. The parties had many discussions in which Hurt explained to Jennings his disappointment at his own failure in marriage and his family's history in terms of failed marriages. Hurt frequently discussed his belief that marriage was a promise or a commitment to "God" and that he was experiencing "dismay about having broken that promise." Because of his feelings and pain relating to this subject, Hurt explained that marriage was "not in the cards" for him. This is corroborated by Hurt's conversation with Mary Beth Hurt when he asked for a divorce. Jennings herself stated "he wanted me to know that he did not necessarily mean a marital commitment. . . ."

In the Spring of 1982 Jennings became pregnant. Hurt's counsel began drafting an agreement governing the parties' financial arrangements of living together and for the support of the expected child. The earliest of these agreements is dated May 1982. The pregnancy prompted Hurt to commence divorce proceedings to terminate his marriage to Mary Beth Hurt. In September, 1982, Hurt went to see his former wife to tell her he wanted to finalize the divorce since "Sandy is having a baby."

On October 31, 1982, Jennings joined Hurt in South Carolina where he was already engaged in the filming of the "Big Chill." During their stay in South Carolina from October 31, 1982 to January 10, 1983, the parties lived in the same house and shared a bed. Their social circle consisted of the cast and others connected with the film project. During this period as well as earlier and later times, their relationship was volatile and permeated by arguments.

On December 3, 1982, Hurt's divorce became final. He learned this sometime later from counsel. Jennings testified that she learned of his divorce on December 27, 1982 when he approached her with another version of the "pre-nuptial agreement" that had been the subject of negotiations between the parties and their counsel. That on that date he said they should sign the agreement, have blood tests and get married. Parenthetically, it is noted that South Carolina does not require blood tests in order to obtain a marriage license. She testified that they then

went to a Notary Public to get the agreement signed and returned home.
Hurt then spoke to his attorney and after that conversation a fight ensued in which he stated Jennings had tricked him, that the agreement
was not valid because she did not have legal counsel. Jennings then allegedly went into the bedroom and started packing to go home to her
mother, whereupon Hurt, according to Jennings,

> . . . threw my suitcase on the ground and we had a huge fight and he
> ended up telling me that it didn't matter because as far as he was con-
> cerned we were married in the eyes of God and we had a spiritual mar-
> riage and this didn't matter. We were more married than married people.

Jennings' claim to be Hurt's common-law wife is based inter alia, on
these events. . . .

Documents admitted in evidence indicate that shortly after December 23, 1982, Hurt received another draft of an agreement the parties
had been discussing with each other and with counsel; that on December 27, 1982 Hurt's signature was notarized on the document entitled
"Paternity Acknowledgment"; that on December 28, 1982, Jennings' signature was notarized on a sublease for her New York apartment, and
that on December 28, 1982, Jennings spoke with someone at her attorneys' telephone number for 17 minutes.

The Notary Public and attorney whose notary appears on both documents, present recollection of having seen the parties only once and yet
having witnessed Hurt and Jennings' signature on the "prenuptial agreement" is weakened by these facts. Moreover, the undisputed fact that
Hurt signed a paternity acknowledgment on that date is inconsistent
with any immediate intention to marry, but is consistent with Hurt's testimony that though his commitment to his child was unequivocal, he had
deep reservations about his relationship with Jennings.

The only evidence introduced of a holding forth as husband and
wife while the parties were in South Carolina was a conversation with
[some persons] in connection with the parties' renting of accommodations for their stay in South Carolina in which Hurt allegedly referred
to Jennings as his wife and a telephone call by Hurt to Jennings' obstetrician, Dr. Credle's office, in which he asked about his "wife." The conversation with the [lessors] occurred on October 31, 1982 and thus is
irrelevant because it predates the removal of the impediment to marriage. The date of the conversation with Mrs. Credle is unknown but in
any event is of little significance.

It is clear from the testimony of [various persons connected with the
"Big Chill"] that the community with whom the parties socialized knew
Jennings and Hurt were not married. Nor is there a preponderance of
credible evidence that the parties held themselves out as husband and
wife after December 27, 1982. There is no evidence that Jennings filed

tax returns or other forms as married. Significantly, the one document on which Jennings is alleged to have her name "Sandra Cronsberg Hurt" is clearly an altered xerox copy of the original with "Hurt" added afterwards and the document re-xeroxed. Indeed, documents signed by Hurt prior to the commencement of a lawsuit, i.e., will, pension, jury form — all indicated he considered himself single. Hurt's accountant testified that but for one tax return, where by error, the box "married" was checked, all taxes have been filed by Hurt as "single."

The testimony of persons who worked for Jennings for several months, years ago, and who each remember one isolated incident of Hurt referring to Jennings as his "wife" is unbelievable and even if true is barely relevant to prove a holding forth as husband and wife. Scheible, Hurt's employee's testimony is rejected as totally unworthy of belief. She appears as a disgruntled former employee attempting to get even as well as protect her own interests in a lawsuit. . . .

The courts of South Carolina [are] reluctant to declare a common-law marriage unless the proof of such marriage is shown by strong and competent testimony. . . . Jennings's claim that a common-law marriage existed stems, to a large extent, from her present recollection of Hurt's alleged utterance after an argument on December 27, 1983, about seven years ago, that as far as he was concerned they were married in the eyes of God and had a spiritual marriage. To which utterance Jennings says she agreed.

Even were this court to find this testimony credible, the event described by Jennings and the words allegedly spoken do not evince an "intent" to solemnize a marriage but rather the kind of words used by one desiring to continue the parties' present state of living together, i.e., in a relationship short of marriage. . . .

Moreover, where as in this case, the relationship began while one of them was already married, a subsequent divorce does not per se transform this illicit relationship into a common-law marriage. Instead the prior relationship is presumed to continue and the party claiming a common-law marriage must show by a preponderance of the evidence that the relationship underwent some fundamental change following the removal of the impediment. . . .

Accordingly, it would be incumbent on Jennings to show an agreement to enter a common-law marriage after the impediment was removed. . . . The evidence shows a paucity of any "declaration or acknowledgement of the parties" of a marital state. Not one friend of either of the parties testified that the parties held themselves out as married.

Indeed, [a cast member] testified that at his wedding Jennings "wished us luck and that we have a good marriage and expressed the hope that she would be next." This statement belies any change in the relationship of the parties having taken place on December 27 or 28,

1982. It indicates that the prior illicit relationship continued although a hope, at least by one of the parties, to one day marry existed. . . .

. . . For all the foregoing reasons the court finds that Sandra Jennings is not the common-law wife of William Hurt.

## Notes and Questions

1. *Epilogue.* Jennings brought the above action as a prelude to seeking an equitable distribution of Hurt's assets, estimated at between $5 and $7 million. Following their separation, Hurt began paying approximately $60,000 annually in child support. (Jennings had requested $192,000, which was denied in an earlier ruling.) In March 1989 Hurt married bandleader Skitch Henderson's daughter Heidi. Subsequently, an appellate court affirmed the judgment in favor of William Hurt. 554 N.Y.S.2d 220, 221 (App. Div. 1990).

2. *Historical background.* American jurisdictions, which adopted common law marriage, followed early English ecclesiastical law. Following the Norman Conquest, when ecclesiastical authorities regulated marriage in England, the Church recognized two types of informal marriage: (1) the exchange of promises to be husband and wife from the present moment; and (2) the exchange of promises to be husband and wife in the future followed by sexual intercourse. Under the second form, the marriage became valid on subsequent consummation. Such marriages were recognized until the enactment of Lord Hardwicke's Act, 26 Geo. II, c. 33, in 1753, which required formalities of church ceremony, publication of banns, and a license. Subsequently, informal marriages continued to be valid only beyond the statute's jurisdiction in Scotland (hence the importance of the first town across the border, Gretna Green) and Ireland.

Professor Lawrence Friedman explains the history of common law marriage in this country:

> [Common-law marriage had a] more solid basis in the social context: the intellectual climate, and the felt needs of the population. [T]here was a shortage of clergymen of every faith. Most of the population lived outside the cities; and many parts of the country were thinly populated. More important, there were large numbers of ordinary people who owned houses and farms, and who had a stake in the economy, and therefore in the legal system. There were, apparently, couples who lived together after makeshift ceremonies, or no ceremony at all. These couples raised flocks of children. The doctrine of common-law marriage allowed the law to treat these "marriages" as holy and valid.
>
> [Joel] Bishop, a shrewd observer of law and morals, felt that the early settlers were inclined to make a virtue of necessity, or at least come to terms with it. Despite their "pure morals and stern habits," the settlers

could not tolerate a strict adherence to the English marriage laws (or their American imitations), which did not suit American conditions. The stringent marriage laws of Pennsylvania, for example, were "ill adapted to the habits and customs of society;" a "rigid execution of them," remarked Justice John Bannister Gibson in 1833, "would bastardize a vast majority of the children which have been born within the state for half a century." Hence the need for common-law marriage.

The laxity of its form did not escape opposition. Some people denounced it as a "strange and monstrous crossbreed between a concubinage and a marriage." There were other problems, too. An informal marriage was, most likely, also a fairly secret marriage; common-law marriage thus might lead to disputes over property rights, to public scandal, and to the perils of bigamy. . . .

Lawrence M. Friedman, A History of American Law 203-204 (1985). See also Michael Grossberg, Governing the Hearth: Law and the Family in Nineteenth-Century America 69-75 (1985); 2 Frederick Pollock & Frederic William Maitland, The History of English Law Before the Time of Edward I 364-399 (S. F. C. Milson ed., 1968 (1898)); Cynthia Grant Bowman, A Feminist Proposal to Bring Back Common Law Marriage, 75 Or. L. Rev. 709, 718-744 (1996); Ariela R. Dubler, Wifely Behavior: A Legal History of Acting Married, 100 Colum. L. Rev. 957, 957-1010 (2000).

3. *Requirements.* Common law marriage has four elements: capacity to enter a marital contract, present agreement to be married, cohabitation, and holding out to the community as husband and wife. Only 11 states and the District of Columbia currently recognize common law marriage. Dubler, supra, at 1011. Ohio abolished common law marriage in 1991, Oklahoma in 1994, and Georgia in 1996. Bowman, supra, at 715 n.24. Texas continues to recognize the doctrine but has limited its application. See Tex. Fam. Code Ann. §2.401 (West 1998) (requiring a proponent of a common law marriage to file suit to establish the marriage within two years after the parties' separation or else to overcome a rebuttable presumption that no agreement to marry existed).

Did Jennings and Hurt hold themselves out as married? What is the evidence pro and con? The main reason for the requirement of a public reputation as man and wife is to prevent fraud. Although an agreement between the parties is necessary, the agreement may be inferred from cohabitation or other circumstantial evidence. In terms of the standard of proof, South Carolina to the contrary, many states require clear and convincing evidence. Homer H. Clark, Jr., The Law of Domestic Relations in the United States 48 (2d ed. 1988).

*Jennings* also discusses the problem of an impediment: A valid common law marriage cannot come into existence while a prior marriage exists on the part of one spouse. Why? Many jurisdictions require that the parties must renew their "agreement" and meet the other requirements following the removal of the impediment (in Hurt's case, following his divorce). For a discussion of the split of authority on when and how such relationships ripen into valid common law marriages, see Prevatte v. Prevatte, 377 S.E.2d 114, 117 (S.C. 1989).

4. Many cases arise on the dissolution of the relationship, as in *Jennings,* or on death when the survivor attempts to claim inheritance or health insurance benefits, workers' compensation, or social security benefits. See, e.g., In re Landolfi, 724 N.Y.S.2d 470 (App. Div. 2001) (plaintiff filed suit against "husband's" estate claiming common law marriage after 26 years of cohabitation). One problem in attempting to establish a common law marriage after the death of one party is the Dead Man's Act. How is a surviving "spouse" to establish a common law marriage in the face of a statute that precludes testimony concerning communications or transactions with a deceased? See In re Estate of Stauffer, 476 A.2d 354 (Pa. 1984) (widow who claimed spouse's elective share could not testify under exception to Dead Man's Act to establish status as common law spouse).

5. *Choice of law.* Can a couple, domiciliaries in a non-common law jurisdiction, obtain marital status by virtue of residing in another jurisdiction that does recognize common law marriage and then returning to the non-common law state? Why did the New York court look to South Carolina law to determine whether the two New Yorkers had entered a common law marriage, given New York's abolition of common law marriage?

A common misconception is that the parties must cohabit for a specified period of time. How long a stay in the nondomiciliary state is sufficient to confer common law marital status? A few days? Compare In re Estate of Bivans, 652 P.2d 744 (N.M. Ct. App. 1982), *cert. quashed,* 652 P.2d 1213 (N.M. 1982), and Kennedy v. Damron, 268 S.W.2d 22 (Ky. 1954) (both holding that mere visits are not enough), with Madewell v. United States, 84 F. Supp. 329 (E.D. Tenn. 1949) (cohabitation for "number of days and nights" sufficient), and Metropolitan Life Ins. Co. v. Holding, 293 F. Supp. 854 (E.D. Va. 1968) (one year sufficient). Courts are influenced by the equities of the situation.

6. Should common law marriage be revived, as some commentators urge? See Bowman, supra, at 712 n.7 (citing authority); Hon. John B. Crawley, Is the Honeymoon Over for Common-Law Marriage: A Consideration of the Continued Viability of the Common-Law Marriage Doctrine, 29 Cumb. L. Rev. 399 (1998-1999) (arguing that doctrine should be retained). In support of the doctrine, Professor Weyrauch notes that it avoids hardship, protects the poor and the ignorant, benefits some innocent spouses after removal of impediments to a prior formal marriage, and protects children from the stigma of illegitimacy. Walter O. Weyrauch, Informal and Formal Marriage — An Appraisal of the Trend in Family Organization, 28 U. Chi. L. Rev. 88, 101 (1960).

Professor Bowman adds that nonrecognition has a significant negative impact on women, especially those who have been widowed, abandoned, are victims of domestic violence, and are African Americans, Mexican Americans, or Native Americans. Bowman, supra, at 769-770.

The arguments against common law marriage include modern social conditions (urbanization) that have eliminated the need for the doctrine, prevention of fraud in the transmission of property, the desire to protect marriage and the family from immoral sexual unions, confusion of the public records, the difficulty of surmounting problems of proof, eliminating evasion of a jurisdiction's statutory requirements, desire to enforce health-related marital requirements through the licensing process, and administrative and judicial efficiency. See Bowman, supra; Ruth L. Deech, The Case Against Legal Recognition of Cohabitation, 29 Intl. & Comp. L.Q. 480, 484 (1980). Which arguments are more convincing?

In the face of this debate, UMDA takes no position on the validity of common law marriage. The drafters of the act include alternative provisions of §211, preferring to leave the choice to the states. 9A U.L.A. (pt. 1) 195-197 (1998).

7. *Privacy.* To what extent does the constitutional right to privacy limit the state's ability to abolish common law marriage? Does Griswold v. Connecticut, supra Chapter 1, imply a concept of marriage that exists independently of state law? See Ellen Kandoian, Cohabitation, Common Law Marriage, and the Possibility of a Shared Moral Life, 75 Geo. L.J. 1829, 1852-1853 (1987). Does the demise of common law marriage signify a trend toward decreased privatization within the family (i.e., less recognition for private ordering)? See Naomi R. Cahn, Models of Family Privacy, 67 Geo. Wash. L. Rev. 1225, 1228 (1997).

## Problems

1. Sandra, a university student, begins dating baseball player Dave Winfield. The couple spends frequent time in California, New Jersey, and Texas. After Sandra becomes pregnant, they discuss marriage. Dave, concerned about his image as fathering a nonmarital child, tells Sandra he wants a private (just the two of them) ceremony. He instructs Sandra to make a reservation at the Amfac Hotel under the name "Mr. & Mrs. David Winfield." After a three-day stay in the honeymoon suite, Sandra tells her mother she and Dave are married. She rents a condo in Houston for them; the name "Winfield" is on the mailbox. Dave pays for rent, food, furniture, medical, and travel expenses. Pursuant to Dave's instructions, Sandra continues to use her surname and signs the baby's birth certificate with her name.

A neighbor, who gave a party in their honor, is prepared to testify that she thought they were married. Further, when the couple vacations in the Bahamas, a local newspaper describes them as husband and wife, as does an announcer at a softball game. Dave does not ask for retractions. Sandra files income tax returns and health insurance forms as single, per Dave's instructions. She does not wear a wedding ring. While living with Sandra, Dave is dating other women, one of whom he eventually marries. Sandra files for divorce, claiming she is his common law wife. Dave testifies that he never agreed to be married, bought the condo to provide for his child and, further, does not recall staying at the Amfac Hotel. Texas recognizes common law marriage, although California and New Jersey do not. What result? Winfield v. Renfro, 821 S.W.2d 640 (Tex. Ct. App. 1991).

2. Maurice and Ann meet at a restaurant where Anne works as a waitress. Soon thereafter, they move into a home purchased by Maurice and titled in his name. Maurice gives Anne an engagement ring and matching wedding band and asks her to marry him (although the wedding never takes place). Anne wears the engagement ring but not the wedding band because she does not believe that she has the right to do so without a formal ceremony. A sign outside their home reads "Hunsakers, Home of the Classics" (referring to the classic car business they operate together). The telephone answering message states "This is the Hunsaker residence." A grandfather clock, displayed in the living room, has the letters "A," "M," and "H" intertwined. Anne is listed as Maurice's spouse on his insurance policy. They own shares of stock and a time-share condominum as joint tenants. They keep separate bank accounts because Maurice has poor credit; they file income tax returns that list themselves as single. Maurice is listed as Anne's "significant other" on two hospital consent forms that Anne signed. Shortly before his death, Maurice tells his attorney that he wants to leave his entire estate to Anne, whom he refers to as his common law wife. He says that if he does not have a will, his family will "eat [Anne] alive." However, before the will can be drafted, Maurice dies. His surviving sister and brothers claim his estate. Anne claims she was his common law wife based on their ten years' cohabitation. The jurisdiction recognizes common law marriage. What result? In re Estate of Hunsaker, 968 P.2d 281 (Mont. 1998).

*(ii) The Putative Spouse Doctrine and Other
Curative Devices*

Courts and legislatures often strain to recognize marriages that fail to comply with the formal requirements. In so doing, they have developed a variety of curative or mitigative devices — so-called because they cure or mitigate the harsh consequences of invalidity.

The most important of these mitigative devices is the putative spouse doctrine. This doctrine recognizes the marriage of an individual who participated in a marriage ceremony in good faith, in the belief that a valid marriage took place, and in ignorance of an impediment making the marriage void or voidable (for example, a preexisting marriage or a disability such as nonage). Homer H. Clark, Jr., The Law of Domestic Relations in the United States 55 (2d ed. 1988). In some situations, a putative marriage will be recognized even in the absence of a ceremony, as when the state allows common law marriage or when the party asserting the doctrine in good faith believed no ceremony was required. See id. at 55 n.64. On later removal of the impediment, the de facto marriage becomes a valid de jure union. Id. at 55.

Section 209 of UMDA, 9A U.L.A. (pt. 1) 192-194 (1998), takes the following approach:

> Any person who has cohabited with another to whom he is not legally married in the good faith belief that he was married to that person is a putative spouse until knowledge of the fact that he is not legally married terminates his status and prevents acquisition of further rights. A putative spouse acquires the rights conferred upon a legal spouse, including the right to maintenance following termination of his status, whether or not the marriage is prohibited (Section 207) or declared invalid (Section 208). If there is a legal spouse or other putative spouses, rights acquired by a putative spouse do not supersede the rights of the legal spouse or those acquired by other putative spouses, but the court shall apportion property, maintenance, and support rights among the claimants as appropriate in the circumstances and in the interests of justice.

In addition, presumptions can sometimes function as curative devices. Rules of evidence in some states raise a presumption of a valid marriage based on a couple's "holding out" as husband and wife, even if the jurisdiction has abolished common law marriage by statute. See e.g., Thompson v. Thompson, 163 S.W.2d 792 (Mo. Ct. App. 1942). Similarly, some states attach a presumption of validity to the later of two (or the latest in a series of) marriages. Thus, for example, if A, who is already married to B, marries C, this second marriage, although bigamous and void, may be presumed valid. To rely on this presumption, one must introduce evidence that the later marriage occurred, and to rebut it one must show "cogent and conclusive" evidence that the earlier marriage continues. Clark, supra, at 72-73. According to Clark, this presumption rests on policies favoring validation of marriages and "the need to make good the parties' expectations." Id. at 71.

Other courts have developed other equitable remedies that, while not creating valid or even de facto marriages, allow some of the incidents of marriage to follow the nonmarital union. See, e.g., Kasey v. Richardson, 331 F. Supp. 580 (W.D. Va. 1971), aff'd, 462 F.2d 757 (4th Cir. 1972) (children's insurance benefits under Social Security Act). Some courts have created "marriage by estoppel." For example, in Danes v. Smith, 104 A.2d 455 (N.J. Super. Ct. App. Div. 1954), the court estopped a man from questioning the validity of his marriage to a woman whom he knew at the time of the ceremony had a living husband. Finally, in another curative device, some courts hold that a common law marriage, even if null and void, will legitimize any issue. See Murphy v. Holland, 377 S.E.2d 363 (Va. 1989).

To what extent should courts apply any of the above devices in cases in which the parties openly cohabit without any belief or reputation that they were married? To what extent should courts apply these remedies to unions ineligible for marriage, such as lesbian or gay cohabitation? To what extent do these curative and mitigative devices belong at all today?

## Problem

When Dr. Norman J. Lewiston, a renown expert in cystic fibrosis at Stanford University, dies of a heart attack in 1991, three women claim to be his widow. Records reveal that he married Diana Lewiston in 1960 in Connecticut, naming her in a 1966 will as his sole heir. (He suffers his fatal heart attack in the home they share in Palo Alto, California.) They have three children, all now adults. Katy Mayer-Lewiston, who marries him in 1985, attends university events with him. His colleagues believe that she is his wife. The two own a house in a town ten miles away. Robin Phelps of San Diego marries Dr. Lewiston in 1989 during his sabbatical in that city. Believing that he plans to retire soon in San Diego, Robin remains there. See Katherine Bishop, Respected Doctor, Professor and Family Man — 3 Families, in Fact, N.Y. Times, Oct. 23, 1991, at A7. Assume that California's community property law would give half of Dr. Lewiston's property acquired during marriage to the surviving spouse. If all three purported widows seek a share of his estate, to what extent do any of the curative and mitigative devices, discussed above, help resolve their claims? See also In re Estate of Vargas, 111 Cal. Rptr. 779 (Ct. App. 1974).

# III

# Being Married: Regulation of the Intact Marriage

## A. INTRODUCTION: THE CHANGING NATURE OF MARRIAGE

Marriage and the family have evolved over time. Marriage has become more companionate.[1] The family has lost some of its functions.[2] Significantly, these and other changes have contributed to an increase in family privacy[3] — not always with positive consequences. The cases and materials that follow focus on the changing nature of marital rights, roles, and responsibilities.

[1]. See Ernest Watson Burgess & Harvey James Locke, The Family: From Institution to Companionship (1953).

[2]. William Fielding Ogburn & Meyer Francis Nimkoff, Technology and the Changing Family (1955).

[3]. For classic historical studies of family privacy, see Philippe Aries, Centuries of Childhood: A Social History of Family Life (1962); David H. Flaherty, Privacy in Colonial New England (1972); Barbara Laslett, The Family as a Public and Private Institution: An Historical Perspective, 35 J. Marriage & Fam. 480, (August 1973); John Modell & Tamara Hareven, Urbanization and the Malleable Household: An Examination of Boarding and Lodging in American Families, 35 J. Marriage & Fam. 467 (August 1973).

**245**

## ■ MARY BETH NORTON, LIBERTY'S DAUGHTERS: THE REVOLUTIONARY EXPERIENCE OF AMERICAN WOMEN, 1750-1800
*65-68 (1996)*

. . . In order to learn about a female slave's marital life, [it is necessary] to rely on the letters and papers of white planters and overseers.

Plantation records demonstrate that, although most black women married, matrimony was probably not as universal an experience for them as it was for whites. . . . The cause of this phenomenon rested in the slave system itself. Women who lived on isolated small farms and plantations must have found it difficult to locate satisfactory marital partners, for in some regions the black population was thinly scattered. Where most white families owned only one or two slaves — who were purchased for their work skills, not for their compatibility by age or sex to other nearby blacks — the development of long-term marriages would have been difficult indeed. On larger plantations, despite their sizable populations of slaves, heavily imbalanced sex or age ratios could prevent the formation of families, even leaving aside the question of personal preference. What is striking about the evidence from plantation registers, therefore, is the fact that, against all odds, they show the existence of high proportions of marriages. . . .

The problems that could confront black couples parted by divergent ownership can be illustrated by reference to the courtship and marriage of Juliet and Jack, who were Massachusetts residents. In 1769, Jack, who belonged to Elizabeth Murray Smith, began to pay court to Juliet, the property of Christian Barnes and her husband, Henry. By December, Jack had had a pair of earrings made for his loved one, and in February 1770 Mrs. Barnes reported, "I believe they have consented to take each other for Better for worse in their own way." . . . Juliet soon became pregnant. . . . One wonders how Jack and Juliet felt when Mrs. Barnes quickly "disposed of" their daughter by giving her to a woman who lived about three miles away. . . .

Slave women who lived on large plantations . . . could establish more permanent marital relationships than could Juliet and Jack and others similarly separated in both the North and the South. Thomas Jefferson's records make this especially clear. [O]nce marriages were established between men and women on Jefferson's holdings, they persisted until broken by death.

Jefferson recognized the value of having couples thus united under his ownership. The policy not only reduced casual absenteeism, it also prevented the trouble that would ensue if another planter decided to sell the spouse of a particularly valuable slave. As a result, although he grumbled about blacks who "imprudently married out of their respective families," he still indicated his willingness "to indulge connections seriously formed by those people, where it can be done reasonably." He lived up to his words on a number of occasions, buying slaves he did not need or selling those he would have preferred to retain in order to keep husbands and wives together. Jefferson never assigned spouses to different quarters, and he also took special steps to encourage marriages within his plantations. . . . Other planters, though, were not as respectful of black marriages as was Thomas Jefferson. . . .

■ **THEODORE CAPLOW ET AL.,**
**THE QUALITY OF MARRIAGE**
**IN MIDDLETOWN: 1924-1976**
*in Middletown Families: Fifty Years of Change and Continuity*
*116, 117, 118, 120, 121, 124-125, 126, 127, 135 (1982)*

. . . It has been argued that the obsolete traditional family stifles, rather than fosters, the happiness of married people. This chapter will assess the validity of such claims by exploring the quality of Middletown marriages [a fictional name for a midwestern city] in the 1920s, 1930s, and 1970s. . . .

### MARRIAGE IN THE 1920S

[T]he average marriage in the Middletown of the 1920s was a dreary one, especially for the working class. Marriage for many husbands meant weariness from trying to provide for their families, numerous children, and wives weary from doing other people's washing. For many wives, marriage meant poverty, cruelty, adultery, and abandonment. [M]ost families, although less than happy, were held together by community values discouraging divorce. . . . Married life was disappointing, but the prospect of a divorce was even more painful. . . .

Observations of husbands and wives revealed that most of them developed a relationship with limited companionship. In the social and recreational activities of the 1920s, the sexes were separated more often than not. At dinners, parties, and other social gatherings, men and women seemed to form separate groups so that the men could talk about business, sports and politics and the women could discuss children, dress styles, and local gossip. Men's leisure activities generally excluded women. Business-class husbands played golf or cards at their clubs without their wives. . . . The one recreational activity that husbands and wives shared was card playing with friends in their homes. . . . The limited communication between husbands and wives and the trivial nature of their conversation left many of them isolated in their separate worlds, his pertaining to work and friends and hers to the children and the home.

In many marriages, they shared a house, each other's bodies, and little else.

. . . Lack of information about birth control and the prejudice against its use made babies the inevitable consequence of physical intimacy for most working-class couples. The uncertainty of employment often made another child an unwanted burden. The conflict between not wanting more children and needing the physical pleasures of marriage, and the resulting stress placed on the marriage, were evident. [C]omments provide considerable insight into Middletown's working-class marriages of the 1920s. The fact that a wife might not dare ask her husband what he thought about birth control, let alone what he felt about practicing it, shows how shallow some of the relationships were. . . .

### Marriage in the 1930s

The Great Depression was thought by Middletown people to have mixed effects on marital happiness. On the one hand, they spoke of how married couples spent more time together and became more dependent on each other, and this enforced togetherness was perceived as strengthening the quality of Middletown's marriages. [T]he Depression did increase the amount of time husbands and wives spent together by making outside activities unaffordable. [On the other hand,] [a]lthough couples spent more time together, they often reacted to economic pressures by mutual recrimination. The wives were quick to reproach their husbands for failing to provide for the family's needs, and the husbands were equally quick to defend their wounded egos by lashing out at wives and children. Despite these mounting tensions, the typical marital relationship during the depression was similar to that of the 1920s. . . .

### Marriage in the 1970s . . .

[We] have witnessed a major change in the style of communication between husbands and wives. [Women have been encouraged to assert their needs and preferences.] Marriage-enrichment programs . . . have purported to teach thousands of American couples how to communicate with each other more effectively. The women's rights movement [has] fostered a more equal marriage relationship in which the needs and wishes of the wife are considered to be at least as important as those of the husband.

It is difficult to imagine many contemporary wives who would be afraid to discuss birth control with their husbands, particularly after the couple has had several children. The taboo on discussing financial matters observed in the 1920s has almost disappeared, and today nearly all wives play an active role in the management of family finances, especially when they work and contribute to the family income. . . .

Not only are contemporary husbands and wives talking to each other, they are engaging in a great deal of leisure activity together. Shopping; eating out; going for drives and to movies, sporting events, fairs, and musical presentations; and taking part in physical fitness activities are frequently shared by husbands and wives. . . . In contemporary American society, television has become an integral part of daily life, a source of news as well as of recreation. . . .

There is additional evidence suggesting that the quality of the average marital relationship has improved over the past 50 years — the number of wives who mentioned their husbands as a source of strength during difficult times. [W]hen a 1924 sample of Middletown housewives was asked the question "What are the thoughts and plans that give you courage to go on when thoroughly discouraged?" not a single wife mentioned her husband as a source of reassurance. . . . The data suggest again that the marital relationship has deepened since the 1920s and that husbands and wives share each other's burdens and provide emotional support to a greater degree now than then. . . .

All things considered, the quality of marriage seems to have improved substantially in Middletown during the past half a century. Such dismal marriages as the Lynds [the researchers] described as typical in the 1920s are now relatively rare. The overwhelming majority of contemporary husbands and wives say that their marriages are happy and fulfilling.

We do not mean to imply that all marriages in Middletown are happy. The data indicate that most are, but the divorce rate is a reminder that many unhappy marriages occur. Indeed, the high divorce rate is one important reason why contemporary marriages are so happy; most of the unhappy ones have been terminated. . . .

---

For recent studies of the history of marriage, see Nancy F. Cott, Public Vows: A Political History of Marriage in the United States (2000); Hendrik Hartog, Man and Wife in America: A History (2000); Marilyn Yalom, A History of the Wife (2001).

■ **ADRIENNE RICH, COMPULSORY HETEROSEXUALITY AND LESBIAN EXISTENCE**
*in Blood, Bread, and Poetry: Selected Prose 1979-1985*
*23, 27, 50-51, 59-60, 63-64, 67 (1986)*

. . . A feminist critique of compulsory heterosexual orientation for women is long overdue. . . . The assumption that "most women are innately heterosexual" stands as a theoretical and political stumbling block for feminism. It remains a tenable assumption partly because lesbian existence has been written out of history or catalogued under disease, partly because it has been treated as exceptional rather than intrinsic, partly because to acknowledge that for women heterosexuality may not be a "preference" at all but something that has had to be imposed, managed, organized, propagandized, and maintained by force is an immense step to take if you consider yourself freely and "innately" heterosexual. Yet the failure to examine heterosexuality as an institution is like failing to admit that the economic system called capitalism or the caste system of racism is maintained by a variety of forces, including both physical violence and false consciousness. To take the step of questioning heterosexuality as a "preference" or "choice" for women — and to do the intellectual and emotional work that follows — will call for a special quality of courage in heterosexually identified feminists. . . .

. . . Women have married because it was necessary, in order to survive economically, in order to have children who would not suffer economic deprivation or social ostracism, in order to remain respectable, in order to do what was expected of women, because coming out of "abnormal" childhoods they wanted to feel "normal" and because heterosexual romance has been represented as the great female adventure, duty, and fulfillment. . . .

[This] apparent acquiescence to an institution founded on male interest and prerogative . . . has been characteristic of female experience. . . . The denial of reality and visibility to women's passion for women, women's choice of women as allies, life companions, and community, the forcing of such relationships into dissimulation and their disintegration under intense pressure have meant an incalculable loss to the power of all women *to change the social relations of the sexes, to liberate ourselves and each other.* The lie of compulsory female heterosexuality today afflicts not just feminist scholarship [but also] every relationship or conversation over which it hovers. . . .

The lie is many-layered. In Western tradition, one layer — the romantic — asserts that women are inevitably, even if rashly and tragically, drawn to men. [It is] an organic imperative. In the tradition of the social sciences it asserts that primary love between the sexes is "normal," that women *need* men as social and economic protectors, for adult sexuality, and for psychological completion; that the heterosexually constituted family is the basic social unit; that women who do not attach their primary intensity to men must be, in functional terms, condemned to an even more devastating outsiderhood than their outsiderhood as women. . . .

The question inevitably will arise: Are we then to condemn all heterosexual relationships, including those which are least oppressive? I believe this question, though often heartfelt, is the wrong question here. We have been stalled in a maze of false dichotomies that prevents our apprehending the institution as a whole: "good" versus "bad" marriages. . . . Within the institution exist, of course, qualitative differences of experience; but the absence of choice remains the great unacknowledged reality, and in the absence of choice, women will remain dependent upon the chance or luck of particular relationships and will have no collective power to determine the meaning and place of sexuality in their lives. . . .

■ **JESSIE BERNARD, THE FUTURE OF MARRIAGE**
*16-18, 26-28, 40-41, 49-50 (1982)*

There are few findings more consistent, less equivocal, more convincing than the sometimes spectacular and always impressive superiority on almost every index — demographic, psychological, or social — of married over never-married men. Despite all the jokes about marriage in which men indulge, all the complaints they lodge against it, it is one of the greatest boons of their sex. Employers, bankers, and insurance companies have long since known this. And whether they know it or not, men need marriage more than women do. As Samuel Johnson said, marriage is, indeed "the best state for man in general; and every man is a worse man in proportion as he is unfit for the married state."

The research evidence is overwhelmingly convincing. Although the physical health of married men is no better than that of never-married men until middle age, their mental health is far better, fewer show serious symptoms of psychological distress, and fewer of them suffer mental health impairments. [Research has] shown that marriage is an asset in a man's career, including his earning power. The value of marriage for sheer male survival is itself remarkable. It does, indeed, pay men to be married. . . . Men . . . profit greatly from having a wife to help them to take care of their health. . . . In the United States, the suicide rate for single men is almost twice as high as for married men. . . .

The actions of men with respect to marriage speak far louder than words; they speak, in fact, with a deafening roar. Once men have known marriage, they can hardly live without it. Most divorced and widowed men remarry. At every age, the marriage rate for both divorced and widowed men is higher than the rate for single men. Half of all divorced white men who remarry do so within three years after divorce. Indeed, it might not be farfetched to conclude that the verbal assaults on marriage indulged in by men are a kind of compensatory reaction to their dependence on it. . . .

[I]t is hard for us to see how different the wife's marriage really is from the husband's, and how much worse. But, in fact, it is. There is a very considerable research literature reaching back over a generation which shows that: more wives than husbands report marital frustration and dissatisfaction; more report negative feelings; more wives than husbands report marital problems; more wives than husbands consider their marriages unhappy, have considered separation or divorce, have regretted their marriages; and fewer report positive companionship. [Yet it is not] the complaints of wives that demonstrate how bad the wife's marriage is, but rather the poor mental and emotional health of married women as compared not only to married men's but also to unmarried women's.

Although the physical health of married women, as measured by absence of chronic conditions or restricted activity, is as good as, and in the ages beyond sixty-five even better than, that of married men, they suffer far greater mental-health hazards and present a far worse clinical picture. [Research has] found that more married women than married men have felt they were about to have a nervous breakdown; more experience psychological and physical anxiety; more have feelings of inadequacy in their marriages and blame themselves for their own lack of general adjustment. Other studies report that more married women than married men show phobic reactions, depression, and passivity; greater than expected frequency of symptoms of psychological distress; and mental-health impairment. . . .

[W]ives make more of the adjustments called for in marriage than do husbands. . . . One of the most poignant adjustments that wives have to make is in the pattern of emotional expression between themselves and their husbands. Almost invariably, they mind the letdown in emotional expression that comes when the husband's job takes more out of him, or the original warmth subsides. Lee Rainwater found in marriages between men and women in the lower-lower classes that wives tended to adopt their husbands' taciturnity and lack of demonstrativeness rather than insist on winning him over to theirs. . . . The psychological and emotional costs of all these adjustments show up in the increasing unhappiness of wives with the passage of time and in their increasingly negative and passive outlook on life. One measure of these costs can be found in the increasing rate of alcoholism with time. . . .

The problem is not why do young women marry, but why, in the face of all the evidence, do more married than unmarried women report themselves as happy? [One way] to look at the seeming anomaly involved here . . . is that happiness is interpreted in terms of conformity. Wives may, in effect, be judging themselves happy by definition. They are conforming to expectations and are therefore less vulnerable to the strains accompanying nonconformity. The pressures to conform are so great that few young women can resist them. Better, as the radical women put it, dead than unwed. Those who do not marry are made to feel inferior, failures. [S]tereotypes of . . . unmarried women [include] the conventional image of a frustrated, repressed, purse-lipped, unnatural being. . . . Escape from being "an old maid" is one definition of happiness.

Such conformity to the norm of marriage does not have to be imposed from the outside. Women have internalized the norms prescribing marriage so completely that the role of wife seems the only acceptable one. And since marriage is set up as the *summum bonum* of life for women, they interpret their achievement of marriage as happiness, no matter how unhappy the marriage itself may be. They have been told that their happiness depends on marriage, so, even if they are miserable, they *are* married, aren't they? . . .

_____

To what extent do you think Jessie Bernard's findings are still true today?

## B.  ROLES AND RESPONSIBILITIES IN MARRIAGE

### 1. *The Common Law View*

#### ■ 1 WILLIAM BLACKSTONE, COMMENTARIES
*\*442-445*

By marriage, the husband and wife are one person in law: that is, the very being or legal existence of the woman is suspended during the marriage, or at least is incorporated and consolidated into that of the husband: under whose wing, protection, and *cover,* she performs everything; and is therefore called in our law-french a *feme-covert;* is said to be *covert-baron,* or under the protection and influence of her husband, her baron, or lord; and her condition during her marriage is called her *coverture.* Upon this principle, of a union of person in husband and wife, depend almost all the legal rights, duties, and disabilities, that either of them acquire by the marriage. . . . For this reason, a man cannot grant anything to his wife, or enter into covenant with her: for the grant would be to suppose her separate existence; and to covenant with her, would be only to covenant with himself: and therefore it is also generally true, that all compacts made between husband and wife, when single, are voided by the intermarriage. . . . The husband is bound to provide his wife with necessities by law, [and] if she contracts debts for them, he is obliged to pay them: but for anything besides necessaries, he is not chargeable. . . . If the wife be indebted before marriage, the husband is bound afterwards to pay the debt; for he has adopted her and her circumstances together. If the wife be injured in her person or her property, she can bring no action for redress without her husband's concurrence, and in his name, as well as her own: neither can she sue or be sued, without making the husband a defendant. . . . In criminal prosecutions, it is true, the wife may be indicted and punished separately; for the union is only a civil union. But, in trials of any sort, they are not allowed to be evidence for, or against, each other: partly because it is impossible their testimony should be indifferent; but principally because of the union of person: and therefore, if they were admitted to be witnesses for each other, they would contradict one maxim of law, ["One ought not be a witness in his own cause"]; and if against each other, they would contradict another maxim, ["No one is bound to accuse himself "]. . . .

But, though our law in general considers man and wife as one person, yet there are some instances in which she is separately considered; as inferior to him, and acting by his compulsion. And therefore all deeds executed, and acts done, by her, during her coverture, are void, or at least voidable; except it be a fine, or the like matter of record, in which case she must be solely and secretly examined, to learn if her act be voluntary. She cannot by will devise lands to her husband, [because] she is supposed to be under his coercion. And in some felonies, and other inferior crimes, committed by her, through constraint of her husband, the law excuses her: but this extends not to treason or murder.

The husband also (by the old law) might give his wife moderate correction. For, as he is to answer for her misbehavior, the law thought it reasonable to entrust him with this power of restraining her, by domestic chastisement, in the same moderation that a man is allowed to correct his servants or children; for whom the master or parent is also liable in some cases to answer. But this power of correction was confined within reasonable bounds; and the husband was prohibited to use any violence to his wife [other than what is reasonably necessary to the discipline and correction of the wife]. . . .

These are the chief legal effects of marriage during the coverture; upon which we may observe, that even the disabilities, which the wife lies under, are for the most part intended for her protection and benefit. So great a favorite is the female sex of the laws of England.[4]

---

[4]. For a famous critique of Blackstone's views and scholarship, see Mary Beard, Woman as Force in History: A Study in Tradition and Realities (1946). See also Berenice Carroll, On Mary Beard's Woman as Force in History: A Critique, in Liberating Women's History 26 (Berenice Carroll ed., 1976).

## 2. *Marital Property Regimes*

### a. Introduction

The state, through its treatment of marital property, regulates certain rights of the spouses upon marriage. According to historian Sir William Holdsworth:

> No legal system which deals merely with human rules of conduct desires to pry too closely into the relationship of husband and wife. Dealings between husband and wife are for the most part privileged. But some rules it must have to regulate the proprietary relationships of the parties. . . .[5]

Two marital property regimes exist in the United States: (1) the common law approach and (2) the community property approach. Each reflects a different philosophy. In the common law system, followed by most jurisdictions, the husband and wife own all property separately. During marriage, property belongs to the spouse who acquired it (traditionally, the wage-earning husband) unless he chooses another form of ownership.

On the other hand, in the community property system, the husband and wife own some property jointly. "Equality is the cardinal precept of the community property system."[6] The community property system is characterized by the concept of a community of ownership under which the spouses are partners. Each spouse has a present, undivided, one-half interest in all property acquired by the efforts of either spouse during marriage. Unlike the common law system, community property recognizes the contributions, for example, of the homemaker spouse. Moreover, the community property system respects each spouse's separate property. Property that each brought to the marriage remains the property of that spouse. Property acquired by a spouse during the marriage by means of gift or inheritance also constitutes separate property.[7] The community property system is in effect in nine states.[8]

[5]. 3 W. S. Holdsworth, A History of English Law 404 (2d ed. 1909). The law of husband and wife was referred to, historically, as the law of "baron et feme." 2 Frederick Pollock & Frederic William Maitland, The History of English Law Before the Time of Edward I 406 (S. F. C. Milsom ed., 1968) (1898).

[6]. William Q. deFuniak & Michael J. Vaughn, Principles of Community Property §1 (2d ed. 1971).

[7]. Note, however, that some states' equitable distribution schemes take separate property into account in awarding the marital property. See Chapter 6, section B.

[8]. Five American states (Arizona, California, Louisiana, New Mexico, and Texas) adopted the community property system because of Spanish, Mexican, or French heritage. The four remaining states (Idaho, Nevada, Washington, and Wisconsin) had different reasons. Wisconsin, the most recent convert, was influenced by the divorce reform movement and the Uniform Marital Property Act (UMPA), 9A U.L.A. (pt. 1) 97 (1983). See Howard S. Erlanger & June M. Weisberger, From Common Law Property to Community Property: Wisconsin's Marital Property Act Four Years Later, 1990 Wis. L. Rev. 769, 770 n.5. For historical background, see W. S. McClanahan, Community Property Law in the United States ch. 3 (1982 & Cum. Supp. 1991).

In the Middle Ages the division between the two marital property systems was not clear-cut. Thirteenth-century England adopted a separate property system; France took another path more beneficial to married women.[9] This divergence is all the more remarkable given the countries' many similarities: agrarian, feudal societies, whose clerical and lay elite shared a common language and culture.[10]

### b. Common Law Disabilities

The common law and community property systems reflect fundamental differences concerning the position of married women. Until the mid-nineteenth century, Blackstone's famous quotation on coverture, supra, described the status of married women at common law. The common law imposed on a married woman many disabilities, summarized as follows.[11]

(1) *Wife's Real Property.* The husband acquired an estate in the wife's real property for the duration of the marriage. In the process, the wife lost all power over her real property during the marriage. The husband's interest, termed *jure uxoris,* entitled him to sole possession and control of any real property that the wife owned in fee — whether acquired by her before or after the marriage. If a child was born of the marriage, the husband's rights became a life estate.

Further, the husband could alienate the wife's real property without her consent. She had no similar power. The means of conveyance of real property was the "fine," by which both husband and wife joined in a fictitious lawsuit. A judge secured testimony (in private) of a wife to substantiate the absence of a husband's coercion in her execution of the deed.[12]

(2) *Dower.* During marriage the wife's primary protection from her husband's conveyances consisted of her right of dower — her life estate of one-third of any land of which the husband was seised in fee at any

[9]. Pollock & Maitland, supra note [5], at 405, 407; Charles Donahue, Jr., What Causes Fundamental Legal Ideas? Marital Property in England and France in the Thirteenth Century, 78 Mich. L. Rev. 59, 61 (1979).

[10]. Donahue, supra note [9], at 61. Donahue sums up the different property systems thus: "the English system seems to have favored the individual [by unifying control in one person so as to pass it intact to the next generation] and suppressed the wife's interest in the process, while the French favored the lineage and enhanced the wife's interest as a result." Id. at 81. Scholars debate the reasons England chose a different property system than France. See Holdsworth, supra note [5], at 408; Pollock & Maitland, supra note [5], at 402 (pointing to the royal courts' surrender of jurisdiction over succession to personal property to the ecclesiastical courts, and upper-class influences). But cf. Donahue, supra note [9], at 83-87 (arguing instead that the family and community were stronger in France than in England, whereas the English monarchy was more powerful than the French).

[11]. Pollock & Maitland, supra note [5], at 403-405.

[12]. Mary Lynn Salmon, Women and the Law of Property in Early America 17 (1986). See also Pollock & Maitland, supra note [5], at 404.

time during the marriage.[13] The husband could not bar her dower right without her consent. She came into enjoyment of her life estate upon surviving her husband.

(3) *Wife's Personal Property.* The wife, similarly, had no right to possess personal property. Whatever personal property she owned before marriage, or might acquire thereafter, became her husband's. She also lacked a right of testamentary disposition over any property.[14]

(4) *Wife's Lack of Rights to Husband's Personal Property.* During the marriage, the husband had the power of disposition (inter vivos or by will) over his personal property. Similarly, all his personal property (including what we might think of as the wife's property) was subject to his creditors. The only exception was the wife's necessary clothes. The husband even could sell or give away his wife's jewels, trinkets, or ornaments (termed her "paraphernalia") during his lifetime.

(5) *Husband's Liability.* The husband was liable for the wife's premarital debts, as well as for torts she committed before or during the marriage.

(6) *Wife's Contracts.* During the marriage the wife could not enter into contracts except as her husband's agent.[15]

Some New England colonies treated married women even more harshly than England. A few colonies, for example, gave male heads of household considerably more control over family property.[16] This harsh treatment of married women was mitigated somewhat by equitable jurisdiction over women's separate estate. However, the majority of women could not take advantage of such equitable reforms.[17]

[13]. Dower, not to be confused with dowry, is an inchoate property interest of a married woman that comes into beneficial enjoyment upon widowhood. Dowry refers to goods with which some women, historically, were endowed in anticipation of marriage.

[14]. As Holdsworth points out: "The logical consequence of the views of the common lawyers was the denial to married women of all testamentary capacity, for it is useless to say that a person may make a will if she has nothing to leave." Holdsworth, supra note [5], at 425-426.

[15]. Peggy Rabkin points out these disabilities evolved from a feudal society based on land tenure. "The irrationality of the common law status of married women became increasingly clear as the economy became more commercial." Peggy A. Rabkin, The Origins of Law Reform: The Social Significance of the Nineteenth-Century Codification Movement and Its Contribution to the Passage of the Early Married Women's Property Acts, 24 Buff. L. Rev. 683, 689 (1975). See also Peggy A. Rabkin, Fathers to Daughters: The Legal Foundations of Female Emancipation (1980).

[16]. Salmon, supra note [12], at 6. For example, Massachusetts, Pennsylvania, and New York dispensed with the need for the wife's private examination upon conveyance of real property. Id. at 22. Salmon attributes this reform not to a desire to deny women property rights, but rather to simplify English marital property law to achieve more efficient land management. Id. at 6, 22.

[17]. Id. at 81. A premarital trust placed funds in the control of a trustee who owed a fiduciary duty (enforceable by the chancery court) to the wife as beneficiary. Most women did not have sufficient property to take advantage of this loophole. In addition, the subsequent abolition of chancery court jurisdiction in several colonies (e.g., Connecticut, Massachusetts, and Pennsylvania) eliminated this means of protection for married women. Id. at 81-82.

The legal status of married women changed little until the mid- to late nineteenth century when many states passed "married women's property acts." This legislation enabled women to own property that they brought to the marriage or acquired thereafter by gift or inheritance. The movement began in Mississippi in 1839 with a statute stipulating that the wife could continue to possess slaves she owned prior to marriage or thereafter acquired (although the husband continued to manage them and reap the profits of their labor).[18] New York legislation, the most progressive, enabled married women to sue and to retain their own earnings.[19] By 1865, 29 states had married women's property acts.[20]

Historians point to several contributing factors to legislative reform:[21]

(1) economic antebellum problems contributing to a desire to protect family property by exempting women's property from attachment by husbands' creditors; (2) the codification/law reform; and (3) a desire to improve women's status. Although historians disagree on the primacy of each factor, most concur that the legislation constituted a significant liberalization in the rules to which married women had been subject for centuries.[22]

### c. Managerial Rules

The husband as master of the household was an entrenched common law principle. Paradoxically, the community property system also reflected this rule because statutes placed management of community property in the husband's hands.[23] Limited exceptions to male management and control did exist. For example, in many community property states, the wife retained management and control of her earnings.

---

[18]. Norma Basch, In the Eyes of the Law: Women, Marriage and Property in Nineteenth-Century New York 27 (1982). Scholars disagree about the first legislation. See Richard H. Chused, Married Women's Property Law: 1800-1850, 71 Geo. L.J. 1359, 1361 n.3, 1398 n.200 (1983) (suggesting Arkansas and Florida predated Mississippi).

[19]. Basch, supra note [18], at 28.

[20]. Id.

[21]. See, e.g., Lawrence M. Friedman, A History of American Law 208-211 (2d ed. 1985); Linda Speth, The Married Women's Property Acts, 1839-1865: Reform, Reaction or Revolution?, in 2 Women and the Law: The Social Historical Perspective 69 (D. Kelly Weisberg ed., 1982); Joan Hoff Wilson, Hidden Riches: Legal Records and Women, 1750-1825, in Woman's Being, Woman's Place: Female Identity and Vocation in American History (Mary Kelley ed., 1979); Chused, supra note [18]; Rabkin, Origins of Law Reform, supra note [15].

[22]. Buf cf. Lawrence M. Friedman, Law Reform in Historical Perspective, 13 St. Louis U. L.J. 351, 362-363 (1969) (arguing that the legislation worked no significant liberalization because practice had already departed from the common law).

[23]. DeFuniak & Vaughn, supra note [6], at §113. The concept of management and control must be distinguished from ownership. Thus, one spouse may own property that is subject to another spouse's right to management and control of that property. Ownership rights in that property are not relinquished, however, by another spouse's management and control.

And the joinder requirement for the conveyance or encumbrance of community real property gave the wife some control.[24] The Supreme Court marked the end of such gender-based rules in Kirchberg v. Feenstra, 450 U.S. 455 (1981), which invalidated, on equal protection grounds, a Louisiana statute designating the husband "head and master" of the community.

Three different, facially gender-neutral rules emerged in response to the unconstitutionality of male managerial rules: (1) extension of the separate property philosophy to link management to the source of earnings; (2) joint control (requiring the consent of both spouses for community property transactions); and (3) equal control (either may manage community property regardless of the source of earnings or without securing the other's consent).[25] Most community property jurisdictions follow the last approach.

Reforms have narrowed the gap between the common law and community property systems. Most common law states have adopted an equitable distribution approach upon divorce (discussed in Chapter 6). Equitable distribution, which attempts to divide marital property in a fair or equitable manner based on a number of factors, has presaged more equal treatment of women.

Another significant modern development, the Uniform Marital Property Act (UMPA) §5, 9A U.L.A. (pt. 1) 114 (1987), imposes a sharing rule from the beginning of the marriage. Under UMPA, absent an agreement, a spouse acting alone can manage and control marital property held in that spouse's name alone, that not held in the name of either spouse, and that held in the name of both spouses in the alternative. Spouses must act together with respect to marital property otherwise held in name of both.

## 3. Duty of Support

### ■ McGUIRE v. McGUIRE
*59 N.W.2d 336 (Neb. 1953)*

MESSMORE, Justice.

The plaintiff, Lydia McGuire, brought this action . . . against Charles W. McGuire, her husband . . . to recover suitable maintenance and support money. [A] decree was rendered in favor of the plaintiff.

[24]. Id. at §115.1.

[25]. Susan Westerberg Prager, The Persistence of Separate Property Concepts in California's Community Property System, 1849-1975, 24 UCLA L. Rev. 1, 70-71 (1976). Despite its facial neutrality, the rule of equal management has been criticized for its gender-based application. See, e.g., Susan Kalinka, Taxation of Community Income, It Is Time for Congress to Override *Poe v. Seaborn*, 58 La. L. Rev. 73, 85 (1997) (pointing out that, in reality, "equal management statutes generally give management and control over community income to the spouse who earns it").

The record shows that the plaintiff and defendant were married in Wayne, Nebraska, on August 11, 1919. At the time of the marriage the defendant was a bachelor 46 or 47 years of age and had a reputation for more than ordinary frugality, of which the plaintiff was aware. She had visited in his home and had known him for about 3 years prior to the marriage. [P]laintiff had been previously married. Her first husband . . . died intestate, leaving 80 acres of land in Dixon County. The plaintiff and each of [their two] daughters inherited a one-third interest therein. At the time of the marriage of the plaintiff and defendant the plaintiff's daughters were 9 and 11 years of age. By working and receiving financial assistance from the parties to this action, the daughters received a high school education in Pender. One daughter attended Wayne State Teachers College for 2 years and the other daughter attended a business college in Sioux City, Iowa, for 1 year. [Both] are married and have families of their own. . . .

At the time of trial plaintiff was 66 years of age and the defendant nearly 80 years of age. No children were born to these parties. . . .

The plaintiff testified that she was a dutiful and obedient wife, worked and saved, and cohabited with the defendant until the last 2 or 3 years. She worked in the fields, did outside chores, cooked, and attended to her household duties such as cleaning the house and doing the washing. For a number of years she raised as high as 300 chickens, sold poultry and eggs, and used the money to buy clothing, things she wanted, and for groceries. She further testified that the defendant was the boss of the house and his word was law; that he would not tolerate any charge accounts and would not inform her as to his finances or business; and that he was a poor companion. . . . On several occasions the plaintiff asked the defendant for money. He would give her very small amounts, and for the last 3 or 4 years he had not given her any money nor provided her with clothing, except a coat about 4 years previous. . . . The defendant had not taken her to a motion picture show during the past 12 years. They did not belong to any organizations or charitable institutions, nor did he give her money to make contributions to any charitable institutions. . . . For the past 4 years or more, the defendant had not given the plaintiff money to purchase furniture or other household necessities. Three years ago he did purchase an electric, wood-and-cob combination stove which was installed in the kitchen, also linoleum floor covering for the kitchen. [T]he house is not equipped with a bathroom, bathing facilities, or inside toilet [or kitchen sink]. Hard and soft water is obtained from a well and cistern. She has a mechanical Servel refrigerator, and the house is equipped with electricity. . . . She had requested a new furnace but the defendant believed the one they had to be satisfactory. She related that the furniture was old and she would like to replenish it, at least to be comparable with some of her neighbors; . . . that one of her daughters was good about furnishing her clothing, at least a dress a year, or sometimes two; that the defendant owns a 1929 Ford coupe equipped with a heater which is not efficient, and on the average of every 2 weeks he drives the plaintiff to Wayne to visit her mother; and that he also owns a 1927 Chevrolet pickup which is used for different purposes on the farm. The plaintiff was privileged to use all of the rent money she wanted to from the 80-acre farm, and when she goes to see her daughters, which is not frequent, she uses part of the rent money for that purpose, the defendant providing no funds for such use. . . . At the present time the plaintiff is not able to raise chickens and sell eggs. [P]laintiff has had three abdominal operations for which the defendant has paid. [P]laintiff further testified that . . . use of the telephone was restricted, indicating that defendant did not desire that she make long distance calls. . . .

It appears that the defendant owns 398 acres of land with 2 acres deeded to a church, the land being of the value of $83,960; that he has bank deposits in the sum of $12,786.81 and government bonds in the amount of $104,500; and that his income, including interest on the bonds and rental for his real estate, is $8,000 or $9,000 a year. . . .

[Defendant appeals, alleging that the decree is not supported by sufficient evidence, and is contrary to law.] The plaintiff relies upon the following cases. [In] Earle v. Earle, 27 Neb. 277, 43 N.W. 118 [(1889)], the plaintiff's petition alleged, in substance, the marriage of the parties, that one child was born of the marriage, and that the defendant sent his wife away from him, did not permit her to return, contributed to her support and maintenance separate and apart from him, and later refused and ceased to provide for her support and the support of his child. The wife instituted a suit in equity against her husband for maintenance and support without a prayer for divorce or from bed and board. The question presented was whether or not the wife should be compelled to resort to a proceedings for a divorce, which she did not desire to do, or from bed and board. On this question, in this state the statutes are substantially silent and at the present time there is no statute governing this matter. The court stated that it was a well-established rule of law that it is the duty of the husband to provide his family with support and means of living — the style of support, requisite lodging, food, clothing, etc., to be such as fit his means, position, and station in life — and for this purpose the wife has generally the right to use his credit for the purchase of necessaries. The court held that if a wife is abandoned by her husband, without means of support, a bill in equity will lie to compel the husband to support the wife without asking for a decree of divorce. . . .

In the case of Brewer v. Brewer, 79 Neb. 726, 113 N.W. 161 [(1907)], the plaintiff lived with her husband and his mother. The mother dominated the household. The plaintiff went to her mother. She stated she would live in the same house with her husband and his mother if she could have control of her part of the house. The defendant did not offer to accede to these conditions. The court held that a wife may bring a suit in equity to secure support and alimony without reference to whether the action is for divorce or not; that every wife is entitled to a home corresponding to the circumstances and condition of her husband over which she may be permitted to preside as mistress; and that she does not forfeit her right to maintenance by refusing to live under the control of the husband's mother. . . .

In the instant case the marital relation has continued for more than 33 years, and the wife has been supported in the same manner during this time without complaint on her part. The parties have not been separated or living apart from each other at any time. In the light of the cited cases it is clear, especially so in this jurisdiction, that to maintain an action such as the one at bar, the parties must be separated or living apart from each other.

The living standards of a family are a matter of concern to the household, and not for the courts to determine, even though the husband's attitude toward his wife, according to his wealth and circumstances, leaves little to be said in his behalf. As long as the home is maintained and the parties are living as husband and wife it may be said that the husband is legally supporting his wife and the purpose of the marriage relation is being carried out. Public policy requires such a holding. It appears that the plaintiff is not devoid of money in her own right. She has a fairsized bank account and is entitled to use the rent from the 80 acres of land left by her first husband, if she so chooses. . . . Reversed and remanded with directions to dismiss.

## Notes and Questions

1. *McGuire* illustrates two doctrines. First, *McGuire* reflects the common law duty of support. At common law, a husband had a duty to provide support to his wife; the wife had a correlative duty to render domestic services. Second, the common law *doctrine of nonintervention* specifies that the state rarely will adjudicate spousal responsibilities in an ongoing marriage. Thus, marital support obligations are enforceable only *after* separation or divorce. This principle of family privacy stems from judicial reluctance to disrupt marital harmony or to interfere with the husband's authority. Was there any marital harmony in the McGuire's marriage to disrupt? Should stereotypical rationale trump spousal welfare?

2. The common law *doctrine of necessaries* was the basis of the lower court opinion in Mrs. McGuire's favor. This doctrine imposed liability on a husband to a merchant who supplied necessary goods to a wife. "Necessaries" generally include food, clothing, shelter, and medical care. Many American jurisdictions codified the common law duty of support

of dependents via so-called family expense statutes, which render both spouses liable for the support of family members. Such statutes are broader than the common law doctrine (that is, applying to "family expenses" rather than merely "necessaries").

3. Why should the state permit a creditor, but not a spouse, a remedy for support? Professor Shultz argues that "the presence of third party interests, even though minimal compared to the spouses' duties to one another, has been viewed as sufficient to allow disruption of the domestic harmony that could not be disturbed for the sake of resolving the spouses' own problems." Marjorie Maguire Shultz, Contractual Ordering of Marriage: A New Model for State Policy, 70 Cal. L. Rev. 207, 238 (1982). Further, Shultz points out, the necessaries doctrine encourages dealings with a creditor behind the back of the other spouse. Does this approach promote marital harmony?

4. Feminist commentators have been especially critical of the doctrine of nonintervention. Professors Nadine Taub and Elizabeth Schneider note:

> The state's failure to regulate the domestic sphere is now often justified on the ground that the law should not interfere with emotional relationships involved in the family realm because it is too heavy-handed. Indeed, the recognition of a familial privacy right in the early twentieth century [Meyer v. Nebraska, 262 U.S. 390 (1923); Pierce v. Society of Sisters, 268 U.S. 510 (1925)] has given this rationale a constitutional dimension. The importance of this concern, however, is undercut by the fact that the same result was previously justified by legal fictions, such as the woman's civil death on marriage. [T]he argument reflects and reinforces powerful myths about the nature of family relations. It is not true that women perform personal and household services purely for love. The family is the locus of fundamental economic exchanges, as well as important emotional ties.
>
> Isolating women in a sphere divorced from the legal order contributes directly to their inferior status by denying them the legal relief that they seek to improve their situations and by sanctioning conduct of the men who control their lives. . . . But beyond its direct, instrumental impact, the insulation of women's world from the legal order also conveys an important ideological message to the rest of society. Although this need not be the case in all societies, in our society the law's absence devalues women and their functions. . . .

Nadine Taub & Elizabeth M. Schneider, Women's Subordination and the Role of Law, in The Politics of Law: A Progressive Critique 328, 333 (David Kairys ed., 1998). For a symposium on privacy and the family, with critical commentary on the doctrine of nonintervention, see 67 Geo. Wash. L. Rev. 1207 (1999) (including articles by Naomi R. Cahn, Martha Albertson Fineman, and Barbara Bennett Woodhouse).

5. The gender-based common law necessaries doctrine poses equal protection problems. The issue has arisen, increasingly, when creditor-health care providers attempt to impose liability on a wife for services rendered prior to the husband's death. Courts adopt one of three approaches. First, some abolish the doctrine (thereby holding only the incurring spouse liable for the debt). E.g., Account Specialists & Credit Collections v. Jackman, 970 P.2d 202 (Okla. Ct. App. 1998); Schilling v. Bedford County Mem. Hosp., 303 S.E.2d 905 (Va. 1983). In response to judicial abolition, some legislatures codified the common law doctrine to impose liability on both spouses. E.g., Va. Code Ann. §55-37 (Michie 1995).

Second, some jurisdictions make the rule gender-neutral (applying the rule equally to both spouses). E.g., St. Luke's Episcopal-Presbyterian Hosp. v. Underwood, 957 S.W.2d 496 (Mo. Ct. App. 1997). Third, other jurisdictions place primary liability on one spouse and secondary liability on the other (requiring the creditor to exhaust the financial resources of one spouse before looking to the other spouse). Among this last category, some jurisdictions impose primary liability on the husband (irrespective of whether he incurred the debt). See Marshfield Clinic v. Discher, 314 N.W.2d 326 (Wis. 1982). Other jurisdictions that follow this approach impose primary liability on the spouse who incurred the debt. See, e.g., Jersey Shore Med. Ctr.-Fitkin Hosp. v. Estate of Baum, 417 A.2d 1003 (N.J. 1980).

Which approach comports with our modern view of marriage? With economic reality? Which better protects women's interests? Is it possible to formulate a gender-neutral rule while, at the same time, to protect dependent or needy spouses? See Margaret M. Mahoney, Economic Sharing During Marriage: Equal Protection, Spousal Support and the Doctrine of Necessaries, 22 J. Fam. L. 22 (1983-1984); Mary Elizabeth Borja, Note, Functions of Womanhood: The Doctrine of Necessaries in Florida, 47 U. Miami L. Rev. 397, 425 (1992).

6. Mrs. McGuire's request for attorneys' fees was denied (as not authorized by statute). Should legal fees be considered a "necessary"? See, e.g., Missoula YWCA v. Bard, 983 P.2d 933 (Mont. 1999) (holding that whether an item is a "necessary" depends on case-by-case analysis but finding that a husband may be liable for wife's legal fees to obtain order of protection).

7. What additional remedies might Mrs. McGuire have? Civil remedies include suits for separate maintenance based either on statute or equity jurisdiction. A party may seek this remedy if the couple is living apart. Criminal remedies also exist: in all states for nonsupport of a child and in nearly half the states with respect to spouses. Homer Clark, Law of Domestic Relations in the United States 269 (2d ed. 1988). What purposes do criminal remedies serve? Would you advise Mrs. McGuire to pursue these?

8. *The good provider role.* One source of marital difficulty in *McGuire* was the husband's neglect of his role of "good provider." How did this gender-linked role develop, and what are its consequences? Consider the excerpt that follows.

## Problem

Husband and Wife marry in 1977. During the course of their marriage, Wife pays for most household expenses, although Husband occasionally contributes to the utility and grocery bills. After 12 years of marriage, Wife informs Husband that she wants a divorce and asks him to leave. She informs him that she is going to, and does, remove him from her health insurance policy. Husband refuses to leave and makes no effort to secure his own coverage. Two years later, in March 1991, Wife files for divorce. On June 3, 1991, they sign an agreement whereby each takes responsibility for his or her own debts. Two days later, Husband is admitted to the hospital with a terminal condition. He submits an outdated insurance card from Wife's policy. Finding it unnecessary to pursue the divorce, Wife instructs her attorney to dismiss the proceedings. Husband dies, leaving a hospital debt of $150,000. The hospital files an action to recover payment from Wife. The jurisdiction has a spousal liability statute providing that both spouses shall be liable "for all debts contracted for necessaries for themselves, one another, or their family during the marriage." What result? Queen's Medical Ctr. v. Kagawa, 967 P.2d 686 (Haw. Ct. App. 1998).

## ■ JESSIE BERNARD, THE GOOD-PROVIDER ROLE: ITS RISE AND FALL
*36 Am. Psychol. 2-10 (Jan. 1981)*

I have not searched the literature to determine when the concept of the good provider entered our thinking. The term *provider* entered the English language in 1532, but was not yet male sex typed, as the older term *purveyor* already was in 1442. Webster's second edition defines the good provider as "one who provides, especially, colloq., one who provides food, clothing, etc. for his family; as, he is a good or an adequate provider." More simply, he could be defined as a man whose wife did not have to enter the labor force. The counterpart to the good provider was the housewife. However the term is defined, the role itself delineated relationships within a marriage and family in a way that added to the legal, religious and other advantages men had over women. . . .

The good provider as a specialized male role seems to have arisen in the transition from subsistence to market — especially money — economies that accelerated with the industrial revolution. The good-provider role for males emerged in this country roughly, say, from the 1830s, when de Tocqueville was observing it, to the late 1970s, when the 1980 census declared that a male was not automatically to be assumed to be head of household. This gives the role a life span of about a century and a half. Although relatively short-lived, while it lasted the role was a seemingly rock-like feature of the national landscape.

As a psychological and sociological phenomenon, the good-provider role had wide ramifications for all of our thinking about families. It marked a new kind of marriage. It did not have good effects on women: The role deprived them of many chips by placing them in a peculiarly vulnerable position. Because she was not reimbursed for her contribution to the family in either products or services, a wife was stripped to a considerable extent of her access to cash-mediated markets. By discouraging labor force participation, it deprived many women, especially affluent ones, of opportunities to achieve strength and competence. It deterred young women from acquiring productive skills. They dedicated themselves instead to winning a good provider who would "take care" of them. . . .

. . . The good-provider role, as it came to be shaped [was] restricted in what it was called upon to provide. Emotional expressivity was not included in that role. One of the things a parent might say about a man to persuade a daughter to marry him, or a daughter might say to explain to her parents why she wanted to, was not that he was a gentle, loving, or tender man but that he was a good provider. He might have many other qualities, good or bad, but if a man was a good provider, everything else was either gravy or the price one had to pay for a good provider. . . . Loving attention and emotional involvement in the family were not part of a woman's implicit bargain with the good provider. . . .

. . . To be a man one had to be not only a provider but a *good* provider. Success in the good-provider role came in time to define masculinity itself. The good provider had to achieve, to win, to succeed, to dominate. He was a bread*winner.* . . . The good provider became a player in the male competitive macho game. What one man provided for his family in the way of luxury and display had to be equaled or topped by what another could provide. . . .

The psychic costs could be high. . . . One individual became responsible for the support of the whole family. Countless stories portrayed the humiliation families underwent to keep wives and especially mothers out of the labor force, a circumstance that would admit to the world the male head's failure in the good-provider role. . . .

[I]n an increasing number of cases the wife has begun to share this role. . . . For some men the relief from the strain of sole responsibility for the provider role has been welcome. But for others the feeling of degradation resembles the feeling reported 40 years earlier in the Great

Depression. It is not that they are no longer providing for the family but that the role-sharing wife now feels justified in making demands on them. The good-provider role with all its prerogatives and perquisites has undergone profound changes. It will never be the same again. Its death knell was sounded when, as noted above, the 1980 census no longer automatically assumed that the male member of the household was its head.

Among the new demands being made on the good-provider role, two deserve special consideration, namely, (1) more intimacy, expressivity, and nurturance — specifications never included in it as it originally took shape — and (2) more sharing of household responsibilities and child care. . . .

## Note: Constitutional Limits on Sex-Stereotyped Role Assignments

Constitutional law reflects the common law's prescription of appropriate gender roles for husbands and wives. In the late nineteenth and early twentieth century, the Supreme Court upheld discrimination against women in employment based on the "separate spheres doctrine" (that is, women occupy the private sphere of home and family while men occupy the public arena of work and politics). Thus, for example, the Court upheld rules barring married women from the practice of law[26] and laws giving working women special legislation to protect them in their childbearing capacity.[27]

The women's movement in the 1960s triggered major reform in constitutional doctrine. In 1971, the Supreme Court first held that sex discrimination violated the Fourteenth Amendment's Equal Protection Clause. In Reed v. Reed, 404 U.S. 71 (1971), the Court invalidated an Idaho law that gave preference to men over women as administrators of intestate estates. The Court reasoned that the statute, which was based on stereotypical gender roles, lacked a rational basis. Reed heralded the beginning of an era of equal protection challenges to sex-based legislation.

The Court announced the applicable level of constitutional scrutiny for gender-based distinctions in 1976. Craig v. Boren, 429 U.S. 190 (1976), challenged the constitutionality of an Oklahoma statute proscribing different ages for men and women to drink beer. The Court applied an intermediate standard of review, maintaining that the classification must serve *important* governmental objectives and must be *substantially* related to achievement of those objectives. This standard, although lower than the strict scrutiny applied to race discrimination

[26]. Bradwell v. Illinois, 83 U.S. (16 Wall.) 130 (1873).
[27]. Muller v. Oregon, 208 U.S. 412 (1908).

("necessary to a compelling state interest"), was higher than the rational basis test ("rationally related to a legitimate governmental objective") applied to most social legislation. The Supreme Court later elevated the standard of review slightly and now requires an "exceedingly persuasive justification" for gender classifications.[28]

Over the years, the Court has wrestled with the meaning of "equal treatment" for men and women in many different contexts. Several cases invalidated gender-based distinctions between widows and widowers in terms of government benefits and, thereby, rejected the gender-based assumption that the husband was the breadwinner and the wife the dependent.[29] The Court had far more difficulty applying equal protection when confronted with classifications that it interpreted to reflect "real" differences.[30]

Our abstract standard of equality, based on the Aristotelian notion, guarantees that likes (that is, "those similarly situated") will be treated alike. But how does one treat women like men in the face of biological differences? And should men provide the norm? Difficulties arose particularly in the Court's treatment of pregnancy (discussed in this chapter). Further, the Court's preference for analyzing cases about reproduction under the Fourteenth Amendment's Due Process Clause ("privacy") left this strand of equal protection doctrine incomplete.[31] In other cases, the Court treated socially imposed differences (for example, the male as aggressor) as biological differences to justify differential treatment. Thus, despite disclaimers, the Court relied on gender-based stereotypes to exclude women from combat[32] and certain employment (for example, prison guards),[33] and to uphold criminal laws applicable to only one sex (for example, statutory rape laws).[34] Scholars criticize the consequences of the Court's equality jurisprudence for women. See Feminist Legal Theory: Foundations 211-331 (D. Kelly Weisberg ed., 1993) (essays by Mary Becker, Patricia Cain, Ruth Colker, Christine Littleton, Catharine MacKinnon, Diana Majury, and Martha Minow).

[28]. United States v. Virginia, 518 U.S. 515 (1996). See also Nguyen v. INS, 121 S. Ct. 2053, 2056 (2001). Some states go farther, applying strict scrutiny to gender-based classifications. See, e.g., Sail'er Inn v. Kirby, 485 P.2d 529 (Cal. 1971).

[29]. See, e.g., Califano v. Goldfarb, 430 U.S. 199 (1977); Weinberger v. Wiesenfeld, 420 U.S. 636 (1975); Frontiero v. Richardson, 411 U.S. 677 (1973).

[30]. See Michael M. v. Superior Court, 450 U.S. 464, 469 (1981) (stating that Court has upheld gender classifications that "realistically reflect[ ] the fact that the sexes are not similarly situated in certain circumstances").

[31]. See Sylvia A. Law, Rethinking Sex and the Constitution, 132 U. Pa. L. Rev. 955, 1007 (1984).

[32]. Rostker v. Goldberg, 453 U.S. 57 (1981).

[33]. Dothard v. Rawlinson, 433 U.S. 321 (1977).

[34]. Michael M. v. Superior Court, 450 U.S. 464 (1981). See also Orr v. Orr, 440 U.S. 268 (1979) (discussed in Chapter 6).

*4. Names in the Family*

## ■ NEAL v. NEAL
### 941 S.W.2d 501 (Mo. 1997)

COVINGTON, Judge.

Melissa J. Neal appeals the trial court's refusal to restore her maiden name. . . . Melissa J. Neal and Bruce L. Neal were married on September 10, 1994. They separated in February of 1995. Wife was pregnant. She filed a petition for dissolution of marriage in March, in which she requested, inter alia, orders relative to the minor child yet to be born and restoration of her maiden name. Husband answered, denying that the marriage was irretrievably broken and requesting nothing other than a dismissal of Wife's petition. On July 16, 1995, Wife gave birth to the parties' child, a son. On the birth certificate she denominated her maiden name, Gintz, as the child's surname. She did not include the name of Husband on the birth certificate. The parties were divorced by a decree of dissolution filed on September 14, 1995. [After making orders for custody, visitation and support], [t]he court also ordered correction of the Certificate of Live Birth to reflect that Husband is the natural father of the minor child and ordered the surname of the minor child changed to Neal. Wife appealed. . . .

The first issue is Wife's claim of trial court error in refusing to restore her maiden name, Gintz. Matter of Natale, 527 S.W.2d 402 (Mo. App. 1975), controls disposition of the issue. In *Natale,* the Missouri Court of Appeals, Eastern District, provided a thorough summary of the common law and statutory rights to change of name. In that case, Judith Natale, with her husband's consent, petitioned pursuant to section 527.270, RSMo 1969, and Rule 95.01 to have her maiden name restored. She desired to change her name for purposes of professional and personal identity and convenience to her husband and herself in carrying out their professional careers. The trial court denied the petition for change of name. The trial court's refusal was based upon the fact that the petitioner was lawfully married and residing with her legal spouse. Under such circumstances, the trial court reasoned, the granting of the petition could be detrimental to others in the future.

In reversing the judgment, the court of appeals provided historical background of the common law right to change of name, regardless of marital status. The court noted that the common law and statutory methods of changing names coexist for the reason that no constitutional or statutory mandate has invalidated the common law. The court of appeals found that, although it is within the trial court's discretion to find a change of name to be detrimental, the scope of discretion in the trial court to deny a petition for change of name is narrow, even within the marital relationship.

Following the teachings of *Natale,* the court of appeals in Miller v. Miller, 670 S.W.2d 591 (Mo. App. 1984), addressed precisely the issue presented here, a request pursuant to a dissolution proceeding that wife's maiden name be restored. Because there were two children born to Mr. and Mrs. Miller, the trial court refused to change Mrs. Miller's name. As the court of appeals stated in reversing the trial court, no law presumes that it is detrimental for a child to have a name that is different from the parent. Id. at 593. A general concern of possible detriment is insufficient to deny a petition for change of name in light of the obvious legislative intent that such a procedure be available, and by reason of the teachings of *Natale*.

In the present case, the trial court provided no reason for its declination to order restoration of Wife's maiden name. There is no substantial evidence to support the trial court's decision. . . . Under the teachings of *Natale* and *Miller*, the trial court erred in refusing to restore Wife's maiden name. . . .

Wife next contends the trial court erred in granting Husband's request to change the child's name to Neal, Husband's surname. Wife attacks the trial court's decision on abuse of discretion grounds; however, there is a threshold issue that must be decided, and that issue is dispositive. . . .

To hold that the trial court in a dissolution proceeding has authority to change the name of a minor child does not, however, confer upon the trial court authority to change a child's name in the absence of proper procedure. Proper procedure first requires that notice be given by the party seeking to have the child's name changed. Notice is required because in changing a child's name, the trial court's discretion is guided by a determination of what is in the best interests of the child. . . .

In the present case, there was no notice to Wife of Husband's intent to change the name of the minor child. . . . Because the trial court erred in granting Husband's request to change the child's name to Neal for the reasons stated above, it is unnecessary to reach the question of whether there was sufficient evidence in the record to prove that the name change was in the best interest of the child. . . . The judgment of the trial court is reversed and the case is remanded.

---

Does state regulation of naming children treat men and women differently?

■ **HENNE v. WRIGHT**
*904 F.2d 1208 (8th Cir. 1990)*, cert. denied, *498 U.S. 1032 (1991)*

BRIGHT, Senior Circuit Judge.
. . . Plaintiffs brought this action under 42 U.S.C. §1983 individually and as next friends to their daughters alleging that Neb. Rev. Stat. §71-

640.01 (1986) unconstitutionally infringes their fundamental fourteenth amendment right to choose surnames for their daughters. . . .

On April 4, 1985, Debra Henne gave birth to Alicia Renee Henne at a hospital in Lincoln, Nebraska. Following Alicia's birth, Debra completed a birth certificate form at the request of a hospital employee. Debra listed Gary Brinton as the father and entered the name Alicia Renee Brinton in the space provided for the child's name. Brinton, also present at the hospital, completed and signed a paternity form.

At the time of the birth, Debra was still married to Robert Henne. Although Debra and Robert Henne had filed for a divorce prior to Alicia's birth, the decree dissolving the marriage did not become final until after the birth. As a result of her marital status, hospital personnel, acting on instructions from the Department of Health, informed Debra that she could not surname her daughter "Brinton." Debra then filled out a second birth certificate form, entering the child's name as Alicia Renee Henne and leaving blank the space provided for the father's name. Robert Henne has never claimed to be Alicia's father and, pursuant to the divorce decree, pays no child support for her.

[O]n February 4, 1988, Debra Henne went in person to the Bureau of Vital Statistics of the Nebraska Department of Health and requested that Alicia's surname be changed to Brinton and that Gary Brinton be listed on the birth certificate as the father. . . . She also presented a signed acknowledgement of paternity from Gary Brinton and a letter from him requesting that the birth certificate be changed. Personnel at the Bureau of Vital Statistics, acting indirectly at the direction of defendants [Dr. Gregg F. Wright, M.D., Director of the Nebraska Department of Health, and Stanley S. Cooper, Director of the Nebraska Bureau of Vital Statistics], denied Debra's request. . . .

On June 17, 1988, at St. Elizabeth's Hospital in Lincoln, Nebraska, Linda Spidell gave birth to a daughter, Quintessa Martha Spidell. Linda wished to give Quintessa the surname "McKenzie," the same surname as her other two children, who were born in California. Hospital personnel, acting upon instructions from the Department of Health, informed Linda that Quintessa could not be surnamed McKenzie and that if Linda did not complete the birth certificate form the hospital would enter Quintessa's last name as Spidell. Linda completed the form, entering "Spidell" as Quintessa's surname and leaving blank the space provided for the father's name.

Linda surnamed her other children McKenzie simply because she liked that name and not because of any familial connection. For that reason, and because she wishes all three children to share the same name, she wants Quintessa surnamed McKenzie. Linda was not married at the time of Quintessa's birth or at the time of this action and there has been no judicial determination of paternity. At trial, however, both Linda and Ray Duffer, who lives with Linda and her children, testified that Duffer is Quintessa's biological father. . . .

Defendants contend that the district court erred in holding Neb. Rev. Stat. §71-640.01[5] unconstitutional. The district court held that an extension of the fourteenth amendment right of privacy protects a parent's right to name his or her child and that the statute failed to survive even minimal scrutiny. We determine that the fourteenth amendment right of privacy does not protect the specific right at issue here and that the statute rationally furthers legitimate state interests.

This case presents the issue whether a parent has a fundamental right to give a child a surname at birth with which the child has no legally established parental connection. We frame the issue this way because each plaintiff wishes to enter on her daughter's birth certificate a surname proscribed by section 71-640.01. [W]hile section 71-640.01 requires that a child have some legally established parental connection to the surname entered on the birth certificate, it does not prevent either plaintiff from ever giving her daughter the desired surname.[7] The district court overlooked this important distinction. . . .

We now turn to the question whether the right at issue is fundamental. A long line of Supreme Court cases have established that "liberty" under the fourteenth amendment encompasses a right of personal privacy to make certain decisions free from intrusive governmental regulation absent compelling justification [citing Zablocki v. Redhail; Moore v. City of East Cleveland; Roe v. Wade; Loving v. Virginia]. Two of the earliest right to privacy cases, Meyer v. Nebraska, 262 U.S. 390 (1923), and Pierce v. Society of Sisters, 268 U.S. 510 (1925), established the existence of a fundamental right to make child rearing decisions free from unwarranted governmental intrusion. *Meyer* and *Pierce* do not, however, establish an absolute parental right to make decisions relating to children free from government regulation.

In determining whether a right not enumerated in the Constitution qualifies as fundamental, we ask whether the right is "deeply rooted in this Nation's history and tradition," Moore v. City of East Cleveland, 431

5. Section 71-640.01 states: . . . (1) If the mother was married at the time of either conception or birth of the child, or at any time between conception and birth, . . . the surname of the child shall be entered on the certificate as being (a) the same as that of the husband, unless paternity has been determined otherwise by a court of competent jurisdiction, (b) the surname of the mother, (c) the maiden surname of the mother, or (d) the hyphenated surname of both parents; (2) If the mother was not married at the time of either conception or birth of the child, or at any time between conception and birth, the name of the father shall not be entered on the certificate without the written consent of the mother and the person named as the father, in which case and upon the written request of both such parents the surname of the child shall be that of the father or the hyphenated surname of both parents; . . . (4) In all other cases, the surname of the child shall be the legal surname of the mother. . . .

7. Debra Henne could enter the surname Brinton on her daughter's birth certificate by obtaining a judicial determination of paternity on the part of Gary Brinton. Linda Spidell could enter the surname McKenzie on her daughter's birth certificate only by first changing her own surname to McKenzie. Nebraska law provides a procedure, however, whereby either child's name could later be changed. . . .

U.S. at 503. . . . While *Meyer* and *Pierce* extended constitutional protection to parental decisions relating to child rearing, the parental rights recognized in those cases centered primarily around the training and education of children. . . . By contrast, the parental decision in this case relates to the choice of a child's surname. This subject possesses little, if any, inherent resemblance to the parental rights of training and education recognized by *Meyer* and *Pierce*. Thus, as the district court rightly recognized, constitutional protection for the right to choose a non-parental surname at birth must flow, if at all, from an extension of *Meyer* and *Pierce*. Furthermore, any logical extension of *Meyer* and *Pierce* has to be grounded in the tradition and history of this nation. Given this standard, we necessarily conclude that plaintiffs have presented no fundamental right.

The custom in this country has always been that a child born in lawful wedlock receives the surname of the father at birth, and that a child born out of wedlock receives the surname of the mother at birth. While some married parents now may wish to give their children the surname of the mother or a hyphenated surname consisting of both parents' surname, and some unmarried mothers may wish to give their children the surname of the father, we can find no American tradition to support the extension of the right of privacy to cover the right of a parent to give a child a surname with which that child has no legally recognized parental connection. Plaintiffs therefore have not asserted a right that is fundamental under the fourteenth amendment right of privacy and Neb. Rev. Stat. §71-640.01 need only rationally further legitimate state interests to withstand constitutional scrutiny. . . .

[T]he law rationally furthers at least three legitimate state interests: the state's interest in promoting the welfare of children, the state's interest in insuring that the names of its citizens are not appropriated for improper purposes and the state's interest in inexpensive and efficient record keeping. Specifically, a reasonable legislature could believe that in most cases a child's welfare is served by bearing a surname possessing a connection with at least one legally verifiable parent. Furthermore, the legislature could reasonably perceive that in the absence of a law such as section 71-640.01, the name of a non-parent could be improperly appropriated to achieve a deliberately misleading purpose, such as the creation of a false implication of paternity. Finally, the legislature could reasonably conclude that it is easier and cheaper to verify and index the birth records of a person who has a surname in common with at least one legally verifiable parent. . . . Although the Nebraska legislature could perhaps tailor the statute to more closely serve these purposes, we cannot say that section 71-640.01 bears no rational relationship to the state's legitimate interests. . . .

ARNOLD, Circuit Judge, concurring in part and dissenting in part.

. . . I respectfully dissent. The fundamental right of privacy, in my view, includes the right of parents to name their own children, and the

State has shown no interest on the facts of these cases sufficiently compelling to override that right. . . .

Debra Henne wants to give her daughter the surname of the little girl's father. . . . Linda Spidell wants to name her daughter "McKenzie." . . . The government, in the person of the State of Nebraska, says no to both mothers. The most plausible reason it offers is administrative convenience. Records are easier to keep and use if every person has the surname of "at least one legally verifiable parent." This interest is legitimate, and the statute under challenge is rationally related to it. If the appropriate level of constitutional scrutiny were the rational-basis test, I would agree that the law is valid. But if a fundamental right is at stake, the State must show a compelling interest, which it has wholly failed to do. . . .

The real question is . . . how do you tell what [the right of privacy] includes? The limits of the right remain controversial, and no doubt they will continue to be tested by litigation. Precedent tells us at least this much, though: family matters, including decisions relating to child rearing and marriage, are on almost everyone's list of fundamental rights. The right to name one's child seems to me, if anything, more personal and intimate, less likely to affect people outside the family, than the right to send the child to a private school, or to have the child learn German. We know, moreover, from Roe v. Wade, 410 U.S. 113 (1973), that these women had a fundamental right to prevent their children from being born in the first place. It is a bizarre rule of law indeed that says they cannot name the children once they are born. If there was ever a case of the greater including the less, this ought to be it. . . .

## Notes and Questions

1. *Name retention.* The feminist movement highlighted the impact of involuntary name changes, upon marriage, on a woman's identity. Most modern courts hold that adoption of the husband's surname was a custom, and not a requirement of the common law. Cases typically involve married women who seek to have their birth name (formerly "maiden name") entered on voting records, automobile registration, or driver's licenses. See, e.g., State v. Taylor, 415 So. 2d 1043 (Ala. 1982); Davis v. Roos, 326 So. 2d 226 (Fla. Dist. Ct. App. 1976); Traugott v. Petit, 404 A.2d 77 (R.I. 1979).

2. Two methods of name change exist: the common law method of consistent, nonfraudulent use and a statutorily prescribed judicial procedure. Most women change their name upon marriage by the first method. Would a requirement of name retention be less confusing and pose less risk of fraud to creditors?

3. Do men and women view surnames differently? One commentator suggests that for women, surnames are markers of family member-

ship and a surname change is natural, whereas for men, surnames implicate identity and a surname change is aberrational. See Merle H. Weiner, We Are Family: Valuing Associationalism in Disputes Over Children's Surnames, 75 N.C. L. Rev. 1625, 1761-1766 (1997).

Men occasionally adopt their wives' surnames. Do such men face reverse discrimination? See Ester Suarez, A Woman's Freedom to Change Her Surname: Is It Really a Matter of Choice?, 18 Women's Rts. L. Rep. 233, 238 (1997) (presenting such anecdotal evidence).

4. *Postdivorce name resumption.* Statutes often provide for a woman to resume her birth name upon divorce. As *Neal* illustrates, early cases wrestled with whether a denial of the wife's request could rest on possible detriment to children from having a different last name. Cf. Cal. Fam. Code §2081 (West 1994 & Supp. 1997) (restoration of surname shall not be denied "(a) on the basis that the wife has custody of a minor child who bears a different name, or (b) for any other reason other than fraud"). How significant is this problem for children? Should courts consider the possibility of embarassment to the child from bearing a different surname?

In *Neal,* the wife failed to secure her husband's consent to restore her surname. Is a wife required to do so? Might Mrs. Neal face additional difficulties in attempting to resume her birth name? One commentator points out that the need for court approval means that women must "endur[e] the time, expense, and inconvenience of doing so." Suarez, supra, at 237. In addition, women may lose any credit history they have accrued during the marriage. Id.

Some married couples adopt a hyphenated surname. In response to this practice, many statutes now confer upon the husband the right to resume his premarriage name upon divorce. See, e.g., N.C. Gen. Stat. §50-12 (1996).

5. Given that the choice of surname reflects personal values, do restrictions abridge free speech? See Comment, A Woman's Right to Her Name, 21 UCLA L. Rev. 665 (1973). Other constitutional rights also may be implicated. See, e.g., Forbush v. Wallace, 341 F. Supp. 217 (M.D. Ala. 1971) (statute mandating name change not violative of equal protection).

6. Naming practices in the United States reflect the dominance of Anglo-Saxon culture. In contrast, Latin American and Spanish custom dictates use of a two-part surname that represents the lineage of both parents. One commentator urges increased governmental sensitivity to this problem in official forms. See Yvonne M. Cherena Pacheco, Latino Surnames: Formal and Informal Forces in the United States Affecting the Retention and Use of the Maternal Surname, 18 T. Marshall L. Rev. 1 (1992). See also Stanley Lieberson & Kelly S. Mikelson, Distinctive African American Names: An Experimental, Historical, and Linguistic Analysis of Innovation, 60 Am. J. Soc. 929 (1995).

7. Is upholding custom a legitimate state interest if custom reflects gender discrimination and stereotypical beliefs? Custom has remarkable vitality as the following account reveals:

> [Federal district court judge Hubert Teitelbaum ordered attorney Barbara Wolvovitz to use the last name of her husband, University of Pittsburgh law professor Jules Lobel.] When she objected, he continued, "Do what I tell you or you're going to sleep in the county jail tonight. You can't tell me how to run my courtroom." [The judge sentenced co-counsel Jon Pushinsky to 30 days in jail for contempt when he objected.]
>
> The exchange began when Pushinsky was questioning a witness in a racial discrimination case to see if he had reported a matter to a manager he called "Ms. Burke." The judge interrupted, asking Pushinsky to refer to the woman as "Mrs. Burke."
>
> The judge then asked Wolvovitz whether she preferred "Ms." to "Mrs." and whether she used her maiden name. Teitelbaum told Wolvovitz the law required her to receive court permission to use her maiden name. In [a subsequent] apology, Teitelbaum said he had made a mistake as to the law. . . .

Debra Cassens Moss, The Judge Mrs. the Point, 74 A.B.A. J. 35 (Sept. 1, 1988).

8. *Children's surnames.* Most American children born in wedlock are given their father's name. In response to the women's movement, statutes increasingly give parents the right to choose the husband's name, the mother's birth name or a hyphenated surname. Nonmarital children, historically, took the mother's name absent the father's consent or a judicial determination of paternity. Currently, in name disputes between parents, courts usually apply one of three standards: a custodial parent presumption, a presumption favoring the status quo, or the best interests of the child test. Weiner, supra, at 1692.

Early cases addressed whether a father has a common law right to determine a child's surname. Some cases concluded that he did. See, e.g., Carroll v. Johnson, 565 S.W.2d 10 (Ark. 1978). See also Jay M. Zitter, Annotation, Rights and Remedies of Parents Inter Se with Respect to the Names of Their Children, 40 A.L.R.5th 697 (1996). A frequently given reason is the need to preserve the father-child bond (especially following divorce). See, e.g., In re Marriage of Presson, 465 N.E.2d 85 (Ill. 1984); West v. Wright, 283 A.2d 401 (Md. 1971). Is this rationale persuasive?

To what extent does *Neal* and the law of surnames, generally, reflect Blackstone's regime with its connotation of men's property interests in their wives and children? In the view of one commentator, all current name-change standards continue to reflect paternal bias. Weiner, supra, at 1753-1760. In the modern blended family, how should a court determine name-change petitions if paternal rights conflict? That is, suppose the child desires a hyphenated surname that combines the surnames of her father and her stepfather. Does the biological father have a right to have the daughter bear his name? See Leadingham ex rel. Smith v. Smith, 56 S.W.3d 420 (Ky. Ct. App. 2001) (so holding).

Weiner, supra, suggests an innovative reform, i.e., the adoption of the custodial parent's preference in name change petitions — if the child would bear the name of the custodial mother or a sibling — unless the noncustodial parent shows, by clear and convincing evidence, that serious harm would result to the child from the name change. Weiner, supra, at 1761-66. What do you think of this proposal?

9. *Constitutional issues.* The *Henne* majority determines that the right to choose a child's surname is not "fundamental." Does this parental decision "possess[ ] little, if any, inherent resemblance to the parental rights of training and education recognized by *Meyer* and *Pierce*"?

Does a paternal preference in naming violate the Fourteenth Amendment and/or state equal rights amendments? See Weiner, supra, at 1753-1760 (discussing equal protection issues). In a recent Canadian case, an unmarried mother refused to name the father on the triplets' birth certificates to avoid giving them his surname. He sought an order that the provisions of the British Columbia Vital Statistics Act (that permit a mother to "unacknowledge" the father and also confer upon her unilateral decisionmaking power over naming) constitute gender discrimination under the Canadian Charter of Rights and Freedoms (similar to the U.S. Equal Protection Clause). The British Columbia Court of Appeal upheld the lower court ruling dismissing the father's petition, finding no gender discrimination. Trociuk v. Attorney Gen. of British Columbia, 2001 B.C.D. Civ. LEXIS 743 (B.C. C.A. 2001).

10. Parental autonomy regarding naming has special significance in the African-American community, given the history of slavery. See generally Peggy Cooper Davis, Contested Images of Family Values: The Role of the State, 107 Harv. L. Rev. 1348 (1994). Some European societies regulate even first names of children. French officials may reject a name if they determine it to be contrary to the child's best interests. Lieberson & Mikelson, supra, at 944 n.17. Far Eastern countries have quite different regulations about names. For example, Thai citizens change their first names and surnames frequently in an effort to ward off misfortune. Sarah Strickland, What's in a Name? The Number Nine, If You Want to Improve Your Luck, The Independent (London), May 3, 2001, at 15. Japanese law prohibits wives' having different surnames from their husbands. As a result, some couples divorce whenever it is necessary to file for official documents such as drivers' licenses or passports. One woman politician (who married the same man five times and divorced him four times) is trying to change the law. Yumiko Ono, In Japan to Keep Your Maiden Name, You Get a Divorce, Wall St. J., June 29, 2000, at A1.

11. In *Henne*, both sets of parents agreed to the proposed surname. Whose wishes should prevail in the event of parental disagreement? Many states use a best interest standard to decide name disputes. One court suggests the following guidelines in the best interests determination: the

child's preference, the effect of the name change on parent-child relationships, how long the child has had the surname, community respect
associated with the name, social difficulties the child might encounter,
and the presence of any parental misconduct or neglect. Huffman v.
Fisher, 987 S.W.2d 269, 274 (Ark. 1999). Do you agree that such factors
are important? What other factors might be relevant?

12. *Henne* concludes that the statute furthers the state's interest in
child welfare. What are the psychological consequences for children of
recognizing a parent's constitutional right to name children? Consider
the following:

> . . . Parents are making use of little-known laws that allow them to bestow
> upon their children the surname of their choice. [I]n Pennsylvania, one set
> of parents gave their boy the surname "Sue." A couple in North Carolina
> dignified their baby with a nine-page last name. . . .
>
> Some parents even pick different surnames for different children. For
> instance, Pierce Barker and Carol Frost . . . gave their first born the last name
> "Roth-Tubman," in honor of author Philip Roth and abolitionist Harriet Tub-
> man; their second child, the name "Smith-Cook," after maternal and pater-
> nal ancestors; and their youngest, the name "Woods," after the child's
> maternal great-great-grandmother. . . . Teddy Roth-Tubman, now 12 years
> old, [when asked] whether he likes having a last name that doesn't match his
> parents', he says, "I guess so. It sure is a lot different than other kids."
>
> Would he do the same with his children? "I don't think so," he re-
> sponds, after some thought. "It's kind of peculiar."

Rifka Rosenwein, What's in a Surname? Genealogists Fear Family Tree
Trouble, Wall St. J., Feb. 11, 1987, at 1.

## Problems

1. A married couple, Barbara and John Smith, who are each the
fifth child in their respective families, decide to call their newborn daughter by the name of "5 + 5." They agree to call her "5" for short. When
Barbara attempts to enter that name on the birth certificate, hospital
personnel (acting on instructions from the Department of Health) inform Barbara that she cannot do so based on a state statute that limits
the choice of a child's surname to that of the mother's birth name, father's surname, or a combination of the two. What arguments would you
make on Barbara's and John's behalf? See In re Ritchie III, 206 Cal.
Rptr. 239 (Ct. App. 1984) (request to change name to "III"); In re
Change of Name of Ravitch, 754 A.2d 1287 (Pa. Super. Ct. 2000) (request to change name to the letter "R").

2. Lori Andrews, a divorced mother of 22-month-old twins, Audrey
and Holly, petitions the divorce court to restore her birth name of

"Brydl" and, simultaneously, to change her daughters' surname of "Andrews" to "Brydl-Andrews" (a hyphenated name incorporating her birth name and her husband's). Lori desires to teach the children to appreciate their Czech heritage and to avoid confusion on medical records. Her ex-husband objects, arguing that the proposed name is burdensome, confusing, and confers no benefit on the children. What result? See In re Andrews, 454 N.W.2d 488 (Neb. 1990).

3. Jennifer Bicknell and Belinda Priddy have been partners for nine years. They have made a verbal commitment to each other and have exchanged rings. Recently, Jennifer underwent artificial insemination. She is expecting a child whom they plan to rear jointly. Jennifer and Belinda petition the court to change their last names to the word "Rylen," which is a combination of several letters in their last names. They also desire a court order permitting their unborn child to share the new surname. A magistrate rules that granting the request would violate public policy. On appeal, what arguments should the women advance? See In re Bicknell, 2001 WL 121147 (Ohio Ct. App. 2001).

## 5. Employment

### ■ BRADWELL v. ILLINOIS
### 83 U.S. (16 Wall.) 130 (1873)

[Mrs. Myra Bradwell, a resident of Illinois, applied to the Illinois State Supreme Court for a license to practice law. Accompanying her petition was the requisite certificate attesting to her good character and qualifications. The Supreme Court of Illinois denied her application. The United States Supreme Court affirmed. Justice Bradley's concurring opinion below is a classic statement of separate spheres ideology.]

Mr. Justice BRADLEY [joined by Justices Swayne and Field], concurring: . . .

. . . The Supreme Court of Illinois denied the application on the ground that [the legislature] had simply provided that no person should be admitted to practice as attorney or counsellor without having previously obtained a license for that purpose from two justices of the Supreme Court, and that no person should receive a license without first obtaining a certificate from the court of some county of his good moral character. In other respects it was left to the discretion of the court to establish the rules by which admission to the profession should be determined. The court, however, regarded itself as bound by at least two limitations. One was that it should establish such terms of admission as would promote the proper administration of justice, and the other that it should not admit any persons, or class of persons, not intended by the legislature to be admitted, even though not expressly excluded by statute. In view of this latter limitation the court felt compelled to deny the application of females to be admitted as members of the bar. Being contrary to the rules of the common law and the usages of Westminster Hall from time immemorial, it could not be supposed that the legislature had intended to adopt any different rule.

The claim . . . under the fourteenth amendment of the Constitution, which declares that no State shall make or enforce any law which shall abridge the privileges and immunities of citizens of the United States . . . assumes that it is one of the privileges and immunities of women as citizens to engage in any and every profession, occupation, or employment in civil life.

It certainly cannot be affirmed, as an historical fact, that this has ever been established as one of the fundamental privileges and immunities of the sex. On the contrary, the civil law, as well as nature herself, has always recognized a wide difference in the respective spheres and destinies of man and woman. Man is, or should be, woman's protector and defender. The natural and proper timidity and delicacy which belongs to the female sex evidently unfits it for many of the occupations of civil life. The constitution of the family organization, which is founded in the divine ordinance, as well as in the nature of things, indicates the domestic sphere as that which properly belongs to the domain and functions of womanhood. The harmony, not to say identity, of interest and views which belong, or should belong, to the family institution is repugnant to the idea of a woman adopting a distinct and independent career from that of her husband. So firmly fixed was this sentiment in the founders of the common law that it became a maxim of that system of jurisprudence that a woman had no legal existence separate from her husband, who was regarded as her head and representative in the social state; and, notwithstanding some recent modifications of this civil status, many of the special rules of law flowing from and dependent upon this cardinal principle still exist in full force in most States. One of these is, that a married woman is incapable, without her husband's consent, of making contracts which shall be binding on her or him. This very incapacity was one circumstance which the Supreme Court of Illinois deemed important in rendering a married woman incompetent fully to perform the duties and trusts that belong to the office of an attorney and counsellor.

It is true that many women are unmarried and not affected by any of the duties, complications, and incapacities arising out of the married state, but these are exceptions to the general rule. The paramount destiny and mission of woman are to fulfill the noble and benign offices of wife and mother. This is the law of the Creator. And the rules of civil society must be adapted to the general constitution of things, and cannot be based upon exceptional cases. . . .

## Notes and Questions

1. The Illinois Supreme Court denied Mrs. Bradwell's application to the bar, in part, based on married women's inability to contract. Why, then, could *unmarried* women not practice law?

2. The Supreme Court determined that *admission* to the bar was a matter reserved to the states and not one of the privileges and immunities belonging to citizens. Thus, the Court found inapplicable the privilege and immunities guarantees of both Article IV and the Fourteenth Amendment. In so doing, the Court failed to consider the applicability to women of the Equal Protection Clause. When the Fourteenth Amendment was ratified in 1868, it engrafted the word "male" in the Constitution for the first time, causing considerable concern to nineteenth-century feminists. The Equal Protection Clause was not applied to invalidate gender-based discrimination until Reed v. Reed, 404 U.S. 71 (1971).

3. What authority does Justice Bradley cite in his concurrence to support his recognition of women's separate spheres? What is the danger of relying on history when considering the expansion of constitutional rights? See Aviam Soifer, Complacency and Constitutional Law, 42 Ohio St. L.J. 383, 409 (1981) ("To settle for the constitutionalization of the status quo is to bequeath a petrified forest").

---

Early cases denying women admission to the bar rested on legal and social rationales directed at married women in particular, as the following article reveals.

## ■ D. KELLY WEISBERG, BARRED FROM THE BAR: WOMEN AND LEGAL EDUCATION IN THE UNITED STATES 1870-1890
*28 J. Legal Educ. 485, 488-493 (1977)*

One of the paramount concerns of any skilled profession is the regulation of access to the profession. As Chroust has pointed out, in colonial America any person desiring to be admitted to the legal profession had four major avenues of entry.

He might, by his own efforts and through self-directed reading and study, acquire whatever scraps of legal information were available in books, statutes, or reports; he could work in the clerk's office of some court of record; he could serve as an apprentice or clerk in the law library of a reputable lawyer, preferably one with a law library; or he could enter one of the four Inns of Court in London and receive there the 'call to the bar.'[1]

Chroust's use of the masculine pronoun above is not entirely without significance. "Any" person in colonial America did have four avenues of legal education open to him, provided that that person was male. The first hundred years of American legal education were characterized by a glaring absence of woman lawyers. . . .

The struggle for women to gain entrance to the legal profession began in the late 1860's with Ada Kepley the first woman to graduate from the Union College of Law (now Northwestern) in 1870 and Arabella Mansfield the first woman to be admitted to the bar of any state (Iowa, 1869). However, the battle was by no means over; in reality it had just begun.

Scarcely two months after Arabella Mansfield was admitted to the Iowa bar, Myra Bradwell passed an examination for the Chicago bar, but the Illinois Supreme Court refused to grant her a license to practice law on the grounds of her sex. When the case was taken on a writ of error to the United States Supreme Court, she was once again unsuccessful. In other landmark cases Lavinia Goodell was refused admission to the Wisconsin bar in 1875 [In re Goodell, 39 Wis. 232 (1875)], Lelia Josephine Robinson was refused admission to the bar of Massachusetts in 1881 [Ex parte Robinson, 131 Mass. 375 (1881)], and Belva Lockwood, although admitted to the District of Columbia bar and admitted to practice before the United States Supreme Court, was still refused admission to the Virginia bar in the 1890's because of her sex [In re Lockwood, 154 U.S. 116 (1893)].

Even after the turn of the century when women were admitted to the bar of almost every state, the battle continued for women's admission to law school. Columbia University first admitted women law students in 1929, Harvard University in 1950 (although women had first applied to Harvard in the 1870's),[8] the University of Notre Dame in 1969, and the last male bastion Washington and Lee University in 1972. . . .

1. Chroust, The Rise of the Legal Profession in America 173 (1965).

8. When M. Fredrika Perry and Ellen Martin applied to the Harvard Law School in the 1870's, the reason given for denying their applications for admission was that "it was not considered practicable to admit young men and young women to the Law Library at the same time, and it was not considered fair to admit to the Law School without giving the privileges of the Library." Cited in Martin, Admission of Women to the Bar, 1 Chic. L.T. 83 (1886). . . .

[A] common rationale utilized to bar women from the legal profession was the argument that the impediments growing out of women's legal status at the common law prevented them from gaining access to the profession. [T]he most serious common law disability which would interfere with women practicing law, or so women's opponents maintained, concerned married women's inability to contract.

This legal rationale was based on the fact that married women at this time were disqualified from entering into contracts with third persons without their husband's consent. In both the *Bradwell* and *Lockwood* decisions, it was held that because of this disability at common law, married women could not be permitted to gain admission to the bar.

However, in some decisions which admitted women to the bar, it was held that married women's inability to contract was not an insurmountable obstacle. In the *Kilgore* decision in Pennsylvania (admitting Mrs. Kilgore), Justice Thayer held that the essential basis of the relationship between lawyer and client was not in contract.

> But what difference does it make if she cannot be sued as upon a contract. There are other adequate remedies for neglect of duty, infidelity, or misbehavior in office, which are provided by law and to which she would undoubtedly be amenable. . . . These laws are an ample security for the client in dealing with an attorney, even if she be a married woman.[18]

[Another] social rationale utilized to bar women from the legal profession centered on woman's traditional role in the family. The professional role of the lawyer was seen to be in direct conflict with the traditional roles of woman as wife and mother. In both the *Bradwell* and *Goodell* decisions, the judges delivered a lengthy discourse on woman's "sphere." The proper sphere for woman, they maintained, citing by way of authority the law of nature and the law of the Creator, was in the home. . . .

Woman's traditional role conflicted with the professional role of lawyer in terms of the divergent sets of priorities of the role sets. The socially approved role for woman as wife and mother had duties associated with it which were expected to be woman's first and primary obligation, superseding any other claim. For the lawyer, obviously, his occupation was intended to be his first priority. Or, as Justice Ryan had asserted in *Goodell:* "The profession enters largely into the well being of society; and to be honorably filled and safely to society, exacts the devotion of life."[34] . . . The requisite personality attributes of the lawyer, moreover, were seen as incompatible with those necessary for the role of wife and mother.

---

18. [14 Wkly. Notes 466 (1883).] Cited in Women as Advocates, 18 Am. L. Rev. 479 (1884).

34. [In re Goodell, 39 Wis. at 244-245.]

The lawyer was supposed to be aggressive — a skilled combatant in the juridical conflicts of the courtroom. Woman was seen as nurturant, gentle, tender. In short, she possessed personality attributes required for the fulfillment of the role of wife and mother. . . .

. . . For the single woman who was not engaged in fulfilling the role of "her destiny," the law was still not to be considered as a possible occupation. The court in *Goodell* had this to say:

> The cruel chances of life sometimes baffle both sexes, and may leave women free from the peculiar duties of their sex. These may need employment. . . . But it is public policy to provide for the sex, not for its superfluous members; and not to tempt women from the proper duties of their sex by opening to them duties peculiar to ours. There are many employments in life not unfit for female character. The profession of law is surely not one of these.[35]

The single woman, thus, was free to enter some other occupation to provide for herself. The legal profession, women's opponents stoutly maintained, should remain forever barred both to her and to her married sisters. . . .

---

On Myra Bradwell and her famous case, see Jane M. Friedman, America's First Woman Lawyer, The Biography of Myra Bradwell (1993); Elizabeth Wheaton, Myra Bradwell, First Woman Lawyer (1997); Richard L. Aynes, *Bradwell v. Illinois:* Chief Justice Chase's Dissent and the "Sphere of Women's Work," 59 La. L. Rev. 521 (1999).

### Note: Married Woman's Domicile

Domicile is, essentially, a person's home. Domicile establishes an individual's legal relationship to the state.[35] Domicile is relevant to determine marriage validity, the award of a divorce, custody, adoption, tax liability, probate and guardianship, as well as the right to vote, to hold and run for public office, to receive state benefits, or to qualify for tuition benefits at state colleges and universities.

---

35. Id.

[35]. See generally Homer H. Clark, Jr., Law of Domestic Relations in the United States (1968), esp. ch. 4 "Domicile in Domestic Relations," at 144-155. Domicile is also treated comprehensively in treatises on the conflict of laws. On the domicile of married women, see Albert A. Ehrenzweig, A Treatise on the Conflict of Laws §72 (1962); Robert A. Leflar et al., American Conflicts Law §11 (4th ed. 1986); Eugene F. Scoles et al., Conflict of Laws §§4.33-4.35 (3d ed. 2000).

Domicile requires two elements: presence plus intent to remain. A "domicile of choice" is acquired by persons who have legal capacity. A "domicile by operation of law" is assigned to those without legal capacity — traditionally, a category that included married women. At common law, the fiction of marital unity led to the assignment to a married woman of her husband's legal domicile. The Restatement of Conflicts codified this rule.[36]

The common law rule caused married women considerable hardship and inconvenience. The rule began to change in the 1970s. "The harshness of the common law rule . . . first became apparent in the field of divorce."[37] Constitutional challenges contributed to the rule's demise.[38] Finally, in 1988, the American Law Institute (ALI) revised the Restatement to confer upon married women the ability to acquire a domicile of choice.[39] Case law currently recognizes that neither spouse has a paramount right to select the marital domicile. See Szumanski v. Szumanska, 611 N.Y.S.2d 737 (Sup. Ct. 1994) (wife's refusal to join husband does not constitute abandonment for divorce purposes because a wife should have the same right as husband to choose a domicile).

■ **ROSS v. STOUFFER HOTEL CO.**
*816 P.2d 302 (Haw. 1991)*

PADGETT, Justice. . . .
On May 27, 1986, Amfac Hotels adopted a policy which read in part:

> [T]he Waiohai/Poipu Beach Hotel's policy with regard to the hiring of relatives is revised as follows: . . . 3. Two direct relatives [direct relative is defined as spouse] will not work in the same department together. If they marry after being employed here, one of the two will be asked to transfer or resign. . . .

On August 1, 1986, appellant Harvey Ross was hired as a massage therapist. Viviana Treffry was employed as the principal massage therapist at the Waiohai Hotel. At the time of his hire, appellant and Treffry had been cohabiting for two years and they married eleven days after he was hired. [The manager of the fitness spa knew that they had cohabited and married.]

---

[36]. Restatement of Conflict of Laws §§26, 27, 30, 40 (1934). Only a wife living apart from her husband but *not* guilty of desertion could have a separate domicile. Id. at §38.

[37]. Restatement (Second) of Conflict of Laws §28 cmt. a. (Tent. Draft No. 2, 1954).

[38]. See, e.g., Samuel v. University of Pittsburgh, 375 F. Supp. 1119 (W.D. Pa. 1974), *decision to decertify class vacated*, 538 F.2d 991 (3d Cir. 1976) (invalidating, on equal protection grounds, university residency rules that assigned the husband's domicile to the wife for determination of tuition).

[39]. Restatement (Second) of Conflict of Laws §21 (Supp. 1988) ("rules for the acquisition of a domicile of choice are the same for both married and unmarried persons").

A little over a year later, on August 24, 1987, Stouffer Hotels acquired the hotel and, on October 16, 1987, made a decision to enforce the no-spouse rule against appellant. The rule allowed either party to transfer out of the department but they declined to do so. Appellant was therefore terminated. Appellant brings this action claiming that his termination violated HRS §378-2, which provides in pertinent part: It shall be an unlawful discriminatory practice: (1) For an employer to refuse to hire or employ or to bar or discharge from employment, or otherwise to discriminate against any individual in compensation or in the terms, conditions, or privileges of employment because of race, sex, age, religion, color, ancestry, physical handicap, marital status, or arrest and court record. [The circuit court granted the employer's motion for a summary judgment. Plaintiff appealed.]

There is some indication in the record that because appellant's wife was his superior, she had a duty under the pertinent statutes and regulations governing massage to report any infractions of the statutes and regulations by appellant, and that appellees were concerned with the inherent possibility of conflict in that situation. On the other hand, there is some indication in the record that appellant's wife offered to step down from her supervisory position in order to meet that concern. . . . In our view, it is the fact of marriage which caused the termination. Apparently continued cohabitation without going through a marriage ceremony would not have been a violation of the policy.

Appellant and appellees have characterized the policy as a "no nepotism" rule. That however is a mischaracterization. Nepotism is defined in Black's Law Dictionary 1039 (6th ed. 1990) as: Bestowal of patronage by public officers in appointing others to positions by reason of blood or marital relationship to appointing authority. In Webster's Third New International Dictionary 1518 (1986), nepotism is defined as: favoritism shown to nephews and other relatives (as by giving them positions because of their relationship rather than on their merits). [The term] deals with hiring someone because of that person's relationship to the hirer. Nothing of that sort is involved in this policy.

Our statute, HRS §378-2 is not unique. Many other states have similar, or identical, statutory provisions and litigation over the meaning of the term "marital status" as used in such statutes has resulted, with a marked split among the courts passing on whether a discriminatory policy such as that with which we are faced violates the statute. New Jersey, New York, and Michigan have all adopted the view that such policies, as the one under which appellant was terminated, do not violate the prohibition against discrimination because of marital status. Basically their reasoning is that the termination was not because of the person's marital status but because of whom the person married.

On the other hand, Washington, Minnesota, and Montana have held that such policies violate the statutory provisions, reasoning that it is the marital status which causes the termination, or the refusal to hire, since by not entering into the marital relationship, or by obtaining a divorce, the disqualification would be removed, and the policy inapplicable. . . .

The problem raised by the conflict between company policies prohibiting married persons from working for the same company, or in the same department, or in a supervisor/supervisee relationship, has also been the subject of scholarly comment. See Wexler, Husbands and Wives: The Uneasy Case for Antinepotism Rules, 62 B.U. L. Rev. 75, 125-139 (1982); Note, Challenging No-Spouse Employment Policies as Marital Status Discrimination: A Balancing Approach, 33 Wayne L. Rev. 1111 (1987). Those two studies, in substance, adopt the position of the Washington and Minnesota courts that a flat out prohibition against employees being married, such as is the case of the policy we are here dealing with, violates the prohibition against discrimination by reason of marital status. However, where an employer can show that the marital status of the employees has a relationship to the statutory exception for bona fide occupational qualifications, then a refusal to hire, or a termination, can be upheld.

The public policy argument behind encouraging marital relationships, enunciated in those opinions and comments seems to us persuasive as applied to the facts of this case. Appellant and his wife are licensed masseurs residing on the island of Kauai. Given the smallness of the community, obviously their opportunity to pursue their licensed occupation is limited. The employer's invocation of the policy a year after they had entered into a marital relationship left them with a Hobson's choice of one of them either giving up his or her employment, or their seeking a divorce, and continuing to live together and being employed in their chosen occupation. We hold the statute in question prohibits forcing a married couple to make such a choice, absent some statutory exception to the rule. . . .

## Notes and Questions

1. *Epilogue.* The Hawaii Supreme Court in *Ross* vacated the summary judgment for defendant and remanded. The court then entered a judgment for the employer. When plaintiff appealed, the Hawaii Supreme Court held that the no-relative policy, as applied to plaintiff, violated the state statute unless the termination was based on a statutory exception, such as business necessity. The court remanded for this determination. Ross v. Stouffer Hotel, 879 P.2d 1037 (Haw. 1994).

2. *Background.* Derived from the Latin word for "nephew," the word "nepotism" was coined during the Middle Ages to describe Pope

Calixtus III's appointment of his unqualified nephews as cardinals.[40] Papal bulls and decrees eventually outlawed this common practice. Nepotism also played a role in American history. President Abraham Lincoln gave government appointments to supporters' relatives; President John Kennedy appointed his brother Robert as attorney general; then-Senator Lyndon Johnson also appointed family members to government positions. After Robert Kennedy's appointment, Congress enacted an antinepotism statute, 5 U.S.C. §3110 (1994), prohibiting public officials from appointing a relative to a position over which the official exercises jurisdiction. Nonetheless, former President Clinton appointed his wife Hillary Rodham Clinton to chair (without pay) the President's Task Force on National Health Care Reform, and a distant cousin to provide travel arrangements for the White House Press Corps.[41]

3. *"No-spouse rules."* Most antinepotism litigation targets the private sector or local government. Some antinepotism policies limit employment specifically of "spouses"; others limit that of "close relatives." Some prohibit hiring, employment in the same department, or supervision of the other's work. Policies may affect spouses in a number of situations. Both spouses may apply to the same employer at the same time. More commonly, one spouse may seek work from an employer who currently employs the other. Or employees of the same employer may marry subsequently.

The increasing number of women in the labor force enhances these possibilities. The problem is acute in small communities (especially those dominated by a single industry) and in narrow specialties where the lack of employment alternatives may make one spouse unemployable. Do female employees disproportionately bear the burden of the no-spouse rule? How do such policies affect the freedom to marry and the right to privacy?

4. *Business rationale.* Antinepotism policies attempt to ensure that unqualified relatives are not hired. Yet, paradoxically, they ban qualified relatives from being hired as well. Cases and commentators present the following arguments *for* antinepotism policies: married individuals will bring quarrels to work; a married couple may form a coalition to advance their own interests, leading to complaints of favoritism and disgruntlement; employment of spouses promotes dual absenteeism because both partners want the same vacation or shifts; and, in an emergency, spouses may harm others to protect each other.

[40]. Joan G. Wexler, Husbands and Wives: The Uneasy Case for Antinepotism Rules, 62 B.U. L. Rev. 75, 75 (1982). Some "nephews" may actually have been illegitimate sons. Id. at 75 n.3 (citing W. Durant, The Renaissance 382 (1953)).

[41]. The press dubbed this latter appointment "Travelgate." Bill Turque, Judgment Calls, Newsweek, May 31, 1993, at 18-19. Newsweek published a political cartoon with a member of the press quizzically asking the "First Cousin": "You don't have anything without a layover in Arkansas?"

Opposing arguments include: the best candidate should not be passed over (or fired) simply because of marriage to an employee; willingness to hire couples will enable firms in lesser-known locations to hire the "star" who otherwise would go to a large town where the spouse would be able to find employment; personnel benefits for employee-spouses are less costly than for unrelated individuals; no-spouse restrictions violate public policy by encouraging cohabitation; no-spouse policies discriminate against women by leading to discharge of women who usually have less seniority than the men they marry.[42]

In an omitted dissent in *Ross*, Justice Wakatsuki argues that antinepotism policies should be left to the legislature, and also that civil rights statutes are not an appropriate remedy in such cases. Which arguments are most persuasive? Least? Which are equally applicable to employees who cohabit or date? What policy would protect the workplace from possible abuses while allowing qualified spouses to work together?

5. *Causes of action.* Both federal and state grounds exist to challenge some antinepotism policies.

(a) *Constitutional challenges — marriage as a fundamental right.* To date, challenges under Zablocki v. Redhail have not proven successful.[43] This cause of action is available only to state employees. And, although *Zablocki* does protect marriage as a fundamental right, only those regulations that "directly and substantially" interfere merit heightened scrutiny. When might a state employer's no-spouse rule "directly and substantially" interfere with the right to marry?

(b) *Title VII.* Title VII of the Civil Rights Act of 1964, 42 U.S.C. §2000e-2(a)(1) (1994), a major weapon to combat gender discrimination in the workplace, has provided an important avenue of attack on antinepotism policies.[44] Title VII prohibits discrimination based on race, color, religion, sex, or national origin (but not marital status). Sex discrimination under Title VII may be categorized either as disparate treatment (that is, express classifications) or disparate impact. Most antinepotism litigation under Title VII is based on disparate impact, challenging policies that do not facially distinguish between employees but, in practice, adversely affect a particular class of employees. To establish disparate impact, a plaintiff must demonstrate statistically the

[42]. On these arguments, see EEOC v. Rath Packing Co., 787 F.2d 318, 332 (8th Cir.), *cert. denied*, 479 U.S. 910 (1986); Yuhas v. Libbey-Owens-Ford Co., 411 F. Supp. 77 (N.D. Ill. 1976), *rev'd*, 562 F.2d 496 (7th Cir. 1977), *cert. denied*, 435 U.S. 934 (1978); Sally M. Avelenda, Love and Marriage in the American Workplace: Why No-Spouse Policies Don't Work, 1 U. Pa. J. Lab. & Emp. L. 691 (1998).

[43]. See, e.g., Parks v. City of Warner Robins, 43 F.3d 609 (11th Cir. 1995); Wright v. MetroHealth Med. Ctr., 58 F.3d 1130 (6th Cir. 1995).

[44]. Given the importance of Title VII, it is interesting to note the serendipitous manner in which the word "sex" was added to the legislation. See Flora Davis, Moving the Mountain: The Women's Movement in America Since 1960, at 38-43 (1991).

adverse effect of an employment practice.[45] The proof requirement may prove unworkable in firms with perhaps only one woman affected.[46] After a plaintiff has presented the requisite statistical evidence, an employer in a disparate impact action has the opportunity to show that the practice is justified, (for example, by business necessity).[47]

Should Title VII be broadened to include marital status discrimination? See Nicole Buonocore Porter, Marital Status Discrimination: A Proposal for Title VII Protection, 46 Wayne L. Rev. 1 (2000) (arguing that Title VII's inclusion of "marital status" would be a more effective way of eliminating marital status discrimination and would provide uniformity among the states).

(c) *Challenges under state civil rights statutes.* The most common attack on antinepotism policies alleges violations of state civil rights statutes that prohibit discrimination on the basis of marital status. Cases turn on expansive versus restrictive judicial interpretations of the statutory term "marital status." As in *Ross,* some states interpret "marital status" broadly to include the identity of the individual's spouse.[48] Other states construe "marital status" narrowly to refer only to the state of being married, single, divorced, or widowed.[49]

6. *Spousal identity.* How broadly should courts define marital status? Specifically, can an employee invoke marital status discrimination if terminated because of an employer's hostility towards the employee's spouse? In Donato v. AT&T, 767 So. 2d 1146 (Fla. 2000), a husband sued AT&T claiming marital status discrimination when he was terminated shortly after his wife, a former AT&T employee, filed suit against the company. The court refused to recognize a cause of action for marital status discrimination, reasoning that marital status "does not include the specific identity or actions of an individual's spouse," and the plain meaning of the term and legislative history referred only to one's status with respect to marriage. Id. at 1155. See also Bammert v. Laboratory & Indus. Review Comm'n, 606 N.W.2d 620 (Wis. Ct. App. 1999) (accord). But cf. Magula v. Benton Franklin Title Co., 930 P.2d 307 (Wash. 1997).

7. *Sexual fraternization.* Do no-dating policies in the workplace constitute employment discrimination? See New York v. Wal-Mart Stores,

---

[45]. 42 U.S.C. §2000e-2k (1994). See Griggs v. Duke Power Co., 401 U.S. 424 (1971); Markey v. Tenneco Oil Co., 635 F.2d 497 (5th Cir. 1981).

[46]. See, e.g., Thomas v. Metroflight, 814 F.2d 1506, 1508 (10th Cir. 1987).

[47]. See, e.g., EEOC v. Rath Packing Co., 787 F.2d 318 (8th Cir. 1986) (invalidating no-spouse policy based on business necessity). But cf. Yuhas v. Libbey-Owens-Ford Co., 562 F.2d 496 (7th Cir. 1977), *cert. denied,* 435 U.S. 934 (1978).

[48]. Maryland Comm'n on Human Relations v. Baltimore Gas & Elec. Co., 459 A.2d 205 (Md. 1983); Thompson v. Board of Trustees, 627 P.2d 1229 (Mont. 1981). Minnesota offers explicit statutory protection. See, e.g., Minn. Stat. Ann. §363.01(24) (West 1991 & Supp. 1997).

[49]. See, e.g., Muller v. BP Exploration, 923 P.2d 783 (Alaska 1996); Boaden v. Department Law Enforcement, 664 N.E.2d 61 (Ill. 1996).

621 N.Y.S.2d 158 (App. Div. 1995); McCavitt v. Swiss Reinsurance Am. Corp., 237 F.3d 166 (N.Y. 2001). Should employers adopt such rules? Compare Anna M. DePalo, Antifraternizing Policies and At-Will Employment: Counseling for a Better Relationship, 96 Ann. Surv. Am. L. 59 (1996) (criticizing policies) with Gary M. Kramer, Limited License to Fish Off the Company Pier: Toward Express Employer Policies on Supervisor-Subordinate Fraternization, 22 W. New Eng. L. Rev. 77 (2000) (policies maximize morale and efficiency).

One commentator notes that people are spending more hours at work than in the past and that employers, increasingly, are hosting and encouraging work-related social events. The natural result is that more relationships are being formed in the workplace. Does this imply that anti-nepotism policies are not in sync with the realities of today's workforce? See Randi Wolkenbreit, In Order to Form a More Perfect Union: Applying No-Spouse Rules to Employees Who Meet at Work, 31 Colum. J.L. & Soc. Probs. 119, 124 (1997).

Should universities bar fraternization between faculty and students? Several universities have adopted or at least considered, such policies.[50] See Billie Wright Dziech et al., "Consensual" or Submissive Relationships: The Second-Best Kept Secret, 6 Duke J. Gender L. & Pol'y 83, 88 (1999). What legal problems do nonfraternization policies raise? On fraternization in the military, see Martha Chamallas, The New Gender Panic: Reflections on Sex Scandals and the Military, 83 Minn. L. Rev. 305 (1998).

8. *Professional responsibility problems.* Marriage between lawyers poses special problems. To what extent should ethical obligations result in restrictions on employment for married lawyers? Should a per se rule bar lawyer spouses or their firms from representing different interests? See Gelman v. Hilal, 607 N.Y.S.2d 853 (N.Y. Sup. Ct. 1994). Do an attorney's obligations to avoid breaches of confidentiality, conflicts of interest, and appearances of impropriety require such automatic disqualification? Should lawyers who are living together or dating one another be governed by the same restrictions?

The American Bar Association's Model Rules of Professional Conduct (1996) provide in Rule 1.8:

> (i) A lawyer related to another lawyer as parent, child, sibling or spouse shall not represent a client in a representation directly adverse to a person who the lawyer knows is represented by the other lawyer except upon consent by the client after consultation regarding the relationship.

---

[50]. Harvard University was the first in 1984 to ban sexual relations between faculty (including graduate instructors) and their students. The University of Iowa and the University of Virginia followed. Jane Gross, Love or Harassment? Campuses Bar (and Debate) Faculty-Student Sex, N.Y. Times, Apr. 14, 1993, at B9; Eileen Wagner, Colleges Need Outright Bans on Sexual Fraternization, Chron. Higher Educ., May 26, 1993, at B1. The University of California's proposed adoption of a ban met with strong opposition. Telephone conversation with Carmen McKines, Title IX Compliance Officer, U.C. Berkeley, July 15, 1993.

Does client consent mitigate this problem? See Blumenfeld v. Borenstein, 276 S.E.2d 607 (Ga. 1981) (emphasizing client's right to counsel of choice). On professional responsibility problems facing lawyer-spouses, see generally Thomas K. Byerley, "'Til Conflict Do Us Part,'" 80 Mich. B.J. 68 (May 2001); Deena L. Buchanan, Strange Bedfellows? Married Lawyers and Conflicts of Interest, 11 Geo. J. Legal Ethics 753 (1988).

Lawyer-judge marriages pose additional problems. Several states' ethics boards have considered the appropriate conduct for judges whose husbands or wives have professional ties to pending cases.[51] See generally Mark M. Brandsdorfer, Lawyers Married to Judges: A Dilemma Facing State Judiciaries — A Case Study of the State of Texas, 6 Geo. J. Legal Ethics 635 (1993). See also St. B. Mich. Comm'n on Prof'l and Jud. Ethics, Formal Op. R-003 (1989) (applying conflict-of-interest rules to lawyers and judges who cohabit as couples); Judges' Wives on Payroll Ruled Ethical Under Code, Cincinnati Enquirer, May 22, 1998, at C1B (ruling that judges' hiring their wives as legal secretaries did not violate ethical standards).

## Problems

1. Jim and Coleen are state troopers in the same squad in a small Illinois town. Their district is patrolled by three one-person squads (each person patrols in a separate car). The squads rotate every eight hours. Jim and Coleen date and decide to marry. When they notify their supervisor, he informs them of an unwritten policy that prohibits spouses from working on the same shift in the patrol area. Jim and Coleen could remain in the same patrol area on different shifts, or one could transfer to a different patrol area and work the same shift. Jim chooses the latter. After their marriage, they challenge the no-spouse policy under state law, which prohibits employers from discriminating against an employee based on marital status (defined as "the legal status of being married, single, separated, divorced, or widowed"). What result? See Boaden v. Department of Law Enforcement, 664 N.E.2d 61 (Ill. 1996).

2. New Jersey law bars judges from political activity. Judge Gaulkin's wife seeks election to the board of education. She asks the New Jersey Supreme Court to change the rule of disqualification that extends to a judge's spouse. The court agrees to reconsider this rule. In doing so, should it lift all restrictions on political activities by a judge's spouse? Or should it permit political activities by a judge's spouse but only with restrictions, such as prohibiting the use of all marital assets for the "polit-

[51]. Robb London, Setting Up Ethics Codes for Lawyers and Judges Married to Each Other, N.Y. Times, Oct. 25, 1991, at B6. See also State of Washington Ethics Advisory Comm., Op. No. 91-18 (1991); Washington Code of Judicial Conduct, Canon 3(D)(1)(c) and (d), reprinted in Natl. Rep. on Legal Ethics (Univ. Pub. Am.) (1993).

ical spouse's" campaign as well as the marital home for this spouse's political meetings and fundraisers? See In re Gaulkin, 351 A.2d 740 (N.J.
1976).

## 6. Parenting

### a. Pregnancy Leave

■ **CLEVELAND BOARD OF EDUCATION v.
LaFLEUR**
*414 U.S. 632 (1974)*

Mr. Justice STEWART delivered the opinion of the Court. . . .
Jo Carol LaFleur and Ann Elizabeth Nelson . . . are junior high
school teachers employed by the Board of Education of Cleveland, Ohio.
Pursuant to a rule first adopted in 1952, the school board requires every
pregnant school teacher to take maternity leave without pay, beginning
five months before the expected birth of her child. . . . The teacher on
maternity leave is not promised re-employment after the birth of the
child; she is merely given priority in reassignment to a position for which
she is qualified. Failure to comply with the mandatory maternity leave
provisions is ground for dismissal.
Neither Mrs. LaFleur nor Mrs. Nelson wished to take an unpaid maternity leave; each wanted to continue teaching until the end of the
school year.[2] Because of the mandatory maternity leave rule, however,
each was required to leave her job in March 1971. The two women then
filed separate suits. . . .
[Another petitioner] Susan Cohen, was employed by the School
Board of Chesterfield County, Virginia. That school board's maternity
leave regulation requires that a pregnant teacher leave work at least four
months prior to the expected birth of her child. Notice in writing must
be given to the school board at least six months prior to the expected
birth date. A teacher on maternity leave is declared re-eligible for employment when she submits written notice from a physician that she is
physically fit for re-employment, and when she can give assurance that
care of the child will cause only minimal interference with her job responsibilities. The teacher is guaranteed re-employment no later than
the first day of the school year following the date upon which she is declared re-eligible.
Mrs. Cohen informed the Chesterfield County School Board in November 1970, that she was pregnant and expected the birth of her child

---

2. Mrs. LaFleur's child was born on July 28, 1971; Mrs. Nelson's child was born during August of that year.

about April 28, 1971. She initially requested that she be permitted to continue teaching until April 1, 1971. The school board rejected the request, as it did Mrs. Cohen's subsequent suggestion that she be allowed to teach until January 21, 1971, the end of the first school semester. Instead, she was required to leave her teaching job on December 18, 1970. She subsequently filed this suit under 42 U.S.C. §1983. . . .

We granted certiorari in both cases, in order to resolve the conflict between the Courts of Appeals regarding the constitutionality of such mandatory maternity leave rules for public school teachers.[8]

This Court has long recognized that freedom of personal choice in matters of marriage and family life is one of the liberties protected by the Due Process Clause of the Fourteenth Amendment. As we noted in Eisenstadt v. Baird, 405 U.S. 438, 453, there is a right "to be free from unwarranted governmental intrusion into matters so fundamentally affecting a person as the decision whether to bear or beget a child."

By acting to penalize the pregnant teacher for deciding to bear a child, overly restrictive maternity leave regulations can constitute a heavy burden on the exercise of these protected freedoms. Because public school maternity leave rules directly affect "one of the basic civil rights of man," Skinner v. Oklahoma, [316 U.S. 535, 541 (1942)], the Due Process Clause of the Fourteenth Amendment requires that such rules must not needlessly, arbitrarily, or capriciously impinge upon this vital area of a teacher's constitutional liberty. The question before us in these cases is whether the interests advanced in support of the rules of the Cleveland and Chesterfield County School Boards can justify the particular procedures they have adopted.

The school boards in these cases have offered two essentially overlapping explanations for their mandatory maternity leave rules. First, they contend that the firm cutoff dates are necessary to maintain continuity of classroom instruction, since advance knowledge of when a pregnant teacher must leave facilitates the finding and hiring of a qualified substitute. Secondly, the school boards seek to justify their maternity rules by arguing that at least some teachers become physically incapable of adequately performing certain of their duties during the latter part of pregnancy. By keeping the pregnant teacher out of the classroom during these final months, the maternity leave rules are said to protect the health of the teacher and her unborn child, while at the same time

8. . . . The practical impact of our decision in the present cases may have been somewhat lessened by several recent developments. At the time that the teachers in these cases were placed on maternity leave, Title VII . . . did not apply to state agencies and educational institutions. On March 24, 1972, however, the Equal Employment Opportunity Act of 1972 amended Title VII to withdraw those exemptions. Shortly thereafter, the Equal Employment Opportunity Commission promulgated guidelines providing that a mandatory leave or termination policy for pregnant women presumptively violates Title VII. While the statutory amendments and the administrative regulations are, of course, inapplicable to the cases now before us, they will affect like suits in the future. . . .

assuring that students have a physically capable instructor in the class-room at all times.[9]

It cannot be denied that continuity of instruction is a significant and legitimate educational goal. [W]hile the advance-notice provisions in the Cleveland and Chesterfield County rules are wholly rational and may well be necessary to serve the objective of continuity of instruction, the absolute requirements of termination at the end of the fourth or fifth month of pregnancy are not. Were continuity the only goal, cutoff dates much later during pregnancy would serve as well as or better than the challenged rules, providing that ample advance notice requirements were retained. Indeed, continuity would seem just as well attained if the teacher herself were allowed to choose the date upon which to com-mence her leave, at least so long as the decision were required to be made and notice given of it well in advance of the date selected.

In fact, since the fifth or sixth month of pregnancy will obviously be-gin at different times in the school year for different teachers, the pres-ent Cleveland and Chesterfield County rules may serve to hinder attainment of the very continuity objectives that they are purportedly designed to promote. For example, the beginning of the fifth month of pregnancy for both Mrs. LaFleur and Mrs. Nelson occurred during March of 1971. Both were thus required to leave work with only a few months left in the school year, even though both were fully willing to serve through the end of the term. Similarly, if continuity were the only goal, it seems ironic that the Chesterfield County rule forced Mrs. Co-hen to leave work in mid-December 1970 rather than at the end of the semester in January, as she requested.

We thus conclude that the arbitrary cutoff dates embodied in the mandatory leave rules before us have no rational relationship to the valid state interest of preserving continuity of instruction. As long as the teachers are required to give substantial advance notice of their condi-tion, the choice of firm dates later in pregnancy would serve the boards' objectives just as well, while imposing a far lesser burden on the women's exercise of constitutionally protected freedom.

---

9. The records in these cases suggest that the maternity leave regulations may have originally been inspired by other, less weighty, considerations. For example, Dr. Mark C. Schinnerer, who served as Superintendent of Schools in Cleveland at the time the leave rule was adopted, testified in the District Court that the rule had been adopted in part to save pregnant teachers from embarrassment at the hands of giggling schoolchildren; the cutoff date at the end of the fourth month was chosen because this was when the teacher "began to show." Similarly, at least several members of the Chesterfield County School Board thought a mandatory leave rule was justified in order to insulate schoolchildren from the sight of conspicuously pregnant women. . . .

The school boards have not contended in this Court that these considerations can serve as a legitimate basis for a rule requiring pregnant women to leave work; we thus note the comments only to illustrate the possible role of outmoded taboos in the adoption of the rules.

The question remains as to whether the cutoff dates at the beginning of the fifth and sixth months can be justified on the other ground advanced by the school boards — the necessity of keeping physically unfit teachers out of the classroom. There can be no doubt that such an objective is perfectly legitimate, both on educational and safety grounds. . . .

The mandatory termination provisions of the Cleveland and Chesterfield County rules surely operate to insulate the classroom from the presence of potentially incapacitated pregnant teachers. But the question is whether the rules sweep too broadly. That question must be answered in the affirmative, for the provisions amount to a conclusive presumption that every pregnant teacher who reaches the fifth or sixth month of pregnancy is physically incapable of continuing. There is no individualized determination by the teacher's doctor — or the school board's — as to any particular teacher's ability to continue at her job. [T]he Due Process Clause requires a more individualized determination.

. . . While the medical experts in these cases differed on many points, they unanimously agreed on one — the ability of any particular pregnant woman to continue at work past any fixed time in her pregnancy is very much an individual matter. Even assuming, arguendo, that there are some women who would be physically unable to work past the particular cut-off dates embodied in the challenged rules, it is evident that there are large numbers of teachers who are fully capable of continuing work for longer than the Cleveland and Chesterfield County regulations will allow. Thus, the conclusive presumption embodied in these rules . . . is neither "necessarily (nor) universally true," and is violative of the Due Process Clause.

The school boards have argued that the mandatory termination dates serve the interest of administrative convenience, since there are many instances of teacher pregnancy, and the rules obviate the necessity for case-by-case determinations. Certainly, the boards have an interest in devising prompt and efficient procedures to achieve their legitimate objectives in this area. . . . While it might be easier for the school boards to conclusively presume that all pregnant women are unfit to teach past the fourth or fifth month or even the first month, of pregnancy, administrative convenience alone is insufficient to make valid what otherwise is a violation of due process of law.[13] The Fourteenth Amendment requires

13. This is not to say that the only means for providing appropriate protection for the rights of pregnant teachers is an individualized determination in each case and in every circumstance. We are not dealing in these cases with maternity leave regulations requiring a termination of employment at some firm date during the last few weeks of pregnancy. We therefore have no occasion to decide whether such regulations might be justified by considerations not presented in these records — for example, widespread medical consensus about the "disabling" effect of pregnancy on a teacher's job performance during these latter days, or evidence showing that such firm cutoffs were the only reasonable method of avoiding the possibility of labor beginning while some teacher was in the classroom, or proof that adequate substitutes could not be procured without at least some minimal lead time and certainty as to the dates upon which their employment was to begin.

the school boards to employ alternative administrative means, which do not so broadly infringe upon basic constitutional liberty, in support of their legitimate goals. . . .

In addition to the mandatory termination provisions, both the Cleveland and Chesterfield County rules contain limitations upon a teacher's eligibility to return to work after giving birth. Again, the school boards offer two justifications for the return rules — continuity of instruction and the desire to be certain that the teacher is physically competent when she returns to work. As is the case with the leave provisions, the question is not whether the school board's goals are legitimate, but rather whether the particular means chosen to achieve those objectives unduly infringe upon the teacher's constitutional liberty. . . .

The respondents . . . do not seriously challenge either the medical requirements of the Cleveland rule or the policy of limiting eligibility to return to the next semester following birth. The provisions concerning a medical certificate or supplemental physical examination are narrowly drawn methods of protecting the school board's interest in teacher fitness; these requirements allow an individualized decision as to the teacher's condition, and thus avoid the pitfalls of the presumptions inherent in the leave rules. Similarly, the provision limiting eligibility to return to the semester following delivery is a precisely drawn means of serving the school board's interest in avoiding unnecessary changes in classroom personnel during any one school term.

The Cleveland rule, however, does not simply contain these reasonable medical and next-semester eligibility provisions. In addition, the school board requires the mother to wait until her child reaches the age of three months before the return rules begin to operate. The school board has offered no reasonable justification for this supplemental limitation, and we can perceive none. To the extent that the three-month provision reflects the school board's thinking that no mother is fit to return until that point in time, it suffers from the same constitutional deficiencies that plague the irrebuttable presumption in the termination rules. The presumption, moreover, is patently unnecessary, since the requirement of a physician's certificate or a medical examination fully protects the school's interests in this regard. And finally, the three-month provision simply has nothing to do with continuity of instruction, since the precise point at which the child will reach the relevant age will obviously occur at a different point throughout the school year for each teacher.

Thus, we conclude that the Cleveland return rule, insofar as it embodies the three-month age provision, is wholly arbitrary and irrational, and hence violates the Due Process Clause of the Fourteenth Amendment. The age limitation serves no legitimate state interest, and unnecessarily penalizes the female teacher for asserting her right to bear children.

We perceive no such constitutional infirmities in the Chesterfield County rule. In that school system, the teacher becomes eligible for re-employment upon submission of a medical certificate from her physician; return to work is guaranteed no later than the beginning of the next school year following the eligibility determination. The medical certificate is both a reasonable and narrow method of protecting the school board's interest in teacher fitness, while the possible deferring of return until the next school year serves the goal of preserving continuity of instruction. . . .

■ **JO CAROL LAFLEUR, "GO HOME
AND HAVE YOUR BABY"**
*in The Courage of Their Convictions 320-328*
*(Peter Irons ed., 1988)*

I learned around January of 1971 that I was pregnant, with the child due to be born around the end of July. Teaching out the school year made perfect sense to me. . . . I thought I was actually contributing, partly by being a good role model [being] a married woman, having a baby, going to a doctor, getting good care. . . . Little did I know that you could not teach in the Cleveland schools past the fourth month of pregnancy.

[The principal, Mr. Wilkins, called Ms. LaFleur to his office about the first of March.] Mr. Wilkins said, I understand you're having a baby in August. . . . You've got to go on maternity leave; you've got to fill out your papers. I said, I don't have to do that, because I'm not leaving. I'm just going to teach until the end of the year. He said, You can't do that; we have rules. I said, My baby isn't scheduled to be born until the summer. I just want to teach school. This class that you just put me in has already lost one teacher. And I teach students who are pregnant. . . . He said, You're a good teacher. I'm not going to fire you, but you've got to take this leave. Mr. Wilkins filled out the maternity leave papers for me, because I wouldn't fill them out. . . . I couldn't believe that anybody would yank from an inner-city school a person who was specially trained to teach there and who *wanted* to teach. . . .

I really thought initially that I could talk Mr. Wilkins out of it, but he would not be moved. [She then asked the teachers' union for help.] The union leader, who was a man said, Oh, Mrs. LaFleur, just go home and have your baby. I said, No! I want to have my baby, but I don't knit, I don't crochet, I don't want to sit home, I just want to teach. It was clear the union had no interest or sympathy whatever. . . . [Later, she called the Women's Equity Action League, who referred her to a constitutional law professor, Jane Picker.] The first time we ever met, Jane said, This child will probably be old enough to read the decision before we ever get a final verdict in this case. No matter the outcome, it's going to end up at the U.S. Supreme Court. . . .

Mr. Wilkins had given me a deadline to leave — near the end of March. . . . Jane tried to get an injunction in the federal court against the schools, to prevent them from barring me from my class. This district court judge, whose name was Connell — elderly, in his seventies — said at the injunction hearing, Mrs. LaFleur will get exactly what she deserves, and she doesn't deserve an injunction. Since we knew he was the trial judge, Jane said, This doesn't bode well. . . .

. . . The school board put on a doctor, a male obstetrician, whose testimony I found really annoying. He was talking about all of the horrible complications that were possible with pregnancy, like placenta previa. There was absolutely *no* data that showed that the act of teaching made it more likely that you would have one of these conditions. In fact, if I were not teaching, I would be home by myself. And if I had a placenta previa and my placenta tore loose, I would much rather be in a school with people who can help me than be in my own home and all of a sudden start hemorrhaging and maybe pass out before I got to a telephone. So if they're worried about your health, putting you in a place of isolation — I remember thinking that their logic didn't make a lot of sense.

It was almost hilarious, in a very pathetic sense, listening to testimony about all of the possible complications of pregnancy. It's a wonder women *ever* have babies, if all of these horrible things happen. . . . The week before my son was born, I played nine holes of golf and I played a set of tennis. The only thing I didn't do was jump the net. . . .

After Judge Connell ruled against me, we filed an appeal with the Sixth Circuit Court of Appeals. . . . Jane had asked me to bring my son, Michael, down to the argument. She said, It can't hurt, if people see that this child is healthy and looks loved. When we got to the courthouse, Michael and I and my husband rode up in the elevator with this older gentleman. He was saying, He's a cute little guy, and I said, He's a sweetheart. When the court comes in, it was Justice Tom Clark of the Supreme Court! I'm going, Oh my gosh. It's a good thing I wasn't yelling at Michael or he wasn't having a tantrum. . . . We won in the court of appeals. . . . The Supreme Court was much iffier. [T]he Court had become much more conservative than in the Earl Warren years. . . .

I remember Justice Blackmun asking the question of Jane Picker, whether she really saw any difference between a man losing his job because he refuses to shave his beard, and a woman losing her job because she's pregnant. And she stood up there, and she put her hands on both hips and she said, Your Honor, that analogy is ludicrous. Simply *ludicrous*. What's the remedy for a man? You shave! For a woman it's abortion, to get rid of the problem. It's a little different, Your Honor. And I could see her husband at counsel table, with his head in his hands — Jane, you shouldn't *say* such things. But Blackmun voted for us. . . .

... I remember the day the decision came down. I was teaching a social studies class [with a guest speaker], and we were discussing death and dying. ... I got called out of the class for a telephone call from a radio station that wanted my opinion on the decision. ... I called Jane's office. They said, The only thing we know is that you won. ...

I went running back to my class, doing these *jetes,* these giant leaps down the hall. I went into my class and I calmed down, and I said, Mr. Smith, could I have just one moment? I need to tell the class something. They knew I had been waiting every day. *We won!* Thank you, please resume. He doesn't know what's going on. The kids are screaming, *All right!* ...

Looking back, I'm not quite sure why I started my case. ... When I got pregnant, I knew I wasn't sick. I knew I wasn't ill. How could a male-dominated school system say to me, Even though you're not ill, and pregnancy is a perfectly normal condition, you are unfit to teach. The fundamental unfairness of it seemed morally wrong, not just stupid but wrong. ...

---

*Postscript.* Jo Carol LaFleur left high school teaching and attended the University of Utah Law School. After graduation, she practiced in the Utah public defender's office and became counsel for the state bar association.

*Pregnancy Discrimination Act of 1978.* The Pregnancy Discrimination Act of 1978 (PDA) amends, as follows, the definitional section of Title VII of the Civil Rights Act of 1964 that prohibits, inter alia, sex discrimination in employment:

> The terms "because of sex" or "on the basis of sex" include, but are not limited to, because of or on the basis of pregnancy, childbirth, or related medical conditions; and women affected by pregnancy, childbirth, or related medical conditions shall be treated the same for all employment-related purposes, including receipt of benefits under fringe benefit programs, as other persons not so affected but similar in their ability or inability to work....

42 U.S.C. §2000e(k) (1994).

## ■ CALIFORNIA FEDERAL SAVINGS & LOAN ASSOCIATION v. GUERRA
*479 U.S. 272 (1987)*

Justice MARSHALL delivered the opinion of the Court.

The question presented is whether Title VII of the Civil Rights Act of 1964, as amended by the Pregnancy Discrimination Act of 1978, preempts a state statute that requires employers to provide leave and reinstatement to employees disabled by pregnancy.

California's Fair Employment and Housing Act (FEHA), Cal. Gov't. Code Ann. §12900 et seq. (West 1980 and Supp. 1986), is a comprehensive statute that prohibits discrimination in employment and housing. In September 1978, California amended the FEHA to proscribe certain forms of employment discrimination on the basis of pregnancy. Subdivision (b)(2) — the provision at issue here — is the only portion of the statute that applies to employers subject to Title VII. It requires these employers to provide female employees an unpaid pregnancy disability leave of up to four months. Respondent Fair Employment and Housing Commission, the state agency authorized to interpret the FEHA, has construed §12945(b)(2) to require California employers to reinstate an employee returning from such pregnancy leave to the job she previously held, unless it is no longer available due to business necessity. In the latter case, the employer must make a reasonable, good faith effort to place the employee in a substantially similar job. The statute does not compel employers to provide paid leave to pregnant employees. Accordingly, the only benefit pregnant workers actually derive from §12945(b)(2) is a qualified right to reinstatement.

Title VII of the Civil Rights Act of 1964, also prohibits various forms of employment discrimination, including discrimination on the basis of sex. However, in General Electric Co. v. Gilbert, 429 U.S. 125 (1976), this Court ruled that discrimination on the basis of pregnancy was not sex discrimination under Title VII. In response to the *Gilbert* decision, Congress passed the Pregnancy Discrimination Act of 1978 (PDA), 42 U.S.C. §2000e(k). The PDA specifies that sex discrimination includes discrimination on the basis of pregnancy.

Petitioner California Federal Savings and Loan Association (Cal. Fed.) is a federally chartered savings and loan association based in Los Angeles; it is an employer covered by both Title VII and §12945(b)(2). Cal. Fed. has a facially neutral leave policy that permits employees who have completed three months of service to take unpaid leaves of absence for a variety of reasons, including disability and pregnancy. Although it is Cal. Fed.'s policy to try to provide an employee taking unpaid leave with a similar position upon returning, Cal. Fed. expressly reserves the right to terminate an employee who has taken a leave of absence if a similar position is not available.

Lillian Garland was employed by Cal. Fed. as a receptionist for several years. In January 1982, she took a pregnancy disability leave. When she was able to return to work in April of that year, Garland notified Cal. Fed., but was informed that her job had been filled and that there were no receptionist or similar positions available. Garland filed a complaint with respondent Department of Fair Employment and Housing. . . . [Prior to the hearing before the Fair Housing and Employment Commission,

Cal. Fed. brought this action.] They sought a declaration that §12945(b)(2) is inconsistent with and pre-empted by Title VII and an injunction against enforcement of the section. [The district court granted petitioners' motion for summary judgment; the Ninth Circuit Court of Appeals reversed.] We granted certiorari, and we now affirm.

. . . In order to decide whether the California statute requires or permits employers to violate Title VII, as amended by the PDA, or is inconsistent with the purposes of the statute, we must determine whether the PDA prohibits the States from requiring employers to provide reinstatement to pregnant workers, regardless of their policy for disabled workers generally.

Petitioners argue that the language of the federal statute itself unambiguously rejects California's "special treatment" approach to pregnancy discrimination, thus rendering any resort to the legislative history unnecessary. They contend that the second clause of the PDA forbids an employer to treat pregnant employees any differently than other disabled employees. Because "[t]he purpose of Congress is the ultimate touchstone" of the pre-emption inquiry, however, we must examine the PDA's language against the background of its legislative history and historical context. . . .

It is well established that the PDA was passed in reaction to this Court's decision in General Electric Co. v. Gilbert, 429 U.S. 125 (1976). . . . By adding pregnancy to the definition of sex discrimination prohibited by Title VII, the first clause of the PDA reflects Congress' disapproval of the reasoning in *Gilbert*. Rather than imposing a limitation on the remedial purpose of the PDA, we believe that the second clause was intended to overrule the holding in *Gilbert* and to illustrate how discrimination against pregnancy is to be remedied. Accordingly, subject to certain limitations, we agree with the Court of Appeals' conclusion that Congress intended the PDA to be "a floor beneath which pregnancy disability benefits may not drop — not a ceiling above which they may not rise."

The context in which Congress considered the issue of pregnancy discrimination supports this view of the PDA. Congress had before it extensive evidence of discrimination against pregnancy, particularly in disability and health insurance like those challenged. . . . The reports, debates, and hearings make abundantly clear that Congress intended the PDA to provide relief for working women and to end discrimination against pregnant workers. In contrast to the thorough account of discrimination against pregnant workers, the legislative history is devoid of any discussion of preferential treatment of pregnancy,[20] beyond ac-

20. The statement of Senator Brooke, quoted in the dissent, merely indicates the Senator's view that the PDA does not itself require special disability benefits for pregnant workers. It in no way supports the conclusion that Congress intended to prohibit the States from providing such benefits for pregnant workers.

knowledgments of the existence of state statutes providing for such preferential treatment. Opposition to the PDA came from those concerned with the cost of including pregnancy in health and disability benefit plans and the application of the bill to abortion, not from those who favored special accommodation of pregnancy.

In support of their argument that the PDA prohibits employment practices that favor pregnant women, petitioners and several amici cite statements in the legislative history to the effect that the PDA does not *require* employers to extend any benefits to pregnant women that they do not already provide to other disabled employees. . . . On the contrary, if Congress had intended to *prohibit* preferential treatment, it would have been the height of understatement to say only that the legislation would not *require* such conduct. It is hardly conceivable that Congress would have extensively discussed only its intent not to require preferential treatment if in fact it had intended to prohibit such treatment.

We also find it significant that Congress was aware of state laws similar to California's but apparently did not consider them inconsistent with the PDA. . . . Title VII, as amended by the PDA, and California's pregnancy disability leave statute share a common goal. The purpose of Title VII is "to achieve equality of employment opportunities and remove barriers that have operated in the past to favor an identifiable group of . . . employees over other employees." Rather than limiting existing Title VII principles and objectives, the PDA extends them to cover pregnancy. As Senator Williams, a sponsor of the Act, stated: "The entire thrust . . . behind this legislation is to guarantee women the basic right to participate fully and equally in the workforce, without denying them the fundamental right to full participation in family life." 123 Cong. Rec. 29658 (1977).

Section 12945(b)(2) also promotes equal employment opportunity. By requiring employers to reinstate women after a reasonable pregnancy disability leave, §12945(b)(2) ensures that they will not lose their jobs on account of pregnancy disability. . . . California's pregnancy disability leave statute allows women, as well as men, to have families without losing their jobs.

Thus, petitioners' facial challenge to §12945(b)(2) fails. The statute is not pre-empted by Title VII, as amended by the PDA, because it is not inconsistent with the purposes of the federal statute. . . .

Justice WHITE, with whom THE CHIEF JUSTICE and Justice POWELL join, dissenting. . . .

The second clause [of the PDA] could not be clearer: it mandates that pregnant employees "shall be treated the same for all employment-related purposes" as nonpregnant employees similarly situated with respect to their ability or inability to work. This language leaves no room for preferential treatment of pregnant workers. . . . In sum, preferential treatment of pregnant workers is prohibited by Title VII, as amended by the PDA. Section 12945(b)(2) of the California Gov't. Code, which extends preferential benefits for pregnancy, is therefore pre-empted. . . .

■ **WENDY W. WILLIAMS, EQUALITY'S RIDDLE: PREGNANCY AND THE EQUAL TREATMENT/SPECIAL TREATMENT DEBATE**
*13 N.Y.U. Rev. L. & Soc. Change 325, 333-349 (1984-1985)*

The treatment of pregnancy and maternity under the law developed in stages. . . .

### A. STAGE ONE: 1870 TO 1970

[W]omen's "maternal functions" formed the basis of a dual system of law. The system treated women differently than men under the claim that it sought to accommodate to and provide for women's special needs. [Williams first describes the era of protective labor legislation during the late nineteenth and early twentieth centuries.]

[T]here were, beginning in the 1940's, a very few provisions dealing specifically with pregnancy. In the early 1940's, the Women's Bureau of the U.S. Department of Labor recommended that pregnant women not work for six weeks before and two months after delivery. Some states adopted laws prohibiting employers from employing women for a period of time before and after childbirth to protect the health of women and their offspring during that vulnerable time. Where leaves were not accompanied by a guarantee of job security or wage replacement, they "protected" pregnant women right out of their jobs, as the Women's Bureau conceded. At the same time, the unemployment insurance laws of many states rendered otherwise eligible women workers ineligible for unemployment insurance if they were pregnant or had recently given birth. Women unemployed because of state laws or employer policies of mandatory unpaid leave thus were precluded from the resources available to other unemployed workers. Four states, including California, created disability insurance programs to provide partial wage replacement to temporarily disabled workers, but those programs either excluded pregnancy-related disabilities altogether or provided restricted benefits. The absence of legislation concerning pregnancy and employment meant that the issue was left to employers (and, where there were unions, to collective bargaining).

By 1960, the dawn of a new decade that would usher in Title VII, many employers simply fired women who became pregnant. Others provided unpaid maternity leaves of absence, frequently accompanied by loss of seniority and accrued benefits. Few provided job security, much less allowed paid sick leave and vacation time to be used for maternity leave. Payment of disability benefits for childbirth was, at best, restricted, and employer sponsored medical insurance provided, at most, limited coverage of pregnancy-related medical treatment and hospitalization.

Pervasively, pregnancy was treated less favorably than other physical conditions that affected workplace performance. The pattern of rules telegraphed the underlying assumption: a woman's pregnancy signaled her disengagement from the workplace. Implicit was not only a factual but a normative judgment: when wage-earning women became pregnant they did, and should, go home.

## B. STAGE TWO: 1970-1976

By 1970, women were in the workforce in unprecedented numbers. Moreover, an increasing number of them were staying after the birth of children.[40] . . . Suits were filed under Title VII and the equal protection clause on the theory that treating pregnancy disabilities differently and less favorably than other disabilities discriminates on the basis of sex. . . .

In 1974, however, the United States Supreme Court eliminated the Equal Protection Clause as a vehicle for an "equal treatment" attack on legislation singling out pregnancy for special treatment. The state statute challenged in Geduldig v. Aiello [417 U.S. 484 (1974)] created a state disability fund, providing temporary, partial wage replacement to private sector workers who became physically unable to work. The statute was liberally interpreted to cover every conceivable work disability, including, according to the record in the case, disability arising from cosmetic surgery, hair transplants, skiing accidents and prostatectomies. It excluded only one type of work disability from coverage — those "arising out of or in connection with" pregnancy. . . .

Justice Stewart, on behalf of a majority of the court, [stated] that the case did not involve discrimination based on gender as such: "The California insurance program does not exclude anyone from benefit eligibility because of gender but merely removes one physical condition — pregnancy — from the list of compensable disabilities." Translated, this means that the statute bases the exclusion on pregnancy, not on sex itself (a point made evident, the court noted, by the fact that the persons covered by the program — disabled nonpregnant persons — included women). This mechanical parsing was apparently reasoning enough for the Court. . . .

40. Between 1950 and 1970, the labor force participation rate for women with children under six years old increased from 12 to 30%. Dept. of Labor, Women's Bureau, Economic Report of the President 93 (1971). By 1979 the rate was 56.1%. U.S. Dept. of Labor, Perspectives on Working Women: A Databook, Table 34, 34 (1980).

The conclusion that discrimination on the basis of pregnancy was not sex discrimination freed the Court from the obligation to engage in the more activist review it reserves for sex discrimination cases. Indulging the strong presumption of constitutionality appropriate to rational basis review, it concluded that a legislature legitimately could exclude a costly disability. . . . The Court's explanation that exclusion was rational because the "additional" cost of covering pregnancy would upset the pre-established contribution rate or benefit level would apply to any frequent or prolonged disability that had been excluded from the program, however arbitrarily. . . .

Justice Brennan, joined in dissent by Justices Marshall and Douglas, adopted the plaintiffs' position in its entirety. Women disabled by pregnancy-related causes were comparable to other disabled workers for purposes of the California program. . . . Moreover, the exclusion of pregnancy-related disabilities constituted sex discrimination. . . .

[Yet,] when the Court struck down the pregnancy policies in [Cleveland Board of Education v. LaFleur, 414 U.S. 632 (1974)], it invoked not the sex discrimination cases decided under the equal protection clause, but rather, the reproductive choice cases, such as Eisenstadt [v. Baird, 405 U.S. 438 (1972)] and Roe v. Wade [410 U.S. 113 (1973)]. . . . The doctrinal distinction between due process and equal protection analysis of pregnancy issues represented by *LaFleur* and *Geduldig* is in a sense a reiteration of the special treatment/equal treatment dichotomy. To oversimplify, the due process approach is not troubled by and, indeed, invokes a form of special treatment analysis. The liberty interest at stake, defined as the right to choose whether to bear or beget a child without undue state interference, is recognized as "fundamental" precisely because of the central and unique importance to the individual of reproductive choice. The characterization of pregnancy discrimination as sex discrimination, by contrast, requires the comparative analysis of the equal protection mode. Its emphasis is on what is not unique about the reproductive process of women. . . .

### C. Stage Three: 1976-1978

In General Electric Company v. Gilbert, [429 U.S. 125 (1976)], decided in December of 1976, the Supreme Court dropped the other shoe. Relying heavily on *Geduldig v. Aiello*, it interpreted Title VII as it had the equal protection clause: it held that discrimination on the basis of pregnancy was not sex discrimination. *Gilbert*, on its facts, was very similar to *Geduldig*. It involved a private employer's disability insurance plan almost identical to the California state plan both in its general scope and in its exclusion of pregnancy-related disabilities. . . .

Under Title VII, rules that are "neutral" but have a disproportionate sex-based effect may also violate the Act. However, the particular "neutral" General Electric pregnancy disability rule, said Justice Rehnquist [writing for the majority,] could not even be viewed as having a discriminatory *effect* on women. Men and women, he said, are both covered by the disability program. Moreover, they are covered for the disabilities common to both sexes. Pregnancy disabilities are therefore an "*additional* risk, unique to women." Failure to compensate women for them does not upset the basic sex equality of the program. In a footnote, he drove home the point: Title VII does not require "that 'greater economic benefit[s]' . . . be paid to one sex or the other because of their differing roles in the 'scheme of human existence.' " This conclusion makes breathtakingly explicit the underlying philosophy of the majority of the justices in *Geduldig* and *Gilbert*. Pregnancy, for Rehnquist, is an "extra," an add-on to the basic male model for humanity. Equality does not contemplate handing out benefits for extras — indeed, to do so would be to grant special benefits to women, possibly discriminating against men. The fact that men were compensated under the program for disabilities unique to their sex troubled his analysis not at all.

Justice Brennan, in his dissent in *Geduldig*, almost grasped the essence of the problem when he observed that "the State has created a double standard for disability compensation; a limitation is imposed upon the disabilities for which women workers may recover, while men receive full compensation for all disabilities suffered, including those that affect only or primarily their sex. . . ." What eluded even Justice Brennan was that the statute did not create a "double" standard. Rather, it made man the standard (whatever disabilities men suffer will be compensated) and measured women against that standard (as long as she is compensated for anything he is compensated for, she is treated equally).

For Rehnquist, as long as women are treated in the same way as men in the areas where they are like men — in the disability program this would mean coverage for things like heart attacks, broken bones, appendicitis — that's equality. To the extent the Court will consider the equities with respect to childbearing capacity, it will consider them only in the category where they belong — extra, separate, different. A family, marital or reproductive right — yes, in appropriate circumstances. A public matter of equality and equal protection of women — no. . . .

### D. STAGE FOUR: 1978-PRESENT

In reaction to *Gilbert* and [a subsequent case, Nashville Gas Co. v. Satty, 434 U.S. 136 (1977)], Congress in 1978 passed the Pregnancy Discrimination Act (PDA) as an amendment to Title VII, quite plainly requiring that pregnancy be treated under the equality model. [This] equal treatment approach, despite its rocky progress in the Supreme Court, has transformed employer pregnancy policies. . . .[101]

---

101. Terminations still occur, no longer on the basis of an overt policy of terminating pregnant women, but in other guises. In such cases, plaintiffs must, like any Title VII plaintiff alleging covert discrimination, demonstrate that the employer intended to discriminate — in these cases because of pregnancy. . . .

## Notes and Questions

1. *LaFleur,* decided before the Pregnancy Discrimination Act, was based on due process. Why did the Supreme Court choose due process rather than equal protection (used by the courts below)?

2. The PDA does not mandate pregnancy leave. Rather, it contains an antidiscrimination rule insisting that pregnancy be treated similarly to other physical conditions in terms of leave and other employment benefits. As *Cal. Fed.* illustrates, some states also require employers to provide job-protected unpaid leaves to pregnant employees. E.g., Cal. Gov't Code §12945(b) (West 1992 & Supp. 2001); Mont. Code Ann. §49-2-310(2) (1999). In addition, some states' temporary disability programs provide partial wage replacement to cover pregnancy. E.g., Cal. Unemp. Ins. Code §2626(b)(1) (West Supp. 2001); Haw. Rev. Stat. §393-32(a) (1996).

3. How does an employer treat pregnant women *similarly* to "other persons not so affected but similar in their ability or inability to work"? See Jamie L. Clanton, Note, Toward Eradicating Pregnancy Discrimination at Work: Interpreting the PDA to "Mean What It Says," 86 Iowa L. Rev. 703 (2001) (pointing out that courts differ in their interpretation).

4. Despite the PDA, workers continue to report pregnancy discrimination (termed "new mom discrimination"). See Diane E. Lewis, Out in the Field; Parents Say They Fear Pregnancy Backlash, Boston Globe, Apr. 8, 2001, at J2 (noting that more than 40 percent of 700 parents fear that announcing their pregnancy will lead to repercussions at work). Because the PDA makes pregnancy discrimination illegal, employers may offer other reasons for discharge or demotion. See, e.g., Craig v. Exxon Corp., 2000 WL 283962 (N.D. Ill. 2000). Some Title VII cases may make it more difficult, however, to prove that an employer's reasons are a pretext for discrimination. See, e.g., St. Mary's Honor Ctr. v. Hicks, 509 U.S. 502 (1993).

5. As Professor Williams explains, the plaintiffs lost in *Geduldig* and *Gilbert* because the Supreme Court determined that pregnancy discrimination did not constitute sex discrimination. However, in a subsequent case, Nashville Gas Co. v. Satty, 434 U.S. 136 (1977), the plaintiff prevailed in her challenge to a pregnant woman's loss of accumulated seniority (upon her return from a maternity leave). If pregnancy discrimination does not amount to sex discrimination in one context (disability insurance coverage), can it in another (loss of seniority)? See David L. Kirp & Dorothy Robyn, Pregnancy, Justice and the Justices, 57 Tex. L. Rev. 947, 954 (1979); cf. Sylvia A. Law, Rethinking Sex and the Constitution, 132 U. Pa. L. Rev. 955, 983 (1984).

6. The Court has held that the PDA protects male employees from unfavorable treatment. In Newport News Shipbuilding & Dry Dock Co. v. EEOC, 462 U.S. 669 (1983), the Court invalidated a medical insurance

plan providing less coverage for the pregnancies of employees' spouses than for other medical conditions of dependents. Can you reconcile this case with *Cal. Fed.*?

7. Is it fair to protect the job of an employee who misses work because of pregnancy but not one who misses work because of a broken leg? To what extent will the "special treatment" required under California law compromise women's employment opportunities? Might it revitalize early twentieth-century attitudes that women needed protective labor legislation (limiting the hours women could work because of women's childbearing potential)? See Muller v. Oregon, 208 U.S. 412 (1908). On the other hand, without "special treatment," what will happen to female employees, of whom approximately 80 percent are likely to require some time off from work because of pregnancy?[52] Do such data mean that the law must require pregnancy-related leaves? See Herma Hill Kay, Equality and Difference: The Case of Pregnancy, 1 Berkeley Women's L.J. 1 (1985). On the equal treatment-special treatment debate, see Feminist Legal Theory: Foundations 121-207 (D. Kelly Weisberg ed., 1993).

8. Do state parental leave statutes violate the right to privacy by compelling men and women to jeopardize job security in order to have children? If so, should these regulations be subject to a higher level of constitutional scrutiny? See Catherine G. Meier, Protecting Parental Leave, A Fundamental Rights Model, 33 Willamette L. Rev. 177 (1997) (so arguing).

9. Should the PDA cover discrimination against women who miss work to undergo infertility treatments? Is infertility "a pregnancy-related medical condition" covered by Title VII? Or is infertility distinct from issues of pregnancy? See Cintra D. Bentley, Note, A Pregnant Pause: Are Women Who Undergo Fertility Treatment to Achieve Pregnancy Within the Scope of Title VII's Pregnancy Discrimination Act?, 73 Chi.-Kent L. Rev. 391 (1998). See also LaPorta v. Wal-Mart Stores, 163 F. Supp.2d 758 (W.D. Mich. 2001).

10. *Fetal protection policies.* Sometimes, pregnancy discrimination derives from the employer's concern about its potential liability for harm to the fetus. May an employer refuse to allow women (both pregnant and non-pregnant) from working in an occupation that might pose harm to the (or a potential) fetus? See International Union, UAW v. Johnson Controls, Inc., 499 U.S. 187 (1991). May an employer lay off a pregnant employee who previously suffered a miscarriage out of fear that she will harm her fetus by continuing to work? Require all pregnant employees to take leaves for the same reason? See Peralta v. Chromium

---

[52]. See Brief for the Amici Curiae, California Dept. of Fair Employment and Housing, Employment Law Center, and Equal Rights Advocates, Inc., Miller-Wohl v. Commissioner, 515 F. Supp. 1264 (D. Mont. 1981), No. 81-3333, at 23.

Plating & Polishing Corp., 2000 U.S. Dist. LEXIS 17416 (E.D.N.Y. 2000). See generally Mary E. Becker, From *Muller v. Oregon* to Fetal Vulnerability Policies, 53 U. Chi. L. Rev. 1219 (1986); Suzanne U. Samuels, The Fetal Protection Debate Revisited: The Impact of *U.A.W. v. Johnson Controls* on the Federal and State Courts, 17 Women's Rts. L. Rep. 209 (1996). See also Diane Frederick, Expectant Mother Ready to Fight Fires, Indianapolis Star, Feb. 7, 1998, at NO1 (reporting case of pregnant firefighter who was relieved of active duty because of employer's concern about potential occupational hazards).

## Problem

Hunter Tylo is a soap opera star on prime-time television. On "Melrose Place," she plays a happily married woman who suddenly begins an affair. Shortly after she accepts the job, Hunter becomes pregnant. She informs her employer Spelling Entertainment Group. One month later, she is fired. Spelling informs her that they have a contractual right to terminate her if there was a "material change in [her] appearance." Further, Spelling argues that her pregnancy does not conform to the character she portrays. Tylo alleges a violation of the Pregnancy Discrimination Act. What result? See Tylo v. Superior Court, 64 Cal. Rptr.2d 731 (Ct. App. 1997).

### b. Balancing Work and Family

### ■ CALDWELL v. HOLLAND OF TEXAS, INC.
*208 F.3d 671 (8th Cir. 2000)*

BRIGHT, Circuit Judge.

[Juanita] Caldwell is a single mother, working to support herself and her three-year-old son, Kejuan. Before she was summarily fired, Caldwell worked for Holland, which owns and operates several Kentucky Fried Chicken restaurants in Texarkana, Arkansas. Caldwell worked for Holland for three years, and during that time, she developed an excellent record working at the Kentucky Fried Chicken on Hickory Street.

On Saturday, June 7, 1997, Kejuan awoke with a high fever, pain in his ears, and congestion. Caldwell promptly notified Assistant Manager Loyce, prior to the start of her morning shift, that she would be absent because Kejuan required immediate medical attention. Loyce gave Caldwell permission to miss her shift. That morning, a doctor at an emergency clinic diagnosed Kejuan as having an acute ear infection. During this visit, the doctor prescribed a ten-day course of antibiotics and a two-day decongestant for Kejuan. At the same time, the treating physician informed Caldwell that her son's condition probably would require surgery if her son was to avoid permanent hearing loss, and he recommended that Caldwell schedule a follow-up examination with her son's regular pediatrician, Dr. Mark Wright.

Later that Saturday night, upon the request of an assistant manager, Caldwell worked an evening shift at one of Holland's other restaurant locations. While Caldwell was working, her elderly mother cared for her son and administered his medications. Caldwell did not have any shifts on Sunday. When Caldwell returned to her regular work on Monday morning, June 9, 1997, Mark Monholland, a manager at the Hickory Street restaurant, abruptly fired Caldwell without discussing her absence of June 7, 1997.

The supplemental affidavit of Ms. Caldwell, Kejuan's mother, asserts that Kejuan suffered "incapacity" for more than three consecutive days following his trip to the clinic and recites that Kejuan did not participate in his "normal activities," remained inside the house, and was kept in bed as much as possible. He remained under the care of either his mother or grandmother who administered prescribed medications during "this entire time." During a follow-up visit on July 1, 1997, Dr. Wright prescribed a second ten-day course of antibiotics for Kejuan in an attempt to treat his "persistent ear infection." On July 17, 1997, Kejuan had surgery to remove his adenoids and tonsils and to place tubes in his ears. Following surgery, Kejuan received another course of antibiotics and orders to remain in bed for one week. His mother and grandmother kept him inside following the operation and restricted him from engaging in normal activities.

Caldwell sued and argued that her termination violated the FMLA. . . .

The FMLA allows eligible employees to take up to a total of twelve workweeks of leave per year for, among other things, "serious health conditions" that afflict their immediate family members. See 29 U.S.C. §2612(a)(1)(C) ("to care for the spouse, or son, daughter, or parent, of the employee [who] has a serious health condition"). The employee must show that her family member suffered a serious health condition and that her absence was attributable to the family member's serious health condition.

A "serious health condition" occurs, under the regulations, when the family member suffers an "illness, injury, impairment, or physical or mental condition" that requires "inpatient care" or "continuing treatment" by a health care provider. See 29 C.F.R. §825.114(a). Here, the parties agree that Kejuan never received inpatient care. The pertinent issue is whether Kejuan received continuing treatment. A family member receives continuing treatment if the person experiences "[a] period of *incapacity* . . . of more than three consecutive calendar days" and then receives subsequent treatment, or experiences further incapacity relating to, the same condition. 29 C.F.R. §825.114(a)(2)(i). The subsequent treatment must include, either "[t]reatment two or more times by a health care provider . . . ," or "[t]reatment by a health care provider on at least one occasion which results in a regimen of continuing treatment under the supervision of the health care provider." 29 C.F.R. §825.114(a)(2)(i)(A)-(B). . . .

The applicability of the FMLA, here, turns on whether Caldwell can prove a two-pronged inquiry: first, she must show that Kejuan suffered "a period of incapacity of more than three consecutive calendar days"; second, she must show that Kejuan subsequently received continued, supervised treatment relating to the same condition. . . .

In assessing the first prong of Caldwell's case, we note at the outset that the question of what constitutes incapacity of a three-year-old raises an issue not directly addressed by the regulations. The regulations state that incapacity may be determined based on an individual's "inability to work, attend school or perform other regular daily activities due to the serious health condition, treatment therefor, or recovery therefrom." See 29 C.F.R. §825.114(a)(2)(i). Because most three-year-old children do not work or attend school, the standard offered by the regulations is an insufficient guide. The fact finder must determine whether the child's illness demonstrably affected his normal activity. In making this determination, the fact finder may consider a variety of factors, including but not limited to: whether the child participated in his daily routines or was particularly difficult to care for during that period, and whether a daycare facility would have allowed a child with Kejuan's illness to attend its sessions.

Caldwell avers that Kejuan's ear infection, which was severe enough to warrant emergency treatment, required constant care for a period of more than three days. She states in her supplemental affidavit that Kejuan was incapacitated beginning Saturday, June 7, 1997, for more than three consecutive days. She further states:

> He [Kejuan] remained inside the house and was kept in bed as much as possible. He did not participate in any of his normal activities. He was under the constant care of me (his mother) and his grandmother, and both the prescribed medications and a fever reducer were administered to him during this entire time.

In addition to Caldwell's affidavit, the medical records show that Kejuan's ear infection was a continuing, persistent condition that could only be treated by surgery. Kejuan's period of incapacity, therefore, may be measured over the entire time during which he was suffering from this illness and being treated for it. We note that Kejuan was treated for his condition for ten days following his first visit to the emergency clinic. The medical records state that the condition did not improve, and as a result, Dr. Wright, his regular physician, prescribed another ten-day course of antibiotics. Despite the two medical treatments, Kejuan's condition continued to persist until Dr. Trone, a surgical specialist, performed surgery to remove his tonsils and adenoids on July 17, 1997. This entire period, from June 7-July 17, 1997, may constitute Kejuan's period of incapacity if his illness and these various treatments disrupted his basic daily routines, and if, as the record suggests, his ongoing treatment was not successfully alleviating his condition of disability. . . .

Alternatively, the ten-day period beginning on June 7, 1997 could constitute Kejuan's period of incapacity. As we have noted, his mother's supplemental affidavit refers to constant care and administration of prescribed medications during "this entire time.". . . Even if Kejuan did not sustain "incapacity" under the regulations *prior* to his surgery, the record clearly shows that the inflammation and infection in his ears resulted in a period of incapacity that lasted more than three days once he had the tonsillectomy and adenoidectomy. . . .

FMLA's purpose is to help working men and women balance the conflicting demands of work and personal life. The law requires courts to consider the seriousness of the afflicted individual's condition because the law was designed to prevent individuals like Juanita Caldwell from having to choose between their livelihood and treatment for their own or their family members' serious health conditions. Upon examining the seriousness of Kejuan's ear infection, which required surgery to prevent deafness, we hold that there is at least a question of fact as to whether Kejuan's condition was "serious" under the regulations. . . .

On the second prong of the threshold inquiry, we believe that Caldwell has generated a genuine issue of fact regarding whether Kejuan received "subsequent treatment." Here, after the first ten-day antibiotic treatment, Kejuan was treated by Dr. Wright and later by Dr. Trone in surgery. . . . Furthermore, the record shows at least two post-operative medical visits to monitor Kejuan's condition. . . .

For the reasons stated above, the district court erred in granting a summary judgment of dismissal. Accordingly, we reverse and remand for further proceedings.

■ **FAMILY AND MEDICAL LEAVE ACT**
*29 U.S.C. §§2601, 2611, 2612, 2614 (1994)*

### §2601. FINDINGS AND PURPOSES

(a) Findings. The Congress finds that

(1) the number of single-parent households and two-parent households in which the single parent or both parents work is increasing significantly; . . .

(3) the lack of employment policies to accommodate working parents can force individuals to choose between job security and parenting; . . .

(5) due to the nature of the roles of men and women in our society, the primary responsibility for family caretaking often falls on women, and such responsibility affects their working lives more than it affects the working lives of men; and

(6) employment standards that apply to one gender only have serious potential for encouraging employers to discriminate against employees and applicants for employment who are of that gender.

(b) Purposes. It is the purpose of this Act

(1) to balance the demands of the workplace with the needs of families, to promote stability and economic security of families, and to promote national interests in preserving family integrity;

(2) to entitle employees to take reasonable leave for medical reasons, for the birth or adoption of a child, and for the care of a child, spouse, or parent who has a serious health condition;

(3) to accomplish such purposes . . . in a manner which accommodates the legitimate interests of employers;

(4) to accomplish such purposes . . . in a manner that, consistent with the Equal Protection Clause of the Fourteenth Amendment, minimizes the potential for discrimination on the basis of sex by ensuring generally that leave is available for eligible medical reasons (including maternity-related disability) and for compelling family reasons, on a gender-neutral basis; and

(5) to promote the goal of equal employment opportunity for women and men, pursuant to such clause.

### §2611. DEFINITIONS . . .

(2)(A) "[E]ligible employee" means an employee who has been employed
(i) for at least 12 months by the employer with respect to whom leave is requested under section 2612; and
(ii) for at least 1,250 hours of service with such employer during the previous 12-month period. . . .
(4)(A) "[E]mployer"
(i) means any person engaged in commerce or in any industry or activity affecting commerce who employs 50 or more employees [within a 75-mile radius of the worksite] . . .
(5) "[E]mployment benefits" means all benefits provided or made available to employees by an employer, including group life insurance, health insurance, disability insurance, sick leave, annual leave, educational benefits, and pensions. . . .
(7) "[P]arent" means the biological parent of an employee or an individual who stood in loco parentis to an employee when the employee was a son or daughter. . . .

(11) "[S]erious health condition" means an illness, injury, impairment, or physical or mental condition that involves

(A) inpatient care in a hospital, hospice, or residential medical care facility; or

(B) continuing treatment by a health care provider.

(12) "[S]on or daughter" means a biological, adopted, or foster child, a stepchild, a legal ward, or a child of a person standing in loco parentis, who is [under 18, or mentally or physically disabled].

(13) "[S]pouse" means a husband or wife, as the case may be.


### §2612. LEAVE REQUIREMENT

(a) In General.

(1) Entitlement to leave. [A]n eligible employee shall be entitled to a total of 12 workweeks of leave during any 12-month period for one or more of the following:

(A) Because of the birth of a son or daughter of the employee and in order to care for such son or daughter.

(B) Because of the placement of a son or daughter with the employee for adoption or foster care.

(C) In order to care for the spouse, or a son, daughter, or parent, of the employee, if such spouse, son, daughter, or parent has a serious health condition.

(D) Because of a serious health condition that makes the employee unable to perform the functions of the position of such employee. . . .

(b) [Leave generally shall not be taken intermittently.]

(c) Unpaid Leave Permitted. Except as provided in subsection (d), leave granted under subsection (a) may consist of unpaid leave. . . .

(d) Relationship to Paid Leave.

(1) Unpaid leave. If an employer provides paid leave for fewer than 12 workweeks, the additional weeks of leave necessary to attain the 12 workweeks of leave required under this subchapter may be provided without compensation.

(2) Substitution of paid leave.

[The employee may choose, or the employer may require, accrued paid leave or sick leave be substituted for the unpaid 12-week leave.]

(e) Foreseeable Leave. [If leave is foreseeable based on birth or placement, employee shall provide employer with 30 days notice. If leave based on birth or adoption is not foreseeable, then employee shall provide such notice as is practicable.]

(f) Spouses Employed by the Same Employer. [If husband and wife] are employed by the same employer, the aggregate number of workweeks of leave to which both may be entitled may be limited to 12 workweeks during any 12-month period. . . .

§2614. Employment and Benefits Protection

(a) Restoration to Position

(1) In general. Except as provided in subsection (b), any eligible employee who takes leave under section 2612 for the intended purpose of the leave shall be entitled, on return from such leave

(A) to be restored by the employer to the position of employment held by the employee when the leave commenced; or

(B) to be restored to an equivalent position with equivalent employment benefits, pay, and other terms and conditions of employment.

[The taking of leave shall not result in the loss of any employment benefit accrued prior to the date on which the leave commenced but the restored employee has no right to the accrual of any seniority benefits during any period of leave.]

(b) Exemption Concerning Certain Highly Compensated Employees.

(1) Denial of restoration. An employer may deny restoration under subsection (a) to any eligible employee described [if]

(A) such denial is necessary to prevent substantial and grievous economic injury to the operations of the employer; . . .

(2) Affected employees. An eligible employee described in paragraph (1) is a salaried eligible employee who is among the highest paid 10 percent of the employees employed by the employer within 75 miles of the facility at which the employee is employed.

(c) [Employer is required to maintain health benefits for the duration of the leave.]

## Notes and Questions

1. *Background.* The public outcry for family leave dates to the 1970's, after the women's liberation movement led to expanding employment opportunities for women. The number of mothers who were working outside the home dramatically increased. The largest increase occurred in the numbers of mothers with preschool children. "Between 1959 and 1974, the employment rate for mothers with children under three more than doubled, from 15 to 31 percent." Marie Richmond-Abbott, Women Wage Earners, in Feminist Philosophies 135, 136 (Janet A. Kourany et al. eds., 1992). By 1999, 79 percent of mothers in the labor force had children between the ages of 14 to 17, and 64 percent had children under the age of six. Michele Himmelberg, Back to Work; After Many Lengthy Absences, Many Women are Re-Entering the Job Market, San Diego Union-Trib., Apr. 2, 2001, at D-1.

2. The FMLA became law after a lengthy battle. First proposed in 1985, the act was twice passed by Congress but vetoed by President

Bush. President Clinton signed the act in February 1993. Since then, 24 million people have taken advantage of its provisions. Bonnie Erbe, Will Congress Leave Leave Alone?, Working Woman, Dec./Jan. 2000, at 25. How does the FMLA redress the PDA's shortcomings? See Patricia Schroeder, Parental Leave: The Need for a Federal Policy, in The Parental Leave Crisis: Toward a National Policy 326-332 (Edward F. Zigler & Meryl Frank eds., 1988). Recall the purpose clause of the FLMA. To what extent does the FMLA accomplish these purposes? See Michael Selmi, The Limited Vision of the Family and Medical Leave Act, 44 Vill. L. Rev. 395, 405-411 (1999) (criticizing FMLA).

Opponents of the FMLA originally charged that it would have a significant negative impact on industry. An empirical study commissioned by Congress (based on 7 million worksites) reveals that, in fact, the FMLA has had little impact in terms of cost or disruption to employers. U.S. Comm'n on Leave, A Workable Balance: Report to Congress on Family and Medical Leave Policies (May 1996).

3. According to the congressional findings supra, the FMLA is especially important for those persons who risk losing their jobs to care for a sick relative. But does the FMLA serve this need? Are the working poor able to take *unpaid* leaves? See Emily A. Hayes, Bridging the Gap Between Work and Family: Accomplishing the Goals of the Family and Medical Leave Act of 1993, 42 Wm. & Mary L. Rev. 1507, 1524 (2001). In response to public demand, approximately 25 states are exploring ways to offer paid leaves. Some states (i.e., California, Hawaii, New Jersey, New York, and Rhode Island) already tap state disability funds to provide partial pay. Of these states, New Jersey and New York are considering expanding their disability program to fathers and other caretakers. Thirteen states are proposing using unemployment funds to provide family leave. See Debra Rosenberg, We Have to Sacrifice: States Offer to Pick Up the Tab for Unpaid Leave, Newsweek, Aug. 27, 2001, at 46.

Conversely, does the FMLA accommodate the needs of highly paid employees? See, e.g., Poppo v. AON Risk Servs. Co., 2001 WL 392543 (S.D.N.Y. 2001). See also Angie K. Young, Assessing the Medical and Family Leave Act in Terms of Gender Equality, Work/Family Balance, and the Needs of Children, 5 Mich. J. Gender & L. 113, 143-144 (1998). In trying to achieve fairness for working parents, does the FMLA create unfairness for the childless?

4. How well does the FMLA address the needs of gay and lesbian parents? See Ruth Colker, The Anti-Subordination Principle: Applications, 3 Wis. Women's L.J. 59, 74-75 n.46 (1987) (criticizing FLMA for its "family-oriented language" that reinforces benefits to traditional family). But cf. Young, supra, at 138 (FMLA, at least, suggests flexible understanding of parent-child relationships). How well does the FMLA address the needs of single parents? Of fathers? In Knussman v.

Maryland, 2001 WL 1379871 (4th Cir. 2001), a federal appellate court vacated a $375,000 jury verdict to a state trooper whose supervisors refused him FMLA leave to care for his newborn but affirmed the judgment against a personnel officer on equal protection grounds (for relying on the irrebutable presumption that only mothers can be primary caregivers). See also Martin H. Malin, Fathers and Parental Leave Revisited, 19 N. Ill. U. L. Rev. 25 (1998).

5. To date, almost all federal litigation concerning the FMLA involves claims of job restoration (i.e., cases in which the employee was not reinstated or not reinstated to an equivalent position) or damages (rather than leave denials). Telephone interview with Malcolm Poist, Wage and Hour Compliance Specialist, FMLA Team, Department of Labor (Sept. 5, 2001).

6. Employees may have rights to family and medical leave under state law as well as under the FMLA. Many states provide maternity, family, or medical leave. Does the FMLA preempt these state statutes? Recall *Cal. Fed.*, supra. Similarly, some employees may have overlapping rights under the Americans with Disabilities Act, 42 U.S.C. §§12101-12213 (1994 & Supp. 1998).

However, note that state employees may face difficulties enforcing their rights. Many circuit courts have held that the FMLA does not apply to state employees, based on recent United States Supreme Court decisions[53] barring suits under the Eleventh Amendment in federal court by state employees to recover money damages by reason of the state's failure to comply with some federal statutes. See, e.g., Laro v. New Hampshire, 259 F.3d 1 (1st Cir. 2001); Lizzi v. Alexander, 255 F.3d 128 (4th Cir. 2001); Townsel v. Missouri, 233 F.3d 1094 (8th Cir. 2000). But cf. Cornforth v. University of Oklahoma Board of Regents, 263 F.3d 1129 (10th Cir. 2001) (holding that an injunction requiring supervisor to reinstate employee under the FMLA was not barred by university's Eleventh Amendment immunity).

7. Because rights under the FMLA may be co-extensive with rights under state law or under an employer's sick leave policy, must the employee specifically refer to FMLA to invoke the statute's protection when notifying an employer of the need for a leave? See Ragsdale v. Wolverine Worldwide, Inc., 218 F.3d 933 (8th Cir. 2000) (holding that employer's failure to designate company leave as FMLA leave does not preclude employer's subsequent denial of FMLA leave), *cert. granted*, 121 S. Ct. 2548 (2001).

8. Given that the employer may need to solicit information from an employee's health care providers to ascertain whether the leave qualifies under the FMLA, does such inquiry invade the employee's privacy? See Lisa Bornstein, Inclusion and Exclusion in Work-Family Policy: The

---

[53]. See, e.g., Kimel v. Florida Bd. of Regents, 528 U.S. 62 (2000) (applying to suits based on the Americans with Disabilities Act), and Board of Trustees of the Univ. of Ala. v. Garrett, 531 U.S. 356 (2001) (applying to suits based on the Rehabilitation Act).

Public Values and Moral Code Embedded in the Family and Medical Leave Act, 10 Colum. J. Gender & L. 77, 104-105 (2000).

9. Until the FMLA, the United States was one of two industrialized countries (with South Africa) without national family leave. Other industrialized countries, as well as less developed countries, guarantee such leave. Many provide paid leave, often for extended periods. For example, Austria provides either parent paid leave from the end of the maternity leave until the child turns two; Sweden provides 18 months of paid leave to either parent. Cara A. McCaffrey & Austin Graff, Note, European Union Directive on Parental Leave: Will the European Union Face the Same Problems as Those Faced by the United States Under the 1993 Family and Medical Leave Act?, 17 Hofstra Lab. & Emp. L.J. 229, 230-231, 244-251 (1999). Why has the United States lagged so far behind in pregnancy leaves and parental leaves? See Joseph P. Allen, European Infant Care Leaves: Foreign Perspectives on the Integration of Work and Family Roles, in The Parental Leave Crisis, supra, at 270-271.

## Problems

1. Martha and Michael Smith are expecting quadruplets (as a result of fertility treatments). Martha is a schoolteacher; Michael works at a computer company. During the fifth month of Martha's pregnancy, her physician advises complete bedrest. Martha has no difficulty taking time off from work because this is summer vacation. However, she will need someone to take care of her (fix her meals, run errands, and so forth). Michael, as well as her sister Miriam (who works for a brokerage firm), consider taking leave under the FMLA to care for Martha for the remainder of her pregnancy. What advice would you give them about the likelihood that their requests will be granted?

2. Catherine Marzano is hired by Computer Science Co. (CSC) as a "junior technical recruiter." She is promoted several times. Shortly after her assignment to Mr. Marzi's unit, she learns that she is pregnant. She is reluctant to tell Mr. Marzi because seven employees previously were terminated after taking maternity leave. She does tell him and plans to take leave. However, she notices that Mr. Marzi speaks as "if she wasn't coming back." During her leave, her unit begins experiencing losses (despite the stellar financial performance of CSC). Mr. Marzi eliminates Catherine's position and nine others. He notifies Catherine by saying that she "would be better off if [she] stays home with the baby and collects unemployment." Catherine alleges pregnancy discrimination and unlawful interference with her rights under the FMLA. What result? Marzano v. Computer Science Corp., 91 F.3d 497 (3d Cir. 1996).

Prior to the FMLA, men occasionally litigated the lack of paternity leave. See, e.g., Danielson v. Board of Higher Educ., 358 F. Supp. 22 (S.D.N.Y. 1972). What barriers prevent fathers from taking family leaves?

## ■ MARTIN H. MALIN, FATHERS AND PARENTAL LEAVE
### 72 Tex. L. Rev. 1047, 1049-1052, 1057-1058, 1064, 1072-1075, 1077-1079 (1994)

During the mid-1980s, the research group Catalyst conducted an extensive study of family leave policies and practices among large employers. Catalyst found that thirty-seven percent of the 322 employers that responded offered unpaid parental leave to men. However, only nine companies were able to report that even one male employee ever took such a leave. More recent evidence confirms the Catalyst finding that it is rare for fathers to take parental leave. . . . A 1993 Bureau of National Affairs survey found that only seven percent of male workers would take a twelve-week unpaid leave following the birth or adoption of a child whereas forty-three percent of working women would do so. Even liberal estimates place the participation rate of American fathers in parental leave programs at less than ten percent. . . .

Largely missing from the debate over maternal work-family conflicts is any discussion of paternal work-family conflicts. The two, however, are linked to a significant extent. Just as the absence of adequate maternal leave policies has been a barrier to women's roles in the workplace, the absence of adequate paternal leave policies has been a barrier to men's roles in the home. Furthermore, as long as parental leave remains de facto maternal leave, work-family conflicts will remain a significant barrier to women's employment and a significant source of discrimination against women. . . .

Sweden provides the most extensive parental leave benefits for men of any country. The Swedish parental leave law was first enacted in 1974, providing parental leave at ninety percent of base pay up to a stated maximum. The leave is paid from a fund that is financed through payroll taxes. Fathers may take ten days of leave immediately after childbirth, colloquially referred to as "daddy days." Couples may also divide between them a generous amount of parental leave, provided that only one parent may be on leave at anytime. Initially parents were able to divide six months between them. . . . Effective January 1, 1995, couples in which only one parent takes leave will receive one month at ninety percent of base pay and ten months at eighty percent. When both parents take leave, each will receive one month at ninety percent and may divide ten months at eighty percent of base pay.

The typical Swedish father takes advantage of his ten daddy days. During 1991, eighty-five percent of all eligible fathers took an average of 9.7 days. Because fathers and mothers are forced to compete for the use of the remaining parental leave, Swedish women still dominate its use. . . .

The most recently published study by sociologist Linda Haas focused on couples in Gothenborg, an industrial city of 500,000 that is Sweden's largest port. Haas found that fathers who took parental leave were significantly more likely to share in child-care responsibilities and in performing specific child-care tasks, including preparing food, shopping, doing laundry, diapering, bathing, getting up at night, reading, comforting, and taking the child to the doctor. The effects of paternal leave were magnified when the father took at least twenty percent of all leave taken by the couple. . . .

### BARRIERS TO PATERNAL USE OF PARENTAL LEAVE . . .

#### 1. AVAILABILITY . . .

Prior to the FMLA, [the lack of paternal leave policies] posed an absolute barrier for many working men. Employers were much more likely to provide childbirth leave to women than men. . . . Even when leave was made available to employed fathers, pre-FMLA employer policies tended to hide it from them. For example, Catalyst found that ninety percent of large companies that offered parental leave for men did so under the rubric of personal leaves of absence and made no attempt to inform their workforce that the leaves were available to new fathers. It was rare for a company expressly to advise male employees of the availability of paternity or parental leave. Consequently, many men failed to take parental leave because they were completely unaware that it was an available option. Instead, fathers tended to create make-shift leaves of short duration by using accrued vacation and personal days. . . .

#### 2. FINANCING PARENTAL LEAVE

Paid paternal leave policies are extremely rare. When parental leave is available to men, it is almost always without pay. Many mothers, on the other hand, are able to take the initial part of a leave following childbirth as disability leave, which often includes full or partial income replacement benefits. The rarity of paid leave for fathers means that almost all working parents face one of two situations: initial paid leave available to the mother coupled with unpaid leave available to the father or unpaid leave available to both parents. In both cases, the absence of pay poses a major barrier to the father's ability to take leave.

When the leave available to the mother is paid and the leave available to the father is not, it sends a signal to the parents that the mother is expected to take leave and the father is not. It becomes easy for the father not to take leave by reasoning that the children will be cared for with little or no drop in household income if only the mother stays home.

When the leave available to both parents is unpaid, the situation is worsened. Because very few families can afford to have no one bringing home a paycheck, unpaid leave forces fathers to compete with mothers for its use. Traditional sex roles that assign primary caregiving responsibilities to mothers and primary breadwinning responsibilities to fathers ensure that when both parents compete for taking leaves, the mother will tend to monopolize the leave. The decision to allocate the unpaid leave to the mother is also economically rational for many couples in which the father earns the higher income.

The birth of a child usually results in an increase in household expenses and is often accompanied by a decrease in maternal contribution to household income. This exacerbates the effects of the lack of adequate funding for paternal parental leaves. . . .

. . . Sweden's experience suggests that funding parental leave greatly increases paternal participation. [T]he history of the Swedish program has been marked by increased use of leave by fathers. Fewer than three percent of Swedish fathers took parental leave in 1974, the first year it was available, as compared with ninety-eight percent of Swedish mothers. In 1975, the amount of paid leave available to be shared by the couple was increased from six to seven months and paternal participation began to increase. By 1977, it had increased to ten percent. . . . In 1989, Sweden increased the almost fully paid leave to twelve months. [F]athers' participation initially jumped to forty-four percent. Another report shows paternal participation at thirty percent. . . . A reasonable conclusion from Sweden's experience is that removal of financial barriers greatly increases fathers' participation in parental leave.

### 3. WORKPLACE HOSTILITY

Employer sensitivity to the need to accommodate workers' family responsibilities is increasing steadily. Unfortunately, many employers' willingness to make such accommodations is limited to women workers. Men's accommodation requests are often met by, "Your wife should handle it."

The Catalyst survey graphically illustrates the extent of employer hostility to male employees taking parental leave. Large employers are least likely to experience negative financial effects from fathers taking parental leave. Yet, Catalyst found that sixty-three percent of large employers considered it unreasonable for a man to take any parental leave, and another seventeen percent considered paternal leave reasonable only if limited to two weeks or less. Even among large employers providing paternal leave, an amazing forty-one percent considered it unreasonable for a man to actually use it, and another twenty-three percent considered a reasonable leave for a man to be two weeks or less! It appears that many employers extend parental leave to fathers so that they can give the appearance of gender-neutral policies, but never intend for fathers to use it.

The Catalyst survey responses show glaring and pervasive employer hostility toward men taking parental leave. Confirmation of this problem may be found in other sources. For example, when Catalyst interviewed human resource and other managers, it found them quite candid in their assessments that their companies would take a very negative view of fathers who might take leave to care for their children. Another study found executives more likely to accommodate the family needs of women employees than similarly situated men, including being more likely to grant a female accountant's request for a one-month child-care leave than a male's. Fathers who take parental leave justifiably fear for their jobs and their families' financial security.

Employers are not the only source of workplace hostility. Co-worker hostility can generate powerful peer pressure. Such peer pressure can intimidate and deter fathers from taking leave.

Even when leave is available and communicated to employees and financial barriers are removed, workplace hostility can deter many fathers from taking leave. . . .

———————————

See also Martin H. Malin, Fathers and Parental Leave Revisited, 19 N. Ill. U. L. Rev. 25 (1998) (examining continued barriers to paternal use of parental leave, especially in terms of collective bargaining agreements and unemployment compensation statutes).

## ■ DIKE v. SCHOOL BOARD
*650 F.2d 783 (5th Cir. 1981)*

GODBOLD, Chief Judge:

Janice Dike, a teacher in the Orange County (Florida) School System, sued the school board and the superintendent of schools under 42 U.S.C. §1983, challenging the board's refusal to permit her to breastfeed her child. . . .

Dike is employed by the school board as a kindergarten teacher at an elementary school. After giving birth to her child she returned to her teaching post. Having chosen to breastfeed her child, Dike wished to feed the child in this manner at all feedings, including the one feeding necessary during the school day. She sought a means of doing so that would not disrupt the education of children attending the school or interfere with her discharge of work responsibilities.

324 III ■ Being Married: Regulation of the Intact Marriage

Dike therefore arranged for her husband or her babysitter to bring the child to school during her lunch period, when she was free from any duties. Dike would then nurse the child in privacy in a locked room into which other persons could not see. On occasions when the school asked Dike to perform duties during her lunch period she would hand the infant to her husband or babysitter. She was thus always available for work even during her duty-free hour. She alleges that this routine did not disrupt the educational process at the school or her work performance.

After three months of this routine without disruption or incident the school principal directed Dike to stop nursing her child on campus, citing a school board directive prohibiting teachers from bringing their children to work with them for any reason. The rule's stated rationale is to avoid possible disruptions by the children of teachers and to avoid the possibility of the children having an accident and subjecting the school board to litigation. The principal threatened disciplinary action should Dike continue to nurse the child at school.

Dike heeded these warnings and stopped nursing her child during the school day. But because the child developed an allergic reaction to formula milk, Dike had to artificially extract milk with a breast pump and leave it for the child's mid-day feeding. Dike asserts this new routine caused the child to develop observable psychological changes that also affected her own emotional well-being. She requested permission to resume her earlier procedure, alternatively requesting permission to nurse the child off campus during her non-duty time or to nurse the child in her camper van in the school parking lot. The school board denied these requests, apparently relying on another policy prohibiting teachers from leaving school premises during the school day.

A short time later the infant began refusing to nurse from a bottle. Dike thus had no choice but to breastfeed the child. Because the school board denied her permission to breastfeed on campus or off, Dike was compelled to take an unpaid leave of absence for the remainder of the school term.

Dike sued the board, alleging that it had unduly interfered with a constitutionally protected right to nurture her child by breastfeeding. [The district court, deeming the action frivolous, dismissed her complaint and awarded attorneys' fees to the defendants.]

The Constitution protects from undue state interference citizens' freedom of personal choice in some areas of marriage and family life. These protected interests have been described as rights of personal privacy or as "fundamental" personal liberties. . . . Among these protected liberties are individual decisions respecting marriage [citing *Zablocki* and *Loving*], procreation [citing *LaFleur* and *Skinner*], contraception [citing *Griswold* and *Eisenstadt*], abortion [citing Roe v. Wade], and family relationships. The Supreme Court has long recognized that parents' interest in nurturing and rearing their children deserves special protection against state interference [citing Pierce v. Society of Sisters, and Meyer v. Nebraska].

Breastfeeding is the most elemental form of parental care. It is a communion between mother and child that, like marriage, is "intimate to the degree of being sacred," Griswold v. Connecticut, 381 U.S. at 486. Nourishment is necessary to maintain the child's life, and the parent may choose to believe that breastfeeding will enhance the child's psychological as well as physical health. In light of the spectrum of interests that the Supreme Court has held specially protected we conclude that the Constitution protects from excessive state interference a woman's decision respecting breastfeeding her child.

Our conclusion that Dike's interest in breastfeeding is a protected liberty interest, however, is the beginning rather than the end of the constitutional inquiry. . . . The Constitution does not prohibit all restrictions of protected liberties, and the school board may establish by appropriate pleading and proof that its regulations prohibiting teachers from leaving campus or bringing children to school, as applied to teachers who wish to breastfeed their children during non-duty time, further sufficiently important state interests and are closely tailored to effectuate only those interests. . . . The school board's interests in avoiding disruption of the educational process, in ensuring that teachers perform their duties without distraction, and in avoiding potential liability for accidents are presumably legitimate. Whether these or other interests are strong enough to justify the school board's regulations, and whether the regulations are sufficiently narrowly drawn, must be determined at trial. . . .

## Notes and Questions

1. One commentator estimates that more than one million women annually are forced to choose between breastfeeding and keeping their jobs. See Henry Wyatt Christrup, Litigating a Breastfeeding and Employment Case in the New Millennium, 12 Yale J.L. & Feminism 263, 263 (2000). How should *Dike* be decided under the PDA? Under the FMLA? As a state employee might Ms. Dike face particular difficulties litigating her FMLA claim in federal court? Under Title VII (i.e., does breastfeeding discrimination constitute employment discrimination)? Under the Americans with Disabilities Act? Can an employer grant special treatment for breastfeeding mothers without providing parental leaves to fathers or to nonbreastfeeding women? See generally Christrup, supra (reviewing the extent of protection offered by these statutes).

2. Professor Sylvia Law staunchly supports reproductive rights. However, she opposes special treatment for nursing mothers. She elaborates as follows:

Does the policy have a substantial impact in perpetuating inequality? It seems that it does. Either parent, or a stranger, is biologically capable of caring for a child. Limiting the childrearing to nursing women reinforces the cultural expectation that "the paramount destiny and mission of woman are to fulfill the noble and benign offices of wife and mother."[271] Such a policy would have to be struck down because it could not withstand strict scrutiny; the state's interest in promoting the physical or psychic benefits of nursing is not sufficiently substantial to justify the burden upon men and women who would choose to take child care leave but who cannot nurse. Also, the oppressive effect upon women who would prefer not to nurse but are compelled to do so in order to qualify for the leave is not justified by the state's interest.

Sylvia A. Law, Rethinking Sex and the Constitution, 132 U. Pa. L. Rev. 955, 1033-1034 (1984). Do you agree?

3. *Epilogue. Dike*'s holding that breastfeeding is a constitutional right based on the right of privacy has been narrowed by subsequent case law. For example, the district court dismissed Dike's claim on remand, finding that the school board's policy was narrowly tailored and based on compelling state interests. In addition, Shahar v. Bowers (discussed infra Chapter IV), overruled *Dike* insofar as it implicated strict scrutiny review of a government employee's freedom of intimate association claim and upheld, instead, the balancing-test approach. Finally, another federal court of appeals narrowed *Dike* by holding it inapplicable to prison inmates. See Southerland v. Thigpen, 784 F.2d 713 (5th Cir. 1986). See generally Christrup, supra, at 272 (discussing these developments).

4. States providing statutory protection for breastfeeding take three different approaches: (a) exempting breastfeeding from public nudity and other criminal statutes, (b) providing an affirmative right to breastfeed wherever mothers and babies are otherwise authorized to be present, or (c) protecting breastfeeding via civil rights remedies. Danielle M. Shelton, When Private Goes Public: Legal Protection for Women Who Breastfeed in Public and at Work, 14 Law & Ineq. J. 179, 186-187 (1995). Florida (site of *Dike*) followed the first two approaches when it became the first state in 1993 to guarantee the right to breastfeed in public. Legislation was introduced by Rep. Miguel de Grandy (R., Miami) after a security guard harassed a nursing mother at a shopping center.[54] See, e.g., Fla. Stat. Ann §800.02-04 & §847.001 (West 2000) (exempting breastfeeding from definitions of "obscene" and "sexual conduct," unnatural and lascivious acts, exposing or exhibiting sexual organs in public, and lewd or lascivious offenses committed upon or in the presence of persons less than 16 years of age). New York adopts the third approach by permitting private suits enforced through the state Division of Human Rights. Shelton, supra, at 189. For discus-

---

271. Bradwell v. Illinois, 83 U.S. (16 Wall.) 130, 141 (1873).
[54]. Cited in Florida Legislature Guarantees Right to Breast-Feed in Public, S.F. Chron., Mar. 4, 1993, at A3.

sion of other instances of harassment, see Corey Silberstein Shdaimah, Why Breastfeeding Is (Also) a Legal Issue, 10 Hastings L.J. 409, 415 (1999).

5. Is an employer's unfavorable treatment of a nursing mother who has a need or desire to *pump* breast milk at her place of employment a form of gender discrimination? Should breast pumping be afforded protected status in the workplace? If so, how? See, e.g., Haw. Rev. Stat. §378-2 (Supp. 2000) (protecting "lactating women" from employment discrimination); Minn. Stat. §181.929 (1998) (requiring employers to provide unpaid break time to nursing mothers to express breast milk). But cf. Martinez v. NBC Inc., 49 F. Supp. 2d 305 (S.D.N.Y. 1999) (holding that breast pumping is not a disability under the ADA). Or, is breastfeeding just a private lifestyle choice that should not merit such protection? See Jendi B. Reiter, Accommodating Pregnancy and Breastfeeding in the Workplace: Beyond the Civil Rights Paradigm, 9 Tex. J. Women & L. 1, 2 (1999).

6. How do professional women experience the work-family conflict? Data reveal that most male lawyers are married with children and have non-working wives. In contrast, however, women lawyers with children constitute a minority in the profession; almost all are married to men who work full-time. See Nancy E. Dowd, Resisting Essentialism and Hierarchy: A Critique of Work/Family Strategies for Women Lawyers, 16 Harv. BlackLetter L.J. 185, 198 (2000). In response to the work-family conflict, women lawyers develop three strategies: some forego marriage and children, some choose areas of practice that better accommodate the family, and some follow male models of work and family by pairing with a nurturing male who serves as a full-time caregiver or by hiring caregivers. Id. at 200-201. For a study of the working poor's experience with the work-family conflict, see Jonathan Kozol, Rachel and Her Children: Homeless Families in America (1988).

7. Do men and women equally share family responsibilities?

# ■ ARLIE HOCHSCHILD & ANN MACHUNG, THE SECOND SHIFT
*2-10 (1999)*

How well do couples [work two full-time jobs and raise young children]? The more women work outside the home, the more central this question. The number of women in paid work has risen steadily since before the turn of the century, but since 1950 the rise has been staggering. . . . We don't know how many women with children under the age of one worked outside the home in 1950; it was so rare that the Bureau of Labor kept no statistics on it. Today half of such women do. [The author interviewed 50 working couples to determine the allocation of such household tasks as cooking, vacuuming, making beds, sewing, gardening and plant care, sending holiday cards, washing the car, household repairs, tax preparation, household planning, noticing when a child's fingernails need clipping, and caring about how the house looked or about a change in a child's mood.]

[I] discovered that women worked roughly fifteen hours longer each week than men. Over a year, they worked an *extra month of twenty-four-hour days a year.* . . . Just as there is a wage gap between men and women in the workplace, there is a "leisure gap" between them at home. Most women work one shift at the office or factory and a "second shift" at home. . . .

It was a woman who first proposed to me the metaphor, borrowed from industrial life, of the "second shift." She strongly resisted the *idea* that homemaking was a "shift." Her family was her life and she didn't want it reduced to a job. But as she put it, "You're on duty at work. You come home, and you're on duty. Then you go back to work and you're on duty." After eight hours of adjusting insurance claims, she came home to put on the rice for dinner, care for her children, and wash laundry. Despite herself her home life *felt* like a second shift. That was the real story and that was the real problem.

Men who shared the load at home seemed just as pressed for time as their wives, and as torn between the demands of career and small children. . . . But the majority of men did not share the load at home. Some refused outright. Others refused more passively, often offering a loving shoulder to lean on, an understanding ear as their working wife faced the conflict they both saw as hers. But I came to realize that those husbands who helped very little at home were often indirectly just as deeply affected as their wives by the need to do that work, through the resentment their wives feel toward them, and through their need to steel themselves against that resentment. Evan Holt, a warehouse furniture salesman [did] very little housework and played with his four-year-old-son, Joey, at his convenience. . . . His wife did the second shift, but resented it keenly, and half-consciously expressed her frustration and rage by losing interest in sex and becoming overly absorbed with Joey. . . .

One reason women take a deeper interest than men in the problems of juggling work with family life is that even when husbands happily shared the hours of work, their wives felt more *responsible* for home and children. More women kept track of doctors' appointments and arranged for playmates to come over. More mothers than fathers worried about the tail on a child's Halloween costume or a birthday present for a school friend. They were more likely to think about their children while at work and to check in by phone with the baby-sitter.

Partly because of this, more women felt torn between one sense of urgency and another, between the need to soothe a child's fear of being left at daycare, and the need to show the boss she's "serious" at work. More women than men questioned how good they were as parents. . . .

As masses of women have moved into the economy, families have been hit by a "speed-up" in work and family life. There is no more time in the day than there was when wives stayed home, but there is twice as much to get done. It is mainly women who absorb this "speed-up." Twenty percent of the men in my study shared housework equally. Seventy percent of men did a substantial amount (less than half but more than a third), and 10 percent did less than a third. Even when couples share more equitably in the work at home, women do two-thirds of the *daily* jobs at home, like cooking and cleaning up — jobs that fix them into a rigid routine. Most women cook dinner and most men change the oil in the family car. But, as one mother pointed out, dinner needs to be prepared every evening around six o'clock, whereas the car oil needs to be changed every six months, any day around that time, any time that day. Women do more childcare than men, and men repair more household appliances. A child needs to be tended daily while the repair of household appliances can often wait "until I have time." Men thus have more control over *when* they make their contributions than women do. . . .

Another reason women may feel more strained than men is that women more often do two things at once — for example, write checks and return phone calls, vacuum and keep an eye on a three-year-old, fold laundry and think out the shopping list. Men more often cook dinner *or* take a child to the park. Indeed, women more often juggle three spheres — job, children, and housework — while most men juggle two — jobs and children. For women, two activities compete with their time with children, not just one.

Beyond doing more at home, women also devote *proportionately more* of their time at home to housework and proportionately less of it to childcare. Of all the time men spend working at home, more of it goes to childcare. . . . Since most parents prefer to tend to their children than clean house, men do more of what they'd rather do. More men than women take their children on "fun" outings to the park, the zoo, the movies. Women spend more time on maintenance, feeding and bathing children, enjoyable activities to be sure, but often less leisurely or "special" than going to the zoo. Men also do fewer of the "undesirable" household chores: fewer men than women wash toilets and scrub the bathroom.

As a result, women tend to talk more intently about being overtired, sick, and "emotionally drained." Many women I could not tear away from the topic of sleep. . . . These women talked about sleep the way a hungry person talks about food.

All in all, if in this period of American history, the two-job family is suffering from a speed-up of work and family life, working mothers are its primary victims. It is ironic, then, that often it falls to women to be the "time and motion expert" of family life. Watching inside homes, I noticed it was often the mother who rushed children, saying "Hurry up! It's time to go." . . . Sadly enough, women are more often the lightning rods for family aggressions aroused by the speed-up of work and family life. They are the "villains" in a process of which they are the primary victims. More than the longer hours, the sleeplessness, and feeling torn, this is the saddest cost to women of the extra month a year.

---

See also Stewart D. Friedman & Jeffrey H. Greenhaus, Work and Family — Allies or Enemies? (2000); Arlie Hochschild, The Time Bind: When Work Becomes Home and Home Becomes Work (1997); Joan Williams: Unbending Gender: Why Family and Work Conflict and What to Do About It (2000).

8. Given the disproportionate impact of the work-family conflict, should employers have separate employment tracks for different women? In a classic article, Felice Schwartz (founder of Catalyst, a nonprofit consulting firm) proposes such a solution. Her point of departure is that women in management are more costly for the corporation because these women often interrupt their careers for family responsibilities.[55] Schwartz contends that corporations should distinguish between "career-primary" and "career-and-family" women, by identifying the former early, giving them the same opportunities as men, accepting them as valued members of management, and recognizing that they face sex stereotypes. On the other hand, the corporation should recognize the need to retain "career-and-family" women and provide them with parental leave, support during relocation, flexible benefits, and good, affordable child care. See Felice N. Schwartz, Management Women and the New Facts of Life, 67 Harv. Bus. Rev. 65 ( Jan.-Feb. 1989).

What would be the consequences for women, in general, and "mommies" in particular, of the "mommy track" (the nickname given by media to Schwartz's proposal)? For children? Fathers? The family? The employer? Does the "mommy track" remedy the problems posed in *The Second Shift*? Professor Karen Czapanskiy addresses some of these issues:

> An ideology of unequal labor allocation is not benign for fathers, either. By permitting employers to assume that every male worker has a female partner caring for the home and children, employers are freed to burden workers with schedules and demands that are inconsistent with family responsibilities or enjoyment. Men are denied social support for developing

---

[55]. Some commentators dispute Schwartz's point of departure that women in management are most costly to employ. See Barbara Ehrenreich & Deirdre English, Blowing the Whistle on the "Mommy Track," Ms. 56 ( July-Aug. 1989).

close relationships with their children. In the event of divorce, men may find themselves deprived of a realistic claim to custody because they have not provided daily care for their children nor learned to be fully competent and involved parents.

Children may be victimized the most by gendered parenting and its second shift consequences. First, they experience and learn to replicate exploitative, antidemocratic family lives. [T]hey will learn that boys fulfill a role which includes very little nurturing behavior, and that girls fulfill one loaded with nurturing, but at a high cost when the nurturing is done by one who also works for money. [B]oth boys and girls may conclude, with substantial logic, that a life without responsibility for nurturing the young is a life worth living. Once they draw that conclusion, they may decide not to have children. Alternatively, they may decide that someone else, either a wife or a daycare worker, will have to take care of any children they have. Because their gendered parents have modelled ways to allocate household labor through exploitation, rather than through mutual respect, negotiation, and power sharing, the relationship of the grownup child from the gendered household with a spouse or daycare worker is also likely to be unequal and exploitative. . . .

Karen Czapanskiy, Volunteers and Draftees: The Struggle for Parental Equality, 38 UCLA L. Rev. 1415, 1455-1456 (1991). Is the "mommy track" sound policy? Is it legal? See generally Rebecca Korzec, Working on the "Mommy-Track": Motherhood and Women Lawyers, 8 Hastings L.J. 117 (1997). On fathers' experience with the work-family conflict, see Keith Cunningham, Note, Father Time: Flexible Work Arrangements and the Law Firm's Failure of the Family, 53 Stan. L. Rev. 967 (2001).

9. To what extent might one argue that employers' failure to provide childcare constitutes sex discrimination? See Catherine L. Fisk, Employer-Provided Child Care Under Title VII: Toward an Employer's Duty to Accommodate Child Care Responsibilities of Employees, 2 Berkeley Women's L.J. 89 (1986).

## Problem

Diane McCourtney's employer, Seagate Technology, dismisses the accounts clerk for excessive absenteeism. McCourtney's absences stem from her inability to find affordable day care for her infant who suffers frequent respiratory ailments. Following her dismissal, she files a claim for unemployment benefits, which is contested by Seagate and denied by the state Jobs and Training Department. She appeals. Minnesota, similar to many states, requires claimants to show that they are "available" for work, although such availability may be restricted for "good cause." To what extent is McCourtney available for work? Do the restrictions on her availability reflect "good cause"? Should the result depend on the availability for childcare of McCourtney's husband? See McCourtney v.

Imprimis Tech., 465 N.W.2d 721 (Minn. Ct. App. 1991). Cf. Phillips v. Martin Marietta Corp., 400 U.S. 542 (1971).

## C. TORT AND CRIMINAL LAW

### 1. Tort Actions Against Third Parties

#### a. Alienation of Affections and Criminal Conversation

■ **HUTELMYER v. COX**
*514 S.E.2d 554 (N.C. Ct. App. 1999)*

TIMMONS-GOODSON, Judge.

. . . Plaintiff brought this action against defendant [for] alienating the affections of her husband and for criminal conversation. Plaintiff's evidence tended to show the following facts. Plaintiff and Joseph Hutelmyer were married on 14 October 1978 and lived together with their three children until 5 January 1996, when Mr. Hutelmyer left the marital home to live with defendant. Plaintiff and Mr. Hutelmyer subsequently divorced, and on 15 May 1997, he and defendant were married. . . .

During the marriage, Mr. Hutelmyer was employed at Seaboard Underwriters, and defendant began work as his secretary in 1986. According to her co-workers, defendant's demeanor when she began her employment was "matronly." She wore predominantly dark clothing and long skirts. Then, in May of 1992, defendant separated from her husband, and she, thereafter, became openly flirtatious and spent increasingly more time alone with Mr. Hutelmyer. Defendant's co-workers testified that she changed her appearance. She cut and dyed her hair and wore short skirts, low-cut blouses, and tight clothing to the office. At or near the same time, defendant and Mr. Hutelmyer began to arrive at work together or within minutes of each other, to dine together alone, and to work late hours at the office. Many nights, defendant and Mr. Hutelmyer were the only employees working late. The testimony of defendant's co-workers also revealed that although defendant rarely traveled in connection with her employment prior to 1990, in 1992, she began accompanying Mr. Hutelmyer on business trips.

Plaintiff's evidence further showed that beginning in 1993, Mr. Hutelmyer began to spend a considerable amount of time at defendant's home. Defendant's former neighbor testified that she frequently saw Mr. Hutelmyer's vehicle parked at defendant's home overnight, from approximately 9:00 P.M. until 5:30 A.M. the following morning. . . .

As defendant and Mr. Hutelmyer became closer, he began to spend less time with his wife and family. Plaintiff testified that their sexual relationship began to deteriorate because Mr. Hutelmyer began to lose interest in her sexually. . . . When she asked him what was wrong, he claimed to be experiencing work-related pressures but maintained that he was still very much in love with her. Plaintiff further testified that Mr. Hutelmyer began coming home very late at night, and when he went to their children's evening soccer games, he would not come home with the family after the games were over, claiming that he had to go back to work.

Plaintiff also recalled that in 1992, Mr. Hutelmyer stopped allowing her to travel with him on business trips. [H]e told her that there had been a change in the company policy which excluded spouses from work-related trips. Despite the changes in Mr. Hutelmyer's behavior, plaintiff believed that her husband still loved her. She continued to regard their marriage as strong and loving, until 1994, when Mr. Hutelmyer lost all desire to have sex with plaintiff and their sexual relationship ceased. The couple, nonetheless, remained together until 5 January 1996, when Mr. Hutelmyer told plaintiff that he was leaving. . . .

[Finding defendant liable for both alienation of affections and criminal conversation, the jury awarded plaintiff $500,000 in compensatory damages and $500,000 in punitive damages.] Defendant, by her first assignment of error, contends [that] the evidence was insufficient as a matter of law to show that she acted maliciously in alienating the affections of plaintiff's husband. We must disagree. . . .

To survive a motion for directed verdict or j.n.o.v. on a claim for alienation of affections, the plaintiff must present evidence to show that: "(1) plaintiff and [her husband] were happily married and a genuine love and affection existed between them; (2) the love and affection was alienated and destroyed; and (3) the wrongful and malicious acts of defendant produced the alienation of affections" [Chappell v. Redding, 313 S.E.2d 239, 241 (N.C. Ct. App. 1984)]. A defendant is not liable for the tort simply because she has "becom[e] the object of the affections that are alienated from a spouse." "There must be active participation, initiative or encouragement on the part of the defendant in causing one spouse's loss of the other spouse's affections for liability to arise" [Peake v. Shirley, 427 S.E.2d 885, 887 (N.C. Ct. App. 1993)]. However, it is not necessary that the malicious conduct of the defendant, by itself, provoke the alienation of affections. All that is necessary to establish the tort is to show that the wrongful acts of the defendant were "the controlling or effective cause of the alienation, even though there were other causes, which might have contributed to the alienation" [Heist v. Heist, 265 S.E.2d 434, 436 (N.C. Ct. App. 1980)]. . . .

Taken in the light most favorable to plaintiff, the evidence tended to show that prior to 1993, plaintiff and Mr. Hutelmyer had "a fairy tale marriage." They traveled together, volunteered in church and community organizations together, and coached their children's soccer teams together. In addition, Mr. Hutelmyer often expressed his love and affection for plaintiff through sentimental poetry. One such poem, written in 1990 and entitled "Why I Love You, II," read as follows:

> Three little angels, trips for two each May; lunch with couch potato, a rocking horse, sleigh, hunting eggs at Easter, puzzles on the wall; Indians in summer, soccer spring and fall; sleepy eyes at sunrise, T.V. time at nine; volunteer extraordinaire, play games at any time; special gift with children, sound sleep without end; patience and understanding, my very, very best friend. Happy Valentine's Day. Love, Joe.

Plaintiff's evidence also tended to show that the love and affection that once existed between her and her husband was alienated and destroyed by defendant's conduct. . . . As he spent more time with defendant, plaintiff's husband began to spend increasingly less time with plaintiff and their children. Accordingly, we hold that plaintiff presented sufficient evidence to overcome defendant's motions for directed verdict and j.n.o.v., and the trial court properly submitted plaintiff's claim for alienation of affections to the jury.

With her next assignment of error, defendant challenges the sufficiency of the evidence to support the award of punitive damages for alienation of affections and criminal conversation. . . . In an action for alienation of affections, punitive damages are recoverable "where the defendant's conduct was willful, aggravated, malicious, or of a wanton character." *Chappell,* 313 S.E.2d at 243. . . .

[As] to the additional circumstances of aggravation justifying punitive damages, the evidence tended to show that defendant publicly displayed the intimate nature of her relationship with plaintiff's husband. A coworker of defendant and Mr. Hutelmyer testified that the paramours often held hands in the workplace, and defendant frequently straightened Mr. Hutelmyer's ties and brushed lint from his suits at business functions. Another co-worker testified that in 1994, during a work outing at a Putt-Putt facility, defendant stood very close to plaintiff's husband and ate ice out of his drinking cup. Defendant's behavior toward Mr. Hutelmyer was such that most of their co-workers knew of their affair.

The evidence further showed that defendant welcomed plaintiff's husband into her home at all hours of the day and night, despite her knowledge of the harm that their relationship would cause his wife and three young children. [D]efendant in the present case "was audacious enough to call plaintiff's home [on Thanksgiving Day in 1995] to discover her husband's whereabouts." Therefore, we hold that plaintiff presented sufficient additional circumstances of aggravation to warrant submission of the punitive damages issue to the jury on plaintiff's claim for alienation of affections. We hold similarly regarding the issue of punitive damages on plaintiff's claim for criminal conversation. . . .

Defendant next assigns as error the trial court's failure to grant a new trial on the issue of compensatory and punitive damages for alienation of affections and criminal conversation. . . . [T]his Court described the injuries for which compensatory damages are appropriate in an alienation of affections action:

> In a cause of action for alienation of affections of the husband from the wife, the measure of damages is the present value in money of the support, consortium, and other legally protected marital interests lost by her through the defendant's wrong. In addition thereto, she may also recover for the wrong and injury done to her health, feelings, or reputation.

[Sebastian v. Kluttz, 170 S.E.2d 104 (N.C. Ct. App. 1969)]. As for criminal conversation, . . . the jury "may consider the loss of consortium, mental anguish, humiliation, injury to health, and loss of support [.]" Id. at 116. Consortium is defined as the " '[c]onjugal fellowship of husband and wife, and the right of each to the company, co-operation, affection, and aid of the other in every conjugal relation.' " Id. at 115 (quoting Black's Law Dictionary, 4th ed.). . . .

In addition to plaintiff's evidence showing a loss of income, life insurance, and pension benefits resulting from the actions of defendant, there was plenary evidence that plaintiff likewise suffered loss of consortium, mental anguish, humiliation, and injury to health. . . . The evidence further showed that plaintiff became physically and emotionally ill after Mr. Hutelmyer left the marital home. She had problems sleeping, and she lost twenty pounds due to her lack of appetite. To cope with the emotional pain and stress she and her children were experiencing, she sought counseling at a Women's Resource Center. Therefore, we conclude that plaintiff presented sufficient evidence to support the $500,000 award of compensatory damages for alienation of affections and criminal conversation. We turn, then, to the issue of punitive damages. [T]here was evidence before the jury concerning "[t]he reprehensibility of the defendant's motives and conduct," "[t]he likelihood . . . of serious harm," "[t]he degree of the defendant's awareness of the probable consequences of its conduct," "[t]he duration of the defendant's conduct," and "[t]he actual damages suffered by the claimant." N.C.G.S. §1-35(2). [W]e cannot say that the amount of punitive damages was excessive as a matter of law. . . .

By her final assignment of error, defendant argues that our Supreme Court's decision in Cannon v. Miller, 313 N.C. 324, 327 S.E.2d 888 (1985), refusing to abolish the torts of alienation of affections and criminal conversation should be reconsidered. While defendant's arguments are skillfully presented, "it is not our prerogative to overrule or ignore clearly written decisions of our Supreme Court." *Kinlaw v. Long Mfg.*, 40 N.C. App. 641, 643, 253 S.E.2d 629, 630, *rev'd on other grounds*, 298 N.C. 494, 259 S.E.2d 552 (1979). . . . Based upon the foregoing, we conclude that defendant enjoyed a fair trial, free of prejudicial error.

## ■ OSBORNE v. PAYNE
### 31 S.W.3d 911 (Ky. 2000)

WINTERSCHEIMER, Justice.

. . . Payne and his wife were experiencing marital difficulties and went to Osborne, their parish priest, for counseling. Ultimately, Payne and his wife were divorced following his discovery of a 45-day adulterous relationship between his wife and Osborne. . . . Payne sued the former priest for the tort of outrageous conduct and the Diocese of Owensboro under a vicarious liability theory for its alleged negligent training, screening and supervision of Osborne. . . . Payne testified that as a result of discovering the adulterous affair, he suffered a nervous breakdown, lost his religion, lost his house and lost his job as well as his wife. . . .

Craft v. Rice, 671 S.W.2d 247 (Ky. 1984), is the seminal case involving the tort of intentional infliction of emotional distress or outrageous conduct in Kentucky. In order to establish such a claim, the plaintiff must prove the following elements: The wrongdoer's conduct must be intentional or reckless; the conduct must be outrageous and intolerable in that it offends against the generally accepted standards of decency and morality; there must be a causal connection between the wrongdoer's conduct and the emotional distress and the distress suffered must be severe. [T]he tort is not available for "petty insults, unkind words and minor indignities" [Kroger Company v. Willgruber, 920 S.W.2d 61 (Ky. 1996)]. . . . Rather, it is intended to redress behavior that is truly outrageous, intolerable and which results in bringing one to his knees.

The circuit court summarily dismissed the claim against the former priest for failure to allege misconduct that was sufficient to satisfy the outrageous element of the tort, relying on Whittington v. Whittington, 766 S.W.2d 73 (Ky. Ct. App. 1989). In that case, the claim of the wife was dismissed under CR 12.02 for failure to state a claim upon which relief can be granted; the circuit court concluded that ordinary fraud and adultery can never reach the status of outrageous conduct.

Here, the most important element of the complaint by Payne, as demonstrated by his deposition testimony, is that he was injured as a result of the misconduct of Osborne while in a special relationship as priest and counselor. Moreover, the alleged exploitation of that relationship occurred in a situation when the former priest was aware that the marriage partners were most vulnerable. . . . The establishment of the existence of a special relationship between the parties can make conduct outrageous. The use of a confidential relationship between Payne and his priest counselor is the heart of his lawsuit. . . . For the purpose of summary judgment, it is evident that the former priest used his relationship with the husband and the wife to obtain a sexual affair with the wife. Conduct and relationship can form the basis for outrageous conduct. . . .

The mere fact that in recent years there has been apparently an increasing number of claims against clergy for sexual misconduct does not make the behavior any less outrageous or disgraceful or otherwise actionable. Some jurisdictions have denied relief under a theory of intentional infliction of emotional distress after concluding that the claims were merely an attempt to bring amatory actions which were no longer viable. See Strock v. Pressnell, 38 Ohio St.3d 207, 527 N.E.2d 1235 (1988). However, we are persuaded by the reasoning used in the cases noted by the Court of Appeals including Destefano v. Grabrian, 763 P.2d 275, 285 (Colo. 1988), in which it was stated that: a plaintiff will not be able to mask one of the abolished actions . . . behind a common law label. However, if the essence of the complaint is directed to a cause of action other than one which has been abolished, that claim is legally cognizable. See also Figueiredo-Torres v. Nickel, 321 Md. 642, 584 A.2d 69 (1991).

We note that this Court abolished the action for breach of promise to marry in Gilbert v. Barkes, 987 S.W.2d 772 (Ky. 1999), but stated that it in no way prohibited other remedies, such as claims for breach of contract and intentional infliction of emotional distress, should a party be able to make such a case. It should be emphasized that these claims must be approached on a case-by-case basis, and there is no blanket or automatic imposition of a cause of action in the clergy/counselor relationship.

Payne next argues that Osborne, as a priest, was engaging in an activity sanctioned by the church and ordinarily performed by a priest, that is, marriage counseling. He argues that it was because Osborne was a priest that he was called upon by them; that his help was sought and that he was invited into the home. Payne reasons that the diocese should be vicariously liable for the actions of Osborne. We cannot agree. To accept such a theory would in effect require the diocese to become an absolute insurer for the behavior of anyone who was in the priesthood and would result in strict liability on the part of the diocese for any actionable wrong involving a parishioner. We must conclude that such an argument is absurd. Certainly, the scope of employment of a priest could include marriage counseling, but it clearly does not include adultery. . . .

Here, Payne has failed to present any evidence in the record that Osborne had a history of sexual misconduct involving parishioners or that the diocese had any knowledge that Osborne might conceivably engage in such misconduct. Consequently, we must conclude that the summary judgment granted by the circuit court and affirmed by the Court of Appeals as to the diocese was correct. . . .

We conclude that members of the clergy can be liable for damages resulting [from] their intentional tortious conduct, commonly called the tort of outrage, when it constitutes the intentional infliction of emotional distress. It is a combination of relationship and conduct that distinguishes this kind of behavior from adultery which has been effectively abolished as a tort claim in Kentucky. Thus, Payne is allowed to proceed with his claim in circuit court against Osborne. However, there is nothing to support a claim of vicarious liability for the conduct of the former priest against the diocese, and it cannot be held vicariously liable in this matter. The judgment of the Court of Appeals is affirmed and this matter is remanded for proceedings consistent with this opinion.

## Notes and Questions

1. The common law made interference with the marital relationship remediable by a tort action for alienation of affections and criminal conversation. Alienation of affections requires: (1) a valid marriage; (2) wrongful conduct by the defendant with the plaintiff's spouse; (3) the loss of affection or consortium; and (4) a causal connection between the defendant's conduct and the deprivation of affection. Restatement (Second) of Torts §683 (1977).

Unlike alienation of affections, criminal conversation requires sexual intercourse. Restatement (Second) of Torts §685 (1977). Dan D. Dobbs, The Law of Torts §442 (2000). Criminal conversation has been called a strict liability tort because the only defenses are the plaintiff's (that is, injured spouse's) consent and the statute of limitations. That is, the participating spouse's consent is not a defense.

2. Many jurisdictions have abolished these tort actions by anti-heart balm legislation. North Carolina (where *Hutelmyer* took place) is one of only six states to recognize alienation of affections. See Kathryn Quigley, Costly Love Affair for Florida Physician, S.F. Chron., June 9, 2001, at A3. In a subsequent North Carolina case, a jury awarded $1.4 million ($910,000 in compensatory damages and $500,000 in punitive damages) in a husband's suit for alienation of affections and criminal conversation. The ex-wife later married her paramour, a Florida family physician, who was her former high school sweetheart. See id. (describing the case). See also Ward v. Beaton, 539 S.E.2d 30 (N.C. Ct. App. 2000) (awarding ex-wife $52,000 in compensatory damages and $43,000 in punitive damages). See generally Jill Jones, Comment, Fanning an Old Flame: Alienation of Affections and Criminal Conversation Revisited, 26 Pepperdine L. Rev. 61 (1999); Jennifer E. McDougal, Comment, Legislating

Morality: The Actions of Alienation of Affections and Criminal Conversation in North Carolina, 33 Wake Forest L. Rev. 163 (1998).

3. What are the various rationales for retaining alienation of affections and criminal conversation? Formerly, tort liability rested, in part, on the view of the wife as her husband's property. Does the fact that women, like Mrs. Hutelmyer, now resort to these claims militate against abolition? See Bland v. Hill, 735 So. 2d 414, 421 (Miss. 1999) (dissenting judge so arguing). Does abolition "send the message that we are devaluing the marriage relationship"? Gorman v. McMahon, 792 So. 2d 307 (Miss. Ct. App. 2001). Should divorce, instead of tort damages, provide the remedy? Some jurisdictions have abolished criminal conversation but retained alienation of affections. See, e.g., Saunders v. Alford, 607 So. 2d 1214 (Miss. 1992); Norton v. Macfarlane, 818 P.2d 8 (Utah 1991). Is this approach preferable?

4. The first Mrs. Hutelmyer in the principal case was awarded $500,000 in compensatory damages and $500,000 in punitive damages. In a subsequent North Carolina case (discussed supra), a jilted husband was awarded $910,000 in compensatory damages and $500,000 in punitive damages. Are such awards excessive? If so, does that argue for or against retention of tort liability?

5. *Alternative theories.* As *Osborne* reveals, abolition of alienation of affections and criminal conversation left an unanswered question: whether jilted spouses could recover under alternative theories, such as intentional infliction of emotional distress (IIED). Some cases permit such claims despite abolition of the amatory torts. See, e.g., Scamardo v. Dunaway, 650 So. 2d 417 (La. Ct. App. 1995). More courts, however, hold that the action is barred as a disguised suit for alienation of affections. See, e.g., McDermott v. Reynolds, 530 S.E.2d 902, 904 (Va. 2000) (noting that "our conclusion is in accord with the decisions of a majority of jurisdictions").

How does intentional infliction differ from alienation of affections and criminal conversation? Do you agree with the court in *Osborne* that extramarital conduct in the context of a fiduciary relationship increases the degree of outrageousness of the conduct to qualify for a claim of IIED? See also Rosenthal v. Erven, 17 P.3d 558, 562 (Or. Ct. App. 2001) (accord). (Criticisms of the role of intentional infliction claims in the context of no-fault divorce are discussed in Chapter V.)

In addition, some jilted spouses assert other theories (for example, breach of fiduciary duty). See, e.g., Cherepski v. Walker, 913 S.W.2d 761 (Ark. 1996) (barring claim). In some cases of sexual conduct involving employees in the workplace, another possible theory of recovery is sexual harassment. See Robert Schwaneberg, Love's Wounded Sue for Damages, Star-Ledger (Newark), Feb. 13, 2000, at 001 (describing several recent cases).

6. Courts also impose liability (but only for the patient) for mental health professionals' sexual relationships with patients. See

generally Paul A. Clark, Tort Law: Applying Respondeat Superior to Psychotherapist-Patient Sexual Relationships, 21 Am. J. Trial Advoc. 439 (1997); Ronald J. Maurer, Ohio Psychotherapist Civil Liability for Sexual Relations with Former Patients, 26 U. Tol. L. Rev. 547 (1995). On divorce lawyers' sexual relationships with clients, see Chapter V, section F3.

## Problems

1. In a jurisdiction that recognizes alienation of affections and criminal conversation, a wife in a dissolution proceeding claims a share (as marital property) in the sums recovered by her husband in his claim for alienation of affections and criminal conversation from the man with whom she had been having an affair. Should she prevail? See T.B.G. v. C.A.G. (C.A.M.), 772 S.W.2d 653 (Mo. 1989).

2. Joe, vice president of Helena Laboratories, has an affair with his secretary, Pam. Joe's wife Allison and Pam's husband Bob sue Helena Laboratories for negligently interfering with their respective marital relations by failing to take action to prevent the affair between Joe and Pam. What result? See Helena Lab. Corp. v. Snyder, 886 S.W.2d 767 (Tex. 1994). See also Mercier v. Davies, 533 S.E.2d 877 (N.C. Ct. App. 2000).

3. Edna and Robert Destefano, both Catholic, seek marriage counseling from their priest Dennis Grabrian. Grabrian becomes sexually involved with Edna. Grabrian has previously engaged in sexual relations with other women who came to him for counseling. Following the couple's divorce, they sue Grabrian (for negligence, intentional infliction of emotional distress, and breach of fiduciary duty) and the diocese (for breach of its duty to supervise). Grabrian counters that the First Amendment precludes tort liability. The jurisdiction has abolished actions for alienation of affections and criminal conversation. What result? Destefano v. Grabrian, 763 P.2d 275 (Colo. 1988). Cf. Langford v. Roman Catholic Diocese of Brooklyn, 677 N.Y.S.2d 436 (N.Y. 1998). See also Lindsey Rosen, Constitutional Law — In Bad Faith: Breach of Fiduciary Duty by the Clergy — F.G. v. MacDonell, 696 A.2d 697 (N.J. 1997), 71 Temp. L. Rev. 743, 748-754 (1998) (discussing cases accepting and rejecting claims of clergy malpractice).

### b. Loss of Consortium

■ **RODRIGUEZ v. BETHLEHEM STEEL CORP.**
525 P.2d 669 (Cal. 1974)

Mosk, J.

In this case we are called upon to decide whether California should continue to adhere to the rule that a married person whose spouse has been injured by the negligence of a third party has no cause of action for loss of "consortium," i.e., for loss of conjugal fellowship and sexual relations. . . .

On May 24, 1969, Richard and Mary Anne Rodriguez were married. Both were gainfully employed. In their leisure time they participated in a variety of social and recreational activities. They were saving for the time when they could buy their own home. They wanted children, and planned to raise a large family.

Only 16 months after their marriage, however, their young lives were shattered by a grave accident. While at work, Richard was struck on the head by a falling pipe weighing over 600 pounds. The blow caused severe spinal cord damage which has left him totally paralyzed in both legs, totally paralyzed in his body below the midpoint of the chest, and partially paralyzed in one of his arms.

The effects of Richard's accident on Mary Anne's life have likewise been disastrous. It has transformed her husband from an active partner into a lifelong invalid, confined to home and bedridden for a great deal of time. Because he needs assistance in virtually every activity of daily living, Mary Anne gave up her job and undertook his care on a 24-hour basis. Each night she must wake in order to turn him from side to side, so as to minimize the occurrence of bedsores. Every morning and evening she must help him wash, dress and undress, and get into and out of his wheelchair. She must help him into and out of the car when a visit to the doctor's office or hospital is required. Because he has lost all bladder and bowel control, she must assist him in the difficult and time-consuming processes of performing those bodily functions by artificial inducement. Many of these activities require her to lift or support his body weight, thus placing a repeated physical strain on her.

Nor is the psychological strain any less. Mary Anne's social and recreational life, evidently, has been severely restricted. She is a constant witness to her husband's pain, mental anguish, and frustration. Because he has lost all capacity for sexual intercourse, that aspect of married life is wholly denied to her: as she explains in her declaration, "To be deeply in love with each other and have no way of physically expressing this love is most difficult physically and mentally." For the same reason she is forever denied the opportunity to have children by him — she is, for all practical purposes, sterilized: again she explains, "I have lost what I consider is the fulfillment of my existence because my husband can't make me pregnant so as to bear children and have a family." The consequences to her are predictable: "These physical and emotional frustrations with no outlet have made me nervous, tense, depressed and have caused me to have trouble sleeping, eating and concentrating." In short, Mary Ann says, "Richard's life has been ruined by this accident. As his partner, my life has been ruined too."

At the time of the accident Richard was 22 years old and Mary Anne was 20. The injuries, apparently, are permanent. . . .

. . . Richard and Mary Anne jointly filed an amended complaint against Richard's employer and various subcontractors. In the first cause of action, predicated on his own injuries, Richard prayed for substantial general damages, past and future medical expenses, and compensation for the loss of his earnings and earning capacity. In the second cause of action Mary Anne alleged the consequences to her of Richard's injuries, and prayed for general damages in her own right, the reasonable value of the nursing care she furnishes her husband, and compensation for the loss of her earnings and earning capacity. Defendants filed general demurrers to the second cause of action on the ground that no recovery for any such loss is permitted in California under the authority of Deshotel v. Atchison T. & S.F. Ry. Co. (1958), 50 Cal. 2d 664, 328 P.2d 449.

When the demurrers came on for hearing the trial court emphasized the rule, recognized in *Deshotel,* that in a wrongful death case a widow can recover damages for the loss of her deceased husband's society, comfort, and protection. The court criticized the contrary rule applicable when, as here, the husband is severely injured but does not die. . . . Addressing Mary Anne's counsel, the court made it clear that it would have ruled in his client's favor but for the precedent of *Deshotel.* [T]he Court of Appeal likewise indicated its dissatisfaction with the *Deshotel* rule. . . .

A careful reading of the *Deshotel* opinion discloses [several] distinct grounds of decision. [E]ach of these reasons has been rendered untenable by developments subsequent to *Deshotel.*

### STARE DECISIS AND THE ROLE OF THE LEGISLATURE . . .

First and foremost, the *Deshotel* court emphasized that the "overwhelming weight of authority" supports the common law rule. . . . In the [years] since *Deshotel* was decided, however, there has been a dramatic reversal in the weight of authority on this question. . . . In these circumstances we may fairly conclude that the precedential foundation of *Deshotel* has been not only undermined but destroyed. . . .

The second principal reliance of the *Deshotel* opinion was that any departure from the then-settled rule denying the wife recovery for loss of consortium "should be left to legislative action," and defendants in the case at bar echo that plea. But in the years since *Deshotel* the argument has fared badly in our decisions. . . . Although the Legislature may of course speak to the subject, in the common law system the primary instruments of this evolution are the courts, . . .

### THE INJURY IS INDIRECT, THE DAMAGES SPECULATIVE, AND THE CAUSE OF ACTION WOULD EXTEND TO OTHER CLASSES OF PLAINTIFFS

Under this heading we group three arguments relied on in *Deshotel* which could be invoked against any proposed recognition of a new cause of action sounding in tort. . . .

First the *Deshotel* court asserted that "Any harm [the wife] sustains occurs *only indirectly* as a consequence of the defendant's wrong to the husband." The argument was negated 10 years after *Deshotel* in Dillon v. Legg (1968), 68 Cal. 2d 728, 69 Cal. Rptr. 72, 441 P.2d 912. There the issue was whether a driver who negligently runs over a small child in the street is also liable to the child's mother for emotional shock and resulting physical disorders suffered by the latter when she personally witnessed the occurrence of the accident. Finding such liability, we in effect rejected the argument that the injury to the mother was too "indirect." The critical question, we explained was foreseeability. . . . The foreseeable risk need not be of an actual physical impact, but may be of emotional trauma alone. Whether a risk is sufficiently foreseeable to give rise to a duty of care depends on the circumstances of each case, including the relationship of the parties and the nature of the threatened injury. . . .

[W]e conclude in the case at bar that one who negligently causes a severely disabling injury to an adult may reasonably expect that the injured person is married and that his or her spouse will be adversely affected by that injury. In our society the likelihood that an injured adult will be a married man or woman is substantial, clearly no less than the likelihood that a small child's mother will personally witness an injury to her offspring. And the probability that the spouse of a severely disabled person will suffer a personal loss by reason of that injury is equally substantial. . . .

The next rationale of the *Deshotel* court was that "the measurement of damage for the loss of such things as companionship and society would involve conjecture since their value would be hard to fix in terms of money." This argument, too, has fared badly in our subsequent decisions. Although loss of consortium may have physical consequences, it is principally a form of mental suffering. . . .

[R]ecently, we observed that under the concept of pain and suffering "a plaintiff may recover not only for physical pain but for fright, nervousness, grief, anxiety, worry, mortification, shock, humiliation, indignity, embarrassment, apprehension, terror or ordeal." Admittedly these terms refer to subjective states, representing a detriment which can be translated into monetary loss only with great difficulty. But the detriment, nevertheless, is a genuine one that requires compensation, and the issue generally must be resolved by [jurors]. Indeed, mental suffering frequently constitutes the principal element of tort damages. . . .

The third argument of this group set forth in *Deshotel* is that if the wife's cause of action were recognized "on the basis of the intimate relationship existing between her and her husband, other persons having a close relationship to the one injured, such as a child or parent, would likely seek to enforce similar claims, and the courts would be faced with the perplexing task of determining where to draw the line with respect to which claims should be upheld." . . . We rejected this argument in *Dillon* on the ground that "the alleged inability to fix definitions for recovery on the different facts of future cases does not justify the denial of recovery on the specific facts of the instant case; in any event, proper guidelines can indicate the extent of liability for such future cases." Those guidelines, as noted hereinabove, are the general principles of negligence law limiting liability to persons and injuries within the scope of the reasonably foreseeable risk. . . .

### THE FEAR OF DOUBLE RECOVERY . . .

[T]he *Deshotel* court expressed the concern that "A judgment obtained by a husband after he is injured by a third person might include compensation for any impairment of his ability to participate in a normal married life, and, if his wife is allowed redress for loss of consortium in a separate action, there would be danger of double recovery." Virtually every decision granting the wife the right to recover for loss of consortium since *Deshotel* has considered and rejected this argument calling it "fallacious." [C]ases have made it crystal clear that, in the quoted words of *Deshotel*, recovery of damages for impairment of "his" ability to participate in a normal married life does not necessarily compensate for the impairment of "her" ability to participate in that life.

It is true the rule against double recovery forecloses the wife from recovering for the loss of her husband's financial support if he is compensated for his loss of earnings and earning power. . . . But there is far more to the marriage relationship than financial support. . . . Perhaps the most undeniable proof of the separate and distinct losses of husband and wife is seen when, as in the case at bar, there is impairment or destruction of the sexual life of the couple. "Today, at least, it is unquestioned that the desire to have children and the pleasures of sexual intercourse are mutually shared. If the husband's potency is lost or impaired, it is both the man and woman who are affected." [Deems v. Western Md. Ry. Co., 231 A.2d 514, 522 (Md. 1967).]

Nor is the wife's personal loss limited to her sexual rights. [C]onsortium includes "conjugal society, comfort, affection, and companionship." An important aspect of consortium is thus the *moral* support each spouse gives the other through the triumph and despair of life. A severely disabled husband may well need all the emotional strength he has just to survive the shock of his injury, make the agonizing adjustment to his new and drastically restricted world, and preserve his mental health through the long years of frustration ahead. He will often turn inwards, demanding more solace for himself than he can give to others. Accordingly, the spouse of such a man cannot expect him to share the same concern for *her* problems that she experienced before his accident. As several of the cases have put it, she is transformed from a happy wife into a lonely nurse. Yet she is entitled to enjoy the companionship and moral support that marriage provides no less than its sexual side, and in both cases no less than her husband. If she is deprived of either by reason of a negligent injury to her husband, the loss is hers alone. . . .

All that is necessary to avoid double recovery [is to insure] that the wife's recovery does not include any damages for loss of her husband's financial support or other items for which *he* is primarily entitled to be compensated. There is no mystery about how this can be accomplished . . . by requiring that such items be carefully identified at trial [and by encouraging joinder of both spouses' causes of action].

We therefore overrule *Deshotel,* and declare that in California each spouse has a cause of action for loss of consortium as defined herein, caused by a negligent or intentional injury to the other spouse by a third party. . . .

## Notes and Questions

1. Early authorities recognized the husband's right for loss of consortium caused by the defendant's assault, battery, or imprisonment. In time the doctrine was extended to include negligence. Homer H. Clark, Jr., The Law of Domestic Relations in the United States 390 (2d ed. 1988). Finally, Hitaffer v. Argonne Co., 183 F.2d 811 (D.C. Cir. 1950), became the first court to permit a wife to recover for negligent injury to her husband. The majority of jurisdictions followed. As *Rodriguez* explains, at common law the wife had no cause of action for intentional or negligent injuries to her husband. How does *Rodriguez* respond to the objections against consortium actions?

2. Because both husband and wife may now recover when a third party's negligence causes a loss of consortium, should the injured spouse's contributory negligence bar the claim? Should the action be available for injuries caused by defective products? Infliction of emotional distress? Defamation? See Fanelle v. LoJack Corp., 79 F. Supp. 2d 558 (E.D. Pa. 2000) (permitting wife's claim for loss of consortium stemming from injuries that her husband suffered to his reputation).

3. *Rodriguez* points to several elements for which plaintiff can recover damages in a loss of consortium action. What are they? Other courts include deprivation of social and family activities and effect on the marriage relationship (such as separation or divorce). Clark, supra, at 396-397.

4. Must a claim for loss of consortium be brought in conjunction with a primary cause of action by the injured spouse? Suppose an injured spouse cannot or will not sue on his or her own behalf? See, e.g., Jacoby v. Brinckerhoff, 735 A. 347 (Conn. 1999) (holding that absent a primary claim by the injured spouse, no loss of consortium claim can be brought by other spouse).

## Problems

1. Wendy and Daniel Sostock file a complaint against Harmswood Stables North seeking damages for personal injuries sustained by Wendy. One month before her marriage to Daniel, Wendy was injured in a fall from a horse allegedly caused by defendants' negligence. In addition to Wendy's claim regarding her injuries, Daniel seeks recovery for the loss of his wife's affection, society, companionship, and consortium. What result? See Sostock v. Reiss, 415 N.E.2d 1094 (Ill. App. Ct. 1980).

2. A father sues Fox Valley Systems and Crown Cork & Seal Co. on behalf of his two children, Megan and Ryan, for injuries they suffered stemming from their father's blindness. The father was injured by an explosion of spray paint allegedly manufactured defectively by the defendants. He sues to recover damages to the children from their loss of his parental care, love, and guidance. Should the action for loss of consortium extend to a child for injury to a parent? See Klaus v. Fox Valley Sys., 912 P.2d 703 (Kan. 1996). See also id. at 705 (noting that 22 jurisdictions reject the child's cause of action while 19 recognize it). Should it matter if the children are minors or adults? See Rolf v. TriState Motor Transit Co., 745 N.E.2d 424 (Ohio 2001). If recovery is allowed, does this mean that liability is potentially limitless?

## 2. Tort Actions Between Spouses

### a. Interspousal Immunity Doctrine

■ **BOONE v. BOONE**
*546 S.E.2d 191 (S.C. 2001)*

Burnett, Justice:

The question presented by this appeal is whether interspousal immunity from personal injury actions violates the public policy of South Carolina. . . .

Appellant Juanita Boone was injured in a car accident in Georgia. At the time of the accident, Wife was a passenger in a vehicle driven by her husband Respondent Freddie Boone. Wife and Husband reside in South Carolina.

Wife brought this tort action against Husband in South Carolina. Concluding Georgia law which provides interspousal immunity in personal injury actions was applicable, the trial judge granted Husband's motion to dismiss. Wife appeals. . . .

Does Georgia law providing interspousal immunity in personal injury actions violate the public policy of South Carolina?

### DISCUSSION

Interspousal immunity is a common law doctrine based on the legal fiction that husband and wife share the same identity in law, namely that of the husband. 92 A.L.R.3d 901 (1979). Accordingly, at common law, it was "both morally and conceptually objectionable to permit a tort suit between two spouses." Id. at 906.

With the passage of Married Women's Property Acts in the mid-nineteenth century, married women were given a legal estate in their own property and the capacity to sue and be sued. Under this legislation, a married woman could maintain an action against her husband for any tort against her property interest such as trespass to land or conversion. Since the legislation destroyed the "unity of persons," a husband could also maintain an action against his wife for torts to his property.

For a long time, however, the majority of courts held Married Women's Property Acts did not destroy interspousal immunity for personal torts. Courts adopted two inconsistent arguments in favor of continued immunity. First, they theorized suits between spouses would be fictitious and fraudulent, particularly against insurance companies. Second, they claimed interspousal suits would destroy domestic harmony.

In the twentieth century, most courts either abrogated or provided exceptions to interspousal immunity [citations omitted]. South Carolina has abolished the doctrine of interspousal immunity from tort liability for personal injury. Pardue v. Pardue, 167 S.C. 129, 166 S.E. 101 (1932). . . .

Very few jurisdictions now recognize interspousal tort immunity [citations omitted]. Georgia continues to recognize the common law doctrine of interspousal immunity. See Ga. Code Ann. §19-3-8 (1999). Under Georgia law, interspousal tort immunity bars personal injury actions between spouses, except where the traditional policy reasons for applying the doctrine are absent, i.e., where there is no marital harmony to be preserved and where there exists no possibility of collusion between the spouses. Shoemake v. Shoemake, 200 Ga. App. 182, 407 S.E.2d 134 (1991).

Under traditional South Carolina choice of law principles, the substantive law governing a tort action is determined by the lex loci delicti, the law of the state in which the injury occurred. However, foreign law may not be given effect in this State if "it is against good morals or natural justice . . ." . . . Accordingly, under the "public policy exception," the Court will not apply foreign law if it violates the public policy of South Carolina. . . .

It is the public policy of our State to provide married persons with the same legal rights and remedies possessed by unmarried persons. Had the parties to this action not been married to each other, Wife could have maintained a personal injury action against Husband. We find it contrary to "natural justice," to hold that because of their marital status, Wife is precluded from maintaining this action against Husband. Accordingly, we conclude application of the doctrine of interspousal immunity violates the public policy of South Carolina.

Moreover, the reasons given in support of interspousal immunity are simply not justified in the twenty-first century. There is no reason to presume married couples are more likely than others to engage in a collusive action. Whether or not parties are married, if fraudulent conduct is suspected, insurers can examine and investigate the claim and, at trial, cross-examine the parties as to their financial stakes in the outcome of the suit. Fraudulent claims would be subject to the trial court's contempt powers and to criminal prosecution for perjury and other crimes. It is unjustified to prohibit all personal injury tort suits between spouses simply because some suits may be fraudulent.

Additionally, we do not agree that precluding spouses from maintaining a personal injury action against each other fosters domestic harmony. Instead, we find marital harmony is promoted by allowing the negligent spouse, who has most likely purchased liability insurance, to provide for his injured spouse. . . . In our opinion, marital disharmony will not increase because married persons are permitted to maintain a personal injury action against each other. . . .

Because interspousal immunity violates the public policy of South Carolina, we will no longer apply the lex loci delicti when the law of the foreign state recognizes the doctrine.


■ **G.L. v. M.L.**
*550 A.2d 525 (N.J. Super. Ct. Ch. Div. 1988)*

Krafte, J.S.C.

Do sexual relations between spouses constitute "marital or nuptial privileges" . . . thereby entitling any sexual tort committed by one spouse upon the other to interspousal immunity? This court finds that they do not.

The plaintiff in this matter filed for divorce on November 2, 1984. Included in her complaint were four separate counts for personal injury alleging that her husband, the defendant, transmitted genital herpes to her during their marriage. The defendant's insurance carrier, defending against the negligence claim and the defendant's attorney in the matrimonial proceeding defending against the intentional tort claim now join together in bringing a motion for summary judgment dismissing the personal injury counts. . . .

Our highest court examined and incorporated the history and nature of interspousal immunity in Merenoff v. Merenoff, 76 N.J. at 539-547, 388 A.2d 951 and abrogated the doctrine regarding tortious conduct stating, ". . . where personal injuries are tortiously inflicted by one spouse upon another, it is just and fair that compensation in appropriate circumstances be afforded the wronged and injured party and, to this end, a suit be allowed to effectuate such recovery." Id. at 557, 388 A.2d [951]. The *Merenoff* court recognized that there was a range of activity in a marital relationship, characterized as "special matters of privacy and familiarity" beyond the reach of the law of torts because they "fall outside the bounds of a definable and enforceable duty of care" and are encompased [sic] by a marital or nuptial privilege. Id. at 557, 388 A.2d [951]. These areas were not left intact, however, were seen as potential exceptions to the otherwise abrogated doctrine and were to be ultimately defined and developed on a case-by-case basis by future courts. . . .

In the present action, the plaintiff alleges that the defendant continued to have sexual relations with her even after discovering that he had herpes, the result of an extramarital relationship. It is argued by the defendant that sexual intercourse between spouses is by its very nature an act which falls within the scope of a marital or nuptial privilege and therefore his conduct should be shielded from liability. This Court does not agree. It is unconscionable that a person could escape liability for infecting a spouse with genital herpes or other sexually transmitted disease by merely claiming that the transmission occurred during privileged sexual relations of marriage. . . .

Defendant misconstrues the meaning of marital privilege and furthermore destroyed any that may have existed by his own intentional involvement in an extramarital relationship. Defendant cannot simultaneously breach his marital relationship by engaging in extramarital intercourse, and claim nuptial immunity for consequences flowing from his own wilful and intentional conduct. . . .

As to the intentional aspect of the personal injury claim, it is clear that the abolition of the interspousal immunity doctrine pertains to intentional tortious conduct as well as conventional negligence. Plaintiff first observed symptoms of the herpes simplex virus on defendant's body in February 1983, but accepted his explanations to the contrary. Defendant argued that he never intended to inflict the plaintiff with herpes as he was never officially diagnosed until 1987, almost three years after the filing of the complaint. However defendant admitted in his deposition that he told plaintiff of his extramarital affair prior to the couple's separation. It was also stated by the parties' former housekeeper that defendant told plaintiff that he had contracted herpes as a result of this affair and was sorry to have infected her. Defendant has since denied this conversation. Regardless, the intentional act was not that of knowingly transmitting herpes to plaintiff but, rather, it was the act of sexual intercourse with the plaintiff after sexual relations with someone else with whom he carried on a two year relationship. Such behavior on defendant's part placed plaintiff at risk of physical harm.

There remains a duty of care to one's spouse and the threat of physical harm cannot be excused. "Consent to sexual intercourse vitiated by one partner's fraudulent concealment of the risk of infection with venereal disease is equally applicable today, whether or not partners involved are married to each other." Kathleen K. v. Robert B., 150 Cal. App. 3d 992, 198 Cal. Rptr. 273, 277 (Ct. App. 1984). The Supreme Court of New York has also indicated its willingness to consider a personal injury action for the transmission of genital herpes between spouses. See Maharam v. Maharam, 510 N.Y.S.2d 104, 123 A.D.2d 165 (App. Div. 1986). While allowing that interspousal immunity may exist as a narrow exception in some areas, the [New Jersey] Court was very clear that it ". . . should not be viewed as a catalyst which renders wrongful acts innocuous." *Tevis*, 79 N.J. at 429, 400 A.2d 1189, citing Merenoff v. Merenoff, and Long v. Llandy, 35 N.J. 44, 171 A.2d (1961). Indeed, at one time, states considered the transmission of syphilis by husband to wife a criminal assault. See State v. Lankford, 29 Del. 1594, 102 A. 63, 64 (Ct. Gen. Sess. 1917). Although a criminal charge is not being addressed, the defendant can not be allowed to hide behind the veil of marital privilege.

This Court holds that the marital privilege of sexual relations does not include immunity to personal injury suits between spouses based upon the transmittal of a sexual disease. Motion for summary judgment is denied. . . .

## Notes and Questions

1. The history of the doctrine of interspousal immunity reflects a century of primarily judicial, rather than legislative, reform. The movement for abrogation occurred first for intentional acts and, subsequently, for negligence. The doctrine currently is a minority rule. Carl Tobias, Interspousal Tort Immunity in America, 23 Ga. L. Rev. 359, 383 (1989). Among the most common interspousal tort actions are assault, battery, false imprisonment, and intentional infliction of emotional distress. Robert G. Spector, Marital Torts: Actions for Tortious Conduct Occurring During the Marriage, 5 Am. J. Fam. L. 71, 72-73 (1991). Often, these actions stem from spousal abuse. See, e.g., Waite v. Waite, 618 So. 2d 1360 (Fla. 1993); Burns v. Burns, 518 So. 2d 1205 (Miss. 1988).

2. Spouses often pursue interspousal tort litigation only on separa-
tion or divorce. As a result, statutes of limitations may bar their claims.
See, e.g., Dubovsky v. Dubovsky, 725 N.Y.S.2d 832 (N.Y. Sup. Ct. 2001).
Should separation be a prerequisite to recovery?

3. To what extent should interspousal liability, which first emerged
in cases of negligent driving, extend to household accidents? See Brown
v. Brown, 409 N.E.2d 717 (Mass. 1980) (wife sustained injuries as a result of husband's allegedly negligent removal of snow). Are there aspects
of marital life that should not give rise to liability? Consider the following (posed by the husband's attorney in *Brown*): (1) Wife puts too much
salt in meals; Husband gets high blood pressure. (2) Husband wants to
have children; Wife does not. She gets pregnant. (3) Husband normally
takes out the garbage. He forgets; Wife lifts the heavy bag and hurts her
back. 6 Fam. L. Rep. (BNA) 1162 (Aug. 26, 1980).

4. Do special reasons support interspousal immunity only for sexual
torts? Is there more "family privacy" to preserve in this context? Does
the rationale for preserving interspousal immunity become especially
persuasive in cases of sexual torts?

5. Since the early twentieth century, courts have recognized tort liability for transmission of venereal disease. See, e.g., Crowell v. Crowell,
105 S.E. 206 (N.C. 1920). Some cases, although recognizing the tort of
negligent transmission, barred recovery based on interspousal immunity. See, e.g., Bandfield v. Bandfield, 75 N.W. 287 (Mich. 1898). The
erosion of the interspousal immunity doctrine has permitted a proliferation of such cases. Most courts, as in *G.L.,* currently extend interspousal
liability to cover the transmission of herpes. Theories of liability include
negligence (and negligence per se), battery, deceit, fraudulent misrepresentation, and intentional infliction of emotional distress.

6. The Restatement of Torts postulates that a spouse has a duty to
disclose physical conditions that make cohabitation dangerous. Restatement (Second) of Torts §554 (1977). Does an infected spouse have an affirmative duty to disclose a sexually transmitted condition? See Maharam
v. Maharam, 510 N.Y.S.2d 104 (App. Div. 1986) (31-year marriage gives
rise to affirmative duty to disclose herpes). Does the infected spouse's ignorance of his disease preclude liability? See McPherson v. McPherson,
712 A.2d 1043 (Me. 1998) (denying recovery to wife because husband,
who had an affair, did not know he was infected).

7. Do spouses have a duty to disclose to each other their HIV- or
AIDS-related status? In the first case to raise the issue, a wife claimed
that her husband's failure to disclose past homosexual liaisons caused
her to suffer "AIDS phobia." Granting the husband's motion to dismiss,
the court distinguished the case from *Maharam,* supra, stating that the
wife alleged only possible exposure to AIDS, whereas the defendant in
*Maharam* contracted and transmitted the disease. Doe v. Doe, 519
N.Y.S.2d 595 (Sup. Ct. 1987). In AIDS-phobia cases, courts are divided

about permitting recovery in the absence of physical injury. See Jill Trachtenberg, Living in Fear: Recovering Negligent Infliction of Emotional Distress Damages Based on the Fear of Contracting AIDS, 2 DePaul J. Health Care L. 529 (1999) (surveying case law).

Given a duty to disclose HIV status, at what level of knowledge should a defendant foresee potential harm to a plaintiff to trigger the duty? If defendant has experienced symptoms? Has or has had sexual contact with an individual diagnosed with HIV? Engaged in high-risk conduct that may result in exposure to HIV? Has had unprotected sexual relations with multiple partners? See Delay v. Delay, 707 So. 2d 400 (Fla. Ct. App. 1998). See generally Josette M. LeDoux, Interspousal Liability and the Wrongful Transmission of HIV-AIDS: Argument for Broadening Legal Avenues for the Injured Spouse and Further Expanding Children's Rights to Sue Their Parents, 34 New Eng. L. Rev. 392 (2000). Do children have legal rights against a parent when that parent wrongfully transmits a sexual disease to the other parent? See id.

8. Does the obligation to disclose extend to disclosure by third parties? (Mandatory disclosure statutes do require reporting of a variety of conditions to state health agencies.) One commentator proposes mandatory notification (by physicians and state health officials) of spouses of HIV-infected individuals. See Sten L. Gustafson, Comment, No Longer the Last to Know: A Proposal for Mandatory Notification of Spouses of HIV Infected Individuals, 29 Hous. L. Rev. 991 (1992). Would you support such legislation? What are the competing policy concerns?

9. Many feminist legal theorists criticize interspousal tort immunity as an example of the lack of legal protection for women in the "private sphere" of family life. See, e.g., Katherine O'Donovan, Sexual Divisions in Law 59-158 (1985); Nadine Taub & Elizabeth M. Schneider, Perspectives on Women's Subordination and the Role of the Law, in The Politics of Law: A Progressive Critique 328 (David Kairys ed., 1998); Elizabeth M. Schneider, The Violence of Privacy, 23 Conn. L. Rev. 973 (1991).

## Problem

Wife has an extramarital affair with a doctor. She contracts an unspecified venereal disease from her lover and transmits the disease to Husband. Husband sues Wife alleging that she was negligent in failing to notify him that she had had an extramarital affair and therefore was at risk of passing a sexually transmissible disease to him. Husband also sues the lover for negligence in failing to notify Wife that he had a sexually transmissible disease and might transmit the disease to her, knowing that Wife was married and at risk of infecting her spouse. The lover defends by asserting that the action is barred by anti-heart balm legislation. How should the court rule on Husband's claim and the lover's defense? See Mussivand v. David, 544 N.E.2d 265 (Ohio 1989).

## b. Wiretapping

■ **KIRKLAND v. FRANCO**
*92 F. Supp. 2d 578 (E.D. La. 2000)*

FALLON, District Judge.

. . . Plaintiff Alice Christina Poe Kirkland and defendant Dennis B. Franco were formerly married. Prior to their separation, they had three children and lived in Slidell, Louisiana. When Franco suspected that Kirkland was having an extramarital affair, he purchased a telephone recording device from Radio Shack and placed it on an extension telephone in the couple's bedroom from August 1, 1998 until August 3, 1998 without the knowledge of his wife.

The tape recordings detail conversations between Kirkland and [her lover] Jones but apparently do not reveal explicit information concerning Kirkland's affair. Kirkland, however, admitted to her affair with Jones when confronted by Franco with the tapes. Franco also discussed the nature of the tapes with Kirkland's pastor, employer, mother, and during a child-custody hearing.

Kirkland and Jones sued Franco in this Court alleging claims under both federal and state law. First, plaintiffs argue that Franco violated the Federal Omnibus Crime Control and Safe Streets Act which prohibits intentionally intercepting electronic communications. See 18 U.S.C. §2510, *et seq.* Second, plaintiffs contend that Franco violated Louisiana's Electronic Surveillance Act which similarly bars willful interception and disclosure of electronic communications. See La. Rev. Stat. Ann. §15:1303. Franco responds that he is entitled to summary judgment because the Fifth Circuit has created an exception for spouses to the Omnibus Act. See Simpson v. Simpson, 490 F.2d 803 (5th Cir. 1974). . . .

### FEDERAL OMNIBUS CRIME CONTROL AND SAFE STREETS ACT CLAIMS

Plaintiffs contest that defendant violated the Federal Omnibus Crime Control and Safe Streets Act ("Omnibus Act"), which prohibits intentionally intercepting electronic communications between two or more individuals, by recording their telephone conversation without their knowledge or consent. See 18 U.S.C. §2510, *et seq.* . . . For violations of the Omnibus Act, plaintiffs are entitled to appropriate declaratory and equitable relief, actual or statutory damages, and reasonable attorney's fees and litigations costs.[1] Both plaintiffs and defendant admit that no

---

1. The court may assess either actual or statutory damages depending upon whichever is the greater: the sum of the actual damages suffered by the plaintiff and any profits made by the violator as a result of the violation or statutory damages consisting of the greater, $100 a day for each day of violation, or $10,000.

genuine issue of material fact exists concerning liability. They argue, respectively, that summary judgment is appropriate as a matter of law.

First, defendant contends that he is entitled to summary judgment because of the interspousal exception to the Omnibus Act created by the Fifth Circuit. See *Simpson*, 490 F.2d at 805-6. In *Simpson*, the Fifth Circuit held that while the Omnibus Act appears to apply by its terms to spouses, "Congress did not intend such a far reaching result, one extending into areas normally left to states, those of the marital home and domestic conflicts." Id.

The *Simpson* court, however, did not rule without reservation. *See* id. (explaining that "we are not without doubts about our decision" which "is, of course, limited to the specific facts of this case"). The Fourth, Sixth, Eighth and Tenth Circuits further criticize the result and reasoning of *Simpson*. See Pritchard v. Pritchard, 732 F.2d 372, 374 (4th Cir. 1984) (finding no express or implied exception for willful, unconsented electronic surveillance between spouses); United States v. Jones, 542 F.2d 661, 666 (6th Cir. 1976) (interpreting legislative history to find no interspousal exception); Kempf v. Kempf, 868 F.2d 970 (8th Cir. 1989) (rejecting the statutory interpretation of *Simpson*); Heggy v. Heggy, 944 F.2d 1537, 1540 (10th Cir. 1991) (rejecting both statutory analysis and legislative interpretation of *Simpson*); see also Kratz v. Kratz, 477 F.Supp. 463, 471-474 (E.D. Pa. 1979) (holding that no exception exists for interspousal wiretapping and rejecting the extension phone exemption). But see Anonymous v. Anonymous, 558 F.2d 677, 679 (2nd Cir. 1977) (supporting *Simpson* and applying telephone extension exception).

While the *Simpson* court itself, as well as other circuits, find fault with the *Simpson* decision, it remains the law that governs the courts of the Fifth Circuit. Kirkland raises well-reasoned arguments, but it is not appropriate for a district court to question clear precedent in a case involving nearly identical facts. Therefore, Franco's motion for summary judgment is granted with respect to Kirkland's claim against him under the Omnibus Act, and Kirkland's motion for summary judgment against Franco under the Omnibus Act is accordingly denied.

[The court holds that Jones, unlike Kirkland, does have a valid claim against Franco and, therefore, is entitled to summary judgment under the Omnibus Act.]

### Louisiana's Electronic Surveillance Act Claims

Plaintiffs also raise claims against Franco under Louisiana's Electronic Surveillance Act. . . . Defendant again does not raise a genuine issue of material fact concerning his liability under Louisiana's Electronic Surveillance Act. In fact, he makes no argument and offers no case law either supporting his claim for summary judgment or refuting plaintiffs' motion for summary judgment for their causes of action under state law.

Franco also cannot rely upon his prior citation of *Simpson* to shield him from plaintiffs' state law claims because *Simpson* examines federal and not state law. Accordingly, defendant's claim for summary judgment on the claims brought under Louisiana's Electronic Surveillance Act is denied.

The Louisiana Supreme Court has not decided whether the Louisiana Electronic Surveillance Act creates an exception for spouses. This Court, therefore, must [determine as best it can] what the Louisiana Supreme Court would decide. . . . Other states that have enacted wiretapping statutes have determined that they do not contain interspousal exceptions. See Markham v. Markham, 272 So. 2d 813 (Fla. 1973); Ransom v. Ransom, 253 Ga. 656, 324 S.E.2d 437 (1985); Standiford v. Standiford, 89 Md. App. 326, 598 A.2d 495 (Ct. Spec. App. 1991). Florida and Georgia have held that their statutory language does not provide an exception for spouses. See *Markham,* 272 So. 2d at 814; *Ransom,* 324 S.E.2d at 438. Maryland has also found no exemption for spouses because the statute created no explicit exception. See *Standiford,* 598 A.2d at 499-500. In addition, states have concluded that the doctrine of interspousal tort immunity does not apply to interspousal wiretapping. See Burgess v. Burgess, 447 So. 2d 220, 223 (Fla. 1984).

[T]his Court finds that Louisiana's Electronic Surveillance Act does not create an interspousal exception. Louisiana courts interpret the statute literally and look to federal case law to analyze provisions similar to the Omnibus Act. The majority of precedent from federal and other state courts has found no interspousal exception for wiretapping. Defendant offers no support other than the discredited *Simpson* to imply that Louisiana would interpret its statute differently from the majority of states. Therefore, because of the plain-meaning of the Electronic Surveillance Act and the defendant's failure to raise a genuine issue of material fact as to his liability, plaintiffs are entitled to summary judgment on their state law claims. . . .

## Notes and Questions

1. Unauthorized eavesdropping may occur in matrimonial disputes to discover evidence of a spouse's extramarital affair. Two primary issues arise. The first concerns the existence of interspousal civil or criminal liability under federal law. *Kirkland* (following *Simpson*) represents the minority rule, refusing to impose liability under federal law. The second issue concerns the admissibility of illegally obtained evidence in divorce proceedings. This issue has receded in importance with the advent of no-fault divorce. However, admissibility issues still arise in the custody context. See, e.g., Scheib v. Grant, 22 F.3d 149 (7th Cir.), *cert. denied,* 513 U.S. 929 (1994).

2. Title III ("the Wiretap Act") was enacted to protect individuals from nonconsensual interception of wire or oral communications. With certain exceptions (for example, law enforcement officers by court order and agents of the communications common carrier to protect the property rights of the carrier), the act imposes civil and criminal liability by the creation of a new tort, a new crime, and evidentiary rules excluding use of the contents. The act entitles an injured party to recover actual damages of a minimum of $100 per day for each day of violation or $10,000, whichever is greater, plus punitive damages, reasonable attorneys' fees, and litigation costs. 18 U.S.C. §2520(c)(2)(B) (1994).

3. Professor Anita Allen points out that some international guarantees are more explicit than our Constitution about the right to privacy in the home. The United Nations Universal Declaration of Human Rights states: "No one shall be subjected to arbitrary interference with his privacy, family home or correspondence, nor to attacks upon his honour and reputation. Everyone has the right to protection of the law against such interference or attacks." Similarly, the European Convention on Human Rights, Article 8, provides: "Everyone has the right to respect for his private and family life, his home, and his correspondence." Anita L. Allen, Uneasy Access: Privacy for Women in a Free Society 59, 191 n.12 (1988).

4. Why impose liability for interspousal invasions of privacy? To discourage or punish eavesdropping? To penalize revelation to third parties? How are wiretapping and taping different from eavesdropping on an extension phone (which is not prohibited)? Professor Allen describes three forms of domestic privacy: "The first two domestic privacies are inaccessibility of the person in the senses of seclusion and anonymity. . . . The third is inaccessibility of personal information, especially the non-disclosure, through secrecy and confidentiality, of personal facts, opinions, or creative expressions contained in documentary form." Allen, supra, at 60. Does this classification help identify the problem in the wiretapping cases?

5. A number of states have passed statutes similar to the federal law. See, e.g., Ohio Rev. Code Ann. §2933.52 (Banks-Baldwin 1997); Va. Code Ann. §§19.2-62, 19.2-69 (Michie 2000). The American Bar Association also has developed a model civil statute that differs from the Wiretap Act in requiring that the defendant know the surveillance was unlawful; it also has no provision for liquidated or punitive damages. ABA Standards for Criminal Justice Standard 2-2.2 (2d ed. 1980).

Should a spouse be entitled to a "good faith" defense based on the belief that there was nothing illegal about tapping a home phone? Would you recommend adoption of the ABA Standard that would not impose liability in such circumstances? See also Fultz v. Gilliam, 942 F.2d 396 (6th Cir. 1991); Young v. Young, 536 N.W.2d 254 (Mich. Ct. App. 1995).

6. Should liability arise for interceptions of communications between the other spouse and the couple's children? In Newcomb v. Ingle,

944 F.2d 1534 (10th Cir. 1991), *cert. denied,* 502 U.S. 1044, *reh'g denied,* 503 U.S. 915 (1992), a divorced mother had custody of Brent and a younger brother. She recorded her husband's telephone conversations, including one in which the husband instructed Brent and his brother as they set fire to their home. The recordings led to the husband's conviction for arson and to juvenile proceedings against the children. On reaching majority, Brent brought suit. The court held that the son had no cause of action under Title III.

Is spousal wiretapping qualitatively different from parental interceptions? Is a minor's expectation of privacy reduced? Consider the following:

> Once the desire for privacy develops in small children, their parents may justifiably deny them their desired levels of privacy on paternalistic grounds to assure discipline and safety. Teenagers living at home are typically allowed greater privacy than small children. But they may find that their phone calls and visitors are monitored, their bedrooms shared with younger siblings, and their diaries read. In a related vein, they may find that their sexual and reproductive preferences, their "decisional privacy," is effectively pre-empted. . . .

Allen, supra, at 62.

Consent precludes imposition of liability under Title III. Can a parent vicariously consent for a child? In Pollock v. Pollock, 154 F.3d 601 (6th Cir. 1998), the Sixth Circuit first adopted the vicarious consent doctrine for parental wiretapping. A mother, who was granted custody of the couple's three children, recorded her daughter's conversations with her father and his new wife. When the father and ex-wife brought an action under the federal wiretap statute, the mother successfully argued that she acted in the best interests of the child stemming from her concern that her ex-husband was subjecting the daughter to psychological abuse. *Accord* D'Onofrio v. D'Onofrio, 780 A.2d 593 (N.J. Super. Ct. 2001). Should parents always be entitled to the vicarious consent exemption, or should courts intervene in some cases to protect children's privacy rights? See Debra Bogosavljevic, Can Parents Vicariously Consent to Recording a Telephone Conversation on Behalf of a Minor Child?: An Examination of the Vicarious Consent Exception Under Title III of the Omnibus Crime Control and Safe Streets Act of 1968, 2000 U. Ill. L. Rev. 321 (2001) (critizing the exemption on privacy grounds).

## Problems

1. Attorney William T. Wuliger is retained by David Ricupero to represent him in a divorce. Ricupero records his wife's telephone conversations, including those with her priest, marriage counselor, attorney,

and friends. He gives the tapes to Wuliger, informing Wuliger falsely of his wife's knowledge. Wuliger transcribes the tapes and has summaries prepared. Mrs. Ricupero learns of the taping in a hearing on her charges of domestic violence. Wuliger uses the tapes to impeach her, to question her lover (whom she later married), and to examine her about her alleged concealment of marital funds. Mrs. Ricupero charges Wuliger with violations of Title III. What result? Should attorneys receive special treatment under the act? See United States v. Wuliger, 981 F.2d 1497 (6th Cir. 1992), *cert. denied,* 510 U.S. 1191, *reh'g denied,* 511 U.S. 1101 (1994).

2. After Husband and Wife decide to divorce, Husband begins sleeping in the family's sun room. Wife and the couple's three children continue to use the room regularly because the room contains the family computer and entertainment center. When Wife discovers a letter from Husband's girlfriend in the sun room, she hires an investigator to copy Husband's files from the computer's hard drive. (Husband mistakenly believes that his e-mail cannot be read without his Internet Service Provider password.) In the couple's subsequent custody dispute, Wife seeks to introduce e-mail messages (both received and sent that were saved on Husband's hard drive) between Husband and his girlfriend. Husband argues for suppression of the evidence as a wrongful invasion of his privacy and a violation of the state wiretap act that prohibits a spouse from intercepting the electronic communications of the other without authorization. What result? See White v. White, 781 A.2d 85 (N.J. Super. Ct. 2001).

### 3. Domestic Violence: Wife Beating[56]

#### a. Introduction

■ **RICHARD J. GELLES & MURRAY A. STRAUS, INTIMATE VIOLENCE**
*84, 88-96 (1988)*

. . . The range of homes where wife beating occurs seems to defy categorization. One can pick up a newspaper and read of wife beating in a lower-class neighborhood and then turn the page and read that the wife of a famous rock musician has filed for divorce claiming she was beaten. . . .

---

[56]. Although both husbands and wives are victims of domestic violence, the Editors use the term "wife beating" (rather than "spousal abuse") based on the feminist view that gender-neutral terms obscure the nature of this social problem. See Michele Bograd, Feminist Perspectives on Wife Abuse: An Introduction, in Feminist Perspectives on Wife Abuse 13 (Kersti Yllo & Michele Bograd eds., 1988).

The profile of those who engage in violence with their partners is quite similar to the profile of the parents who are abusive toward their children. The greater the stress, the lower the income, the more violence. Also, there is a direct relationship between violence in childhood and the likelihood of becoming a violent adult. Again, we add the caution that although there is a relationship, this does not predetermine that all those who experience violence will grow up to be abusers.

One of the more interesting aspects of the relationship between childhood and adult violence is that *observing* your parents hit one another is a more powerful contributor to the probability of becoming a violent adult than being a victim of violence. The learning experience of seeing your mother and father strike one another is more significant than being hit yourself. Experiencing, and more importantly observing, violence as a child teaches three lessons:

1. Those who love you are also those who hit you, and those you love are people you can hit.
2. Seeing and experiencing violence in your home establishes the moral rightness of hitting those you love.
3. If other means of getting your way, dealing with stress, or expressing yourself do not work, violence is permissible. . . .

Lurking beneath the surface of all intimate violence are confrontations and controversies over power. Our statistical evidence shows that the risk of intimate violence is the greatest when all the decision making in a home is concentrated in the hands of one of the partners. . . .

It goes without saying that intimate violence is most likely to occur in intimate settings. Occasionally couples will strike one another in the car. Husbands sometimes grab their wives at a party or on the street. Husbands or wives rarely slap their partners in public. The majority of domestic combat takes place in private, behind closed doors. . . .

[T]he bedroom is the most lethal room in the house. The criminologist Marvin Wolfgang reported that 20 percent of *all* victims of criminal homicide are killed in the bedroom. The kitchen and dining room are the other frequent scenes of lethal violence between family members.

After 8:00 P.M. the risk for family violence increases. This is almost self-evident, since this is also the time when family members are most likely to be together in the home. . . . The temporal and spatial patterns of intimate violence support our notion that privacy is a key underlying factor that leads to violence. Time and space constrain the options of both the offender and the victim. As the evening wears on, there are fewer places to run to, fewer places to hide. . . .

. . . When we looked at which day of the week violence was most likely to occur, we found that [w]eekends are when families spent the most time together and when the potential for [conflict] is greatest. Not surprisingly, seven out of ten violent episodes we talked about with family members took place on either Saturday or Sunday. Weekends after a payday can be especially violent. . . .

Common sense would not suggest that violence is most likely to erupt at times of the year when families celebrate holidays and the spirit of family togetherness. Yet, contrary to common sense, it is the time from Thanksgiving to New Year's Day and again at Easter that violence in the home peaks. . . .

A number of factors may contribute to the likelihood of domestic violence and abuse during the Christmas season. This is a time when families can assume tremendous financial burdens. Purchasing Christmas gifts can either take a toll on a family's resources or plunge a family into debt. Stress can also come from *not* buying gifts and presents. . . . Holidays also create nonfinancial stress. Christmas and Easter holidays project images of family harmony, love, and togetherness. Songs, advertisements, and television specials all play up the image of the caring, loving, and even affluent family. A family with deep conflict and trouble may see these images in sad and frustrating contrast with their own lives. . . .

Time of day and time of year analysis supports the notion that privacy and stress are important structural components to domestic violence. . . .

■  **PATRICIA TJADEN & NANCY THOENNES,
EXTENT, NATURE AND CONSEQUENCES
OF INTIMATE PARTNER VIOLENCE:
FINDINGS FROM THE NATIONAL
VIOLENCE AGAINST WOMEN SURVEY**
*iii-v, 52-53 (July 2000)*

This report presents findings from the National Violence Against Women Survey on the extent, nature, and consequences of intimate partner violence in the United States. [Research consisted of telephone surveys of 8,000 men and 8,000 women.]

Intimate partner violence is pervasive in U.S. society. Nearly 25 percent of surveyed women and 7.6 percent of surveyed men said they were raped and/or physically assaulted by a current or former spouse, cohabiting partner, or date at some time in their lifetime; 1.5 percent of surveyed women and 0.9 percent of surveyed men said they were raped and/or physically assaulted by a partner in the previous 12 months. According to these estimates, approximately 1.5 million women and 834,732 men are raped and/or physically assaulted by an intimate partner annually in the United States. . . .

Stalking by intimates is more prevalent than previously thought. Almost 5 percent of surveyed women and 0.6 percent of surveyed men reported being stalked by a current or former spouse, cohabiting partner, or date at some time in their lifetime; 0.5 percent of surveyed women and 0.2 percent of surveyed men reported being stalked by such a partner in the previous 12 months. . . .

Women experience more intimate partner violence than do men. . . . These findings support data from the Bureau of Justice Statistics' National Crime Victimization Survey, which consistently show women are at significantly greater risk of intimate partner violence than are men. . . .

Rates of intimate partner violence vary significantly among women of diverse racial backgrounds. The survey found that Asian/Pacific Islander women and men tend to report lower rates of intimate partner violence than do women and men from other minority backgrounds, and African-American and American Indian/Alaska Native women and men report high rates. . . . More research is needed to determine how much of the difference in intimate partner prevalence rates among women and men of different racial and ethnic backgrounds can be explained by the respondent's willingness to disclose intimate partner violence. . . .

Most intimate partner victimizations are not reported to the police. Approximately one-fifth of all rapes, one-quarter of all physical assaults, and one-half of all stalkings perpetrated against female respondents by intimates were reported to the police. Even fewer rapes, physical assaults, and stalkings perpetrated against male respondents by intimates were reported. The majority of victims who did not report their victimization to the police thought the police would not or could not do anything on their behalf. . . .

Information from the NVAW Survey shows that violence perpetrated against women by intimates is rarely prosecuted. Only 7.5 percent of the women who were raped by an intimate, 7.3 percent of the women who were physically assaulted by an intimate, and 14.6 percent of the women who were stalked by an intimate said their attacker was criminally prosecuted. . . . [V]iolence against men by intimates is even less likely to be criminally prosecuted. . . .

■ **BEVERLY HORSBURGH, LIFTING THE VEIL OF SECRECY: DOMESTIC VIOLENCE IN THE JEWISH COMMUNITY**
*18 Harv. Women's L.J. 171, 172-173 (1995)*

. . . You can't know my life. My story would be a bestseller. He hit me before we married — chased me around the room when I refused to marry him. After we married it was much worse. He drank a lot and took drugs. He became even more violent when he was drinking. He was two different people. In public he was the famous doctor, holier than God, loved by all. In private, he was a monster. He controlled absolutely everything. At our home in Miami Beach he wanted the air-conditioning at 72 degrees. If I changed it, he would scream, hit, carry on so. The radio station he liked had to be on in every room. I wasn't allowed to touch it. It was his way or no way. He also beat the children. We have six children. When the children talked in bed past bedtime he would make them do push-ups. Those poor little kids, trying to do push-ups, so young. If they stopped, he would get out the strap or a hanger from the closet. I couldn't interfere. I would get such a smack across the face, my nose would bleed.

I couldn't leave him. It would break my parents' hearts to know that I was unhappy. I had six children. I was not educated. I didn't speak good English. I had no job skills. Where could I go with six kids? I told no one. If I told the rabbi, he would want to talk to my husband and then he would really kill me. I was raised not to complain about your personal problems. You don't hang your dirty laundry outside. It would hurt his practice if I told our friends. Besides, he threatened if I left him he would kill me, himself, and the children. Also, he told me he would disappear and I would never see a cent. Once he showed me a newspaper article about a husband who murdered his wife. He told me he would do this too. . . .

### b. Battered Woman Syndrome

■ **HAWTHORNE v. STATE**
*408 So. 2d 801 (Fla. Dist. Ct. App. 1982)*

PER CURIAM. . . .
This was appellant's second trial for the murder of her husband. Her first conviction, for first degree murder, was reversed by this court in Hawthorne v. State, 377 So. 2d 780 (Fla. 1st DCA 1979). [Defendant's husband was shot to death in the early morning hours of January 28, 1977, in the Hawthorne home by bullets fired from a number of weapons belonging to the deceased.] The last argument by appellant that warrants discussion is that the trial court erred in disallowing the testimony of Dr. Lenore Walker, a clinical psychologist who would have testified as an expert with regard to the battered-woman syndrome. The purpose of such testimony would have been to give the jury a basis for considering whether appellant suffered from the battered-woman syndrome, not in order to establish a novel defense, but as it related to her claim of self-defense. We are aware of the conflicting decisions of various jurisdictions as to the admissibility of this type of expert testimony. See, e.g., Smith v.

State, 247 Ga. 612, 277 S.E.2d 678 (1981); State v. Thomas, 66 Ohio St. 2d 518, 423 N.E.2d 137 (1981); Buhrle v. State, 627 P.2d 1378, 1378 (Wyo. 1981); Ibn-Tamas v. United States, 407 A.2d 626 (D.C. App. 1979). The courts that have considered the admissibility of this type of expert testimony have generally analyzed it to see whether it meets three basic criteria: (1) the expert is qualified to give an opinion on the subject matter; (2) the state of the art or scientific knowledge permits a reasonable opinion to be given by the expert; and (3) the subject matter of the expert opinion is so related to some science, profession, business, or occupation as to be beyond the understanding of the average layman. Basically, the same criteria are applicable in the instant case.

The few case authorities which have considered the admissibility of this type of expert testimony disagree primarily with regard to (1) whether the study of the battered-woman syndrome is an area sufficiently developed to permit an expert to assert a reasonable opinion, and (2) whether the battered-woman syndrome is beyond the knowledge and experience of most laymen.

In *Ibn-Tamas* and *Smith,* the courts concluded that the expert testimony should have been allowed, inasmuch as the subject matter was "beyond the ken of the average layman." 277 S.E.2d at 683. "[T]he expert's testimony explaining why a person suffering from battered woman's syndrome would not leave her mate, would not inform police or friends, and would fear increased aggression against herself, would be such conclusions that jurors could not ordinarily draw for themselves." Id. The court in *Ibn-Tamas* also concluded that the expert could provide "an interpretation of the facts which differed from the ordinary lay perception," therefore the subject matter was "beyond the ken of the average layman." 407 A.2d at 635. The *Ibn-Tamas* court determined, however, that the trial court had not ruled on whether the expert, Dr. Lenore Walker, was sufficiently qualified to give an opinion or whether "the state of the pertinent art or scientific knowledge" would permit an expert opinion. 407 A.2d at 635. The court said that this third criterion depended on "whether Dr. Walker's methodology for identifying and studying battered women" was generally accepted. 407 A.2d at 638. The question whether the second and third criteria were satisfied was remanded to the trial court.

In State v. Thomas, the Ohio Supreme Court determined that expert testimony by a psychiatric social worker was properly excluded because the battered-woman syndrome was within the jury's understanding and also that the syndrome "is not sufficiently developed, as a matter of commonly accepted scientific knowledge, to warrant testimony under the guise of expertise." 423 N.E.2d at 140.

In Buhrle v. State, the Wyoming Supreme Court in rejecting Dr. Walker's testimony on the syndrome said that "we are not saying that this type of expert testimony is not admissible; we are merely holding that the state of the art was not adequately demonstrated to the court, and because of inadequate foundation the proposed opinions would not aid the jury." 627 P.2d at 1378.

We agree with the view expressed by the Georgia Supreme Court in Smith v. State insofar as it concluded that jurors would not ordinarily understand "why a person suffering from battered-woman's syndrome would not leave her mate, would not inform police or friends, and would fear increased aggression against herself. . . ." 277 S.E.2d at 683. In the instant case, however, there has been no determination below as to the adequacy of Dr. Walker's qualifications or the extent to which her methodology is generally accepted indicating that the subject matter can support a reasonable expert opinion. Our determination that this expert testimony would provide the jury with an interpretation of the facts not ordinarily available to them is subject to the trial court determining that Dr. Walker is qualified and that the subject is sufficiently developed and can support an expert opinion.

Appellee argues that to admit this type of expert testimony would violate the rule . . . that "testimony regarding the mental state of a defendant in a criminal case is inadmissible in the absence of a plea of not guilty by reason of insanity," [Zeigler v. State, 402 So. 2d 365, 373 (Fla. 1981)]. In this case, a defective mental state on the part of the accused is not offered as a defense as such. Rather, the specific defense is self-defense which requires a showing that the accused reasonably believed it was necessary to use deadly force to prevent imminent death or great bodily harm to herself or her children. The expert testimony would have been offered in order to aid the jury in interpreting the surrounding circumstances as they affected the reasonableness of her belief. . . . Appellant did not seek to show through the expert testimony that the mental and physical mistreatment of her affected her mental state so that she could not be responsible for her actions; rather, the testimony would be offered to show that because she suffered from the syndrome, it was reasonable for her to have remained in the home and, at the pertinent time, to have believed that her life and the lives of her children were in imminent danger. It is precisely because a jury would not understand why appellant would remain in the environment that the expert testimony would have aided them in evaluating the case. . . .

Reversed and remanded for a new trial.

## ■ DR. LENORE WALKER, TERRIFYING LOVE: WHY BATTERED WOMEN KILL AND HOW SOCIETY RESPONDS
*23-41 (1989)*

I first met Joyce Hawthorne three years after [husband] Aubrey's death.

An ordinary-looking woman of forty, about 5'3" tall, weighing about 150 lbs., she didn't attract much attention. Her smile was rare but sweet; her eyes sparkled when she laughed. She looked just like the church-going mother of five that she was. Judging by her appearance alone, no one would have known that she'd killed a man much larger than herself, firing five guns in the process, even if sometimes her facial expression, at rest, revealed her fear and unhappiness. . . .

Joyce never denied that she'd fired the fatal shots; rather, although she had no memory of it, she claimed that she had been justified in firing them because she had wanted to protect herself and her family from assault, rape, and death. . . . Although she did not remember shooting her husband, she had initially confessed to doing it in order to get the police to release her five children, who were being held for questioning at the time.* [Her prior conviction of first degree murder was reversed because evidence of her husband's alleged abuse toward her and the children was improperly excluded.]

In reversing the judge's previous decision, an appellate court had ruled that evidence about the extensive family abuse in this case could be introduced in the upcoming trial; but nothing had been specifically stated about the permissibility of allowing an expert witness to explain what Joyce's behavior had meant. . . .

Battered Woman Syndrome had not previously been used in the state of Florida to support a self-defense argument (although several other states had, by that time, permitted such testimony in courts of law). Before, it would have been much more common for a woman like Joyce to plead insanity, arguing that her husband's terrible abuse had rendered her temporarily insane. . . . Shortly after Aubrey's death, Joyce Hawthorne had been examined by a psychiatrist, who had found that she knew right from wrong, the legal standard for Florida's insanity plea. I, too, would find that Joyce Hawthorne was legally sane — but terrified that she and her family would be slaughtered, just as Aubrey had threatened. In my opinion, her belief that she and her children were in danger that night had been reasonable, and reasonable perception of imminent physical danger is the legal standard for acting in self-defense.

. . . I agreed with [defense attorney] Leo Thomas that a second jury would have to be carefully educated as to how and why this soft-spoken, church-going mother of five had been able to kill the father of her children. . . . Leo knew that, without understanding the long history of marital abuse Joyce had endured, the average person sitting on a jury could not be expected to comprehend why she had believed her husband would kill her when she refused his sexual advances. . . .

*Two years later, the appellate court ruled that the police should not have promised to release her children in order to force her to give a statement, especially after she and her attorney had already exercised her right not to talk to the detectives. It is never considered a "voluntary" statement when someone is forced to talk under duress. . . .

But Battered Woman Syndrome would provide the appropriate explanation; it would delineate the perception of imminency,[**] and show how that perception was affected by the woman's state of mind. It would make her state of mind comprehensible, because battered women are always afraid of being hurt; any crisis situation may be perceived as a matter of life or death. . . .

Leo Thomas realized that he would have to educate this second jury . . . to make them understand why Joyce hadn't divorced Aubrey despite the daily horror of their marriage; he would have to corroborate Joyce's reports of domestic violence, even if no one else had seen Aubrey beat her; he would have to introduce convincing evidence to demonstrate that Joyce's fear had been reasonable on the night she finally killed him. All this would mean persuading the jury that Aubrey Hawthorne's repeated abuse of his wife had so affected her state of mind that she'd believed she needed to shoot him, to stop him from hurting her — as she perceived him coming toward her, even before he'd actually touched her — on that night in January 1977. Leo would have to help Joyce persuade the jury that her acute state of terror had induced her to use no less than five guns that night, firing at least nine bullets into her husband's body; that, in fact, her behavior had been a demonstration not of anger but of fear. . . .

. . . Most women are at a serious disadvantage when facing an attack from a man who is not only physically stronger but more ready and willing to fight. And battered women who kill are really like battered women who don't kill — they endure the same harassment, the same psychological torture; they experience the same terror — except that they have partners who are ready, able, and willing to kill them. When a battered woman kills her abuser, she has reached the end of the line. She is absolutely desperate, in real despair. She believes, with good reason, that if she does not kill, she will be killed. . . .

After being sworn in, I [found myself] the silent center of a swirling legal argument. . . .

"Dr. Walker is not being presented to testify as to Joyce Hawthorne's mental status," I heard Leo say. "We are not trying to test Florida's insanity standards under the law." . . .

"If Dr. Walker tells the jury what effect the Battered Woman Syndrome had on Joyce Hawthorne's state of mind at the time she killed Aubrey Hawthorne, then she will be testifying as to a mental condition," Ron Johnson countered. "No notice of an insanity plea has been received, and therefore she shouldn't be permitted to testify. The state has the right to examine the defendant if an insanity plea is filed; therefore, we would have been denied that right." . . .

---

**The term *imminent* as it is defined in self-defense statutes usually means "to be on the brink of," not "immediate," as is its more common interpretation.

"Judge, this is justifiable homicide we are arguing, not excusable homicide, which would have been a mental health defense. Dr. Walker can testify as to the reasonableness of Joyce Hawthorne's perception that she was in imminent danger when she shot her husband. We say she acted in self-defense, not out of a disturbed mental condition." . . .

Ron Johnson assumed a threatening stance. "If you let her testify, Judge, then she takes away the role of the jury to decide if Joyce Hawthorne's perceptions of danger were reasonable. You'll open the door to allow any woman to kill a man she doesn't like, and get away with it!" . . .

"She is a noted feminist," Johnson continued, "she admits to it right here on page 15 of the introduction to her book *The Battered Woman,* so we all know she's biased against men. This woman would have decent people justify the actions of any woman who kills a man, just because he tells her to obey him. It will be open season on killing men, your honor, and you mustn't allow it!" . . .

I knew of no feminists who'd advocated killing men as a way to equalize power. . . . I heard Leo Thomas echo some of my thoughts to the judge.

"Dr. Walker will not be invading the jury's province. The appellate court judges in the case of *Ibn-Tamas vs. the United States* ruled that they needed a psychologist to explain the defendant's state of mind. This is not a feminist issue, your honor. It is about what happens to a woman when she lives with a man whom she loves and who beats her." . . .

## Notes and Questions

1. English common law recognized the right of husbands to discipline their wives by physical force. Recall Blackstone, supra page 250. American common law followed this tradition, although gradually restrictions evolved. Divorce, rather than criminal sanctions, was considered the appropriate remedy. Further, the interspousal immunity doctrine precluded tort recovery.

In the mid-1800s, courts began to repudiate the right of husbands physically to chastise their wives. During the late nineteenth century, most courts declared wife beating illegal. See generally Linda Gordon, Heroes of Their Own Lives: The Politics and History of Family Violence, Boston, 1880-1960 (1988); Elizabeth Pleck, Domestic Tyranny: The Making of Social Policy Against Family Violence from Colonial Times to the Present (1987); Elizabeth M. Schneider, Battered Women and Feminist Lawmaking (2000); Reva B. Siegel, "The Rule of Love": Wife Beating as Prerogative and Privacy, 105 Yale L.J. 2117, 2121-2142 (1996).

2. Battered women who kill their husbands increasingly rely on evidence of the battered woman syndrome (BWS), a theory of behavior

that characterizes a relationship of physical abuse. BWS derives from the research of psychologist Lenore Walker, who posits: (1) the "cycle theory of violence" and (2) the theory of "learned helplessness." Walker theorizes that abuse occurs within a three-phase cycle: (1) the tension-building phase — a gradual escalation of tension during which the batterer displays hostility and dissatisfaction and the woman attempts to placate him; (2) the acute battering incident in which the batterer explodes into uncontrollable rage (often out of proportion to the situation); and, (3) the contrition phase in which the batterer shows remorse and promises to end the abuse. Despite the promises, the cycle inevitably begins anew.

The theory of "learned helplessness" explains why women stay in a battering relationship even though they could have left their spouses. Relying on a theory formulated by Martin Seligman (Helplessness: On Depression, Development, and Death (1975)) with regard to shocks in laboratory animals, Walker explains that a battered woman becomes so depressed from the repeated battering that she loses motivation to respond or leave. Lenore Walker, The Battered Woman Syndrome 117-118, 126-127 (2000).

3. Expert testimony has been used to support two types of defenses. Early cases offered syndrome evidence to prove insanity or diminished capacity. Subsequently, BWS was introduced to support a claim of self-defense (as in the principal case). Traditionally, the battered woman who kills her husband faces difficulties in using self-defense because (1) a person must use only proportional force against unlawful armed force; (2) the victim must reasonably fear that she is in imminent danger of bodily harm; (3) the victim cannot have been the aggressor; and (4) in some jurisdictions, the victim must seek to retreat before using deadly defensive force.[57]

The following problems arise: First, the woman may use lethal force (a gun or knife) against a man who has attacked with his hands. Second, the victim may not pose an imminent threat because he may be incapacitated at the time of the killing (for example, he is asleep or drunk). Third, the woman appears to be the aggressor in the fatal attack. Finally, her husband is a lawful occupant of the dwelling. See generally Cynthia K. Gillespie, Justifiable Homicide: Battered Women, Self-Defense, and the Law (1989).

BWS evidence overcomes these problems by addressing the reason[chableness of the perception of the imminence and seriousness of the danger. Applying Walker's theory, the woman experiences the grow-

---

[57]. See Douglas A. Orr, *Weiand v. State* and Battered Spouse Syndrome: The Toothless Tigress Can Now Roar, 3 Fla. Coastal L.J. 125, 130 (2000) (discussing the "castle doctrine" and noting that Florida recently joined the majority of states by deciding that the duty to retreat does not apply when the defendant and victim are occupants of the same home).

ing tension of phase one and acute battering of phase two. In response, she develops a constant fear of serious bodily harm that she perceives as imminent partially because of the unpredictability of her spouse's rage. Further, the cycle theory also addresses the element of the reasonableness of the amount of force necessary to repel the attack by suggesting that the woman perceives herself trapped in a cycle of potentially deadly violence and feels compelled to use deadly force to preempt the attack of the more powerful, even though perhaps unarmed, aggressor.

4. As the principal case reveals, states initially were resistant to the admission of evidence on BWS. Currently, all 50 states and the District of Columbia admit such evidence, at least to some degree, either by statute or case law. Janet Parrish, U.S. Dept. of Justice, Trend Analysis: Expert Testimony on Battering and Its Effects on Criminal Cases 12-17 (1996). See also David L. Faigman et al., Modern Scientific Evidence: The Law and Science of Expert Testimony, The Battered Woman Syndrome and Other Psychological Effects of Domestic Violence Against Women: The Legal Relevance of Research on Domestic Violence Against Women §8-1.0 (1997 & Supp. 2000) (maintaining that BSW has received greater acceptance by courts "than perhaps any other area of psychological research").

To determine the admissibility of novel scientific evidence, federal courts traditionally relied on the "general acceptance" standard set forth in Frye v. United States, 293 F. 1013 (D.C. Cir. 1923). *Frye* permitted the admission of evidence if it has become generally accepted by scientists in the particular field of study. This classic formulation was superseded by Daubert v. Merrell Dow Pharmaceuticals, Inc., 509 U.S. 579 (1993), which adopted Federal Rule of Evidence 702. Under the *Daubert* standard, evidence may be admitted if it is helpful to the trier of fact and also, if the methodology is scientifically valid. Does BWS evidence meet this standard? Although *Daubert* technically applies only to federal courts, many state courts now adhere to it. For a post-*Daubert* case, see Fowler v. State, 958 S.W.2d 853, 863-864 (Tex. Ct. App. 1997) (finding that state failed to show sufficient evidence of the scientific validity of BWS).

5. Problems sometimes arise for prosecutors because corroboration of battering may be difficult (as it takes place in private), and victims may not be able to testify (due to fear, unwillingness, or death). Should there be a special exception to the hearsay rule for domestic violence to aid prosecution? See Neal A. Hudders, Note, The Problem of Using Hearsay in Domestic Violence Cases: Is a New Exception the Answer?, 49 Duke L.J. 1041 (2000). Also, does the increasing acceptance of BWS testimony open the doors for a lesser standard of imminence in other criminal contexts? See Martin E. Veinsreideris, The Prospective Effects of Modifying Existing Law to Accommodate Preemptive Self-Defense by Battered Women, 149 U. Pa. L. Rev. 613, 614 (2000).

6. States have split over whether to apply objective or subjective rules to the battered woman's self-defense claim. Under the objective standard, the defendant must have a reasonable belief (traditionally measured by the "reasonable man" test) that deadly force was necessary for self-defense. The subjective standard measures reasonableness from the perceptions of the particular individual. Admission of syndrome evidence can enable the judge or jury to understand better the perspective of the battered woman. Compare People v. Humphrey, 921 P.2d 1 (Cal. 1996) (adopting the subjective standard) with State v. Edwards, 2001 WL 567612 (Mo. Ct. App. 2001) (adopting the objective standard).

7. The federal government has played an increasing role in domestic violence. Although legislation was first proposed in 1977, Congress finally enacted the Family Violence Prevention and Services Act in 1984, which furnished funds for shelters and programs. In 1994 Congress enacted the Violence Against Women Act (VAWA), Pub. L. No. 103-322, 108 Stat. 1796 (1994). Title II, Safe Homes for Women, creates a federal remedy for crossing a state line with intent to injure or harass a spouse or intimate partner (18 U.S.C. §2261 (1994 & Supp. 1999)) and provides for interstate enforcement of protection orders (18 U.S.C. §2265 (1994)). Title III created a federal civil rights remedy for victims of gender-motivated violent crimes (codified at 42 U.S.C. §13981 (1994)). In United States v. Morrison, 529 U.S. 598 (2000), the United States Supreme Court invalidated VAWA's civil rights remedy as an unconstitutional exercise of Congress's power under both Section 5 of the Fourteenth Amendment and the Commerce Clause. Although Title III is no longer a remedy for victims, other VAWA provisions continue to provide financial incentives for states to address domestic violence (via education, prevention, and support programs). See generally Jennifer R. Hagan, Can We Lose the Battle and Still Win the War?: The Fight Against Domestic Violence After the Death of Title III of the Violence Against Women Act, 50 DePaul L. Rev. 919 (2001).

Federal legislation also addresses battering of immigrant women. Regulations of the Immigration and Naturalization Service (INS) formerly required that resident-husbands petition the INS to establish legal residence status for their immigrant wives. Battered wives were at particular risk — alone in a new environment, without family and friends, and with poor language skills. They were often forced to stay with their abusers to avoid deportation and to obtain legal residence. The VAWA amended the Immigration and Nationality Act to provide for self-petitioning for battered spouses and to permit such spouses to apply for suspension of deportation. See Illegal Immigration Reform and Immigrant Responsibility Act of 1996, §204(a)(1), 8 U.S.C.A. §1154(a)(1)(A)(iii) (West 1994 & Supp. 1999) (self-petitioning); 8 U.S.C.A. §1254(a)(3) (West Supp. 1997) (deportation).

On the problem of battering and women of color, see generally Mary Ann Dutton et al., Characteristics of Help-Seeking Behaviors, Resources and Service Needs of Battered Immigrant Latinas: Legal and Policy Implications, 7 Geo. J. Poverty L. & Pol'y 245 (2000); Cecilia M. Espenoza, No Relief for the Weary: VAWA Relief Denied for Battered Immigrants Lost in the Intersections, 83 Marq. L. Rev. 163 (1999).

8. BWS enables the criminal justice system to respond more sympathetically to the experiences of women. Does admission of BWS violate equal protection?

9. Walker's research on battered women is not without its critics. Among these is Professor David Faigman who criticizes her research design (interviewers' rating incidents as part of a cycle), the failure to use a control group, the use of leading questions, and the failure to place the cycle phases within a definite time frame. He also criticizes Walker for misapplication of the learned helplessness theory.

> [She] uses the theory in a way that overlooks a crucial finding of Seligman's original research. In Seligman's experiment, once the dogs were rendered helpless, researchers found it extremely difficult, and in some cases impossible, to retrain the dogs to exercise control over their environment. Thus, from a theoretical perspective one would predict that if battered women suffered from learned helplessness they would not assert control over their environment; certainly one would not predict such a positive assertion of control as killing the batterer. . . .

David Faigman, Note, the Battered Woman Syndrome and Self-Defense: A Legal and Empirical Dissent, 72 Va. L. Rev. 619, 640-641 (1986). See also David Faigman, The Battered Woman Syndrome in the Age of Science, 39 Ariz. L. Rev. 67 (1997).

One commentator notes the following arguments by feminists and other critics regarding BWS evidence: (1) it promotes stereotypes of women as helpless, (2) it inaccurately portrays women as mentally ill and hysterical, (3) it fails to explain that victims respond in different ways, (4) it disadvantages minorities, (5) it provides special treatment to defendants in violation of equal treatment and antidiscrimination ideals, and (6) its use as a defense is subject to sexist applications by judges and juries. Sharan K. Suri, Note, A Matter of Principle and Consistency: Understanding the Battered Woman and Cultural Defenses, 7 Mich. J. Gender & L. 107, 126-127 (2000). See also Rebecca S. Cornia, Current Use of Battered Woman Syndrome: Institutionalization of Negative Stereotypes About Women, 8 UCLA Women's L.J. 99 (1997).

Is homicide an assertion of control by a battered woman over her environment or a recognition of her lack of control? See Martha Mahoney, Victimization or Oppression? Women's Lives, Violence, and Agency, in The Public Nature of Private Violence (Martha Fineman ed.,

1994); Elizabeth M. Schneider, Feminism and the False Dichotomy of Victimization and Agency, 38 N.Y.L. Sch. L. Rev. 387 (1993).

One commentator proposes use of guardianship proceedings to protect a battered woman until she is able to make decisions for herself. See Ruth Jones, Guardianship for Coercively Controlled Battered Women: Breaking the Control of the Abuser, 88 Geo. L.J. 605, 609-612 (2000). What do you think of this suggestion?

10. One of the most difficult issues for jurors to understand is why the battered woman killed her husband instead of merely leaving him. Below Mahoney attempts to shed some light on this issue:

> The "shopworn question" [why didn't she leave?] reveals several assumptions about separation: that the right solution is separation, that it is the woman's responsibility to achieve separation, and that she could have separated. . . .
>
> When we ask the woman, "Exactly what did you do in your search for help?" the answer often turns out to be that she left — at least temporarily. In [one] study, more than seventy percent of the women had left home at some time in response to violence, though only fourteen percent had gone to shelters. Of the women Walker studied, about one quarter left temporarily after each battering incident. . . .
>
> [T]he assumption that the woman's first separation should be permanent ignores the real dangers that the man will seek actively — and sometimes violently — to end the separation. . . .
>
> [We ask], "What did he do when you left?" . . . Often, a woman has left several times before she finally ends a marriage. Or, she may have been restrained from leaving by violent or coercive means: by being held prisoner in her home, by being threatened with custody suits, by having her savings taken away before she could depart. [W]e need to reckon with the dangers she faces. . . . The story of the violent pursuit of the separating woman must become part of the way we understand domestic violence to help eliminate the question "Why didn't she leave?" from our common vocabulary.

Martha Mahoney, Legal Images of Battered Women: Redefining the Issue of Separation, 90 Mich. L. Rev. 1, 61-63 (1991).

11. All jurisdictions have criminal and/or civil remedies for spouse abuse, including protective orders, civil and criminal liability for assault and battery, and tort liability for intentional infliction of emotional distress. Civil protection orders restrain a respondent from committing further acts of violence or harassment. They may be issued immediately and without notice. Once served, the adverse party becomes subject to action by local law enforcement upon violation. Protective orders may include temporary awards of custody, visitation, and child support, spousal support, as well as attorneys' fees and costs, and possession of the family home. Does the ex parte nature of these orders deprive a defendant of due process? See State ex rel. Williams v. Marsh, 626 S.W.2d 223 (Mo. 1982) (en banc).

How effective are restraining orders? A federally funded study reports that 17.1 percent of battered women obtained them. Victims resort to restraining orders not as a form of early intervention but rather as an act of desperation. Further, the study confirms that most temporary restraining orders are violated: More than two-thirds of orders involving rape or stalking were violated compared to one-half of those orders involving physical assault. Patricia Tjaden & Nancy Thoennes, Extent, Nature and Consequences of Intimate Partner Violence: Findings from the National Violence Against Women Survey 52-53 (July 2000). What are the implications of these findings for public policy?

12. *Epilogue.* Joyce Hawthorne's conviction (for first degree murder) was reversed because of, inter alia, the introduction of illegally obtained confessions and the exclusion of testimony about the decedent's violent actions, 377 So. 2d 780 (Fla. Dist. Ct. App. 1979). Her second conviction (for second degree murder) was reversed when the appellate court remanded for a determination of the admissibility of evidence of BWS (the principal case here). Upon rehearing, the trial court rejected the evidence, reasoning that its scientific basis was not sufficiently accepted. The appellate court affirmed, 470 So. 2d 770 (Fla. Dist. Ct. App. 1985). After Hawthorne was again charged with murder, her attorney successfully argued that retrial (her fourth) would constitute cruel and unusual punishment.

13. One famous battered spouse case involved abuse by Securities and Exchange Commission official John Fedders during an 18-year marriage. Amidst the ensuing publicity, Fedders resigned from his prestigious post. Although one circuit court (granting the divorce) noted that the husband was guilty of "excessively vicious conduct," another court, surprisingly, decreased the wife's alimony by one-third and awarded the husband 25 percent of the profits from his wife's book, Shattered Dreams: The Story of Charlotte Fedders (1987). Women's groups and family violence experts soundly criticized the ruling. Georgia Dullea, A Battered Wife's Fight, In and Out of Court, N.Y. Times, Nov. 9, 1987, at C15. On another famous battered spouse case (involving O. J. Simpson), see generally 67 U. Colo. L. Rev. (1996); 6 Hastings Women's L.J. (1995) (both symposia).

Battering in same-sex relationships is discussed in Chapter IV, section C4d, and cohabitants' relationships generally in Chapter IV, section C.

## Problem

Ann and her husband Jeff are having drinks at a bar. When Jeff goes to the bathroom, Greg begins talking to Ann. Jeff returns, becomes jealous and argues with Greg. Jeff leaves with Ann and retrieves two handguns from home. They return to the bar. Greg is shot when he exits. The police charge Jeff with murder. However, the grand jury reindicts both Ann and Jeff after Ann tells police that she fired the fatal shot accidentally during a struggle between the two men. A jury convicts Ann and Jeff of first degree murder; they are sentenced to life imprisonment. Ann files an application for postconviction relief, alleging that, as a victim of BWS, her husband forced her to relate a false account. She claims that he beat her, over an 18-month period, if she failed to rehearse the story or relate it to his satisfaction. What result? McMaugh v. State, 612 A.2d 725 (R.I. 1992). See also Kelly Grace Monacella, Supporting a Defense of Duress: The Admissibility of Battered Woman Syndrome, 70 Temple L. Rev. 699 (1997).

---

Historically, law enforcement personnel have been reluctant to interfere in domestic disputes. This reluctance has precipitated a number of civil suits such as the following.

### c. Duties of Law Enforcement

## ■ FAJARDO v. COUNTY OF LOS ANGELES
### 179 F.3d 698 (9th Cir. 1999)

PREGERSON, Circuit Judge:

[At 10:30 p.m. on August 27, 1989, Maria Navarro was celebrating her birthday with her relatives and friends in her home in East Los Angeles when she received a telephone call from the brother of her estranged husband, Raymond Navarro, warning her that Raymond was on his way to her house to kill her and any others present. Maria immediately dialed 911 to request emergency assistance. She told the 911 dispatcher that she had just received a warning that her estranged husband was on his way to kill her, that she believed that he was in fact on his way to kill her, and that he was under a restraining order.

When Maria stated that her estranged husband had not yet arrived, but that she believed he would definitely come to her house, the dispatcher responded, "O.K., well, the only thing to do is just call us if he comes over there . . . I mean, what can we do? We can't have a unit sit there to wait and see if he comes over." Fifteen minutes after the 911 call, Raymond Navarro entered through the rear of Maria Navarro's house, shot and killed Maria Navarro and four other people, and injured two others.] [This synopsis is from Navarro v. Block, 72 F.3d 712, 713-714 (9th Cir. 1995), referred to below as *Navarro I.*]

## DISCUSSION. . .

The Navarros claim that the County carried out a policy and practice of not treating 911 requests for assistance relating to domestic violence as "emergency" calls. The Navarros rely primarily on the deposition of Helen Pena, the 911 dispatcher who answered Maria Navarro's call. In her deposition, Helen Pena testified that it was the practice of the Sheriff's Department not to classify domestic violence 911 calls as Code 2 or "emergency procedure" calls.

Denise Navarro and other relatives of decedent Maria Navarro appeal the district court's grant of judgment on the pleadings in favor of the defendants. . . . The Navarros sued Defendants under 42 U.S.C. §1983 for allegedly giving lower priority to domestic-violence 9-1-1 calls than to non-domestic-violence 9-1-1 calls.

This case is before us for the second time. . . . In *Navarro I*, we held that the Navarros had established a genuine issue of material fact for trial by offering evidence that 9-1-1 "dispatchers in practice treat domestic violence calls differently from non-domestic violence calls." [72 F.3d at 715.] We also held that the Navarros' equal protection claim survived summary judgment because "they could prove that the domestic violence/non-domestic violence classification fails even the rationality test" under the Equal Protection Clause. Id. at 717. Accordingly, we reversed and remanded. . . .

## ANALYSIS

On remand, the district court ruled that Defendants' practice of treating domestic-violence calls differently from non-domestic-violence calls passed the rational basis test as a matter of law because (1) it is rational to limit emergency response to in-progress calls, and (2) "9-1-1 emergency assistance is provided for individuals who are severely injured and near death and domestic violence *rarely* reaches this level of injury." Defendants argue that these rationales justify discriminating against domestic-violence crimes.

It does not matter whether it is rational to distinguish between in-progress calls and not-in-progress calls because that was not the distinction that Defendants allegedly made. The Navarros allege that Defendants distinguished between domestic-violence 9-1-1 calls and non-domestic-violence 9-1-1 calls regardless of whether the violence was in progress.

Moreover, whether domestic violence "rarely" results in death or severe injury does not, by itself, end the matter. The critical issue is whether domestic-violence crimes result in severe injury or death less frequently than non-domestic-violence crimes that *are* considered 9-1-1 emergencies. Nothing in the pleadings suggests that victims of domestic violence are less likely to suffer severe injury or death than are victims of other 9-1-1 emergency crimes.

Additionally, if the Navarros can prove at trial that Defendants dispatch peace officers to prevent crimes that pose less (or equal) risk of death or severe injury than that posed by domestic violence crimes, then the Navarros would establish that Defendants' asserted justification is a pretext. If Defendants' justification for discriminating against domestic-violence crimes is nothing more than pretextual, then Defendants' actions are arbitrary and violate the Equal Protection Clause.

Hence, the district court erred by equating domestic violence calls with not-in-progress calls and equating non-domestic violence calls with in-progress calls, and by assuming that domestic-violence crimes are less injurious than non-domestic-violence crimes. Because these assumptions formed the basis of the district court's conclusion, the district court also erred when it concluded, as a matter of law, that Defendants' domestic-violence/non-domestic-violence classification was rational and reasonable under equal-protection analysis. . . .

The separate concurrence reasons that (1) there is no evidence of a domestic violence/non-domestic violence classification, and (2) that even if such a classification were proved, it would not violate equal protection.

The concurrence overlooks the evidence cited in our first opinion. See *Navarro I*, 72 F.3d at 715 & n.4 (noting that a 9-1-1 dispatcher had testified that it was the practice of the Sheriff's department not to classify domestic violence calls as emergency procedure calls). . . .

The concurrence also cites six cases for the proposition that, absent evidence of sex discrimination as a motivating factor, there is no constitutional claim. But the foundational case, Watson v. City of Kansas, 857 F.2d 690 (10th Cir. 1988), is in perfect harmony with our disposition in this case. In *Watson*, the district court granted summary judgment to the defendants on the question whether the police violated a domestic abuse victim's rights to equal protection by failing to provide the same police protection to victims of domestic violence that they provided to victims of non-domestic violence. On appeal, the Tenth Circuit found that the plaintiff had failed to state a prima facie case for *sex-based* discrimination and affirmed the district court's grant of summary judgment on *this* ground. But the Tenth Circuit also held that, because there were disputed issues of material fact concerning whether the police had a "policy or custom of affording less protection to victims of domestic violence than to victims of nondomestic attacks," the district court erred in granting summary judgment to the defendants on *that* basis. . . .

[T]he Navarros sued Defendants for allegedly giving lower priority to 9-1-1 domestic-violence calls than to non-domestic-violence calls. Here, there are disputed issues of material fact on the question whether Defendants had such a policy. In our earlier opinion, we reversed the district court's grant of summary judgment on this ground, and we now reverse the district court's grant of judgment on the pleadings.

Reversed and remanded for a hearing to determine first, whether the city had a policy or custom of giving lower priority to domestic-violence calls than to non-domestic-violence calls, and second, if such a policy or custom exists, whether that policy or custom has a rational basis.

## Notes and Questions

1. *Background.* *Fajardo* was one of a number of cases instituted by battered women, beginning in the late 1970s, to force local police departments to treat complaints seriously. Similar to the suit in *Fajardo,* many claims were brought under the Federal Civil Rights Act, 42 U.S.C. §1983 (1994). Remedies under §1983 require the plaintiff to show a deprivation under color of law of a constitutional right. Generally, no right to police protection exists for private acts of violence. Thus, a cause of action arises only if the state discriminates in providing protection to the public in violation of the Equal Protection Clause or if the state has a "special relationship" to an individual such that the state has an affirmative duty to act.

The parameters of the special relationship doctrine (as applied to battered spouses) were explored in Balistreri v. Pacifica Police Department, 855 F.2d 1421 (9th Cir. 1988). In *Balistreri,* the district appellate court held that the plaintiff satisfied the special relationship doctrine, thereby imposing a duty of protection on the police, because the police had repeated notice of the husband's assaults and plaintiff had a restraining order. However, DeShaney v. Winnebago, 489 U.S. 189 (1989), severely limited the scope of the special relationship doctrine by holding that a special relationship arises only in a custodial context. (*DeShaney* is discussed in Chapter VIII, section B4b.) Subsequently, the Ninth Circuit Court of Appeals amended its earlier opinion in *Balistreri* to deny the victim's due process claim (because no custodial context was involved) but to allow her to amend her complaint to clarify her equal protection claim.

2. *DeShaney* had a devasting impact on suits by battered women. See Barbara E. Armacost, Affirmative Duties, Systemic Harms, and the Due Process Clause, 94 Mich. L. Rev. 982, 1040 (1996); G. Kristian Miccio, Notes From the Underground: Battered Women, the State, and Conceptions of Accountability, 23 Harv. Women's L.J. 133, 155 (2000) (both pointing out influence of *DeShaney*). Post-*DeShaney*, plaintiffs must bring suits against state officials based on different theories of liability, claiming (1) exceptions to *DeShaney* (such as the existence of a custodial relationship); (2) a violation of procedural, rather than substantive, due

process (that is, an entitlement to procedural safeguards); (3) a violation of equal protection; and (4) liability under state tort theories. Developments in the Law: Legal Responses to Domestic Violence, Making State Institutions More Responsive, 106 Harv. L. Rev. 1551, 1560 (1993).

3. The nonarrest policy of many police departments potentially violates equal protection by (1) denying battered spouses the protection given to victims abused by strangers, and (2) reflecting a policy of sex discrimination because women are usually the victims of domestic violence.

4. Several factors explain police nonintervention: (1) the police perception that the battered spouse merely wants to scare the abuser, get him out of the house, or obtain transportation to a hospital; (2) the family cannot afford the economic impact of arrest; (3) the acceptability of the abuse in the spouses' culture; (4) a concern that the abuser may retaliate after release; (5) the fear that criminal justice intervention might dissolve the family; (6) the concern that prosecutors will not prosecute because of the high attrition rate, and finally (7) the belief that "a man's home is his castle." Raymond I. Parnas, The Police Response to the Domestic Disturbance, 1967 Wis. L. Rev. 914. What role should such concerns play in arrest policies?

5. Another factor that explains police reluctance to intervene is the difficulty of securing the battered woman's cooperation. Battered women sometimes request that the batterer not be arrested and, subsequently, refuse to testify against him. What role should her decision play?

An evidentiary privilege of spousal disqualification prevents a prosecutor from compelling a reluctant spouse to testify against the defendant-spouse. (See discussion of *Trammel*, infra page 389.) At common law, some exceptions to this privilege developed for cases of severe spousal violence (for example, assaults, rape, and attempted murder). The majority of American jurisdictions, similarly, adopt spousal violence exceptions to the privilege either by case law or statute. See Malinda L. Seymoure, Isn't It a Crime: Feminist Perspectives on Spousal Immunity and Spousal Violence, 90 Nw. U. L. Rev. 1032, 1052-1061 (1996) (survey of jurisdictions). Should courts permit a battered spouse to testify if she so desires but not compel her to do so? Or should courts compel her to testify on the theory that the dynamics of battering (fear, self-blame, and so forth) prevent her sound judgment? See generally Cheryl Hanna, No Right to Choose: Mandated Victim Participation in Domestic Violence Prosecutions, 109 Harv. L. Rev. 1850 (1996). Does compelling the victim to testify, despite her objections, signal a continued policy of disrespect of the woman's wishes? Does spousal immunity in domestic violence cases reflect the antiquated idea that the law does not belong in the private sphere of the family? See Seymoure, supra, at 1072.

6. What type of evidence is required to show a discriminatory police policy? In McKee v. City of Rockwall, 877 F.2d 409 (5th Cir. 1989),

*cert. denied,* 493 U.S. 1023 (1990), an alleged statement by the police chief was not sufficient.

> [Plaintiff] McKee contends that the police officers would have arrested Harry Streetman but for a city policy which discouraged officers from making arrests in domestic violence cases. In an effort to present evidence of such a policy, McKee relied on an affidavit from her mother [asserting]: Within one or two days of the assault upon my daughter, my husband Roy McKee and I had a conversation with Chief Beaty of the Rockwall Police Department. During that conversation we asked the Chief why Harry Streetman had not been arrested when our daughter first called the police and reported his assault upon her. The Chief responded that his officers did not like to make arrests in domestic assault cases since the women involved either wouldn't file charges or would drop them prior to trial. . . .
>
> We have already quoted in full the only evidence which McKee produced to support her allegation of a discriminatory policy. This evidence, however, is completely without probative weight. . . . Officers may do things — indeed, they may be required by policy to do things — that they do not like to do. Nor, for that matter, is one officer's dislike binding upon another. It is possible that most, or even nearly all, of the officers in the Rockwall Police Department disliked making arrests in domestic violence cases, but that Officers Fleetwood and Parrish did not share this dislike. In this respect, too, a dislike is different from a policy, which is binding on all officers regardless of their sentiments.

Id. at 411, 414, 415. Does failure to remedy a known pattern of discriminatory behavior constitute a discriminatory policy?

7. *Mandatory arrest.* Mandatory arrest practices are a controversial approach to battering. Approximately 15 states and the District of Columbia have enacted such laws. Marion Wanless, Note, Mandatory Arrest: A Step Toward Eradicating Domestic Violence, But Is It Enough?, 1996 U. Ill. L. Rev. 533, 534. States have enacted these laws to shield themselves from potential liability from battered women, to address the complaints of activists and legislators, and to effectuate an alternative solution to mediation that poses dangers to abused spouses. Id. at 538.

The benefits and detriments of mandatory arrest remain contested. Advocates of mandatory arrest argue that (1) it communicates to offenders that society will not tolerate their behavior; (2) it protects victims more effectively by immediate relief; (3) it empowers the victim to change a situation she may not feel capable of changing herself; (4) it equalizes the position of women; (5) it clarifies the role of police by providing guidelines; and (6) it decreases police injuries during domestic disturbances. Carol Wright, Comment, Immediate Arrest in Domestic Violence Situations: Mandate or Alternative, 14 Cap. U. L. Rev. 243, 253-254 (1984); Dennis P. Saccuzzo, How Should the Police Respond to Domestic Violence?: A Therapeutic Jurisprudence Analysis of Mandatory

Arrest, 39 Santa Clara L. Rev. 765, 775-779 (1999). However, opponents question the effectiveness.

Empirical findings on the effectiveness of mandatory arrest are inconclusive. An early study (1980-1984) by the National Institute of Justice (NIJ) found that fewer batterers who were arrested were involved in repeat episodes (10 percent compared to 19 percent of those who received mediation and 24 percent of those who were ordered to leave the premises). Wanless, supra, at 554 (citing NIJ findings). Subsequently, the NIJ conducted follow-up studies in six cities. In three studies, researchers found that arrest was an effective deterrent. However, in three other cities, arrest increased abuse among some abusers (for example, those unemployed) and had a disparate effect on certain races. Id. at 555. In the face of these inconclusive findings, how should legislators respond?

Does the existence of a mandatory arrest policy give rise to a private cause of action against police for failure to protect the victim? Compare Latiolais v. Guillory, 747 So. 2d 675 (La. Ct. App. 1999) (holding that police were not liable under the Louisiana Protection from Family Violence Act) with Nearing v. Weaver, 670 P.2d 137 (Or. 1983) (holding that police were liable under state's Family Abuse Prevention Act).

8. The seemingly gender-neutral policy of nonintrusion into marital privacy is justified sometimes by the desire to preserve family harmony. Does nonintervention promote family harmony? Does nonintervention respect the rights of all family members equally, particularly when one has asked for help? Or does it preserve the freedom of more powerful family members at the expense of weaker members? How much discretion, if any, should law enforcement officials, such as prosecutors, have in filing charges in wife beating cases? Should prosecutorial discretion be treated differently from police discretion? See generally Sally F. Goldfarb, Violence Against Women and the Persistence of Privacy, 61 Ohio St. L.J. 1 (2000). Is a no-drop policy required by the Equal Protection Clause? See Kaylani Robbins, No-Drop Prosecution of Domestic Violence: Just Good Policy, or Equal Protection Mandate?, 52 Stan. L. Rev. 205, 206-208 (1999).

### d. Crimes: Marital Rape

### ■ PEOPLE v. LIBERTA
*474 N.E.2d 567 (N.Y. 1984),* **cert. denied,**
*471 U.S. 1020 (1985)*

WACHTLER, Judge.

[Defendant charges that the marital rape exemption in New York's rape and sodomy statutes renders those statutes violative of the Equal Protection Clause.]

## I

Defendant Mario Liberta and Denise Liberta were married in 1978. Shortly after the birth of their son, in October of that year, Mario began to beat Denise. In early 1980 Denise brought a proceeding in the Family Court in Erie County seeking protection from the defendant. On April 30, 1980 a temporary order of protection was issued to her by the Family Court. Under this order, the defendant was to move out and remain away from the family home, and stay away from Denise. The order provided that the defendant could visit with his son once each weekend.

On the weekend of March 21, 1981, Mario, who was then living in a motel, did not visit his son. On Tuesday, March 24, 1981 he called Denise to ask if he could visit his son on that day. Denise would not allow the defendant to come to her house, but she did agree to allow him to pick up their son and her and take them both back to his motel after being assured that a friend of his would be with them at all times. The defendant and his friend picked up Denise and their son and the four of them drove to defendant's motel.

When they arrived at the motel the friend left. As soon as only Mario, Denise, and their son were alone in the motel room, Mario attacked Denise, threatened to kill her, and forced her to perform fellatio on him and to engage in sexual intercourse with him. The son was in the room during the entire episode, and the defendant forced Denise to tell their son to watch what the defendant was doing to her.

The defendant allowed Denise and their son to leave shortly after the incident. Denise, after going to her parents' home, went to a hospital to be treated for scratches on her neck and bruises on her head and back, all inflicted by her husband. She also went to the police station, and on the next day she swore out a felony complaint against the defendant. On July 15, 1981 the defendant was indicted for rape in the first degree and sodomy in the first degree.

## II

Section 130.35 of the Penal Code provides in relevant part that "A male is guilty of rape in the first degree when he engages in sexual intercourse with a female . . . by forcible compulsion." "Female," for purposes of the rape statute, is defined as "any female person who is not married to the actor" (Penal Law, §130.00, subd. 4). Section 130.50 of the Penal Law provides in relevant part that "a person is guilty of sodomy in the first degree when he engages in deviate sexual intercourse with another person . . . by forcible compulsion." "Deviate sexual intercourse" is defined as "sexual conduct between persons not married to each other consisting of contact between the penis and the anus, the mouth and penis, or the mouth and the vulva" (Penal Law, §130.00, subd. 2). Thus, due to the "not married" language in the definitions of "female" and "deviate sexual intercourse," there is a "marital exemption" for both forcible rape and forcible sodomy. The marital exemption itself, however, has certain exemptions. For purposes of the rape and sodomy statutes, a husband and wife are considered to be "not married" if at the time of the sexual assault they [are living apart pursuant to a court order or a separation agreement].

Defendant moved to dismiss the indictment, asserting that because he and Denise were still married at the time of the incident[1] he came within the "marital exemption" to both rape and sodomy. The People [contended] that the temporary order of protection required Mario and Denise to live apart, and they in fact were living apart, and thus were "not married" for purposes of the statutes. [The trial court dismissed the indictment, holding that the marital exemption applied. The appellate court reversed and remanded, finding that the couple was "not married" for purposes of the statute. The defendant was convicted and appealed. He asserted that both statutes are unconstitutional.]

## IV

The defendant's constitutional challenges to the rape and sodomy statutes are premised on his being considered "not married" to Denise and are the same challenges as could be made by any unmarried male convicted under these statutes. The defendant's claim is that both statutes violate equal protection because they are underinclusive classifications which burden him, but not others similarly situated. . . .

### A. THE MARITAL EXEMPTION

As noted above, under the Penal Law a married man ordinarily cannot be convicted of forcibly raping or sodomizing his wife. This is the so-called marital exemption for rape. . . . The assumption, even before the marital exemption was codified, that a man could not be guilty of raping his wife, is traceable to a statement made by the 17th century English jurist Lord Hale, who wrote: "[T]he husband cannot be guilty of a rape committed by himself upon his lawful wife, for by their mutual matrimonial consent and contract the wife hath given up herself in this kind unto her husband, which she cannot retract" (1 Hale, History of Pleas of the Crown, p.629). Although Hale cited no authority for his statement it was relied on by State Legislatures which enacted rape statutes with a marital exemption and by courts which established a common-law exemption for husbands. . . .

---

1. The defendant and Denise were divorced several months after the assault in the motel room.

Presently, over 40 States still retain some form of marital exemption for rape. While the marital exemption is subject to an equal protection challenge, because it classifies unmarried men differently than married men, the equal protection clause does not prohibit a State from making classifications, provided the statute does not arbitrarily burden a particular group of individuals. Where a statute draws a distinction based upon marital status, the classification must be reasonable and must be based upon "some ground of difference that rationally explains the different treatment" (Eisenstadt v. Baird, 405 U.S. 438 [(1972)]).

We find that there is no rational basis for distinguishing between marital rape and nonmarital rape. The various rationales which have been asserted in defense of the exemption are either based upon archaic notions about the consent and property rights incident to marriage or are simply unable to withstand even the slightest scrutiny. . . .

Lord Hale's notion of an irrevocable implied consent by a married woman to sexual intercourse has been cited most frequently in support of the marital exemption. Any argument based on a supposed consent, however, is untenable. Rape is not simply a sexual act to which one party does not consent. Rather, it is a degrading, violent act which violates the bodily integrity of the victim and frequently causes severe, long-lasting physical and psychic harm. To ever imply consent to such an act is irrational and absurd. Other than in the context of rape statutes, marriage has never been viewed as giving a husband the right to coerced intercourse on demand. Certainly, then, a marriage license should not be viewed as a license for a husband to forcibly rape his wife with impunity. A married woman has the same right to control her own body as does an unmarried woman. . . .

The other traditional justifications for the marital exemption were the common-law doctrines that a woman was the property of her husband and that the legal existence of the woman was "incorporated and consolidated into that of the husband" (1 Blackstone's Commentaries [1966 ed.], p.430). . . . Both these doctrines, of course, have long been rejected in this State. . . .

Because the traditional justifications for the marital exemption no longer have any validity, other arguments have been advanced in its defense. The first of these recent rationales, which is stressed by the People in this case, is that the marital exemption protects against governmental intrusion into marital privacy and promotes reconciliation of the spouses, and thus, that elimination of the exemption would be disruptive to marriages. While protecting marital privacy and encouraging reconciliation are legitimate State interests, there is no rational relation between allowing a husband to forcibly rape his wife and these interests. The marital exemption simply does not further marital privacy because this right of privacy protects consensual acts, not violent sexual assaults (see Griswold v. Connecticut, 381 U.S. 479, 485-486 [(1965)]). Just as a husband cannot invoke a right of marital privacy to escape liability for beating his wife, he cannot justifiably rape his wife under the guise of a right to privacy.

Similarly, it is not tenable to argue that elimination of the marital exemption would disrupt marriages because it would discourage reconciliation. [I]f the marriage has already reached the point where intercourse is accomplished by violent assault it is doubtful that there is anything left to reconcile. . . .

Another rationale sometimes advanced in support of the marital exemption is that marital rape would be a difficult crime to prove. A related argument is that allowing such prosecutions could lead to fabricated complaints by "vindictive" wives. The difficulty of proof argument is based on the problem of showing lack of consent. Proving lack of consent, however, is often the most difficult part of any rape prosecution, particularly where the rapist and the victim had a prior relationship. Similarly, the possibility that married women will fabricate complaints would seem to be no greater than the possibility of unmarried women doing so. The criminal justice system, with all of its built-in safeguards, is presumed to be capable of handling any false complaints. Indeed, if the possibility of fabricated complaints were a basis for not criminalizing behavior which would otherwise be sanctioned, virtually all crimes other than homicides would go unpunished.

The final argument in defense of the marital exemption is that marital rape is not as serious an offense as other rape and is thus adequately dealt with by the possibility of prosecution under criminal statutes, such as assault statutes, which provide for less severe punishment. [T]here is no evidence to support the argument that marital rape has less severe consequences than other rape. On the contrary, numerous studies have shown that marital rape is frequently quite violent and generally has *more* severe, traumatic effects on the victim than other rape (see, generally [Diana Russell, Rape in Marriage 190-199 (1982); Martin D. Schwartz, The Spousal Exemption for Criminal Rape Prosecution, 7 Vt. L. Rev. 33, 45-46 (1982); Thomas R. Bearrows, Abolishing the Marital Exemption for Rape: A Statutory Proposal, 1983 U. Ill. L. Rev. 201, 209)].

Among the recent decisions in this country addressing the marital exemption, only one court has concluded that there is a rational basis for it (see People v. Brown, 632 P.2d 1025 (Colo. 1981)). We agree with the other courts which have analyzed the exemption, which have been unable to find any present justification for it [citations omitted]. Justice Holmes wrote: "It is revolting to have no better reason for a rule of law than that so it was laid down in the time of Henry IV. It is still more revolting if the grounds upon which it was laid down have vanished long since, and the rule simply persists from blind imitation of the past" (Holmes, The Path of the Law, 10 Harv. L. Rev. 457, 469 [(1897)]). This statement is an apt characterization of the marital exemption; it lacks a rational basis, and therefore violates the equal protection clauses of both the Federal and State Constitutions. . . .

### B. THE EXEMPTION FOR FEMALES

Under the Penal Law only males can be convicted of rape in the first degree.[11] [The court then proceeds to examine the sex-based classification to determine whether it is substantially related to the achievement of an important governmental objective.]

The first argument advanced by the People in support of the exemption for females is that because only females can become pregnant the State may constitutionally differentiate between forcible rapes of females and forcible rapes of males. This court and the United States Supreme Court have upheld statutes which subject males to criminal liability for engaging in sexual intercourse with underage females without the converse being true (Michael M. v. Sonoma County Superior Court, 450 U.S. 464 [(1981)]). The rationale behind these decisions was that the primary purpose of such "statutory rape" laws is to protect against the harm caused by teenage pregnancies, there being no need to provide the same protection to young males.

There is no evidence, however, that preventing pregnancies is a primary purpose of the statute prohibiting forcible rape, nor does such a purpose seem likely. Rather, the very fact that the statute proscribes "forcible compulsion" shows that its overriding purpose is to protect a woman from an unwanted forcible, and often violent sexual intrusion into her body. Thus, due to the different purposes behind forcible rape laws and "statutory" (consensual) rape laws, the cases upholding the gender discrimination in the latter are not decisive with respect to the former, and the People cannot meet their burden here by simply stating that only females can become pregnant.

The People also claim that the discrimination is justified because a female rape victim "faces the probability of medical, sociological, and psychological problems unique to her gender." This same argument, when advanced in support of the discrimination in the statutory rape laws, was rejected by this court [previously], and it is no more convincing in the present case. . . .

Finally, the People suggest that a gender-neutral law for forcible rape is unnecessary, and that therefore the present law is constitutional, because a woman either cannot actually rape a man or such attacks, if possible, are extremely rare. Although the "physiologically impossible" argument has been accepted by several courts, it is simply wrong. The argument is premised on the notion that a man cannot engage in

11. The sodomy statute applies to any "person" and is thus gender neutral. Defendant's gender-based equal protection challenge is therefore addressed only to the rape statute.

sexual intercourse unless he is sexually aroused, and if he is aroused then he is consenting to intercourse. "Sexual intercourse" however, "occurs upon any penetration, however slight" (Penal Law, §130.00); this degree of contact can be achieved without a male being aroused and thus without his consent.

As to the "infrequency" argument, while forcible sexual assaults by females upon males are undoubtedly less common than those by males upon females this numerical disparity cannot by itself make the gender discrimination constitutional. Women may well be responsible for a far lower number of all serious crimes than are men, but such a disparity would not make it permissible for the State to punish only men who commit, for example, robbery. . . .

[Because a gender-neutral law would better serve the state's objective of deterring and punishing forcible sexual assaults,] we find that section 130.35 of the Penal Law violates equal protection because it exempts females from criminal liability for forcible rape. [I]t is now the law of this State that any person who engages in sexual intercourse or deviate sexual intercourse with any other person by forcible compulsion is guilty of either rape in the first degree or sodomy in the first degree. Because the statutes under which the defendant was convicted are not being struck down, his conviction is affirmed. . . .

## Notes and Questions

1. When *Liberta* was decided, most states had statutes exempting husbands from prosecution for rape. In contrast, almost all states today have changed their marital rape laws. In large part, the movement resulted from feminists' call in the 1970s for reform of rape laws. Susan Estrich, Real Rape 80 (1987).

2. Ironically, most states retain some form of special treatment for marital rapists despite the law reform movement. One commentator points out that the majority of states manifest elements of the common law regime by (1) criminalizing a narrower range of offenses if committed within marriage, (2) subjecting marital rape to less serious sanctions, and/or (3) creating special procedural hurdles for marital rape prosecutions (such as reporting requirements to designated professionals or within certain time periods). Jill Elaine Hasday, Contest and Consent: A Legal History of Marital Rape, 88 Calif. L. Rev. 1373, 1375 (2000). She concludes that "the current state of the law represents a confusing mix of victory and defeat for the exemption's contemporary feminist critics." Id. What is the justification for such statutory distinctions? Do these distinctions survive equal protection?

3. As *Liberta* reveals, prior to the reform movement, a few states permitted prosecution only if the spouses were living apart at the time of

incident or if one spouse had initiated legal proceedings at the time of the rape. Some states required both conditions. See Sallee Fry Waterman, Note, For Better or For Worse: Marital Rape, 15 N. Ky. L. Rev. 611, 622-623 nn.77-80 (1988) (citing statutes).

Why should it matter whether the husband and wife are living apart? Does this requirement help establish the "legitimacy" of the women as victims? "Legitimacy has to do with whether a victim can successfully persuade the police that she is 'deserving' of the status of rape victim." Susan Carol Randall & Vicki McNickle Rose, Barriers to Becoming a "Successful" Rape Victim, in Women and Crime in America 342 (Lee H. Bowker ed., 1981). What additional factors in *Liberta* establish Denise Liberta's legitimacy as a victim? For a rare case permitting prosecution when the married couple were living together without a decree of separation or dissolution or a temporary restraining order, see State v. Rider, 449 So. 2d 903 (Fla. Dist. Ct. App. 1984).

4. *Liberta* is one of the few cases to address the role of the right to privacy in marital rape exemptions. Was the court focusing on family privacy, marital privacy, or individual privacy? Why does *Liberta* say that the exemption does not further marital privacy? In contrast, one commentator argues that the marital right to privacy should prevail over prosecuting spousal rapists:

> [I]t appears unseemly to permit the public to examine the intimacies of a marital relationship. Allowing the public this examination is to encourage a type of public voyeurism. Second, one or both of the spouses may feel embarrassed about having the details of their private marital life exposed to the public view. Furthermore, it is questionable whether the complaining spouse alone has the right to waive the marital privacy right of the couple by presenting the matter before the courts and the public. . . .

Michael Gary Hilf, Marital Privacy and Spousal Rape, 16 N. Eng. L. Rev. 31, 34 (1980). Is such reasoning persuasive? See also People v. DeStefano, 467 N.Y.S.2d 506, 517 (Suffolk Cty. Ct. 1983) (exemption interferes with marital privacy by giving husband control over wife's bodily integrity). Recall Planned Parenthood v. Danforth, discussed in Chapter 1. Can the marital right to privacy supersede the individual right to privacy? Why?

Does *Griswold*, with its recognition of marital privacy, support the abolition of the marital rape exemption, as *Liberta* suggests, or bolster its retention? Has the Supreme Court held that the marital right to privacy supersedes the individual's right to privacy? Recall Eisenstadt v. Baird, discussed in Chapter 1.

5. *Empirical evidence.* Marital rape is a form of domestic violence. Sociologist Diana Russell notes that 14 percent of married women have been raped by their husbands. Diana Russell, Rape in Marriage 57 (2d ed. 1990). Many wives (10 percent) are both battered and raped.

Russell, supra, at 89. Professor Russell suggests that marital rape is frequently quite violent and has more severe and traumatic effects on the victim than nonmarital rape. She found that 52 percent of marital rape victims suffer extreme long-term effects. Id. at 193. She also noted that 31 percent of the women who had been raped by their husbands were raped over 20 times. Id. at 111. In 91 percent of the cases, the rape occurred in a private setting but in many of these cases it occurred within earshot of others or in front of the children. Id. at 113. See also Lisa R. Eskow, Note, The Ultimate Weapon?: Demythologizing Spousal Rape and Reconceptualizing Its Prosecution, 48 Stan. L. Rev. 67, 684-689 (1996) (discussing the implications of Russell's study).

6. In *Liberta*, the couple's young son was forced to watch his father rape his mother. What might have been the effect of this on him? Evidence suggests that merely observing domestic violence has negative effects on children. For a fuller discussion, see Chapter 8, section B.

## Problem

Mr. & Mrs. Adair have been married for six years and have two children. Two children from Mrs. Adair's prior marriage also live with them. Marital problems arise and result in Mrs. Adair's sleeping in the basement. In the early evening hours of September 27, Mrs. Adair is awakened by Mr. Adair who sexually assaults her. The district attorney charges him with two counts of third degree criminal sexual conduct based on her allegations of digital-anal penetration and digital oral penetration against her will. Mr. Adair denies that the incidents occurred. Further, he attempts to introduce evidence of specific instances of Mrs. Adair's subsequent consensual sexual relations with him. The prosecutor seeks to exclude such evidence as barred by a "rape-shield statute" that precludes admission of the victim's past sexual conduct "unless material to a fact at issue" and "unless its prejudicial effect is outweighed by its probative value." How should the court rule? See People v. Adair, 550 N.W.2d 505 (Mich. 1996).

## Note: Property Crimes Between Spouses

Damage to a spouse's property may be inflicted as part of the phenomenon of spousal abuse. Batterers have been known to inflict such damage as destroying furniture; breaking windows and/or skylights; damaging walls, roofs, and garages; injuring or killing a family pet; damaging the spouse's clothing or car; and damaging items of sentimental value to the spouse. Commentators urge that criminal mischief laws be more frequently applied to such instances of spousal abuse. See Victoria

L. Lutz & Cara M. Bonomolo, My Husband Just Trashed Our Home:
What Do You Mean That's Not a Crime?, 48 S.C. L. Rev. 641 (1997).

A central dilemma concerns whether an abusive spouse can be prosecuted for damaging the victim-spouse's property when that property is
jointly owned. Most courts have yet to address this issue. However, a few
courts have determined that a batterer can be charged for such offenses.
Id. at 656. For example, in People v. Kahanic, 241 Cal. Rptr. 722 (Ct.
App. 1987), the court held that a wife who threw a bottle at her husband's Mercedes, while it was parked at his woman friend's home, may
be prosecuted for vandalism even though the car was community property. Interpreting Cal. Penal Code §594(a), which criminalizes damage
to property "not his own," the court ruled that the statute excludes liability "only when the actor-defendant is involved with property wholly
his or her own. . . . The essence of the crime is in the physical acts
against the ownership interest of another, even though that ownership
is less than exclusive." 241 Cal. Rptr. at 725.


## 4. Evidentiary Privileges Arising from the Marital Relationship

■ **TRAMMEL v. UNITED STATES**
*445 U.S. 40 (1980)*

Mr. Chief Justice BURGER delivered the opinion of the Court.

We granted certiorari to consider whether an accused may invoke
the privilege against adverse spousal testimony so as to exclude the voluntary testimony of his wife. . . .


### I

On March 10, 1976, petitioner Otis Trammel was indicted with two
others . . . for importing heroin into the United States from Thailand
and the Philippine Islands and for conspiracy to import heroin in violation of 21 U.S.C. §§952(a), 962(a), and 963. The indictment also named
six unindicted co-conspirators, including petitioner's wife Elizabeth Ann
Trammel.

According to the indictment, petitioner and his wife flew from the
Philippines to California in August 1975, carrying with them a quantity
of heroin. . . . Elizabeth Trammel then traveled to Thailand where she
purchased another supply of the drug. On November 3, 1975, with four
ounces of heroin on her person, she boarded a plane for the United
States. During a routine customs search in Hawaii, she was searched, the
heroin was discovered, and she was arrested. After discussions with Drug

Enforcement Administration agents, she agreed to cooperate with the Government.

Prior to trial on this indictment, petitioner . . . advised the court that the Government intended to call his wife as an adverse witness and asserted his claim to a privilege to prevent her from testifying against him. At a hearing on the motion, Mrs. Trammel was called as a Government witness under a grant of use immunity. She testified that she and petitioner were married in May 1975 and that they remained married.[1] She explained that her cooperation with the Government was based on assurances that she would be given lenient treatment.[2] She then described, in considerable detail, her role and that of her husband in the heroin distribution conspiracy.

After hearing this testimony, the District Court ruled that Mrs. Trammel could testify in support of the Government's case to any act she observed during the marriage and to any communication "made in the presence of a third person"; however, confidential communications between petitioner and his wife were held to be privileged and inadmissible. . . .

At trial, Elizabeth Trammel testified within the limits of the court's pretrial ruling; her testimony, as the Government concedes, constituted virtually its entire case against petitioner. He was found guilty on both the substantive and conspiracy charges. [On appeal], petitioner's only claim of error was that the admission of the adverse testimony of his wife, over his objection, contravened this Court's teaching in Hawkins v. United States, [358 U.S. 74 (1958)], and therefore constituted reversible error. The Court of Appeals rejected this contention. . . .

## II

The privilege claimed by petitioner has ancient roots. Writing in 1628, Lord Coke observed that "it hath beene resolved by the Justices that a wife cannot be produced either against or for her husband." 1 E. Coke, A Commentarie upon Littleton 6b (1628). This spousal disqualification sprang from two canons of medieval jurisprudence: first, the rule that an accused was not permitted to testify in his own behalf because of his interest in the proceeding; second, the concept that husband and wife were one, and that since the woman had no recognized separate legal existence, the husband was that one. From those two now long-abandoned doctrines, it followed that what was inadmissible from the lips of the defendant-husband was also inadmissible from his wife.

---

1. In response to the question whether divorce was contemplated, Mrs. Trammel testified that her husband had said that "I would go my way and he would go his."

2. The Government represents to the Court that Elizabeth Trammel has not been prosecuted for her role in the conspiracy.

Despite its medieval origins, this rule of spousal disqualification remained intact in most common-law jurisdictions well into the 19th century. . . . Indeed, it was not until 1933, in Funk v. United States, 290 U.S. 371, that this Court abolished the testimonial disqualification in the federal courts, so as to permit the spouse of a defendant to testify in the defendant's behalf. *Funk,* however, left undisturbed the rule that either spouse could prevent the other from giving adverse testimony. The rule thus evolved into one of privilege rather than one of absolute disqualification.

The modern justification for this privilege against adverse spousal testimony is its perceived role in fostering the harmony and sanctity of the marriage relationship. Notwithstanding this benign purpose, the rule was sharply criticized. Professor Wigmore termed it "the merest anachronism in legal theory and an indefensible obstruction to truth in practice." 8 Wigmore §2228, at 221. The Committee on Improvements in the Law of Evidence of the American Bar Association called for its abolition. 63 American Bar Association Reports 594-595 (1938). In its place, Wigmore and others suggested a privilege protecting only private marital communications, modeled on the privilege between priest and penitent, attorney and client, and physician and patient. See 8 Wigmore §2332 et seq.[5]

These criticisms influenced the American Law Institute, which, in its 1942 Model Code of Evidence advocated a privilege for marital confidences, but expressly rejected a rule vesting in the defendant the right to exclude all adverse testimony of his spouse. See American Law Institute, Model Code of Evidence, Rule 215 (1942). In 1953 the Uniform Rules of Evidence, drafted by the National Conference of Commissioners on Uniform State Laws, followed a similar course. . . . Several state legislatures enacted similarly patterned provisions into law. In Hawkins v. United States, 358 U.S. 74 (1958), this Court considered the continued vitality of the privilege against adverse spousal testimony in the federal courts. [*Hawkins*] left the federal privilege for adverse spousal testimony where it found it, continuing "a rule which bars the testimony of one spouse against the other unless both consent." Id., at 78. Accord, Wyatt v. United States, 362 U.S. 525, 528 (1960). . . .

---

5. This Court recognized just such a confidential marital communications privilege in Wolfle v. United States, 291 U.S. 7 (1934), and in Blau v. United States, 340 U.S. 332 (1951). In neither case, however, did the Court adopt the Wigmore view that the communications privilege be substituted in place of the privilege against adverse spousal testimony. The privilege as to confidential marital communications is not at issue in the instant case. . . .

**III**

[T]he long history of the privilege suggests that it ought not to be casually cast aside. That the privilege is one affecting marriage, home, and family relationships — already subject to much erosion in our day — also counsels caution. At the same time, we cannot escape the reality that the law on occasion adheres to doctrinal concepts long after the reasons which gave them birth have disappeared and after experience suggest the need for change. . . .

Since 1958, when *Hawkins* was decided, support for the privilege against adverse spousal testimony has been eroded further. Thirty-one jurisdictions, including Alaska and Hawaii, then allowed an accused a privilege to prevent adverse spousal testimony. 358 U.S., at 81, n.3 (Stewart, J., concurring). The number has now declined to 24. . . .

[W]e must decide whether the privilege against adverse spousal testimony promotes sufficiently important interests to outweigh the need for probative evidence in the administration of criminal justice.

It is essential to remember that the *Hawkins* privilege is not needed to protect information privately disclosed between husband and wife in the confidence of the marital relationship — once described by this Court as "the best solace of human existence." Stein v. Bowman, 13 Pet., at 223. Those confidences are privileged under the independent rule protecting confidential marital communications. The *Hawkins* privilege is invoked, not to exclude private marital communications, but rather to exclude evidence of criminal acts and of communications made in the presence of third persons.

No other testimonial privilege sweeps so broadly. The privileges between priest and penitent, attorney and client, and physician and patient limit protection to private communications. These privileges are rooted in the imperative need for confidence and trust. . . . The *Hawkins* rule stands in marked contrast to these three privileges. Its protection is not limited to confidential communications; rather it permits an accused to exclude all adverse spousal testimony. As Jeremy Bentham observed more than a century and a half ago, such a privilege goes far beyond making "every man's house his castle," and permits a person to convert his house into "a den of thieves." 5 Rationale of Judicial Evidence 340 (1827). It "secures, to every man, one safe and unquestionable and ever ready accomplice for every imaginable crime." Id., at 338.

The ancient foundations for so sweeping a privilege have long since disappeared. Nowhere in the common-law world — indeed in any modern society — is a woman regarded as chattel or demeaned by denial of a separate legal identity and the dignity associated with recognition as a whole human being. Chip by chip, over the years those archaic notions have been cast aside. . . .

The contemporary justification for affording an accused such a privilege is also unpersuasive. When one spouse is willing to testify against the other in a criminal proceeding — whatever the motivation — their relationship is almost certainly in disrepair; there is probably little in the way of marital harmony for the privilege to preserve. In these circumstances, a rule of evidence that permits an accused to prevent adverse spousal testimony seems far more likely to frustrate justice than to foster family peace.[12] Indeed, there is reason to believe that vesting the privilege in the accused could actually undermine the marital relationship. For example, in a case such as this the Government is unlikely to offer a wife immunity and lenient treatment if it knows that her husband can prevent her from giving adverse testimony. If the Government is dissuaded from making such an offer, the privilege can have the untoward effect of permitting one spouse to escape justice at the expense of the other. It hardly seems conducive to the preservation of the marital relation to place a wife in jeopardy solely by virtue of her husband's control over her testimony.

Our consideration of the foundations for the privilege and its history satisfy us that "reason and experience" no longer justify so sweeping a rule as that found acceptable by the Court in *Hawkins*. Accordingly, we conclude that the existing rule should be modified so that the witness-spouse alone has a privilege to refuse to testify adversely; the witness may be neither compelled to testify nor foreclosed from testifying. This modification — vesting the privilege in the witness-spouse — furthers the important public interest in marital harmony without unduly burdening legitimate law enforcement needs.

Here, petitioner's spouse chose to testify against him. That she did so after a grant of immunity and assurances of lenient treatment does not render her testimony involuntary. [T]he judgment of the Court of Appeals is [a]ffirmed.

## Notes and Questions

1. At common law, special evidentiary rules existed regarding competence of spouses as witnesses and the privacy of communications between spouses. A spouse of a party was not considered a competent witness. From this notion followed a rule of disqualification preventing a spouse from testifying for or against the other in civil or criminal proceedings.

Further, special privileges protected the privacy of spousal communications. Most spouses would be particularly concerned about the

---

12. It is argued that abolishing the privilege will permit the Government to come between husband and wife, pitting one against the other. That, too, misses the mark. Neither *Hawkins,* nor any other privilege, prevents the Government from enlisting one spouse to give information concerning the other or to aid in the other's apprehension. It is only the spouse's testimony in the courtroom that is prohibited.

admission of adverse spousal testimony. Such testimony might include confidential marital communications as well as communications made to the spouse in the presence of third parties.

Note the difference between the privileges. Under the confidential marital communications privilege, private communications between husband and wife are privileged absolutely; either spouse may invoke this privilege. This rule is independent of the privilege at issue in *Trammel:* the ability of a spouse to exclude evidence by the other spouse of criminal acts and of communications in the *presence of third persons. Trammel* left the former privilege untouched in the federal courts. Should courts and legislatures also vest the confidential marital communications privilege in the witness spouse alone? Abolish it?

2. *Trammel* had several consequences. First, different rules now apply in the federal (and many state) courts concerning the two different types of spousal communications. Second, at the time *Trammel* was decided, 24 states permitted a spouse to prevent adverse spousal testimony. Now, only 13 do so. Milton C. Regan, Jr., Spousal Privilege and the Meanings of Marriage, 81 Va. L. Rev. 2045, 2060-2061 (1995).

3. In vesting the adverse spousal testimony privilege in the witness-spouse, *Trammel* makes much of the fact that Mrs. Trammel gave her testimony voluntarily. The Court reasons, because her testimony was voluntary, there was little marital harmony to preserve. Was her testimony voluntary? Was there little marital harmony to preserve?

4. What images of marriage and the family does *Trammel* reflect? See, e.g., Michael W. Mullane, *Trammel v. United States:* Bad History, Bad Policy, and Bad Law, 47 Me. L. Rev. 105, 147-152 (1995). Further, how does vesting the privilege in the witness spouse "further the important public interest in marital harmony"? Alternatively, how does vesting it in the defendant spouse "actually undermine the marital relationship"? Doesn't the rule in *Trammel* put the government in the position of "forc[ing] or encourag[ing] testimony which might alienate husband and wife, or further inflame existing domestic differences" (*Hawkins,* 358 U.S. at 79) (cited in *Trammel*)? Is this an appropriate governmental role? For arguments that *Trammel* encourages the government to turn spouses against each other, see Richard O. Lempert, A Right to Every Woman's Evidence, 66 Iowa L. Rev. 725 (1981).

5. Should the adverse spousal testimony privilege be abolished altogether? Because the privilege is riddled with exceptions, it provides many avenues for appeal. Moreover, whether the privilege furthers its avowed purpose remains uncertain. In Vance v. Rice, 524 F. Supp. 1297 (S.D. Iowa 1981), to prevent use of the privilege, a federal court upheld an injunction preventing a couple from marrying despite the woman's pregnancy. Do such results further the rule's objective? For arguments favoring abolition, see David Medine, The Adverse Testimony Privilege: Time to Dispose of a "Sentimental Relic," 67 Or. L. Rev. 519 (1988);

Amanda H. Frost, Updating the Marital Privileges: A Witness-Centered Rationale, 14 Wis. Women's L.J. 1 (1999).

6. Does the adverse spousal privilege have a disparate impact on women? See Regan, supra, at 2144 (suggesting that the privilege prevents women, rather than men, from testifying).

7. For a case in which the defendant arguably got too much of a good thing, see People v. Vermeulen, 438 N.W.2d 36 (Mich. 1989). The court upheld application of the spousal communication privilege invoked by a man, charged with first degree murder of his second wife, who had confided in his first wife that he planned to kill his second wife whom he had married before the divorce from the first became final.

8. Suppose the witness-spouse invokes the privilege examined in *Trammel.* Would his or her joint participation in the criminal activity warrant an exception to the marital privilege? Some courts have so held, reasoning (a) that the goal of preserving the family "does not justify assuring a criminal that he can enlist the aid of his spouse in a criminal enterprise without fear that by recruiting an accomplice or co-conspirator, he is creating another potential witness," United States v. Van Drunen, 501 F.2d 1393, 1396 (7th Cir.), *cert. denied,* 419 U.S. 1091 (1974); (b) that the marriage of joint participants in criminal activity is unlikely to be "an important institution contributing to the rehabilitation of the defendant spouse," id. at 1397; and (c) that such marriages are unlikely to be devoted. *Accord* United States v. Clark, 712 F.2d 299 (7th Cir. 1983); *contra,* Appeal of Malfitano, 633 F.2d 276 (3d Cir. 1980).

What implications might *Trammel* have for a joint participation exception? (The court below in *Trammel* admitted the adverse testimony, holding that the privilege does not apply when the spouses jointly participate in crime. 583 F.2d 1166, 1169 (10th Cir. 1978).) See also In re Grand Jury Subpoena United States, 755 F.2d 1022, 1026 (2d Cir. 1985), *vacated,* 475 U.S. 133 (1986). In this case, the government was attempting to determine whether Karel Koecher was engaged in a conspiracy to share defense documents with Czechoslovakia. Subpoenaed, his wife, an alleged courier, refused to testify "on the ground that to do so could adversely affect the interest of my husband . . . and I might destroy the harmony of our 21 years of marriage." Id. at 1023. What result? Although the Supreme Court had agreed to hear the case (*cert. granted,* 474 U.S. 815 (1985)), it became moot when the United States agreed to release the Koechers in return for the release of Soviet human rights activist Anatoly Shcharansky. See Henry J. Reske, Suspected Spy Leaves Country, Court Case, U.P.I., Feb. 12, 1986.

Assuming one spouse is willing to testify, should the courts or legislatures recognize a joint participation exception to the confidential marital communications privilege? See United States v. Estes, 793 F.2d 465 (2d Cir. 1986).

## Problems

1. Kenneth Taylor, a police officer, is charged with aggravated battery of his girlfriend Glenda Richard. The battery consisted of a severe beating with his fists, police flashlight, and service revolver. After Glenda's hospitalization, she agrees to testify against Kenneth and provides a typed statement, an affidavit expressing her desire to prosecute and a video tape affirming that desire. Ten days before the trial, Glenda marries Kenneth. At trial, when the prosecutor calls Glenda as a victim-witness of the assault, she refuses to testify, invoking the spousal privilege for adverse testimony. Louisiana has no spousal crime exception to the privilege. What arguments would you advance on behalf of Glenda? On behalf of the prosecution? See Louisiana v. Taylor, 642 So. 2d 160 (La. 1994).

2. President Bill Clinton is accused of having an extramarital affair with former White House intern Monica Lewinsky and of having committed perjury by denying it before a grand jury investigating his liaison with another woman, Paula Jones. To help build a case against Clinton, independent counsel Kenneth Starr calls Marcia Lewis, the mother of Lewinsky, to testify before a federal grand jury regarding her discussions with her daughter about Lewinsky's relationship with Clinton. The resultant controversy (regarding the wisdom of compelling a mother to testify against her daughter) evokes a demand for an adverse testimonial privilege for parents and children. Do the rationales employed by *Trammel* with respect to the adverse spousal testimonial privilege apply with equal force to parents and children? See Amee A. Shah, The Parent-Child Testimonial Privilege — Has the Time for It Finally Arrived?, 47 Clev. St. L. Rev. 41, 43 & nn.14-15 (1999) (pointing out that nine federal circuits have rejected such a privilege although four states recognize it).

# IV

# *Alternative Families*

The American family has been experiencing dramatic changes. The traditional nuclear family is on the decline. Currently, only one in four families fits this family type.[1] In contrast, alternative family forms (such as unmarried heterosexual couples, gay and lesbian couples, and single parents) are proliferating.

This chapter explores the law's response to these alternative family forms. First, the materials focus on the changing legal meaning of "family." To what extent is a "family" limited to ceremonially initiated or biologically based relationships? Does this definition apply for some purposes but not others? Second, the chapter explores the extent to which legal treatment of these families differs from that of the traditional family. In the cases and materials that follow, consider how the law should treat alternative families. Should the state define and impose a

---

[1]. According to Census Bureau data, in 1970, 40 percent of households consisted of married couples with their own children under age 18. During the next three decades, the percentage of nuclear families decreased, to 31 percent in 1980, 26 percent in 1990, and 24.6 percent in 1998. Bureau of the Census, U.S. Dept. of Commerce, Current Population Reports, Household and Family Characteristics: March 2000, at 3 (2001); Bureau of the Census, U.S. Dept. of Commerce, Current Population Reports, Household and Family Characteristics: March 1998, at 1 (1998).

legal meaning of "family" on all persons without exception? Or should the state honor private choices, so long as a given unit acts like a family and performs familial functions?

## A. COMMUNAL LIVING ARRANGEMENTS

### 1. *Is a Commune a Family for Zoning Purposes?*

### ■ VILLAGE OF BELLE TERRE v. BORAAS
### 416 U.S. 1 (1974)

Mr. Justice DOUGLAS delivered the opinion of the Court.

Belle Terre is a village on Long Island's north shore of about 220 homes inhabited by 700 people. Its total land area is less than one square mile. It has restricted land use to one-family dwellings excluding lodging houses, boarding houses, fraternity houses, or multiple-dwelling houses. The word "family" as used in the ordinance means,

(o)ne or more persons related by blood, adoption, or marriage, living and cooking together as a single housekeeping unit, exclusive of household servants. A number of persons but not exceeding two (2) living and cooking together as a single housekeeping unit though not related by blood, adoption, or marriage shall be deemed to constitute a family.

Appellees, the Dickmans, are owners of a house in the village and leased it in December 1971 for a term of 18 months to Michael Truman. Later Bruce Boraas became a colessee. Then Anne Parish moved into the house along with three others. These six are students at nearby State University at Stony Brook and none is related to the other by blood, adoption, or marriage. When the village served the Dickmans with an "Order to Remedy Violations" of the ordinance, the owners plus three tenants thereupon brought this action under 42 U.S.C. §1983 for an injunction and a judgment declaring the ordinance unconstitutional. . . .

This case brings to this Court a different phase of local zoning regulations from those we have previously reviewed. [In] Village of Euclid v. Ambler Realty Co., 272 U.S. 365 [(1926)], [t]he Court sustained the zoning ordinance under the police power of the State, saying that the line "which in this field separates the legitimate from the illegitimate assumption of power is not capable of precise delimitation. It varies with circumstances and conditions." Id., at 387. . . . The main thrust of [*Euclid*] was in the exclusion of industries and apartments, and . . . the desire to keep residential areas free of "disturbing noises"; "increased traffic"; the hazard of "moving and parked automobiles"; the "depriving children of the privilege of quiet and open spaces for play, enjoyed by those in more favored localities." Id., at 394. . . .

The present ordinance is challenged on several grounds: that it interferes with a person's right to travel; that it interferes with the right to migrate to and settle within a State; that it bars people who are uncongenial to the present residents; that it expresses the social preferences of the residents for groups that will be congenial to them; that social homogeneity is not a legitimate interest of government; that the restriction of those whom the neighbors do not like trenches on the newcomers' rights of privacy; that it is of no rightful concern to villagers whether the residents are married or unmarried; that the ordinance is antithetical to the Nation's experience, ideology, and self-perception as an open, egalitarian, and integrated society.

We find none of these reasons in the record before us. It is not aimed at transients. It involves no procedural disparity inflicted on some but not on others. . . . It involves no "fundamental" right guaranteed by the Constitution, such as voting; the right of association; the right of access to the courts; or any rights of privacy, cf. Griswold v. Connecticut, 381 U.S. 479 [(1965)]; Eisenstadt v. Baird, 405 U.S. 438, 453-454 [(1972)]. We deal with economic and social legislation where legislatures have historically drawn lines which we respect against the charge of violation of the Equal Protection Clause if the law be "reasonable, not arbitrary" and bears "a rational relationship to a (permissible) state objective." Reed v. Reed, 404 U.S. 71, 76.

It is said, however, that if two unmarried people can constitute a "family," there is no reason why three or four may not. But every line drawn by a legislature leaves some out that might well have been included. That exercise of discretion, however, is a legislative, not a judicial, function.

It is said that the Belle Terre ordinance reeks with an animosity to unmarried couples who live together. There is no evidence to support it; and the provision of the ordinance bringing within the definition of a "family" two unmarried people belies the charge.

The ordinance places no ban on other forms of association, for a "family" may, so far as the ordinance is concerned, entertain whomever it likes.

The regimes of boarding houses, fraternity houses, and the like present urban problems. More people occupy a given space; more cars rather continuously pass by; more cars are parked; noise travels with crowds.

A quiet place where yards are wide, people few, and motor vehicles restricted are legitimate guidelines in a land-use project addressed to family needs. This goal is a permissible one. . . . The police power is not confined to elimination of filth, stench, and unhealthy places. It is ample to lay out zones where family values, youth values, and the blessings

of quiet seclusion and clean air make the area a sanctuary for people.
. . . Reversed.

Mr. Justice MARSHALL, dissenting. . . .

My disagreement with the Court today is based upon my view that
the ordinance in this case unnecessarily burdens appellees' First Amendment freedom of association and their constitutionally guaranteed right
to privacy. Our decisions establish that the First and Fourteenth Amendments protect the freedom to choose one's associates. NAACP v. Button,
371 U.S. 415, 430 (1963). Constitutional protection is extended, not only
to modes of association that are political in the usual sense, but also to
those that pertain to the social and economic benefit of the members.
The selection of one's living companions involves similar choices as to
the emotional, social, or economic benefits to be derived from alternative living arrangements.

The freedom of association is often inextricably entwined with the
constitutionally guaranteed right of privacy. The right to "establish a
home" is an essential part of the liberty guaranteed by the Fourteenth
Amendment [citing Meyer v. Nebraska and Griswold v. Connecticut]. And
the Constitution secures to an individual a freedom "to satisfy his intellectual and emotional needs in the privacy of his own home." Stanley v.
Georgia, 394 U.S. 557, 565 (1969). Constitutionally protected privacy is,
in Mr. Justice Brandeis' words, "as against the Government, the right to
be let alone . . . the right most valued by civilized man." Olmstead v.
United States, 277 U.S. 438, 478 (1928) (dissenting opinion). The choice
of household companions — of whether a person's "intellectual and emotional needs" are best met by living with family, friends, professional
associates, or others — involves deeply personal considerations as to the
kind and quality of intimate relationships within the home. That decision
surely falls within the ambit of the right to privacy protected by the Constitution [citing, inter alia, *Roe, Eisenstadt,* and *Griswold*].

The instant ordinance discriminates on the basis of just such a personal lifestyle choice as to household companions. It permits any number of persons related by blood or marriage, be it two or twenty, to live
in a single household, but it limits to two the number of unrelated persons bound by profession, love, friendship, religious or political affiliation, or mere economics who can occupy a single home. Belle Terre
imposes upon those who deviate from the community norm in their
choice of living companions significantly greater restrictions than are applied to residential groups who are related by blood or marriage, and
compose the established order within the community. The village has, in
effect, acted to fence out those individuals whose choice of lifestyle differs from that of its current residents.

This is not a case where the Court is being asked to nullify a town-
ship's sincere efforts to maintain its residential character by preventing

the operation of rooming houses, fraternity houses, or other commercial or high-density residential uses. Unquestionably, a town is free to restrict such uses. Moreover, as a general proposition, I see no constitutional infirmity in a town's limiting the density of use in residential areas by zoning regulations which do not discriminate on the basis of constitutionally suspect criteria. This ordinance, however, limits the density of occupancy of only those homes occupied by unrelated persons. It thus reaches beyond control of the use of land or the density of population, and undertakes to regulate the way people choose to associate with each other within the privacy of their own homes. . . .

Because I believe that this zoning ordinance creates a classification which impinges upon fundamental personal rights, it can withstand constitutional scrutiny only upon a clear showing that the burden imposed is necessary to protect a compelling and substantial governmental interest [and that] no less intrusive means will adequately protect the compelling state interest. . . . It is claimed that the ordinance controls population density, prevents noise, traffic and parking problems, and preserves the rent structure of the community and its attractiveness to families. [T]hese are all legitimate and substantial interests of government. But I think it clear that the means chosen to accomplish these purposes are both overinclusive and underinclusive, and that the asserted goals could be as effectively achieved by means of an ordinance that did not discriminate on the basis of constitutionally protected choices of lifestyle. The ordinance imposes no restriction whatsoever on the number of persons who may live in a house, as long as they are related by marital or sanguinary bonds — presumably no matter how distant their relationship. Nor does the ordinance restrict the number of income earners who may contribute to rent in such a household, or the number of automobiles that may be maintained by its occupants. In that sense the ordinance is underinclusive. On the other hand, the statute restricts the number of unrelated persons who may live in a home to no more than two. It would therefore prevent three unrelated people from occupying a dwelling even if among them they had but one income and no vehicles. While an extended family of a dozen or more might live in a small bungalow, three elderly and retired persons could not occupy the large manor house next door. Thus the statute is also grossly overinclusive to accomplish its intended purposes.

[The village could address density] problems by limiting each household to a specified number of adults, two or three perhaps, without limitation on the number of dependent children. The burden of such an ordinance would fall equally upon all segments of the community. It would surely be better tailored to the goals asserted by the village than the ordinance before us today, for it would more realistically restrict population density and growth and their attendant environmental costs. Various other statutory mechanisms also suggest themselves as solutions to Belle Terre's problems — rent control, limits on the number of vehicles per household, and so forth, but, of course, such schemes are matters of legislative judgment and not for this Court. Appellants also refer to the necessity of maintaining the family character of the village. There is not a shred of evidence in the record indicating that if Belle Terre permitted a limited number of unrelated persons to live together, the residential, familial character of the community would be fundamentally affected. . . .

## Notes and Questions

1. Zoning ordinances control land use by protecting a family's residential use from interference by commercial or industrial users. As the definition of the family has changed, however, groups of unrelated individuals (such as those in *Belle Terre*) increasingly are challenging ordinances that restrict single-family dwellings to traditional families.

In *Belle Terre*, Justice Douglas analogizes the student commune to "boarding houses, fraternity houses, and the like" because of their residential density, traffic congestion and noise. Is the comparison apt? Do groups of unrelated persons cause more urban problems than traditional families?

2. Is *Belle Terre* a dispute about the meaning of "family" or "family values"? How does the student group threaten family values? Does the group threaten the family value of permanency? See Laurence H. Tribe, American Constitutional Law 1403 (2d ed. 1988) (so arguing). Given the high divorce rate, is permanency a family value that the state should protect? Would less restrictive alternatives, suggested by Justice Marshall, meet the state's objectives?

3. Justice Douglas maintains that *Belle Terre* involves no fundamental right, such as association or privacy. Do you agree? Cf. City of Santa Barbara v. Adamson, 164 Cal. Rptr. 539 (Cal. 1980) (invalidating zoning restriction based on right to privacy in state constitution). For a rebuttal, see Kenneth L. Karst, The Freedom of Intimate Association, 89 Yale L.J. 624 (1980). Based on this view, Douglas uses rational basis review. Would the ordinance have survived strict scrutiny?

4. Justice Douglas does not analyze the provision requiring a "single housekeeping unit." Would plaintiffs' household comply? In a subsequent New Jersey case, ten college students challenged an ordinance that limits occupancy by defining a "family" as:

one or more persons occupying a dwelling unit as a single non-profit housekeeping unit, who are living together as a stable and permanent living unit, being a traditional family unit or the functional equivalency thereof.

Borough of Glassboro v. Vallorosi, 568 A.2d 888, 889 (N.J. 1990). The *Vallerosi* ordinance, similar to that in *Belle Terre,* aimed to preserve stable, permanent housing. Influenced by state precedents equating "single family" with "single housekeeping unit," the New Jersey Supreme Court adopted a functional standard and held that the group complied because they planned to live together for three years, ate together, shared household tasks and expenses. Is *Vallerosi*'s functional standard superior to *Belle Terre*'s focus on associational ties?

5. State courts are divided on the issue of the constitutionality of single-family zoning ordinances as applied to groups. Most follow *Belle Terre,* finding that the ordinances meet the rational basis test. A few, however, decline to adopt *Belle Terre*'s reasoning on the basis of state constitutional rights to either due process or privacy. See Katia Brener, Note, *Belle Terre* and Single-Family Home Ordinances: Judicial Perceptions of Local Government and the Presumption of Validity, 74 N.Y.U. L. Rev. 447, 456-463 (1999) (discussing cases).

6. The Belle Terre zoning ordinance contained an exception permitting two unrelated persons to constitute a family. Plaintiffs argued that the ordinance "reeks with animosity to unmarried couples" and asked why more than two unmarried persons could not constitute a family. How does Justice Douglas respond? Does his response imply that the Court would strike down a zoning ordinance that excluded unmarried couples? See City of Ladue v. Horn, 720 S.W.2d 745 (Mo. Ct. App. 1986) (rejecting couple's constitutional challenge).

7. *Belle Terre* (and *Vallerosi,* supra) illustrate the elasticity of the definition of "family" in the use of zoning as an agent of social control. The Supreme Court again examined an ordinance that excluded a group home in City of Cleburne v. Cleburne Living Center, 473 U.S. 432 (1985). The city denied an exemption from the local ordinance to a home for the mentally retarded. The group then alleged that the ordinance violated equal protection. The Court held the ordinance invalid as applied, reasoning that the denial rested on irrational prejudice. Did the Belle Terre ordinance, as applied, rest on "irrational prejudice" against students? See also City of Edmonds v. Oxford House, 514 U.S. 725 (1995) (challenging land use restriction as applied to group of substance abusers). Is resort to the police power appropriate to exclude "undesirables" from the community?

## Problems

1. A "co-housing movement," originating in Scandinavia, is attracting adherents in California and Washington. Karen and Tom Smith and their two preschoolers move into a development in Seattle that features privately owned homes, common childcare facilities, and a communal

dining area and kitchen. Supporters of the co-housing movement claim it responds to contemporary housing needs, specifically, mothers working outside the home and the isolation of the contemporary family. Suppose Seattle attempts to exclude the residents via a zoning ordinance similar to that of *Belle Terre* or *Vallerosi*. Do the residents constitute a "single family"? See generally Charles Durrett & Kataryn McCamant, Cohousing: A Contemporary Approach to Housing Ourselves (2d ed. 1994); Richard Paoli, So Happy Together: Cohousing Developments Offer Residents the Chance to Share Life, S.F. Chron. (Real Estate Section), July 15, 2001, at 1.

2. The Jones family, a polygamous Morman "extended family," desire to move to a community with a zoning ordinance similar to that of *Belle Terre* or *Vallerosi*. How might they fare in a zoning challenge?

## 2. Is a Commune a Family for Other Purposes?

### ■ U.S. DEPARTMENT OF AGRICULTURE v. MORENO
*413 U.S. 528 (1973)*

Mr. Justice BRENNAN delivered the opinion of the Court.

This case requires us to consider the constitutionality of §3(e) of the Food Stamp Act of 1964, 7 U.S.C. §2012(e) [established] in 1964 in an effort to alleviate hunger and malnutrition among the more needy segments of our society. Eligibility for participation in the program is determined on a household rather than an individual basis. An eligible household purchases sufficient food stamps to provide that household with a nutritionally adequate diet. The household pays for the stamps at a reduced rate based upon its size and cumulative income. The food stamps are then used to purchase food at retail stores, and the Government redeems the stamps at face value, thereby paying the difference between the actual cost of the food and the amount paid by the household for the stamps.

As initially enacted, §3(e) defined a "household" as "a group of related or non-related individuals, who are not residents of an institution or boarding house, but are living as one economic unit sharing common cooking facilities and for whom food is customarily purchased in common." In January 1971, however Congress redefined the term "household" so as to include only groups of related individuals. Pursuant to this amendment, the Secretary of Agriculture promulgated regulations rendering ineligible for participation in the program any "household" whose members are not "all related to each other."

Appellees in this case consist of several groups of individuals who allege that, although they satisfy the income eligibility requirements for federal food assistance, they have nevertheless been excluded from the program solely because the persons in each group are not "all related to each other." Appellee Jacinta Moreno, for example is a 56-year-old diabetic who lives with Ermina Sanchez and the latter's three children. They share common living expenses, and Mrs. Sanchez helps to care for appellee. Appellee's monthly income, derived from public assistance, is $75; Mrs. Sanchez receives $133 per month from public assistance. The household pays $135 per month for rent, gas and electricity, of which appellee pays $50. Appellee spends $10 per month for transportation to a hospital for regular visits, and $5 per month for laundry. That leaves her $10 per month for food and other necessities. Despite her poverty, appellee has been denied federal food assistance solely because she is unrelated to the other members of her household. Moreover, although Mrs. Sanchez and her three children were permitted to purchase $108 worth of food stamps per month for $18, their participation in the program will be terminated if appellee Moreno continues to live with them.

Appellee Sheilah Hejny is married and has three children. Although the Hejnys are indigent, they took in a 20-year-old girl, who is unrelated to them because "we felt she had emotional problems." The Hejnys receive $144 worth of food stamps each month for $14. If they allow the 20-year-old girl to continue to live with them, they will be denied food stamps by reason of §3(e).

Appellee Victoria Keppler has a daughter with an acute hearing deficiency. The daughter requires special instruction in a school for the deaf. The school is located in an area in which appellee could not ordinarily afford to live. Thus, in order to make the most of her limited resources, appellee agreed to share an apartment near the school with a woman who, like appellee, is on public assistance. Since appellee is not related to the woman, appellee's food stamps have been, and will continue to be, cut off if they continue to live together.

These and two other groups of appellees instituted a class action . . . seeking declaratory and injunctive relief against the enforcement of the 1971 amendment of §3(e) and its implementing regulations. In essence, appellees contend, and the District Court held, that the "unrelated person" provision of §3(e) creates an irrational classification in violation of the equal protection component of the Due Process Clause of the Fifth Amendment. We agree. . . .

The challenged statutory classification (households of related persons versus households containing one or more unrelated persons) is clearly irrelevant to the stated purposes of the Act. As the District Court recognized, "(t)he relationships among persons constituting one economic unit and sharing cooking facilities have nothing to do with their abilities to stimulate the agricultural economy by purchasing farm surpluses, or with their personal nutritional requirements." 345 F. Supp., at 313.

Thus, if it is to be sustained, the challenged classification must rationally further some legitimate governmental interest. . . . Regrettably, there is little legislative history to illuminate the purposes of the 1971 amendment of §3(e). The legislative history that does exist, however, indicates that that amendment was intended to prevent so-called "hippies" and "hippie communes" from participating in the food stamp program. See H.R. Conf. Rep. No. 91-1793, p.8; 116 Cong. Rec. 44439 (1970) (Sen. Holland). The challenged classification clearly cannot be sustained by reference to this congressional purpose. For if the constitutional conception of "equal protection of the laws" means anything, it must at the very least mean that a bare congressional desire to harm a politically unpopular group cannot constitute a legitimate governmental interest. . . .

Although apparently conceding this point, the Government maintains that the challenged classification should nevertheless be upheld as rationally related to the clearly legitimate governmental interest in minimizing fraud in the administration of the food stamp program.[7] In essence, the Government contends that, in adopting the 1971 amendment, Congress might rationally have thought (1) that households with one or more unrelated members are more likely than "fully related" households to contain individuals who abuse the program by fraudulently failing to report sources of income or by voluntarily remaining poor; and (2) that such households are "relatively unstable," thereby increasing the difficulty of detecting such abuses. But even if we were to accept as rational the Government's wholly unsubstantiated assumptions concerning the differences between "related" and "unrelated" households we still could not agree with the Government's conclusion that the denial of essential federal food assistance to all otherwise eligible households containing unrelated members constitutes a rational effort to deal with these concerns.

At the outset, it is important to note that the Food Stamp Act itself contains provisions, wholly independent of §3(e), aimed specifically at the problems of fraud. . . . The existence of these provisions necessarily casts considerable doubt upon the proposition that the 1971 amendment could rationally have been intended to prevent those very same abuses.

7. The Government initially argued to the District Court that the challenged classification might be justified as a means to foster "morality." In rejecting that contention, the District Court noted that "interpreting the amendment as an attempt to regulate morality would raise serious constitutional questions." 345 F. Supp. 310, 314. Indeed, citing this Court's decisions [in Griswold v. Connecticut, Stanley v. Georgia, and Eisenstadt v. Baird], the District Court observed that it was doubtful at best, whether Congress, "in the name of morality, could 'infringe the rights to privacy and freedom of association *in the home*." 345 F. Supp., at 314. (Emphasis in original.) Moreover, the court also pointed out that the classification established in §3(e) was not rationally related "to prevailing notions of morality, since it in terms disqualifies all households of unrelated individuals, without reference to whether a particular group contains both sexes." 345 F. Supp., at 315. The Government itself has now abandoned the "morality" argument.

[I]n practical operation, the 1971 amendment excludes from participation in the food stamp program, not those persons who are "likely to abuse the program," but, rather, only those persons who are so desperately in need of aid that they cannot even afford to alter their living arrangements so as to retain their eligibility. Traditional equal protection analysis does not require that every classification be drawn with precise "mathematical nicety." But the classification here in issue is not only "imprecise," it is wholly without any rational basis. The judgment of the District Court holding the "unrelated person" provision invalid under the Due Process Clause of the Fifth Amendment is therefore affirmed. . . .

Mr. Justice DOUGLAS, concurring. . . .

. . . As the facts of this case show, the poor are congregating in households where they can better meet the adversities of poverty. This banding together is an expression of the right of freedom of association that is very deep in our traditions.

Other like rights have been recognized that are only peripheral First Amendment rights — the right to send one's child to a religious school, the right to study the German language in a private school, the protection of the entire spectrum of learning, teaching, and communicating ideas, the marital right of privacy. As the examples indicate, these peripheral constitutional rights are exercised not necessarily in assemblies that congregate in halls or auditoriums but in discrete individual actions such as parents placing a child in the school of their choice. Taking a person into one's home because he is poor or needs help or brings happiness to the household is of the same dignity.

Congress might choose to deal only with members of a family of one or two or three generations, treating it all as a unit. Congress, however, has not done that here. Concededly an individual living alone is not disqualified from the receipt of food stamp aid, even though there are other members of the family with whom he might theoretically live. Nor are common-law couples disqualified: they, like individuals living alone, may qualify under the Act if they are poor — whether they have abandoned their wives and children and however antifamily their attitudes may be. In other words, the "unrelated" person provision was not aimed at the maintenance of normal family ties. It penalizes persons or families who have brought under their roof an "unrelated" needy person. It penalizes the poorest of the poor for doubling up against the adversities of poverty.

But for the constitutional aspects of the problem, the "unrelated" person provision of the Act might well be sustained as a means to prevent fraud. . . . I could not say that this "unrelated" person provision has no "rational" relation to control of fraud. We deal here, however, with the right of association, protected by the First Amendment. People who are desperately poor but unrelated come together and join hands with the aim better to combat the crises of poverty. The need of those living together better to meet those crises is denied, while the need of households made up of relatives that is no more acute is serviced. Problems of the fisc, as we stated in Shapiro v. Thompson, 394 U.S. 618, 633 [(1969)], are legitimate concerns of government. But government "may not accomplish such a purpose by invidious distinctions between classes of its citizens." Ibid. . . .

The right of association, the right to invite the stranger into one's home is too basic in our constitutional regime to deal with roughshod. If there are abuses inherent in that pattern of living against which the food stamp program should be protected, the Act must be "narrowly drawn," to meet the precise end. The method adopted and applied to these cases makes §3(e) of the Act unconstitutional by reason of the invidious discrimination between the two classes of needy persons. . . .

Mr. Justice REHNQUIST, with whom THE CHIEF JUSTICE concurs, dissenting.

[O]ur role is limited to the determination of whether there is any rational basis on which Congress could decide that public funds made available under the food stamp program should not go to a household containing an individual who is unrelated to any other member of the household. . . . I do not think it is unreasonable for Congress to conclude that the basic unit which it was willing to support with federal funding through food stamps is some variation on the family as we know it — a household consisting of related individuals. This unit provides a guarantee which is not provided by households containing unrelated individuals that the household exists for some purpose other than to collect federal food stamps. . . .

## Notes and Questions

1. In *Moreno*, the Supreme Court was willing to include unrelated persons in a definition of "household" for food stamp purposes. In contrast, in *Belle Terre*, the Court was unwilling to confer recognition on a similar household for zoning purposes. Are the cases distinguishable? How can you explain Justice Douglas's concurrence in *Moreno*, given his majority opinion in *Belle Terre*?

2. How do the Court's views of the households in *Belle Terre* and *Moreno* differ? For example, *Belle Terre* reveals concerns about transiency, overcrowding, and congestion. Yet, *Moreno* is skeptical about the government's "unsubstantiated assumptions" about the instability of households of unrelated persons. Was the outcome different because the *Moreno* plaintiffs conformed more to our concept of the traditional family?

3. In Dutton v. Department of Social Welfare, 721 A.2d 109 (Vt. 1998), the Vermont Supreme Court addressed whether elderly home-owners and their boarders should be counted as a single household for purposes of state and federal subsidies for energy costs. Is *Dutton* more closely analogous to *Belle Terre* or *Moreno*?

4. Commentators criticize *Moreno* for its unwillingness to address the degree to which the Constitution protects the right to choose with whom to share a home. J. Harvie Wilkinson III & G. Edward White, Consti-tutional Protection for Personal Lifestyles, 62 Cornell L. Rev. 563, 584 (1977). If *Moreno* and *Belle Terre* raise the right to associate in the home with unrelated individuals, is there a comparable right *not* to associate with relatives? Cf. Robinson v. Block, 869 F.2d 202 (3d Cir. 1989) (co-resident siblings have burden of establishing separateness, under food stamp amendments, to avoid classification as a single household).

# B. THE EXTENDED FAMILY

## ■ MOORE v. CITY OF EAST CLEVELAND
### *431 U.S. 494 (1977)*

Mr. Justice POWELL announced the judgment of the Court, and de-livered an opinion in which Mr. Justice BRENNAN, Mr. Justice MARSHALL, and Mr. Justice BLACKMUN joined.

East Cleveland's housing ordinance, like many throughout the coun-try, limits occupancy of a dwelling unit to members of a single family. But the ordinance contains an unusual and complicated definitional sec-tion that recognizes as a "family" only a few categories of related indi-viduals, §1341.08.[2] Because her family, living together in her home, fits none of those categories, appellant stands convicted of a criminal of-fense. The question in this case is whether the ordinance violates the Due Process Clause of the Fourteenth Amendment.

Appellant, Mrs. Inez Moore, lives in her East Cleveland home to-gether with her son, Dale Moore Sr., and her two grandsons, Dale, Jr., and John Moore, Jr. The two boys are first cousins rather than brothers; we are told that John came to live with his grandmother and with the elder and younger Dale Moores (sic) after his mother's death.

---

2. Section 1341.08 (1966) provides:

"Family" means a number of individuals related to the nominal head of the house-hold or to the spouse of the nominal head of the household living as a single house-keeping unit in a single dwelling unit, [including spouse, parent, or unmarried children, provided the unmarried children have no co-resident children, but] a family may include not more than one dependent married or unmarried child of the nominal head of the household or of the spouse of the nominal head of the household and the spouse and dependent children of such dependent child. . . .

In early 1973, Mrs. Moore received a notice of violation from the city, stating that John was an "illegal occupant" and directing her to comply with the ordinance. When she failed to remove him from her home, the city filed a criminal charge. [She claimed that the ordinance was facially unconstitutional. She was convicted and sentenced to 5 days in jail and a $25 fine.]

The city argues that our decision in Village of Belle Terre v. Boraas, 416 U.S. 1 (1974), requires us to sustain the ordinance attacked here. . . . But one overriding factor sets this case apart from *Belle Terre*. The ordinance there affected only *unrelated* individuals. It expressly allowed all who were related by "blood, adoption, or marriage" to live together, and in sustaining the ordinance we were careful to note that it promoted "family needs" and "family values." East Cleveland, in contrast, has chosen to regulate the occupancy of its housing by slicing deeply into the family itself. This is no mere incidental result of the ordinance. On its face it selects certain categories of relatives who may live together and declares that others may not. In particular, it makes a crime of a grandmother's choice to live with her grandson in circumstances like those presented here.

When a city undertakes such intrusive regulation of the family, neither *Belle Terre* nor *Euclid* governs; the usual judicial deference to the legislature is inappropriate. "This Court has long recognized that freedom of personal choice in matters of marriage and family life is one of the liberties protected by the Due Process Clause of the Fourteenth Amendment." Cleveland Board of Education v. LaFleur, 414 U.S. 632, 639-640 (1974). A host of cases, tracing their lineage to Meyer v. Nebraska, 262 U.S. 390, 399-401 (1923), and Pierce v. Society of Sisters, 268 U.S. 510, 534-535 (1925), have consistently acknowledged a "private realm of family life which the state cannot enter." Prince v. Massachusetts, 321 U.S. 158, 166 (1944). Of course, the family is not beyond regulation. See Prince v. Massachusetts, supra, 321 U.S. at 166. But when the government intrudes on choices concerning family living arrangements, this Court must examine carefully the importance of the governmental interests advanced and the extent to which they are served by the challenged regulation.

When thus examined, this ordinance cannot survive. The city seeks to justify it as a means of preventing overcrowding, minimizing traffic and parking congestion, and avoiding an undue financial burden on East Cleveland's school system. Although these are legitimate goals, the ordinance before us serves them marginally, at best. For example, the ordinance permits any family consisting only of husband, wife, and unmarried children to live together, even if the family contains a half dozen licensed drivers, each with his or her own car. At the same time it forbids an adult brother and sister to share a household, even if both faithfully use public transportation. The ordinance would permit a grandmother to live with a single dependent son and children, even if his school-age children number a dozen, yet it forces Mrs. Moore to find another dwelling for her grandson John, simply because of the presence of his uncle and cousin in the same household. . . .

The city would distinguish the cases based on *Meyer* and *Pierce*. It points out that none of them "gives grandmothers any fundamental rights with respect to grandsons," . . . and suggests that any constitutional right to live together as a family extends only to the nuclear family, essentially a couple and their dependent children.

To be sure, these cases did not expressly consider the family relationship presented here. They were immediately concerned with freedom of choice with respect to childbearing, or with the rights of parents to the custody and companionship of their own children, or with traditional parental authority in matters of child rearing and education. But unless we close our eyes to the basic reasons why certain rights associated with the family have been accorded shelter under the Fourteenth Amendment's Due Process Clause, we cannot avoid applying the force and rationale of these precedents to the family choice involved in this case. . . .

Substantive due process has at times been a treacherous field for this Court. There *are* risks when the judicial branch gives enhanced protection to certain substantive liberties without the guidance of the more specific provisions of the Bill of Rights. As the history of the *Lochner* era demonstrates, there is reason for concern lest the only limits to such judicial intervention become the predilections of those who happen at the time to be Members of this Court. That history counsels caution and restraint. But it does not counsel abandonment, nor does it require what the city urges: cutting off any protection of family rights at the first convenient, if arbitrary boundary — the boundary of the nuclear family.

Appropriate limits on substantive due process come not from drawing arbitrary lines but rather from careful "respect for the teachings of history (and), solid recognition of the basic values that underlie our society." Griswold v. Connecticut, 381 U.S., at 501. Our decisions establish that the Constitution protects the sanctity of the family precisely because the institution of the family is deeply rooted in this Nation's history and tradition. It is through the family that we inculcate and pass down many of our most cherished values, moral and cultural.

Ours is by no means a tradition limited to respect for the bonds uniting the members of the nuclear family. The tradition of uncles, aunts, cousins, and especially grandparents sharing a household along with parents and children has roots equally venerable and equally deserving of constitutional recognition. Over the years millions of our citizens have grown up in just such an environment, and most, surely, have profited from it. Even if conditions of modern society have brought about a decline in extended family households, they have not erased the accumulated wisdom of civilization, gained over the centuries and honored throughout our history, that supports a larger conception of the family. Out of choice, necessity, or a sense of family responsibility, it has been common for close relatives to draw together and participate in the duties and the satisfactions of a common home. Decisions concerning child rearing, which *Yoder, Meyer, Pierce* and other cases have recognized as entitled to constitutional protection, long have been shared with grandparents or other relatives who occupy the same household, indeed who may take on major responsibility for the rearing of the children. Especially in times of adversity, such as the death of a spouse or economic need, the broader family has tended to come together for mutual sustenance and to maintain or rebuild a secure home life. This is apparently what happened here.[16]

Whether or not such a household is established because of personal tragedy, the choice of relatives in this degree of kinship to live together may not lightly be denied by the State. [T]he Constitution prevents East Cleveland from standardizing its children and its adults by forcing all to live in certain narrowly defined family patterns. . . .

Mr. Justice BRENNAN, with whom Mr. Justice MARSHALL joins, concurring.

I join the plurality's opinion. . . . I write only to underscore the cultural myopia of the arbitrary boundary drawn by the East Cleveland ordinance in the light of the tradition of the American home that has been a feature of our society since our beginning as a Nation. . . .

. . . The "extended family" that provided generations of early Americans with social services and economic and emotional support in times of hardship, and was the beachhead for successive waves of immigrants who populated our cities, remains not merely still a pervasive living pattern, but under the goad of brutal economic necessity, a prominent pattern virtually a means of survival for large numbers of the poor and deprived minorities of our society. For them compelled pooling of scant resources requires compelled sharing of a household.

The "extended" form is especially familiar among black families.[6] We may suppose that this reflects the truism that black citizens, like gen-

---

16. We are told that the mother of John Moore, Jr., died when he was less than one year old. He, like uncounted others who have suffered a similar tragedy, then came to live with the grandmother to provide the infant with a substitute for his mother's care and to establish a more normal home environment.

6. B. Yorburg, [The Changing Family 108 (1973)]. The extended family often plays an important role in the rearing of young black children whose parents must work. Many such children frequently "spend all of their growing-up years in the care of extended kin. . . . Often children are 'given' to their grandparents, who rear them to adulthood. . . . Many children normally grow up in a three-generation household and they absorb the influences of grandmother and grandfather as well as mother and father." J. Ladner, Tomorrow's Tomorrow: The Black Woman 60 (1972).

erations of white immigrants before them, have been victims of economic and other disadvantages that would worsen if they were compelled to abandon extended, for nuclear, living patterns. . . . In black households whose head is an elderly woman, as in this case, . . . 48% of such black households, compared with 10% of counterpart white households, include related minor children not offspring of the head of the household.[9]

I do not wish to be understood as implying that East Cleveland's enforcement of its ordinance is motivated by a racially discriminatory purpose: The record of this case would not support that implication. But the prominence of other than nuclear families among ethnic and racial minority groups, including our black citizens, surely demonstrates that the "extended family" pattern remains a vital tenet of our society. It suffices that in prohibiting this pattern of family living as a means of achieving its objectives, appellee city has chosen a device that deeply intrudes into family associational rights that historically have been central, and today remain central, to a large proportion of our population. . . .

[The concurring opinion of Justice Stevens, emphasizing Mrs. Moore's right to use her property as she sees fit, has been omitted.]

Mr. Justice STEWART, with whom Mr. Justice REHNQUIST joins, dissenting. . . .

The *Belle Terre* decision . . . disposes of the appellant's contentions to the extent they focus not on her blood relationships with her sons and grandsons but on more general notions about the "privacy of the home." Her suggestion that every person has a constitutional right permanently to share his residence with whomever he pleases, and that such choices are "beyond the province of legitimate governmental intrusion," amounts to the same argument that was made and found unpersuasive in *Belle Terre*. . . .

The appellant is considerably closer to the constitutional mark in asserting that the East Cleveland ordinance intrudes upon "the private realm of family life which the state cannot enter." Prince v. Massachusetts, 321 U.S. 158, 166. Several decisions of the Court have identified specific aspects of what might broadly be termed "private family life" that are constitutionally protected against state interference.

Although the appellant's desire to share a single-dwelling unit also involves "private family life" in a sense, that desire can hardly be equated with any of the interests [which we have previously protected]. The ordinance about which the appellant complains did not impede her choice to have or not to have children, and it did not dictate to her how her own children were to be nurtured and reared. The ordinance clearly does not prevent parents from living together or living with their unemancipated offspring.

9. [R. Hill, The Strengths of Black Families 5-6 (1972)].

But even though the Court's previous cases are not directly in point, the appellant contends that the importance of the "extended family" in American society requires us to hold that her decision to share her residence with her grandsons may not be interfered with by the State. This decision, like the decisions involved in bearing and raising children, is said to be an aspect of "family life" also entitled to substantive protection under the Constitution. Without pausing to inquire how far under this argument an "extended family" might extend, I cannot agree. . . . To equate [Moore's] interest with the fundamental decisions to marry and to bear and raise children is to extend the limited substantive contours of the Due Process Clause beyond recognition.

The appellant also challenges the single-family occupancy ordinance on equal protection grounds [an issue which the majority did not reach]. Her claim is that the city has drawn an arbitrary and irrational distinction between groups of people who may live together as a "family" and those who may not. . . . I do not think East Cleveland's definition of "family" offends the Constitution. The city has undisputed power to ordain single-family residential occupancy. And that power plainly carries with it the power to say what a "family" is. Here the city has defined "family" to include not only father, mother, and dependent children, but several other close relatives as well. The definition is rationally designed to carry out the legitimate governmental purposes identified in the *Belle Terre* opinion. . . .

Obviously, East Cleveland might have as easily and perhaps as effectively hit upon a different definition of "family." But a line could hardly be drawn that would not sooner or later become the target of a challenge like the appellant's. If "family" included all of the householder's grandchildren there would doubtless be the hard case of an orphaned niece or nephew. If, as the appellant suggests, a "family" must include all blood relatives, what of longtime friends? . . .

## Notes and Questions

1. *The tradition of the extended family.* Justice Powell's plurality opinion invalidates the East Cleveland ordinance based on the historical importance of the extended family. In fact, this view is a myth. The Cambridge Group for the History of Population and Social Structure documented, based on computer analysis, that the nuclear (rather than the extended) family predominated before industrialization. See Household and Family in Past Time (Peter Laslett ed., 1972); Peter Laslett, The World We Have Lost Further Explored 97-99 (3d ed. 1984). See also William J. Goode, World Revolution and Family Patterns 6 (1970) (referring to the extended family as the "family form of Western nostalgia"). Would such knowledge have changed the outcome in *Moore*?

2. Do Justice Powell's plurality opinion and Justice Brennan's concurrence rest on a mythical model of *white* families? Although demographical data supports the mythical status of the extended family among whites, empirical research supports the prevalence of this family form among African-Americans. See Robert Joseph Taylor et al., Developments in Research on Black Families: A Decade Review, in Family in Transition: Rethinking Marriage, Sexuality, Child Rearing, and Family Organization 439, 445-446 (Arlene S. Skolnick & Jerome H. Skolnick eds., 7th ed. 1992). Latino culture encompasses a similar multigenerational view of family. See Ana Novoa, American Family Law: History and Whostory, 19 Chicano-Latino L. Rev. 265, 266-267 (1998). See generally Vern L. Bengtson, Beyond the Nuclear Family: The Increasing Importance of Multigenerational Bonds, 63 J. Marriage & Fam. 1 (2001).

3. Belle Terre *distinguished*. In applying a stricter standard of review than it used in *Belle Terre*, the Court treats *Moore* as involving not zoning, but rather family privacy. Why does the Belle Terre ordinance serve "family needs" and "family values" but the East Cleveland ordinance "slic[es] deeply into the family itself"? Is the latter ordinance directed at the same ends (eliminating traffic congestion and overcrowding) or at other family values? Professor Robert Burt responds:

> The plurality did not consider that the purpose of the ordinance was quite straightforward: to exclude from a middle-class, predominantly black community, that saw itself as socially and economically upwardly mobile, other black families most characteristic of lower-class ghetto life.
>
> Perhaps the Court did not see this purpose or, if it did, considered this an "illegitimate goal," though in other cases the Court had been exceedingly solicitous of white middle-class communities' attempts to preserve a common social identity — "zones," as the Court had put the matter [in *Belle Terre*] — "where family values, youth values, and the blessings of the quiet seclusion and clean air make the area a sanctuary for people." . . . I find in [Justice Brennan's] characterization of the East Cleveland ordinance, as "senseless" and "eccentric," precisely what he alleges in it: "a depressing insensitivity toward the economic and emotional needs" of the current majority of residents in East Cleveland.

Robert A. Burt, The Constitution of the Family, 1979 Sup. Ct. Rev. 329, 389.

In an omitted dissent, Justice White disputes the idea that Mrs. Moore's interest in living with her grandchildren is protected by the Due Process Clause. He reasons that the ordinance prevents Mrs. Moore from living only in East Cleveland but that she is free to move elsewhere in Cleveland. Does his suggestion respond to Professor Burt's criticism above?

Justice Brennan, in his concurrence, justifies constitutional protection by noting the devastation that severing an extended family may cause. Might a definition of "family" that prevents unrelated persons from living together have the same consequences?

4. Are blood and legal ties conclusive evidence of a family? Suppose John Moore, Jr. is an adult grandchild who is employed, financially independent, pays rent to his grandmother but seldom interacts with her. Or suppose that Inez Moore takes into her home her neighbor's child when the friend becomes terminally ill. Does a blood relationship merit protection of John Jr.'s residential right but not the child's? What factors, other than consanguinity and marriage, are suggestive of the existence of a family? A parent-child relationship? What problems does this approach perpetuate? See Developments in the Law — The Constitution and the Family, 93 Harv. L. Rev. 1156, 1270-1289 (1980).

5. Federal benefit schemes often distinguish among relatives who function as an economic unit. For example, in Lyng v. Castillo, 477 U.S. 635 (1986), the Supreme Court upheld a statute presuming parents, children, and siblings functioned as a single economic unit for food stamp purposes. More distant relatives and unrelated persons were not so presumed, resulting in their larger allotment. Upholding the statute as rational, the Court decided that the distinction did not violate equal protection or burden any fundamental right. Is *Lyng* reconcilable with *Moreno* or *Moore?* See also Bowen v. Gilliard, 483 U.S. 587 (1987).

## Problem

States may remove children from parental custody because of abuse or neglect and place them in foster care. State and federal legislation (for example, Title IV-E of the Social Security Act, 42 U.S.C. §§670-676 (1994 & Supp. V 1999)) often provide foster care subsidies. Title IV-E provides funds without regard to whether foster parents are relatives. However, Oregon provides subsidies only to unrelated foster parents for children who are ineligible under Title IV-E. Relatives now wish to care for three Oregon children who were removed from their parents. Sheri Lipscomb's aunt and uncle, who do not have medical coverage for Sheri (who has multiple disabilities) and who do not receive state foster care payments or medical benefits because they are related to her, fear that they will have to give her up. Two other children's foster parents (also relatives) do give them up for lack of state subsidies. The state then places these latter two children with unrelated foster parents and provides benefits. Sheri and the other children challenge the constitutionality of the state's denial of aid to children whose relatives act as foster parents. What result? See Lipscomb v. Simmons, 884 F.2d 1242 (9th Cir. 1989), *reh'g en banc granted*, 907 F.2d 114 (9th Cir. 1990), decided en banc, 962 F.2d 1374 (9th Cir. 1992). See generally Elizabeth Killackey, Kinship Foster Care, 26 Fam. L.Q. 211 (1992)[2]; Randi Mandelbaum, Trying to Fit Square Pegs into Round Holes: The Need for a New Funding Scheme for Kinship Caregivers, 22 Fordham Urb. L.J. 907 (1995).

## C. COHABITATION: UNMARRIED COUPLES

### 1. Introduction

■ **RICHARD J. GELLES, CONTEMPORARY FAMILIES: A SOCIOLOGICAL VIEW**
*176-178 (1995)*

Cohabitation is the pattern of two unmarried persons of the opposite sex with a romantic interest in each other sharing a residence. It is an increasingly common phenomenon. . . . Thirty years ago, cohabitation as a form of courtship was frowned upon, and participants were subjected to negative social sanctions. Eleanor Macklin, writing about cohabitation in 1972, noted that in 1962 a graduate student at Cornell University was suspended for having a woman living in his apartment. The Cornell University Faculty Council on Student Conduct considered "overnight unchaperoned mixed company" a violation of "sexual morality."

Eight years after Cornell's reprimand to students for cohabitation, there were about 450,000 couples living together in the United States. . . . In 1992, there were 3.3 million unmarried-couple households. . . .

There are a number of reasons why cohabitation has become a more popular and socially acceptable form of relationship in the past 30 years. First, evidence from the Scandinavian countries, such as Denmark and Sweden, where cohabitation is much more common suggests that cohabitation does not undermine or destroy the family. . . . Second, modern advances in contraception make it possible for couples to cohabitate without the complications of pregnancy. Changing gender roles and the status of women have somewhat freed woman from the double standard whereby women who cohabitated were seen as immoral and not suitable marriage partners. Colleges, like Cornell, have changed their views, values, and rules regarding student behavior. The concept of *in loco parentis* (in place of the parents) that dominated college rules and regulations

---

[2]. Note that federal welfare reform legislation requires states to "give preference to an adult relative over a non-related caregiver when determining a placement for a child, provided that the relative caregiver meets all relevant State child protection standards." See Personal Responsibility and Work Opportunity Reconciliation Act of 1996, 42 U.S.C. §671 (1994 & Supp. 1999).

in the 1950s and 1960s and that led to curfews, sign-ins, and other regulations has been eliminated. Campuses now have coeducational residence halls, classes on sex education, and dispense birth control pills and condoms (the latter may be more a concession to the threat of AIDS than a change in attitude about premarital sex).

Off college campuses, the increase in the divorce rate has produced a large pool of single individuals of all ages who seek heterosexual relations without immediately committing to a marriage. . . .

———————————

Data reveal that unmarried heterosexual couples constitute a small but significant percentage of American couples. Currently, there are 3,822,000 unmarried-heterosexual-partner households compared with 55,311,000 married-couple households.[3] Demographers view cohabitation as a stage in the family life cycle rather than a rejection of marriage.[4] According to a recent Census Bureau report, about half of couples marrying today have lived together. About 40 percent of unmarried couples will marry within seven years. Among unmarried couples (compared to married couples), the woman is likely to be older than the man, the couple is more likely to be interracial, the woman is likely to be more highly educated, and there is a smaller earnings gap between the man and the woman. More unmarried-couple households now include children.[5] See generally The Ties That Bind: Perspectives on Marriage and Cohabitation (Linda J. Waite, ed., 2000) (essays on cohabitation).

Official estimates of the numbers of gay and lesbian households also exist (although estimates may be low because many gays and lesbians are reluctant to identify themselves). In 1990, the Bureau of the Census began gathering such information. As of 1998, same-sex partner households made up 28 percent of unmarried partner households.[6]

Cohabitation among gays and lesbians, as a visible social phenomenon, may be traced to the emergence of a gay community in New York City between 1890 and World War II.[7] The second wave of gay ac-

[3]. Bureau of the Census, supra note [1] at 13.
[4]. Bureau of the Census, U.S. Dept. of Commerce, American Families Resilient After 50 Years of Change 2 (Jan. 2001).
[5]. Id.
[6]. Bureau of the Census, U.S. Dept. of Commerce, Household and Family Characteristics (tbl.) (1998). Preliminary data for the 2000 Census reveal that gay male and lesbian couples are evenly divided nationwide, although gay male couples tend to cluster in big cities whereas lesbian couples, who are more likely to have children, prefer suburban and rural areas. Carol Ness, Census 2000: S.F. Upstaged as Gay Mecca, S.F. Chron., Aug. 8, 2001, at A1.
[7]. George Chauncey, Gay New York: Gender, Urban Culture, and the Making of a Gay Male World, 1890-1940, at 1 (1994).

tivism, following the Stonewall rebellion in 1969 in New York City, also led to an increase in the numbers of gay and lesbian cohabitants. Recently, the threat of AIDS has spurred an increasing number of gay men to seek long-term monogamous relationships.

## 2. Traditional Response: Criminal Sanctions

### ■ DOE v. DULING
*782 F.2d 1202 (4th Cir. 1986)*

WILKINSON, Circuit Judge.

Plaintiffs brought suit under the pseudonyms Jane Doe and James Doe challenging the constitutionality of Virginia statutes prohibiting fornication and cohabitation. . . .

Plaintiffs (appellees in this action) are unmarried adults who maintain separate residences in the City of Richmond. [T]hey state that they have engaged in sexual intercourse in the city with unmarried members of the opposite sex. Jane Doe further alleges that she has engaged in unlawful cohabitation. The Does believe that fornication and cohabitation are "common forms of conduct in society generally and in the City of Richmond in particular" and that an arrest for such activity could cause them "considerable personal embarrassment" and affect professional standing. Though neither has ever been arrested or threatened with arrest for violation of these statutes, the Does maintain each has abstained from sexual intercourse and cohabitation since they learned of the laws in question for fear of prosecution. Finally, each expresses a desire to engage in private, consensual heterosexual activity free from government intrusion.

Virginia has prohibited fornication since at least 1819. The current code provides that "[a]ny person, not being married, who voluntarily shall have sexual intercourse with any other person shall be guilty of fornication," Va. Code §18.2-344 (1982). The last reported conviction for fornication in Virginia was in 1849.

Cohabitation is prohibited under §18.2-345 of the current code: "If any persons, not married to each other, lewdly and lasciviously associate and cohabit together, or whether married or not, be guilty of open and gross lewdness and lasciviousness, each of them shall be guilty of a . . . misdemeanor." This section contains two distinct prohibitions, the second of which involves open and conspicuous lewd behavior. The cohabitation offense presumably requires no such openness. Virginia has maintained its statutory prohibition on cohabitation for well over 100 years. The last recorded conviction for private, consensual cohabitation occurred in 1883.

The Does introduced depositions of police officers and arrest records that purportedly reveal a pattern of current enforcement on which their fears of prosecution are grounded. Four current or former members of the Richmond vice division testified in general terms that all laws are enforced and specifically stated that they would investigate complaints of fornication and cohabitation if time and personnel limitations allowed. None of the officers, however, recalled any arrests for fornication in a private, consensual setting except for those involving prostitution. . . . None of the officers recalled a cohabitation arrest since 1976. [Lieutenant] Carlson stated his belief that cohabitation had to involve open sexual conduct before it fell within the prohibitions of the statute.

The arrest records [of several fornication cases] entered into evidence bear this testimony out. The parties stipulated that none of these arrests involved fornication in a private residence. [A]ll involved public conduct. Two arrests, for example, were of individuals in a car; three arrests occurred in a public park.

The district court . . . found that the Does had standing [Doe v. Duling, 603 F. Supp. at 964]. Recognizing that there must be "a threat of prosecution sufficient to make this controversy ripe for review," id., the court held that the general policy of enforcing criminal laws, coupled with recent enforcement of the challenged statutes, established a credible threat, making the case ripe for review. On the merits, the court found that "the constitutional right to privacy extends to a single adult's decision whether to engage in sexual intercourse." Id. at 967. Finding no compelling state interest, it struck down the fornication statute and that portion of §18.2-345 prohibiting cohabitation. It found the prohibition in §18.2-345 of "open and gross lewdness and lasciviousness" within the state's proper sphere of regulation. . . .

The Supreme Court has made it abundantly clear that one challenging the validity of a criminal statute must show a threat of prosecution under the statute to present a case or controversy. . . . The record in this case establishes that the Does face only the most theoretical threat of prosecution. . . .

The Does maintain, however, that they are fearful of cohabiting or engaging in sexual intercourse since they have learned of the statutes in question. Such subjective fear of prosecution does not establish an objective threat. . . . Every criminal law, by its very existence, may have some chilling effect on personal behavior. That was the reason for its passage. . . .

There is no better example of the need for judicial circumspection than the instant case. In the absence of a threat of prosecution, this action represents no more than an abstract debate, albeit a volatile one. . . . The briefs before this court present instead the clash of argument in the abstract that would be better suited to a campaign for public office or a legislative hearing.

We are not concerned that this unenforced statute may escape the attention of the political process. Nor are we persuaded by the argument that if quaint statutes are never enforced, then defendants' constitutional rights will never be tested, and the Does lack any meaningful remedy. The absence of a "remedy" works no injustice on those who have never suffered so much as the threat of an injury. Furthermore, statutes whose status may be largely symbolic are appropriate subjects for political debate.

The instant case well illustrates this point. To many, the Virginia statutes here compromise the sacred component of privacy in sexual expression. They represent the potential intrusion of the state into the sanctity of the home or apartment, the potential for police action on nothing more than pretext and suspicion, and the imposition of antiquated attitudes about sex that bear little relevance to the diversity of individual lifestyles in a contemporary world. To others, these statutes express the value society places upon the life of the family and the institution of marriage, upon the realization of love through the encouragement of sexual fidelity, and upon the prevention of sexually transmitted diseases brought on by promiscuity. They discern in old laws renewed relevance as traditional values come under siege.

Each view has its adherents, and the pendulum of social conscience will doubtless swing between the two indefinitely. It is, however, for state legislatures, not federal courts, to face that political choice. . . .

■ **BOWERS v. HARDWICK**
*478 U.S. 186 (1986)*

Review pages **50-51.**

## Notes and Questions

1. *Historical background.* Traditionally, nonmarital fornication and cohabitation were considered deviant behavior and subject to criminal sanctions. See Edwin Powers, Crime and Punishment in Early Massachusetts 1620-1692: A Documentary History *passim* (1966). Efforts to revise or repeal these criminal statutes took place against a backdrop of national reforms. The drafters of the Model Penal Code first proposed criminalizing cohabitation only if "open and notorious." Model Penal Code §207.1 (Tent. Draft No. 4, 1955). Subsequently, the ALI Council voted to delete the section because the law was seldom enforced, inconsistent with the widespread policy of nonenforcement of moral standards, without deterrent value, and prone to discriminatory enforcement. Id. at cmt.

2. The legal response to sexual activity between gays and lesbians, similarly, has been punitive. Criminal prohibitions on sodomy (consensual

oral or anal sex) exist in 18 states. Aimee D. Dayhoff, Sodomy Laws: The Government's Vehicle to Impose the Majority's Social Values, 27 Wm. Mitchell L. Rev. 1863, 1864 (2001). How do such laws, if unenforced, harm gays and lesbians? See Christopher R. Leslie, Creating Criminals: The Injuries Inflicted by "Unenforced" Sodomy Laws, 35 Harv. C.R.-C.L. L. Rev. 103 (2000).

Reform efforts have targeted state sodomy laws. In 1955 (when all states had prohibitions), the ALI recommended decriminalization. Model Penal Code §207.5 (Tent. Draft No. 4, 1955). See also Model Penal Code §213.2 (Prop. Off. Draft 1962). In response, more than 20 state legislatures repealed their laws. Paula A. Brantner, Note, Removing Bricks from a Wall of Discrimination: State Constitutional Challenges to Sodomy Laws, 19 Hastings Const. L.Q. 495 (1992). More recently, gays and lesbians have achieved a measure of success by challenging sodomy laws on state constitutional grounds. Indeed, in Powell v. State, 510 S.E.2d 18 (Ga. 1998), the Georgia Supreme Court declared the state's sodomy statute (at issue in Bowers v. Hardwick) violative of due process under the state constitution. But cf. Lawrence v. State, 41 S.W.3d 349 (Tex. Crim. App. 2001) (upholding conviction of gay men for engaging in consensual sex in their home, reasoning that Texas sodomy statute does not violate equal protection or right to privacy).

3. Why distinguish between private and public ("open and notorious") acts as the basis for sanctions? Why are such acts offensive? The drafters of the Model Penal Code believed that the public nature of cohabitation might provoke violence. Is this concern realistic?

4. If the appellate court in *Duling* had addressed the right to privacy, what should be the outcome? The district court, which upheld the Does' challenge, focused on the Supreme Court's affirmation (in *Griswold, Eisenstadt,* and *Roe*) of the right to privacy regarding childbearing. Should the decision to have (or not to have) children determine the applicability of privacy rights? Is the district court correct that the right to sexual privacy is limited to procreational rights? If so, how does one explain Stanley v. Georgia, 394 U.S. 557 (1969) (upholding the right to possess pornography)? But see Osborne v. Ohio, 495 U.S. 103 (1990) (upholding conviction for possession of child pornography in the home). One commentator has quipped: "One would be hard pressed to claim ingenuously that the right to possess pornography in one's home, indeed to use it as one's sexual stimulation, even for a lifetime, was essentially a form of family planning." Richard D. Mohr, Mr. Justice Douglas at Sodom: Gays and Privacy, 18 Colum. Hum. Rts. L. Rev. 43, 82 (1986).

5. The plaintiffs in *Duling* attacked the fornication and cohabitation statutes as violations of their right to privacy as well as freedom of association and expression (although the district court only addressed the privacy claim). What is the relationship between the First Amendment

and privacy? Professor Kenneth Karst argues that "[t]he intimacies threatened in *Griswold* were another form of expressive conduct, 'the speech of loving.'" Kenneth L. Karst, The Freedom of Intimate Association, 89 Yale. L.J. 624, 653 (1980). Karst contends that *Griswold* established not a right to privacy but a right to intimate association that protects familial-like relationships. He speculates that courts may avoid deciding cases on this ground because "[a]lmost everything we do is expressive in one way or another. . . . The First Amendment would, in short, be stretched to cover all our constitutional freedoms." Id. at 654. Gays and lesbians also argue that governmental restrictions on homosexuals implicate the First Amendment's protection of expressive conduct. See David Cole & William N. Eskridge, Jr., From Hand-Holding to Sodomy: First Amendment Protection of Homosexual (Expressive) Conduct, 29 Harv. C.R.-C.L. L. Rev. 319 (1994).

6. Do cohabitation statutes violate equal protection? See Martha L. Fineman, Law and Changing Patterns of Behavior: Sanctions on Non-Marital Cohabitation, 1981 Wis. L. Rev. 275, 314-315 (so arguing).

7. *Law and morality.* The relationship between law and morality has prompted considerable philosophical debate. John Stuart Mill, a staunch opponent of state paternalism, asserted that the only rationale for state restriction on liberty is to prevent harm to others. John Stuart Mill, On Liberty 13 (Gateway ed. 1959). Are cohabitation, fornication, and sodomy "victimless crimes," or do they cause harm? See Fineman, supra, at 303 (characterizing potential harm from cohabitation). What justifies criminal sanctions? Is the prevention of such social problems as illegitimacy and/or disease a proper object of legislation? Are these problems sufficiently important to outweigh the right to privacy? See generally Jerome H. Skolnick, Coercion to Virtue: The Enforcement of Morals, 41 S. Cal. L. Rev. 588 (1968).

A critic of Mill, Sir Patrick Devlin, counters that society is entitled to prevent harm perpetrated by the "weakness or vice of too many of its members." Patrick Devlin, The Enforcement of Morals 104 (1965). Do cohabitation bans safeguard society? Participants? Women? Is such paternalism justifiable? Advisable? Might such sexual conduct have positive consequences? Might suppressive measures produce socially undesirable effects?

8. In *Duling* the district court and the court of appeals reached different conclusions on the threat of prosecution. How realistic is this threat? Limited empirical data reveal that situations most likely to prompt prosecution for cohabitation include (1) welfare fraud; (2) domestic violence complaints; (3) complaints by cohabitants' family members; and (4) investigation of unrelated criminal conduct. Fineman, supra, at 287-293 (study of prosecution rates in Wisconsin during a five-year period that reported 90 prosecutions in 12 counties). Do these findings support the views of the ALI Council, supra, that these laws are seldom enforced,

have no deterrent value, and result in discriminatory enforcement? Wisconsin subsequently abolished criminal sanctions for cohabitation.

By the same token, sodomy laws are seldom enforced. (Recall in *Bowers* that the district attorney decided not to take the matter to the grand jury.) If this is so, why do many gays and lesbians earnestly seek to repeal such laws?

9. Should law reformers direct their efforts to the repeal of prohibitions against sexual conduct or adopt other approaches? Professor Karst writes that "[t]he more serious questions concerning marriage-like relationships do not concern laws forbidding fornication or adultery, which largely go unenforced in any event, but the conditioning of various benefits on marital status, or on the termination of unmarried cohabitation." Karst, supra, at 674. Should civil and/or criminal penalties be abolished?

10. Prosecutors have found a new use for fornication laws. In Idaho prosecutors are bringing fornication charges against pregnant teens and their boyfriends in an attempt to prevent teen pregnancies. (Most of the girls were arrested after they applied for state assistance.) Is this an appropriate use of such statutes? See Heidi Meinzer, Idaho's Throwback to Elizabethan England: Criminalizing a Civil Proceeding?, 34 Fam. L.Q. 165 (2000).

## 3. Unmarried Couples' Rights Inter Se

■ **MARVIN v. MARVIN**
*557 P.2d 106 (Cal. 1976)*

Tobriner, Justice.

During the past 15 years, there has been a substantial increase in the number of couples living together without marrying. Such nonmarital relationships lead to legal controversy when one partner dies or the couple separates. Courts of Appeal, faced with the task of determining property rights in such cases, have arrived at conflicting positions. . . . We take this opportunity to resolve that controversy and to declare the principles which should govern distribution of property acquired in a nonmarital relationship. . . .

. . . In the instant case plaintiff and defendant lived together for seven years without marrying; all property acquired during this period was taken in defendant's name. When plaintiff sued to enforce a contract under which she was entitled to half the property and to support payments, the trial court granted judgment on the pleadings for defendant, thus leaving him with all property accumulated by the couple during their relationship. . . .

Since the trial court rendered judgment for defendant on the pleadings, we must accept the allegations of plaintiff's complaint as true, determining whether such allegations state, or can be amended to state, a cause of action. We turn therefore to the specific allegations of the complaint.

Plaintiff avers that in October of 1964 she and defendant "entered into an oral agreement" that while "the parties lived together they would combine their efforts and earnings and would share equally any and all property accumulated as a result of their efforts whether individual or combined." Furthermore, they agreed to "hold themselves out to the general public as husband and wife" and that "plaintiff would further render her services as a companion, homemaker, housekeeper and cook to . . . defendant."

Shortly thereafter plaintiff agreed to "give up her lucrative career as an entertainer [and] singer" in order to "devote her full time to defendant . . . as a companion, homemaker, housekeeper and cook"; in return defendant agreed to "provide for all of plaintiff's financial support and needs for the rest of her life."

Plaintiff alleges that she lived with defendant from October of 1964 through May of 1970 and fulfilled her obligations under the agreement. During this period the parties as a result of their efforts and earnings acquired in defendant's name substantial real and personal property, including motion picture rights worth over $1 million. In May of 1970, however, defendant compelled plaintiff to leave his household. He continued to support plaintiff until November of 1971, but thereafter refused to provide further support. . . .

[D]efendant offers some four theories to sustain the ruling. . . . Defendant first and principally relies on the contention that the alleged contract is so closely related to the supposed "immoral" character of the relationship between plaintiff and himself that the enforcement of the contract would violate public policy.[4] He points to cases asserting that a contract between nonmarital partners is unenforceable if it is "involved in" an illicit relationship. A review of the numerous California decisions concerning contracts between nonmarital partners, however, reveals that the courts have not employed such broad and uncertain standards to strike down contracts. The decisions instead disclose a narrower and more precise standard: a contract between nonmarital partners is unenforceable only *to the extent* that it *explicitly* rests upon the immoral and illicit consideration of meretricious sexual services. . . .

---

4. Defendant also contends that the contract was illegal because it contemplated a violation of former Penal Code section 269a, which prohibited living "in a state of cohabitation and adultery." (§269a was repealed by Stats. 1975, ch. 71, eff. Jan. 1, 1976.) Defendant's standing to raise the issue is questionable because he alone was married and thus guilty of violating section 269a. . . . The numerous cases discussing the contractual rights of unmarried couples have drawn no distinction between illegal relationships and lawful nonmarital relationships. Moreover, even if we were to draw such a distinction . . . plaintiff sought to amend her complaint to assert that the parties reaffirmed their contract after [his] divorce.

Although the past decisions hover over the issue in the somewhat wispy form of the figures of a Chagall painting, we can abstract from those decisions a clear and simple rule. The fact that a man and woman live together without marriage, and engage in a sexual relationship, does not in itself invalidate agreements between them relating to their earnings, property, or expenses. Neither is such an agreement invalid merely because the parties may have contemplated the creation or continuation of a nonmarital relationship when they entered into it. Agreements between nonmarital partners fail only to the extent that they rest upon a consideration of meretricious sexual services. Thus the rule asserted by defendant, that a contract fails if it is "involved in" or made "in contemplation" of a nonmarital relationship, cannot be reconciled with the decisions. . . .

The principle that a contract between nonmarital partners will be enforced unless expressly and inseparably based upon an illicit consideration of sexual services not only represents the distillation of the decisional law, but also offers a far more precise and workable standard than that advocated by defendant. [A] standard which inquires whether an agreement is "involved" in or "contemplates" a nonmarital relationship is vague and unworkable. Virtually all agreements between nonmarital partners can be said to be "involved" in some sense in the fact of their mutual sexual relationship, or to "contemplate" the existence of that relationship. Thus defendant's proposed standards, if taken literally, might invalidate all agreements between nonmarital partners, a result no one favors. Moreover, those standards offer no basis to distinguish between valid and invalid agreements. By looking not to such uncertain tests, but only to the consideration underlying the agreement, we provide the parties and the courts with a practical guide to determine when an agreement between nonmarital partners should be enforced.

Defendant secondly relies upon the ground suggested by the trial court: that the 1964 contract violated public policy because it impaired the community property rights of Betty Marvin, defendant's lawful wife. . . . In the present case Betty Marvin, the aggrieved spouse, had the opportunity to assert her community property rights in the divorce action. The interlocutory and final decrees in that action fix and limit her interest. Enforcement of the contract between plaintiff and defendant against property awarded to defendant by the divorce decree will not impair any right of Betty's, and thus is not on that account violative of public policy.

Defendant's third contention is . . . that enforcement of the oral agreement between plaintiff and himself is barred by Civil Code section 5134, which provides that "All contracts for marriage settlements must be in writing. . . ." A marriage settlement, however, is an agreement in contemplation of marriage. . . . The contract at issue here does not conceivably fall within that definition. [The court also rejected, as a "rather strained contention," defendant's fourth argument that plaintiff was asserting a claim for breach of promise to marry, barred by statute.]

In summary, we base our opinion on the principle that adults who voluntarily live together and engage in sexual relations are nonetheless as competent as any other persons to contract respecting their earnings and property rights. Of course, they cannot lawfully contract to pay for the performance of sexual services, for such a contract is, in essence, an agreement for prostitution and unlawful for that reason. . . . So long as the agreement does not rest upon illicit meretricious consideration, the parties may order their economic affairs as they choose, and no policy precludes the courts from enforcing such agreements.

In the present instance, plaintiff alleges that the parties agreed to pool their earnings, that they contracted to share equally in all property acquired, and that defendant agreed to support plaintiff. The terms of the contract as alleged do not rest upon any unlawful consideration. We therefore conclude that the complaint furnishes a suitable basis upon which the trial court can render declaratory relief. The trial court consequently erred in granting defendant's motion for judgment on the pleadings. . . .

As we have noted, both causes of action in plaintiff's complaint allege an express contract; neither assert any basis for relief independent from the contract. In In re Marriage of Cary, [109 Cal. Rptr. 862 (1973)], however, the Court of Appeal held that, in view of the policy of the Family Law Act, property accumulated by nonmarital partners in an actual family relationship should be divided equally. . . . Although our conclusion that plaintiff's complaint states a cause of action based on an express contract alone compels us to reverse the judgment for defendant, resolution of the *Cary* issue will serve both to guide the parties upon retrial and to resolve a conflict presently manifest in published Court of Appeal decisions.

Both plaintiff and defendant stand in broad agreement that the law should be fashioned to carry out the reasonable expectations of the parties. Plaintiff, however, presents the following contentions: that the decisions prior to *Cary* rest upon implicit and erroneous notions of punishing a party for his or her guilt in entering into a nonmarital relationship, that such decisions result in an inequitable distribution of property accumulated during the relationship, and that *Cary* correctly held that the enactment of the Family Law Act in 1970 overturned those prior decisions. Defendant in response maintains that the prior decisions merely applied common law principles of contract and property to persons who have deliberately elected to remain outside the bounds of the community property system. *Cary*, defendant contends, erred in holding that the Family Law Act vitiated the force of the prior precedents.

[T]he truth lies somewhere between the positions of plaintiff and defendant. The classic opinion on this subject is Vallera v. Vallera, [134 P.2d

761 (Cal. 1943)]. Speaking for a four-member majority, Justice Traynor posed the question: "whether a woman living with a man as his wife but with no genuine belief that she is legally married to him acquires by reason of cohabitation alone the rights of a co-tenant in his earnings and accumulations during the period of their relationship." [T]he majority answered that question "in the negative." *Vallera* explains that "Equitable considerations arising from the reasonable expectation of the continuation of benefits attending the status of marriage entered into in good faith are not present in such a case." (134 P.2d at 763.) In the absence of express contract, *Vallera* concluded, the woman is entitled to share in property jointly accumulated only "in the proportion that her funds contributed toward its acquisition." . . .

The majority opinion in *Vallera* did not expressly bar recovery based upon an implied contract, nor preclude resort to equitable remedies. But *Vallera*'s broad assertion that equitable considerations "are not present" in the case of a nonmarital relationship led the Courts of Appeal to interpret the language to preclude recovery based on such theories. . . .

Consequently, when the issue of the rights of a nonmarital partner reached this court in Keene v. Keene, [371 P.2d 329 (Cal. 1962)], the claimant forwent reliance upon theories of contract implied in law or fact. Asserting that she had worked on her partner's ranch and that her labor had enhanced its value, she confined her cause of action to the claim that the court should impress a resulting trust on the property derived from the sale of the ranch. The court limited its opinion accordingly, rejecting her argument on the ground that the rendition of services gives rise to a resulting trust only when the services aid in acquisition of the property, not in its subsequent improvement. . . .

Thus in summary, the cases prior to *Cary* exhibited a schizophrenic inconsistency. By enforcing an express contract between nonmarital partners unless it rested upon an unlawful consideration, the courts applied a common law principle as to contracts. Yet the courts disregarded the common law principle that holds that implied contracts can arise from the conduct of the parties. Refusing to enforce such contracts, the courts spoke of leaving the parties "in the position in which they had placed themselves," just as if they were guilty parties "in pari delicto."

Justice Curtis noted this inconsistency in his dissenting opinion in *Vallera*, pointing out that "if an express agreement will be enforced, there is no legal or just reason why an implied agreement to share the property cannot be enforced." (134 P.2d at 764; see Bruch, Property Rights of De Facto Spouses Including Thoughts on the Value of Homemakers' Services (1976) 10 Family L.Q. 101, 117-121.) And in Keene v. Keene, [371 P.2d 329 (1962),] Justice Peters observed that if the man and woman "were not illegally living together . . . it would be a plain business relationship and a contract would be implied." [371 P.2d at 338 (diss. opn.).]

Still another inconsistency in the prior cases arises from their treatment of property accumulated through joint effort. To the extent that a partner had contributed *funds* or *property*, the cases held that the partner obtains a proportionate share in the acquisition, despite the lack of legal standing of the relationship. Yet courts have refused to recognize just such an interest based upon the contribution of *services*. As Justice Curtis points out "Unless it can be argued that a woman's services as cook, housekeeper, and homemaker are valueless, it would seem logical that if, when she contributes money to the purchase of property, her interest will be protected, then when she contributes her services in the home, her interest in property accumulated should be protected." (Vallera v. Vallera, 134 P.2d at 764 (diss. opn.).)

Thus as of 1973, the time of the filing of In re Marriage of Cary, the cases apparently held that a nonmarital partner who rendered services in the absence of express contract could assert no right to property acquired during the relationship. The facts of *Cary* demonstrated the unfairness of that rule.

Janet and Paul Cary had lived together, unmarried, for more than eight years. They held themselves out to friends and family as husband and wife, reared four children, purchased a home and other property, obtained credit, filed joint income tax returns, and otherwise conducted themselves as though they were married. Paul worked outside the home, and Janet generally cared for the house and children.

In 1971 Paul petitioned for "nullity of the marriage." Following a hearing on that petition, the trial court awarded Janet half the property acquired during the relationship, although all such property was traceable to Paul's earnings. The Court of Appeal affirmed the award [reasoning that prior cases that denied relief were based] upon a policy of punishing persons guilty of cohabitation without marriage. The Family Law Act, the court observed, aimed to eliminate fault or guilt as a basis for dividing marital property. But once fault or guilt is excluded, the court reasoned, nothing distinguishes the property rights of a nonmarital "spouse" from those of a putative spouse. Since the latter is entitled to half the "quasi marital property" (Civ. Code §4452), the Court of Appeal concluded that, giving effect to the policy of the Family Law Act, a nonmarital cohabitator should also be entitled to half the property accumulated during an "actual family relationship."

*Cary* met with a mixed reception in other appellate districts. [W]e agree [with the view] that *Cary* distends the act. No language in the Family Law Act addresses the property rights of nonmarital partners, and nothing in the legislative history of the act suggests that the Legislature considered that subject. [A]lthough we reject the reasoning of *Cary* . . . , we share the perception . . . that the application of former precedent in the factual setting of those cases would work an unfair distribution of the property accumulated by the couple. . . .

The principal reason why the pre-*Cary* decisions result in an unfair distribution of property inheres in the court's refusal to permit a nonmarital partner to assert rights based upon accepted principles of implied contract or equity. We have examined the reasons advanced to justify this denial of relief, and find that none have merit.

First, we note that the cases denying relief do not rest their refusal upon any theory of "punishing" a "guilty" partner. Indeed, to the extent that denial of relief "punishes" one partner, it necessarily rewards the other by permitting him to retain a disproportionate amount of the property. Concepts of "guilt" thus cannot justify an unequal division of property between two equally "guilty" persons.

Other reasons advanced in the decisions fare no better. The principal argument seems to be that "[e]quitable considerations arising from the reasonable expectation of . . . benefits attending the status of marriage . . . are not present (in a nonmarital relationship)." (Vallera v. Vallera, 134 P.2d at 763.) But, although parties to a nonmarital relationship obviously cannot have based any expectations upon the belief that they were married, other expectations and equitable considerations remain. The parties may well expect that property will be divided in accord with the parties' own tacit understanding and that in the absence of such understanding the courts will fairly apportion property accumulated through mutual effort. We need not treat nonmarital partners as putatively married persons in order to apply principles of implied contract, or extend equitable remedies; we need to treat them only as we do any other unmarried persons.

The remaining arguments advanced from time to time to deny remedies to the nonmarital partners are of less moment. There is no more reason to presume that services are contributed as a gift than to presume that funds are contributed as a gift; in any event the better approach is to presume, as Justice Peters suggested, "that the parties intend to deal fairly with each other." [Keene v. Keene, 371 P.2d at 339 (diss. opn.).]

The argument that granting remedies to the nonmarital partners would discourage marriage must fail; as *Cary* pointed out, "with equal or greater force the point might be made that the pre-1970 rule was calculated to cause the income producing partner to avoid marriage and thus retain the benefit of all of his or her accumulated earnings." [109 Cal. Rptr. at 866.] Although we recognize the well-established public policy to foster and promote the institution of marriage, perpetuation of judicial rules which result in an inequitable distribution of property accumulated during a nonmarital relationship is neither a just nor an effective way of carrying out that policy.

In summary, we believe that the prevalence of nonmarital relationships in modern society and the social acceptance of them, marks this as a time when our courts should by no means apply the doctrine of the unlawfulness of the so-called meretricious relationship to the instant case. As we have explained, the nonenforceability of agreements expressly providing for meretricious conduct rested upon the fact that such conduct, as the word suggests, pertained to and encompassed prostitution. To equate the nonmarital relationship of today to such a subject matter is to do violence to an accepted and wholly different practice.

We are aware that many young couples live together without the solemnization of marriage, in order to make sure that they can successfully later undertake marriage. This trial period, preliminary to marriage, serves as some assurance that the marriage will not subsequently end in dissolution to the harm of both parties. We are aware, as we have stated, of the pervasiveness of nonmarital relationships in other situations.

The mores of the society have indeed changed so radically in regard to cohabitation that we cannot impose a standard based on alleged moral considerations that have apparently been so widely abandoned by so many. Lest we be misunderstood, however, we take this occasion to point out that the structure of society itself largely depends upon the institution of marriage, and nothing we have said in this opinion should be taken to derogate from that institution. The joining of the man and woman in marriage is at once the most socially productive and individually fulfilling relationship that one can enjoy in the course of a lifetime.

We conclude that the judicial barriers that may stand in the way of a policy based upon the fulfillment of the reasonable expectations of the parties to a nonmarital relationship should be removed. As we have explained, the courts now hold that express agreements will be enforced unless they rest on an unlawful meretricious consideration. We add that in the absence of an express agreement, the courts may look to a variety of other remedies in order to protect the parties' lawful expectations.[24]

The courts may inquire into the conduct of the parties to determine whether that conduct demonstrates an implied contract or implied agreement of partnership or joint venture, or some other tacit understanding between the parties. The courts may, when appropriate, employ principles of constructive trust. Finally, a nonmarital partner may recover in quantum meruit for the reasonable value of household services rendered less the reasonable value of support received if he can show that he rendered services with the expectation of monetary reward.[25]

24. We do not seek to resurrect the doctrine of common law marriage, which was abolished in California by statute in 1895. Thus we do not hold that plaintiff and defendant were "married," nor do we extend to plaintiff the rights which the Family Law Act grants valid or putative spouses; we hold only that she has the same rights to enforce contracts and to assert her equitable interest in property acquired through her effort as does any other unmarried person.

25. Our opinion does not preclude the evolution of additional equitable remedies to protect the expectations of the parties to a nonmarital relationship in cases in which existing remedies prove inadequate; the suitability of such remedies may be determined in later cases in light of the factual setting in which they arise.

Since we have determined that plaintiff's complaint states a cause of action for breach of an express contract, and, as we have explained, can be amended to state a cause of action independent of allegations of express contract,[26] we must conclude that the trial court erred in granting defendant a judgment on the pleadings. [R]eversed and . . . remanded for further proceedings consistent with the views expressed herein.

## ■ M. v. H.
### [1999] 2 S.C.R. 3 [Canadian Supreme Court]

CORY, J.:

. . . The question to be resolved is whether the extension of the right to seek [spousal] support to members of unmarried opposite-sex couples infringes §15(1) of the Charter* [Canada's equivalent to the U.S. Constitution's Equal Protection Clause] by failing to provide the same rights to members of same-sex couples.

### FACTUAL BACKGROUND

M. and H. are women who met while on vacation in 1980. It is agreed that in 1982 they started living together in a same-sex relationship that continued for at least five years. That relationship may have lasted ten years, but that figure is disputed by H. During that time they occupied a home which H. had owned since 1974. H. paid for the upkeep of the home, but the parties agreed to share living expenses and household responsibilities equally. At the time, H. was employed in an advertising firm and M. ran her own company.

In 1982, M. and H. started their own advertising business. The business enjoyed immediate success and was the main source of income for the couple during the relationship. H.'s contribution to this company was greater than that of M. [The trial judge] observed that this disparity was probably due to the fact that M. had no previous experience in advertising, and, as time went on, she was content to devote more of her time to domestic tasks rather than the business. Nevertheless, the parties continued to be equal shareholders in the company.

In 1983, M. and H. purchased a business property together. In 1986, they purchased as joint tenants a vacation property in the coun-

---

26. We do not pass upon the question whether, in the absence of an express or implied contractual obligation, a party to a nonmarital relationship is entitled to support payments from the other party after the relationship terminates.

*Charter of Rights and Freedoms: §15. "(1) Every individual is equal before and under the law and has the right to the equal protection and equal benefit of the law without discrimination and, in particular, without discrimination based on race, national or ethnic origin, colour, religion, sex, age or mental or physical disability."

try. They later sold the business property and used the proceeds to finance the construction of a home on the country property.

As a result of a dramatic downturn in the advertising business in the late 1980s, the parties' debt increased significantly. H. took a job outside the firm and placed a mortgage on her home to pay for her expenses and those of M. M. also tried to find employment but was unsuccessful. Her company, which she had continued to run on a casual basis throughout the relationship, produced very little income.

By September of 1992, M. and H.'s relationship had deteriorated. H. was concerned about what she perceived to be an unfair disparity in their relative financial contributions. H. presented M. with a draft agreement to settle their affairs. The same day that the agreement was presented, M. took some of her personal belongings and left the common home. Upon M.'s departure, H. changed the locks on the house.

The parties did not divide the personal property or household contents. M. alleged that she encountered serious financial problems after the separation. In October 1992, M. sought an order for [partition and sale of the house, a share of the business, and a claim for support under the Family Law Act (FLA). She also challenged the constitutionality of Section 29 of the Act (explained below). H.'s motion for summary judgment was dismissed.]

Analysis

To begin, it may be useful to review briefly the structure of the FLA and the rights and obligations it establishes. First and foremost, it is of critical importance to recognize that the FLA contains more than one definition of "spouse." The first definition is set out in §1(1) [the definitional section of the FLA] and includes only persons who are actually married, or who have entered into a void or voidable marriage in good faith. This definition applies to all parts of the Act.

The second definition is found in §29, and extends the meaning of "spouse," but only for certain purposes. Specifically, unmarried opposite-sex couples who have cohabited for at least three years, or who are the natural or adoptive parents of a child and have also cohabited in a relationship of "some permanence," bear a mutual obligation of support under Part III of the FLA. They also have the right to enter into cohabitation agreements to regulate their relationship under Part IV, and may bring a claim for dependants' relief in tort under Part V. . . .

In other words, the FLA draws a distinction by specifically according rights to individual members of unmarried cohabiting opposite-sex couples, which by omission it fails to accord to individual members of same-sex couples who are living together. It is this distinction that lies at the heart of the §15 analysis. The rights and obligations that exist between married persons play no part in this analysis. The legislature did not extend full marital status, for the purposes of all the rights and obligations under the FLA, to those unmarried cohabitants included in §29 of the Act. Rather, the definition of "spouse" in §29 only applies for certain purposes. Specifically, it allows persons who became financially dependent in the course of a lengthy intimate relationship some relief from financial hardship resulting from the breakdown of that relationship. It follows that this provision was designed to reduce the demands on the public welfare system. . . .

It is true that women in common law relationships often tended to become financially dependent on their male partners because they raised their children and because of their unequal earning power. But the legislature drafted §29 to allow either a man or a woman to apply for support, thereby recognizing that financial dependence can arise in an intimate relationship in a context entirely unrelated either to child rearing or to any gender-based discrimination existing in our society. . . .

It is thus apparent that in this appeal there is no need to consider whether same-sex couples can marry, or whether same-sex couples must, for all purposes, be treated in the same manner as unmarried opposite-sex couples. The only determination that must be made is whether, in extending the spousal support obligations set out in Part III of the FLA to include unmarried men or women in certain opposite-sex relationships, the legislature infringed the equality rights of men or women in similar same-sex relationships. . . .

[The FLA provides that "spousal support" is available to those members of unmarried couples who meet the minimum criteria of a three-year cohabitation or parenthood.] Same-sex relationships are capable of meeting the last two requirements. Certainly same-sex couples will often form long, lasting, loving and intimate relationships. The choices they make in the context of those relationships may give rise to the financial dependence of one partner on the other. . . .

Molodowich v. Penttinen (1980), 17 R.F.L. (2d) 376 (Ont. Dist. Ct.), sets out the generally accepted characteristics of a conjugal relationship. They include shared shelter, sexual and personal behaviour, services, social activities, economic support and children, as well as the societal perception of the couple. However, it was recognized that these elements may be present in varying degrees and not all are necessary for the relationship to be found to be conjugal. . . . Obviously the weight to be accorded the various elements or factors to be considered in determining whether an opposite-sex couple is in a conjugal relationship will vary widely and almost infinitely. The same must hold true of same-sex couples. Courts have wisely determined that the approach to determining whether a relationship is conjugal must be flexible. . . . In these circumstances, the Court of Appeal correctly concluded that there is nothing to suggest that same-sex couples do not meet the legal definition of "conjugal."

Since gay and lesbian individuals are capable of being involved in conjugal relationships, and since their relationships are capable of meeting the FLA's temporal requirements, the distinction of relevance to this appeal is between persons in an opposite-sex, conjugal relationship of some permanence and persons in a same-sex, conjugal relationship of some permanence. . . .

[T]he first broad inquiry in the §15(1) analysis determines whether there is differential treatment imposed by the impugned legislation between the claimant and others. It is clear that there is differential treatment here. Under §29 of the FLA, members of opposite-sex couples who can meet the requirements of the statute are able to gain access to the court-enforced system of support provided by the FLA. It is this system that ensures the provision of support to a dependent spouse. Members of same-sex couples are denied access to this system entirely on the basis of their sexual orientation. . . .

In [Law v. Canada (Minister of Employment and Immigration), [1999] 1 S.C.R. 497], Iacobucci J. explained that there are a variety of contextual factors that may be referred to by a §15(1) claimant in order to demonstrate that legislation demeans his or her dignity . . . :

> As has been consistently recognized throughout this Court's jurisprudence, probably the most compelling factor favouring a conclusion that differential treatment imposed by legislation is truly discriminatory will be, where it exists, pre-existing disadvantage, vulnerability, stereotyping, or prejudice experienced by the individual or group [citations omitted]. These factors are relevant because, to the extent that the claimant is already subject to unfair circumstances or treatment in society by virtue of personal characteristics or circumstances, persons like him or her have often not been given equal concern, respect, and consideration. It is logical to conclude that, in most cases, further differential treatment will contribute to the perpetuation or promotion of their unfair social characterization, and will have a more severe impact upon them, since they are already vulnerable.

In this case, there is significant pre-existing disadvantage and vulnerability, and these circumstances are exacerbated by the impugned legislation. The legislative provision in question draws a distinction that prevents persons in a same-sex relationship from gaining access to the court-enforced and -protected support system. This system clearly provides a benefit to unmarried heterosexual persons who come within the definition set out in §29, and thereby provides a measure of protection for their economic interests. This protection is denied to persons in a same-sex relationship who would otherwise meet the statute's requirements, and as a result, a person in the position of the claimant is denied a benefit regarding an important aspect of life in today's society. Neither common law nor equity provides the remedy of maintenance that is made available by the FLA. The denial of that potential benefit, which may impose a financial burden on persons in the position of the claimant, contributes to the general vulnerability experienced by individuals in same-sex relationships.

A second contextual factor that was discussed in *Law* as being potentially relevant to the §15(1) inquiry is the correspondence, or the lack of it, between the ground on which a claim is based and the actual need, capacity, or circumstances of the claimant or others. [T]he focus of the inquiry must always remain upon the central question of whether, viewed from the perspective of the claimant, the differential treatment imposed by the legislation has the effect of violating human dignity. However, the legislation at issue in the current appeal fails to take into account the claimant's actual situation. As I have already discussed, access to the court-enforced spousal support regime provided in the FLA is given to individuals in conjugal relationships of a specific degree of permanence. Being in a same-sex relationship does not mean that it is an impermanent or a non-conjugal relationship.

A third contextual factor . . . is the question of whether the impugned legislation has an ameliorative purpose or effect for a group historically disadvantaged in the context of the legislation. [T]he existence of an ameliorative purpose or effect may help to establish that human dignity is not violated where the person or group that is excluded is more advantaged with respect to the circumstances addressed by the legislation. Gonthier J. [the dissenting judge] argues that the legislation under scrutiny in the present appeal is just such ameliorative legislation — that it is meant to target women in married or opposite-sex relationships. He proceeds to argue that in this legal context, women in same-sex relationships are not similarly disadvantaged. [W]e disagree with this characterization of the legislation. Accordingly, we reject the idea that the allegedly ameliorative purpose of this legislation does anything to lessen the charge of discrimination in this case.

A fourth contextual factor specifically adverted to by Iacobucci J. in *Law*, at para. 74, was the nature of the interest affected by the impugned legislation. [T]he discriminatory calibre of differential treatment cannot be fully appreciated without considering whether the distinction in question restricts access to a fundamental social institution, or affects a basic aspect of full membership in Canadian society, or constitutes a complete non-recognition of a particular group. In the present case, the interest protected by §29 of the FLA is fundamental, namely the ability to meet basic financial needs following the breakdown of a relationship characterized by intimacy and economic dependence. Members of same-sex couples are entirely ignored by the statute, notwithstanding the undeniable importance to them of the benefits accorded by the statute.

The societal significance of the benefit conferred by the statute cannot be overemphasized. The exclusion of same-sex partners from the benefits of §29 of the FLA promotes the view that M., and individuals in same-sex relationships generally, are less worthy of recognition and protection. It implies that they are judged to be incapable of forming intimate relationships of economic interdependence as compared to opposite-sex couples, without regard to their actual circumstances. [S]uch exclusion perpetuates the disadvantages suffered by individuals in same-sex relationships and contributes to the erasure of their existence.

Therefore I conclude that an examination of the four factors outlined above, in the context of the present appeal, indicate that the human dignity of individuals in same-sex relationships is violated by the impugned legislation. In light of this, I conclude that the definition of "spouse" in §29 of the FLA violates §15(1). . . .

## Notes and Questions on *Marvin* and *M. v. H.*

1. *Epilogue.* On remand in *Marvin*, the trial court found: (1) no express contract was negotiated by the parties, and (2) the conduct of the parties did not give rise to an implied contract. Despite these findings, the trial judge awarded the plaintiff $104,000 as "rehabilitative alimony," reasoning:

> The court is aware that Footnote 25 urges the trial court to employ whatever equitable remedy may be proper under the circumstances. The court is also aware of the recent resort of plaintiff to unemployment insurance benefits to support herself and of the fact that a return of plaintiff to a career as a singer is doubtful. Additionally, the court knows that the market value of defendant's property at the time of separation exceeded $1,000,000. In view of these circumstances, the court in equity awards plaintiff $104,000 for rehabilitation purposes so that she may have the economic means to re-educate herself and to learn new, employable skills or to refurbish those utilized, for example, during her most recent employment and so that she may return from her status as companion of a motion picture star to a separate, independent but perhaps more prosaic existence.

5 Fam. L. Rep. (BNA) 3079, 3085 (Apr. 24, 1979). The trial judge arrived at the amount by fixing the award (for a two-year period) at the highest salary plaintiff had earned as a singer prior to the cohabitation. On appeal, the Court of Appeals deleted the award, maintaining:

> [T]he special findings in support of the challenged rehabilitation award merely established plaintiff's need therefor and defendant's ability to respond to that need. This is not enough. The award, being nonconsensual in nature, must be supported by some recognized underlying obligation in law or in equity.

... A court of equity admittedly has broad powers, but it may not create totally new substantive rights under the guise of doing equity. [I]n view of the already-mentioned findings of no damage (but benefit instead), no unjust enrichment and no wrongful act on the part of defendant with respect to either the relationship or its termination, it is clear that no basis whatsoever, either in equity or in law, exists for the challenged rehabilitative award.

176 Cal. Rptr. 555, 559 (Ct. App. 1981).

2. Jurisdictions have adopted different approaches to claims by heterosexual cohabitants. The majority follow *Marvin* in recognizing express and implied agreements as well as equitable remedies. However, some jurisdictions recognize only express agreements whereas others recognize express and implied agreements (but not equitable remedies). Finally, a few jurisdictions refuse to recognize property rights between these cohabitants on public policy grounds (e.g., Hewitt v. Hewitt, discussed below). Katherine C. Gordon, Note, The Necessity and Enforcement of Cohabitation Agreements: When Strings Will Attach and How to Prevent Them — A State Survey, 37 Brandeis L.J. 245, 248-254 (1998-1999).

3. *Empirical research.* How frequently do unmarried couples have written agreements? In a survey of 169 heterosexual and same-sex couples, social scientists found that 74 percent had no such agreements. Jennifer K. Robbennolt & Monica Kirkpatrick Johnson, Legal Planning for Unmarried Committed Partners: Empirical Lessons for a Preventative and Therapeutic Approach, 41 Ariz. L. Rev. 417 (1999). What factors might characterize couples that do execute written agreements? See id.

4. *Marvin* permits recovery for cohabitants based on express agreements, and in the absence thereof, implied-in-fact and implied-in-law agreements. Note that *Marvin*'s statements regarding implied agreements are dicta because the plaintiff pleaded an express agreement. Because most agreements between cohabitants are not express, *Marvin*'s importance rests on this dictum and on the suggestion (in footnote 25) of "other equitable remedies." Implied-in-fact remedies are applicable when a court infers contractual intent from the parties' conduct. Implied-in-law remedies are impressed judicially to prevent unjust enrichment, regardless of the parties' intent. Thus, the latter, of course, are not really contracts.

What guidelines does the court give for determining the existence of implied agreements or the application of additional equitable remedies? Does the court assume that the parties have identical expectations? In reality, don't parties' expectations frequently vary? In addition, the court advocates adherence to a presumption that the parties intend to deal fairly with each other. What facts should raise the presumption? Does this presumption interfere with freedom of contract and constitute impermissible state intervention?

5. In *Marvin*, the defendant argued that recognition of a contract would violate public policy by impairing the rights of his ex-wife (to whom he was married during part of the cohabitation). Should a cohabitant be disqualified by, preferred to, or share property equally with, a lawful spouse? Does legal recognition of the rights of both women result in equating cohabitation with polygamy? See Ruth Deech, The Case Against Legal Recognition of Cohabitation, in Marriage and Cohabitation 1 Contemporary Societies 300, 306 (John M. Eekelaar & Sanford N. Katz eds., 1980).

6. *Homemaking services.* In *Marvin*, the plaintiff asserts that she provided homemaking services, among other services, in return for the defendant's promise of support. Courts currently disagree about whether homemaker services are sufficient consideration for an agreement between cohabitants. Gordon, supra, at 247. Under traditional contract doctrine, domestic services fail to provide such consideration because of the rationales that (1) the woman acted from affection rather than expectation of gain, (2) she intended her actions as a gift, or (3) her services are offset by the man's companionship and services. Should such services constitute consideration? If so, how do we value them? Apportion them?

Does provision of homemaking services fulfill the element of "unjust enrichment" that restitutionary theory requires? Specifically, has the plaintiff conferred a benefit on the defendant at her expense? Was the enrichment "unjust"? Professor Robert C. Casad responds:

> . . . The parties cohabit fully aware of the relevant facts, and the indicia of unjustness found in the fraud, duress, and mistake circumstances are therefore absent. [The parties] probably contemplated that the benefits they would receive — material and non-material — would offset the burdens they undertook. Neither party anticipated paying for the material benefits received from the other except by contributing to the relationship. . . . Under those assumptions, neither party's contributions could unjustly enrich the other. . . .

Robert C. Casad, Unmarried Couples and Unjust Enrichment: From Status to Contract and Back Again, 77 Mich. L. Rev. 47, 55 (1978).

7. *Sexual services. Marvin,* interpreting prior case law to stand for the rule that express contracts are enforceable except when founded on sexual services, assumes that the cohabitants' agreement can be separated from the sexual relationship. How does a plaintiff show that the claim is independent from the sexual relationship? Aren't sexual services always an implicit part of an agreement between cohabitants? Or is that confusing the contractual terms with the motive for entering the contract? See Leonard Wagner, Note, Recognizing Contract and Property Rights of Unmarried Cohabitants in Wisconsin: Watts v. Watts, 1988 Wis. L. Rev. 1092, 1113.

By refusing to recognize sexual services as consideration, is a court simply saying that it refuses to confer value on these services for policy reasons? Would recognition of sexual services implicate an invasion of privacy? Professor Fran Olsen counters:

> To make "whisperings across the pillows," sacred, private, and unrepeatable is to support the sexual status quo. . . . Sex is private in part because the state makes it private and because keeping sex private seems to serve the interests of those with power. . . .

Frances E. Olsen, The Myth of State Intervention in the Family, 18 U. Mich. J.L. Reform 835, 857 n.57 (1985). See also David L. Chambers, The "Legalization" of the Family: Toward a Policy of Supportive Neutrality, 18 U. Mich. J.L. Reform 805, 822-825 (1985) (discussing privacy implications of *Marvin*).

8. *Hewitt's hard line*. A few jurisdictions refuse to recognize agreements between cohabitants. See Gordon, supra, at 253 (discussing cases in Georgia, Illinois, and Louisiana). In the classic case of Hewitt v. Hewitt, 394 N.E.2d 1204 (Ill. 1979), the Illinois Supreme Court refused to recognize, on public policy grounds, an agreement between cohabitants. Victoria and Robert Hewitt resided together for 15 years, holding themselves out as husband and wife, and had three children. The couple began living together as college students after the woman became pregnant; the man told her that no formal ceremony was necessary and that the law considered them as husband and wife. At dissolution, the plaintiff alleged that the couple had an express oral agreement to share property equally. In rejecting the woman's claim, the court reasoned that recognition of cohabitants' property rights would equate cohabitation with the abolished doctrine of common law marriage and would undermine marriage. The court deferred to the legislature as a more appropriate body to address the recognition of same-sex relationships.

*Hewitt* did not signal a total refusal of Illinois courts to recognize cohabitants' claims. In a subsequent case, a court recognized the claim of a cohabitant who furnished almost all the consideration and obtained financing for several vehicles that were purchased during a six-year cohabitation and titled in defendant's name "for insurance purposes." See Spafford v. Coats, 455 N.E.2d 241 (Ill. App. Ct. 1983).

Both *Marvin* and *Hewitt* address the potential impact of cohabitation on the institution of marriage. Which view is more persuasive? Both courts also consider the relationship between cohabitation and common law marriage. How do the legal consequences differ? Both cases implicitly deplore a return to common law marriage. Why? Would resurrection of the doctrine help cohabitants? Support or weaken marriage? See Cynthia Grant Bowman, A Feminist Proposal to Bring Back Common Law Marriage, 75 Or. L. Rev. 709 (1996). Do you agree with *Hewitt* that the legislature is the more appropriate body for law reform?

9. *Gender equality.* Does recognition of cohabitants' rights alleviate gender inequality? Is *Marvin* an advance or a setback for women? What is the effect for women of denying relief? One commentator points out that "courts can justify the failure to enforce cohabitation agreements as mere nonintervention, overlooking the fact that the superior position in which the non-action tends to leave the male partner is at least in part a product of the legal system." Clare Dalton, An Essay in the Deconstruction of Contract Doctrine, 94 Yale L.J. 997, 1107 (1985). On the other hand, some commentators argue that the imposition of remedies undermines gender equality by presuming the woman needs protection. See Deech, supra, at 303. Which view is more persuasive?

10. *Marriage as the standard.* Should the economic consequences of cohabitation imitate the rights and duties of marriage? For example, on remand in *Marvin,* the trial court awarded "rehabilitative alimony," using the traditional factors for spousal support of need versus ability to pay. Should cohabitants be entitled to "spousal support" regardless of contractual intent?

11. *Contract or status principles. Marvin* disapproved the status approach in In re Marriage of Cary, 109 Cal. Rptr. 862 (Ct. App. 1973), which treated cohabitants like married persons by granting them half the accumulated property, based on an extension of no-fault divorce and community property principles. Washington became the first community property state to adopt this approach. See Connell v. Francisco, 898 P.2d 831 (Wash. 1995). Commentators have also proposed variations of the status-based approach to operate independently of the parties' intentions. See, e.g., Grace Ganz Blumberg, Cohabitation Without Marriage: A Different Perspective, 28 UCLA L. Rev. 1125, 1167-1168 (1981). Blumberg recommends, for purposes of support and property division, treating cohabitants similarly to married persons if they have remained together for two years. She rejects durational requirements if a child is born to the parties or, for inheritance purposes, if the relationship remains intact until the death of one partner. What do you think of such a proposal?

12. *Same-sex couples.* How should the law treat same-sex couples upon termination of their relationships? Vermont's civil union law equates same-sex couples to married couples for all purposes, including "spousal support" at the end of the relationship. In contrast, reciprocal beneficiaries in Hawaii and domestic partners in California may terminate their relationship without consequences. Greg Johnson, Vermont Civil Unions: The New Language of Marriage, 25 Vt. L. Rev. 15, 42-43 (2000); Greg Lucas, Domestic Partner Rights Ok'd by Assembly Panel, S.F. Chron., Mar. 29, 2000, at A3.

Scandinavia and the Netherlands also protect cohabitants upon termination of the relationship. William N. Eskridge, Jr., Comparative Law and the Same-Sex Marriage Debate: A Step-by-Step Approach Toward

State Recognition, 31 McGeorge L. Rev. 641 (2000); Caroline Forders, European Models of Domestic Partnership Law: The Field of Choice, 17 Can. J. Fam. L. 371, 375-381 (2000); Nancy G. Maxwell, Opening Civil Marriage to Same-Gender Couples: A Netherlands-United States Comparison, 18 Ariz. J. Int'l & Comp. L. 141 (2001).

13. In *M. v. H.*, why did the Canadian Supreme Court hold that the exclusion of same-sex couples from the definition of "spouse" in the Family Law Act (for purposes of support upon termination of the relationship) violates the Canadian Charter of Rights and Freedoms?

Is adoption of such an approach likely in this country? See generally Patrick J. Dooley, Note, I Am Who I Am, or Am I? A Comparison of the Equal Protection of Sexual Minorities in Canadian and U.S. Courts: Immutability Has Only Found a Home North of the Border, 17 Ariz. J. Int'l & Comp. L. 371 (2000). See also Kathleen A. Lahey, Are We 'Persons' Yet?: Law and Sexuality in Canada (1999).

14. *M. v. H.* prompted widespread law reform in Canada. Following the case, several provinces adopted legislation to amend their definitions of "spouse" by prohibiting discrimination against gays and lesbians in terms of pensions, benefits, support requirements, and death benefits. Some provinces also revised their laws to permit same-sex partners to adopt children. Gilles Marchildon, Gay, Lesbian Community Has Reason to Be Shocked, Winnipeg Free Press, June 26, 2001, at A11 (suggesting that reforms only partially redress discrimination).

15. *ALI.* The American Law Institute's Principles of the Law of Family Dissolution apply the same rules to the financial claims of domestic partners (same-sex or heterosexual) as to marital couples upon dissolution of their relationship. ALI, Principles of the Law of Family Dissolution: Analysis and Recommendations (2002), Chapter 6: Domestic Partners. To qualify as a domestic partner under ALI §§6.03(3) and (4), two persons must maintain a "common household" by which they share a primary residence only with each other and other family members for a continuous period established by a rule of statewide application. (If unrelated persons are present in the household, the partners must act "jointly . . . with respect of management of the household," according to §6.03(4)). A presumption of a domestic partnership arises if the persons have maintained a common household with their common child for a requisite period or if they have simply maintained the common household for the requisite period. If neither presumption applies, a person may establish that the relationship constitutes a domestic partnership by proof of certain factors (i.e., statements made to each other or jointly to a third party, intermingling finances, economic dependence, emotional or physical intimacy, community reputation as a couple, participation in a commitment ceremony, naming each other as beneficiary of life insurance or of a will, or joint assumption of parenthood). §6.03(7)(a) to (m). (Not surprisingly, these provisions reflect features of Professor Grace Blumberg's status-based approach because she served as one of the Re-

porters for the ALI project.) See generally Martha M. Ertman, The ALI Principles' Approach to Domestic Partnership, 8 Duke J. Gender L. & Pol'y 107 (2001).

16. In one of the few reported cases involving the property rights of same-sex cohabitants, the NewYork Supreme Court upheld a written separation agreement between two lesbians at the end of their 14-year relationship that guaranteed one ex-partner pay the other a "salary" for five years in return for the other's agreement to vacate the apartment and give up claims to any property. Silver v. Starrett, 674 N.Y.S.2d 915 (Sup. Ct. 1998). See also Posik v. Layton, 695 So. 2d 759 (Fla. 1997) (upholding prenuptial agreement of lesbian couple regarding support after the end of the relationship). Note that the ALI Principles regarding premarital, marital, and separation agreements also apply to individuals who are, or plan to become, domestic partners (same-sex and opposite-sex). See ALI Principles, supra, §§7.01, 7.02.

For a symposium on the legacy of *Marvin,* see 76 Notre Dame L. Rev. (2001) (including articles by Margaret Brinig, Ira Ellman, Thomas Oldham, and Milton Regan).

## Problems

1. Patricia brings an action for breach of contract against her long-term paramour, noted criminal defense attorney Johnnie L. Cochran, Jr. (who successfully defended O.J. Simpson in Simpson's double murder trial). The couple's 17-year relationship began in 1966 when Johnnie was still married to his first wife (whom he divorced in 1978). In 1973, Patricia and Johnnie have a son, and the next year, purchase a house together. Many people believe that the couple is married, especially after Patricia changes her surname to Cochran. Johnnie manages Patricia's finances and, at various times, directs her to quit her jobs and forego her career in order to take care of him and their child. During his first marriage and until 1985 when Johnnie informs Patricia that he is remarrying another woman, he lives with Patricia from 2 to 4 nights per week (staying at his other home the rest of the week). After his remarriage, he never again spends the night at Patricia's, although he visits frequently and takes meals there. Patricia contends that, in 1983, Johnnie orally promised to support her for the rest of her life, and that he did so until 1995 when he became angry after she discussed their relationship on television. Johnnie, citing Marvin v. Marvin, argues that the support agreement is unenforceable because the couple was not living together full-time when the promise was made and also contends that it is violative of public policy because he was married. He characterizes the relationship as little more than "dating." What result? See Cochran v. Cochran, 106 Cal. Rptr.2d 899 (Ct. App. 2001). Cf. Bergen v. Wood, 18 Cal. Rptr.2d 75 (Ct. App. 1993).

2. Anita and Larry begin living together. A few months later, Larry suggests that they jointly build a home. He promises that title will be in joint tenancy with the right of survivorship and that Anita will receive half the equity of the house if the relationship ends. Relying on Larry's promises, Anita obligates herself to pay a $48,000 mortgage. For three years when Larry is unemployed, Anita pays most of the mortgage, taxes, and insurance. When the relationship dissolves ten years later, she discovers that title is in Larry's name. Larry refuses to pay Anita half of the equity in the house. Anita files suit alleging breach of contract and unjust enrichment. Suppose that both *Hewitt* and Spafford v. Coats, supra, are precedents in this jurisdiction. What result? See Ayala v. Fox, 564 N.E.2d 920 (Ill. Ct. App. 1990).

■ **KIRK JOHNSON, GAY DIVORCE:**
  **FEW MARKERS IN THIS REALM**
  *N.Y. Times, Aug. 12, 1994, at A16*

Gay couples who want the right to be legally married make news these days, but consider for a moment the more quietly anguished plight of Bill and Elliot, who only want a divorce.

They lived together for 18 years near Kansas City, Mo. They were co-owners of a small business and a home filled with expensive antiques. They wanted a court system that had never legally recognized their union to dissolve it fairly and equitably, amid the bitter storm of recrimination that was sweeping over their lives as their relationship foundered.

"We had a Dickens of a time even getting a judge to listen to us," said Michael J. Albano [who represented one of the men]. Mr. Albano said he had gone through three judges before finding one who would hear the case. And while the fourth judge finally granted a divorce decree, Mr. Albano said the record was sealed. "No one was sure it was legal or appropriate," he added. . . . Just about every gay divorce is like that: loaded with ambiguities and unknowns, conducted in a court system that lawyers and clients say is hostile at worst and indifferent at best. Because gay people cannot be legally married anywhere in the United States, there is, for starters, no access to divorce court. . . .

People familiar with family law and gay issues say that the number of homosexuals who seek legal help in dissolving their relationships is unknown, because most such cases are settled quietly out of court. High-profile disputes, like Martina Navratilova's noisy legal separation from her longtime companion, Judy Nelson, remain rare. . . . Some lawyers contend that the complexities of gay divorce will eventually prove the strongest argument yet for gay marriages, since it would establish the right to a fair process when those relationships fall apart. . . .

## 4. Unmarried Couples, Third Parties, and the State

### a. Tort Recovery

■ **DUNPHY v. GREGOR**
*642 A.2d 372 (N.J. 1994)*

HANDLER, J. . . .

Eileen Dunphy and Michael T. Burwell became engaged to marry in April 1988 and began cohabitating two months later. The couple set a date of February 29, 1992, for their wedding. On September 29, 1990, the couple responded to a friend's telephone call for assistance in changing a tire on Route 80 in Mount Arlington. As Michael changed the left rear tire of the friend's car on the shoulder of the roadway, he was struck by a car driven by defendant, James Gregor. [H]is body was either dragged or propelled 240 feet. Eileen, who had been standing approximately five feet from Michael, witnessed the impact, and ran to him immediately. Realizing that he was still alive, she cleared pebbles and blood from his mouth to ease his breathing. She attempted to subdue his hands and feet as they thrashed about, all the while talking to him in an effort to comfort him. The following day, after a night-long vigil at Dover General Hospital, Eileen was told that Michael Burwell had died as a result of his injuries. Since the accident, Eileen has undergone psychiatric and psychological treatment for depression and anxiety. She instituted an action seeking to recover damages for the "mental anguish, pain and suffering" experienced as a result of witnessing the events that led to the death of her fiance.

Eileen testified at her deposition that both she and Michael had taken out life-insurance policies making each other beneficiaries. They had maintained a joint checking account from which they had paid their bills, and also they had jointly purchased an automobile. In addition, Michael had asked her several times to elope with him, and he had introduced her in public as his wife.

[The trial court ruled that an action for negligent infliction of emotional distress was not available to a cohabitant. The Appellate Division ruled that a jury should be allowed to determine whether the plaintiff's relationship was the functional equivalent of an intimate familial relationship.]

In Portee v. Jaffee, 84 N.J. 88, 417 A.2d 521 (1980), this Court first recognized a cause of action for the negligent infliction of emotional injury experienced by a bystander who witnessed the wrongful death of another person. A mother suffered horrendous emotional trauma as a result of watching her seven-year-old son suffer a slow and agonizing death after becoming trapped in an elevator. The Court sustained the mother's right to bring a negligence action for the infliction of emotional injury against the landlord and the elevator company, although she herself had not been subjected to any risk of physical harm. In recognizing a bystander's cause of action for the negligent infliction of emotional injury, the Court cited approvingly to Dillon v. Legg, 68 Cal. 2d 728, 69 Cal. Rptr. 72, 441 P.2d 912 (1968), in which the California Supreme Court allowed a mother to recover damages for the emotional injury she had suffered from witnessing the wrongful death of her daughter. The California court, acknowledging that the mother had been a mere bystander to the tragedy, specifically noted that the horror of the event bore uniquely on her because the victim had been her own daughter and because she had been near the accident and had actually observed its occurrence. Those considerations shaped the standard adopted by the court to govern a cause of action for the infliction of emotional injury.

In *Portee*, we adopted a similar standard. *Portee* set out a four-factor test for determining a cause of action for negligent infliction of emotional distress. For a bystander-claimant to prevail, the claimant must demonstrate "(1) the death or serious physical injury of another caused by defendant's negligence; (2) a marital or intimate, familial relationship between the plaintiff and the injured person; (3) observation of the death or injury at the scene of the accident; and (4) resulting severe emotional distress." . . .

[T]he California court, which authored *Dillon*, supra, has since refused to extend the cause of action for negligently-inflicted emotional distress to persons in a cohabitant relationship. [Elden v. Sheldon, 758 P.2d 582 (Cal. 1988).] [T]he plaintiff and the decedent in *Elden* were cohabitants and were involved in a relationship that the plaintiff claimed was similar to a marital relationship. They were riding together in a car when it was struck by the defendant's car, throwing the decedent from the vehicle and fatally injuring him. The plaintiff brought an action to recover for the negligent infliction of emotional distress resulting from witnessing her fiance's fatal injuries.

In rejecting the cohabitant's claim, the California Supreme Court stressed the need for a "sufficiently definite and predictable test to allow for consistent application from case to case." [Id. at 587.] It reasoned that to allow recovery for emotional distress to those outside of the victim's immediate family "would result in the unreasonable extension of the scope of liability of a negligent actor." [Id. at 588.] It determined that it must draw a "bright line" to limit the scope of liability of a negligent actor, and it therefore restricted bystander liability to persons who were legally married or related.

The court in *Elden* was reacting to the experience of the California courts with bystander liability under the *Dillon* standard. After *Dillon*, California courts had expanded nearly all the boundaries of liability set out in the several prongs of the *Dillon* analysis. See, e.g., Ochoa v. Superior Court, 39 Cal. 3d 159, 216 Cal. Rptr. 661, 703 P.2d 1 (1985) (permitting recovery even though injury-producing event was not sudden or accidental); Molien v. Kaiser Foundation Hospitals, 27 Cal. 3d 916, 167 Cal. Rptr. 831, 616 P.2d 813 (1980) (eliminating "sudden occurrence element" for "direct victim" plaintiffs); Krouse v. Graham, 19 Cal. 3d 59, 137 Cal. Rptr. 863, 562 P.2d 1022 (1977) (ruling that plaintiff need not visually perceive third-party injury to recover); Nazaroff v. Superior Court, 80 Cal. App. 3d 553, 145 Cal. Rptr. 657 (Ct. 1978) (broadening concept of contemporaneous observation). *Elden* thus came after a marked expansion of the applicability of bystander liability. . . .

Our own experience does not parallel that of California. In general, our courts have applied all the elements of the *Dillon-Portee* test restrictively. . . . Nothing in our experience with bystander liability counsels a departure from our accustomed application of the traditional principles of tort law. Rather, we are convinced that the solution to the posed question lies not in a hastily-drawn "bright line" distinction between married and unmarried persons but in the "sedulous application" of the principles of tort law, which inform our ultimate determination that a particular claimant is owed a duty of care.

Although a foreseeable risk is the indispensable cornerstone of any formulation of a duty of care, not all foreseeable risks give rise to duties. The imposition of a duty is the conclusion of a rather complex analysis that considers the relationship of the parties, the nature of the risk — that is, its foreseeability and severity — and the impact the imposition of a duty would have on public policy. Ultimately, whether a duty exists is a matter of fairness. . . .

Although novel, applying the standard of an intimate familial relationship to an unmarried cohabitant such as Eileen Dunphy and affording her the protections of bystander liability is hardly unfair. She represents an eminently foreseeable but clearly discrete class of potential plaintiffs. Moreover, the other elements of the bystander cause of action under *Portee* — contemporaneous observation, death or serious injury to the victim, and severe emotional injury to the plaintiff — structure the kind of "particularized foreseeability" that ensures that the class is winnowed even further and that limitless liability is avoided.

One can reasonably foresee that people who enjoy an intimate familial relationship with one another will be especially vulnerable to emotional injury resulting from a tragedy befalling one of them. . . . Persons engaged to be married and living together may foreseeably fall into that category of relationship. . . .

Nor can we discern any additional, unfair burden that would be placed on potential wrongdoers in general, or, as in this case, negligent drivers. The identical acts of reasonable care that would have prevented the fatal accident that claimed the life of Michael Burwell would have preserved the emotional security of Eileen Dunphy. Certainly the extension of such a duty of care to an engaged cohabitant as a foreseeable and protectable person does not increase the burden of care or extend it beyond what is ordinarily expected and appropriate for reasonable drivers.

Most recently, the Court in [Carey v. Lovett, 622 A.2d 1279 (N.J. 1993)] employed traditional tort doctrine in addressing bystander liability, stating that under common-law-negligence principles, "the scope of duty depends generally on the foreseeability of the consequences of a negligent act, as limited by policy considerations and concerns for fairness." 132 N.J. at 57, 622 A.2d 1279. Such an approach, as stated by Justice Broussard in his dissent in *Elden,* recognizes that those in an intimate and familial relationship are "foreseeably and genuinely injured by a negligent defendant's acts," and allowing for their recovery "both advances the goals of tort compensation and sufficiently limits liability. To that end, a standard based on the significance and stability of the plaintiff's relationship is workable and fair." *Elden,* supra, 250 Cal. Rptr. at 265, 758 P.2d at 593 (Broussard, J., dissenting). We agree.

Central to a claim under bystander liability is the existence of an intimate familial relationship and the strength of the emotional bonds that surround that relationship. The harm precipitating emotional distress must be so severe that it destroys the emotional security derived from a relationship that is deep, enduring, and intimate. The quality of the relationship creates the severity of the loss. As we said in *Portee,* "no loss is greater than the loss of a loved one, and no tragedy is more wrenching than the helpless apprehension of death or serious bodily injury to one of those whose very existence is a precious treasure." 84 N.J. at 97, 417 A.2d 521.

Our courts have shown that the sound assessment of the quality of interpersonal relationships is not beyond a jury's ken and that courts are capable of dealing with the realities, not simply the legalities, of relationships to assure that resulting emotional injury is genuine and deserving of compensation. [T]his critical determination must be guided as much as possible by a standard that focuses on those factors that identify and define the intimacy and familial nature of such a relationship. That standard must take into account the duration of the relationship, the degree of mutual dependence, the extent of common contributions to a life together, the extent and quality of shared experience, and, as expressed by the Appellate Division, "whether the plaintiff and the injured person were members of the same household, their emotional reliance on each other, the particulars of their day to day relationship, and the manner in which they related to each other in attending to life's mundane requirements." 261 N.J. Super. at 123, 617 A.2d 1248.

[W]e are unpersuaded by the concerns of the California court expressed in *Elden* . . . that without a "bright line" definition of the bystander-victim relationship, courts will not be able to counteract fraudulent and meretricious claims. That consideration does not outweigh the need to recognize claims that are legitimate and just. . . . The California court also feared that the allowance of a cause of action under such circumstances would intrude on the privacy of the parties. Of course, even if the persons are married, probing inquiry into the nature of their relationship will nonetheless occur. [T]he fact that people are unmarried does not make that inquiry any more intrusive or problematic.

The imposition of a duty of care, we have said, must not only be fair, it must accord with sound public policy. We do not find that bystander liability in favor of unmarried persons who enjoy an intimate familial relationship that is substantial, stable, and enduring is inimical to concerns of public policy.

We reject California's belief that the State's strong interest in promoting marriage will be subverted if unmarried cohabitants are given the same rights as married persons with respect to the right to recover for the negligent infliction of emotional injury. *Elden,* supra, 250 Cal. Rptr. at 258-59, 758 P.2d at 586. In his dissent, Justice Broussard correctly argues that allowing recovery will not undermine the State's interest in promoting marriage, because "[p]resumably, a person who would not otherwise choose to marry would not be persuaded to do so in order to assure his or her legal standing in a future personal injury action should that person have the misfortune of witnessing the serious injury of his or her spouse." Id. 250 Cal. Rptr. at 263, at 591. . . .

We concur in that view. . . . We conclude that under the circumstances of this case an unmarried cohabitant should be afforded the protections of bystander liability for the negligent infliction of emotional injury. . . . The judgment of the Appellate Division is affirmed.

## Notes and Questions

1. *Dunphy* represents the minority view. In extending tort recovery for relationship injuries to cohabitants, *Dunphy* rejects the concerns expressed by the California Supreme Court in Elden v. Sheldon (which rejected a cohabitant's claims for emotional injury and loss of consortium). Which court has a more persuasive argument regarding these concerns? Are the objectives of the tort system met by the extension of liability in this context?

2. Justice Garibaldi, in an omitted dissent in *Dunphy,* raises additional policy concerns. She protests that the exclusion of cohabitants conforms to societal expectations that spouses should be treated differently and also is consistent with nonrecognition of common law marriage (which, she asserts, is an ephemeral arrangement that may dissolve at any time). She also charges that permitting recovery will cause confusion because spouses are treated differently from cohabitants in many legal

areas (for example, intestacy, alimony, loss of consortium). She adds that a clear rule is especially important for causes of action for negligent infliction of emotional distress because emotional injuries are hard to define and potential claimants are limitless. Finally, she claims that the cohabitant-plaintiff has a distinct advantage over the tortfeasor in proving the quality of the relationship because only the bystander survivor is available to testify regarding details of the relationship. Are these arguments persuasive?

3. *Quality or status.* Prior to *Dunphy*, several commentators endorsed recovery for bystander emotional harm and/or loss of consortium based on the quality of the relationship rather than its legal status. See, e.g., John David Burley, Comment, *Dillon* Revisited: Toward a Better Paradigm for Bystander Cases, 43 Ohio St. L.J. 931 (1982); Kris Treu, Comment, Loss of Consortium and Engaged Couples: The Frustrating Fate of Faithful Fiancees, 44 Ohio St. L.J. 219 (1983). Yet, how is a plaintiff to prove the quality of the relationship? What evidence would a defendant introduce to minimize the quality of the relationship? How workable is the specific standard adopted by *Dunphy*, that is, the duration of the relationship, the degree of mutual dependence, the extent of common contributions to a life together, the extent and quality of shared experience, and their membership in the same house — "their emotional reliance on each other, the particulars of their day to day relationship, and the manner in which they related to each other in attending to life's mundane requirements"? Is a "no marriage-no recovery" rule preferable?

How easy is *Dunphy*'s test to administer in the following situations: (a) Mary and Joe are engaged when Mary is killed because of defendant's negligence. However, the couple is not living together because of opposition from Mary's parents (although the couple spends several nights per week together). They share all assets and expenses. (b) Carol and Paul live together with their infant for six months before Carol is killed in an automobile accident caused by defendant's negligence. The couple had no plans to marry and kept all accounts separate. Should recovery be allowed? Suppose a relationship is not monogamous. Should that preclude recovery? How is "emotional reliance" determined?

Following *Dunphy*, some commentators introduced proposals for refining the standard for recognition of cohabitants' claims. One commentator suggests that courts should afford married bystanders who witness a spouse's death or injury a rebuttable presumption that a close relationship exists. However, for cohabitants, courts should apply a rebuttable presumption suggesting that their relationship does not meet the "close relationship" standard. David Sampedro, When Living as Husband and Wife Isn't Enough: Reevaluating *Dillon*'s Close Relationship in Light of *Dunphy v. Gregor*, 25 Stetson L. Rev. 1085, 1117 (1996).

Another commentator suggests giving weight to such elements as: a bystander in the zone of danger who has shared the victim's household for more than two years; a bystander who has had a monogamous relationship with the victim for more than one year with evidence of plans to marry; and a bystander who has had a monogamous relationship with the victim for more than one year and has had children with the victim. Dennis G. Bassi, Note, It's All Relative: A Graphical Reasoning Model for Liberalizing Recovery for Negligent Infliction of Emotional Distress Beyond the Immediate Family, 30 Val. U. L. Rev. 913 (1996). Do these proposals make *Dunphy*'s approach more workable?

4. If recovery is to be permitted based on the "functional equivalency" test, should courts permit recovery by gay cohabitants? What does *Dunphy* suggest? In the only case to date to address this issue, a California appellate court denied recovery to a gay partner. See Coon v. Joseph, 237 Cal. Rptr. 873, 877 (Ct. App. 1987). Does the denial of recovery to same-sex partners violate equal protection? See Laura M. Raisty, Bystander Distress and Loss of Consortium: An Examination of the Relationship Requirements in Light of *Romer v. Evans*, 65 Fordham L. Rev. 2647, 2648 (1997) (so arguing).

5. The majority in *Elden*, the California case that denied liability, contends that it is self-evident that morality is not at issue. Are you convinced? Does the view that only a marital relationship represents a cognizable interest reflect a moral stance? See also Bulloch v. United States, 487 F. Supp. 1078 (D.N.J. 1980) (denial of action for loss of consortium could be construed as punishment for not having legal marriage).

6. *Marvin distinguished.* Has California adopted a paradoxical position toward unmarried couples? Does it make sense to allow recovery by cohabitants in contract (*Marvin*) but not tort (*Elden*)? Is it significant that *Marvin* resolved a dispute between the parties while *Elden* presented a claim against third parties?

7. *Engaged couples.* In *Dunphy*, plaintiff and the victim were engaged to marry almost two years in the future. Does this factor strengthen plaintiff's claim? See, e.g., Miller v. Curtis, 1999 WL 1013222 (Conn. Super. Ct. 1999); Garrett v. Watson, 2001 WL 238196 (E.D. La. 2001). Should the length of the engagement matter? Suppose Michael Burwell was injured rather than killed. The couple marries after the accident. Should Dunphy be allowed to recover for the loss of consortium she subsequently experienced stemming from the premarital injury? Compare Harris v. Sherman, 708 A.2d 1348 (Vt. 1998) (denying recovery), with Sutherland v. Auch Inter-Borough Transit Co., 366 F. Supp. 127 (E.D. Pa. 1973) (permitting recovery). See generally Paul Davis Fancher, To Have and Not Hold: Applying the Discovery Rule to Loss of Consortium Claims Stemming from Premarital, Latent Injuries, 53 Vand. L. Rev. 685, 694 (2000).

Most courts deny recovery to parties who marry subsequent to the injury on the ground that the claimant knowingly married into the loss of consortium. In those jurisdictions that permit recovery, however, from when should recovery commence — the date of the marriage or the date of the injury? See *Sutherland,* supra (date of marriage).

Is a cohabitant's claim entitled to more weight than that of an *engaged* person? Professor Grace Blumberg argues that it is:

> Strictly speaking, a cohabitant's claim is distinguishable. The cohabitant was enjoying consortium at the time of the injury. More importantly, the underlying rationale of the betrothal cases seems incorrect. It is socially prudent to encourage fiances and cohabitants to remain with the injured victims of tortfeasors. Denying them loss of consortium recovery on the ground that they were not legally bound to the injured person would seem to sanction and to encourage abandonment of the injured. . . . In this sense, fiances and cohabitants are similarly situated: neither is bound to be virtuous. Moreover, the advent of freely available divorce weakens the traditional distinction between the spouse and the fiance. Like the fiance who is not legally required to marry into loss of consortium, the spouse practically speaking, is free to dissolve a burdensome marriage whenever he wishes.

Grace Ganz Blumberg, Cohabitation Without Marriage: A Different Perspective, 28 UCLA L. Rev. 1125, 1138-1139 n.80 (1981).

8. Both *Dunphy* and *Marvin* note the dramatic increase in the numbers of unmarried couples. To what extent do demographic data support the arguments for (or against) legal recognition of cohabitants? That is, should legal reality mirror social reality, or should other considerations come into play?

### b. Employment

### ■ SHAHAR v. BOWERS
*114 F.3d 1097 (11th Cir. 1997)*

EDMONDSON, Circuit Judge:

In this government-employment case, Plaintiff-Appellant contends that the Attorney General of the State of Georgia violated her federal constitutional rights by revoking an employment offer because of her purported "marriage" to another woman. . . .

. . . Plaintiff Robin Joy Shahar is a woman who has "married" another woman in a ceremony performed by a rabbi within the Reconstructionist Movement of Judaism. According to Shahar, though the State of Georgia does not recognize her "marriage" and she does not claim that the "marriage" has legal effect, she and her partner consider themselves to be "married."

Since August 1981, Defendant-Appellee Michael J. Bowers has been the Attorney General [hereafter the "Department"] of the State of Georgia, a statewide elective office. . . .

While a law student, Shahar spent the summer of 1990 as a law clerk with the Department. In September 1990, the Attorney General offered Shahar the position of Staff Attorney when she graduated from law school. Shahar accepted the offer and was scheduled to begin work in September 1991.

In the summer of 1990, Shahar began making plans for her "wedding." Her rabbi announced the expected "wedding" to the congregation at Shahar's synagogue in Atlanta. Shahar and her partner invited approximately 250 people, including two Department employees, to the "wedding." The written invitations characterized the ceremony as a "Jewish, lesbian-feminist, out-door wedding." The ceremony took place in a public park in South Carolina in June 1991.

In November 1990, Shahar filled out the required application for a Staff Attorney position. In response to the question on "marital status," Shahar indicated that she was "engaged." She altered "spouse's name" to read "future spouse's name" and filled in her partner's name: "Francine M. Greenfield." In response to the question "Do any of your relatives work for the State of Georgia?" she filled in the name of her partner as follows: "Francine Greenfield, future spouse."

Sometime in the spring of 1991, Shahar and her partner were working on their "wedding" invitations at an Atlanta restaurant. [While there, they met a paralegal and staff attorney, Susan Rutherford, from the Attorney General's office and mentioned to them the wedding preparations.] In June 1991, Shahar told Deputy Attorney General Robert Coleman that she was getting married at the end of July, changing her last name, taking a trip to Greece and, accordingly, would not be starting work with the Department until mid-to-late September. At this point, Shahar did not say that she was "marrying" another woman. Senior Assistant Attorney General Jeffrey Milsteen, who had been co-chair of the summer clerk committee, was in Coleman's office at the time and heard Coleman congratulate Shahar. Milsteen later mentioned to Rutherford that Shahar was getting married. Rutherford then told Milsteen that Shahar was planning on "marrying" another woman. This revelation caused a stir.

Senior aides to the Attorney General became concerned about what they viewed as potential problems in the office resulting from the Department's employment of a Staff Attorney who purported to be part of a same-sex "marriage." As the Attorney General was out of the office that week, the five aides held several meetings among themselves to discuss the situation.

Upon the Attorney General's return to the office, he was informed of the situation. He held discussions with the senior aides, as well as a few other lawyers within the Department. After much discussion, the Attorney General decided, with the advice of his senior lawyers, to withdraw Shahar's job offer. In July 1991, he did so in writing. The pertinent letter stated that the withdrawal of Shahar's offer:

> has become necessary in light of information which has only recently come to my attention relating to a purported marriage between you and another woman. As chief legal officer of this state, inaction on my part would constitute tacit approval of this purported marriage and jeopardize the proper functioning of this office.

[Shahar then instituted suit seeking damages, injunctive relief, and "reinstatement." She argued that revocation of the employment offer violated the rights to free exercise and association, equal protection, and substantive due process. The district court granted the Attorney General's motion for summary judgment.]

Even when we assume, for argument's sake, that either the right to intimate association or the right to expressive association or both are present, we know they are not absolute. Georgia and its elected Attorney General also have rights and duties which must be taken into account, especially where (as here) the State is acting as employer. We also know that because the government's role as employer is different from its role as sovereign, we review its acts differently in the different contexts. In reviewing Shahar's claim, we stress that this case is about the government acting as employer.

Shahar argues that we must review the withdrawal of her job offer under strict scrutiny. The only precedent to which Shahar refers us for the proposition that strict scrutiny is to be applied to the government as employer is Dike v. School Board, 650 F.2d 783 (5th Cir. 1981). In *Dike,* the Fifth Circuit — our predecessor — implied that a school district's refusal to allow a teacher to breast-feed her child on her lunch hour must withstand strict scrutiny. To the extent that *Dike* might be interpreted as requiring strict scrutiny review of a government employee's freedom of intimate association claim, it misstates the appropriate standard; and we overrule it now. . . .

We conclude that the appropriate test for evaluating the constitutional implications of the State of Georgia's decision — as an employer — to withdraw Shahar's job offer based on her "marriage" is the same test as the test for evaluating the constitutional implications of a government employer's decision based on an employee's exercise of her right to free speech, that is, the *Pickering* [Pickering v. Board of Ed., 391 U.S. 563 (1968)] balancing test. . . .

We must decide whether Shahar's interests outweigh the disruption and other harm the Attorney General believes her employment could cause. . . . To decide this case, we are willing to accord Shahar's claimed associational rights (which we have assumed to exist) substantial weight. But, we know that the weight due intimate associational rights, such as, those involved in even a state-authorized marriage, can be overcome by a government employer's interest in maintaining the effective functioning of his office.

In weighing her interest in her associational rights, Shahar asks us also to consider the "non-employment related context" of her "wedding" and "marriage" and that "[s]he took no action to transform her intimate association into a public or political statement." In addition, Shahar says that we should take into account that she has affirmatively disavowed a right to benefits from the Department based on her "marriage."

To the extent that Shahar disclaims benefits bestowed by the State based on marriage, she is merely acknowledging what is undisputed, that Georgia law does not and has not recognized homosexual marriage. We fail to see how that technical acknowledgment counts for much in the balance.

If Shahar is arguing that she does not hold herself out as "married," the undisputed facts are to the contrary. Department employees, among many others, were invited to a "Jewish, lesbian-feminist, out-door wedding" which included exchanging wedding rings: the wearing of a wedding ring is an outward sign of having entered into marriage. Shahar listed her "marital status" on her employment application as "engaged" and indicated that her future spouse was a woman. She and her partner have both legally changed their family name to Shahar by filing a name change petition with the Fulton County Superior Court. They sought and received the married rate on their insurance. And, they, together, own the house in which they cohabit. These things were not done secretly, but openly. . . .

[T]he Attorney General's worry about his office being involved in litigation in which Shahar's special personal interest might appear to be in conflict with the State's position [is] not unreasonable. In addition, the Department, when the job offer was withdrawn, had already engaged in and won a recent battle [Bowers v. Hardwick, 478 U.S. 186 (1986)] about homosexual sodomy — highly visible litigation in which its lawyers worked to uphold the lawful prohibition of homosexual sodomy. This history makes it particularly reasonable for the Attorney General to worry about the internal consequences for his professional staff (for example, loss of morale, loss of cohesiveness and so forth) of allowing a lawyer, who openly — for instance, on her employment application and in statements to coworkers — represents herself to be "married" to a person of the same sex, to become part of his staff. . . .

Shahar also argues that, at the Department, she would have handled mostly death penalty appeals and that the *Pickering* test requires evidence of potential interference with these particular duties. Even assuming Shahar is correct about her likely assignment within the

Department, a particularized showing of interference with the provision of public services is not required. In addition, the Attorney General must be able to reassign his limited legal staff as the needs of his office require. . . . In a similar way, it is not for this court to tie the Department's hands by telling it which Staff Attorneys may be assigned to which cases or duties or to force upon the Attorney General a Staff Attorney of limited utility. Such an interference by the federal judiciary into the internal organization of the executive branch of a state government is almost always unwarranted.

. . . Shahar argues that [the Attorney General] may not justify his decision by reference to perceived public hostility to her "marriage." We have held otherwise about the significance of public perception when law enforcement is involved [citing McMullen v. Carson, 754 F.2d 936, 938 (11th Cir. 1985)]. In this case, the Attorney General was similarly entitled to consider any "deleterious effect on [his] ability to enforce the law of the community," [id. at 938,] and that "[u]nder our system of Government, that duty [law enforcement] can be performed only with the consent of the vast majority. . . . Efficient law enforcement requires mutual respect, trust and support." Id. at 939. . . .

Public perception is important; but, at the same time, it is not knowable precisely. That the public (which we know is rarely monolithic) would not draw the Attorney General's anticipated inferences from Shahar's "marriage" or, at least, would not attribute such perceptions to the Department or the Attorney General is a possibility. But assessing what the public perceives about the Attorney General and the Law Department is a judgment for the Attorney General to make in the day-to-day course of filling his proper role as the elected head of the Department, not for the federal judiciary to make with hindsight or from a safe distance away from the distress and disturbance that might result if the decision was mistaken. We must defer to Georgia's Attorney General's judgment about what Georgians might perceive unless his judgment is definitely outside of the broad range of reasonable views. . . .

Shahar says that by taking into account these concerns about public reaction, the Attorney General impermissibly discriminated against homosexuals; and she refers us to the Supreme Court's recent decision in Romer v. Evans, 116 S. Ct. 1620 (1996). In *Romer*, the Supreme Court struck down an amendment to a state constitution as irrational because the amendment's sole purpose was to disadvantage a particular class of people (to "den[y] them protection across the board," id. at 1628) and because the government engaged in "classification of persons undertaken for its own sake, something the Equal Protection Clause does not permit." Id. at 1629.

*Romer* is about people's condition; this case is about a person's conduct. And, *Romer* is no employment case. Considering (in deciding to revoke a job offer) public reaction to a future Staff Attorney's conduct in taking part in a same-sex "wedding" and subsequent "marriage" is not the same kind of decision as an across-the-board denial of legal protection to a group because of their condition, that is, sexual orientation or preference.

This case is about the powers of government as an employer, powers which are far broader than government's powers as sovereign. In addition, the employment in this case is of a special kind: employment involving access to the employer's confidences, acting as the employer's spokesperson, and helping to make policy. This kind of employment is one in which the employer's interest has been given especially great weight in the past. Furthermore, the employment in this case is employment with responsibilities directly impacting on the enforcement of a state's laws: a kind of employment in which appearances and public perceptions and public confidence count a lot.

Particularly considering this Attorney General's many years of experience and Georgia's recent legal history, we cannot say that he was unreasonable to think that Shahar's acts were likely to cause the public to be confused and to question the Law Department's credibility; to interfere with the Law Department's ability to handle certain controversial matters, including enforcing the law against homosexual sodomy; and to endanger working relationships inside the Department. We also cannot say that the Attorney General was unreasonable to lose confidence in Shahar's ability to make good judgments as a lawyer for the Law Department.

We stress in this case the sensitive nature of the pertinent professional employment. And we hold that the Attorney General's interest — that is, the State of Georgia's interest — as an employer in promoting the efficiency of the Law Department's important public service does outweigh Shahar's personal associational interests. . . .

Georgia's Attorney General has made a personnel decision which none of the asserted federal constitutional provisions prohibited him from making. . . .

## Notes and Questions

1. *Background.* Following plaintiff's appeal from the district court's summary judgment in favor of the attorney general, the court of appeals initially held that the plaintiff's intimate association with the woman whom she planned to marry was protected by the First Amendment, and that strict scrutiny and the compelling state interest test (rather than the *Pickering* balancing test) applied. 70 F.3d 1218 (11th Cir. 1995). The court subsequently granted a rehearing en banc and vacated the previous panel's opinion. 78 F.3d 499 (11th Cir. 1996). The court of appeals ultimately applied the *Pickering* test to reach the conclusion in the principal case.

2. In *Shahar,* plaintiff claims violation of her constitutional rights because she lost her offer of employment at the hands of a state actor. The appellate court relies on the *Pickering* balancing test because the state-employer has special interests. Would plaintiff's marriage have interfered with the performance of her daily duties? How many cases involving homosexual unions might be handled regularly by the defendant's office? What role should public perception play in employment decisions involving state actors? See Michele L. Booth, *Shahar v. Bowers:* Is Public Opinion Transformed into a Legitimate Government Interest When Government Acts as Employer?, 78 B.U. L. Rev. 1235 (1998).

3. Assuming (as the court does, "for argument's sake") that Shahar has a constitutionally protected right to intimate association, how can one reconcile this case with Bowers v. Hardwick? Does an inference of illegal conduct follow from same-sex marriage?

4. Does *Shahar* imply that plaintiff lost her employment only because she made "public" her relationship? How "private" would plaintiff have had to keep this information to prevent defendant from establishing a sufficiently countervailing state interest? Does *Shahar* suggest that the Constitution affords more protection to those relationships "in the closet"? See also McConnell v. Anderson, 451 F.2d 193, 195 (8th Cir. 1971) (affirming denial of employment to university librarian after employee applied for a marriage license with his same-sex partner because of his "activist role in implementing his unconventional ideas"); Singer v. U.S. Civil Serv. Comm'n, 530 F.2d 247, 249 (9th Cir. 1976), *vacated,* 429 U.S. 1034 (1977) (clerk typist fired for "flaunting" homosexuality by embracing another male at place of employment). See generally William N. Eskridge, Gaylaw: Challenging the Apartheid of the Closet (1999); Todd Brower, Of Courts and Closets: A Doctrinal and Empirical Analysis of Gay Identity in the Courts, 38 San Diego L. Rev. 565 (2001).

The judicial attitude that penalizes an employee for certain behavior (for example, same-sex marriage, public displays of affection to a member of the same sex, and activism) has prompted one commentator to point out:

> what is seen as extravagant flaunting on the part of gay men and lesbians is routine, even expected behavior for heterosexuals in this society. Heterosexuals are free to reveal their status and preferences through public displays of affection as diverse as holding hands and sending out wedding announcements. Conversations among heterosexuals about "the process of forming couples" and one's life with one's partner are "expected and appropriate . . . in social and work settings."

Mary Anne Case, Couples and Coupling in the Public Sphere: A Comment on the Legal History of Litigating for Lesbian and Gay Rights, 79 Va. L. Rev. 1643, 1672 (1993) (quoting Marc A. Fajer, Can Two Real Men

Eat Quiche Together? Storytelling, Gender-Role Stereotypes, and Legal Protection for Lesbians and Gay Men, 46 U. Miami L. Rev. 511, 604 (1992)).

5. Gays and lesbians may face explicit threats of discharge if they reveal their sexual orientation. The most famous example is the military's policy of "don't ask-don't tell." See generally Janet E. Halley, Don't: A Reader's Guide to the Military's Anti-Gay Policy (1999). See also Brower, supra, at 569 n.23 (discussing case of lesbian coach/teacher who was threatened with termination if she discussed her sexual orientation with students, staff, or parents).

6. Unmarried heterosexual couples who are public employees may face similar problems. Compare Kukla v. Village of Antioch, 647 F. Supp. 799 (N.D. Ill. 1986) (upholding the discharge of a male police sergeant and female dispatcher for cohabitation); Hollenbaugh v. Carnegie Free Library, 436 F. Supp. 1328 (W.D. Pa. 1977), aff'd, 578 F.2d 1374 (3d Cir.), cert. denied, 439 U.S. 1052 (1978) (upholding dismissal of librarian and janitor for cohabiting) with LaSota v. Town of Topsfield, 979 F. Supp. 45 (D. Mass. 1997) (holding that discharge of teacher because of her cohabitation with a child abuser violated her privacy right).

7. *Employment-related health benefits.* Increasingly, gay and lesbian couples are seeking employment-related health benefits that are available to legal spouses. In Tanner v. Oregon Health Sciences University, 971 P.2d 435 (Or. App. 1998), three lesbian employees sued the university over the denial of health and insurance benefits to domestic partners. The court held that OHSU did not violate the Oregon statute prohibiting discrimination on the basis of sex or marital status because both heterosexual and homosexual couples were denied health and insurance benefits. The court did hold, however, that OHSU's denial of health and insurance benefits to domestic partners violated the privileges and immunities clause of the state constitution. Most jurisdictions, however, have not extended employment-related benefits to gay and lesbian couples. See generally Frances N. Balonwu, Rights and Entitlement of Same-Sex Cohabitants: Should Gays and Lesbians Have a Right to Their Partner's Employment Benefits?, 23 T. Marshall L. Rev. 483 (1998).

8. *Epilogue.* One week after the ruling in *Shahar,* former state attorney general Michael Bowers confessed his 15-year adulterous affair with a former employee. Shahar filed a motion for rehearing. She argued that because Bowers's sexual conduct similarly was prohibited by Georgia law, that undermined the court's conclusion that Bowers did not treat Shahar differently simply because she was a lesbian. The Eleventh Circuit denied her petition, saying that she was not terminated because of her sexual conduct but because of her marriage. Wendy Kaminer, Gay Rights, American Prospect, Feb. 28, 2000, at 67. Shahar later took a job as an attorney with the city of Atlanta. Joyce Murdoch & Deb Price, Courting Justice: Gay Men and Lesbians v. the Supreme Court 494

(2001). Michael Bowers resigned as state attorney general in 1998 to become a Republican gubernatorial candidate. After his unsuccessful bid for office, he returned to private practice as a partner with the Atlanta firm of Meadows, Ichter and Trigg. Lyle V. Harris, Out of the Wrestling Ring, Into the Courtroom, Atlanta J. & Const., Mar. 3, 2000, at G1 (describing case involving Bowers's law firm).

## Problem[8]

Peter, a camera crewman at Onstage Productions, has been living with his partner Austin for 14 years. They jointly own real and personal property and name each other as beneficiaries of their life insurance policies and wills, as well as appointees of each other's health care proxy (conferring medical decisionmaking power in the event of disability). They participate in a "commitment ceremony" and are open about their relationship. Carolyn, another Onstage employee, lives with her two children and her partner Gordon, for two years. She and Gordon are beneficiaries under each other's life insurance policy and will. Peter asks his benefits manager to consider a welfare and pension benefits policy for employees with same-sex partners. The human resources committee considers two approaches: the "Lotus Alternative," named after a Cambridge, Massachusetts, software firm that was the first private corporation to grant benefits to same-sex partners but not to heterosexual cohabitants; and the "Ben and Jerry" model, named after the Vermont ice cream maker that offers health coverage to the unmarried partners of both heterosexual and homosexual employees. Considering cost, the potential for abuse, and the effects on morale and productivity, what approach should the committee adopt? (Assume that neither approach would violate ERISA.) If a governmental employer (for example, a state university) were exploring similar options, what problems should it consider?

## ■ MacGREGOR v. UNEMPLOYMENT INSURANCE APPEALS BOARD
*689 P.2d 453 (Cal. 1984)*

REYNOSO, Justice. . . .
Plaintiff Patricia MacGregor worked as a waitress [in] California from July 7, 1978 through December 31, 1979. On January 1, 1980, she

---

[8]. This problem is a slightly modified version of the problem in Alice Rickel, Extending Employee Benefits to Domestic Partners: Avoiding Legal Hurdles While Staying in Tune with the Changing Definition of the Family, 16 Whittier L. Rev. 737, 739-742 (1995).

began a six-month pregnancy leave of absence. According to the terms of her leave, she was to return to work in June of 1980.

MacGregor was engaged to and lived with Dick Bailey, the father of her expected child. Their daughter Leanna was born February 29, 1980. The three continued to live together as a family. Bailey acknowledged that he was Leanna's father.

In April, Bailey decided the family should move to New York to live with and care for his 76-year-old father. At the time, his father was under medical care for a variety of serious ailments and anticipated surgery later that summer. Because of his ill health he no longer wished to live alone. No relatives lived nearby and Bailey was the only child. Bailey's father asked if Bailey, MacGregor and their daughter would come to live with and care for him. In May MacGregor informed her employer that she would not be returning to work.

MacGregor, Bailey and their daughter moved into Bailey's father's home in June. When MacGregor was unable to find work, she applied for unemployment insurance benefits. Her claim was referred to the California Employment Development Department (Department), which determined that she had quit voluntarily without good cause and was thus ineligible for benefits. (Unemp. Ins. Code, §1256.)

MacGregor appealed this decision. [An administrative law] judge determined MacGregor had left her most recent work voluntarily without good cause and was thus disqualified from receiving benefits. Although the judge found evidence in the record indicating that Bailey had to return to New York to care for his father who was ill, the judge concluded that "it [was] not apparent why it was essential for the claimant to follow." Since there was no marriage, no plans to marry at a certain future date, and no assurance the relationship would continue for any particular period of time, the judge found there was no family unit to be preserved. . . .

[On appeal, the court found that MacGregor's three-year relationship, formation of a family unit with a child, and her decision to relocate established good cause for employment termination and that she was therefore entitled to receive benefits. While the Board's appeal was pending, the California Supreme Court decided Norman v. Unemployment Insurance Appeals Board, 663 P.2d 904 (Cal. 1983).]

. . . Section 1256 provides that "an individual is disqualified for unemployment compensation benefits if the director finds that he or she left his or her most recent work voluntarily without good cause [or has been discharged for misconduct]. Good cause may exist for reasons which are personal and not connected to the employment situation, but those reasons must be imperative and compelling in nature. . . . Precedent decisions of the Board have long recognized that the circumstances attendant upon a worker's decision to leave employment in order to accompany a spouse and family to a new home may be so compelling as to constitute good cause for quitting within section 1256. . . .

In 1982 the Legislature added the fourth paragraph to section 1256 which recognizes that the desire to preserve a marital relationship, or a relationship in which marriage is imminent, may constitute good cause within the meaning of the statute. The Legislature explicitly stated that the amendment was intended to overturn the Court of Appeal decision in Norman v. Unemployment Ins. Appeals Bd. (which had found good cause based on a nonmarital relationship). . . .

[In *Norman* the California Supreme Court] found that a claimant who had left California to preserve her relationship with the man she planned to marry had not established good cause. The record contained no indication that the couple's marriage was imminent and lacked sufficient indications of the need to preserve a permanent and lasting familial relationship. Citing a line of appellate decisions declining to equate nonmarital relationships with marriage for all purposes, the *Norman* opinion concluded that "[t]he Legislature's decision to give weight to marital relationships in the determination of 'good cause' supports public policy encouraging marriage and is a reasonable method of alleviating otherwise difficult problems of proof." (663 P.2d 904.)

[Nonetheless, *Norman* permitted an exception if an applicant could establish compelling circumstances that made her voluntary leave "akin to involuntary departure."] Using a hypothetical which foresaw the claim now before us, the *Norman* court suggested that some significant factor in addition to the nonmarital relationship might provide the necessary compelling circumstance: "Thus, for example, where there are children of a nonformalized relationship, and an employee leaves his or her position to be with a nonmarital loved one and their children, good cause might be shown." (Ibid.). . . .

The evidence here amply supports the trial court's findings that MacGregor had "established a family unit consisting of herself, her fiance and their child" and that she "chose to relocate to New York with her fiance and their child in order to maintain and preserve their family unit." . . . It is difficult to conceive of a more fundamental familial relationship than one which is created when two parents establish a home with their natural child. . . .

Leanna was only two months old when Bailey decided his father's illness required him to move to New York. The need for MacGregor to follow — which the administrative law judge could not fathom — is in our view manifest. The intimate nature of the family bond among these three individuals would have been forever altered had MacGregor decided that she, or she and Leanna, should not accompany Bailey to New York.

The Board's arguments here, like the administrative decisions below, focus on the lack of a legal marriage relationship between plaintiff and Bailey. The Board urges that leaving work to join a spouse should be deemed good cause only where there is a marriage to be preserved. This rule, according to the Board, is consistent with the public policy favoring marriage and with laws which afford special benefits and protections to that institution. The rule would also avoid the difficulties and dangers which would accompany a requirement that administrative agencies and the courts make individualized determination of the "true nature" of intimate personal relationships.

This court considered similar arguments in Norman v. Unemployment Ins. Appeals Bd., supra. There, although we declined to find good cause based solely on a nonmarital relationship in which marriage was not imminent, we explicitly declined to hold that a legal marriage is a prerequisite for establishing good cause where other indices of compelling familial obligations exist. Today we reaffirm the principle that the lack of a legally recognized marriage does not prevent a claimant from demonstrating that compelling familial obligations provided good cause for leaving employment.[5] . . . The state's policy in favor of maintaining secure and stable relationships between parents and children is equally as strong as its interest in preserving the institution of marriage. . . . The problems of proof which concerned this court in the *Norman* case are not substantial in this situation where the basis for the familial relationship is clear and objectively verifiable. . . .

## Notes and Questions

1. The lower court in *MacGregor* based its finding of a lack of a family unit largely on the absence of plans to marry or the assurance that the relationship would endure. Do plans to marry reliably indicate the requisite "permanence and lasting family relationship"?

2. In 1988 the unemployment insurance code examined in *MacGregor* was amended to specify that "[f]or the purposes of this section 'spouse' includes a person to whom marriage is imminent." Cal. Unemp. Ins. Code §1256 (West 1996 & Supp. 2001). What showing would satisfy this requirement? Does the use of such definition suggest legislative intent to deny recovery to someone in MacGregor's situation?

3. The California Supreme Court contrasts *MacGregor* with an earlier case, Norman v. Unemployment Insurance Appeals Board. Is the court saying that the presence of a child adds a requisite degree of "permanence" to cohabitation? Makes a relationship more worthy of preservation? Solves administrative problems because the "basis for the familial relationship is clear and objectively verifiable"? *MacGregor* leaves open the question whether unmarried cohabitants without children will ever

---

5. In light of this decision we need not resolve plaintiff's contention that a nonmarital rule unconstitutionally infringes her right of privacy in the matters of marriage and reproduction.

be able to establish good cause. What additional factors might prove compelling?

4. The California Supreme Court fails to reach the issue whether the challenged rule infringes MacGregor's right of privacy (see footnote 5). Does it?

5. Almost two decades after *MacGregor*, the California state Senate voted to pass legislation (AB25) that would permit a registered same-sex partner to relocate with the other partner without losing unemployment benefits. Christopher Heredia & Greg Lucas, State Senate Oks Milestone Domestic Partners Bill, S.F. Chron., Sept. 11, 2001, at A1. The legislation (to amend Cal. Unemp. Ins. Code §1256) was signed by the governor in October 2001.

### c. Health

### ■ IN RE GUARDIANSHIP OF KOWALSKI (KOWALSKI III)
*478 N.W.2d 790 (Minn. Ct. App. 1991)*

Davies, Judge. . . .

Sharon Kowalski is 35 years old. On November 13, 1983, she suffered severe brain injuries in an automobile accident which left her in a wheelchair, impaired her ability to speak, and caused severe loss of short-term memory.

At the time of the accident, Sharon was sharing a home in St. Cloud with her lesbian partner, appellant Karen Thompson. They had exchanged rings, named each other as insurance beneficiaries, and had been living together as a couple for four years. Sharon's parents were not aware of the lesbian relationship at the time of the accident. Sharon's parents and siblings live on the Iron Range, where Sharon was raised.

In March of 1984, both Thompson and Sharon's father, Donald Kowalski, cross-petitioned for guardianship. Thompson, expecting that she would have certain visitation rights and input into medical decisions, agreed to the appointment of Mr. Kowalski as Sharon's guardian. The guardianship order, however, gave complete control of visitation to Kowalski, who subsequently received court approval to terminate Thompson's visitation rights on July 25, 1985. Kowalski immediately relocated Sharon from a nursing home in Duluth to one in Hibbing.

In May of 1988, Judge Robert Campbell ordered specialists at Miller-Dwan Medical Center to examine Sharon to determine her level of functioning and whether Sharon could express her wishes on visitation. The doctors concluded that Sharon wished to see Thompson, and the court permitted Thompson to reestablish visitation in January of 1989. The doctors also recommended in 1989 that Sharon be relocated to Trevilla at Robbinsdale, where she currently resides. After Sharon's move, Thompson was permitted to bring Sharon to her St. Cloud home for semi-monthly weekend visits.

In late 1988, Kowalski notified the court that, due to his own medical problems, he wished to be removed as Sharon's guardian. The court granted his request [and] Thompson, on August 7, 1989, filed a petition for appointment as successor guardian of Sharon's person and estate. No competing petition was filed. [At the hearing] Thompson called approximately 16 medical witnesses, all of whom had treated Sharon and had firsthand knowledge of her condition and care. The court also heard testimony from three witnesses in opposition to Thompson's petition: Debra Kowalski, Sharon's sister; Kathy Schroeder, a friend of Sharon and the Kowalskis; and [Karen Tomberlin, a Kowalski family friend]. These witnesses had no medical training, each had visited Sharon infrequently in recent years, and none had accompanied Sharon on any outings from the institution. Sharon's parents chose not to attend the hearing.

[T]he trial court denied Thompson's petition for guardianship and simultaneously appointed Tomberlin as guardian. . . . The only issue on appeal is the court's choice of guardian and its findings and conclusions on the comparative qualifications of Thompson and Tomberlin.

[Minn. Stat. §525.551(5) provides that the standard for appointment of a guardian is the best interests of the ward. The statute also enumerates certain criteria, discussed below, relevant in that determination.]

### 1. THE WARD'S EXPRESSED PREFERENCE

The court heard testimony from its appointed evaluation team at Miller-Dwan about Sharon's ability to express a reliable preference as to where and with whom she wanted to be. [T]he doctor overseeing the evaluation submitted the following recommendation to the court:

> We believe Sharon Kowalski has shown areas of potential and ability to make rational choices in many areas of her life and she has consistently indicated a desire to return home. And by that, she means to St. Cloud to live with Karen Thompson again. Whether that is possible is still uncertain as her care will be difficult and burdensome. We think she deserves the opportunity to try.

All the professional witnesses concurred in this conclusion, including Sharon's current treating physician. No contradictory evidence was provided from any professionals who worked with Sharon.

The three lay witnesses who opposed Thompson's petition were skeptical that Sharon could reliably express her wishes, saying that Sharon changed her mind too often to believe what she said, given her impaired short-term memory.

Despite the uncontradicted medical testimony about Sharon's capability to make choices in her life, the trial court concluded that Sharon could not express a reliable preference for guardianship. This court finds that, in the absence of contradictory evidence about Sharon's decision-making capacity from a professional or anyone in daily contact with her, the trial court's conclusion was clearly erroneous. . . .

### 2. PETITIONER'S QUALIFICATIONS

The medical professionals were all asked about Thompson's qualifications with respect to the statutory criteria. The testimony was consistent that Thompson: (1) achieves outstanding interaction with Sharon; (2) has extreme interest and commitment in promoting Sharon's welfare; (3) has an exceptional current understanding of Sharon's physical and mental status and needs, including appropriate rehabilitation; and (4) is strongly equipped to attend to Sharon's social and emotional needs.

Sharon's caretakers described how Thompson has been with Sharon three or more days per week, actively working with her in therapy and daily care. They described Thompson's detailed knowledge of Sharon's condition, changes, and needs.

The doctors unanimously testified that their long-term goal for Sharon's recovery is to assist her in returning to life outside an institution. It is undisputed that Thompson is the only person willing or able to care for Sharon outside an institution. In fact, Thompson has built a fully handicap-accessible home near St. Cloud in the hope that Sharon will be able to live there. On the other hand, Sharon's sister testified that none of her relatives is able to care for Sharon at home, and that her parents can no longer take Sharon for overnight visits. Tomberlin testified that she is not willing or able to care for Sharon at home and is in a position only to supervise Sharon's needs in an institution. . . .

The medical witnesses also testified about Thompson's effectiveness with Sharon's rehabilitation. They all agreed that Sharon can be stubborn and will often refuse to cooperate in therapy. They testified, however, that Thompson is best able to get Sharon motivated to work through the sometimes painful therapy. Moreover, Thompson is oftentimes the only one who can clean Sharon's mouth and teeth, since Sharon is apparently highly sensitive to invasion of her mouth. Oral hygiene is crucial to prevent recurrence of a mouth fungus which can contribute to pain and tooth loss, further inhibiting Sharon's communication skills and her ability to eat solid foods. . . .

The trial court concluded that "constant, long-term medical supervision in a neutral setting, such as a nursing home . . . is the ideal for Sharon's *long-term* care," and that "Ms. Thompson is incapable of providing, as a single caretaker, the necessary health care to Sharon at Thompson's home in St. Cloud." (Emphasis in original.) These conclusions are without evidentiary support and clearly erroneous as they are directly contradicted by the testimony of Sharon's doctors and other care providers. . . .

### 3. THE COURT'S CHOICE OF A "NEUTRAL" GUARDIAN

The trial court recognized Thompson and Sharon as a "family of affinity" and acknowledged that Thompson's continued presence in Sharon's life was important. In its guardianship decision, however, the court responded to the Kowalski family's steadfast opposition to Thompson being named guardian. Debra Kowalski testified that her parents would refuse ever to visit Sharon if Thompson is named guardian. The trial court likened the situation to a "family torn asunder into opposing camps," and concluded that a neutral third party was needed as guardian.

The record does not support the trial court's conclusion that choosing a "neutral" third party is now necessary. Thompson testified that she is committed to reaching an accommodation with the Kowalskis whereby they could visit with Sharon in a neutral setting or in their own home. . . . Thompson's appointment as guardian would not, of itself, result in the family ceasing to visit Sharon. The Kowalskis are free to visit their daughter if they wish. It is not the court's role to accommodate one side's threatened intransigence, where to do so would deprive the ward of an otherwise suitable and preferred guardian.

The court seized upon Tomberlin as a neutral party in this case. This decision, however, is not supported by sufficient evidence in the record as to either Tomberlin's suitability for guardianship or her neutrality. [G]iven that Tomberlin rarely visited Sharon, it is unlikely that [the] witnesses would have been able to comment knowledgeably on Tomberlin's qualifications. . . . There was equally little evidence establishing Tomberlin's neutrality in this case. . . . Tomberlin lives near the Kowalskis and helped facilitate the appearance at the hearing of Schroeder and Debra Kowalski in opposition to Thompson. Both in her deposition and at the hearing, Tomberlin testified that her first and primary goal as guardian was to relocate Sharon to the Iron Range, close to her family. This testimony undermines the one "qualification" relied on by the trial court in appointing Tomberlin — her role as an impartial mediator.

### 4. COURT-IDENTIFIED DEFICIENCIES IN APPELLANT'S PETITION

. . . The court found fault with Thompson on several issues the court viewed as contrary to Sharon's best interest. [T]he court suggested that Thompson's statement to the family and to the media that she and Sharon are lesbians was an invasion of privacy, perhaps rising to the level of an actionable tort. The court also took issue with Thompson taking

Sharon to public events, including some gay and lesbian-oriented gatherings and other community events where Thompson and Sharon were featured guests. Finally, the court concluded that Thompson's solicitation of legal defense funds and her testimony that she had been involved in other relationships since Sharon's accident raised questions of conflicts of interest with Sharon's welfare.

The record does not support the trial court's concern on any of these issues. First, while the extent to which Sharon had publicly acknowledged her sexual preference at the time of the accident is unclear, this is no longer relevant. Since the accident, Sharon's doctors and therapists testified that Sharon has voluntarily told them of her relationship with Thompson. Moreover, Sharon's doctor testified that it was in Sharon's best interest for Thompson to reveal the nature of their relationship promptly after the accident because it is crucial for doctors to understand who their patient was prior to the accident, including that patient's sexuality.

Second, there was no evidence offered at the hearing to suggest that Sharon is harmed or exploited by her attendance at public events. In fact, the court authorized Sharon to travel with Thompson to receive an award at the National Organization for Women's annual convention. A staff person who accompanied Sharon to one of these events testified that Sharon "had a great time" and interacted well with other people. . . . The only negative testimony about these outings consisted of speculation from Schroeder and Debra Kowalski that they did not think Sharon would enjoy the events, particularly those that were gay and lesbian-oriented in nature. They were, however, never in attendance and had no opportunity to evaluate Sharon's reaction firsthand.

Finally, there is no evidence in the record about a conflict of interest over Thompson's collection of defense funds or her other personal relationships. The evidence showed the money was raised in Thompson's own name to help defray the cost of years of litigation and that none of it was used for her personal expenses. Thompson testified that whatever extra money raised was used to purchase special equipment for Sharon, such as her voice machine, motorized wheelchair, hospital bed, and a special lift for transfers. . . .

Appellant also challenges the process by which Tomberlin was named guardian. She points out that Tomberlin never submitted a formal petition and that the court never held a hearing on her qualifications. [T]his court is troubled by the trial court's failure to give notice and its naming of Tomberlin in this manner. . . .

While the trial court has wide discretion in guardianship matters, this discretion is not boundless. [I]t appears the trial court clearly abused its discretion in denying Thompson's petition and naming Tomberlin guardian instead. . . . We reverse the trial court and grant Thompson's petition. . . .

## Notes and Questions

1. *Background and epilogue.* Immediately after the accident (caused by a drunk driver), relations between Karen and Sharon's parents were cordial. Hostility developed because of Karen's devotion and frequent hospital visits. On a psychologist's advice, Karen disclosed the women's relationship to the Kowalskis. The family was appalled, denied Sharon's lesbianism, and limited Karen's visitation. Animosity continued as Karen questioned their choice of a nursing home rather than a rehabilitation facility with state-of-the-art brain injury treatment. Sharon's parents moved her to a distant nursing home where she was not permitted an electric wheelchair, typewriter or computer (she could type short sentences); was confined to bed; and was denied visitation by her friends. Contrary to guardianship requirements, her father refused competency testing for three years.

During the eight-year separation from Sharon, Karen fell in love with, and began living with, a teacher. Nonetheless, Karen remained devoted to her ex-partner. After the principal case, Sharon came to live with both women, who care for her in their home. See generally Joyce Murdoch & Deb Price, Courting Justice: Gay Men and Lesbians v. the Supreme Court 260-270 (2001); Karen Thompson & Julie Andrzejewski, Why Can't Sharon Kowalski Come Home? (1988).

2. *Functional versus formalistic definitions.* The principal case, the third litigated dispute between Karen and the Kowalskis, rests on a clash between a functional versus formalistic definition of "family." In *Kowalski I*, 382 N.W.2d 861 (Minn. Ct. App.), *cert. denied*, 475 U.S. 1085 (1986), Karen petitioned for appointment as guardian, arguing that she was best suited based on her intimate relationship and Sharon's preference. Sharon's father, relying on the biological relationship, countered that his "unconditional parental love" supported his appointment.

The trial court, influenced by a formalistic definition of "family," confirmed Sharon's father and gave him power to determine her visitors. At the same time, the court rejected application of the substituted judgment standard, which would have given effect to Sharon's choices and ruled, instead, that the best interests standard should apply (that is, "best interests" as determined by the court). Further, the appellate court determined that Sharon's brain injuries precluded her expression of a reliable preference. The animosity between Karen and the Kowalskis continued. Acting on the advice of Sharon's physician, Mr. Kowalski moved to terminate Karen's visitation. In *Kowalski II*, 392 N.W.2d 310 (Minn. Ct. App. 1986), Karen unsuccessfully petitioned to find Mr. Kowalski in contempt for terminating her visitation and to remove him as guardian.

Both *Kowalski I* and *II* strongly affirm the role of legal family members as guardians with broad powers over incompetents. Moreover, both cases are laden with assumptions and stereotypes about the disabled (for example, reducing Sharon to a child, discounting her preferences, denying her sexuality) and about homosexuals and homosexuality (for example, questioning Sharon's lesbianism, characterizing Karen as sexually abusive and exploitative, stating the need for Sharon to be "protected" from her lover). See Amy L. Brown, Note, Broadening Anachronistic Notions of "Family" in Proxy Decisionmaking for Unmarried Adults, 41 Hastings L.J. 1029, 1059-1062 (1990). How does *Kowalski III,* the principal case, address these issues?

3. In a guardianship conflict between the family and a gay or lesbian partner, what relevance, if any, should attach to:

(a) the potential guardian's views of homosexuality? For example, Mr. Kowalski reportedly said, "On the farm and in the Army we called them queers and fruits" and also stated that Karen would never be granted guardianship because "there ain't a law in the United States that allows a lesbian relationship." Nancy Livingston, A Bitter Love Triangle: The Fight Between Family and Lover to Control a Woman's Future, S.F. Chron., Sept. 11, 1988 (This World), at 10.

(b) the manner in which the couple held themselves out? For example, Sharon never told her family of her relationship.

(c) the emotions experienced by the ward following the partner's visits? *Kowalski II* relied in part on Sharon's despondency following visits. Would the battle over guardianship have differed had Kowalski's partner been male?

4. *Medical decisionmaking.* One difficulty faced by Karen after the accident was an inability to acquire information about Sharon's medical condition and to make medical decisions. For example, Karen was told that medical personnel could only release information to "immediate family members." Thompson & Andrzejewski, supra, at 4. This issue has become increasingly serious for same-sex partners with the prevalence of AIDS. What might cohabitants do, prior to becoming incapacitated, to ensure they play a role in medical decisionmaking?

Traditionally, the common law included a preference for family members as guardians of incompetents to serve as proxy medical decisionmakers. Statutes and courts contain strict definitions of affinity and consanguinity in such determinations. Many states, however, now broaden common law preferences by permitting an incompetent to designate a proxy decisionmaker by means of a "durable power of attorney for health care decisionmaking." Such a designation is especially important for gay and lesbian couples.

A related problem arises after death as to the decisionmaker for disposition of the body. Because statutes give preference to a deceased's legal spouse (then to children, parents, and siblings), conflicts may arise between the surviving partner and family members. See generally Jennifer E. Horan, "When Sleep at Last Has Come": Controlling the Disposition of Dead Bodies for Same-Sex Couples, 2 J. Gender, Race & Just. 423 (1999).

## Problem

Karen and John live together with Karen's son from a prior marriage. When Karen becomes pregnant, she and John attend a natural childbirth class. They receive permission from Karen's physician for John to be present during labor and delivery. However, Mercy Memorial Hospital (the only hospital in the county equipped to deliver babies) refuses permission because John is not a member of Karen's "immediate family." Hospital policy limits the mother's support personnel to immediate family members. Karen and John allege that the policy violates the state civil rights act prohibiting discrimination in public accommodations and public services because of marital status. What result? See Whitman v. Mercy Mem. Hosp., 339 N.W.2d 730 (Mich. Ct. App. 1983).

### d. Domestic Violence

■ **STATE v. YADEN**
*1997 WL 106343 (Ohio Ct. App. 1997)*

PAINTER, J.
We are asked to decide whether a person living in a same-sex relationship may be guilty of domestic violence against the other person in violation of R.C. 2919.25. This is an issue of first impression in this district. . . .

In late April 1996, Dave Thompson, Joe Fields, Fields's son, Joe Jr., and defendant-appellant Ronnie Yaden went to a flea market. Fields and Yaden began to argue and the group returned to Fields's apartment. Thompson and Joe Jr. left the apartment temporarily. As the argument became louder, Fields threatened to call the police unless Yaden quieted down. Fields testified that Yaden ripped the phone from the wall and threw it, striking Fields in the forehead. Yaden then allegedly punched Fields in the stomach. . . . Yaden denied hitting Fields either in the head or in the stomach.

Fields and Yaden had been living together as a same-sex couple for approximately four years, but had broken up shortly before this incident. . . . After the breakup, Yaden continued to keep personal belongings in Fields's apartment and would stay with Fields when he had no other place to stay. . . .

[T]he trial court found Yaden guilty of a violation of R.C. 2919.25(A), domestic violence. Yaden has appealed, [arguing] that the trial court erred when it found that a same-sex relationship falls within the statutory definition of "living as a spouse." Yaden asserts that people who are not permitted legally to marry cannot live as though a marriage has occurred.

R.C. 2919.25(A) states that "[n]o person shall knowingly cause or attempt to cause physical harm to a family or household member." R.C. 2919.25(E)(1)(a)(i) defines "family or household member" in pertinent part as "[a] spouse, a person living as a spouse, or a former spouse of the offender." R.C. 2919.25(E)(2) further defines "living as a spouse" as "a person who is living or has lived with the offender in a common law marital relationship, who otherwise is cohabiting with the offender, or who otherwise has cohabited with the offender within one year prior to the date of the alleged commission of the act in question." Thus, Yaden asserts that he and Fields did not "cohabit" when they were living together for the four years prior to the incident, because, in his view, same-sex couples cannot "cohabit."

. . . The definition of "cohabitation" in the context of domestic violence in a same-sex relationship controls our decision on this issue. Jurists across the country have struggled to provide guidance. . . . Each unique set of facts giving rise to each court's focus on certain aspects over other aspects illustrates the complexity, difficulty and danger in creating some all-encompassing definition to describe intimate relationships.

In Alabama, cohabitation means "some permanency of relationship coupled with more than occasional sexual activity between the cohabitants." In California, cohabitation means "an unrelated man and woman living together in a substantial relationship manifested principally by a [sic] permanence, or sexual, or amorous intimacy." In Delaware, the alimony statute defines cohabitation as "regularly residing with an adult of the same or opposite sex, if the parties hold themselves out as a couple, and regardless of whether the relationship confers a financial benefit. . . ." In New Jersey, cohabitation is "generally residing together in a common residence . . . where they generally engage in some, but not necessarily all of the following: meals taken together at the residence; departing from and returning to the residence of the other for employment and/or social purposes; maintaining clothing at the other's residence; sleeping together at the residence, or the residence of the other; and receiving telephone calls at the residence or the residence of the other."

Other definitions include: "living together as husband and wife" (Illinois); "a significant live-together relationship" (Iowa); . . . "living together as husband and wife without a legal marriage having been performed" (Maryland); "living together as man and wife, though not necessarily implying sexual relations" (North Carolina); "living together in the same house" (South Carolina); "dwelling or living together; community of life . . ." (Texas); "doing things ordinarily done by spouses"

(Texas); and "liv[ing] together permanently or for an indefinite period and assum[ing] the duties and obligations normally attendant with a marital relationship." (Virginia). [Citations omitted.] . . .

Against this backdrop of definitions, we turn to Ohio jurisprudence in this area. Cohabitation has not been defined by the Ohio Supreme Court. [This court has held] that "cohabitation" is "a man and a woman living together in the same household and behaving as would a husband and wife." But the context of our decision and the decision upon which it was based concerned opposite-sex relationships and did not involve same-sex cohabitation. . . .

The seminal Ohio case with facts describing domestic violence in a same-sex relationship is State v. Hadinger [573 N.E.2d 1191 (Ohio Ct. App. 1991)]. In *Hadinger,* the Tenth District Court of Appeals compiled various definitions given for cohabitation and stated that the only common thread among those definitions was simply "living together in an intimate relationship." The Hamilton County Municipal Court has agreed with *Hadinger* that same-sex couples are subject to the domestic violence statute [State v. Linner, 665 N.E.2d 1180 (Hamilton Cty. Mun. Ct. 1996)]. . . .

In short, definitions of "cohabitation" have two fact-specific prongs: financial support and consortium. Factors that establish financial support include shelter, food, clothing, utilities, and perhaps co-mingled assets. Factors that establish consortium include mutual respect, fidelity, emotional support, affection, society, cooperation, solace, comfort, aid of each other, friendship, conjugal relations and companionship. The facts that rise to the level of "cohabitation" are unique to each case, and can only be sifted on a case-by-case basis by triers of fact.

The *Hadinger* court concluded that, under the language of R.C. 2919.25, the legislature intended the statute to protect persons who are cohabiting, regardless of sex. It is true that same-sex couples are not permitted to be "spouses" with each other. But the definition of "living as a spouse" includes a larger segment of couples — not only "spouses" but also "cohabitors." Opposite-sex couples who "cohabit" are protected. We can see no tangible benefit to withholding this statutory protection from same-sex couples. . . .

## Notes and Questions

1. All states have civil and/or criminal legislation addressing domestic violence. See Chapter III, section C3. Such legislation often includes provisions for protective orders, such as restraining orders and orders allowing the victim exclusive possession of the dwelling. Many of these statutes include broad definitions that protect cohabitants. Should such statutes be limited to cohabitants of the opposite sex? To cohabitants

with children? Cf. N.Y. Crim. Proc. Law §530.11 (McKinney 1995 & Supp. 2001) (applies to "persons who have a child in common, regardless whether such persons have been married or have lived together at any time").

2. Some statutes permit ex parte orders (issued without notice or a hearing) that restrain the offender from entering the victim's dwelling. E.g., Mich. Ct. Rules 3.207 (2001). The theory is that the victim, who is usually the woman, is more likely to be the financially dependent party. Leaving the batterer would therefore be more burdensome. Should this remedy be extended to unmarried cohabitants who may be less likely than spouses to have a property interest in the home?

3. Does broad statutory interpretation, as adopted by *Yaden*, result in difficulties for arresting officers who must determine whether a victim is "cohabiting" with the offender?

## Problem

Mary lives in a small hotel room without kitchen facilities. A friend, Joe, comes to stay during June. In July, Joe rents another motel room, taking his belongings with him. He comes to live with Mary for the last two weeks of August. Joe returns to the hotel room after long days at work only to shower and sleep. Mary and Joe do not cook together and rarely eat together. They have sex occasionally. Mary describes the relationship as that of friends and roommates. Joe admits sleeping in Mary's bed (explaining that there was no other bed) but states that he slept on top of the covers, with his pants on. Joe does not have a key to Mary's room; she leaves the door unlocked. Mary and Joe do not share rent, have a joint bank account, make joint purchases, or hold themselves out as husband and wife. On August 29, Joe beats and terrorizes Mary. He is charged with inflicting corporal injury on a cohabitant under the following penal code provision:

> Any person who willfully inflicts upon his or her spouse, or any person who willfully inflicts upon any person of the opposite sex with whom he or she is cohabiting, corporal injury resulting in a traumatic condition, is guilty of a felony, and upon conviction thereof shall be punished by imprisonment in the state prison for 2, 3 or 4 years. . . . (b) Holding oneself out to be the husband or wife of the person with whom one is cohabiting is not necessary to constitute cohabitation as the term is used in this section.

Joe argues that the provision is void for vagueness by not defining "cohabiting." What result? See People v. Holifield, 252 Cal. Rptr. 729 (Ct. App. 1988).

■ **RUTHANN ROBSON, LAVENDER BRUISES:**
**INTRA-LESBIAN VIOLENCE, LAW AND**
**LESBIAN LEGAL THEORY**
*20 Golden Gate U. L. Rev. 567, 570-581 (1990)*

The legal sanctions in cases of intra-lesbian violence have often been directed more at the "lesbian" sexual component than at the act(s) of violence. [A]nother legal response to intra-lesbian violence which implicitly privileges sexuality over violence is the insistence on the erasure of lesbianism. . . . Thus, the lesbianism may be denied or it may be "hetero-relationized."[6] . . .

Not only does hetero-relationality impact upon legal responses to intra-lesbian violence, but homophobia does as well. In a very recent and unreported trial apparently involving the first use of the "battered woman syndrome" defense in a lesbian relationship, Annette Green was convicted of the first degree murder of her lover Ivonne Julio by a Palm Beach County, Florida, jury. The judge allowed the "battered woman syndrome defense," construing it as a "battered person defense."[13] The prosecutor had argued that the defense was inappropriate, despite his admission that defendant Green had been "battered." "She was shot at before by the victim. She had a broken nose, broken ribs." Nevertheless, even with the complicated issues presented by the "battered person" defense before the jury, it took only two and one-half hours to return a guilty verdict. Green's defense attorney attributed this to homophobia, noting that it usually takes a jury much longer to deliberate, even in routine cases. One jury member related an incident to the judge in which two venire members spoke in the women's restroom about their desire to be selected as jurors in order to "hang that lesbian bitch."

[T]he legal help available to battered lesbians may be chimerical. In Florida, where Annette Green was surviving abuse before she killed her lover, Green was not within the statutory definitions of a victim of domestic abuse. Annette Green was not entitled to shelter or services from "domestic violence centers," partially funded by the state, because domestic violence is defined as violence "by a person against the person's spouse." [Fla. Stat. §415.602(3) (1989).] Further, Annette Green was not entitled to avail herself of the judicial system to obtain an injunction for protection against domestic violence. . . .

Even where legal assistance is statutorily available, applications for restraining orders may be denied by courts because of the parties' lesbianism. The courts may reason that the situation is one of "mutual

---

6. This phrase is from Janice Raymond's concept of the re-definition of women in "hetero-relational terms" to fit prevailing models of heterosexuality and patriarchy. See J. Raymond, A Passion for Friends 64-66 (1986).

13. Telephone conversation with William Lasley, attorney for Annette Green (Nov. 13, 1989).

combat." The term "mutual combat" indicates a situation where the parties are "really just fighting" rather than one in which abuse is occurring. . . . "[M]utual combat" is a myth, and a dangerous one. . . . Many judges and legal officials have been educated in domestic violence issues in ways which emphasize the dominant/submissive patriarchal arrangement based on objective criteria such as gender. When such factors are absent, judges may be more likely to feel inadequate to determine against whom the restraining order should issue. In the face of such inadequacy, such judges may either deny the restraining order or issue a mutual restraining order.

The denying of a restraining order has obvious import: the violence is legally sanctioned. The issuing of a mutual restraining order may have a less obvious significance. To be "restrained" from doing some act one has never done and apparently has no desire to do, appears insignificant. Yet this very irrelevance conveys the message of its relevance. . . . In addition to its rhetoric, the mutual restraining order has practical legal effects. [P]enalties are applied to persons against whom restraining orders have been issued [such as disqualification from] employment with mental health facilities, alcohol treatment facilities, drug treatment facilities, nursing homes, or child care facilities, or from working with the developmentally disabled, working with youth services or providing foster care. . . .

[T]he silence about intra-lesbian violence, both intimate and nonintimate, is founded on an acute — and very real — awareness of societal homophobia. Internalized homophobia also impacts upon the reactions of individuals within the lesbian community, often in complex and contradictory ways. For example, internalized homophobia may lead one to become rigidly defensive about one's lesbianism and thus susceptible to denying intra-lesbian violence even when witnessed or experienced. . . .

---

See also Krisana M. Hodges, Comment, Trouble in Paradise: Barriers to Addressing Domestic Violence in Lesbian Relationships, 9 Law & Sexuality 311 (2000).

### e. Familial Benefits: Housing, Inheritance, Adoption

■ **BRASCHI v. STAHL ASSOCIATES CO.**
*543 N.E.2d 49 (N.Y. 1989)*

TITONE, Judge. . . .
Appellant, Miguel Braschi, was living with Leslie Blanchard in a rent-controlled apartment located at 405 East 54th Street from the sum-

mer of 1975 until Blanchard's death in September of 1986. [R]espondent, Stahl Associates Company, the owner of the apartment building, served a notice to cure on appellant contending that he was a mere licensee with no right to occupy the apartment since only Blanchard was the tenant of record [and threatened eviction proceedings]. The present dispute arises because the term "family" is not defined in the rent-control code and the legislative history is devoid of any specific reference to the noneviction provision. All that is known is the legislative purpose underlying the enactment of the rent-control laws as a whole.

Rent control was enacted to address a "serious public emergency" created by "an acute shortage in dwellings," which resulted in "speculative, unwarranted and abnormal increases in rents" (L. 1946 ch. 274, codified, as amended, at McKinney's Uncons. Laws of N.Y. §8581 et seq.). These measures were designed to regulate and control the housing market so as to "prevent exactions of unjust, unreasonable and oppressive rents and rental agreements and to forestall profiteering, speculation and other disruptive practices tending to produce threats to the public health [and] to prevent uncertainty, hardship and dislocation" (id.). [The legislation was] initially designed as an emergency measure to alleviate the housing shortage attributable to the end of World War II. . . .

To accomplish its goals, the Legislature recognized that not only would rents have to be controlled, but that evictions would have to be regulated and controlled as well. Hence, section 2204.6 of the New York City Rent and Eviction Regulations, which authorizes the issuance of a certificate for the eviction of persons occupying a rent-controlled apartment after the death of the named tenant, provides, in subdivision (d), noneviction protection to those occupants who are either the "surviving spouse of the deceased tenant or *some other member of the deceased tenant's family* who has been living with the tenant [of record]" (emphasis supplied).

[R]espondent argues that the term "family member" as used in 9 NYCRR 2204.6(d) should be construed, consistent with this State's intestacy laws, to mean relationships of blood, consanguinity and adoption in order to effectuate the over-all goal of orderly succession to real property. Under this interpretation, only those entitled to inherit under the laws of intestacy would be afforded noneviction protection. [R]espondent relies on our decision in Matter of Robert Paul P., 63 N.Y.2d 233, 481 N.Y.S.2d 652, 471 N.E.2d 424 [(1984)], arguing that since the relationship between appellant and Blanchard has not been accorded legal status by the Legislature, it is not entitled to the protections of section 2204.6(d). . . . Finally, respondent contends that our construction of the term "family member" should be guided by the recently enacted noneviction provision of the Rent Stabilization Code (9 NYCRR 2523.5[a], [b][1], [2]) [which includes a precise definition of family members based on the existence of marital or blood ties].

However, as we have continually noted, the rent-stabilization system is different from the rent-control system in that the former is a less onerous burden on the property owner, and thus the provisions of one cannot simply be imported into the other. Respondent's reliance on Matter of Robert Paul P. is also misplaced, since [that case] was based solely on the purposes of the adoption laws and has no bearing on the proper interpretation of a provision in the rent-control laws.

We also reject respondent's argument that the purpose of the noneviction provision of the rent-control laws is to control the orderly succession to real property in a manner similar to that which occurs under our State's intestacy laws. The noneviction provision does not concern succession to real property but rather is a means of protecting a certain class of occupants from the sudden loss of their homes. . . . Moreover, such a construction would be inconsistent with the purposes of the rent-control system as a whole, since it would afford protection to distant blood relatives who actually had but a superficial relationship with the deceased tenant while denying that protection to unmarried lifetime partners. . . .

Contrary to all of these arguments, we conclude that the term family, as used in 9 NYCRR 2204.6(d), should not be rigidly restricted to those people who have formalized their relationship by obtaining, for instance, a marriage certificate or an adoption order. The intended protection against sudden eviction should not rest on fictitious legal distinctions or genetic history, but instead should find its foundation in the reality of family life. In the context of eviction, a more realistic, and certainly equally valid, view of a family includes two adult lifetime partners whose relationship is long term and characterized by an emotional and financial commitment and interdependence. This view comports both with our society's traditional concept of "family" and with the expectations of individuals who live in such nuclear units. In fact, Webster's Dictionary defines "family" first as "a group of people united by certain convictions or common affiliation" (Webster's Ninth New Collegiate Dictionary 448 [1984]). Hence, it is reasonable to conclude that, in using the term "family," the Legislature intended to extend protection to those who reside in households having all of the normal familial characteristics. Appellant Braschi should therefore be afforded the opportunity to prove that he and Blanchard had such a household. . . .

The determination as to whether an individual is entitled to noneviction protection should be based upon an objective examination of the relationship of the parties. In making this assessment, the lower courts of this State have looked to a number of factors, including the exclusivity and longevity of the relationship, the level of emotional and financial commitment, the manner in which the parties have conducted their everyday lives and held themselves out to society, and the reliance placed upon one another for daily family services. These factors are most helpful, although it should be emphasized that the presence or absence of one or more of them is not dispositive since it is the totality of the relationship as evidenced by the dedication, caring and self-sacrifice of the parties which should, in the final analysis, control. Appellant's situation provides an example of how the rule should be applied.

Appellant and Blanchard lived together as permanent life partners for more than 10 years. They regarded one another, and were regarded by friends and family, as spouses. The two men's families were aware of the nature of the relationship, and they regularly visited each other's families and attended family functions together, as a couple. Even today, appellant continues to maintain a relationship with Blanchard's niece, who considers him an uncle.

In addition to their interwoven social lives, appellant clearly considered the apartment his home. He lists the apartment as his address on his driver's license and passport, and receives all his mail at the apartment address. Moreover, appellant's tenancy was known to the building's superintendent and doormen, who viewed the two men as a couple.

Financially, the two men shared all obligations including a household budget. The two were authorized signatories of three safe-deposit boxes, they maintained joint checking and savings accounts, and joint credit cards. In fact, rent was often paid with a check from their joint checking account. Additionally, Blanchard executed a power of attorney in appellant's favor so that appellant could make necessary decisions — financial, medical and personal — for him during his illness. Finally, appellant was the named beneficiary of Blanchard's life insurance policy, as well as the primary legatee and coexecutor of Blanchard's estate. Hence, a court examining these facts could reasonably conclude that these men were much more than mere roommates. [The court concludes] that appellant has demonstrated a likelihood of success on the merits [and remands the case].

■  **NORTH DAKOTA FAIR HOUSING COUNCIL
v. PETERSON**
*625 N.W.2d 551 (N.D. 2001)*

SANDSTROM, Justice.

In 1999, an unmarried couple tried to rent from David and Mary Peterson. The Petersons refused because the unmarried couple were seeking to cohabit. The North Dakota Fair Housing Council and Robert and Patricia Kippen — the unmarried couple, who had since married — sued, claiming housing discrimination in violation of the North Dakota Human Rights Act. . . .

[The landlords moved to dismiss the Housing Council on the ground that they lacked standing, and the district court granted the motion. The

Housing Council appealed. The district court also granted summary judgment in favor of the Petersons. The Kippens appealed.]

We are asked to decide whether refusing to rent to an unmarried couple because they are seeking to cohabit violates the discriminatory housing practices provision of the North Dakota Human Rights Act, N.D.C.C. §14-02.4-12. The question is one of statutory interpretation. . . . The pertinent human rights statute in effect at the time of the alleged violation, North Dakota Century Code §14-02.4-12 (1995), provided:

> Discriminatory housing practices by owner or agent. It is a discriminatory practice for an owner of rights to housing or real property [to]:
>
>     Refuse to transfer an interest in real property or housing accommodation to a person because of race, color, religion, sex, national origin, age, physical or mental disability, or status with respect to marriage or public assistance . . .

We have not previously addressed the relationship between N.D.C.C. §§12.1-20-10 [the prohibition of cohabitation] and 14-02.4-12 [above]. The issue, however, has been addressed in a formal attorney general's opinion and in two federal district court opinions. We begin with a review of the history of the legislation.

North Dakota has prohibited unlawful cohabitation since statehood. The provision, as codified in 1895, remained essentially unchanged until the 1970s. . . . The 1971 legislative assembly provided for an interim committee to draft a new criminal code. The interim committee considered whether to recommend repeal of the prohibition on unlawful cohabitation. . . . Because sexual offenses were a controversial portion of the proposed new criminal code, alternative provisions were submitted to the 1973 legislature in three separate bills. All three bills contain the same language on unlawful cohabitation [with somewhat different penalties]. The new criminal code [retaining the prohibition] was approved by the 1973 legislature. . . .

The 1983 legislature adopted the North Dakota Human Rights Act. 1983 N.D. Sess. Laws ch. 173. The legislative history reflects no discussion of the cohabitation statute.

The issue of a claimed conflict between the cohabitation statute and the Human Rights Act was presented to the attorney general in 1990. In a formal opinion, the attorney general wrote: . . .

> The North Dakota Supreme Court has not ruled on the apparent conflict between N.D.C.C. §§14-02.4-12's protection of a person's right to housing notwithstanding the person's marital status, and N.D.C.C. §12.1-20-10's prohibition against allowing unmarried couples to live as a married couple. However, there has been similar litigation in other states whose laws prohibit both cohabitation and discriminatory housing prac-

tices based on marital statutes. In McFadden v. Elma Country Club, 26 Wash. App. 146 [195], 613 P.2d 146 (1980), the court held that, notwithstanding a statute prohibiting discrimination based upon marital status, a country club could refuse to admit to membership an unmarried woman cohabiting with a man. Id. at 152. The court's holding was based upon the fact the statute prohibiting cohabitation was not repealed when the discrimination statute was enacted. This fact the court said "would vitiate any argument that the legislature intended 'marital status' discrimination to include discrimination on the basis of a couple's unwed cohabitation." Id. at 150.

As in the *McFadden* case, N.D.C.C. §12.1-20-10 was not repealed when N.D.C.C. §14-02.4-12 was enacted. Thus, the continuing existence of the unlawful cohabitation statute after the enactment of N.D.C.C. §14-02.4-12 vitiates "any argument that the legislature intended 'marital status' discrimination to include discrimination on the basis of a couple's unwed cohabitation." *McFadden* at 150. . . .

Attorney General's Opinion 90-12 (1990).

In 1991, House Bill 1403, a measure to repeal the cohabitation statute, was introduced, with the legislator who had requested the 1990 attorney general's opinion as the primary sponsor. . . . The House of Representatives defeated the bill by a vote of 27 yeas and 78 nayes.

In 1999, the United States District Court for North Dakota decided a case involving the alleged conflict between the cohabitation statute and the Human Rights Act and concluded it was not unlawful to refuse to rent to an unmarried couple seeking to cohabit. . . . North Dakota Fair Housing Council, Inc. v. Haider, No. A1-98-077 (D.N.D. 1999). In 2000, the United States District Court for North Dakota decided a suit similar to this one brought by the Housing Council. North Dakota Fair Housing Council v. Woeste, No. A1-99-116 (D.N.D. 2000). The federal court, analyzing North Dakota law and distinguishing federal cases relied on by the Housing Council, concluded the Housing Council lacked standing to sue under the North Dakota Human Rights Act. . . .

With this historical background, we turn to the framework for analyzing statutes and claimed conflicts between statutes. . . . We now consider the meaning of the cohabitation statute and the meaning of the Human Rights Act discriminatory housing practices provision. . . . North Dakota's cohabitation statute, N.D.C.C. §12.1-20-10, states:

A person is guilty of a class B misdemeanor if he or she lives openly and notoriously with a person of the opposite sex as a married couple without being married to the other person.

The 1973 amendment of the statute removed the language "cohabits as husband or wife" and added "lives openly and notoriously with a person of the opposite sex as a married couple."

Varying definitions of cohabitation exist. The 1996 edition of Merriam Webster's Dictionary of Law defines cohabit as "to live together as a married couple or in the manner of a married couple." The 1999 edition of Black's Law Dictionary, at page 254, defines cohabitation as "[t]he fact or state of living together, esp. as partners in life, usu. with the suggestion of sexual relations." Notorious cohabitation is the "act of a man and a woman openly living together under circumstances that make the arrangement illegal under statutes that are now rarely enforced."[4] Id. The Minnesota Supreme Court has defined "cohabit" as living "together in a sexual relationship when not legally married." State by Cooper v. French, 460 N.W.2d 2, 4 n.1 (Minn. 1990) (citing The American Heritage Dictionary of the English Language 259 (1980) (New College Dictionary)). . . .

The Housing Council asserts that North Dakota has decriminalized all sexual relations among consenting adults. The assertion is contradicted by the cohabitation statute as well as the criminal penalties for adultery, bigamy, prostitution, or incest, notwithstanding the consent of the parties. . . .

At issue is the term "status with respect to marriage," which is undefined under the Human Rights Act. Analyzing other definitions under North Dakota law, the district court concluded the "Legislature intended the phrase to mean being married, single, separated or divorced." The Housing Council and the Kippens argue "status with respect to marriage" is simple: a person is either married or not married. Although it is unlawful to deny housing based solely on whether a person is or is not married, the relevant inquiry is whether a person is divorced, widowed, or separated, rather than simply married or unmarried.

The Petersons argue that although it is true that under the discriminatory housing provision a person cannot be discriminated against because of marital status, the Kippens were denied housing not because they were single, but because they were unmarried and were seeking to live together as if they were married. . . .

Numerous courts have addressed language similar to "status with respect to marriage," the language at issue here. Those courts disagree regarding the appropriate weight to give to words with an import similar to "status with respect to marriage." In McCready v. Hoffius, 222 Mich. App. 210, 564 N.W.2d 493, 495-96 (1997), the court differentiated marital status from conduct by concluding the term "marital status" was legislatively intended to prohibit discrimination "based on *whether* a person is married" (quoting Miller v. C.A. Muer Corp., 420 Mich. 355, 362 N.W.2d 650 (1984)).

---

4. Although it is argued cohabitation statutes are rarely enforced, this Court has held the lack of enforcement to be of no significance.

The Wisconsin Supreme Court has also concluded refusal to rent to unmarried tenants who choose to live together is based on conduct rather than status. See County of Dane v. Norman, 174 Wis.2d 683, 497 N.W.2d 714 (1993). On the other hand, Alaska, Massachusetts, and California have concluded refusal to rent to unmarried cohabitants is based upon status rather than conduct. [Smith v. Fair Employment & Housing Comm'n, 913 P.2d 909 (Cal. 1996), *cert. denied*, 521 U.S. 1129 (1997); Swanner v. Anchorage Equal Rights Comm'n, 874 P.2d 274 (Alaska 1994), *cert. denied*, 513 U.S. 979 (1994); Attorney General v. Desilets, 636 N.E.2d 233 (Mass. 1994)]. . . .

When the legislature enacted the Human Rights Act, it is presumed to have known of the existing criminal cohabitation statute. [B]y suggesting the Human Rights Act requires that housing be provided regardless of compliance with the criminal code, the Housing Council and the Kippens are asking us to repeal or to give new meaning to the cohabitation statute. We are then confronted with the well-established rule precluding amendment or repeal of legislation by implication. . . . The cohabitation statute and the discriminatory housing provision are harmonized by recognizing that the cohabitation statute regulates conduct, not status. The opposite interpretation would render the prohibition against cohabitation meaningless.

Like Michigan, Wisconsin, and Minnesota, we conclude these two provisions may be harmonized while still giving each of them full effect. It is unlawful to openly and notoriously live together as husband and wife without being married. It is unlawful to deny housing based on a person's status with respect to marriage (i.e., married, single, divorced, widowed, or separated). It is not unlawful to deny housing to an unmarried couple seeking to openly and notoriously live together as husband and wife. . . . Under the words of the statute, the rules of statutory construction, and the legislative, administrative, and judicial history, we conclude it is not an unlawful discriminatory practice under N.D.C.C. §14-02.4-12 to refuse to rent to unmarried persons seeking to cohabit. Summary judgment was therefore appropriate. . . .

## Notes and Questions

1. *Braschi*, like *Dunphy*, adopts a functional definition of family. The significance of this definition for the recognition of the rights of gay and lesbian partners cannot be underestimated. As one commentator remarks:

> Both *Braschi* and *Dunphy* illustrate the greatest advantage and benefit of pursuing recognition of lesbian and gay families from the functional perspective. These cases promote an examination of the purpose for which

the law was adopted and ask whether adhering to formalized definitions of family furthers or obstructs the law's goals. In so doing, the courts paved the way for many types of families to receive long overdue support.

Paula L. Ettelbrick, Wedlock Alert: A Comment on Lesbian and Gay Family Recognition, 5 J.L. & Pol'y 107, 142 (1996). How determinative is the functional definition of "family" in *Smith*?

2. *Braschi* states that the legislature intended to protect those who reside in households "having all of the normal familial characteristics." Which "normal familial characteristics" did the Braschi household exhibit? Which did it not? Recall the question posed at the beginning of the chapter: Should the state define and impose a legal meaning of "family" on all persons without exception, or should the law honor private choices, so long as a given unit acts like a family and performs familial functions? See generally Note, Looking for a Family Resemblance: The Limits of the Functional Approach to the Legal Definition of Family, 104 Harv. L. Rev. 1640 (1991). See also Martha L. Minow, Redefining Families: Who's In and Who's Out?, 62 U. Colo. L. Rev. 269 (1991).

Does *Braschi* sanction legal distinctions between those same-sex couples who do and those who do not fit the traditional family model? For example, suppose one of the partners is not monogamous? See Picon v. O.D.C. Assocs., No. 86-22894 (Sup. Ct. N.Y. Co., Jan. 28, 1991) (minimizing relevance of sexual affair for surviving tenant's occupancy claim because "peccadillos of this nature seem not to be uncommon, even in the marital life of normally married couples"). Suppose the couple keeps their finances separate? See Kath Weston, Families We Choose: Lesbians, Gays, Kinship 113-114 (1991) (reporting empirical findings that lesbian and gay partners tend to manifest more financial independence than do heterosexual couples).

Although many gay and lesbian commentators applaud the result in *Braschi*, some criticize its implications. For example, Professor Mary Ann Case writes:

> In *Braschi*, the court held, in effect, that if you behave like Ozzie and Harriet, or alternatively like Baron and Feme [husband and wife], then you are a couple and can receive the succession rights of family members under the New York rent control laws. The Court of Appeals, in determining whether the household Braschi had shared with his deceased lover . . . focused on things like sexual fidelity, sharing a domicile, and commingling finances as the evidence of commitment it required before recognizing the couple.
>
> Married couples in this society are not required to do the rather conservative things the Court of Appeals required of Braschi and his lover. . . .

Mary Ann Case, Couples and Coupling in the Public Sphere: A Comment on the Legal History of Litigating for Lesbian and Gay Rights, 79

Va. L. Rev. 1643 (1993). Do you agree with Professor Case's criticism that *Braschi* may be "more oppressive for feminists, whatever their sexual preference, than gay marriage would be for anyone"? Id. at 1666.

3. *Braschi* suggests factors to determine whether an individual qualifies as a family member for noneviction protection. Do you agree with the dissent that these factors "produce[ ] an unworkable test that is subject to abuse" and leads to extended litigation "focusing on such intangibles as the strength and duration of the relationship and the extent of the emotional and financial interdependency"? Does *Braschi*'s necessity of proof of financial interdependence cause more difficulty for low-income cohabitants? One commentator notes that recipients of government benefits programs "often are forced to down play their interconnectedness with a co-occupant in order to maximize their benefit levels." Paris Baldacci, Litigation Succession Rights Cases of Nontraditionally Recognized Families in Rent-Controlled/Stabilized Housing in New York State: Some Evidentiary and Procedural Issues, 242 Practising L. Inst./Est. 89, 117 (Dec. 1995).

4. Social forces historically play a role in the development of landlord-tenant law. For example, the civil rights movement and the Vietnam War influenced the "revolution" in tenant rights in the late 1960s and 1970s. Edward H. Rabin, The Revolution in Residential Landlord-Tenant Law: Causes and Consequences, 69 Cornell L. Rev. 517, 546, 550 (1984). What social forces might have played a role in *Braschi*?

5. New York distinguishes between "rent control" and "rent stabilization."[9] As *Braschi* reveals, different definitions of "family" apply for rent control versus rent stabilization purposes. The former provides protection against eviction for the co-resident surviving spouse or "some other (co-resident) member of the deceased tenant's family." The latter provision includes a more precise definition, limiting family members to husband, wife, son, daughter, steprelationships, nephew, niece, uncle, aunt, grandparents, grandchildren, and in-law relationships. Further, different definitions apply for inheritance purposes and zoning purposes. How does the *Braschi* majority treat the existence of these conflicting definitions? What is the effect of granting legal recognition for some purposes but not others?

Shortly after *Braschi*, a similar case arose under the rent stabilization legislation. Robert Wells and Stuart Goldstein lived together in a rent

---

[9]. Both rent stabilization and rent control impose ceilings on rent increases, with minor differences. A vacancy in a rent controlled apartment permits a landlord to return the apartment to market rent; a vacancy in a rent stabilized apartment permits a landlord to re-rent at a slightly higher rate. Rent control generally applies to buildings built before 1947. See G. Samuel Zucker, Insurance for Eviction Without Cause: A Middle Path for Tenant Tenure Rights and a New Remedy for Retaliatory Eviction, 28 Urb. Law. 113, 118 n.18 (1996).

stabilized apartment from 1977 to 1987 when Goldstein, the named tenant on the lease, died of AIDS. When the landlord attempted to evict Wells to re-rent at a higher price, Wells argued that *Braschi* applied. The Appellate Division agreed, finding similar purposes behind the two code sections, and ruled that Wells was protected despite the statutory limitations to named family members. The court concluded that the relationship met the *Braschi* standard, noting:

> Both of these individuals demonstrated a high level of emotional commitment to one another and took care of each other's day-to-day needs. They were open about their relationship, and their devotion to one another as life partners was apparent to their family and friends, as is reflected in affidavits by Goldstein's mother and son, who considered Wells to be a part of their family and have characterized the relationship of their son and father and that of a spouse to Wells.

East 10th St. Assocs. v. Estate of Goldstein, 552 N.Y.S.2d 257, 257 (App. Div. 1990).

6. Case law reveals considerable incongruity in the treatment of cohabitants' rights. For example, in Trombetta v. Conkling, 593 N.Y.S.2d 670 (App. Div. 1993), a niece witnessed an accident in which her aunt was killed by a tractor-trailer. Although the two women did not reside in the same household, the aunt had cared for the plaintiff after the plaintiff's mother's death when the plaintiff was 11 years old. The two saw each other daily and the plaintiff asserted that the aunt was the most important person in the plaintiff's life. The court dismissed plaintiff's claim based on its concern with limiting liability. For another incongruous result in the same jurisdiction, see *Alison D.* in Chapter 7, section B3.

7. *Braschi*, like *Dunphy*, presents a dispute not of cohabitants inter se (as *Marvin*), but rather a dispute involving third parties. Does the presence of third parties dictate different treatment of cohabitants in the housing and tort contexts?

Further, how relevant is the fact that *Braschi* did *not* present the court with two openly gay litigants in a contentious dispute? One commentator responds:

> [F]or the equanimity of the New York court's mind . . . , the [*Braschi*] plaintiff was not, after all, in a living gay relation — owing to the death of his life-partner. [C]ourts may give rights to gays by ones, but they will not give rights to gays by twos. . . . So when the courts do on occasion give rights to gays by ones — they do so in spite of rather than because of their gayness. And in giving rights to gays by ones only, the courts, even as they hand out a right, destroy the very basis and idea of gayness, that it is a relation between people.

Richard D. Mohr, Gay Ideas: Outing and Other Controversies 82 (1992). See also William Rubenstein, We Are Family: A Reflection on the Search for Legal Recognition of Lesbian and Gay Relationships, 8 J.L. & Pol'y 89 (1991) (discussing role of stereotypes in *Braschi*).

8. In response to *Braschi,* the State Division of Housing and Community Renewal (DHCR) amended administrative regulations to conform the provisions governing lease succession rights and anti-eviction protections. DHCR promulgated an emergency rule broadening the definition of "family" in accordance with *Braschi* and eliminated the distinction between the tenant of record's death and departure. See N.Y. Comp. Codes R. & Regs. tit. 9, §2204.6(d)(3)(i) (Supp. 1996). Landlords' organizations successfully sought to enjoin the rule's implementation. Following *Goldstein,* the Appellate Division of the State Supreme Court vacated the preliminary injunction. Rent Stabilization Assn. v. Higgens, 562 N.Y.S.2d 962 (App. Div. 1990). Subsequently, the Appellate Division reaffirmed the validity of the regulations (592 N.Y.S.2d 255 (App. Div. 1993)) and the Court of Appeals affirmed (608 N.Y.S.2d 930 (1993)).

9. Is housing an appropriate context in which to implement social goals? Is zoning? Recall Village of Belle Terre v. Boraas, supra. Are the contexts distinguishable?

10. *Peterson* reveals that because federal law (the Fair Housing Act of 1968, amended by the Fair Housing Amendments Act of 1988, 42 U.S.C. §§3601-3619, 3631 (1994 & Supp. V 1999)) does not prohibit marital status discrimination, unmarried cohabitants must resort to state law for protection. Most states, however, fail to address marital status discrimination. A few states explicitly exclude unmarried cohabitants from coverage. Among those states with specific prohibitions against marital status discrimination, jurisdictions are split as to whether the term "marital status" applies to unmarried cohabitants. Michael V. Hernandez, The Right of Religious Landlords to Exclude Unmarried Cohabitants: Debunking the Myth of the Tenant's "New Clothes," 77 Neb. L. Rev. 494, 500-506 (1998). Because many states (in this last category) have no definition of "marital status," courts (like *Peterson*) must turn to legislative and judicial history.

11. What is the status/conduct distinction referred to in *Peterson*? Is it a meaningful distinction? See Barbara Endoy, Irreconcilable Cohabitation Statutes and Statutory Proscriptions Against Marital Status Discrimination: *McCready v. Hoffius* and the Unworkable Status-Conduct Distinction, 44 Wayne L. Rev. 1809 (1999).

12. Suppose a landlord refuses to rent to unmarried couples on religious grounds. Is the First Amendment a defense against the landlord's violation of state housing discrimination laws? See Smith v. Fair Employment & Housing Comm'n, 913 P.2d 909 (Cal. 1996). See also Hernandez, supra. How relevant is the presence or absence of a statutory prohibition against cohabitation and fornication? Should it matter that these statutes are rarely, if ever, enforced?

13. In one of the few reported cases of housing discrimination involving same-sex couples, two lesbians challenged a university housing policy. In Levin v. Yeshiva University, 754 N.E.2d 1099 (N.Y. 2001), two medical students applied to have their respective same-sex partners live with them in university housing. The university denied their requests based on a rule permitting only spouses (subject to proof of marriage) and dependent children to reside in university housing. The medical students sued the university, alleging a violation of the state prohibitions against marital status discrimination and housing discrimination. The court rejected their marital status claim, arguing that the university was not preventing the medical students from living in university housing and was not discriminating based on the students' status of being single, married, divorced, or widowed. However, the court ruled that the students' claim of housing discrimination based on sexual orientation could proceed.

14. How likely are *Braschi* and *Peterson*, respectively, to influence landlords' behavior? Might some landlords use "covert" tactics to give effect to their religious beliefs?

## Problems

1. Jay rents a New York City apartment. Ten years later he desires to share his residence with his partner James. Jay receives the landlord's permission to occupy the adjoining apartment as well. Although Jay continues to be the tenant of record on both units, James also lives there and shares rent. After 16 years, the men split up. Jay vacates the apartments. The landlord then serves a "notice of termination of license and/or notice to quit" on James. James refuses to vacate, and the landlord commences eviction proceedings questioning James' right to remain. James asserts, as affirmative defenses, that the landlord, by accepting his rent, has waived the right to object to James' occupancy and, also, that by virtue of his familial relationship with Jay, James is a legal tenant. What result? Should *Braschi* apply? (Assume that the New York court has not yet ruled on the constitutionality of the administrative regulations that protect family members both on the death or departure of the tenant of record.) See Park Holding Co. v. Power, 554 N.Y.S.2d 861 (App. Div. 1990).

2. Suppose instead that Jay and James decide to move to another jurisdiction. They inform a prospective landlord of their desire to live together. The landlord notifies them that it is against his religious beliefs to rent to homosexuals. The jurisdiction has a statute prohibiting housing discrimination based on marital status. However, no case law has yet interpreted that provision to apply to gay and lesbian couples. What arguments would you advance on behalf of the landlord? What counter-

arguments on behalf of Jay and James? Of what relevance is Romer v. Evans, 517 U.S. 620 (1996) (holding that equal protection was violated by a Colorado constitutional amendment that prohibited legislative, executive, or judicial action designed to protect homosexuals from discrimination)?

■ **VASQUEZ v. HAWTHORNE**
*994 P.2d 240 (Wash. Ct. App. 2000)*

BRIDGEWATER, C.J.

[Frank] Vasquez and [Robert] Schwerzler lived together from 1967 to 1995, with the exception of two years during which they lived in different apartments in the same building. When Schwerzler died, he had several assets in his name including: the house he and Vasquez shared, a life insurance policy, two automobiles, and a checking account. No will for Schwerzler was found.

Vasquez filed a claim against the estate, asserting that he and Schwerzler had been homosexual life-partners and that he was entitled under the case law for division of property in meretricious relationships to a share of the community property. Joseph Hawthorne, the appointed personal representative for the estate, denied Vasquez's claim. Vasquez took his claim to superior court and the court ruled in his favor, awarding nearly all of the property to Vasquez on partial summary judgment. . . . Hawthorne appeals.

### I. MERETRICIOUS RELATIONSHIP

Hawthorne contends that the trial court erred by treating Vasquez's relationship with Schwerzler as a meretricious relationship because as a matter of law, a same-sex relationship cannot be a meretricious relationship. This is an issue of first impression in Washington.

The term "meretricious relationship" is a term of art in Washington, and has been defined as "a stable, marital-like relationship where both parties cohabit with knowledge that a lawful marriage between them does not exist." Connell v. Francisco, 127 Wash.2d 339, 346, 898 P.2d 831, 69 A.L.R. 5th 705 (1995). In the first major case dealing with the division of property at the end of a meretricious relationship, the Supreme Court of Washington applied a bright-line rule regarding the property rights of intimate, unmarried cohabitants. In Creasman v. Boyle, 31 Wash.2d 345, 347-49, 196 P.2d 835 (1948), the couple cohabited for seven years, holding themselves out as husband and wife until the woman's death. [During their cohabitation, the woman purchased their home, in part, by using some of the man's personal property. She took title in her name alone but made mortgage payments from joint funds. When she died, he sought to obtain title. The trial court awarded him a one-half interest in the property. The state supreme court reversed, holding that the property was not community property if the couple was not married and that title created a presumption of ownership.]

The Supreme Court later rejected the *Creasman* presumption in In re Marriage of Lindsey, 101 Wash.2d 299, 678 P.2d 328 (1984). Instead, the court adopted two new theories: (1) that courts may apply community property laws by analogy to determine property ownership at the end of a meretricious relationship, and (2) that courts could distribute property acquired during such a relationship on a just and equitable basis.

Further explanation and expansion of the meretricious relationship body of law came in Connell v. Francisco, which also involved the division of property between an unmarried man and a woman who had lived together. The court did not precisely define when a meretricious relationship exists. Instead, it left the question to the courts, as a question of application of law to fact to be determined on a case-by-case basis. According to *Connell*'s definition, a relationship must satisfy three elements to be meretricious: (1) it must be "stable," (2) it must be "marital-like," and (3) the parties must "cohabit with knowledge that a lawful marriage between them does not exist." *Connell*, 127 Wash.2d at 346, 898 P.2d 831.

It is only after the trial court determines according to the factors that a meretricious relationship exists that the couple will be accorded "pseudo" community property treatment.

> [T]he trial court then: (1) evaluates the interest each party has in the property acquired during the relationship, and (2) makes a just and equitable distribution of the property. Lindsey, 101 Wash.2d at 307, 678 P.2d 328; Community Property Deskbook §2.64. The critical focus is on property that would have been characterized as community property *had the parties been married.*

*Connell*, 127 Wash.2d at 349, 898 P.2d 831 (emphasis added). The court in *Connell* also stated that in a "meretricious relationship," the parties have chosen not to get married and the court will not change that. The court was very clear in distinguishing a meretricious relationship from a marriage:

> Until the Legislature, as a matter of public policy, concludes meretricious relationships are the legal equivalent to marriages, we limit the distribution of property following a meretricious relationship to property that would have been characterized as community property *had the parties been married.*

*Connell*, 127 Wash.2d at 350, 898 P.2d 831 (emphasis added).

We deduce from *Connell* and its predecessors that a "meretricious relationship" is one where the parties may legally marry. And it is clear that these courts implicitly assumed that a meretricious relationship can only exist between a man and a woman. In Washington, there are statutory limitations on who may marry. We hold that these limitations are relevant in determining whether a relationship is sufficiently "marital-like" to be meretricious. To marry, parties must be over the age of 18 and mentally competent. *See* RCW 26.04.010(1). Further, neither party may be married to another person, *the parties must be of the opposite sex,* and the parties must not be nearer of kin than second cousins. *See* RCW 26.04.020 (emphasis added).

Although the Legislature only recently amended the marriage statute to explicitly exclude same-sex marriage, the law has been interpreted that way for many years. *See* Singer v. Hara, 11 Wash. App. 247, 522 P.2d 1187, *review denied,* 84 Wash.2d 1008 (1974).

A meretricious relationship is a "quasi-marital" relationship. . . . By holding that a meretricious relationship is a "quasi-marital" one, we accord some of the protections of marriages and community property law. We find no precedent for applying the marital concepts, either rights or protections, to same-sex relationships; all of the reported cases concerning "meretricious relationships" have been between men and women, and community property law clearly applies only to opposite-sex relationships. Vasquez argued that a meretricious relationship could exist between father-son, mother-daughter, or any relationship. Indeed, he maintained that the court had established a different type of property ownership based upon the "meretricious criteria." We disagree. We find no legal basis for judicially extending the rights and protections of marriage to same-sex relationships. Such an extension of the law is for the Legislature to decide, not the courts. Furthermore, we note that Vasquez potentially has other legal recourse in the form of constructive trust and implied partnership. . . .

We hold that a same-sex relationship cannot be a meretricious relationship because such persons do not have a "quasi-marital" relationship. Same-sex persons may not legally marry and such a relationship is not entitled to the rights and protections of a quasi-marriage, such as community property-like treatment. . . . The order of partial summary judgment is reversed.

■ **IN RE ADOPTION OF SWANSON**
*623 A.2d 1095 (Del. 1993)*

MOORE, Justice. . . .
When Richard Sorrels sought to adopt James Swanson, his companion of 17 years, they were, respectively, 66 and 51 years of age. The

adoption had two purposes — to formalize the close emotional relationship that had existed between them for many years and to facilitate their
estate planning. Apparently, they sought to prevent collateral claims on
their respective estates from remote family members, and to obtain the
reduced inheritance tax rate which natural and adopted children enjoy
under Delaware law. Admittedly, there was no pre-existing parent-child
relationship between them, and on that basis the Family Court denied
the petition.

Adult adoptions in Delaware are governed by our Domestic Relations Law, 13 Del. C. §§951 through 956. Section 953 provides that "[i]f
the petition complies with the requirements of §§951 and 952 of this title, and if the person or persons to be adopted appear in court and consent to the adoption, the Family Court *may* render a decree ordering the
issuance of a certificate of adoption to the petitioner." 13 Del. C. §953
(emphasis added). Although the statute mentions no other requirements
beyond those listed in Sections 951-952, the Family Court sua sponte
concluded that approval of an adult adoption was contingent upon a
pre-existing family relationship. . . . As a result, we are faced with a simple question of statutory construction — did the Family Court err as a
matter of law in formulating or applying legal principles when it interpreted Section 953 to require a preexisting parent-child relationship?

We begin with the basic rule of statutory construction that requires
a court to ascertain and give effect to the intent of the legislature. If the
statute as a whole is unambiguous and there is no reasonable doubt as
to the meaning of the words used, the court's role is limited to an application of the literal meaning of those words. However, where, as here,
the Court is faced with a novel question of statutory construction, it must
seek to ascertain and give effect to the intention of the General Assembly as expressed by the statute itself.

There is no reference in Section 953 to any condition of a pre-
existing parent-child relationship. Instead, the statute only compels a
person seeking an adult adoption to sign and file a petition containing
certain basic personal data. If, after having done so, the adoptee appears
in court and consents to the adoption, the Family Court may grant the
petition for adoption. [T]he relevant adult adoption statute, has existed
in equivalent form since 1915, without any material change by the General Assembly. That is indicative of legislative satisfaction with the provisions of the statute.

Regardless of one's views as to the wisdom of the statute, our role as
judges is limited to applying the statute objectively and not revising it.
A court may not engraft upon a statute language which has been clearly
excluded therefrom. Thus, where, as here, provisions are expressly included in one part of a statute, but omitted from another, it is reasonable to conclude that the legislature was aware of the omission and
intended it. As a result, the omission from the adult adoption procedure

for investigation and supervision of prospective placements, found in the requirements for adopting minors, persuades us that it was not the result of an accident. If anything, it is the best evidence of a legislative policy against imposing unnecessary conditions upon the adult adoption process.

Many jurisdictions limit inquiry into the motives or purposes of an adult adoption. However, most recognize that adult adoptions for the purpose of creating inheritance rights are valid. K. M. Potraker, Annotation, Adoption of Adult, 21 A.L.R.3d 1012, 1029-1030 (1968). In one of the earliest cases, the Supreme Judicial Court of Massachusetts upheld an adoption of three adults, aged 43, 39 and 25 respectively, by a 70 year old person who intended the adoption to operate in lieu of a will. Collamore v. Learned, Mass. Supr., 171 Mass. 99, 50 N.E. 518 (1898). The court ruled that motive, although proper in that case, had no effect on the validity of the adoption. . . .

Cases upholding adoptions for the purpose of improving the adoptee's inheritance rights continue to grow. . . . The general disinclination to examine the motives of the petitioner has been extended beyond the area of inheritance rights. In 333 East 53rd Street Associates v. Mann, 1st Dept., 121 A.D.2d 289, 503 N.Y.S.2d 752 (1986), a petitioner adopted an adult woman in order to ensure that she would succeed to the tenancy of a rent controlled apartment. The building's owner sought a declaratory judgment that the adoptee had no rights in the apartment. The appellate court found nothing inherently wrong with an adoption intended to confer an economic benefit on the adopted person.

On the other hand, the New York Court of Appeals ruled that a fifty-seven year old man could not adopt a fifty year old male with whom he shared a homosexual relationship. Matter of Adoption of Robert Paul P., 63 N.Y.2d 233, 481 N.Y.S.2d 652, 471 N.E.2d 424 (1984). The court reasoned that adoption is not a quasi-matrimonial device to provide unmarried partners with a legal imprimatur for their sexual relationship. The court also determined that New York's adult adoption process requires the adoption to be in the best interests of the adoptee, and thus, the financial and emotional condition of the petitioner must still be investigated. Delaware's adult adoption process clearly abandons the requirement for such an investigation. It suggests no corresponding need to determine that an adult adoption be in the best interests of the adoptee. We also note the compelling dissent in Matter of Adoption of Robert Paul P., 481 N.Y.S.2d at 656, 471 N.E.2d at 428 (Meyer, J., dissenting), taking the majority to task for imposing limitations on the process that are not found in New York's adult adoption statute.

There are, of course, common sense limitations on any adult adoption. That is why our statute, 13 Del. C. §953, appears to confer reasonable discretion upon the Family Court's approval of an adult adoption. Solely by way of example, no court should countenance an adoption to effect a fraudulent, illegal or patently frivolous purpose. See, e.g., In re Jones, 122 R.I. 716, 411 A.2d 910 (1980), where an older married man sought to adopt his 20-year-old paramour to the economic detriment of his wife and family. Delaware law is not necessarily inconsistent with the results in Adoption of Robert Paul P. and In re Jones, supra. Adult adoptions intended to foster a sexual relationship would be against public policy as violative of the incest statute. See 11 Del. C. §766(b), which defines the crime of incest to include sexual intercourse between a parent and child "without regard to . . . relationships by adoption."

A statute cannot be construed to produce an absurd, meaningless or patently inane result. However, where, as here, the petition contemplates an adoption that is not only within the scope of the statute, but which is also widely recognized as a proper exercise of the authority granted by the statute, we can divine no reason why this petition should be denied. . . .

## Notes and Questions

1. Inheritance law constitutes a context in which cohabitants (both heterosexual and homosexual) are treated differently from spouses. As a general rule, unmarried cohabitants cannot inherit from their partner by intestate succession. See Mary Louise Fellows et al., Committed Partners and Inheritance: An Empirical Study, 16 Law & Ineq. J. 1, 15 (1998); Gary Spitko, The Expressive Function of Succession Law and the Merits on Non-Marital Inclusion, 41 Ariz. L. Rev. 1063, 1065 (1999). Only Hawaii and Vermont permit a surviving non-marital partner who is a registered same-sex partner to take a share of the decedent's intestate estate. See Haw. Rev. Stat. Ann. §560:2-102 (1999); Vt. Stat. Ann. tit. 15 §1204(e)(1)(2000). On the other hand, New Hampshire provides intestacy rights for those unmarried persons who are "cohabiting and acknowledging each other as husband and wife, and generally reputed to be such, for the period of three years, and until the decease of one of them." N.H. Rev. Stat. Ann. §457:39 (West 2001). See Spitko, supra, at 1065 n.10 (discussing Hawaii and New Hampshire laws).

2. *Epilogue.* When Robert Schwerzler died at the age of 78, he had lived with Frank Vasquez (then age 64) for almost 27 years. The two men worked together in the burlap-bag business that Schwerzler owned and operated in their home. Vasquez, disabled from a childhood head injury, cooked and took care of the couple's home. According to his lawyer, Vasquez is illiterate and unsophisticated. "His name isn't on anything because he trusted Bob to handle everything." Daniel B. Kennedy, Til Death Do Us Part, 87 A.B.A. J. 22 (Jan. 2001). After Schwerzler's death, his siblings took over the business and the couple's residence. "They lit-

erally wanted to put Mr. Vasquez out on the street with nothing," said
Vasquez's attorney. Paul Queary, New Trial Ordered in Gay Rights Case,
Nov. 2, 2001 (n.p.). Schwerzler's relatives deny that their brother was
gay and insist that Vasquez merely served as a housekeeper and boarder.
Following the principal case herein, the Washington Supreme Court
granted review (11 P.3d 825 (Wash. 2000)), and ordered a new trial for
Vasquez to prove the nature of the men's relationship. Women's groups
are closely watching the case because of its implications for unmarried
heterosexual couples. See Natalie M. Perry, Nine Critical Documents for
Every Gay and Lesbian Couple, Mondaq Bus. Briefing, June 11, 2001
(n.p.); Queary, supra.

3. Several decades prior to *Vasquez*, the issue of the inheritance
rights of same-sex partners was addressed in In re Will of Kaufmann,
247 N.Y.S.2d 664 (App. Civ. 1964), *aff'd*, 205 N.E.2d 864 (N.Y. 1965).
Millionaire Robert Kaufmann lived with his partner, lawyer Walter Weiss,
in New York City for ten years. While Walter managed the household
and finances, Robert pursued his interest in painting. In his numerous
wills, Robert gradually increased Walter's share in his estate. When
Robert died, his brother challenged the last will on the ground of undue influence. Two juries found undue influence, a finding that was ultimately affirmed by the New York Court of Appeals. On the *Kaufmann*
case, see Thomas L. Shaffer, Death, Property, and Lawyers: A Behavioral
Approach 243-257 (1970); Ray D. Madoff, Unmasking Undue Influence,
8 Minn. L. Rev. 571, 592-600 (1997); Jeffrey G. Sherman, Undue Influence and the Homosexual Testator, 42 U. Pitt. L. Rev. 225, 239-248
(1981).

Research has led Professor Jeffrey Sherman to conclude that "the
lover-legatee of a homosexual testator faces a more difficult task at probate than does his heterosexual counterpart." Sherman, supra, at 246.
Sherman cites the tendency of juries in will contests to return verdicts
"more in keeping with their prejudices than with the facts." Id. at 246
n.102. An empirical study in California determined that the jury finds
for the contestant in over 75 percent of the cases. Note, Will Contests on
Trial, 6 Stan. L. Rev. 91 (1953). Sherman speculates that there would be
more litigation involving same-sex partners were it not for the pressure
to settle because the parties fear bias against homosexuals. Sherman,
supra, at 233 n.43.

4. In *Vasquez*, if Frank Vasquez had been a woman, would the result
have been different?

5. *Estate planning for gay clients. Vasquez* highlights some of the estate
planning problems for same-sex partners. Attorney and gay rights activist Roberta Achtenberg elaborates:

> Early in the estate planning process the lawyer should inquire as to
> the client's concerns about a will contest and should discuss the grounds

for such contests and their applicability, if any, to the client's situation. This discussion should serve both to identify potential contestants (if there are any) and in most cases to reduce the client's fears. In this regard it is important to the lawyer to have an accurate picture of the kind of emotional relationship the testator has with her or his biological family. Does the family know the testator is homosexual, or that the testator has a lover or friend whom she or he intends to benefit through the will? Does the testator hold property of such value that a contest by the biological family would be predictable? Is there anything the testator can do during her or his lifetime to minimize the shock which members of the biological family might experience if they were to discover that the bulk of the testator's estate was being left to an "unrelated" person?

[T]he lawyer should not presume that just because a client is lesbian or gay, she or he does not have a legal spouse from whom she or he was never divorced. Also, the lawyer should ascertain whether the client has any children. [If there are any such individuals] to whom no bequests are intended, a statement of specific omission must be made in the will.

Special caution must be exercised where the client is terminally ill or otherwise in a weakened mental or physical state. Any documents executed under such circumstances will probably be more susceptible to attack than documents executed when the client is healthy and clearly competent. . . .

Sexual Orientation and the Law §4.04 (Roberta Achtenberg ed., 1991).

AIDS raises additional issues, emphasizing the importance of planning for illness, incapacity, and death, including the execution of nominations of conservator (or guardian), powers of attorney to cover asset management and personal care, directives to physicians (for example, living wills), and determination of eligibility for public benefit programs that will pay necessary medical, food, and personal support costs. See generally id. at §§13.03[1]-13.04[3].

6. An inter vivos transaction provides an alternative means to ensure that an estate will pass to a lover. For example, Robert Schwerzler might have made Frank Vasquez the beneficiary of an inter vivos trust instead of a will. See, e.g., Knowles v. Binford, 298 A.2d 862 (Md. 1973) (inter vivos trust leaving life estate to man's female partner). Robert might have executed a contract to devise property to Frank (perhaps in exchange for Frank's services during Robert's lifetime). What are the advantages and disadvantages of such devices? See Lewis H. Parham, Jr., Note, Wills and Contracts — Degree of Mental Capacity Requisite for Each, 34 N.C. L. Rev. 155 (1955); Note, Undue Influence in Inter Vivos Transactions, 41 Colum. L. Rev. 707 (1941).

7. Because gays and lesbians cannot marry, another vehicle for ensuring inheritance rights is adult adoption. Not all jurisdictions allow adult adoption. See, e.g., Ariz. Rev. Stat. Ann. §8-102 (West 1999); Appeal of Ritchie, 53 N.W.2d 753 (Neb. 1952). If permitted by a given jurisdiction, however, adult adoption creates a legally recognized family relationship that facilitates, inter alia, (1) establishment of inheritance

rights; (2) access to information limited to family members (such as in medical decisionmaking); (3) evasion of housing and zoning restrictions; (4) access to insurance and unemployment benefits; and (5) immigration into the United States. Peter N. Fowler, Comment, Adult Adoption: A "New" Legal Tool for Lesbians and Gay Men, 14 Golden Gate U. L. Rev. 667, 679-688 (1984). In California, approximately 200 to 300 adult adoptions occur each year, of which 30 to 40 percent involve lesbians or gay men. Id. at 702. See also Mandi Rae Urban, The History of Adult Adoption in California, 11 J. Contemp. Legal Issues 612 (2000).

8. Judicial attitudes toward homosexual adult adoption have ranged from support to condemnation. For example, a case cited in *Swanson, Robert Paul P.,* overruled two New York decisions that allowed the practice (In re Adoption of Adult Anonymous I, 435 N.Y.S.2d 527 (Fam. Ct. 1981); In re Adoption of Adult Anonymous II, 452 N.Y.S.2d 198 (App. Div. 1982)). See also Walter Wadlington, Adoption of Adults: A Family Law Anomaly, 54 Cornell L. Rev. 566, 579 (1969) (questioning the practice of adult adoptions, pointing to "instances in which adult adoption might be put to undesirable social uses. Classic examples include . . . a homosexual's adoption of his similarly-inclined mate.").

9. The court in *Swanson* refused to accept the premise that a preexisting sexual relationship between the parties precludes an adult adoption because any sexual intimacy is repugnant to the parent-child relationship. If a person has adopted a child (whether of the same or opposite sex), does their subsequent sexual activity (after the adoptee reaches adulthood) constitute incest? On this issue, the *Anonymous II* court reasoned:

> Incest is only a makeweight issue in this case. The New York incest statute is limited and does not proscribe a relationship such as here. DRL §5 prohibits relations only between ancestor and descendant; brother and sister; and aunt/ uncle-niece/nephew. Incest in general involves blood relatives. And, of course, the taboo against incest, grounded in eugenics . . . has little application in a relationship which can hardly result in offspring.

452 N.Y.S.2d at 201.

10. Would denial of the adoption in *Swanson* promote morality? See Adult Anonymous I, 435 N.Y.S.2d at 531 (arguing that it would not). Would granting the adoption signal state approval of the sexual relationship?

11. *Swanson* reveals that some states require a finding that the adoption would serve the best interests of the adoptee, even for adult adoptees. What does "best interests" mean in the context of an adoption between consenting adults? Should a court or legislature intervene to question what the adoptee claims to want? Does this requirement reflect legal paternalism? See In re Adoption of A, 286 A.2d 751 (N.J. Super. Ct. 1972);

Adult Anonymous I, 435 N.Y.S.2d at 530. Procedures for adult adoption are generally simpler than for adoption of children. Wadlington, supra, at 572. Often home investigations are not performed, parental consent is not required, support obligations do not apply, and the adoptee does not change his name or life in any way. William M. McGovern, Jr., et al., Wills, Trusts and Estates Including Taxation and Future Interests 96-97 (2d ed. 2001).

12. *Other state restrictions.* Until recently, two states (Florida and New Hampshire) prohibited adoptions by gays and lesbians. Fla. Stat. Ann. §63.042(3) (West 1997); N.H. Rev. Stat. Ann. §170-B:4 (1994). In 1999, the New Hampshire legislature repealed its statute. The Florida statute thus far has withstood constitutional attack. See Lofton v. Kearney, 157 F. Supp.2d 1372 (S.D. Fla. 2001) (granting summary judgment to defendant-state agency regarding gay foster parents' claims for violations of their rights to due process and equal protection).

On the other hand, a few states have co-residence, consanguinity, or age restrictions that preclude a gay or lesbian adopting a partner. For example, some states include requirements that the adoptee be the adoptor's niece, nephew, stepchild, or natural child. E.g., Va. Code Ann. §63.1-219.50 (Michie Supp. 2000). Other states require that the adoptee's relationship be commenced during the latter's minority. E.g., Idaho Code §16-1501 (1979 & Supp. 2000). Finally, some states require that the adoptee be some statutorily specified age younger than the adoptor. E.g., Idaho Code §16-1502 (1979 & Supp. 2000) (15 years); N.J. Stat. Ann. §2A:22-2 (West 2000) (10 years).

13. Adoption, even if permitted for same-sex lovers, may not ensure inheritance rights. Professor Sherman notes that relatives have standing to contest an adoption for undue influence even after the adoptor's death.

> It might still be advantageous for the homosexual testator to adopt his lover, however, if he promptly informs his prospective heirs of the adoption. A number of states have statutes of limitations requiring that actions to vacate adoption decrees be brought within a certain period of time. [I]f the homosexual adoptor informs his prospective heirs of the adoption as soon as it occurs, it is likely that they will be compelled either to object to the adoption then and there or to acquiesce in it permanently, and they may be most unwilling to challenge the adoptor face to face.

Sherman, supra, at 260-261.

## Problems

1. Jerri Blanchard becomes a tenant in a New York City apartment in 1940. In 1970 Helen Mann moves into Jerri's apartment. In 1983

Jerri (83) adopts Helen (67). Jerri dies one year later. The owner of the building seeks to evict Helen and subsequently contests the adoption. Helen pleads she is a co-resident "member of the deceased tenant's family" and thereby protected by New York's rent control legislation. What result? See 333 East 53rd St. Assocs. v. Mann, 503 N.Y.S.2d 752 (App. Div. 1986), *aff'd*, 512 N.E.2d 541 (N.Y. 1987).

2. Mary Freeman, an American widow living in Paris, meets a young man, Thomas Russell, and grows very fond of him. She requests him to come live at the same residential hotel where she has resided for many years. He occupies a room on the same floor as her apartment for a few months and then, again at her request, accompanies her on a ship to America. They again take communicating rooms at a residential hotel in Philadelphia until her death a short time later. Russell has a homosexual lover who resided with him while at the hotel in Paris. In Philadelphia, the lover resides a short distance away. When Mrs. Freeman attempts to adopt Russell, she is age 71, he is 32. Should a court grant the adoption? See In re Adoption of Russell, 85 A.2d 878 (Pa. Super. Ct. 1952).

3. You are the legislative intern for a state senator who wishes to make recommendations for revisions to the state inheritance laws. In particular, the senator is concerned that existing laws may not adequately protect domestic partners. The senator wishes you to draft a memo exploring the manner in which inheritance laws could better meet the changing definitions of "family." What recommendations would you make, and why? See generally Susan N. Gary, Adapting Intestacy Laws to Changing Families, 18 Law & Ineq. J. 1 (2000).

### f. New Approaches: Domestic Partnership Statutes and Ordinances

Currently, three states provide for registration of domestic partners by statute (California, Hawaii, and Vermont). California established a statewide registry that accords domestic partners many rights that formerly were afforded only to married couples, such as the right to sue for wrongful death and negligent infliction of emotional distress, to adopt a partner's child using the stepparent adoption process, to make health care decisions for a partner, to administer a partner's estate, to use sick leave to care for a partner, and to receive unemployment benefits for leaving work to accompany a domestic partner. Hawaii has established a registry for "reciprocal beneficiaries" that provides such benefits as hospital visitation rights, the right to make health care decisions for a partner, the right to sue in tort as a spouse, and the right to be named as beneficiary of a partner's life insurance policy. Vermont, in legislation that goes further than either California or Hawaii, creates "civil unions" that enable same-sex couples to receive all the benefits and protections that the state extends to married couples, including the right to be treated as a spouse with respect to property rights, adoption, insurance benefits, hospital visitation, and intestacy laws.

California's domestic partnership legislation applies to same-sex couples as well as to those heterosexual cohabiting couples who are over 62 years old and eligible for Social Security. Cal. Fam. Code §297(b)(6) (2000). Hawaii's "reciprocal beneficiaries" legislation applies to "couples composed of two individuals who are legally prohibited from marrying one another under state law." Haw. Rev. Stat. Ann. §572C-1. (The legislation also offers benefits to other individuals who have significant personal, emotional, and economic relations with another individual yet who are prohibited from marrying, such as a widowed mother and her unmarried son.) Haw. Rev. Stat. Ann. §572C-2 (2000). In contrast, Vermont's "civil union" law applies only to same-sex couples. Vt. Stat. Ann. tit. 15 §1202(2) (2000).

In addition to these states, several cities confer significant rights on unmarried couples by domestic partnership ordinances. Among these municipalities are New York City, Minneapolis, Chicago, San Francisco, Austin, New Orleans, Boulder, Iowa City, St. Louis, Ann Arbor, Boston, Hartford, Chapel Hill, Seattle, and Philadelphia. The ordinances differ significantly in terms of (1) the definition of domestic partners, (2) the range of benefits offered, and (3) the partners' legal responsibilities to each other (for example, liability for living expenses). Challenges to the validity of domestic partner benefit ordinances have upheld those ordinances. See Slattery v. City of New York, 686 N.Y.S.2d 683 (N.Y. Sup. Ct. 1999); Crawford v. City of Chicago, 710 N.E.2d 91 (Ill. App. Ct. 1999); City of Atlanta v. Morgan, 492 S.E.2d 193 (Ga. 1997). But cf. Connors v. City of Boston, 714 N.E.2d 335 (Mass. 1999).

Opposition to the San Francisco ordinance illustrates the difficulties faced by gay rights' advocates. The San Francisco domestic partnership ordinance, first signed into law on June 5, 1989, extends a full range of benefits to city employees and their partners. It bans discrimination against live-in lovers who formally register as domestic partners. Under the measure, city employees and their unmarried partners have the same rights as married employees to hospital visitation, sick leave, bereavement leave, and maternity leave.

The same day that the new domestic partners law was to take effect in 1989, City Attorney Louise Renne suspended it in response to a petition drive. Religious leaders condemned the law as a threat to the family. (The city charter states that, if referendum petitions are submitted before an ordinance takes effect, the board of supervisors must either repeal the measure or send it to the voters.) In 1989, voters rejected the measure by a narrow margin. Subsequently, a substantially similar measure appeared on the ballot. This measure succeeded, becoming effective on Valentine's Day in 1991. On the first day of registration, most couples who registered were gays and lesbians.

In June 1994, the San Francisco City Council voted to add health benefits for members of unmarried couples who were municipal employees. To qualify, employees must sign an affidavit stating that their domestic partnership has been in effect for at least one year. Three years later, the San Francisco Board of Supervisors unanimously approved the first measure (effective June 1, 1997) to require companies doing business in the city to provide domestic partnership benefits to their employees if the companies provided similar benefits to legal spouses. The measure does not apply to state or federal contracts. The requirement may be waived if compliance would economically disadvantage a company or if the company is the sole provider of a particular service. Companies not complying are punishable by fine or rescission of their contracts with the city. To date, more than 3,200 companies that do business with the city now offer domestic partner benefits. Further, other cities (e.g., Los Angeles, Seattle, Berkeley) have replicated the law. Christopher Heredia, Equal-Benefit Law in S.F., Has Big Impact Across U.S., S.F. Chron., Nov. 4, 2001, at A23.

On June 14, 2001, the Ninth Circuit upheld San Francisco's ordinance requiring all contractors doing business with the city to provide domestic partnership benefits to their employees. S.D. Myers v. City and County of San Francisco, 253 F.3d 461 (9th Cir. 2001). The court held that the ordinance was valid under the Commerce Clause, Due Process Clause, and California law. The court noted that the ordinance only affects out-of-state entities that affirmatively chose to subject themselves to the ordinance by contracting with the city.

In 2001 in San Francisco, Sharon Smith, the domestic partner of Diane Whipple, filed a wrongful death suit against the owners of two dogs who attacked and mauled her partner to death. At the time, standing was conferred only upon legal spouses; California did not allow domestic partners to sue in tort as a spouse. Smith's case, however, prompted the California legislature to expand domestic partners' rights to allow this cause of action.

See generally Heidi Eischen, For Better or Worse: An Analysis of Recent Challenges to Domestic Partner Benefits Legislation, 31 U. Tol. L. Rev. 527 (2000); Greg Johnson, Vermont Civil Unions: The New Language of Marriage, 25 Vt. L. Rev. 15 (2000); Paul R. Lynd, Domestic Partner Benefits Limited to Same-Sex Couples: Sex Discrimination Under Title VII, 6 Wm. & Mary J. Women & Law 561 (2000).


# Problem


Irene, a public interest attorney, and her long-time partner, Lorna, desire to effectuate law reform regarding gay and lesbian rights. The women are uncertain whether to challenge the state law on marriage, or to attempt to formulate a citywide (or possibly statewide) domestic partnership initiative, or to propose an antidiscrimination measure explicitly covering sexual orientation. You are a legislative aide to a legislator who is sympathetic to their desires. Consider the advantages and disadvantages of each approach. For example, do domestic partnership initiatives provide a meaningful alternative to marriage for both heterosexual and homosexual couples? What would you advise the legislator?

## D. PARENTS' AND CHILDREN'S RIGHTS IN THE NONMARITAL FAMILY

In recent decades the family has witnessed a steady increase in the number of single-parent families. For example, families headed by women (with no husband present) have more than doubled in the last 25 years.[10] This dramatic increase is attributable largely to changing social values, in particular, the decreasing stigma attached to illegitimacy.

The single-parent family has its share of problems, usually economic.[11] Because most such families are headed by women, families must survive on the income of only a working mother. Economic difficulties are inevitable, stemming both from gender discrimination (for example, lower salaries than men) and racial discrimination.[12] This section explores some of the legal problems faced by single-parent families: the support rights of nonmarital children and limitations on the rights of parents of nonmarital children. Subsequent chapters address support rights in general (Chapter 6), as well as other problems experienced by single-parent families, such as custody (Chapter 7) and adoption (Chapter 9).

---

[10]. Bureau of the Census, supra note [1], at 2 (the number of female-householder families increased from 5.5 million to 12.6 million compared to the rise in male-householder families from 1.2 million to 4.0 million). Male-householder families also increased during the same period. Although fewer such families exist, the number of male-headed single families grew from 393,000 in 1970 to 2 million in 2000. Id.

[11]. Id. at 8.

[12]. Many single-parent heads-of-households are women of color. For example, in 2000, 65 percent of Black female householders have never been married, compared to 44 percent for Hispanics and 30 percent for whites. Id. at 4. One commentator points out that unmarried women with children comprise one of the truly "hard core poor" groups in the United States. Nancy Moore Clatworthy, The Non-Traditional Family and the Child, 12 Cap. U. L. Rev. 345, 347 (1983).

## 1. Support Rights of Nonmarital Children

### ■ CLARK v. JETER
486 U.S. 456 (1988)

Justice O'CONNOR delivered the opinion of the Court.

Under Pennsylvania law, an illegitimate child must prove paternity before seeking support from his or her father, and a suit to establish paternity ordinarily must be brought within six years of an illegitimate child's birth. By contrast, a legitimate child may seek support from his or her parents at any time. . . .

On September 22, 1983, petitioner Cherlyn Clark filed a support complaint in the Allegheny County Court of Common Pleas on behalf of her minor daughter, Tiffany, who was born out of wedlock on June 11, 1973. Clark named respondent Gene Jeter as Tiffany's father. The court ordered blood tests, which showed a 99.3% probability that Jeter is Tiffany's father.

Jeter moved to dismiss the complaint on the ground that it was barred by the 6-year statute of limitations for paternity actions. In her response, Clark contended that this statute is unconstitutional under the Equal Protection and Due Process Clauses. . . .

[The trial court upheld the statute of limitations and Clark appealed. Before the court decided her case, however, the legislature enacted an 18-year statute of limitations for actions to establish paternity to comply with the federal Child Support Enforcement Amendments of 1984 requiring all states participating in the federal child support program to have procedures to establish the paternity of any child who is less than 18 years old. 42 U.S.C. §666(a)(5) (1982 ed., Supp. IV). The Superior Court concluded that Pennsylvania's new 18-year statute of limitations did not apply retroactively, and it affirmed the trial court's conclusions that the 6-year statute of limitations was constitutional. The Court granted Clark's petition for certiorari.]

In considering whether state legislation violates the Equal Protection Clause of the Fourteenth Amendment, we apply different levels of scrutiny to different types of classifications. . . . Between [the] extremes of rational basis review and strict scrutiny lies a level of intermediate scrutiny, which generally has been applied to discriminatory classifications based on sex or illegitimacy.

To withstand intermediate scrutiny, a statutory classification must be substantially related to an important governmental objective. Consequently we have invalidated classifications that burden illegitimate children for the sake of punishing the illicit relations of their parents, because "visiting this condemnation on the head of an infant is illogical and unjust." Weber v. Aetna Casualty & Surety Co., 406 U.S. 164, 175 (1972). Yet, in the seminal case concerning the child's right to support, this Court acknowledged that it ~~might be appropriate to treat illegiti-~~ ~~mate children differently in the support context because of "lurking~~ ~~problems with respect to proof of paternity.~~" Gomez v. Perez, 409 U.S. 535, 538 (1973).

*FRAMEWORK* *OF EVALUATION* This Court has developed a particular framework for evaluating equal protection challenges to statutes of limitations that apply to suits to establish paternity, and thereby limit the ability of illegitimate children to obtain support.

> First, the period for obtaining support . . . must be sufficiently long in du-
> ration to present a reasonable opportunity for those with an interest in
> such children to assert claims on their behalf. Second, any time limitation
> placed on that opportunity must be substantially related to the State's in-
> terest in avoiding the litigation of stale or fraudulent claims.

Mills v. Habluetzel, 456 U.S., at 99-100.

*1 YR TOO* *SHORT*   In *Mills*, we held that Texas' 1-year statute of limitations failed both steps of the analysis. We explained that paternity suits typically will be brought by the child's mother, who might not act swiftly amidst the emotional and financial complications of the child's first year. And, it is unlikely that the lapse of a mere 12 months will result in the loss of evidence or appreciably increase the likelihood of fraudulent claims. A concurring opinion in *Mills* explained why statutes of limitations longer than one year also may be unconstitutional. Id., at 102-106 (O'Connor, J., joined by Burger, C.J., and Brennan and Blackmun, JJ., and joined as to Part I by Powell, J., concurring). First, the State has a countervailing interest in ensuring that genuine claims for child support are satisfied. Second, the fact that Texas tolled most other causes of action during a child's minority suggested that proof problems do not become overwhelming during this period. Finally, the practical obstacles to filing a claim for support are likely to continue after the first year of the child's life.

*2 YR TOO* *SHORT*   In Pickett v. Brown, 462 U.S. 1 (1983), the Court unanimously struck down Tennessee's 2-year statute of limitations for paternity and child support actions brought on behalf of certain illegitimate children. Adhering to the analysis developed in *Mills,* the Court first considered whether two years afforded a reasonable opportunity to bring such suits. The Tennessee statute was relatively more generous than the Texas statute considered in *Mills* because it did not limit actions against a father who had acknowledged his paternity in writing or by furnishing support; nor did it apply if the child was likely to become a public charge. Nevertheless, the Court concluded that the 2-year period was too short in light of the persisting financial and emotional problems that are likely to afflict the child's mother. Proceeding to the second step of the analysis, the Court decided that the 2-year statute of limitations was not substantially related to Tennessee's asserted interest in preventing stale and fraudulent claims. The period during which suit could be brought was only a year longer than the period considered in *Mills,* and this incremental difference would not create substantially greater proof and fraud problems. . . . Finally, scientific advances in blood testing had alleviated some problems of proof in paternity actions. For these reasons, the Tennessee statute failed to survive heightened scrutiny under the Equal Protection Clause.

In light of this authority, we conclude that Pennsylvania's 6-year statute of limitations violates the Equal Protection Clause. Even six years does not necessarily provide a reasonable opportunity to assert a claim on behalf of an illegitimate child. "The unwillingness of the mother to file a paternity action on behalf of her child, which could stem from her relationship with the natural father or . . . from the emotional strain of having an illegitimate child, or even from the desire to avoid community and family disapproval, may continue years after the child is born. The problem may be exacerbated if, as often happens, the mother herself is a minor." *Mills,* supra, at 105, n.4 (O'Connor, J., concurring). Not all of these difficulties are likely to abate in six years. A mother might realize only belatedly "a loss of income attributable to the need to care for the child," *Pickett,* supra, at 12. Furthermore, financial difficulties are likely to increase as the child matures and incurs expenses for clothing, school, and medical care. Thus it is questionable whether a State acts reasonably when it requires most paternity and support actions to be brought within six years of an illegitimate child's birth.

We do not rest our decision on this ground, however, for it is not entirely evident that six years would necessarily be an unreasonable limitations period for child support actions involving illegitimate children. We are, however, confident that the 6-year statute of limitations is not substantially related to Pennsylvania's interest in avoiding the litigation of stale or fraudulent claims. In a number of circumstances, Pennsylvania permits the issue of paternity to be litigated more than six years after the birth of an illegitimate child [for example, for intestate succession purposes, in paternity actions initiated by the father, and tolls the limitation during minority in other civil actions as well]. In *Pickett* and *Mills* similar tolling statutes cast doubt on the State's purposed interest in avoiding the litigation or fraudulent claims.

A more recent indication that Pennsylvania does not consider proof problems insurmountable is the enactment by the Pennsylvania Legislature in 1985 of an 18-year statute of limitations for paternity and support actions. 23 Pa. Cons. Stat. §4343(b) (1985). To be sure the legislature did not act spontaneously, but rather under the threat of losing some federal funds. Nevertheless, the new statute is a tacit concession that proof problems are not overwhelming. The legislative history of the federal Child Support Enforcement Amendments explains why Congress thought such statutes of limitations are reasonable. Congress adverted to the problem of stale and fraudulent claims, but recognized that increasingly sophisticated tests for genetic markers permit the exclusion of over 99% of those who might be accused of paternity, regardless of the age of the child. This scientific evidence . . . is an additional reason to doubt that Pennsylvania had a substantial reason for limiting the time within which paternity and support actions could be brought.

We conclude that the Pennsylvania statute does not withstand heightened scrutiny under the Equal Protection Clause. We therefore find it unnecessary to reach Clark's due process claim. . . .

## Notes and Questions

1. *Clark* reflects the trend of increasing constitutional protection of nonmarital children. Traditionally, the law regarded the nonmarital (or "illegitimate") child as *filius nullius* and a bastard.[13] That status affected the child's right to both support and inheritance. Absent a statute to the contrary, the mother, but not the father, had a common law duty of support for a nonmarital child. In Gomez v. Perez, 409 U.S. 535 (1973), the Supreme Court held that a state cannot grant marital children a statutory right to paternal support while denying this right to nonmarital children. Although modern statutes require both parents to support the child regardless of legitimacy, distinctions still exist in terms of inheritance (explained below).

2. At the time of *Clark,* many states had statutes of limitations that restricted the time within which paternity suits could be brought. States justified these short statutory periods to prevent the filing of stale claims and to discourage fraud. Several Supreme Court decisions prior to *Clark* invalidated short statutes of limitations. E.g., Pickett v. Brown, 462 U.S. 1 (1983); Mills v. Habluetzel, 456 U.S. 91 (1982). Thereafter, many states substantially lengthened their statutory periods. Congress also addressed statutes of limitations in paternity establishment, as *Clark* explains. To improve child support enforcement, Congress enacted the Child Support Enforcement Amendments of 1984 requiring states (as a condition for receipt of federal funds) to extend their statutes of limitations to permit paternity establishment for 18 years after birth. 42 U.S.C. §666(a)(5)(A)(ii) (1994).

Subsequently, the Family Support Act (FSA) of 1988, 42 U.S.C. §1305 (1994), requires states to permit paternity establishment for children whose paternity actions were dismissed previously under short statutes of limitations. The FSA also requires states to have procedures by which the state can order all parties in a contested case (including the child) to

---

[13]. See Harry D. Krause, Illegitimacy: Law and Social Policy 22 (1971). See also 1 William Blackstone, Commentaries *454-459.

submit to genetic tests. The legislation provides for a limited exception for individuals who can establish good cause for refusing to cooperate. 42 U.S.C. §602(a)(26)(B) (1994). On the circumstances constituting good cause, see Christa Anders, State Intervention into the Lives of Single Mothers and Their Children: Toward a Resolution of Maternal Autonomy and Children's Needs, 8 Law & Ineq. J. 567, 583 (1990).

The FSA also sets performance standards for state programs establishing paternity. States must meet a specified "paternity establishment percentage." 42 U.S.C. §652(g) (1994 & Supp. V 1999). See id. at §654(4)(A). The federal legislation also makes available to state officials seeking to enforce child support obligations the federal "Parent Locator Service," which uses social security numbers to locate absent parents, even in the absence of court-ordered support. Id. at §653(c). A state must make its paternity determination services available, for a fee, to those not receiving public assistance. Id. at §654(6). The Personal Responsibility and Work Opportunity Reconciliation Act (discussed infra pages 511, 512) also addresses paternity establishment.

3. The Supreme Court first held discrimination against nonmarital children unconstitutional in the late 1960s. In Levy v. Louisiana, 391 U.S. 68 (1968), the Court ruled that Louisiana's Wrongful Death Act violated the Equal Protection Clause by denying recovery to a nonmarital child for the death of the mother. In Glona v. American Guarantee & Liability Insurance Co., 391 U.S. 73 (1968), the Court reached a similar result, permitting recovery by a mother for the death of her nonmarital child.

In Weber v. Aetna Casualty & Surety Co., 406 U.S. 164 (1972), the Court extended this approach to permit recovery by a nonmarital child for the father's death under a state workers' compensation law. The Court rejected the argument that the denial of recovery would promote the state's interest in "legitimate family relationships." Id. at 173. As the Court explained:

> The status of illegitimacy has expressed through the ages society's condemnation of irresponsible liaisons beyond the bonds of marriage. But visiting this condemnation on the head of an infant is illogical and unjust. Moreover, imposing disabilities on the illegitimate child is contrary to the basic concept of our system that legal burdens should bear some relationship to individual responsibility or wrongdoing. Obviously, no child is responsible for his birth and penalizing the illegitimate child is an ineffectual — as well as an unjust — way of deterring the parent. Courts are powerless to prevent the social opprobrium suffered by these hapless children, but the Equal Protection Clause does enable us to strike down discriminatory laws relating to status of birth where — as in this case — the classification is justified by no legitimate state interest, compelling or otherwise.

Id. at 175-176.

4. Although the Supreme Court minimized many differences in legal treatment of nonmarital and marital children, the Court declined to invalidate all discrimination against nonmarital children, especially inheritance rights. Many state laws treat nonmarital and marital children differently in terms of the right to intestate succession in their father's estate (if the father dies without a will). In Labine v. Vincent, 401 U.S. 532 (1971), the Court held that the denial of the right of intestate succession to a nonmarital child who had been publicly acknowledged by her father did not violate equal protection or due process. The Court rested its opinion on the state's interest in the promotion of family life and regulating property disposition.

The Court appeared willing to soften its position in Trimble v. Gordon, 430 U.S. 762 (1977). Deta Mona Trimble was the nonmarital child of Jessie Trimble and Sherman Gordon. The couple lived together until Gordon died as the victim of a homicide. Prior to Gordon's death, the mother obtained a paternity order. Later, she sought to establish Deta Mona's right to inherit Gordon's estate. Under Illinois law, nonmarital children could inherit by intestate succession only from their mothers but marital children could inherit from both parents. For a nonmarital child to inherit intestate from a putative father, the Illinois statute required that the parents must marry (that is, subsequent to the child's birth) and that the father must acknowledge the child. The Supreme Court held that this statutory distinction between nonmarital and marital children violated equal protection as not rationally related to the state's objective in effectuating the accurate disposition of property at death. The Court reasoned that the proof of paternity here (the judicial determination of paternity) was sufficient to effectuate the state's interest.

However, the next year the Court retreated. Lalli v. Lalli, 439 U.S. 259 (1978), upheld a New York statute requiring a judicial order of filiation to establish paternity during the putative father's lifetime in order for a nonmarital child to inherit intestate from the father. Robert Lalli, although openly acknowledged by his father in a notarized document consenting to Robert's marriage, was excluded from inheriting from his father. Robert could not meet this high level of proof. Upholding the statute, the plurality reasoned that the law did not pose an insurmountable barrier (in contrast to Trimble's requirement of parental marriage plus acknowledgement). Further, the plurality reasoned, preclusion was justified by the state interest in the orderly disposition of property at death, rather than by a goal of influencing parental behavior or shaping societal norms. Many states subsequently liberalized the inheritance rights of nonmarital children. E.g., Ala. Code §43-8-48 (1991); Mass. Ann. Laws ch. 190, §7 (West 1990 & Supp. 2001). See generally Ralph C. Brashier, Children and Inheritance in the Nontraditional Family, 1996 Utah L. Rev. 93, 103-147.

Is identification of the father more difficult in intestacy, rather than support, cases? Why then, as noted in *Clark*, does Pennsylvania's *intestacy* statute permit a nonmarital child to establish paternity at any time after the child's birth?

Should the rights of children be dependent on the actions of their parents (that is, the initiation of a judicial proceeding within a specified time period)? Should the state use the concept of legitimacy to discourage nonmarital relationships so that children can be raised by "state-sanctioned" families?

5. Both the Uniform Parentage Act and the Uniform Probate Code significantly broaden the rights of nonmarital children. The Uniform Parentage Act, 9B U.L.A. 287 (1987), which is primarily concerned with paternity establishment, does not contain a legitimacy-illegitimacy distinction. Rather, the act introduces the status of a presumed "parent and child relationship" that operates regardless of the parents' marital status. It applies to those children who have been received by the father into his home and "held out" as his children or have been acknowledged in writing by the father (which acknowledgment has been filed with the appropriate court or administrative agency). Unif. Parentage Act §4. An action to establish a "parent and child relationship" must be brought before the father's estate is closed in order for the child to inherit. Unif. Parentage Act §§6 and 7. See statute infra pages 529-530.

The Uniform Probate Code permits a nonmarital child to inherit intestate from either natural parent if certain conditions are met: if paternity is established by an adjudication prior to the parent's death by clear and convincing evidence or has been established under the Uniform Parentage Act, if the natural parent has openly treated the child as his or hers, and if the natural parent has not refused to support the child during the parent's lifetime. Unif. Probate Code §2-109(2)(ii), 8 U.L.A. (pt. 1) 91 (1998).

## Note on Paternity Establishment

Proceedings to establish the identity of the biological father are often necessary for child support as well as inheritance purposes. At common law, a presumption of legitimacy operated on behalf of children of married women. This presumption (irrebuttable, in many states) held that the mother's husband was the father of the child. Courts justified the presumption on the ground that it promoted marital harmony (see Michael H. v. Gerald D., infra). For the nonmarital child, paternity or filiation proceedings provide the vehicle for identifying the fathers. Such proceedings raise a number of issues.

a. *Jurisdiction.* To establish the paternity of an out-of-state putative father, a court must obtain personal jurisdiction over him. Courts use different theories to extend long-arm bases of jurisdiction: failure to support constitutes the "commission of a tortious act," the breach of a contractual obligation within the state, or "doing business" in the state. See, e.g., Jones v. Chandler, 592 So. 2d 966 (Miss. 1991) (finding all three bases of jurisdiction within long-arm statute). See also Unif. Parentage Act §8, 9B U.L.A. 309-310 (1987); Unif. Interstate Family Support Act §201, 9 U.L.A. (pt. 1A) 170 (1999) (providing that one who has sexual intercourse within the state thereby submits to jurisdiction regarding any ensuing child). On multistate child support cases, see also Chapter 6, section F3.

b. *Admissible evidence.* Concerns about fraudulent claims of paternity led to rules about the admissibility of evidence. Before the development of scientific methods, some courts permitted the jury's visual comparison of the baby and the alleged father. See, e.g., Berry v. Chaplin, 169 P.2d 442 (Cal. Dist. Ct. App. 1946). Subsequent medical tests provided increasingly accurate evidence. The Human Leukocyte Antigens (HLA) blood-test system detects markers, or antigens, on white blood cells. When used in combination with red blood cell tests, the HLA test can exclude a defendant as the father with a 97.3 percent accuracy rate.[14] In contrast, modern scientific improvements, including electrophoresis tests that examine serum proteins and cell enzymes, when used in combination with previous tests, can establish a 99 percent probability of paternity.[15] Testing can be performed even after a defendant's death. See In re Estate of Greenwood, 587 A.2d 749 (Pa. Super. Ct. 1991). For an expansive approach to the admissibility of evidence, see Unif. Parentage Act §12(5), 9B U.L.A. 317 (1987) (permitting liberal admission of evidence of sexual intercourse at any possible time of conception, expert testimony regarding the probability of paternity, blood test results and other medical evidence, and "all other evidence relevant to the issue of paternity").

c. *Plaintiffs.* Traditionally, paternity actions were brought by the mother. Increasingly, states permit such actions by the child or the child's representative. For many decades, states also have permitted public welfare authorities to bring a paternity suit, especially if the child was likely to become a public charge. This practice stemmed from federal interest in the identification of the father for child support enforcement. For over 60 years, the federal government assisted needy children through the Aid to Families with Dependent Children (AFDC) program, which was enacted in 1935 as part of the Social Security Act. The program provided welfare payments for needy children (and others in the child's household) who were deprived of support because a parent was absent,

[14]. Lisa Wilson-Caddes, The Determination of Paternity and Its Consequences for the Illegitimate Child, 8 J. Juv. L. 486, 488 (1984).

[15]. See Paula Roberts, Establishing a Family: Blood Tests and the Paternity Determination Process, 26 Clearinghouse Rev. 1019, 1024 (1993).

incapacitated, deceased, or unemployed. Under this "entitlement" program, federal statutes determined eligibility, although states decided the amount of benefits and administered the program. Federal provisions required states (as a condition for receipt of federal funds) to undertake paternity establishment procedures (for example, requiring mothers on AFDC to cooperate in paternity establishment and securing support).

Welfare reform legislation, the Personal Responsibility and Work Opportunity Reconciliation Act of 1996, 42 U.S.C. §603 (Supp. V 1999), replaced AFDC with a block grant to the states. To address the problem of nonmarital births, the legislation offers financial rewards to states that are most successful in reducing such births. 42 U.S.C. §603(a)(2) (Supp. V 1999).

d. *Indigent defendants.* Indigent defendants sometimes lack financial resources to pay for genetic tests that might disprove paternity. The Supreme Court has explored the scope of indigents' due process rights in paternity proceedings. In Little v. Streater, 452 U.S. 1 (1981), the Court held that the Due Process Clause guarantees indigent defendants seven groups of blood tests. Applying the balancing test of Mathews v. Eldridge, 424 U.S. 319 (1976), the Court weighed the private interests at stake, the risk of erroneous results as well as the value of the procedural safeguard, and the governmental interest. The Court concluded that the state's monetary interest in finding fathers does not outweigh the defendant's and the child's interest in accurate paternity determinations and that, without blood tests, paternity defendants face high risk of error.

Commentators and some case law also suggest that due process mandates an indigent defendant's right to counsel in paternity actions. See Allen v. Division of Child Support Enforcement ex rel. Ware, 575 A.2d 1176 (Del. 1990); Mark Esterle, *Gideon's Trumpet* Revisited: Protecting the Rights of Indigent Defendants in Paternity Actions, 24 J. Fam. L. 1 (1985-1986); Paula Roberts & John Ott, The Right to Counsel in Paternity Proceedings, 18 Clearinghouse Rev. 1170 (1985).

e. *Jury composition.* The Supreme Court has also addressed the composition of a jury that is adjudicating a paternity dispute. In J.E.B. v. Alabama ex rel. T.B., 511 U.S. 127 (1994), the Court held that when the state, suing on behalf of the child, uses its peremptory challenges purposely to exclude all men from the jury, it violates the Equal Protection Clause.

f. *Standard of proof.* The Supreme Court has held that due process requires only the "preponderance of the evidence" standard of proof in paternity proceedings. In Rivera v. Minnich, 483 U.S. 574 (1987), Jean Marie Minnich, an unmarried woman, filed for child support for her three-week-old son, alleging that Gregory Rivera was the father. Rivera argued that due process required that the standard of proof for paternity establishment be "clear and convincing" evidence, relying on

Santosky v. Kramer, 455 U.S. 745 (1982) (mandating the higher standard for termination of parental rights). Rejecting the higher standard, the Court distinguished the state's imposition of parent-child obligations from the termination of those obligations because of the latter's severe consequences (that is, the elimination of preexisting rights). Justice Brennan, dissenting, argued that paternity proceedings result in "the imposition of a lifelong relationship with significant financial, legal, and moral dimensions." 483 U.S. at 583.

g. *Voluntary paternity establishment.* Finally, a significant development is the transformation from judicial to voluntary establishment of paternity. Beginning in 1992, a few states adopted voluntary paternity establishment programs that targeted mothers at birthing facilities. For example, Virginia provided for an in-hospital affidavit that had the same effect as a judgment; Washington provided for a similar affidavit that established a rebuttable presumption of paternity. See Paula Roberts, Paternity Establishment: An Issue for the 1990s, 26 Clearinghouse Rev. 1019, 1020 (1993) (discussing Va. Code Ann. §20-49.1 (1992) and Wash. Rev. Code Ann. §70.58-080 (1992)). The success of these programs prompted Congress to include a requirement for all states to adopt in-hospital programs in the Omnibus Budget Reconciliation Act of 1993, 42 U.S.C. §666(a)(5)(C) (1994 & Supp. V 1999). The Personal Responsibility and Work Opportunity Reconciliation Act of 1996, 42 U.S.C. §666 (1994 & Supp. V 1999), expands the scope of such programs (for example, by establishing voluntary acknowledgments as legal findings subject to rescission within 60 days), and requires states to streamline their paternity procedures (for example, blood tests). See generally Paul K. Legler, The Coming Revolution in Child Support Policy: Implications of the 1996 Welfare Act, 30 Fam. L.Q. 519, 532-533 (1996).

## ■ L. PAMELA P. v. FRANK S.
*449 N.E.2d 713 (N.Y. 1983)*

Wachtler, Judge.

The issue on this appeal is whether a father, whose paternity of a child has been established, may assert, as a defense to his support obligation the deliberate misrepresentation of the mother concerning her use of contraception. . . .

Family Court found that petitioner had purposely deceived respondent with regard to her use of contraception and that this wrongful conduct should weigh in respondent's favor in determining the parents' respective support obligations. Thus, the Family Court held that the general rule that the apportionment of child support obligations between parents is to be based upon the parents' means would not be applicable to the present case; rather, it held that an order of support would be entered against the father only in the amount by which the mother's means were insufficient to meet the child's needs.[1]

The Appellate Division modified the Family Court's order, striking the defense of fraud and deceit and increasing the child support award accordingly. Noting that the only factors to be considered by Family Court in fixing an award of child support are the needs of the child and the means of the parents, the Appellate Division held that the father's allegations concerning the mother's fraud and deceit had no relevance to the determination of his obligation to support the child.

Although at one time the objective of paternity proceedings was merely to prevent a child born out of wedlock from becoming a public charge, it is now well established that the appropriate emphasis must be upon the welfare of the child. The primary purpose of establishing paternity is to ensure that adequate provision will be made for the child's needs, in accordance with the means of the parents.

This overriding concern for the child's welfare is reflected in the provisions of article 5 of the Family Court Act. Once paternity is established, section 545 requires the court to "direct the parent or parents possessed of sufficient means or able to earn such means to pay . . . a fair and reasonable sum according to their respective means as the court may determine and apportion for such child's support and education, until the child is twenty-one." . . . The statute does not require, nor, we believe, does it permit, consideration of the "fault" or wrongful conduct of one of the parents in causing the child's conception. . . .

Respondent argues, however, that petitioner's intentional misrepresentation that she was practicing birth control deprived him of his constitutional right to decide whether to father a child. Recognizing that petitioner herself engaged in no State action by her conduct, respondent urges that imposition of a support obligation upon him under these circumstances constitutes State involvement sufficient to give vitality to his constitutional claim.

Assuming, without deciding, that sufficient State action is present in this case we conclude that respondent's contentions fall short of stating any recognized aspect of the constitutional right of privacy.

Clearly, respondent has a constitutionally protected right to decide for himself whether to father a child (Carey v. Population Servs. Int., 431 U.S. 678 [(1977)]; Eisenstadt v. Baird, 405 U.S. 438, 453 [(1972)]). This

---

1. Family Court after a further hearing ordered respondent father to pay $790 per month toward the child's support, whose needs had been found to require expenditures totaling $945 per month.

Although the court expressed an intent to adhere to its prior determination that the mother should, so far as possible, bear the burden of support, an examination of the mother's financial circumstances apparently convinced the court that she could not bear a large part of this burden without substantially diminishing her ability to meet her own needs. Respondent, on the other hand, stipulated to his ability to provide whatever amount of support the court ordered.

right is deemed so fundamental that governmental interference in this area of decision-making may be justified only by compelling State interests. Yet, the interest protected has always been stated in terms of governmental restrictions on the individual's access to contraceptive devices [citing *Griswold, Eisenstadt,* and *Carey*]. It involves the freedom to decide for oneself, without unreasonable governmental interference, whether to avoid procreation through the use of contraception. This aspect of the right of privacy has never been extended so far as to regulate the conduct of private actors as between themselves. Indeed, as the Appellate Division recognized, judicial inquiry into so fundamentally private and intimate conduct as is required to determine the validity of respondent's assertions may itself involve impermissible State interference with the privacy of these individuals.

The interest asserted by the father on this appeal is not, strictly speaking, his freedom to choose to avoid procreation, because the mother's conduct in no way limited his right to use contraception. Rather, he seeks to have his choice regarding procreation fully respected by other individuals and effectuated to the extent that he should be relieved of his obligation to support a child that he did not voluntarily choose to have. But respondent's constitutional entitlement to avoid procreation does not encompass a right to avoid a child support obligation simply because another private person has not fully respected his desires in this regard. However unfairly respondent may have been treated by petitioner's failure to allow him an equal voice in the decision to conceive a child, such a wrong does not rise to the level of a constitutional violation. . . .

## Notes and Questions

1. Should the support obligation rest on a biological or social relationship to the child? Should either relationship alone be enough? Should the obligation depend on whether the child's parents are married?

2. Suppose Frank knew that Pamela had sought to conceive a child but that the two had entered into a written agreement relieving him of support. Would such contract have compelled a different outcome? See Straub v. B.M.T., 626 N.E.2d 848 (Ind. Ct. App. 1993) (refusing to enforce such a written agreement, reasoning that parents cannot contract away the rights of their children and that the state has an interest in keeping children off the welfare rolls).

3. To what extent does the mother in *L. Pamela P.* have a duty to mitigate damages? Would the result change if the alleged father had offered to pay for an abortion? See People in the Interest of S.P.B., 651 P.2d 1213 (Colo. 1982). What if the defendant had used birth control that failed? Does any man who engages in sexual intercourse "assume the

risk" with all attendant duties? If so, why should actual paternity matter — why not impose shared liability on all men who might have fathered a particular child? Cf. Smith v. Cole, 553 So. 2d 847 (La. 1989) (upholding continued validity of dual paternity concept, imposing support duty on biological father but recognizing mother's husband as legal father).

4. Can an unwilling father, such as Frank, recover in tort? How much is the emotional harm of unwanted fatherhood worth? See Wallis v. Smith, 22 P.3d 682 (N.M. Ct. App. 2001) (denying father's claims for fraud, conversion, and breach of contract to recoup financial parental obligations). What result if the mother sues for "wrongful birth" of a healthy baby based on the father's false statement that he had a vasectomy? See C.A.M. v. R.A.W., 568 A.2d 556 (N.J. Super. Ct. App. Div. 1990).

5. Does the father have any constitutional claims? Would the right to privacy support or prohibit recognition of tort claims, for example? Does the father have a constitutional right to avoid fatherhood? Is the Fourteenth Amendment violated if the woman has the right to choose parenthood after conception via abortion or adoption but the man has no corresponding right? See Sorrel v. Henson, 1998 WL 886561 (Tenn. Ct. App. 1998).

6. How can the state deter the birth of nonmarital children? Even if it remains "illogical and unjust" to punish children for the misconduct of their parents, how far can the state go in penalizing the unmarried parents themselves? To what extent will such penalties inevitably affect the children as well?

## 2. Limitations on Unmarried Parents' Rights

### ■ STANLEY v. ILLINOIS
### 405 U.S. 645 (1972)

Mr. Justice WHITE delivered the opinion of the Court.

Joan Stanley lived with Peter Stanley intermittently for 18 years during which time they had three children. When Joan Stanley died, Peter Stanley lost not only her but also his children. Under Illinois law the children of unwed fathers become wards of the State upon the death of the mother. Accordingly, upon Joan Stanley's death, in a dependency proceeding instituted by the State of Illinois, Stanley's children were declared wards of the State and placed with court-appointed guardians. Stanley appealed, claiming that he had never been shown to be an unfit parent and that since married fathers and unwed mothers could not be deprived of their children without such a showing, he had been deprived of the equal protection of the laws guaranteed him by the Fourteenth Amendment. . . .

Stanley presses his equal protection claim here. The State continues to respond that unwed fathers are presumed unfit to raise their children. . . . We granted certiorari to determine whether this method of procedure by presumption could be allowed to stand in light of the fact that Illinois allows married fathers — whether divorced, widowed, or separated — and mothers — even if unwed — the benefit of the presumption that they are fit to raise their children.

We must [examine this question]: Is a presumption that distinguishes and burdens all unwed fathers constitutionally repugnant? We conclude that, as a matter of due process of law, Stanley was entitled to a hearing on his fitness as a parent before his children were taken from him and that by denying him a hearing and extending it to all other parents whose custody of their children is challenged, the State denied Stanley the equal protection of the laws guaranteed by the Fourteenth Amendment.

Illinois has two principal methods of removing nondelinquent children from the homes of their parents. In a dependency proceeding it may demonstrate that the children are wards of the State because they have no surviving parent or guardian. Ill. Rev. Stat., c. 37, §§702-1, 702-5. In a neglect proceeding it may show that children should be wards of the State because the present parent(s) or guardian does not provide suitable care. Ill. Rev. Stat., c. 37, §§702-1, 702-4.

The State's right — indeed duty — to protect minor children through a judicial determination of their interests in a neglect proceeding is not challenged here. Rather, we are faced with a dependency statute that empowers state officials to circumvent neglect proceedings on the theory that an unwed father is not a "parent" whose existing relationship with his children must be considered. "Parents," says the State, "means the father and mother of a legitimate child, or the survivor of them, or the natural mother of an illegitimate child, and includes any adoptive parent," Ill. Rev. Stat., c. 37, §701-14, but the term does not include unwed fathers.

Under Illinois law, therefore, while the children of all parents can be taken from them in neglect proceedings, that is only after notice, hearing, and proof of such unfitness as a parent as amounts to neglect, an unwed father is uniquely subject to the more simplistic dependency proceeding. By use of this proceeding, the State, on showing that the father was not married to the mother, need not prove unfitness in fact, because it is presumed at law. Thus, the unwed father's claim of parental qualification is avoided as "irrelevant."

In considering this procedure under the Due Process Clause, we recognize, as we have in other cases, that due process of law does not require a hearing "in every conceivable case of government impairment of private interest." Cafeteria Workers v. McElroy, 367 U.S. 886 (1961). [That case] firmly established that "what procedures due process may require under any given set of circumstances must begin with a determination of the precise nature of the government function involved as well as of the private interest that has been affected by governmental action." . . .

The private interest here, that of a man in the children he has sired and raised, undeniably warrants deference and, absent a powerful countervailing interest, protection. . . . The Court has frequently emphasized the importance of the family. The rights to conceive and to raise one's children have been deemed "essential," Meyer v. Nebraska, 262 U.S. 390, 399 (1923), "basic civil rights of man," Skinner v. Oklahoma, 316 U.S. 535, 541 (1942), and "[r]ights far more precious . . . than property rights," May v. Anderson, 345 U.S. 528, 533 (1953). . . .

Nor has the law refused to recognize those family relationships unlegitimized by a marriage ceremony. The Court has declared unconstitutional a state statute denying natural, but illegitimate, children a wrongful-death action for the death of their mother, emphasizing that such children cannot be denied the right of other children because familial bonds in such cases were often as warm, enduring, and important as those arising within a more formally organized family unit. Levy v. Louisiana, 391 U.S. 68, 71-72 (1968). "To say that the test of equal protection should be the 'legal' rather than the biological relationship is to avoid the issue. For the Equal Protection Clause necessarily limits the authority of a State to draw such 'legal' lines as it chooses." Glona v. American Guarantee Co., 391 U.S. 73, 75-76 (1968). These authorities make it clear that, at the least, Stanley's interest in retaining custody of his children is cognizable and substantial.

For its part, the State has made its interest quite plain: Illinois has declared that the aim of the Juvenile Court Act is to protect "the moral, emotional, mental, and physical welfare of the minor and the best interests of the community" and to "strengthen the minor's family ties whenever possible, removing him from the custody of his parents only when his welfare or safety or the protection of the public cannot be adequately safeguarded without removal . . ." Ill. Rev. Stat., c. 37, §701-2. These are legitimate interests well within the power of the State to implement. We do not question the assertion that neglectful parents may be separated from their children.

But we are here not asked to evaluate the legitimacy of the state ends, rather, to determine whether the means used to achieve these ends are constitutionally defensible. What is the state interest in separating children from fathers without a hearing designed to determine whether the father is unfit in a particular disputed case? We observe that the State registers no gain towards its declared goals when it separates children from the custody of fit parents. Indeed, if Stanley is a fit father, the State spites its own articulated goals when it needlessly separates him from his family. . . .

It may be, as the State insists, that most unmarried fathers are unsuitable and neglectful parents. It may also be that Stanley is such a parent and that his children should be placed in other hands. But all unmarried fathers are not in this category; some are wholly suited to have custody of their children. This much the State readily concedes, and nothing in this record indicates that Stanley is or has been a neglectful father who has not cared for his children. Given the opportunity to make his case, Stanley may have been seen to be deserving of custody of his offspring. Had this been so, the State's statutory policy would have been furthered by leaving custody in him. . . .

It may be argued that unmarried fathers are so seldom fit that Illinois need not undergo the administrative inconvenience of inquiry in any case, including Stanley's. The establishment of prompt efficacious procedures to achieve legitimate state ends is a proper state interest worthy of cognizance in constitutional adjudication. But the Constitution recognizes higher values than speed and efficiency. . . .

Procedure by presumption is always cheaper and easier than individualized determination. But when, as here, the procedure forecloses the determinative issues of competence and care, when it explicitly disdains present realities in deference to past formalities, it needlessly risks running roughshod over the important interests of both parent and child. It therefore cannot stand.

. . . The State's interest in caring for Stanley's children is de minimis if Stanley is shown to be a fit father. It insists on presuming rather than proving Stanley's unfitness solely because it is more convenient to presume than to prove. Under the Due Process Clause that advantage is insufficient to justify refusing a father a hearing when the issue at stake is the dismemberment of his family.

The State of Illinois assumes custody of the children of married parents, divorced parents, and unmarried mothers only after a hearing and proof of neglect. The children of unmarried fathers, however, are declared dependent children without a hearing on parental fitness and without proof of neglect. Stanley's claim in the state courts and here is that failure to afford him a hearing on his parental qualifications while extending it to other parents denied him equal protection of the laws. We have concluded that all Illinois parents are constitutionally entitled to a hearing on their fitness before their children are removed from their custody. It follows that denying such a hearing to Stanley and those like him while granting it to other Illinois parents is inescapably contrary to the Equal Protection Clause. . . .

## ■ MICHAEL H. v. GERALD D.
### *491 U.S. 110, reh'g denied, 492 U.S. 937 (1989)*

Justice SCALIA announced the judgment of the Court and delivered an opinion, in which THE CHIEF JUSTICE joins, and in all but note 6 of which Justice O'CONNOR and Justice KENNEDY join.

Under California law, a child born to a married woman living with her husband is presumed to be a child of the marriage. Cal. Evid. Code Ann. §621 (West Supp. 1989). The presumption of legitimacy may be rebutted only by the husband or wife, and then only in limited circumstances. The instant appeal presents the claim that this presumption infringes upon the due process rights of a man who wishes to establish his paternity of a child born to the wife of another man, and the claim that it infringes upon the constitutional right of the child to maintain a relationship with her natural father.

The facts of this case are, we must hope, extraordinary. On May 9, 1976, in Las Vegas, Nevada, Carole D., an international model, and Gerald D., a top executive in a French oil company, were married. The couple established a home in Playa del Rey, California, in which they resided as husband and wife when one or the other was not out of the country on business. In the summer of 1978, Carole became involved in an adulterous affair with a neighbor, Michael H. In September 1980, she conceived a child, Victoria D., who was born on May 11, 1981. Gerald was listed as father on the birth certificate and has always held Victoria out to the world as his daughter. Soon after delivery of the child, however, Carole informed Michael that she believed he might be the father.

In the first three years of her life, Victoria remained always with Carole, but found herself within a variety of quasi-family units. In October 1981, Gerald moved to New York City to pursue his business interests, but Carole chose to remain in California. At the end of that month, Carole and Michael had blood tests of themselves and Victoria, which showed a 98.07% probability that Michael was Victoria's father. In January 1982, Carole visited Michael in St. Thomas, where his primary business interests were based. There Michael held Victoria out as his child. In March, however, Carole left Michael and returned to California, where she took up residence with yet another man, Scott K. Later that spring, and again in the summer, Carole and Victoria spent time with Gerald in New York City, as well as on vacation in Europe. In the fall, they returned to Scott in California.

In November 1982, rebuffed in his attempts to visit Victoria, Michael filed a filiation action in California Superior Court to establish his paternity and right to visitation. In March 1983, the court appointed an attorney and guardian ad litem to represent Victoria's interests. Victoria then filed a cross-complaint asserting that if she had more than one psychological or de facto father, she was entitled to maintain her filial relationship, with all of the attendant rights, duties, and obligations, with both. In May 1983, Carole filed a motion for summary judgment. During this period, from March through July 1983, Carole was again living with Gerald in New York. In August, however, she returned to California, became involved once again with Michael, and instructed her attorneys to remove the summary judgment motion from the calendar.

For the ensuing eight months, when Michael was not in St. Thomas he lived with Carole and Victoria in Carole's apartment in Los Angeles and held Victoria out as his daughter. In April 1984, Carole and Michael signed a stipulation that Michael was Victoria's natural father. Carole left Michael the next month, however, and instructed her attorneys not to file the stipulation. In June 1984, Carole reconciled with Gerald and joined him in New York, where they now live with Victoria and two other children since born into the marriage.

In May 1984, Michael and Victoria, through her guardian ad litem, sought visitation rights for Michael *pendente lite*. To assist in determining whether visitation would be in Victoria's best interests, the Superior Court appointed a psychologist to evaluate Victoria, Gerald, Michael, and Carole. The psychologist recommended that Carole retain sole custody, but that Michael be allowed continued contact with Victoria pursuant to a restricted visitation schedule. The court concurred and ordered that Michael be provided with limited visitation privileges *pendente lite*.

On October 19, 1984, Gerald, who had intervened in the action, moved for summary judgment on the ground that under Cal. Evid. Code §621 there were no triable issues of fact as to Victoria's paternity. This law provides that "the issue of a wife cohabiting with her husband, who is not impotent or sterile, is conclusively presumed to be a child of the marriage." The presumption may be rebutted by blood tests, but only if a motion for such tests is made, within two years from the date of the child's birth, either by the husband or, if the natural father has filed an affidavit acknowledging paternity, by the wife.

On January 28, 1985, having found that affidavits submitted by Carole and Gerald sufficed to demonstrate that the two were cohabiting at conception and birth and that Gerald was neither sterile nor impotent, the Superior Court granted Gerald's motion for summary judgment, rejecting Michael's and Victoria's challenges to the constitutionality of §621. The court also denied their motions for continued visitation pending the appeal under Cal. Civ. Code §4601, which provides that a court may, in its discretion, grant "reasonable visitation rights . . . to any . . . person having an interest in the welfare of the child." Cal. Civ. Code Ann. §4601 (West Supp. 1989). It found that allowing such visitation would "violate the intention of the Legislature by impugning the integrity of the family unit." [Michael and Victoria appeal.]

Before us, Michael and Victoria both raise equal protection and due process challenges. We do not reach Michael's equal protection claim, however, as it was neither raised nor passed upon below. . . . We address first the [due process] claims of Michael. At the outset, it is necessary to clarify what he sought and what he was denied. California law, like nature itself, makes no provision for dual fatherhood. Michael was seeking to be declared the father of Victoria. The immediate benefit he evidently sought to obtain from that status was visitation rights. But if Michael were successful in being declared the father, other rights would follow — most importantly, the right to be considered as the parent who should have custody. . . . All parental rights, including visitation, were automatically denied by denying Michael status as the father. . . .

Michael contends as a matter of substantive due process that, because he has established a parental relationship with Victoria, protection of Gerald's and Carole's marital union is an insufficient state interest to support termination of that relationship. This argument is, of course, predicated on the assertion that Michael has a constitutionally protected liberty interest in his relationship with Victoria. . . .

In an attempt to limit and guide interpretation of the [Due Process] Clause, we have insisted not merely that the interest denominated as a "liberty" be "fundamental" (a concept that, in isolation, is hard to objectify), but also that it be an interest traditionally protected by our society. . . . This insistence that the asserted liberty interest be rooted in history and tradition is evident, as elsewhere, in our cases according constitutional protection to certain parental rights. Michael reads the landmark case of Stanley v. Illinois, 405 U.S. 645 (1972), and the subsequent cases of Quilloin v. Walcott, 434 U.S. 246 (1978), Caban v. Mohammed, 441 U.S. 380 (1979), and Lehr v. Robertson, 463 U.S. 248 (1983), as establishing that a liberty interest is created by biological fatherhood plus an established parental relationship — factors that exist in the present case as well. We think that distorts the rationale of those cases. As we view them, they rest not upon such isolated factors but upon the historic respect — indeed, sanctity would not be too strong a term — traditionally accorded to the relationships that develop within the unitary family.[3] . . .

Thus, the legal issue in the present case reduces to whether the relationship between persons in the situation of Michael and Victoria has been treated as a protected family unit under the historic practices of our society, or whether on any other basis it has been accorded special protection. We think it impossible to find that it has. In fact, quite to the contrary, our traditions have protected the marital family (Gerald, Car-

---

3. Justice Brennan asserts that only "a pinched conception of 'the family'" would exclude Michael, Carole, and Victoria from protection. We disagree. The family unit accorded traditional respect in our society, which we have referred to as the "unitary family," is typified, of course, by the marital family, but also includes the household of unmarried parents and their children. Perhaps the concept can be expanded even beyond this, but it will bear no resemblance to traditionally respected relationships — and will thus cease to have any constitutional significance — if it is stretched so far as to include the relationship established between a married woman, her lover, and their child, during a 3-month sojourn in St. Thomas, or during a subsequent 8-month period when, if he happened to be in Los Angeles, he stayed with her and the child.

ole, and the child they acknowledge to be theirs) against the sort of claim Michael asserts.[4]

The presumption of legitimacy was a fundamental principle of the common law. Traditionally, that presumption could be rebutted only by proof that a husband was incapable of procreation or had had no access to his wife during the relevant period. As explained by Blackstone, nonaccess could only be proved "if the husband be out of the kingdom of England (or, as the law somewhat loosely phrases it, *extra quatuor maria* [beyond the four seas]) for above nine months. . . ." 1 Blackstone's Commentaries 456 ( J. Chitty ed. 1826). And, under the common law both in England and here, [neither parent could testify to bastardize the child]. The primary policy rationale underlying the common law's severe restrictions on rebuttal of the presumption appears to have been an aversion to declaring children illegitimate, thereby depriving them of rights of inheritance and succession, and likely making them wards of the state. A secondary policy concern was the interest in promoting the "peace and tranquillity of States and families," a goal that is obviously impaired by facilitating suits against husband and wife asserting that their children are illegitimate. . . .

We have found nothing in the older sources, nor in the older cases, addressing specifically the power of the natural father to assert parental rights over a child born into a woman's existing marriage with another man. Since it is Michael's burden to establish that such a power (at least where the natural father has established a relationship with the child) is so deeply embedded within our traditions as to be a fundamental right, the lack of evidence alone might defeat his case. But the evidence shows that even in modern times — when, as we have noted, the rigid protection of the marital family has in other respects been relaxed — the ability of a person in Michael's position to claim paternity has not been generally acknowledged. . . .

Moreover, even if it were clear that one in Michael's position generally possesses, and has generally always possessed, standing to challenge the marital child's legitimacy, that would still not establish Michael's case. As noted earlier, what is at issue here is not entitlement to a state pronouncement that Victoria was begotten by Michael. It is no conceivable denial of constitutional right for a State to decline to declare facts unless

---

4. Justice Brennan insists that in determining whether a liberty interest exists we must look at Michael's relationship with Victoria in isolation, without reference to the circumstance that Victoria's mother was married to someone else when the child was conceived, and that that woman and her husband wish to raise the child as their own. We cannot imagine what compels this strange procedure of looking at the act which is assertedly the subject of a liberty interest in isolation from its effect upon other people — rather like inquiring whether there is a liberty interest in firing a gun where the case at hand happens to involve its discharge into another person's body. The logic of Justice Brennan's position leads to the conclusion that if Michael had begotten Victoria by rape, that fact would in no way affect his possession of a liberty interest in his relationship with her.

some legal consequence hinges upon the requested declaration. What Michael asserts here is a right to have himself declared the natural father and *thereby to obtain parental prerogatives*. What he must establish, therefore, is not that our society has traditionally allowed a natural father in his circumstances to establish paternity, but that it has traditionally accorded such a father parental rights, or at least has not traditionally denied them. . . . What counts is whether the States in fact award substantive parental rights to the natural father of a child conceived within, and born into, an extant marital union that wishes to embrace the child. We are not aware of a single case, old or new, that has done so. This is not the stuff of which fundamental rights qualifying as liberty interests are made.[6] . . .

We do not accept Justice Brennan's criticism that this result "squashes" the liberty that consists of "the freedom not to conform." It seems to us that reflects the erroneous view that there is only one side to this controversy — that one disposition can expand a "liberty" of sorts without contracting an equivalent "liberty" on the other side. Such a happy choice is rarely available. Here, to provide protection to an adulterous natural father is to deny protection to a marital father, and vice versa. If Michael has a "freedom not to conform" (whatever that means), Gerald must equivalently have a "freedom to conform." One of them will pay a price for asserting that "freedom." . . . Our disposition does not choose between these two "freedoms," but leaves that to the people of California. Justice Brennan's approach chooses one of them as the constitutional imperative, on no apparent basis except that the unconventional is to be preferred.

We have never had occasion to decide whether a child has a liberty interest, symmetrical with that of her parent, in maintaining her filial relationship. We need not do so here because, even assuming that such a right exists, Victoria's claim must fail. Victoria's due process challenge is, if anything, weaker than Michael's. Her basic claim is not that California has erred in preventing her from establishing that Michael, not Gerald,

---

6. Justice Brennan criticizes our methodology in using historical traditions specifically relating to the rights of an adulterous natural father, rather than inquiring more generally "whether parenthood is an interest that historically has received our attention and protection." . . .

We do not understand why, having rejected our focus upon the societal tradition regarding the natural father's rights vis-à-vis a child whose mother is married to another man, Justice Brennan would choose to focus instead upon "parenthood." Why should the relevant category not be even more general — perhaps "family relationships"; or "personal relationships"; or even "emotional attachments in general"? Though the dissent has no basis for the level of generality it would select, we do: We refer to the most specific level at which a relevant tradition protecting, or denying protection to, the asserted right can be identified. If, for example, there were no societal tradition, either way, regarding the rights of the natural father of a child adulterously conceived, we would have to consult, and (if possible) reason from, the traditions regarding natural fathers in general. But there is such a more specific tradition, and it unqualifiedly denies protection to such a parent. . . .

should stand as her legal father. Rather, she claims a due process right
to maintain filial relationships with both Michael and Gerald. This assertion merits little discussion, for, whatever the merits of the guardian
ad litem's belief that such an arrangement can be of great psychological
benefit to a child, the claim that a State must recognize multiple fatherhood has no support in the history or traditions of this country. Moreover, even if we were to construe Victoria's argument as forwarding the
lesser proposition that, whatever her status vis-à-vis Gerald, she has a liberty interest in maintaining a filial relationship with her natural father,
Michael, we find that, at best, her claim is the obverse of Michael's and
fails for the same reasons.

Victoria claims in addition that her equal protection rights have
been violated because, unlike her mother and presumed father, she had
no opportunity to rebut the presumption of her legitimacy. We find this
argument wholly without merit. We reject, at the outset, Victoria's suggestion that her equal protection challenge must be assessed under a
standard of strict scrutiny because, in denying her the right to maintain
a filial relationship with Michael, the State is discriminating against her
on the basis of her illegitimacy. See Gomez v. Perez, 409 U.S. 535, 538
(1973). Illegitimacy is a legal construct, not a natural trait. Under California law, Victoria is not illegitimate, and she is treated in the same
manner as all other legitimate children: she is entitled to maintain a filial relationship with her legal parents. . . . Since it pursues a legitimate
end [protecting the integrity of the marital family] by rational means,
California's decision to treat Victoria differently from her parents is not
a denial of equal protection. . . .

[In an omitted concurring opinion, Justice O'Connor, joined by Justice Kennedy, objects that the plurality's historical analysis might foreclose the identification of future liberty interests. In a separate concurring
opinion, Justice Stevens concludes that the trial court had given Michael
H. his constitutionally protected right to be heard.]

Justice BRENNAN, with whom Justice MARSHALL and Justice BLACK-
MUN join, dissenting. . . .

Today's plurality . . . does not ask whether parenthood is an interest
that historically has received our attention and protection; the answer to
that question is too clear for dispute. Instead, the plurality asks whether
the specific variety of parenthood under consideration — a natural father's relationship with a child whose mother is married to another man
— has enjoyed such protection.

If we had looked to tradition with such specificity in past cases, many
a decision would have reached a different result. Surely the use of contraceptives by unmarried couples, or even by married couples; the freedom from corporal punishment in schools; . . . and even the right to
raise one's natural but illegitimate children, were not "interest[s] tradi-

tionally protected by our society" at the time of their consideration by this Court. . . .

In construing the Fourteenth Amendment to offer shelter only to those interests specifically protected by historical practice, moreover, the plurality ignores the kind of society in which our Constitution exists. We are not an assimilative, homogeneous society, but a facilitative, pluralistic one, in which we must be willing to abide someone else's unfamiliar or even repellant practice because the same tolerant impulse protects our own idiosyncracies. Even if we can agree, therefore, that "family" and "parenthood" are part of the good life, it is absurd to assume that we can agree on the content of those terms and destructive to pretend that we do. In a community such as ours, "liberty" must include the freedom not to conform. The plurality today squashes this freedom by requiring specific approval from history before protecting anything in the name of liberty. . . .

. . . This is not a case in which we face a "new" kind of interest, one that requires us to consider for the first time whether the Constitution protects it. On the contrary, we confront an interest — that of a parent and child in their relationship with each other — that was among the first that this Court acknowledged in its cases defining the "liberty" protected by the Constitution [citing Meyer v. Nebraska, Skinner v. Oklahoma, Prince v. Massachusetts].

The evidence is undisputed that Michael, Victoria, and Carole did live together as a family; that is, they shared the same household, Victoria called Michael "Daddy," Michael contributed to Victoria's support, and he is eager to continue his relationship with her. Yet they are not, in the plurality's view, a "unitary family," whereas Gerald, Carole, and Victoria do compose such a family. The only difference between these two sets of relationships, however, is the fact of marriage. . . . However, the very premise of *Stanley* and the cases following it is that marriage is not decisive in answering the question whether the Constitution protects the parental relationship under consideration. . . .

The plurality's exclusive rather than inclusive definition of the "unitary family" is out of step with other decisions as well. This pinched conception of "the family," crucial as it is in rejecting Michael's and Victoria's claims of a liberty interest, is jarring in light of our many cases preventing the States from denying important interests or statuses to those whose situations do not fit the government's narrow view of the family. From Loving v. Virginia, 388 U.S. 1 (1967), to Levy v. Louisiana, 391 U.S. 68 (1968), and Glona v. American Guarantee & Liability Ins. Co., 391 U.S. 73 (1968), and from Gomez v. Perez, 409 U.S. 535 (1973), to Moore v. East Cleveland, 431 U.S. 494 (1977), we have declined to respect a State's notion, as manifested in its allocation of privileges and burdens, of what the family should be. Today's rhapsody on the "unitary family" is out of tune with such decisions. . . .

## Notes and Questions

1. To what extent does *Stanley* recognize substantive rights for unwed fathers? Whose rights are being vindicated? The father's? The children's? To what extent does *Stanley* accord equal status to unwed fathers and mothers?

2. The Court addressed the constitutional claims of unmarried fathers in three cases decided after *Stanley* but before *Michael H.:*

(a) In Quilloin v. Walcott, 434 U.S. 246 (1978), the Court unanimously upheld a Georgia adoption statute requiring only the consent of the mother unless the father had legitimated the child by marriage and acknowledgment or by court order. The mother in *Quilloin,* shortly after her child's birth, married a man who was not the child's father. The mother's new husband petitioned for adoption after the child had lived with him for approximately nine years. The biological father, who had been given notice of the adoption proceeding, responded by requesting that the adoption be denied, that he be declared the child's legitimate father and that he be granted visitation. The natural father, although he never lived with the mother and child and never legitimated the child, had made some support payments and had visited the child on several occasions. The child expressed a desire to be adopted.

The Supreme Court affirmed the stepparent adoption as consistent with the child's best interests. The Court denied the father's procedural due process and equal protection claims. Rejecting the father's argument that due process prohibited termination of his parental rights without a finding of unfitness, the Court noted that the father had received a hearing when he sought to legitimate the child in response to the adoption petition and also distinguished the need for a hearing in this case from the need in *Stanley* because of this father's failure ever to have or seek child custody. The Court also rejected the father's equal protection claim (that is, that the distinction between unmarried and married fathers was unconstitutional) on the ground that his interests were distinguishable from those of a married father because the latter had borne legal responsibility for the rearing of his children. "[L]egal custody of children is, of course, a central aspect of the marital relationship, and even a father whose marriage has broken apart will have borne full responsibility for the rearing of his children during the period of the marriage." Id. at 256.

(b) In Caban v. Mohammed, 441 U.S. 380 (1979), an unmarried father brought a successful equal protection challenge to a New York law that permitted the adoption of his children, without his consent, by the husband of the children's mother. Abdiel Caban had lived with Maria Mohammed for five years and had fathered their two children. When the couple separated, the mother began living with another man whom she eventually married. Caban continued to see his children frequently, contributed to their support, and at one point had custody of them. After the mother and her new husband petitioned for adoption, Caban and his new wife cross-petitioned.

The Supreme Court found the statute, which required the consent of only the mother of a nonmarital child, an overbroad gender-based generalization. The Court rejected the state's asserted justifications for the statute: a mother has a closer relationship with her children and the state has an interest in promoting adoption of nonmarital children. The Court pointed out that in this case, both the mother and father had participated in the children's care and support, and also that the state's interest in promoting adoption was not advanced in cases such as this. The Court elaborated:

> In those cases where the father never has come forward to participate in the rearing of his child, nothing in the Equal Protection Clause precludes the State from withholding from him the privilege of vetoing the adoption of that child. . . . But in cases such as this, where the father has established a substantial relationship with the child and has admitted his paternity, a State should have no difficulty in identifying the father even of children born out of wedlock. Thus, no showing has been made that the different treatment afforded unmarried fathers and unmarried mothers under [the statute] bears a substantial relationship to the proclaimed interest of the State in promoting the adoption of illegitimate children.

Id. at 392-393.

(c) Finally, in Lehr v. Robertson, 463 U.S. 248 (1983), the Court upheld another New York adoption statute dispensing with notice of adoption proceedings for some fathers of nonmarital children. In *Lehr*, Lorraine Robertson married Richard Robertson eight months after the birth of her nonmarital child. The biological father, Jonathan Lehr, had never contributed to the child's support and had seen her only infrequently. When the child was two, the Robertsons filed an adoption petition. Lehr claimed that the Due Process and Equal Protection Clauses, as interpreted in *Stanley*, gave him a right to notice and an opportunity to be heard. New York law required notice for fathers who had registered with a "putative father registry," as well as those who were adjudicated to be the father, identified on the birth certificate, lived openly with the child and the child's mother, or were married to the mother before the child was six months old. Lehr fit none of these categories. Unanswered by *Quilloin* and *Caban* was the extent of constitutional protection required for a father, such as Lehr, who manifests only a biological relationship with his child. That is, was he entitled to notice and an opportunity to be heard before the child could be adopted?

The Supreme Court rejected both of Lehr's constitutional challenges. The Court concluded that due process does not require notice to a biological father if he has not assumed any responsibility for the care of his child.

The significance of the biological connection is that it offers the natural father an opportunity that no other male possesses to develop a relationship
with his offspring. If he grasps that opportunity and accepts some measure of responsibility for the child's future, he may enjoy the blessings of
the parent-child relationship and make uniquely valuable contributions to
the child's development. If he fails to do so, the Federal Constitution will
not automatically compel a state to listen to his opinion of where the child's
best interests lie.

Id. at 262. Further, the Court reasoned that the statute did not constitute a denial of equal protection because it did not distinguish between
a mother and father who were similarly situated. Lehr had never established a custodial, personal, or financial relationship with the child. "If
one parent has an established custodial relationship with the child and
the other parent has either abandoned or never established a relationship, the Equal Protection Clause does not prevent a state from according the two parents different legal rights." Id. at 267-268. The Court
distinguished "between the developed parent-child relationship that was
implicated in *Stanley* and *Caban,* and the potential relationship involved
in *Quilloin* and this case. . . ." Id. at 261.

A troublesome issue, raised by the dissent in *Lehr* but unaddressed
by the majority, concerns the degree of constitutional protection to be
afforded if the mother actually prevents the father from establishing a
relationship with the child. The dissenting opinion in *Lehr* points out
that Lehr's efforts to establish a parent-child relationship were thwarted
by the mother who concealed her whereabouts from him after the birth.
See Chapter 9 section B2.

The *Quilloin-Caban-Lehr* trilogy of cases stand for the principle that
an unwed father is entitled to constitutional protection of his parental
rights so long as he is willing to accept the responsibilities of parenthood
(the "biology plus test"). The extent of this constitutional protection
varies according to the degree to which the unwed father manifests a
custodial, personal, or financial relationship with the child ("the indicia
of parenthood"). To what extent is *Michael H.* consistent with these
precedents?

3. Professor Janet L. Dolgin sees familial relationships as the determinative variables in these cases:

[T]he unwed father cases, from *Stanley* through *Michael H.,* delineate three
factors that make an unwed man a father. These are the man's biological
relation to the child, his social relation to the child, and his relation to the
child's mother. . . . In this regard, *Michael H.* clarifies the earlier cases. A
biological father does protect his paternity by developing a social relationship with his child, but this step demands the creation of a family, a step
itself depending upon an appropriate relationship between the man and
his child's mother.

Janet L. Dolgin, Just A Gene: Judicial Assumptions About Parenthood, 40 UCLA L. Rev. 637, 671 (1993).

4. Like Moore v. City of East Cleveland, supra, which overturned the city's definition of "family," both *Stanley* and *Michael H.* test the government's power to write its own definition of certain terms: "parent" in *Stanley* and "father" in *Michael H.* Can you reconcile *Michael H.* with the two earlier cases? Is footnote 3 in the plurality opinion persuasive?

p. 521

5. Michael Grossberg has traced the history of the presumption of legitimacy to the strong reluctance to stigmatize illegitimate children in the post-Revolutionary period. He adds that this reluctance ultimately found expression in the creation of common law marriage, the exclusion of evidence that would bastardize the child of a married woman, the recognition of the offspring of annulled marriages as legitimate, and the adoption of the doctrine of putative marriage. As Grossberg elaborates:

> In the agonizing conflict between a man's right to limit his paternity only to his actual offspring and the right of a child born to a married woman to claim family membership, the common law, first in England and then in America, generally made paternal rights defer to the larger goal of preserving family integrity.

Michael Grossberg, Governing the Hearth: Law and the Family in Nineteenth-Century America 201-202 (1985).

6. Given the decreasing stigma of illegitimacy and the increasing accuracy of paternity determinations, how strong is the case for retention of presumptions?

The Uniform Parentage Act replaces the traditional presumption of legitimacy with the following presumption. Is this an improvement?

### §4. [Presumption of Paternity]

(a) A man is presumed to be the natural father of a child if:

(1) he and the child's natural mother are or have been married to each other and the child is born during the marriage, or within 300 days after the marriage is terminated by death, annulment, declaration of invalidity, or divorce, or after a decree of separation is entered by the court;

(2) before the child's birth, he and the child's natural mother have attempted to marry each other by a marriage solemnized in apparent compliance with law, although the attempted marriage is or could be declared invalid, and,

(i) if the attempted marriage could be declared invalid only by a court, the child is born during the attempted marriage, or within 300 days after its termination by death, annulment, declaration of invalidity, or divorce; or

(ii) if the attempted marriage is invalid without a court order, the child is born within 300 days after the termination of cohabitation;

(3) after the child's birth, he and the child's natural mother have married, or attempted to marry, each other by a marriage solemnized in apparent compliance with law, although the attempted marriage is or could be declared invalid, and

(i) he has acknowledged his paternity of the child in writing filed with the [appropriate court or Vital Statistics Bureau];

(ii) with his consent, he is named as the child's father on the child's birth certificate; or

(iii) he is obligated to support the child under a written voluntary promise or by court order;

(4) while the child is under the age of majority, he receives the child into his home and openly holds out the child as his natural child; or

(5) he acknowledges his paternity of the child in a writing filed with the [appropriate court or Vital Statistics Bureau], which shall promptly inform the mother of the filing of the acknowledgment, and she does not dispute the acknowledgment within a reasonable time after being informed thereof, in a writing filed with the [appropriate court or Vital Statistics Bureau]. If another man is presumed under this section to be the child's father, acknowledgment may be effected only with the written consent of the presumed father or after the presumption has been rebutted.

(b) A presumption under this section may be rebutted in an appropriate action only by clear and convincing evidence. If two or more presumptions arise which conflict with each other, the presumption which on the facts is founded on the weightier considerations of policy and logic controls. The presumption is rebutted by a court decree establishing paternity of the child by another man.

9B U.L.A. 298-299 (1987). How would *Michael H.* have been decided under this rule?

7. *Revised Uniform Parentage Act.* In August 2000, the National Conference of Commissioners on Uniform State Laws approved a revised Uniform Parentage Act. Reform was necessitated by the increasing number of nonmarital children, improved accuracy of paternity determinations, and the development of assisted reproduction. The revised act changed Article 4 (above) to eliminate subsections 4 and 5: the presumption of paternity that arises from a man receiving the child into his home and openly holding out the child as his, and the presumption of paternity that arises if a man submits a written acknowledgment with an agency that is not disputed by the mother. The commissioners rejected the first presumption in the belief that genetic testing is a superior means of determining paternity. They eliminated the latter presumption because it conflicted with another provision of the new act under which a valid acknowledgment establishes paternity rather than a presumption of paternity. Unif. Parentage Act (2000), §204, 9B U.L.A. 311 cmt. (2001). How would *Michael H.* be decided under the revised Uniform Parentage Act?

The revised UPA makes another significant change. Recall that *Lehr*, in contrast to *Stanley*, requires an affirmative act on the biological father's part before he is entitled to notice of a hearing to terminate his parental rights. The revised UPA emphasizes the infant's rights in the balancing of rights. When the mother favors the adoption, the new act requires that the biological father must register before birth or within 30 days thereafter (UPA §402(a), 9B U.L.A. 322 (2001)), unless the man begins a paternity proceeding before the court moves to terminate his rights (UPA §402(b)(2)). (In the latter case, similar to the *Lehr* situation, the alternate proceeding would alert the court to the need for notice to the father.) The short period is intended to facilitate adoptions.

8. If the dissenters would afford constitutional protection to Michael's interests because he, Carole, and Victoria lived together as a family, would they afford similar protection to any interests asserted by Scott, another man with whom Carole and Victoria lived?

9. How relevant is the fact that when Victoria was born, Carole was apparently still *physically* residing with Gerald? In Brian C. v. Ginger K., 92 Cal. Rptr.2d 294 (Ct. App. 2000), Ginger was married to (but separated from) her husband when she gave birth to a daughter, the product of an affair with Brian. Although living with her husband at the time of the affair, Ginger moved out a few months before the birth. She and the baby then lived with Brian for about a year. When Ginger reconciled with her husband, they resisted Brian's attempts to maintain a relationship with the child. After Brian petitioned to establish a parent-child relationship, the court of appeal held that the conclusive presumption of the husband's paternity did not apply. The court ruled that Brian had a constitutionally protected liberty interest in continuation of his relationship with the child, reasoning that (in contrast to the facts in *Michael H.*) this child was not born into "an extant marital family" because Ginger had left her husband before the birth. Id. at 309. Is the distinction persuasive?

10. *Michael H.* was decided by a sharply divided court. In an omitted portion of the dissenting opinion, Justice Brennan ( joined by Justices Marshall and Blackmun) highlights the divisions, pointing out that five Justices refuse to foreclose the possibility that a natural father in Michael's position might ever have a constitutionally protected interest, four Justices agree that Michael has a liberty interest, and five Justices believe that the flaw is procedural.

Discomfort with the plurality's decision is evident in judicial and legislative responses to the case. California amended its presumption of legitimacy to allow either a presumed father who is not the child's mother's husband or the child to move for blood tests within two years of birth. Cal. Fam. Code §7541(b) (West 1994). The statute also permits an award of custody or visitation *pendente lite* when blood tests show a parent-child relationship and such award would promote the child's best interests. Id.

at §7604. The statutory definition of presumed father (Cal. Fam. Code §7611 (West 1994)) parallels that of the Uniform Parentage Act.

Some states, by case law, now depart from strict adherence to the presumption. See, e.g., Johnson v. Studley-Preston, 812 P.2d 1216 (Idaho 1991) (putative father has standing to rebut presumption); K.B. v. D.B., 639 N.E.2d 725 (Mass. App. Ct. 1994) (relieving social father from support obligation to child fathered during the marriage by another man). Other states depart from the presumption based on the child's best interests. See, e.g., N.A.H. v. S.L.S., 9 P.3d 354 (Colo. 2000). See generally Diane S. Kaplan, Why Truth Is Not a Defense in Paternity Actions, 10 Tex. J. Women & L. 69, 73-81 (2000) (describing different state approaches).

11. *Nonmarital children and immigration*. The United States Supreme Court recently decided another case concerning the paternity of nonmarital children. In Nguyen v. INS, 200 U.S. 321 (2001), the Supreme Court rejected a claim that different requirements for a nonmarital child's acquisition of citizenship, depending on the gender of the citizen-parent, violate equal protection. According to INS regulations, nonmarital children born abroad to citizen mothers become citizens based on a short residency requirement for the mother. However, additional requirements exist for nonmarital children born abroad to citizen fathers: The father has to act affirmatively to establish paternity before the child reaches the age of 18. The Court reasoned that the distinction satisfied the important governmental interest in assuring that children have a biological and social attachment to their citizen parent: Attachment to the mother is established by the pregnancy and birth, unlike for the father, who has to act affirmatively. The Court was unconvinced by the petitioners' argument that the statutory distinction rested on problems of paternity establishment that were obviated by the reliability of DNA testing. Was the Court's ruling based on stereotypical notions of gender roles? Note that the Court's gender-based stereotypes are belied by the facts: The child's Vietnamese mother abandoned the child soon after birth, whereas the American father brought him to the United States.

## Problem

When Stephanie marries Jeffrey, she is not motivated by love but by a desire to obtain military benefits and to share rent. Thereafter, Stephanie begins an intimate relationship with Paul and bears his child. Before the birth, they move in together. During the two years in which they live together, Paul holds the child out as his son. Subsequently, Stephanie and Paul break up. At that time, Stephanie lies to Paul, telling him that he might not be the father. Paul files suit to establish paternity in California after the legislature has amended the statute (discussed supra) in response to *Michael H.* Stephanie defends, alleging that Jeffrey is the child's father based on the statutory presumption of legitimacy. What result? Comino v. Kelley, 30 Cal. Rptr. 728 (Ct. App. 1994).

# V

■

# *Divorce*

## A. INTRODUCTION

### 1. *Divorce as a Historical Phenomenon*

■ **LAWRENCE M. FRIEDMAN, A HISTORY
OF AMERICAN LAW**
*204-208, 498-504 (2d ed., 1988)*

England had been a "divorceless society," and remained that way until 1857. There was no way to get a judicial divorce. The very wealthy might squeeze a rare private bill of divorce out of Parliament. Between 1800 and 1836 there were, on the average, three of these a year. For the rest, unhappy husbands and wives had to be satisfied with annulment (no easy matter), or divorce from bed and board *(a mensa et thoro)*, a form of legal separation, which did not entitle either spouse to marry again. The most common solutions, of course, when a marriage broke down, were adultery and desertion.

In the colonial period, the South was generally faithful to English tradition. . . . In New England, however, courts and legislatures occasionally granted divorce. In Pennsylvania, Penn's laws of 1682 gave

**533**

spouses the right to a "Bill of Divorcement" if their marriage partner was convicted of adultery. Later, the governor or lieutenant governor was empowered to dissolve marriages, on grounds of incest, adultery, bigamy, or homosexuality. There is no evidence that the governor ever used this power. Still later, the general assembly took divorce into its own hands. The English privy council disapproved of this practice, and in the 1770's disallowed legislative divorces in Pennsylvania, New Jersey, and New Hampshire. The Revolution, of course, put an end to the privy council's power.

After Independence, the law and practice of divorce began to change, but regional differences remained quite strong. In the South, divorce continued to be unusual. The extreme case was South Carolina. Henry William Desaussure, writing in 1817, stated flatly that South Carolina had never granted a single divorce. He was right. . . . In other Southern states, legislatures dissolved marriages by passing private divorce laws. The Georgia constitution of 1798 allowed legislative divorce, on a two-thirds vote of each branch of the legislature — and after a "fair trial" and a divorce decree in the superior court. . . . Between 1798 and 1835, there were only 291 legislative divorces in Georgia. The frequency curve was rising toward the end of the period. Twenty-seven couples were divorced legislatively in 1833. . . .

North of the Mason-Dixon line, courtroom divorce became the normal mode rather than legislative divorce. Pennsylvania passed a general divorce law in 1785, Massachusetts one year later. Every New England state had a divorce law before 1800, along with New York, New Jersey, and Tennessee. Grounds for divorce varied somewhat from state to state. New York's law of 1787 permitted absolute divorce only for adultery. Vermont, on the other hand, in 1798 allowed divorce for impotence, adultery, intolerable severity, three years' willful desertion, and long absence with presumption of death (1798). Rhode Island allowed divorce for "gross misbehaviour and wickedness in either of the parties, repugnant to and in violation of the marriage covenant." In New Hampshire, it was grounds for divorce if a spouse joined the Shaker sect — not an unreasonable rule, since the Shakers did not believe in sexual intercourse.

This efflorescence of divorce laws must reflect a real increase in demand for legal divorce. The size of the demand doomed the practice of divorce by statute. Like corporate charters, private divorce bills became a nuisance, a pointless drain on the legislature's time. . . .

. . . The divorce rate in the nineteenth century, of course, was the merest trickle in comparison to the rate in more recent times. Still it was noticeable and it was growing, and to some self-appointed guardians of national morals, it was an alarming fire bell in the night, a symptom of moral dry rot, and a cause in itself of still further moral decay. . . .

. . . Nor was the rising divorce rate so obviously a sign that the family was breaking down. The family was indeed changing. There were new strains on marital relationships. William O'Neill put it this way:

"when families are large and loose, arouse few expectations, and make few demands, there is no need for divorce." That need arises when "families become the center of social organization." At this point, "their intimacy can become suffocating, their demands unbearable, and their expectations too high to be easily realizable. Divorce then becomes the safety valve that makes the system workable." Moreover, a divorceless state is not a state without adultery, prostitution, fornication. It may be, rather, a place sharply divided between zones of official law and zones of unofficial behavior. A country with rare or expensive divorce is a country with two kinds of family laws, one for the rich, and one for the poor. . . . Divorce was simplest to obtain and divorce laws most advanced in those parts of the country — the West especially — least stratified by class. . . .

[By 1880, legislative divorce was abolished. From 1850 to 1870, many states adopted highly liberal divorce laws.] After 1870, the tide began to turn. Influential moral leaders had never stopped attacking loose divorce laws. Horace Greeley thought that "easy divorce" had made the Roman Empire rot. A similar fate lay in store for America. [In 1881, a New England Divorce Reform League was formed which later became the National Divorce Reform League. By 1882, the Connecticut law had been repealed.] Maine's law fell in 1883. A more rigorous divorce law replaced it, with tougher grounds, a six-month wait before decrees became "absolute," and a two-year ban on remarriage of the plaintiff without court permission; as for the guilty defendant, he or she could never remarry without leave of the court.

Naturally, there were two sides to the question. Militant feminists took up the cudgels for permissive divorce. A furious debate raged in New York. Robert Dale Owen, son of the Utopian reformer, went into battle against Horace Greeley. Owen . . . felt that strict divorce laws, not lax ones, led to adultery. . . .

[A dramatic increase occurred in the divorce rate between 1867-1886 despite the stricter divorce laws.] How is that fact to be accounted for? There are two possibilities. Either dry rot had affected family life; or more people wanted *formal* acceptance of the fact that their marriages were dead. Those who prattled about Babylon and chastity believed in the first explanation. But the second seems far more likely. Just as more of the middle class wanted, and needed, their deeds recorded, their wills made out, [and] their marriages solemnized, so they wanted the honesty and convenience of divorce, the right to remarry in bourgeois style, to have legitimate children with their second wife (or husband), and the right to decent, honest disposition of their worldly goods. . . . "Divorce rings" operated practically in the open. Manufactured adultery was a New York specialty. Henry Zeimer and W. Waldo Mason, arrested in 1900, had hired young secretaries and other enterprising girls for this business. The girls would admit on the witness stand that they knew the plaintiff's husband, then blush, shed a few tears, and leave the rest to the judge. Annulments, too, were more common in New York than elsewhere; they were a loophole in the divorce laws, less distasteful, though less certain, than trumped-up adultery. Friendly divorces were a simple matter in those states which allowed "cruelty" as grounds for divorce. . . .

The migratory divorce, for people with money and the urge to travel, was another detour around strict enforcement of divorce law. To attract the "tourist trade," a state needed easy laws and a short residence period. Indiana was one of these states, before the 1870's. . . . Finally, Nevada became the place. . . . Nevada remained quite impervious to moral arguments; its career as national divorce mill lasted longer than any other state's.

Plainly, in the late 19th century, the number of married people who *wanted* divorce was greater than before. [This was] an era of national panic over morality, eugenics, the purity of the bloodline and the future of old-fashioned white America. To prophets of doom the whore, divorce, had to be contained. The result of this clash of opinion was, as often, a stalemate — or compromise. . . . The national law of divorce was a hodgepodge. South Carolina still allowed no divorces at all. New York allowed divorce, practically speaking, only for adultery. Most states had a broader list. In a few jurisdictions, the innocent party might remarry, the guilty party not. . . . In the strict states, the compromise took this form: the moralists had their symbolic victory, a stringent law strutting proudly on the books. At the same time, enforcement of these laws was defective. A cynical traffic in runaway and underground divorce flourished in the shadows. Divorce law stood as an egregious example of a branch of law tortured by contradictions in public opinion, [and] in a federal system with freedom of movement back and forth . . . beyond the power and grasp of any single state.

---

World War II brought higher divorce rates. This consequence stemmed from the effects of separation during war (such as wartime adultery) and the difficulties of postwar adjustment to married life. Divorce rates stabilized in the 1950s for about ten years.[1] Rates began rising again in 1964 and continued to increase through the early 1970s and early 1980s with the advent of no-fault divorce.[2] After peaking in 1981,

[1]. Roderick Phillips, Putting Asunder: A History of Divorce Law in Western Society 557-564 (1988). See also Norma Basch, Framing American Divorce: From the Revolutionary Generation to the Victorians (1999) (history of divorce from 1770 to 1870).

[2]. U.S. Dept. of Health & Human Servs., Nat'l Center for Health Statistics, Monthly Vital Statistics Report, Divorces and Annulments and Rates, 1940-1990, at 1 (1995) (table 1). On the effect of no fault on the divorce rate, compare Ira Mark Ellman, Divorce Rates, Marriage Rates, and the Problematic Persistence of Traditional Marital Roles, 34 Fam. L.Q. 1 (2000) (arguing that rise in divorce rate predated no fault) with Margaret F. Brinig & F.H. Buckley, No-Fault Laws and At-Fault People, 18 Int'l Rev. L. & Econ. 325 (1998) (presenting data to support theory that no fault resulted in higher divorce rate).

the divorce rate began to decline steadily until 1998 when it reached the lowest rate since 1972.[3]

## 2. Divorce as a Social Phenomenon

### ■ PAUL BOHANNON, THE SIX STATIONS OF DIVORCE
*in Divorce and After 29-32 (Paul Bohannon ed., 1970)*

The complexity of divorce arises because at least six things are happening at once. They may come in a different order and with varying intensities, but there are at least these six difference experiences. . . .

I have called these six overlapping experiences (1) the emotional divorce, which centers around the problem of the deteriorating marriage; (2) the legal divorce, based on grounds [and now, on no fault]; (3) the economic divorce, which deals with money and property; (4) the coparental divorce, which deals with custody, single-parent homes, and visitation; (5) the community divorce, surrounding the changes of friends and community that every divorcee experiences; and (6) the psychic divorce, with the problem of regaining individual autonomy.

The first visible stage of a deteriorating marriage is likely to be what psychiatrists call emotional divorce. This occurs when the spouses withhold emotion from their relationship because they dislike the intensity or ambivalence of their feelings. They may continue to work together as a social team, but their attraction and trust for one another have disappeared. . . . The natural and healthy "growing apart" of a married couple is very different. As marriages mature, the partners grow in new directions, but also establish bonds of ever greater interdependence. With emotional divorce, people do not grow together as they grow apart — they become, instead, mutually antagonistic and imprisoned, hating the vestiges of their dependence. Two people in emotional divorce grate on each other because each is disappointed. . . .

The economic divorce must occur because in Western countries husband and wife are an economic unit. . . . While technically the couple is not a corporation, they certainly have many of the characteristics of a legal corporation. At the time the household is broken up by divorce, an economic settlement must be made, separating the assets of the "corporation" into two sets of assets, each belonging to one person. This is the property settlement. Today it is vastly complicated by income tax law. . . .

The coparental divorce is necessary if there are children. When the household breaks up, the children have to live somewhere. Taking care

[3]. Bureau of the Census, U.S. Dept. of Commerce, Statistical Abstract of the United States: 2000, at 101 (2000) (table 77).

of the children requires complex arrangements for carrying out the obligations of parents.

All divorced persons suffer more or less because their community is altered. Friends necessarily take a different view of a person during and after divorce — he ceases to be a part of a couple. Their own inadequacies, therefore, will be projected in a new way. Their fantasies are likely to change as they focus on the changing situation. In many cases, the change in community attitude — and perhaps people too — is experienced by a divorcee as ostracism and disapproval. For many divorcing people, the divorce from community may make it seem that nothing in the world is stable.

Finally comes the psychic divorce. It is almost always last, and always the most difficult. Indeed, I have not found a word strong or precise enough to describe the difficulty of the process. Each partner to the ex-marriage, either before or after the legal divorce — usually after, and sometimes years after — must turn himself or herself again into an autonomous social individual. People who have been long married tend to have become socially part of a couple or a family; they lose the habit of seeing themselves as individuals. . . .

Divorce is an institution that nobody enters without great trepidation. In the emotional divorce, people are likely to feel hurt and angry. In the legal divorce, people often feel bewildered — they have lost control, and events sweep them along. In the economic divorce, the reassignment of property and the division of money (there is *never* enough) may make them feel cheated. In the parental divorce, they worry about what is going to happen to the children; they feel guilty for what they have done. With the community divorce, they may get angry with their friends and perhaps suffer despair because there seems to be no fidelity in friendship. In the psychic divorce, in which they have become autonomous again, they are probably afraid and are certainly lonely. However, the resolution of any or all of these various six divorces may provide an elation of victory that comes from having accomplished something that had to be done and having done it well. . . . I know a divorced man who took great comfort in the fact that one of his business associates asked him, when he learned of his divorce, "Do I feel sorry for you or do I congratulate you?" He thought for a moment and said — out of bravado as much as conviction — "Congratulate me." It was, for him, the beginning of the road back.

---

Men and women experience marriage differently, as we saw in Chapter III. Below, men and women report different perceptions of the causes of divorce.

■ **CATHERINE K. RIESSMAN, DIVORCE TALK:**
**WOMEN AND MEN MAKE SENSE**
**OF PERSONAL RELATIONSHIPS**
*65-72 (1990)*

. . . For women, marriage flounders because husbands fail to be emotionally intimate in the ways wives expect them to be. This element of the companionate marriage is the centerpiece in women's accounts, working class and middle class alike. For men, the explanatory schema is very different: particularly for more economically advantaged men, the marriage failed because other relationships — with children, kin, and friends — were not subordinated to it; the marital relationship was not self-contained or was not primary enough to the wife. For both husbands and wives there was a failure in companionship; yet the particular activities women and men wanted to "do together" are strikingly different, especially in working-class marriages. And both women and men lament acts of sexual infidelity and incompatibility, though the interpretations they place on these events are not the same. For women, infidelity is an act of betrayal, living proof the marriage is over. Men have complex and differentiated views of infidelity, even as sex is central to their definition of what a good marriage should provide.

Some might argue that these different constructions arise out of the very different personality structures of women and men. Feminist psychological theory suggests that masculinity becomes defined through separation, whereas femininity becomes defined through relationships.[1] Women and men, in bringing these different orientations into marriage, put severe strains on it. Women define the institution of marriage interpersonally. The relationship with the spouse is one of a series of interpersonal ties that coexist for them — not without conflict, of course. Yet at the same time women want marriage to be emotionally intimate through talking about feelings, problems, and daily experiences, and through understandings that go beyond words. Further, they expect talk to be reciprocal: their husbands will disclose to them at the same time as they share with their husbands. Divorced women's accounts describe men who could not or did not express love in these ways, or whose needs for separation, some might argue, precluded this kind of emotional intimacy.

Men want something very different from marriage. Especially prominent is their desire for the undivided attention of their wives. [Men]

1. See Nancy Chodorow, The Reproduction of Mothering: Psychoanalysis and the Sociology of Gender (Berkeley: University of California Press, 1978); Carol Gilligan, In a Different Voice: Psychological Theory and Women's Development (Cambridge: Harvard University Press, 1982); Jean Baker Miller, Toward a New Psychology of Women (Boston: Beacon Press, 1976).

want the marital relationship to be exclusive and primary; women in contrast, add it to their other relational investments. Men value the autonomy of the marital pair rather than its interconnectedness. They expect to achieve emotional closeness with their wives through sex and a particular kind of companionship. It is these "doing" aspects of marriage that they emphasize. [T]he masculine style of love emphasizes practical help, shared physical activities, spending time together, and sex — manifestations of love that achieve connection through action rather than talk, just as providing for a family does. This style of love fits well with cultural expectations for men more generally, for achievement, responsibility, instrumentality. . . .

Neither the women nor the men interviewed, whether working class or middle class, questioned the ideology of the companionate marriage. It was the failure of their particular partners to live up to the ideal that was defined as the problem, not the dream itself. . . .

## B. FAULT-BASED GROUNDS FOR DIVORCE

### 1. Adultery

■ **LICKLE v. LICKLE**
*52 A.2d 910 (Md. 1947)*

DELAPLAINE, Judge.

William F. Lickle, an insurance agent, of Towson, is appealing here from a decree of the Circuit Court for Baltimore County granting his wife, Margaret Lee Lickle, a divorce a vinculo matrimonii. He contends that the evidence fails to support her charge of adultery.

The parties were married in 1917. They had three children, who are now adults. Appellant, a captain in the First World War, is now over 55. The parties have not cohabited as man and wife for many years, although they resided in the same house. In 1937 appellant met A. Gordon Boone, a young Towson lawyer, and his wife, Edith Flint Boone, the co-respondent in this case. Appellant frequently visited their home on Bellona Avenue, went to parties with them, and accompanied them to the races. . . .

In July 1942, Boone received a commission in the United States Navy. . . . During the years when Boone was in the service [overseas], appellant became increasingly intimate with Mrs. Boone. She changed her residence four times during that period. . . . But in each of these homes appellant was a frequent visitor. One of Mrs. Boone's maids testified that he was at the home at Owings Mills "most of the time." Another maid testified that he visited Mrs. Boone in her homes at Riderwood and Ruxton on numerous occasions, staying all night several times a week, and eating many meals there. She also testified that appellant and Mrs. Boone often went motoring together, returning late at night.

Twice during the summer of 1943 appellant and Mrs. Boone vacationed together at Ocean City, Maryland. The first time was early in June, when they stopped at the Delmar Hotel. On that occasion appellant was accompanied by one of his sons, while Mrs. Boone and her elder son, Gordon, Jr., then ten years old, had rooms across the hall. The second trip was entirely different. Appellant and Mrs. Boone, traveling together in an automobile, arrived in Ocean City on July 23. They were unaccompanied. Mrs. Boone had sent her ten-year-old son to camp, and had left her one-year-old son at home with a nurse. Appellant registered at the Ambassador Apartments for both himself and Mrs. Boone, and during the next two weeks they occupied rooms on the third floor of the building. The first night they occupied adjoining rooms with connecting bathroom. After the first night appellant took another room across the hall, but they visited each other's room frequently, sometimes until after midnight. It further appears that in September, 1944, appellant drove Mrs. Boone and her two boys on a trip to Cumberland, and at the Fort Cumberland Hotel, where they spent the night, appellant registered for the party as "William F. Lickle and family."

Boone testified that he had not had sexual relations with his wife since September, 1943. In October, 1943, when he was home on a furlough, she repulsed his advances without any explanation. Three other times — when he returned from Europe in 1944, in June, 1945, and in October, 1945 — she again refused to have relations with him. He then accused her of being fond of another man, and he suspicioned that it was Lickle. In January, 1945, he was ordered to Chicago to act as instructor in amphibious warfare at Northwestern University. He pleaded with her to go with him to Chicago, but she refused even to visit him at any time during the year. . . . He returned home in October, and received his honorable discharge in December, 1945. Several days after Christmas Boone confronted Lickle with the charge that he had committed adultery with Mrs. Boone. Lickle denied that there had been any improper conduct. . . .

In a suit for divorce the burden of proof is on the complainant, but the charge of adultery as a ground for divorce need not be proved beyond a reasonable doubt. . . . However, it is broadly stated that the evidence sufficient to prove the charge of adultery must be so clear, satisfactory and convincing as to lead the unprejudiced mind of a reasonable and prudent man to that conclusion. We have also stated that circumstantial evidence required to prove a charge of adultery in a divorce case must show (1) an opportunity to commit the offense, and (2) a disposition to commit it.

In the instant case appellant and the co-respondent had innumerable opportunities to commit adultery. . . . It is appellant's contention that the evidence fails to show an adulterous disposition. He claims that he cultivated merely a Platonic friendship, which began about ten years ago. He says that he enjoyed talking with Boone's father, and that he helped the family in locating new homes and in various other ways while Boone was overseas. [W]hile opportunity to commit adultery is not in itself sufficient to justify a finding of its commission, in the absence of evidence of a disposition to commit it, such a disposition may be inferred from the conduct of the parties and the surrounding circumstances. . . .

It is our conclusion that the conduct of appellant, a married man, and Mrs. Boone, a married woman, was not consistent with innocence. After carefully considering the evidence, we find no reason to disturb the chancellor's decree. . . .

## Notes and Questions

1. At common law, the *crime* of adultery could be committed only with a married woman. For divorce, however, adultery is the voluntary sexual intercourse of a married person with someone other than that person's spouse. Case law holds that same-sex sexual acts also constitute adultery for divorce purposes. See, e.g., Owens v. Owens, 274 S.E.2d 484 (Ga. 1981); S.B. v. S.J.B., 609 A.2d 124 (N.J. Super. Ct. Ch. Div. 1992).

Although case law once required actual intercourse, subsequent decisions appear to follow the English view that considers noncoital acts as adultery. See, e.g., Bonura v. Bonura, 505 So. 2d 143 (La. Ct. App. 1987). But cf. Glaze v. Glaze, 1998 WL 972306 (Va. Cir. Ct. 1998) (holding that a woman cannot commit adultery with another woman because there is no actual intercourse).

2. Corrobation was widely required to prove acts of marital misconduct for purposes of divorce. The purpose of the requirement was to prevent collusion. Homer H. Clark, Jr., The Law of Domestic Relations 400, 401 (1968). This requirement necessitated eye-witness testimony (sometimes, acquired by private detectives) and contributed to the adversarial nature of divorce proceedings. Despite the usual requirement of corroboration, courts permitted the introduction of circumstantial evidence to prove adultery. What explains the relaxation of the rule? Wiretapping sometimes also provides proof of adultery, although it presents other problems (discussed in Chapter 3).

The applicable standard of proof may reflect adultery's status as a crime. What standard does *Lickle* follow? See also Cutlip v. Cutlip, 383 S.E.2d 273, 275 (Va. Ct. App. 1989).

3. A double standard once governed adultery. A wife had to prove "course of conduct" to obtain a divorce; a husband could prove a wife's

single act. The criminal requirement of a married woman's participation reveals a similar bias. A British sociologist suggests two explanations for this rule: (1) a married woman was considered her husband's property (that is, adultery was regarded as a form of theft), and (2) adultery of a married woman threatened the lineage. Annette Lawson, Adultery: An Analysis of Love and Betrayal 41 (1988). See also Laura Hanft Korobkin, Criminal Conversations: Sentimentality and Nineteenth Century Legal Stories of Adultery (1998).

4. Why did Mr. Lickle so strongly contest his wife's charge?

5. Until the 1970s, adultery was a ground for divorce in all states — in New York the *only* ground until 1967. Approximately 28 states make adultery a ground for divorce. Matthew Butler, Grounds for Divorce: A Survey, 11 J. Contemp. Legal Issues 164, 170, 172 (2000) (listing divorce grounds in the various jurisdictions). See 2 Lynn D. Wardle et al., Contemporary Family Law, Divorce — Fault Grounds — Adultery, §19.02 (1988 & Supp. 1989) (27 states).

6. *Empirical evidence.* The "Kinsey Report" estimated that half of married men have extramarital affairs. Alfred C. Kinsey et al., Sexual Behavior in the Human Male 585 (1948). For married women, the proportion was 26 percent. Kinsey et al., Sexual Behavior in the Human Female 416 (1953). Despite the prevalence of adultery, other fault grounds proved more popular. See Glenda Riley, Divorce: An American Tradition 124 (1991) (from 1887-1906, adultery accounted for 16.3 percent of divorces, cruelty 21.8 percent, and desertion 38.9 percent). What explains the small percentage for adultery?

Studies reveal that the gender gap is closing. The National Health and Social Life Survey reports that approximately 25 percent of married men, but 15 percent of married women, have had affairs. Edward O. Laumann et al., The Social Organization of Sexuality: Sexual Practices in the United States 216 (table 5.15) (1994). Another difference: Almost 12 percent of men but less than 3 percent of women had more than two sexual partners while they were married. Id. at 208.

7. Criminal charges for adultery are occasionally brought. See Charlie Goodyear, Air Force Set to Try Travis Pilot Over Affair; Accused Captain Could Get 27 Years, S.F. Chron., Feb. 12, 1999, at A21. While criminal trials for adultery have been decreasing, military prosecutions have "exploded." What might explain this phenomenon? See C. Quince Hopkins, Rank Matters But Should Marriage?: Adultery, Fraternization, and Honor in the Military, 9 UCLA Women's L.J. 177, 178 (1999). See also Martha Chamallas, The New Gender Panic: Reflections on Sex Scandals and the Military, 83 Minn. L. Rev. 305 (1998).

With the evolution of sexual mores and views of marital fault, should adultery be decriminalized? Do adultery prohibitions violate the right to privacy? See City of Sherman v. Henry, 928 S.W.2d 464 (Tex. 1996) (holding that state and federal privacy rights do not include protection for adultery), *cert. denied*, 519 U.S. 1156 (1997).

## Problems

1. Diane Goydan, the married mother of two, "meets" Ray on the Internet. Diane and Ray (whose online nickname is "The Weasel") begin a torrid online affair. Diane neglects her job, her husband John, and her children. John notices Diane's long hours online and the increasing monthly charges. He monitors Diane's online conversations and saves them on his hard drive. Eight months after Diane's affair begins, John files for divorce on the ground of adultery. What result? See James Langton, "We Just Clicked" as the Internet Buzzes with On-line Romance, James Langton Offers Some Words of Warning, Sun Telegraph, Mar. 3, 1996, at 5. See also Christina Tavella Hall, Sex Online: Is This Adultery?, 20 Hastings Commun. & Ent. L.J. 201 (1997).

2. Armand and his wife Doris have been married for 28 years. Armand meets a woman at a meeting of Alcoholics Anonymous. Although Doris has no evidence of Armand's infidelity, she confronts him. He confesses. They separate, reconcile briefly, and finally Armand leaves home. During their separation, Doris observes Armand's truck parked in front of the woman's apartment at night. Armand petitions for divorce; Doris counterpetitions on the ground of adultery. The jurisdiction permits divorce on either irreconcilable differences or fault-based grounds (including adultery). According to statute, when alternative grounds exist, a court must determine the "primary cause" of the breakup before awarding the divorce. Armand argues that adultery did not cause the breakdown of the marriage because it began only after his departure and his filing for divorce. What result? See Yergeau v. Yergeau, 569 A.2d 237 (N.H. 1990). See also Barnes v. Barnes, 428 S.E.2d 294 (Va. Ct. App. 1993).

---

If rarely enforced, why do adultery prohibitions remain? The excerpt below suggest possible answers.

## ■ RICHARD A. WASSERSTROM, IS ADULTERY IMMORAL?
*in Today's Moral Problems 209-211, 213, 217-219*
*(Richard A. Wasserstrom ed., 3d ed. 1985)*

One argument for the immorality of adultery might go something like this: what makes adultery immoral is that it involves the breaking of a promise, and what makes adultery seriously wrong is that it involves the breaking of an important promise. [W]hen one of the parties has sexual intercourse with a third person he or she breaks that promise about sexual relationships which was made when the marriage was en-

tered into, and defeats the reasonable expectations of exclusivity enter- *broken promise*
tained by the spouse. [A]dherence to this promise may be of much
greater importance to the parties than is adherence to many of the other
promises given or received by them in their lifetime. . . .

Another argument for the immorality of adultery focuses not on the
existence of a promise of sexual exclusivity but on the connection be- *deception*
tween adultery and deception. According to this argument, adultery involves deception. And because deception is wrong, so is adultery. . . .

What might be said in response to the foregoing arguments? The
first thing that might be said is that the account of the connection between sexual intimacy and feelings of affection is inaccurate. [T]he view
I have delineated may describe reasonably accurately the concepts of the
sexual world in which I grew up, but it does not capture the sexual
*weltanschauung* of today's youth at all. . . . Second, the argument leaves
to be answered the question of whether it is desirable for sexual intimacy
to carry the sorts of messages described above. For those persons for
whom sex does have these implications, there are special feelings and
sensibilities that must be taken into account. But it is another question
entirely whether any valuable end — moral or otherwise — is served by
investing sexual behavior with such significance. . . .

. . . The remaining argument that I wish to consider [is] a more in- *maintain*
strumental one. It seeks to justify the prohibition by virtue of the role *nuclear*
that it plays in the development and maintenance of nuclear families. [I]t *family*
is easy to see how the prohibition upon extramarital sex helps to hold
marriage together. At least during that period of life when the enjoyment of sexual intercourse is one of the desirable bodily pleasures, persons will wish to enjoy those pleasures. If one consequence of being
married is that one is prohibited from having sexual intercourse with
anyone but one's spouse, then the spouses in marriage are in a position
to provide an important source of pleasure for each other that is unavailable to them elsewhere in the society.

The point emerges still more clearly if this rule of sexual morality is *get + stay*
seen as of a piece with the other rules of sexual morality. When this pro- *married*
hibition is coupled, for example, with the prohibition on nonmarital sexual intercourse, we are presented with the inducement both to get
married and to stay married. For if sexual intercourse is only legitimate
within marriage, then persons seeking that gratification which is a feature of sexual intercourse are furnished explicit social directions for its
attainment; namely marriage. . . . Adultery is wrong, in other words, because a prohibition on extramarital sex is a way to help maintain the institutions of marriage and the nuclear family. [However,] instrumental *? ?*
prohibitions are within the domain of morality only if the end they serve
or the way they serve it is itself within the domain of morality.

What this should help us see, I think, is the fact that the argument
that connects the prohibition on adultery with the preservation of

marriage is at best seriously incomplete. Before we ought to be convinced by it, we ought to have reasons for believing that marriage is a morally desirable and just institution. . . .

---

For a rebuttal to Wasserstrom, see Michael J. Wreen, What's Really Wrong with Adultery, in The Philosophy of Sex 179 (Alan Soble ed., 2d ed. 1991).

## 2. Cruelty

### ■ MUHAMMAD v. MUHAMMAD
*622 So. 2d 1239 (Miss. 1993)*

BANKS, Justice, for the Court: . . .

Robert J. Muhammad and Debra Muhammad, formerly Robert and Debra Wilson, were married on September 17, 1983, in Flint, Michigan. They resided in Flint until 1987, when they relocated to an Islamic community in French Lick, Jefferson County, Mississippi, known as the University of Islam. . . .

In July 1987, Debra Muhammad and the couple's two month old child, Radeyah, relocated to the University. With the agreement of Debra, Robert remained in Flint for a few more months before permanently relocating to the University himself in October of 1987. Robert sold the couple's house to Debra's father and sold and disposed of some personal property, including a car. A substantial portion of the proceeds was given to the New Nation of Islam.

A second child, Raheem, was born to Robert and Debra Muhammad on August 4, 1988. Robert and Debra lived together with their two children at the University of Islam until October 13, 1989. While Robert was asleep during the late night hours of that date, Debra took the two children and went back to Flint, Michigan. She and the children were transported by Debra's mother, who had come down from Flint, Michigan, to take them back after Debra had communicated to her by phone that Debra was extremely unhappy with life at the University. Robert still resides at the University.

Robert and Debra had been experiencing marital difficulties before moving to the University. Debra indicated to at least one person at the University that she had tried Islam and moved to the University with Robert in an effort to save her marriage. Debra testified that she had been unhappy in the lifestyle at the University from the moment she arrived there.

The University of Islam is comprised of members of the New Nation of Islam [who] practice the "Black Muslim" religion . . . under the leadership of Mr. Marvin Muhammad. To his followers, Marvin Muhammad is . . . accepted as their savior in the sense that he provides them with the spiritual guidance necessary to attaining salvation. The chief earthly mission of the New Nation is to unite peoples of the African diaspora and establish a nation outside the United States that they themselves would govern. . . .

Virtually every aspect of life of the University is impacted by religious doctrine. The social and family structure is strongly paternal. Men are viewed as the maintainers of their wives and children. Women are required to submit to their husbands. The role of the woman is viewed primarily as being the helpmate of her husband. Child care is one of her chief responsibilities. Women make no decisions. They cannot leave the confines of the community without the permission of their husband. Members of the faith are not allowed to ingest alcohol, tobacco, drugs or other intoxicating substances. Neither are they allowed to eat red meat. Although the food supply is adequate in quantity, the diet at the University is fairly limited to beans, broccoli, fish, bread, cauliflower, and sometimes corn. Meals are restricted to one per day for adults. Fasting from these meals periodically occurs. Women are required to breastfeed their children. . . . Mail is subject to being censored. . . .

Robert . . . contends that the trial court erred in granting a divorce to Debra on the ground of "habitual cruel and inhuman treatment." He argues that insufficient evidence was presented at trial. . . . He claims that the chancellor's findings only indicate at best that Debra was unwilling to follow the precepts of the Muslim religion.

The chancellor set forth the following discussion in his opinion with respect to a finding of habitual cruel and inhuman treatment:

> While the most devout and dedicated female followers of Islam apparently do not mind the conditions that exist in the community, the Defendant and Counter-Plaintiff did. She, her husband and two children lived in one room of a small house. There was a lack of privacy. She was unable to go into town or to travel as she pleased. She had no control of personal finances. She had telephone calls withheld from her and her mail was censored. She complained about her diet and the lack of food. Curiously, although the members of the community disdain the government of the United States and its political subdivisions, they allowed the Defendant and Cross-Plaintiff to participate in the WIC Program to secure milk and juice for her children. However, the milk was used in the bakery, and the Defendant had to seek permission from Marvin Muhammad to get diapers for her children. Finally, the Defendant suffered physical abuse at the hands of the Plaintiff. She left Jefferson County in the middle of the night with her children, and the Plaintiff has had very little contact with them since that time.

It is my opinion that these conditions constitute habitual cruel and inhuman treatment. . . . This Court has defined cruel and inhuman treatment in this vein as "conduct endangering life, limb, or health, or creating reasonable apprehension of danger, or unnatural and infamous conduct making the marital relation revolting." . . . Despite the standard's general demand for endangerment to one's health, this Court has held on numerous occasions that the harm . . . need not derive from physical attack by the offending spouse. . . .

[T]he case at bar . . . presents a claim of a nature not squarely confronted by this Court before. The Missouri Court of Appeals decided a similar case in Rogers v. Rogers, 430 S.W.2d 305 (Mo. 1968). In that case, a husband filed for divorce on the ground of "indignities," a statutory ground in that state, after he became deeply dissatisfied with life in a religious community known as the Zion's Order of the Sons of Levi, and his wife preferred to stay in the community. . . . [T]he husband came to resent the authoritarian nature of the organization and objected to the Order's health practices, dietary practices, and policy of arrogating all of the members' work pay into the organization's common fund. The husband eventually left the community and went home. By the time he left, he was very thin and suffered from nervous condition and tularemia. The Missouri Court of Appeals held that the husband was entitled to a divorce [on the ground of general indignities].

[A]s with other cruelty divorce cases, the polestar consideration continues to be the intolerableness of the plight created for the nonoffending spouse. . . . The most common scenario for this type of action is undoubtedly where one spouse engages in overt physical or verbal actions of such a harsh and continuing nature that the other spouse cannot continue to cohabit with the offending spouse without threat of physical or mental harm. In the instant case, Debra Muhammad only testified to one incident where her husband used physical force against her, and that incident was arguably provoked by her. . . .

Nevertheless, Debra's case presents a compelling set of circumstances for a grant of divorce by way of habitual cruel and inhuman treatment. Although, Robert himself physically did little to harm Debra, the rules and social order of the University relegated Debra to a status and set of living conditions that would be unbearable to a great many, if not a majority, of the women living in our modern society. Debra's mother indicated that her daughter was on the verge of a nervous breakdown. For Debra, staying in her marital relationship meant continuing to endure the lot which she found oppressive. The only way she could escape these conditions was to leave her marital relationship. Therefore, if a spouse's actions which cause deep personal misery that has no foreseeable end is the gravamen of the action for divorce by reason of habitual cruel and unusual treatment, we cannot say that the chancellor's determination that Debra's case warranted a divorce was "manifestly wrong." . . .

SMITH, Justice, dissenting: . . .

[I]t is clear that it was manifest error to grant the divorce on habitual cruel and inhuman grounds. There is no testimony that indicated Debra was ever in reasonable apprehension of danger to life, limb, or health. Debra's complaints were not with her husband specifically but with the living conditions in the community they chose to live in. These circumstances were not imposed on or directed at her by her husband. [T]he "physical abuse" was one isolated incident in which Debra was not without fault. The chancellor has not set out any conduct by Robert that fits within the criteria required by our law for granting this divorce on habitual, cruel and inhuman treatment. Debra's general dissatisfaction with the community lifestyle is not sufficient. [T]he chancellor should have considered Robert's complaint for divorce on desertion or allowed the parties to consider irreconcilable differences grounds. . . .

## Notes and Questions

1. *Elements.* Cruelty, termed "indignities" or "cruel and inhuman treatment," has provided a ground for divorce in most states. Courts generally require a course of conduct of cruel behavior that creates an adverse health effect. What is a "course of conduct"? "Adverse health effect"? The Mississippi court explained:

> [T]he charge of cruel and inhuman treatment . . . means something more than unkindness or rudeness or mere incompatibility or want of affection. It has been said that: "The conduct of the offending spouse must be so unkind as to be cruel, that is, so unreasonably harsh and severe as to be inhumane, so lacking in human qualities, so unfeeling or brutal as to endanger, or put one in reasonable apprehension of danger to life, limb, or health. And finally, such conduct must be habitual, that is, done so often, or continued so long, that its recurrence may be reasonably expected whenever occasion or opportunity presents itself."

Kergosien v. Kergosien, 471 So. 2d 1206, 1210 (Miss. 1985) (citing Wires v. Wires, 297 So. 2d 900, 902 (Miss. 1974)). How did the wife in *Muhammad* establish the requisite elements? Was Debra's unhappiness with the religious practices sufficient to establish "habitual cruel and inhuman treatment" by Robert?

Numerous courts maintain that one incident will not satisfy the "course of conduct" requirement. Some courts have ruled, however, that a single incident may suffice if the act is particularly brutal, e.g., Carroll v. Carroll, 577 So. 2d 1140, 1144 (La. Ct. App. 1991) (attempted strangling of spouse); McDowell v. McDowell, 386 S.E.2d 468 (S.C. Ct. App. 1989) (attempt to shoot spouse).

2. In the nineteenth century, divorce on grounds of cruelty was often the only remedy available to battered spouses. See generally Elizabeth Pleck, Domestic Tyranny: The Making of Social Policy Against Family Violence from Colonial Times to the Present (1987).

3. *Mental cruelty.* English ecclesiastical courts required actual or threatened bodily harm. Courts gradually expanded the definition to include mental cruelty. Many jurisdictions require that cruelty be sufficiently severe as to threaten physical or mental health. See David N. Levine, Marital Cruelty: New Wine in Old Bottles, 2 Fam. L.Q. 296, 306 (1968).

What acts establish mental cruelty? Cruel conduct toward a child? See Denisi v. Denisi, 135 N.E.2d 668 (Mass. 1956) (divorce denied despite incest). Unreasonable sexual demands? See Jizmejian v. Jizmejian, 492 P.2d 1208 (Ariz. App. 1972) (refusal of intercourse); Goldstein v. Goldstein, 235 A.2d 498 (N.J. Super. Ct. Ch. Div. 1967) (insistence on birth control). Does this last present constitutional problems? See also Garriga v. Garriga, 770 So. 2d 978 (Miss. Ct. App. 2000) (drunken rampages, refusal to let family eat fast food, abandonment in parking lot at night); Richard v. Richard, 711 So. 2d 884 (Miss. 1998) (false accusations of infidelity and incest, watching home shopping network all day, and buying items therefrom instead of paying household bills); Ginn v. Ginn, 175 N.E.2d 848 (Ohio Ct. App. 1961) (baseless commitment proceedings); Langan v. Langan, 279 S.W.2d 680 (Tex. Civ. App. 1955) (failure to support); Metcalf v. Metcalf, 310 P.2d 254 (Wash. 1957) (constant denigration).

4. Courts traditionally have shown concern about the ease of establishing cruelty in an effort to avoid facilitating divorce. The requirement of "adverse health effect" addresses this concern. How difficult is this requirement to establish? See Breckinridge v. Breckinridge, 478 N.Y.S.2d 136 (App. Div. 1984) (husband's uncommunicativeness, excessive criticism, and deliberate frightening of wife insufficient; wife's depression might also have resulted from sister's death).

Some jurisdictions requires a higher degree of proof of cruelty for divorce from a long-term marriage. See, e.g., William M.M. v. Kathleen M.M., 611 N.Y.S.2d 317 (App. Div. 1994). What purpose is served thereby? Is this rule sound?

5. Adultery was more widely alleged as a nineteenth-century ground for divorce than cruelty. In the mid 1960s the trend reversed. Possible reasons include: liberalized interpretation of divorce grounds and acceptance of the companionate marriage. See Jessie Bernard, No News, but New Ideas, in Divorce and After 16-20 (Paul Bohannon ed., 1970). The advent of no-fault divorce and remedies for domestic violence lessened the frequency of cruelty-based divorces. Currently, 27 states provide for cruelty as a ground for divorce. Matthew Butler, Grounds for Divorce: A Survey, 11 J. Contemp. Legal Issues 164, 170, 172 (2000).

# Problems

1. Beulah files for a divorce from her husband (J.H.) on grounds of "general indignities." She testifies that he moved his daughter from a nonmarital relationship into the house against her wishes. She claims that after the daughter moved in, J.H. never invited her to go places with them so that she felt lonely. She complains that he "tongue-lashed" her on several occasions so that she feared for her life. She also alleges that he refused to take her to the hospital when she had an allergic reaction to penicillin. J.H. contends that Beulah failed to offer sufficient proof to establish cruelty. What result? Hornbeck v. Hornbeck, 1996 WL 633323 (Ark. Ct. App. 1996).

2. Robert and Olga have been trying for several years to have children. Robert claims that Olga subjected him to verbal abuse over their inability to conceive. Olga claims that Robert finally told her to do "whatever she wanted to do" to become pregnant, at which point she underwent in vitro fertilization procedure. Olga became pregnant by using donor eggs and sperm that had been mixed from donor sperm and Robert's sperm. She forged Robert's signature on the medical consent form. Olga subsequently gives birth to twin girls. Genetic testing determines that Robert is the father. Robert files for divorce on the grounds of cruel and inhuman treatment. What result? See McDonald v. McDonald, 684 N.Y.S.2d 414 (Sup. Ct. 1999).

## 3. Desertion

### ■ REID v. REID
375 S.E.2d 533 (Va. Ct. App. 1989)

KOONTZ, Chief Judge.

[Judith N. Reid sought a divorce on the ground of constructive desertion. Dr. Robert Reid responded seeking a divorce on the ground of desertion. When the commissioner recommended denial of the divorce on fault grounds but the entry of a no-fault divorce decree, both parties filed exceptions and a motion requesting preservation of the issue of fault for appeal. This appeal by Dr. Reid followed.]

The parties were married on June 26, 1965, in Denver, Colorado. Mrs. Reid had obtained a degree in medical technology and was employed at a local hospital. Dr. Reid was in medical school. In 1966, the first of their four children was born. In 1967 the parties moved to New York City where Dr. Reid completed his internship and residency. [Following Dr. Reid's stint in the Navy,] the parties moved to Charlottesville, Virginia, where Dr. Reid obtained a position at the University. He ultimately became tenured, head of his division, and director of the nurse practitioner program. [He subsequently left the university position to establish a medical corporation.]

During the first years of the marriage in which the parties' remaining children were born, Mrs. Reid was a homemaker. In 1980 she began part-time employment with [her husband's corporation] and ultimately became its controller. In 1985 Mrs. Reid and two other individuals, with the concurrence of Dr. Reid, formed King Travel, Inc., a travel agency, [and became president].

In his report, the commissioner reflected: "The testimony of Dr. Reid and Mrs. Reid rarely conflicts. They were talking about two different aspects [perceptions] of what were actually separate lives." The record amply supports the appropriateness of this statement. Mrs. Reid testified in detail as to the gradual breakdown in the marital relationship during this nineteen year marriage. The commissioner concluded that in each specific instance Mrs. Reid identified a marital problem, Dr. Reid did not perceive a problem. In fact, almost to the very end of the marriage, as if they lived separate lives, Dr. Reid considered himself happily married, while Mrs. Reid considered her emotional health endangered.

[Mrs. Reid] does not challenge the chancellor's finding that Dr. Reid did not constructively desert her. [Rather, she asserts she was justified in leaving her husband when she moved out in 1984 because her emotional health was endangered by virtue of the following marital problems]: (1) sexual inactivity, (2) Dr. Reid's excessive work habits, (3) Dr. Reid's failure to assist in the disciplining and rearing of their children, and (4) a lack of "intimacy within the marriage." . . .

It is apparent from the record and particularly Mrs. Reid's testimony that, following the birth of their first child in 1966, the sexual pattern which developed between the couple can best be described as infrequent. While three additional children were conceived and born over the ensuing years, many months passed between acts of sexual intercourse. These periods of abstinence gradually increased until no intercourse occurred for approximately two to three years prior to the final separation. It is also apparent that Dr. Reid suffered periods of sexual impotency, and that the infrequency of intercourse was more a concern to Mrs. Reid than to Dr. Reid.

Compounding this difficult situation, Mrs. Reid described the work pattern of Dr. Reid which she considered excessive. From the beginning of the marriage, Dr. Reid held more than one job. During the Navy years, he worked at night conducting insurance physicals. After accepting the position at the University of Virginia, he worked at night at the emergency room of a nearby hospital, opened a nearby clinic with two other doctors, and ultimately formed Commonwealth Clinical. There is no dispute that these activities severely limited the time available for Dr. Reid to spend at home with his wife and children. . . . Mrs. Reid felt that Dr. Reid was not appropriately supportive of her efforts to discipline [one child in particular] and, rather, conveyed to her the sense that this problem was solely her responsibility.

Mrs. Reid's description of the lack of "intimacy within the marriage," while conceptually understandable, is nebulous at best. On brief, she partially summarizes it as Dr. Reid's refusal "to talk to her about their lives with its joys and its sorrows, about the family and where it was and where it was going, or any other matter not directly related to one of the family financial concerns." . . . It is fair to say that while Dr. Reid was financially supportive, Mrs. Reid bore the major responsibility for raising the children and maintaining the home. In the process she became unhappy and felt unfulfilled. We accept the commissioner's conclusion that this condition was due in major part to Dr. Reid's denial or lack of recognition of the needs and feelings of Mrs. Reid.

While not specifically asserted by Mrs. Reid as a justification for her leaving, it is clear from the evidence that the marital problems of this couple were compounded by the additional responsibilities assumed by Mrs. Reid when she undertook her duties at Commonwealth Systems and eventually King Travel. These activities were encouraged by Dr. Reid, but they did not produce the personal satisfaction or the lessening of Mrs. Reid's frustration as they both apparently had hoped. Finally, the purchase of a large sailing boat and Mrs. Reid's enthusiastic involvement in sailing without Dr. Reid, in turn, merely added more stress to the marriage.

. . . The issue remains, however, whether as a matter of law these circumstances provide a justification for leaving the marriage. In that regard, the additional facts surrounding her leaving become critical.

In April, 1983, in what she describes as an effort to get Dr. Reid's attention, Mrs. Reid informed Dr. Reid that she could no longer endure the stress created by the problems in their marriage. As a result, the parties underwent counseling, which was unsuccessful. Mrs. Reid asserts that at that point she was totally committed to saving the marriage, but that Dr. Reid did not perceive the extent of their problems. The record supports this assertion. Subsequently, in October of that year, Mrs. Reid went on a month long sailing cruise to the Virgin Islands. Upon returning she advised Dr. Reid that she wanted a separation. The separation was delayed because Mrs. Reid underwent a gallbladder operation and she did not want to upset the children at Christmas. . . . Mrs. Reid testified that she eventually made a deposit on an apartment and on a Friday night again discussed the marriage with Dr. Reid. There was no agreement for a mutual separation. She described this conversation as "not being intimate" but rather, "a superficial sort of thing." On the following Monday, without Dr. Reid's knowledge, Mrs. Reid moved to this apartment. She testified that her intent in leaving the marital home was to make Dr. Reid realize that they had a problem, and that she "couldn't go on with it without doing something about it." This separation occurred on April 16, 1984. Mrs. Reid filed her suit for divorce on June 13, 1984. The chancellor sustained the commissioner's finding that as a matter of law Mrs. Reid did not intend to desert the marriage. We disagree. . . .

"Proof of an actual breaking off of matrimonial cohabitation combined with the intent to desert . . . constitutes desertion as grounds for divorce. However, reasons for leaving the marriage other than an intent to desert may justify discontinuance of the relationship without giving rise to grounds for divorce." [Citations omitted.] Under the law existing at the time of the present suit, fault, such as desertion, was a bar to spousal support. . . .

Mrs. Reid's description of her feelings and emotional condition are understandable in terms of human experience. The *cause* of her feelings and emotional condition, however, cannot be attributed factually or legally solely to the conduct of Dr. Reid. Rather, the evidence established that the pattern of conduct, indeed the entire marital relationship, established by both parties in this marriage resulted in her frustration and guided her decision to terminate the marriage. Mrs. Reid's complaints that Dr. Reid absented himself from the home and his proper share of the child discipline while working to provide financially for her and the family cannot serve as the justification for leaving him. Mrs. Reid would have us draw a fine line between where perhaps he excelled in one duty to the family at a sacrifice of another duty. This we cannot do. Her complaint of a "lack of intimacy in the marriage" is, in the final analysis, no more than a reflection of the different personalities of these marital partners and their method of relating to each other. It can be considered no more than a general complaint of unhappiness on the part of one spouse, which is the regrettable risk in all marriages. Finally, her complaint of the infrequency of sexual intercourse was a pattern developed uniquely between them almost from the beginning of the marriage. Moreover, Dr. Reid's periodic impotency was a mutual problem; the solution to which, obviously, was not within his sole control.

Under these circumstances, the most that can be concluded is that there was a gradual breakdown in the marriage relationship. As a result, Mrs. Reid understandably became unhappy and believed her emotional health was endangered. Her response to this problem was to terminate matrimonial cohabitation. The fact that she filed for divorce within two months thereafter belies an intent for a temporary separation. In so doing, she legally deserted the marriage and forfeited her right to spousal support. For these reasons, the commissioner erred in his conclusions of law. . . .

## Notes and Questions

1. Virginia permits divorce on no-fault grounds (a year's separation) as well as fault-based grounds (adultery, conviction of a felony, cruelty,

desertion or abandonment, or causing reasonable apprehension of bodily harm). Va. Code Ann. §20-91 (Michie 2000). If both fault-based and no-fault grounds exist, the judge may use discretion to select the most appropriate ground. Zinkhan v. Zinkhan, 342 S.E.2d 658 (Va. Ct. App. 1986). When *Reid* was filed, fault barred spousal support. Subsequently, the legislature eliminated fault as a bar to spousal support in all cases except adultery. Va. Code Ann. §20-107.1 (Michie 2000).

2. *Epilogue.* Following the principal case, the husband petitioned for restitution of spousal support paid to Mrs. Reid under the decree that was reversed and set aside on appeal. A trial judge denied the husband's motion; a panel of the court of appeals affirmed. The court of appeals subsequently granted a rehearing en banc. On rehearing, the appellate court concluded that restitution could be ordered and remanded for a determination of the amount. On appeal, the Virginia Supreme Court held that the trial court lacked the statutory authority to order restitution of spousal support. Reid v. Reid, 419 S.E.2d 398 (Va. Ct. App. 1992), *rev'd*, 429 S.E.2d 208 (Va. 1993).

3. Desertion constitutes a ground for divorce in 26 jurisdictions. Matthew Butler, Grounds for Divorce: A Survey, 11 J. Contemp. Legal Issues 164, 170, 172 (2000). 2 Lynn D. Wardle et al., Contemporary Family Law, §19.11 n.15 (1988). A spouse's mere departure is not sufficient to prove desertion. Desertion requires a cessation of cohabitation, without cause or consent, but with intent to abandon, continuing for a statutory period.

Although intent to desert, abandon, or terminate the relationship is essential, separation and intent need not occur contemporaneously. Separation without the requisite intent will not constitute desertion; subsequent intent formed after a separation will suffice, however. The desertion, then, dates from the time the intention is formed. Did Mrs. Reid satisfy the requisite elements? Desertion must also occur without justification. Why did the court deem Mrs. Reid's desertion unjustified?

Some statutes require that desertion be voluntary. Does desertion caused by imprisonment suffice? See generally Necessity of Voluntariness, 24 Am. Jur. 2d Divorce and Separation §65 (1998). Must the abandonment be total? See Jeffries v. Jeffries, 138 N.W.2d 882, 884 (Iowa 1965) (husband's regular support barred wife's action).

Does refusal to engage in sexual relations constitute desertion? See, e.g., Davis v. Davis, 1998 WL 281330 (Va. Ct. App. 1998) (affirming trial court's refusal to find constructive desertion based on wife's refusal of sexual intercourse). Suppose the refusal is "justified" because of health reasons? Religious beliefs? Objections to the other spouse's sexual practices? Would desertion have occurred in *Muhammad*, supra, if Debra had refused to follow Robert to the University of Islam or when she left him there? If so, who would have deserted whom?

4. *Constructive desertion distinguished.* Recall that Mrs. Reid filed for divorce on the ground of constructive desertion. Dr. Reid cross-complained

for desertion. Constructive desertion constitutes intolerable conduct by one spouse toward an innocent spouse that causes the innocent spouse to leave the marital abode. Thus, if Dr. Reid's conduct gives the plaintiff justification for leaving the home, then Mrs. Reid is not guilty of desertion. Under this ground, a spouse (in this case, Dr. Reid) need not specifically intend that the plaintiff leave. Did Dr. Reid provide just cause for Mrs. Reid to leave?

5. To what extent does *Reid* exemplify Catherine Riessman's thesis, supra, about the gender differences in divorce experiences? How does the judge interpret the facts? Compare the court's description of Dr. Reid's work, requiring absence from the home, as "excel[ling] in one duty," with its assessment of Mrs. Reid's work, which the court found "[compounded] the marital problems of this couple."

6. Why require a statutory period of desertion for divorce? Should parties be able to file once intent is expressed? Does a statutory period assist courts in determining a party's intent?

7. *Other fault-based grounds.* Additional statutory fault-based grounds include willful nonsupport of wife by husband (e.g., R.I. Gen. Laws §15-5-2 (1996)); criminal conviction or imprisonment (e.g., Ala. Code §30-2-1(a)(4) (1998)); drunkenness and drug addiction (e.g., Tenn. Code Ann. §36-4-101 (1996 & Supp. 2000)); impotence (e.g., Miss. Code §93-5-1 (1999)); and insanity (e.g., Utah Code Ann. §30-3-1(3)(i) (1998)). See also Homer H. Clark, Jr., The Law of Domestic Relations 354-358 (1968).

## C. FAULT-BASED DEFENSES

### 1. Recrimination

### ■ PARKER v. PARKER
*519 So. 2d 1232 (Miss. 1988)*

LEE, Chief Justice.

[Carolyn Moody Parker appeals the denial of a divorce from James Charles Parker based on recrimination.] The parties were married June 24, 1966, and they lived in Winston County until their separation occurred in February, 1984. No children were born of the marriage. Appellant operated a beauty shop, and appellee operated a garage, both located on three acres of land upon which the parties lived.

. . . Appellant called a number of witnesses [who testified as follows] to establish her ground for divorce of habitual cruel and inhuman treatment. . . .

. . . Charles watched the beauty shop with binoculars while Carolyn was cutting the hair of a male customer. . . . Carolyn arrived home one night to discover Charles and a woman exiting his garage. . . . Charles offered $100.00 to his friend's wife in return for sexual favors. . . . Charles falsely accused Carolyn of "going with" the church song leader and having sex with other men. . . . Charles would check the mileage on Carolyn's car to determine if she had been anywhere while he was gone. . . . Charles had a vision in which the Lord told him that if Carolyn went out on a certain weekend, her face "would not be fit to be seen anymore on the earth . . ." . . . When Charles saw Carolyn dancing with another man at a birthday party, he shoved her into their car, bruising her leg in the process, and called her a "sorry, low-down slut." . . . Charles fired a pistol outside Carolyn's beauty shop. . . . Some of Carolyn's beauty shop customers quit doing business with Carolyn because of her difficulties with Charles. The beauty shop has since gone out of business.

Appellant's physician testified that, at the time of the separation, appellant required hospitalization for "severe anxiety" caused by "family problems" which left her "almost hysterical." She remained hospitalized for four days.

Appellee pled the affirmative defense of recrimination, e.g., that appellant had committed adultery. At the conclusion of the trial, the chancellor remarked . . . :

> The Court finds by clear and convincing evidence that the Plaintiff has been guilty of adultery and that the defense of recrimination does prohibit and preclude the granting of a divorce in this case. . . .

In order for a divorce to be granted on the ground of habitual cruel and inhuman treatment, there must be proof of systematic and continuous behavior on the part of the offending spouse which goes beyond mere incompatibility. . . . We think the evidence fully supported a divorce for appellant on the ground of habitual cruel and inhuman treatment.

. . . The doctrine of recrimination is founded on the basis that the equal guilt of a complainant bars his/her right to divorce, and the principal consideration is that the complainant must come into court with clean hands. The complainant's offense need not be the same offense charged against his spouse, but it must be an offense sufficient to constitute a ground for divorce.

[Professor Marvin Moore states the following reasons for the defense of recrimination:]

> At least four policy-oriented justifications of the doctrine may be found in judicial opinions: (a) By rendering divorces more difficult to procure, recrimination promotes marital stability. (b) The rule tends to deter immorality, since a spouse is less likely to commit adultery (or any other marital offense) if he knows that his misdeed may bar him from obtaining

a divorce at some future time. (c) The doctrine serves to protect the wife's economic status. (d) Recrimination prevents persons who are obviously poor marriage risks from being freed to contract — and probably ruin — another marriage.

[Marvin M. Moore, An Examination of the Recrimination Doctrine, 20 S.C. L. Rev. 685, 714-715 (1968).]

These reasons for recrimination offered are impractical and fail with the mores of present times, particularly insofar as they affect the case sub judice. . . . There is no marital stability in the present case, and the marriage has deteriorated to the point where there is no marriage. . . . The record here reflects that the appellant wife did not commit adultery during the time the parties lived together and cohabited as husband and wife, but only after the separation and dissolution of the marriage relationship.

The economic status of the appellant wife here is not protected, but, on the other hand, for practical purposes has been destroyed. The undisputed evidence indicates . . . that appellant's troubles with appellee have adversely affected her business. . . . It is apparent that the public interest in promoting appellant's financial security would be served, not by denying appellant a divorce, but by granting one along with a property settlement sufficient to permit her to resume the operation of her own business.

The State's interest in preventing bad marriages is acknowledged, and it is possible that denial of a divorce in this case will prevent subsequent bad marriages involving these parties. However, it is practically certain that denial of divorce in the present case under these facts would perpetuate an already-existing bad marriage.

While this Court is not suggesting condonation of the conduct of the appellant wife after the separation of the parties, when we balance out the uncontradicted evidence that the conduct of the appellee was responsible for the separation of the parties and the dissolution of their marriage; that the misconduct of the appellant wife occurred after the destruction of the marriage; and that the legislature has, in the least, greatly weakened the defense of recrimination; we are of the opinion that the learned chancellor erred in denying a divorce to appellant. . . .

## Notes and Questions

1. Recrimination "prevents the dissolution of those very marriages most appropriate for dissolution." Homer H. Clark, Jr., The Law of Domestic Relations in the United States 527 (2d ed. 1988). Should divorce be granted only to "innocent" parties? Did the *Parker* court abandon the doctrine?

2. Suppose that Carolyn had taken a lover upon learning of Charles's adultery. Would the result have been the same? How determinative was Charles's cruelty?

3. One commentator points out that the defense of recrimination tended to be raised "as an issue only when one party was dissatisfied with the property arrangements." J. Herbie DiFonzo, Alternatives to Marital Fault: Legislative and Judicial Experiments in Cultural Change, 34 Idaho L. Rev. 1, 19 (1997). What considerations may have influenced Charles's use of the defense?

4. The court cites protection of the wife's economic status as a reason to grant the divorce. If the wife is equally culpable, why should the court concern itself with this issue? In the cited article, Professor Moore asks: "Is it realistic to suppose that a spouse who is induced to commit adultery, cruelty, or some other marital offense is likely to desist out of fear that his actions will enable his mate at some future time to defeat his petition for divorce?" 20 S.C. L. Rev. at 718. What purpose does recrimination serve?

5. If recrimination were abolished as a fault-based defense, should it be retained, nonetheless, to determine alimony? That is, should fault trump financial need?

6. Recrimination still surfaces occasionally as a divorce defense. See Wright v. Phipps, 712 A.2d 606 (Md. Ct. Spec. App. 1998); Harmon v. Harmon, 757 So. 2d 305 (Miss. Ct. App. 1999). On the history of the doctrine, see J. G. Beamer, The Doctrine of Recrimination in Divorce, 10 UMKC L. Rev. 213 (1942); DiFonzo, supra, at 18-19.

## 2. Condonation

### ■ HAYMES v. HAYMES
*646 N.Y.S.2d 315 (App. Div. 1996)*

MAZZARELLI, Justice. . . .

Gail and Stephen Haymes were married in 1965 and lived together, without interruption, until 1987. They are the parents of two adult children, born in 1967 and 1975. According to plaintiff's allegations, beginning in December 1984, defendant refused to have sexual relations with her, rejecting her repeated overtures. In September 1987, defendant moved out of the couple's home, an act which plaintiff maintains was without her consent and without justification. The plaintiff claimed that defendant engaged in several adulterous relationships with women identified in the complaint. Defendant retained legal counsel, who wrote to plaintiff, suggesting that she retain her own matrimonial lawyer. This action for divorce and related relief was commenced [by wife] in September of 1988. . . .

The couple attempted a reconciliation between November 18, 1988 and January 4, 1989, during which time they resumed residing unhappily together. According to Ms. Haymes, her husband expressed neither remorse for his adultery nor any affection for her during this six-week period. Unable to resolve their problems, Gail and Stephen Haymes returned to living apart and pursuing their respective marital claims. Indeed, in January 1989, defendant asserted his own counterclaim for divorce.

On January 23, 1995, on the eve of the trial herein, defendant moved in open court for dismissal [of wife's causes of action for abandonment and constructive abandonment]. He urged that these claims were precluded because of the wife's admission, during a wholly separate conversion action, that she and the husband resumed living together briefly between November 18, 1988 and January 4, 1989. The wife also conceded that during this time period, while on a family vacation in Vail, Colorado, she and her husband had engaged in sexual relations at least once. According to defendant, upon returning from the family vacation, plaintiff informed him that the attempted reconciliation was a failure and that he was not to come back to the marital home. [T]he parties had later visited Acapulco, Mexico, together in 1990. Plaintiff, in response, argued that a single unsuccessful effort at reconciliation after the matrimonial action had already been commenced is hardly sufficient to defeat, as a matter of law, her claims founded in abandonment. . . .

[T]here is a dearth of current appellate authority in this state directly addressing the legal question presented by this dispute, whether a relatively brief attempt at a reconciliation . . . should require plaintiff to forfeit these otherwise facially valid causes of action for divorce. . . . In our view, common sense teaches that it is consistent with the public policy of this state that couples enduring marital disharmony should be encouraged to attempt reconciliation, particularly when, as here, the marriage is one of long duration. That the courts should, when practicable, encourage the preservation of families, in all their permutations, is so painfully obvious, that the lack of appellate authority so declaring can only be explained by the failure heretofore of anyone to contest such a basic proposition.

The extant case law does not point to a contrary result. . . . Although not exactly on all fours with this case, we find that the authorities relied on by plaintiff, in that they discuss the effect of reconciliation attempts on causes of action other than abandonment, are at least supportive of her position. Moreover, we agree with plaintiff that there is more than an implication in several of the cases that an effort to reconcile is meaningless without a showing that it was made in good faith.

. . . In the case at bar, by granting the motion for summary judgment just prior to opening statements, the trial court prevented plaintiff from endeavoring to prove that defendant did not make a good faith effort to reconcile. The court held plaintiff's abandonment claims were forfeited as a matter of law by the fact she engaged in sexual relations with her husband during the failed reconciliation attempt. However, we view the extant record as ambiguous as to the frequency of those relations and whether they were entered into in good faith by the defendant husband. The prevailing legal authority, even if sparse, seems to hold that cohabitation by itself is insufficient to invalidate a separation agreement or an accrued claim for divorce. . . . Furthermore, in the context of a cruel and inhuman treatment cause of action, it has been held that a short period of cohabitation does not amount to condonation of the cruel and inhuman treatment asserted as the basis of a divorce. [Lowe v. Lowe, 324 N.Y.S.2d 229 (Sup. Ct. 1970), aff'd, 322 N.Y.S.2d 975 (App. Div. 1971).]

As long ago as 1928 this court declared, and the Court of Appeals agreed, in the context of a cause of action for cruel and inhuman treatment, that "[w]e are not in accord with defendant's argument that cohabitation after acts of cruelty may be considered as condonation, in the sense in which it would be after an act of adultery. We rule that endurance of unkind treatment in an effort to overcome its practice and continuance of cohabitation does not condone a course of inhuman conduct" [Fisher v. Fisher, 227 N.Y.S. 345 (Sup. Ct. 1928), aff'd, 165 N.E. 460 (N.Y. 1929)]. Today, we hold that an estranged couple's attempt at a reconciliation, even where it involves the brief and isolated resumption of cohabitation and/or sexual relations, after a matrimonial action has already been commenced, does not, as a matter of law, preclude an entry of judgment in favor of the spouse who originally had an otherwise valid claim for abandonment. Rather, the trial court should examine the totality of the circumstances surrounding the purported reconciliation, before determining its effect, if any, upon the pending marital proceeding. Among the many factors for the trial court to consider are whether the reconciliation and any cohabitation were entered into in good faith, whether it was at all successful, who initiated it and with what motivation. Although concededly more difficult to apply than a rule which automatically results in the forfeiture of abandonment claims upon the parties making even the most hollow attempt at reconciliation, we conclude that the approach we adopt is not only consonant with human experience and common sense, but with the public policy and law of our State as well. . . .

## Notes and Questions

1. Under the principle of condonation, "a spouse who has once condoned a marital transgression by his mate is thereafter barred from using that transgression as grounds for divorce." Marvin M. Moore, An Examination of the Condonation Doctrine, 2 Akron L. Rev. 75 (1969). Grounds that may be condoned include adultery, cruelty, habitual

drunkenness, and, as in *Haymes,* desertion (termed here "abandon-ment"). However, as *Haymes* explains, some courts limit the application of the condonation defense to adultery.

2. Does condonation require both forgiveness of marital misconduct and resumption of sexual intercourse? See Hoffman v. Hoffman, 762 A.2d 766 (Pa. Super. Ct. 2000) (holding that husband's resumption of sexual relations was evidence of his condonation of wife's infidelity despite his re-fusal to withdraw the custody action). Is resumption of cohabitation suffi-cient to establish condonation or must the cohabitation include sexual relations? See Nemeth v. Nemeth, 481 S.E.2d 181 (S.C. Ct. App. 1997) (finding no condonation because spouses spent two nights together with-out sexual relations after wife confessed adultery). Is it appropriate to as-sume that the resumption of sexual relations constitutes forgiveness by one party? Does the doctrine raise constitutional issues of family privacy?

3. Should condonation serve as grounds for denying divorce, or merely affect the granting of fault-based alimony?

4. With the advent of no fault (discussed in the next section), many jurisdictions abolished the fault-based defenses. Nonetheless, as *Haymes* reveals, some jurisdictions continue to recognize some or all of these de-fenses. See Ga. Code Ann. §19-5-4 (1999) (recognizing collusion, con-nivance, recrimination, and condonation). A few jurisdictions that have abolished recrimination as a defense still preserve the defense of condo-nation. See, e.g., 750 Ill. Comp. Stat. Ann. 5/403 (West 1999); Tex. Fam. Code Ann. §6.008 (West 1998).

5. The traditional condonation doctrine was harsh in its application to the forgiving spouse. One commentator notes:

> The practical effect of the rule of condonation is to impose a "do-or-die" decision upon the innocent spouse in the hour of crisis. Confronted suddenly with the knowledge of his partner's infidelity, he must decide promptly whether to pack his suitcase and leave what may have been and could be a very happy home, or to continue marital relations thereby for-feiting the right to dissolve the marriage if it should subsequently cease to be viable. The penalizing effect of the rule is to trap in a cancerous mar-riage those parties who have made laudable, although unsuccessful, at-tempts to reconcile.

Arthur L. Fox II, Condonation: An Obstruction to Reconciliation, 2 Fam. L.Q. 259, 259-260 (1969). Is the approach adopted by *Haymes* an improvement?

## Problem

Marian and Henry marry in 1964. During the early years of their marriage, they have two sons (both now adults). However, during the past ten years, the parties have engaged in a sexual relationship on only one occasion. At the time they had sexual relations, Henry told Marian that he fantasized about being gay and that she was the only one who could "save" him. Subsequently, Marian finds a hotel receipt that reveals her husband spent the weekend with another man. She also finds letters from a gay pen pal club and pornographic videos and paraphernalia depicting homosexual acts. She files a petition for divorce on the grounds of cruelty. Henry answers, contending that the trial court erred in granting the divorce on the ground of cruelty and that Marian had condoned his homosexual behavior. What result? Thomas v. Thomas, 1996 WL 679985 (Va. Ct. App. 1996).

## Note: Other Fault-Based Defenses

In the fault-based era, other common defenses to divorce were connivance and collusion. Connivance constitutes express or implied consent by the plaintiff to the misconduct alleged. 27A C.J.S. *Divorce* §85 (1986). Courts have offered three reasons why connivance is a defense to divorce: First, according to the Latin maxim *Volenti non fit injuria*, "He who consents cannot receive an injury." Second, a petitioner with unclean hands is not entitled to equitable relief. Third, some states limited divorce to the innocent party, and a conniving spouse was not an innocent party. See Marvin M. Moore, An Analysis of Collusion and Connivance, Bars to Divorce, 36 UMKC L. Rev. 193, 196-197 (1968).

Collusion is an agreement between husband and wife to: (1) commit a marital offense in order to obtain a divorce, (2) introduce false evidence of a transgression not actually committed, or (3) suppress a valid defense. Id. at 194-195. Before no-fault divorce "[t]he collusive divorce, so far from being a rare phenomenon, appears to be the norm." Id. at 226.

Courts sometimes have difficulty distinguishing collusion from connivance. See, e.g., Furst v. Furst, 78 N.Y.S.2d 608 (Sup. Ct. 1948), *modified*, 91 N.Y.S.2d 202 (App. Div. 1949). Professor Moore explains the distinctions:

> Although related in concept and function, collusion and connivance differ in two significant respects: First, connivance requires only the corrupt consent of the plaintiff, while collusion requires that of both spouses; and secondly, connivance cannot occur without the actual commission of a marital offense, while collusion can take place without either party's ever actually giving the other cause for divorce.

Moore, supra, at 195.

Finally, insanity provided a ground for divorce as well as a defense. See Rutherford v. Rutherford, 414 S.E.2d 157 (S.C. 1992). Because divorce required a "guilty" party, mental illness served to relieve the defendant from liability for acts of marital misconduct. See generally J. Herbie DiFonzo, Alternatives to Marital Fault: Legislative and Judicial Experiments in Cultural Change, 34 Idaho L. Rev. 1 (1997); Lawrence M. Friedman, A Dead Language: Divorce Law and Practice Before No-Fault, 86 Va. L. Rev. 1497 (2000) (both providing historical accounts of divorce prior to no fault).

## Problem

Mrs. Hollis seeks a divorce on the ground of adultery. Mr. Hollis alleges the defense of connivance. He contends that his wife urged him to date other women. He introduces into evidence a handwritten note to him, stating her hope that he would fall in love with another woman so that Mrs. Hollis could leave the marriage. After the husband began an affair, the wife again wrote to him that she hoped that he and his new love would live together for some time (prior to marriage). Further, the husband testifies that when he and his new woman friend first had sexual relations at a hotel, they received flowers and a card from the wife saying, "My very best wishes to you both today, to your new beginning." What result? See Hollis v. Hollis, 427 S.E.2d 233 (Va. Ct. App. 1993).

## D. NO-FAULT DIVORCE

### 1. Divorce Reform

All states currently offer some form of no-fault divorce. Considerable variation exists, however, as to that form. Two common models, the California Family Law Act and the Uniform Marriage and Divorce Act, are discussed below.

### ■ ALLEN M. PARKMAN, GOOD INTENTIONS GONE AWRY: NO-FAULT DIVORCE AND THE AMERICAN FAMILY
*72-75, 79-81 (2000)*

The nation's unequivocal no-fault law became effective in California in 1970. . . . It is impossible to identify exactly when the reform movement began, but the California legislature took its first steps in that direction in 1963. In that year, a House Resolution was passed that initiated a study of the laws on divorce, and an interim committee began the study. . . . Four major themes emerged from the 1964 hearings in the California Assembly which set the agenda for the legislative proposals that followed. There were widespread concerns about:

1. the high divorce rate,
2. the adversary process creating hostility, acrimony, and trauma,
3. a need to recognize the inevitability of divorce for some couples and attempt to make the legal process less destructive for them and their children, and
4. charges made by divorced men that the divorce law and its practitioners worked with divorced women to acquire an unfair advantage over former husbands.

The hearings reached no conclusions, nor was any legislation proposed; the interim committee disbanded. In 1966, Governor Edmund G. Brown, who was enthusiastic about divorce law reform, established a twenty-two member Commission on the Family. This commission consisted of one minister, four legislators, six lawyers, four judges, three psychiatrists, two law professors, one medical doctor, and one member of the State Social Welfare Board. . . .

The commission reviewed the condition of the family and made recommendations in two areas: First, it suggested revisions in the substantive law of divorce. Second, it examined the feasibility of establishing a system of family courts. The commission proposed legislation in the form of a model Family Court Act that would have created a family court, eliminated fault as a ground for divorce, and revised the community property distribution rules. The family court proposal included both the creation of a family court system and the establishment of procedures to encourage the parties to use the court's conciliation and counseling services. The commission also recommended that dissolution should be granted whenever the court found that the legitimate objectives of the marriage had been destroyed and that there was no reasonable likelihood that the marriage could be saved.

[The commission's recommendations served as a working model for subsequent bills.] The major objection raised to these bills was the potentially high cost of the counseling. No definitive action was taken on these bills in 1967, but they were reintroduced in 1968. . . .

James A. Hayes, a member of the Assembly Judiciary Committee, independently put together another proposal that eliminated the major cost-incurring features — a separate family court system and mandatory counseling structure — but kept the marriage-breakdown theory of divorce. [A subsequent bill, drafted by a conference committee of which he was a member, was enacted as the Family Law Act of 1969.]

The new Family Law Act established two grounds for marital dissolution, "irreconcilable differences which have caused the irremediable breakdown of the marriage" and incurable insanity. [The new act had no provision for a family court system or counseling.] Other changes emphasized a new orientation in divorce proceedings. The term *divorce* was replaced by *dissolution of marriage*. A neutral petition form, *In re the Marriage of Mrs. Smith and Mr. Smith*, replaced the adversarial form *Smith v. Smith*. The parties were called "petitioner" and "respondent" rather than "plaintiff" and "defendant,". . .

Under the prior law, the property division was unequal when the grounds for divorce were adultery, extreme cruelty, or incurable insanity, with the innocent party allocated a disproportionately large share of the community property. Under the new act, community property usually was to be divided equally, with no regard for fault, unless the division would impair the value of the property, such as a business, or when community funds had been deliberately squandered or misused by one spouse to the extent that an equal division of the remaining assets would no longer be equitable. Alimony was redefined as "support" and was determined by fairness rather than fault. . . .

. . . Often ignored in the histories of no-fault divorce in California was the special interest that Hayes brought to his advocacy of no-fault. James A. Hayes was involved in a bitter divorce action during the evolution of no-fault in the California legislature. [Lawyer Hayes divorced his homemaker wife in 1969, after 25 years of marriage and four children. The final decree was fairly generous to his wife. Three years later, in 1972, Hayes petitioned to end his financial obligations to his wife because he had remarried and assumed new financial obligations.] Hayes's brief in support of his request included a quotation from the 1969 California Assembly Judiciary Committee Report on the new California Family Law Act, which he helped write. Part of the quotation included:

> When our divorce law was originally drawn, woman's role in society was almost totally that of mother and homemaker. She could not even vote. Today, increasing numbers of married women are employed, even in the professions. In addition, they have long been accorded full civil rights. Their approaching equality with the male should be reflected in the law governing marriage dissolution. . . .

When the judge's decision was handed down in March 1973, James Hayes prevailed. Child support was ended, and alimony was gradually reduced to $300 per month [from the previous award of $650]. [A year later Hayes again requested a reduction in alimony. His wife's alimony was further reduced, and the judge told Hayes's 53-year-old ill ex-wife to find employment. That decision was overruled subsequently as an abuse of discretion.]

. . . Hayes was obviously not a casual observer. He was instrumental in enacting no-fault divorce in California; after its passage, in the report that rationalized its passage, he emphasized the equality between men and women. He then used the law and the report to attempt to reduce the financial arrangements to which he had agreed as a condition for his divorce. . . .

In most histories of the passage of the law, James Hayes's role is given only passing notice. If anything, he is pictured as a very active public servant. But the passage of no-fault in California bears witness to the process of legislative self-interest. . . . This is a law that was passed by a legislature dominated by men . . . reenforced by the lobbying efforts of men's interest groups and maneuvered through the California legislature by a man who personally had a great deal to gain from a reduction in the negotiating power of married women. . . .

■ **LYNNE CAROL HALEM, DIVORCE
REFORM: CHANGING LEGAL AND
SOCIAL PERSPECTIVES**
*269-277 (1980)*

### [THE UNIFORM MARRIAGE AND DIVORCE ACT]

The idea of a national marriage and divorce statute, either in the form of an amendment to the Constitution or a singular law to be adopted by each state, was first proposed in 1884 and continued to spark debates for many years. [T]he Uniform Marriage and Divorce Act [was] ratified by the National Conference of Commissioners on Uniform State Laws in 1970. [The original intent was to remove the concept of fault by substituting the term "irretrievable breakdown" for fault-based grounds and to reject the no-fault ground of separation because it might be construed as a form of punishment.]

The critical blow came from the members of the Family Law Section of the American Bar Association. Whereas in the past, the ABA had been most supportive of the commissioners' bills, this statute proved to be the exception. Without discrediting the concept of no-fault, the Bar attacked the statute on three grounds: the ease and speed with which a divorce could be granted; the absence of conciliation provisions or other brakes on hasty divorce; and the lack of specificity in the regulations governing property division. . . . Using standard conservative arguments, the ABA charged that passage of the act would legalize "easy" or "quickie" divorces. It may be that this position reflected the fear of an insidious plot to minimize the role of legal counsel. . . .

[The commissioners drafted three versions of the statute before they received ABA endorsement in 1974. The 1973 version of the act reintroduced notions of fault.] If the commissioners' capitulation was not total it was, nonetheless, significant. The new statute introduced a clause

568 V ■ Divorce

for the no-fault ground of separation even if the waiting period was abbreviated to 180 days; the term "marital discord" was implicitly linked to the ground of "cruel and inhuman treatment" even if "marital misconduct" was not mentioned; references to reconciliation were more obtrusive even if they were not clearly defined; and the ABA's denouncement of demand divorce received credence through the addition of new safeguards even if they were weak and inoperable.

In other ways, however, the Uniform Marriage and Divorce Act was more progressive than California's law. Issues of marital misconduct were considered irrelevant to custody. . . . [Evidence of fault was relevant to custody in early versions of the California statute but not after 1993.] The effort to discourage spousal maintenance by basing awards on the needs and resources of the parties might eventually prove a more realistic and less acrimonious approach to the problem of post-divorce economics.

Further, incurable insanity and irreconcilable differences did not appear as grounds for dissolution. Whereas the former was largely superfluous in the California act, the latter troubled some purists who objected to the multiplicity of possible translations. Quite obviously the uniform bill had other vagaries. The term "irretrievably broken" was not defined, nor were precise directives furnished to curtail the discretionary powers of the judiciary. Hence many of the indeterminacies in the California model were duplicated in this statute. But in California the reformers could predict fairly accurately the court's interpretation would be liberal. This was not the case with the Uniform Act. . . .

---

Many states follow the California[4] or UMDA models. Other jurisdictions have taken different approaches (illustrated below).

■ **CALIFORNIA FAMILY CODE §§2310, 2311, 2335**
*(West 1994) (formerly California Civil Code §§4506,*
*4507, 4509)*

### §2310. GROUNDS FOR DISSOLUTION OR LEGAL SEPARATION

Dissolution of the marriage or legal separation of the parties may be based on either of the following grounds, which shall be pleaded generally:

[4]. Approximately 17 states are "pure" no-fault jurisdictions, i.e., they have abolished all fault-based grounds for dissolution. See National Survey of State Laws 362-377 (Richard A. Leiter, ed. 1999).

(a) Irreconcilable differences, which have caused the irremediable breakdown of the marriage.

(b) Incurable insanity.

### §2311. IRRECONCILABLE DIFFERENCES DEFINED

Irreconcilable differences are those grounds which are determined by the court to be substantial reasons for not continuing the marriage and which make it appear that the marriage should be dissolved.

### §2335. MISCONDUCT; ADMISSIBILITY OF SPECIFIC ACTS OF MISCONDUCT

Except as otherwise provided by statute, in a pleading or proceeding for dissolution of marriage or legal separation of the parties, including depositions and discovery proceedings, evidence of specific acts of misconduct is improper and inadmissible.

## ■ UNIFORM MARRIAGE AND DIVORCE ACT
### §§302, 305
*9A U.L.A. (pt. I) 200 (1998)*

### §302. [DISSOLUTION OF MARRIAGE; LEGAL SEPARATION]

(a) The [_____] court shall enter a decree of dissolution of marriage if: . . .

(2) the court finds that the marriage is irretrievably broken, if the finding is supported by evidence that (i) the parties have lived separate and apart for a period of more than 180 days next preceding the commencement of the proceeding, or (ii) there is serious marital discord adversely affecting the attitude of one or both of the parties toward the marriage. . . .

### §305. [IRRETRIEVABLE BREAKDOWN]

(a) If both of the parties by petition or otherwise have stated under oath or affirmation that the marriage is irretrievably broken, or one of the parties has so stated and the other has not denied it, the court, after hearing, shall make a finding whether the marriage is irretrievably broken.

(b) If one of the parties has denied under oath or affirmation that the marriage is irretrievably broken, the court shall consider all relevant factors, including the circumstances that gave rise to filing the petition and the prospect of reconciliation, and shall:

(1) make a finding whether the marriage is irretrievably broken; or

(2) continue the matter for further hearing not fewer than 30 nor more than 60 days later, or as soon thereafter as the matter may be reached on the court's calendar, and may suggest to the parties that they seek counseling. The court, at the request of either party shall, or on its own motion may, order a conciliation conference. At the adjourned hearing the court shall make a finding whether the marriage is irretrievably broken.

(c) A finding of irretrievable breakdown is a determination that there is no reasonable prospect of reconciliation.

## ■ NEW YORK DOMESTIC RELATIONS LAW §170
*(McKinney 1999)*

An action for divorce may be maintained by a husband or wife to procure a judgment divorcing the parties and dissolving the marriage on any of the following grounds:

(1) The cruel and inhuman treatment of the plaintiff by the defendant such that the conduct of the defendant so endangers the physical or mental well being of the plaintiff as renders it unsafe or improper for the plaintiff to cohabit with the defendant.

(2) The abandonment of the plaintiff by the defendant for a period of one or more years.

(3) The confinement of the defendant in prison for a period of three or more consecutive years after the marriage of plaintiff and defendant.

(4) The commission of an act of adultery. . . .

(5) The husband and wife have lived apart pursuant to a decree or judgment of separation for a period of one or more years after the granting of such decree or judgment, and satisfactory proof has been submitted by the plaintiff that he or she has substantially performed all the terms and conditions of such decree or judgment.

(6) The husband and wife have lived separate and apart pursuant to a written agreement of separation, . . . for a period of one or more years after the execution of such agreement and satisfactory proof has been submitted by the plaintiff that he or she has substantially performed all terms and conditions of such agreement. . . .

## 2. *Legal Problems Raised by No-Fault Divorce*

### a. What Is No Fault?

### ■ IN RE MARRIAGE OF McKIM
*493 P.2d 868 (Cal. 1972)*

WRIGHT, C.J. . . .

The parties were married in July 1968 and separated in September 1968. There were no children of the marriage. On October 21, 1968, the wife filed her verified complaint for divorce on the ground of extreme cruelty. On November 11, 1968, the parties stipulated that the wife "may proceed to procure a default divorce." The stipulation provided for a division of property, the wife waived alimony, and the husband agreed to pay all community obligations. The husband's default was entered in December 1968. . . .

On January 1, 1970, by operation of statute and rule the pending action for divorce became a proceeding under the Family Law Act for dissolution of marriage on the ground of irreconcilable differences.

On February 17, 1970, the proceeding came on for hearing. The wife was not present, and her counsel did not explain her absence or mention producing her testimony by affidavit or other means. The husband did not appear as a party but attended the hearing under subpoena as a witness for the wife. Under examination by the wife's counsel the husband testified as to the parties' irreconcilable differences. . . .[3] The trial court indicated that in its opinion the proceeding could not go forward on the basis of the husband's testimony. . . .

---

3. "*Q.* Mr. McKim, you are the respondent in this case; is that correct?
"*A.* Right.
"*Q.* At the time the petition in this matter was filed, was it your belief that there were irreconcilable differences between you and your wife?
"*A.* Right.
"*Q.* Since that time, have you and your wife attempted to resolve these differences?
"*A.* Yes.
"*Q.* In fact, you reconciled for a period of time; is that correct?
"*A.* Yes.
"*Q.* That reconciliation did not work out?
"*A.* No.
"*Q.* Is it your opinion that at the present time there are irreconcilable differences?
"*A.* Right.
"*Q.* Is it your opinion that any further waiting period of conciliation would assist in saving this marriage?
"*A.* No.
"*Q.* As far as you are concerned, there is no longer a marriage?
"*A.* No."

[It] appears from the record that the trial court's judgment [on May 8, 1970] denying dissolution was based on its determinations that the wife was required to appear personally at the hearing of the proceeding for dissolution of marriage and that the grounds of dissolution could not be proved by the testimony of her husband whose default had been entered. Neither the Family Law Act nor the Family Law Rules adopted by the Judicial Council pursuant to the act expressly require the personal appearance and testimony of the petitioner or expressly forbid proof of irreconcilable differences by testimony of a respondent. Therefore, we look to the overall purposes of the act in order to determine whether the requirements imposed by the trial court were proper. . . .

By eliminating faults and wrongs as substantive grounds for dissolution and "By requiring the consideration of the marriage as a whole and making the possibility of reconciliation the important issue, the intent is to induce a conciliatory and uncharged atmosphere which will facilitate resolution of the other issues and perhaps effect a reconciliation." [4 Assem. J. (1969) p. 8058.]

Although the Legislature intended that as far as possible dissolution proceedings should be nonadversary, eliminating acrimony, it did not intend that findings of the existence of irreconcilable differences be made perfunctorily. . . .

Section 4511 [now §2336 of the Family Code] is derived from the provision of former section 130 that "No divorce can be granted upon the default of the defendant . . . but the court must . . . require proof of the facts alleged, and such proof, if not taken before the Court, must be upon written questions and answers."

A principal purpose of the rule stated in former section 130 was to prevent the parties . . . from obtaining a divorce by collusion. . . .

We cannot accept the wife's understanding of the purposes and operation of the act. . . . Under the wife's theory, . . . it would be proper for the parties to agree that one of them would present false evidence that their differences were irreconcilable and their marriage had broken down irremediably. . . . Under the Family Law Act the court, not the parties, must decide whether the evidence adduced supports findings that irreconcilable differences do exist and that the marriage has broken down irremediably and should be dissolved. [W]hen the petitioner does not appear and testify personally . . . , the trial court in its sound discretion may well remain unconvinced by the evidence that the parties' differences are truly irrecon[chcilable and have led to the irremediable breakdown of their marriage.

The trial court here, however, did not deny a dissolution because it was not persuaded that the marriage had broken down irremediably. Instead it failed to reach that crucial question of fact because the petitioning wife did not appear personally and because it was of the opinion that the testimony of the defaulting husband as a matter of law was not competent evidence on the issue of irreconcilable differences. . . .

[W]e hold that a trial court must require the petitioner to appear personally and testify at the hearing unless, in exceptional circumstances where an explanation of petitioner's absence is shown to the satisfaction of the court, the court in its sound discretion permits the requisite proof to be made by affidavit as recognized by section 4511. We further hold that in exceptional cases where the court deems it warranted, it may receive in lieu of petitioner's testimony or affidavit the testimony of other competent witnesses including the respondent. Such testimony, of course, must be sufficient to enable the court to make the required findings as hereinabove set forth.

Unnecessary hardship would result from denying relief to the wife because she sought to establish grounds for dissolution solely by the testimony of her husband and was unaware that the trial court in its discretion could require that she testify in person or, if exceptional circumstances were shown, by affidavit.

The judgment is reversed and the cause is remanded for further proceedings consistent with this opinion. . . .

Mosk, J. [dissenting]. . . .

The California Legislature took a giant leap forward in the field of domestic relations with adoption of the Family Law Act, operative as of January 1, 1970. Regrettably my colleagues in the majority take a step backward as they judicially legislate potentially burdensome requirements not contained in the statute. . . .

The fundamental error of the majority is in looking backward to the old divorce practice. Because trial judges previously *as a matter of policy* required the plaintiff to appear personally and testify in court, the majority can see nothing in the new law that "suggests an intention to depart from the former practice." This, of course, completely disregards the . . . innovative spirit and intent of the Family Law Act, as well as the precise language of new Civil Code section 4511, which significantly departs from the previous law (§130) in providing that "No decree of dissolution can be granted upon the default of one of the parties . . . but the court must . . . require proof of the grounds alleged, and such proof, *if not taken before the court, shall be by affidavit.*" [Emphasis added.] What the Legislature clearly intended was that the trial court shall hold a hearing, but that proof of the parties' irreconcilable differences, if not presented before the court by in-person testimony, *shall* be by affidavit. There is no reference to unusual circumstances or to compulsory attendance by the petitioning party. . . . It is not appropriate for this court to encompass trial judges in procedural strait-jackets not contemplated by the Legislature. . . .

■ **NIETERS v. NIETERS**
*815 S.W.2d 124 (Mo. Ct. App. 1991)*

PUDLOWSKI, Presiding Judge. . . .

Husband filed his verified petition for dissolution of marriage on June 12, 1989. . . . Wife filed her answer to husband's petition on May 4, 1990, denying that the marriage was irretrievably broken. . . .

[A]t trial, husband testified that the couple had been separated since September, 1988. He also testified concerning the problems the couple had during the marriage and his current relationship with a woman named Cindy Yates. [Wife] stated that there were differences about how the children should be raised and that she donated some money she earned to televangelists. Both parties testified concerning their property, children, and incomes.

[The trial court dissolved the marriage, divided the marital property, awarded primary custody of the children to the wife, and awarded the wife child support and attorneys' fees.]

On October 24, 1990, wife filed her motion to amend judgment or in the alternative to order a new trial alleging that husband had not provided sufficient evidence to sustain a finding that the marriage was irretrievably broken. The trial court denied wife's motion. [Wife appeals.]

Under the Missouri Dissolution of Marriage Statute §452.320.2, RSMo 1986, when one party denies that the marriage is irretrievably broken, the court after considering all the relevant factors and hearing the evidence, must be satisfied that petitioner has established one of the following five facts in order to find that the marriage is irretrievably broken:

(a) That the respondent has committed adultery and the petitioner finds it intolerable to live with the respondent;
(b) That the respondent has behaved in such a way that the petitioner cannot reasonably be expected to live with the respondent;
(c) That the respondent has abandoned the petitioner for a continuous period of at least six months preceding the presentation of the petition;
(d) That the parties to the marriage have lived separate and apart by mutual consent for a continuous period of twelve months immediately preceding the filing of the petition;
(e) That the parties to the marriage have lived separate and apart for a continuous period of at least twenty-four months preceding the filing of the petition. . . .

In her first point, wife argues that the trial court erred in finding the marriage irretrievably broken. She contends that there was no substantial evidence to support a finding that one of the five facts was established.

We agree that the trial court's decree was against the weight of the evidence and unsupported by substantial evidence. The trial court should not have found the marriage irretrievably broken because the evidence does not establish any of the five fact situations necessary when one party denies that the marriage is irretrievably broken.

The first three fact situations require wrongdoing by the respondent. None of these are established because there is nothing in the transcript to evidence that wife committed adultery, that she behaved in such a way that husband could not reasonably be expected to live with her, or that she abandoned husband for a continuous period of six months before the petition. Husband's trial testimony, that there were "several occasions where we just could not get along" and that "it got somewhat violent on both parts" over the last three or four years, does not provide substantial evidence of these three situations. Also, the fact that there were differences about raising the children and wife's donating some of her own money to televangelists is not behavior that one could not be reasonably expected to live with. In fact, husband's behavior, concerning his new companion and living arrangements, is more characteristic of behavior one would not be reasonably expected to live with.

The last two situations for rendering the marriage irretrievably broken are not supported by the record. There is no evidence that the parties lived apart by mutual consent for twelve months preceding the filing of the petition. Also, there is no evidence that husband and wife lived separate for a continuous period of at least twenty-four months preceding the filing of the petition. . . . The parties' separation for, at the most, ten months, was clearly not sufficient to satisfy either of the last two circumstances for finding the marriage irretrievably broken.

We are persuaded by In re Marriage of Mitchell, 545 S.W.2d 313 (Mo. App. 1976). In that case, wife denied that the marriage was irretrievably broken. After discussing the society-preserving objectives of Missouri's "modified no fault" divorce law, the court went on to find that none of the five fact circumstances were established by substantial evidence. The parties were only separated for nine months and the husband could reasonably be expected to live with the wife's behavior. The instant case evokes the same concern that the *Mitchell* court noted: This marriage may well be beyond saving, and in holding as we do that there is not sufficient evidence in this record to support the finding of the trial court that this marriage is irretrievably broken within the terms of §452.320.2(1) we are but delaying the inevitable; nevertheless, we as an appellate court, construe and apply the law, we do not make it. *Mitchell,* 545 S.W.2d at 320.

We hold that the record does not provide substantial evidence that the marriage of the parties was irretrievably broken. . . .

## Notes and Questions

1. What must petitioner show to get a no-fault divorce? In requiring a divorce petitioner to make a personal appearance, *McKim* ended the practice of at least one California county to permit divorce by affidavit at the discretion of the trial judge. Does legislative history or statutory interpretation suggest why a spouse's pleadings, substantiated by the other's testimony, are not sufficient to support a finding of irremediable breakdown? Would perfunctory testimony from petitioner paralleling that from respondent (see footnote 3) suffice?

2. Does no-fault divorce eliminate all standards so long as both spouses agree? Was *McKim* concerned about the possibility of "collusion"? Should collusion play a role in a no-fault regime?

3. Does New York's use of separation as a no-fault ground avoid the problems that concerned the *McKim* court? What disadvantages does it present?

4. *Summary Dissolution.* California ultimately dispensed with the need for an appearance in some cases. In 1978 the legislature enacted a summary dissolution procedure (a simple procedure that permits dissolution in a short period of time upon mutual consent) if the parties: (1) have no children, (2) were married less than 5 years, (3) do not own real property, (4) have debts (excluding automobiles) totaling less than $4,000, (5) have no more than $25,000 in community property and separate property, and (6) waive spousal support. Cal. Fam. Code §2400 (West 1994). Similar procedures exist in many jurisdictions.

5. *Nieters* (and the Missouri statute) reflect discomfort with unilateral divorce. In this regard, does Missouri's approach differ from that of California or UMDA? Cf. In re Marriage of Dunn, 511 P.2d 427, 429 (Or. Ct. App. 1973) (reading statute patterned on California's to require difference "that reasonably appears to the court to be in the mind of the petitioner an irreconcilable one [which] need not necessarily be so viewed by both parties").

Even without a statutory directive like Missouri's, some courts resisted no-fault dissolution over the objection of one party. For example, in Shearer v. Shearer, 356 F.2d 391 (3d Cir. 1965), *cert. denied*, 384 U.S. 940 (1966), the court reversed the divorce granted to a husband. Despite the couple's constant bickering, their six-year separation initiated by the husband (and his overcoming alcoholism only after the separation), the court concluded that the finding of "incompatibility" was clearly erroneous. The majority emphasized the wife's interest in continuing the marriage and the couple's 10 years' cohabitation.

The ground of "incompatibility" was the precursor to modern no-fault dissolution. The Virgin Islands was the first American jurisdiction (almost 50 years before California) to adopt the no-fault basis of incompatibility, derived from Scandinavian law. (The Virgin Islands was a former Danish territory.) Six other jurisdictions followed suit between 1920 and 1969. See J. Herbie DiFonzo, Alternatives to Marital Fault: Legislative and Judicial Experiments in Cultural Change, 34 Idaho L. Rev. 1, 29 (1997).

6. A number of other problems plagued early no-fault legislation. Opponents unsuccessfully challenged the legislation on such constitutional grounds as vagueness, impairment of contract, equal protection, and freedom of religion. See, e.g., In re Walton's Marriage, 104 Cal. Rptr. 472 (Ct. App. 1972); In re Marriage of Franks, 542 P.2d 845 (Colo. 1975).

## Problem

Blackacre recently simplified its divorce procedure. A newly enacted statute authorizes divorce-by-mail decrees. Such decrees allow petitioners to divorce without making a personal appearance if: (1) the couple has no minor children and the wife is not pregnant, (2) neither party has real property, (3) neither party desires spousal support, (4) the couple's debts do not exceed $10,000, and (5) the marital property totals less than $15,000. See Ariz. R. Civ. P. Ann. 55(b)(1)(ii) (West 2001). Mary Jones, a Blackacre legislator, is concerned that cutbacks in legal services have resulted in vast numbers of persons whose needs for divorce are not being met. She would like to propose that the simplified procedure be extended. You are her legislative intern. What do you advise?

## ■ BENNINGTON v. BENNINGTON
### 381 N.E.2d 1355 (Ohio Ct. App. 1978)

McCormac, Judge.

Mary Bennington commenced an action for alimony only, claiming gross neglect of duty and abandonment without just cause as grounds therefor. Larry Bennington answered, denying grounds for alimony, and counterclaimed for divorce alleging gross neglect of duty and extreme cruelty. His counterclaim was later amended asserting the grounds for divorce of living separate and apart for at least two years without cohabitation. . . .

Plaintiff and defendant were married in 1946. No children have been born to the marriage. In 1963, plaintiff suffered a stroke rendering her permanently and totally disabled and causing her left side to become paralyzed. There have been no sexual relations between the parties since that time.

In 1974, Larry Bennington moved out of the house and into a travel van located adjacent to the house on the same premises. His primary reason for moving into the van was that his wife kept the heat in the house at about 85 to 90 degrees Fahrenheit. He was also irritated about the fact that his wife locked and bolted the door to the house and, when he arrived home from work, it frequently took her fifteen to twenty minutes to come to the door to let him into the house. Her reason for locking the door was apparently for security purposes. There were also other areas of conflict between the parties. However, there was no intention on the part of Larry Bennington to abandon his marital responsibilities when he moved from the house to the van in 1974. On the contrary, he continued to help his disabled wife with household chores, pretty much the same as before moving into the travel van. There was a conflict as to whether he ever slept inside the house again after moving to the van, or whether he used the house otherwise for his comfort and enjoyment. It is clear, however, that he did enter the house regularly to assist his disabled wife.

On November 26, 1976, Larry Bennington finally became thoroughly disenchanted with the entire arrangement and decided to leave home. He went to Arizona for about one month. He then returned, regaining his job. After his return, he lived off of the premises in the van for about three months and then obtained an apartment elsewhere.

R.C. 3105.01(K) provides grounds for divorce ". . . [w]hen husband and wife have, without interruption for two years, lived separate and apart without cohabitation. . . ."

The trial court found that when the husband moved from the house to the van located on the same premises that he was living separate and apart without cohabitation. . . .

The trial court erroneously included the time that the husband lived in the van adjacent to the house as part of the two-year period, as the parties were not living "separate and apart" during that time. During that time there was no cessation of marital duties and relations between the wife and husband. Approximately the same duties were performed by the husband to the wife and by the wife to the husband as prior to the time that the husband moved outside of the house to the van. . . . While the parties were living apart in a limited sense, they were not living separately in a marital sense. . . .

Judgment reversed.

## Notes and Questions

1. With the movement toward no fault, many states merely added no-fault grounds (for example, living separate and apart) to their traditional fault-based grounds. Thus, a large number of states reflect a "mixed" fault/no-fault regime. This approach contrasts with "pure" no-fault laws in some jurisdictions, such as California.

Statutes reflect three types of "living separate and apart" provisions. Homer H. Clark, Jr., The Law of Domestic Relations in the United States 518 (2d ed. 1988). First, parties must live apart under a judicial decree or separation agreement for a prescribed period. Second, parties must live apart "willingly" or "voluntarily" (that is, by mutual consent). The third, and least restrictive, merely requires proof that the parties lived apart for the statutory period. E.g., UMDA §302(a)(2), 9 U.L.A. (pt. I) 200 (1998). Which type is the statute in *Bennington*?

2. *Historical background.* Many states had living-apart statutes prior to California's adoption of no fault. J. Herbie DiFonzo, Alternatives to Marital Fault: Legislative and Judicial Experiments in Cultural Change, 34 Idaho L. Rev. 1, 39 (1997) (citing 23 states). However, such statutes were aimed at forestalling, rather than facilitating, divorce. In addition, the requisite statutory periods were so long (generally five to ten years) that the statutes were seldom utilized. Id. at 42, 44.

3. Durational periods for "living separate and apart" now range from six months (for example, UMDA §302(2)) to three years. See Linda D. Elrod & Robert G. Spector, A Review of the Year in Family Law: Children's Issues Take the Spotlight, 29 Fam. L.Q. 741, 769 (1996) (listing durational provisions). In jurisdictions that require lengthy separations before filing for a no-fault divorce, an unhappy spouse must thereby resort to traditional fault-based grounds. What purposes do lengthy separation requirements serve? Do they undermine the purposes of no fault?

4. Why does the court conclude the parties were not "living separate and apart"? Suppose the van were not adjacent to the house. Down the street? Across town? Is the geographic location determinative? Suppose Mr. Bennington obtained an apartment in 1974, yet still returned daily to assist his wife. Is he living separate and apart? May parties who separate to reside in different bedrooms ever establish that they are "living separate and apart"? See In re Marriage of Uhls, 549 S.W.2d 107, 112 (Mo. Ct. App. 1977) (statute "does not necessarily mean separate roofs but rather means separate lives" for couple residing in separate bedrooms who had ceased sexual relations for four years).

5. Did Mrs. Bennington's acts constitute sufficient cruelty for divorce? How did her disability affect the outcome? Were Mr. Bennington's chores in the household after moving to the van "marital duties and relations" or caretaking of a disabled person? Should Mr. Bennington's altruistic behavior preclude his divorce?

6. How is living separate and apart similar to, and different from, fault-based grounds, particularly desertion? Why is a statutory period required? What difference does it make when it commences? What should toll the statutory period? Suppose the Benningtons were intimate once during the statutory period. Recall the condonation defense. Should fault-based defenses be available?

7. Should a party wishing to separate be forced to vacate the marital home, even if not financially able? See Carol Bruch, The Legal Import of Informal Marital Separations: A Survey of California Law and a Call for Change, 65 Cal. L. Rev. 1015 (1977) (requirement causes financial hardship).

8. One commentator suggests that living-apart statutes spared parties "the intrusion into their privacy which fault divorce proceedings mandated." DiFonzo, supra, at 39. Is this an apt characterization of the proceedings in *Bennington*?

9. *Legal separation distinguished.* Legal separations, constituting an alternative to divorce, were quite common during the fault-based era when divorce was difficult to obtain. Such separations were once called "divorce from bed and board" (from the Latin *divorce a mensa et thoro*) to be distinguished from absolute divorce (or *divorce a vinculo matrimonii* from the bonds of marriage). Decrees of legal separation do not free the parties to remarry but do relieve them from cohabitation. Today, decrees of separation are still necessary in some states to satisfy statutory requirements for the divorce ground of "living separate and apart."

## Note: Abolition of Fault-Based Defenses

One important legal issue after the adoption of no fault was the status of fault-based defenses. Many states abolished them legislatively. See, e.g., Colo. Rev. Stat. Ann. §14-10-107(5) (West 1997); Fla. Stat. Ann. §61.044 (West 1997); Minn. Stat. Ann. §518.06 (West 1990); Mont. Code Ann. §40-4-105(4) (1999). Some states abolished them judicially. See Flora v. Flora, 337 N.E.2d 846, 852 (Ind. Ct. App. 1975). On the other hand, some states that added no-fault divorce to their fault grounds still maintain the defenses. See, e.g., Me. Rev. Stat. Ann. tit. 19-A, §902(3) (recrimination), §902(4) (condonation) (West 1998). Fault-based defenses become important in jurisdictions with lengthy separation requirements (which force parties who want a speedier divorce to resort to traditional fault-based grounds) or in those jurisdictions in which fault continues to play a role in spousal support or property division.

### b. What Role for Fault?

■ **TWYMAN v. TWYMAN**
*855 S.W.2d 619 (Tex. 1993)*

Cornyn, Justice.
In this case we decide whether a claim for infliction of emotional distress can be brought in a divorce proceeding. . . .

Sheila and William Twyman married in 1969. Sheila filed for divorce in 1985. She later amended her divorce petition to add a general claim for emotional harm without specifying whether the claim was based on negligent or intentional infliction of emotional distress. In her amended petition, Sheila alleged that William "intentionally and cruelly" attempted to engage her in "deviate sexual acts."[7] Following a bench trial, the court rendered judgment dissolving the marriage . . . and awarding Sheila $15,000 plus interest for her claim for emotional distress. William appealed that portion of the judgment based on emotional distress, contending that interspousal tort immunity precluded Sheila's recovery for negligent infliction of emotional distress. . . .

[While the case was pending, the Texas Supreme Court refused to recognize the tort of negligent infliction of emotional distress. The court, therefore, considered the alternative ground of intentional infliction of emotional distress.]

[T]he elements of the tort [of intentional infliction of emotional distress] as expressed in the Restatement (Second) of Torts §46 (1965) [are]: 1) the defendant acted intentionally or recklessly, 2) the conduct was extreme and outrageous, 3) the actions of the defendant caused the plaintiff emotional distress, and 4) the emotional distress suffered by the plaintiff was severe. Id. According to the Restatement, liability for outrageous conduct should be found "only where the conduct has been so outrageous in character, and so extreme in degree, as to go beyond all possible bounds of decency, and to be regarded as atrocious, and utterly intolerable in a civilized community." Id. cmt. d. . . .

We now consider whether the cause of action for intentional infliction of emotional distress may be brought in a divorce proceeding. In Bounds v. Caudle, this court unanimously abolished the doctrine of interspousal immunity for intentional torts. 560 S.W.2d 925 (Tex. 1977). Ten years later, we abrogated interspousal immunity "completely as to any cause of action," including negligence actions for personal injuries. Price v. Price, 732 S.W.2d 316, 319 (Tex. 1987). Under [these precedents], there appears to be no legal impediment to bringing a tort claim in a divorce action based on either negligence or an intentional act such as assault or battery.

The more difficult issue is when the tort claim must be brought and how the tort award should be considered when making a "just and right" division of the marital estate. See Tex. Fam. Code §3.63(b). Of the

---

7. At trial, Sheila testified that William pursued sadomasochistic bondage activities with her, even though he knew that she feared such activities because she had been raped at knife-point before their marriage. The trial court found that William "attempted to emotionally coerce [Sheila] in 'bondage' on an ongoing basis. . . ." and "engaged in a continuing course of conduct of attempting to coerce her to join in his practices of 'bondage' by continually asserting that their marriage could be saved only by [Sheila] participating with him in his practices of 'bondage.' "

states that have answered this question, several have held that the tort case and the divorce case must be litigated separately. See, e.g. Walther v. Walther, 709 P.2d 387, 388 (Utah 1985); Windauer v. O'Connor, 107 Ariz. 267, 485 P.2d 1157 (1971); Simmons v. Simmons, 773 P.2d 602, 605 (Colo. Ct. App. 1988). Other states require joinder of the two actions. See, e.g. Tevis v. Tevis, 79 N.J. 422, 400 A.2d 1189, 1196 (1979); Weil v. Lammon, 503 So. 2d 830, 832 (Ala. 1987).

We believe that the best approach lies between these two extremes. As in other civil actions, joinder of the tort cause of action should be permitted, but subject to the principles of res judicata. Of course, how such claims are ultimately tried is within the sound discretion of the trial court. But joinder of tort claims with the divorce, when feasible, is encouraged. Resolving both the tort and divorce actions in the same proceeding avoids two trials based at least in part on the same facts, and settles in one suit "all matters existing between the parties."

When a tort action is tried with the divorce, however, it is imperative that the court avoid awarding a double recovery. [A] spouse should not be allowed to recover tort damages and a disproportionate division of the community estate based on the same conduct. Therefore, when a factfinder awards tort damages to a divorcing spouse, the court may not consider the same tortious acts when dividing the marital estate. . . .

Sheila Twyman cannot recover based on the findings of fact made by the trial court in this case. It is likely, however, that this case proceeded on a theory of negligent infliction of emotional distress. . . . When, as here, a party presents her case in reliance on precedent that has been recently overruled, remand is appropriate. Therefore, in the interest of justice, we reverse the judgment of the court of appeals and remand this cause to the trial court for a new trial.

PHILLIPS, Chief Justice, concurring and dissenting.

. . . In recognizing [the tort of intentional infliction of emotional distress], I would not extend it to actions between spouses or former spouses for conduct occurring during their marriage. . . . To recover damages Sheila must prove that William's conduct was outrageous — that is, "extreme," "beyond all possible bounds of decency," "atrocious," and "utterly intolerable in a civilized community." . . .

The sexual relationship is among the most intimate aspects of marriage. People's concepts of a beneficial sexual relationship vary widely, and spouses may expect that some accommodation of each other's feelings will be necessary for their mutual good. Any breach of such an intimate and essential part of marriage may be regarded as outrageous by the aggrieved spouse and will often be the cause of great distress. There are many other aspects of marriage which are likewise sensitive. How money is to be spent, how children are to be raised, and how time is to be allocated are only a few of the many areas of conflict in a marriage.

Not infrequently disagreements over these matters are deep and contribute to the breakup of the marriage. If all are actionable, then tort claims will be commonplace in divorce cases, and judges and juries with their own deeply felt beliefs about what is proper in a marital relationship will face the hard task of deciding whether one spouse or another behaved outrageously with no standards but their own to guide.

The inquiry which must be made to determine whether a spouse's conduct is outrageous entails too great an intrusion into the marital relationship. Although courts are already called upon to consider fault in divorce actions, allowance of tort claims requires a more pervasive inspection of spouses' private lives than should be permissible. In this case the parties were called to testify in detail and at length about the most private moments of their marriage. If the court's only concern were the degree to which a spouse's fault had contributed to the demise of the marriage, the inquiry into each spouse's conduct need not have been so detailed. To recover damages, however, Sheila was required to testify at length before a jury, and to rebut her claim, William was obliged to answer in equal detail. The prospect of such testimony in many divorces is too great an invasion of spouses' interests in privacy, and promises to make divorce more acrimonious and injurious than it already is.

The plurality opinion's justification for allowing the tort of intentional infliction of emotional distress between spouses is that this represents a middle ground among the various positions taken by Members of this Court. But being in the middle does not equate to being right. . . .

## Notes and Questions

1. Several factors contribute to new applications of tort theories in divorce, including the abolition of interspousal immunity, awareness of the problem of domestic violence, and the demise of fault-based divorce. Does plaintiff's attempt to recover tort damages in divorce resurrect fault-based grounds such as cruelty? See Harry D. Krause, On the Danger of Allowing Marital Fault to Re-Emerge in the Guise of Torts, 73 Notre Dame L. Rev. 1355, 1363-1366 (1998); Robert G. Spector, Marital Torts: The Current Legal Landscape, 33 Fam. L.Q. 745, 746 (1999).

2. With the abolition of interspousal immunity, should tort claims for marital misconduct be treated similarly to other torts? Or, should special rules apply? For example, should statutes of limitations be tolled for victims of spousal abuse who frequently endure years of abuse before filing for divorce? See Giovine v. Giovine, 663 A.2d 109 (N.J. Super. Ct. App. Div. 1995) (relying on battered women's syndrome to extend statute of limitations). See also Clare Dalton, Domestic Violence, Domestic Torts and Divorce: Constraints and Possibilities, 31 N. Eng. L. Rev. 319, 339-346 (1997); David E. Poplar, Comment, Tolling the Statute

of Limitations for Battered Women after *Giovine v. Giovine:* Creating Equitable Exceptions for Victims of Domestic Abuse, 101 Dick. L. Rev. 161 (1996).

3. On remand, how should the trial court rule? Under the Restatement, was the husband's conduct so extreme and outrageous? Was his conduct intended to inflict harm?

4. *Twyman* presents two issues: whether courts should permit interspousal actions for intentional infliction and, if so, whether courts should require joinder of tort claims and divorce claims. Do you agree with *Twyman*'s resolution of these issues? Do interspousal claims for emotional distress "present a more complicated picture than does battery" so as to "caution against their recognition"? Ira Mark Ellman, The Place of Fault in a Modern Divorce Law, 28 Ariz. St. L.J. 773, 793, 802 (1996). See also Ira Mark Ellman & Stephen D. Sugarman, Spousal Emotional Abuse as a Tort?, 55 Md. L. Rev. 1268, 1285-1289 (1996) (expressing concerns that recognition of emotional distress claims will undermine no-fault divorce law and disserve goals of tort law).

5. Do you find Justice Phillips's views in *Twyman* persuasive that notions of privacy should militate against recognition of intentional infliction claims?

6. As *Twyman* reveals, courts that permit interspousal actions for intentional infliction of emotional distress adopt different positions regarding joinder. What benefits follow from joinder? Professor Andrew Schepard responds:

> Divorce litigation comprises a major portion of the caseload of many large state court systems. The policy interest in conserving scarce judicial resources by concentrating all claims between the divorcing couple into a single proceeding is thus great. . . .
>
> There is also a related social interest in reducing the private transaction costs (the most significant component of which is legal fees) of settling marital differences. Divorce is generally a zero sum economic transaction: there is not enough money in the marital settlement pot for both spouses to live postdivorce at the same standard of living as before the divorce. Increasing the transaction costs of the divorce settlement by reopening proceedings reduces further the total resources available for the postdivorce family to live on. . . .
>
> Also weighing in favor of [joinder] is the policy of repose that underlies [res judicata]. Divorce is a wrenching, all-consuming emotional experience. [The husband's and wife's] well-being, and their continued productive functioning as members of society, require that their emotional stability be reestablished quickly and firmly by a final settlement of marital differences.

Andrew Schepard, Divorce, Interspousal Torts, and Res Judicata, 24 Fam. L.Q. 127, 131-132 (1990). See also Barbara H. Young, Note, Interspousal Torts and Divorce: Problems, Policies, Procedures, 27 J. Fam. L. 489, 493-499 (1988-1989) (arguing that joinder should be permissible rather than mandatory).

Which approach to joinder does *Twyman* adopt? Which do you favor? If a court does not permit joinder, is a plaintiff without remedy? May she pursue a separate action? Must she? If she does pursue a separate action after the divorce, may her husband raise the affirmative defense of res judicata? Compare Brinkman v. Brinkman, 966 S.W.2d 780 (Tex. Ct. App. 1998) (holding that wife's assault claim was barred by her divorce action based on ground of cruelty) with Sotirescu v. Sotirescu, 52 S.W.3d 1 (Mo. Ct. App. 2001) (holding that wife's postdissolution assault claim was not barred by divorce court finding that neither party engaged in marital misconduct). See also McCulloh v. Drake, 24 P.3d 1162 (Wyo. 2001) (refusing to permit joinder because wife's right to jury trial on tort claim would delay determination of custody and support issues; also holding that res judicata was unavailable to husband).

7. What is the purpose of, and legal theory behind, a tort action? Do the different legal theories of tort and divorce militate against joinder? Do the different procedural characteristics? See Stuart v. Stuart, 421 N.W.2d 505, 508 (Wis. 1988). If joinder is required, how should a court resolve the problem of attorneys' fees (contingent fees are not permitted in divorce actions)? Access to jury trials (normally permitted in tort actions)? See Brennan v. Orban, 678 A.2d 667, 677 (N.J. 1996) (suggesting that certain factors, such as child welfare, may suggest a nonjury trial of a marital tort case but that "society's interest in vindicating a marital tort through the jury process" may dictate otherwise). If a jury trial is ordered, where shall the claim be litigated — in family court or a trial court? See id. at 677 (discussing respective advantages and disadvantages).

8. Following *Twyman,* the Texas Supreme Court adjudicated a different tort claim in the context of divorce. In Schlueter v. Schlueter, 975 S.W.2d 584 (Tex. 1998), the court held that no independent tort action existed in a divorce proceeding for a spouse's fraudulent depletion of community assets. In so ruling, the court permitted joinder in divorce actions for personal injury torts but not for economic torts. Does this rule make sense? See generally Cynthia S. Schiffer, Note, The Allowance of Independent Tort Causes of Action in Divorce Proceedings in Light of *Schlueter v. Schlueter,* 51 Baylor L. Rev. 1063 (1999). In a similar action involving a husband who created an elaborate scheme to hide his income, another court considered whether a RICO claim (under the Racketeer Influenced and Corrupt Organizations Act) could be brought in the context of divorce. See Perlberger v. Perlberger, 1999 WL 79503 (E.D. Pa. 1999), *aff'd,* 242 F.3d 371 (3d Cir. 2000) (holding that wife's RICO claim survived summary judgment). See generally Erin Alexander, Comment, The Honeymoon Is

Definitely Over: The Use of Civil RICO in Divorce, 37 San Diego L.
Rev. 541 (2000).

## Problem

Jane and John Doe have been married for seven years and have a
son and twin girls. Unbeknownst to John, his wife had a sexual affair
during the marriage with her art professor. John discovers a letter that
reveals to him that the children may have been fathered by the professor. DNA testing confirms that John is father of the son but not the twins.
The next day John petitions for divorce, alleging adultery, fraud, and
intentional infliction of emotional distress. Should he be permitted to
bring the tort claim in the divorce proceeding? Should his tort claim be
barred by the interspousal immunity doctrine? Does the wife's conduct
satisfy the requirements for intentional infliction? Are there any considerations that distinguish this case from *Twyman*? See Doe v. Doe, 712
A.2d 132 (Md. Ct. Spec. App. 1998). See generally Linda L. Berger, Lies
Between Mommy and Daddy: The Case for Recognizing Emotional Distress Claims Based on Domestic Deceit That Interferes with Parent-
Child Relationships, 33 Loy. L.A. L. Rev. 449 (2000).

## 3. Assessment of the No-Fault "Revolution"

### a. Divorce Reform in the United States

■ **DEBORAH L. RHODE & MARTHA MINOW,
REFORMING THE QUESTIONS,
QUESTIONING THE REFORMS: FEMINIST
PERSPECTIVES ON DIVORCE LAW**
*in Divorce Reform at the Crossroads 191-199, 209-210
(Stephen D. Sugarman & Herma Hill Kay eds., 1990)*

Our central premise is that the legal issues surrounding divorce
have been conceived too narrowly. Reform initiatives have too often
treated divorce as a largely private dispute and have not adequately addressed its public dimensions. . . .

The leading proponents of initial no-fault reform were lawyers,
judges, and law professors. Their primary focus was on the legal grounds
for divorce; their primary purposes were to reduce expense, acrimony,
and fraud in resolving matters envisioned as essentially private concerns.
What is, perhaps, most revealing about these original efforts are the is-

sues that were not on the agenda. Early reform strategies neglected gender equality and public responsibilities.

Although no-fault initiatives coincided with the resurgence of a women's rights movement, proponents of these reforms generally were not seeking to remedy women's disadvantages under traditional family policies. Indeed, to the extent that gender equity appeared at all in discussions among decision makers, the focus involved equity for men. The dominant concern was beleaguered ex-husbands, crippled by excessive alimony burdens, and threats of blackmail. Although this problem was grossly exaggerated, the absence of systematic data allowed policymakers to rely on anecdotal experiences to formulate the problem they sought to reform.

In part, the absence of women's concerns from the debate reflected the absence of women. Those with greatest influence in policy-making — practicing attorneys, politicians, and family law experts — were overwhelmingly male. The newly emerging women's rights movement was not significantly involved with early divorce reforms, in part because it was understaffed and overextended during this period, but more important, because the implications of such reforms were not yet apparent. Only as the divorce rate escalated and scholars concerned with women's issues began to chronicle its impact did the focus of debate begin to change.

Even when reformers identified gender equality as an objective, they relied almost exclusively on gender-neutral formulations. For example, they succeeded in eliminating explicitly sex-linked provisions (such as those granting alimony only to wives) and in reformulating rules for marital property distribution to require "equal" or "equitable" division of assets. Yet . . . such provisions have secured equality in form, but not equality in fact.

The assumptions underlying early reforms also marginalized the public implications of divorce doctrine. No-fault initiatives began from the premise that decisions involving the termination of marriage should rest with private parties; the public's responsibility was simply to provide efficient legal rules for processing their agreement and resolving any disputes. Within this framework, a couple's allocation of financial and child-rearing obligations appeared to be primarily matters for private ordering. If parties failed to reach agreement, their differences would be resolved under broad discretionary standards mandating equality or equity between the spouses in financial matters and the best interest of the child in custody contests. Public norms about the kinds of resolutions society should endorse receded to the background. As a result, the state was given little responsibility for guiding, enforcing, or supplementing judicial awards.

Paradoxically, this move toward private ordering failed adequately to acknowledge the diversity of private family circumstances. Those who framed and interpreted legal doctrine often overlooked the fact that marriages of different durations, formed during different decades with different expectations, could leave divorcing parties in sharply divergent situations. One single, discretionary standard was thought adequate to deal with circumstances ranging from a couple married for one year while the parties finished college to a couple married for twenty-five years while the woman worked in the home and the husband held paid employment.

Early no-fault reforms gave no special attention to the concerns of particularly vulnerable groups such as displaced homemakers with limited savings, insurance, and employment options; families with inadequate income to support two households (a problem disproportionately experienced by racial minorities); or couples with no children, no significant property, and no need for a formal adjudicative procedure. Nor was child support central to the reform agenda; it appeared only as a side issue, buried within custody and other financial topics.

It bears emphasis what such a limited conception of public responsibility left out. The early reform agenda did not specify clear public norms concerning financial and child-care responsibilities to guide parties' decision making or judicial review. Nor did it mandate effective, affordable enforcement procedures for spousal and child support awards, or state subsidies where private resources were inadequate. Reformers also neglected the impact of postdivorce property divisions — such as the forced sale of the family home — on dependent children. And what was most critical, no-fault initiatives omitted criteria for assessing the outcomes of divorce, outcomes affecting not only the parties and their children but subsequent marriages, stepfamilies, and public welfare responsibilities.

In noting what was absent from the no-fault agenda, we do not mean to devalue its central objective. Reducing the acrimony, expense, and fraud associated with fault-based procedures was a goal worth pursuing on its own right. Given the opposition to liberalizing grounds for divorce, reformers may have been justifiably wary about raising other related issues. But we also believe that the limitations of the original reform movement reflect not only what was politically expedient at that historical moment but also more fundamental conceptual inadequacies. By remaining wedded to traditional public/private distinctions, early divorce reform tended to amplify rather than redress gender inequalities. . . .

. . . Norms governing termination of a marriage should be consistent with the ideal to which marriage aspires — that of equal partnerships between spouses who share resources, responsibilities, and risks. . . . Gender equality and child welfare should become priorities in practice, not just theory, under contemporary divorce law. . . .

b. **Divorce Reform: The Comparative-Law Perspective**

■ **NAOMI NEFT & ANN D. LEVINE, WHERE WOMEN STAND: AN INTERNATIONAL REPORT ON THE STATUS OF WOMEN IN 140 COUNTRIES**
*98 (1997)*

Divorce is now legal in nearly every country, and as marriage rates have been declining, divorce rates have been rising, even in some predominantly Roman Catholic countries where divorce has long been a contentious political issue. In Spain divorce was not legalized until 1981. In Brazil, although divorce became legal in 1977, each person was allowed only one divorce during his or her lifetime, a stipulation that was not removed until 1988. In 1995 Ireland became the last major European country to legalize divorce [in situations in which] the couple have been separated for four of the last five years.

The Philippines, also predominantly Roman Catholic, is one of the few countries where divorce is still prohibited. Yet a 1987 law greatly extended the grounds for legal separation and allowed marriages to be easily annulled on psychological grounds. Chile, too, permits legal separation and annulment but not divorce. In both these countries, people who wish to remarry must seek an annulment, and since an annuled marriage never legally existed, the wives in these situations are not legally entitled to alimony or child support from their husbands.

Among developed countries, Russia has the highest divorce rate, for every 100 couples who get married each year, 60 couples get divorced. Other developed countries with high divorce rates include the United States, the Scandinavian countries, and the United Kingdom.

One of the reasons divorce rates are rising around the world is that since the 1970s many countries — among them Argentina, Australia, Canada, India, and Japan — have liberalized their divorce laws to provide divorce by mutual consent or on a no-fault basis. . . .

---

See also Mary Ann Glendon, Abortion and Divorce in Western Law 61-81 (1987) (finding that many Western countries that chose to add no-fault grounds to traditional fault grounds nonetheless provided safeguards by permitting courts to deny no-fault divorces in cases of extreme hardship for nonconsenting innocent spouses); William J. Goode, World Changes in Divorce Patterns (1993) (analyzing world trends in divorce and concluding that increasing divorce rates represent a socioeconomic problem for women and children).

## Note: The Return of Fault

A movement is afoot to reintroduce fault in the dissolution process. Since 1997, 25 states have considered laws to repeal or revise their no-fault laws. In three states (Louisiana, Arizona, and Arkansas), the reform movement led to adoption of "covenant marriage" acts making it more difficult for couples to obtain no-fault divorces.[5]

Louisiana became the first state in 1997 to allow couples to choose a "covenant marriage," instead of a traditional marriage, when they applied for a marriage license. According to La. Rev. Stat. Ann. §9:272 (West 2000), couples who choose covenant marriage must sign a declaration of intent that indicates they have received premarital counseling on the "nature, purpose and responsibilities" of marriage, and that they promise to seek marriage counseling in the event of marital problems. Divorce is permitted only for adultery, conviction of a felony resulting in death or imprisonment, desertion for at least one year, physical or sexual abuse of a spouse or child, or after a two-year separation without reconciliation. Id. at §9:307.

Arizona adopted a similar measure in 1998. However, the Arizona statute allows for divorce subject to the parties' mutual consent. Ariz. Rev. Stat. Ann. §25-901 (West 2000). The most recent state to pass a covenant marriage statute, Arkansas, did so in 2001. That legislation was enacted in response to the fact that Arkansas currently has the second highest rate of divorce in the United States, after Nevada.[6]

Covenant marriages have not been as popular as supporters originally hoped. In Louisiana, 400 already-married couples signed up for covenant marriages in 1998. However, in 1999, that number dropped to less than 5. In 2000, of 4,148 marriage license applications, only 115 of those were for covenant marriages.[7]

In 1999, of the 17 states that considered covenant marriage bills, most states adopted less stringent variations, such as reducing marriage license fees for couples who attend premarital counseling.[8] Other proposed bills would permit divorce only for fraud (California); permit divorce only in the case of adultery (Mississippi); enact lengthy waiting periods before obtaining a no-fault divorce (Missouri and Minnesota); enact strict premarital counseling requirements (Alabama, Nebraska,

[5]. Lynne Marie Kohm, A Comparative Study of Covenant Marriage Proposals in the United States, 12 Regent U. L. Rev. 31, 41 (1999).

[6]. Blaine Harden, Bible Belt Couples "Put Asunder" More, Despite New Efforts, N.Y. Times, May 21, 2001, at A1.

[7]. Covenant Marriages on the Decline, Couples Opting for Traditional Unions, Sunday Advocate (Baton Rouge, La.), Feb. 4, 2001, at 23.

[8]. See H. J. Cummins, "I Do" . . . Really; "Super Vows" Aim to Strengthen Marriages, Chi. Sun-Times, Jan. 9, 2000, at 27.

and Minnesota); require marital counseling, mediation, and arbitration before permitting a suit for divorce (Colorado); and limiting suits in tort between spouses (Missouri).[9]

Supporters of covenant marriages criticize no-fault divorce for harming children by increasing divorce rates and leaving many single parents with few financial and emotional resources for their children.[10] Advocates hope that covenant marriages will make prospective spouses consider marital commitments more seriously and that the adoption of covenant marriage acts will spark a "children first" movement in the United States.[11] Critics argue, however, that these reforms raise constitutional concerns (e.g., placing an undue burden on the right to make decisions regarding family life), conflict-of-laws and choice-of-law questions (possibly forcing non-covenant marriage states to recognize covenant marriages and denying no-fault divorces to spouses who seek them outside of their home state), practice of law problems (requiring clergy marriage counselors to counsel couples regarding the "nature and purpose" of marriage), and policy debates (the effect of covenant marriages on preserving the family, protecting women and children, and lowering juvenile crime rates).[12] Furthermore, some worry that covenant marriages may make it more difficult for victims of domestic violence to exit from abusive marriages.[13]

On the return-to-fault movement, see generally Allen M. Parkman, Good Intentions Gone Awry: No-Fault Divorce and the American Family 151-200 (2000); Ira Mark Ellman & Sharon Lohr, Marriage as Contract, Opportunistic Violence, and Other Bad Arguments for Fault-Based Divorce, 1997 Ill. L. Rev. 719 (1997); Eric Rasmusen & Jeffrey Evans Stake, Lifting the Veil of Ignorance: Personalizing the Marriage Contract, 73 Ind. L.J. 453 (1998). On covenant marriage, see Samuel Pyeatt Menefee, The "Sealed Knot": A Preliminary Bibliography of "Covenant Marriage," 12 Regent U. L. Rev. 145 (1999); Katherine Shaw Spaht, Louisiana's Covenant Marriage: Social Analysis and Legal Implications, 59 La. L. Rev. 63 (1998); Katherine Shaw Spaht, What's Become of Louisiana Covenant Marriage Through the Eyes of Social Scientists, 47 Loy. L. Rev. 709 (2001).

[9]. Kohm, supra note [5], at 42-47.
[10]. Robert M. Gordon, The Limits of Limits on Divorce, 107 Yale L.J. 1435, 1436 (1998).
[11]. Kohm, supra note [5], at 38.
[12]. See Jay Macke, Note, Of Covenants and Conflicts — When 'I Do' Means More Than It Used to, But Less Than You Thought, 59 Ohio St. L.J. 1377 (1998).
[13]. Gordon, supra note [10], at 1447-1449.

# E. ACCESS TO DIVORCE

## 1. *Economic Obstacles*

## ■ BODDIE v. CONNECTICUT
### 401 U.S. 371 (1971)

Mr. Justice HARLAN delivered the opinion of the Court.

Appellants, welfare recipients residing in the State of Connecticut, brought this action in the Federal District Court for the District of Connecticut on behalf of themselves and others similarly situated, challenging, as applied to them, certain state procedures for the commencement of litigation, including requirements for payment of court fees and costs for service of process, that restrict their access to the courts in their effort to bring an action for divorce.

It appears from the briefs and oral argument that the average cost to a litigant for bringing an action for divorce is $60. Section 52-259 of the Connecticut General Statutes provides: "There shall be paid to the clerks of the supreme court or the superior court, for entering each civil cause, forty-five dollars. . . ." An additional $15 is usually required for the service of process by the sheriff, although as much as $40 or $50 may be necessary where notice must be accomplished by publication.

There is no dispute as to the inability of the named appellants in the present case to pay either the court fees required by statute or the cost incurred for the service of process. The affidavits in the record establish that appellants' welfare income in each instance barely suffices to meet the costs of the daily essentials of life and includes no allotment that could be budgeted for the expense to gain access to the courts in order to obtain a divorce. . . .

[Appellants challenged the constitutionality of the statute and sought an injunction to permit them to proceed without payment of fees and costs. A three judge court found the statute constitutional.] We now reverse. Our conclusion is that, given the basic position of the marriage relationship in this society's hierarchy of values and the concomitant state monopolization of the means for legally dissolving this relationship, due process does prohibit a State from denying, solely because of inability to pay, access to its courts to individuals who seek judicial dissolution of their marriages. . . .

. . . Without [the Fifth and Fourteenth Amendments'] guarantee that one may not be deprived of his rights, neither liberty nor property, without due process of law, the State's monopoly over techniques for binding conflict resolution could hardly be said to be acceptable under our scheme of things. . . .

Such [due process] litigation has, however, typically involved rights of defendants — not, as here, persons seeking access to the judicial process in the first instance. This is because our society has been so structured that resort to the courts is not usually the only available, legitimate means of resolving private disputes. . . .

. . . As this Court on more than one occasion has recognized, marriage involves interests of basic importance in our society [citing *Loving, Skinner,* Meyer v. Nebraska]. It is not surprising, then, that the States have seen fit to oversee many aspects of that institution. Without a prior judicial imprimatur, individuals may freely enter into and rescind commercial contracts, for example, but we are unaware of any jurisdiction where private citizens may covenant for or dissolve marriages without state approval. Even where all substantive requirements are concededly met, we know of no instance where two consenting adults may divorce and mutually liberate themselves from the constraints of legal obligations that go with marriage, and more fundamentally the prohibition against remarriage, without invoking the State's judicial machinery.

Thus, although they assert here due process rights as would-be plaintiffs, we think appellants' plight, because resort to the state courts is the only avenue to dissolution of their marriages, is akin to that of defendants faced with exclusion from the only forum effectively empowered to settle their disputes. Resort to the judicial process by these plaintiffs is no more voluntary in a realistic sense than that of the defendant called upon to defend his interests in court. For both groups this process is not only the paramount dispute-settlement technique, but, in fact, the only available one. In this posture we think that this appeal is properly to be resolved in light of the principles enunciated in our due process decisions that delimit rights of defendants compelled to litigate their differences in the judicial forum.

[P]recedent has firmly embedded in our due process jurisprudence two important principles upon whose application we rest our decision in the case before us. [First,] due process requires, at a minimum, that absent a countervailing state interest of overriding significance, persons forced to settle their claims of right and duty through the judicial process must be given a meaningful opportunity to be heard. . . . Our cases further establish that a statute or a rule may be held constitutionally invalid as applied when it operates to deprive an individual of a protected right although its general validity as a measure enacted in the legitimate exercise of state power is beyond question. . . .

No less than these rights, the right to a meaningful opportunity to be heard within the limits of practicality, must be protected against denial by particular laws that operate to jeopardize it for particular individuals. . . . Just as a generally valid notice procedure may fail to satisfy due process because of the circumstances of the defendant, so too a cost requirement, valid on its face, may offend due process because it operates to foreclose a particular party's opportunity to be heard. The State's obligations under the Fourteenth Amendment are not simply generalized ones; rather, the State owes to each individual that process which, in light of the values of a free society, can be characterized as due.

Drawing upon the [these] principles . . . we conclude that the State's refusal to admit these appellants to its courts, the sole means in Connecticut for obtaining a divorce, must be regarded as the equivalent of denying them an opportunity to be heard upon their claimed right to a dissolution of their marriages, and, in the absence of a sufficient countervailing justification for the State's action, a denial of due process.

The arguments for this kind of fee and cost requirement are that the State's interest in the prevention of frivolous litigation is substantial, its use of court fees and process costs to allocate scarce resources is rational, and its balance between the defendant's right to notice and the plaintiff's right to access is reasonable.

In our opinion, none of these considerations is sufficient to override the interest of these plaintiff-appellants in having access to the only avenue open for dissolving their allegedly untenable marriages. Not only is there no necessary connection between a litigant's assets and the seriousness of his motives in bringing suit, but it is here beyond present dispute that appellants bring these actions in good faith. Moreover, other alternatives exist to fees and cost requirements as a means for conserving the time of courts and protecting parties from frivolous litigation, such as penalties for false pleadings or affidavits, and actions for malicious prosecution or abuse of process, to mention only a few. In the same vein we think that reliable alternatives exist to service of process by a state-paid sheriff if the State is unwilling to assume the cost of official service. This is perforce true of service by publication which is the method of notice least calculated to bring to a potential defendant's attention the pendency of judicial proceedings. We think in this case service at defendant's last known address by mail and posted notice is equally effective as publication in a newspaper. . . .

In concluding that the Due Process Clause of the Fourteenth Amendment requires that these appellants be afforded an opportunity to go into court to obtain a divorce, we wish to re-emphasize that we go no further than necessary to dispose of the case before us, a case where the bona fides of both appellants' indigency and desire for divorce are here beyond dispute. We do not decide that access for all individuals to the courts is a right that is, in all circumstances, guaranteed by the Due Process Clause of the Fourteenth Amendment so that its exercise may not be placed beyond the reach of any individual, for, as we have already noted, in the case before us this right is the exclusive precondition to the adjustment of a fundamental human relationship. The requirement that these appellants resort to the judicial process is entirely a state-created matter. Thus we hold only that a State may not, consistent with the obligations imposed on it by the Due Process Clause of the Fourteenth Amendment, pre-empt the right to dissolve this legal relationship without affording all citizens access to the means it has prescribed for doing so. . . .

Mr. Justice DOUGLAS, concurring in the result. . . .

. . . The Court today puts "flesh" upon the Due Process Clause by concluding that marriage and its dissolution are so important that an unhappy couple who are indigent should have access to the divorce courts free of charge. Fishing may be equally important to some communities. May an indigent be excused if he does not obtain a license which requires payment of money that he does not have? How about a requirement of an onerous bond to prevent summary eviction from rented property? The affluent can put up the bond, though the indigent may not be able to do so. Is housing less important to the mucilage holding society together than marriage? The examples could be multiplied. I do not see the length of the road we must follow if we accept my Brother Harlan's invitation. . . .

An invidious discrimination based on poverty is adequate for this case. While Connecticut has provided a procedure for severing the bonds of marriage, a person can meet every requirement save court fees or the cost of service of process and be denied a divorce. Connecticut says in its brief that this is justified because "the State does not favor divorces; and only permits a divorce to be granted when those conditions are found to exist in respect to one or the other of the named parties, which seem to the legislature to make it probable that the interests of society will be better served and that parties will be happier, and so the better citizens, separate, than if compelled to remain together."

Thus, under Connecticut law divorces may be denied or granted solely on the basis of wealth. . . . Affluence does not pass muster under the Equal Protection Clause for determining who must remain married and who shall be allowed to separate.

## Notes and Questions

1. Some jurisdictions permit indigents to avoid filing fees by proceeding *in forma pauperis*. When *Boddie* was decided, approximately 32 states (excluding Connecticut), as well as the District of Columbia and the federal government, had *in forma pauperis* statutes. Charles Brooks, Note, *Boddie v. Connecticut:* The Rights of Indigents in a Divorce Action, J. Fam. L. 121, 122 n.5 (1971).

2. Justice Harlan notes, "There is no dispute as to the inability of the named appellants [to pay]" and, later, "it is here beyond present dispute that appellants bring these actions in good faith." Thus, the holding is limited to plaintiffs who make a showing of indigency and who seek a divorce in good faith. How does an indigent demonstrate these requirements?

3. The majority rests its opinion on "the basic position of the marriage relationship in this society's hierarchy of values and the concomitant state monopolization of the means for legally dissolving this relationship." Are both aspects necessary to the result, or are they independent grounds?

4. If *Boddie* rests on both premises (societal values and monopoly), does an indigency exemption for other divorce expenses (for example, attorneys' fees) follow? Should it matter if the fees are paid to the court or to third parties? How meaningful is a right of access without an attorney? See In re Smiley, 330 N.E.2d 53 (N.Y. 1975). Do the advent of no-fault divorce and pro se divorce kits alter your views? See Robert B. Yegge, Divorce Litigants Without Lawyers, 28 Fam. L.Q. 407 (1994) (recommendations based on ABA studies on pro se family law litigants).

5. How far does *Boddie* protect indigents' rights? If *Boddie* rests on a monopoly rationale, then *Boddie* might guarantee access in civil cases generally. But cf. United States v. Kras, 409 U.S. 434 (1973) (no constitutional right to free bankruptcy discharge); Ortwein v. Schwab, 410 U.S. 656 (1973) (no constitutional right to waive filing fees for welfare appeals). How is divorce distinguishable from bankruptcy and welfare? Does *Boddie* mandate waiver of fees in other family law matters (for example, annulment, separation, paternity, custody, and adoption)? Marriage license fees?

6. Recently, one jurisdiction decided, based on state law rather than constitutional grounds, that an indigent divorce petitioner has the right to appointed counsel. Sholes v. Sholes, 732 N.E.2d 1252 (Ind. Ct. App. 2000).

7. How sound is *Boddie*'s approach? For example, what criteria does the Court suggest for determining which interests are fundamental for due process purposes? Is equal protection a superior approach, as Justice Douglas suggests (as does Justice Brennan in an omitted concurrence)? See Jeffreys v. Jeffreys, 296 N.Y.S.2d 74 (Sup. Ct. 1968) (state court costs for divorce violate indigents' state and federal rights to equal protection), *rev'd on other grounds*, 300 N.Y.S.2d 550 (App. Div. 1972) (requiring state, but not city, to pay such costs in absence of statutory authorization).

8. *Epilogue.* On remand, the court ordered state officials to waive filing fees. Boddie v. Connecticut, 329 F. Supp. 844 (D. Conn. 1971).

## Problems

1. Blackacre has an explicit provision in its state constitution protecting the right to privacy. The Blackacre legislature has just repealed its no-fault laws and reintroduced fault. The Blackacre Family Code per-

mits divorce only for adultery, cruelty, and desertion. John and Jane Doe, a married couple, challenge the statute, alleging that it violates their constitutional right of privacy by disallowing divorce by mutual consent. What result? Does *Boddie* guarantee a constitutional right to divorce, similar to the constitutional right to marry? See Ferrer v. Commonwealth, 4 Fam. L. Rep. (BNA) 2744 (Sept. 26, 1978) (deciding a somewhat similar issue based on Puerto Rican law). See generally Kenneth L. Karst, The Freedom of Intimate Association, 89 Yale L.J. 624, 671-672 (1980).

2. Public interest groups in Arkansas, Arizona, and Louisiana argue that "covenant marriage" laws are unconstitutional in light of *Boddie*. What arguments would they make? See generally David M. Wagner, The Constitution and Covenant Marriage Legislation: Rumors of a Constitutional Right to Divorce Have Been Greatly Exaggerated, 12 Regent U.L. Rev. 53 (1999).

## Note: Pro Se Divorce

In the fault-based system, lawyers were essential to prove the existence (or lack) of marital fault. No fault resulted in a diminished role for lawyers and the growth of pro se divorce. Divorce self-help kits and services began proliferating in many states, sparking concerns by the organized bar about the unauthorized practice of law.

Less than a decade after the advent of no fault, researchers conducted studies of the effectiveness of pro se divorce. One study by Yale law students found that most clients, themselves, resolve property, support, and custody issues. The authors questioned whether counsel was necessary for reasons of judicial efficiency or public welfare considerations.[14]

Psychologists, who conducted a subsequent empirical study of pro se divorce funded by the American Bar Association, came to a different conclusion. By comparing a broad sample of self-represented versus attorney-represented cases, these researchers pointed out that pro se divorce has several shortcomings, including that (1) pro se litigants are less satisfied with the terms of their divorces as their cases become more complex, (2) they are less likely to receive tax advice or information about alternative dispute resolution, and (3) many petitioners and respondents encounter difficulties that are never resolved.[15]

[14]. Ralph C. Cavanaugh & Deborah L. Rhode, Project, The Unauthorized Practice of Law and Pro Se Divorce: An Empirical Analysis, 86 Yale L.J. 104, 128-129 (1976).
[15]. Bruce D. Sales et al., Is Self-Representation a Reasonable Alternative to Attorney Representation in Divorce Cases?, 37 St. Louis U. L.J. 553 (1993).

Now, the number of pro se litigants appears to be increasing.[16] Lawyers and judges continue to express concerns that pro se representation compromises litigants' legal rights and interferes with judicial efficiency.[17] In response, courts and legal service programs are developing many new forms of assistance. Efforts include simplifying legal forms and instructions, creating self-help centers, developing Internet-based forms of assistance, conducting clinics for litigants, subsidizing paid paralegals to help litigants, and providing limited legal assistance on discrete tasks.[18] In addition, some legal services programs are offering courses to train persons to represent themselves in divorces.[19] One commentator, however, questions the effectiveness of such training courses, worrying whether several factors (i.e., cursory screening and advice, and the devaluing of women's issues) jeopardize "client empowerment, protect[ing] clients' rights in divorce, or even produc[ing] divorce decrees."[20]

## 2. Social and Cultural Obstacles

### ■ LITTLEJOHN v. ROSE
*768 F.2d 765 (6th Cir. 1985),* cert. denied,
*475 U.S. 1045 (1986)*

KEITH, Circuit Judge. . . .
Appellant Linda Littlejohn was a non-tenured teacher in the Calloway County school system. Appellant was originally hired as a substitute teacher and librarian, and held a teaching certificate that qualified her to teach all subjects in elementary grades 1 through 8. In the 1980-81 and 1981-82 school years, Littlejohn was employed as a full-time fifth grade teacher.

[16]. Elizabeth McCulloch, Let Me Show You How: Pro Se Divorce Courses and Client Power, 48 Fla. L. Rev. 481 (1996) (citing ABA study). This finding is not surprising given that domestic relations cases are the fastest growing segment of state court civil caseloads. See Jessica Pearson, Court Services: Meeting the Needs of Twenty-First Century Families, 33 Fam. L.Q. 617 (1999).

[17]. See Raul V. Esquivel III, Comment, The Ability of the Indigent to Access the Legal Process in Family Law Matters, 1 Loy. J. Pub. Interest L. 79, 92-93 (2000) (describing judges' concern regarding their role in helping pro se litigants through procedural difficulties as well as the general perception that pro se litigants clog court dockets).

[18]. See, e.g., Margaret Martin Barry, Accessing Justice: Are Pro Se Clinics a Reasonable Response to the Lack of Pro Bono Legal Services and Should Law School Clinics Conduct Them?, 67 Fordham L. Rev. 1879, 1884, 1892-1893 (1999) (describing a Maricopa County, Arizona, program); Genie Miller Gillespie, Volunteer Opportunity: Provide Assistance for Pro Se Litigants in Domestic Relations Division, CBA (Chicago Bar Association) Record 43 (Jan. 2001) (describing Cook County program).

[19]. Pearson, supra note [16], at 627.

[20]. McCulloch, supra note [16], at 504.

According to her principal, Bobby Allen, Littlejohn was an "excellent" teacher. She had good evaluations for the two years she taught. . . .

Under Kentucky law, non-tenured teachers are automatically rehired for the following school year unless they receive written notice to the contrary by April 30. The Calloway County School System could not definitely determine its hiring needs for the next school year by April 30. Therefore, in order to avoid automatic renewal, each April the Calloway County school system would notify the non-tenured teachers that their contracts would not be renewed. During the summer, the superintendent would recommend the appropriate number of non-tenured teachers for rehire.

In April 1982, Littlejohn and other non-tenured teachers received written notice that their contracts would not be renewed for the 1982-83 school year. Subsequently, Littlejohn and her husband of nine years separated, and were eventually divorced in July 1982.

During the summer of 1982, defendant Jack Rose, Superintendent of the Calloway County Schools, began making recommendations for the reemployment of the non-tenured teachers for the 1982-83 school year. Despite Principal Allen's decision to strongly recommend Littlejohn for rehire, Rose determined not to do so. . . .

Appellant contended that the failure of the superintendent to recommend the renewal of her teaching contract was based upon the status of her marital relationship, specifically, her impending divorce, in violation of her constitutional rights of privacy and liberty. The suit, based on 42 U.S.C. §1983, sought reinstatement, back pay, and other damages and relief. [The district court directed a verdict in favor of defendants; plaintiff appealed.]

The fundamental right violated here is Ms. Littlejohn's right to privacy regarding her marital status. After analyzing Supreme Court rulings, the district court concluded that the right to privacy is only recognized when certain fundamental rights such as liberty or property rights are also affected. The district court is incorrect. [Roe v. Wade] clearly established the existence of a constitutionally protected right to privacy which includes matters relating to procreation and marriage. . . .

By focusing on whether Littlejohn had any right to employment, the district court missed the key inquiry of this case: Whether the school board or Superintendent Rose could, without sufficient justification, deny public employment because of involvement in constitutionally protected activity. . . . The Supreme Court has generally rejected the theory that a government benefit, such as public employment, to which employees have no contractual right, may be denied for any reason. Keyishian v. Board of Regents, 385 U.S. 589, 605 (1967). . . .

In the case at bar, allowing the board to refuse to renew a teaching contract because a teacher is undergoing divorce could possibly subject untenured teachers to painful consequences from the state board due to their marriage decisions. It is clear from the Supreme Court's analysis in [Perry v. Sindermann, 408 U.S. 593, 597 (1972)] that a person's involvement in activity shielded by the constitutionally protected rights of privacy and liberty constitutes an impermissible reason for denying employment. . . .

In the instant case it is clear that the district court's grant of a directed verdict was incorrect. Viewing the record before us, it is clearly possible for a reasonable jury to find in favor of Ms. Littlejohn. The testimony below includes statements by appellant's superiors adequate to support the theory that her divorce was the motivating factor in the superintendent's refusal to recommend her for rehire. In direct testimony, Ms. Littlejohn's principal stated his positive opinion of her skills, then went on to detail a conversation with Superintendent Rose regarding appellant's reappointment:

*Q.* During the summer of 1982, did you have an occasion to have a conference with Superintendent Jack Rose concerning the employment of various teachers, including Linda Littlejohn?

*A.* Yes, I did. . . .

*Q.* Was it your desire and did you make any type of recommendation concerning Linda Littlejohn for her following year's employment?

*A.* Yes, I did. I recommended her back.

*Q.* All right. And did you have any conversation with Doctor Rose about that recommendation?

*A.* Yes. As I recall, Doctor Rose mentioned to me that he had gotten some phone calls, something about some lady in the community had called that was concerned about the divorcees. And we did have a couple or three divorcees in the East school. I don't think that's that uncommon, but we did have. And she expressed some concern about it, as well.

*Q.* All right. And what was his comment to you about the divorce?

*A.* Well, as nearly as I can recall now — this has been two years ago, but as near as I can recall, I asked him what the reason was for Linda's not being recommended back, and he stated to me that it was the divorce and the rumors of, you know, that was being circulated about the divorce, or whatever, or the phone call, I suppose, and the image that it would present in the community with the Eastwood Christian School being located in our community and we had some students from all three schools that had filtered over into the Eastwood Christian School. And that was of some concern to Dr. Rose, I think.

*Q.* All right. If you would, retrace for the jury so they can clearly understand how that conversation came about.

*A.* Well, we were talking about filling the position, and he just informed me — and it kind of caught me as a surprise — that he wasn't going to recommend Linda back. And I just said, "Well, why not?" And he stated to me then, "Because of the divorce, the phone call, and the image that we would present in the community." . . .

In our view, Mr. Allen's testimony was sufficient to create an issue of fact for the jury. . . . Accordingly, we reverse the district court's grant of a directed verdict and remand the case for a new trial not inconsistent with the reasoning herein. . . .

## Notes and Questions

1. What fundamental right did the defendants violate? Are precedents based on marriage, procreation, or contraception relevant here?

2. What attitudes does Superintendant Rose's decision reveal about divorce and divorced persons? Considerable stigma attached to divorce in previous eras, as one commentator illustrates:

> [Divorce studies] shared a common theme, perhaps best stated by psychiatrist Edmund Bergler:
>
>> Divorce is a *neurotic* procedure of neurotic people. In the great majority of cases divorce is not a chance occurrence but unconsciously self-provoked, even if only by the choice of a neurotic partner. . . . There is less chance in the choice of marriage partners than is generally assumed. Two neurotics unconsciously seek and find each other. . . .
>
> Augmenting these clinical diagnoses were the data generated by empirical studies on the relationships between mental illness and divorce. Loeb and Price and Blumenthal reported that divorced and separated parents had more emotional disturbances than the nondivorced. Although such studies were not conclusive or unchallenged, the affiliation between psychopathology and divorce was not to be broken. . . .
> In many respects it was this prognosis that brought divorce therapy into the arena of marriage counseling. Ostensibly the purpose behind clinical treatment was not chiefly to effect reconciliation but rather to help the divorced or the would-be divorced "to understand the causes of failure, to grow and to mature . . . , and to become potentially better candidates for some marriage in the future." . . .

Lynne Halem, Divorce Reform: Changing Legal and Social Perspectives 181-183 (1980).

3. Would the superintendent have reached the same conclusion had Littlejohn been male? For research reviews on gender differences at divorce, see Women and Divorce/Men and Divorce: Gender Differences in Separation, Divorce and Remarriage (Sandra S. Volgy ed., 1991). See also Terry Arendell, Gender Bias in Divorce, in Mothers and Divorce: Legal, Economic, and Social Dilemmas 150-151, 155-156 (1986).

### 3. Access to Alternatives to Divorce

To what extent do religious considerations compel the state to provide access to alternatives to dissolution?

■ **AFLALO v. AFLALO**
*685 A.2d 523 (N.J. Super. Ct. Ch. Div. 1996)*

FISHER, J.S.C. . . .

This case requires the court to visit an issue that has previously troubled our courts in matrimonial actions involving Orthodox Jews — a husband's refusal to provide a "get."[1] [T]he parties were married on October 13, 1983 in Ramle, Israel, and have one child, Samantha. Plaintiff Sondra Faye Aflalo has filed a complaint seeking a dissolution of the marriage. . . . Henry does not want a divorce and has taken action with The Union of Orthodox Rabbis of the United States and Canada in New York City (the "Beth Din"[2]) to have a hearing on his attempts at reconciliation. [Sondra did not appear in response to the summons forwarded to her by the Beth Din.]

[At a settlement conference before trial, Henry asserted his refusal to provide Sondra with a "get."] Unlike what the court faced in Segal v. Segal, 278 N.J. Super. 218, 650 A.2d 996 (App. Div. 1994) and Burns v. Burns, 223 N.J. Super. 219, 538 A.2d 438 (Ch. Div. 1987), Henry was not using his refusal to consent to the "get" as a means of securing a more favorable resolution of the issues before this court. That type of conduct the *Burns* court rightfully labelled "extortion." On the contrary, Henry's position (as conveyed during the settlement conference) was that regardless of what occurs in this court he will not consent to a Jewish divorce.

Henry's position spun off an unexpected problem; it caused his attorney to move to be relieved as counsel. Arguing that since he, too, is a practicing Orthodox Jew, Henry's counsel claims that he would "definitely have a religious problem representing a man who at the conclusion of a divorce proceeding refused, without reason, to give his wife a Get." [His counsel] indicated, upon questioning from the court, that his religious quandary comes not from Henry's use of his consent to a Jewish divorce as leverage in negotiations (which was not occurring), but in the blanket refusal of his client to give a "get" without reason.

---

1. A "get" is a bill of divorce which the husband gives to his wife to free her to marry again. The word "get" apparently signifies the number 12, the "get" being a twelve-lined instrument. The word is a combination of "gimel" (which has a value of three) together with "tet" (which has a value of nine).

2. The "Beth Din" is a rabbinical tribunal having authority to advise and pass upon matters of traditional Jewish law.

Henry opposed his attorney's motion. . . . Henry stated under oath that while he desires a reconciliation he would follow the recommendations of the Beth Din [that is, should reconciliation fail] and give the "get" if that was the end result of those proceedings. The court finds Henry both credible and sincere in this regard; his position clearly eliminates his counsel's stated concerns. . . .

Sondra claims that this court, as part of the judgment of divorce which may eventually be entered in this matter, may and should order Henry to cooperate with the obtaining of a Jewish divorce upon pain of Henry having limited or supervised visitation of Samantha or by any other coercive means. She claims that Minkin v. Minkin, 180 N.J. Super. 260, 434 A.2d 665 (Ch. Div. 1981) authorizes this court to order Henry to consent to the Jewish divorce. . . .

[T]he Free Exercise Clause prohibits governmental regulation of religious beliefs but does not absolutely prohibit religious conduct. Second, to pass constitutional muster, a law must have both a secular purpose and a secular effect. That is, a law must not have a sectarian purpose; it must not be based upon a disagreement with a religious tenet or practice and must not be aimed at impeding religion. Only when state action passes these threshold tests is there a need to balance the competing state and religious interests. . . . Here, the relief Sondra seeks from this court so obviously runs afoul of the threshold tests of the Free Exercise Clause that the court need never reach the delicate balancing normally required in such cases.

The court will first endeavor to describe precisely what it is that Sondra seeks. . . .

"When a man takes a wife and possesses her, if she fails to please him because he finds something obnoxious about her, then he writes her a bill of divorcement, hands it to her, and sends her away from his house." Deuteronomy 24:1-4. From this biblical verse, the Jewish law and tradition that the "power of divorce rests exclusively with the husband" has its genesis. . . . Without such a divorce, the wife remains an "agunah" (a "tied" woman) and may not remarry in the eyes of Jewish law. If she remarries without a "get" she is considered to be an adulteress because she is still halakhically married to her first husband; any subsequent children are considered to be "mamzerim" (illegitimate) and may not marry other Jews.

The court is not unsympathetic to Sondra's desire to have Henry's cooperation in the obtaining of a "get." She, too, is sincere in her religious beliefs. Her religion, at least in terms of divorce, does not profess gender equality. But does that mean that she can obtain the aid of this court of equity to alter this doctrine of her faith? That the question must be answered negatively seems so patently clear that the only surprising aspect of Sondra's argument is that it finds some support in the few cases on the subject.

In *Minkin,* the trial court requested the testimony of several distinguished rabbis. The court viewed the issue as whether a state court could order specific performance of the "ketubah." The "ketubah" is the marriage contract in which the couple is obligated to comply with the laws of Moses and Israel. [It also contains the parties' agreement to recognize the authority of the Beth Din.] In determining that it could specifically enforce the "ketubah," *Minkin* relied on a New York decision [that specific performance would not compel the husband to practice any religion but would merely require him to do what he voluntarily agreed to do]. Analyzing the case against the test used to determine whether state action violates the Establishment Clause . . . , the *Minkin* court said:

> Relying upon credible expert testimony that the acquisition of a get is not a religious act, the court finds that the entry of an order compelling defendant to secure a get would have the clear secular purpose of completing a dissolution of the marriage. Its primary effect neither advances nor inhibits religion since it does not require the husband to participate in a religious ceremony or to do acts contrary to his religious beliefs. Nor would the order be an excessive entanglement with religion.

[180 N.J. Super. at 266, 434 A.2d 665.]

Also, in reliance upon the expert testimony found credible, the *Minkin* court concluded that an order compelling a husband to acquire a "get" is "not a religious act." The court apparently relied on one of the rabbis who testified "that Jewish law cannot be equated with religious law, but instead is comprised of two components — one regulating a man's relationship with God and the other regulating the relationship between man and man. The get, which has no reference to God but which does affect the relationship between two parties, falls into the latter category and is, therefore, civil and not religious in nature." 180 N.J. Super. at 265-266, 434 A.2d 665.

*Minkin*'s approach that the "ketubah" may be specifically enforced without violating the First Amendment is in accord with the decisional law of New York, [Avitzur v. Avitzur, 446 N.E.2d 136 (N.Y. 1983)]; Illinois, [In re Marriage of Goldman, 554 N.E.2d 1016 (Ill. App. Ct. 1990)] and Delaware, Scholl v. Scholl, 621 A.2d 808, 810-812 (Del. Fam. Ct. 1992), and at odds with Arizona, Victor v. Victor, 177 Ariz. 231, 866 P.2d 899, 901-902 (App. 1993) and, now, this court. *Minkin* and its followers (including the New Jersey trial court in *Burns*) are not persuasive for a number of reasons.

First, [*Minkin*] examined the problem against the backdrop of the Establishment Clause and not the Free Exercise Clause. The Establishment Clause prohibits government from placing its support behind a particular religious belief. The Free Exercise Clause, obviously implicated here, prohibits government from interfering or becoming entangled in the practice of religion by its citizens.

Second, the conclusion that an order requiring the husband to provide a "get" is not a religious act nor involves the court in the religious beliefs or practices of the parties is not at all convincing. It is interesting that the court was required to choose between the conflicting testimony of the various rabbis to reach this conclusion. The one way in which a court may become entangled in religious affairs, which the court in *Minkin* did not recognize, was in becoming an arbiter of what is "religious." . . .

Third, the conclusion that its order concerned purely civil issues is equally unconvincing. . . . No matter how one semantically phrases what was done in *Minkin,* the order directly affected the religious beliefs of the parties. By entering the order, the court empowered the wife to remarry in accordance with her religious beliefs and also similarly empowered any children later born to her. . . . Nor is it sound to argue that religion involves only one's relation to the creator and not one's relation to other persons, as may be obligated by religious traditions or teachings. . . . *Minkin* draws too fine a line in its rejection of the latter as an area constituting "religion" to command this court's assent to its holding.

Fourth, *Minkin* fails to recognize that coercing the husband to provide the "get" would not have the effect sought. The "get" must be phrased and formulated in strict compliance with tradition, according to the wording given in the Talmud. The precisely worded "get" states that the husband does "willingly consent, being under no restraint, to release, to set free, and put aside thee, my wife." . . . What value then is a "get" when it is ordered by a civil court and when it places the husband at risk of being held in contempt should he follow his conscience and refuse to comply? . . .

*Minkin* ultimately conjures the unsettling vision of future enforcement proceedings. Should a civil court fine a husband for every day he does not comply or imprison him for contempt for following his conscience? [S]hould visitation of Samantha be limited pending Henry's cooperation? . . . Should this court enjoin Henry — no matter how imperfect he may be pursuing it [an apparent reference to the fact that Henry has not paid the Beth Din fees] — from moving for reconciliation in that forum and order other relief which the Beth Din apparently cannot give? . . . The spectre of Henry being imprisoned or surrendering his religious freedoms because of action by a civil court is the very image which gave rise to the First Amendment.

It may seem "unfair" that Henry may ultimately refuse to provide a "get." But the unfairness comes from Sondra's own sincerely-held religious beliefs. When she entered into the "ketubah" she agreed to be obligated to the laws of Moses and Israel. Those laws apparently include the tenet that if Henry does not provide her with a "get" she must remain an "agunah." That was Sondra's choice and one which can hardly be remedied by this court. . . .

The First Amendment was designed to protect [against] unwarranted, unwanted and unlawful steps over the "wall of separation between Church and State." This court will not assist Sondra in her attempts to lower that wall. . . .

## Notes and Questions

1. Commentators have estimated that 15,000 Orthodox Jewish women in New York alone are civilly divorced but unable to obtain a "get." Heather Lynn Capell, Comment, After the Glass Has Shattered: A Comparative Analysis of Orthodox Jewish Divorce in the United States and Israel, 33 Tex. Int'l L.J. 331, 337 (1998). The religious doctrine governing the "get" applies to Orthodox and Conservative, but not Reform, Jews.

2. Many husbands use the threat of denying a "get" to extract concessions during divorce. See, e.g., Perl v. Perl, 512 N.Y.S.2d 372, 374 (App. Div. 1987) (husband wanted all jointly owned securities, $65,000, deed to marital home, title to wife's car, and her personal jewelry). Mr. Aflalo has not paid the Beth Din fees (in conjunction with his request for reconciliation) and also is in arrears on his child support obligation. Is it so clear that his motives are "pure"? Should a husband's motives affect the outcome?

3. Is the ketubah a valid prenuptial agreement that is enforceable pursuant to contract law or part of a religious marriage ceremony, outside the purview of secular law? Are the court's views in *Aflalo* or *Minkin* more persuasive? See Michelle Greenberg-Kobrin, Civil Enforceability of Religious Prenuptial Agreements, 32 Colum. J.L. & Soc. Probs. 359, 371 (1999) (arguing that courts should infer a prior contractual commitment on husband's part to give wife a "get" if ketubah is signed prior to religious ceremony).

4. Under traditional Jewish law, only the husband may grant a "get." Some rabbis may apply subtle pressure or the threat of community ostracism to recalcitrant husbands. Under a recent law of the Israeli Parliament (the "Knesset"), such husbands can be refused employment, a driver's license, or banking privileges. Capell, supra, at 334. In the United States, however, the availability of civil divorce has increased a husband's bargaining power, while at the same time reducing rabbinical leverage. Does the state have a legitimate interest in preventing a husband from taking advantage of his wife's religious beliefs or in correcting a disparity in spousal bargaining power? See

Debbie E. Sreter, Nothing to Lose But Their Chains: A Survey of the Aguna Problem in American Law, 28 J. Fam. L. 703, 721 (1989-1990) (so suggesting).

5. Many courts avoid constitutional issues (as *Aflalo* explains) by relying on contract or tort principles. Although most successful cases rely on contract principles, tort remedies are also possible. One commentator suggests the remedy of intentional infliction of emotional distress. Greenberg-Kobrin, supra, at 389. What do you think of her suggestion?

In response to *Avitzur* (the most famous "get" case), New York passed in 1983 a "get" statute (N.Y. Dom. Rel. Law §253 (McKinney 1999)), providing that no final judgment of divorce may be ordered unless the party who commences the proceeding alleges that he or she has taken or will take (prior to entry of judgment) "all steps" within his or her power to "remove any barrier" to the remarriage of defendant. Would the statute help Mrs. Aflalo, the moving party?

Commentators have questioned the constitutionality of the "get" statute on several grounds. Section 253(7) allows the rabbi who performed the marriage to deny that all barriers had been removed, thus unconstitutionally giving a clerical authority the right to block a civil divorce. The constitutional validity of a statute addressing the problems of a single religion is also questionable. See, e.g., Chambers v. Chambers, 471 N.Y.S.2d 958 (Sup. Ct. 1983) (avoiding due process concerns by deciding the case on narrower contract grounds). The constitutional arguments in *Aflalo* regarding possible Establishment Clause violations apply with equal force to New York's "get" statute because a husband may be compelled to participate in what he considers to be a religious practice to obtain a civil divorce.

Despite widespread doubts as to the statute's constitutionality, the New York legislature extended the application of the statute in 1992. The legislature amended the equitable distribution law to permit a judge to consider the effect of any "barrier to remarriage" in postdivorce decisionmaking regarding property distribution and spousal support. N.Y. Dom. Rel. Law §236B(5)(h) (McKinney 1999). Unlike N.Y. Dom. Rel. §253, this statute takes into account the actions of both spouses in regard to removing barriers to remarriage. Is this sound policy?

6. Does judicial refusal to order a "get" violate principles of international human rights law that guarantee equal access to marriage and divorce for men and women? See Erica R. Clinton, Chains of Marriage: Israeli Women's Fight for Freedom, 3 J. Gender, Race & Just. 283 (1999) (so suggesting).

7. Similar legal issues arise regarding contracts in marriage ceremonies in other religions. See, e.g., Aziz v. Aziz, 488 N.Y.S.2d 123 (Sup. Ct. 1985) (marital agreement based on Islamic law).

## F. THE ROLE OF COUNSEL

### 1. Emotional Aspects of Divorce

■ **ANDREW WATSON, THE LAWYER
AND HIS CLIENT: THE PROCESS
OF EMOTIONAL INVOLVEMENT**
*in Psychiatry for Lawyers 1-36 (2d ed. 1978)*

It is often suggested that only trial lawyers or attorneys specializing in Criminal or Domestic Relations Law need know anything of formal psychological theory. Nothing could be further from fact. . . .

Psychoanalytic therapy developed as an offshoot of Sigmund Freud's early exploration of the hypnotic technique. . . . From the time of Freud's collaboration with Breuer in the "Case of Anna," he was aware of the importance of the relationship of patient and doctor as a therapeutic tool as well as hazard. . . . Freud, in his 1910 lecture at Clark University, said, "In every psycho-analytic treatment of a neurotic patient the strange phenomenon that is known as 'transference' makes its appearance. The patient, that is to say, directs towards the physician a degree of affectionate feeling (mingled, often enough, with hostility) which is based on no real relation between them and which — as is shown by every detail of its emergence — can only be traced back to old wishful fantasies of the patient's." From these early beginnings, stems the present concept of transference. . . .

Whenever one makes an acquaintance, there is an immediate flood of perceptions about the newly encountered person. This includes such things as physical characteristics, interests, estimates of various personality traits, and other impressions about his nature. These new, mainly unconscious impressions are associated with many past personal encounters, especially with members of one's immediate family. There is a powerful unconscious tendency to generalize the nature of the new acquaintance so that instead of perceiving a face which is reminiscent of father's face, or a manner of speech which is like brother's, there is the feeling that this new person is *like* father or *like* brother. In other words, from the similarity of a part, the new person is given the whole characteristic of the past figure. Thus, at best, part of the reaction to the new person is inappropriate. While this distortion may be helpful in establishing a close relationship with great rapidity, it can just as likely cause coolness and withdrawal, depending on the nature of the past relationships from which the transference is made. At any rate, the reaction is *not* based on a realistic appraisal of the nature of the new person, and the way is laid open for future problems which can be formidable and difficult to untangle. We must regard this kind of projection as universal and hold it responsible for at least some difficulty in all interpersonal relationships. . . .

The concept of *countertransference* was somewhat later to be discovered, formulated, and understood. . . . Originally, countertransference was defined as the doctor's transference to the patient. In other words, those irrational projections which the patient's character precipitated in the doctor were called countertransference. However, [the term now includes] all of the doctor's reactions and feelings toward his patient and toward all his work with that patient. . . . Transference and countertransference are the two halves in a circle of dynamic interaction between the personalities of the two individuals in the relationship. . . . It is important for professional persons engaged in close personal relationships with clients or patients to understand the nature of this dynamic interaction. . . .

[L]et us turn to some of the specific places in which lawyers might, through a broader understanding of the interview and counseling process, achieve their professional goals more effectively. . . . The question may well be raised as to whether or not it is appropriate or even legitimate for lawyers to embark on the treacherous ground of counseling. However, this is a purely academic question since, for better or for worse, the very nature of a lawyer's activities forces him into this role. . . . For example, a man might arrive in his lawyer's office in a state of marked agitation, demanding that counsel take action to help him gain custody of his three children who "are being ruined by their mother," his former wife. He pours forth his anguished tale about how his oldest son, a boy of superior intelligence with a keen interest in science, is being "allowed to go through school with just passing grades. In addition he spends most of his time sitting around with his friends listening to that deafening rock music crap. She always did want to indulge him and she couldn't care less about whether or not he makes it in this world where a man has to know how to put his best foot forward. She has always acted like success just falls into a person's lap and all you have to do is wait and pick it up." . . .

The traditional response to this kind of request would be for the lawyer to figure out how to make a case for removing the children from the mother, thus satisfying the client's desire to gain custody. Unfortunately, such a course would overlook significant "facts" in the case. [I]t takes counseling skill for a lawyer to help his client bring [the client's] motives into conscious awareness. Counsel must be able to help the father openly evaluate the negative effects of litigation on the children and their parental relationships, as well as the "gains" he is seeking. In place of litigation, alternative routes of problem solving between the parents have to be found and facilitated. All too often counsel's knee-jerk response in matters like this is to reach for the weapon of litigation, a sure route to overkill with no real problem-solving effect. . . .

Let us consider the specific ways in which clients' conscious and unconscious attitudes toward lawyers may impinge upon the professional relationship. First of all, when a client seeks help from a lawyer, he is generally ignorant of the technical aspects of law. His ordinary techniques for judging persons or situations must be suspended, for he has no way of adequately testing the competency of the lawyer he chooses. He may make inquiries about him, and he may be able to investigate past successes and failures; but, generally, he is unable to make any realistic appraisal of skill and trustworthiness. Of necessity, then, he must place himself under the authority and assistance of the lawyer, essentially in blind trust. By virtue of this fact, all the client's previous attitudes toward authority and dependency will be stirred up, usually eliciting a certain amount of irrational fear and concern. He will feel impotent to broach these fears and will conceive of the relationship to his attorney as one of helplessness although, in reality, he is free to procure a new lawyer any time he wishes.

With such an attitude, the client may harbor certain magical expectations, for instance, that the lawyer is able to accomplish any manipulation or transaction that the client desires. Failure to demonstrate such omnipotence generally provokes anger which, since it is irrational and generally unconscious, may only be expressed in distorted ways. A lawyer can deal with this source of trouble more easily by knowing in advance that he is going to be assigned this authority role. . . .

In most law schools there is little opportunity for students to deal directly and consciously with these problems. . . . The law practitioner who takes the time to help his clients disentangle primarily psychological problems is performing as valuable a service as giving legal advice. . . .

■  **KENNETH KRESSEL ET AL.,**
   **PROFESSIONAL INTERVENTION IN**
   **DIVORCE: THE VIEWS OF LAWYERS,**
   **PSYCHOTHERAPISTS, AND CLERGY**
   *in Divorce and Separation 246, 250-255 (George Levinger &*
   *Oliver C. Moles eds., 1979)*

Much more frequently than either therapists or clergy, [divorce lawyers in our sample] mentioned sources of stress inherent in the nature of their work. . . . Let us set forth the major sources of role strain reflected in the lawyer interviews.

*The adversary nature of the legal proceedings.* Despite many changes in recent years, divorce remains largely an adversary process in the eyes of the law. [T]he law's formal bias, the availability of legal threats and counter-threats, as well as the emotional agitation of clients, may push even the most cooperative of lawyers toward serious escalation of conflict. (No-fault divorce has not removed the problem; couples still file bitter suits and countersuits over who shall have custody, how much child support shall be paid, etc.)

*The one-sidedness of the lawyer's view.* The lawyer's objective appraisal of the marital situation is greatly limited by the professional injunction that lawyers deal with only one of the spouses. Our respondents referred frequently to the difficulty of ascertaining the true state of affairs from the perspective provided by their own clients. Hearing only one side, the lawyer is more easily led to overidentify with the client's point of view — and the client may have strong motives, conscious or unconscious, for wishing to use the adversary system as a vehicle for retribution.

*The shortage of material resources.* Since two households cannot be supported as cheaply as one, it is highly unlikely that both parties to a divorce will be happy with the terms of the economic settlement. The attorney, therefore, is often in the position of being the bearer of bad news. . . .

*The economics of the law office.* "There are some lawyers who want to litigate, litigate. They get better fees that way — the taxicab with the meter running." How widespread this phenomenon is nobody knows. It represents nonetheless a serious potential conflict of interest between lawyer and client.

Another potential source of conflict stems from the fact that it is generally the husband who pays the wife's legal costs. The lawyer who represents the wife, therefore, is in the anomalous position of having his fee paid by the opposing side. Unconscious pressures may thus be created for a less than totally effective representation of the wife's interests. The wife herself may have doubts about the degree of allegiance which she can expect from the arrangement.

*The non-legal nature of many of the issues.* In major areas of their activity, lawyers are operating largely outside the domain of law or legal training. Relatively few of the issues that arise are strictly "issues of law." Moreover, even many legal and financial issues engage psychological judgment and expertise, or personal values (e.g., custody or visitation arrangements that would best meet the emotional needs of both children and parents). Unfortunately, the training of lawyers poorly equips them to understand or handle the psychological and interpersonal issues in divorce, even though such issues may be crucial for creating equitable and workable agreements.

*The difficulties in the lawyer-lawyer relationship.* Almost universally the lawyers noted that a crucial determinant of divorce outcomes is the relationship between the two opposing attorneys. Indeed, for some respondents a constructive divorce was defined as one in which the two attorneys "come to operate within each other's framework." . . .

[The authors identify six roles that lawyers adopt in response to the problems of divorce practice.]

1. *The Undertaker.* This metaphor (supplied, incidentally, by one of our respondents) rests on two assumptions: that the job is essentially

thankless and messy; and that the clients are in a state of emotional "derangement." This stance is also characterized by a general cynicism about human nature and the doubt that good or constructive divorces are ever possible. . . .

2. *The Mechanic.* This is a pragmatic, technically oriented stance. It assumes that clients are basically capable of knowing what they want. The lawyer's task primarily involves ascertaining the legal feasibility of doing what the client wants. . . . A good outcome lies in producing "results" for the client, "results" usually understood in financial terms. . . .

3. *The Mediator.* This stance is oriented toward negotiated compromise and rational problem solving, with an emphasis on cooperation with the other side and, in particular, the other attorney. . . . Unlike the Undertaker and Mechanic, but like the following three stances, the Mediator tends to downplay the adversary aspect of his role. [A] good outcome is a "fair" negotiated settlement that both parties can "live with" (a frequently used phrase). . . .

4. *The Social Worker.* This stance centers around a concern for the client's post-divorce adjustment and overall social welfare. Regarding women clients in particular, there may be an emphasis on the client's "marketability."

> The main thing is to fully explore her ability to contribute to her own support. I have had agreements where I have been able to get money for college or a business course — or, in one case, a course in cooking.

Even though the attorney represents only one of the parties, there may also be a tendency to consider the interests of the entire family [such as the children]. This stance is also frequently associated with the view that, contrary to many clients' expectations, divorce is not usually an easy solution to marital unhappiness. The involvement of therapists or clergy is welcome. [A] "good" outcome is perceived to be one in which the client achieves social reintegration.

5. *The Therapist.* This stance involves active acceptance of the fact that the client is in a state of emotional turmoil. There is a concomitant assumption that the legal aspects of a divorce situation can be adequately dealt with only if the emotional aspects are engaged by the lawyer. Correspondingly, there is an orientation toward trying to understand the client's motivations. . . . A "good" outcome is conceptualized more or less as it would be in a therapeutically oriented crisis-intervention situation: personal reintegration of the client after a trying, stressful period. Predictably enough, this is also a stance that welcomes involvement of psychotherapists and in which clients may be encouraged to seek such assistance.

6. *The Moral Agent.* In this final stance there is a more or less explicit rejection of neutrality; it is assumed that the lawyer should not hesitate

to use his or her sense of "right" and "wrong." This stance appears to be particularly salient when the divorcing couple has children, with the lawyer attempting to serve as a kind of guardian and protector of the children's interests. . . . A constructive outcome is one in which the lawyer's sense of "what is right" is satisfied, not only in relation to the client, but to the other spouse and the children.

We have sought to explain this typology of lawyer stances largely as a product of the role strains characteristic of matrimonial practice. . . .

■ **MOSES v. MOSES**
*1 Fam. L. Rep. (BNA) 2604 ( July 22, 1975),* aff'd, *344 A.2d 912 (Pa. Super. Ct. 1975)*

Cercone, J.

This appeal has been taken by the husband, Dr. Lawrence Moses, from the lower court's award of attorney's fees and expenses to his wife's counsel. . . .

From December 16, 1968 until February 4, 1969, Mrs. Moses consumed many of the hours for which Mr. Fox billed Dr. Moses in personal and telephonic conversations of staggering numbers. Although the content of those conversations is privileged, there are indications in the record that large parts of the discussions are based upon Mr. Fox's friendship with both Dr. and Mrs. Moses, as well as his professional relationship with Mrs. Moses. Her phone calls to Mr. Fox at all hours of the day and night eventually grew so burdensome that they were apparently the principal case of Mr. Fox's withdrawal from the case in favor of Mr. Robinson.

After his withdrawal, Mr. Fox tendered a bill for $4,842 in counsel fees (121 hours and 5 minutes at $40 per hour) and expenses of $112.10. Only fifty-six days elapsed from the time that Mr. Fox began consulting with Mrs. Moses until he withdrew on February 10, 1969, so that he averaged two hours every day, including weekends and holidays, working on Mrs. Moses' problems. The only tangible result of this labor was the support award for Mrs. Fox and the children of $275 weekly. Indeed, to this day the parties are not divorced. . . .

The difficulty in the instant case is that there can be little doubt that Mr. Moses is able to pay, and Mrs. Moses is unable to pay, the fees charged by Mr. Fox. We also do not dispute the finding by the lower court that Mr. Fox actually spent 121 hours on the case, and that $40 per hour is a fair hourly charge for those services. We do challenge, however, the propriety of Mr. Fox investing so much time in this case. We feel that there is an obligation upon counsel, if he expects his fee to be paid by the other spouse, to control excessive demands upon his time, energy and intellect by the dependent spouse. We find that Mr. Fox failed to exercise such control in the instant case. [C]ase law in other jurisdictions . . . supports our view herein. . . .

Finally, our decision is supported by the American Bar Association's Code of Professional Responsibility, Disciplinary Rule 2-106 (1970), which sets forth the factors that counsel should consider in determining the reasonableness of his fee: "(1) The time and labor required, the novelty and difficulty of the questions involved, and the skill requisite to perform the legal service properly. (2) The likelihood, if apparent to the client, that the acceptance of the particular employment will preclude other employment by the lawyer. (3) The fee customarily charged in the locality for similar legal services. (4) The amount involved and the results obtained. (5) The time limitations imposed by the client or by the circumstances. (6) The nature and length of the professional relationship with the client. (7) The experience, reputation, and ability of the lawyer or lawyers performing the services. (8) Whether the fee is fixed or contingent."

We find that the time and labor required, the results obtained, and the nature and length of Mr. Fox's professional relationship with Mrs. Moses, all militate against the allowance of fees and expenses of roughly $5,000 in the instant case. [T]he allowance for attorney's fees and expenses is reduced to $3,000. . . .

## Notes and Questions

1. The *Moses* case reveals the overlap between the divorce attorney's role as advocate and psychological counselor. Given the court's advice, how would you recommend that an attorney "control [such] excessive demands upon his time, energy and intellect"?

2. If the divorce attorney believes that a client should consult a trained therapist, should the attorney so suggest? How can the attorney do so in a nonthreatening manner? Might such a suggestion conceivably backfire? If the client refuses to heed the advice, should the attorney withdraw from the case?

3. Many divorce lawyers provide less emotional support than the attorney in *Moses*. An empirical study of 40 divorce cases in California and Massachusetts (characterizing representation as a conversational tug-of-war) explains that clients seek to include a "broader picture of their lives, experiences, and needs" (especially regarding the failure of their marriage). Divorce lawyers resist these efforts. "[Lawyers] are interested only in those portions of the client's life that have tactical significance for the prospective terms of the divorce settlement or the conduct of the case." Austin Sarat & William L. F. Felstiner, Divorce Lawyers and Their Clients: Power and Meaning in the Legal Process 144 (1995). Thus, the lawyers "did not act as 'counselors for the situation' nor did they try to provide

psychological, emotional, or moral support or guidance for their clients." In fact, lawyers tend to emphasize communicating their legal knowledge in order to move clients toward positions that the lawyers deem reasonable and realistic. Id. at 145.

These findings accord with those of a small-scale empirical study by sociologist Terry Arendell. Arendell reports that 53 (of 60) women had strong complaints about their lawyers. Many complaints focused on the different perceptions of the lawyers' role.

> Most of the women said their attorneys had showed little interest in their present or future problems and had not tried to keep them informed about divorce legalities and the overall legal process. Although they had been sought out as counselors in a personal life crisis, these lawyers soon appeared to be bureaucratic technicians, more concerned with forms, figures, and procedures than with a client's history, fears, or future well-being. . . .
>
> Oversights by attorneys provoked a great deal of anger and frustration. Failure to return phone calls, the most frequent complaint, eroded the attorney-client relationship and increased the woman's sense of stress. . . .

Terry Arendell, Mothers and Divorce: Legal, Economic, and Social Dilemmas 10-11 (1986).[21]

4. The emotionally charged divorce context can present danger for attorneys and judges when clients occasionally discharge their frustration by resorting to violence against legal professionals. Some psychologists and divorce lawyers believe that the rash of violence is prompted by the movement to no fault, which makes litigants more angry and anxious to lash out at the legal system. Joan M. Cheever & Joanne Naiman, The Deadly Practice of Divorce, Natl. L.J., Oct. 12, 1992, at 1. See also Henry J. Reske, Domestic Relations, Escalating Violence in the Family Courts, A.B.A. J., July 1993, at 48.

## 2. Conflicts of Interest

### ■ FLORIDA BAR v. DUNAGAN
#### 731 So. 2d 1237 (Fla. 1999)

PER CURIAM.

. . . After a formal hearing in this matter, the referee found the following facts. In July 1992, [Attorney] Dunagan prepared a bill of sale

---

[21]. Of the seven women in Arendell's study who had no complaints, three prepared and filed their own divorce papers, three negotiated a spousal agreement before retaining an attorney, and the remaining woman was a law student! Arendell, at 13.

purporting to transfer certain assets of a restaurant business, "Biscuits 'N' Gravy 'N' More" ("B & G"), to the joint ownership of William and Paula Leucht. Dunagan also prepared the fictitious name filing for this business but, according to a letter sent by him to the Leuchts, inadvertently omitted Paula Leucht's name on the registration form.

Subsequently, a commercial lease dispute arose between B & G and Bay-Walsh Properties (Florida) Inc., d/b/a/ Nova Village Market Partnership ("Bay-Walsh"). The suit filed by Bay-Walsh named B & G, William Leucht, and Paula Leucht as defendants. Dunagan represented B & G and the Leuchts in this action and specifically moved to dismiss Paula Leucht as an improper party to the suit.

Later in 1994, Dunagan was involved in negotiations between the Leuchts and a third party to open another B & G restaurant in Daytona Beach and, in 1994 and 1995, also represented B & G and the Leuchts in an eminent domain suit against the Florida Department of Transportation.

On or about February 23, 1996, Dunagan sent a letter to the Port Orange Police Department and city attorney in which he stated that he represented William Leucht, that William Leucht was the sole owner of B & G, and that although there was a bill of sale which was "considered to put the business in the name of William and Paula Leucht," this "instrument and the legal consequences thereof were duly considered, and it was determined with deliberation that William Leucht would remain the sole owner." The letters further advised that Mr. Leucht intended to fire two employees, after which they would no longer be welcome on the premises of the restaurant, and that if they entered the premises, they would be ejected. The letters purported to notify the police "in order to prevent a breach of the peace from occurring."

Several days after sending these letters, Dunagan filed a petition for dissolution of marriage on behalf of William Leucht against Paula Leucht. A few days later, Paula Leucht called B & G restaurant and was told by an employee that William Leucht was the sole owner and she could not come to the restaurant. Ms. Leucht went to the restaurant anyway and was arrested for disorderly conduct and forcibly removed from the premises. Prior to, during, and after her arrest, Ms. Leucht informed the police that she co-owned the restaurant.

Finally, on May 2, 1996, the judge in the divorce proceeding ordered that William and Paula Leucht were to share equally in the net proceeds from both B & G restaurants, and on October 31, 1996, Dunagan filed a motion to withdraw from representation of William Leucht in the divorce proceeding after Paula Leucht hired an attorney to file a malpractice lawsuit against him. [Dunagan seeks review of the referee's findings and recommendation.]

## I. CONFLICT OF INTEREST

Dunagan first argues that the referee erred in finding that his representation of William Leucht in the divorce proceeding after having jointly represented William and Paula Leucht in matters relating to their business presented a conflict of interest. Dunagan argues that the business matters in which he represented the Leuchts were completely unrelated to the dissolution of marriage and that ownership of the business was not a central issue in the divorce; therefore, he reasons, there was no conflict of interest. This argument is without merit.

Rule 4-1.9(a) of the Rules Regulating The Florida Bar prohibits a lawyer who has formerly represented a client from representing another person "in the same or a substantially related matter" where that person's interests are materially adverse to the former client's interests. Whether two legal matters are substantially related depends upon the specific facts of each particular situation or transaction. Further, the comment to rule 4-1.9 states that "[w]hen a lawyer has been directly involved in a specific transaction, subsequent representation of other clients with materially adverse interests clearly is prohibited.". . .

[H]ere Dunagan represented William and Paula Leucht in the formation of their business and, specifically, prepared a bill of sale transferring assets of the business to their joint ownership. Because the business was begun during the marriage, it was a marital asset and as such was inherently an issue in the divorce. Additionally, the petition for dissolution of marriage filed by Dunagan on William Leucht's behalf specifically raised the issue of the ownership of the business and impliedly disputed the validity of the bill of sale prepared by Dunagan in that it alleged that William Leucht "is the sole owner of the restaurant known as 'Biscuits 'N' Gravy 'N' More'." While ownership of the business may not have been a hotly contested issue, it was still an issue involved in the divorce; therefore, at least one prior matter in which Dunagan jointly represented the Leuchts was substantially related to the divorce. Therefore, we find that Dunagan's representation of William Leucht in the divorce proceeding against Paula Leucht constituted a conflict of interest and approve the referee's finding in this regard.

## II. CONSENT

Dunagan next argues that the referee erred in finding that Paula Leucht did not consent to Dunagan's representation of William Leucht in the dissolution of marriage action. Under certain circumstances, a lawyer may be permitted to represent a client despite a conflict of interest, but only if he or she obtains the consent of the appropriate party or parties after consultation. *See* R. Regulating Fla. Bar 4-1.7(a)-(b); 4-1.9(a). Here, the referee found that "no disclosure of the conflict or waiver of same took place, given the uncontested fact that no testimony was provided that the respondent ever consulted with Paula Leucht as to the circumstances which led him to represent William Leucht in the divorce, and to what her position was vis-a-vis his representing William Leucht." This finding is supported by the evidence.

Without consulting with or obtaining Paula Leucht's consent, Dunagan filed a petition for dissolution of marriage against her and on behalf of William Leucht. Shortly thereafter, Paula Leucht arrived home from a trip and discovered that the dissolution petition had been filed. Only then, after first calling Mr. Dunagan's office, did Paula Leucht seek and retain another attorney to represent her in the divorce. Only after she had retained an attorney of her own did Dunagan claim he sought her consent through her attorney.

Dunagan testified that he contacted Ms. Leucht's original and subsequent attorneys who gave their consent as attorneys for her. Ms. Leucht's original attorney, Mr. Beck, submitted an affidavit stating that "pursuant to a conference with my client, Paula K. Leucht, it was agreed that there would be no objection raised to the Respondent, Walter B. Dunagan, Esq., representing William Leucht." Paula Leucht acknowledged that she discussed Dunagan's representation of William Leucht with Beck and he advised her that there were better attorneys to be up against; so, she testified, "we never did say anything about him representing me." However, Ms. Leucht also testified that Beck never clearly advised her of her rights or the possible prejudice Dunagan's representation of her ex-husband presented. Accordingly, Ms. Leucht's and her attorney's failure to affirmatively object cannot be construed as "consent after consultation" as required by the rules.

Dunagan makes much of the fact that he could not personally consult with and obtain Ms. Leucht's consent because she was represented by counsel. However, there was no reason that Dunagan could not have consulted with and attempted to obtain Paula Leucht's consent prior to filing the dissolution petition on behalf of William Leucht and, therefore, prior to the time Paula Leucht retained other counsel to represent her in the divorce. This, in fact, would have been the most appropriate course of action. Although the rules do not specifically state that consultation with and consent from the client or former client must be obtained before the attorney may undertake the conflicting representation, clearly they contemplate as much. The rules state that an attorney *shall not represent* conflicting interests unless the client consents. Especially where the conflict exists prior to the beginning of the representation, this can only mean that the necessary consent should be obtained before the attorney agrees to represent the conflicting interest. This was clearly not done in this case. . . .

### III.  VIOLATION OF RULE 4-1.9(b)

Dunagan also argues that the referee erred in concluding that his letters to the Port Orange police and city attorney violated rule 4-1.9(b). As discussed above, those letters stated that Dunagan represented William Leucht, that William Leucht was the sole owner of B & G, and that although there was a bill of sale which was "considered to put the business in the name of William and Paula Leucht," this "instrument and the legal consequences thereof were duly considered, and it was determined with deliberation that William Leucht would remain the sole owner." "[I]n order to prevent a breach of the peace from occurring," the letters further purported to notify the police that William Leucht intended to fire two employees who would then no longer be welcome on the restaurant premises.

Rule 4-1.9(b) prohibits a lawyer from using information relating to the representation of a former client to the former client's disadvantage except as permitted by rule 4-1.6 or when the information has become generally known. Dunagan essentially argues that the information in the letter was not used to Paula Leucht's disadvantage because it only addressed who had the right to sole possession of the premises, and Paula Leucht was arrested for disorderly conduct, not trespassing. Therefore, he argues, the letters did not cause her to be arrested.

However, the evidence supports the referee's finding that the letters contributed, at least to some degree, to Ms. Leucht's being arrested and forcibly removed from the premises of the business. Ms. Leucht testified that on the morning of her arrest, she called the restaurant and was told by an employee that Mr. Leucht had shown papers from Dunagan saying that Mr. Leucht was the sole owner of the restaurant and she was not welcome there. Ms. Leucht then went to the restaurant, where she was told by the police that she had to leave because William Leucht owned the restaurant, and was ultimately arrested. Although she was charged with disorderly conduct, the arrest report filled out by the police officer clearly shows that the police officers relied on the letter from Dunagan. [B]ecause Dunagan clearly used information relating to his representation of Paula Leucht to her disadvantage and such disclosures were not permitted under rule 4-1.6, we approve the referee's conclusion that the letters at issue violated rule 4-1.9(b).

Finally, Dunagan argues that the recommended discipline, a ninety-one-day suspension, is too harsh. . . . We find that the recommended suspension is appropriate. [T]he Court has imposed similar suspensions for similar conduct. . . .

## Notes and Questions

1. The divorce lawyer may face several ethical problems, including conflicts of interest. In *Dunagan,* what was the nature of the conflict of interest? Why does the court reject Dunagan's arguments that no conflict of interest existed? For example, how were the couple's business matters and divorce related? How were Mr. Leucht's interests materially adverse to his ex-wife's interests?

2. Many courts have wrestled with the issue how broadly to interpret the term "conflict of interest" for disciplinary or disqualification purposes. See, e.g., Jones v. Jones, 369 S.E.2d 478 (Ga. 1988) (reversing disqualification of husband's divorce attorney who was married to wife's divorce attorney; actual impropriety must be shown); Burton v. Burton, 527 N.Y.S.2d 53 (App. Div. 1988) (appearance of impropriety based on husband's previous consultation with wife's counsel compels disqualification); Davis v. Stansbury, 824 S.W.2d 278 (Tex. App. 1992) (abuse of discretion in granting husband's motion to disqualify wife's attorney based on attorney's partner's limited representation of husband in same matter in which unprivileged information had been communicated).

3. *Joint representation.* Is joint representation permissible? If so, when? According to current ethical rules (i.e., Model Code of Professional Responsibility and Model Rules of Professional Conduct), joint representation is permitted if the attorney reasonably believes he or she can adequately represent both clients' interests and if both clients consent after full disclosure of the risks of such representation. The American Law Institute's recently adopted Restatement (Third) of the Law Governing Lawyers §128 (2000) reaffirms this rule.

On the other hand, some states condemn the practice of joint representation via disciplinary rules, case law, or state bar opinions (as illustrated below). See Debra Lyn Bassett, Three's a Crowd: A Proposal to Abolish Joint Representation, 32 Rutgers L.J. 387, 426 & n. 173 (2001) (pointing to such opinions in Connecticut, Mississippi, New Hampshire, New Jersey, Oregon, South Carolina, Vermont, West Virginia, and Wisconsin). The American Academy of Matrimonial Lawyers (a voluntary association of lawyers and judges that establishes ethical standards for family law practitioners that exceed those of the ABA and most state ethics codes) also admonishes against joint representation, even if clients consent. Which point of view do you find more persuasive?

4. Did Mrs. Leucht consent to Mr. Dunagan's representation of her ex-husband in the dissolution action? Why did the Florida supreme court hold that her "failure to affirmatively object" could not be construed as consent pursuant to the state bar rules?

■ **ETHICS COMMITTEE, MISSISSIPPI STATE
   BAR OPINION 80**
   *Laws. Man. on Prof. Conduct (ABA/BNA) 801:5104*
   *(Mar. 25, 1983)*

An attorney may not represent both parties in a no-fault divorce. The interests of the parties are conflicting, inconsistent, diverse, and otherwise discordant, no matter what the parties themselves believe. Serving one client's interest may result in not adequately representing the other client's interest. The lawyer's loyalty will be divided. DRs 5-105(A)(C); ECs 5-14, 5-15.

■ **ETHICS COMMITTEE, STATE BAR OF
   MONTANA, OPINION 10**
   *Laws. Man. on Prof. Conduct (ABA/BNA) 801:5401*
   *(Dec. 1980)*

A lawyer may represent both spouses in a joint petition for dissolution as a nonadversary procedure. A lawyer may represent both spouses if it is obvious that he can adequately represent the interest of each after each consents to the representation after full disclosure of the possible effect of such representation on the exercise of his independent professional judgment on behalf of each. DRs 5-104; Canon 5.

■ **ROBERT G. SPECTOR, THE DO'S
   AND DON'TS WHEN ONE LAWYER
   REPRESENTS BOTH PARTIES**
   *Family Advocate, Spring 1991, at 16-18*

Representing both parties in an uncontested divorce has traditionally been viewed as an inherent conflict of interest and has been prohibited. However, the past decade has witnessed considerable disagreement over whether it is permissible for a lawyer to perform the role of the intermediary in a "friendly divorce." Many states still view divorce as a real conflict, despite any appearance of harmony [and prohibit joint representation]. Other states have ethics opinions that allow an attorney to represent both husband and wife, albeit under restrictive circumstances. . . .

The perils into which you advance in this situation are quite clear. If something goes wrong with the agreement that has been drafted, it may be set aside. In such a case, you may be sued for malpractice, particularly if the client believes that you truly represented only one of the parties. If that occurs, the existence of the attorney-client re-lationship may well be a jury question. Or you might be subject to discipline.

Despite all the potential trouble, however, lawyers do take on joint representation and must know how to proceed. In jurisdictions that have adopted the Model Rules of Professional Conduct and that do not otherwise prohibit joint representation, compliance with the strictures of the rule can present problems.

Model Rule 2.2, Intermediary, provides:

> a) A lawyer may act as intermediary between clients if:
>     1) the lawyer consults with each client concerning the implications of the common representation, including the advantages and risks in-volved, and the effects on the attorney-client privilege, and obtains each client's consent to the common representation;
>     2) the lawyer reasonably believes that the matter can be resolved on terms compatible with the clients' best interests, that each client will be able to make adequately informed decisions in the matter, and that there is little risk of material prejudice to the interests of the clients if the contemplated resolution is unsuccessful; and
>     3) the lawyer reasonably believes that the common representation can be undertaken impartially and without improper effect on other responsibilities the lawyer has to any of the clients.
>     b) While acting as intermediary, the lawyer shall consult with each client concerning the decisions to be made and the considerations rele-vant in making them, so that each client can make adequately informed decisions.
>     c) A lawyer shall withdraw as intermediary if any of the clients so re-quests, or if any of the conditions stated in paragraph (a) is no longer satisfied. Upon withdrawal, the lawyer shall not continue to represent any of the clients in the matter that was the subject of intermediation.

The comment to Rule 2.2 specifically notes that this rule does not apply when you are acting as a mediator or arbitrator — roles the clients may not understand precisely. At the initial interview, you should explain the differences between a mediator, an arbitrator, an interme-diary, and an advocate. If one of the clients mistakenly believes that he or she is engaging an advocate, the inevitable result will be an unhappy client and risk for you. . . .

If, in spite of all the warnings, you decide to act as an intermedi-ary, . . . Model Rule 2.2(a)(2), (3) requires that you make three objec-tive determinations: that the matter can be resolved on terms compatible with the clients' best interests with little risk of material prejudice, that the clients are able to make informed decisions, and that the common representation can be undertaken impartially. Once you have made these determinations and have made full disclosure to the clients, you must still obtain each client's consent. Rule 2.2 (a)(1). In essence, Rule 2.2(a)(3) requires that you consider whether advocacy will be needed by one of the parties and whether an independent counsel will be required for each party. To determine if that is the case, consider the following factors:

1) The parties' social and economic relationship — When one party dominates another, it is unlikely that the dominated spouse will be able to make an informed decision in his or her best interest. The dominated party needs an independent advocate, not an intermediary.

2) Each party's emotional condition — Most parties to a divorce are under great stress. If either spouse is emotionally disturbed, it will impair his or her ability to make informed decisions. If you believe that this is the case, you should decline intermediary representation.

3) Each party's understanding of divorce law — The parties cannot arrive at an informal decision that is in their best interests unless they know the law that governs their relationship. . . .

4) The extent of disclosure of assets and liabilities — If there has not been full disclosure, an informed decision is impossible. If the parties balk at disclosure, obviously advocacy and independent counsel are needed.

5) The agreement that has been reached — If the parties have reached a general agreement on the various issues of their divorce, you can help them work out the detailed legal problems. However, be sure that the parties have discussed all the issues. If they have not discussed and agreed on most of the issues (you should have a list), contentious negotiations are likely. If this occurs, the spouses need advocates, not an intermediary.

6) The existence of minor children and substantial assets or debts, and the need for alimony or maintenance — The presence of these factors indicates that the divorce is likely to involve complexities. The more complex the divorce, the less likely it is that the parties have adequately discussed the issues. In some states, in fact, the existence of any of the above factors will prohibit your acting as an intermediary.

7) Your relationship with either party — Rule 2.2(a)(3) requires your independent judgment that you can impartially undertake joint representation without its affecting any other responsibilities to the clients. In practice, this means that if you have a close relationship with one of the parties, either personal or professional, you should decline joint representation. A lawyer who has previously represented one of the spouses may have to be disqualified anyway, on the basis of Rule 1.9, Former Client. Even if disqualification under Rule 1.9 would not be required, a lawyer can hardly be thought of as neutral when he or

she has benefitted from one of the parties as a client or may do so in the future.

## CLIENT CONSENT

Rule 2.2(a)(1) requires that you consult with each client about the implications of common representation and that you get each client's consent to the representation. To obtain consent, follow these guidelines:

1) Get separate consent for each client — Rule 2.2 explicitly requires separate [written] consent from each client. . . .

2) Explain attorney-client privilege in joint representation — Tell clients that the normal attorney-client confidentiality provisions of Rule 1.6 do not apply to jointly represented parties. If you are later forced to withdraw from the case, either party will be able to call you to testify to communications made to you. The comment to Rule 2.2 notes that during common representation, you are still required to keep clients adequately informed and to maintain confidentiality of information. This balance is impossible to maintain. When acting as intermediator, you must maintain full communication with both clients. Rule 2.2(b) requires you to consult with each client concerning the decisions to be made. To ensure that the clients fully understand this point, clearly explain that you will communicate with them only together, never separately.

3) Point out problems of advice — Acknowledge to the clients that an attorney who is not acting as an advocate for either party will not be able to present the best position for either party. This is a point that many clients do not understand. Many of the suits that follow joint representation — either against the lawyer for malpractice or to set aside the agreement — allege that the attorney did not advise the client of the best position to take on certain issues.

4) Explain withdrawal and its problems — Tell the clients that if serious disagreement develops regarding any issue, you will have to withdraw from joint representation. If that occurs, you will not be able to represent either party, and each will have to hire new counsel. It's best to illustrate this with an example — to say, perhaps, that if you discover that one party has not made and does not intend to make full disclosure of assets, you will have to withdraw. . . .

5) Communicate problems of fees — The clients should know that even if you have to withdraw from the case, you will expect to be paid for the time expended. You should also tell them that if you have to withdraw and the clients hire separate counsel, the total fees for the divorce will be higher than if the clients had hired separate counsel at the outset.

6) Explain the benefits of obtaining separate counsel — The difficulties of joint representation are such that some courts have required that you suggest [the possibility and desirability of seeking independent legal advice].

7) Discuss the finality of any agreement — The parties should be informed that any agreement they conclude will likely be as binding as an agreement concluded with independent counsel. Even if a court later decides that the intermediary representation was unwise, the agreement may still be sustained. . . .

## 3. Sexual Ethics

### ■ IN RE TSOUTSOURIS
*748 N.E.2d 856 (Ind. 2001)*

PER CURIAM.

The respondent, James V. Tsoutsouris, engaged in a sexual relationship with his client while he was representing her in a dissolution matter. He claims such a relationship was not improper. Alternatively, he argues that even if it were, it merits only a private reprimand. We disagree. . . .

[A] client hired the respondent [to] represent her in a dissolution action against her second husband [and in a child support action against her first husband]. While the respondent was representing the client in the fall of 1994, the respondent and the client began dating and engaged in consensual sexual relations several times. The respondent did not inform the client how a sexual relationship between them might impact his professional duties to her or otherwise affect their attorney/client relationship.

The respondent ended the sexual relationship a few weeks after it began in 1994. The client hired the respondent for a third legal matter in 1996. In 1997, the client sought psychological treatment. One of the subjects discussed during that treatment was her personal relationship with the respondent three years earlier.

[T]he respondent contends his consensual sexual relationship with his client during his representation of her does not violate the *Rules of Professional Conduct.* He bases that argument on the lack of evidence establishing that his sexual relationship with the client impaired his ability to represent the client effectively. The respondent contends that a sexual relationship between attorney and client in Indiana is professional misconduct only when it affects the quality of the attorney's representation of the client. The respondent also suggests that Indiana law in 1994 was ambiguous with respect to the impropriety of sexual relations between attorney and client. Therefore, he argues a finding of misconduct would be inappropriate because he was unaware of his obligations to avoid sexual contact with his client at the time of such contact.

Rule 1.7(b) prohibits representation of a client if the representation "may be materially limited . . . by the lawyer's own interests." Although

the rule contains general exceptions in instances where the lawyer reasonably believes that the representation will not be adversely affected
and the client consents after consultation, these exceptions will not generally avail when the "lawyer's own interests" at issue are those related
to a lawyer/client sexual relationship. In effect, the respondent argues
that sexual relationships between lawyers and clients ought to be authorized unless there is evidence of impaired representation. We decline to
adopt that position.

Twenty-five years ago this Court suspended a lawyer for sexual misconduct with clients and warned of the professional conflicts such intimate associations create. Matter of Wood, 265 Ind. 616, 358 N.E.2d 128
(1976) (finding a violation of Rule 5-101(A) of the *Code of Professional Responsibility* — the predecessor to Rule 1.7(b) of the Rules of Professional
Conduct). In a subsequent case involving the same attorney accused of
similar misconduct, this Court ruled that the intermeshing of a lawyer's
professional duties with the lawyer's personal sexual interests creates a
situation where "the exercise of professional judgment on behalf of
a client would be affected by personal interests" in violation of Rule
5-101(A). Matter of Wood, 489 N.E.2d 1189, 1190 (Ind. 1986).

Six years after our second *Wood* decision, the American Bar Association issued an ethics opinion on the subject of sexual relationships between attorneys and clients. ABA Formal Ethics Opinion No. 92-364,
*Sexual Relations with Client.* The ABA made it clear that attorneys should
avoid sexual contact with their clients.[3] This position is further bolstered by the recent proposed revisions of the ABA *Model Rules of Professional Conduct* [that] include a proposed new rule explicitly declaring
that "A lawyer shall not have sexual relations with a client unless a consensual sexual relationship existed between them when the client-lawyer
relationship commenced." Proposed Model Rule 1.8(j). The proposed

---

3. While the ABA *Model Rules of Professional Conduct* do not explicitly prohibit a sexual relationship between an attorney and client, we note that such relationships have been
unequivocally discouraged, as noted in ABA Ethics Opinion 92-364:

First, because of the dependence that so often characterizes the attorney-client relationship, there is a significant possibility that the sexual relationship will have resulted from the exploitation of the lawyer's dominant position and influence and,
thus, breached the lawyer's fiduciary obligation to the client. Second, a sexual relationship with a client may affect the independence of the lawyer's judgment. Third,
the lawyer's engaging in a sexual relationship with a client may create a prohibited
conflict between the interests of the lawyer and those of the client. Fourth, a non-
professional, yet emotionally charged, relationship between attorney and client may
result in confidences being imparted in circumstances where the attorney-client
privilege is not available, yet would have been, absent the personal relationship. We
believe the better practice is to avoid all sexual contact with clients during the
representation.

rule is further supported by commentary reflecting important policy considerations.[4] . . .

In Matter of Grimm, 674 N.E.2d 551 (Ind. 1996), this Court found an attorney's "sexual relationship with his client during the pendency of dissolution and post-dissolution matters materially limited his representation of her," thereby violating Prof. Cond. R. 1.7(b). Grimm, 674 N.E.2d at 554. We explained:

> In their professional capacity, lawyers are expected to provide emotionally detached, objective analysis of legal problems and issues for clients who may be embroiled in sensitive or difficult matters. Clients, especially those who are troubled or emotionally fragile, often place a great deal of trust in the lawyer and rely heavily on his or her agreement to provide professional assistance. Unfortunately, the lawyer's position of trust may provide opportunity to manipulate the client for the lawyer's sexual benefit. Where a lawyer permits or encourages a sexual relationship to form with a client, that trust is betrayed and the stage is set for continued unfair exploitation of the lawyer's fiduciary position. Additionally, the lawyer's ability to represent effectively the client may be impaired. Objective detachment, essential for clear and reasoned analysis of issues and independent professional judgment, may be lost.

Id., 674 N.E.2d at 554.

*Grimm* is one of several cases decided under the *Rules of Professional Conduct* in which this Court has held that consensual sexual relationships with clients constitute professional misconduct. In Matter of Hawkins, 695 N.E.2d 109 (Ind. 1998), we found a violation of Rule 1.7(b) and held that, by "having sexual relations with his client, the respondent promoted and served his own interests and thereby threatened material limitation of his representation of her.". . . We hold that the respondent

---

4. Proposed Comment 17 to Rule 1.8 states:

The relationship between lawyer and client is a fiduciary one in which the lawyer occupies the highest position of trust and confidence. The relationship is almost always unequal; thus, a sexual relationship between lawyer and client can involve unfair exploitation of the lawyer's fiduciary role, in violation of the lawyer's basic ethical obligation not to use the trust of the client to the client's disadvantage. In addition, such a relationship presents a significant danger that, because of the lawyer's emotional involvement, the lawyer will be unable to represent the client without impairment of the exercise of independent professional judgment. Moreover, a blurred line between the professional and personal relationships may make it difficult to predict to what extent client confidences will be protected by the attorney-client evidentiary privilege, since client confidences are protected by privilege only when they are imparted in the context of the client-lawyer relationship. Because of the significant danger of harm to client interests and because the client's own emotional involvement renders it unlikely that the client could give adequate informed consent, this Rule prohibits the lawyer from having sexual relations with a client regardless of whether the relationship is consensual and regardless of the absence of prejudice to the client.

violated Prof. Cond. R. 1.7(b) and prejudiced the administration of justice in violation of Prof. Cond. R. 8.4(d).

Given our finding of misconduct, we must determine an appropriate sanction. In doing so, we consider the misconduct, the respondent's state of mind underlying the misconduct, the duty of this court to preserve the integrity of the profession, the risk to the public in allowing the respondent to continue in practice, and any mitigating or aggravating factors. As a mitigating factor only, we find no evidence that the respondent's sexual relationship with his client actually impaired his representation of her. In fact, the client hired the respondent to handle another legal matter for her after the sexual relationship ended but before disciplinary charges were filed against the respondent. Moreover, the respondent has not been disciplined previously during his 33 years of practicing law. Given these mitigating factors, we conclude a 30-day suspension from the practice of law is warranted.

## Notes and Questions

1. *Tsoutsouris* represents a minority position, particularly in its strong disapproval of attorney-client sexual conduct and its acceptance of the premises that such conduct jeopardizes clients' rights and poses an inherent conflict of interest. Does the divorce context call for special rules on attorney-client sexual relationships? Are divorce clients uniquely vulnerable? How does the lawyer's role here differ from that in other stressful legal contexts (for example, personal injury or criminal cases)?

2. Does the consensual nature of the relationship militate against the imposition of sanctions? Should it matter if the client, rather than the attorney, initiates the sexual relationship? See Committee on Professional Ethics and Conduct v. Hill, 436 N.W.2d 57 (Iowa 1989) (suspending attorney even though client initiated sexual relationship, reasoning that attorney should have recognized the potential negative effects on her case). Some commentators argue that attorney-client sex can never be voluntary because of the power imbalance and the client's emotional and financial status. Jennifer Tuggle Crabtree, Does Consent Matter? Relationships Between Divorce Attorneys and Clients, 23 J. Legal Prof. 221, 229-232 (1998). Do you agree?

3. Tsoutsouris argues that his sexual relationship with his client did not impair his ability to represent her. In cases in which no prejudice results to the client's case, what is the harm of attorney-client sexual conduct? To the profession? To the client? What are the dangers inherent in a situation in which the attorney is sexually involved with a client whom he is representing in proceedings involving custody, child support, or property distribution? See, e.g., In re DiSandro, 680 A.2d 73 (R.I. 1996) (calling for withdrawal from representation in such cases).

See generally William K. Shirley, Dealing with the Profession's "Dirty Little Secret": A Proposal for Regulating Attorney-Client Sexual Relations, 13 Geo. J. Legal Ethics 131, 135-148 (1999) (discussing variety of harms).

Although no empirical studies investigate the effects of lawyers' sexual misconduct with clients, the effects of sexual relations between therapists and clients are well documented. For example, 90 percent of patients in one study (n=559) suffered negative effects, including loss of motivation, impaired social adjustment, suicidal feelings or behavior, and increased substance abuse. Jacqueline Bouhoutsos et al., Sexual Intimacy Between Psychotherapists and Patients, 14 Prof. Psychol.: Res. & Prac. 185, 191 (1983). How is the attorney-client relationship similar to, and different from, the psychotherapist-client relationship? See, e.g., Suppressed v. Suppressed, 565 N.E.2d 101, 105 (Ill. App. Ct. 1990) (distinguishing professions), *appeal denied*, 571 N.E.2d 156 (Ill. 1991). Are similar effects to clients likely?

Regulations currently prohibit sexual conduct between psychotherapists and clients. See, e.g., Cal. Bus. & Prof. Code §726 (West 1994 & Supp. 2001). Some statutes limit prohibitions to conduct within two years of termination of therapy (e.g., Cal. Civil Code §43.93 (West Supp. 2001)); other statutes contain absolute prohibitions (e.g., Fla. Stat. Ann. §491.0112 (West 1991 & Supp. 2001)). See Kenneth M. Austin et al., Confronting Malpractice: Legal and Ethical Dilemmas in Psychotherapy 145 (1990).

4. If rules regulating sexual conduct between lawyer and client are adopted, should they exempt sexual relationships that predate the professional relationship? Sexual relationships that result in cohabitation and/or marriage?

5. Should special censure be reserved for an attorney's conditioning the exchange of legal services for sexual services? In re Ashy, 721 So. 2d 859 (La. 1998). For coercing or misleading a client into having sexual relations?

6. The issue of attorney-client sexual misconduct has prompted considerable debate. Most states do not prohibit sexual relations between lawyers and clients. States that disapprove of such conduct take a variety of approaches. A few states (e.g., Indiana in *Tsoutsouris*, and Colorado) take the strictest approach, prohibiting all sexual relationships between attorneys and clients. Other states (e.g., Minnesota, Oregon, and Wisconsin) ban attorney-client sexual relations, except when the relationship predates the representation. New York limits the ban to domestic relations attorneys. Some states prohibit only those relationships that negatively affect the practice of law. See generally Linda Fitts Mischler, Personal Morals Masquerading as Professional Ethics: Regulations Banning Sex Between Domestic Relations Attorneys and Their Clients, 23 Harv. Women's L.J. 1 (2000); Abed Awad, Attorney-Client Sex Should Always Be Off Limits, N.J. L.J., Mar. 13, 2000.

7. Different types of sanctions might apply to sexual misconduct, such as those for violations of state business and professions codes. Suspensions and disbarrment are possible sanctions. Civil tort remedies, such as intentional infliction of emotional distress or malpractice, might apply (e.g., McDaniel v. Gile, 281 Cal. Rptr. 242 (Ct. App. 1991)). See also Doe v. Roe, 681 N.E.2d 640 (Ill. Ct. App. 1997) (client may pursue claim for breach of fiduciary duty against her divorce lawyer who coerced her into a sexual relationship). Criminal statutes also might be relevant. What relief do you favor?

8. Does regulation of the sexual aspects of the attorney-client relationship invade privacy? In Committee on Professional Ethics and Conduct v. Hill, 436 N.W.2d 57 (Iowa 1989), an attorney had sexual intercourse, purportedly in exchange for money, with a divorce client involved in child custody litigation. The attorney argued that the court's consideration of his conduct violated his right to privacy, protecting private acts between two consenting adults. How should the court rule?

9. Several famous lawyers' affairs have received publicity. See, e.g., William Vogeler, They Are Trying to Destroy Me, 103 L.A. Daily J., May 2, 1990, at 11 (reporting allegations of sexual misconduct against Marvin Mitchelson). Attorney Melvin Belli went on record saying that sex between a lawyer and client is the "lawyer's prerogative." See Thomas Lyon, Sexual Exploitation of Divorce Clients: The Lawyer's Prerogative?, 10 Harv. Women's L.J. 159 (1987).

10. Not all sexual misconduct involves a male attorney and female client. After public attention focused on the California state bar rule (discussed infra), the assemblywoman who proposed the legislation began receiving calls from heterosexual men complaining about advances by female attorneys and also from gay men complaining about their male attorneys. Michele Fuetsch, Bar OK's Limits on Lawyer, Client Sex, L.A. Times, Apr. 21, 1991, at A-3.

11. *Background.* California was the first state whose bar association approved a rule proscribing attorney-client sexual relationships. Cal. R. Prof. Conduct 3-120 prohibits an attorney from: (1) requiring or demanding sexual relations as a condition of representation, (2) employing coercion, intimidation, or undue influence in entering into sexual relations, or (3) continuing to represent a client after having sexual relations with that client if the sexual relationship causes the attorney to perform legal services incompetently. The rule does not apply to sexual relationships predating the initiation of the lawyer-client relationship. Controversial proposed language, eventually eliminated, would have effectuated a presumption that an attorney who engages in sexual relations with a client has violated the rule. See Calif. Sex-with-Clients Rule, 7 Laws. Man. on Prof. Conduct (ABA/BNA) 279, 280 (Sept. 11, 1991).

12. *ABA proposal.* In March 1999, in response to the growing number of complaints against lawyers, the American Bar Association Ethics

2000 Commission proposed the following per se prohibition of attorney-client sexual relations: "A lawyer shall not have sexual relations with a client unless a consensual sexual relationship existed between them when the lawyer-client relationship commenced." See Model Rules of Professional Conduct, Proposed Rule 1.8 (Ethics Commission on the Evaluation of Professional Conduct) (November 2000). See Ralph H. Brock, Sex, Clients, and Legal Ethics, 64 Tex. B.J. 234, 238-239 (2001) (discussing the proposed prohibition). The ABA House of Delegates approved the proposed rule in August 2001. Final approval of the entire Ethics 2000 Report is expected at the meeting in August 2002.

## Problems

1. Recently you receive a telephone call from a former law school friend. He asks for your advice, explaining that he is very attracted to a woman he is representing in a contentious divorce case. Although he is eager to become romantically involved, he would like to know more about potential ethical issues. He confesses that he is so smitten that he has lost his objectivity. Nonetheless, he believes he can continue to represent her effectively even if they begin to see each other romantically.[22] What would you advise?

2. Cheryl retains Attorney Drucker to represent her in her divorce. At trial she testifies that during her initial consultation, she discussed her marriage, conjugal relations, and her psychiatric treatment for an anxiety disorder. On her second visit, she alleges that Drucker held her hand, embraced her, and told her of his stressful marriage. When he apologized and offered to refer her to another lawyer, she declined. She was not anxious to retell her personal history. Drucker called her at home that day to tell her he is attracted to her. On three subsequent visits Cheryl alleges that they engaged in sexual activity. Although unable to remember dates, Cheryl pinpoints two of the encounters based on surrounding events (that is, Drucker's daughter was ill, a particular client was in the office). After Drucker ends the relationship, Cheryl's husband discovers her love letters and diary. He confronts her in the presence of their son, who is the subject of a custody dispute. Drucker denies the sexual relationship. The Committee on Professional Conduct files a petition to suspend Drucker from the practice of law. What result? See Drucker's Case, 577 A.2d 1198 (N.H. 1990).

[22]. This problem is posed in Ethics: Affairs of the Heart, A.B.A. J., June, 1990, at 82.

## G. DIVORCE JURISDICTION

### 1. Over the Plaintiff and Defendant

### ■ IN RE MARRIAGE OF KIMURA
*471 N.W.2d 869 (Iowa 1991)*

LAVORATO, Justice. . . .

Ken and Fumi Kimura were married in Japan in 1965. Both are Japanese citizens. They have a daughter and a son. The daughter, Izumi, was twenty-three at the time of the dissolution hearing. The son, Naoki, was twenty-one. Ken and Fumi have lived apart since September 1973.

Ken graduated from Kobe University Medical School in Japan. Currently, he is a pediatric surgeon at the University of Iowa Hospitals and Clinics in Iowa City.

In July 1986 Ken was invited to come to the United States where he took a position at the Long Island Jewish Medical Center in New Hyde Park, New York. When he came to the States, Ken had an H-1 visa. Such a visa is a temporary one, issued to persons with special talents or abilities that may be useful to the United States. [The center filed an application on Ken's behalf for permanent residency status, which he received in October 1987. Subsequently, he was hired at the University of Iowa as an Associate Professor of Medicine.]

In March 1988 Ken filed a divorce mediation proceeding with the family court in Japan. In July he withdrew from the proceeding. Apparently he could not attend that court's reconciliation proceeding between himself and Fumi because of his work.

In December Ken filed a petition for dissolution of marriage in Johnson County District Court. He alleged that he had resided in Iowa for more than one year. He further alleged that his residency was not just for the purpose of obtaining a dissolution. Finally, he alleged a breakdown of the marital relationship.

Because personal service was not possible on Fumi in Iowa, a copy of the petition was mailed to her in Japan. In addition, notice of the petition was published in the Iowa City Press Citizen on December 14, December 21, and December 28.

In February 1989 Fumi filed a preanswer motion in which she contested the district court's subject matter and personal jurisdiction. [Her affidavit pointed out that Ken could not obtain a divorce under Japanese law because his conduct caused the marital problems. At final hearing, Fumi did not personally appear but her attorney did. After testimony about Ken's employment, residence status, and the breakdown of the marriage, the court concluded Ken satisfied residency requirements and dissolved the marriage. Fumi appealed.]

## II. THE DUE PROCESS CHALLENGE

Fumi poses the issue this way: "Iowa's assertion of jurisdiction over respondent (who has no contacts with Iowa) or her marriage based solely on petitioner's alleged residence in Iowa violates the due process clauses of the United States and Iowa Constitutions." . . .

Early on, due process required the personal presence of the defendant in the forum state as a condition for rendering a binding personal or in personam judgment against the defendant. Pennoyer v. Neff, 95 U.S. 714, 733 (1878). The rule was expanded in International Shoe Co. v. Washington, 326 U.S. 310 (1945). Now due process does not require such personal presence. Due process only requires that the defendant have certain minimum contacts with the forum state. However, those contacts must be such "that the maintenance of the suit does not offend traditional notions of fair play and substantial justice." *International Shoe*, 326 U.S. at 316. Simply put, there must be a connection among the forum, the litigation, and the defendant.

Fumi relies on [Shaffer v. Heitner, 433 U.S. 186 (1977),] in support of her contention that jurisdiction to grant the dissolution must be tested by the minimum contacts standard of *International Shoe*. A footnote in *Shaffer* suggests her reliance is misplaced. See *Shaffer*, 433 U.S. at 208 n.30. One commentator seems to agree:

> Although the *Shaffer* Court concluded that all assertions of state-court jurisdiction must conform to the standards of *International Shoe* and, thus, be based upon a nexus among the forum, the litigation, and the defendant, the nexus requirement is unlikely to apply to cases in which status provides the basis of the asserted jurisdiction. The power to dissolve the marriage status in an ex parte proceeding normally is thought to stem, at least in part, from the perception of the marriage status as a res, and thus, as a "thing" to which the court's jurisdiction can attach. Despite the obvious analogy between in rem and quasi in rem jurisdiction based on the presence of property and ex parte-divorce jurisdiction based on the presence of a res (marriage status), the Court specifically noted in a footnote [n.30] that it was not suggesting "that jurisdictional doctrines other than those discussed in text, such as the particularized rules governing adjudications of status, are inconsistent with the standard of fairness." The all-inclusive language of the *Shaffer* conclusion, therefore, may not include cases in which status is the basis of the asserted jurisdiction. As far as the *Shaffer* holding is concerned, the forum-litigation-plaintiff nexus recognized as sufficient by the Court in Williams v. North Carolina seems to remain a valid basis of jurisdiction for ex parte divorces.

State-Court Jurisdiction, 63 Iowa L. Rev. at 1005-06 (citations omitted).

In Williams v. North Carolina, 317 U.S. 287 (1942) [hereinafter *Williams I*], the question was whether full faith and credit had to be given to a foreign divorce decree where only one spouse was domiciled in the foreign state and the other spouse had never been there. *Williams I,* 317 U.S. at 298-99. The Supreme Court held that the foreign state's high interest in the marital status of its domiciliaries required that full faith and credit be given such a decree. The Court did require, however, that substituted service on the absent spouse meet due process standards, that is, reasonably calculated to give the absent spouse actual notice and an opportunity to be heard.

In *Williams I* the Court had difficulty classifying dissolution proceedings. Though it did not view such proceedings as in rem actions neither did it view them as mere in personam actions. According to the Court, domicile of one spouse within the forum state gave that state the power to dissolve the marriage regardless of where the marriage occurred. This court too has deemed domicile as essential to dissolution of marriage jurisdiction.

The cases generally adopt the following explanation of the components for a dissolution of marriage proceeding:

> It is commonly held that an essential element of the judicial power to grant a divorce, or jurisdiction, is domicile. A court must have jurisdiction of the res, or the marriage status, in order that it may grant a divorce. The res or status follows the domiciles of the spouses; and therefore, in order that the res may be found within the state so that the courts of the state may have jurisdiction of it, one of the spouses must have a domicile within the state.

24 Am. Jur. 2d Divorce & Separation §238, at 336 (1983).

Williams v. North Carolina reached the Supreme Court a second time. The Court held that while the finding of domicile by the state that granted the decree is entitled to prima facie weight, it is not conclusive in a sister state but might be relitigated there. Williams v. North Carolina, 325 U.S. 226, 238-39 (1945) [*Williams II*].

The divisible divorce doctrine emerged in Estin v. Estin, 334 U.S. 541, 549 (1948). In *Estin* the Court held that Nevada in an ex parte divorce proceeding could change the marital status of those domiciled within its boundaries. The power to do so stems from Nevada's "considerable interest in preventing bigamous marriages and in protecting the offspring of marriages from being [illegitimate]." *Estin,* 334 U.S. at 546. But Nevada could not wipe out the absent spouse's claim for alimony under a New York judgment in a prior separation proceeding because Nevada had no personal jurisdiction over the absent spouse. So New York did not have to give full faith and credit to that part of the Nevada decree which purported to eliminate the support obligation of its domiciliary. [The Supreme Court reaffirmed *Estin* in Vanderbilt v. Vanderbilt, 354 U.S. 416, 417-418 (1957). *Vanderbilt* differed in the fact that the absent spouse's right to alimony had not been determined before the ex parte divorce in Nevada.]

The divisible divorce doctrine simply recognizes the court's limited power where the court has no personal jurisdiction over the absent spouse. In these circumstances the court has jurisdiction to grant a divorce to one domiciled in the state but no jurisdiction to adjudicate the incidents of the marriage, for example, alimony and property division. In short, the divisible divorce doctrine recognizes both the in rem and in personam nature of claims usually raised in dissolution of marriage proceedings.

We conclude that the all-inclusive language of the *Shaffer* conclusion does not include dissolution of marriage proceedings. In other words, jurisdiction to grant such a dissolution is not to be tested by the minimum contacts standard of *International Shoe*.

We further conclude that domicile continues to be the basis for a court's jurisdiction to grant a dissolution of marriage decree. So the courts of this state have the power to grant dissolution of marriage decrees provided the petitioner is domiciled in this state. Such power exists even though the petitioner's spouse is absent from this state, has never been here, and was constructively rather than personally served. [W]e are left with the question whether Ken established his domicile or residency in this state. . . .

### III. CHALLENGE TO DOMICILE OR RESIDENCY

The district court adjudicated only the marital status. And that was done based on Ken being domiciled in this state. None of the incidents of the marriage — for example, alimony and property division — were adjudicated because the court did not have personal jurisdiction over Fumi. . . .

Fumi contends that even if minimum contacts were not the standard, Ken still had to establish that he met the residency requirements of this state before the court could dissolve the marriage. She argues that Ken failed to establish those requirements and so the district court should not have dissolved the marriage. For reasons we discuss, we disagree. . . .

According to [Iowa Code §598.6] Ken had to establish the following: (1) he resided in Iowa for at least one year before the petition was filed; and (2) his residence here was in good faith and not just for the purpose of obtaining a marriage dissolution.

Residence for the purpose of section 598.6 has the same meaning as domicile. To have a residence or domicile within the meaning of this section, "one must have a fixed habitation with no intention of" leaving it.

Once a domicile is established, it continues until a new one is established. A new domicile is established if all of the following things happen: (1) the former domicile is abandoned; (2) there is an actual removal to, and physical presence in the new domicile; and (3) there is a bona fide intention to change and to remain in the new domicile permanently or indefinitely. This intention must be a present and fixed intention and not dependent on some future or contingent event. . . .

We think Ken amply proved that he met the residency requirements of section 598.6. . . . In the affidavit he swore to a number of facts showing that he had abandoned his domicile in Japan in favor of the one here. For example, he swore that he had no other permanent residence other than his residence in Johnson County. In addition, he swore that since moving to Iowa he had obtained an Iowa driver's license and had opened bank accounts at local banks. Finally, he swore that he intends to remain here for an indefinite period so long as his employment at the university is satisfactory to him and the university. . . .

We see nothing in the evidence to support Fumi's contention that Ken's residence here was in bad faith and only for the purpose of obtaining a dissolution of marriage. It may be that one reason Ken came here was — as Fumi suggests — because of our liberal dissolution marriage law as compared to Japan's. But that fact is not sufficient to preclude Ken from establishing a domicile or residence in Iowa, especially in light of his intention to remain here indefinitely.

Nor does Ken's continued Japanese citizenship preclude such a domicile or residence. A foreign citizenship does not — standing alone — bar one from establishing a domicile or residence for dissolution of marriage purposes. . . .

### IV. CHALLENGE TO COURT'S RULING REFUSING TO DECLINE JURISDICTION BASED ON FORUM NON CONVENIENS DOCTRINE

[Fumi contends the district court should have declined jurisdiction based on forum non conveniens, arguing] that Japan is the more convenient forum and is the nation with the most significant contacts to the marital status of the parties. . . . Forum non conveniens is a facet of venue. This doctrine presupposes at least two forums in which jurisdiction and venue are proper. Under the doctrine a court may decline to proceed with an action though venue and jurisdiction are proper. The doctrine is a self-imposed limit on jurisdictional power that can be used to avoid unfair, vexatious, oppressive actions in a forum away from the defendant's domicile. . . .

What the moving party must show is that the relative inconveniences are so unbalanced that jurisdiction should be declined on an equitable basis. Factors that bear on this determination include the following: the relative ease of access to sources of proof; the availability of compulsory process for attendance of unwilling, and the cost of obtaining attendance of willing, witnesses; the possibility of view of the premises, if view would be appropriate to the action; the enforceability of the judgment if one is obtained; and all other practical problems that make trial of a case easy, expeditious, and inexpensive. All of these factors pertain to the private interest of the litigant.

Factors of public interest are also considered. They include the administrative difficulties for courts, trial in the forum that is the home of the state law which governs the case, and the burden of jury duty imposed on citizens of a forum with no relation to the litigation. Residency of the plaintiff is also considered but only as one of the many factors in the balancing process.

Whether to apply the doctrine of forum non conveniens lies in the sound discretion of the district court. . . . In deciding whether the district court abused its discretion in this case, we think it would be helpful to look at the divorce process in Japan. Japan has a variety of ways to dissolve a marriage [in contested cases] . . . : divorce through mediation in the family court, divorce by judicial decree in the family court, and divorce by judicial decree in the district court. A person seeking a divorce by judicial decree in the district court must prove fault. . . .

The family court may grant a divorce without proof of such grounds. But a divorce by judicial decree in the family court is rare because if either party objects, the divorce becomes invalid. So a decree of divorce by judicial decision usually issues from the district court.

Before the parties may proceed to the district court they must attempt mediation in the family court. Divorce can be effected without resort to litigation if the parties can agree on terms. If the parties fail to reach agreement, a divorce petition may then be submitted to and processed by the district court. Mediators in family court have no power to arbitrate disputes and are likely to oppose the idea of divorce. As a practical matter, a failure to agree to terms in mediation may mean no divorce in district court.

A divorce in Japan means the severance of all ties between the parties — they virtually become strangers. Usually a lump sum property settlement occurs. Because of enforcement problems, a settlement involving installment payments is rare. Alimony and other postdivorce maintenance payments are not available under Japanese law. Indeed, there is no legal requirement that property be divided or that support be paid. . . .

It has been suggested that divorce in Japan is quick and easy if a party can bribe, coerce, threaten, or persuade the other party to a divorce by mutual consent. A nonconsensual divorce is difficult, if not impossible, to obtain. . . .

For several reasons, the district court here could have determined that Japan is the more convenient forum for the parties. First, Japan has complete jurisdiction over the marital status of the parties and over all the incidents of the marriage. Second, a Japanese court has a societal interest in the marital status of its citizens. Third, given the nature of the divorce proceedings in Japan, Fumi's bargaining power in a family court mediation may be reduced by permitting a dissolution of marriage here. Fourth, Fumi may be at a cultural disadvantage with regard to customs and language in an Iowa proceeding. Last, Iowa is an inconvenient forum in relation to her residence.

On the other hand we think the district court was well within its discretion to deny Fumi's request to decline jurisdiction. Iowa too has an interest in the marital status of its residents. Right or wrong, our legislature has opted for no-fault divorce. One reason, we suspect, was to eliminate the extortion leverage an "innocent" spouse had over a "guilty" spouse. Had the district court honored Fumi's request, Ken — an Iowa resident — would have been denied the protection of Iowa's dissolution law. In short, a ruling in Fumi's favor may have resulted in no dissolution at all for one of this State's residents.

In addition we are impressed with the vigorous representation Fumi enjoyed in the district court and here. We doubt there would be any less representation in a postdissolution action for alimony and property division. . . . Our liberal discovery rules should allow Fumi to discover all of Ken's assets and his income in such an action. This is in contrast to Japan where it is difficult to discover a party's assets in divorce proceedings. Given our liberal rules on alimony and property division, we suspect Fumi might even fare better here than in Japan. . . . The district court did not violate Fumi's rights under either the federal or state constitutions. . . .

## Notes and Questions

1. *Kimura* reveals that special jurisdictional rules, unlike those in other civil actions, apply to divorce. To terminate a marriage, the plaintiff must be domiciled in the forum state. Personal jurisdiction over the defendant is not required. (Although personal jurisdiction is not required merely to terminate the marriage, it is required to resolve the financial incidents of the marriage.) However, *notice* to the defendant that complies with due process *is* required to inform the defendant of the pendency of the action. A divorce without proper notice may be challenged for lack of jurisdiction. On the history of the domicile rule in England and colonial America, see Rhonda Wasserman, Divorce and Domicile: Time to Sever the Knot, 39 Wm. & Mary L. Rev. 1, 8-19 (1997).

2. *Ex parte divorces.* As *Kimura* indicates, some divorce decrees issued in one state may be collaterally attacked in another state for want of jurisdiction. Williams v. North Carolina, 317 U.S. 287 (1942), established

that the domiciliary state of one spouse may grant an ex parte divorce (that is, one in which the forum lacks jurisdiction over the respondent-spouse) entitled to full faith and credit in all other states. Because divorce courts routinely apply local substantive law, the ruling in *Williams I* reinforced the practice of migratory divorce during the fault era, when unhappy spouses often traveled to a new "domicile" to seek a divorce under the forum state's more permissive grounds. See generally Max Rheinstein, Marriage Stability, Divorce, and the Law 63-81 (1972).

In *Williams II*, however, the Supreme Court limited that holding. Williams v. North Carolina, 325 U.S. 226 (1945). *Williams II* held that, although the full faith and credit obligation assumes the forum has valid jurisdiction as the domicile of the petitioner, a subsequent showing of lack of domicile will allow sister states to refuse to recognize the divorce. The holding thus allowed North Carolina to prosecute for bigamy two North Carolina residents who purported to establish a domicile in Nevada where each got a divorce, married each other, and then immediately returned home. See Thomas Reed Powell, And Repent at Leisure: An Inquiry into the Unhappy Lot of Those Whom Nevada Hath Joined Together and North Carolina Hath Put Asunder, 58 Harv. L. Rev. 930 (1945).

What rationale underlies the judicial willingness to recognize ex parte divorces? Is the ex parte divorce fair to the "stay-at-home spouse"? To the state whose laws the migratory petitioning-spouse seeks to evade?

3. *Bilateral divorce.* In another line of cases, the Supreme Court has indicated that, when the forum has personal jurisdiction over both spouses in a migratory divorce, the principles of full faith and credit forbid collateral attack. See, e.g., Johnson v. Muelberger, 340 U.S. 581 (1951); Sherrer v. Sherrer, 334 U.S. 343 (1948). If the petitioning spouse has not genuinely established a domicile in the divorce forum (a jurisdictional prerequisite for all divorces, ex parte and bilateral alike), why should personal jurisdiction over the respondent spouse prevent collateral attack, say, by way of a bigamy prosecution? What good is a state's restrictive divorce law if a resident spouse can simply cross state lines, purport to establish a new domicile and — after the personal appearance of the other spouse — obtain a divorce immune from collateral attack?

4. *Transitory presence.* The Supreme Court elaborated the standards for in personam jurisdiction over a defendant in Burnham v. Superior Court, 495 U.S. 604 (1990), which held that a defendant's transitory presence can satisfy due process even when the defendant has no substantial connection to the forum. The Court upheld California's assertion of general jurisdiction over a New Jersey resident who was personally served during a brief trip to conduct business and visit his children in California, his wife's new home. The plurality determined that due process was satisfied because (1) the minimum-contacts/fairness approach

to jurisdiction (initiated by *International Shoe*) addresses only absent (not present) defendants, and (2) the long-standing rule conferring jurisdiction upon a defendant personally served in the forum accords with "traditional notions of fair play and substantial justice."

One concurrence ( Justice White) rejected the need to entertain individual claims of unfairness for a defendant whose presence in the forum is intentional. Another concurrence ( Justices Brennan, Marshall, Blackmun, and O'Connor) insisted on a "fairness" inquiry even for nonresident defendants personally served in the forum, but found such fairness in Mr. Burnham's purposeful, albeit brief, availment of California's benefits (for example, police protection, roads). Then why is it not fair, as Justice Scalia asks in his plurality opinion, to serve a defendant *after* he has left the forum and returned to his home state if receipt of benefits proves determinative?

Note that, as a result of the Court's holding in *Burnham,* the divorce action in *Burnham* becomes a bilateral, rather than an ex parte, proceeding, allowing the forum to resolve the financial incidents of the dissolution.

5. *Foreign country divorces.* In the fault era, disputes arose about divorces obtained in foreign countries by U.S. residents seeking to evade restrictive laws. American courts do not owe full faith and credit to decrees from foreign countries, although they may recognize such divorces under principles of "comity." E.g., Rosenstiel v. Rosenstiel, 209 N.E.2d 709 (N.Y. 1965). Because comity is discretionary, some states refuse to apply the doctrine to recognize foreign divorces. See, e.g., Warrender v. Warrender, 190 A.2d 684 (N.J. Super. Ct. App. Div. 1963), *aff'd,* 200 A.2d 123 (N.J. 1964). For a modern application of comity principles in the divorce context, see In re Marriage of Goode, 997 P.2d 244 (Or. Ct. App. 2000) (recognizing wife's Dominican Republic divorce).

6. Has an attorney in a restrictive state violated ethical principles by facilitating the client's out-of-state or foreign-country divorce? See, e.g., In re Donnelly, 470 N.W.2d 305 (Wis. 1991) (suspending an attorney's license for two years for advertising in national publications his arrangement of Dominican Republic divorces, without always cautioning prospective clients about the questionable validity of such decrees).

## Problem

A man sends his wife an e-mail via the Internet, informing her that he is divorcing her. The husband relies on Internet notice because he is studying then in a foreign country on a scholarship. Based on that notice, the wife subsequently remarries. After his studies, when the husband returns home, he changes his mind about the divorce and threatens to sue the wife if she will not leave her new husband. The wife requests the court to rule on the sufficiency of the notice. What result? See Egypt Dismisses Net Divorce Case (AP) (visited June 1, 2000) <http://daily news.yahoo.com/h/ap/20000601/tc/egypt_internet_divorce_1.html>. Would such notice comply with the requirements of due process?

## 2. Durational Residency Requirements

### ■ SOSNA v. IOWA
*419 U.S. 393 (1975)*

Mr. Justice REHNQUIST delivered the opinion of the Court.

Appellant Carol Sosna married Michael Sosna on September 5, 1964, in Michigan. They lived together in New York between October 1967 and August 1971, after which date they separated but continued to live in New York. In August 1972, appellant moved to Iowa with her three children, and the following month she petitioned the District Court of Jackson County, Iowa, for a dissolution of her marriage. Michael Sosna, who had been personally served with notice of the action when he came to Iowa to visit his children, made a special appearance to contest the jurisdiction of the Iowa court. The Iowa court dismissed the petition for lack of jurisdiction, finding that Michael Sosna was not a resident of Iowa and appellant had not been a resident of the State of Iowa for one year preceding the filing of her petition. In so doing the Iowa court applied the provisions of Iowa Code §598.6 (1973) requiring that the petitioner in such an action be "for the last year a resident of the state." . . .

The durational residency requirement under attack in this case is a part of Iowa's comprehensive statutory regulation of domestic relations, an area that has long been regarded as a virtually exclusive province of the States. Cases decided by this Court over a period of more than a century bear witness to this historical fact. . . . In Pennoyer v. Neff, 95 U.S. 714, 734-735 (1878), the Court said: "The State . . . has absolute right to prescribe the conditions upon which the marriage relation between its own citizens shall be created, and the causes for which it may be dissolved." . . .

The imposition of a durational residency requirement for divorce is scarcely unique to Iowa, since 48 States impose such a requirement as a condition for maintaining an action for divorce. As might be expected, the periods vary among the States and range from six weeks to two years. The one-year period selected by Iowa is the most common length of time prescribed.

Appellant contends that the Iowa requirement of one year's residence is unconstitutional for two separate reasons: *first,* because it establishes two classes of persons and discriminates against those who have recently exercised their right to travel to Iowa, thereby contravening the

Court's holdings in Shapiro v. Thompson, 394 U.S. 618 (1969); Dunn v. Blumstein, 405 U.S. 330 (1972); and Memorial Hospital v. Maricopa County, 415 U.S. 250 (1974); and, *second,* because it denies a litigant the opportunity to make an individualized showing of bona fide residence and therefore denies such residents access to the only method of legally dissolving their marriage.

State statutes imposing durational residency requirements were, of course, invalidated when imposed by States as a qualification for welfare payments, *Shapiro,* supra; for voting, *Dunn,* supra; and for medical care, *Maricopa County,* supra. But none of those cases intimated that the States might never impose durational residency requirements. . . . What those cases had in common was that the durational residency requirements they struck down were justified on the basis of budgetary or record-keeping considerations which were held insufficient to outweigh the constitutional claims of the individuals. But Iowa's divorce residency requirement is of a different stripe. Appellant was not irretrievably foreclosed from obtaining some part of what she sought, as was the case with the welfare recipients in *Shapiro,* the voters in *Dunn,* or the indigent patient in *Maricopa County.* She would eventually qualify for the same sort of adjudication which she demanded virtually upon her arrival in the State. Iowa's requirement delayed her access to the courts, but, by fulfilling it, she could ultimately have obtained the same opportunity for adjudication which she asserts ought to have been hers at an earlier point in time.

Iowa's residency requirement may reasonably be justified on grounds other than purely budgetary considerations or administrative convenience. A decree of divorce is not a matter in which the only interested parties are the State as a sort of "grantor," and a divorce petitioner such as appellant in the role of "grantee." Both spouses are obviously interested in the proceedings, since it will affect their marital status and very likely their property rights. Where a married couple has minor children, a decree of divorce would usually include provisions for their custody and support. With consequences of such moment riding on a divorce decree issued by its courts, Iowa may insist that one seeking to initiate such a proceeding have the modicum of attachment to the State required here.

Such a requirement additionally furthers the State's parallel interests both in avoiding officious intermeddling in matters in which another State has a paramount interest, and in minimizing the susceptibility of its own divorce decrees to collateral attack. [See Williams v. North Carolina, 325 U.S. 226 (1945).] A State such as Iowa may quite reasonably decide that it does not wish to become a divorce mill for unhappy spouses who have lived there as short a time as appellant had when she commenced her action in the state court after having long resided elsewhere. . . .

Nor are we of the view that the failure to provide an individualized determination of residency violates the Due Process Clause. . . . An individualized determination of physical presence plus the intent to remain, which appellant apparently seeks, would not entitle her to a divorce even if she could have made such a showing. For Iowa requires not merely "domicile" in that sense, but residence in the State for a year in order for its courts to exercise their divorce jurisdiction.

In Boddie v. Connecticut, [401 U.S. 371 (1971)] this Court held that Connecticut might not deny access to divorce courts to those persons who could not afford to pay the required fee. Because of the exclusive role played by the State in the termination of marriages, it was held that indigents could not be denied an opportunity to be heard "absent a countervailing state interest of overriding significance." 401 U.S., at 377. But the gravamen of appellant Sosna's claim is not total deprivation, as in *Boddie,* but only delay. . . . Affirmed.

Mr. Justice MARSHALL, with whom Mr. Justice BRENNAN joins, dissenting. . . .

The Court omits altogether what should be the first inquiry: whether the right to obtain a divorce is of sufficient importance that its denial to recent immigrants constitutes a penalty on interstate travel. In my view, it clearly meets that standard. The previous decisions of this Court make it plain that the right of marital association is one of the most basic rights conferred on the individual by the State. The interests associated with marriage and divorce have repeatedly been accorded particular deference [citing *Loving* and *Boddie*]. . . .

Having determined that the interest in obtaining a divorce is of substantial social importance, I would scrutinize Iowa's durational residency requirement to determine whether it constitutes a reasonable means of furthering important interests asserted by the State. . . .

. . . Iowa's residency requirement, the Court says, merely forestalls access to the courts; applicants seeking welfare payments, medical aid, and the right to vote, on the other hand, suffer unrecoverable losses throughout the waiting period. This analysis, however, ignores the severity of the deprivation suffered by the divorce petitioner who is forced to wait a year for relief. The injury accompanying that delay is not directly measurable in money terms like the loss of welfare benefits, but it cannot reasonably be argued that when the year has elapsed, the petitioner is made whole. The year's wait prevents remarriage and locks both partners into what may be an intolerable, destructive relationship. . . . The Court cannot mean that Mrs. Sosna has not suffered any injury by being foreclosed from seeking a divorce in Iowa for a year. It must instead mean that it does not regard that deprivation as being very severe.

I find the majority's second argument no more persuasive. The Court forgoes reliance on the usual justifications for durational residency requirements — budgetary considerations and administrative convenience. . . . In their place, the majority invokes a more amorphous justification — the magnitude of the interests affected and resolved by a divorce proceeding. Certainly the stakes in a divorce are weighty both for the individuals directly involved in the adjudication and for others immediately affected by it. The critical importance of the divorce process, however, weakens the argument for a long residency requirement rather than strengthens it. . . .

The Court's third justification seems to me the only one that warrants close consideration. Iowa has a legitimate interest in protecting itself against invasion by those seeking quick divorces in a forum with relatively lax divorce laws, and it may have some interest in avoiding collateral attacks on its decrees in other States. These interests, however, would adequately be protected by a simple requirement of domicile — physical presence plus intent to remain — which would remove the rigid one-year barrier while permitting the State to restrict the availability of its divorce process to citizens who are genuinely its own. . . .

## Notes and Questions

1. As *Sosna* explains, many states require a divorce petitioner to reside in the state for a period of time. In some states, residence alone suffices for divorce jurisdiction. Other jurisdictions mandate both durational residence and domicile requirements.[23]

2. Justices Rehnquist and Marshall disagree about the significance of delay in petitions for dissolution and the consequences of such delay. Whose argument is more persuasive? Justice Rehnquist also distinguishes a one-year delay for permitting dissolution of marriage from a delay for voting, welfare benefits, and medical aid. Is it distinguishable?

3. Justice Rehnquist distinguishes *Boddie* by claiming the filing fee foreclosed access while the residency requirement in *Sosna* imposes "only delay." Do you agree that indigent plaintiffs have a stronger claim than recent immigrants? Would your analysis change upon a showing that women predominate among recent immigrants (moving for jobs, proximity to parents, or a new relationship)?

4. Justice Marshall, dissenting, intimates that the state's real goal is to avoid becoming known as a "divorce mill." During the fault era, Nevada, Florida, Idaho, and Arkansas developed the reputation of divorce mills. Max Rheinstein, Marriage Stability, Divorce, and the Law 76

---

[23]. However, *Williams*, discussed in *Sosna*, makes clear that domicile is necessary for full faith and credit, regardless of the statutory language. In some instances, durational residency requirements may provide evidence of domicile.

(1972). Why does such a reputation pose problems? How important are problems of migratory divorce and divorce mills in the no-fault era? See Helen Garfield, The Transitory Divorce Action: Jurisdiction in the No-Fault Era, 58 Tex. L. Rev. 501, 546 (1980).

5. One student commentator points out that *Sosna* was decided a decade before *Zablocki*. "The case is therefore not indicative either of how the Court would decide the right to divorce issue today nor how it should decide it." She explains further: "[P]etitioners did not raise any challenges on substantive due process grounds or right to privacy grounds." Laura Bradford, Note, The Counterrevolution: A Critique of Recent Proposals to Reform No-Fault Divorce Laws, 49 Stan. L. Rev. 607, 636 n.112 (1997). How do you think *Sosna* would be decided today? Note Justice Marshall's view that the right to divorce is equivalent to the right to marry.

6. In our increasingly mobile society, does it make sense to limit divorce jurisdiction to the state of the parties' domicile? See Rhonda Wasserman, Divorce and Domicile: Time to Sever the Knot, 39 Wm. & Mary L. Rev. 1 (1997) (arguing that the domicile rule fails to preserve state sovereignty or assure the convenience of the parties and that federal legislation would be a better approach to ensure interstate recognition of divorce decrees).

7. How much deference do the majority and dissent give to the state's exclusive control over family law matters? The parameters of federal versus state authority are reflected in the case below.

## 3. Domestic Relations Exception to Diversity Jurisdiction

■ **ANKENBRANDT v. RICHARDS**
*504 U.S. 689 (1992)*

Justice WHITE delivered the opinion of the Court. . . .

Petitioner Carol Ankenbrandt, a citizen of Missouri, brought this lawsuit . . . on behalf of her daughters L.R. and S.R. against respondents Jon A. Richards and Debra Kesler, citizens of Louisiana, in the United States District Court for the Eastern District of Louisiana. Alleging federal jurisdiction based on the diversity-of-citizenship provision of §1332, Ankenbrandt's complaint sought monetary damages for alleged sexual and physical abuse of the children committed by Richards and Kesler. Richards is the divorced father of the children and Kesler his female companion. [T]he District Court granted respondents' motion to dismiss this lawsuit [concluding] that this case fell within what has become known as the "domestic relations" exception to diversity jurisdiction, and that it lacked jurisdiction over the case. . . .

We granted certiorari limited to the following questions: "(1) Is there a domestic relations exception to federal jurisdiction? (2) If so, does it permit a district court to abstain from exercising diversity jurisdiction over a tort action for damages?" . . . We address each of these issues in turn.

The domestic relations exception upon which the courts below relied to decline jurisdiction has been invoked often by the lower federal courts. The seeming authority for doing so originally stemmed from the announcement in Barber v. Barber, 21 How. 582 (1859), that the federal courts have no jurisdiction over suits for divorce or the allowance of alimony. In that case, the Court heard a suit in equity brought by a wife (by her next friend) in Federal District Court pursuant to diversity jurisdiction against her former husband. She sought to enforce a decree from a New York state court, which had granted a divorce and awarded her alimony. The former husband thereupon moved to Wisconsin to place himself beyond the New York courts' jurisdiction so that the divorce decree there could not be enforced against him; he then sued for divorce in a Wisconsin court, representing to that court that his wife had abandoned him and failing to disclose the existence of the New York decree. In a suit brought by the former wife in Wisconsin Federal District Court, the former husband alleged that the court lacked jurisdiction. The court accepted jurisdiction and gave judgment for the divorced wife.

On appeal [in *Barber*], it was argued that the District Court lacked jurisdiction on two grounds: first, that there was no diversity of citizenship because although divorced, the wife's citizenship necessarily remained that of her former husband; and second, that the whole subject of divorce and alimony, including a suit to enforce an alimony decree, was exclusively ecclesiastical at the time of the adoption of the Constitution and that the Constitution therefore placed the whole subject of divorce and alimony beyond the jurisdiction of the United States courts. Over the dissent of three Justices, the Court rejected both arguments. After an exhaustive survey of the authorities, the Court concluded that a divorced wife could acquire a citizenship separate from that of her former husband and that a suit to enforce an alimony decree rested within the federal courts' equity jurisdiction. The Court reached these conclusions after summarily dismissing the former husband's contention that the case involved a subject matter outside the federal courts' jurisdiction. In so stating, however, the Court also announced the following limitation on federal jurisdiction:

> Our first remark is — and we wish it to be remembered — that this is not a suit asking the court for the allowance of alimony. That has been done by a court of competent jurisdiction. The court in Wisconsin was asked to interfere to prevent that decree from being defeated by fraud.

We disclaim altogether any jurisdiction in the courts of the United States upon the subject of divorce, or for the allowance of alimony, either as an original proceeding in chancery or as an incident to divorce *a vinculo,* or to one from bed and board.

*Barber,* supra, at 584. . . .

The statements disclaiming jurisdiction over divorce and alimony decree suits, though technically dicta, formed the basis for excluding "domestic relations" cases from the jurisdiction of the lower federal courts, a jurisdictional limitation those courts have recognized ever since. . . . Because we are unwilling to cast aside an understood rule that has been recognized for nearly a century and a half, we feel compelled to explain why we will continue to recognize this limitation on federal jurisdiction.

Counsel argued in *Barber* that the Constitution prohibited federal courts from exercising jurisdiction over domestic relations cases. An examination of Article III, *Barber* itself, and our cases since *Barber* makes clear that the Constitution does not exclude domestic relations cases from the jurisdiction otherwise granted by statute to the federal courts.

Article III, §2, of the Constitution . . . delineates the absolute limits on the federal courts' jurisdiction. But in articulating three different terms to define jurisdiction — "Cases, in Law and Equity," "Cases," and "Controversies" — this provision contains no limitation on subjects of a domestic relations nature. Nor did *Barber* purport to ground the domestic relations exception in these constitutional limits on federal jurisdiction. The Court's discussion of federal judicial power to hear suits of a domestic relations nature contains no mention of the Constitution, and it is logical to presume that the Court based its statement limiting such power on narrower statutory, rather than broader constitutional, grounds. Subsequent decisions confirm that *Barber* was not relying on constitutional limits in justifying the exception. . . .

. . . The dissenters in *Barber* [suggested] that the federal courts had no power over certain domestic relations actions because the court of chancery lacked authority to issue divorce and alimony decrees. . . . We have no occasion here to join the historical debate over whether the English court of chancery had jurisdiction to handle certain domestic relations matters. . . . We thus are content to rest our conclusion that a domestic relations exception exists as a matter of statutory construction not on the accuracy of the historical justifications on which it was seemingly based, but rather on Congress' apparent acceptance of this construction of the diversity jurisdiction provisions in the years prior to 1948, when [Congress last amended the rules applicable to federal diversity jurisdiction]. Considerations of *stare decisis* have particular strength in this context, where "the legislative power is implicated, and Congress remains free to alter what we have done." . . .

In the more than 100 years since this Court laid the seeds for the development of the domestic relations exception, the lower federal courts have applied it in a variety of circumstances. Many of these applications go well beyond the circumscribed situations posed by *Barber* and its progeny. *Barber* itself disclaimed federal jurisdiction over a narrow range of domestic relations issues involving the granting of a divorce and a decree of alimony, and stated the limits on federal-court power to intervene prior to the rendering of such orders:

> It is, that when a court of competent jurisdiction over the subject-matter and the parties decrees a divorce, and alimony to the wife as its incident, and is unable of itself to enforce the decree summarily upon the husband, that courts of equity will interfere to prevent the decree from being defeated by fraud. The interference, however, is limited to cases in which alimony has been decreed; then only to the extent of what is due, and always to cases in which no appeal is pending from the decree for the divorce or for alimony.

Id., at 591.

The *Barber* Court thus did not intend to strip the federal courts of authority to hear cases arising from the domestic relations of persons unless they seek the granting or modification of a divorce or alimony decree. The holding of the case itself sanctioned the exercise of federal jurisdiction over the enforcement of an alimony decree that had been properly obtained in a state court of competent jurisdiction. . . .

Subsequently, this Court expanded the domestic relations exception to include decrees in child custody cases. In a child custody case brought pursuant to a writ of habeas corpus, for instance, the Court held void a writ issued by a Federal District Court to restore a child to the custody of the father. "As to the right to the control and possession of this child, as it is contested by its father and its grandfather, it is one in regard to which neither the Congress of the United States nor any authority of the United States has any special jurisdiction." In re Burrus, [136 U.S. 586, 594 (1890)].

Although In re Burrus technically did not involve a construction of the diversity statute, as we understand *Barber* to have done, its statement that "[t]he whole subject of the domestic relations of husband and wife, parent and child, belongs to the laws of the States and not to the laws of the United States," id., at 593-594, has been interpreted by the federal courts to apply with equal vigor in suits brought pursuant to diversity jurisdiction. This application is consistent with *Barber*'s directive to limit federal courts' exercise of diversity jurisdiction over suits for divorce and alimony decrees. We conclude, therefore, that the domestic relations exception, as articulated by this Court since *Barber*, divests the federal courts of power to issue divorce, alimony, and child custody decrees.

Given the long passage of time without any expression of congressional dissatisfaction, we have no trouble today reaffirming the validity of the exception as it pertains to divorce and alimony decrees and child custody orders.

Not only is our conclusion rooted in respect for this long-held understanding, it is also supported by sound policy considerations. Issuance of decrees of this type not infrequently involves retention of jurisdiction by the court and deployment of social workers to monitor compliance. As a matter of judicial economy, state courts are more eminently suited to work of this type than are federal courts, which lack the close association with state and local government organizations dedicated to handling issues that arise out of conflicts over divorce, alimony, and child custody decrees. Moreover, as a matter of judicial expertise, it makes far more sense to retain the rule that federal courts lack power to issue these types of decrees because of the special proficiency developed by state tribunals over the past century and a half in handling issues that arise in the granting of such decrees.

By concluding, as we do, that the domestic relations exception encompasses only cases involving the issuance of a divorce, alimony, or child custody decree, we necessarily find that the Court of Appeals erred by affirming the District Court's invocation of this exception. This lawsuit in no way seeks such a decree; rather, it alleges that respondents Richards and Kesler committed torts against L.R. and S.R., Ankenbrandt's children by Richards. Federal subject-matter jurisdiction pursuant to §1332 thus is proper in this case. . . .

## Notes and Questions

1. Under the "domestic relations exception to federal jurisdiction," federal courts traditionally declined to exercise jurisdiction over matters of domestic relations even in cases in which plaintiffs could establish the requisite diversity of citizenship and amount in controversy. The rationale was that domestic relations cases involve matters of peculiarly state, rather than federal, law. *Ankenbrandt* narrowed this exception, that is, limiting the types of cases that federal courts could refuse to adjudicate. After *Ankenbrandt,* federal courts could decline jurisdiction only over those cases involving the issuance of divorce decrees and the issuance or modification of child custody or alimony.

2. *Ankenbrandt* left open an alternative means by which federal courts can still "slam shut" the federal courthouse door to some domestic relations matters that do not involve divorce, alimony or custody. In an omitted portion of the opinion, the Court holds that neither the domestic relations exception nor the "abstention doctrine" bars Ankenbrandt's tort claim. The abstention doctrine, delineated in Younger v.

Harris, 401 U.S. 37 (1971), and Burford v. Sun Oil Co., 319 U.S. 315 (1943), is founded on principles of federalism. It provides that federal courts may refuse to adjudicate civil proceedings that involve important state interests or substantial policy concerns. *Ankenbrandt* concluded, by way of dicta, that abstention might be proper

> when a case presents "difficult questions of state law bearing on policy problems of substantial public importance whose importance transcends the result in the case then at bar" (citation omitted). Such might well be the case if a federal suit were filed prior to effectuation of a divorce, alimony, or child custody decree, and the suit depended on a determination of the status of the parties.

*Ankenbrandt,* 504 U.S. 689, 705 (1992).

3. Why did Carol Ankenbrandt prefer to litigate her tort claim alleging sexual abuse in a federal, rather than state, court? What are the benefits, as well as detriments, that will ensue from *Ankenbrandt* for litigants? Families? Society?

4. Various considerations favor federal courts' declining jurisdiction, such as recognition of special state expertise, disdain toward family law, and federal docket congestion. Countervailing considerations include the "growing national nature of family law, traditional diversity concerns of averting prejudice toward out-of-state claimants, the general institutional duty of courts to adjudicate cases within their purview, and the protection of federal rights." Michael Ashley Stein, The Domestic Relations Exception to Federal Jurisdiction: Rethinking an Unsettled Federal Courts Doctrine, 36 B.C. L. Rev. 669, 705 (1995). Which considerations do you find most persuasive?

Does the policy set forth in *Ankenbrandt* (that is, deference to state expertise) support the application of the exception in cases of divorce, custody, and alimony? Is it a wise policy to delegate sovereignty to the state over family law matters? Professor Anne Dailey, writing in defense of state sovereignty, notes:

> [N]ational authority over family law raises a serious threat of governmental tyranny over the moral identities of developing citizens. To begin with, a politics of the good family life entails a degree of civic engagement and a sense of shared community identity unattainable at the national level. Although family law does not require the moral homogeneity characteristic of strong communitarian cultures, it does demand a political discourse built upon the normative commitments of a specific historical community. States . . . are far better situated than the national government to develop and sustain a normative political discourse on family. Moreover, regulatory diversity among the fifty states preserves some measure of individual and family choice in matters touching upon the formative conditions of human identity.

Anne C. Dailey, Federalism and Families, 143 U. Pa. L. Rev. 1787, 1791-1792 (1995). Professor Naomi Cahn counters:

> Throughout the country, family law has traditionally reflected community norms, [and] the federal courts have attempted to protect the local character of domestic relations law. . . .
>
> The belief in local control over family law, however, beyond suggesting an inevitability to this means of family regulation, also overlooks the negative aspects of the community. While community can be a powerfully positive force, it can also be an extremely confining form of authority. The courts' examination of whether certain customs are based in community traditions, for instance, may enshrine majoritarian conventions such as a ban on gay marriage or certain consensual sex. Within certain communities, expectations are that women will be confined within traditional roles, thus hindering women's efforts to achieve equality. The many and various state regulations held unconstitutional by the Supreme Court provide yet further examples of the danger of trusting family law to community mores.

Naomi R. Cahn, Family Law, Federalism, and the Federal Courts, 79 Iowa L. Rev. 1073, 1123 (1994). Which argument is more persuasive?

5. Is the use of federal court jurisdiction, signaled by *Ankenbrandt,* consistent with the trend of increasing congressional regulation of family law?

## Problems

1. Jeanne sues in state court, charging that Joseph (the man with whom she has been cohabiting) breached his agreement to provide financial support for the rest of her life. Joseph removes the case to federal court on the basis of diversity. The court raises, on its own motion, the issue whether this "palimony" case falls within the domestic relations exception to federal jurisdiction requiring remand to state court. See Anastasi v. Anastasi, 544 F. Supp. 866 (D.N.J. 1982). How would this case be decided after *Ankenbrandt?* For a post-*Ankenbrandt* case, see Johnson v. Thomas, 808 F. Supp. 1316 (W.D. Mich. 1992).

2. When Kimberly and James divorce, their separation agreement, which is incorporated into the divorce decree, provides that James shall sell the marital home. The house fails to sell, Kimberly believes, because of James's efforts. Kimberly then files a motion in federal court, alleging breach of an agreement for the sale of real estate. Federal jurisdiction is predicated on diversity (she has relocated to another state). The court dismisses Kimberly's action for lack of federal subject matter jurisdiction, reasoning that the domestic relations exception precludes jurisdiction. Kimberly appeals. What result? See McLaughlin v. Cotner, 193 F.3d 410 (6th Cir. 1999).

# VI

■

# Financial Consequences of Dissolution

Approximately one million couples divorce annually.[1] These dissolutions often entail a division of property and an award of spousal support (formerly called "alimony" and now often referred to as "maintenance"). In marriages with children, a divorce decree also includes provision for their support.

Termination of marriage thus gives the state significant opportunities for intervention in matters left to private resolution in the intact family. Private choices have a role upon dissolution, however. Increasingly, the law defers to "private ordering" — allowing divorcing parties to negotiate their own financial arrangements in separation agreements and premarital contracts.

This chapter combines theory and practice. It explores traditional and evolving approaches to property division, spousal support, and child support, emphasizing the distinct theoretical bases for each. It also shows that, in practice, different financial issues typically arise together and their resolution often blurs these theoretical distinctions. Finally, it examines the roles of the parties and the state in allocational decisions.

[1]. U.S. Census Bureau, Statistical Abstract of the United States 104 (2000) (data showing 850,800 in 1998).

## A. INTRODUCTION: THE DEMISE OF FAULT?

Although every state now has some form of no-fault divorce, sharp differences persist about the role of fault in dividing property and determining spousal support.[2] California's early adoption of "pure no-fault"[3] laws prompted a famous study by sociologist Dr. Lenore J. Weitzman.[4]

According to Weitzman's 1985 book, *The Divorce Revolution: The Unexpected Social and Economic Consequences for Women and Children in America,* fault previously played a dual role in determining the economic consequences of divorce. First, marital misconduct provided a rationale for judicial awards and settlements, requiring a "guilty" husband to "pay for his transgressions with alimony" or with an additional portion of marital property.[5] Second, fault offered valuable leverage to an "innocent" spouse who could obtain financial concessions in exchange for cooperation.

Weitzman found that California's transition to a no-fault regime had unexpectedly impoverished women and children because family homes, formerly awarded to "innocent wives," were now being sold (and children displaced) so the proceeds could be divided equally between the spouses. Likewise, support awards were shrinking for women, primarily mothers and homemakers, who were now expected to be self-sufficient. And even a "guilty" spouse could now divorce unilaterally, eliminating the bargaining power of the resisting spouse, often the wife.

Weitzman's empirical study concluded that, just one year after divorce, men were experiencing a 42 percent improvement in their standard of living and women a 73 percent decline.[6] These dramatic figures

---

[2]. According to a survey by the American Law Institute (ALI), 20 states decide the financial consequences of dissolution without regard to marital misconduct; 5 disregard fault for property division and, as a practical matter, almost always do so for support; 3 almost never consider fault in financial matters although they could do so under their statutes; 7 disregard fault for property division but consider it in support awards; and 15 states consider misconduct in both areas. American Law Institute, Principles of the Law of Family Dissolution: Analysis and Recommendations, Chapter 1, Topic 2 (2002) (Summary of Existing Law). See also Linda D. Elrod & Robert G. Spector, A Review of the Year in Family Law: Redefining Families, Reforming Custody Jurisdiction, and Refining Support Issues, 34 Fam. L.Q. 607, 653 (2001) (listing 23 jurisdictions in which fault is not considered in alimony cases and 30 where it is relevant); Peter Nash Swisher, Reassessing Fault Factors in No-Fault Divorce, 31 Fam. L. Q. 269, 297 (1999) (11 of 17 states confronting the issue allow consideration of fault in property division and alimony).

[3]. The term describes states that, by statute, disregard marital misconduct in deciding both property division and support. See ALI Principles, supra note [2].

[4]. Professors Weitzman and Ruth Dixon studied the social and economic effects of divorce law reform by collecting and analyzing random samples of 2,500 court dockets over a 10-year period and by interviewing 169 family law attorneys, 44 family law judges, and 228 divorced men and women approximately one year after their divorces. Lenore J. Weitzman, The Divorce Revolution: The Unexpected Social and Economic Consequences for Women and Children in America (1985).

[5]. Id. at 12-13.

[6]. Id. at 339.

proved enormously influential, prompting not only a feminist critique of no-fault divorce[7] but also the passage of 14 new laws in California.[8] Subsequent empirical studies have substantiated Weitzman's general finding that men's standard of living rises after divorce, while that of women and children declines,[9] but not her oft-quoted 42/73 percent statistic. Weitzman's work also provoked a spate of criticisms. Some critics question her attempt to generalize from findings based on the California experience.[10] Others find flaws in her data[11] (which Weitzman now concedes[12]) and report a less significant decrease in women's standard of living.[13] Commentators also take Weitzman to task for failing to recognize the extent of adverse economic consequences for women under the fault regime.[14] Weitzman's work has received so much attention that it has become a part of popular culture.[15]

[7]. See Herma Hill Kay, From the Second Sex to the Joint Venture: An Overview of Women's Rights and Family Law in the United States During the Twentieth Century, 88 Cal. L. Rev. 2017, 2066-2068 (2000).

[8]. Lenore J. Weitzman, The Economic Consequences of Divorce Are Still Unequal: Comment on Peterson, 61 Am. Soc. Rev. 537, 538 (1996). See also Sanford L. Braver, The Gender Gap in Standard of Living After Divorce: Vanishingly Small?, 33 Fam. L.Q. 111, 113 (1999) ("impossible to overestimate how influential Weitzman's" figures were); Fred R. Shapiro, The Most-Cited Legal Books Published Since 1978, 29 J. Legal Stud. 397, 405 (2000) (listing Weitzman's book as the seventh most cited nonlegal book, published since 1978, in legal periodicals).

[9]. See, e.g., Terry Arendell, Mothers and Divorce 37 (1986); Andrea H. Beller & John W. Graham, Small Change: The Economics of Child Support 59 (1993); Eleanor E. Maccoby & Robert H. Mnookin, Dividing the Child: Social and Legal Dilemmas of Custody 128, 259 (1992) (finding also that the economic discrepancy continued in the subsequent three-year period). For an empirical study prior to Weitzman's that reports similar adverse effects, see Karen Seal, A Decade of No-Fault Divorce, 1 Fam. Advoc. 10 (Spring 1979).

[10]. See, e.g., Marsha Garrison, Good Intentions Gone Awry: The Impact of New York's Equitable Distribution Law on Divorce Outcomes, 57 Brook. L. Rev. 621, 724 (1991) (New York experience); Herbert Jacob, Faulting No-Fault, 1986 Am. B. Found. Res. J. 773.

[11]. Using her data, Richard Peterson was unable to replicate Weitzman's findings. Richard R. Peterson, A Re-Evaluation of the Economic Consequences of Divorce, 61 Am. Soc. Rev. 528 (1996).

[12]. Weitzman, supra note [8].

[13]. See, e.g., Richard R. Peterson, Women, Work, and Divorce 106 (1989) (finding 30-40 percent decrease, which abates over the long term to 5-20 percent); Saul D. Hoffman & Greg J. Duncan, What Are the Economic Consequences of Divorce?, 25 Demography 641 (1988) (suggesting that a finding of 33 percent decrease is more realistic); Peterson, supra note [11], at 652 (finding 27 percent decline for women and 10 percent increase for men). See also Richard R. Peterson, Statistical Errors, Faulty Conclusions, Misguided Policy: Reply to Weitzman, 61 Am. Soc. Rec. 539 (1996).

[14]. See, e.g., Stephen D. Sugarman, Dividing Financial Interests on Divorce, in Divorce Reform at the Crossroads 130, 132-135 (Stephen D. Sugarman & Herma Hill Kay eds., 1990); Marygold S. Melli, Constructing a Social Problem: The Post-Divorce Plight of Women and Children, 1986 Am. B. Found. Res. J. 759, 770 (pointing out adverse consequences of fault regime for women and children).

[15]. See Susan Faludi, Backlash: The Undeclared War Against American Women 19 (1991) (accusing Weitzman's work of sending women the message that they should remain in bad marriages to avoid the economic consequences of divorce).

Since California initiated no-fault divorce, attention has focused on three questions about the economic consequences of dissolution: First, what role should fault play? Second, what rationales for dividing property and awarding alimony might take the place of fault? Third, has no-fault divorce financially burdened women (and children) as a class while economically benefiting men? The next two sections address these questions by presenting a variety of materials that examine modern rationales for property division and spousal support awards, respectively.

## B. PROPERTY DISTRIBUTION: FROM TITLE THEORY TO CONTRIBUTION

What property can a court allocate between the spouses at dissolution? What theory determines how much to award to each?

■ **FERGUSON v. FERGUSON**
*639 So. 2d 921 (Miss. 1994) (en banc)*

PRATHER, Presiding Justice. . . .

[Linda Ferguson, age 44, and Billy Cleveland Ferguson, Sr., age 48, were married in 1967 and separated in 1991. They had two children. During their 24 years of marriage, Linda worked both as a homemaker and as a cosmetologist/beautician. Billy, employed by South Central Bell as a cable repair technician, installed and maintained local telephone service. Linda filed for divorce, which the chancellor awarded to her on the ground of Billy's adultery. The chancellor also awarded her custody of the 14-year-old son and $300 a month child support as well as the marital home and its contents, four acres of land comprising the homestead, with title to the marital home to be divested from Billy and vested in Linda, debt free; one-half interest in Billy's pension plan, stock ownership plan, and savings and security plan; and periodic alimony in the amount of $400 per month and lump sum alimony in the sum of $30,000 to be paid at the rate of $10,000 annually beginning on January 1, 1992. Billy appeals.]

States have devised various methods to divide marital assets at divorce, and approaches have usually followed one of three systems [separate property, equitable distribution, and community property.] Mississippi, Florida, South Carolina, Virginia, and West Virginia previously followed the separate property system, which was a system that merely determined title to the assets and returned that property to the title-holding spouse.

Our separate property system at times resulted in unjust distributions, especially involving cases of a traditional family where most property was titled in the husband, leaving a traditional housewife and mother with nothing but a claim for alimony, which often proved unenforceable. In a family where both spouses worked, but the husband's resources were devoted to investments while the wife's earnings were devoted to paying the family expenses or vice versa, the same unfair results ensued. The flaw of the separate property system, however, is not merely that it will occasionally ignore the financial contributions of the non-titlehold-ing spouse. The system . . . is also unable to take account of a spouse's non-financial contribution. In the case of many traditional housewives such non-financial contributions are often considerable.[2] Thus, to allow a system of property division to ignore non-financial contributions is to create a likelihood of unjust division of property.

The non-monetary contributions of a traditional housewife have been acknowledged by this Court, and to some extent, case law has helped lessen the unfairness to a traditional housewife in the division of marital property. [T]his Court has allowed lump sum alimony as an ad-justment to property division to prevent unfair division. The lump sum award has been described as a method of dividing property under the guise of alimony. . . .

Courts have acknowledged that the power and authority of the chancery court to award alimony and child support have been histori-cally derived from the legal duty of the husband to support the family. As to division of marital assets, it is the broad inherent equity powers of the chancery court that give it the authority to act. General equity prin-ciples of fairness undergird this authority. That duty was codified in Miss. Code. Ann. §93-5-23 (Supp. 1993). . . . This Court, therefore, holds that the chancery court is within its authority and power to equitably di-vide marital assets at divorce. . . .

[T]his Court recognizes the need for guidelines to aid chancellors in their adjudication of marital property division. Therefore, this Court di-rects the chancery courts to evaluate the division of marital assets by the following guidelines. [The court lists, inter alia: substantial contribution to the accumulation of the property, the market and emotional value of the assets, tax and other economic consequences of the distribution, the parties' needs, and any other factor that in equity should be considered.]

[F]airness is the prevailing guideline in marital division. . . . All prop-erty division, lump sum or periodic alimony payment, and mutual obli-gations for child support should be considered together. "Alimony and equitable distribution are distinct concepts, but together they command the entire field of financial settlement of divorce. Therefore, where one expands, the other must recede." [LaRue v. LaRue, 304 S.E.2d 312, 334

---

2. The persistent attempts made to put a monetary value on a homemaker's contri-bution are likely to undervalue the magnitude of such contributions. Nonetheless, esti-mates of replacement loss are made as high as $40,000 per year. . . .

(W. Va. 1983) (Neely, J., concurring).] Thus, the chancellor may divide marital assets, real and personal, as well as award periodic and/or lump sum alimony, as equity demands. To aid appellate review, findings of fact by the chancellor, together with the legal conclusions drawn from those findings, are required. . . .

. . . Billy contends that he owned all the interest in the pension plan, stock, and savings [obtained through his employer, Bell South], and that it was his separate property. On appeal [of the chancellor's allocation of one-half these asssets to Linda], Billy claims Linda in no way contributed to the acquisition of this property, and nothing was ever issued in her name. . . .

When a couple has been married for twenty-four years, yet the only retirement benefits accumulated throughout the marriage are titled in the name of only one spouse, is it equitable to find only one spouse entitled to financial security upon retirement when both have benefitted from the employer funded plan along the way? When one spouse has contributed directly to the fund, by virtue of his/her labor, while the other has contributed indirectly, by virtue of domestic services and/or earned income which both parties have enjoyed rather than invested, the spouse without retirement funds in his/her own name could instead have been working outside the home and/or investing his/her wages in preparation for his/her own retirement. When separate plans for each spouse are not in existence, it is only equitable to allow both parties to reap the benefits of the one existing retirement plan, to which both parties have materially contributed in some fashion. . . .

[In addition,] Billy contends the chancellor lacked the authority to order him to convey, free of all encumbrances, his one-half interest in the jointly owned four acres on which the marital home was situated. . . . "A spouse who has made a material contribution toward the acquisition of property which is titled in the name of the other may claim an equitable interest in such jointly accumulated property incident to a divorce proceeding." Jones v. Jones, 532 So. 2d 574, 580 (Miss. 1988) (citing Watts v. Watts, 466 So. 2d 889 (Miss. 1985)). [W]e said that "[i]f 'contribution' toward the acquisition of assets is proven by a divorcing party, then the court has the authority to divide these 'jointly' accumulated assets." Jones, 532 So. 2d at 580. . . .

[There were two mortgages on the marital home.] This Court holds that under existing case law the chancellor was within his authority to order Billy to effect a transfer of title to Linda to the marital home and the surrounding four acres [free and clear of any liens] to accomplish an equitable division. . . . Nonetheless, this issue is remanded for consideration together with the other assets [for equitable] division to be guided by the factors promulgated today. . . .

The chancellor stated on the record that he tended to believe the testimony of [Billy's paramour that he] had withdrawn $30,000.00 from his Bell South Savings and Security Plan and put it where nobody could get to it or find it. He awarded this amount to Linda as lump sum alimony to be paid in three installments. . . . Linda worked and contributed to Billy's financial status, but had no assets of her own; her separate estate pales in comparison to Billy's. This award of lump sum alimony may have been made by the chancellor to give Linda financial security. An explanation of the basis of this award will help this Court determine whether the distribution represents an abuse of discretion or a division supported by the record. Therefore, a remand is warranted on this issue. . . .

## ■ UNIFORM MARRIAGE AND DIVORCE ACT §307
*9A U.L.A. (pt. I) 288 (1998)*

### (ALTERNATIVE A)

### [DISPOSITION OF PROPERTY]

(a) [T]he court, without regard to marital misconduct, [in a dissolution] shall, and in a proceeding for legal separation may, finally equitably apportion between the parties the property and assets belonging to either or both however and whenever acquired, and whether the title thereto is in the name of the husband or wife or both. In making apportionment the court shall consider the duration of the marriage, and prior marriage of either party, antenuptial agreement of the parties, the age, health, station, occupation, amount and sources of income, vocational skills, employability, estate, liabilities, and needs of each of the parties, custodial provisions, whether the apportionment is in lieu of or in addition to maintenance, and the opportunity of each for future acquisition of capital assets and income. The court shall also consider the contribution or dissipation of each party in the acquisition, preservation, depreciation, or appreciation in value of the respective estates, and the contribution of a spouse as a homemaker or to the family unit. . . .[16]

---

[16]. Alternative B, designed for community property states, directs the court to assign separate property to the spouse-owner and to effect a "just" division of the community property, without regard to fault and "after considering all relevant factors including" the contribution of each spouse to the acquisition of marital property, including a homemaker's contribution; the value of the property set aside to each; marriage duration; and the economic circumstances of each spouse, including the desirability of awarding the family home to the custodial parent. 9A U.L.A. (pt. I) at 288-289. These two alternatives replaced the original version of §307, reprinted infra page 663.

■ STEPHEN D. SUGARMAN, DIVIDING
FINANCIAL INTERESTS ON DIVORCE
*in Divorce Reform at the Crossroads 130, 136-141 (Stephen D.*
*Sugarman & Herma Hill Kay eds., 1990)*

[The author attempts to identify a theoretical framework or legal analogy for understanding the financial incidents of divorce. He rejects fault as a suitable principle, given the high social cost imposed. He also rejects the notion of "marriage as contract," in part because modern no-fault, unilateral divorce leaves no room for "the concept of breach and resultant damages." He then considers partnership law.]

Perhaps a better legal analogy to no-fault divorce can be found in partnership law. The idea is that through marriage the man and woman have joined together (50-50?) in an economic partnership, which, like partnerships generally, can be dissolved by either party. On the ending of the marriage partnership, like other partnerships, there is to be a winding up of the partnership's activities and a distribution of the partnership assets. . . .

Under the partnership analogy all earnings generated by the couple during the marriage would seem to belong to the partnership, as would any things bought with those earnings and any earnings left unspent and saved or invested. . . . In the marriage setting [unlike in traditional financial partnerships], it is as though, as a general rule, all the extra income and asset appreciation of the partnership is simply retained and reinvested in the partnership. . . .

[J]ust as financial partners contribute only some of their property to the typical partnership, certain items of property belonging to the husband and wife could be seen as outside the marital partnership and not subject to division on the marriage's termination. They might include assets the parties bring to the marriage and do not commingle with other marital property, and those gifts and inheritances separately received by either party during the marriage and maintained separately.

If marriage under no-fault is to be seen as a conventional partnership, no formal distinctions would be made between long- and short-duration marriages; to be sure, in long-duration marriages, there might be more assets to distribute. So, too, the family home would not be treated differently from any other asset. The implication of minor children would be ambiguous since there is no obvious counterpart in ordinary partnerships. Does gaining custody mean that you have obtained a partnership asset, or merely that you have assumed a partnership liability for which you should be compensated?

Most important, under the partnership analogy, there would be no spousal support. That is, in the traditional partnership, even though the partners agree to make their earning capacity available to the partnership during its lifetime, they ordinarily just walk away from the dissolved partnership with all their own human capital. This applies both to the human capital they brought to the partnership and to any enhanced human capital they gained during the operation of the partnership. . . .

Traditional financial partners, of course, may anticipate certain problems of partnership breakup and, if they wish, enter into alternative arrangements at the outset. . . . They [even] might agree to be other than 50-50 partners originally. Perhaps married couples could also be encouraged to make specific agreements in advance. But, in fact, nowadays nearly no one does so. . . .

## ■ AMERICAN LAW INSTITUTE, PRINCIPLES OF THE LAW OF FAMILY DISSOLUTION: ANALYSIS AND RECOMMENDATIONS §4.12
*(2002)*

### RECHARACTERIZATION OF SEPARATE PROPERTY AS MARITAL PROPERTY AT THE DISSOLUTION OF LONG-TERM MARRIAGES

(1) In marriages that exceed a minimum duration specified in a uniform rule of statewide application, a portion of the separate property that each spouse held at the time of their marriage should be recharacterized at dissolution as marital property.

(a) The percentage of separate property that is recharacterized as marital property under Paragraph (1) should be determined by the duration of the marriage, according to a formula specified in a rule of statewide application.

(b) The formula should specify a marital duration at which the full value of the separate property held by the spouses at the time of their marriage is recharacterized at dissolution as marital property.

(2) A portion of separate property acquired by each spouse during marriage should be recharacterized at dissolution as marital property if, at the time of dissolution, both the marital duration, and the time since the property's acquisition (the "holding period"), exceed the minimum length specified for each in a rule of statewide application.

(a) The percentage of separate property that is recharacterized as marital property under Paragraph (2) should be determined by a formula, specified in a rule of statewide application, that takes into account both the marital duration and the holding period of the property in question.

(b) The formula should specify a marital duration and holding period at which the full value of the property is recharacterized at dissolution as marital property.

(3) For the purpose of this section, any appreciation in the value of separate property, or income from it, that would otherwise itself be separate property is treated as having been acquired at the same time as the underlying asset, and any asset acquired in exchange for separate property is treated as having been acquired as of the time its predecessor asset was acquired.

(4) A spouse should be able to avoid the application of this section to gifts or inheritances received during marriage by giving written notice of that intention to the other spouse within the time period following the property's receipt that is specified in a rule of statewide application.

(5) The provision of a will or deed of gift specifying that a bequest or gift is not subject to claims under this section should be given effect.

(6) This section should not apply to separate property if, as set forth in written findings of the trial court . . . , preservation of the property's separate character is necessary to avoid substantial injustice.

## Notes and Questions on the Theory of Property Division

1. *Development of equitable distribution.* Most American states follow the common law approach to spousal ownership of property during marriage. Eight use a community property approach derived from their French or Spanish heritage; Wisconsin's system is modeled on the Uniform Marital Property Act, 9A U.L.A. (pt. I) 103 (1998). See Chapter III, page 255.

The common law scheme reflects "title theory." Title to property, as evidenced in a deed, for example, determines ownership between the spouses. Property acquired or earned during marriage belongs to the acquiring or earning spouse, unless that spouse acts affirmatively to create joint ownership (for example, buying a house titled jointly in the names of both spouses). Upon divorce, the court assigns property to the owner. In the 1980s, after adopting no-fault grounds and witnessing a rising divorce rate, many states began abandoning the title system in favor of a system of "equitable distribution" applicable at the end of marriage. In *Ferguson,* Mississippi became the last state to abandon the title system. See generally Deborah H. Bell, Equitable Distribution: Implementing the Marital Partnership Theory Through the Dual Classification System, 67 Miss. L. J. 115 (1997) (examining *Ferguson's* background, implementation, and difficulties in classifying property subject to equitable division).

Before the development of equitable distribution laws, statutes permitting a court to divide property upon divorce were limited, and some states had no such statutes at all. In a few states courts used the doctrine of "special equities" to award a wife who had made substantial contributions a share of her husband's property or applied other equitable remedies, such as resulting trust, constructive trust, or unjust enrichment. See Brett R. Turner, Equitable Distribution of Property §1.02 (2d ed. 1994 & Supp. 2000).

One influential model was the original 1970 version of the Uniform Marriage and Divorce Act (UMDA). Using definitions typical of community property systems, UMDA distinguished separate property from marital property and listed factors courts should consider in making a "just" division of the latter:

### §307. [Disposition of Property]

(a) [The court in a dissolution or legal separation proceeding] shall assign each spouse's property to him. It also shall divide the marital property without regard to marital misconduct in just proportions considering all relevant factors including:

(1) contribution of each spouse to acquisition of the marital property, including contribution of a spouse as homemaker;

(2) value of the property set apart to each spouse;

(3) duration of the marriage; and

(4) economic circumstances of each spouse when the division of property is to become effective, including the desirability of awarding the family home or the right to live therein for reasonable periods to the spouse having custody of any children.

(b) For purposes of this Act, "marital property" means all property acquired by either spouse subsequent to the marriage except:

(1) property acquired by gift, bequest, devise, or descent;

(2) property acquired in exchange for property acquired before the marriage or in exchange for property acquired by gift, bequest, devise, or descent;

(3) property acquired by a spouse after a decree of legal separation;

(4) property excluded by valid agreement of the parties; and

(5) the increase in value of property acquired before the marriage.

(c) All property acquired by either spouse after the marriage and before a decree of legal separation is presumed to be marital property, regardless of whether title is held individually or by the spouses in some form of co-ownership such as joint tenancy, tenancy in common, tenancy by the entirety, and community property. The presumption of marital property is overcome by a showing that the property was acquired by a method listed in subsection (b).

9A U.L.A. (pt. I) 289-290 (1998). Laws following this model bring common law states much closer to community property states in the treatment of property after divorce. That is, equitable distribution laws in common law states create a "deferred community property" system, with the concept of marital property becoming effective upon divorce. See Turner, supra, §1.02 n.44.

Although most states adopted equitable distribution by statute (often modeled on UMDA), Mississippi did so by judicial decision in *Ferguson*. What is the source of *Ferguson*'s authority to adopt a new property distribution system? Does the ruling deprive Billy Ferguson of his property without due process? Are the court's "guidelines" really "judicial legislation" in disguise? See *Ferguson*, 639 So. 2d at 940 (Lee, P.J., concurring and dissenting).

2. *Homemaker services.* A significant criticism of the title theory, as *Ferguson* reveals, pertains to its treatment of the traditional homemaker. As one commentator notes: "[The title system] has increasingly been understood to be unfair as clearly favoring the market actor who has economic assets with which to accumulate property and devaluing the non-economic activities of homemakers." Martha Albertson Fineman, The Illusion of Equality 202 n.22 (1991). This traditional devaluation of homemakers' activities followed from the common law doctrine of coverture, including the wife's duty to perform household services and the husband's rights to her property and earnings.

How does UMDA treat homemaker services? With UMDA as an influential example, states gradually began recognizing that such services have value.

3. *Contribution.* Does *Ferguson*'s contribution theory treat marriage as a partnership, the approach examined by Professor Sugarman? What is the difference? Does the partnership analogy, first developed in community property states, provide fair outcomes for homemakers? See Bea Ann Smith, The Partnership Theory of Marriage: A Borrowed Solution Fails, 68 Tex. L. Rev. 689 (1990). But see Cynthia Starnes, Divorce and the Displaced Homemaker: A Discourse on Playing with Dolls, Partnership Buyouts and Dissociation Under No-Fault, 60 U. Chi. L. Rev. 67 (1993) (proposing contemporary partnership model). What property is subject to division under a contribution rationale? Only property acquired during marriage?

4. *Marital property versus "hotchpot."* Note how UMDA identifies the property that is subject to division. Alternative A of revised §307 (a model proposed for common law states) gives the court authority to divide the great "hotchpot" of assets owned by either spouse, whenever and however acquired. See Linda D. Elrod & Robert G. Spector, A Review of the Year in Family Law: Redefining Families, Reforming Custody Jurisdiction, and Refining Support Issues, 34 Fam. L. Q. 607, 657 (2001) (listing 21 jurisdictions that do not limit property division to marital assets only). Can partnership or contribution theories explain judicial authority to divide property acquired before marriage or received by one spouse as a gift?

More states, instead, follow the original version of UMDA, directing division of "marital property" only. These statutes define marital property as that acquired by either spouse during the marriage, except when acquired by gift, inheritance, or in exchange for nonmarital or "separate property"; such statutes often presume that all property acquired during the marriage is marital. E.g., Ky. Rev. Stat. Ann. §403.190 (Michie 1999); Mo. Rev. Stat. §452.330 (2000). Why did UMDA's drafters replace the "marital property" with the "hotchpot" approach? See Joan M. Krauskopf, A Theory for "Just" Division of Marital Property in Missouri, 41 Mo. L. Rev. 165, 173-174 (1976) (ABA Family Law Section feared complexity of classifying property as separate or marital). See also Ralph J. Podell, The Case for Revision of the Uniform Marriage and Divorce Act, 7 Fam. L.Q. 169, 175 (1973) (division of all property more equitable).

Under yet another approach, a "hybrid system," the court distributes nonmarital property only after the distribution of marital property, if equity requires. Which approach does *Ferguson* follow? Does the court identify what property is subject to division?

5. *The ALI's approach: recharacterizing separate property.* The American Law Institute's Principles of the Law of Family Dissolution (ALI Principles) seek to guide states in addressing divorce-related questions. The ALI Principles reconceptualize dissolution's financial consequences to enhance consistency among outcomes and to clarify rationales. The ALI Principles propose the use of presumptive formulae ("rules of statewide application") that will allow prediction of judicial outcomes, in turn facilitating settlement at dissolution or encouraging premarital contracts. These presumptive formulae serve as default rules applicable in the absence of agreement by the parties. Courts can depart from the outcomes yielded by the formulae only on written findings that substantial injustice would result.

Does ALI Principles §4.12's recharacterization split the difference between those states dividing only marital property and those using the "hotchpot" approach? Why should duration of marriage itself transform separate property into marital property (which the ALI Principles subject to presumptively equal division)? Do the ALI Principles provide for greater predictability than laws modeled on UMDA, which make the marriage's length one factor in an equitable division? In addition to promoting predictability, §4.12 claims to reflect the reasonable expectations of spouses. The comments explain:

> After many years of marriage, spouses typically do not think of their separate-property assets as separate, even if they would be so classified under the technical property rules. Both spouses are likely to believe, for example, that such assets will be available to provide for their joint retirement, for a medical crisis of either spouse, or for other personal emergencies. The longer the marriage the more likely it is that the spouses will have made decisions about their employment or the use of their marital assets that are premised in part on such expectations about the separate property of both spouses. If the marriage ends with the death of the wealthier spouse, the common law has traditionally provided the remedy of a forced

share for survivors not otherwise provided for. The 1990 revision of the Uniform Probate Code gradually enlarges the spouse's forced share with the duration of the marriage according to a mechanical formula. Section 4.12 of these Principles provides an analogous remedy when the marriage ends with dissolution rather than death.

ALI Principles §4.12 cmt. a. Given that the explanation cites no empirical studies of spousal attitudes about property ownership in long marriages, what is the basis of this approach?

6. *"Equitable" distribution.* Once a court determines the property subject to division and its value, how does the court determine the amount each party should get? Alternative A of UMDA's revised §307 directs an "equitable" apportionment according to a wide-ranging list of factors of unidentified weight. Other statutes direct the court to divide such property "in just proportions." E.g., 750 Ill. Comp. Stat. §5/503(d) (West Supp. 2001). Are these standards too vague to be helpful?

7. *Debts.* Courts generally allocate debts as well as assets. For example, *Ferguson* addresses responsibility for mortgages. Usually the same principles of classification (that is, separate or marital) govern property and debts, and the same factors guide distribution of both. E.g., In re Marriage of Speirs, 956 P.2d 622, 623 (Colo. Ct. App. 1997) (classifying wife's student loans as marital debt).

8. *Fault.* Should marital misconduct play a role in the equitable or just division of property? To what extent does the husband's adultery in *Ferguson* explain the court's departure from title theory? Was the court punishing him for his "fault"? Does consideration of fault in dividing property mitigate the harsh effects of no-fault divorce found by Dr. Lenore Weitzman, supra, page 664? Even if dissolution should be available without regard to fault, does it follow that the law should not impose economic rewards and punishments for behavior during marriage? See Peter Nash Swisher, Reassessing Fault Factors in No-Fault Divorce, 31 Fam. L.Q. 269 (1999).

Approximately 15 states consider fault in dividing property at dissolution. ALI Principles, supra, at Chapter 1, Topic 2 (Summary of Existing Law). Some states consider fault but disallow giving it "excessive weight." E.g., McDougal v. McDougal, 545 N.W.2d 357, 362 (Mich. 1996) ("fault is an element in the search for an equitable division . . . not a punitive basis for an inequitable division"). In contrast, in some states one spouse's misconduct can justify awarding all marital assets to the other spouse. E.g., Bell v. Bell, 540 N.W.2d 602 (N.D. 1995) (based on both economic and noneconomic misconduct). What position does UMDA take?

9. *Equal division.* Community property principles, explicitly recognizing marriage as a partnership, give each spouse an undivided one-half interest in property acquired by spousal labor during the marriage. Most, but not all, community property states apply a rule or presumption of equal division at dissolution. E.g., Putterman v. Putterman, 939

P.2d 1047 (Nev. 1997) (equal division absent "compelling reasons"). Equal division contemplates equality in value, not dividing an asset in half.

The ALI Principles dictate a presumption of equal division of marital property in §4.09. This approach disregards fault, in part to achieve predictability and facilitate settlement. Like UMDA, however, the ALI Principles in §4.10 include an exception for financial misconduct with marital assets. Unlike other marital misconduct, financial misconduct can be predictably measured, for example, one spouse's gift of $10,000 in marital property to a lover. Under §4.10, the misconduct must occur within a time period before serving the dissolution petition, specified in a rule of statewide application.

For an equitable distribution, should a court use an equal division as a starting point? Do partnership and contribution rationales presume equal participation by both spouses? See In re Marriage of Massee, 970 P.2d 1203, 1209-1211 (Or. 1999) (analyzing presumption of equal contributions by homemaker and breadwinner).

Does the absence of a presumption of equal division constitute sex discrimination? Will courts disproportionately favor breadwinners over homemakers if given unfettered discretion to achieve an equitable or fair division of property? See Wendt v. Wendt, 757 A.2d 1225, 1241-1245 (Conn. App. Ct. 2000) (rejecting wife's challenge under state ERA).

10. *Need.* Does *Ferguson's* reliance on a contribution rationale leave room to divide property based on need? On what basis did Linda Ferguson "need" the marital home and the other property that was titled to her husband but awarded to her? Is need compatible with contribution and partnership rationales? Some evidence suggests a "glass ceiling," reflected in decreasing percentage awards for wives as the amount of marital property increases. Professor Mary Moers Wenig discerns in such cases the "enough is enough" principle, based on the notion that need cannot not justify an award above a certain amount. Mary Moers Wenig, The Marital Property Law of Connecticut, Past, Present and Future, 1990 Wis. L. Rev. 807, 873 & n.289. In response, Professor Joan Williams wonders: "In this country we do not ordinarily condition ownership on whether the owners 'need' their property. Why treat wives differently?" Joan Williams, Do Wives Own Half? Winning for Wives After *Wendt,* 32 Conn. L. Rev. 249, 250 (1999).

Surveying the factors listed by legislatures and courts to guide equitable division, Professor Martha Fineman categorizes four under the concept of "contribution" and five under "need." Martha L. Fineman, Societal Factors Affecting the Creation of Legal Rules for Distribution of Property of Divorce, 23 Fam. L.Q. 279 (1989). She explains the inconsistency in these rationales for property division:

... The fact that within any system the factors are often combined and exist simultaneously reflects the tension between two incompatible contemporary images of marriage — the egalitarian partnership and the dependency models. In fact, the partnership image gives rise to the idea of contribution; each person contributes a different but valuable set of benefits to the good of the whole, and the whole should be divided to reflect these contributions if it is dissolved. Need has no role to play in a true partnership of equals. The dependency image, in contrast, anticipates that a woman has been "victimized" to some extent in marriage. She is viewed as having sacrificed career goals and ambitions for the marriage. At divorce she is dependent and that dependency will continue. She, therefore, has needs that should be compensated. . . .

[Under the equality conceptualization of marriage, divorce is] seen as an economic adjustment between partners, with the ideal solution being an equal division of the assets and liabilities amassed as a result of their equally valued contribution. . . . Contribution operates at the expense of inquiry into possible future needs.

Id. at 290, 292. Alternatively, does need make more sense as a rationale for spousal support than for property division? In the materials that follow consider whether existing theories of alimony address Fineman's concerns.

## Problem

Rolando and Julieta separate only two years after marrying. During the separation, Rolando sends money to their children (all born before the marriage) and pays for Julieta's surgery. Eight years after separating, they reconcile for four years. In subsequent divorce proceedings, Rolando challenges the court's classification of assets he acquired during the separation as marital property. Assuming the 1970 version of UMDA governs, what result and why? See Rodriguez v. Rodriguez, 908 P.2d 1007 (Alaska 1995). Alternatively, suppose the assets in question had been acquired by Rolando premaritally, while he and Julieta were cohabiting as a prelude to their marriage? See In re Rolf, 16 P.3d 345, 351 (Mont. 2000); Northrop v. Northrop, 622 N.W.2d 219 (N.D. 2001).

## C. SPOUSAL SUPPORT: THEORIES OF NEED, SELF-SUFFICIENCY, AND BEYOND

The concept of divorce as the dissolution of a partnership leaves unexplained the duty to provide future support for a former spouse. What is the rationale for spousal support? How should the amount be determined? How long should the duty continue?

## ■ ORR v. ORR
*440 U.S. 268 (1979)*

Mr. Justice BRENNAN delivered the opinion of the Court.

The question presented is the constitutionality of Alabama alimony statutes which provide that husbands, but not wives, may be required to pay alimony upon divorce.

On February 26, 1974, a final decree of divorce was entered, dissolving the marriage of William and Lillian Orr. That decree directed appellant, Mr. Orr, to pay appellee, Mrs. Orr, $1,240 per month in alimony. On July 28, 1976, Mrs. Orr initiated a contempt proceeding . . . alleging that Mr. Orr was in arrears in his alimony payments. [A]t the hearing on Mrs. Orr's petition, Mr. Orr submitted in his defense a motion requesting that Alabama's alimony statutes be declared unconstitutional. . . .

In authorizing the imposition of alimony obligations on husbands, but not on wives, the Alabama statutory scheme "provides that different treatment be accorded . . . on the basis of . . . sex; it thus establishes a classification subject to scrutiny under the Equal Protection Clause," Reed v. Reed, 404 U.S. 71, 75 (1971). The fact that the classification expressly discriminates against men rather than women does not protect it from scrutiny. "To withstand scrutiny" under the Equal Protection Clause, " 'classifications by gender must serve important governmental objectives and must be substantially related to achievement of those objectives.' " Califano v. Webster, 430 U.S. 313, 316-317 (1977). We shall, therefore, examine the three governmental objectives that might arguably be served by Alabama's statutory scheme.

[The Court rejected as a legitimate purpose the state's preference for traditional sex-based roles in marriage.] "No longer is the female destined solely for the home and the rearing of the family, and only the male for the marketplace and the world of ideas," [Stanton v. Stanton, 421 U.S. 7, 14-15 (1975).]

The opinion of the Alabama Court of Civil Appeals . . . states that the Alabama statutes were "designed" for "the wife of a broken marriage who needs financial assistance," 351 So. 2d [904, 905 (Ala. Civ. App. 1977)]. This may be read as asserting either of two legislative objectives. One is a legislative purpose to provide help for needy spouses, using sex as a proxy for need. The other is a goal of compensating women for past discrimination during marriage, which assertedly has left them unprepared to fend for themselves in the working world following divorce. We concede, of course, that assisting needy spouses is a legitimate and important governmental objective. We have also recognized "[r]eduction of the disparity in economic condition between men and women caused by the long history of discrimination against women . . . as . . . an important governmental objective," Califano v. Webster, supra, 430

U.S., at 317. It only remains, therefore, to determine whether the classi-fication at issue here is "substantially related to achievement of those objectives."

Ordinarily, we would begin the analysis of the "needy spouse" ob-jective by considering whether sex is a sufficiently "accurate proxy," Craig v. Boren, 429 U.S. 190, 204 (1976), for dependency to establish that the gender classification rests " 'upon some ground of difference having a fair and substantial relation to the object of the legislation,' " Reed v. Reed, supra, 404 U.S., at 76. Similarly, we would initially ap-proach the "compensation" rationale by asking whether women had in fact been significantly discriminated against in the sphere to which the statute applied a sex-based classification, leaving the sexes "not similarly situated with respect to opportunities" in that sphere.

But in this case, even if sex were a reliable proxy for need, and even if the institution of marriage did discriminate against women, these fac-tors still would "not adequately justify the salient features of" Alabama's statutory scheme, Craig v. Boren, supra, 429 U.S., at 202-203. Under the statute, individualized hearings at which the parties' relative financial circumstances are considered already occur. There is no reason, there-fore, to use sex as a proxy for need. Needy males could be helped along with needy females with little if any additional burden on the State. In such circumstances, not even an administrative-convenience rationale exists to justify operating by generalization or proxy. Similarly, since in-dividualized hearings can determine which women were in fact discrim-inated against vis-à-vis their husbands, as well as which family units defied the stereotype and left the husband dependent on the wife, Al-abama's alleged compensatory purpose may be effectuated without plac-ing burdens solely on husbands. . . .

Moreover, use of a gender classification actually produces perverse results in this case. As compared to a gender-neutral law placing alimony obligations on the spouse able to pay, the present Alabama statutes give an advantage only to the financially secure wife whose husband is in need. Although such a wife might have to pay alimony under a gender-neutral statute, the present statutes exempt her from that obligation. Thus, "[t]he [wives] who benefit from the disparate treatment are those who were . . . nondependent on their husbands," Califano v. Goldfarb, 430 U.S. 199, 221 (1977) (Stevens, J., concurring in judgment). They are precisely those who are not "needy spouses." . . .

Legislative classifications which distribute benefits and burdens on the basis of gender carry the inherent risk of reinforcing the stereotypes about the "proper place" of women and their need for special protec-tion. Thus, even statutes purportedly designed to compensate for and ameliorate the effects of past discrimination must be carefully tailored. Where, as here, the State's compensatory and ameliorative purposes are as well served by a gender-neutral classification as one that gender classifies and therefore carries with it the baggage of sexual stereotypes, the State cannot be permitted to classify on the basis of sex.

[Reversed and remanded.]

## ■ UNIFORM MARRIAGE AND DIVORCE ACT §308
### 9A U.L.A. (pt. I) 446 (1998)

[MAINTENANCE]

(a) [The court in a dissolution or legal separation proceeding] may grant a maintenance order for either spouse only if it finds that the spouse seeking maintenance:

(1) lacks sufficient property to provide for his reasonable needs; and

(2) is unable to support himself through appropriate employment or is the custodian of a child whose condition or circumstances make it appropriate that the custodian not be required to seek employment outside the home.

(b) The maintenance order shall be in amounts and for periods of time the court deems just, without regard to marital misconduct, and after considering all relevant factors including:

(1) the financial resources of the party seeking maintenance, including marital property apportioned to him, his ability to meet his needs independently, and the extent to which a provision for support of a child living with the party includes a sum for that party as custodian;

(2) the time necessary to acquire sufficient education or training to enable the party seeking maintenance to find appropriate employment;

(3) the standard of living established during the marriage;

(4) the duration of the marriage;

(5) the age and the physical and emotional condition of the spouse seeking maintenance; and

(6) the ability of the spouse from whom maintenance is sought to meet his needs while meeting those of the spouse seeking maintenance.

## ■ IRA MARK ELLMAN, THE THEORY OF ALIMONY
### 77 Cal. L. Rev. 1, 3, 5-6, 40-43, 49-51 (1989)

Why do we have alimony? . . . One might question how alimony could have survived thus far without a satisfactory explanation for its existence. The answer is that alimony's form has remained the same while its function has changed. Originally, alimony was a remedy of the English ecclesiastical courts which accompanied a legal separation — divorce "from bed and board" — at a time when complete divorces were available only by special legislative action, and gender roles in marriage were rigid and unquestioned. The husband had a legal and customary duty to support his wife. This duty continued after "divorce" because there was no divorce in the modern sense, only legal separation. When judicial divorce became available in the eighteenth and nineteenth century, alimony remained as a remedy. Courts and legislatures still viewed alimony as proper because women remained dependent and society expected husbands to support their wives. It was believed that the "innocent" wife gained "the apparent right to perpetual support as if the marriage had remained intact."[9] Indeed, following this rationale, some jurisdictions allowed alimony claims only by "innocent" wives divorcing "guilty" husbands. But any justification such a system might have provided for an alimony remedy has been undermined completely by the modern divorce reform movement of the last twenty years, which makes fault irrelevant and rejects gender roles. A new rationale is therefore required. . . .

If contract [and partnership rationales do not work], then what principles can we look to in fashioning alimony rules? The question is fundamental, for by shifting away from contract we necessarily shift away from a conception of alimony as a claim based on promise or commitment, to one grounded in some other policy. What should that policy be? Examination of analogous commercial arrangements may be instructive. . . .

The first goal is to encourage the durability of the relationship. Marriage is usually intended to be a long-term arrangement. The typical commercial arrangement is not; although it may in fact continue over many years, in most cases there is no agreement legally binding the parties over a long term. In some cases, however, parties make a long-term commitment. One reason they do is relevant here: A contracting party might seek a long-term commitment because the relationship requires that party to make an investment that he cannot otherwise justify.

For example, the owner of a building might be willing to modify it for a prospective tenant only if that tenant signs a long-term lease; a supplier to IBM might be willing to invest the capital necessary to produce a part only if it is assured that IBM will not change suppliers the next year. . . . The traditional marriage bears many similarities to this arrangement. It is a relationship in which the wife makes many initial investments of value only to her husband, investments a self-interested bargainer would make only in return for a long-term commitment. [T]he

9. J. Eekelaar & M. Maclean, [Maintenance After Divorce 14 (1986)]. This rule was fueled by the belief that such a remedy would deter people from immoral conduct. . . .

traditional wife makes her marital investment early in the expectation of a deferred return: sharing in the fruits of her husband's eventual market success. The traditional husband realizes his gains from the marriage in its early years, in the form of increased earning capacity and the production of children; his contribution is deferred until the marriage's later years when he shares the fruits of his enhanced earning capacity with his wife. In any relationship in which the flow of payments and benefits to the parties is not symmetrical over time, there is a great temptation to cheat. The party who has already received a benefit has an incentive to terminate the relationship before the balance of payments shifts. The traditional marriage, like the machinery necessary for the production of a customized part, is a risky investment in the absence of an enforceable long-term contract.

Non-economic factors exacerbate the wife's difficulty. The spouses' respective marriageability, if they divorce and seek new partners, follows a different pattern as they age. Prevailing social mores, relatively universal and apparently intractable, cause the woman's appeal as a sexual partner to decline more rapidly with age than does the man's. Moreover, even though the man's appeal as a sexual partner also declines with age, the financial assets he brings to a marriage typically increase, somewhat softening the decline in his marriageability. The more precipitous decline in the woman's sexual appeal, on the other hand, is worsened by another social convention: In general women marry men who are of the same age or older, but do not marry men significantly younger than themselves. The woman seeking a second husband thus operates in a constricted marriage market. . . .

. . . We have now identified [the loss that alimony is intended to compensate]. It is the "residual" loss in earning capacity that arises from . . . economically rational marital sharing. . . . This is a residual loss in the sense that it survives the marriage. . . . When one conceives of alimony as compensation for [this] particular kind of loss, rather than as a general claim to relieve need, it is much more possible to explain why liability should fall on the former spouse. . . .

The function of alimony [is thus] to reallocate the postdivorce financial consequences of marriage in order to prevent distorting incentives. Because its purpose is to reallocate, it is necessarily a remedy by one spouse against the other.[143] While such a theory of alimony might seem excessively economic, its rationale does not assume that wealth maximization is in fact the only purpose of marriage. To the contrary, by eliminating any financial incentives or penalties that might otherwise flow from different marital lifestyles, this theory maximizes the parties'

143. Such a reallocation gives each spouse an appropriate economic stake in the survival of that marriage, thereby reducing the incentive to terminate it as the marriage ages and the "balance of payments" shifts. Under modern divorce laws, a marriage will end if either spouse wishes, regardless of the other's desires. . . .

freedom to shape their marriage in accordance with their nonfinancial preferences. They can allocate domestic duties according to these preferences without putting one spouse at risk of a much greater financial loss than the other if the marriage fails. . . .

■ **AMERICAN LAW INSTITUTE, PRINCIPLES OF THE LAW OF FAMILY DISSOLUTION: ANALYSIS AND RECOMMENDATIONS §5.04**
*(2002)*

COMPENSATION FOR LOSS OF MARITAL LIVING STANDARD

(1) A person married to someone of significantly greater wealth or earning capacity is entitled at dissolution to compensation for a portion of the loss in the standard of living he or she would otherwise experience, when the marriage was of sufficient duration that equity requires the loss be treated as the spouses' joint responsibility.

(2) Entitlement to an award under this section should be determined by a rule of statewide application under which a presumption of entitlement arises in marriages of specified duration and spousal-income disparity.

(3) The value of the award made under this section should be determined by a rule of statewide application that sets a presumptive award of periodic payments calculated by applying a specified percentage to the difference between the incomes the spouses are expected to have after dissolution. This percentage [referred to as the *durational factor*] should increase with the duration of the marriage until it reaches a maximum value set by the rule. . . .

## Notes and Questions on the Rationales for Postdissolution Support

1. *Need and gender.* Why should a duty of spousal support continue after a marriage ends? *Orr* suggests "need" furnishes the underlying rationale but rejects gender as a proxy for need. Does Professor Ellman's analysis also rely on archaic sex-based generalizations or "real" economic and social differences for men and women after divorce? Cf. June R. Carbone, Economics, Feminism, and the Reinvention of Alimony, 43 Vand. L. Rev. 1463, 1465 (1990). Some divorce courts still invoke gender stereotypes. See Vann v. Vann, 495 S.E.2d 370, 372 (N.C. Ct. App. 1998) (reversing trial court finding that husband, as provider, had a higher duty to preserve marriage than wife).

Why should a former spouse (rather than parents, children, or the state) have responsibility for meeting the other spouse's postdissolution need? How does Ellman respond?

2. *Need or contract?* Does the marriage contract explain why the duty of spousal support continues after divorce? According to one classic treatment, although "alimony and marriage cannot be separated, [alimony] would seem to be most readily justified on the ground that it places the obligation to support a spouse who is in need upon the party who has undertaken to share the responsibilities and pleasures of such spouse by entering into the solemn compact of marriage, rather than upon the state." 2 Chester G. Vernier, American Family Laws 259, 262 (1932). Does this explanation suggest that part of the marriage contract remains binding after divorce? Or that alimony serves as a remedy for breach of this contract? See Elizabeth S. Scott & Robert E. Scott, Marriage as Relational Contract, 84 Va. L. Rev. 1225, 1309-1310 (1998) (theorizing alimony as legally enforceable insurance payments, under analysis of marriage as long-term relational contract).

Professor Mary Becker writes that need is an unsound basis for alimony, using as an illustration In re Marriage of Otis, 299 N.W.2d 114 (Minn. 1980). Ms. Otis, a skilled executive secretary with a substantial income, had left her job upon marriage. Upon divorce 24 years later, she received rehabilitative maintenance for four years, rather than the permanent alimony she sought.

> Ms. Otis's need — in and of itself — is the weakest imaginable reason for awarding her post-divorce transfer payments. Her current need reflects her investment in her husband's career, an investment from which he will continue to profit. Her need reflects the reliance loss she sustained by not working in order to raise their son and further her husband's career (and in order to avoid embarrassing him by typing). . . . Her needs should be met because a reasonable term of their arrangement, with its traditional division of labor, is that in exchange for her reliance in engaging exclusively in non-wage domestic production and reproduction and contributing to his career rather than her own, she would receive a reasonable share of the profit brought in by her husband's career and a reasonable share of the financial security accumulated for their old age. . . .

Mary E. Becker, Prince Charming: Abstract Equality, 1987 Sup. Ct. Rev. 201, 221. Does Becker's analysis suggest a contractual rationale for alimony? Is this Ellman's approach as well, despite his disclaimers?

3. *"A residual role for fault?"*[17] If alimony provides a remedy in contract, how does a court determine who breached? Does the contractual rationale require consideration of fault?

---

[17]. Professor Sugarman poses this question. Sugarman, supra note [14], at 136.

Does it follow from the reasons for divorce reform that courts should ignore fault in awarding spousal support? Put differently, should courts use doctrines such as "clean hands" in fashioning postdissolution equitable remedies? Should domestic violence trigger additional postdissolution support? Should one's misconduct (for example, adultery) preclude, or at least reduce, an award? Do you agree with the argument, supra section A, that the elimination of fault has hurt women and children? Would consideration of fault correct such sex-specific inequities? See Jane C. Murphy, Rules, Responsibility, and Commitment to Children: The New Language of Morality in Family Law, 60 U. Pitt. L. Rev. 1111, 1145-1150 (1999) (alimony awards so low in fault era that their "moral force . . . was very weak"). Compare, e.g., Hammonds v. Hammonds, 597 So. 2d 653 (Miss. 1992) (adulterous husband to pay only limited alimony to long-term wife because of her adultery); R.G.M. v. D.E.M., 410 S.E.2d 564 (S.C. 1991) (wife's extramarital lesbian activities bar spousal support), with Rodriguez v. Rodriguez, 13 P.3d 415 (Nev. 2000) (wife's affair should not bar or reduce alimony). One tabulation shows 30 states where fault is relevant in alimony cases. Linda D. Elrod & Robert G. Spector, A Review of the Year in Family Law: Redefining Families, Reforming Custody Jurisdiction, and Refining Support Issues, 34 Fam. L.Q. 607, 653 (2001).

Should no-fault regimes at least allow consideration of egregious misconduct? If so, what conduct meets the test? Battering? Would a preferable approach remit such questions to tort actions between the spouses? E.g., Brennan v. Orban, 678 A.2d 667 (N.J. 1996); Ira Mark Ellman, The Place of Fault in a Modern Divorce Law, 28 Ariz. L.J. 773, 792-802 (1996). See Chapter V, section D2b.

For a feminist dialogue on whether to consider fault in divorce's financial consequences, see Barbara Bennett Woodhouse with Comments by Katharine T. Bartlett, Sex, Lies, and Dissipation: The Discourse of Fault in a No-Fault Era, 82 Geo. L.J. 2525 (1994). Woodhouse laments:

> The traditional fault paradigm, still dominant in some states, reflected an obsession with controlling women and their sexuality. It had the virtue, however, of protecting (at least in theory) those conventionally "virtuous" spouses who worked hard and kept the promises that their partner failed to keep. By contrast, the new no-fault paradigm tends to reduce marriage to a calculus that considers economic harms, but not violations of physical integrity, intimacy, or trust.

Id. at 2526. See also Katharine B. Silbaugh, Gender and Nonfinancial Matters in the ALI Principles of the Law of Family Dissolution, 8 Duke J. Gender L. & Pol'y 203 (2001).

4. *Standard of living.* What does "need" mean for purposes of computing a support award? Does it refer only to necessities of life? The standard of living during the marriage? See, e.g., In re Marriage of Mc-

Naughton, 194 Cal. Rptr. 176 (Ct. App. 1983) (though wife got marital property worth $3 million, court upholds $3,500 per month for support based on lavish lifestyle during 32-year marriage, her needs, and husband's ability to pay); Crews v. Crews, 751 A.2d 524, 527 (N.J. 2000) (standard of living during marriage "serves as the touchstone" for alimony award). Is this what UMDA means by "reasonable needs"? Should the marital standard of living determine the level of support even after a brief marriage? One tabulation shows that 42 jurisdictions consider the marital standard of living in setting alimony. Elrod & Spector, supra, at 653.

5. *Rehabilitation for self-sufficiency.* How does UMDA frame the parameters of "need"? Note this model statute makes maintenance a remedy of last resort, to be awarded only when a spouse's "reasonable needs" remain unmet because of the absence of sufficient property or income from appropriate employment. Why did UMDA's drafters make maintenance a disfavored remedy, to be awarded only when equitable distribution of property fails to achieve economic justice? Once this need threshold is satisfied, however, the court has discretion to order support in an amount and duration that is "just," based on all relevant factors.

Jurisdictions following UMDA view self-sufficiency as an important objective, making support a temporary, transitional measure. E.g., Beeler v. Beeler, 820 S.W.2d 657, 661 (Mo. Ct. App. 1991). Some courts refer to such support as "rehabilitative alimony." E.g., In re Fowler, 764 A.2d 916, 919 (N.H. 2000). Weitzman criticizes this approach as "unrealistic" in many cases and partly responsible for the economic harm women and children have suffered from no-fault divorce. See Lenore J. Weitzman, Women and Children Last: The Social and Economic Consequences of Divorce Law Reforms, in Feminism, Children, and the New Families 212, 224-229 (Sanford M. Dornbusch & Myra H. Strober eds., 1988).

How does the rehabilitation principle change the traditional stereotypes underlying alimony, reviewed in *Orr*? What are the purposes of rehabilitative alimony? To spur women to financial independence? To relieve former husbands of long-term support obligations? To foster equality between spouses?

How long should rehabilitation take? Is permanent alimony ever justified? Suppose the recipient refuses to become rehabilitated? See In re Marriage of Hecker, 568 N.W.2d 705 (Minn. 1997) (willful failure to rehabilitate does not automatically preclude all permanent maintenance). To what standard of living should rehabilitation aim? What is "appropriate employment" under UMDA? How costly can the rehabilitative training be?

6. *Loss compensation.* Ellman's critique of existing justifications for alimony focuses instead on "loss compensation." As Chief Reporter for the ALI Principles, Ellman makes loss compensation the objective of the formulations for "compensatory spousal payments." This term covers

"residual" financial awards (financial awards other than for child support or property division). See ALI Principles §5.01 cmt. a. The notion of loss compensation also helps explain the gradual recharacterization of separate property as marital property because this process protects a long-term spouse from the unexpected loss of assets. See supra pages 661-662.

How might a legislature draft a law (or a court fashion a rule) based on ALI Principles §5.04? The following illustration is provided:

> *A presumption arises that a spouse is entitled to an award under this section whenever that spouse has been married five years or more to a person whose income at dissolution is expected to be at least 25 percent greater than the claimant's. The presumptive award shall equal the difference in the spouses' expected incomes at dissolution, multiplied by the appropriate durational factor. The durational factor is equal to the years of marriage multiplied by .01, but shall in no case exceed .4.*

Id. §5.04 cmt. a, illus. 1. The comment continues by explaining:

> Under the illustrative provision, the maximum durational factor would be reached after 40 years of marriage, since .01 × 40 = .4. If at that time Spouse A's expected monthly income were $5,000, and Spouse B's were $3,000, the award would equal .4 × $2,000, or $800 per month, leaving Spouse A with $4,200 monthly and providing Spouse B with $3,800 monthly. If Spouse A earned $3,000 and Spouse B could only be expected to earn $1,000 monthly after dissolution, the award would still equal .4 × $2,000, or $800, leaving A with $2,200 and B with $1,800. These awards would be proportionately less for marriages of shorter duration. . . .

Id.

Is "loss compensation" just another way of saying that marriage is a contract with liquidated damages as the remedy for breach? See Allen M. Parkman, Reforming Divorce Reform, 41 Santa Clara L. Rev. 379, 417 (2001). Does In re Marriage of Otis, as described by Professor Becker, supra, exemplify the rationale for "compensatory payments"? In what other situations does dissolution impose losses that merit compensation? See ALI Principles §§5.05 (child care responsibilities), 5.11 (care of certain third parties), and 5.13 (certain losses of premarital living standard after short marriage).

7. *Equal income sharing.* Professor Jane Rutherford proposes adding the incomes of the former couple and dividing the total equally among all those to be supported — an alternative approach she calls "income sharing." Jane Rutherford, Duty in Divorce: Shared Income as a Path to Equality, 58 Fordham L. Rev. 539, 578 (1990). Thus, a former husband's annual salary of $100,000 and his former wife's of $50,000 would result in $75,000 for each of them per year. Rutherford explains:

> [T]he theoretical basis for income sharing is quite different from that of alimony. Income sharing is not based on need, pre-divorce standard of

living, prior contributions, or fault. Instead, it represents a conscious effort to achieve equality between spouses who have divided their labors during marriage. If spouses have not divided the labor, either because they were not married long enough, or because they did not have children, then income sharing should not apply. . . .

Income sharing has four distinct advantages. First, it fosters the kind of sharing and caring that should typify families. Second, income sharing offers a way out of the fault conundrum. Third, income sharing empowers the financially disadvantaged who may be economically trapped in destructive relationships. . . .

Finally, income sharing provides a route to actual financial equality between the spouses. Currently, there is a vast difference in the financial impact of divorce on men and women. Income sharing would eliminate that difference. . . . Income sharing, however, will work even when the millennium comes and both sexes have equal earning power. . . .

Id. at 578-584. What are the advantages of Rutherford's proposal over UMDA? Over the ALI Principles? The disadvantages?

8. *Alimony, race, and feminism.* Does the quest for a modern theory of alimony rest on racial stereotypes (that is, an economically powerful husband and a wife who has chosen to give priority to her family over her career) that exclude most African-American marriages? See Twila L. Perry, Alimony: Race, Privilege and Dependency in the Search for Theory, 82 Geo. L.J. 2481, 2493 (1994). Does alimony contribute to the racial hierarchy among women and encourage economic dependence by women of privilege? See id. at 2504.

## Problems

1. Brian, a 48-year-old commercial pilot, and Ruth, a 47-year-old schoolteacher, divorce after 27 years of marriage. They have no children. Brian's annual salary is $75,000; Ruth's is $43,000. The trial court divides the marital property equally and awards Ruth half the difference in their incomes for two years to enable her to obtain additional university credits. All alimony will cease at the end of the two-year period. Ruth appeals, asking for a higher monthly award and alimony for at least 12 years. She claims that even a doctorate degree would not significantly increase her income as a teacher and Brian will continue to have much greater income than she can ever expect. Brian also appeals, arguing that Ruth does not need support and she never expressed interest in additional education before divorce. What result under UMDA and why? Under the illustration showing how §5.05 of the ALI Principles works? Under an income-equalization approach? See Gardner v. Gardner, 881 P.2d 645 (Nev. 1994).

2. John and Connie divorce after six months of marriage. John is a civil engineer earning $40,000 annually. Connie, who has a high school

diploma, earns $12,000 as an employee of Citibank. Before marriage Connie earned an additional $400 per month by working the nightshift at Citibank and cleaning houses during the day; at John's urging, upon marriage she switched to the lower paying dayshift and ended her house-cleaning job. The court grants Connie a divorce on the basis of John's "extreme mental cruelty" because of his inability to engage in satisfactory intercourse with Connie, John's "homosexual tendencies," and his "incessant and inappropriate passing of gas." The trial court returns the property that each spouse brought into the marriage but orders John to pay Connie's premarital credit card debt of $5,000 and to pay her alimony of $450 monthly for 15 months. John appeals, challenging the allocation of Connie's premarital debt to him and the alimony award. What outcome would be "fair"? Which of the facts should be considered? Excluded from consideration? Which different approaches to property division and support, respectively, would best achieve a fair result? See Osman v. Keating-Osman, 521 N.W.2d 655 (S.D. 1994).

## D. "WINDING UP" A MARRIAGE: APPLYING THEORIES OF PROPERTY AND SUPPORT

Despite the different theoretical bases, courts typically confront property and support questions together, along with related questions such as attorneys' fees, tax liability, and pension rights. The following cases present specific factual contexts for applying the theories explored above while illustrating the interconnections among all of dissolution's financial incidents.

### 1. Two Couples' Stories

■ **MICHAEL v. MICHAEL**
*791 S.W.2d 772 (Mo. Ct. App. 1990)*

PUDLOWSKI, Judge. . . .
[A]ppellant and respondent were married in August 1972 and separated in April 1987. There were no children born of this marriage. . . . Appellant [husband] holds a baccalaureate degree in political science and a master's degree in journalism. Respondent [wife] holds a baccalaureate degree in journalism and a master's degree in public administration.

In 1972, on the day following the parties' marriage, the couple moved to Little Rock, Arkansas where respondent was going to work for Southwestern Bell Corporation. While living in Little Rock, appellant was employed as a reporter for a local newspaper.

In June 1974, respondent received a promotion and was transferred back to St. Louis. In St. Louis, appellant worked for APC Skills Company and then for Maritz, Inc. In 1978, appellant was fired from Maritz, Inc. [T]he couple agreed that appellant would not seek outside employment but instead would devote time to writing fiction. [Respondent then] received another transfer and the couple moved to Oklahoma City.

While living in Oklahoma, appellant continued to pursue a writing career, however, later abandoned this endeavor without ever having written a chapter in a book or a scene in a play. After giving up the attempt at writing, appellant worked briefly in a food store and spent 8-9 months working free-lance public relations. When appellant was not employed outside of the home, the couple agreed that appellant would be responsible for the general upkeep of the house and also for the preparation of the evening meal. Appellant spent several hours a day preparing the couple's dinner. Respondent claimed that appellant's other domestic chores were very lax. For two years while the couple was living in Oklahoma appellant drove respondent to and from work. However, for the rest of the mornings, appellant slept until 10 or 11:00 A.M.

In 1984 respondent was again transferred to St. Louis. After moving to St. Louis, appellant continued to cook the couple's dinner. He also periodically took the respondent to work but did not seek outside employment.

Throughout the marriage, the couple's lifestyle improved and they had a significant amount of disposable income. They were able to purchase homes whenever respondent accepted a job transfer and the couple took many trips including visits to Europe. . . .

At the time of trial, respondent had been working for Southwestern Bell for more than 15 years and was earning over $70,000 per year [and had vested pension benefits equal to $1,169.58 monthly.] Appellant's statement of income and expenses provides that he receives no income from employment, however he receives $75 per month in interest, and his share of the gross income on the previous year's Federal Income Tax Return was $1200.

It is with some interest that we note the gender roles of the parties in this marriage are reversed from the more traditional roles of husband and wife. . . . However, certainly the sex of the parties should have no bearing on the division of marital property or on the allowance or prohibition of maintenance.

The trial court allocated $51,347 or 75.5% of the parties' marital property to respondent and $14,128 or 21.5% to appellant. The court granted appellant no maintenance but allowed appellant $500 for attorney's fees. . . . Appellant claims that the trial court abused its discretion. . . .

Section 452.330 RSMo 1988 directs the trial court to divide the marital property in a just manner, after considering all relevant factors including [each spouse's economic circumstances; the contribution of each to the acquisition of the marital property, including homemaker contributions; the value of the nonmarital property of each; and the conduct during the marriage].

There are two guiding principles inherent in §452.330: "[F]irst property division should reflect the concept of marriage as a shared enterprise similar to a partnership; and, second property division should be utilized as a means of providing future support for an economically dependent spouse." Krauskopf, A Theory for "Just" Division of Marital Property in Missouri, 41 Mo. L. Rev. 165 (1976).

When applying these guiding principles inherent in §452.330 to the present case we find that the trial court abused its discretion in its division of marital property. [First, throughout] the course of the marriage, appellant has become economically dependent on the respondent. At the time of the dissolution of marriage, appellant was unemployed, had not been employed in his chosen field of journalism for fifteen years, and had not been employed full-time since 1978. Conversely, at the time of dissolution of marriage, respondent had elevated herself. . . .

With regard to the second statutory factor [contribution], the trial court found that the respondent, for the greater part of the marriage, had been the sole financial support of the parties and the funds used to acquire the marital property had been earned almost solely by her. Also, the court found that the appellant made no substantial contribution to the marriage as a homemaker because he showed a marked disinclination to undertake the normal domestic duties of a homemaker, engaging only in those duties, such as cooking the evening meal, which he found fulfilling, stimulating and interesting.

Although appellant did not work outside of the home for the majority of the years of the marriage, he did have outside employment for nearly one-third of the marriage. For two additional years appellant drove respondent to work and picked her up from work in the evening. While the appellant's performance of traditional domestic chores was oftentimes lax, he did prepare dinner for himself and respondent throughout the duration of the marriage. We are not finding that appellant's contributions entitled him to an equal division of the marital property, however, we do hold that the trial court's division of property is against the weight of the evidence and therefore an abuse of discretion.

In his second point appellant claims that the trial court erred and abused its discretion in awarding no maintenance to appellant. . . . Appellant does not claim that he is completely unable to support himself. However, due to the extended period of time that appellant has been out of the work force in his field, he requires a period of rehabilitative maintenance during which time he can obtain the necessary education and retraining to allow him to gain satisfactory employment in the field of journalism. Appellant argues that he would require an additional two and one half or three years of education to take course work that would enable him to be self-supporting as a journalist.

We have said that maintenance is awarded when one spouse has detrimentally relied on the other spouse to provide the monetary support during the marriage. If the relying spouse's withdrawal from the marketplace so injures his/her marketable skills that he/she is unable to provide for his/ her reasonable needs maintenance may be awarded. . . . Rehabilitative maintenance is appropriate where there is substantial evidence that the party seeking maintenance will or should become self-supporting. . . .

[The trial court erred.] Appellant's need to acquire fresh skills in order to re-enter the field of journalism is reasonable. Journalism is a competitive field. Every year newly graduated students enter the job market with fine skills. . . . Appellant's plan to return to school in order to increase his marketability as a journalist would ensure that he become self-sufficient. . . .

CRANDALL, Judge, dissenting:
I dissent from that portion of the majority opinion which finds error in the division of the marital property and the denial of maintenance to husband. . . . If we accept the concept of marriage as a shared enterprise similar to a partnership, husband had a negative impact on that partnership. Husband did not sacrifice his career for wife, rather he was a hindrance to her progress. On the issue of maintenance, husband has simply shown that he is unwilling, rather than unable, to support himself through appropriate employment. . . .

■ **ROSENBERG v. ROSENBERG**
*497 A.2d 485 (Md. Ct. Spec. App.), cert. denied, 501 A.2d*
*845 (Md. 1985)*

BELL, J.
Large fortunes beget large problems, which engender predictable issues when the holders of those fortunes enter the domestic relations arena. . . . Eleanor Kantor and Henry A. Rosenberg, Jr., were married on June 22, 1952, in Charleston, West Virginia. Their three sons are all emancipated. On November 1, 1981, Mr. Rosenberg left home with the purpose of ending the marriage. The divorce decree followed a lengthy and highly publicized trial and ended almost thirty-two years of marriage. [The chancellor found, in part, that Mr. Rosenberg had committed adultery on many occasions and Mrs. Rosenberg had done so once, two years after they separated.]

### ROSENBERG FAMILY BACKGROUND

[Henry A. Rosenberg, Jr., was a descendant of the family that started the American Trading and Production Corporation (ATAPCO) in 1931.] ATAPCO originally consisted of a little less than fifty percent interest in Crown Central Petroleum Corporation (Crown) and twenty-five percent in American Oil Company. A subsequent merger of American Oil Company with Standard Oil of Indiana produced the large stock holdings of the latter company now held by ATAPCO. . . . ATAPCO continued to hold approximately 50% of the Crown voting stock and ATAPCO stock was owned wholly by family members.

### MR. AND MRS. ROSENBERG

In 1954, after a short stint in the service, appellant returned to work at Crown, where his father was President. In 1955, his father died suddenly. To assist [his mother], appellant and his family moved into the large family home, where they remained for two and one-half years.

In 1955, appellant also became a director of Crown and Assistant to the President. His career continued to flourish. [He later became Chairman of the board and Chief Executive Officer of Crown.] When Jacob Blaustein [appellant's uncle] died in 1970, appellant succeeded him as the ATAPCO representative on the Union Trust Board; ATAPCO is the largest shareholder in Union Trust Bank. Over the years, ATAPCO formed subsidiaries for its increasing holdings, and appellant became a director of all but one of them. . . .

Crown and ATAPCO prospered through the years and appellant's income soared; his assets swelled, and he adopted and maintained an opulent lifestyle for himself, his wife and his family. In 1983, his cash income exceeded $850,000, and his total annual income including noncash benefits was far more. ATAPCO provided him with free legal, accounting and investment services estimated at more than $50,000 for one year, and Crown supplied a new Cadillac automobile biannually. . . . At the time of the divorce, the chancellor found appellant's net worth was approximately $33 million.

Eleanor Rosenberg, appellee, shared her husband's aspirations and made significant contributions to his success. . . . For instance, in 1955, when the first two of the parties' children were infants, appellant asked appellee to give him "his freedom" to pursue his business career. The witnesses overwhelmingly agreed that she undertook virtually the entire burden of raising the children and of maintaining and managing the family household. Appellant admitted that the single-minded pursuit of his business career led him to neglect his wife and family; he absented himself from the home on weekends and was even late for his 25th wedding anniversary party, a particularly sore point. Witnesses told of leaving the party before appellant's midnight arrival and of appellee's humiliation and embarrassment.

During the marriage, appellee also entertained frequently for her husband's benefit. She routinely invited business associates and community leaders to their home for large parties and intimate dinners. [S]he headed the wives' group [of a large national organization of petroleum refiners] and performed her duties skillfully, diligently and graciously.

The parties owned and occupied a 20-room mansion, maintained by a staff of four, in an exclusive area of Baltimore. Appellant also purchased and furnished two other homes at a combined cost of approximately $550,000. [They vacationed frequently, often traveling in the Crown corporate jet which was at appellant's disposal.]

Appellant's largest asset, and that which experienced the greatest growth, was his ownership interest in ATAPCO. . . .

Over the years, the relationship between appellant and appellee deteriorated. He found interests outside the home, as did she. A substantial difference, however, was that his interests involved, at least in part, other women, while she became prominent in community and charitable enterprises.

In the late 1970's appellee began to abuse alcohol and prescription drugs. Appellant also abused alcohol, but did not suffer the same effects. The situation reached a climax in July 1981, when she admitted herself to Springwood Hospital for drug treatment. He visited his wife at the hospital to announce that he was leaving home and to secure her signature on a separation agreement. She refused and then underwent a brief psychotic episode. As a result, her hospitalization was prolonged by about a month and a half. After her discharge from the hospital, appellant remained in the marital home and continued his efforts to have her sign the separation agreement. He ultimately moved out on November 1, 1981.

### TRIAL COURT PROCEEDINGS

In 1983, Mrs. Rosenberg filed a Bill of Complaint for Divorce A Vinculo Matrimonii, alleging adultery, abandonment and desertion as grounds for the divorce. Mr. Rosenberg filed an Answer and Cross-Bill of Complaint for Divorce A Vinculo Matrimonii, relying on a two-year separation of the parties as grounds for the divorce. The case came to trial in April 1984 and lasted approximately four weeks. [The chancellor granted a divorce and determined that the husband had given the wife all her jewelry and her interest in the marital residence as gifts. The chancellor ordered the parties to sell the home; the husband to pay the wife a monetary award of $1,520,000, plus any difference between $230,000 and the wife's share of the proceeds from the sale of the house; the husband to pay the wife alimony in the amount of $275,000 per year, at the rate of $22,916.66 per month, to cease upon her remarriage or the death of either party; and the husband pay the wife's attorneys' fees of $224,579.95. Mr. Rosenberg appealed, challenging the monetary award, award of alimony, counsel fees, and expenses. Mrs. Rosenberg cross-appealed, challenging the failure to classify as marital property the increases in value of her husband's ATAPCO stock.]

## MONETARY AWARD

The chancellor meticulously catalogued the assets of the parties, designated the marital property and then valued it. Items of marital property included: (1) an interest-free promissory note from Dorothy Bohny [the new Mrs. Rosenberg]; (2) the interest foregone on that note; and (3) the amount of various cash advances to Dorothy Bohny between June 2, 1982, and April 1, 1984. The chancellor found that these items dissipated the marital property. [Maryland case law regards intentional dissipation as a fraud on marital rights and considers the dissipated property as extant marital property.]

The chancellor in the case sub judice found that appellant had dissipated the marital property by making [a $150,000] loan and cash advances to Dorothy Bohny [after he informed appellee he intended to end the marriage]. We conclude that the evidence supports this finding. [T]he lost interest was also a dissipation of the marital property. . . .

[The chancellor classified the appellant's interests in the family trusts as nonmarital assets because they were acquired by gift. The chancellor accepted the valuation of appellee's experts that appellant's interest in the trust created by his grandfather was worth $4.2 million and his interest in the four trusts created by his mother and grandmother was worth $24 million.]

Following identification of the marital property and its valuation, the statute directs the chancellor to consider nine factors before determining the amount of the monetary award, if any, and the method of payment. . . . A plain reading of the statutory language indicates that the chancellor is not restricted to the categories listed. Rather, he may take into account "[s]uch factors as the court deems necessary or appropriate to consider in order to arrive at a fair and equitable monetary award." Md. Cts. & Jud. Proc. Code Ann., §3-6A-05.

[Appellant complains here that the chancellor erred in applying several factors listed in the statute, as follows:]

"(1) The contributions, monetary and nonmonetary, of each party to the well-being of the family."

Appellant argues that there was no evidence to support the chancellor's conclusions that: (1) appellee "was forced to accept the full responsibility for the sons' upbringing"; and (2) he "admitted that he neglected his family obligations . . . even to the point of foregoing all but the last hour of his twenty-fifth wedding anniversary. . . ." We disagree. There was such evidence. . . .

"(4) The circumstances and facts which contributed to the estrangement of the parties."

Appellant alleges that there was not a scintilla of evidence presented that he "virtually supported [appellee's] dependency on drugs [and] for at least the last fifteen or so years, [he] maintained liaisons with other women. . . ." Although appellant may not agree with the chancellor's conclusions, there was evidence to that effect. . . .

"(7) How and when specific marital property was acquired, including the effort expended by each party in accumulating the marital property."

The chancellor stated that appellee "contributed, though non-monetarily, substantially more than [appellant] toward the marital property." Appellant complains that the chancellor failed to specify the efforts appellee expended in accumulating the marital property and that the evidence did not indicate any efforts by her. Moreover, he contends that the largest part of the marital property consists of his interests in Crown [pension] benefit plans, and that all of these are attributable to his service as an executive officer of Crown. . . . Appellant declares that "[w]hile [appellee's] effort as the homemaker may have enabled [him] to devote more of his time to earning income, this is not a sufficient basis for a conclusion that [appellee] contributed substantially more than [he] toward the marital property." We simply do not agree.

[T]he basic goal of what has come to be called "The Marital Property Act" is to achieve a fair and equitable distribution. If we were to adopt appellant's legalistic proposition, it would follow that one who does not earn cash can never contribute substantially more than the one who does. This flies in the face of the very purpose of the Act. The conclusion by the chancellor that appellee contributed substantially more toward accumulating the marital property than did appellant, while limited to the unusual situation here presented, is far from clearly erroneous. . . .

One error is apparent, however. [A supplemental opinion designating the jewelry as a gift owned solely by appellee would reduce the joint personal property by $89,000 and increase appellee's individual assets by that amount.] This [error] should be addressed on remand. . . .

Appellee/Cross-Appellant also seeks review of the monetary award on appeal. [S]he essentially claims only one error — that the chancellor failed to include the increased value of the ATAPCO stock as marital property. She explains that at various times Mr. Rosenberg became the beneficiary of life interests or residuary interests in several trusts [created by his mother and grandmother]. The corpus of the four life interest trusts was comprised largely of ATAPCO stock. ATAPCO, in turn, held about 50% of the voting stock of Crown. It is these four trusts which here concern us. They were all gifts or inheritances and, admittedly, non-marital property at the inception. Through the efforts of appellant, his family and other influences, the value of the trusts grew substantially during the marriage. Hence, appellee claims Mr. Rosenberg's interest in that increased value should have been included as marital property.

Marital property is "all property, however titled, acquired by either or both spouses during their marriage. It does not include property acquired prior to the marriage, property acquired by inheritance or gift from a third party, or property excluded by valid agreement or property directly traceable to any of these sources." Md. Cts. & Jud. Proc. Code Ann., §3-6A-01(e), supra. When property is paid for over a period of time, it is deemed to have been the subject of a continuing acquisition. Thus, if the funds used are partly marital and partly non-marital, the property retains the same character based on the source of those funds, i.e., it is considered partly marital and partly non-marital. . . .

[In his opinion, the chancellor found that appellee had not proven that appellant's personal efforts at Crown or as a member of the Board of Directors of ATAPCO either directly or indirectly contributed to the increase in value of appellant's life interests in ATAPCO; rather ATAPCO's worth increased as the result of factors other than appellant's personal efforts in either Company.]

Appellee . . . claims the facts established that there was a joint venture by the family, and therefore, each was the agent for the other and an increase for one is an increase for all. Although an interesting theory, that is not the test. Appellant only had one voice on these various boards. The chancellor's findings were not clearly erroneous.

### ALIMONY

In his brief, appellant asserts that "[t]he Chancellor abused his discretion in determining the amount of [the] alimony award and its duration." . . .

Under the current statute, the principal function of alimony is rehabilitation. . . . The court may award alimony for an indefinite period of time, however, when it finds that:

"(i) The party seeking alimony, by reason of age, illness, infirmity, or disability, cannot reasonably be expected to make substantial progress toward becoming self-supporting; or

"(ii) Even after the receiving party will have made as much progress toward self-support as can reasonably be expected, the respective standards of living of the two parties will be unconscionably disparate."

Md. Code Ann., Art. 16, §1(c)(1), supra.

In the case sub judice the chancellor found that appellant

"will continue as a high level executive at Crown and will most probably become more involved at ATAPCO. He will reap the benefits of his family's history of investment in ATAPCO and Crown for the rest of his life. In all, [appellant's] life will not be financially altered a great deal after his divorce is granted."

He further found that appellee

"is in a totally different situation. She needs money for her everyday living expenses and has been totally dependent upon [appellant] for such funds for almost thirty-two years . . . [She] alone will never become sufficiently self-supporting to allow her to continue the life style she shared with her husband for over thirty years . . . [She] has no specialized skills to enable her to enter the workplace at a level which would allow her to attain her married standard of living, and it is unlikely that she will develop such skills at this stage of her life." . . .

In any event, we hold that the court did not err in awarding appellee indefinite alimony.

Appellant next contends that the court's alimony award to appellee of $275,000 a year is "grossly excessive." In support of this argument, he asserts that during the marriage he provided her with a monthly household allowance of $6,000 per month and that after the separation he "voluntarily increased this amount to $7,000 per month. . . ." He concludes that these amounts reflect the parties' standard of living and, therefore, the court erred in awarding her "as alimony 3.27 times the amount of money she received before the divorce." . . .

In determining the amount and duration of alimony, the court must consider all relevant factors, [including, inter alia, need, contributions, standard of living, and circumstances leading to dissolution]. Md. Code Ann., Art. 16, §1(b), supra. We note at the outset that the record shows appellee estimated her actual monthly expenses for 1984 at $10,088 per month. In addition, she deferred expenses of $7,881, which included contributions, car leasing, furnishings, household maintenance, vacation and travel, furs, insurance, clothing, dental expenses, legal and accounting fees. The amount of alimony sought would have carried an income tax expense of $14,000 a month, making her total expenses $31,969 per month. Appellee was awarded approximately $22,900 per month. Because she was receiving only $7,000 each month from appellant, she borrowed funds to pay some of her expenses, deferred payment on expenses already incurred and delayed incurring any obligation on still others. The fact that appellant was giving her a household allowance during the marriage of $6,000 a month and was paying her $7,000 a month after the separation is in no way indicative of her total needs. . . .

The chancellor reduced the alimony sought by . . . $9,000 a month. He was required to take into account, among other things, her actual expenses and her needs. He was also required specifically to consider any monetary award. . . . As the Court of Appeals noted in McAlear v. McAlear, 298 Md. 320, [327,] 469 A.2d 1256 (1984):

> "We recognize . . . that there is an interrelationship between a monetary award . . . and an award of alimony. . . . [I]n determining the amount of a monetary award, equity courts must consider any award of alimony, while in determining the amount of alimony, equity courts must consider any monetary award." . . .

We cannot be positive from the chancellor's opinion whether he considered the income that would accrue from the monetary award. [W]e remand to the chancellor to determine the financial needs and resources of appellee including the effect of the monetary award and all other income. Based on these findings, the chancellor must then review the alimony award.

### FEES AND COSTS

The large fortune involved in this case resulted in each issue and potential issue being fought every inch of the way. As a consequence, the lengthy and broad discovery, the long trial and the numerous post-trial hearings generated substantial attorneys' fees and litigation costs for both parties. Over vehement objections, appellee's counsel was awarded $430,390 in attorneys' fees and $224,579 for costs.

Appellant challenges these awards. . . . According to Md. Code Ann., Art. 16, §3, supra, [the court may award a reasonable amount for "reasonable and necessary expenses" after considering the parties' resources and needs.] The award of fees and costs is within the "sound discretion of the trial court, and such an award should not be modified unless it is arbitrary or clearly wrong." Gravenstine v. Gravenstine, [58 Md. App. 158, 182 (1984)]. [T]here is no basis for . . . modification of these fees and costs on remand. . . .

## Notes and Questions

1. Questions of property division and spousal support typically arise together in divorce litigation, as *Michael* and *Rosenberg* illustrate. As *Ferguson,* supra, observes: " 'Alimony and equitable distribution are distinct concepts, but together they command the entire field of financial settlement of divorce. Therefore, where one expands, the other must recede.' " 639 So. 2d at 929 (quoting LaRue v. LaRue, 304 S.E.2d 312, 334 (W. Va. 1983)). See also Smith v. Smith, 752 A.2d 1023, 1031 (Conn. 1999) (financial orders at dissolution are "entirely interwoven"

and constitute "a carefully crafted mosaic, each element of which may be dependent on the other").

The analysis generally addresses property first, considering the following questions: "1. Is it in fact 'property' (the identification question)? 2. Is it marital or nonmarital (the characterization question)? 3. How much is it worth (the valuation question)? 4. How much of it does each spouse get (the distribution question)?" Robert J. Levy, An Introduction to Divorce-Property Issues, 23 Fam. L.Q. 147, 147 (1989).

2. On the "characterization question," *Rosenberg* presents the common situation of a spouse working in the family business in which he or she had a premarital ownership interest (thus making it separate property); during the marriage the value of this property increases. Why did *Rosenberg* refuse to classify as divisible marital property the increase in value of appellant's ATAPCO stock? Why wasn't it enough for Mrs. Rosenberg to show her husband's role at Crown and ATAPCO during marriage or her own efforts as hostess and "corporate wife"? What arguments support treating the increases as marital property? As separate property? Should income from such separate property be treated the same way as appreciation in value? See generally Mary Moers Wenig, Increase in Value of Separate Property During Marriage: Examination and Proposals, 23 Fam. L.Q. 301 (1989).

Most community property jurisdictions follow the "American rule," which classifies as separate property appreciation and income from separate property. See ALI Principles, supra, §4.04 cmt. a. This approach "traces" existing assets to their source: Assets traceable to separate property are treated as separate property, while those traceable to marital funds are treated as marital. The original 1970 version of UMDA §307, supra, reflects this rule. The minority approach, the "Spanish rule," treats as community property any income generated during marriage, even income from separate property.

Equitable distribution states often treat income or appreciation from separate property as marital, based on "marital efforts" or the "contribution" of either spouse. E.g., Knowles v. Knowles, 588 A.2d 315 (Me. 1991); Hartog v. Hartog, 647 N.E.2d 749 (N.Y. 1995). Did *Rosenberg* reject this approach or simply find no "marital efforts" on the facts? Why is acquisition during marriage, without more, insufficient? Cf. In re Marriage of Massee, 970 P.2d 1203, 1212 (Or. 1999). The classification of income or appreciation from separate property proves particularly important when the breadwinner spouse works in a family or other closely held business and can decide what portion of the business earnings to take as salary (marital property) and what portion to retain or reinvest in the company. See, e.g., Smith v. Smith, 475 S.E.2d 881 (W. Va. 1996). Cf. Watkins v. Watkins, 924 S.W.2d 542 (Mo. Ct. App. 1996).

Similarly, the ALI Principles would classify such income and appreciation as marital property to the extent attributable to spousal labor.

ALI Principles, supra, §4.04. In addition, the income and appreciation from separate property recharacterized as marital property under §4.12, supra, is to be divided as marital property.

3. *Dissipation.* The *Rosenberg* court counted as marital property funds that the husband had "intentionally dissipated." Although Mr. Rosenberg's loans and cash advances to his paramour present an easy illustration, what other kinds of expenditures might constitute dissipation? See, e.g., In re Marriage of O'Neill, 563 N.E.2d 494 (Ill. 1990) (unsuccessful defense of attempted rape charge is not dissipation, which requires purpose unrelated to marriage). What time period is relevant? Suppose Mr. Rosenberg made the loans years before the marriage ended? Should dissolution trigger an accounting of all losses and unwise expenditures throughout the marriage? Can a court following a strict no-fault approach consider dissipated assets? (Recall that under ALI Principles §4.10, supra, financial misconduct within a specified time period is considered in division of property.)

4. After valuing the assets, which often requires expert testimony, the court must distribute the property to be divided. How did *Rosenberg* approach distribution? To what extent did the statutory factors help determine an equitable award? On what basis did the court decide that Mrs. Rosenberg's contribution exceeded her husband's? Does contribution provide a satisfactory explanation for her property award? In examining another "corporate wife" case, Professor Joan Williams proposes a joint property theory and emphasis on family work, instead of direct contributions. See Joan Williams, Do Wives Own Half? Winning for Wives After *Wendt*, 32 Conn. L. Rev. 249, 267-268 (2000). See generally Debra Baker, Wealthy Wives' Tales: High-Asset, High-Profile Divorces Are Changing the Way Judges Look at Partnership, 84 A.B.A. J., July 1998, at 72.

What role does fault play in the property distribution in *Rosenberg*? How much, in terms of property, is adultery worth? Emotional abandonment of one's family? Substance abuse? Is the theory of property division underlying *Rosenberg* the same as that followed in *Michael*? What division of property is "just" in each case? Would the equal-division presumption used in some community property states and in the ALI Principles have provided a better outcome in either?

5. Does *Rosenberg* take a sound approach to issues of support? How does the court arrive at an amount? Why does the Maryland statute make contribution a factor for determining alimony (as well as property division)? What theory of alimony does the opinion reflect? Note how the court requires consideration of property division (the monetary award) in determining alimony.

Why must Mr. Rosenberg make large support payments *indefinitely*? *Rosenberg* reveals that, despite the modern emphasis on self-sufficiency, courts still consider this goal inappropriate in some cases. What criteria dictate permanent alimony? Marriage duration? Chronic health problems? Caring for young children? Fault?

In *Michael*, why is Mr. Michael a candidate for support? For how long? Cf. Or. Rev. Stat. §107.407 (1999) (after paying support payments for ten years, payor can petition court to set obligation aside if recipient has not made reasonable effort to become self-sufficient). How would the loss-sharing proposal of the ALI's Principles apply in *Michael* and *Rosenberg*? The income-sharing proposal of Professor Rutherford?

6. How typical are the applications of the law exemplified in *Michael* and *Rosenberg*? What patterns does the exercise of judicial discretion in divorce cases reveal? For a legal and empirical analysis of alimony awards by the judge who wrote *Rosenberg*, see Rosalyn B. Bell, Alimony and the Financially Dependent Spouse in Montgomery County, Maryland, 22 Fam. L.Q. 225 (1988). Judge Bell found courts are not awarding alimony to men; the husband's income and the duration of the marriage are the most significant factors in alimony awards for wives, followed by the wife's income and occupation; women at fault cannot get court-ordered alimony of any type; and permanent alimony cases usually involve women over 50. Id. at 267, 299, 316. See also Marsha Garrison, How Do Judges Decide Divorce Cases? An Empirical Analysis of Discretionary Decision Making, 74 N.C. L. Rev. 401, 452, 467 (1996) (under New York's equitable distribution statute, judges tend to divide marital property equally, and spousal income and marital duration are best predictors of alimony).

7. In economic analysis, legal rules are incentives that influence choices. Thus, the legal rules of divorce may affect future behavior by shaping the expectations of those entering marriage. "A nonpunitive, nonsexist, and nonpaternalistic framework for marriage dissolution, then, should begin with recommendations that encourage sharing behavior during marriage without penalizing such behavior at divorce." Herma Hill Kay, Beyond No-Fault: New Directions in Divorce Reform, in Divorce Reform at the Crossroads 6, 31 (Stephen D. Sugarman & Herma Hill Kay eds., 1990). Do you agree with this goal? What does it mean in practice? Does the outcome in *Rosenberg* help achieve such objectives? Does *Michael*?

Some feminists criticize Ellman's *The Theory of Alimony*, supra, for relying "on the premise that women *should* specialize in domestic matters to the extent they earn less than . . . men *because* they have historically borne the major childrearing role." June R. Carbone, Economics, Feminism, and the Reinvention of Alimony: A Reply to Ira Ellman, 43 Vand. L. Rev. 1463, 1464-1465 (1990). Ellman's approach to increasing specialization "will ratify existing gender inequalities" "by increasing women's economic dependence on their husbands." Id. at 1465. See also Cynthia Lee Starnes, Victims, Breeders, Joy, and Math: First Thoughts on Compensatory Spousal Payments Under the Principles, 8 Duke J.

Gender L. & Pol'y 137 (2001) (ALI approach casts women as victims and favors "breeder" wives).

Does *Rosenberg* support such criticism? What outcome and analysis would have avoided this problem? What impact on future behavior and "gender inequalities" does *Michael* have? Was the determinative factor Mr. Michael's "contribution" or his "need"? To what extent does "fault" play a role in either case? What effect will each court's stance on fault have for the future?

8. *Attorneys' fees and costs.* Courts often require one spouse to pay the other's attorneys' fees and litigation costs. For example, *Michael* (in an omitted section) and *Rosenberg* both affirm such awards. Historically, a gender-based rule premised on the duty to provide necessaries prevailed. Today, many jurisdictions impose responsibility for fees on the spouse in the superior financial position, treating the award as an additional distribution of property or a species of spousal support. See, e.g., 750 Ill. Comp. Stat. 5/508 (West 1999). See also, e.g., Rosen v. Rosen, 696 So. 2d 697 (Fla. 1997). When the spouses occupy similar financial positions, they now pay their own fees and costs.

The appropriate *amount* of fees often generates dispute, given the emotional climate of divorce proceedings. Jurisdictions divide on whether contingent fee agreements in divorce litigation are permissible. Compare, e.g., Davis v. Taylor, 344 S.E.2d 19 (N.C. Ct. App. 1986) (such agreements violate public policy), with Alexander v. Inman, 974 S.W.2d 689, 693 (Tenn. 1998) (contingent fees "begrudgingly permitted"). See generally Restatement (Third) of the Law Governing Lawyers §35 cmt. g (2000) (examining underlying policies).

## 2. Special Problems in Achieving a Fair Dissolution

With courts attempting to divide property "equitably" and to award "just" support, general considerations of fairness often overshadow theoretical distinctions between the two remedies. Given the practice of blurring these lines, what difference does it make whether a particular payment represents property or support? Will the purpose of the payment as property distribution or support always be clear? Should the label used by the court control? If not, what considerations should govern?

### a. Changing Circumstances

■ **KELLER v. O'BRIEN**
*652 N.E.2d 589 (Mass. 1995)*

Liacos, C.J.

This case involves the modification of an alimony judgment [ordering plaintiff husband to pay defendant wife $500 per week in alimony. After defendant remarried,] the plaintiff filed a complaint for modification seeking to terminate his alimony obligation because the defendant's remarriage constituted a material change of circumstances. . . .

. . . The parties were married for twenty-six years prior to their divorce. During the marriage, the defendant stayed at home to raise their children. The plaintiff was a successful bank executive whose income in 1990, at the time of the divorce, was $158,327.12. In contrast, the defendant, who had completed only two years of college prior to the marriage, had limited employability and was qualified for only unskilled, entry level positions at minimum wage.

After the divorce, the defendant found part-time employment as a medical assistant, with earnings of $90 a week. [At the time of the modification hearing, both parties had remarried.] [Wife's] present spouse earned $28,000 per year, $7,800 of which he paid to a former wife as child support. The defendant's present spouse had a net take-home pay of $184.43 a week. He contributed $300 a month to the defendant's income tax expenses. The defendant had expenses of $588.81 per week, excluding income tax expenses on alimony payments received from the plaintiff. At the time of the modification hearing, the plaintiff's income had increased to more than $180,000. The value of his assets had increased substantially. He had weekly expenses of $1,527, including the $500 weekly alimony obligation.

. . . On appeal, the principal issues raised by the plaintiff are whether this court should adopt a rule automatically terminating alimony on the remarriage of the recipient spouse (in the absence of an agreement to the contrary), and whether the probate judge's [findings that the defendant was still in need of support and her remarriage] did not constitute a material change of circumstances [are] clearly erroneous.

. . . General Laws c. 208, §37, provides for modification of alimony awards, but does not specifically address whether remarriage requires the termination of alimony payments.[3] Although the statute does not make clear provision for the termination of the obligation to pay alimony on the recipient spouse's remarriage, this court has held that remarriage is prima facie evidence of a material change of circumstance which would warrant termination. . . .

. . . The majority of States have statutes providing that alimony payments automatically terminate on the recipient spouse's remarriage. In those States that do not have statutes that specifically address whether alimony payments should terminate on remarriage of the recipient spouse,

---

3. General Laws c. 208, §37 (1992 ed.), provides in relevant part: "After a judgment for alimony or an annual allowance for the spouse or children, the court may, from time to time, upon the action for modification of either party, revise and alter its judgment relative to the amount of such alimony or annual allowance and the payment thereof, and may make any judgment relative thereto which it might have made in the original action."

We have held that, in order to obtain modification of a judgment for alimony, a petitioner must demonstrate a material change of circumstances since entry of the earlier judgment.

statutes generally allow for modification of alimony obligations when changed circumstances warrant. A small number of States have statutes that, like G.L. c. 208, §37, merely allow for modification and leave to the courts the determination as to when modification is appropriate.

In States where legislation does not specifically address the issue, [most] courts have held that the recipient spouse's remarriage does not automatically terminate alimony, but that it creates a strong presumption or a prima facie case that alimony will cease in the absence of extraordinary circumstances. In a few States, the courts have adopted an automatic termination rule.

We believe the preferable rule is that, where not otherwise provided in the judgment of divorce or in an agreement between the parties, a recipient spouse's remarriage does not of itself automatically terminate alimony. Instead, the recipient spouse's remarriage makes a prima facie case which requires the court to end alimony, absent proof of some extraordinary circumstances, established by the recipient spouse, warranting its continuation. . . . For example, if a remarried recipient spouse becomes a public charge, a judge may order the former spouse to continue making alimony payments. Although this may burden the payor spouse, we believe that he or she should not be relieved of the obligation to pay alimony if the result would be to burden the taxpayers of this Commonwealth with support of the remarried recipient spouse.

In so holding, we recognize that, except in extraordinary circumstances, it is "illogical and unreasonable" that a spouse should receive support from a current spouse and a former spouse at the same time. The new spouse does, after all, assume a duty to support on marriage. We believe that "the remarriage should serve as an election between the support provided by the alimony award and the legal obligation of support embodied in the new marital relationship." Voyles v. Voyles, 664 P.2d 847, 849 (Alaska 1982). . . .

[I]t is not apparent from the record that the defendant satisfied her burden of showing that extraordinary circumstances warranted requiring her former husband to continue paying alimony. The mere fact that, without alimony, the defendant would not be able to live with her second husband in the way in which she lived prior to her marriage to him is not a valid reason to continue alimony. [W]e vacate the judgment of dismissal [and] remand this case for further proceedings consistent with this opinion. . . .

### Notes and Questions

1. Distributions of property upon divorce are final, even if the parties' circumstances change significantly after dissolution. By contrast, support awards typically allow modification upon a showing of changed circumstances. UMDA is illustrative:

### §316. [Modification and Termination of Provisions for Maintenance, Support, and Property Disposition]

(a) [T]he provisions of any decree respecting maintenance or support may be modified only as to installments accruing subsequent to the motion for modification and only upon a showing of changed circumstances so substantial and continuing as to make the terms unconscionable. The provisions as to property disposition may not be revoked or modified, unless the court finds the existence of conditions that justify the reopening of a judgment under the laws of this state.

(b) Unless otherwise agreed in writing or expressly provided in the decree, the obligation to pay future maintenance is terminated upon the death of either party or the remarriage of the party receiving maintenance. . . .

9A U.L.A. (pt. II) 102 (1998). See also UMDA §307, supra. Which theories of property division and support awards best explain the finality of the former and the modifiability of the latter?

2. Why did Massachusetts enact a statute without an automatic termination provision like UMDA's? Without any explicit requirement of changed circumstances? Is it ever fair for a former spouse to pay support after the recipient's remarriage? *Keller* notes the "illogic" of receiving support from a former and a current spouse simultaneously. Further, if alimony is a transitional remedy, then remarriage may provide the surest path to "self-sufficiency" for divorced women, according to an empirical study by a British scholar:

> So for women who have access to a man with reasonable earning capacity, remarriage is a far better economic alternative to increasing hours of paid work. The women who didn't remarry — particularly the urban black women — included many whose earning capacity was steadier than that of any available potential new partners. Compared with welfare, former partner support, or unskilled women's earnings, remarriage to an employed man is an attractive option. It adds a second income to yield a viable household package, presents an opportunity to cut down hours of work, and is now the most usual eventual outcome for American women after divorce. In the UK there is similar evidence of the economic benefits of remarriage. . . .

Mavis Maclean, Surviving Divorce 69, 75-77 (1991).

Is *Keller* nonetheless persuasive that support should sometimes continue despite remarriage? Under what circumstances? See, e.g., Campitelli v. Johnson, 761 A.2d 369 (Md. Ct. Spec. App. 2000) (prior agreement of parties); Dow v. Adams, 707 A.2d 793 (Me. 1998) (recipient's medical condition and absence of hardship for obligor). Should the purpose of the support award matter? See N.J. Stat. Ann. §2A:34-25 (West 2000) (remarriage terminates permanent and limited duration, but not rehabilitative or reimbursement, alimony).

3. *Epilogue*. When the plaintiff sued for restitution of payments made after his former wife's remarriage, the court held that the rule in the principal case applies prospectively only, given the lack of advance notice to the wife of the consequences of remarriage. Keller v. O'Brien, 683 N.E.2d 1026 (Mass. 1997).

4. When should changes in the *obligor*'s circumstances warrant reduction or termination of spousal support? Suppose the obligor retires? Compare Pimm v. Pimm, 601 So. 2d 534 (Fla. 1992), with Jameson v. Jameson, 600 N.W.2d 577 (S.D. 1999). Changes careers? See, e.g., Mizrachi v. Mizrachi, 683 A.2d 137 (D.C. 1996); Gastineau v. Gastineau, 573 N.Y.S.2d 819 (Sup. Ct. 1991). Assumes new family responsibilities through remarriage? See, e.g., Butts v. Butts, 906 S.W.2d 859 (Mo. Ct. App. 1995); McCarthy v. McCarthy, 610 N.Y.S.2d 619 (App. Div. 1994).

5. What occurrences warrant an *increase* in spousal support? The recipient's deteriorating health? See, e.g., In re Marriage of Perlmutter, 772 P.2d 621 (Colo. 1989); In re Marriage of Wessels, 542 N.W.2d 486 (Iowa 1995). A substantial increase in the obligor's ability to pay? Compare Bedell v. Bedell, 583 So. 2d 1005 (Fla. 1991), with Crews v. Crews, 751 A.2d 524 (N.J. 2000). See also In re Marriage of Monslow, 912 P.2d 735 (Kan. 1996) (approving inclusion of automatic "escalator clause" in maintenance award to give wife share of anticipated increase in husband's income).

6. With the advent of modern short-term maintenance, a recipient who did not achieve self-sufficiency during the maintenance period had the burden of seeking modification to extend postdissolution support. Yet in such cases, circumstances had not changed since the initial award, precluding the necessary showing. In response, some courts shifted the burden of modification to the obligor by ordering permanent alimony for the recipient. See, e.g., Colucci v. Colucci, 392 So. 2d 577 (Fla. Dist. Ct. App. 1980). See also Cal. Fam. Code §4336(b) (West 1994) (continuing judicial jurisdiction over support after a marriage "of long duration"). But see Dobrin v. Dobrin, 569 N.W.2d 199, 201-203 (Minn. 1997).

7. According to conventional wisdom, an attorney should always ask the court to award at least $1 in support to provide a basis for jurisdiction to modify in the event of future changed circumstances; the absence of a maintenance award was thought to preclude jurisdiction. Some modern courts have found the practice an unnecessary formality. See, e.g., Mulling v. Mulling, 912 S.W.2d 934 (Ark. 1996); Saxvik v. Saxvik, 544 N.W.2d 177 (S.D. 1996).

## Problem

State X's statute, modeled on UMDA §316, automatically terminates maintenance upon the recipient's remarriage. As a result, according to a lobby of ex-husbands, alimony recipients often elect not to remarry but to cohabit. As a legislator, would you support expanding the statute to treat cohabitation relationships just like remarriage? All cohabitation relationships? If not, which ones? What constitutes cohabitation? Should any sexual relationship of the recipient suffice? See, e.g., Pence v. Pence, 401 S.E.2d 727 (Ga. 1991); In re Marriage of Herrin, 634 N.E.2d 1168 (Ill. App. Ct. 1994); Gilman v. Gilman, 956 P.2d 761 (Nev. 1998); Pearson v. Pearson, 606 N.W.2d 128 (N.D. 2000). See also Kripp v. Kripp, 784 A.2d 158 (Pa. Super. Ct. 2001); ALI Principles, supra, §5.09.

### b. Bankruptcy

■ **DEICHERT v. DEICHERT**
*587 A.2d 319 (Pa. Super. Ct. 1991)*

MONTEMURO, Judge. . . .
Appellee, Eleanor M. Deichert, filed a Complaint in Divorce against appellant, Dr. Robert Deichert. . . . Approximately eight months after the final [divorce decree], appellant filed a voluntary petition for Chapter VII bankruptcy in the United States Bankruptcy Court [describing] himself as married but separated. Appellee was not listed as a creditor in any required Schedule A statements (concerning debtor liabilities), and appellant listed the marital residence and a 1980 Oldsmobile station wagon as real and exempt assets respectively, although both of these items had been granted to appellee pursuant to [the divorce decree].

[Subsequently,] the Honorable Thomas C. Gibbons, Bankruptcy Judge, entered a Discharge of Debtor Order releasing appellant from all personal liability for debts existing on the date the bankruptcy case was instituted. Debts determined non-dischargeable were not included. . . . At the hearing on appellee's enforcement petition, [appellant argued] that his obligations had been discharged by the Bankruptcy Court. [The court designated various marital obligations in the divorce decree and order as dischargeable or nondischargeable in bankruptcy and imposed a $1,000 per day fine for failure to comply with the nondischargeable obligations.]

Appellant's basic contention is that none of his obligations under the [divorce decree] were properly determined to be non-dischargeable in bankruptcy. In the . . . amended order, which determined dischargeability, it was found that: (1) appellant's equity interest in the medical building, valued at $25,000, and the husband's interest in his pension, valued at $45,114.58, were dischargeable; and, (2) all other dispositions . . . remained with appellee as non-dischargeable obligations.

The governing provision of the Bankruptcy Code, 11 U.S.C.S. §523(a) (5), states:

### §523. Exceptions to Discharge

(a) A discharge under section 727, 1141, or 1328(b) of this title [11 U.S.C.S. §727, 1141, or 1328(b)] does not discharge an individual debtor from any debt — . . .

   (5) to a spouse, former spouse, or child of the debtor, for alimony to, maintenance for, or support of such spouse or child, in connection with a separation agreement, divorce decree, or other order of a court of record or property settlement agreement, but not to the extent that — . . .

      (B) such debt includes a liability designated as alimony, maintenance, or support, unless such liability is actually in the nature of alimony, maintenance, or support. . . .

Preliminary, it must be noted that ". . . bankruptcy courts and state courts exercise concurrent jurisdiction over the question of whether a particular [marital] obligation is dischargeable under section 523(a)(5) of the Bankruptcy Code." [Buccino v. Buccino, 397 Pa. Super. 241, 247-248 n.6, 580 A.2d 13, 16 n.6 (1990).] Further, "What constitutes alimony, maintenance or support is to be determined according to federal bankruptcy law, not state law." [Citations omitted.] However, since there is no federal domestic relations law, and since the state court formulated the original marital obligations pursuant to state law, "it would be impossible to disregard state domestic relations law in determining the nature of an obligation the very existence of which is dependent on state law." *Buccino,* supra 397 Pa. Super. at p.249, 580 A.2d at p.17. Therefore, when determining dischargeability under the Bankruptcy Code, the court is to follow federal law, employing state law considerations in its analysis. . . .

Analysis of the facts and the law must be made in conjunction with two countervailing principles: (a) the bankruptcy court's fundamental goal of providing an economic "fresh start" to the honest debtor; and, (b) the congressional policy of giving first priority to the adequate financial maintenance of a debtor's children and ex-spouse. The basis of an inquiry into dischargeability under section 523(a)(5) is to question whether the particular debt (obligation) was created to perform a support function. To be taken into account in this determination are all relevant economic and non-economic factors, including the living standards of the parties. The substance and function of the debt are to control the determination, rather than the form or title given the debt. Further, ". . . if a specific obligation in connection with a divorce is labelled property division or 'equitable distribution,' such designation will not preclude a finding that the debt is, in fact, in the nature of alimony or support and, consequently, not dischargeable." *Buccino*, supra 397 Pa. Super. at 251, 580 A.2d at 18, citing In re Shine, 802 F.2d 583 (1st Cir. 1986) (citations omitted). A court is to look at both the intent of the parties and/or the divorce court and the effect/function of the obligation. [T]he trial court's determination that the marital residence, furnishings and 1980 station wagon were maintenance and support is correct under the principles enunciated in *Buccino*.

With regard to the residence and furnishings, appellee suffered considerable economic disadvantage during the marriage. She put her nursing career on hold for approximately twenty years in order to be wife, mother and homemaker. Further, her financial resources are considerably less than those of the appellant, and are likely to remain that way. These considerations warrant a finding that the marital residence and furnishings were a means of shelter, a necessary aspect of support.

Further, as transportation can be classified as maintenance, for purposes of non-dischargeability, the trial court was correct in holding that the 1980 Oldsmobile station wagon was non-dischargeable. [R]eliable transportation is an essential item for a family and children. The vehicle can provide necessary support for a family. As appellant received the parties' other automobile, appellee should not be deprived of transportation, as it is a necessary adjunct to support her reasonable needs as mother and homemaker.

Appellant's court ordered payment of the mortgage on the marital residence is also a non-dischargeable debt under section 523(a)(5). As stated in *Buccino*, "Bankruptcy courts have consistently held that the assumption of mortgage debts by a debtor-spouse which enables the creditor-spouse to provide for or remain in the marital residence are not dischargeable in bankruptcy because they are in the nature of support, alimony or maintenance." *Buccino*, supra 397 Pa. Super. at 260, 580 A.2d at 22. (An obligation to maintain and support a family includes the obligation to keep a roof over their heads.) Further, the trial court was correct in holding the $100,000 lien on appellant's medical building non-dischargeable, as the lien was used to ensure compliance with the obligation to provide alimony and property to appellee for her support, obligations appellant has consistently attempted to avoid.

Finally, regarding appellant's responsibility for the parties' joint debts, the trial court properly took into account such factors as the economic disparity between the parties, the employability and educational levels of the parties and the economic disadvantage to the creditor spouse as a result of the marriage in finding this obligation as support to appellee. Based upon those findings, the joint debts are non-dischargeable and the trial court's classification as maintenance and support was not error. . . .

In concluding, we would note that appellant has succeeded in abusing the procedures of the courts of this state and has effectively delayed performing the obligations imposed upon him by marriage and subsequent divorce. Such actions amount to a flagrant abuse of the administration of justice, and, further, create undue hardship and injustice to his wife and children.[9] [We affirm.]

## Notes and Questions

1. Under the Bankruptcy Code, when an individual petitions for bankruptcy, the debtor's property becomes part of the bankrupt's "estate," 11 U.S.C. §541 (1994), distributed among creditors. To further bankruptcy's protective policy, the debtor may claim exemption for certain property (for example, a home or car). The Code also allows a debtor spouse to be discharged from certain obligations. The general rule allows discharge of obligations for property division but not spousal or child support. The nondischargeability of spousal support obligations derives from judicial origin (Audubon v. Shufeldt, 181 U.S. 575 (1901)). The rule was subsequently codified and extended to child support in 1903 amendments to the Bankruptcy Act of 1898. Jana B. Singer, Divorce Obligations and Bankruptcy Discharge: Rethinking the Support/Property Distinction, 30 Harv. J. Legis. 43, 47, 53 (1993).

The Bankruptcy Reform Act of 1994 (BRA), which adds §523(a)(15) to the Code, makes divorce-related property obligations nondischargeable but only if the creditor spouse complies with strict procedural requirements, including filing within 60 days of the first date set for the creditors' meeting. The debtor spouse can still discharge these obligations, however, by showing they can be satisfied only from resources needed for the debtor's own support, dependents' support, or business.[18] Or, if the debtor proves the benefit of discharge outweighs the

---

9. We must also note the apparent discrepancy between the intent of the bankruptcy court, to provide relief for an honest debtor, and the intent of the state's divorce code, to give first priority to the adequate financial maintenance of a debtor's children and ex-spouse. In the instant case, appellant has shown himself to be far less than honest in his dealings with the court. Yet we are constrained to affirm the discharge of certain debts (namely the pension and interest in the medical partnership) which are under the principles of equitable distribution due and owing to appellee, but for appellant's access to the bankruptcy courts. Husband's actions, in effect, amount to an attempt to nullify the divorce decree. Our state court system has provided an adequate remedy for such challenges pursuant to either party's right to appeal a final order in divorce. Allowing appellant the opportunity to avoid the final order and distribution by filing for bankruptcy is inconsistent with the intention of both the bankruptcy and domestic relations statutes. However, until this ploy is legislatively rendered impossible, our decision must stand.

[18]. Courts have divided on whether the creditor or debtor has the burden of proof on these issues. Compare, e.g., In re Braslett, 233 B.R. 177 (Bankr. D. Me. 1999), with In re Jodoin, 209 B.R. 132 (B.A.P. 9th Cir. 1997). See Hui Yu, Note, Allocating the Burden of Establishing Nondischargeability in Bankruptcy of Property Settlement Obligations under §523(a)(15), 83 Iowa L. Rev. 861 (1998).

creditor spouse's detriment, the debt will be discharged. 11 U.S.C. §523(a)(15)(B) (1994). Further, property division (but not maintenance and support) obligations remain dischargeable if the debtor spouse files a Chapter 13 bankruptcy (providing for debt restructuring by wage earners). See generally Bernice B. Donald & Jennie D. Latta, The Dischargeability of Property Settlement and Hold Harmless Agreements in Bankruptcy: An Overview of §523(a)(15), 31 Fam. L.Q. 409 (1997); Yvonne M. Lada, Comment, Something Every Divorce Lawyer Should Know About Bankruptcy Law, 23 S. Ill. U. L.J. 735 (1999).

An empirical study finds that under §523(a)(15) bankruptcy courts have held the debt discharged in half the cases. Richard H. W. Maloy, Using Bankruptcy Court to Modify Domestic Relations Decrees: Problems Created by §523(a)(15), 31 Fam. L.Q. 433, 436 (1997).

2. The different treatment of support and property in bankruptcy law highlights the importance of classifying obligations. This task is problematic for several reasons, however, despite the help of the "intent-function" test that *Deichert* and most federal courts use. First, tax considerations often dictate the language of awards. Second, divorce courts, which usually resolve all the economic issues together, often use property to achieve the purpose of support. Third, as *Deichert* notes, in bankruptcy the property-support distinction rests on federal law, which in turn uses state law considerations. Finally, the function prong of the test merely gives the debtor-spouse another chance to reargue issues of fairness and need that he lost in the divorce case. Singer, supra, at 61-64. See, e.g., Cummings v. Cummings, 244 F.3d 1263 (11th Cir. 2001). See also Meredith Johnson, Note, At the Intersection of Bankruptcy and Divorce: Property Division Under the Bankruptcy Reform Act of 1994, 97 Colum. L. Rev. 91, 105-107 (1997).

3. Does the debtor spouse's discharge of property obligations constitute a changed circumstance, allowing the divorce court to increase support payments to the creditor spouse? See Dickson v. Dickson, 474 S.E.2d 165 (Va. Ct. App. 1996); Sheryl L. Scheible, Bankruptcy and the Modification of Support: Fresh Start, Head Start, or False Start?, 69 N.C. L. Rev. 577, 619-625 (1991). Would such modification, in effect, change the division of property, a final award? See In re Trickey, 589 N.W.2d 753 (Iowa 1998).

4. Does the problem in *Deichert* derive not from the difficulty in distinguishing support from property but rather from the dischargeability of property division obligations? See Allen M. Parkman, Bringing Consistency to the Financial Arrangements at Divorce, 87 Ky. L.J. 51, 89-91 (1999). How far does the BRA go in resolving this problem? Does it eliminate the necessity for enlarging the definition of "support," as in *Deichert*? See generally Sheryl L. Scheible, Defining "Support" Under Bankruptcy Law: Revitalization of the "Necessaries" Doctrine, 41 Vand. L. Rev. 1 (1988). Does it create a "Catch-22" for the creditor spouse who

must, in effect, claim that obligations do not constitute true alimony or support under §523(a)(5) (see *Deichert*) in order to rely on §523(a)(15) to attempt to block a discharge? Does it address the particular difficulties bankruptcy law creates for women creditors? See Peter C. Alexander, Divorce and the Dischargeability of Debts: Focusing on Women as Creditors in Bankruptcy, 43 Cath. U. L. Rev. 351 (1994).

5. To what extent did *Deichert*'s outcome rest on appellant's "flagrant abuse of the administration of justice" and "attempt to nullify the divorce decree"? Does the BRA solve this problem? See In re Butler, 186 B.R. 371, 372-373 (Bankr. D. Vt. 1995) ("Congress enacted §523(a)(15) because obligors were able to craftily draft settlement agreements to be in property rather than alimony terms and then discharge their marital obligations in bankruptcy"). Should marital fault, such as fraudulent diversion of assets or spouse abuse, militate against dischargeability? Does such conduct justify dismissing the debtor's bankruptcy action altogether? See In re Huckfeldt, 39 F.3d 829 (8th Cir. 1994) (dismissing bankruptcy petition filed in "bad faith" to frustrate divorce decree).

6. One common method of securing an obligation to an ex-spouse is to impose a lien on the obligor's property in favor of the obligee. In Farrey v. Sanderfoot, 500 U.S. 291 (1991), Gerald Sanderfoot attempted to avoid his ex-wife's judicial lien (imposed to secure his obligation to pay her for her share of the marital assets) against the real estate that the court had allocated to him, by declaring bankruptcy and listing the real estate as exempt homestead property. Although noting that the Bankruptcy Code, 11 U.S.C. §522(f)(1), allows the debtor to avoid the fixing of some judicial liens on exempt property, the Court held that a debtor cannot use this provision to avoid a lien on an interest acquired *after* the lien attached. In other words, to use this provision, the debtor must possess the interest to which the lien fixes, before it fixes. 500 U.S. at 299. Turning to state law (Wisconsin), the Court determined Sanderfoot could not avoid Farrey's lien because he did not acquire his fee simple interest before Farrey acquired her lien against this interest.

The BRA of 1994 changes the provision applied in *Farrey* so that a debtor can avoid fixing a judicial lien on exempt property only when it does not "secure a debt to a spouse, former spouse or a child" for alimony, maintenance, or support. 11 U.S.C. §522(f)(1)(A)(i) (1994). See Margaret Howard, Avoiding Powers and the 1994 Amendments to the Bankruptcy Code, 69 Am. Bank. L.J. 259, 277-279 (1995); Sheryl Scheible Wolf, Divorce, Bankruptcy, and Metaphysics: Avoidance of Marital Liens Under §522(f) of the Bankruptcy Code, 31 Fam. L.Q. 513 (1997).

7. Are awards of attorneys' fees against one spouse for the benefit of the other dischargeable in bankruptcy, or are they "in the nature of alimony" — that is, functionally equivalent to support? Suppose the obligor is ordered to pay them directly to the other spouse's attorney?

See In re Kline, 65 F.3d 749 (8th Cir. 1995) (fee awards in nature of support nondischargeable despite statutory exemption from discharge only for debts for support "to a spouse").

## Note: The Family Home

Frequently, the family home is the most significant marital asset and becomes the focus of the court's effort to effect an equitable distribution of property. Yet this property often serves a support function for the dependent spouse and children.

When one spouse owns the home premaritally as separate property, the other spouse's contributions (financial or homemaking) to its preservation and appreciation can make the increased equity achieved during marriage a divisible asset. See, e.g., Cohen v. Cohen, 937 S.W.2d 823, 833 (Tenn. 1996).

Rules requiring or favoring equal division of marital property often result in the sale of the family home. If the couple has no asset of comparable value to allocate to the spouse not to be awarded the home, the home must be sold so the proceeds can be shared. Dr. Lenore Weitzman helped publicize that such rules disadvantage children. Lenore J. Weitzman, The Divorce Revolution: The Unexpected Social and Economic Consequences of Divorce 384-387 (1985). To remedy this problem, some states allow courts to award the family home, at least temporarily, to the custodial parent, treating use of the residence as a form of child support and reflecting reluctance to uproot the children. See, e.g., Cal. Fam. Code §3802 (West 1994); Mo. Rev. Stat. §452.330.1(1) (2000).

Building on the California statute, the ALI Principles of the Law of Family Dissolution say that child support rules should provide for judicial orders deferring sale of the family residence and that a court may make such order only if it finds that deferral is "economically feasible and would avoid significant detriment to the child." ALI Principles, supra, §3.11. The Principles resolve any conflict between this approach and the presumption of equal division of marital property, supra page 667, by treating as additional child support "any resulting enhancement in the residential parent's property share" and requiring no adjustment or offset. Id. §4.09(3).

Some commentators would go further. Weitzman, for example, urges legislative directives *requiring* judges to delay the sale of the family residence in the interests of maintaining a stable home for children. Weitzman, supra, at 384-387. See also Martha F. Davis, Comment, The Marital Home: Equal or Equitable Distribution?, 50 U. Chi. L. Rev. 1089 (1983).

When the family home represents a liability (because of a large mortgage), the court can allocate responsibility for the debts. This allocation can occur in the distribution of property. Alternatively, monthly maintenance obligations can include mortgage payments on behalf of a former spouse.

### c. Pensions and Employee Benefits

■ **COHEN v. COHEN**
*937 S.W.2d 823 (Tenn. 1996)*

WHITE, J. . . .

[Pamela Cohen and Jay Cohen married on September 1, 1982.] During the parties' marriage, Mr. Cohen was employed by Nashville Metropolitan Fire Department as a paramedic. In April, 1987, the department began making monthly contributions to the retirement plan on Cohen's behalf.

In January, 1992, Mrs. Cohen filed for divorce. . . . The trial court declined to award the wife any interest in the husband's unvested retirement benefits. The Court of Appeals reversed. . . .

Prior to determining whether unvested retirement benefits are marital property under our statute, we will review the concepts. An employee has a "vested" retirement right when the employee has completed the requisite term of employment necessary to be entitled to receive retirement benefits at some future time. A "vested" right matures when an employee reaches retirement age and elects to retire. Frequently, vested, but immature rights, are conditioned upon the employee reaching retirement age. An "unvested" retirement account is one in which the time period requirements have not been fulfilled.

Our analysis begins with Tennessee Code Annotated Section 36-4-121 which defines marital and separate property:

> (b)(1)(A) "Marital Property" means all real and personal property, both tangible and intangible, acquired by either or both spouses during the course of the marriage up to the date of the final divorce hearing . . . including any property to which a right was acquired up to the date of the final divorce hearing, and valued as of a date as near as reasonably possible to the final divorce hearing date.
>
> (B) "Marital property" includes income from, and any increase in value during the marriage, of property determined to be separate property in accordance with subdivision (b)(2) if each party substantially contributed to its preservation and appreciation and the value of vested pension, retirement or other fringe benefit rights accrued during the period of the marriage. . . .
>
> (2) "Separate property" means:
>
> (A) All real and personal property owned by a spouse before marriage;
>
> (B) Property acquired in exchange for property acquired before the marriage;

> (C) Income from and appreciation of property owned by a spouse before marriage except when characterized as marital property under subdivision (b)(1); and
>
> (D) Property acquired by a spouse at any time by gift, bequest, devise or descent.

Tenn. Code Ann. §36-4-121(b)(1)(A),(B) & (2) (1991 Repl.).

First, we must determine whether the right to an unvested retirement benefit fits within the statutory definition of marital property. In construing statutes, we look to the plain language and give effect to the ordinary meaning of the words. . . . In applying [the] rules of statutory construction, we conclude that the legislature intended to include unvested retirement benefits as marital property. First, the definition of marital property found in subsection (A) is virtually all inclusive. That broad definition clearly includes unvested retirement benefits. Second, subsection (B), which serves to append to subsection (A's) definition "vested pension, retirement, or other fringe benefit rights" and certain forms of separate property does not exclude unvested retirement benefits. Third, we note that unvested retirement benefits are not included in the definition of separate property. . . .

Our conclusion based on these rules of construction is consistent with the legislative intent behind these statutes. Specifically, the legislative definitions of marital and separate property were "to codify existing case law, to define marital property more clearly, and to recognize a homemaker's contributions." Kendrick v. Kendrick, 902 S.W.2d 918, 922 (Tenn. App. 1994). . . .

Though not necessary to our conclusion, we note that courts of other states and our own Court of Appeals are in accord with our conclusion that unvested retirement benefits accruing during the marriage constitute marital property. [R]etirement benefits have been described as part of the consideration earned by an employee and as a form of deferred compensation provided by the employer for work already performed. Since the benefits are acquired with the fruits of the wage earner's labor, were it not deferred it could benefit the parties during the marriage. . . .

Retirement benefits, vested or unvested, are important assets. Many married couples consider these benefits as substitutes for savings or investments. As the date of vesting grows nearer, the benefit may be the most valuable asset of the marriage, particularly if economic circumstances have prevented couples from saving or investing a portion of their income. A spouse who is primarily a homemaker would be seriously disadvantaged by the inability to claim a portion of the retirement benefits that accrued during the course of the marriage. Even when both spouses are publicly employed and have accrued retirement benefits, the spouse who has devoted more time to homemaking and child-rearing will frequently have greatly reduced benefits. In order to obtain an equitable distribution of marital property as contemplated by the legislature, the trial court must be able to consider the distribution of all retirement benefits.

We, therefore, conclude that marital property includes retirement benefits, both vested and unvested which accrue during the marriage. . . . We are aware that the [few] states that do not recognize unvested retirement benefits as marital property do so largely because of the contingent and speculative nature of the benefit. . . . Contingencies should be considered on the issue of method of distribution, perhaps, but not on the determination of classification.

Further, the difficulty in determining the value of the benefits should not affect the classification of the property. . . . The difficulty in dividing future benefits is aided by the use of elastic, equitable approaches. Most courts use one of two techniques [the present cash value method or the "deferred distribution" method]. The choice of valuation method remains within the sound discretion of the trial court to determine after consideration of all relevant factors and circumstances. While the parties are entitled to an equitable division of their marital property, that division need not be mathematically precise. It must, however, reflect essential fairness in light of the facts of the case.

In this case, Mr. Cohen earned approximately six years of retirement benefits during the marriage. Those benefits are marital property subject to equitable division by the court. . . . After hearing the evidence, the trial court shall determine the appropriate valuation method and shall make appropriate orders. . . .

## Notes and Questions

1. *Cohen* exemplifies the majority rule that nonvested, as well as vested, pensions are marital property subject to division upon dissolution. See also, e.g., Janssen v. Janssen, 331 N.W.2d 752 (Minn. 1983); Majauskas v. Majauskas, 463 N.E.2d 15 (N.Y. 1984); Grode v. Grode, 543 N.W.2d 795 (S.D. 1996). After *Cohen,* the legislature clarified the definition of marital property by adding a reference to unvested pension rights. See Tenn. Code Ann. §36-4-121 (LEXIS, through 2001 slip laws).

2. What arguments support recognition of vested pensions as marital assets? Nonvested pensions? Are pension benefits "gifts" by the employer? See Daigre v. Daigre, 83 So. 2d 900 (La. 1955). Do they constitute mere expectancies, rather than property interests? Should a court consider such contingent interests in determining support rather than property distribution? Does the nonemployee spouse suffer a compensable loss under the ALI Principles, supra, when divorce thwarts the opportunity to enjoy these future benefits?

The landmark case In re Marriage of Brown, 544 P.2d 561 (Cal. 1976), established the majority rule. In *Brown*, a couple divorced after a 24-year marriage, but 3 years prior to the husband's eligibility for retirement. The husband argued that his nonvested pension rights were not divisible as a community asset. In ruling for the wife, *Brown* overturned a long line of decisions holding nonvested pension rights a "mere expectancy" not subject to division. Justice Tobriner described pension benefits as a form of "deferred compensation" based on the employment contract, a form of property. Id. at 565. *Brown* also noted the unfairness of classifying unvested pensions as separate property. Alimony cannot rectify this unfairness because the spouse "should not be dependent on the discretion of the court . . . to provide her with the equivalent of what should be hers as a matter of absolute right." 544 P.2d at 567.

Courts now use identical analysis to treat unvested stock options as divisible property. See, e.g., Fisher v. Fisher, 769 A.2d 1165 (Pa. 2001). See also DeJesus v. DeJesus, 687 N.E.2d 1319 (N.Y. 1997).

3. Pension plans increasingly play an important role upon dissolution as an asset subject to distribution or as a source of funds for meeting support obligations. Pension benefits (in addition to the marital home) constitute the most significant marital asset for many couples. Nonetheless, courts recognize that equitable division requires considering the speculative and nonmarketable nature of pension rights, regardless of their value. See Blanchard v. Blanchard, 731 So. 2d 175 (La. 1999) (holding inequitable an award of residence to husband and pension rights to wife despite similar value).

(a) *Types of plans.* A pension plan is a mechanism by which an employer facilitates an employee's accumulation of savings for retirement. Pension plans may be "qualified" or "nonqualified."[19] Under a qualified plan, the employee defers taxation on the employer's contribution until the funds are distributed during retirement.

Deferred compensation plans may be either defined benefit plans or defined contribution plans. The former provide a fixed dollar amount, usually monthly, payable to the participant upon retirement. The exact benefit is defined by formulae that take into account such factors as age, length of service, and average salary (often the highest average salary for a three- or five-year period).

In contrast, defined contribution plans (of which one popular type is called a "401(k) plan," pursuant to the relevant provision of the Internal Revenue Code), do not provide for payment of a fixed sum upon retirement. Rather, these benefits are based on the employer's (and

---

[19]. The former simply describes a private plan that qualifies for favorable tax treatment under the Internal Revenue Code, I.R.C. §401(a) (West Supp. 2001 & Pamphlet No. 1 Sept. 2001). Under such plans, the employer gets an immediate deduction of the employer's contribution, and investments of earnings accumulate tax free.

sometimes the participant's) contributions to the plan. Unlike defined benefit plan funds, defined contribution plan funds are held in a separate account for each participant. The contribution formulae for these plans vary. Some promise a specified annual contribution (for example, a money-purchase plan providing 10 percent of current compensation), while profit-sharing plans may tie the employer's total contribution to current or accumulated profits or may leave the amount to the discretion of the board of directors.

(b) *Federal regulation of private pension plans: ERISA.* The Employee Retirement Income Security Act of 1974 (ERISA), 29 U.S.C. §§1001 et seq. (1994 & Supp. V 1999), protects employee retirement benefits through comprehensive federal regulation of private pension plans. The statute expressly preempts state law. With important exceptions for government and church plans, ERISA applies to (1) plans that systematically defer cash compensation until termination of employment or longer ("employee pension benefit plans") and (2) plans providing, inter alia, health care benefits, death and disability benefits, day care centers, and prepaid legal services ("employee welfare benefit plans"). See Peter J. Wiedenbeck, Implementing ERISA: Of Policies and "Plans," 72 Wash. U. L.Q. 559, 564-565 (1994).

(c) *REA: QDROs.* Under ERISA, as originally enacted, a nonemployee spouse (for example, the wife of a covered employee) had limited rights to share in the employee's pension upon dissolution,[20] as the result of an "anti-alienation rule" barring assignment or alienation of pension plan benefits (although not welfare plan benefits). See ERISA §206(d)(1), 29 U.S.C. §1056(d)(1) (1994). This protective policy ensures that the participant cannot consume retirement savings before retirement. ERISA made no exceptions for domestic relations claims against an employee's pension plan. In the wake of ERISA, federal and state courts split on whether the anti-alienation rule barred distribution of pension benefits to a nonemployee spouse upon divorce.

The Retirement Equity Act of 1984 (REA or REAct) sought to remedy this and other problems experienced particularly by women. REA mandates that ERISA's anti-alienation rule must yield to certain state domestic relations decrees and permits a court to divide pension benefits in the same manner as other marital assets. That is, REA amends ERISA to provide for the enforcement of "qualified domestic relations orders" or QDROs and removes such orders from ERISA's preemption scheme. See ERISA §§206(d)(3), 514(b)(7), 29 U.S.C. §§1056(d)(3), 1144(b)(7) (1994 & Supp. V 1999). QDROs facilitate the enforcement of awards of

---

[20]. ERISA, similarly, failed to protect the spouse of a plan participant who died before reaching the plan's retirement age. REA amendments extended protection by providing a "qualified preretirement survivor annuity" or QPSA when the employee spouse had any vested benefits. ERISA §205(a)(2), 29 U.S.C. §1055 (1994 & Supp. V 1999).

spousal support and child support by authorizing retirement plan administrators to make payments directly to a former spouse.

Under the act, "qualified domestic relations order" means a domestic relations order "which creates or recognizes the existence of an alternate payee's right to, or assigns to an alternate payee the right to, receive all or a portion of the benefits payable with respect to a participant under a plan"; for purposes of this provision, a domestic relations order is a judgment, decree, or order "which relates to the provision of child support, alimony payments, or marital property rights to a spouse, former spouse, child, or other dependent of a participant," made "pursuant to a State domestic relations law (including a community property law)." ERISA §206(d)(3)(B), 29 U.S.C. §1056(d)(3)(B) (1994).

A QDRO thus recognizes the right of another person (the "alternate payee") to receive benefits under a pension plan. That is, the "alternate payee" is treated as a beneficiary under the plan. REA defines an "alternate payee" as "any spouse, former spouse, child, or other dependent of a participant who is recognized by a domestic relations order as having a right to receive all, or a portion of, the benefits payable under a plan with respect to such participant." ERISA §206(d)(3)(K), 29 U.S.C. §1056(d)(3)(K) (1994).

To qualify as a plan beneficiary under a QDRO, the nonemployee spouse must obtain a state court decree (not merely a separation agreement), which specifies the plan participant's liability for pension assets. Note that pension assets can be distributed under a QDRO not only for property division (the question in *Cohen*) but also for spousal and child support obligations. Although QDROs facilitate collection of divorce awards by directing retirement plan administrators to make payments directly to the "alternate payee," QDROs have several limitations. The extent of the nonemployee spouse's benefits is governed by those of the employee spouse — that is, the former spouse may not obtain a lump sum distribution, for example, if such an option is not available to the employee spouse. Similarly, if the nonemployee spouse is divorced from a previously divorced spouse already subject to a QDRO, the first ex-spouse will prevail.

(d) *Federal pension benefits.* Federal retirement benefit plans cover certain government employees. Both the United States Supreme Court and Congress have addressed the question whether state divorce laws apply to benefits under these plans or whether federal law preempts the field. The Court initially favored federal preemption, with the result that state divorce courts could not award any benefits to the nonemployee spouse. See Hisquierdo v. Hisquierdo, 439 U.S. 572 (1979) (railroad employees' benefits); McCarty v. McCarty, 453 U.S. 210 (1981) (military retirement benefits). Congress, however, later enacted corrective legislation. 45 U.S.C. §231a(c)(4)(1994) (amendments to Railroad Retirement Act extending benefits to divorced spouses married to railroad employee for at least ten years, among other conditions); 10 U.S.C. §1408 (1994 & Supp. V 1999) (Uniformed Services Former Spouses Protection Act over-ruling retroactively *McCarty* to permit state courts to apply their laws to military retirement benefits upon divorce, with enforcement mechanism available under certain conditions). Feminist commentators have been especially critical of the initial preemption policy. To what extent does this policy reflect gender bias, protecting pensioners (usually husbands) at the expense of needy spouses (usually wives) and reflecting the tradi-tional belief that assets belong only to the spouse who earns them? See, e.g., Sylvia Law, Families and Federalism, 4 Wash. U. J.L. & Pol'y 175, 203 (2000).[21]

(e) *Pension valuation.* Pension valuation presents complex problems often requiring the assistance of actuarial experts. One method of valu-ation (most useful for plans funded by employee contributions) calcu-lates the employee's marital contributions to the plan, plus interest, and awards the nonemployee spouse an appropriate share.

A second method (the most common for defined benefit plans) cal-culates the present value of the prospective benefits while discounting this value for contingencies such as mortality and vesting. This process entails identifying the amount of retirement benefits to be paid at some future date, assuming that the participant continues employment. The court determines what part of this amount is marital property and then awards the former spouse a lump sum of the appropriate proportion of the marital interest, often in the form of equivalent property, with the employee receiving the pension when it becomes payable. This method of valuation is the most speculative because it involves so many uncer-tain variables and assumptions.

Under a third valuation method, the reserved jurisdiction approach (also called deferred distribution settlement or the "if, as, and when" ap-proach), the court determines the spousal shares by a percentage or for-mula at the time of divorce, but retains jurisdiction, delaying the division until the employee spouse receives the payments. Courts disfavor this approach because it frustrates finality and forces ex-spouses to remain financially interdependent. This method also arguably allows the non-employee spouse to benefit from compensation the employee spouse earns after divorce, which is generally not marital property.

See generally Joyce Hens Green et al., Dissolution of Marriage 414 (1986); John H. Langbein & Bruce A. Wolk, Pension and Employee Ben-efit Law 599-600 (3d ed. 2000); Brett Turner, Equitable Distribution of Property §6.12 (2d ed. 1994 & Supp. 2000).

---

[21]. Note that some statutes exempt certain state employees' pensions from classifi-cation as marital property, e.g., teachers' pensions. See Susan J. Prather, Comment, Char-acterization, Valuation, and Distribution of Pensions at Divorce, 15 J. Am. Acad. Matrim. Law. 443, 449-451 (1998).

4. *Pensions and bankruptcy.* Should the obligation to share retirement benefits be included in the debtor spouse's bankruptcy estate and be subject to discharge? Some courts treat the debtor spouse's obligation to pay a portion of retirement benefits as dischargeable property division; others treat the obligation as nondischargeable support. Margaret Dee McGarity, Who Gets the Retirement Plan?, 14 Fam. Advoc. 53, 54 (1992). In addition, even if characterized as property, the nonemployee spouse's share of pension benefits will not be dischargeable if the divorce decree impressed a constructive trust on the pension for the nonemployee spouse. Under this approach, the affected share of the benefits is no longer the property of the employee spouse and thus not part of the employee's bankruptcy estate. See In re MacCafferty, 96 F.3d 192 (6th Cir. 1996). See generally Mary A. Throne, Pension Awards in Divorce and Bankruptcy, 88 Colum. L. Rev. 194 (1988).

## Problems

1. Karen and Robert divorced after 26 years of marriage. Karen, a part-time secretary for a church, was earning $645 per month; Robert, an employee of Miller Brewing Co., was earning $2,900 per month. In the division of marital property, Robert got his pension, valued at $11,355, and Karen got other property of roughly the same value (but no interest in Robert's pension). The court ordered Robert to pay Karen $600 per month maintenance. After taking voluntary retirement at age 55, Robert now seeks to terminate maintenance payments, arguing he has no income available. Karen seeks to continue maintenance, arguing that the $2,700 per month Robert gets from his pension is income available for maintenance. What result and why? Is it unfair "double-counting" to consider Robert's pension plan both as an asset in the property division and as income for maintenance payments? See In re Marriage of Olski, 540 N.W.2d 412 (Wis. 1995); In re Marriage of Wettstaedt, 625 N.W.2d 900 (Wis. Ct. App. 2001).

2. David, an employee of the Boeing Corporation in Washington, designated his wife, Donna, as the beneficiary of both a life insurance policy and a pension plan provided by his employer. The couple divorced, and two months later David died intestate in an automobile accident, without ever having changed the beneficiary designation. Under Washington law, however, divorce automatically revokes the designation of a spouse as the beneficiary of a nonprobate asset.

When benefits are paid to Donna under the plans, David's children from a previous marriage sue, invoking the Washington statute and claiming that they should receive the benefits as David's heirs at law. ERISA governs both of the employee benefit plans in question. ERISA's express preemption clause, which Donna argues applies, says that ERISA

"shall supercede any and all State laws insofar as they may now or hereafter relate to any employee benefit plan" covered by ERISA. What result
and why? As a matter of policy, is the question one that federal or state
legislation should control? On these facts, what role, if any, should the
REA's purpose of protecting divorced spouses play? See Egelhoff v. Egelhoff, 532 U.S. 141 (2001). See also Boggs v. Boggs, 520 U.S. 833 (1997).

### Note: Medical Coverage Following Dissolution (COBRA)

An important issue for many spouses upon dissolution, especially
homemakers, is securing the continuation of medical benefits. Congressional concern about the high cost of medical insurance and its unavailability for dependent ex-spouses resulted in the 1985 enactment of the
Consolidated Omnibus Budget Reconciliation Act (COBRA), adding
§§601-608 to ERISA and subsequent amendments thereto. See 29 U.S.C.
§§1161-1168 (1994 & Supp. V 1999).

COBRA requires, inter alia, employers of more than 20 employees
to offer continued medical coverage at group rates to "qualified beneficiaries" who would otherwise lose benefits upon the occurrence of certain "qualified events." Qualified beneficiaries (a class including
employees and their dependents) may make "elections" for continuation
of the same coverage. A "qualified event" includes divorce or legal separation. A spouse is entitled to continued coverage for 36 months following the date of divorce or legal separation. Coverage may not be
conditioned on evidence of insurability. The qualified beneficiary must
pay the required premiums after the COBRA election.

### d. Investments in a Spouse's Future Success: Degrees, Earning Capacity, and Goodwill

### ■ IN RE MARRIAGE OF ROBERTS
*670 N.E.2d 72 (Ind. Ct. App. 1996)*

GARRARD, Judge. . . .

[Matthew and Leigh Anne Roberts] were married on June 24, 1989.
In the fall of 1990, Matthew began attending the Valparaiso University
Law School as a full-time student. Before law school, Matthew had been
employed at Society Bank in South Bend, Indiana and had been earning a salary of $30,000.00 per year at the time he left employment.
Matthew and Leigh Anne agreed that Matthew should quit working
and attend school full-time while Leigh Anne continued to work to
support them. Leigh Anne also assumed primary responsibility for

running the household so that Matthew could devote all of his time to his studies.

Two months before Matthew's graduation Leigh Anne learned that she was pregnant, and thereafter the couple separated. Matthew finished third in his graduating class and also served as editor-in-chief of the Valparaiso Law Review. After graduation, he took an associate position with a large law firm in Chicago, Illinois. He filed his petition for dissolution of marriage on August 4, 1993.

The major asset of the parties was the marital home, valued at $70,000.00 with a mortgage of $63,245.00. The parties also owned certain personal property and each had 401(k) accounts and IRA accounts. The court determined that Matthew's law degree could not be considered a marital asset subject to distribution. However, the court did include Matthew's student loans, totaling $22,500.00, in valuing the marital estate, and the court found repayment to be the sole responsibility of Matthew. The court determined that, based upon the student loans, the disproportionate earnings history and the earning potential of the parties, the presumption of equal distribution had been rebutted. The court [allocated to Matthew $22,084.96 total assets and $24,500 total debts, resulting in a net debt of $2,415.04; it allocated to Leigh Anne $90,779.98 total assets and $65,245.00 total debts, amounting to net assets of $25,534.98].

Leigh Anne first argues that the trial court should have included Matthew's law degree as a marital asset subject to distribution. . . .

The specific issue of whether a degree obtained during a marriage by one party may be considered marital property upon divorce was addressed in Prenatt v. Stevens, 598 N.E.2d 616 (Ind. Ct. App. 1992), *trans. denied.* In *Prenatt,* the trial court found that the wife's doctoral degree in English, which was obtained during the marriage, was a marital asset. This determination was reversed on appeal, with the court relying upon Wilcox v. Wilcox, 173 Ind. App. 661, 365 N.E.2d 792 (1977) and In re Marriage of McManama, 272 Ind. 483, 399 N.E.2d 371 (1980). In *Wilcox,* the court first noted that any award over and above the assets of the marriage must represent some form of support or maintenance. The court then held that the husband's future earnings could not be considered a marital asset as there was no vested present interest in such income. In *McManama,* the trial court had awarded the wife a lump sum in the amount she had contributed to help her husband obtain his advanced degree on the theory that there had been a dissipation of marital property. Our supreme court reversed, finding that the award was in actuality an award to be paid from the husband's future income. Such an award of future income could only be proper as either support or maintenance, and there was no evidence of any incapacity to support such an award.

Based upon this precedent, *Prenatt* concluded that, despite the legislature's intent for "property" to be interpreted as broadly inclusive, a degree simply does not possess the common characteristics of property:

> A degree is an intangible which is personal to the holder. It is a piece of paper and has no real value except for what the holder chooses to pursue with it. Potential worth is dependent upon choice and availability of work, whether the holder is good at what she does, or a myriad of other potentialities.
>
> Valuation of a degree is fraught with uncertainty because of the personal factors described above. Even if valuation could be made certain, such valuation, whether based on future earning capacity or upon cost of acquisition, would ultimately result in an award beyond the actual physical assets of the marriage. As noted in *Wilcox* and *McManama,* such award is improper.

*Prenatt,* 598 N.E.2d at 620.

The only statutory exception is I.C. §31-1-11.5-11(d), which states:

> When the court finds there is little or no marital property, it may award either spouse a money judgment not limited to the property existing at the time of final separation. However, this award may be made only for the financial contribution of one (1) spouse toward tuition, books, and laboratory fees for the higher education of the other spouse.

Thus, a spouse may be reimbursed, even above the assets of the marital estate, but reimbursement is strictly limited.

We agree with the finding in *Prenatt* that a degree does not constitute marital property. While the maintenance statute does not permit any type of "reimbursement maintenance," the enhanced earning ability of a degree-earning spouse may certainly be considered in making a division of the marital assets. See I.C. §31-1-11.5-11(c)(3), (5) (factors which court may consider in rebutting presumption of an equal division of property include the economic circumstances of each spouse and the earnings or earning ability of the parties); see also *Prenatt,* 598 N.E.2d at 622 (Garrard, J., concurring) ("It should be pointed out that the educational achievements and potential earning life referred to by the court in its findings *do* constitute a valid consideration and basis for determining the appropriate disposition of the marital assets. . . .") (emphasis in original).

Therefore, while Indiana does not permit a degree to be included as marital property, and further will not allow an award of future earnings unless the spouse qualifies for maintenance, nevertheless the earning ability of the degree-earning spouse may be considered in determining the distribution of the marital estate. . . .

Leigh Anne also argues that the trial court should have made an award to compensate her for the dissipation of the marital estate by Matthew as a result of the income which the family was deprived of while Matthew attended law school and the contributions Leigh Anne made toward Matthew's education and the household living expenses. [W]e must respond that in employing the term "dissipation," our legislature intended that it carry its common meaning denoting "foolishly" or "aimlessly." Thus, under the circumstances of this case it cannot be said that the money expended in order to secure Matthew's law degree was dissipated, even though Leigh Anne did not receive the benefits she expected therefrom. . . .

Finally, Leigh Anne argues that, if Matthew's law degree is not to be considered a marital asset then, correspondingly, Matthew's student loans should not be considered marital liabilities. We disagree. The student loans were contracted during the marriage and were properly considered as part of the marital estate. Moreover, the court quite properly determined that Matthew should be solely responsible for their repayment. Leigh Anne suffered no harm whatever from their inclusion in the marital pot and the order that Matthew be solely responsible for their repayment. . . .

We affirm the judgment. . . .

## ■ JOAN WILLIAMS, IS COVERTURE DEAD? BEYOND A NEW THEORY OF ALIMONY
### 82 Geo. L.J. 2227, 2267-2272, 2274-2275 (1994)

Despite some early support for using the language of property to address the issue of post-divorce impoverishment, it is an article of faith among many family law courts and scholars today that property language is out of place and inherently unconvincing in this context. This dismissal is ironic because . . . conclusions about ownership are inevitable; the only question is whether the family wage will continue to be awarded one-sidely to the husband. The disagreement is not over whether the family wage will be owned, but over who shall own it.

[T]he courts' and commentators' rejection of property language in this context reflects its linkage with arguments of human capital theorists. Such arguments generally have failed to persuade courts, leading many family law scholars to conclude that property rhetoric has failed them. In fact, property rhetoric is not the problem; human capital theory is. . . .

The typical degree case involves a wife who supported her husband through professional school and who claims "property in his degree" when he divorces her shortly after graduation. Courts, with few exceptions, have rejected wives' claims that the degrees are marital property, often using broad language to the effect that human capital does not have the attributes traditionally associated with property. To justify this rejection, courts rely on the traditional Blackstonian image of property rights as the absolute dominion of people over things. This imagery, however, was never an accurate description of property law, and was formally abandoned in the First Restatement of Property in 1936. The 1936 Restatement adopted instead Wesley Hohfeld's view that property rights defined the relationships among people with respect to some valuable interest. The image is not of "absolute" ownership but of an evolving set of claims, in which courts attach the name "property" as a signal they have accepted someone's claim. . . .

[In most degree cases, the] court starts out with a pre-defined notion of what "property" entails. It then inquires whether a degree "fits" that image. Upon deciding that it does not, it concludes that no property right exists in the wife. . . . In contrast to the Hohfeldian view's message that "property" is a word courts use to signal their legal conclusion that someone has an entitlement, the [court's] language sends the message that judges play no active role in determining entitlements. But they do. Conclusions about property are legal conclusions, made in a context where the court has to allocate the asset to someone. . . .

Many modern property rights . . . clash with a model of absolute, alienable, inheritable, and exchangeable entitlements. Examples are pensions and goodwill which are widely recognized as property despite their lack of heritability and their status as income streams provided by "many years of . . . hard work." . . . Courts' refusal to recognize "new property" rights in the context of the family stems not from the logic of property, but from unstated assumptions about who is entitled to what. . . .

If the courts' projected image of property rights is so inaccurate and their property theory half a century out of date, why have the degree cases proved so convincing? . . . Family court judges, almost by definition, are successful lawyers. Most are men who have conformed to an ideal worker pattern in a profession notorious for long hours. This workaholic culture tends to marginalize the ideal workers' wives, as they assume more and more family responsibilities to allow for their husbands' "success." It is also the (upper-middle) class context in which the ideology of gender equality is strongest. In short, the judges in degree cases are heavily invested in the polite fiction — observed in most intact marriages — that the husband's career success and the wife's marginalization both result not from a system that privileges ideal workers who can command a flow of domestic services from women, but from the idiosyncracies of two individuals residing in the republic of choice.[231]

231. [See Joan Williams, Gender Wars: Selfless Women in the Republic of Choice, 66 N.Y.U. L. Rev. 1559, 1562-1608 (1991).] The relatively few female judges may be high-human-capital women who may not be sympathetic to the claims of mothers marginalized by motherhood. Id. at 1597-98, 1605-06.

The degree cases also reflect judges' sense that they worked long and hard for their degrees. Their reaction is colored by their struggles in law school and their sense that they have earned everything they have achieved through their own hard work. That degree holders worked long and hard is not the issue. So did their wives, both in the home and (often) at boring, dead-end jobs, passing up opportunities for better positions. The issue is not who worked hard, but whose hard work gives rise to entitlements. . . .

## Notes and Questions

1. *Roberts* follows the majority of courts in refusing to treat advanced degrees and professional licenses, as well as the enhanced earning capacity therefrom, as property. Hence, the supporting spouse's contribution does not make them divisible assets upon divorce. See, e.g., Simmons v. Simmons, 708 A.2d 949 (Conn. 1998); Stevens v. Stevens, 492 N.E.2d 131 (Ohio 1986); Becker v. Perkins-Becker, 669 A.2d 524 (R.I. 1996). Is Professor Williams's explanation for this rule persuasive? See also Alicia Brokars Kelly, The Marital Partnership Pretense and Career Assets: The Ascendancy of Self Over the Marital Community, 81 B.U. L. Rev. 59 (2001) (critiquing law's rejection of "sharing principles" for career assets).

*Roberts* states, however, that Matthew's enhanced earning capacity is a factor in the distribution of property and approves a disproportionate division favoring Leigh Anne. Is this approach fair? Suppose the couple had spent everything on the husband's degree, without accumulating any assets? Does the statute quoted in *Roberts* (now Ind. Code Ann. §31-15-7-6 (West 1999)) solve the problem?

2. If the couple has no assets to divide, should a court recognize the supporting spouse's contribution by awarding maintenance? Does Leigh Anne *need* support? See also Hodge v. Hodge, 520 A.2d 15, 18 (Pa. 1986) (purpose of alimony is "rehabilitation not reimbursement"). In contrast to *Roberts*, other cases have used maintenance to provide a remedy. E.g., Guy v. Guy, 736 So.2d 1042 (Miss. 1999) (lump sum alimony); Mahoney v. Mahoney, 453 A.2d 527 (N.J. 1982) ("reimbursement alimony").

3. Some courts have used a frankly flexible approach, stating that achieving a fair result is more important than whether a traditional "property" or "alimony" label fits. In Washburn v. Washburn, 677 P.2d 152 (Wash. 1984) (en banc), the court declined to identify the husband's veterinary degree as property but went on to say:

> . . . A professional degree confers high earning potential upon the holder. The student spouse should not walk away with this valuable advantage without compensating the person who helped him or her obtain it.

[T]he supporting spouse may be compensated through a division of property and liabilities. In many cases, however, the wealth of the marriage will have been spent toward the cost of the professional degree, leaving few or no assets to divide. Where the assets of the parties are insufficient to permit compensation to be effected entirely through property division, a supplemental award of maintenance is appropriate.

[W]e recognize that the spouse who is capable of supporting someone through school will in most cases also be capable of supporting him or herself after the marriage is dissolved. However, under the extremely flexible provisions of [the statute], a demonstrated capacity of self-support does not automatically preclude an award of maintenance. Indeed, the ability of the spouse seeking maintenance to meet his or her needs independently is only one factor to be considered. . . . Moreover, the factors listed in the statute are not exclusive. . . .

Under our opinion today, Mrs. Washburn may be entitled to an award as compensation for her contribution to her husband's education. Such compensation may be effected through property division, maintenance or a combination of both. . . .

Id. at 158, 161. Despite the Washington Supreme Court's lack of concern about the "label" for Mrs. Washburn's award, what difference will the label make? Suppose Mrs. Washburn remarries? Suppose her former husband declares bankruptcy?

4. Does the limited remedy of reimbursement for financial contributions (under the statute quoted in *Roberts*) result in unjust enrichment for the supported spouse? Does an analysis based on unjust enrichment require consideration of fault? Does the supporting spouse deserve compensation not just for financial contributions but also for the loss of a return on the investment in the supported spouse's career? How should a court treat debts from the supported spouse's student loans? See generally Milton C. Regan Jr., Alone Together: Law and the Meanings of Marriage 148-161 (1999); Margaret F. Brinig, Property Distribution Physics: The Talisman of Time and Middle Class Law, 31 Fam. L.Q. 93 (1997); Jana B. Singer, Husbands, Wives and Human Capital: Why the Shoe Won't Fit, 31 Fam. L.Q. 119 (1997).

5. Under the more flexible approach approved in *Washburn*, how does a judge compute a fair result? One court approved the following approaches: (a) a "cost value approach" by which the court calculates the supporting spouse's contributions (including services) during the marriage; (b) an "opportunity-costs approach" under which the court considers income sacrificed because the student spouse attended school instead of working; (c) a return on investment theory that compensates the supporting spouse according to the present value of the student spouse's enhanced earning capacity; and (d) consideration of the supporting spouse's contribution at one-half of the student spouse's enhanced yearly earning power for the time during which the supporting

spouse supported the other spouse. Haugan v. Haugan, 343 N.W.2d 796, 802-803 (Wis. 1984). The concurrence in *Haugan* rejected the third approach because of its reliance on future earning potential. Cf. Katherine Wells Meighan, For Better or For Worse: A Corporate Finance Approach to Valuing Educational Decrees at Divorce, 5 Geo. Mason L. Rev. 193 (1997); Elizabeth S. Scott & Robert E. Scott, Marriage as Relational Contract, 84 Va. L. Rev. 1225, 1275-1277, 1319-1323 (1998).

6. What remedy would married individuals themselves find fair? According to an empirical study of professional students and their spouses:

> [W]hen a spouse 1) provides monetary support, 2) makes a personal sacrifice, 3) divorces shortly after the spouse attains a degree, leaving few assets to divide, and 4) possesses a lower earning capacity than the professional spouse, participants feel that the supporting spouse deserves recompense. Furthermore, the results show that if some or all of these factors are present in a marriage, *both* spouses think that the supporting spouse should be compensated.

Rebecca Redosh Eisner & Ruth Zimmerman, Note, Individual Entitlement to the Financial Benefits of a Professional Degree: An Empirical Study of the Attitudes and Expectations of Married Professional Students and Their Spouses, 22 U. Mich. J.L. Ref. 333, 363 (1989).

7. In contrast to the majority approach, New York treats degrees and professional licenses as property subject to equitable division, based on the legislature's definition of marital property. In O'Brien v. O'Brien, 489 N.E.2d 712 (N.Y. 1985), the court explained:

> [The statute] provides that in making an equitable distribution of marital property, "the court shall consider: . . . (6) any equitable claim to, interest in, or direct or indirect contribution made to the acquisition of such marital property by the party not having title, including joint efforts or expenditures and contributions and services as a spouse, parent, wage earner and homemaker, and *to the career or career potential* of the other party [and] . . . (9) the impossibility or difficulty of evaluating any component asset or any interest in a business, corporation or *profession*" (Domestic Relations Law §236[B][5][d][6], [9] [emphasis added]). Where equitable distribution of marital property is appropriate but "the distribution of an interest in a business, corporation or *profession* would be contrary to law" the court shall make a distributive award in lieu of an actual distribution of the property (Domestic Relations Law §236[B][5][e] [emphasis added]). The words mean exactly what they say: that an interest in a profession or professional career potential is marital property which may be represented by direct or indirect contributions of the non-title-holding spouse, including financial contributions and nonfinancial contributions made by caring for the home and family.

Id. at 715-716. Under this approach, the supporting spouse should get an "equitable portion" of this property, based on the present value of "the enhanced earning capacity it affords the holder." Id. at 718. Few other courts define property so expansively. E.g., Postema v. Postema, 471 N.W.2d 912 (Mich. Ct. App. 1991); In re Marriage of Denton, 951 P.2d 693 (Or. 1998).

8. Consistent with majority rule, the ALI Principles reject the treatment of earning capacity as divisible property. Instead, they provide for "compensatory payments" to reimburse the supporting spouse for the financial contributions made to the other spouse's education or training. ALI Principles, supra, §§4.07, 5.12. For compensation under §5.12, the education must have been completed in less than a specified number of years (set out in a rule of statewide application) before the filing of the dissolution petition.

The ALI formulation resembles an earlier California statute, which provides for reimbursement of the community "for community contributions to education or training of a party that substantially increases the earning capacity of the party." Cal. Fam. Code §2641(b)(1) (West 1994). This statute contains a rebuttable presumption "that the community has not substantially benefited from community contributions to the education or training made less than 10 years before the commencement of the proceeding, and that the community has substantially benefited from community contributions to the education or training made more than 10 years before the commencement of the proceeding." Id. at §2641(c). This statute provides the exclusive remedy for community contributions to education or training but does not limit consideration of such contributions for purposes of support orders. Id. at §2641(d). For another statutory approach, see, e.g., Iowa Code Ann. §598.21-3h (West Supp. 2001) (in ordering support, court should consider any mutual agreement made by the parties concerning financial contributions "with the expectation of future reciprocation or compensation").

9. *Comparing pensions and goodwill.* The advanced degree cases test the limits of the "new property." See, e.g., Lenore J. Weitzman, The Divorce Revolution: The Unexpected Social and Economic Consequences for Women and Children in America 110-142 (1985). Weitzman's definition of the term includes "tangible and intangible assets that are acquired as part of either spouse's career or career potential," id. at 110, and encompasses pensions and other retirement benefits, the goodwill value of a business or profession, insurance benefits, as well as professional degrees and licenses, id. at 110-142. Given that courts routinely treat pensions and retirement funds as marital property, what explains their reluctance to afford similar treatment to professional degrees and licenses?

With respect to professional goodwill, the majority approach regards it as marital property but only if the goodwill exists independently of the professional's reputation. See, e.g., Thompson v. Thompson, 576 So. 2d 267 (Fla. 1991); Dugan v. Dugan, 457 A.2d 1 (N.J. 1983). But see Powell

v. Powell, 648 P.2d 218 (Kan. 1982) (professional practice is personal, not divisible). If professional goodwill constitutes a divisible asset, how should courts value it? Eslami v. Eslami, 591 A.2d 411, 418 (Conn. 1991), insists upon a valuation method that differentiates "between the goodwill of the practice as a saleable entity and the practitioner's own earning power as enhanced by such goodwill. . . ." Without this distinction, a court might mistakenly count such goodwill twice, first as a divisible asset and again as a measure of earning capacity for purposes of awarding support. Cf. Alicia Brokars Kelly, Sharing a Piece of the Future Post-Divorce: Toward a More Equitable Distribution of Professional Goodwill, 51 Rutgers L. Rev. 569, 626 (1999) (proposing awarding "a percentage share in the income stream that good will produces post-divorce").

The ALI Principles in §4.07 follow the majority approach on goodwill while excluding human capital from the definition of property. See Allen M. Parkman, The ALI Principles and Marital Quality, 8 Duke J. Gender L. & Pol'y 151 (2001) (criticizing exclusion).

10. *Awards for lost future earnings.* There is considerable authority for treating as divisible property personal injury awards designed to compensate for lost future earnings. See, e.g., Dalessio v. Dalessio, 570 N.E.2d 139 (Mass. 1991) (personal injury award for lost earning capacity and medical expenses divisible); Wren v. Wren, 785 P.2d 1164 (Wyo. 1990) (division of damages for violation of wife's civil rights). On what theory?

Professor Grace Blumberg, finding the case law in disarray, proposes an analysis that classifies "awards according to the nature of the assets they replace. Thus, compensation for wages lost during coverture is marital property and compensation for wages lost after marriage is separate property." See Grace Ganz Blumberg, Marital Property Treatment of Pensions, Disability Pay, Workers' Compensation, and Other Wage Substitutes: An Insurance, or Replacement, Analysis, 33 UCLA L. Rev. 1250, 1282 (1986). This analysis can also be applied to life insurance, disability pay, and workers' compensation awards. See generally id. Why isn't a worker's disabled body considered separate property? Alternatively, why shouldn't the determinative question be whether the benefits in question were acquired through a spouse's labor during marriage? See, e.g., Doucette v. Washburn, 766 A.2d 578 (Me. 2001); Thompson v. Thompson, 642 A.2d 1160 (R.I. 1994) (reviewing case law).

Can a court divide a spouse's accrued vacation time or sick leave upon dissolution? See Lesko v. Lesko, 457 N.W.2d 695 (Mich. Ct. App. 1990); Hurd v. Hurd, 848 P.2d 185 (Wash. Ct. App. 1993). An early retirement incentive package accepted by the employee spouse after divorce? See Olivo v. Olivo, 624 N.E.2d 151 (N.Y. 1993). An attorney's contingent fees for cases started during marriage? See McDermott v. McDermott, 986 S.W.2d 843 (Ark. 1999).

## Problems

1. Upon dissolution of the 17-year marriage of New York opera singer Frederica von Stade Elkus, her husband argues that her career and celebrity status constitute marital property subject to equitable distribution. At the time of their marriage in 1973, von Stade had just begun her career and was performing minor roles with the Metropolitan Opera Company. During the marriage, she became a highly successful concert and television performer and international recording artist. Although in the first year of the marriage she earned $2,250, by 1989 she earned $621,878.

During the marriage von Stade's husband served as her voice coach and photographer, traveling with her, critiquing her performance, and photographing her for albums and magazine articles. He claims he sacrificed his own career as an opera teacher and singer to devote himself to her career and to their two children. As a result of his efforts, Elkus contends that he is entitled to equitable distribution of the appreciation of the value of her career and her celebrity status as marital property.

According to New York Domestic Relations Law (see *O'Brien*, supra), marital property is defined as property acquired during the marriage "regardless of the form in which title is held." In enacting the Equitable Distribution Law, the legislature broadly defined the term "marital property" to give effect to the "economic partnership" concept of marriage.

What result and why? See Elkus v. Elkus, 572 N.Y.S.2d 901 (App. Div. 1991). Is celebrity status distinguishable from reputation, which courts in professional goodwill cases have held is not divisible? See also Golub v. Golub, 527 N.Y.S.2d 946 (Sup. Ct. 1988). How should a court rule in a state without New York's expansive definition of property? See Piscopo v. Piscopo, 555 A.2d 1191 (N.J. Super. Ct. Ch. Div. 1988), *aff'd*, 557 A.2d 1040 (N.J. Super. Ct. App. Div.), *cert. denied*, 564 A.2d 875 (N.J. 1989).

2. John and Margaret divorced when he was Manager of Municipal Markets at Merrill Lynch and she was a housewife. The court equally divided their substantial assets and ordered John to pay half his monthly salary as alimony. After John became ill and lost his job, he successfully sought to reduce his alimony obligation, based on the changed circumstances.

Margaret now appeals this modification, contending that the court underestimated John's ability to pay by ignoring his "experience as a savvy investor." She claims that John's "sophisticated investment skills are to him what Luciano Pavarotti's voice is to him: the 'asset' that is capable of earning a significant amount of money." She asks the court to measure John's ability to pay on the basis of the higher yield investments available to him, not his actual income. What result and why? See Miller v. Miller, 734 A.2d 752 (N.J. 1999). But cf. Clark v. Clark, 779 A.2d 42, 47 & n.3 (Vt. 2001).

### e. Taxation

Divorce raises tax issues that affect the fairness of a given financial disposition. The tax consequences thus often become a factor in determining both property division and support.

Suppose Nancy, a schoolteacher, and Dick, an accountant, divorce after 21 years. They have three children, ages 10, 15, and 20. Upon their dissolution, the parties agree that Dick will pay Nancy $25,000 per year for 3 years as spousal support. In addition, Dick will pay $3,000 per year per child as child support, until each turns 21. What information should an attorney provide to them concerning the tax implications of the termination of their marriage?

#### (i) Spousal Support

Congress includes Nancy's spousal support, termed "alimony" in the Internal Revenue Code,[22] in her gross income just like her salary.[23] Thus, Nancy must pay tax on the entire amount of alimony she receives from Dick. She may be able to offset her tax liability through the use of various deductions and credits, however.

Simultaneously, the Code allows Dick a deduction for the full amount of alimony he pays Nancy.[24] In fact, I.R.C. §62 specifically lists alimony as a deduction used to arrive at "adjusted gross income." The inclusion of alimony in §62 means that Dick will receive a dollar-for-dollar deduction in his gross income and then can take, in addition, a standard deduction, if beneficial. As a result, he may avoid paying the greater tax rate applicable to the portion of his income that would otherwise fall into a higher tax bracket.[25]

Regardless of how state law defines alimony, however, Dick's payments must meet specific federal criteria to qualify as deductible alimony under the Code. I.R.C. §71(b) requires the payments in cash, not property or services.[26] Second, the payments must be received by or on behalf of Nancy,[27] according to a divorce or separation instrument (decree or written separation agreement).[28] Third, in the case of a decree of

[22]. I.R.C. §71 (1994).
[23]. Id. at §61(a). The definition of gross income lists "alimony and separate maintenance payments" as one of 15 nonexclusive examples of income. Id.
[24]. Id. at §§62, 215.
[25]. See id. at §1.
[26]. Treas. Reg. §1.71-1T(b) (1984).
[27]. Payments of cash to a third party, such as rent, mortgage, or tuition liabilities, may be made if on behalf of Nancy, but any payments to maintain property owned by Dick, even if used by Nancy, will not qualify. Id.
[28]. I.R.C. §71(b)(2) (1994).

divorce or separate maintenance, the parties cannot cohabit in the same residence nor file a joint return once payments commence.[29] Fourth, Dick's liability for spousal support must terminate upon Nancy's death (for example, there can be no provision for postdeath payments).[30] The decree or separation agreement may provide, however, that Dick's payments will continue and remain deductible in the event that Nancy remarries.

The attorney must advise Nancy and Dick that they are not obligated to treat spousal support as alimony under §71.[31] Depending on their respective incomes and tax rates, treating the payments as nontaxable to Nancy and nondeductible to Dick may be more advantageous. If the deduction does not save Dick as much money as it costs Nancy in taxes, they can choose to treat the payments as nontaxable and nondeductible.[32] To effectuate this option, the parties must so provide in their divorce or separation instrument and must attach a copy of the instrument to Nancy's (the recipient's) tax return.[33]

If Dick attempts to disguise property distribution payments as alimony by making "excess alimony payments" during the first two postseparation years, I.R.C. §71(f) provides for recomputation to "recapture" the excess deductions over the amount permitted by the statute. Significantly, it is Dick's *front-loading* of alimony payments that triggers the recapture of the excess, not his effort to disguise property distribution.[34] Thus, if Nancy were willing to spread out evenly her receipt of the property distribution over the first three postseparation years, Dick could avoid the recapture by paying Nancy her alimony plus one-third of his property obligation during each of these years.

---

[29]. Id. at §71(b)(1)(C). This requirement does not apply in cases of couples who have only a written separation agreement.

[30]. Id. at §71(b)(1)(D). Thus, any specified term of payments (e.g., three years) must provide that the payments will stop upon Nancy's death if it occurs during the payment period.

[31]. Id. at §71(b)(1)(B).

[32]. For example, if Nancy is in the 31 percent tax bracket and Dick in the 15 percent, then it would be disadvantageous to invoke §71. See I.R.C. §1(c) (1994). Use of §71 would have no tax effect if Nancy and Dick are in the same bracket.

[33]. Treas. Reg. §1.71-1T(b) (1984).

[34]. For additional detail, see Douglas A. Kahn, Federal Income Tax: A Student's Guide to the Internal Revenue Code §§2.1420-2.1430 (4th ed. 1999). Critics have noted that the law's complexities create a trap for the unwary, inviting taxpayers inadvertently to trigger recapture and generally handicapping those without adequate representation. E.g., Laurie L. Malman, Unfinished Reform: The Tax Consequences of Divorce, 61 N.Y.U. L. Rev. 363, 404 (1986).

### (ii) Transfers of Property to Spouse

For most transfers of property between spouses or former spouses if "incident to the divorce," no gain or loss will be recognized.[35] I.R.C. §1041(b) treats the property transferred as a gift to the recipient. As a result, the value of the gift, or property, is excluded from the recipient's income. Further, the recipient takes the donor's basis in the property. For example, suppose the divorce instrument instructs Dick to transfer to Nancy their home (which Dick owns), which originally cost $100,000. Currently, the fair market value of the home is $150,000. When Dick transfers the home to Nancy, he will not recognize gain, and Nancy will not receive income. Nancy will take the property at Dick's basis ($100,000), rather than the fair market value, deferring recognition of the gain. If Nancy subsequently sells this property, the Code allows her to exclude as much as $250,000 gain from her gross income, so long as during the five-year period preceding the sale she or Dick owned and used the property as a principal residence for periods aggregating two years or more.[36] For §1041 to apply to former spouses, the transfers must occur within one year after the date of the divorce or must be related to the cessation of the marriage.[37] Applicable regulations create a rebuttable presumption that a transfer not pursuant to a divorce or separation instrument and any transfer more than six years after the marriage ends is not "related to the cessation of the marriage."[38] (The same general analysis would apply if Dick and Nancy had owned the home as joint tenants, but then Dick would only be transferring his one-half to Nancy.)

After Dick transfers the home to Nancy, suppose the couple agree that, while Nancy lives in the home, Dick will be responsible for paying the mortgage of $1,500 and annual property taxes of $2,000. Whether these expenses qualify as spousal support payments on behalf of Nancy depends on whether Dick completely relinquished ownership of the home. By transferring title of the home to Nancy, Dick's payments qualify as deductible

---

[35]. I.R.C. §1041(a) (1994). See also id. at §1041(e) (rule does not apply to transfers in trusts for the benefit of a spouse when liabilities exceed the basis). Property transfers cannot be "alimony" because they are not cash transfers; a cash transfer will constitute a "property settlement" if it does not meet the other requirements for "alimony" described above.

At one time, the tax consequences of property transfers varied depending upon state law, either community property or common law, under United States v. Davis, 370 U.S. 65 (1962). According to *Davis*, distributions in community property jurisdictions were nontaxable divisions, simply reflecting the preexisting co-ownership of the two spouses, while a distribution in a common law jurisdiction was a taxable transfer in satisfaction of a legal obligation. As a result, in common law states the distribution became the time to tax the transferor spouse on any gain realized between the initial acquisition of the property and the transfer to the recipient spouse.

[36]. I.R.C. §121 (West Supp. 2001 & Pamphlet No. 1 Sept. 2001). For purposes of determining the five-year period for Nancy, the predivorce period during which Dick owned the home in which the couple resided is counted. Id. at §121(d)(3)(A).

[37]. I.R.C. §1041(c) (1994).

[38]. Treas. Reg. §1.1041-1T(b) (1984).

spousal support made to a third party.[39] If, however, Dick retains ownership of the home during Nancy's occupancy, the identical payments do not qualify as spousal support, even if made pursuant to the divorce instrument. In short, spousal support payments must be made on behalf of the spouse; if Dick owns the home, he is paying his own expenses.[40]

### (iii) Child Support

In contrast to alimony, child support payments are nontaxable and nondeductible under I.R.C. §71(c). Suppose that Dick attempts to disguise his child support payments as spousal support in order to receive larger deductions. Accordingly, instead of awarding $25,000 in alimony, the divorce instrument sets the amount at $34,000 per year until the date when the oldest child turns 21, when the sum drops to $31,000. When the second child reaches 21, the sum drops to $28,000 and drops again to $25,000 when the youngest reaches that age. Because I.R.C. §71(c) classifies child support payments as "fixed" sums specifically designated by the divorce instrument to be reduced by the happening of a contingency relating to the payor's children, only $25,000 per year will be treated as alimony. Further, if Dick ever pays less than the total amount specified in the divorce instrument for both spousal and child support, the money received will first be regarded as child support, with only the excess treated as deductible spousal support.[41]

An attorney should inform Nancy and Dick that careful planning can ensure that child support payments are treated as alimony. First, the divorce instrument should not contain a "fixed" sum payable for the support of the payor's children. Second, the support should not be reduced by any event relating to the children (such as attaining majority age or marriage). Third, dates relating to the reduction or termination of child support should not occur within six months before or after any child reaches majority.[42]

### (iv) Other Tax Considerations

In addition to spousal and child support, an attorney must alert Nancy and Dick to the tax consequences of changing their marital status. Because they can no longer file joint returns, they must decide to file as either head of household or as unmarried.[43] Between the two op-

---

[39]. Treas. Reg. §1.71-1T(b) (1984).

[40]. See supra note [27].

[41]. Id. at §71(c)(3).

[42]. Treas. Reg. §1.71-1T(c) (1984) treats this period as being "clearly associated with the happening of a contingency relating to a child of the payor."

[43]. They can file a joint return if they have only a written separation or support decree but then I.R.C. §71(e) (1994) makes the favorable treatment of alimony unavailable. In addition, unless I.R.C. §7703(b) (1994) applies, they may need to file as married individuals filing separate returns.

tions, head of household is more advantageous, but it requires that the taxpayer must be unmarried on the last day of the taxable year and maintain as his or her home a household constituting the principal residence for an unmarried descendant or dependent for more than half of the year. Thus, assuming Nancy receives custody of her children, she can file as head of household as long as the children live with her for more than half the year.[44] Because Nancy and Dick have more than one child, it would benefit Dick if the court awarded him custody of at least one child, so he could also enjoy the preferential status of head of household.

The taxpayer's filing status determines the amount of the standard deduction he will receive under I.R.C. §63(c). The standard deduction is a flat amount provided to all taxpayers of similar status. Deducted from the adjusted gross income, it operates with the personal exemptions (discussed next) to determine taxable income. If Dick satisfies the head of household requirements, he can take the standard deduction, a figure adjusted annually for cost-of-living according to §63(c)(4). Conversely, if Nancy maintains the household for all three children, Dick must file as unmarried. This status offers a lower deduction, again a figure adjusted annually for cost-of-living adjustments.[45] Thus, the standard deduction illustrates how filing status can directly affect tax liability.

Besides the standard deduction, Nancy and Dick will also be permitted personal exemptions to lower their taxable income. I.R.C. §151 allows an exemption for the taxpayer as well as for any eligible dependents. The dependent must be under 19 years of age, or under 24 years if a student, to be eligible under §151(c). Assuming that Nancy and Dick's oldest child attends college, they can claim three additional exemptions. Generally, a taxpayer may claim a dependency exemption if he provides over one-half of the dependent's support.[46] However, §152(e) specifically refers to children of divorced parents and treats the custodial parent as providing over one-half of the child's support (regardless of actual contribution). Assuming that Nancy retains custody of all three children, Dick cannot take any additional personal exemptions. Nevertheless, Nancy could sign a written declaration releasing her claim to one or more of her dependency deductions, enabling Dick to take advantage of the available exemptions.[47]

Unlike the standard deduction, §151(d) provides for a "phaseout"[48] of the personal exemptions if the taxpayer's adjusted gross income

---

[44]. Id. at §2(b).

[45]. Id. at §63(c)(2), (4) (West Supp. 2001 & Pamphlet No. 1 Sept. 2001).

[46]. I.R.C. §§151(c), 152(a) (1994).

[47]. Id. at §152(e)(2). State courts have split on the question whether they have the power to award the federal exemption to a noncustodial parent. Compare Bradley v. Bradley, 512 S.E.2d 248 (Ga. 1999) (disallowing award), with Macias v. Macias, 968 P.2d 814 (N.M. Ct. App. 1998) (allowing award).

[48]. The phaseout expires in stages until its termination in 2010. I.R.C. §151(d)(3) (West Supp. 2001 & Pamphlet No. 1 Sept. 2001).

exceeds a certain "threshold" amount. As a tax strategy, Nancy and Dick should allocate the exemptions by comparing their incomes with the threshold amounts. Suppose Nancy's high income risks the phaseout of her exemptions. Rather than waste these deductions, she should allocate them to Dick so all three exemptions are fully utilized.

After tax liability has been determined, additional tax preferences, known as credits, are available to qualifying taxpayers to reduce final tax liability on a dollar-for-dollar basis. Section 24 allows some taxpayers up to $600 credit for each child under 17 for whom the taxpayer is entitled to a dependency deduction (with the figure rising in stages to $1,000 in 2010).[49] Suppose Nancy has custody of all three children and continues to work full-time. She would also be entitled to a childcare credit under I.R.C. §21, equal to the applicable percentage of childcare expenses she incurs to remain employed. However, she is only entitled to the expenses she incurs for the care of "qualifying individuals," which §21(b) defines as dependents under the age of 13. Thus, she cannot deduct expenses for the care of her two older children. Because there is only one qualifying individual, §21(c) allows Nancy to take a maximum credit of $1,050, subject to certain phaseout limitations.[50]

## E. CHILD SUPPORT

### 1. Imposing Support Obligations: From Discretion to Guidelines

A child support award typically requires the periodic transfer of funds from the noncustodial parent to the custodial parent for the benefit of their child. At one time, courts determined child support in the same way they set alimony — using open-ended standards to reach unpredictable results. Now, however, the regime of judicial discretion has given way to a new approach, the use of mathematical formulae called

[49]. I.R.C. §24 (West Pamphlet No. 1 Sept. 2001).

[50]. I.R.C. §21(a)(2) (1994). Section 21(a) allows a credit for 35 percent of expenses, reduced (but not below 20 percent) by 1 percent for each $2,000 or fraction thereof by which the taxpayer's adjusted gross income exceeds $15,000. The limit on creditable expenses considered is $3,000 for one qualifying individual and $6,000 for two or more qualifying individuals. For an analysis of feminist perspectives on this credit, see Anne L. Alstott, Tax Policy and Feminism: Competing Goals and Institutional Choices, 96 Colum. L. Rev. 2001, 2056-2059 (1996).

Another credit, the earned income credit, although targeted to low-income individuals, gives a larger credit to those with a qualifying child under the age of 19, or 24 if a student. Id. at §32(c)(3). I.R.C. §32(b) provides phaseout percentages based on income, increased in stages for joint returns. (West Pamphlet No. 1 Sept. 2001).

"guidelines." In the following materials, consider what objectives a child support award should seek to achieve and whether the move to guidelines serves these goals.

■ **DOWNING v. DOWNING**
   *45 S.W.3d 449 (Ky. Ct. App. 2001)*

KNOPF, Judge:
[Donald R. Downing and Sharon A. Downing divorced in 1992. Sharon received sole custody of their two children. In 1998, she filed a motion to increase Donald's child support obligations, based on a substantial increase in his income. The Domestic Relations Commissioner found that Donald's monthly income had increased by $40,000, to $57,000.] In the DRC's recommendations he noted the difficulties in setting child support when the parents' income greatly exceeds the highest level set in the child support guidelines:

> When child support is set outside of the Guidelines, the Court is required to exercise discretion in arriving at a fair and equitable amount of support. . . . A review of the Child Support Guidelines under the column headed for two children indicates that at the high income end, child support increases at the rate of about 4% of combined income. Taking into account the Respondent's income and the Petitioner's income using $57,000.00 per month for the Respondent and $1,500.00 per month for the Petitioner, and projecting the Guidelines, the base monthly support would calculate to $3,584.00 per month of which the Respondent would have a 97% responsibility. This calculates to $3,475.00 per month[2] [, which I recommend].

2. In reaching this calculation, the DRC applied the child support guidelines to the first $15,000.00 of the parties' combined monthly income. The DRC set additional child support by multiplying the excess income by 4%, as follows:

|   |   |   |
|---|---|---|
|   | $58,500.00 | combined monthly income of the parties |
| − | $15,000.00 | highest income provided by the Guidelines |
|   | $43,500.00 | amount the parents' income exceeds the Guidelines |
| × | .04 | percentage applied to income in excess of the Guidelines |
|   | $ 1,740.00 | projected base monthly support obligation for two children for the amount of income exceeding the Guidelines |
| + | $ 1,844.00 | base monthly support obligation for two children for parents' combined monthly income of $15,000.00 |
|   | $ 3,584.00 | projected base monthly support obligation for two children with combined parental monthly income of $58,500.00 |
| × | .97 | Donald's percentage of parents' combined monthly income |
|   | $ 3,476.48 | Donald's projected child support obligation. |

The child support guidelines set out in KRS 403.212 serve as a rebuttable presumption for the establishment or modification of the amount of child support. Courts may deviate from the guidelines only upon making a specific finding that application of the guidelines would be unjust or inappropriate. However, KRS 403.211(3)(e) specifically designates that "combined monthly adjusted parental gross income in excess of the Kentucky child support guidelines" is a valid basis for deviating from the child support table. Furthermore, the trial court may use its judicial discretion to determine child support in circumstances where combined adjusted parental gross income exceeds the uppermost level of the guidelines table [$15,000 per month.]

. . . The DRC set out three considerations for his determination of the appropriate level of support: (1) the reasonable needs of the children; (2) the standard of living enjoyed by the parents; and (3) a mathematical projection of the child support guidelines. Donald agrees that the first two criteria are appropriate. [He contends, however, hat the DRC found little evidence on (1) and (2) and relied exclusively on (3).]

[T]he Kentucky Child Support Guidelines are based on the "Income Shares Model." The basic premise of this model is that a child should receive the same proportion of parental income that the child would have received if the parents had not divorced. A review of the Kentucky child support table further shows that it is based upon the assumption that as parental income increases, the proportion of income spent on child support decreases.[14]

. . . Sharon takes the position that this Court should adopt a "share the wealth" approach. [Under this approach, while] support must be reasonable under the circumstances, what amount is "reasonable" is defined in relation to a child's "needs" and varies with the circumstances and resources of the parties. The standard of living to which a child is entitled will be measured in terms of the standard of living attainable by the income available to the parents rather than by evidence of the manner in which the parents' income is expended and the parents' resulting lifestyle. . . .

We reject this approach. . . . An increase in child support above the child's reasonable needs primarily accrues to the benefit of the custodial

---

14. An examination of the child support table in KRS 403.212 bears out this model. Where the combined monthly adjusted parental gross income is $1,000.00, the base child support for two children is $303.00, or 30.3%; At $5,000.00, the base child support is $1,010.00, or 20.2%; At $10,000.00, the base child support is $1,515.00, or 15.15%; And at the highest income on the chart, $15,000.00 per month, the base child support is $1,844.00, or 12.23%. In this case, the DRC's calculation of the base monthly support works out to approximately 6.1% of Donald and Sharon's combined gross income ($3,584.00 / (57,000 + 1,500) = .0612). This percentage of income is about one-half of the percentage used at the highest income level of the child support table.

parent rather than the children. In addition, this approach effectively transfers most of the discretionary spending on children to the custodial parent. . . . Beyond a certain point, additional child support serves no purpose but to provide extravagance and an unwarranted transfer of wealth. [C]hild support must be set in an amount which is reasonably and rationally related to the realistic needs of the children. This is sometimes referred to as the "Three Pony Rule." That is, no child, no matter how wealthy the parents, needs to be provided more than three ponies.

We recognize that the DRC did not use a straight-line extrapolation to calculate Donald's child support obligation. . . . Nevertheless, the DRC set child support based almost entirely on the mathematical calculation. In the absence of any other supporting findings or evidence in the record, we must conclude that the amount set by the DRC was arbitrary.

We do not agree with Donald that the highest applicable amount set by the guidelines is the presumptively correct amount of support. To the contrary, once the trial court finds a valid basis under KRS 403.211(3) for deviating from the guidelines chart it has considerable discretion in setting child support above the guidelines . . . based primarily on the child's needs, as set out in specific supporting findings. There was no evidence that the needs of the children [had changed].

Any assessment of the child's reasonable needs should also be based upon the parents' financial ability to meet those needs [and the standard of living during the marriage]. [W]hile a trial court may take a parent's additional resources into account, a large income does not require a noncustodial parent to support a lifestyle for his children of which he does not approve.[24] [Vacated and remanded.]

## Notes and Questions

1. *History.* Blackstone described the duty of parents to provide for the support of their children as "a principle of natural law."[51] Traditionally, American divorce laws provided only vague guidance on post-dissolution child support, using terms such as "just," "reasonable," or "necessary" to direct courts how to set an award.[52] Later, statutes listed factors to be considered, among others, in the exercise of judicial

---

24. Donald claims that the trial court "usurped his parental authority to make lifestyle choices for his children." Yet a child is not expected to live at a minimal level of comfort while the noncustodial parent is living a life of luxury. Moreover, Donald has not provided any evidence that his standard of living has diminished, or what lifestyle he would deem appropriate for his children.

[51]. 1 William Blackstone, Commentaries *447-448.

[52]. 2 Chester G. Vernier, American Family Laws 193 (1932).

discretion to determine child support obligations,[53] much like the approach many states use for property distribution and spousal support.

Vague standards and judicial discretion resulted in inadequate (or sometimes nonexistent) awards, inconsistency from case to case, disrespect for support orders, and unpredictability, in turn discouraging settlement. Illinois and Maine responded by enacting optional guidelines.[54]

But the difficulties also prompted federal concern as the federal AFDC program (Aid to Families with Dependent Children) faced increasing burdens in meeting the needs of children left unmet by their parents. Seeking to limit these fiscal burdens, in 1984 Congress mandated that by 1987 states use child support guidelines as rebuttable presumptions in so-called Title IV-D cases (in which the state seeks to recover from an absent parent payments made to support a needy child). The guidelines requirement was extended to all cases by the Family Support Act of 1988 (FSA), 42 U.S.C. §667(a)-(b) (1994). Congress imposed these requirements on the states by making compliance a condition for receiving federal AFDC funds.

2. *Objectives.* The unpredictability of a system entrusted entirely to judicial discretion was exacerbated by the absence of any clear theory or objective for child support awards. What purposes should an award seek to achieve? Fairness to the noncustodial parent? Prevention of child poverty? Support to the full extent possible? Continuation of the marital standard of living? Equalization of the standard of living in the custodial and noncustodial households? Then how should child support relate to alimony? In other words, does ensuring a standard of living for the child guarantee the same for the custodial parent? How should in-kind contributions of the custodial parent be evaluated? On the difficulty identifying the goals of the past and current approaches to child support, see generally Marsha Garrison, Autonomy or Community? An Evaluation of Two Models of Parental Obligation, 86 Cal. L. Rev. 41 (1999); Marsha Garrison, The Goals and Limits of Child Support Policy, in Child Support: The Next Frontier 16 (J. Thomas Oldham & Marygold S. Melli eds., 2000).

In contrast to the traditional way of thinking about child support *after* property division and alimony, Professor Mary Ann Glendon pro-

---

[53]. For example, §309 of the Uniform Marriage and Divorce Act directs courts to set an amount "reasonable or necessary," considering "all relevant factors including: (1) the financial resources of the child; (2) the financial resources of the custodial parent; (3) the standard of living the child would have enjoyed had the marriage not been dissolved; (4) the physical and emotional condition of the child and his educational needs; and (5) the financial resources and needs of the noncustodial parent." 9A U.L.A. (pt. I) 573 (1998).

[54]. Beller & Graham, supra note [9], at 165.

poses a "children first" approach under which property division and spousal support would be addressed only after the children's needs have been met. Mary Ann Glendon, Abortion and Divorce in Western Law 94-95 (1987).

What objectives for child support does *Downing* identify? The federal Advisory Panel on Child Support Guidelines recommended that states should adhere to the following principles in developing guidelines: Both parents should share responsibility for child support; parental subsistence needs should be considered (but child support should virtually never be set at zero); child support should cover a child's basic needs while allowing enjoyment of a parent's higher standard of living; each child has an equal right to share in a parent's income, subject to factors such as age, income, and other dependents; child support determinations should not depend on gender or the marital status of the parents; guidelines should not create economic disincentives for remarriage or work; and guidelines should encourage the involvement of both parents in the child's life. See Laura W. Morgan, Child Support Guidelines: Interpretation and Application §1.02(d) (1996 & Supp. 2001).

The American Law Institute's Principles of the Law of Family Dissolution list nine general objectives, including the child's ability to enjoy both a "minimum decent standard of living" when possible to achieve without impoverishing either parent and a "standard of living not grossly inferior to that of the child's higher income parent," protection of the child from "loss of important life opportunities," fairness to both parents, avoidance of disincentives that discourage parents from working or training for work, as well as fostering cooperation and minimizing parental conflict. ALI Principles, supra, §3.04. See Grace Ganz Blumberg, Balancing the Interests: The American Law Institute's Treatment of Child Support, 33 Fam. L.Q. 39 (1999).

3. Reliance on guidelines achieves uniformity and predictability, as *Downing* suggests, by identifying a precise amount that the court presumptively orders. Jurisdictions have complied with the federal mandate in different ways. Twenty-five jurisdictions adopted guidelines by statute, eight by administrative regulations, and eighteen by court rule or decision. See Morgan, supra, at §1.03.

The income-shares model is the most popular approach, used by 35 states. As *Downing* shows, these states rely on a chart that lists the share of combined parental income allocated for child support at different income levels; parents share the obligation in proportion to their incomes. Sixteen jurisdictions use, with some variation, the percentage-of-income model, which allocates a fixed fraction of the noncustodial parent's income for child support. Only two states follow Delaware's use of the Melson formula, which prorates between parents the child's support needs based on available net income. See id. For a more detailed summary of each approach, see Robert G. Williams, Implementation of the Child

Support Provisions of the Family Support Act: Child Support Guidelines, Updating of Awards, and Routine Income Withholding, in Child Support and Child Well-Being, 93, 96-98 (Irwin Garfinkel et al. eds., 1994).

Building on states' experience under different models, particularly the version of the percentage-of-income approach used in Massachusetts, the ALI Principles have developed a second-generation formula. It starts with marginal expenditure percentages, representing what families spend on their children. It then adjusts the obligation up or down in light of each parent's ability to enjoy basic economic adequacy and each parent's relative ability to support the child. See Blumberg, supra, at 44.

4. What are the advantages and disadvantages of the various approaches?

> The primary advantage of [the percentage-of-income model] is its simplicity. But, its simplicity also forms the basis for criticism because the obligor will pay the same dollar amount whether the custodial parent earns no income or an amount equal to that of the obligor. Advocates have countered that the model contains the implicit assumption that the custodial parent contributes his or her share of financial support directly. . . .
>
> In addition to designating that both parents make a monetary contribution, the [income-shares] model is flexible in allowing for the apportionment between the parents of additional basic expenses such as work-related child care, extraordinary medical expenses, and a variety of custody arrangements. A disadvantage . . . is that it may reduce the incentive for the custodial parent to increase her work effort because the increased income may lower child support payments. Moreover, it can bring about what may seem like perverse changes in the noncustodial parent's contribution. An increase in the noncustodial parent's income could result in a decrease in the amount of child support owed, and a decrease in income could result in an increase in the amount owed. Any version of this model may be criticized for not acknowledging the nonmonetary contribution of the custodial parent in directly caring for the children. [The] Melson model involves the most complex calculations. . . .

Andrea H. Beller & John W. Graham, Small Change: The Economics of Child Support 200-201 (1993).

The ALI Principles' formula purports to effect the most satisfactory balance of competing interests of the child, the parents, and society. It would probably increase awards, "particularly those involving small families of modest means in which the residential parent, usually the mother, has a lower income than the nonresidential parent." Leslie Joan Harris, The Proposed ALI Child Support Principles, 35 Willamette L. Rev. 717, 718 (1999) (using Oregon as example).

5. Given the federal goals for child support guidelines, why has Congress not adopted a *national* guideline? Linda Henry Elrod, The

Federalization of Child Support Guidelines, 6 J. Am. Acad. Matrim. Law. 103, 128-129 (1990). Advantages of fully federalizing the standards for child support would include eliminating the variability of awards from state to state, improving processing for interstate child support, and ensuring that actual awards meet adequate levels relative to any federally funded child support benefit. See Williams, supra, at 107. What disadvantages would a national guideline pose?

6. Child support guidelines create a rebuttable presumption of the appropriate award. Courts must explicitly justify deviations from the guideline amount. A frequently litigated issue asks what findings justify rebutting the presumption. See, e.g., Hamiter v. Torrence, 717 N.E.2d 1249 (Ind. Ct. App. 1999). *Downing* addresses a version of this question in determining appropriate child support in high-income families. Why does *Downing* decide that extrapolations from the guidelines do not apply? Does the court's emphasis on "reasonable needs" revive the judicial discretion that guidelines were designed to displace? Given the premise of the income-shares model, why does the court reject the "share the wealth" approach? What is the appropriate weight to accord a parent's right to determine the child's lifestyle (footnote 24)? See also, e.g., Harris v. Harris, 714 A.2d 626, 632 (Vt. 1998) (upholding discretion above guidelines). But see Laurie Dichiara, Note & Comment, Heeding the Call of *Cassano v. Cassano,* The Need to Amend the Child Support Standards Act, 17 Pace L. Rev. 405 (1997) (advocating elimination of a cap).

Empirical evidence suggests a lack of uniformity in judicial application of guidelines in cases of both very high and very low incomes. Most states have responded to the latter by setting floors below which the guidelines do not apply. Beller & Graham, supra, at 202.

7. Now that guidelines have transformed child support, what explains the absence of similar formulae for property distribution and spousal support? A few jurisdictions are moving in this direction. See Gregory J.M. v. Carolyn A.M., 442 A.2d 1373, 1377 (Del. 1982); Ball v. Minnick, 648 A.2d 1192 (Pa. 1994). Indeed, child support guidelines provide the model for the formulaic approach to property distribution and "compensatory payments" proposed by the ALI. See ALI Principles, supra, at Chapter 1, Topic 1 (overview of Chapters 4 and 5, IIc) (introductory discussion on the "value of statewide rules establishing presumptive results"). See Ira Mark Ellman, Inventing Family Law, 32 U.C. Davis L. Rev. 855 (1999).

Who will benefit from the trend toward greater consistency and predictability reflected in the adoption of numerical formulae? Cf. Jane C. Murphy, Eroding the Myth of Discretionary Justice in Family Law: The Child Support Experiment, 70 N.C. L. Rev. 209, 218 (1991) (greater tolerance of discretion in family law than in commercial law attributable to gender of parties seeking relief).

8. Can mathematical formulae adequately address the variations and complexities of modern allocations of parental responsibility?

Increasingly, courts must consider how to apply guidelines to joint custody and other shared parenting arrangements. Do such arrangements justify a deviation from the guidelines? See, e.g., Guillot v. Munn, 756 So. 2d 290 (La. 2000) (stating what obligor must show for deviation). Should each joint custodian be treated as a support obligor for the time the child spends with the other parent? See, e.g., Rogers v. Rogers, 622 N.W.2d 813, 815-816 (Minn. 2001) (so holding except when one parent has sole physical custody and other provides significant physical care). Does joint custody warrant a special formula? See, e.g., Wright v. Osburn, 970 P.2d 1071, 1073-1074 (Nev. 1998) (Springer, C.J., dissenting) (criticizing majority for creating one). See generally Marygold S. Melli, Guideline Review: Child Support and Time Sharing by Parents, 33 Fam. L.Q. 219 (1999).

Should travel expenses for visitation be included in the guidelines amount or ordered as an "add-on" to such award? Or should they be subtracted from the parental income available for child support? Compare In re Marriage of Gigliotti, 39 Cal. Rptr. 2d 367 (Ct. App. 1995), with In re Marriage of Fini, 31 Cal. Rptr. 2d 749 (Ct. App. 1994). Should employment-related childcare expenses be treated the same way? See, e.g., Fitzgerald v. Fitzgerald, 629 N.W.2d 115 (Minn. Ct. App. 2001) (allocating child care costs in proportion to parental net income, after calculating support).

9. *Family home.* The ALI Principles, supra, §3.05(8), explicitly treat use of the family home by the residential (custodial) parent as a form of additional child support beyond that resulting from the formula, apportioning the costs according to relative parental income and other equities. Under §3.11, an order deferring the sale of the family residence is justified only to avoid "significant detriment to the child" — an assessment based on all relevant factors including, for example, the time the child has lived there, the child's grade in school, and facilitation of the parent's employment. How can you explain the additional benefit the custodial parent will enjoy by living in the family home, given the ALI Principles' strict formulaic approach to property division, compensatory spousal payments, and child support?

10. *Health care coverage.* Federal law now requires state child support guidelines to allocate health care costs (see 42 U.S.C. §652(f) (Supp. V 1999); 45 C.F.R. §302.56 (2001)). Congress also mandates health care coverage for children otherwise ineligible under an employer-sponsored benefit plan (see 42 U.S.C. §1396g-1 (1994)). State responses vary, with many "income shares states includ[ing] extraordinary medical expenses as an add-on to the basic child support award and thus prorat[ing] them between the parents." Irwin Garfinkel et al., Child Support Orders: A Perspective on Reform, The Future of Children, Spring 1994, at 84, 89.

11. *Empirical research.* Empirical research has explored the effect of guidelines. Tentative findings from the period when guidelines were

first adopted reveal they raise awards as intended — but only for divorced and separated non-Black mothers, not for the never-married and African-American mothers. Economists Beller and Graham speculate that the older guidelines may have had loopholes that resulted in fewer awards for the latter populations. Beller & Graham, supra, at 192, 194.

A subsequent study compares the effects of guidelines in three jurisdictions (Colorado's income-shares, Hawaii's Melson formula, and Illinois's percentage-of-income approaches). This study concludes that the guidelines modestly achieved the congressional objectives of increased award levels, award consistency, and case processing efficiency. No single model produces consistently lower or higher awards, however. Nancy Thoennes et al., The Impact of Child Support Guidelines on Award Adequacy, Award Variability, and Case Processing Efficiency, 25 Fam. L.Q. 325, 345 (1991). Some attribute the modest impact to widespread deviations from the guidelines. Irwin Garfinkel et al., Child Support and Child Well-Being: What Have We Learned, in Child Support and Child Well-Being 1, 9 (Irwin Garfinkel et al. eds., 1994).

Recent analyses reach even more guarded conclusions. The poverty rate for families with a noncustodial parent remains higher than that for other families, and custodial mothers continue to be three times more likely to be poor than custodial fathers.[55] Under existing guidelines, awards fail to meet the estimated childrearing expenditures calculated by the U.S. Department of Agriculture, a reasonable approximation of actual expenditures on children.[56] Although federal policy on guidelines appears settled (with no changes included in Congress's sweeping 1996 welfare reform), states likely will continue to experiment, using more finely tuned models such as that in the ALI Principles.

## Problem

Denise appeals from the trial court's order requiring her former husband, Kevin, to pay $816 monthly child support (instead of the presumptive amount of $1,121 required by the guidelines, based on Kevin's

[55]. Poverty rates for custodial parents decreased between 1993 and 1997 (from 33.3 to 28.9 percent), but the poverty rate for families with a noncustodial parent remained much higher than that for all families with related children (15.7 percent), and custodial mothers were still three times more likely to be poor than custodial fathers (32.1 versus 10.7 percent, respectively). Timothy Grall, U.S. Department of Commerce, U.S. Census Bureau, Current Population Reports, Child Support for Custodial Mothers and Fathers 2 (2000). See also Irwin Garfinkel et al., A Brief History of Child Support Policies in the United States, in Fathers Under Fire: The Revolution in Child Support Enforcement 22, 24 (Irwin Garfinkel et al. eds., 1998) (describing actual effect of guidelines as modest, despite large potential effects).

[56]. See Laura W. Morgan & Mark C. Lino, A Comparison of Child Support Awards Calculated Under States' Child Support Guidelines with Expenditures on Children Calculated by the U.S. Department of Agriculture, 33 Fam. L.Q. 191, 218 (1999).

net disposable income). At the time of the order, Kevin was spending only one hour per week with the couple's two young daughters, subject to an order of supervised visitation, stemming from allegations of sexual abuse. In deviating from the guideline, the trial judge explained:

> Presumably the Legislature did not intend to create certain shortfalls in a payor's standard of living solely for the purpose of providing absolute windfalls to the payee parent's and children's standard of living. A child support order of $816 per month will allow Kevin to meet his monthly needs while yet providing Diane and the children with a surplus of $833 over her and the children's stated needs. Such a child support order is in the children's best interest, because to order a guidelines amount providing them with an even larger surplus while leaving Kevin unable to meet his own monthly cost of living would teach them disrespect for the fairness of the legislative and judicial branches of government.

What result when Diane appeals, seeking an award of $1,211 monthly? Was the deviation from the guideline justified? To what extent is the parents' division of time with the children (1 percent for Kevin and 99 percent for Diane) relevant? See In re Marriage of Denise and Kevin C., 67 Cal. Rptr. 2d 508 (Ct. App. 1997).

## 2. Postmajority Support

■ **CURTIS v. KLINE**
*666 A.2d 265 (Pa. 1995)*

Justice ZAPPALA. . . .
The issue now before us is whether [Act 62] violates the equal protection clause of the Fourteenth Amendment of the United States Constitution. [This legislation allows a court to order separated, divorced or unmarried parents to provide equitably for educational costs of a child, even after the child has reached 18.]
    . . . Appellee filed a petition to terminate his [child] support obligation as to Amber, a student at Kutztown University, and Jason, a student at West Chester University. After Act 62 was promulgated, Appellee was granted leave to include a constitutional challenge to the Act as a basis for seeking relief from post-secondary educational support. . . .
    [W]e are satisfied that Act 62 neither implicates a suspect class nor infringes upon a fundamental right. Neither the United States Constitution nor the Pennsylvania Constitution provides an individual right to post-secondary education. . . . Consequently, Act 62 must be upheld if there exists any rational basis for the prescribed classification. . . .
    Act 62 classifies young adults according to the marital status of their parents, establishing for one group an action to obtain a benefit en-

forceable by court order that is not available to the other group. . . . It will not do to argue that this classification is rationally related to the legitimate governmental purpose of obviating difficulties encountered by those in non-intact families who want parental financial assistance for post-secondary education, because such a statement of the governmental purpose assumes the validity of the classification. Recognizing that within the category of young adults in need of financial help to attend college there are some having a parent or parents unwilling to provide such help, the question remains whether the authority of the state may be selectively applied to empower only those from non-intact families to compel such help. We hold that it may not. . . .

It is not inconceivable that in today's society a divorced parent, e.g., a father, could have two children, one born of a first marriage and not residing with him and the other born of a second marriage and still residing with him. Under Act 62, such a father could be required to provide post-secondary educational support for the first child but not the second, even to the extent that the second child would be required to forego a college education. Further, a child over the age of 18, of a woman whose husband had died would have no action against the mother to recover costs of a post-secondary education, but a child over the age of 18, of a woman who never married, who married and divorced, or even who was only separated from her husband when he died would be able to maintain such an action. These are but two examples demonstrating the arbitrariness of the classification adopted in Act 62. . . .

The underlying premise upon which the New Hampshire Supreme Court [in LeClair v. LeClair, 624 A.2d 1350 (N.H. 1993)] undertook its constitutional analysis of the post-secondary educational support scheme was that the legislation created two classifications: married parents and divorced parents. . . . The result is a heightened judicial involvement in the financial and personal lives of divorced families with children that is not necessary with intact families with children. The New Hampshire Supreme Court concluded that because of the unique problems of divorced families, the legislature could rationally conclude that absent judicial involvement, children of divorced families may be less likely than children of intact families to receive post-secondary educational support from both parents.

With all due respect to our sister state, we must reject the New Hampshire Supreme Court's analysis in *LeClair*. The discriminatory classification adopted by our legislature is not focused on the parents but rather the children. The question is whether similarly situated young adults, i.e., those in need of financial assistance, may be treated differently. [W]e can conceive of no rational reason why those similarly situated with respect to needing funds for college education should be treated unequally. Accordingly, [we] conclude that Act 62 is unconstitutional. . . .

Mr. Justice MONTEMURO [dissenting].

Act 62 . . . operates on the assumption that divorce necessarily involves a disadvantage to the children of broken families, and is intended to assure that children who are thus disadvantaged by the divorce or separation of their parents are not deprived of the opportunity to acquire post secondary school education. In effect, it attempts to maintain the children of divorce in the same position they would have been in had their parents' marriage remained intact. . . .

It would be difficult to argue successfully that the payment of child support is, in general, an obligation freely acknowledged and willingly undertaken by non-custodial parents. The extraordinary amount of time, attention and money devoted by courts, government agencies and legislatures to fashioning and enforcing support orders is testament to the unfortunate fact that the opposite is true. . . .

It has also been widely acknowledged that among the negative effects of divorce on children are those which concern higher education. Courts faced with cases similar to the one at bar have also noted, over and over again, that in divorce, the normative rules of behavior may no longer apply. Ex Parte Bayliss, 550 So. 2d 986 (Ala. 1989); Kujawinski v. Kujawinski, 71 Ill. 2d 563, 376 N.E.2d 1382, 17 Ill. Dec. 801 (1978); Neudecker v. Neudecker, 577 N.E.2d 960 (Indiana 1991); Vrban v. Vrban, 293 N.W.2d 198 (Iowa 1980). Whether because they lose concern for their children's welfare, or out of animosity toward the custodial parent, non-custodial parents frequently become reluctant to provide financial support for any purpose, but are particularly determined to avoid the costs of a college education. Then the custodial parent, who typically has less money than the non-custodial parent, most often becomes the de facto bearer of most, if not all, of the burden of educational expenses, even where the non-custodial parent possesses both resources and background which would inure to the child's benefit were the parents still married. Such parents, are, in addition, even less inclined to assist with the educational expenses of daughters than of sons.

The courts addressing the issue have uniformly decided that equal protection is not offended by an attempt to equalize the disparate situation faced by children of divorce. . . . If the Majority's view prevails, there is no recourse for these children, who will be victimized twice, first by the disruptions, both financial and psychological, of their parents' divorce, and again by the system which is theoretically designed to protect them. Moreover, such a course will not benefit the children of intact marriages in which, because of a parental disinterest in education or a view that non-support encourages the work ethic, the parents will also refuse to assist their children. The result will be no improvement for anyone. . . .

## Notes and Questions

1. The problem of parental responsibility for postmajority education arose because of the national trend to lower the age of majority in the wake of the Vietnam War. The trend resulted from widespread public sentiment that youth who could enter combat should be able to drink, vote, and exercise other rights. In response, most statutes lowered the age of majority from 21 to 18. See Kathleen Conrey Horan, Postminority Support for College Education — A Legally Enforceable Obligation in Divorce Proceedings?, 20 Fam. L.Q. 589 (1987). This change created a "windfall" for noncustodial fathers who, previously, had to support children for a longer period of minority.

States responded to the ensuing problem of postmajority educational support in a variety of ways. Some legislatures explicitly addressed the question. In some states, courts took the lead by construing existing statutory terms such as "children" and "education" broadly to fashion doctrines of extended dependency and deferred emancipation. See, e.g., Ex parte Bayliss, 550 So. 2d 986 (Ala. 1989). Some used this approach to continue support past minority for high school but not college students. See e.g., Blue v. Blue, 616 A.2d 628 (Pa. 1992). Other states rigidly enforced statutes authorizing support for "minor children" only. See, e.g., Smith v. Smith, 447 N.W.2d 715 (Mich. 1989). Most states still do not authorize postmajority educational support. See Laura W. Morgan, Child Support Guidelines: Interpretation and Application §4.05[d] (1996 & Supp. 2001) (state-by-state list). Under §3.12 of the ALI Principles, supra, courts may require parents to provide for a child's "life opportunities."

2. Why did *Curtis* focus on the law's classification of children instead of its classification of parents? Does the court's analysis jeopardize laws allowing courts to order divorced parents to pay child support to minors — a protection not provided to minors in intact families? In contrast to *Curtis*, other courts have examined the different treatment among parents and rejected constitutional challenges. See, e.g., In re Marriage of Kohring, 999 S.W.2d 228 (Mo. 1999) (rejecting equal protection and parental autonomy challenges); In re Marriage of Crocker, 22 P.3d 759 (Or. 2001) (statute survives equal protection review). See also In re Marriage of McGinley, 19 P.3d 954, 960 (Or. Ct. App. 2001) (rejecting argument that divorced parents constitute a suspect class, despite unfavorable depiction in books, movies, and campaigns to collect child support).

The statute struck down in *Curtis* responded to an earlier decision of the state supreme court, declining to recognize a duty of postmajority support for college in the absence of legislative action. *Blue*, 616 A.2d 628. What should the legislature do in response to *Curtis*? Must it include intact families in authorizing court-ordered postmajority educational support? Can it? See Chapter VIII, section A.

3. At common law the child had a right to support; the parent had a right to the child's services and earnings. See 1 William Blackstone, Commentaries on the Laws of England *453. Although divorce may prevent fulfillment of this reciprocal relationship, the principle that child support is an individual parental responsibility still controls. Professor Harry Krause, however, suggests that family disruption has diminished this reciprocity, with far-reaching consequences:

> . . . When Blackstone formulated the support obligation for the common law world, he was looking at a world that was centered on the ongoing family. Divorce did not exist. . . . Choosing to rest most of his case on natural law and what we now call sociobiology, Blackstone did not say that the support obligation was founded on the reciprocal relationship of parent and child in the ongoing family, but I think it was. This reciprocity had an economic and a social component.
>
> Economically, the support-obligated parent was entitled to the child's earnings until the child reached majority. More important, economic reciprocity extended to the parent's old age. Support received by the young child morally and legally obligated the adult child to support the aged parent. Thus, before we had Social Security, child support was an "investment" the parent made, to be recovered if needed. . . . Socially, parent and child reciprocity involved an ongoing family life. . . .
>
> The point is that the absent parent may fairly claim that he is not getting his money's worth for the support he is obligated to pay, not on the economic or social level. Today's enlarged child support obligation does not resemble what Blackstone was talking about. . . .

Harry D. Krause, Child Support Reassessed: Limits of Private Responsibility and the Public Interest, in Divorce Reform at the Crossroads 166, 178-180 (Stephen D. Sugarman & Herma Hill Kay eds., 1990). Does increased reliance on public support follow from Krause's analysis? Or unmet needs for children?

Alternatively, should the law treat a parent's assumption of post-majority educational expenses as a form of intergenerational wealth transmission that parents may avoid, just as they can disinherit their children? See Judith G. McMullen, Father (or Mother) Knows Best: An Argument Against Including Post-Majority Educational Expenses in Court-Ordered Child Support, 34 Ind. L. Rev. 343 (2001).

4. *Empirical research.* Although empirical research is limited, one small-scale study of 49 children in Marin County, California, found that after high school, many middle-class noncustodial fathers cease financial support, maintain it at minimal levels, or attach burdensome strings. See Judith S. Wallerstein & Shauna B. Corbin, Father-Child Relationships After Divorce: Child Support and Educational Opportunity, 20 Fam. L.Q. 109 (1986). See also Judith S. Wallerstein et al., The Unexpected

Legacy of Divorce: A 25 Year Landmark Study 247-250, 335-336 (2000)
(finding 30 percent of youngsters from divorced families receive some
college support, compared to 90 percent from intact families).

## Problem

Patrick, the son of Cherry and John, was 12 at the time of their divorce. When Patrick turns 18, Cherry (who has custody) files a petition
to increase John's child support payments to include $30,000 in com-
bined tuition and expenses at Trinity College, a private college where
Patrick has gained admission. Cherry shows that John's net worth exceeds $1 million. Assuming the court has the authority to order post-
majority support for education, what result on Cherry's petition and
why? What additional evidence, if any, might be relevant in order for the
court to decide?

Should the court consider the quality of the relationship between the
noncustodial parent and child? See McKay v. McKay, 644 N.E.2d 164
(Ind. Ct. App. 1994); In re Pendergast, 565 N.W.2d 354 (Iowa Ct. App.
1997). Cf. McKay v. McKay, 671 N.E.2d 194 (Ind. Ct. App. 1996).
Parental disapproval of the college chosen? Cf. Jones v. Jones, 450 S.E.2d
762 (Va. Ct. App. 1994). What should be the extent of the noncustodial
parent's financial burden — public higher education? Private higher education? Graduate school? What facts must support the determination?
Parent(s)' educational background? Academic talent? A wealthy noncustodial parent? See, e.g., Ex parte Bayliss, 550 So. 2d 986 (Ala. 1989), *appeal after remand*, 575 So. 2d 1117 (Ala. Civ. App. 1990).

## 3. Modification of Child Support

### a. Remarriage and New Families

### ■ POHLMANN v. POHLMANN
703 So. 2d 1121 (Fla. Ct. App. 1997)

PETERSON, J. . . .

[The former husband unsuccessfully petitioned to reduce his child
support obligation, alleging that this modification was justified by
changed circumstances, including a permanent decrease in his income,
his remarriage and his three children from this marriage, and his former wife's remarriage. He appeals.]

We first address the former husband's argument that subsection 61.30(12) is unconstitutional. The subsection provides:

### 61.30 Child Support Guidelines. — ...

(12) A parent with a support obligation may have other children living with him or her who were born or adopted after the support obligation arose. The existence of such subsequent children should not as a general rule be considered by the court as a basis for disregarding the amount provided in the guidelines. The parent with a support obligation for subsequent children may raise the existence of such subsequent children as a justification for deviation from the guidelines. However, if the existence of such subsequent children is raised, the income of the other parent of the subsequent children shall be considered by the court in determining whether or not there is a basis for deviation from the guideline amount. *The issue of subsequent children may only be raised in a proceeding for an upward modification of an existing award and may not be applied to justify a decrease in an existing award.*

(Emphasis added). [W]e apply the rational basis standard of review because neither a suspect classification nor a fundamental right is involved. See Feltman v. Feltman, 434 N.W.2d 590 (S.D. 1989). Under the rational basis standard of review, a statute is presumed valid and will be upheld if the classification under the law bears some reasonable relationship to the achievement of a legitimate state purpose. [W]e find that subsection 61.30(12) furthers a legitimate state interest and affirm the trial court's finding of constitutionality. The statute assures that noncustodial parents will continue to contribute to the support of their children from their first marriage notwithstanding their obligation to support children born during a subsequent marriage. Granting priority of child support to children of an earlier first marriage, the *Feltman* court determined that the South Dakota statute provided a fair and logical prioritization of claims against a noncustodial parent's income. *Feltman* at 592. "Without prioritization, the children from the first family might find their standard of living substantially decreased by the voluntary acts of a noncustodial parent. A noncustodial parent who elects to become responsible for supporting the children of a second marriage does so with the knowledge of a continuing responsibility to the children of the first marriage." Id.

We also affirm the trial court's finding that the former husband failed to show a substantial change of circumstances. . . . In an attempt to manufacture a substantial change in circumstances, the former husband and his current wife produced the latter's petition for separate maintenance [and child support] which tellingly was filed only two weeks before trial. The current wife testified that while she filed such petition in order to assure that her three children would be provided for, nothing in their marital relationship has changed. The trial court did not abuse its discretion in finding that the former husband failed to meet his burden of proving a permanent, involuntary, and substantial change in circumstances. . . .

HARRIS, J., dissenting.

The issue in this case, quite simply, is whether it is a "legitimate government interest" for the State, through its legislative process, to prefer certain children over others. . . . It is our obligation, under the constitution of this state, to determine whether the state has the right under any circumstance (even if recommended by a commission) to discriminate between children born to the same parent. There is no doubt that if parents are required to support their children by a second marriage to the same extent that they must support their children from an earlier marriage, the standard of living of all of the children will be affected. But so too will the standard of living of the first-born child in an intact marriage be affected by the birth of the second child. . . . It is not appropriate for the state to punish the children of a second marriage because their parent was involved in a previous divorce.

Although the state should not involve itself with the divorced parent's decision regarding remarriage, our statute is designed to discourage a parent from having a second family unless he or she is willing to support the second family at a lesser standard. . . . At least the parent has assumed the risk of state discrimination. But the children of the later marriage were not aware of the statutory provision nor did they consent to be born into state-mandated poverty. ["Obviously, no child is responsible for his birth and penalizing the . . . child is an ineffectual — as well as unjust — way of deterring the parent." [Plyler v. Doe, 457 U.S. 202, 220 (1982).]

[W]e should keep in mind that we are not here dealing with state funds. The state is mandating a disproportionate allocation of the parent's income. . . . The state's current approach is Cinderellian — it makes noncustodial parents appear as wicked stepparents to their own children by requiring them to provide new ball gowns for their first born while supplying hand-me-downs to their later children. . . . The children of the first marriage simply have no more veto power over the noncustodial parent's future reproductive decisions than a child of an intact marriage has over his parents' decision to have additional children. . . . Because the state has no business discriminating between children based solely on the fact of a divorce, there is no legitimate state purpose in requiring a parent to allocate his or her income more to one child than another. . . .

## Notes and Questions

1. A number of factors occurring after dissolution, such as remarriage, may affect a parent's support obligations. The increasing incidence of multiple and "blended" families raises questions about the role subsequent family obligations should play in applying support guidelines to children of a prior marriage. What are the rationale and implications of *Pohlmann*'s approach, sometimes called the "first mortgage" approach? See, e.g., In re Marriage of Ladely, 469 N.W.2d 663 (Iowa 1991); Elizabeth S. Scott & Robert E. Scott, Parents as Fiduciaries, 81 Va. L. Rev. 2401, 2466-2468 (1995). But see Martha Minow, How Should We Think About Child Support Obligations?, in Fathers Under Fire: The Revolution in Child Support Enforcement 302, 313-318 (Irwin Garfinkel et al. eds., 1998) (examining conflicting intuitions on support priorities in successive families).

In applying the rule in *Pohlmann*, should "subsequent" refer to a child's age or the date of a support order? See In re Marriage of Potts, 696 N.E.2d 1263, 1266 (Ill. App. Ct. 1998). Why did the current wife in *Pohlmann* attempt to get a child support order? How should the court calculate the former husband's support obligation to his children with this wife, if they were to divorce? See, e.g., Moreland v. Hartman, 39 S.W.3d 23 (Ark. Ct. App. 2001) (case of one father, three mothers, and five children); Buncombe Cty. ex rel. Blair v. Jackson, 531 S.E.2d 240 (N.C. Ct. App. 2000) (same).

Can the law restrict the choice to have a second family as a means of protecting the rights of the first family? Does Zablocki v. Redhail, Chapter II, page 156, apply? Constitutional challenges to state child support schedules, such as *Pohlmann*, have generally proven unsuccessful. See also P.O.P.S. v. Gardner, 998 F.2d 764 (9th Cir. 1993).

When Congress enacted the Family Support Act of 1988 (mandating state guidelines), it left to the states the weight to be given to a parent's financial obligations to successive families. See generally Misti Nelc, Inequitable Distribution: The Effect of Minnesota's Child Support Guidelines on Prior and Subsequent Children, 17 Law & Ineq. J. 97 (1999). In contrast to *Pohlmann*, some courts follow a "second family first" doctrine, deducting the support needed for the second family to determine the parent's available income before applying the guidelines for the first family's support. See Irwin Garfinkel et al., Child Support Orders: A Perspective on Reform, The Future of Children, Spring 1994, at 84, 90. Is this a better approach? Suppose that states following this approach allow the obligor to invoke support of the subsequent family defensively (to show why the court should not increase his present obligation to his prior family), but not offensively (to reduce support to the prior family)? See, e.g., Schuyler v. Briner, 13 P.3d 738 (Alaska 2000). See generally Laura W. Morgan, Positive Parenting and Negative Contributions: Why

Payment of Child Support Should Not Be Regarded as Dissipation of Marital Assets, 30 N.M. L. Rev. 1, 6-7 (2000).

2. *Obligations of stepparents.* What financial responsibilities does the law impose upon stepparents? At common law stepparents had no duty to support their stepchildren either during a marriage or following its dissolution, but courts and legislatures are changing these rules. Margaret M. Mahoney, Support and Custody Aspects of the Stepparent-Child Relationship, 70 Cornell L. Rev. 38 (1984).

Several states have statutes imposing financial responsibility on a stepparent who receives a child into the family, so long as the child remains in the home. E.g., Mo. Rev. Stat. §453.400 (2000). Others simply codify the doctrine of in loco parentis, presuming a stepparent who accepts and supports a child does so as a parent but allowing unilateral termination of that status at any time, e.g., Okla. Stat. Ann. tit. 10, §15 (West 1998) (phrased in terms of husband's support of wife's children by former husband), or look to stepparents only when a child would otherwise become destitute, e.g., Vt. Stat. Ann. tit. 15, §296 (1989). See also Logan v. Logan, 424 A.2d 403 (N.H. 1980) (construing state statute imposing duty of parental support equally for natural children, adopted children, and stepchildren). See generally Margaret M. Mahoney, Stepfamilies and the Law 38-39 (1994). The obligation does not continue, however, upon dissolution of that marriage. See, e.g., Weinand v. Wienand, 616 N.W.2d 1 (Neb. 2000) (ex-stepparent granted visitation not required to pay child support).

3. A related issue concerns whether a court, in computing a parent's child support obligation, should take into account the income of this parent's new spouse. Should it matter whether the remarried parent shares a present ownership interest in the spouse's income, as in community property states? See Rodgers v. Rodgers, 887 P.2d 269 (Nev. 1994). What of the in-kind income contributed by the new spouse or cohabitant, such as the provision of living quarters? See Workman v. Workman, 632 N.W.2d 286 (Neb. 2001). For an examination of the inconsistencies in the way child support rules treat obligations to prior families and the way the law of property division penalizes such payments, see Morgan, Positive Parenting, supra.

4. Do stepparent obligations make sound policy? Professor David Chambers has observed that empirical studies find stepparents play an important family role:

Some empirical evidence suggests that when residential stepparents enter children's lives, the children generally see their absent parents less often than they did before. [D]espite the ambiguities of the stepparent relationship, many individual stepparents do form strong emotional bonds with their stepchildren. They are seen by the child as "parent." And, of course, there is ample corresponding evidence that biologic fathers who do not live with their children will not pay child support unless compelled to do so and that they visit their children less and less as time passes, whether or not the mother remarries. In the future, we may come to view residential stepparents as replacing absent parents and assuming some or all of their responsibilities.

David L. Chambers, Stepparents, Biologic Parents, and the Law's Perceptions of "Family" after Divorce, in Divorce Reform at the Crossroads 102, 117 (Stephen D. Sugarman & Herma Hill Kay eds., 1990).

Given these realities, should the law adjust child support obligations whenever remarriage occurs? See id. at 127-128 (rule would risk encouraging remarriage decisions based on economic consequences or spite). Should a stepparent be responsible for continued child support after the breakup of the subsequent marriage? Chambers suggests relevant factors in this determination include the length of time the stepparent lived with the child, the extent of support the stepparent actually provided, and the extent of support the biologic parents provided during the marriage. Id. at 128.

5. The issue posed by *Pohlmann* typically arises in litigation seeking to modify an existing child support award, because courts can modify child support awards based upon a showing of changed circumstances. The standards for modifying maintenance and child support are the same under UMDA §316, 9A U.L.A. (pt. II) 102 (1998). See supra page 697. Should the obligor's acquisition of a second family have the same impact in both contexts?

6. Most jurisdictions have long disallowed retroactive modification of child support obligations, that is, alterations of payments past due. E.g., Kinsella v. Kinsella, 181 N.W.2d 764 (N.D. 1970). Note that the rule against retroactive modification places the burden on the obligor to seek modification as soon as circumstances change.

Now, federal legislation requires all states to recognize child support obligations as judgments once due, entitled to full faith and credit, and to disallow retroactive modification. 42 U.S.C. §666(a)(9) (1994). Does this requirement mean that states lose the discretion to forgive arrearages even when equity dictates relief for the obligor or the facts show the obligor's inability to pay during the period in question? See Price v. Price, 912 S.W.2d 44 (Ky. 1995); Rutledge v. Barrett, 802 S.W.2d 604 (Tenn. 1991). But see Department of Human Resources v. Fillingane, 761 So. 2d 869 (Miss. 2000). Cf. Harry D. Krause, Child Support Reassessed: Limits of Private Responsibility and the Public Interest, in Divorce Reform at the Crossroads 166, 175 (Stephen D. Sugarman & Herma Hill Kay eds., 1990) (recommending forgiveness of arrears owed to government when obligor has no hope of repayment).

### b. Employment Changes

### ■ ANTONELLI v. ANTONELLI
*409 S.E.2d 117 (Va. 1991)*

COMPTON, J. . . .

The parties were divorced by a May 1987 final decree which incorporated a property settlement agreement obligating the father to pay $1,600 per month for the support of the parties' four minor children. In July 1987, the father voluntarily left a salaried management position with a Richmond stock brokerage firm for a commissioned sales position with another Richmond stock broker. At the time of the change, the father's earnings at the new job had been projected to be about the same as at his former employment. Following the stock market "crash" in October 1987, however, his annual income diminished approximately $10,000 from the sum he had been earning from the first employer.

In January 1989, the father filed a petition . . . alleging a material change in his financial circumstances and seeking a reduction in his child support obligation. That court reduced the obligation to $830 per month. On appeal, the Circuit Court of Henrico County, after a hearing, denied the reduction request and ordered the father to continue to pay the original amount.

The chancellor ruled that the father had proved "there is a financial change in circumstances" and held "that this is a material change of circumstances." The chancellor noted, explicitly relying on Edwards v. Lowry, 232 Va. 110, 348 S.E.2d 259 (1986), that the father must also prove "that the lack of ability to pay is not due to any voluntary act or neglect."

Additionally, the chancellor determined that the father's change from a management position to a sales position was "a voluntary act and a lateral move" with "similar income potential." In making the change, the chancellor found, the father "accepted the risk involved in being a commissioned stockbroker." Concluding, the chancellor decided that the father had failed to meet the requirements of *Edwards* and that he had failed to prove he was entitled to a reduction in the support obligation. The father appealed [and the Court of Appeals reversed].

When invoking the divorce court's continuing jurisdiction under Code §20-108, following entry of a final decree of divorce, a party seeking a change in court-ordered child support has the burden to prove by a preponderance of the evidence a material change in circumstances justifying modification of the support requirement. In discharging this burden, a father seeking a reduction in support payments must also make a full and clear disclosure about his ability to pay, and he must . . . establish that he is not "voluntarily unemployed or voluntarily under employed." Code §20-108.1(B)(3).

The Court of Appeals, in the course of its opinion, elaborated on the *Edwards* statement that the father must show his inability to pay is not due to his "own voluntary act or because of his neglect." . . . The Court of Appeals construed the term "voluntary act" to mean a "willful act done for the purpose of frustrating the feasibility or enforceability of the support obligation." . . .

Applying [*Edwards's*] criteria, the Court of Appeals said that the circuit court found that the father had demonstrated a change of circumstances, but was silent on "the required corollary finding of whether this change justified the reduction sought." The circuit court, according to the Court of Appeals, failed to determine whether the father's voluntary act in changing employment was "a bona fide and reasonable business undertaking or whether it was for the purpose of reducing his ability to support his children." Finding such failure to be error, the Court of Appeals remanded the matter. . . .

We agree with the gloss the Court of Appeals has placed on *Edwards*. We disagree, however, with the Court of Appeals' application of those principles to this case, the effect of which is to afford the father another opportunity to prove what he failed to prove in the first instance. . . .

The effect of the chancellor's decision to deny the reduction was to hold that the father gambled with the children's ability to receive his financial support, and lost. Of course, a father is not prohibited from voluntarily changing employment. But, the chancellor, in the exercise of judicial discretion, implicitly held that when the father who was under court order to pay a certain sum for child support, which he was able to pay given his employment, chose to pursue other employment, albeit a bona fide and reasonable business undertaking, the risk of his success at his new job was upon the father, and not upon the children. . . .

Reversed and remanded.

Justice WHITING, dissenting. . . .

[T]he trial court and the majority treat the allocation of the risk of the father's bona fide job change as an "either/or" proposition, and require the father to assume the entire risk of its success, regardless of whether his job change was a reasonable business decision made in good faith. . . .

[One] relevant factor to be considered should be an allocation of the burden of the father's reduced income between the father and his children, if the evidence already before the trial court establishes that the job change was based on a reasonable business decision, made in good faith. Should the trial court find that a reduction was justified in these circumstances, it need not impose the entire burden of the father's reduced income on either the father or the children. Instead, it should apportion the burden between the two in deciding how much to reduce the father's support obligation.

This seems fair for two reasons. First, if the father had been a custodian of the children, either before or after the marriage terminated,
the children would have shared the benefits and burdens of this risk
with their father.

Second, . . . if the father's job change had increased his income, this
"changed circumstance" might authorize an increase in the support payments due the mother as custodian of the children. Because the children
can share in the benefits resulting from an increase in the father's income, a trial court should consider whether the children should bear
any burden resulting from their noncustodial father's decreased income,
provided his decision to change jobs was made in good faith and was a
reasonable business decision. . . .

## Notes and Questions

1. Courts do not agree on whether the noncustodial parent's decision to change careers or pursue additional education, resulting in an
income reduction, warrants a decrease in child support. See generally
Homer H. Clark, Jr., The Law of Domestic Relations in the United
States 729 (2d ed. 1988). *Antonelli* exemplifies a strict approach. Are all
"voluntary" reductions in income insufficient to justify modification?
What changes does the term "voluntary" encompass? See, e.g., Gastineau
v. Gastineau, 573 N.Y.S.2d 819 (Sup. Ct. 1991) (defendant rejects lucrative professional football contract because of inability to concentrate, resulting from paramour's cancer); Koch v. Williams, 456 N.W.2d 299
(N.D. 1990) (obligor's incarceration for incest).

2. An alternative approach uses a "good faith" test, disallowing modification only when the change in employment reflects an attempt to
evade support obligations. Is this a better standard than that used in *Antonelli*? Who should have the burden of showing the obligor's motive?
See Minnear v. Minnear, 814 P.2d 85 (Nev. 1991) (willful underemploy-
ment creates presumption of purpose to avoid support obligation and
justifies increase in support payments). Another approach employs a
"best interests" standard. See Overbey v. Overbey, 698 So. 2d 811 (Fla.
1997). Finally, some courts use a "balancing test." See Little v. Little, 975
P.2d 108 (Ariz. 1999). See generally Lewis Becker, Spousal and Child
Support and the "Voluntary Reduction of Income" Doctrine, 29 Conn.
L. Rev. 647 (1997).

3. The dissent in *Antonelli* states that an obligor's children would enjoy increases in his income. On what theory? In Graham v. Graham, 597
A.2d 355 (D.C. 1991), the court held that such increase is a changed circumstance justifying upward modification of both alimony and child support. The dissent would distinguish alimony from child support, allowing
modification only for the latter. What explains the dissent's distinction?

4. *Automatic adjustment*. Frequently, a child support award will become inadequate over time. Does this situation warrant an increase in the award, in contrast to the decreases sought in *Pohlmann* and *Antonelli?* The applicable rule is the same, requiring the party seeking to modify to show sufficiently changed circumstances. This rule, which discourages modification to protect courts from the burden of such proceedings, has "impoverishing effects":

> The prevailing American rule for child support modification in many instances requires the custodial parent, usually the mother, to absorb the effects of inflation, the additional cost of raising older children, and changes in the child's needs, regardless of changes in the obligor's income. To remedy these imbalances, she must bear the cost of pursuing a new action and, in most states, prove that a party's circumstances have substantially changed since the date of the original order. Further, she must make this decision with little guidance as to the likelihood of success: she is generally ignorant of the obligor's true financial situation, and the judge's broad discretion to find that circumstances have or have not substantially changed creates even more uncertainty.

J. Thomas Oldham, Abating the Feminization of Poverty: Changing the Rules Governing Post-Decree Modification of Child Support Obligations, 1994 B.Y.U. L. Rev. 841, 843-844.

Guidelines should make awards easier to update than when they were based on judicial discretion. The Family Support Act of 1988 required state review of the guidelines every four years (42 U.S.C. §667(a) (1994)) as well as administrative review of all awards in Title IV-D cases every three years and all other cases when either parent so requests (id. at §666(a)(10)). Empirical studies show, however, only a small percentage of awards are modified.[57]

The Personal Responsibility and Work Opportunity Reconciliation Act of 1996 (welfare reform legislation) gives states three options for reviewing and adjusting awards: the process required under the Family Support Act, a cost-of-living adjustment (using a consumer price index to update the amount periodically), or an automated adjustment (based on tax or other records). 42 U.S.C. §666(a)(10) (Supp. V 1999). The custodial parent still has the burden of requesting review. Often she will avoid doing so because of unfamiliarity with the process or a desire to avoid antagonizing the obligor. See Paul K. Legler, The Coming Revo-

---

[57]. Robert G. Williams, Implementation of the Child Support Provisions of the Family Support Act: Child Support Guidelines, Updating of Awards, and Routine Income Withholding, in Child Support and Child Well-Being 93, 111-112 (Irwin Garfinkel et al., eds., 1994). One problem may be the difficulty of automatic updating under the income-shares guidelines. Irwin Garfinkel et al., Child Support Orders: A Perspective on Reform, The Future of Children, Spring 1994, at 92. Framing child support awards in terms of a percentage of the obligor's income facilitates automatic adjustment.

lution in Child Support Policy: Implications of the 1996 Welfare Act, 30 Fam. L.Q. 519, 557-559 (1996); Oldham, supra.

Should courts respond to this problem by including "escalator clauses" in child support decrees to increase automatically the award as the cost of living increases? Compare Snipes v. Snipes, 454 S.E.2d 864 (N.C. Ct. App. 1995), with Roya v. Roya, 494 A.2d 132 (Vt. 1985).

## Problems

1. Upon the divorce of Cheryl and Charles, the court ordered Charles to make bi-weekly support payments of $345 for the couple's two children, based on his annual salary of $35,000. Thereafter, Charles left his position as a civilian employee of the National Guard to finish college and go to medical school, plans that would take seven years to complete. As a result of his ability to work only part-time, his yearly income dropped to $13,840. Charles now petitions to reduce his child support payments accordingly. Charles states, and Cheryl concedes, that during marriage the couple agreed that Charles would defer his dream of medical school so that he could work and earn income while Cheryl attended college. The children are now 11 and 13. What result and why? See Harvey v. Robinson, 665 A.2d 215 (Me. 1995). See also *Little*, 975 P.2d 108; *Overbey*, 698 So. 2d 811.

2. Upon divorce, the Missouri court awarded custody of the couple's four children to Linda and ordered Elliot, whose yearly income was $105,000, to pay her $562.50 per month per child. Thereafter, Linda, a physician with an average annual salary of $100,000, remarried and moved with the children to her new husband's home in California. She decided not to resume her medical practice right away, explaining:

> The primary reason, this is really the first opportunity I have had to be home with my children. Moving to a new place there is going to be a lot of adjustments. We felt it was very important for me to be home and helping establish a new routine for everyone. I also do not have a license to practice in California at this point.

Thereafter, the court granted Elliot's petition to reduce his child support payments to $308 per month per child, based on the yearly salary of Linda's new husband ($225,000) and Linda's own earning capacity. In applying the guidelines, the court imputed to Linda income of $100,000 although she presently earns nothing. Linda now appeals contending the court erred in (a) treating her new husband's salary as a sufficient changed circumstance to warrant downward modification and (b) imputing income to a custodial parent who chooses to stay home to care for minor children. What result and why? For (a), would the answer change if she were cohabiting without remarriage? Compare Cook v. Eggers, 593 N.W. 2d 781 (N.D. 1999), with Allred v. Allred, 744 A.2d 70 (Md. Spec. Ct. App. 2000). For (b), should the children's ages matter? See Stanton v. Abbey, 874 S.W.2d 493 (Mo. Ct. App. 1994). See also Bailey v. Bailey, 724 So. 2d 335 (Miss. 1998); Tetreault v. Coon, 708 A.2d 571 (Vt. 1998); ALI Principles, supra, §3.15; Catherine Moseley Clark, Comment, Imputing Parental Income in Child Support Determinations: What Price for a Child's Best Interests? 49 Cath. U. L. Rev. 167 (1999); Karl A. W. DeMarce, Note, Devaluing Caregiving in Child Support Calculations: Imputing Income to Custodial Parents Who Stay Home with Children: *Stanton v. Abbey*, 61 Mo. L. Rev. 429 (1996).

## F. ENFORCEMENT

Traditionally, enforcement of the financial consequences of divorce was largely a matter of private responsibility. In recent years, however, states and the federal government have assumed a significant role. Although child support enforcement in particular has become a national priority, problems in enforcing property divisions and alimony awards persist as well.

This section examines enforcement mechanisms, including traditional state-created private remedies and modern measures triggered by the "federalization" of this part of family law. Like the recent developments in this area, this section emphasizes enforcement of child support, but it also notes applications to the other financial consequences of dissolution. Throughout this material, consider first how the law should allocate enforcement responsibilities among individual obligees, the states, and the federal government. Further, consider the extent to which the need for effective enforcement mechanisms trumps even fundamental privacy rights and liberty interests, an issue posed by the following case.

### 1. Imprisonment: Criminal Nonsupport and Contempt of Court

■ **STATE v. OAKLEY**
*629 N.W. 2d 200 (Wis.), reconsideration denied & opinion clarified, 635 N.W. 2d 760 (Wis. 2001)*

JON P. WILCOX, J. . . .
David Oakley (Oakley), the petitioner, was initially charged with intentionally refusing to pay child support for his nine children he has fathered with four different women. The State subsequently charged Oakley with seven counts of intentionally refusing to provide child sup-

port as a repeat offender. [D]uring the relevant time period, Oakley had paid no child support and . . . there were arrears in excess of $25,000. [T]he State argued that Oakley should be sentenced to six years in prison. . . .

After taking into account Oakley's ability to work and his consistent disregard of the law and his obligations to his children, Judge Hazlewood observed that . . . "if Mr. Oakley goes to prison, he's not going to be in a position to pay any meaningful support for these children." [The judge imposed a term of probation and] then imposed the condition at issue here: while on probation, Oakley cannot have any more children unless he demonstrates that he had the ability to support them and that he is supporting the children he already had. After sentencing, Oakley filed for postconviction relief contesting this condition. . . .

Refusal to pay child support by so-called "deadbeat parents" has fostered a crisis with devastating implications for our children. Of those single parent households with established child support awards or orders, approximately one-third did not receive any payment while another one-third received only partial payment.[5] For example, in 1997, out of $26,400,000,000 awarded by a court order to custodial mothers, only $15,800,000,000 was actually paid, amounting to a deficit of $10,600,000,000.[6] These figures represent only a portion of the child support obligations that could be collected if every custodial parent had a support order established. Single mothers disproportionately bear the burden of nonpayment as the custodial parent. On top of the stress of being a single parent, the nonpayment of child support frequently presses single mothers below the poverty line. In fact, 32.1% of custodial mothers were below the poverty line in 1997, in comparison to only 10.7% of custodial fathers. Indeed, the payment of child support is widely regarded as an indispensable step in assisting single mothers to scale out of poverty, especially when their welfare benefits have been terminated due to new time limits.

. . . In addition to engendering long-term consequences such as poor health, behavioral problems, delinquency and low educational attainment, inadequate child support is a direct contributor to childhood poverty. . . . Child support — when paid — on average amounts to over one-quarter of a poor child's family income. There is little doubt that the payment of child support benefits poverty-stricken children the most. Enforcing child support orders thus has surfaced as a major policy directive in our society.

In view of the suffering children must endure when their noncustodial parent intentionally refuses to pay child support, it is not surprising

---

5. Timothy Grall, Child Support for Custodial Mothers and Fathers, Current Population Reports, United States Census Bureau, 4 (October 2000).

6. United States Census Bureau, U.S. Dep't of Commerce, Current Population Survey, Child Support 1997, Table 1 (1998).

that the legislature has attached severe sanctions to this crime. Wis. Stat. §948.22(2). This statute makes it a Class E felony for any person "who intentionally fails for 120 or more consecutive days to provide spousal, grandchild or child support which the person knows or reasonably should know the person is legally obligated to provide. . . ."[19] A Class E felony is punishable with "a fine not to exceed $10,000 or imprisonment not to exceed 2 years, or both." Wis. Stat. §939.50(3)(e). The legislature has amended this statute so that intentionally refusing to pay child support is now punishable by up to five years in prison.

But Wisconsin law is not so rigid as to mandate the severe sanction of incarceration as the only means of addressing a violation of §948.22(2). In sentencing, a Wisconsin judge can take into account a broad array of factors, including the gravity of the offense and need for protection of the public and potential victims. . . . After considering all these factors, a judge may decide to forgo the severe punitive sanction of incarceration and address the violation with the less restrictive alternative of probation coupled with specific conditions. . . . As we have previously observed, "the theory of the probation statute is to rehabilitate the defendant and protect society without placing the defendant in prison." . . .

But Oakley argues that the condition imposed by Judge Hazlewood violates his constitutional right to procreate. This court, in accord with the United States Supreme Court, has previously recognized the fundamental liberty interest of a citizen to choose whether or not to procreate. [Citations omitted.] Accordingly, Oakley argues that the condition here warrants strict scrutiny. That is, it must be narrowly tailored to serve a compelling state interest. Although Oakley concedes, as he must, that the State's interest in requiring parents to support their children is compelling, he argues that the means employed here is not narrowly tailored to serve that compelling interest because Oakley's "right to procreate is not restricted but in fact eliminated." According to Oakley, his right to procreate is eliminated because he "probably never will have the ability to support" his children. Therefore, if he exercises his fundamental right to procreate while on probation, his probation will be revoked and he will face the stayed term of eight years in prison.

. . . We emphatically reject the novel idea that Oakley, who was convicted of intentionally failing to pay child support, has an absolute right to refuse to support his current nine children and any future children that he procreates, thereby adding more child victims to the list. In an analogous case, Oregon upheld a similar probation condition to protect child victims from their father's abusive behavior in State v. Kline, 963

---

19. In Wisconsin, a circuit court typically orders support payments as a percentage of a parent's income, not as an invariable dollar amount. This means that it is within any parent's ability — regardless of his or her actual income or number of children he or she has — to comply with a child support order.

P.2d 697, 699 (Or. Ct. App. 1998). Furthermore, Oakley fails to note that incarceration, by its very nature, deprives a convicted individual of the fundamental right to be free from physical restraint, which in turn encompasses and restricts other fundamental rights, such as the right to procreate. . . .

[The condition of probation is not overly broad. Oakley can satisfy it] by making efforts to support his children as required by law. Judge Hazlewood placed no limit on the number of children Oakley could have. Instead, the requirement is that Oakley acknowledge the requirements of the law and support his present and any future children. If Oakley decides to continue his present course of conduct — intentionally refusing to pay child support — he will face eight years in prison regardless of how many children he has. Furthermore, this condition will expire at the end of his term of probation. He may then decide to have more children, but of course, if he continues to intentionally refuse to support his children, the State could charge him again. . . .

[T]he condition essentially bans Oakley from violating the law again. . . . Accordingly, this condition is reasonably related to his rehabilitation because it will assist Oakley in conforming his conduct to the law. . . .

ANN WALSH BRADLEY, J. [ joined by Shirley S. Abrahamson, C.J., and Diane S. Sykes, J.] (dissenting). . . .

. . . Today's decision makes this court the only court in the country to declare constitutional a condition that limits a probationer's right to procreate based on his financial ability to support his children. . . . While on its face the order leaves room for the slight possibility that Oakley may establish the financial means to support his children, the order is essentially a prohibition on the right to have children. Oakley readily admits that unless he wins the lottery, he will likely never be able to establish that ability. . . . In a similar context, the United States Supreme Court has explained that a statutory prohibition on the right to marry, a right closely aligned with the [fundamental] right at issue, was not a justifiable means of advancing the state's interest in providing support for children. Zablocki v. Redhail, 434 U.S. 374, 388-90 (1978). . . . The narrowly drawn means described by the Supreme Court in *Zablocki* still exist today and are appropriate means of advancing the state's interest in a manner that does not impair the fundamental right to procreate. See, e.g., Wis. Stat. §767.265 (garnishment/wage assignment); §767.30 (lien on personal property); §785.03 (civil contempt). These means, as well as other conditions of probation or criminal penalties, are available in the present case. . . .

[U]pholding a term of probation that prohibits a probationer from fathering a child without first establishing the financial wherewithal to support his children [also] carries unacceptable collateral consequences and practical problems. First, prohibiting a person from having children

as a condition of probation has been described as "coercive of abortion."
. . . Because the condition is triggered only upon the birth of a child [not
upon intercourse], the risk of imprisonment creates a strong incentive
for a man in Oakley's position to demand from the woman the termination of her pregnancy. It places the woman in an untenable position:
have an abortion or be responsible for Oakley going to prison for eight
years. . . .

Second, by allowing the right to procreate to be subjected to financial qualifications, the majority imbues a fundamental liberty interest
with a sliding scale of wealth. . . . Third, the condition of probation is unworkable. . . . The condition of probation will not be violated until the
woman with whom he has sexual relations carries her pregnancy
to term. Then, Oakley will be imprisoned, and another child will go
unsupported. . . .

I, too, am troubled by the societal problem caused by "deadbeat"
parents . . . . Let there be no question that I agree with the majority that
David Oakley's conduct cannot be condoned. It is irresponsible and
criminal. However, we must keep in mind what is really at stake in this
case. The fundamental right to have children, shared by us all, is damaged by today's decision. . . .

## Notes and Questions

1. Does the majority successfully distinguish this case from *Zablocki*,
supra page 156, and other constitutional authorities? Does the immediate availability of a prison sentence distinguish these facts from *Zablocki*'s?
How should a court apply *Zablocki*'s "narrow tailoring" requirement to
a particular obligor after less onerous means of support enforcement
have failed?

The majority emphasizes that the defendant could have been incarcerated for the crime of intentional failure to support his children;
hence, probation with conditions, however demanding, constitutes a less
intrusive alternative. Is Judge Hazlewood's approach a welcome innovation designed to address a difficult social problem? Or does it exemplify "unusual, idiosyncratic, and often quite alarming criminal
sentences" accomplished through the judicial discretion permitted in
fashioning probation conditions? See Andrew Horowitz, Coercion, Pop-
psychology, and Judicial Moralizing: Some Proposals for Curbing Judicial Abuse of Probation Conditions, 57 Wash. & Lee L. Rev. 75, 76,
136-141 (2000). See generally Developments in the Law: Alternatives to
Incarceration, 111 Harv. L. Rev. 1863 (1998).

2. To what extent does the "practical problem" of abortion coercion,
which troubles the dissent, undermine the majority's analysis and conclusion? Suppose the defendant had been a "deadbeat mom." Cf. Stacey

L. Arthur, The Norplant Prescription: Birth Control, Woman Control, or Crime Control, 40 UCLA L. Rev. 11 (1992) (child abuse); Joan Callahan, Contraception or Incarceration: What's Wrong with This Picture?, 7 Stan. L. & Pol'y Rev. 67 (1996) (same).

All four male members of the Wisconsin Supreme Court joined the majority opinion, and all four females dissented. How do you explain this division, particularly given the data about the disproportionate impact on single mothers of unpaid support obligations?

3. *Contempt.* Delinquent support obligors also face incarceration (and/or monetary fines) for contempt of court, that is, the failure to comply with a court's order to make payments specified in a divorce, separation, or paternity decree. Courts exercise the contempt power either to punish the contemnor for past misconduct (criminal contempt) or to coerce compliance with a judicial order (civil contempt). Whether the purpose is punitive or remedial determines the criminal versus civil nature and applicable procedural safeguards, such as the standard and burden of proof. Hicks ex rel. Feiock v. Feiock, 485 U.S. 624, 631 (1998) ("substance of proceeding and character of relief" determinative). See generally Hon. Mark S. Coven, Welfare Reform, Contempt and Child Support Enforcement, 30 Suffolk U. L. Rev. 1067 (1997). Because compliance purges civil contempt, it is often said that civil contemnors "carry the keys of their prison in their own pockets." It follows, then, that imprisonment for civil contempt cannot coerce an obligor unable to comply with the court's order.

The obligor's inability to pay precludes the use of imprisonment for *civil* contempt to enforce a support award. See, e.g., Desai v. Fore, 711 A.2d 822, 825-826 (D.C. 1998). Are all of an obligor's resources considered in assessing ability to pay? See Rose v. Rose, 481 U.S. 619 (1987) (upholding contempt of veteran whose sole support derived from disability-related Veterans' Administration benefits). Present inability to pay also provides a defense to *criminal* contempt.

Should the alleged contemnor be required to establish inability to pay, or must the petitioner prove ability to pay? See *Hicks*, 485 U.S. 624. Compare Powers v. Powers, 653 N.E.2d 1154 (N.Y. 1995) (alleged contemnor has burden of going forward but then petitioner must prove ability to pay), with Moss v. Superior Ct., 950 P.2d 59, 78 (Cal. 1998) ("Inability to comply is an affirmative defense which must be proven by a preponderance of the evidence by the alleged contemnor.").

The federal Deadbeat Parents Punishment Act of 1998, 18 U.S.C. §228(a)(3) (Supp. V 1999), which punishes as a felony willful failure to pay a support obligation for a child living in another state if the obligation has remained unpaid for over two years or exceeds $10,000, creates a presumption of willful nonpayment. See Darrell Baugh, Throw the Book at Deadbeat Parents: Criminal Enforcement of Child Support Cases, Fam. Advoc., Fall 2000, at 49, 50-51 (examining Act).

4. Does imprisonment for failure to pay child support or alimony violate state constitutional prohibitions against imprisonment for debt? See In re Marriage of Nussbeck, 974 P.2d 493, 498-499 (Colo.), *cert. denied*, 528 U.S. 817 (1999). Does employment under threat of imprisonment for violation of a support order constitute involuntary servitude? See *Moss*, 950 P.2d 59.

5. Does the Constitution guarantee obligors who face incarceration for civil contempt a right to counsel? See Mead v. Batchlor, 460 N.W.2d 493 (Mich. 1990) (so holding based on due process, *modifying* Sword v. Sword, 249 N.W.2d 88 (Mich. 1976)); Russell v. Armitage, 697 A.2d 630 (Vt. 1997). Given the distinction between civil and criminal contempt as well as the principle of double jeopardy, can an obligor be punished by imprisonment for failure to make the same payments that previously resulted in incarceration for civil contempt? See Dunagan v. Commonwealth, 31 S.W.3d 928 (Ky. 2000).

6. *Empirical research on effectiveness.* How effective is incarceration as an enforcement tool? Professor David Chambers's study of collection rates in Michigan from 1972-1975 "found a close parallel between payments and jailing: the counties that jailed more did in fact collect more." David L. Chambers, Making Fathers Pay: The Enforcement of Child Support 84 (1979). Although he found incarceration (or the threat of it) effective, however, Chambers does not advocate this remedy:

> . . . Stack up all the dubious aspects of jailing for nonsupport: the offense is an intrafamily one with complex emotional roots; jails are debilitating institutions — they exceed rather than fit this crime; jailing in this setting is difficult, nearly impossible, to administer in an evenhanded manner; when widely used, the prospect of jailing may well affect adversely the relationship between children and the parent under an order of support, even when the parent pays with unflagging regularity. On these grounds taken together, I, were I a legislator, would vote to remove the sanction of jailing for contempt from the permissible range of techniques for enforcing support. Many others, however, . . . would also hear another small voice whispering compellingly in the background, "But jail works." It works not merely in the sense of satisfying a public need for retribution. It works by altering the very behavior toward which it is addressed, an impact so rarely demonstrated for penal sanctions that we may wish to hold on to it for its very rarity — a whooping crane in the criminal justice system.
>
> To my view the effectiveness of jailing is largely irrelevant, if my reasons for deploring jailing are sound. Nonetheless, persons troubled by jailing but strongly moved by its success in extracting dollars should lose much of their enthusiasm for jailing if equitable alternatives exist that permit even more reliable support for children without the unfortunate aspects of jails. And I too would say that if effective alternatives exist — "less restrictive alternatives" than jailing, to borrow a term from constitutional law — it would be immoral for government to continue to rely on jailing.

It would be immoral in much the same sense that it would be immoral to use a sledgehammer to swat a mosquito on a friend's back. . . .

Id. at 253. For critiques, see David C. Baldus, Father in Jail, 78 Mich. L. Rev. 750 (1980); Robert H. Mnookin, Review: Using Jail for Child Support Enforcement, 48 U. Chi. L. Rev. 338 (1981).

7. *Oakley* cites data demonstrating the enormity of the problem of unmet support obligations. Why do noncustodial parents — generally fathers — fail to pay support? Commentators advance several possible answers:

> [M]ost men pay little or no child support because they can get away with it. The gender-based division of labor in the family leads many men to see their children as women's responsibility. . . .
> [Fathers often] begin their postdivorce lives with a strong commitment to support their children. Over time, their resolution weakens as relations with their children become emotionally less rewarding or they acquire a new set of family commitments. In effect these men trade in old obligations for new ones. From their point of view, they are not callously disregarding their family responsibilities but rather redefining them as they move from one marriage to the next. . . .

Frank F. Furstenberg, Jr. & Andrew J. Cherlin, Divided Families: What Happens to Children When Parents Part 59-60 (1991). In addition, Chambers points to the anger, confusion, and depression fathers feel upon divorce; their resentment toward relinquishing part of their earnings; their association of money with marital failure; and their weak attachment to their children. Chambers, supra, at 71-75. The increasing use of joint custody might well address the last point. See Margaret F. Brinig & F. H. Buckley, Joint Custody: Bonding and Monitoring Theories, 73 Ind. L.J. 393 (1998) (empirical data suggesting joint custody gives obligor parent greater incentive to pay support because of greater opportunity to monitor how payments are spent).

## 2. The Transformation of Enforcement: From Private to Public Responsibility

### a. The Traditional Approach

*Oakley* exemplifies the increasingly visible role of government in enforcing financial obligations in nonintact families. Although states have long had statutes criminalizing desertion and nonsupport, prosecutors' heavy caseloads, reservations about the propriety and effectiveness of punishment, and limited applications of such laws meant that in the past little help came from direct intervention by the state.

Instead, under the traditional approach to enforcement as a private responsibility, an obligor's failure to comply with a court-ordered transfer of property or an award of spousal or child support left the obligee to initiate judicial proceedings for enforcement, a time-consuming process requiring an attorney. The long-standing state-created remedies available include (in addition to contempt citations) the imposition of a trust on the obligor's property; reducing past-due payments to a money judgment (if accrued installments do not already constitute final judgments), followed by a lien against the obligor's real estate; requiring the obligor to post security or bond; and garnishment or assignment of the obligor's wages or income. See generally Homer H. Clark, Jr., The Law of Domestic Relations in the United States 269-274, 671-682, 739-743 (2d ed. 1988); Paula G. Roberts, Child Support Orders: Problems with Enforcement, The Future of Children, Spring 1994, at 101, 106.

Several practical problems made all these civil remedies inefficient and unpredictable, however. Judicial discretion prevailed and the adversary nature of enforcement proceedings offered a forum unlikely to induce cooperation and compliance. Enforcement of postdivorce obligations to make periodic payments (that is, alimony and child support) proved particularly problematic because they presented such frequent opportunities for noncompliance.

### b. Congress Intervenes

The same problems that prompted Congress in the 1980s to direct the states to use child support guidelines had even earlier focused federal attention on support enforcement: Among data showing rising rates of divorce and out-of-wedlock births, an escalating number of female-headed single-parent families, and an increasing "feminization of poverty,"[58] statistics indicated widespread noncompliance with child support awards. The federal AFDC program, as well as state public assistance programs, felt the impact. In several enactments, Congress directed the states to implement new and increasingly aggressive enforcement mechanisms.

Federal involvement began in 1967 when Congress imposed on state welfare agencies responsibility for child support enforcement as a condition for receiving federal funding. Congress entered the field by directing states to comply with specific federal requirements and by adopting a program of federal monitoring. Professor Marsha Garrison

---

[58]. Beller & Graham, supra note [9], at 2-3 (study based on U.S. Census Bureau's Current Population Survey). The data consistently reveal the gendered nature of the problem.

continues to trace the history of the federal role under this "carrot and stick" approach:

> Since 1975, through its authority over the Aid for Dependent Children (AFDC) program, Congress has legislated, with bipartisan support, increasingly tough child support requirements. The first congressional enactment established the federal Office of Child Support Enforcement and required each state to establish mechanisms for assisting parents in establishing paternity, obtaining child support awards, and enforcing child support obligations. Although state initiatives in these areas were required for AFDC recipients, they were also made available to families that did not receive welfare benefits. The Child Support Enforcement Amendments of 1984 mandated enhanced state enforcement efforts, including state tax refund interception and automatic wage withholding for overdue payments; the amendments also required the states to develop numerical guidelines that could be used by courts in setting child support awards. . . .

Marsha Garrison, Child Support and Children's Poverty, 28 Fam. L.Q. 475, 476 (1994). See See Irwin Garfinkel et al., A Brief History of Child Support Policies in the United States, in Fathers Under Fire: The Revolution in Child Support Enforcement 22 (Irwin Garfinkel et al. eds., 1998).

Initially, such federal involvement was confined to welfare cases. Under the 1975 enactments, creating Title IV-D of the Social Security Act, all AFDC recipients must assign their support rights to the states for collection. Cases in which such support-rights assignments to the state have been made are often denominated "Title IV-D cases" while all other child-support cases are called "non-Title IV-D" cases.

Significantly, the Family Support Act of 1988 extended this federal involvement to nonwelfare (or non-Title IV-D) cases. See 42 U.S.C. §§651-669 (1994). As noted earlier, this legislation required states to use numerical guidelines as rebuttable presumptions in determining *all* child support awards. It also mandated procedures for establishing paternity of children of unmarried parents. (See Chapter IV, section D1.) Finally, it specified that "each State must have in effect laws requiring the use of the following procedures" for enforcing child support orders: procedures for, inter alia, income withholding, expedited enforcement (administrative processes for establishing and enforcing support obligations), diversion of state income tax refunds, liens against real and personal property for overdue support, posting a bond or giving security for overdue support, and disclosure of overdue support to consumer reporting agencies. These federal directives required each state's law to provide explicitly for such collection devices.

In the Personal Responsibility and Work Opportunity Reconciliation Act of 1996, welfare reform legislation that replaces AFDC with a block-grant system promising states more authority over their welfare programs, Congress imposed new requirements for child support en-forcement. See 42 U.S.C. §§651-669a (Supp. V 1999). The 1996 law re-flects the vision that "support payments should be automatic and inescapable, 'like death or taxes.' " Paul K. Legler, The Impact of Wel-fare Reform on the Child Support Enforcement System, in Child Sup-port: The Next Frontier 46, 49-50 (J. Thomas Oldham & Marygold S. Melli eds., 2000). All states must now adopt measures that Congress found successful in particular state experiments, detailed below, or risk their eligibility for block grants.

### (i) Income Withholding

The Family Support Act of 1988 required states to provide proce-dures for immediate withholding for *all* child support orders issued on or after January 1, 1994, whether or not the child support obligor had fallen in arrears, unless one party shows good cause or the parties have a written agreement providing an alternative. 42 U.S.C. §666(b) (1994). Under typical statutes implementing this federal directive, an obligor's employer must comply with a court order requiring withholding of up to 50 percent of the obligor's disposable earnings to be paid to the at-torney general, court registry, or child support collection office; the em-ployer becomes liable to the obligee for noncompliance and is subject to penalty for discriminatory hiring or discharge based on such order. See, e.g., Tex. Fam. Code Ann. §§158.001-158.405 (Vernon 1996 & Supp. 2001).

The Personal Responsibility and Work Opportunity Reconciliation Act of 1996 strengthens the use of income withholding by establishing a national system to track the employment of delinquent obligors. 42 U.S.C. §§653a (Supp. V 1999); see 42 U.S.C. §666(b) (1994 & Supp. V 1999). Based on an approach pioneered by Washington, all employers in the United States must report new hires to a designated state agency, which will forward the information to a national directory for matching with the Federal Case Registry of Child Support Orders. This reform complements earlier requirements that states obtain each parent's Social Security number upon a child's birth. 42 U.S.C. §405(c)(2)(C)(ii) (Supp. V 1999).

### (ii) Tax Refund Interceptions, Automatic Seizures, and Administrative Procedures

In Title IV-D cases, states can notify the Internal Revenue Service of child support delinquencies and the IRS will intercept any tax refund due to the obligor and forward it to the appropriate state agency. See 42 U.S.C. §664 (1994 & Supp. V 1999). States must have similar mecha-nisms in place to seize state tax refunds.

The Personal Responsibility and Work Opportunity Reconciliation Act of 1996 goes farther. States must impose automatic liens on an obligor's assets, similar to the automatic withholding of income. 42 U.S.C. §666(a)(4) (Supp. V 1999). Following a model developed in Massachusetts, states must have administrative procedures for imposing liens. Id. at §666(a)(2), (c).

This development embodies one facet of "mass case processing," which seeks to use computers, databases, bank account records, and the like for handling efficiently the large volume of child support enforcement cases. In addition, states must have central registries of child support orders and centralized units for collection and disbursement.

Administrative liens also exemplify a larger move away from individual, judicial enforcement proceedings in favor of an approach that triggers enforcement automatically, without any initiation by the obligee or court involvement. States must provide certain expedited procedures for routine cases, but nonwelfare obligees can opt out of any of the enforcement measures made available by the Title IV-D agency. See generally Legler, supra.

### (iii) License and Passport Suspension

Following successful measures in some states,[59] the Personal Responsibility and Work Opportunity Reconciliation Act of 1996 requires all states to have procedures for withholding, suspending, or restricting licenses (including driver's, professional, occupational, and recreational licenses) of obligors owing overdue support. 42 U.S.C. §666(a)(16) (Supp. V 1999). This legislation mandates the Secretary of State to deny a passport for nonpayment of child support and permits revocation or restriction of one previously issued. Id. at §652(k). Also, states must have procedures for reporting delinquencies to credit bureaus. Id. at §666(a)(7). Similarly, the Fair Credit Reporting Act requires inclusion in consumer reports of failure to pay overdue child support. 15 U.S.C. §1681s-1 (1994).

### c. Evaluation: "Small Change"?

Congress's enactment of substantial, new federal requirements as part of welfare reform demonstrates that problems in child support enforcement persist despite 30 years of federally orchestrated efforts. One glimpse of the difficulties emerges in class actions brought by obligees

[59]. See Margaret Graham Tebo, When Dad Won't Pay, 86 A.B.A. J., Sept. 2000, at 54, 56 (reporting Maryland collected $56.8 million in past-due child support in 1999 by threatening to suspend drivers' licenses).

seeking to compel state compliance with federal directives on child support enforcement. Although the Supreme Court has held Title IV-D does not create an enforceable individual federal right to compel compliance with all IV-D requirements, such lawsuits reveal "systemic failures" in some states, including failure to procure wage assignments, failure to disburse support payments in a timely manner, and frequent losses of files. See Blessing v. Freestone, 520 U.S. 329 (1997).

In an influential study conducted prior to the 1996 reforms, economists examined census data to assess the effect of the federal initiatives. Professors Andrea Beller and John Graham found little improvement in child support enforcement despite increased attention to the issue in the 1980s — in short, "small change."[60] Evaluating specific mechanisms, they concluded that income withholding, property liens, bond or security requirements, and criminal penalties have proven most effective.[61] Beller and Graham urged caution, however, in the use of expedited (administrative) processes required by the Family Support Act of 1988 because this enforcement technique appears to produce lower receipt rates for child support. In addition, they encouraged experimentation with innovative techniques such as license seizures.[62] Congress nonetheless has included both new administrative processes and license seizures in its 1996 requirements.

More recent assessments remain mixed. One analysis claims that new measures, such as the directory of new hires and license suspensions, helped increase collections significantly.[63] Yet despite ongoing law reform, billions of dollars more could be collected.[64] *Oakley*, supra, demonstrates that child poverty and collection problems persist,[65] while emphasizing new reliance on criminal sanctions, an avenue Congress has pursued in enacting the Deadbeat Parents Punishment Act of 1998, 18 U.S.C. §228(a)(3) (Supp. V 1999), which makes some child support violations federal felonies with enhanced penalties.

---

[60]. Beller & Graham, supra note [9], at 16, 51-52. Only Black mothers and never-married mothers made notable gains. These gains included some increased award and receipt rates but at the same time these mothers received an increasingly smaller proportion of their awards. Id. at 51-52.

[61]. Id. at 2, 255 (recommendations).

[62]. Id. at 256-257.

[63]. The amount rose to $14.3 billion by 1998 (from $1 billion). Marygold S. Melli, Whatever Happened to Divorce?, 2000 Wis. L. Rev. 637, 639-640.

[64]. One estimate says as much as $34 billion more could be collected. Marsha Garrison, The Goals and Limits of Child Support Policy, in Child Support: The Next Frontier 16, 21 (J. Thomas Oldham & Marygold S. Melli eds., 2000). See also id. at 30, 31.

[65]. See generally id. Census data for 1997 show that only 2,286,000 custodial parents, of the 7,006,000 who were supposed to, received support payments. Grall, supra note [55], at 7.

Visions for the future include proposals to create universal assured child support benefits,[66] to locate responsibility for all children outside the private family while providing supports for caregiving,[67] and to make child support enforcement entirely a federal function (for example, by having the IRS enforce all child support orders).[68] Controversy about the "federalization" of family policy likely will persist, given recent decisions curbing Congress's authority over areas traditionally governed by the states.[69]

## 3. The Challenge of Multistate Cases

A substantial percentage of all child support cases involve parties located in different jurisdictions.[70] Do the special problems raised by these cases, explored below, require federal intervention?

### a. Jurisdictional Limitations on Establishing Awards

■ **KULKO v. SUPERIOR COURT**
*436 U.S. 84 (1978)*

Mr. Justice MARSHALL delivered the opinion of the Court. . . .

Appellant Ezra Kulko married appellee Sharon Kulko Horn in 1959, during appellant's three-day stopover in California en route from a military base in Texas to a tour of duty in Korea. At the time of this marriage, both parties were domiciled in and residents of New York State. Immediately following the marriage, Sharon Kulko returned to New York, as did appellant after his tour of duty. [They lived together in New

---

[66]. Irwin Garfinkel, The Limits of Private Child Support and the Role of an Assured Benefit, in Child Support: The Next Frontier 183 (J. Thomas Oldham & Marygold S. Melli eds., 2000).

[67]. Martha Albertson Fineman, Child Support Is Not the Answer: The Nature of Dependencies and Welfare Reform, in Child Support: The Next Frontier 209 (J. Thomas Oldham & Marygold S. Melli eds., 2000).

[68]. See Jonathon S. Jemison, Note, Collecting and Enforcing Child Support Orders with the Internal Revenue Service: An Analysis of a Novel Idea, 20 Women's Rts. L. Rep. 137 (1999).

[69]. Compare United States v. Morrison, 529 U.S. 598 (2000) (invalidating civil damages provision of Violence Against Women Act), with Kansas v. United States, 214 F.3d 1196 (10th Cir.) (upholding 1996 welfare requirements under Congress's spending power), *cert. denied,* 531 U.S. 1035 (2000). See, e.g., Lynn A. Baker, Conditional Federal Spending After *Lopez,* 95 Colum. L. Rev. 1911 (1995); Laura W. Morgan, The Federalization of Child Support, A Shift in the Ruling Paradigm: Child Support as Outside the Contours of "Family Law," 16 J. Am. Acad. Matrim. Law. 195 (1999).

[70]. See John J. Sampson & Paul M. Kurtz, UIFSA: An Interstate Support Act for the 21st Century, 27 Fam. L.Q. 85, 88 (1993) (estimating one-fourth).

York for13 years and then separated. Ezra remained in New York with their children, Darwin and Ilsa, and Sharon moved to California. Sharon returned briefly to sign a separation agreement, which provided that the children would live in New York with their father but spend Christmas, Easter, and summer vacations in California with their mother.] Ezra Kulko agreed to pay his wife $3,000 per year in child support for the periods when the children were in her care, custody, and control. Immediately after execution of the separation agreement, Sharon Kulko flew to Haiti and procured a divorce there; the divorce decree incorporated the terms of the agreement. She then returned to California, where she remarried and took the name Horn.

The children resided with appellant during the school year and with their mother on vacations, as provided by the separation agreement, until December 1973. At this time, just before Ilsa was to leave New York to spend Christmas vacation with her mother, she told her father that she wanted to remain in California after her vacation. Appellant bought his daughter a one-way plane ticket, and Ilsa left, taking her clothing with her. Ilsa then commenced living in California with her mother during the school year and spending vacations with her father. In January 1976, appellant's other child, Darwin, called his mother from New York and advised her that he wanted to live with her in California. Unbeknownst to appellant, appellee Horn sent a plane ticket to her son, which he used to fly to California where he took up residence with his mother and sister.

Less than one month after Darwin's arrival in California, appellee Horn commenced this action against appellant in the California Superior Court. She sought to establish the Haitian divorce decree as a California judgment; to modify the judgment so as to award her full custody of the children; and to increase appellant's child-support obligations. Appellant appeared specially and moved to quash service of the summons on the ground that he was not a resident of California and lacked sufficient "minimum contacts" with the State under International Shoe Co. v. Washington, 326 U.S. 310, 316 (1945), to warrant the State's assertion of personal jurisdiction over him.

The trial court summarily denied the motion to quash, and appellant sought review. . . . The California Supreme Court . . . sustained the rulings of the lower state courts. 19 Cal. 3d 514, 564 P.2d 353 (1977). It noted first that the California Code of Civil Procedure demonstrated an intent that the courts of California utilize all bases of in personam jurisdiction "not inconsistent with the Constitution." Agreeing with the court below, the Supreme Court stated that, where a nonresident defendant has caused an effect in the State by an act or omission outside the State, personal jurisdiction over the defendant in causes arising from that effect may be exercised whenever "reasonable." It went on to hold that such an exercise was "reasonable" in this case because appellant had "purposely availed himself of the benefits and protections of the laws of California" by sending Ilsa to live with her mother in California. While noting that appellant had not, "with respect to his other child, Darwin, caused an effect in [California]" — since it was appellee Horn who had arranged for Darwin to fly to California in January 1976 — the court concluded that it was "fair and reasonable for defendant to be subject to personal jurisdiction for the support of both children. . . ." [We reverse.]

The Due Process Clause of the Fourteenth Amendment operates as a limitation on the jurisdiction of state courts to enter judgments affecting rights or interests of nonresident defendants. [T]he constitutional standard for determining whether the State may enter a binding judgment against appellant here is that set forth in this Court's opinion in International Shoe Co. v. Washington, supra: that a defendant "have certain minimum contacts with [the forum State] such that the maintenance of the suit does not offend 'traditional notions of fair play and substantial justice.' " 326 U.S., at 316. [A]n essential criterion in all cases is whether the "quality and nature" of the defendant's activity is such that it is "reasonable" and "fair" to require him to conduct his defense in that State. International Shoe Co. v. Washington, [326 U.S.] at 316-317, 319. . . .

In reaching its result, the California Supreme Court did not rely on appellant's glancing presence in the State some 13 years before the events that led to this controversy, nor could it have. Appellant has been in California on only two occasions, once in 1959 for a three-day military stopover on his way to Korea and again in 1960 for a 24-hour stopover on his return from Korean service. To hold such temporary visits to a State a basis for the assertion of in personam jurisdiction over unrelated actions arising in the future would make a mockery of the limitations on state jurisdiction imposed by the Fourteenth Amendment. Nor did the California court rely on the fact that appellant was actually married in California on one of his two brief visits. We agree that where two New York domiciliaries, for reasons of convenience, marry in the State of California and thereafter spend their entire married life in New York, the fact of their California marriage by itself cannot support a California court's exercise of jurisdiction over a spouse who remains a New York resident in an action relating to child support.

Finally, in holding that personal jurisdiction existed, the court below carefully disclaimed reliance on the fact that appellant had agreed at the time of separation to allow his children to live with their mother three months a year and that he had sent them to California each year pursuant to this agreement. [T]o find personal jurisdiction in a State on this basis, merely because the mother was residing there, would discourage parents from entering into reasonable visitation agreements. Moreover, it could arbitrarily subject one parent to suit in any State of the Union where the other parent chose to spend time while having custody of their offspring pursuant to a separation agreement. As we have empha-sized: "The unilateral activity of those who claim some relationship with a nonresident defendant cannot satisfy the requirement of contact with the forum State. [I]t is essential in each case that there be some act by which the defendant purposefully avails him[self] of the privilege of con-ducting activities within the forum State. . . ." Hanson v. Denckla, [357 U.S. 235, 253 (1958)].

The "purposeful act" that the California Supreme Court believed did warrant the exercise of personal jurisdiction over appellant in Cali-fornia was his "actively and fully consent[ing] to Ilsa living in California for the school year . . . and . . . send[ing] her to California for that pur-pose." 19 Cal. 3d, at 524, 564 P.2d, at 358. [Yet, a] father who agrees, in the interests of family harmony and his children's preferences, to allow them to spend more time in California than was required under a sep-aration agreement can hardly be said to have "purposefully availed him-self" of the "benefits and protections" of California's laws.[7] . . .

The circumstances in this case clearly render "unreasonable" Cali-fornia's assertion of personal jurisdiction. . . . The cause of action herein asserted arises, not from the defendant's commercial transactions in in-terstate commerce, but rather from his personal, domestic relations. . . . Furthermore, the controversy between the parties arises from a separa-tion that occurred in the State of New York; appellee Horn seeks mod-ification of a contract that was negotiated in New York and that she flew to New York to sign. [T]he instant action involves an agreement that was entered into with virtually no connection with the forum State.

Finally, basic considerations of fairness point decisively in favor of appellant's State of domicile as the proper forum for adjudication of this case, whatever the merits of appellee's underlying claim. It is appellant who has remained in the State of the marital domicile, whereas it is ap-pellee who has moved across the continent. Appellant has at all times resided in New York State, and, until the separation and appellee's move to California, his entire family resided there as well. As noted above, ap-pellant did not more than acquiesce in the stated preference of one of his children to live with her mother in California. This single act is surely not one that a reasonable parent would expect to result in the substan-tial financial burden and personal strain of litigating a child-support suit in a forum 3,000 miles away, and we therefore see no basis on which it can be said that appellant could reasonably have anticipated being "haled before a [California] court," Shaffer v. Heitner, 433 U.S. [186, 216 (1977)].

---

7. The court below stated that the presence in California of appellant's daughter gave appellant the benefit of California's "police and fire protection, its school system, its hos-pital services, its recreational facilities, its libraries and museums. . . ." 19 Cal. 3d, at 522, 564 P.2d, at 356. But, in the circumstances presented here, these services provided by the State were essentially benefits to the child, not the father, and in any event were not ben-efits that appellant purposefully sought for himself.

To make jurisdiction in a case such as this turn on whether appellant bought his daughter her ticket or instead unsuccessfully sought to prevent her departure would impose an unreasonable burden on family relations, and one wholly unjustified by the "quality and nature" of appellant's activities in or relating to the State of California. International Shoe Co. v. Washington, 326 U.S., at 319.

In seeking to justify the burden that would be imposed on appellant were the exercise of in personam jurisdiction in California sustained, appellee argues that California has substantial interests in protecting the welfare of its minor residents and in promoting to the fullest extent possible a healthy and supportive family environment in which the children of the State are to be raised. These interests are unquestionably important. But while the presence of the children and one parent in California arguably might favor application of California law in a lawsuit in New York, the fact that California may be the " 'center of gravity' " for choice-of-law purposes does not mean that California has personal jurisdiction over the defendant. . . .

■ **STATE EX REL. MAHONEY v. ST. JOHN**
*964 P.2d 1242 (Wyo. 1998)*

TAYLOR, Justice. . . .

On August 24, 1985, Sheree Mahoney (Sheree) was born in Casper, Wyoming, as the issue of Sherrill L. Mahoney (Sherrill) and Benjamin F. St. John, III (appellee). Although Sheree was produced without benefit of parental wedlock, appellee verbally acknowledged fatherhood and visited mother and child regularly during the first several months of Sheree's life. Early in 1986, however, Sherrill and Sheree relocated to the State of Washington. Although gainfully employed, Sherrill remained frequently obliged to secure Aid to Families with Dependent Children (AFDC) in Washington during the late 1980's and early 1990's.

In 1992, the State of Washington, upon Sherrill's relation, brought a paternity action against appellee, who continued to reside in Casper. . . . Perhaps hoping that matrimony might be an alternative to a judgment for $17,396.00 in back child support and maintenance, appellee summoned Sherrill back to Casper, where the two were married in August of 1993.

The couple and their daughter returned to Washington where appellee secured employment and set up housekeeping with his wife and daughter. Less than nine months later, however, the marital bonds had been irretrievably broken and appellee fled back to Casper. Shortly thereafter, Sherrill filed her petition for divorce in Washington, achieving personal service upon appellee in Wyoming on July 11, 1994. Having been personally served in Wyoming pursuant to Wash. Rev. Code

Ann. §4.28.185(1)(f) (West 1988) (hereinafter RCWA), appellee chose to default and judgment was entered against him in Washington for $20,628.00 in child support arrearages, inter alia.

However, when Washington moved to enforce the support obligation in Wyoming pursuant to the Uniform Interstate Family Support Act (UIFSA; formerly the Uniform Reciprocal Enforcement of Support Act or URESA),[1] appellee availed himself of a Wyoming forum to contest Washington's exercise of *in personam* jurisdiction over a Wyoming resident. The Wyoming district court subsequently held that the Washington order was invalid because appellee had not been personally served within the boundaries of Washington (predicated upon the district court's view that service within *our* state's boundaries is requisite to an exercise of *in personam* jurisdiction by a *Wyoming* court). The State of Washington, upon the relation of Sherrill, timely brought this appeal. . . .

. . . The proper inquiry is whether the Washington court had and exercised good and sufficient personal jurisdiction over appellee at the time the decree and order of support were entered. [If the Washington court had jurisdiction, its order is constitutionally entitled to full faith and credit in Wyoming.] This rule . . . is consistent with UIFSA, which requires Wyoming district courts to "recognize and enforce . . . a registered order if the issuing tribunal had jurisdiction." A foreign order becomes a "registered" order upon filing with a Wyoming district court.

. . . Bearing in mind that appellee admits to residing with his wife and child in Washington while gainfully employed there, while Sherrill and Sheree continued to live in Washington after appellee deserted the marriage, the answer [to whether Washington has jurisdiction] is found at RCWA §4.28.185(1)(f):

> (1) Any person, whether or not a citizen or resident of this state, who . . . does any of the acts in this section enumerated, thereby submits said person . . . to the jurisdiction of the courts of this state as to any cause of action arising from the doing of any said acts: . . .
>
> (f) Living in a marital relationship within this state notwithstanding subsequent departure from this state, as to all proceedings authorized by chapter 26.09 RCW [Dissolution of Marriage, etc. (including child support)], so long as the petitioning party has continued to reside in this state. . . ."

Again, we find that the existence of personal jurisdiction pursuant to the foregoing section is entirely consistent with multiple expressions of such to be found in both states' codifications of the UIFSA. For ex-

---

1. Adopted by Washington at RCWA §§26.21.010 *et seq.* (West 1994) and adopted by Wyoming at Wyo. Stat. §§20-4-139 through 20-4-194 (1997 and Supp. 1998) (made retroactive to matters initiated under URESA by Wyo. Stat. §20-4-189 (1997)).

ample, RCWA §26.21.075(3) (West 1997 Supp.), in pertinent portion, is a verbatim reiteration of Wyo. Stat. §20-4-142(a)(iii) (Supp. 1998):

> In a proceeding to establish, enforce or modify a support order or to determine parentage, a tribunal of this state may exercise personal jurisdiction over a nonresident individual . . . if: . . .
>        (3) The individual resided with the child in this state[.]. . . .

[Under the Full Faith and Credit Clause of the Constitution, we must] enforce a support order issued by a foreign court, so long as that court enjoyed personal jurisdiction over the [obligor]. Washington's assumption of personal jurisdiction over appellee was consistent with that state's general laws of jurisdiction as well as the Uniform Interstate Family Support Act as codified by Washington *and* Wyoming. The judgment of the district court is, therefore, reversed, and the case is remanded to the district court with instructions to enforce the support order entered by the Washington court.

## Notes and Questions

1. Under the doctrine of divisible divorce, due process requires personal jurisdiction over both spouses to resolve the financial incidents of dissolution, although one can get an ex parte divorce entitled to full faith and credit. E.g., Estin v. Estin, 334 U.S. 541 (1948); Snider v. Snider, 2001 W. Va. LEXIS 94 (W. Va. 2001). Cf. Abernathy v. Abernathy, 482 S.E.2d 265 (Ga. 1997) (situs of real property has in rem jurisdiction for division at dissolution). Applying this doctrine, *Kulko* finds the father's connections with California insufficient to satisfy due process.

Under this doctrine, Ezra Kulko may remain immune from child-support litigation in California but only until he visits his children there and risks personal service of process. Recall Burnham v. Superior Court (noted Chapter V, page 639). What impact does this rule have on visitation? Why do benefits provided by California to the children not count as benefits to their father? What alternative jurisdictional rules might avoid these practical and policy-based difficulties? See Monica J. Allen, Child-State Jurisdiction: A Due Process Invitation to Reconsider Some Basic Family Law Assumptions, 26 Fam. L.Q. 293 (1992).

2. With the expansion of personal jurisdiction signaled by International Shoe Co. v. Washington, 326 U.S. 310 (1945), states enacted long-arm statutes designed to reach absent defendants. One approach, the "single-act" statute, enumerates specific conduct conferring jurisdiction, such as the commission of a tortious act in the state or the transaction of business there. Some courts have construed these statutes, although enacted with other litigation in mind, to apply in family law cases, reasoning

that failure to pay support constitutes a tortious act in the obligee's domicile or that support rights springing from the marriage contract have financial and business implications. See, e.g., Lozinski v. Lozinski, 408 S.E.2d 310 (W. Va. 1991) (haling husband into court in marital domicile after he moved away).

Under this approach, did Ezra Kulko commit a tortious act in California for purposes of justifying jurisdiction? Any assertion of jurisdiction under single-act statutes must satisfy the Due Process Clause's minimum contacts requirement, explained in *Kulko*. As a result, some states have followed a second approach illustrated by California's statute in *Kulko:* legislation that allows courts to assert jurisdiction whenever due process permits, thus encompassing all the single acts usually listed and any additional jurisdictional bases permitted by the Constitution.

3. More recently, a number of states enacted long-arm statutes explicitly addressing family law cases. The Washington statute quoted in *Mahoney* exemplifies this development. See, e.g., Louise Everett Graham, Starting Down the Road to Reform: Kentucky's New Long-Arm Statute for Family Obligations, 81 Ky. L. Rev. 585 (1993).

How should a court construe the marital-relationship language of the Washington statute? Must the defendant conduct "the daily activities of his marital life" in the forum for a particular time? Cf. Panganiban v. Panganiban, 736 A.2d 190, 194 (Conn. Ct. App. 1999). If St. John had stayed in Washington three months instead of nine, would that suffice? Will a long absence from a state so weaken the contacts with the defendant's previous home that long-arm jurisdiction becomes improper? Cf. Sharp v. Sharp, 765 A.2d 271 (N.J. Super. Ct. App. Div. 2001).

Recall that Ezra Kulko and Sharon Kulko Horn married in California during a brief stopover. Suppose that, after their separation, Ezra visits Sharon in California on occasion and they have sexual intercourse there. Would California have sufficient contacts under a statute like Washington's and the requirements of due process? See State ex rel. Phelan v. Davis, 965 S.W.2d 886 (Mo. Ct. App. 1998) (no). See also Register v. McGloon, 771 So. 2d 488 (Ala. Civ. App. 2000). Suppose, in addition to marrying in California and visiting there occasionally, Ezra also administered his financial affairs from that state, although he never resided there because his business required him to travel all over the world. See Sherlock v. Sherlock, 545 S.E.2d 757 (N.C. Ct. App. 2001) (sufficient minimum contacts if other spouse still resides in this state).

4. *Evolution of UIFSA. Mahoney* invokes UIFSA, the Uniform Interstate Family Support Act, the latest in a series of efforts designed to promote consistency and efficiency in multistate support cases. These efforts began in 1944, when the National Conference of Commissioners on Uniform State Laws proposed the Uniform Support of Dependents Law (USDL). USDL provided a civil procedure requiring out-of-state fathers

to pay support. Only a few states adopted USDL, which assumed each jurisdiction in a case would have the legislation.

The Commissioners' proposal in 1950 of the Uniform Reciprocal Enforcement of Support Act (URESA), 9C U.L.A. 273 (2001), met with more success. URESA (or its amended versions), adopted by virtually every state, became the principal means for establishment and enforcement of interstate support orders assisting obligees, whose obligors leave the state and then refuse to pay support, as well as obligees who relocate to another state. A URESA case entailed a two-state proceeding, with a petition filed in the obligee's state and transmitted to a court elsewhere having personal jurisdiction over the obligor.

Substantial changes in URESA in 1968 resulted in the Revised Reciprocal Enforcement of Support Act (RURESA), 9C U.L.A. 81 (2001). Although URESA and RURESA increased collections from deadbeat parents and lightened the burden on public assistance, problems remained. First, the lack of uniformity among states made the process difficult. Second, the system permitted multiple support orders. See generally Tina M. Fielding, Note, The Uniform Interstate Family Support Act: The New URESA, 20 U. Dayton L. Rev. 425 (1994).

The Commissioners replaced the earlier models with the Uniform Interstate Family Support Act (UIFSA), which they approved in 1992, amended in 1996, and amended again in 2001. 9 U.L.A. (pt. IB) 235, 393 (1999).[71] Although based on URESA and RURESA, UIFSA contains new procedures for establishing, enforcing, and modifying support orders. To assure acceptance by the states, Congress made enactment of UIFSA a condition for federal funding for child support enforcement, under the Personal Responsibility and Work Opportunity Reconciliation Act of 1996. 42 U.S.C. §666(f) (Supp. V 1999). See generally Uniform Interstate Family Support Act (1996) (with More Unofficial Annotations by John J. Sampson), 32 Fam. L.Q. 390 (1998).

Like its predecessors, UIFSA covers both spousal and child support (but not property distribution), see §101(21), 9 U.L.A. (pt. IB) 258 (1999), and spells out procedures for establishing support orders and enforcing them. UIFSA responds to a number of perceived weaknesses in earlier laws, examined below.

5. *Expanding jurisdiction.* Critics claim that traditional jurisdictional rules thwart effective support enforcement. As a result, a federal commission exploring law reform initially proposed attacking *Kulko* to allow jurisdiction in most support cases in the state of the child's domicile. This approach, called "child-state jurisdiction," parallels jurisdiction in the child's home state in custody adjudications under the Uniform Child

---

[71]. For the 2001 amendments, without final style revisions or comments, see <www.nccusl.edu>, visited Nov. 5, 2001. Unless otherwise noted, references in text use the 1996 version.

Custody Jurisdiction Act (UCCJA) and the Parental Kidnapping Prevention Act (PKPA). See infra Chapter VII, pages 916-920.

In drafting UIFSA, the Commissioners narrowly decided to rely on long-arm statutes instead of the broader "child-state" approach. See Sampson, supra, at 421-422 n.56. UIFSA's eight bases for jurisdiction over absent obligors include when the individual resided with the child in the state, the child resides in the state "as the result of acts or directives of the individual," the individual engaged in intercourse in the state and the child may have been conceived therefrom, and there is any other basis consistent with the Constitution for the exercise of personal jurisdiction. 9 U.L.A. (pt. IB) 275 (1999). This expanded long-arm jurisdiction facilitates a one-state proceeding, in place of the two-state approach under URESA.

Is the provision in *Mahoney* narrower or broader than one based on having resided with the child in the state? Why did UIFSA's drafters not use only a catch-all provision, which covers any basis consistent with due process?

Would UIFSA change the result in *Kulko*? Would the "acts or directives" provision apply? Would its application satisfy due process? Why did the drafters fail to adopt the more expansive "child-state" approach? See generally Monica J. Allen, Child-State Jurisdiction: A Due Process Invitation to Reconsider Some Basic Family Law Assumptions, 26 Fam. L.Q. 293 (1992). Is it time to rethink *Kulko*'s limitations on jurisdiction? Compare McCaffrey v. Green, 931 P.2d 407 (Alaska 1997), with Fox v. Fox, 7 S.W.3d 339 (Ark. Ct. App. 1999), and Taylor v. Jarrett, 959 P.2d 807 (Ariz. Ct. App. 1998).

6. *Choice of law.* What law should govern in a multistate support cases? Note that *Kulko* concedes that California law might govern, even though California lacks jurisdiction. But if it is unfair to subject Ezra Kulko to the jurisdiction of California's courts, is it not unfair to subject him to California law? See Linda J. Silberman, *Shaffer v. Heitner:* The End of an Era, 53 N.Y.U. L. Rev. 33, 88 (1978). Under URESA or RURESA, the law of any state where the obligor was present when support was sought applies. UIFSA principally applies the forum's procedural and substantive law (§303). 9 U.L.A. (pt. IB) 303 (1999). See also id. at 357 (under §604, law of issuing state governs in enforcement actions).

## Problem

In *Kulko,* assume that Ezra frequently telephones his children in California, writes to them, provides health insurance for them, pays for their orthodontics, and furnishes them airline tickets so they can visit him in New York. Suppose that Sharon then files a petition to establish a child support award in California (which, if granted, would be the first child support award for this family). Would California have personal jurisdiction over Ezra to order him to pay child support? Why? See In re Marriage of Crew, 549 N.W.2d 527 (Iowa 1996). See also Blanchard v. Blair, 781 So. 2d 228 (Ala. Civ. App. 2000).

### b. Modification and Enforcement

■ **LETELLIER v. LETELLIER**
*40 S.W.3d 490 (Tenn. 2001)*

HOLDER, J. . . .

In May 1989, the Superior Court of the District of Columbia entered an order adjudging Steven G. LeTellier to be the father of Teresa B. LeTellier's child, Nicholas. The court awarded custody of Nicholas to Ms. LeTellier and ordered Mr. LeTellier to pay child support. Ms. LeTellier later moved with Nicholas to Tennessee, and Mr. LeTellier moved to Virginia.

In September 1998, Ms. LeTellier filed petitions in the Juvenile Court of Davidson County, Tennessee, seeking (1) to enroll the District of Columbia order, and (2) to modify the child support award. [A juvenile court granted Mr. LeTellier's motion to dismiss the modification petition on grounds that the Tennessee court lacked subject matter jurisdiction and ordered that the case be transferred to Virginia.]

The Court of Appeals reversed [finding] that the jurisdictional provisions of Tennessee's Uniform Interstate Family Support Act conflict with the Federal Full Faith and Credit for Child Support Orders Act. It held that FFCCSOA preempted UIFSA and conferred jurisdiction upon the Davidson County Juvenile Court. We granted review [and now reverse the Court of Appeals.]

The Uniform Interstate Family Support Act, Tenn. Code Ann. §36-5-2201, et seq., controls the establishment, enforcement, or modification of support orders across state lines. UIFSA is intended to "recognize that only one valid support order may be effective at any one time." Unif. Interstate Family Support Act, U.L.A. (1996) (prefatory notes). Key to promoting UIFSA's intent is the concept of "continuing exclusive jurisdiction." A state that issues a support order has continuing exclusive jurisdiction over that order. No other state may modify that order as long as the issuing state has continuing exclusive jurisdiction.

The issuing state may lose continuing exclusive jurisdiction, however. In this case, the District of Columbia lost continuing exclusive jurisdiction when Mr. LeTellier, Ms. LeTellier, and Nicholas were no longer residents of that state. The District of Columbia "no longer had an appropriate nexus with the parties or the child to justify exercise of jurisdiction to modify." Tenn. Code Ann. §36-5-2205 cmt. . . .

Section 36-5-2611(a) of UIFSA confers subject matter jurisdiction upon Tennessee courts to modify child support orders issued by other states [as follows:]

> (a) After a child support order issued in another state has been registered in this state, the responding tribunal of this state may modify that order only if . . . after notice and hearing it finds that:
>> (1) The following requirements are met:
>>> (i) The child, the individual obligee, and the obligor do not reside in the issuing state;
>>> (ii) *A petitioner who is a nonresident of this state seeks modification;* and
>>> (iii) The respondent is subject to the personal jurisdiction of the tribunal of this state. . . .

Tenn. Code Ann. §36-5-2611(a) (emphasis added).

Because Ms. LeTellier is a resident of Tennessee, she fails to meet [subject-matter jurisdiction] the requirement of §36-5-2611(a)(1)(ii). . . . Ms. LeTellier claims, however, that §36-5-2611(a)(1)(ii) does not preclude the exercise of jurisdiction because §36-5-2201 and §36-5-2202 provide the basis for jurisdiction in this case. Because long-arm jurisdiction was obtained over Mr. LeTellier pursuant to §36-5-2202, [Ms. LeTellier claims this is a one-state proceeding under UIFSA.] The comments to §36-5-2202 . . . describe the one-state proceeding/two-state proceeding dichotomy: "Assertion of long-arm jurisdiction over a nonresident essentially results in a one-state proceeding, notwithstanding the fact that the parties reside in different states."

An effort to establish, enforce, or modify a support decree against an out-of-state resident ordinarily would have an interstate character. An action to establish, enforce, or modify a Tennessee order is transformed into a one-state proceeding when long-arm personal jurisdiction over the out-of-state resident is acquired. . . . Once that is done, the out-of-state resident is no longer out-of-state for purposes of that action, and the action loses its interstate character. [In such one-state cases, the substantive and procedural law of the forum controls. Ms. LeTellier thus argues that the requirements for two-state proceedings, including §35-5-2611(a), do not apply.]

. . . Even assuming [long-arm personal jurisdiction has been satisfied in this case,] the order [Ms. LeTellier] sought to modify was issued by a state other than Tennessee. Tennessee courts lack subject matter jurisdiction to modify out-of-state orders when the provisions of UIFSA are not satisfied. Because this case still retains its interstate character, §36-5-2202 has no application to this case. The remaining provisions of UIFSA, including the subject matter jurisdiction provisions of §36-5-2611(a), still apply. . . .

Moreover, the comments to §36-5-2611 refute any contention that asserting personal jurisdiction over an obligor pursuant to §36-5-2201 is sufficient to confer subject matter jurisdiction to modify an out-of-state decree. The comments also clearly establish that an action to modify an out-of-state support order cannot be brought in the petitioner's home state as Ms. LeTellier attempted:

> The policies underlying the change affected by Subsection (a)(1) contemplate that the issuing State has lost continuing, exclusive jurisdiction and that the obligee may seek modification in the obligor's State of residence, or that the obligor may seek a modification in the obligee's State of residence. This restriction attempts to achieve a rough justice between the parties in the majority of cases by preventing a litigant from choosing to seek modification in a local tribunal to the marked disadvantage of the other party. For example, an obligor visiting the children at the residence of the obligee cannot be validly served with citation accompanied by a motion to modify the support order. Even though such personal service of the obligor in the obligee's home State [confers personal jurisdiction], the motion to modify does not fulfill the requirement of being brought by "a [petitioner] who is a nonresident of this State. . . ." In short, the obligee is required to register the existing order and seek modification of that order in a State which has personal jurisdiction over the obligor other than the state of the obligee's residence. Most typically this will be the State of residence of the obligor. . . .

Ms. LeTellier alternatively alleges that the Federal Full Faith and Credit for Child Support Orders Act, 28 U.S.C. §1738B, confers jurisdiction upon the Juvenile Court for Davidson County, Tennessee. FFCCSOA and UIFSA therefore conflict, and FFCCSOA, as federal law, controls. FFCCSOA provides for modification of out-of-state child support orders as follows:

> (e) Authority to modify orders. — A court of a State may modify a child support order issued by a court of another State if —
> (1) the court has jurisdiction to make such a child support order pursuant to subsection (i); and
> (2)(A) the court of the other State no longer has continuing, exclusive jurisdiction of the child support order because that State no longer is the child's State or the residence of any individual contestant. . . .

28 U.S.C. §1738B(e). Subsection (i), regarding jurisdiction, states as follows:

> (i) Registration for modification. — If there is no individual contestant or child residing in the issuing State, the party or support enforcement agency seeking to modify, or to modify and enforce, a child support order issued in another State shall register that order in a State with jurisdiction over the nonmovant for the purpose of modification.

Subsection (i) differs from UIFSA in that it does not contain the non-resident requirement found at §36-5-2611(a)(ii). Ms. LeTellier contends that jurisdiction is proper in the Tennessee court under FFCCSOA in spite of her status as a resident of Tennessee because of the doctrine of federal preemption. We again disagree.

Application of general rules of federal preemption leads us to conclude that FFCCSOA and UIFSA do not conflict. We begin with a presumption that Congress did not intend to preempt UIFSA. . . . In 1988, Congress established the United States Commission on Interstate Child Support ("Commission") to offer recommendations on the resolution of interstate child support problems. As part of its recommendations, the Commission "declared its support for the Uniform Interstate Family Support Act." H.R. Rep. No. 102-982 (1992). FFCCSOA was signed into law in 1994. From its inception, FFCCSOA was intended to be consistent with UIFSA.

In 1996, Congress enacted a law requiring all fifty states to adopt UIFSA by January 1, 1998. 42 U.S.C. §666(f) (1996). . . . While conflicts between the two laws were recognized, they were characterized as unintentional. Subsequent revisions to FFCCSOA were intended to correct any conflicts and make FFCCSOA consistent with UIFSA. . . .

In the absence of preemption, we apply traditional rules of statutory construction to reconcile both statutes. . . . The word "jurisdiction" as used in FFCCSOA, 28 U.S.C. §1738B(i), is ambiguous. FFCCSOA does not specify whether "jurisdiction" refers to personal jurisdiction alone or to both personal and subject matter jurisdiction. . . .

A consistent reading of UIFSA and FFCCSOA requires only that "jurisdiction" under subsection (i) of FFCCSOA be construed as referring to both personal jurisdiction and subject matter jurisdiction. . . . Accordingly, under FFCCSOA, a state has jurisdiction to modify an out-of-state support order only when the petitioner registers the order in a state having personal and subject matter jurisdiction for the purpose of modification. Since, under §36-5-2611(a) of UIFSA, Tennessee courts do not have subject matter jurisdiction to modify the District of Columbia's order because Ms. LeTellier is a resident of Tennessee, the Juvenile Court for Davidson County did not have "jurisdiction over the non-movant for the purpose of modification" under FFCCSOA. . . .

## Notes and Questions

1. Support awards typically are subject to modification in the rendering state. As a result, some authorities have questioned whether the constitutional full-faith-and-credit requirement applies in such cases or whether other states can refuse to recognize a support award issued elsewhere. Even if the requirement controls, it would allow a sister state as

much room to modify the decree as the rendering state (because "full faith and credit" means that the second forum must treat the decree the same way the rendering state would). In the face of this uncertainty, some jurisdictions based interstate recognition of modifiable support awards on comity. See, e.g., Lowery v. Lowery, 591 A.2d 81 (Vt. 1991). Under URESA and RURESA (which committed enacting states to rules of reciprocal recognition), enforcement of a support award issued elsewhere often required a cumbersome two-state procedure, involving the courts of both states.

UIFSA uses direct enforcement when an order is sent to an obligor's employer in another state, in turn triggering wage withholding (§501), 9 U.L.A. (pt. IB) 336 (1999). Alternatively, UIFSA authorizes direct administrative enforcement of an order issued elsewhere by an agency in the obligor's state (§507), id. at 349. UIFSA includes a registration process (§§601-604), id. at 352-358, allowing courts and agencies in one state to enforce support orders issued in another. UIFSA's requirement that an obligor must contest a foreign order by requesting a hearing within 20 days of notification of the order's registration (§606), id. at 362, has survived due process challenge. Washington v. Thompson, 6 S.W.3d 82 (Ark. 1999). UIFSA explicitly makes visitation irrelevant (§305(d)), 9 U.L.A. (pt. IB) 305-306 (1999). See Clemmons v. Office of Child Support Enforcement, 984 S.W.2d 837 (Ark. 1999) (mother who willfully concealed son, preventing father's visitation, not estopped from recovering support arrearages). See generally Uniform Interstate Family Support Act (1996) (with More Unofficial Annotations by John J. Sampson), 32 Fam. L.Q. 390, 405-406 (1998).

2. Under URESA and RURESA, courts took different positions on whether one state could modify another's support decree and on whether the original state must recognize another's modification. See, e.g., Taylor v. Vilcheck, 745 P.2d 702 (Nev. 1987) (court can enforce reduced amount of support payments awarded in another state, but cannot increase); Stout v. Stout, 534 S.E.2d 776 (W. Va. 2000) (original state need not recognize another's modification); Poirrier v. Jones, 781 P.2d 531 (Wyo. 1989) (when second court enforces reduced amount, obligee can still recover the difference in issuing state). Modification outside the issuing state often produced multiple and conflicting support orders.

UIFSA, which has a "One-Order, One-Time" rule, sought to address such problems through modification limitations explained by LeTellier. How do they work? How would they operate on the facts of Kulko, which — despite its significance for jurisdictional rules generally, including those applicable to establishing an initial support award — concerned a petition to modify child support? How would they work if Ezra Kulko had been the party seeking the modification? UIFSA's 2001 amendments (§201(b)) clarify the distinction between jurisdiction and jurisdiction to modify.

3. The comments to UIFSA, quoted in *LeTellier*, claim that the jurisdictional limitations on modification attempt a "rough justice" between the litigants. See also Linn v. Delaware Support Enforcement, 736 A.2d 954, 961 (Del. 1999). Would these limitations disallow Ezra Kulko from bringing his modification action in New York, given that he remained at the marital domicile and Sharon left the family for California? Recall the Supreme Court's analysis of fairness in that case. Does the expansion of long-arm jurisdiction for establishing initial awards, plus the requirement of "continuing exclusive jurisdiction" in the issuing state (so long as one party remains there), answer this question? To what extent do UIFSA's limitations address, at least in modification cases, the policy problems posed by rules that subject a parent to personal jurisdiction if service of process is accomplished during a visit with a child who resides out of state?

4. *Full faith and credit.* Even before the 1996 welfare reform legislation requiring states to adopt UIFSA, Congress enacted measures to facilitate interstate recognition and enforcement of support orders. The Family Support Act of 1988 required states to adopt procedures insuring finality and full faith and credit for all payments or support obligations once due. 42 U.S.C. §666(a)(9) (1994). This federal legislation prohibits retroactive (as distinguished from prospective) modification everywhere.

As *LeTellier* notes, Congress subsquently enacted the Full Faith and Credit for Child Support Orders Act, 28 U.S.C. §1738B (1994 & Supp. V 1999), incorporating many UIFSA concepts. This legislation imposes duties on states to enforce and not modify (except as authorized) child support orders established by other states, consistently with the act's requirements. It provides for continuing, exclusive jurisdiction by a court that has made an order, so long as the state is the child's state or the residence of any individual contestant, unless a court in another state has modified the order, in accordance with the act. "Child's state" is defined as "the State in which a child resides." For choice of law, the act generally dictates application of the forum's law, but specifies the law of the issuing state for interpreting orders. In 1996, Congress amended the legislation to make it consistent with UIFSA. Courts have construed the statute to apply retroactively to accrued arrearages. See, e.g., Twaddell v. Anderson, 523 S.E.2d 710 (N.C. Ct. App. 1999); Dunn v. Dunn, 738 N.E.2d 81 (Ohio Ct. App. 2000).

5. *Federal parent locator service.* Special problems arise when the obligor's whereabouts are unknown. Solutions such as those examined in *Kulko, Mahoney,* and *LeTellier* assume that obligors can be located, although they might have disappeared to evade support enforcement. Congress responded to this problem by directing the Secretary of Health and Human Services to establish and conduct the "parent locator service." 42 U.S.C. §653 (1994 & Supp. V 1999). This service relies on So-

cial Security numbers to track absent parents. The Personal Responsibility and Work Opportunity Reconciliation Act of 1996 strengthens this service by incorporating the National Director of New Hires and Federal Case Registry of child support orders. See generally Janet Atkinson, Assisting Children and the Courts: The Federal Parent Locator Service, 83 Judicature 26 (1999).

6. *Federal crimes.* The Child Support Recovery Act (CSRA), 18 U.S.C. §228 (Supp. V 1999), criminalizes the willful failure to pay a past-due support obligation for a child who resides in another state. "Past-due support obligation" means any amount determined by a court order or administrative process to be due for the support and maintenance of a child, or a child and the parent with whom the child is living, if the amount has remained unpaid for more than a year or exceeds $5,000. The CSRA does not create a private right of action for obligees. See, e.g., Salahuddin v. Alaji, 232 F.3d 305 (2d Cir. 2000).

Congress amended the CSRA in 1998, with the enactment of the Deadbeat Parents Punishment Act, 18 U.S.C. §228(a)(3) (Supp. V 1999), which makes willful failure to pay a support obligation for a child in another state a felony, if the obligation remains unpaid for over two years or exceeds $10,000. Courts have rejected ex post facto challenges to the enhanced penalties for accrued arrearages, reasoning that the amendments cover only post-enactment willful failures to pay. See United States v. Wilson, 210 F.3d 230 (4th Cir. 2000); United States v. Russell, 186 F.3d 883 (8th Cir. 1999).

Most courts have upheld the CSRA against challenges that it exceeds Congress's authority under the Commerce Clause and the Tenth Amendment. E.g., United States v. Faasse, 265 F.3d 475 (6th Cir. 2001); United States v. Mussari, 95 F.3d 787 (9th Cir. 1996), *cert. denied sub nom.* Schroeder v. United States, 520 U.S. 1203 (1997). These courts have reasoned that the payment of a debt constitutes economic activity and the difference in location of obligor and obligee requires satisfaction of the debt by interstate means. But see United States v. King, 2001 U.S. Dist. LEXIS 1120 (S.D.N.Y. 2001), *rev'd* 2002 U.S. App. LEXIS 54 (2d Cir. 2002). See generally Ann Laquer Estin, Federalism and Child Support, 5 Va. J. Soc. Pol'y & L. 541, 559-576 (1998).

7. *International support enforcement.* Special problems arise when the obligor flees to another country. Compare Haker-Volkening v. Haker, 547 S.E.2d 127 (N.C. Ct. App. 2001) (deeming Switzerland not a "state" under UIFSA), with Foreman v. Foreman, 2001 N.C. App. LEXIS 542 (N.C. Ct. App. 2001) (treating England as "state" under UIFSA). The Personal Responsibility and Work Opportunity Reconciliation Act facilitates international support enforcement by establishing procedures for recognition of "foreign reciprocating countries." 42 U.S.C. §659a (Supp. V 1999). See generally Gary Caswell, International Child Support — 1999, 32 Fam. L.Q. 525 (1998). The 2001 amendments to UIFSA (§§102(20)(ii),

308(b), 615) expand the definition of "state" to permit enforcement of foreign support orders in the United States and to allow states to arrange with foreign countries for reciprocal child support enforcement.

## Problem

Angela and George are the parents of two children born out of wedlock in Louisiana. George, who never disputed paternity, moved to Mississippi four years after the younger child was born. After their separation, a Louisiana court entered a consent judgment awarding Angela custody and ordering George to pay child support. For about two years George complied with the order. Angela and the two children subsequently moved to Ohio.

Six months after moving, before ever registering the Louisiana order in another state, Angela files a petition in Louisiana seeking to increase the child support. George enters a special appearance to challenge Louisiana's jurisdiction and then also seeks a change of custody so that the children can live with him. Can the Louisiana court grant the modification? Why? Does Louisiana retain jurisdiction until some other state acquires it? See Jurado v. Brashear, 782 So. 2d 575 (La. 2001). Cf. Linn v. Delaware Child Support Enforcement, 736 A.2d 954 (Del. 1999). How, if at all, does "continuing" jurisdiction differ from "exclusive" jurisdiction under UIFSA or the federal Full Faith and Credit to Child Support Orders legislation? See Porter v. Porter, 684 A.2d 259, 263 (R.I. 1996).

## G. SEPARATION AGREEMENTS

Most divorcing parties themselves settle the financial issues incident to dissolution. They then present their agreement to the court for approval.[72] The rules governing property division and spousal and child support thus establish the framework within which such "private ordering" takes place.[73] This section examines the legal principles applicable to separation agreements.

---

[72]. Professors Robert Mnookin and Lewis Kornhauser report that "probably less than 10% [of dissolutions] involve disputes that are contested in court." Robert H. Mnookin & Lewis Kornhauser, Bargaining in the Shadow of the Law: The Case of Divorce, 88 Yale L.J. 950, 951 n.3 (1979). In a study of 1,100 California families with children, most reported little conflict concerning financial issues. Maccoby & Mnookin, supra note [9], at 135-136.

[73]. See Mnookin & Kornhauser, supra note [72], at 950-952.

## ■ BALDRIDGE v. LACKS
*883 S.W.2d 947 (Mo. Ct. App. 1994)*

AHRENS, Judge.

In this action seeking damages for legal malpractice, the trial court entered judgment on a jury verdict for plaintiff in the amount of $6,834,926. An amended judgment was subsequently entered by the trial court in the remitted amount of $2,424,966. Defendants appeal. . . .

[Plaintiff retained defendant Lacks to represent her in the dissolution of her marriage to Kenneth Baldridge.] At a July 1988 meeting, plaintiff and defendant Lacks discussed the possibility of settling the divorce. Plaintiff testified that Lacks told her that Baldridge was attempting to prove his entire net worth was composed of non-marital assets because it was attributable to the original million dollars he had prior to the marriage. Plaintiff further testified that Lacks advised her to settle because, if Baldridge were successful in doing so, or if the postnuptial agreement was found to be valid, she "could walk away with nothing from the marriage." Lacks spent the remainder of 1988 negotiating a settlement with Kenneth Baldridge's attorneys. [Lacks then] advised plaintiff that her options were to risk receiving nothing or to settle the case.

[Prior to a hearing on Plaintiff's motion for temporary support, she] met with Lacks, who informed her that Baldridge had offered one million dollars and a condominium in Florida to settle the divorce. Plaintiff testified that Lacks told her that Baldridge was going to prove that "everything you own is separate," and that she should "take [the offer] and run."[1] A dissolution hearing was held. . . . An oral settlement agreement was dictated into the record. Plaintiff testified that she understood the property she would receive under the settlement agreement was her share of the marital property and all she would receive from Kenneth Baldridge. Plaintiff also testified that she was aware that Kenneth Baldridge might have had as much as fifteen million dollars in property and that she was releasing and waiving all rights to any of that property. Plaintiff further testified that she understood that if her divorce were to proceed to trial, the court could give her substantially more than what she was to receive under the settlement agreement. . . . The court later signed and entered a decree of dissolution, finding that the settlement agreement was not unconscionable.

After the dissolution of marriage, plaintiff's ex-husband suggested to plaintiff that she had gotten a bad settlement and that she could have

---

1. This testimony was sharply disputed by Lacks. Lacks testified that he told plaintiff that it was too early to settle the case, but plaintiff ignored his advice and instructed him to settle. He further testified that he told plaintiff that they stood a good chance of getting the postnuptial agreement set aside but that he could not quantify her chances of success because he didn't know what a judge might do.

recovered more money than she had agreed to accept. Plaintiff brought this legal malpractice action against defendant Lacks and his law partners, seeking damages for their allegedly negligent handling of her divorce.

At trial, plaintiff's expert, attorney Allen Russell, testified that Lacks failed to meet the standard of care in regard to the duty to ensure that the client has facts necessary to make a decision as to whether a settlement proposal is acceptable, fair and equitable . . . because Lacks failed to engage in discovery, failed to trace assets and did not know the extent of the marital and nonmarital estates. Russell also opined that Lacks was not equipped with the necessary information to advise his client as to the advantages and disadvantages of a proposed settlement. . . .

Defendants' . . . expert, attorney Charles Todt, testified that an attorney's paramount duty is to do what the client tells him to do and, therefore, defendant Lacks' discovery was sufficient because plaintiff instructed him to settle the case. . . . Todt opined that Lacks met an attorney's standard of care in handling plaintiff's divorce. . . .

[Defendants] claim that the trial court erred in denying their motion for a directed verdict because litigants should not be allowed to file malpractice lawsuits which challenge the adequacy of previous settlements. . . . Their position is that public policy dictates that settlements, once consummated, should not be lightly undone. In addition, they argue that Missouri law encourages the peaceful settlement of disputes. . . .

We agree that public policy strongly favors the peaceful settlement of disputes and that settled cases should not be readily revisited. Particularly in marriage dissolution cases, the statutes seek "to promote amicable settlement of disputes between the parties to a marriage . . ." §452.325.1 RSMo 1986; Dow v. Dow, 732 S.W.2d 906, 908 (Mo. en banc 1987). Balanced against this consideration, however, is the common law right of a client to maintain an action seeking civil liability for negligence.

. . . In essence, defendants ask us to grant attorneys immunity from civil liability in cases where their clients have settled, absent some affirmative misrepresentation or fraud by the attorney. We do not believe it would serve the interests of justice to do so. . . . To prove damages, it was sufficient for plaintiff to include expert testimony as to what she would have received had the underlying action been tried. . . .

[Nonetheless, the court reversed and remanded for a new trial because of an erroneous jury instruction, which allowed a finding of negligence based *solely* on defendant's failure to advise plaintiff of the nature and extent of the marital estate. Defendant had conceded this failure but asserted in defense that the client had insisted on settling without discovery, against his advice.]

# ■ UNIFORM MARRIAGE AND DIVORCE ACT §306
*9A U.L.A. (pt. I) 248-249 (1998)*

[Separation Agreement]

(a) To promote amicable settlement of disputes between parties to a marriage attendant upon their separation or the dissolution of their marriage, the parties may enter into a written separation agreement containing provisions for disposition of any property owned by either of them, maintenance of either of them, and support, custody, and visitation of their children.

(b) In a proceeding for dissolution of marriage or for legal separation, the terms of the separation agreement, except those providing for the support, custody and visitation of children, are binding upon the court unless it finds, after considering the economic circumstances of the parties and any other relevant evidence produced by the parties, on their own motion or on request of the court, that the separation agreement is unconscionable.

(c) If the court finds the separation agreement unconscionable, it may request the parties to submit a revised separation agreement or may make orders for the disposition of property, maintenance, and support.

(d) If the court finds that the separation agreement is not unconscionable as to disposition of property or maintenance, and not unsatisfactory as to support:

(1) unless the separation agreement provides to the contrary, its terms shall be set forth in the decree of dissolution or legal separation and the parties shall be ordered to perform them, or

(2) if the separation agreement provides that its terms shall not be set forth in the decree, the decree shall identify the separation agreement and state that the court has found the terms not unconscionable.

(e) Terms of the agreement set forth in the decree are enforceable by all remedies available for enforcement of a judgment, including contempt, and are enforceable as contract terms.

(f) Except for terms concerning the support, custody, or visitation of children, the decree may expressly preclude or limit modification of terms set forth in the decree if the separation agreement so provides. Otherwise, terms of a separation agreement set forth in the decree are automatically modified by modification of the decree.

## Notes and Questions

1. At one time, separation agreements were held to violate public policy because they facilitated divorce by removing uncertainty about

how a court would resolve the financial incidents. In contrast, UMDA makes the parties' "amicable settlement of disputes" an explicit policy objective. The Missouri statute cited in *Baldridge* is modeled on UMDA §306.

Why does UMDA reject the traditional disfavor of separation agreements? Does the transition from fault to no-fault divorce explain the change? Does the increasing acceptance of premarital agreements? What are the advantages of "private ordering" over judicial resolution? See Robert H. Mnookin, Divorce Bargaining: The Limits on Private Ordering, 18 U. Mich. J.L. Ref. 1015, 1017-1019 (1985). The disadvantages?

The American Law Institute's Principles of the Law of Family Dissolution also favor private ordering. To encourage settlement, the Principles' formulaic approach to the financial consequences of dissolution is designed to enhance the predictability of the outcome a court would reach. See supra page 665. Accordingly, the Principles' treatment of agreements sets out the requirements for parties to "opt out" of the default rules that would otherwise govern. See ALI Principles §7.02 cmt. a. Chapter 7 covers premarital agreements, postnuptial agreements, separation agreements, and agreements for domestic partnerships and their dissolution. From a public policy perspective, should the law show more or less deference to separation agreements, compared to premarital agreements? Why? See id. §7.09 cmt. b. Does the psychological stress associated with divorce call for greater legal protection of parties entering separation agreements than premarital agreements? See Mnookin, supra.

2. Does UMDA's "attendant upon" language require that the parties enter the agreement at the time of separation or dissolution or only that the agreement resolve disputes arising then? See, e.g., Reisenleiter v. Reisenleiter, 926 S.W.2d 914 (Mo. Ct. App. 1996). Might strict timing requirements discourage attempted reconciliations? Compare Williams v. Williams, 463 S.E.2d 815 (N.C. Ct. App. 1995), *aff'd*, 469 S.E.2d 553 (N.C. 1996), with Vaccarello v. Vaccarello, 757 A.2d 909 (Pa. 2000).

3. How does a court determine whether an agreement is "unconscionable"? Does this standard contemplate a substantive evaluation of fairness or only perfunctory judicial review? See, e.g., In re Marriage of Gundmundson, 955 P.2d 648, 653 (Mont. 1998) (judge makes no inquiry on unconscionability). Some authorities claim that the absence of judicial oversight disproportionately disadvantages women. See, e.g., Penelope Eileen Bryan, The Coercion of Women in Divorce Settlement Negotiations, 74 Denv. U. L. Rev. 931, 937-938 (1997).

The ALI Principles make presumptively unenforceable agreements that would substantially change the property rights or compensatory payments otherwise due, when enforcement would substantially impair the economic well-being of either a party with custody of the children or a party with substantially fewer economic resources than the other party. ALI Principles, supra, §7.09(2). What advantages does this standard have over the "unconscionability" test? What disadvantages? See also id. §7.01 (procedural requirements).

4. Consistent with *Baldridge*, other cases have held that policies favoring the settlement of disputes do not preclude malpractice judgments against a divorce attorney who advised a client to sign a separation agreement, so long as the client can show negligence causing an economic injury. See, e.g., Grayson v. Wofsey, Rosen, Kweskin & Kuriansky, 646 A.2d 195 (Conn. 1994); McWhirt v. Heavey, 550 N.W.2d 327 (Neb. 1996). Should the client's agreement serve as a defense in such malpractice cases? Should the court's approval of the separation agreement as "not unconscionable"?

What should an attorney do when a client asserts that the highest priority is resolving the case quickly? Should the emotionally charged nature of divorce proceedings influence the attorney's conduct? The fact that the other party (if economically stronger) will be paying the attorneys' fees? See generally Lewis Becker, Ethical Concerns in Negotiating Family Law Agreements, 30 Fam. L.Q. 587 (1996); Andrew S. Grossman, Avoiding Legal Malpractice in Family Law Cases: The Dangers of Not Engaging in Financial Discovery, 33 Fam. L.Q. 361 (1999).

5. *The bargaining process.* The conventional wisdom depicts the parties bargaining toward a separation agreement in the "shadow of the law." Under this theory, the outcome the judge would order if the spouses did not settle significantly influences the settlement they will reach. See Robert H. Mnookin & Lewis Kornhauser, Bargaining in the Shadow of the Law: The Case of Divorce, 88 Yale L.J. 950, 951 (1979). In predicting the outcome adjudication would yield, however, attorneys necessarily consider the high proportion of cases that settle. Further, empirical studies show that judicial review operates primarily as a rubber stamp of the parties' agreements and that settlements often reflect not genuine agreement but rather " 'the best I can get' solution." Marygold S. Melli et al., The Process of Negotiation: An Exploratory Investigation in the Context of No-Fault Divorce, 40 Rutgers L. Rev. 1133, 1159 (1988). Professor Melli and her co-authors thus conclude that divorce might well represent a system of "adjudication in the shadow of bargaining." Id. at 1147.

6. *Incorporation and merger.* Separation agreements may be "contractual" or "decretal," a distinction with important consequences. Without its incorporation (sometimes called "merger") into a judicial decree, a separation agreement is simply a contract. In one method of incorporation, the judgment recites the essential provisions of the agreement; in the other the judgment refers to the agreement and incorporates its provisions by reference. See Alexander Lindey & Louis I. Parley, 2 Lindey Parley on Separation Agreements and Antenuptial Contracts §83.30 (2d ed. 1998). UMDA §306 creates a presumption of incorporation that parties seeking to avoid must dispel by a clear statement to the contrary.

One consequence that depends on the status of the agreement concerns enforcement. For example, if one party does not perform the terms (say, the obligation to pay support), contempt of court and possible imprisonment provide remedies for noncompliance with a judicial decree. Such remedies are not available for breach of contract. UMDA §306 provides for enforcement remedies for "terms of the agreement set forth in the decree."

Similarly, courts can modify some provisions of a judicial decree if circumstances change (that is, support provisions); courts cannot rewrite the terms of a contract no matter how unfair or inadequate they become. See, e.g., Ex parte Owens, 668 So. 2d 545 (Ala. 1995) (court can modify alimony provisions upon changed circumstances when agreement incorporated into decree); In re Marriage of Dellitt, 571 N.E.2d 523 (Ill. App. Ct. 1991) (agreement not incorporated into decree raises questions of contract law only). Note that UMDA §306 allows the parties to preclude or limit modification (except for terms concerning children). See also, e.g., Day v. Day, 717 A.2d 914 (Me. 1998).

A few courts hold that, even if merged or incorporated into a divorce decree, a separation agreement retains its character as a contract. Hence, the court cannot modify the alimony terms upon a showing of changed circumstances; only the parties can change the terms by agreement. See Rockwell v. Rockwell, 681 A.2d 1017 (Del. 1996). Further, although many jurisdictions treat the terms as synonomous, some jurisdictions distinguish between incorporation and merger, applying the rules of contract law in the absence of true merger. See, e.g., Merl v. Merl, 493 N.E.2d 936, 937 (N.Y. 1986); Nicholson v. Combs, 703 A.2d 407 (Pa. 1997). See also ALI Principles, supra, §7.10.

7. In reaching a separation agreement, the parties resolve a number of incidents of divorce. The bargaining process may entail purely financial tradeoffs, for example, decreased alimony for a greater share of the marital property. Alternatively, it may entail negotiation of financial and nonfinancial interests, for example, decreased alimony for sole child custody. See, e.g., Scott Altman, Lurking in the Shadow, 68 S. Cal. L. Rev. 493 (1995) (examining custody-property trades in negotiations); Margaret F. Brinig & Michael V. Alexeev, Trading at Divorce: Preferences, Legal Rules and Transaction Costs, 8 Ohio St. J. Disp. Resol. 279 (1993) (theoretical and empirical investigation).

Some jurisdictions have special rules for "integrated bargains," agreements in which the consideration exchanged between the parties includes both property rights and support payments. For example, support payments in an integrated bargain incorporated into the divorce decree are not modifiable upon a showing of changed circumstances because modification would necessarily alter the property division and upset the parties' carefully crafted quid pro quo. See, e.g., Beasley v.

Beasley, 707 So. 2d 1107 (Ala. Civ. App. 1997); Holcomb v. Holcomb, 513 S.E.2d 807 (N.C. Ct. App. 1999). Further, some agreements use terms or a payment structure that leaves unclear whether an obligation represents a division of assets, spousal support, or some of both. See, e.g., Sally Burnett Sharp, Step by Step: The Development of the Distributive Consequences of Divorce in North Carolina, 76 N.C. L. Rev. 2017, 2044-2052 (1998) (discussing lump sum alimony in integrated separation agreements).

8. *Vacating the decree.* Orders dividing property are final in the sense that a court cannot modify them upon changed circumstances (see section D2a). Nevertheless, they can be reopened if they form part of an agreement procured by fraud or other improper means. E.g., In re Rossi, 108 Cal. Rptr. 2d 270 (Cal. Ct. App. 2001) (undisclosed lottery jackpot); Shafmaster v. Shafmaster, 642 A.2d 1361 (N.H. 1994) (setting aside property settlement seven years later).

Some courts have vacated divorce judgments based on a stipulated agreement on the ground that the agreement was unconscionable. E.g., Crawford v. Crawford, 524 N.W.2d 833 (N.D. 1994). Should the same standard of unconscionability apply when a party attempts to set aside an agreement after its entry as when the court considers whether to adopt the agreement initially? What does this approach mean for private ordering? The dissenting judge in *Crawford* discerns a troubling new rule in the majority opinion:

> The majority's disregard of our standard of review and its application of a nebulous unconscionability standard invites, even compels, judges to patronizingly and paternalistically meddle in the proposed stipulations of presumptively competent divorcing adults, with very little guidance or principle other than our own personal sense of what feels fair and right. . . . Despite my own impression that [the wife] has been left with the very short end of this marital stick, . . . I am not willing to let this hard case make bad law. . . .

Id. at 837 (Neumann, J., dissenting).

Some commentators claim that wives are more likely than husbands to enter bad divorce bargains because of factors such as wives' financial dependency, their naive trust of their attorneys and the justice system, their ethic of care, and their greater tendency toward depression. See Penelope Eileen Bryan, Women's Freedom to Contract at Divorce: A Mask for Contextual Coercion, 47 Buff. L. Rev. 1153 (1999). See also Amy L. Wax, Bargaining in the Shadow of the Market: Is There a Future for Egalitarian Marriage?, 84 Va. L. Rev. 509 (1998). Do such generalizations call for standards that give judges more room to vacate divorce decrees based on agreements? Does the perfunctory quality of judicial review at the time of divorce call for more permissive standards in subsequent challenges?

The ALI Principles find a middle ground, affording the parties a short opportunity to challenge the terms after experiencing the agreement's operation, when a court finds that both the agreement is "tainted" by noncompliance with the procedural or substantive requirements of §7.09 and "the challenged terms of the decree were substantially less favorable to the moving party than they would have been without the agreement." ALI Principles, supra, §7.11.

9. *Bargaining with child support.* UMDA §306 treats child support, custody, and visitation specially, making the parties' agreement on these issues not binding on the court and also preserving the possibility of future modification, despite agreement to contrary. Other authorities reflect a similar approach. E.g., Reinsch v. Reinsch, 611 N.W.2d 86 (Neb. 2000); Brescia v. Fitts, 436 N.E.2d 518 (N.Y. 1982); ALI Principles, supra, §§7.06, 7.07, 7.09 & cmt. i.

What explains UMDA's special treatment of provisions concerning children? What is the difference between finding property or maintenance provisions "not unconscionable" and finding (child) support provisions "not unsatisfactory?" Does UMDA allow the parties to leave child support, custody, and visitation as purely matters of contract? Should courts defer to the parties' explicit preclusion of modification of child support in the separation agreement? See Portlock v. Portlock, 518 A.2d 116 (D.C. 1986); Harry D. Krause, Child Support in America: The Legal Perspective 18 (1981); Eleanor E. Maccoby & Robert H. Mnookin, Dividing the Child: Social and Legal Dilemmas of Custody 41 (1992). Should a court be less willing to modify an award of child support based on a separation agreement, in deference to the policy favoring private ordering? Are there reasons a court should be more willing to modify in such cases? Compare Tietig v. Boggs, 602 So. 2d 1250 (Fla. 1992), and Solis v. Tea, 468 A.2d 1276, 1282-1283 (Del. 1983), with Boyd v. Boyd, 343 S.E.2d 581, 584-585 (N.C. Ct. App. 1986).

10. What impact will federally mandated child support guidelines have on agreements negotiated by parents? If states adopt more predictable rules for property division and alimony, as recommended by the ALI Principles, supra, will settlement increase? Will such reforms enhance autonomy by lessening dependence on experts? The absence of clear rules and the unpredictability of results have been criticized for putting "the disputants at the mercy of legal experts who know the ropes, who control the process (judges and mediators), or who claim special insights into its workings (the lawyers), and so can pressure the parties into accepting solutions that suit the professionals' goals but that often seem unresponsive to the spouses' personal senses of justice and to their self-defined needs." Inga Markovits, Family Traits, 88 Mich. L. Rev. 1734, 1749 (1990).

# Problem

In the property settlement agreement judicially ratified, affirmed, and incorporated by reference in the divorce decree, David agrees to relinquish all of his equity in the jointly owned marital home (the couple's only asset) in exchange for Marilyn's promise never to request child support. Their agreement explicitly states that Marilyn "has accepted all of David's equity in lieu of requesting child support" and that "should a court ever grant a child support award against David, Marilyn convenants and agrees to pay directly to David any amount of support that he is directed to pay to any party." Pursuant to the agreement, David conveys to Marilyn his equity in the marital home, valued at $40,000, where she and the children continue to live. Marilyn alone supports the children.

Six years later, David petitions for definite periods of visitation with the children. Marilyn then petitions for David to pay child support. He counters by moving the court to order Marilyn to reimburse him for any amount of child support the court orders. What result? See Kelley v. Kelley, 449 S.E.2d 55 (Va. 1994). See also Savarese v. Corcoran, 709 A.2d 829 (N.J. Super. Ct. Ch. Div. 1997), *aff'd,* 709 A.2d 799 (N.J. Super. Ct. App. Div. 1998); ALI Principles, supra, §3.13.

# VII

■

# Child Custody

Custody disputes arise in many different settings: divorce, guardianship, child abuse and neglect, and adoption.[1] This chapter focuses primarily on the first of these settings. Post-divorce custody law is characterized by the dual rationale of private dispute resolution and child protection.[2] The resolution of custody disputes thereby reflects the fundamental tension between respect for family autonomy versus the need for state intervention.

When the parents can agree on child custody, the state generally defers to family autonomy. However, in approximately 10 to 20 percent of divorce cases involving children, the parents cannot agree.[3] For these cases, the important question is how these disputes should be resolved. This chapter begins by exploring empirical evidence regarding the effects of divorce on children.

[1]. On these different "strands" of custody law, see Robert H. Mnookin, Child Custody Adjudication: Judicial Functions in the Face of Indeterminacy, 39 Law & Contemp. Probs. 226, 230-246 (1975). See also Chapter VIII (child abuse) and Chapter IX (adoption and guardianship).

[2]. See Mnookin, supra note [1], at 281.

[3]. Eleanor E. Maccoby & Robert H. Mnookin, Dividing the Child: Social and Legal Dilemmas of Custody 134 (1992); Robert W. Hansen, The Role and Rights of Children in Divorce Actions, 6 J. Fam. L. 1, 2 (1966).

## A. INTRODUCTION: EFFECTS OF PARENTAL DIVORCE

■ **JUDITH S. WALLERSTEIN et al., THE**
   **UNEXPECTED LEGACY OF DIVORCE:**
   **A 25 YEAR LANDMARK STUDY**
   *298-300 (2000)*

From the viewpoint of the children . . . divorce is a cumulative experience. Its impact increases over time and rises to a crescendo in adulthood. . . .

The first upheaval occurs at the breakup. Children are frightened and angry, terrified of being abandoned by both parents, and they feel responsible for the divorce. Most children are taken by surprise; few are relieved. As adults, they remember with sorrow and anger how little support they got from their parents when it happened. They recall how they were expected to adjust overnight to a terrifying number of changes that confounded them. . . . The children concluded early on, silently and sadly, that family relationships are fragile. . . .

As the postdivorce family took shape, their world increasingly resembled what they feared most. Home was a lonely place. The household was in disarray for years. Many children were forced to move, leaving behind familiar schools, close friends, and other supports. What they remember vividly as adults is the loss of the intact family and the safety net it provided, the difficulty of having two parents in two homes, and how going back and forth cut badly into playtime and friendships. Parents were busy with work, preoccupied with rebuilding their social lives. Both moms and dads had a lot less time to spend with their children and were less responsive to their children's needs or wishes. . . . Children soon learned that the divorced family has porous walls that include new lovers, live-in partners, and stepparents. Not one of these relationships was easy for anyone. . . .

Meanwhile, children who were able to draw support from school, sports teams, parents, stepparents, grandparents, teachers, or their own inner strengths, interests, and talents did better than those who could not muster such resources. By necessity, many of these so-called resilient children forfeited their own childhoods as they took responsibility for themselves; their troubled, overworked parents; and their siblings. . . .

But it's in adulthood that children of divorce suffer the most. The impact of divorce hits them most cruelly as they go in search of love, sexual intimacy, and commitment. Their lack of inner images of a man and a woman in a stable relationship and their memories of their parents' failure to sustain the marriage badly hobbles their search, leading them to heartbreak and even despair. [They complain bitterly] that they have no good models on which to build their hopes. . . . Many end up with unsuitable or very troubled partners in relationships that were doomed from the start. . . .

[I]n coping with the normal stresses in a marriage, adults from divorced families were at a grave disadvantage. Anxiety about relationships was at the bedrock of their personalities and endured even in very happy marriages. Their fears of disaster and sudden loss rose when they felt content. And their fear of abandonment, betrayal, and rejection mounted when they found themselves having to disagree with someone they loved. After all, marriage is a slippery slope and their parents fell off it. . . .

_____

The above excerpt is from the 25-year follow-up study of a sample of 131 children in post-divorce families. For the 10-year follow-up study, see Judith S. Wallerstein & Sandra Blakeslee, Second Chances: Men, Women, and Children a Decade after Divorce — Who Wins, Who Loses — and Why (1996).

## B. PARENTAL DISPUTES CONCERNING CHILD CUSTODY

### 1. Standards for Selecting the Custodial Parent: What Should Be the Standard?

#### a. Presumptions?

##### (i) Tender Years Presumption

■ **DEVINE v. DEVINE**
*398 So. 2d 686 (Ala. 1981)*

MADDOX, Justice.

[A]ppellant Christopher P. Devine [and] Appellee, Alice Beth Clark Devine were legally and lawfully married on December 17, 1966, . . . and separated in Calhoun County, Alabama, on March 29, 1979. [They have two sons, Matthew, born in 1972, and Timothy, born in 1975.]

. . . Since [college] graduation in 1962, Mrs. Devine has taught high school. [I]n 1975 [she] commenced employment with the U.S. Army at Fort McClellan, Alabama, where she was employed continuously through the [trial] as an Educational Specialist. [She] was 38 years of age at the time of [trial]. The Appellant/natural father, Christopher P. Devine [age 41] was a member of the faculty and head of the Guidance and

Counseling Department at Jacksonville State University, Jacksonville, Alabama. At the time of the trial, the older son had just completed the first grade at the said University's Elementary Laboratory School and the younger son was enrolled in the said University's Nursery Laboratory School.

[The trial court awarded custody of both boys to the mother based on the tender years presumption.] [T]he trial court . . . offered the following justification for its decision:

> The facts of this case clearly show that either plaintiff or defendant would be a fit and proper person to be vested with the care, custody and control of the parties' minor children. While there was evidence presented at trial which raised questions in the mind of the court as to each parent's suitability, none presented was of such magnitude that it showed either to be unfit. Likewise, evidence was presented to the court showing that each parent possessed certain positive qualities that should be considered in determining which of them would be the proper one to be awarded custody.

At the conclusion of the case, there did not exist a clear preponderance of the evidence for either party regarding child custody. However, there exists in Alabama law a presumption that when dealing with children of tender years, the natural mother is presumed, in absence of evidence to the contrary, to be the proper person to be vested with custody of such children. This presumption, while perhaps weaker now than in the past, remains quite viable today. . . .

The sole issue presented for review is whether the trial court's reliance on the tender years presumption deprived the father of his constitutional entitlement to the equal protection of the law. . . .

At common law, it was the father rather than the mother who held a virtual absolute right to the custody of their minor children. This rule of law was fostered, in part, by feudalistic notions concerning the "natural" responsibilities of the husband at common law. The husband was considered the head or master of his family, and, as such, responsible for the care, maintenance, education and religious training of his children. By virtue of these responsibilities, the husband was given a corresponding entitlement to the benefits of his children, i.e., their services and association. It is interesting to note that in many instances these rights and privileges were considered dependent upon the recognized laws of nature and in accordance with the *presumption* that the father could best provide for the necessities of his children:

> Undoubtedly, the father has primarily, by law as by nature, the right to the custody of his children. This right is not given him solely for his own gratification, but because nature and the law ratifying nature assume that the author of their being feels for them a tenderness which will secure their happiness more certainly than any other tie on earth. Because he is the fa-

ther the presumption naturally and legally is that he will love them most, and care for them most wisely. And, as a consequence of this, it is presumed to be for the real interest of the child that it should be in the custody of its father, as against collateral relatives, and he, therefore, who seeks to withhold the custody against the natural and legal presumption, has the burden of showing clearly that the father is an unsuitable person to have the custody of his child.

Hibbette v. Baines, 78 Miss. 695, 29 So. 80 (1900). As Chief Justice Sharkey more eloquently stated in his dissenting opinion in Foster v. Alston, 7 Miss. (6 How.) 406, 463 (1842):

We are informed by the first elementary books we read, that the authority of the father is superior to that of the mother. It is the doctrine of all civilized nations. It is according to the revealed law and the law of nature, and it prevails even with the wandering savage, who has received none of the lights of civilization.

By contrast, the wife was without any rights to the care and custody of her minor children. By marriage, husband and wife became one person with the legal identity of the woman being totally merged with that of her husband. As a result, her rights were often subordinated to those of her husband and she was laden with numerous marital disabilities. As far as any custodial rights were concerned, Blackstone stated the law to be that the mother was "entitled to no power [over her children], but only to reverence and respect." 1 W. Blackstone, Commentaries on the Law of England 453 (Tucker ed. 1803).

By the middle of the 19th Century, the courts of England began to question and qualify the paternal preference rule. This was due, in part, to the "hardships, not to say cruelty, inflicted upon unoffending mothers by a state of law which took little account of their claims or feelings." W. Forsyth, A Treatise on the Law Relating to the Custody of Infants in Cases of Difference Between Parents or Guardians 66 (1850). Courts reacted by taking a more moderate stance concerning child custody, a stance which conditioned a father's absolute custodial rights upon his fitness as a parent. Ultimately, by a series of statutes culminating with Justice Talfourd's Act, 2 and 3 Vict. c. 54 (1839), Parliament affirmatively extended the rights of mothers, especially as concerned the custody of young children. Justice Talfourd's Act expressly provided that the chancery courts, in cases of divorce and separation, could award the custody of minor children to the mother if the children were less than seven years old. This statute marks the origin of the tender years presumption in England.

In the United States the origin of the tender years presumption is attributed to the 1830 Maryland decision of Helms v. Franciscus, 2 Bl. Ch. (Md.) 544 (1830). In *Helms,* the court, while recognizing the general rights of the father, stated that it would violate the laws of nature to "snatch" an infant from the care of its mother:

> The father is the rightful and legal guardian of all his infant children; and in general, no court can take from him the custody and control of them, thrown upon him by the law, not for his gratification, but on account of his duties, and place them against his will in the hands even of his wife. . . . Yet even a court of common law will not go so far as to hold nature in contempt, and snatch helpless, pulling infancy from the bosom of an affectionate mother, and place it in the coarse hands of the father. The mother is the softest and safest nurse of infancy, and with her it will be left in opposition to this general right of the father.

Thus began a "process of evolution, perhaps reflecting a change in social attitudes, [whereby] the mother came to be the preferred custodian of young children and daughters. . . ." Foster, Life with Father, 11 Fam. L.Q. 327 (1978). . . .

As late as 1946, this Court continued to recognize the paternal preference rule. Brown v. Jenks, 247 Ala. 596, 25 So. 2d 439 (1946); however, by that time the rule was no longer a formidable factor in resolving child custody disputes. The influence of the paternal preference rule had been gradually replaced by a growing adherence to the tender years presumption.

At the present time, the tender years presumption is recognized in Alabama as a rebuttable factual presumption based upon the inherent suitability of the mother to care for and nurture young children. All things being equal, the mother is presumed to be best fitted to guide and care for children of tender years. To rebut this presumption the father must present clear and convincing evidence of the mother's positive unfitness. Thus, the tender years presumption affects the resolution of child custody disputes on both a substantive and procedural level. Substantively, it requires the court to award custody of young children to the mother when the parties, as in the present case, are equally fit parents. Procedurally, it imposes an evidentiary burden on the father to prove the positive unfitness of the mother.

In recent years, the tender years doctrine has been severely criticized by legal commentators as an outmoded means of resolving child custody disputes. . . . In twenty states the doctrine has been expressly abolished by statute or court decision, and in four other states its existence is extremely questionable. . . . In Orr v. Orr, 440 U.S. 268 (1979), the United States Supreme Court held that any statutory scheme which imposes obligations on husbands, but not on wives, establishes a classification based upon sex which is subject to scrutiny under the Fourteenth Amendment. The same must also be true for a legal presumption which imposes evidentiary burdens on fathers, but not on mothers. . . .

Having reviewed the historical development of the presumption as well as its modern status, . . . we conclude that the tender years presumption represents an unconstitutional gender-based classification which discriminates between fathers and mothers in child custody proceedings solely on the basis of sex.

## Notes and Questions

1. Beginning in the mid- to late nineteenth century, the tender years presumption applied to custody determinations. This presumption (also called the "maternal preference") provided that the natural mother of a young child was entitled to custody of the child unless she was found unfit. Courts treated the doctrine as either: (1) a tie-breaker mandating maternal custody if all other factors are equal, or (2) a rule placing the burden of persuasion on the father to show that paternal custody serves the best interests of the child, or (3) a rule affecting the burden of proof that requires the father, in order to prevail, to prove maternal unfitness. Robert F. Cochran, Jr., The Search for Guidance in Determining the Best Interests of the Child at Divorce: Reconciling the Primary Caretaker and Joint Custody Preferences, 20 U. Rich. L. Rev. 1, 10 (1985). Do each of these have constitutional shortcomings?

Professor Mary Becker proposes a "maternal deference" standard that would permit judicial deference to the mother's judgment regarding custody so long as the mother is fit. Would this standard pass constitutional muster? See Mary Becker, Maternal Feelings: Myth, Taboo, and Child Custody, 1 S. Cal. Rev. L. & Women's Stud. 133, 203-223 (1992).

The tender years presumption has been replaced by the purportedly gender-neutral "best-interests-of-the-child" standard. This highly discretionary standard is based on a list of factors (usually statutory) regarding the child's needs.

2. Consider the advantages and disadvantages of the tender years presumption. Like all presumptions, the doctrine offers relative certainty. It thereby avoids the stress of litigation. However, the presumption clearly puts fathers at a disadvantage because they must prove the mother's unfitness before they can gain custody. But, might a gender-neutral presumption disadvantage the mother?

3. Although the Supreme Court never addressed the constitutionality of the presumption, several states (similar to Alabama in *Devine*) declared that the presumption violates the Fourteenth Amendment. See, e.g., Watts v. Watts, 350 N.Y.S.2d 285, 290 (Fam. Ct. 1973); Pusey v. Pusey, 728 P.2d 117 (Utah 1986). Others held that it violates state equal rights amendments. See Phillip E. Hassman, Annotation, Construction and Application of State Equal Rights Amendments Forbidding Determination of Rights Based on Sex, 90 A.L.R.3d 158, 186-190 (1979).

4. *Historical background.* The tender years presumption was introduced early in the nineteenth century, as *Devine* suggests, in an influential case that carved out an exception to the paternal preference for infants. Social conditions facilitated widespread acceptance of the doctrine. Industrialization and urbanization contributed to the increasing privatization of the family, accompanied by a glorification of motherhood and an intense concern with childrearing. See generally Barbara Ehrenreich & Deirdre English, For Her Own Good: 150 Years of the Experts' Advice to Women (1978); Michael Grossberg, Governing the Hearth: Law and the Family in Nineteenth-Century America 234-285 (1985); Richard Sennett, Families Against the Cities: Middle Class Homes of Industrial Chicago, 1872-1890 (1984); Barbara Welter, The Cult of True Womanhood, 1820-1860, 18 Am. Q. 151 (1966).

5. Most jurisdictions now assume that both parents are equally capable of childcare. Yet, despite the abolition of the presumptive effect of the tender years doctrine, some states still consider the child's age as a factor. See, e.g., Mercier v. Mercier, 717 So. 2d 304, 307 (Miss. 1998). See also Unif. Marriage & Divorce Act §402, 9A U.L.A. (pt. II) 282 (1998) (official comments to §402 state that a preference for maternal custody, when all other things are equal, is in the best interests of the child).

6. *ALI.* The American Law Institute's Principles of the Law of Family Dissolution prohibit a court from considering the gender of either the parent or the child in determining custody arrangements. ALI Principles §2.12(1)(b)(2002).

Should the *child's* gender be relevant in custody decisionmaking? That is, should courts award custody of girls to the mother and boys to the father? Most courts award custody irrespective of the child's gender. See, e.g., Giffin v. Crane, 716 A.2d 1029 (Md. Ct. App. 1998) (holding that trial court erred when it assumed that daughter had specific need to be with parent of same gender). Some evidence suggests, however, that children who are awarded to parents of the same sex are better adjusted and have higher self-esteem. See Robert E. Emery, Marriage, Divorce, and Children's Adjustment 85-86 (1988). Should such data affect custody decisionmaking?

7. *Empirical evidence.* Although the maternal presumption no longer operates de jure, empirical evidence suggests that most courts continue to award custody to the mother.[4] Eleanor E. Maccoby & Robert H. Mnookin, Dividing the Child: Social and Legal Dilemmas of Custody 112-113 (1992). Does this practice constitute gender discrimination in application? See Wheeler v. Wheeler, 574 So. 2d 832 (Ala. Civ. App. 1990).

---

[4]. Although some researchers contend that fathers disproportionately obtain custody when they seek it, others find no such paternal bias. See Terry Arendell, Fathers and Divorce 78 (1995) (citing research).

Empirical research also sheds light on the immediate impact of *Devine*. A sociological study in Alabama assessed the impact of the decision on fathers' custody requests, contests, custody grants, and noncustodial father visitation, and found no significant impact. "The number of fathers being granted sole custody remain[ed] relatively small and constant. . . ." Laura E. Santilli & Michael C. Roberts, Custody Decisions in Alabama Before and After the Abolition of the Tender Years Doctrine, 14 Law & Hum. Behav. 123, 134 (1990).

### (ii) *Primary Caretaker Presumption*

For a brief period, the primary caretaker presumption superseded the tender years presumption in some jurisdictions. According to this presumption, the best interests of the child are served by placing the child with the parent who has taken primary responsibility for the child's care. West Virginia first adopted the presumption in Garska v. McCoy, 278 S.E.2d 357 (W. Va. 1981), and enumerated specific caretaking factors to determine primary caretaker status. Minnesota followed in Pikula v. Pikula, 374 N.W.2d 705 (Minn. 1985), but abrogated the presumption a few years later. Minn. Stat. §518.17(1)(a) (Supp. 2001). West Virginia also recently abandoned the presumption. W.V. Code §48-11-201 et seq. (1999).

Although no state currently adheres to the primary caretaker presumption, the primary caretaker doctrine has continued vitality. Many states consider primary caretaker status as one among many factors in determining the child's best interests. See, e.g., Kjelland v. Kjelland, 609 N.W.2d 100 (N.D. 2000); Zepeda v. Zepeda, 628 N.W.2d 48 (S.D. 2001).

Commentators have elaborated on the advantages and disadvantages of the doctrine. A major justification for the presumption is its gender neutrality. The presumption grants custody to the parent who has performed more childcare (and, thereby knows the child better, has the stronger bond, and has demonstrated a commitment to meeting the child's needs) — irrespective of the parent's gender.[5] Yet many criticize the doctrine. Professor David Chambers, for example, charges that the doctrine overemphasizes the importance of attachment in child development by exaggerating the importance of the bond to the primary caretaker in comparison to the other parent. According to Chambers, the doctrine fails to take into account research indicating that children form strong attachments to both parents and that fathers' roles as rule

---

[5]. David L. Chambers, Rethinking the Substantive Rules for Custody Disputes in Divorce, 83 Mich. L. Rev. 477, 478 (1984); Robert F. Cochran, Jr., The Search for Guidance in Determining the Best Interests of the Child at Divorce: Reconciling the Primary Caretaker and Joint Custody Preferences, 20 U. Rich. L. Rev. 1, 37 (1985).

makers enlarge as children age.[6] Chambers also questions whether the doctrine is genuinely gender neutral because women tend to do more childcare, especially for young children.

Professor Mary Becker criticizes the doctrine for minimizing women's contributions while at the same time maximizing men's. She contends that the doctrine's emphases on gender neutrality and caretaking tasks lead courts to discount women's care during childbearing and early infancy (i.e., breastfeeding) and their subsequent emotional caretaking. She also claims that courts tend to give disproportionately greater weight to fathers' smaller contributions to childcare.[7]

Another justification for the presumption is that its bright line rule should reduce litigation. Yet one commentator suggests that the vagueness of the primary caretaker standard increases litigation.[8]

When West Virginia rejected the presumption, legislators there replaced it with a version of the American Law Institute's Principles Governing the Allocation of Custodial and Decisionmaking Responsibility for Children.[9] The ALI requires a party seeking a custody determination to submit a "parenting plan." In this regard, the ALI mirrors statutory developments in an increasing number of jurisdictions[10] that require parents who seek custody to file a written agreement by which the parents specify caretaking and decisionmaking authority for their children as well as the manner in which future disputes are to be resolved.

[6]. Chambers, supra note [5] at 533-535. Based on his study of developmental theory and research, Chambers advocates a primary caretaker preference for children aged six months to five years. For a rebuttal, see Martha L. Fineman, A Reply to David Chambers, 1987 Wis. L. Rev. 165; Martha L. Fineman & Anne Opie, The Uses of Social Science Data in Legal Policymaking: Custody Determinations at Divorce, 1987 Wis. L. Rev. 107. See also David L. Chambers, The Abuses of Social Science: A Response to Fineman and Opie, 1987 Wis. L. Rev. 159.

[7]. Mary E. Becker, Maternal Feelings: Myth, Taboo, and Child Custody, 1 S. Cal. Rev. L. & Women's Stud. 133, 201-202 (1992).

[8]. See Gary Crippen, Stumbling Beyond Best Interests of the Child: Reexamining Child Custody Standard-Setting in the Wake of Minnesota's Four Year Experiment in the Primary Caretaker Preference, 75 Minn. L. Rev. 427, 461(1990) (pointing out this effect in Minnesota).

[9]. Since 1989, the ALI has been involved in a project to reform family law by clarifying its underlying principles and making policy recommendations. The ALI's recommendations on child custody reject the "best interests of the child standard" (discussed on page 807) because of its subjectivity and lack of predictability. Instead, the ALI emphasizes "private ordering," i.e., parental agreements. See ALI Principles of the Law of Family Dissolution: Analysis and Recommendations §§2.06, 2.11-2.12 (2002) (parenting agreements, and limiting and prohibited factors for such plans) (hereafter ALI Principles).

[10]. Washington was one of the first states to adopt parenting plan legislation in 1987. Heather Crosby, The Irretrievable Breakdown of the Child: Minnesota's Move Toward Parenting Plans, 21 Hamline J. Pub. L. & Pol'y 489, 509 (2000). Approximately 15 states provide for parenting plans, although most require parenting plans only in joint custody situations. Mary R. Cathcart & Robert E. Robles, Parenting Our Children: In the Best Interest of the Nation 21, 36 (Report of the U.S. Commission on Child and Family Welfare 1996).

According to the ALI Principles, if the parents agree, the court should enforce their agreement unless the agreement is not voluntary or would be harmful to the child (§2.06(1)(a) & (b)). However, if the parents are unable to agree, the court should award custody based on the allocation of caretaking responsibility prior to the separation (§2.08(1)). The objective is to replicate the division of responsibility that was followed when the family was intact.[11] In a scheme that favors private ordering, such an allocation of decisionmaking gives deference to the arrangements on which the parties once agreed.

Although some might question whether the ALI recommendation implicitly reinstates the primary caretaker presumption, the ALI provision differs in several ways. Unlike the primary caretaking presumption, the ALI Principles contemplate a spectrum of possibilities. For example, the Principles favor an equal allocation of custodial time if the parents in the intact family had allocated caretaking responsibilities equally. In addition, the ALI rule may be rebutted by specific factors such as a prior parental agreement, the child's preference, the need to keep siblings together, harm to the child's welfare (based on emotional attachment to a parent and the parent's ability/availability to meet the child's needs), avoidance of custodial arrangements that would be impractical or interfere with the child's need for stability, and the need to deal with parental relocation (§2.08(1)(a) to (g)).

### b. Best Interests of the Child?

*(i) Introduction*

■ **ROBERT H. MNOOKIN, CHILD-CUSTODY ADJUDICATION: JUDICIAL FUNCTIONS IN THE FACE OF INDETERMINACY**
*39 Law & Contemp. Probs. 226, 233-237, 255-256, 261-264*
*(1975)*

The history of the legal standards governing custody disputes between a child's parents reveals a dramatic movement from rules to a highly discretionary principle. . . . Divorce custody standards now show the overwhelming dominance of the best-interests principle. A majority of the states provide by statute for a best-interests-of-the-child standard. Other states have no statutory standard but have relied on their courts to develop a best-interests standard. . . . In analyzing the custody decision from this perspective, my purpose is not to describe how judges in

---

[11]. This "approximation standard" was first formulated by Elizabeth Scott, Pluralism, Parental Preference, and Child Custody, 80 Cal. L. Rev. 615 (1992).

fact decide custody disputes nor to propose a method of how they should. Instead, it is to expose the inherent <u>indeterminacy of the best-interests standard.</u>

. . . An inquiry about what is best for a child often yields indeterminate results because of the problems of having adequate information, making the necessary predictions, and finding an integrated set of values by which to choose. But some custody cases may still be comparatively easy to decide. While there is no consensus about what is best for a child, there is much consensus about what is very bad (e.g., physical abuse); some short-term predictions about human behavior can be reliably made (e.g., chronic alcoholism or psychosis is difficult quickly to modify). Asking which alternative is in the best interests of a child may have a rather clear-cut answer in situations where one claimant exposes the child to substantial risks of immediate harm and the other claimant already has a substantial personal relationship with the child and poses no such risk. [W]here one alternative plainly risks irreversible effects on the child that are bad and the other does not, there is no need to make longer-term predictions or more complicated psychological evaluations of what is likely to happen to the child's personality.

But to be easy, a case must involve only one claimant who is well known to the child and whose conduct does not endanger the child. If there are two such claimants or none, difficult choices remain. Most custody disputes pose difficult choices. [I]n many private disputes, the court must often choose between parties who each offer advantages and disadvantages, knowing that to deprive the child completely of either relationship will be disruptive. . . .

. . . What are some of the implications of the use of indeterminate standards in custody disputes? Would more precise standards that ask an answerable question be better? . . . More rule-like standards would avoid or mitigate some obvious disadvantages of adjudication by an indeterminate principle. For one thing, the use of an indeterminate standard makes the outcome of litigation difficult to predict. This may encourage more litigation than would a standard that made the outcome of more cases predictable. Because each divorcing parent can often make plausible arguments why a child would be better off with him or her, a best-interests standard probably creates a greater incentive to litigate than would a rule that children should go to the parent of the same sex. . . .

An indeterminate standard raises a number of questions related to fairness that better defined and less discretionary standards could minimize. Inherent in the application of a broad, person-oriented principle is the risk of retroactive application of a norm of which the parties affected will have had no advance notice. This may be unfair because (1) the private parties may have no opportunity to conform their private conduct to the norm subsequently applied by a particular judge; and

(2) during the litigation itself, a party may not have an opportunity to address or question the aspect of the case that the court uses as a basis for decision.

Indeterminate standards also pose an obviously greater risk of vio- ④ lating the fundamental precept that like cases should be decided alike. Because people differ and no two custody cases are exactly alike, the claim can be made that no process is more fair than one requiring res- olution by a highly individualized, person-oriented standard. But with an indeterminate standard, the same case presented to different judges may easily result in different decisions. The use of an indeterminate standard means that state officials may decide on the basis of unarticu- lated (perhaps even unconscious) predictions and preferences that could be questioned if expressed. . . .

. . . While judges may be ill-equipped to develop and evaluate in- formation about the child, having some other state official decide or making various procedural adjustments (such as giving counsel to the child, providing better staff to courts, or making the proceedings more or less formal) will not cure the root problem. The indeterminacy flows from our inability to predict accurately human behavior and from a lack of social consensus about the values that should inform the decision. Procedural adjustments may make the system fairer and more efficient and may avoid some conspicuously erroneous determinations — goals worth pursuing. But neither greater use of existing expertise nor better procedures will make an indeterminate question answerable for an in- dividual case.

Unlike procedural changes, adjudication by a more determinate rule would confront the fundamental problems posed by an indeterminate principle. But the choice between indeterminate standards and more precise rules poses a profound dilemma. The absence of rules removes the special burdens of justification and formulation of standards charac- teristic of adjudication. Unfairness and adverse consequences can result. And yet, rules that relate past events or conduct to legal consequences may themselves create substantial difficulties in the custody area. Our in- adequate knowledge about human behavior and our inability to gener- alize confidently about the relationship between past events or conduct and future behavior make the formulation of rules especially problem- atic. Moreover, the very lack of consensus about values that makes the best-interests standard indeterminate may also make the formulation of rules inappropriate. . . .[12]

---

[12]. For additional criticisms of the best interests standard, see Mary E. Becker, Ma- ternal Feelings: Myth, Taboo, and Child Custody, 1 S. Cal. Rev. L. & Women's Stud. 133, 172-183 (1992); Jon Elster, Solomonic Judgments: Against the Best Interests of the Child, 54 U. Chi. L. Rev. 1 (1987).

# ■ UNIFORM MARRIAGE AND DIVORCE ACT
*9A U.L.A. (pt. II) 282 (1998)*

### §402 [BEST INTEREST OF CHILD]

The court shall determine custody in accordance with the best interest of the child. The court shall consider all relevant factors including:

(1) the wishes of the child's parent or parents as to his custody;

(2) the wishes of the child as to his custodian;

(3) the interaction and interrelationship of the child with his parent or parents, his siblings, and any other person who may significantly affect the child's best interest;

(4) the child's adjustment to his home, school, and community; and

(5) the mental and physical health of all individuals involved.

The court shall not consider conduct of a proposed custodian that does not affect his relationship to the child.

*(ii) Constitutional Factors*

(1) Race

# ■ PALMORE v. SIDOTI
*466 U.S. 429 (1984)*

Chief Justice BURGER delivered the opinion of the Court.

We granted certiorari to review a judgment of a state court divesting a natural mother of the custody of her infant child because of her remarriage to a person of a different race.

### I

When petitioner Linda Sidoti Palmore and respondent Anthony J. Sidoti, both Caucasians, were divorced in May 1980 in Florida, the mother was awarded custody of their three-year-old daughter. In September 1981 the father sought custody of the child by filing a petition to modify the prior judgment because of changed conditions. The change was that the child's mother was then cohabiting with a Negro, Clarence Palmore, Jr., whom she married two months later. Additionally, the father made several allegations of instances in which the mother had not properly cared for the child.

After hearing testimony from both parties and considering a court counselor's investigative report, the court noted that the father had made allegations about the child's care, but the court . . . made a finding that "there is no issue as to either party's devotion to the child, adequacy of housing facilities, or respect[a]bility of the new spouse of either parent."

The court then addressed the recommendations of the court counselor, who had made an earlier report "in [another] case coming out of this circuit also involving the social consequences of an interracial marriage. Niles v. Niles, 299 So. 2d 162." From this vague reference to that earlier case, the court turned to the present case and noted the counselor's recommendation for a change in custody because "[t]he wife [petitioner] has chosen for herself and for her child, a life-style unacceptable to her father *and to society.* . . . The child . . . is, or at school age will be, subject to environmental pressures not of choice."

The court then concluded that the best interests of the child would be served by awarding custody to the father. The court's rationale is contained in the following:

> The father's evident resentment of the mother's choice of a black partner is not sufficient to wrest custody from the mother. It is of some significance, however, that the mother did see fit to bring a man into her home and carry on a sexual relationship with him without being married to him. Such action tended to place gratification of her own desires ahead of her concern for the child's future welfare. *This Court feels that despite the strides that have been made in bettering relations between the races in this country, it is inevitable that Melanie will, if allowed to remain in her present situation and attains school age and thus more vulnerable to peer pressures, suffer from the social stigmatization that is sure to come.*

(Emphasis added.)

The Second District Court of Appeal affirmed without opinion, thus denying the Florida Supreme Court jurisdiction to review the case. We granted certiorari, and we reverse.

## II

The judgment of a state court determining or reviewing a child custody decision is not ordinarily a likely candidate for review by this Court. However, the court's opinion, after stating that the "father's evident resentment of the mother's choice of a black partner is not sufficient" to deprive her of custody, then turns to what it regarded as the damaging impact on the child from remaining in a racially-mixed household. This raises important federal concerns arising from the Constitution's commitment to eradicating discrimination based on race.

The Florida court did not focus directly on the parental qualifications of the natural mother or her present husband, or indeed on the father's qualifications to have custody of the child. The court found that "there is no issue as to either party's devotion to the child, adequacy of housing facilities, or respect[a]bility of the new spouse of either parent."

This, taken with the absence of any negative finding as to the quality of the care provided by the mother, constitutes a rejection of any claim of petitioner's unfitness to continue the custody of her child.

The court correctly stated that the child's welfare was the controlling factor. But that court was entirely candid and made no effort to place its holding on any ground other than race. Taking the court's findings and rationale at face value, it is clear that the outcome would have been different had petitioner married a Caucasian male of similar respectability.

A core purpose of the Fourteenth Amendment was to do away with all governmentally-imposed discrimination based on race. Classifying persons according to their race is more likely to reflect racial prejudice than legitimate public concerns; the race, not the person, dictates the category. [T]o pass constitutional muster, [racial classifications] must be justified by a compelling governmental interest. . . .

The State, of course, has a duty of the highest order to protect the interests of minor children, particularly those of tender years. In common with most states, Florida law mandates that custody determinations be made in the best interests of the children involved. Fla. Stat. §61.13(2)(b)(1) (1983). The goal of granting custody based on the best interests of the child is indisputably a substantial governmental interest for purposes of the Equal Protection Clause.

It would ignore reality to suggest that racial and ethnic prejudices do not exist or that all manifestations of those prejudices have been eliminated. There is a risk that a child living with a step-parent of a different race may be subject to a variety of pressures and stresses not present if the child were living with parents of the same racial or ethnic origin.

The question, however, is whether the reality of private biases and the possible injury they might inflict are permissible considerations for removal of an infant child from the custody of its natural mother. We have little difficulty concluding that they are not. The Constitution cannot control such prejudices but neither can it tolerate them. Private biases may be outside the reach of the law, but the law cannot, directly or indirectly, give them effect. . . .

. . . The effects of racial prejudice, however real, cannot justify a racial classification removing an infant child from the custody of its natural mother found to be an appropriate person to have such custody.

The judgment of the District Court of Appeal is reversed.

## Notes and Questions

1. *Epilogue.* After *Palmore*, the father (who had moved to Texas) filed an application there for a temporary restraining order. The mother subsequently filed, in Texas, a petition for a writ of habeas corpus to recover

the child, and, in Florida, a motion to compel return of the child. The father moved to dismiss the mother's motion in the Florida court. The Florida court declined jurisdiction in favor of the Texas court. Appealing, the mother argued that the Florida court erred in declining to exercise jurisdiction under the Uniform Child Custody Jurisdiction Act. See infra page 916. The mother also argued that, as a result of the Supreme Court's decision, custody should revert to her (that is, the situation prior to the order).

The Court of Appeals of Florida disagreed, stating: "The Supreme Court's decision was that the modification of custody could not be predicated upon the mother's association with a black man. Its opinion did not direct a reinstatement of the original custody decree and the immediate return of the child. The Supreme Court did not say that a Florida court could not defer to a Texas court. . . ." 472 So. 2d 843, 846 (Fla. Dist. Ct. App. 1985). The court concluded, given the passage of time, and the "substantial upheavals of [the child's] life," it would be in the child's best interest to remain in her father's custody. Id. at 847.

2. Prior to *Palmore,* courts adopted different approaches: (1) race was not relevant to custody; (2) race could be considered as one factor in determining a child's best interests; and (3) race could not be used as the determinative factor. Which view does *Palmore* support? See cases cited in Lee R. Russ, Annotation, Race as Factor in Custody Award or Proceedings, 10 A.L.R.4th 796 (1981 & Supp. 2000).

3. How can an appellate court identify race as the unarticulated rationale of a trial court ruling? Professor Katharine Bartlett notes that in several cases involving white mothers who lost custody after their affairs with African-American men, the court used other justifications for the custody modification besides race (e.g., the mother lied about the affair, her sexual activity displayed poor judgment). Bartlett explains: "It is difficult to second-guess these cases under a best-interests test because it is not a test that compels transparency." Katharine T. Bartlett, Comparing Race and Sex Discrimination in Custody Cases, 28 Hofstra L. Rev. 877, 884 & n.35 (2000).

4. *ALI.* The ALI Principles prohibit courts from considering the race or ethnicity of the child, parent, or other member of the household in determining custody arrangements. ALI Principles §212(1)(a)(2002).

On consideration of race in adoption decisionmaking, see Chapter IX.

## Problems

1. Dawn and Kevin and their three children live in South Dakota. Kevin, a member of the Sisseton-Wahpeton Dakota Nation, was adopted at age 7 by a Caucasian couple, the Jones. Dawn, Kevin, and the

children live on the Jones's family farm where Kevin is employed. Kevin's adoptive family is extremely close-knit. Dawn, a homemaker, decides to enroll in a nursing program. Kevin's alcoholism (and verbal and physical abuse while intoxicated) contribute to the breakup of the marriage. At trial, a licensed psychologist and a clinical social worker both testify that Dawn should have custody. Nonetheless, the trial court rules that Kevin should have primary physical custody (provided that he remains alcohol-free) because of Kevin's close relationship with the Jones family and also because, as a Native American, Kevin will be better able to deal with the needs of the children. Dawn appeals. What result? See Jones v. Jones, 542 N.W.2d 119 (S.D. 1996). Cf. In re Custody of M.A.L., 457 N.W.2d 723 (Minn. Ct. App. 1990).

2. Teri and Richard, a Caucasian couple, have been married for five years. They have a one-year-old son, Dylan. After Teri files for divorce, both parents seek custody of Dylan. At trial, Richard argues that the court should award him custody because Teri, a nurse, is having a relationship with the African-American doctor for whom she works. A family nurse practitioner testifies, when asked if it would be harmful for Dylan to be raised in this environment, that it would be harmful. She adds that interracial relationships are more acceptable in large cities, but that it may be harmful for a child to be raised in such an environment in a small town such as theirs. The trial court finds both parents fit but awards custody to Richard, stating that extramarital affairs interfere with the well-being of the child. It orders no contact between the child and the doctor (an order Richard did not even request). Teri appeals. What result? See Parker v. Parker, 986 S.W.2d 557 (Tenn. 1999).

(2) Religion

■ **ABBO v. BRISKIN**
  *660 So. 2d 1157 (Fla. Dist. Ct. App. 1995)*

FARMER, Judge. . . .

This was a second marriage. When they met, the mother was Roman Catholic and the father of the Jewish faith. She already had two young children by her previous marriage, who resided with her and were being raised as Catholics. As the parties considered marrying, they had extended discussions about religion. Ultimately she agreed to convert to Judaism after he insisted that they would not marry unless she did so.[3]

Their daughter was born nearly a year after the marriage. Shortly after her birth, the mother converted back to Catholicism. When the

---

3. The trial judge described her conversion as being with "great reservations . . . because she had a great spiritual attachment to the Catholic faith, after a life-long training and association with the beliefs and traditions of Catholicism."

daughter was 4 1/2 years old, they decided to divorce. The principal dispute at trial was the child's religion. . . . The court recognized that the child would be raised in a home with two other children who were already being raised as Catholics, who would attend mass on Sunday, who were likely to attend parochial school or catechism classes, and who would likely participate in Catholic ceremonies such as First Holy Communion and Confirmation. At the same time, the court also recognized that there was no evidence that the child's best interests would be affected by any order the court might make on the subject of religious preference.

The court enforced the parties' agreement for shared parental custody and ordered that the mother be the primary, custodial parent. Ultimately, the court decided that she would be required to "do everything in her power to assure [the child] shall be raised in the Jewish faith and shall cooperate with [the father] in seeking this result." . . . In an order on a motion for rehearing, the court further explained what it was requiring of the mother: "The Petitioner should not interfere in the development of the child's Jewish religious training and upbringing, nor should she actively influence the religious training of the child in any other direction, other than the Jewish faith. . . ." It is these orders that we review.

We begin by noting that the trial judge's injunction is not expressly founded on any fact relating to the physical or psychological welfare of the child. Rather it seems to flow from the court's finding that the mother had agreed before marriage to convert to the Jewish faith. Thus the restriction is not grounded in a factual finding that an attempt to expose the child to Catholic teachings or to raise the child as Catholic would adversely and detrimentally affect her well-being or welfare. Equally, it is not based on any finding that it would beneficially promote her health or welfare if she were raised in Judaism. It is thus safe to say that the court's order must find its support in something other than the traditional rubric "the best interests of the child." Lurking beneath the order, as we have already hinted, is the suggestion that an oral premarital agreement to convert to Judaism authorizes a judge to enjoin a parent to raise the child in that faith.

American society is frequently described as being diverse in religions. Many of the earliest settlements in the new world were designed as havens for dissenters from religious orthodoxy. Although one or more of the early colonies could accurately be described as theocracies, later settlers came from differing, often opposing, religious backgrounds. By the time of our revolutionary war, religious diversity was a fact of colonial life. Thus, it is no accident that the very first in our Bill of Rights protected the free exercise of religion and barred the government from establishing or supporting any particular religion.

The freedom to choose any religion necessarily comprehends the freedom to change religions. Great changes in religious beliefs by individuals are a feature of Western history; e.g., Saul of Tarsus on the road to Damascus; Constantine and the cross in the sky; Martin Luther and the cathedral door at Worms, to cite a few. We would reduce the right to the free exercise of religion by half if we did not recognize the right to change one's religious mind. At the same time, moreover, the momentous events of a life may bring one to question one's religious views, and the parental aspirations of women and men often evolve after the birth of a child.

We recognize that a person contemplating marriage may properly agree with a prospective spouse on many subjects. Certainly, the law will enforce any such bargain so long as it is not against public policy. We have grave doubts, however, that the law could or should enforce an unwritten premarriage agreement to raise a child in one faith or the other. These doubts are intensified when the parent to be compelled later suffers, as here, a genuine, good faith change of religious conscience.

Quite apart from the obvious human willingness to promise anything when one is in the throes of romantic passion and urgent to commit to marriage, we are concerned about the implications of judges using their contempt powers to preclude a custodial parent whose marriage is being dissolved from doing anything to influence the religious training of a child inconsistently with the faith of the other parent. In this case, the order is even more involved in the free exercise of religion in that it commands the custodial parent to do everything in her power to promote, as it were, a religious belief in the child that the parent is conscience stricken against.

There is no provision in our laws purporting to authorize such judicial enforcement in married parents. In a dissolution of marriage action, the court's powers as to matters relating to the custody of minor children are found in section 61.13(2) and (3), Florida Statutes (1993). . . . Section 61.13 commands parents to confer on all major decisions affecting the welfare of their child and to reach an agreement as to any required decision. When the matter involves the religious training and beliefs of the child, we do not agree that the court may make a decision in favor of a specific religion over the objection of the other parent. . . .

## Notes and Questions

1. With the increasing incidence of intermarriage, courts frequently adjudicate custody disputes regarding children's religious upbringing. Courts take one of three approaches: (1) religion may be one, but not the sole or dominant, factor; (2) religion may be considered only to the extent that it affects the child's secular well-being; or, (3) religion may be considered only for children with ascertainable religious preferences or for whom religion has become an important part of their identity. See

Donald L. Beschle, God Bless the Child?: The Use of Religion as a Factor in Child Custody and Adoption Proceedings, 58 Fordham L. Rev. 383, 398-404 (1989). See generally Carl E. Schneider, Religion and Child Custody, 25 U. Mich. J.L. Reform 879 (1992); Annotation, Religion as Factor in Child Custody and Visitation Cases, 22 A.L.R.4th 971 (1983 & Supp. 1996).

2. Judicial consideration of religion is constrained by constitutional guarantees. According to the First Amendment's Free Exercise Clause, the court may not interfere with a parent's right to practice his or her religion (or not to practice religion). Under the Establishment Clause (requiring separation between church and state and forbidding excessive government entanglement with religion), a court may not weigh the relative merits of parents' religions or favor an observant parent over a nonreligious one. How can judges adjudicate parental disputes without violating these guarantees? Should courts follow a policy of noninterference? See Osteraas v. Osteraas, 859 P.2d 948, 952 (Idaho 1993). What compelling interest might justify interference?

3. In a survey of more than 50 custody cases, one commentator found that courts frequently consider parents' religious beliefs and practices by endorsing one parent's religious training over either the other's lack of training or the other's religious training. In so doing, she continues, "[M]any courts violate the free exercise rights of at least one of the custody contestants and risk violating the Establishment Clause." Jennifer Ann Drobac, Note, For the Sake of the Children: Court Consideration of Religion in Child Custody Cases, 50 Stan. L. Rev. 1609, 1611 (1998). Drobak also found that, in evaluating the effect of religious beliefs and practices, courts use different standards of harm, i.e., actual harm, substantial threat of harm, or some risk of harm. According to Drobac, only the actual harm standard passes constitutional muster. Id. at 1631-1640.

4. What is the appropriate balance between constitutional rights and private ordering, as in *Abbo*, for example, when the parents have a premarital agreement regarding children's religious upbringing? With *Abbo*, compare LeDoux v. LeDoux, 452 N.W.2d 1 (Neb. 1990), and Zummo v. Zummo, 574 A.2d 1130 (Pa. Super. Ct. 1990). Does judicial enforcement of the parental agreement constitute excessive entanglement in religion? See generally Jocelyn E. Strauber, Note, A Deal Is a Deal: Antenuptial Agreements Regarding the Religious Upbringing of Children Should Be Enforceable, 47 Duke L.J. 971 (1998).

5. Mental health professionals Joseph Goldstein, Anna Freud, and Albert J. Solnit advocate a policy of judicial deference to the wishes of the custodial parent in the interests of stability. See Joseph Goldstein et al., Beyond the Best Interests of the Child 38 (1973). Is this a sound solution to the resolution of parents' religious disputes?

6. Although a court may not favor one parent's religion, it may examine the effect of that religion on the child. What risks are relevant?

Physical harm from discipline based on religious beliefs? See, e.g., Varnum v. Varnum, 586 A.2d 1107 (Vt. 1990). How serious must the risk be? Death? Emotional harm? See Quiner v. Quiner, 59 Cal. Rptr. 503 (Ct. App. 1967). Must the harm be actual or merely anticipated? See Osier v. Osier, 410 A.2d 1027 (Me. 1980) (immediate and substantial). If emotional harm is relevant, how can a court be certain that the harm derives from the religious practices rather than the parental conflict? In the evaluation, might adherents of minority religions face a disadvantage? See Carolyn R. Wah, Religion in Child Custody and Visitation Cases: Presenting the Advantage of Religious Participation, 28 Fam. L.Q. 269, 278 (1994).

7. Are religious disputes always harmful to children? See Felton v. Felton, 418 N.E.2d 606, 607-608 (Mass. 1981) (suggesting that "a diversity of religious experience is itself a sound stimulant for a child").

8. If a court adjudicates a dispute about religious upbringing, how should it enforce its decision? Can a court monitor compliance without violating the constitution by becoming entangled in religious dogma? What penalty should the court impose for violations of the order? What are the implications of such judicial involvement for family privacy? See Schneider, supra, at 903-904.

9. *ALI.* The American Law Institute's Principles of the Law of Family Dissolution prohibit a court from considering the "religious practices" of either the parent or child in custody decisionmaking except in the following situations: (a) if the religious practices present "severe and almost certain harm" to the child (and then a court may limit the religious practices only to the minimum degree necessary to protect the child), or (b) if necessary to protect the child's ability to practice a religion "that has been a significant part of the child's life." ALI Principles §212(1)(c) (2002).

## Problem

When Jeffrey (who is Christian) marries Barbara (who is Jewish), they agree to raise their children as Jews. After the birth of their second child, Jeffrey becomes a member of a fundamentalist Christian faith whose adherents believe that non-members are damned to hell. As a result, Jeffrey makes serious efforts to persuade his children to accept his church's teachings. After the birth of their third child, Barbara adopts Orthodox Judaism and the couple becomes enmeshed in "opposite doctrinal extremes." When the parents file for divorce, both seek custody. Barbara seeks to limit the children's exposure to Jeffrey's religion. The court awards joint legal custody but forbids Jeffrey from exposing the children to religious content that will cause them to feel upset or to worry about themselves or their mother. Barbara appeals the joint custody award, asserting that it is inappropriate because the parents cannot come to any agreement on the children's moral and religious development.

What result? Based on the standard adopted in this jurisdiction, would exposure to the father's religion cause "substantial physical or emotional injury" to the children and have a "similar harmful tendency for the future"? What evidence would suffice to establish substantial harm? Is limiting the children's exposure to Jeffrey's religion appropriate? Does the limitation constitute an invasion of privacy? See Kendall v. Kendall, 687 N.E.2d 1228 (Mass. 1997).

*(iii) Fitness*

(1) Sexual Orientation

## ■ DELONG v. DELONG
*1998 WL 15536 (Mo. Ct. App. 1998)*

ULRICH, Chief Judge, Presiding Judge.

. . . Mother and Father were married in June 1985. At the time of the wedding, Mother was 24 years old and beginning her career as a school teacher with an annual income of $13,000. Father was 36 years old and a full-time attorney with his own practice and an average annual income of $80,000. Father was the primary custodian of a son, Joseph DeLong IV, born of a previous marriage.

As a condition of the marriage, Father asked Mother to submit to a psychological evaluation by his psychologist. The stated purpose of the evaluation was to test the parties' compatibility for marriage. During a meeting with the psychologist, Mother revealed that she was sexually attracted to both men and women and that she had engaged in sexual activity with women in the past. Despite these revelations, and based on Mother's expressed commitment to a monogamous relationship, Father was satisfied with Mother's psychological profile. . . .

Three minor children were born of the union: Morgan, born May 25, 1986, Kelsey, born February 23, 1988, and Chase, born April 6, 1990. Mother primarily stayed at home to care for Joseph, who is Father's son, and the three younger children. Father eventually became the principal shareholder and CEO of DeLong's, Inc., the family's bridge-steel fabrication business.

In March 1994, Mother filed a petition for dissolution of marriage in Boone County requesting that her marriage to Father be dissolved, that joint legal custody of the minor children be awarded to her and Father, and that she be designated the primary physical custodian of the children. . . . Father filed an answer [and requested the court dissolve his marriage and] award sole custody of the children to him with restricted visitation to Mother. . . .

At trial, the parties introduced evidence regarding their parental skills and their relationship with the children. Both parties presented custody evaluation reports prepared by psychologists and psychiatrists recommending custody awards.

Evidence was also presented that Mother engaged in homosexual conduct and involved herself in extramarital affairs with women during the marriage. She admitted to two sexual relationships and another brief nonsexual relationship with women beginning in 1991 after concluding that her marriage was irreparable. She also testified to having engaged in sexual conduct with another woman after she and Father separated. Mother testified that all of her sexual encounters were discreet and that the children did not know of the nature of the relationships, although they knew the women as friends of their mother. Father testified that he also had an extramarital sexual relationship with a woman after separation. . . .

The trial court entered its decree of dissolution in April 1996 dissolving the DeLongs' marriage and awarding sole custody of the three minor children to Father. It found that joint custody would not be appropriate and that the children's best interests would be met if they were in their father's custody. In making these findings, the court cited Mother's engagement "in a promiscuous series of four homosexual affairs," her repeated denial and concealment of "her adulterous lesbian activity," her intention to continue "exposing her lesbian lovers to her children," and her "immaturity in seeking after repeated new love relationships." The trial court also restricted Mother's visitation with the children [by ordering her to refrain from having present during visitation any person known by her to be a lesbian or any other female with whom Mother may be living]. The trial court further directed the guardian ad litem to monitor a "telling" session wherein Mother was to tell the two older children that "she is homosexual.". . .

[On appeal, Mother] argues that the court's rulings regarding custody and visitation were not based on the best interests of the children but solely on the fact that "she is homosexual." Mother alleges that instead of a focus on the best interests of the children, "the courtroom became a battleground in which sexual orientation was the principal issue" and that Father and the guardian ad litem became obsessed with dissecting her sexual life, "uncovering every detail of any kiss, touch or other intimate contact she may have engaged in with a member of the same sex.". . .

In Missouri, a court determines custody in a dissolution action in accordance with the best interests of the child. . . . Missouri courts generally deem a good environment and stable home the single most important, relevant consideration in custody matters. Thus, the character, conduct, behavior, morals, and mode of life of the parents are proper considerations for a trial court in awarding custody. . . .

A custody award should not be a reward or punishment of either parent; custody of a minor child is made in the best interests of the child. The issue is not condemnation or approval of a parent's behavior or a moral standard but whether the conduct in question is detrimental to the child's welfare. A parent's behavior, therefore, must affect the child's welfare before it is relevant in a custody dispute. Adultery, promiscuity, or sexual misconduct, while generally condemned by courts, is insufficient, standing alone, to deem a parent an unfit custodian of the parent's child if unaccompanied by evidence that the conduct adversely affected the child. . . .

Considerations in a custody dispute of a parent's moral or sexual activities are not limited to conduct that has detrimentally affected the child. Evidence that a parent's conduct may be expected to have an adverse effect on the child is also considered. Likewise, evidence that a parent's inappropriate conduct may inspire by example or foster by condonation must be considered.

Despite the best interests of the child standard, which requires a fact-based assessment of all factors relevant to the child's welfare, Missouri courts appear to apply a *"per se* rule" in awarding custody where one parent is homosexual. The *per se* rule establishes an irrefutable presumption that a parent who engages in homosexual behavior is unfit to be custodian of his or her child. Without assessing the fitness of the parent who engages in homosexual conduct, the possible unfitness of the parent who does not engage in homosexual conduct, the relationship between each parent and the child, the effect of homosexual conduct on the child, or any other factor relevant to the child's welfare, Missouri courts presume that "placing primary custody of a minor child with the nonhomosexual parent is in the best interests of the child." S.L.H. v. D.B.H., 745 S.W.2d 848, 849 (Mo. App. E.D. 1988).

Since 1980, Missouri appellate courts have decided seven cases involving homosexual conduct and child custody and visitation. [citations omitted]. In all cases, the trial court's award of custody to the heterosexual parent and restrictions on the homosexual parent's visitation rights have been upheld. . . .

To the extent that Missouri case law automatically presumes that a homosexual parent is *per se* unfit to be custodian of his or her child, it is not followed in this case. Such an irrefutable presumption, where a parent's homosexual conduct is, alone, determinative, is inherently inconsistent with the best interests of the child standard, which requires consideration of *all* factors relevant to the child's welfare. In fact, focusing a custody determination on a parent's homosexual conduct, alone, may permit a decision contrary to the best interests of the child in a case where the characteristics of the heterosexual parent are undesirable or possibly harmful. A *per se* approach necessarily ignores the heterosexual parent's fitness to be custodian, and the application of this approach could conceivably result in an award of custody to the heterosexual parent without any evidence regarding his or her inappropriate heterosexual conduct or parenting skills.

Accordingly, a nexus approach is adopted in custody cases involving the issue of a parent's sexual conduct. Under this approach, a connection, or nexus, between a parent's sexual conduct, homosexual or heterosexual, and harm to the child must be established before the parent's sexual conduct is considered relevant to the custody determination. The relevant issue under this approach is not the nature of the parent's sexual activity but whether that activity adversely affects the child. Application of a nexus approach in these cases is consistent with the best interests of the child standard. . . .

Generalizations regarding the possible impact a parent's sexual conduct outside the presence of a child may have on a child are impermissible. Likewise, the disapproval of morals or other personal characteristics, without evidence of how the morals or characteristics adversely impact the child, should not be used to determine the fitness of a parent to care for a child. Pronouncement of a nexus approach is not a comment on whether homosexuality is condoned by this court or community. Rather, it is meant to reconcile custody determinations involving a homosexual parent with the best interests of the child standard. . . .

In the present case, the trial court focused primarily on Mother's homosexual conduct in awarding custody of the children to Father. While evidence was presented regarding the nature of Mother's sexual conduct, no evidence was introduced regarding whether or how it affects the children. The children were unaware of Mother's sexual preference, and Mother never engaged in any sexual or affectionate behavior in the presence of the children. The trial court's order did not include findings that Mother's homosexual conduct harmed or may harm the children. . . .

Although the trial court cited the best interests of the child standard and discussed Father's fitness to be custodian, the court's reliance on Mother's homosexual conduct, absent evidence of the impact such conduct had or may have on the children, was controlling. The order is devoid of discussion of the detrimental effects Mother's homosexual conduct is causing the children now or that can reasonably be anticipated in the future. The trial court, therefore, misapplied the law in awarding custody and restricting visitation based on Mother's homosexual conduct absent evidence of its impact on the children. Accordingly, the custody and visitation award is reversed, and the case is remanded to the trial court for the reception of additional evidence, if any, regarding the effect Mother's homosexual conduct has or may have on the children and for consideration of all factors relevant to the children's welfare. . . .

# Notes and Questions

1. *Epilogue.* The case was transferred to the Missouri Supreme Court. That court affirmed the award of sole custody to the husband. The court reasoned that although a homosexual parent is not per se unfit for custody, it was not error for the trial court to consider the effect of the mother's conduct on the children. The court held further that the trial court erred in restricting visitation so broadly, and therefore approved restrictions only as to those individuals whose "presence and conduct" might be contrary to the children's best interests (rather than all lesbians). The court also refused to review the appropriateness of the trial court order requiring the mother to disclose her homosexuality to the daughters, finding that the issue was mooted because the mother already had made this disclosure. J.A.D. v. F.J.D., 978 S.W.2d 336, 340 (Mo. 1998).

2. *Sexual conduct generally.* A threshold consideration in the determination of the best interests is parental fitness. The focus on fitness traditionally gives considerable weight to extramarital sexual conduct.[13] In the fault era, sexual immorality in the form of adultery or cohabitation often resulted in custodial denials because courts deemed the "guilty party" unfit.[14] Within the past few decades, dramatic changes in social mores have had an impact on custody law. Under the modern view, influenced by the Uniform Marriage and Divorce Act (UMDA), a parent's sexual conduct is relevant to custody determinations only if the conduct has an adverse effect on the child. See UMDA §402, supra page 810. How would *DeLong* be decided under UMDA?

Does judicial consideration of sexual conduct reflect gender bias? In Boles v. Boles, 558 So. 2d 710, 712 (La. Ct. App. 1990), the court approved a change to sole custody by the father, stating: "[The mother's] moral fitness must be assessed in the light of the fact that just three weeks after she met [a new man] she went to Michigan . . . to live with him for six months before marrying him." Id. at 712. The court noted without comment that the father had recently married his fourth wife. Id. at 711. See generally Cynthia A. McNeely, Lagging Behind the Times: Parenthood, Custody, and Gender Bias in the Family Court, 5 Fla. St. U. L. Rev. 891 (1998).

Some courts evaluate sexual conduct (especially the mother's) based on whether the parent has legitimized that conduct (that is, by

---

[13]. See generally Katheryn Katz & Maris Warfman, Custody Disputes Between Parents, in 2 Child Custody and Visitation Law and Practice §10.09 (Sandra Morgan Little, ed., 2000). See also Diane M. Allen, Annotation, Propriety of Provision of Custody or Visitation Order Designed to Insulate Child from Parent's Extramarital Sexual Relationships, 40 A.L.R.4th 812 (1985 & Supp. 2000).

[14]. See, e.g., Jarrett v. Jarrett, 400 N.E.2d 421 (Ill. 1979); Beck v. Beck, 120 N.W.2d 585 (Neb. 1963).

remarriage). See, e.g., In re Marriage of Cripe, 538 N.E.2d 1175 (Ill. App. Ct. 1989). Also, some courts are less tolerant of women in non-monogamous relationships. See, e.g., Boykin v. Boykin, 370 S.E.2d 884, 886 (S.C. Ct. App. 1988) (awarding father custody because mother's relationships with five men during one year were "flagrant promiscuity").

3. *Homosexual conduct.* Sexual conduct with members of the same sex is more likely to lead to denials (or changes) of custody. Available data suggest that significant numbers of homosexuals are parents.[15] Prior to the 1970s, few homosexuals prevailed in custody cases.[16]

Currently, courts take one of three approaches toward homosexual parents. Some courts find homosexuality to be evidence of unfitness per se. See, e.g., Jacobson v. Jacobson, 314 N.W.2d 78 (N.D. 1981); Roe v. Roe, 324 S.E.2d 691 (Va. 1985).[17] Other courts presume adverse impact and require that the parent prove the absence of harm. See, e.g., Thigpen v. Carpenter, 730 S.W.2d 510 (Ark. 1987). Still other courts, the emerging consensus,[18] deny custody only on proof that the parent's sexual orientation has, or will have, an adverse impact on the child. See, e.g., A.C. v. C.B., 829 P.2d 660 (N.M. Ct. App. 1992). This last approach is termed "the nexus test."

4. *ALI.* The ALI Principles of the Law of Family Dissolution prohibit a court from considering either the sexual orientation or the extramarital sexual conduct of a parent except upon a showing that such conduct causes harm to the child. ALI Principles §2.12(1)(d) (sexual orientation) & (e) (extramarital sexual conduct) (2002).

5. Could a homosexual partner ever meet the requisite moral "fitness" standard given that, at the present time, gay and lesbian partners are not permitted to marry?

6. What showing of harm suffices under the nexus test? Emotional harm? Teasing? See, e.g., Doe v. Doe, 452 N.E.2d 293 (Mass. App. Ct. 1983). Is potential harm sufficient? See Pulliam v. Smith, 501 S.E.2d 898, 904 (N.C. 1998). May the court take into account the "social condemnation" accorded to homosexuality? See Bottoms v. Bottoms, 457 S.E.2d

---

[15]. "Between eight and fourteen million children are being raised in homes headed by a lesbian or gay parent. Most of these children are the product of a heterosexual marriage that ended in divorce — with a lesbian or gay parent's 'coming out' or a parent's post-dissolution announcement of a lesbian or gay sexual orientation." Kathryn Kendell, The Custody Challenge: Debunking Myths About Lesbian and Gay Parents and Their Children, 20 Fam. Advoc. 21, 21 (1997).

[16]. Rhonda P. Rivera, Queer Law: Sexual Orientation Law in the Mid-Eighties, 11 U. Dayton L. Rev. 275, 335 (1986).

[17]. Some courts, while they will not deny custody to a homosexual parent, will use it as a reason to select joint custody over sole custody to the homosexual parent. See, e.g., Lundin v. Lundin, 563 So. 2d 1273 (La. Ct. App. 1990).

[18]. Stephen B. Pershing, "Entreat Me Not to Leave Thee": *Bottoms v. Bottoms* and the Custody Rights of Gay and Lesbian Parents, 3 Wm. & Mary Bill Rts. J. 289, 308 (1994).

102, 108 (Va. 1995); Jacoby v. Jacoby, 763 So. 2d 410, 413 (2000). Is harm to the child more likely because a parent is "out" or "in the closet"? See, e.g., Ex Parte J.M.F., 730 So. 2d 1190 (Ala. 1998) (holding that trial court acted within its discretion in modifying custody to husband based on change in wife's lesbian relationship from a discreet affair to a more open relationship).

7. What role do common beliefs about homosexual parents play? Beliefs include: (1) children raised thereby are more likely to become homosexual; (2) a homosexual parent is more likely to molest the child; and (3) children of homosexual parents suffer stigma from peers and the community.[19]

Are these assumptions supported by empirical evidence? Studies of children of gay and lesbian parents uniformly conclude that a parent's sexual orientation is not determinative of the child's sexual preference.[20] Evidence also reveals that child molestation is generally heterosexual in nature.[21] Finally, evidence suggests that peer pressure may not be a significant problem.[22] See generally Mary Becker, Maternal Feelings: Myth, Taboo, and Child Custody, 1 S. Cal. Rev. L. & Women's Stud. 133, 182-183 (1992) (discussing research on lesbian mothers).

8. A heated debate in the legal literature concerns the effects of parents' sexual orientation on children's psychological development. Professor Lynn Wardle contends that the pro-gay bias of researchers taints research findings. Lynn D. Wardle, The Potential Impact of Homosexual Parenting on Children, 1997 U. Ill. L. Rev. 833. He suggests that parents' sexual orientation may be harmful to children and argues that the law should reflect a rebuttable presumption that parenting by homosexuals is not in children's best interests.

[19]. David Cramer, Gay Parents and Their Children: A Review of Research and Practical Implications, 64 J. Counseling & Dev. 504, 504-505 (1986); Note, Custody Denials to Parents in Same-Sex Relationships: An Equal Protection Analysis, 102 Harv. L. Rev. 617, 630-635 (1989).

[20]. See, e.g., Julie Gottman, Children of Gay and Lesbian Parents, in Homosexuality and Family Relations 177, 189 (Frederick W. Bozett & Marvin B. Sussman eds., 1990); Susan Golombok & Fiona Tasker, Do Parents Influence the Sexual Orientation of Their Children? Findings from a Longitudinal Study of Lesbian Families, 32 Dev. Psychol. 3 (1996). See also Charlotte J. Patterson, Children of Lesbian and Gay Parents, 63 Child Dev. 1025 (1992) (review of research).

[21]. An early classic study points out that most sexual child abuse is perpetrated on girls by fathers and stepfathers. See Vincent DeFrancis, Protecting the Child Victim of Sex Crimes Committed by Adults 33 (1969).

[22]. See, e.g., Mary Hotvedt & Jane Barclay Mandel, Children of Lesbian Mothers, in Homosexuality: Social, Psychological, and Biological Issues 275, 282 (W. Paul et al. eds., 1982); Sharon L. Huggins, A Comparative Study of Self-Esteem of Adolescent Children of Divorced Lesbian Mothers and Divorced Heterosexual Mothers, in Homosexuality and the Family 123, 132 (Frederick W. Bozett ed., 1989); Susan Golombok et al., Children in Lesbian and Single-Parent Households: Psychosexual and Psychiatric Appraisal, 24 J. Child Psychol. & Psychiatry 551, 565-567 (1983).

In rebuttal, Carlos Ball and Janice Pea disagree that research suggests that parents' sexual orientation harms children. They contend that Wardle's presumption poses practical, normative, and constitutional problems. They argue that parenting ability rather than sexual orientation should be determinative in decisionmaking. Carlos A. Ball & Janice Farrell Pea, Warring with Wardle: Morality, Social Science, and Gay and Lesbian Parents, 1998 U. Ill. L. Rev. 253 (rebuttal). See also Lynn D. Wardle, Fighting with Phantoms: A Reply to Warring with Wardle, 1998 U. Ill. L. Rev. 629 (surrebuttal).

Two sociologists recently have also entered the fray. After identifying methodological and analytical limitations in existing research, Judith Stacey and Timothy Biblarz challenge the predominant finding that sexual orientation of parents plays no role in child development. Instead, they find some differences: (1) children of same-sex parents develop in less gender-stereotypical ways; (2) their experiences give them greater sensitivity, empathy for social diversity, and capacity to express feelings (because same-sex parents tend to be older, more educated, and self-aware than heterosexual couples); and (3) such children grow up more open to same-sex relationships themselves. Although Stacey and Biblarz disagree that differences are nonexistent, they believe that such differences fail to justify discrimination on the basis of sexual orientation. Judith Stacey & Timothy J. Biblarz, (How) Does the Sexual Orientation of Parents Matter, 66 Am. Soc. Rev. 159 (April 2001).

9. *Constitutional issues.* Do custody denials to gay and lesbian parents pose constitutional issues? Is *Palmore* applicable? Compare S.N.E. v. R.L.B., 699 P.2d 875, 879 (Alaska 1985) (applying *Palmore* to find impermissible the use of real or imagined stigma as a reason for denying custody), with S.E.G. v. R.A.G., 735 S.W.2d 164, 166 (Mo. Ct. App. 1987) (finding *Palmore* inapplicable because homosexuality is not afforded the same constitutional protection as race).

10. *Comparative-law issues.* Several European countries with domestic partnership legislation recognize same-sex partnerships but, nonetheless, disapprove of lesbian and gay parenting. Professor Nancy Polikoff points out reasons for the divergent paths of law reform between some American states and these European countries: European countries are more motivated to ensure equal access to economic security for their lesbian and gay citizens, and domestic adoptions are less frequent in Europe. She notes that this European policy "continues to send, at best, a mixed message about the value of gay and lesbian couples as parents." Nancy D. Polikoff, Recognizing Partners But Not Parents: Gay and Lesbian Family Law in Europe and the United States, 17 N.Y.L. Sch. J. Hum. Rts. 711, 751 (2000).

11. With the increasing incidence of AIDS in the gay male community, fear of HIV infection sometimes becomes an issue in custody disputes. See infra page 857. On fitness of gay and lesbian parents in adoption, see Chapter IX.

(2) Careers

## ■ ROWE v. FRANKLIN
### 663 N.E.2d 955 (Ohio Ct. App. 1995)

GORMAN, Judge:

Appellant, Kimberly Rowe ("mother"), appeals the trial court's decision designating appellee, Donald J. Franklin ("father"), the residential parent and legal guardian of their then five-year-old son. . . .

The parties were married on July 25, 1987. On February 20, 1988, their son was born. In December of 1991, the mother left the marital residence with the child and filed a complaint for divorce. . . . [Each parent requested sole custody.] During May 1992, with the father's knowledge, the mother moved to Versailles, Kentucky, for what she expected to be a short time. She stated that the move was made to be closer to her job as a part-time pilot for the U.S. Army so she could increase her flying time and earn more money. During this same time, she was attending law school, after having earned a four-year degree in international affairs and business and having taken some graduate business classes. . . . The father, an ironworker, was unemployed during that summer.

[The trial court order required that neither parent remove the child from the state without a court order or parental agreement.] On September 10, 1993, the mother filed a motion to modify the court's order to allow her to remove the child to Versailles, Kentucky, and to establish his residence there. She had applied to take classes through the University of Kentucky Law School in July and had become pregnant sometime in May by a man whom she had begun seeing in March, and who was married but separated from his wife. In August she enrolled her son in a private school for the times she would attend law school classes. In response to her motion, the father filed an emergency motion for contempt and for return of the child to Ohio. The trial court denied her motion, held the father's contempt motion in abeyance, and allowed the child to remain with the mother until the completion of a previously ordered custody investigation.

Dr. Cynthia Dember completed a psychological evaluation on May 1, 1992. Parenting specialist Jayne Zuberbuhler completed a pre-decree parenting report on February 18, 1993. . . . Dr. Dember and Ms. Zuberbuhler, while finding both parents adequate, ultimately recommended custody of the child be given to the father. [The trial court awarded custody to the father, and the mother appealed.]

In determining which parent should have custody of a minor child in a divorce proceeding, the trial court is bound to consider the best interests of the child. R.C. 3109.04(F). . . . Concern for a child's well-being or best interests does not, however, provide the court carte blanche to judge the rights and lifestyles of parents by nonstatutory codes of moral or social values. Although a court is not obligated to wear blinders as to a parent's lifestyle and/or morals, including sexual conduct, any state interest in competing lifestyles and accompanying moral values which affect child custody would most equitably be served if limited to a determination of the direct or probable effect of parental conduct on the physical, mental, emotional, and social development of the child, as opposed to a determination of which lifestyle choices made by a parent are "correct." In a society as diverse as the one in which we live a court is ill-equipped to determine which of such choices are "correct." . . .

We first note that the trial court, using the factors enumerated in R.C. 3109.04(F)(1), concluded that both parents had taken a proper parental interest in the child, that the child was very much attached to both parents, that the child interacted appropriately with both parents, that both parents loved and nurtured the child, and that interference with either relationship could hurt the child. The trial court also determined that the child had bonded with his step-brother, had a good relationship with the mother's male companion, and was doing well in the Kentucky school. Even so, the trial court determined that the child should be removed from the mother and custody granted to the father.

The error in the analysis by which the trial court reached its conclusion, however, is apparent from its comparison of the mother's living situation with the father's. The trial court stated that for the first three years of the child's life,

> [u]ntil Dec. 1991, the child lived in the marital residence which is presently occupied by [father]. He is most familiar with the surroundings, the neighborhood, the people in the neighborhood, etc. [The child] has roots in his home in Cincinnati and but for his mother's move to Kentucky, it appears that his home would be one of stability. He has family here both maternal and paternal. He has friends here. He has friends of both parents who care for him here. The only adjustment necessary for [the child] here is that his mother would not be here.

By contrast, the trial court concluded that the mother and the child did not have substantial roots in the Kentucky community, stating it had not been provided with much information regarding that community. The record, however, belies this contention. Uncontested information was available that: the mother had been working in Kentucky for several years, that she had many friends there that she had met at work, that her son was friendly with and associated with her friends' children, that her son had adapted to the school he attended and had friends there, that the child had friends in the neighborhood with whom he played, and that he attended soccer and karate classes in Kentucky.

The trial court then "thoroughly examine[d]" the child's adjustment to his new home. . . . The record does not support the trial court's finding that the home, the mother's work or her school schedule has required "tremendous" adjustment by the child, nor does it indicate what will necessitate future adjustment. . . .

The trial court stated that it had no concerns about either parent's mental health. It found the father to be stable. . . . In contrast it found that the mother made decisions that caused the court to question her stability. Included in these "questionable" decisions were the many moves she made prior to her current situation, the move to Kentucky, and the sudden and complete relationship with her new male companion and the resulting pregnancy. The trial court deemed that these were not decisions in the best interest of the child and concluded that appellant placed her needs before the child's needs.

The trial court failed to recognize that the moves were precipitated by the father refusing, upon advice of counsel, to move from the marital residence, thus forcing the mother to leave the marital residence with the child, if she desired to terminate the marriage, and to live with the child in a variety of makeshift homes for a short transitional period. It entirely discounted how the father's decision subjected the child to changes in the environment. . . .

In examining the parties' commitment to the child, a nonstatutory *factor*, the trial court concluded that

> [p]ersonal accomplishments and career goals are obviously worthwhile undertakings. To accomplish what Ms. Rowe has as far as academics is concerned is very commendable. However this court perceives that this child has paid a price. The evidence has shown that Ms. Rowe returned to a full-time law school curriculum when the child was three (3) weeks old. Ms. Rowe returned to her job with the Kentucky National Guard when the child was six (6) weeks old. Ms. Rowe's time to nurture the child has been limited tremendously as she pursues other matters. The Court is cognizant of the time [the child] has spent with babysitters and at child care. In summation, this Court questions the priorities of Ms. Rowe. The *number of poor choices made by Ms. Rowe as to the best interests of [the child] coupled with her personal agenda* indicates to this court that she may not be as committed to [the child's] best interests as she should be.

(Emphasis added.)

The transcript of the mother's law school classes contained in the record indicates that she did not start law school until the fall of 1990 when the child was over two years old. It was at that time that the child received day-care supervision. She had returned to school earlier to continue the coursework necessary to obtain her undergraduate degree the spring semester of 1988 and began taking graduate courses primarily in the evening the following fall. The child was attended to by the parents, family or friends during this period of time. The record shows that the mother did not return to flying until the child was approximately eight months old. . . .

Although pursuing his career and designated as the primary financial support for the family, the father was deemed by the trial court to be dedicated to the well-being of his child and to have a "willingness to be *a good and proper parent.*" (Emphasis added.)

The trial court also considered the mother's relationship with her male companion and concluded that he appeared to be a "good, dedicated individual." [However,] [t]he trial court did not like that the mother became sexually involved with a man so soon after the breakup of both of their marriages and expressed concern that her companion could handle the stress of so many changes in his life. There is a total absence of evidence in the record to suggest that the mother's relationship had any unfavorable effect on the child, or to support the trial judge's concerns. . . .

Although the trial court explicitly stated that the best interest of the child was its primary consideration, the plain meaning of its reasons in reality constitute use of a "reproval of the mother" test. Therefore, we conclude that the trial court abused its discretion by its reliance on an erroneous standard to justify the designation of the residential parent. [W]e reverse the trial court's judgment and remand this cause for further proceedings in accordance with this Opinion.

## Notes and Questions

1. Today, many divorced mothers work outside the home.[23] Maternal employment sometimes plays a role in the application of the best interests standard. Courts have denied custody to mothers who were medical students, architects, nurses, and brokers, among others. See Burchard v. Garay, 724 P.2d 486 (Cal. 1986) (reversing custody denial to nurse); Lewis v. Lewis, 219 N.W.2d 910 (Neb. 1974) (custody denial to medical student); Fitzsimmons v. Fitzsimmons, 722 P.2d 671 (N.M. Ct. App. 1986) (reversing custody denial to architect); Hansen v. Hansen, 327 N.W.2d 47 (S.D. 1982) (custody denial to broker). A number of cases, similar to *Rowe*, involve women lawyers. See, e.g., Prost v. Greene, 652 A.2d 621 (D.C. 1995); Young v. Hector, 740 So. 2d 1153 (Fla. Dist. Ct. App. 1998), *rev'd en banc* (1999).

2. What are the conflicting role expectations for working mothers versus fathers? What gender stereotypes underlie custody determinations involving working mothers? Might the working mother be perceived as a "bad mother"? See generally Amy D. Ronner, Women Who

---

[23]. Approximately 80 percent of divorced mothers work. Kingsley Davis, Wives and Work: A Theory of the Sex-Role Revolution and Its Consequences, in Feminism, Children, and the New Families 67, 81 (Sanford M. Dornbusch & Myra H. Strober eds., 1988).

Dance on the Professional Track: Custody and the Red Shoes, 23 Harv. Women's L.J. 173 (2000).

In the nineteenth century, women who sought careers were ridiculed as deviant and mentally unstable. See Barbara Ehrenreich & Deirdre English, For Her Own Good: 150 Years of the Experts' Advice to Women 147-148 (1989). How does the *Rowe* trial court evaluate Mrs. Rowe's stability?

3. *Empirical research.* Survey data also substantiate the existence of gender stereotypes in judicial attitudes toward working women. One study reports that half of judges express such stereotypical beliefs as "[m]others should be home when their school-age children get home from school"; and, "[a] preschool child is likely to suffer if his/her mother works." Report of the Gender Bias Study of the Supreme Judicial Court, Commonwealth of Massachusetts 63 (1989).

4. Must working mothers be "supermoms" to prevail in custody disputes? Some commentators believe so. See Lisa Genasci, Working Mothers at Risk in Custody Disputes; Divorce: Scholars Say Courts Often Hold Women to Higher Parenting Standards than Their Ex-Spouses, L.A. Times, Mar. 5, 1995, at A8. Are mothers who work irregular schedules at a disadvantage? See, e.g., Kerkhoff v. Kerkhoff, 400 N.W.2d 752 (Minn. Ct. App. 1987) (awarding custody to father because waitress-mother works nights and is absent at times to play in traveling band).

5. What role should a working mother's day care arrangements play? How did the trial court in *Rowe* assess this factor? In a much-publicized case, an appellate court overturned a custody award to a father that was influenced by day care arrangements. The father's mother could care for the child full-time in her home while the child's mother, a university student, relied on day care. See Ireland v. Smith, 542 N.W.2d 344 (Mich. Ct. App. 1995), *aff'd,* 547 N.W.2d 686 (Mich. 1996). See also Burchard v. Garay, 724 P.2d 486 (Cal. 1986).

Controversy about the effects of day care on children dates to the 1970s when an increasing number of mothers entered the work force. Early studies warned of the likelihood of insecure attachment and cognitive deficits in day care children, especially those placed as infants. More comprehensive recent research from the National Institute of Child Health and Human Development that compares a variety of day care facilities has not substantiated such concerns. See Gwen J. Broude, The Realities of Day Care, Public Interest, Sept. 1, 1996, at 95. See also Susan Faludi, Backlash: The Undeclared War Against American Women 41-45 (1991) (discussing role of backlash against working women in myths that day care poses high risk of child abuse and developmental problems).

6. *Wealth as a factor.* What weight, if any, should be given to a parent's superior earning capacity? Generally, the relative wealth of the parties is not decisive unless one parent is unable to provide adequately for the child. See In re Custody of Pearce, 456 A.2d 597 (Pa. Super. Ct.

1983). Although not a decisive factor, should wealth be a relevant factor? See generally Carolyn J. Frantz, Note, Eliminating Consideration of Parental Wealth in Post-Divorce Child Custody Disputes, 99 Mich. L. Rev. 216 (2000).

7. *ALI.* The ALI Principles prohibit the court from considering parents' relative earning capacities or financial circumstances unless the parents' combined financial resources "set practical limits on the custodial arrangements." ALI Principles §212(1)(f) (2002). Further, the ALI Principles provide that placement of the child in day care does not constitute sufficient changed circumstances to warrant custody modification. Id. at §2.15(3)(c).

8. *Time as a factor.* Should the amount of time a parent has available to spend with a child be a relevant factor?

## ■ D. KELLY WEISBERG, PROFESSIONAL WOMEN AND THE PROFESSIONALIZATION OF MOTHERHOOD: MARCIA CLARK'S DOUBLE BIND[24]
### 6 Hastings Women's L.J. 295, 312-319, 321-322 (1995)

In custody determinations, the governing standard is the best interests of the child. . . . Only occasionally is "time" enumerated as a statutory factor. More often, consideration of parental availability enters into the determination implicitly, either because of vague statutory language or because of the tremendous discretion vested by the best interests standard in decisionmakers' determinations of parental fitness.

[There are] several problems . . . in utilizing time as a determinative, or even, [a] relevant, factor. . . . The quantity of time that a parent has available to spend with a child [does not dictate] the quality of that interaction. [Nor, does it guarantee] that the available time [will] be spent with the child. For example, research on mother-child, compared to father-child, relationships reveals that husbands of working wives spend considerably less time than the working mothers in childcare activities. . . . Research has also suggested that, at the time of divorce, fathers often overestimate the time they say they want to spend with their children. . . . Research that documents visitation patterns over time supports this finding. . . .

. . . In addition, a focus on the quantity of time that a child spends with a parent may detract from more important considerations. For example, in Renee B. [v. Michael B., No. V5272186 (N.Y. Fam. Ct. May 8,

[24]. The title refers to the custody dispute of Marcia Clark (the chief prosecutor in the murder trial of O. J. Simpson) in which her husband sought custody of their two sons for the reason that her demanding career rendered him a more fit custodian.

1992)], a court-appointed expert determined that the unemployed father would be a better custodian than the mother because of his greater availability. In awarding custody to the father, the appellate court gave little weight to the father's character, which had been described by the trial judge as: "cold, pedantic, and humorless, and above all, with a pervasive quality of controlled anger. [E]ven when directly discussing his daughter, there was little sense of the warmth and empathy for her that the mother displayed" [slip op. at 108]. [And, in Prost v. Greene, 652 A.2d 621 (D.C. App. 1995)], by focusing on [the mother's] availability, the trial court minimized allegations of domestic violence by Prost's husband (which had been serious enough to merit a civil protection order). . . .

[Moreover,] societal views have evolved concerning children's need for quantity time. Sociologist Arlie Hochschild writes that in the second half of the nineteenth century, when a woman's place was in the home, child care experts agreed that the child needed a mother's constant care at home. [However, as] women's roles have changed, so has our concept of children's needs: "Nowadays, a child is increasingly imagined to need time with other children, to need 'independence-training,' not to need 'quantity time' with a parent but only a small amount of 'quality time.'"

A second problem regarding consideration of time as a factor in custody decision-making is that a reliance on availability "freezes" the status quo. [That is,] it measures the *present time constraints* of one parent against the *present availability* of the other parent to determine fulfillment of the *present time needs* of a child. Yet, any, or all, of these factors may change significantly over time. . . . Consideration of a parent's current career demands assumes that these constraints are reflective of the career as a whole. [And,] in time, [the non-custodial parent] might be promoted into a more demanding position, accept a different job, [and/or] become involved in a new amorous relationship that would take up more of his time. [Further,] children's demands on a parent's time vary as a function of each developmental stage. For example, once children reach school age, they are absent from home for a large portion of the parent's work day. Moreover, school children's after-school lives may quickly fill with extracurricular activities and friendships, thus lessening their need and desire to be with a parent.

A third criticism of reliance on availability as a factor in custody decision-making rests on an unspoken assumption that availability is an objective and easily measurable criteria. [Yet, such assumptions may be] open to challenge. . . . One problem in emphasizing the more visible caretaking activities is that this tends to minimize all the "invisible" work that mothers might perform [e.g.,] arranging for baby-sitting or housekeeper services, scheduling doctors' appointments, scheduling play dates, determining a child's need for new clothes and haircuts, helping with school work, planning domestic chores and events, making grocery lists, paying bills, [and so forth].

Sociologist Arlie Hochschild [in The Second Shift (1989)] has made visible the extent of the child care and house work that working women perform. [She also] suggests that working mothers may actually do more family work (house work and child care) [when compared to] non-working mothers. [And, in a finding that is suggestive for professional women,] Hochschild points out that those working women who earn more than their husbands tend to participate to a greater extent than other working women in the division of labor. Hochschild attributes this to the women's subconscious desire to restore power to their husbands.

. . . Measurement of availability is complicated by other subtle factors. Mothers and fathers may attach different meanings to the attentiveness required by child care. Or, mothers and fathers may have different standards [that is, one may care more, or less, how the house looks or how clean the children are, and perform more, or fewer, child-care or household tasks accordingly.]

Further, it becomes important to notice how certain tasks are weighted in the measurement of availability. An evaluation of availability [may be based] on gender-based assumptions about the traditional roles of mother and father. . . . The families of [working] women may function [on different assumptions].

. . . A final criticism of reliance on time as a relevant factor in custody decision-making is the subjectivity of the assessment by the parties themselves. Their measurement may be not unbiased, especially given the likelihood of intra-parental conflict and hostility upon divorce. . . . Hochschild's findings suggest that unconscious motivations may also play a role in a parent's measurement of child care contributions. That is, Hochschild suggests that some families participate in "family myths," i.e., delusions that serve some unconscious function. One such myth is that the marriage is egalitarian and that the husband's workload (in terms of housework and child care) is equal to that of the wife. Specifically, Hochschild identifies relationships in which (despite an observable gender-based inequality in the division of labor), *both* the husband and wife refer to the division of labor as "equal" . . . "because equality was so important to [the wife]."

(3) Domestic Violence

■ **SCHUMACHER v. SCHUMACHER**
*598 N.W.2d 131 (N.D. 1999)*

VANDE WALLE, Chief Justice.
. . . Coreen and Kurt married in May 1992. [Their] daughter, Morgan, was born about one month later.

Kurt has worked as a locomotive engineer with the Burlington Northern Santa Fe Railroad for twenty years. His salary is approximately $42,000 per year and he receives health, dental and vision insurance which covers Morgan through his employer. He owns a 4-bedroom home in Minot.

Coreen is presently employed as an assistant manager for a gas station in Vaughn, Montana. She makes approximately $12,000 per year, and after 6 months of employment will receive benefits. She resides in a trailer house owned by her mother. During most of the parties' marriage, Coreen worked full time and her income was used to pay the family's living expenses. Kurt gave Coreen about $50 every two weeks for groceries.

The parties separated in August 1994. An interim order issued by the district court allowed Coreen, Morgan and Bryson, Coreen's son from a previous marriage, to live in the marital home. . . . In August 1997, Coreen moved to Vaughn, Montana with Bryson and Morgan. Coreen wanted to move back to Montana to attend college. Coreen wants to become a licensed practical nurse and obtain a degree in occupational therapy. Coreen stated she did not attend college in Minot because Kurt would not financially assist her, and his income was too high for her to qualify for a loan or grant.

Kurt filed for divorce September 23, 1997. Coreen filed an answer and counterclaim seeking a divorce, custody of Morgan, child support and division of the parties' property and debts. . . .

A trial was held June 19, 1998 and continued on September 30, 1998. Both parties presented evidence concerning domestic violence. Coreen and Bryson testified about an incident which took place shortly after the parties' marriage when she was pregnant with Morgan. Attempting to take the wedding ring from Coreen, Kurt forced Coreen to the ground with his knee in her ribs. He bruised her eye and arms, and tore hair from her head. Kurt also grabbed Bryson by the hair to stop him from calling 911. Coleen Shipp [a friend of the mother] testified she saw the effects of this abuse. Coreen testified about another incident in which Kurt dragged her down a hallway after a pushing match. Coreen further testified Kurt came home intoxicated one evening and literally kicked her out of the bed.

Kurt also presented evidence of domestic violence by Coreen. He testified that in the fall of 1993, Coreen hit him when she became upset. He called the police, but no arrests were made. Kurt also stated he has slapped Coreen a couple of times in self-defense. Kurt presented a letter written by Coreen, before the parties were married, in which she apologizes for slapping him. . . .

[The district court awarded custody of Morgan to Coreen and ordered Kurt to pay spousal support and child support.] Kurt argues the district court's custody determination is erroneous because the Court incorrectly analyzed the evidence concerning domestic violence. . . .

In an initial custody determination, a trial court must decide custody in the best interests and welfare of the child. In doing so, the trial court must consider all factors under the best interests [standard]. N.D.C.C. §14-09-06.2(1)(j) guides trial courts in their evaluation of domestic violence evidence in a custody determination. We have explained the domestic violence presumption in recent cases:

> Section 14-09-06.2(1)(j) was amended in 1993 to create a rebuttable presumption against awarding custody to a parent who had perpetrated domestic violence when the court found "credible evidence that domestic violence has occurred." See 1993 N.D. Sess. Laws ch. 144, §2. In 1997 the Legislature amended the statute again, raising the level of domestic violence required to trigger the presumption. See 1997 N.D. Sess. Laws ch. 147, §2. The presumption is now triggered when the trial court finds: "credible evidence that domestic violence has occurred, and there exists one incident of domestic violence which resulted in serious bodily injury or involved the use of a dangerous weapon or there exists a pattern of domestic violence within a reasonable time proximate to the proceeding."
>
> Once the presumption under section 14-09-06.2(1)(j) is triggered, the issue of domestic violence becomes the "paramount factor" in the trial court's custody decision. The presumption prevents an abusive parent from obtaining custody of the child unless the abusive parent proves "by clear and convincing evidence that the best interests of the child require" the abusive parent to participate in or have custody.

Holtz v. Holtz, 1999 ND 105, §27, 595 N.W.2d 1 [quoting Reeves v. Chepulis, 1999 ND 63, §§11-12, 591 N.W.2d 791]. In doing so, the trial court must consider all [statutory] factors. If the evidence of domestic violence is insufficient to trigger the presumption, it nevertheless remains one of the best-interest factors to be considered by the court under N.D.C.C. §14-09-06.2.

The trial court, in its findings of fact, recited the incidents of domestic violence committed by both Coreen and Kurt and stated: "I find that neither party made any untrue allegation of domestic violence against the other." However, the court determined only the domestic violence of Kurt invoked the rebuttable presumption: "There is credible evidence of domestic violence which resulted in serious bodily injury and there exists a pattern of domestic violence within a reasonable time proximate to the proceeding committed by Kurt." The district court's findings support this conclusion. The court details four incidents of domestic violence by Kurt. Furthermore, the court describes the serious bodily injury which occurred when Kurt attempted to take the wedding ring from Coreen's finger, including the bruised eye and arms and torn hair from Coreen's head.

Kurt contends that if domestic violence has been committed by both parents, the trial court is obligated to measure the amount and extent of the domestic violence inflicted by both parents, citing Krank v. Krank, 529 N.W.2d 844 (N.D. 1995). According to Kurt, the district court made no specific findings with respect to the domestic violence committed by Coreen.

When a trial court addresses whether the evidence of domestic violence triggers the domestic violence presumption, we require the court to make specific and detailed findings regarding the effect the allegations of domestic violence have on the presumption. However, specific factual findings are not required when the evidence of domestic violence does not rise to the level triggering the presumption. The district court concluded that only Kurt's domestic violence invoked the presumption. Accordingly, the district court was not required to make specific factual findings regarding the effect the allegations of domestic violence by Coreen had on the presumption.

The district court's child custody determination was not clearly erroneous. . . . *ok*

## Notes and Questions

1. Should domestic violence be given special consideration in custody decisionmaking? Public concern about spousal abuse has contributed to the passage of legislation addressing the role of domestic violence in custody disputes. States either include domestic violence as a factor in the best interests standard or provide that evidence of domestic violence creates a rebuttable presumption against awarding custody (often including joint custody) to the abusive parent. Amy B. Levin, Comment, Child Witnesses of Domestic Violence: How Should Judges Apply the Best Interests of the Child Standard in Custody and Visitation Cases Involving Domestic Violence, 47 UCLA L. Rev. 813, 827 & nn.31-37 (2000) (current state survey). Some states additionally provide protection for battered spouses in custody mediation. See page 994.

What weight do you think should be attached to domestic violence in custody decisions? Do you agree with the suggestion of the above commentator (Levin, supra, at 855) that courts should prefer other alternatives (e.g., supervised visitation and mandated treatment) to rebuttable presumptions against awarding custody to batterers? See generally Nancy K.D. Lemon, The Legal System's Response to Children Exposed to Domestic Violence, in The Future of Children 67 (Winter 1999).

2. *ALI.* The ALI also addresses the role of domestic violence in custody. According to the ALI Principles, parents and the court share the burden of discovery: Parents must disclose battering in the parenting plan submitted to the court; the court also must have a process to identify abuse. ALI Principles §§2.06, 2.11 (2002). Batterers may not

receive custodial responsibility unless the court orders appropriate measures to ensure protection of the child and other parent (e.g., by mandated counseling). Id. at §§2.11(2)(i). In addition, the Principles broadly define abuse for purposes of custody determinations (i.e., any physical injury or creation of a reasonable fear thereof on the part of a parent, child, or any member of household). Id. at §2.03(7). Finally, the Principles suggest that courts be aware that the abuser might try to use custody or visitation rights to harass the victim-spouse. Id. at §2.11(c) cmt.

How should courts deal with *mutual* acts of domestic violence? For example, what weight should be given to Kurt's allegations that Coreen physically abused him? Some states provide that custody should be awarded to the parent least likely to continue perpetrating the violence. Levin, supra, at 827 n.30. According to the ALI Principles, acts of self-defense do not constitute abuse. Rather, if one spouse's act is more extreme or dangerous, "it may be appropriate for the court to impose limits on the primary aggressor but not on the primary victim." ALI Principles §2.11(c) cmt. How does a court determine who is the primary aggressor or primary victim?

3. Another possible evidentiary problem is gender bias. Studies highlight accounts of lawyers and judges who minimize and disbelieve reports of domestic violence. See generally Jane H. Aiken & Jane C. Murphy, Evidence Issues in Domestic Violence Civil Cases, 34 Fam. L.Q. 43, 44-45 (2000) (suggesting judges and juries continue to "ignore or discount" victims' testimony of abuse).

4. Do custody statutes provide adequate protection for abused spouses? How might statutes facilitate proof of domestic violence? See, e.g., Ariz. Rev. Stat. Ann. §25-403(B) (West 2000); Cal. Fam. Code §3011 (West 1994 & Supp. 2001) (suggesting police reports, medical records, child protective service records, domestic violence shelter records, school records, and testimony of witnesses).

5. Is an abusive spouse by definition an unfit parent? In states with rebuttable presumptions against awards of custody to perpetrators of domestic violence, it becomes important to determine what triggers the operation of the presumption. Some statutes require a criminal conviction. See Family Violence Project, National Council of Juvenile and Family Court Judges, Family Violence in Child Custody Statutes: An Analysis of State Codes and Legal Practice, 29 Fam. L.Q. 197, 209 n.62 (1995) (citing examples).

6. Is it possible that a batterer who kills his wife might be a fit parent? See In re H.L.T., 298 S.E.2d 33, 34 (Ga. Ct. App. 1982); In re Lutgen, 532 N.E.2d 976 (Ill. App. Ct. 1988), *appeal denied*, 537 N.E.2d 811 (Ill. 1989). Should legislatures adopt a presumption that a homicidal spouse abuser is not a fit parent absent clear and convincing evidence? See Lillian Wan, Note, Parents Killing Parents: Creating a Presumption of Unfitness, 63 Alb. L. Rev. 333 (1999).

7. Some courts will not consider domestic violence as a factor in custody determinations unless the violence has been directed at the child. See, e.g., Collinsworth v. O'Connell, 508 So. 2d 744, 746 (Fla. Dist. Ct. App. 1987); Baker v. Baker, 494 N.W.2d 282 (Minn. 1992). Does this distinction make sense? See Nancy Ver Steegh, The Silent Victims: Children and Domestic Violence, 26 Wm. Mitchell L. Rev. 775, 797-801 (2000) (discussing risks faced by children when courts grant unsupervised visitation to an abusive parent). On the effects of domestic violence on children, see Chapter VIII, section Bb.

8. *Friendly parent provisions.* Many statutes contain "friendly parent provisions" mandating that courts favor a custody award to the parent more likely to maintain the child's relationship with the other parent. What problems might such statutes pose for victims of spousal abuse? Similar problems are raised by statutes providing for joint custody. See generally D. Lee Khachaturian, Comment, Domestic Violence and Shared Parental Responsibility: Dangerous Bedfellows, 44 Wayne L. Rev. 1745 (1999).

9. *Failure to protect.* Should women be deemed unfit parents for allowing themselves to be abused or for failing to protect their children from abuse? Professor Mary Becker proposes a higher standard of care for mothers who have been abused themselves "for failing to protect their children from others' abuse and neglect, provided that they knew or had reason to know of the harm to their children." Mary E. Becker, Double Binds Facing Mothers in Abusive Families: Social Support Systems, Custody Outcomes, and Liability for Acts of Others, 2 U. Chi. L. Sch. Roundtable 13, 32 (1995). Is this a sound approach? Or, does it revictimize the victim? See Linda J. Panko, Legal Backlash: The Expanding Liability of Women Who Fail to Protect their Children from their Male Partner's Abuse, 6 Hastings Women's L.J. 67 (1995). On the "failure to protect" as neglect, see Chapter VIII, section Bd.

## Note: Physical Disability

The physical health of the parents is another relevant factor in the best interests determination. Many statutes model UMDA, mandating consideration of "the mental and physical health of all individuals involved." UMDA §402(5), 9A U.L.A. (pt. II) 282 (1998). See Katheryn Katz & Maris Warfman, Custody Disputes Between Parents, in 2 Child Custody and Visitation Law and Practice §10.11 n.1 (Sandra Morgan Little, ed., 2000) (citing statutes).

Public policy currently addresses discrimination against the disabled in many areas of life. For example, the Americans with Disabilities Act of 1990 (ADA), 42 U.S.C. §§12101-12213 (1994), prohibits discrimination against the disabled in employment, public services, public transportation, public accommodations, and telecommunications. However, the ADA does not apply to child custody.

Formerly, many trial courts assumed that a severely physically disabled parent was per se unfit. Ann M. Haralambie, Handling Child Custody, Abuse and Adoption Cases §8.11, at 465 (1993). This judicial presumption manifested itself "in different guises for different types of disabilities: deaf parents are thought to be incapable of effectively stimulating language skills; blind parents cannot provide adequate attention or discipline; and parents with spinal cord injuries cannot adequately supervise their children." Michael Ashley Stein, Mommy Has a Blue Wheelchair: Recognizing the Parental Rights of Individuals with Disabilities, 60 Brook. L. Rev. 1069, 1083 (1994). Courts became concerned especially when the children were not themselves disabled. See id. at 1098.

Appellate courts, however, have rejected this presumption and instead focus on the effects of the parent's disability on the child. Haralambie, supra. In the classic case to announce this principle, Carney v. Carney, 598 P.2d 36 (Cal. 1979), custody was originally awarded to the father. Five years later the father became a quadriplegic as a result of a jeep accident while serving in the military reserve. The mother, who had not visited the children or provided child support in five years, requested a modification in her behalf. The California Supreme Court, reversing the trial court's award for its reliance on a presumption of unfitness based on the father's disability, stated:

> the essence of parenting is not to be found in the harried rounds of daily carpooling endemic to modern suburban life, or even in the doggedly dutiful acts of "togetherness" committed every weekend by well-meaning fathers and mothers across America. Rather, its essence lies in the ethical, emotional, and intellectual guidance the parent gives to the child throughout his formative years, and often beyond. The source of this guidance is the adult's own experience of life; its motive power is parental love and concern for the child's well-being; and its teachings deal with such fundamental matters as the child's feelings about himself, his relationships with others, his system of values, his standards of conduct, and his goals and priorities in life. Even if it were true, as the court herein asserted that William [the father] cannot do "anything" for his sons except "talk to them and teach them, be a tutor," that would not only be "enough" — contrary to the court's conclusion — it would be the most valuable service a parent can render. Yet his capacity to do so is entirely unrelated to his physical prowess: however limited his bodily strength may be, a handicapped person is a whole person to the child who needs his affection, sympathy, and wisdom to deal with the problems of growing up. Indeed, in such matters, his handicap may well be an asset: few can pass through the crucible of a severe physical disability without learning enduring lessons in patience and tolerance.

598 P.2d at 44. Other courts have permitted parents to retain custody who are paraplegic, quadraplegic, stroke victims, epileptic, and deaf. See Haralambie, supra, at 466 n.116; Katz & Warfman, supra, at §10.11[2][b]; Kristine Cordier Karnezis, Annotation, Parent's Physical Disability or Handicap as Factor in Custody Award or Proceedings, 3 A.L.R.4th 1044 (1981 & Supp. 2000) (citing cases).

Professor Michael Stein argues that the protection of the rights of disabled parents requires the evaluation of their performance of parental tasks by a different perspective taking into account that the disabled require more time and structural supports. Stein, supra, at 1092-1095. Stein also advocates improved efforts by social service agencies to assist disabled parents with childcare tasks. Id. at 1098 n.133.

On custody rights of disabled parents, see generally Gerald L. Nissenbaum, Discovery, in 3 Child Custody and Visitation Law and Practice §17.06[1] (Sandra Morgan Little 2000); Paul Bernstein, Termination of Parental Rights on the Basis of Mental Disability: A Problem in Policy and Interpretation, 22 Pac. L.J. 1155 (1991); Duffy Dillon, Comment, Child Custody and the Developmentally Disabled Parent, 2000 Wis. L. Rev. 127 (2000).

### c. Joint-Custody: Presumption, Preference, or Option?

■ **BELL v. BELL**
*794 P.2d 97 (Alaska 1990)*

MATTHEWS, Chief Justice.

Greg and Debra Bell were married in January 1986. They separated sixteen months later in July 1987. Greg filed for divorce on September 14, 1987. A Partial Decree of Divorce was entered on March 4, 1988, leaving matters related to child custody, child support and property division to be determined by a trial which resulted in this appeal.

On appeal, Greg challenges . . . the trial court's award of legal and physical custody of Scott, the parties' child, to Debra. . . .

Gregory "Scott" Bell was born on August 19, 1986. While married, Greg and Debra shared most child rearing tasks on an equal basis. Since both parents were employed, Sharon Nollman babysat Scott part time beginning about December 1986, and then full time in approximately February 1987. She continued to babysit full time until February 1988, then every other week until the trial.

When Greg and Debra separated, they agreed to share custody of Scott, alternating physical custody every week or so. Both used Nollman to babysit. They accommodated each other's employment, social, and vacation schedules and shared babysitting expenses. A two-day interim custody hearing was held before Master Andrew Brown on October 15-16, 1987. Based upon the recommendations of an Alaska Court Custody Investigator, Master Brown issued a report recommending that Scott remain in the babysitting care of Nollman and that the parties continue their weekly alternating schedule of shared physical custody of Scott. The court approved the Master's report.

Greg and Debra cooperated in the weekly custody exchanges for another ten and one-half months until trial on August 26 and 29, 1988. However, in early 1988, Debra unilaterally began placing Scott at the Saakaaya Daycare Center during the weeks that she had physical custody. Greg continued to use Nollman during the weeks that he had physical custody of Scott.

In March 1988, the parties agreed to bifurcate the proceedings. A Partial Decree of Divorce was entered April 4, 1988. All other issues were reserved for a later adjudication or agreement of the parties.

Greg and Debra continued to accommodate each other's schedules and to share physical custody of Scott on an alternating basis. They also cooperated in making major decisions about Scott's medical care. For example, after Scott was hospitalized with asthma in September 1987, Greg and Debra conferred together with medical specialists and agreed to have tubes implanted in Scott's ears.

At trial, Ardis Cry, Custody Investigator, Alaska Court System, recommended that shared legal custody continue. She further recommended that Scott have a primary home and that Debra be the primary physical custodian.

The trial court awarded legal and physical custody of Scott to Debra. The court also allowed Greg visitation with Scott (1) on alternate weekends from Friday afternoon through Monday morning and on Wednesday evening through Thursday mornings and (2) during four one-week periods spread throughout the year until Scott reaches school age.

Greg contends that the trial court erred by not awarding joint custody to both parents pursuant to AS 25.20.060. AS 25.20.060 states, in part: "The court may award shared custody to both parents if shared custody is determined to be in the best interests of the child." . . .

In the present case, the trial court denied joint custody and determined that "the physical and legal custody of [Scott] should be vested with [Debra] subject to [Greg's] rights of visitation. . . ." In reviewing the propriety of the trial court's denial of joint custody, we find it necessary to distinguish between two interrelated aspects of a joint custody arrangement. First, an award of joint custody gives both parents "legal custody" of the child. This means that they "share responsibility in the making of major decisions affecting the child's welfare." 17 A.L.R.4th 1015 n.1. Second, an award of joint custody gives both parents "physical custody" of the child. This means that "each is entitled to the companionship of the child over periodic intervals of time." Id.

In an act amending AS 25.20.060, the legislature drew this distinction and expressed a policy favoring the award of joint legal custody, regardless of the physical custody arrangement. The legislature finds that . . . it is in the public interest to encourage parents to share the rights and responsibilities of child rearing. While actual physical custody may not be practical or appropriate in all cases, it is the intent of the legislature that both parents have the opportunity to guide and nurture their child and to meet the needs of the child on an equal footing beyond the considerations of support or actual custody. An Act Relating to Child Custody, ch. 88 §1(a), SLA 1982.

In light of this expression of legislative intent, and because the controlling factual finding underlying the trial court's ruling is clearly erroneous, we reverse the award of sole legal custody to Debra.

The trial court's award was apparently based on its finding that Greg and Debra "are incapable of meaningful communication and/or negotiation regarding the matters that relate to the best interests of [Scott]."[1] If this finding is correct, joint custody would be inappropriate because "cooperation between the parents is essential if joint custody is to be in the child's best interest." Lone Wolf, 741 P.2d at 1189. Based on our review of the record, however, we hold that this finding is clearly erroneous.

The trial court record and Debra's arguments on appeal indicate only one area of irreconcilable conflict between Greg and Debra — throughout the proceedings below they could not agree on what form of day care would be best for Scott. Greg wanted Scott in Nollman's home, and Debra wanted Scott in Saakaaya Daycare Center.

Given the abundance of contrary evidence indicative of their ability to cooperate in Scott's best interest, however, we think that this one conflict does not warrant the trial court's finding of an "inability" to cooperate. Prior to the trial court ruling, Greg and Debra shared custody of Scott for 14 months, alternating physical custody every week or so. This arrangement was initially reached by mutual agreement. Throughout the 14 months, they accommodated each other's employment, social,

---

1. The trial court did not isolate any of the other AS 25.20.090 or AS 25.24.150(c) factors as being factually subsidiary to its ruling, other than a finding that Debra is a "much more capable" parent. With respect to denying Greg legal custody, however, the dispositive significance of this finding is undercut by the trial court's finding that "both parties can be classified as fit," and that Greg is a "good parent[ ]." The record amply supports this latter finding. The record reflects, for example, that Greg studied child development and consulted with others about Scott's needs. The child custody investigator found that Greg loves Scott and would provide him with good care. Debra also testified that "Greg is a good parent."

and vacation schedules, and cooperated in making major decisions about Scott's medical care.

Furthermore, after interviewing Greg and Debra, the custody investigator recommended "joint legal custody" because she found that they had the "ability . . . to deal with each other in a civil and mutual manner" and thought that they demonstrated "potential to facilitate cooperation and compromise." Both Greg and Debra also testified to their ability to work cooperatively in Scott's best interest. Moreover, Debra generally agreed with the investigator's recommendations and was willing to settle the custody issue under the terms the investigator recommended. Thus, at trial, both parties agreed that joint legal custody was appropriate.

In light of such evidence, we are left with a firm conviction that the trial court's finding of an inability to cooperate was erroneous. We realize that the disagreement over daycare relates to a fundamental child care issue. But resolution of this issue did not require denial of that which the Alaska legislature recognizes as the favored course; i.e., joint legal custody. We therefore reverse the trial court's denial of joint legal custody and remand with instructions to enter an award of joint legal custody. Because we cannot ascertain the extent to which the trial court's erroneous finding influenced its decision regarding physical custody, that portion of its judgment is vacated. On remand, the trial court shall reconsider its physical custody/visitation determination, taking new evidence as may be appropriate. . . .

## Notes and Questions

1. Joint custody is based on the belief that the child benefits from frequent contact with both parents. The doctrine recognizes that fathers, as well as mothers, have an important role to play in childrearing. A nascent fathers' rights movement spearheaded the passage of joint custody legislation in the late 1970s. See Herbert Jacob, The Silent Revolution: The Transformation of Divorce Law in the United States 136-143 (1988). The doctrine caught on quickly. Currently, almost all states have statutes that permit some form of joint custody. See Stephanie B. Goldberg, Make Room for Daddy, 83 A.B.A. J. 48, 49 (Feb. 1997).

Do fathers have a constitutional right to joint custody? See Holly L. Robinson, Joint Custody: Constitutional Imperatives, 54 U. Cin. L. Rev. 27 (1985).

2. *Presumption, preference, or option.* California was one of the first states to adopt joint custody in 1980. See Cal. Fam. Code §3080 (West 1994) (formerly Cal. Civ. Code §4600.5(a)). The California statute became a model for many states. Jacob, supra, at 142. The statute created

CA

a presumption in favor of joint custody if both parents agreed. The CA
statute was amended in 1988 to repeal the presumption and to permit waffles
the court the widest discretion to select a plan in the best interests of the
children. Cal. Civ. Code 4600(d) (West 1989). In 1994, in response to
lobbying by religious groups and fathers' rights groups, the legislature
reinstated the presumption if both parents agree.

Currently, states follow four approaches to joint custody. Some states, 4 APROACHES
following California's lead, create a presumption of joint custody (al- CA
though not all states require parental agreement as a prerequisite). See 1-presumption
Goldberg, supra, at 49 (listing 14 states and the District of Columbia with
a presumption of joint custody). Other states, similar to Alaska in Bell, 2. preference
have a preference for joint custody. Third, and most common, some 3. factor
states make joint custody one factor in the best interests determination. 4. disfavor
See, e.g., Walker v. Walker, 539 N.E.2d 509, 510 (Ind. Ct. App. 1989);
Dunham v. Dunham, 777 P.2d 403, 404 (Okla. Ct. App. 1989). Finally,
some states view joint custody with disfavor. See, e.g., Dormann v. Dormann, 606 N.W.2d 837, 846 (Neb. Ct. App. 2000); Martin v. Martin, 798
P.2d 321, 322 (Wyo. 1990). See generally ALI Principles §2.08 cmt. a ALI
(2002) (discussing statutory and case law treatment of joint custody); Vi-
tauts M. Gulbis, Annotation, Propriety of Awarding Joint Custody of
Children, 17 A.L.R.4th 1013 (1982 & Supp. 2000).

3. A custody award resolves the dual issues of "legal custody" and
"physical custody." Legal custody confers responsibility for major decisionmaking (that is, upbringing, health, welfare, and education). Physical
custody determines the child's residence and confers responsibility for
day-to-day decisions regarding physical care. (Compare the ALI Principles' terms of "decisionmaking responsibility" for legal custody and "custodial responsibility" for physical custody.) In an award of joint legal
custody, both parents share responsibility for major childrearing decisions. In such an award, both parents may share physical custody or only
one parent may be the actual physical custodian. Thus, joint custody is
distinguishable from the traditional award of sole custody, which gave
one parent (normally the mother) both legal control and physical custody, while the other parent (normally the father) had visitation rights.

4. Joint custody signifies a radical departure from conventional psychological wisdom about childrearing. In an influential book in the early
1970s, Professors Goldstein, Freud, and Solnit propounded the view SOLE
that stability and minimization of conflict should guide child placement. CUSTODY
They said that healthy emotional development requires an "omnipo- RATIONALE
tent" parent on whom the child can rely for all important decisions. To
that end, they advocated that custody should be awarded to only one
parent who should have power to decide the extent of the other's contact with the child (even prohibiting it). See Joseph Goldstein et al., Beyond the Best Interests of the Child 38 (1973). Do you find their views
persuasive?

5. *Parental agreement.* One source of debate concerns whether parental agreement should be a prerequisite to joint custody awards. Many states, as indicated in *Bell,* mandate such agreement. However, other courts order joint custody even if a parent objects. Compare In re Aylward, 592 N.E.2d 1247 (Ind. Ct. App. 1992), with Monahan v. Monahan, 577 N.Y.S.2d 709, 710 (App. Div. 1991). Is joint custody to unwilling parents likely to be successful? Can the parties to an acrimonious divorce cooperate on childrearing decisions? See Eleanor E. Maccoby & Robert H. Mnookin, Dividing the Child: Social and Legal Dilemmas of Custody 240-242 (1992) (couples who express considerable hostility immediately upon separation continue to manifest significant animosity at a later point in time).

In a modern statutory development, many states now require that parents seeking custody must file a parenting plan (i.e., a written agreement specifying the caretaking and decisionmaking authority for their children as well as the manner in which future disputes are to be resolved). Among these states, the majority require such plans only in joint custody situations.

6. When is an award of joint custody inappropriate? If the parents are geographically separated? See, e.g., Quinn v. Quinn, 622 P.2d 230 (Mont. 1981); Shepherd v. Metcalf, 794 S.W.2d 348, 351 (Tenn. 1990). What constitutes proximity? Might this consideration place the departing partner at a disadvantage? Does it reinsert notions of marital fault into the custody process?

What kind of time sharing is optimal? Should courts require equal residential time? Compare Mont. Code Ann. §40-4-224(2)(1995) (providing that joint custody should entail substantially equal time with child) with Idaho Code §21-717B(2)(Supp. 1995) (stating that joint physical custody does not mean equal time with child). If courts require equal time, should it be six months with each parent, nine months with one parent and summer vacations with the other, or switching homes every week? Or should courts order the child(ren) to remain in the family home with the parents alternating periods there (i.e., the "bird's nest" model)? See Waits v. Waits, 556 So. 2d 215 (La. Ct. App. 1990). What considerations should influence the arrangement?

7. *Domestic violence and joint custody.* Is joint custody, which requires continuing communication, appropriate in cases of domestic violence? Statutes take domestic violence into account in several ways before joint custody can be awarded. Some consider abuse as a factor in joint custody decisions; some create a rebuttable presumption that joint custody is not in the best interests of the child when there has been abuse; and some prohibit joint custody if evidence of abuse exists. Naomi R. Cahn, Civil Images of Battered Women: The Impact of Domestic Violence on Child Custody Decisions, 44 Vand. L. Rev. 1041, 1064-1068 (1991). See also D. Lee Khachaturian, Domestic Violence and Shared Parental Re-

sponsibility: Dangerous Bedfellows, 44 Wayne L. Rev. 1745 (1999). On the role of domestic violence in mediation, see infra page 944.

8. Joint custody legislation has had a significant impact on custody decisions. Professors Eleanor Maccoby & Robert Mnookin report that in 79 percent of approximately 1,000 families in two California counties (in the late 1980s), the divorce decree provided for joint legal custody. This outcome occurred even in cases where one parent opposed the request. Maccoby & Mnookin, supra, at 107. This figure represents a significant increase from the 25 percent of judgments providing for joint custody in 1979. Id. at 108. Irrespective of the legal label, in the vast majority of families, the children resided with their mother. Id. at 73.

---

How do parents manage the logistics of joint custody? The excerpt below sheds some light on this issue.

# ■ ELEANOR E. MACCOBY & ROBERT H. MNOOKIN, DIVIDING THE CHILD: SOCIAL AND LEGAL DILEMMAS OF CUSTODY
### 177-178, 212-217, 224-225 (1992)

[A]lthough a large majority of boys and girls lived with their mothers initially, boys were more likely to live with their fathers or in dual residence than were girls, who more often lived with their mothers. This situation did not change with time. . . . While we had expected that more boys than girls might shift into father residence, particularly among preteens growing into adolescence, this did not prove to be the case. Although a child's entry into puberty may sometimes be a trigger for a residential move, the move is not more likely to be to the same-sex parent's household. There were some instances in our sample in which a girl of 12 or 13 would move to the father's household when a mother's new partner moved in with the mother, presumably because the presence of the new partner represented an unknown and possibly threatening factor for the daughter. Cases of this kind balanced the small group of boys who moved from mother to father residence for other reasons. Also, teenagers of either sex sometimes moved away from a residential parent's household when parent-child conflict was high, regardless of whether they were living with a same-sex or opposite-sex parent.

[C]hildren's age had some bearing on where they would live. The probability was high, and equally high in all age groups, that children would live with their mothers. However, the probabilities of father residence were higher for older children, and the probabilities of dual residence were higher for children between the ages of 3 and 8 than they were for the preteen and teenage children. Thus, in deciding on the initial residential arrangements, parents evidently took the developmental level of the children into account when other circumstances permitted. Some parents told us they did not find dual-residence arrangements workable for infants and toddlers, for whom they felt a single familiar place to sleep was especially important. Others said that teenagers had a greater voice than younger children in decisions about where they were to live and how much they would visit, and that children of this age tended to avoid arrangements in which they would have to sleep in two different houses. . . .

Certain routine functions (preparing meals, helping young children to bathe and dress, washing clothes) were quite easily replicated in the two parental households, and these routine aspects of child care were carried out in whichever household the children were in at a given time. There was considerable variation, however, in the way the following functions were divided: taking the children to buy everyday clothes; keeping track of shots, checkups, and dental appointments; and supervising homework. [E]ach parent believed that the other was less involved in these activities then the other claimed to be. . . .

Apart from these differing viewpoints of mothers and fathers, certain major trends can be seen: first, as might be expected, the parent with whom the child is living takes more responsibility than the nonresident parent for all three functions, and this is true regardless of which parent is reporting. Second, there is a bias toward mothers doing more of the functions when one statistically controls for residence. Thus, mothers do more for children living with their fathers than fathers do for children living with their mothers. . . .

The carry-over of maternal responsibility into the dual-residence situation is pronounced regarding the children's medical regimen. [I]t is usually the parent who has been responsible before the separation — the mother — who continues to arrange for the child's medical regimen. [I]n a substantial number of families it appears that both parents attempt to be involved in managing the child's medical care. We have encountered instances where two parents had different pediatricians (who maintained separate medical records for the child) and where parents did not know whether a treatment (for example, a course of antibiotics for an ear infection) that was supposed to be continued actually was maintained after the child went to the other household. Evidently, this is a function for which coordination is especially important, but for which it does not always occur.

Moving children back and forth between households called for some form of understanding between the parents concerning where and when the children would be picked up and returned. While a few families tried to remain so flexible that the outside parent could drop by at any time to see or pick up the children without prior notice, most had a schedule agreed upon in advance. Parents did not always live up to their agreements, however. . . . In general, mothers reported somewhat more logistical problems than did fathers, probably indicating that fathers were more likely to initiate schedule changes. . . .

When children were returned from a visit to the other household, parents often wanted to be informed about significant experiences the children might have had during the absence — illnesses, upsetting experiences, and so forth. Many parents commented that the ex-spouse provided little such information upon returning the children, and mothers in particular were concerned about the lack of information which they thought it important to have. . . .

*Does joint legal custody enhance joint decision-making?* When California policymakers embodied a preference for joint legal custody in the revised California divorce law, one purpose was to keep non-custodial parents from dropping out of their children's lives. The hope was not only that they would keep up their child support payments more reliably and see the children more often, but that they would involve themselves in decisions concerning the children's lives. [W]hen the children were living with their mothers, a joint legal custody award made essentially no difference in whether the children's contact with their fathers would be maintained. There is a similar result with respect to the involvement of non-residential fathers in decision-making: when factors (such as income) that affect whether a family will be awarded joint legal custody are controlled, non-residential fathers who have joint legal custody are no more likely to be involved in either day-to-day decisions or major decisions.

---

What are the benefits and detriments of joint custody for children, mothers,[25] and fathers?

## ■ JANA B. SINGER & WILLIAM L. REYNOLDS, A DISSENT ON JOINT CUSTODY
*47 Md. L. Rev. 497, 500-503 (1988)*

Advocates of joint custody believe that an impressive number of benefits result from its use. On their face, these arguments make a strong case.

---

[25]. Some feminists oppose joint custody. Professor Herbert Jacob explains that feminist opposition grew slowly because early second wave feminists focused on federal issues instead (e.g., ratification of the Equal Rights Amendment, reform of federal legislation). Herbert Jacob, The Silent Revolution: The Transformation of Divorce Law in the United States 138 (1988). Opposition began to coalesce in the mid-1980s following the publication of Lenore Weitzman's The Divorce Revolution (1985). See also Hugh McIsaac, California Joint Custody Retrospective, in Joint Custody and Shared Parenting 262, 264 (Jay Folberg ed., 1991).

First, the child benefits from having "meaningful relationships and frequent contact with both psychological parents." This common-sense observation is confirmed by a number of studies. Research shows that children adjust better to divorce if they have frequent contact with both parents, a process hampered by the tendency of the noncustodial father to withdraw following divorce. Joint custody, by ensuring continued contact with the father, counteracts this tendency and thus promotes the child's welfare. Advocates like to quote the statement from Wallerstein and Kelly, prominent child development experts, that "divorcing parents should be encouraged and helped to shape post-divorce arrangements which permit and foster continuity in the child's relations with both parents."

Second, joint custody benefits the parents. . . . Parents in successful joint custody situations feel better about themselves, about each other, and, as a result, they feel better about the child. The child can only benefit from that improvement.

Joint custody is also touted as a solution to the child support problem. . . . The failure of fathers to pay any, much less adequate, child support is a national disgrace. Some believe that at least part of the explanation lies in the fact that divorced fathers lack significant contact with their children under sole custody arrangements. Sharing custody, it is hoped, will encourage fathers to pay more regularly.

Joint custody is also said to reflect modern changes in parental roles. Today's fathers spend more time with their children; today's mothers spend more time in the workplace. Joint custody is thought to be a proper way of reflecting modern reality and ensuring that custody decisions are not based on outmoded gender stereotypes.

Finally, joint custody is said to ease judicial administration. A preference in favor of joint custody avoids the detailed inquiry necessary to determine the best interests of the children in each contest custody case. Where both parents are reasonably fit, determining who will make the "better" custodian is often time-consuming and difficult. Some judges simply are not well-suited, either by training or by temperament, to make this kind of decision. Joint custody makes easier the life of such a judge.

Moreover, the certainty provided by a widespread regime of joint custody will tend to reduce litigation (and relitigation), thus decreasing costs to the parties and the judicial system. And joint custody may also help alleviate some of the terrible uncertainty parents (and children) must feel as they await the decision of the court.

These arguments have had a dramatic impact on custody law. Indeed, commentators have described the rise of joint custody as a "small revolution . . . in child custody law." The basis for this revolution, however, is highly questionable. . . .

None of the arguments advanced by proponents of court-imposed or presumptive joint custody is persuasive. First, proponents of court-imposed joint custody use the term "joint custody" to cover several quite different types of custody arrangements. Most important, they fail to dis-tinguish joint physical custody from joint legal custody, in which the child resides primarily (or exclusively) with one parent — usually the mother — while the nonresidential father retains joint decisionmaking authority over the child's upbringing. Most "joint custody" arrangements — and virtually all courtimposed joint custody decrees — fall into the latter category. This latter category closely resembles the traditional maternal-custody-with-liberal-paternal-visitation arrangement with one essential difference: it accords the nonresidential father almost all of the rights but few of the responsibilities that raising a child entails.

Second, joint custody proponents make an unjustified leap from the common sense proposition that children do better after divorce if they maintain frequent contact with both parents to the startling conclusion that joint custody is the only way to ensure such contact. Neither logic nor data support this leap.

Third, virtually all of the studies relied upon by joint custody proponents involve voluntary rather than court-imposed joint custody arrangements; the limited success of voluntary arrangements simply does not support the imposition of joint custody on parents who oppose it. Moreover, the studies indicate that even voluntary joint custody arrangements produce significant risks for children, and create serious problems for both divorced parents and the judicial system.

The possibility of court-imposed joint custody also introduces significant distortions into the judicial process. Awarding joint custody, particularly joint legal custody, affords judges an easy and fair sounding "fix" for resolving difficult custody disputes. It creates the illusion of equality and Solomonic wisdom and improperly allows a judge to avoid making a difficult — but often necessary — choice between two seemingly fit parents.

Finally, proponents of joint custody presumptions fail to consider the detrimental effect of their proposals on the already lop-sided process of divorce bargaining. Proponents ignore what studies increasingly confirm: divorcing husbands routinely and successfully use the threat of a custody fight to reduce or eliminate alimony and child support obligations. The success of such "custody blackmail" has been identified as a major cause of the impoverishment of divorced women and their children. . . .[26]

---

[26]. But cf. Maccoby & Mnookin, supra note [3], at 154-159 (finding no statistical evidence that mothers who experience more legal conflict have to accept less support in order to obtain their preferred custody outcome). On the detriments of joint custody for women, see also Katharine T. Bartlett & Carol B. Stack, Joint Custody, Feminism and the Dependency Dilemma, 2 Berkeley Women's L.J. 9, 11-14 (1986).

For additional studies on the benefits and burdens of joint custody, see Margaret F. Brinig & F. H. Buckley, Joint Custody: Bonding and Monitoring Theories, 73 Ind. L.J. 393 (1998); Stephanie N. Barnes, Comment, Strengthening the Father-Child Relationship Through a Joint Custody Presumption, 35 Willamette L. Rev. 601, 620-626 (1999) (discussing research).

## 2. Standards Governing the Noncustodial Parent: Visitation

### a. Restrictions on Visitation

### ■ HANKE v. HANKE
*615 A.2d 1205 (Md. Ct. Spec. App. 1992)*

BELL, Judge.

Appellant, Mary Elizabeth Hanke, brings this appeal, asking us to review an order granting her ex-husband, Dan Wolf Hanke, appellee, overnight visitation with the parties' four-year-old daughter. Ms. Hanke's concern for this child stems, in part, from an incident of sexual abuse by Mr. Hanke of one of Ms. Hanke's daughters (stepchild) from a previous marriage. . . .

On August 1, 1990, Mr. and Ms. Hanke were divorced by a judgment of the Circuit Court for Harford County. Ms. Hanke was granted custody of the parties' child and the issue of Mr. Hanke's visitation privileges was reserved for a later hearing. On March 15, 1991, hearings began to consider visitation. On March 18, 1991, the court ordered unsupervised four-hour visitations on alternate Sunday afternoons from noon until 4:00 P.M. On March 20, 1991, the court ordered Mr. Hanke to submit to a mental health examination by Lawrence Raifman, PhD, J.D. . . . The order of the Harford County judge, who transferred custody to Mr. Hanke, has not been enforced, pending the outcome of the investigation by the Kentucky DSS. [The mother had moved to Kentucky, where her family lived, because she was unable to find employment.]

Mr. Hanke has admitted sexually abusing his 11-year-old stepchild in 1986. This particular instance of sexual abuse was one event, but there is overwhelming evidence that other instances of excessive punishment with sexual overtones had occurred prior to this incident. . . . During a therapy session, Mr. Hanke stated that he was drunk when he sexually molested his stepchild. . . . Mr. Hanke feels that he does not "need any therapy for alcoholism." He did, however, secure therapy for the sexual abuse incident.

At the time of the separation, Ms. Hanke was pregnant with the parties' child who is the subject of this case. The parties separated as soon as Ms. Hanke learned from the 11-year-old child that she had been sexually molested by Mr. Hanke. Criminal charges of sexual molestation were brought against Mr. Hanke for the incident involving his stepchild. As part of the plea bargain entered into by Mr. Hanke for a suspended sentence in the criminal case, he agreed to, among other things, supervised visitation with the parties' child. . . .

The trial judge granted Mr. Hanke unsupervised four-hour weekly visitation periods with the child, beginning in March of 1991. After one of these visits, the parties' child reported to a teenage friend of her stepsister that Mr. Hanke "was touching her where he was not supposed to." Ms. Hanke examined the child and found scarring in the genital area. She immediately reported the matter to the Harford County Department of Social Services (DSS). Based on Ms. Hanke's complaint, DSS had the child examined at Mercy Hospital. The examination was conducted on May 23, 1991 by Dr. Reichel at the Mercy Hospital outpatient clinic. His report states ". . . Prior abuse cannot be excluded." Annetta Bloxham, the DSS caseworker investigating the complaint . . . also testified that she had verified the child's report of sexual molestation . . . by the parents of the teenager, to whom the child had reported the molestation, that the child did indeed report the molestation. This family refused, however, to permit the teenager to testify. . . .

Dr. Raifman, who evaluated Mr. Hanke pursuant to a court order, [concluded] that Mr. Hanke stated that he abused his stepchild to "get at her mother"; that the stepchild had been physically abused by Mr. Hanke for a long time before the incident of sexual abuse; that Mr. Hanke should not be placed in a situation where he is alone with his child; that Mr. Hanke should not continue to use alcohol because he was drunk at the time he sexually abused his stepchild; that Mr. Hanke had not come to terms with his abuse of alcohol as a factor in his abuse of his stepchild. [U]ntil these issues are resolved therapeutically, he is at risk and, therefore, his child is at risk.

Ms. Hanke's attorney, the attorney representing the Harford County DSS, and the attorney representing the child were unanimous in their call for supervised visitation. There was, however, also a small amount of contradictory evidence presented, which the judge seemed to favor, that Ms. Hanke was overreacting to the situation and Mr. Hanke was not a potential danger to their child. On March 18, 1991, the court ordered unsupervised visitation and on August 16, 1991, the court ordered visitation overnight, specifying one of four persons who were close to Mr. Hanke to "be present during visitation periods." The judge refused to protect the child further, and he found that overnight visitation was appropriate.

We have reviewed the findings and holdings in this case, bearing in mind that the ultimate test for custody and visitation is the best interests of the child. In most instances the decision of the trial judge is accorded great deference, unless it is arbitrary or clearly wrong. We hold that, given the circumstances presented in this case, the decision of the trial judge was clearly wrong.

It is obvious that the trial judge was annoyed because Ms. Hanke moved to Kentucky with the child and was unwilling to allow visitation. Even if the judge were correct that Ms. Hanke was not acting in compliance with the judge's orders, his primary responsibility was to protect this minor child, and not to punish Ms. Hanke by ordering overnight visitation. Then, when he could not enforce the overnight visitation order, the judge next removed the child from her custody with no provisions to protect the child. Where the evidence is such that a parent is justified in believing that the other parent is sexually abusing the child, it is inconceivable that that parent will surrender the child to the abusing parent without stringent safeguards. The fact that the judge does not agree with that parent's fear is immaterial. This is not a case in which there is no basis for the mother's belief. Past behavior is the best predictor of future behavior, and Ms. Hanke, while perhaps incorrect, is not unjustified in her belief that there may be some unresolved problems.

Assuming without deciding that the trial judge was correct in ruling that the child was at no or minimal risk in the overnight visitation, he abused his discretion in failing to provide a specific place for the supervised visitation designed to protect the child fully with supervisors satisfactory to all parties. He could do no less. . . .

## Notes and Questions

1. Traditionally, a custody award to one parent (typically the mother) was accompanied by an award of visitation rights to the other parent. Some modern custody awards continue to mirror this traditional arrangement. In such cases, the trial judge has considerable discretion to determine the scope of visitation, including placing conditions on visitation by the noncustodial parent. (Conditions on visitation may also occur when the parties have joint custody.) Procedurally, if a parent requests the court to order restrictions on visitation, that parent bears the burden of proof on the need for the restriction.

Visitation rights in cases of sexual abuse (such as *Hanke*) constitute "one of the most pressing judicial and legislative problems in family law." See Doris Jonas Freed & Timothy B. Walker, Family Law in the Fifty States: An Overview, 23 Fam. L.Q. 495, 511 (1990).

2. What constitutional problems emerge in judicial resolution of visitation disputes? Is visitation a constitutionally protected right? See Steven L. Novinson, Post-Divorce Visitation: Untying the Triangular Knot, 1983 U. Ill. L. Rev. 121.

3. Because of public attention on domestic violence, a dramatic growth has occurred in the establishment of programs that offer supervised visitation services. See generally Janet R. Johnston & Robert B. Straus, Traumatized Children in Supervised Visitation: What Do They Need?, 37 Fam. & Conciliation Courts Rev. 135, 135 (1999). Services range from close supervision by a constant observer to more minimal supervision. Sometimes, supervision only takes place on the transfer of the child. Supervised visits might take place at, or away from, a program center. What is the purpose of supervised visitation? To evaluate parenting behavior? To reassure the custodial parent? To protect the child's safety? All of these? See Johnston & Straus, supra.

4. Based on courts' wide discretion in fashioning visitation orders, courts may specify the time, place, and circumstances of visitation. See generally Roland Fancher, Visitation, in 3 Child Custody and Visitation Law and Practice §16 (Sandra Morgan Little, ed., 2000). Supervised visitation gives rise to a host of difficulties framing the order. How frequent should visitation be? Should it include overnights? Should supervised visitation commence only after a parent seeks treatment for substance abuse or sexual abuse? See, e.g., Mary D. v. Watt, 438 S.E.2d 521 (W. Va. 1992). Completes treatment? Should visitation be phased in gradually if a suspension in visitation has occurred?

Who should supervise visitation? A social service worker? A mental health professional? An attorney? A relative? If a relative, should it be a relative of the abuser? Should it matter if the relative denies that the abuse took place? If payment for the supervisor is required, who should pay the fee? Should the supervisor be someone whom the child knows? Should the child's feelings about visitation be taken into account? See Carla Garrity & Mitchell A. Baris, Custody and Visitation: Is it Safe?, 17 Fam. Advoc. 40 (1995) (proposing models for supervised visitation, based on the child's age and other factors).

5. When should supervised visitation give way to unsupervised visitation? Suppose the parent contends that supervised visitation is interfering with the establishment of a good relationship with the child? See Grant v. Grant, 1995 WL 136775 (Ohio Ct. App. 1995).

6. What type of restrictions on visitation are enforceable in cases of sexual abuse? Can a court order an alleged abuser to cooperate with the children's therapist as a condition of visitation? In In re J.G.W., 433 N.W.2d 885 (Minn. 1988), a therapist required the father to admit responsibility for the abuse before she would recommend visitation. When the father objected, the appellate court concluded that this requirement constituted unlawful coercion.

7. Some courts may even terminate visitation in cases of sexual abuse. Because allegations of sexual abuse introduce criminal elements into a civil proceeding, what standard of proof should be required in

termination of parental rights to protect the alleged abuser's constitutional rights? See In re A.C., 643 So. 2d 743 (La. 1994); Mullen v. Phelps, 647 A.2d 714 (Vt. 1994) (both requiring clear and convincing evidence). On termination of parental rights, see Chapter VIII.

8. *Empirical research.* Research reveals that the majority of children who receive supervised visitation are victims of multiple and severe trauma (i.e., physical/sexual abuse and neglect, parental substance abuse, and parents' mental illness). Johnston & Straus, supra, at 135. Although few dissolution cases (about 5 percent) receive supervised visitation, the need far exceeds the demand. Nancy Thoennes & Jessica Pearson, Supervised Visitation: A Profile of Providers, 37 Fam. & Conciliation Courts Rev. 460, 468-469 (1999) (based on a survey of 94 programs in the United States and Canada). Obstacles to more widespread use of supervised visitation include cost, parental resistance, and the perception that supervision is merely a short-term solution. Id. at 470. Thoennes and Pearson conclude that supervised visitation is most effective when combined with other therapeutic interventions. Id. at 476.

9. *Other conditions.* Other parental behavior or practices may also lead to conditions on visitation, to wit:

a. *Religious exercise.* Disputes concerning the children's religion commonly arise. Because visitation often occurs on weekends, attendance at church or Sunday school becomes problematic. Can a parent be required to present the children at a particular religious institution during visitation? Conversely, can the court prohibit a parent from exposing the children to one parent's religion during visitation? Do these conditions violate either parent's constitutional rights? See Brown v. Szakal, 514 A.2d 81 (N.J. Super. Ct. Ch. Div. 1986); Zummo v. Zummo, 574 A.2d 1130 (Pa. Super. Ct. 1990).

b. *Sexual conduct.* Gay and lesbian parents also experience restrictions on their visitation rights. Courts are especially likely to restrict overnight visitation with a noncustodial parent on the condition that the child not be in the presence of the parent's lover. (Recall the restrictions in *DeLong,* supra, at 819.) See also Hertzler v. Hertzler, 908 P.2d 946 (Wyo. 1996). But cf. Boswell v. Boswell, 721 A.2d 662 (Md. 1998). See also Taylor v. Taylor, 47 S.W.3d 222 (Ark. 2001) (ordering removal of same-sex partner from household).

Such restrictions still occur but are less common for heterosexual relationships. See T.K.T. v. F.P.T., 716 So. 2d 1235 (Ala. Civ. App. 1998). But cf. Harrington v. Harrington, 648 So. 2d 543 (Miss. 1994); Carrico v. Blevins, 402 S.E.2d 235 (Va. Ct. App. 1991). See generally Robert G. Bagnall et al., Comment, Burdens on Gay Litigants and Bias in the Court System: Homosexual Panic, Child Custody, and Anonymous Parties, 19 Harv. C.R.-C.L. L. Rev. 497, 525 (1984).

c. *AIDS*. The AIDS epidemic prompted attempts (thus far unsuccessful) by custodial parents to restrict children's visitation with HIV-positive parents. See, e.g., North v. North, 648 A.2d 1025 (Md. Ct. Spec. App. 1994); Steven L. v. Dawn J., 561 N.Y.S.2d 322 (Fam. Ct. 1990). See generally Pierce J. Reed & Laura Davis Smith, HIV, Judicial Logic and Medical Science: Toward a Presumption of Noninfection in Child-Custody and Visitation Cases, 31 N. Eng. L. Rev. 471 (1997).

d. *Smoking*. Attention recently has focused on the dangers of "secondhand" smoke. Should a parent's smoking lead to conditions on that parent's visitation? See, e.g., Pizzitola v. Pizzitola, 748 S.W.2d 568 (Tex. App. 1988). A transfer of custody? See, e.g., Lizzio v. Lizzio, 618 N.Y.S.2d 934 (Fam. Ct. 1994). See generally Merril Sobie, Second Hand Smoke and Child Custody Determinations — A Relevant Factor or a Smoke Screen?, 18 Pace L. Rev. 41 (1997). Do conditions on smoking violate a parent's right to privacy? See generally Michele L. Tyler, Note, Blowing Smoke: Do Smokers Have a Right? Limiting the Privacy Rights of Cigarette Smokers, 86 Geo. L.J. 783 (1998).

10. What should be the penalty if a parent violates the condition on visitation? Contempt? Modification of custody? Temporary suspension of visitation? Denial of visitation?

## Problem

Roxie and Jeffrey separate after two years of marriage. Roxie and the couple's baby move in with Roxie's parents. Because Jeffrey performed limited childcare during the marriage and also because of Jeffrey's "unstable lifestyle" (details unspecified), Roxie requests that Jeffrey's contact be limited to supervised visitation at Roxie's home. Jeffrey does not contest the need for supervised visitation. When Jeffrey moves out-of-state to New Jersey, he requests a different visitation schedule and proposes as "supervisor" his 21-year-old brother and a friend who lives nearby. At the subsequent divorce proceeding, Roxie is awarded custody. The court awards visitation to Jeffrey on "alternative holidays and during the summer vacation provided he gives twenty-four hours notice of his intent to visit [and] that one of the individuals [whom he has suggested] be present during said visitation." Roxie appeals the visitation order, claiming that it is vague and gives no consideration to the qualifications of the visitation supervisors. What result? Would your reasoning change based on the reason for the supervision? Substance abuse? Sexual abuse? Homosexuality? Immaturity? If the court does elaborate further, how should it structure the visitation order (based on each of these possibilities)? See Weber v. Weber, 457 S.E.2d 488 (W. Va. 1995).

### b. Denial of Visitation

■ **TURNER v. TURNER**

*919 S.W.2d 340 (Tenn. Ct. App. 1995)*

KOCH, J.

This appeal involves an acrimonious post-divorce dispute over child support and visitation. . . . This appeal involves the denial of the father's latest petition for modification and the summary suspension of his visitation for not paying child support. . . .

Rebecca Diane Turner (now Turpin) and Charles Daniel Turner were married in September 1984. They had two children before separating in May 1987. After an unsuccessful attempt at reconciliation, Ms. Turner filed for divorce in June 1989. On August 15, 1990, the trial court entered a final order granting Ms. Turner the divorce and awarding her custody of the parties' children. The trial court also granted Mr. Turner visitation rights and ordered him to pay $704.13 per month in child support and to pay for the children's medical insurance. The trial court later denied Mr. Turner's post-trial motion to alter or amend the child support award but granted him additional visitation.

In early November 1990, Ms. Turner sought to have Mr. Turner held in contempt for being $2,166.52 in arrears in his child support. Mr. Turner responded with a petition admitting that he was delinquent in his child support payments and requesting a reduction in his child support because he was financially unable to comply with the August 1990 order. Thereafter, Mr. Turner paid all the child support due through November 30, 1990, and agreed to pay an additional $475 for the children's medical expenses. Following a hearing in January 1991, the trial court entered an order on February 1, 1991, finding Mr. Turner in contempt for failing to pay child support and to obtain medical insurance for his children. The trial court decided not to act on Mr. Turner's petition to modify his child support because "he comes to the Court with unclean hands." In addition, the trial court directed Mr. Turner to begin paying an additional $177 per month to reimburse Ms. Turner for obtaining medical insurance for the children through her group insurance plan at work.

Ms. Turner filed a second petition in May 1991 seeking to hold Mr. Turner in contempt for inappropriate conduct while he was returning her son from visitation. In December 1993, she filed her third contempt petition complaining that Mr. Turner had harassed and abused her and the children and that he was seriously delinquent in his child support obligations. Following an ex parte hearing, the trial court ordered Mr. Turner's arrest and suspended his visitation rights. Mr. Turner responded, as he had in the past, that he was financially unable to meet his child support obligations and again requested the trial court to reduce his child support.

Following a January 1994 hearing, the trial court filed an order on February 14, 1994, finding Mr. Turner in criminal contempt for violating the orders prohibiting him from harassing and abusing Ms. Turner and the children and also finding him in civil contempt for failing to make his child support payments. The trial court sentenced Mr. Turner to ten days for the criminal contempt to be served consecutively with a six-month sentence for civil contempt but determined that Mr. Turner could purge himself of the civil contempt by paying $40,908.86. The trial court also ordered that Mr. Turner's visitation would be summarily suspended if he did not make prompt and timely support payments.

The trial court summarily suspended Mr. Turner's visitation before he was released from jail because he failed to pay his child support. Mr. Turner filed another petition in July 1994 requesting modification of his child support and reinstatement of his visitation. On December 20, 1994, the trial court filed an order denying Mr. Turner's petition. . . .

Mr. Turner . . . takes issue with the trial court's refusal to permit him to visit his children because he is delinquent in paying his child support. While we are not prepared to say that this sanction is never appropriate, we find that the present facts do not warrant suspending Mr. Turner's visitation rights.

Child custody and visitation decisions should be guided by the best interests of the child. They are not intended to be punitive. Pizzillo v. Pizzillo, 884 S.W.2d 749, 757 (Tenn. Ct. App. 1994); Barnhill v. Barnhill, 826 S.W.2d 443, 453 (Tenn. Ct. App. 1991). As a general rule, the most preferable custody arrangement is one which promotes the children's relationships with both the custodial and noncustodial parent.

Ms. Turner argues in her brief that the children are adversely affected by Mr. Turner's failure to support them, and thus their best interests will be served by cutting off their visitation with their father unless he begins supporting them. This assertion would have some merit if the record contained proof to substantiate it. We find no such proof. The record, however, contains some support for concluding that the children are not going without basic necessities because Ms. Turner is presently able to provide for their needs.

The courts may deny or condition continuing visitation on the grounds of parental neglect. See Mimms v. Mimms, 780 S.W.2d 739, 745 (Tenn. Ct. App. 1989) (parental neglect may be considered in relation to the children's best interests). The denial of visitation is warranted, however, only when the noncustodial parent is financially able to support his or her children but refuses to do so. Since the trial court has not conclusively determined that Mr. Turner is at present willfully refusing to support his children even though he is financially able to do so, we have determined that the order curtailing Mr. Turner's visitation rights should likewise be vacated and that this issue should likewise be addressed and definitively decided on remand. Pending the remand hearing, the trial court should enter an interim order permitting Mr. Turner visitation on whatever terms the trial court determines are just and appropriate. . . .

## Notes and Questions

1. Because the Constitution protects the parent-child relationship, courts deny visitation reluctantly. What situations justify such a ban? Physical or sexual abuse? See, e.g., Nelson v. Jones, 781 P.2d 964 (Alaska 1989), *cert. denied*, 498 U.S. 810 (1990). Incarceration? See Knight v. Knight, 680 A.2d 1035 (Me. 1996). Child abduction? Substance abuse? See In re Marriage of DeSantis, 817 P.2d 769 (Or. Ct. App. 1991). Failure to pay child support?

2. What purpose does denial of visitation serve? Protection? Coercion? Punishment? What does *Turner* respond? Is it ever in the child's best interests to deny all contact with a parent? See generally Annotation, Complete Denial of Visitation Rights of Divorced Parent, 88 A.L.R.2d 148 (1963).

3. *Turner* illustrates the general rule: Visitation normally will not be conditioned on payment of child support; nor may support be withheld because an ex-spouse interferes with visitation. Some courts, however, similar to *Turner,* make an exception for willful and intentional failure to pay child support, which is detrimental to the child. See also Peterson v. Jason, 513 So. 2d 1351, 1352 (Fla. Dist. Ct. App. 1987). What explains the reluctance to link the two issues?

4. What are the advantages and disadvantages of disconnecting the issues? Of connecting them? Professor Karen Czapanskiy argues that both approaches limit the custodial parent's need for personal autonomy. She adds that the latter approach invites retaliatory withholding of support payments and limitations on opportunity to spend time with a child. Karen Czapanskiy, Child Support and Visitation: Rethinking the Connections, 20 Rutgers L.J. 619, 619-620 (1989). She also criticizes the application of both rules because they reflect gender-based parental roles. Id. at 644-658.

5. If interference with visitation is not a defense to nonpayment of support, should the former be grounds for modification of custody? Compare In re Marriage of Laird, 831 P.2d 1343 (Kan. Ct. App. 1992), with Webb v. Knudson, 582 A.2d 282, 287 (N.H. 1990).

6. Should a court compel a parent to exercise visitation rights? Compel a child to visit a parent?

---

Does empirical research support the rule that the right to visit and duty to support should not be dependent on each other? Consider the excerpt below.

■ **JESSICA PEARSON & NANCY THOENNES,**
**THE DENIAL OF VISITATION RIGHTS:**
**A PRELIMINARY LOOK AT ITS INCIDENCE,**
**CORRELATES, ANTECEDENTS AND**
**CONSEQUENCES**
*10 Law & Poly. 363, 375-379 (1988)*

This paper explores the nature and incidence of the denial of visitation rights and the non-payment of child support. . . . The analysis reveals that visitation denial is a problem with approximately 22 percent of sample mothers reputedly failing to comply with the visitation terms of their divorce decree. This is consistent with reports of [other studies], however, it should be noted that these levels fall far below the reported levels of non-compliance with child support. Only about half of all custodial parents owed child support receive the full amount of support owed to them in any given year. Even fewer custodians receive all the payments on time.

Estimated levels of visitation denial also fall below levels of non-contact by absent parents noted in previous research. For example, in their longitudinal study of 1,747 households, Furstenburg and North (1983:10) discovered that in cases involving children living in one-parent families where the non-custodian is believed to be alive, "over a third of the children . . . lost contact altogether with the biological parent living outside the home." Hetherington, et al. (1978) report that two years following the divorce, 30 percent of the children saw their fathers about once a month or less. Luepnitz (1982) reports that in 24 percent of the 34 maternal custody families she studied, all of whom had separated at least two years, the non-custodian "never" saw the children. Fulton's (1979) study also notes that after two years, 30 percent of the fathers no longer visit their children. And at the five year follow-up study with their volunteer sample of 60 families, Wallerstein and Kelly (1980) report that only nine percent of the children had no contact with the non-custodian, although another 17 percent were visited only sporadically.

Clearly, it is inaccurate to assume that all of these are cases in which custodians encourage sporadic visitation or deny the non-custodian regular access to the children. Indeed in her study, Luepnitz notes that:

> In half of the cases when the non-custodial father visits rarely or never, it is because the children dislike him and have decided not to see him. But in many other cases, custodial mothers report that their ex had split the scene "in order to evade child support payments."

(Luepnitz, 1982:34).

Further investigation of visitation non-compliance reveals that it rarely stands alone as a post-divorce problem and that such allegations are accompanied by a host of other visitation-related complaints.

Moreover, for most parents visitation difficulties appear to become established fairly early on and fail to deviate over time.

Couples with visitation problems are decidedly more embittered than their compliant counterparts and their lack of cooperation, conflict and anger are apparent at the earliest interview, well before the promulgation of a divorce decree and are corroborated by independent interviewer ratings. Although non-payment of child support cases do not always involve a visitation problem, the two phenomena are related and cases with visitation problems are substantially more likely to involve child support non-payment or disputes over support. Both phenomena appear to stem from conflict patterns between the parents, although we were unable to assess causal order in cases that involved both types of non-compliance. . . .

There is some relationship between compliance and anger level, with couples who are non-compliant on both visitation and support ranking the highest and compliant couples scoring the lowest on interviewer assessments of anger. Predictably, couples with only one area of alleged non-compliance fall mid-way between these two extremes, although there is not a clear pattern of non-compliance on the part of an angry parent. This indicates that other issues of an economic, legal, situational and psychological nature come to play in explaining non-compliance although the extreme patterns of mutual withholding and mutual compliance do appear to be more closely associated with couple dynamics at early stages of the divorce process.

### POLICY CONSIDERATIONS

These findings inspire several policy recommendations. Minimally, there is a need for reliable record keeping of both child support and visitation arrears. Without reliable record keeping, violations are difficult to prove, make-up policies are impossible to establish or supervise. To date, several states require child support payments to be made through the Clerk of the Court rather than directly to the custodial parent. . . . Objective accounts of visitation denial, however, are harder to come by. One model approach is found in a Michigan law which requires the child support enforcement agency, the Friend of the Court, to keep track of alleged visitation denials (with the custodial parent having an opportunity to contest the allegation) and to supervise make-up visitation orders (Mich. Comp. Laws F25.164 (42)(4)-(5)).

Secondly these findings underscore the importance of interventions with divorcing couples aimed at enhancing their communication skills and reducing levels of anger and hostility. [A] preliminary assessment of relationships between the non-custodial parent and his children reveals that conflict between divorced parents is a good prediction of both child support payment, visitation and other types of involvement (Braver et al., 1985). [I]t appears that neglect of therapeutic elements of the process may vastly diminish its potential effectiveness in reducing post-divorce conflict over visitation and support.

A third conclusion of this research is the need to consider child support and visitation issues concurrently. While there is no evidence to suggest that the two issues should be made contingent upon one another so that the denial of one should be a remedy for the withholding of the other, policy should reflect the fact that they co-occur and that grievances in both areas should be jointly aired. This conclusion runs counter to current practice. To date most court based mediation services deal with the issues of contested child custody and/or visitation only. Child support and the other financial issues of divorce are considered to be beyond the purview of the mediation intervention. In the few settings where child support issues are mediated in court settings, they tend to be handled by a separate staff. . . .

A fourth implication of our research is the need to create and evaluate mechanisms for the enforcement of both child support and visitation orders. As previously noted, Michigan law enables the Friend of the Court in each county to formulate a make-up visitation policy, including compensatory visitation. Other states have explored the use of fines, tort remedies, etc. (See Horowitz and Dodson 1985). Improved visitation enforcement is warranted by the observed incidence of interference, the co-occurrence of visitation and child support problems and equity considerations.

---

For additional empirical research on the relationship between custody and support, see Eleanor E. Maccoby & Robert H. Mnookin, Dividing the Child: Social and Legal Dilemmas of Custody (1992) (esp. ch. 10); Jessica Pearson & Nancy Thoennes, Child Custody and Child Support After Divorce, in Joint Custody and Shared Parenting 185 ( Jay Folberg ed., 1991); Jessica Pearson & Nancy Thoennes, Supporting Children After Divorce: The Influence of Custody on Support Levels and Payments, 22 Fam. L.Q. 319 (1988); Judith A. Seltzer et al., Family Ties After Divorce: The Relationship Between Visiting and Paying Child Support, 51 J. Marriage & Fam. 1013 (1989).

### 3. Standards Governing Parent versus Non-Parent Disputes

### ■ TROXEL v. GRANVILLE
*530 U.S. 57 (2000)*

Justice O'CONNOR announced the judgment of the Court and delivered an opinion, in which The Chief Justice, Justice GINSBURG, and Justice BREYER join. . . .

Tommie Granville and Brad Troxel shared a relationship that ended in June 1991. The two never married, but they had two daughters, Isabelle and Natalie. Jenifer and Gary Troxel are Brad's parents, and thus the paternal grandparents of Isabelle and Natalie. After Tommie and Brad separated in 1991, Brad lived with his parents and regularly brought his daughters to his parents' home for weekend visitation. Brad committed suicide in May 1993. Although the Troxels at first continued to see Isabelle and Natalie on a regular basis after their son's death, Tommie Granville informed the Troxels in October 1993 that she wished to limit their visitation with her daughters to one short visit per month.

[Two months later, the Troxels filed this petition for visitation.] At trial, the Troxels requested two weekends of overnight visitation per month and two weeks of visitation each summer. Granville did not oppose visitation altogether, but instead asked the court to order one day of visitation per month with no overnight stay. [T]he Superior Court [ordered] visitation one weekend per month, one week during the summer, and four hours on both of the petitioning grandparents' birthdays.

Granville appealed, during which time she married Kelly Wynn. [Before hearing Granville's appeal, the Washington Court of Appeals remanded the case to the Superior Court, which found that visitation was in the children's best interests. Nine months later, Granville's husband formally adopted the girls. The Court of Appeals reversed the visitation order based on their statutory interpretation that nonparents lack standing unless a custody action is pending.] Having resolved the case on the statutory ground, however, the Court of Appeals did not expressly pass on Granville's constitutional challenge to the visitation statute. . . .

## II.

The demographic changes of the past century make it difficult to speak of an average American family. The composition of families varies greatly from household to household. While many children may have two married parents and grandparents who visit regularly, many other children are raised in single-parent households. In 1996, children living with only one parent accounted for 28 percent of all children under age 18 in the United States. Understandably, in these single-parent households, persons outside the nuclear family are called upon with increasing frequency to assist in the everyday tasks of child rearing. In many cases, grandparents play an important role. For example, in 1998, approximately 4 million children — or 5.6 percent of all children under age 18 — lived in the household of their grandparents.

The nationwide enactment of nonparental visitation statutes is assuredly due, in some part, to the States' recognition of these changing realities of the American family. Because grandparents and other relatives undertake duties of a parental nature in many households, States have sought to ensure the welfare of the children therein by protecting the relationships those children form with such third parties. The States' nonparental visitation statutes are further supported by a recognition, which varies from State to State, that children should have the opportunity to benefit from relationships with statutorily specified persons — for example, their grandparents. The extension of statutory rights in this area to persons other than a child's parents, however, comes with an obvious cost. For example, the State's recognition of an independent third-party interest in a child can place a substantial burden on the traditional parent-child relationship. . . .

The liberty interest at issue in this case — the interest of parents in the care, custody, and control of their children — is perhaps the oldest of the fundamental liberty interests recognized by this Court. More than 75 years ago, in Meyer v. Nebraska, 262 U.S. 390, 399, 401 (1923), we held that the "liberty" protected by the Due Process Clause includes the right of parents to "establish a home and bring up children" and "to control the education of their own." Two years later, in Pierce v. Society of Sisters, 268 U.S. 510, 534-535 (1925), we again held that the "liberty of parents and guardians" includes the right "to direct the upbringing and education of children under their control." We explained in Pierce that "[t]he child is not the mere creature of the State; those who nurture him and direct his destiny have the right, coupled with the high duty, to recognize and prepare him for additional obligations." Id., at 535. We returned to the subject in Prince v. Massachusetts, 321 U.S. 158 (1944), and again confirmed that there is a constitutional dimension to the right of parents to direct the upbringing of their children. "It is cardinal with us that the custody, care and nurture of the child reside first in the parents, whose primary function and freedom include preparation for obligations the state can neither supply nor hinder." Id., at 166.

In subsequent cases also, we have recognized the fundamental right of parents to make decisions concerning the care, custody, and control of their children [citing Stanley v. Illinois, Wisconsin v. Yoder, Quilloin v. Walcott, etc.]. In light of this extensive precedent, it cannot now be doubted that the Due Process Clause of the Fourteenth Amendment protects the fundamental right of parents to make decisions concerning the care, custody, and control of their children.

Section 26.10.160(3), as applied to Granville and her family in this case, unconstitutionally infringes on that fundamental parental right. The Washington nonparental visitation statute is breathtakingly broad. According to the statute's text, "[a]ny person may petition the court for visitation rights at any time," and the court may grant such visitation rights whenever "visitation may serve the best interest of the child." §§26.10.160(3) (emphases added). That language effectively permits any third party seeking visitation to subject any decision by a parent concerning visitation of the parent's children to state-court review. Once the visitation petition has been filed in court and the matter is placed before a judge, a parent's decision that visitation would not be in the child's best interest is accorded no deference. Section 26.10.160(3) contains no requirement that a court accord the parent's decision any presumption of validity or any weight whatsoever. Instead, the Washington statute places the best-interest determination solely in the hands of the judge. Should the judge disagree with the parent's estimation of the child's best interests, the judge's view necessarily prevails. Thus, in practical effect, in the State of Washington a court can disregard and overturn any decision by a fit custodial parent concerning visitation whenever a third party affected by the decision files a visitation petition, based solely on the judge's determination of the child's best interests. . . .

Turning to the facts of this case, the record reveals that the Superior Court's order was based on precisely the type of mere disagreement we have just described and nothing more. The Superior Court's order was not founded on any special factors that might justify the State's interference with Granville's fundamental right to make decisions concerning the rearing of her two daughters. To be sure, this case involves a visitation petition filed by grandparents soon after the death of their son — the father of Isabelle and Natalie — but the combination of several factors here compels our conclusion that §26.10.160(3), as applied, exceeded the bounds of the Due Process Clause.

First, the Troxels did not allege, and no court has found, that Granville was an unfit parent. That aspect of the case is important, for there is a presumption that fit parents act in the best interests of their children. [S]o long as a parent adequately cares for his or her children (i.e., is fit), there will normally be no reason for the State to inject itself into the private realm of the family to further question the ability of that parent to make the best decisions concerning the rearing of that parent's children.

The problem here is not that the Washington Superior Court intervened, but that when it did so, it gave no special weight at all to Granville's determination of her daughters' best interests. More importantly, it appears that the Superior Court [adopted "a commonsensical approach [that] it is normally in the best interest of the children to spend quality time with the grandparent" and placing] on Granville, the fit custodial parent, the burden of *disproving* that visitation would be in the best interest of her daughters. . . .

The decisional framework employed by the Superior Court directly contravened the traditional presumption that a fit parent will act in the best interest of his or her child. In that respect, the court's presumption failed to provide any protection for Granville's fundamental constitutional right to make decisions concerning the rearing of her own daughters. In an ideal world, parents might always seek to cultivate the bonds between grandparents and their grandchildren. Needless to say, however, our world is far from perfect, and in it the decision whether such an intergenerational relationship would be beneficial in any specific case is for the parent to make in the first instance. And, if a fit parent's decision of the kind at issue here becomes subject to judicial review, the court must accord at least some special weight to the parent's own determination.

Finally, we note that there is no allegation that Granville ever sought to cut off visitation entirely. Rather, the present dispute originated when Granville informed the Troxels that she would prefer to restrict their visitation with Isabelle and Natalie to one short visit per month and special holidays. . . . The Superior Court gave no weight to Granville's having assented to visitation even before the filing of any visitation petition or subsequent court intervention. . . . Significantly, many other States expressly provide by statute that courts may not award visitation unless a parent has denied (or unreasonably denied) visitation to the concerned third party.

Considered together with the Superior Court's reasons for awarding visitation to the Troxels, the combination of these factors demonstrates that the visitation order in this case was an unconstitutional infringement on Granville's fundamental right to make decisions concerning the care, custody, and control of her two daughters. The Washington Superior Court failed to accord the determination of Granville, a fit custodial parent, any material weight. In fact, the Superior Court made only two formal findings in support of its visitation order. First, the Troxels "are part of a large, central, loving family, all located in this area, and the [Troxels] can provide opportunities for the children in the areas of cousins and music." App. 70a. Second, "[t]he children would be benefitted from spending quality time with the [Troxels], provided that that time is balanced with time with the childrens' [sic] nuclear family." Ibid. These slender findings, in combination with the court's announced presumption in favor of grandparent visitation and its failure to accord significant weight to Granville's already having offered meaningful visitation to the Troxels, show that this case involves nothing more than a simple disagreement between the Washington Superior Court and Granville concerning her children's best interests. The Superior Court's announced reason for ordering one week of visitation in the summer demonstrates our conclusion well: "I look back on some personal experiences. . . . We always spen[t] as kids a week with one set of grandparents and another set of grandparents, [and] it happened to work out in our family that [it] turned out to be an enjoyable experience. Maybe that can, in this family, if that is how it works out." Verbatim Report 220-221. As we have explained, the Due Process Clause does not permit a State to infringe on the fundamental right of parents to make childrearing decisions simply because a state judge believes a "better" decision could be made. Neither the Washington nonparental visitation statute generally — which places no limits on either the persons who may petition for visitation or the circumstances in which such a petition may be granted — nor the Superior Court in this specific case required anything more. Accordingly, we hold that §26.10.160(3), as applied in this case, is unconstitutional. . . .

Because we rest our decision on the sweeping breadth of §26.10.160(3) and the application of that broad, unlimited power in this case, we do not consider the primary constitutional question passed on by the Washington Supreme Court — whether the Due Process Clause requires all nonparental visitation statutes to include a showing of harm or potential harm to the child as a condition precedent to granting visitation. We do not, and need not, define today the precise scope of the parental due process right in the visitation context. [T]he constitutionality of any standard for awarding visitation turns on the specific manner in which that standard is applied. . . . Because much state-court adjudication in this context occurs on a case-by-case basis, we would be hesitant to hold that specific nonparental visitation statutes violate the Due Process Clause as a *per se* matter. . . .

[In separate omitted concurring opinions, Justice Souter upheld the state court's determination of the statute's facial unconstitutionality, and Justice Thomas noted that strict scrutiny ought to apply. In separate omitted dissenting opinions, Justice Scalia declined to recognize unenumerated constitutional rights, and Justice Kennedy reasoned that the best interest doctrine is not always an unconstitutional standard in visitation cases.]

    Justice STEVENS, dissenting.
    . . . In my view, the State Supreme Court erred in its federal constitutional analysis [when it found the statute facially unconstitutional] because neither the provision granting "any person" the right to petition the court for visitation, nor the absence of a provision requiring a "threshold . . . finding of harm to the child," provides a sufficient basis for holding that the statute is invalid in all its applications. . . . Under the Washington statute, there are plainly any number of cases — indeed, one suspects, the most common to arise — in which the "person" among "any" seeking visitation is a once-custodial caregiver, an intimate relation, or even a genetic parent. Even the Court would seem to agree that in many circumstances, it would be constitutionally permissible for a court to award some visitation of a child to a parent or previous caregiver in cases of parental separation or divorce, cases of disputed custody, cases involving temporary foster care or guardianship, and so forth. As the statute plainly sweeps in a great deal of the permissible, the State Supreme Court majority incorrectly concluded that a statute authorizing "any person" to file a petition seeking visitation privileges would invariably run afoul of the Fourteenth Amendment.

The second key aspect of the Washington Supreme Court's holding — that the Federal Constitution requires a showing of actual or potential "harm" to the child before a court may order visitation continued over a parent's objections — finds no support in this Court's case law. While, as the Court recognizes, the Federal Constitution certainly protects the parent-child relationship from arbitrary impairment by the State, we have never held that the parent's liberty interest in this relationship is so inflexible as to establish a rigid constitutional shield, protecting every arbitrary parental decision from any challenge absent a threshold finding of harm. The presumption that parental decisions generally serve the best interests of their children is sound, and clearly in the normal case the parent's interest is paramount. But even a fit parent is capable of treating a child like a mere possession.

Cases like this do not present a bipolar struggle between the parents and the State over who has final authority to determine what is in a child's best interests. There is at a minimum a third individual, whose interests are implicated in every case to which the statute applies — the child. . . .

[Justice Stevens discusses *Lehr* and *Michael H.* to support his argument that limitations exist to parental liberty interests.] A parent's rights with respect to her child have thus never been regarded as absolute, but rather are limited by the existence of an actual, developed relationship with a child, and are tied to the presence or absence of some embodiment of family. These limitations have arisen, not simply out of the definition of parenthood itself, but because of this Court's assumption that a parent's interests in a child must be balanced against the State's long-recognized interests as parens patriae, and, critically, the child's own complementary interest in preserving relationships that serve her welfare and protection.

While this Court has not yet had occasion to elucidate the nature of a child's liberty interests in preserving established familial or family-like bonds, it seems to me extremely likely that, to the extent parents and families have fundamental liberty interests in preserving such intimate relationships, so, too, do children have these interests, and so, too, must their interests be balanced in the equation. At a minimum, our prior cases recognizing that children are, generally speaking, constitutionally protected actors require that this Court reject any suggestion that when it comes to parental rights, children are so much chattel. The constitutional protection against arbitrary state interference with parental rights should not be extended to prevent the States from protecting children against the arbitrary exercise of parental authority that is not in fact motivated by an interest in the welfare of the child.

This is not, of course, to suggest that a child's liberty interest in maintaining contact with a particular individual is to be treated invariably as on a par with that child's parents' contrary interests. Because our substantive due process case law includes a strong presumption that a parent will act in the best interest of her child, it would be necessary, were the state appellate courts actually to confront a challenge to the statute as applied, to consider whether the trial court's assessment of the "best interest of the child" incorporated that presumption. . . . But presumptions notwithstanding, we should recognize that there may be circumstances in which a child has a stronger interest at stake than mere protection from serious harm caused by the termination of visitation by a "person" other than a parent. The almost infinite variety of family relationships that pervade our ever-changing society strongly counsel against the creation by this Court of a constitutional rule that treats a biological parent's liberty interest in the care and supervision of her child as an isolated right that may be exercised arbitrarily. It is indisputably the business of the States, rather than a federal court employing a national standard, to assess in the first instance the relative importance of the conflicting interests that give rise to disputes such as this. . . .

### ■ ALISON D. v. VIRGINIA M.
*572 N.E.2d 27 (N.Y. 1991)*

#### OPINION OF THE COURT

At issue in this case is whether petitioner, a biological stranger to a child who is properly in the custody of his biological mother, has standing to seek visitation with the child under Domestic Relations Law §70. . . .

Petitioner Alison D. and respondent Virginia M. established a relationship in September 1977 and began living together in March 1978. In March 1980, they decided to have a child and agreed that respondent would be artificially inseminated. Together, they planned for the conception and birth of the child and agreed to share jointly all rights and responsibilities of child-rearing. In July 1981, respondent gave birth to a baby boy, A.D.M., who was given petitioner's last name as his middle name and respondent's last name became his last name. Petitioner shared in all birthing expenses and, after A.D.M.'s birth, continued to provide for his support. During A.D.M.'s first two years, petitioner and respondent jointly cared for and made decisions regarding the child.

In November 1983, when the child was 2 years and 4 months old, petitioner and respondent terminated their relationship and petitioner moved out of the home they jointly owned. Petitioner and respondent agreed to a visitation schedule whereby petitioner continued to see the child a few times a week. Petitioner also agreed to continue to pay one half of the mortgage and major household expenses. By this time, the child had referred to both respondent and petitioner as "mommy."

Petitioner's visitation with the child continued until 1986, at which time respondent bought out petitioner's interest in the house and then began to restrict petitioner's visitation with the child. In 1987 petitioner moved to Ireland to pursue career opportunities, but continued her attempts to communicate with the child. Thereafter, respondent terminated all contact between petitioner and the child, returning all of petitioner's gifts and letters. No dispute exists that respondent is a fit parent. Petitioner commenced this proceeding seeking visitation rights pursuant to Domestic Relations Law §70. . . .

Pursuant to Domestic Relations Law §70 "either parent may apply to the supreme court for a writ of habeas corpus to have such minor child brought before such court; and [the court] may award the natural guardianship, charge and custody of such child to either parent . . . as the case may require." Although the Court is mindful of petitioner's understandable concern for and interest in the child and of her expectation and desire that her contact with the child would continue, she has no right under Domestic Relations Law §70 to seek visitation and, thereby, limit or diminish the right of the concededly fit biological parent to choose with whom her child associates. She is not a "parent" within the meaning of section 70.

Petitioner concedes that she is not the child's "parent"; that is, she is not the biological mother of the child nor is she a legal parent by virtue of an adoption. Rather she claims to have acted as a "de facto" parent or that she should be viewed as a parent "by estoppel." Therefore, she claims she has standing to seek visitation rights. These claims, however, are insufficient under section 70. Traditionally, in this State it is the child's mother and father who, assuming fitness, have the right to the care and custody of their child, even in situations where the non-parent has exercised some control over the child with the parents' consent. "It has long been recognized that, as between a parent and a third person, parental custody of a child may not be displaced absent grievous cause or necessity" (Matter of Ronald FF. v. Cindy GG., [70 N.Y.2d 141, 144 (1987)]. To allow the courts to award visitation — a limited form of custody — to a third person would necessarily impair the parents' right to custody and control. . . .

Section 70 gives parents the right to bring proceedings to ensure their proper exercise of their care, custody and control. Where the Legislature deemed it appropriate, it gave other categories of persons standing to seek visitation and it gave the courts the power to determine whether an award of visitation would be in the child's best interests (see, e.g., Domestic Relations Law §71 [visitation rights for siblings]; §72 [visitation rights for grandparents]). We decline petitioner's invitation to read the term parent in section 70 to include categories of nonparents who have developed a relationship with a child or who have had prior relationships with a child's parents and who wish to continue visitation with the child (accord, Nancy S. v. Michele G., 228 Cal. App. 3d 831, 279 Cal. Rptr. 212 [1st Dist., Mar. 20, 1991]). While one may dispute in an individual case whether it would be beneficial to a child to have continued contact with a nonparent, the Legislature did not in section 70 give such nonparent the opportunity to compel a fit parent to allow them to do so. . . .

KAYE, J. (dissenting).

The Court's decision, fixing biology[1] as the key to visitation rights, has impact far beyond this particular controversy, one that may affect a wide spectrum of relationships — including those of longtime heterosexual stepparents, "common-law" and nonheterosexual partners such as involved here, and even participants in scientific reproduction procedures. [T]he impact of today's decision falls hardest on the children of those relationships, limiting their opportunity to maintain bonds that may be crucial to their development. . . .

[I]t is perhaps helpful to begin with what is not at issue. This is not a custody case, but solely a visitation petition. [T]he sole issue is the relationship between Alison D. and A.D.M., in particular whether Alison D.'s petition for visitation should even be considered on its merits. I would conclude that the trial court had jurisdiction to hear the merits of this petition.

[I]t is uncontested [Virginia M. and Alison D.] shared "financial and emotional preparations" for the birth, and that for several years Alison D. actually filled the role of coparent to A.D.M., both tangibly and intangibly. In all, a parent-child relationship — encouraged or at least condoned by Virginia M. — apparently existed between A.D.M. and Alison D. during the first six years of the child's life.

While acknowledging that relationship, the Court nonetheless proclaims powerlessness to consider the child's interest at all, because the word "parent" in the statute imposes an absolute barrier to Alison D.'s petition for visitation. That same conclusion would follow . . . were the coparenting relationship one of 10 or more years, and irrespective of how close or deep the emotional ties might be between petitioner and child, or how devastating isolation might be to the child. I cannot agree that such a result is mandated by section 70, or any other law. [T]he Domestic Relations Law contains no such limitation. Indeed, it does not define the term "parent" at all. That remains for the courts to do, as often happens when statutory terms are undefined.

The majority insists, however, that, the word "parent" in this case can only be read to mean biological parent; the response "one fit parent" now forecloses all inquiry into the child's best interest, even in vis-

*[handwritten marginalia: even to the → detriment of the child]*

---

1. While the opinion speaks of biological and legal parenthood, this Court has not yet passed on the legality of adoption by a second mother.

itation proceedings. We have not previously taken such a hard line in these matters. . . . Domestic Relations Law §70 [whose objectives include "promoting the best interest of the child"] was amended in 1964 to broaden the category of persons entitled to seek habeas corpus relief. Previously, only a husband or wife living within the State, and legally separated from the spouse, had standing to bring such a proceeding. The courts, however, refused to apply the statute so literally. . . .

As the Court wrote in Matter of Bennett v. Jeffreys (40 N.Y.2d 543, 546) — even in recognizing the superior right of a biological parent to the custody of her child — "when there is a conflict, the best interest of the child has always been regarded as superior to the right of parental custody. Indeed, analysis of the cases reveals a shifting of emphasis rather than a remaking of substance. This shifting reflects more the modern principle that a child is a person, and not a subperson over whom the parent has an absolute possessory interest."

Apart from imposing upon itself an unnecessarily restrictive definition of "parent," and apart from turning its back on a tradition of reading of section 70 so as to promote the welfare of the children, in accord with the parens patriae power, the Court also overlooks the significant distinction between visitation and custody proceedings.

While both are of special concern to the State, custody and visitation are significantly different. Custody disputes implicate a parent's right to rear a child — with the child's corresponding right to be raised by a parent. Infringement of that right must be based on the fitness — more precisely the lack of fitness — of the custodial parent.

Visitation rights also implicate a right of the custodial parent, but it is the right to choose with whom the child associates. Any burden on the exercise of that right must be based on the child's overriding need to maintain a particular relationship. Logically, the fitness concern present in custody disputes is irrelevant in visitation petitions, where continuing contact with the child rather than severing of a parental tie is in issue. . . .

Of course there must be some limitation on who can petition for visitation. . . . Arguments that every dedicated caretaker could sue for visitation if the term "parent" were broadened, or that such action would necessarily effect sweeping change throughout the law, overlook and misportray the Court's role in defining otherwise undefined statutory terms to effect particular statutory purposes, and to do so narrowly, for those purposes only.

[R]ecent decisions from other jurisdictions, for the most part concerning visitation rights of stepparents, are instructive. [In Spells v. Spells, 378 A.2d 879, 881-882 (Pa. Super. Ct. 1977)], the court fashioned a test for "parental status" or "in loco parentis" requiring that the petitioner demonstrate actual assumption of the parental role and discharge of parental responsibilities. It should be required that the relationship with the child came into being with the consent of the biological or legal parent, and that the petitioner at least have had joint custody of the child for a significant period of time. . . . It is not my intention to spell out a definition but only to point out that it is surely within our competence to do so. . . .

I would remand the case to the Supreme Court for an exercise of its discretion in determining whether Alison D. stands in loco parentis to A.D.M. and, if so, whether it is in the child's best interest to allow her the visitation rights she claims.

## Notes and Questions

1. At common law, grandparents had no right to visitation with grandchildren in the face of parental objection. All states now have third-party visitation statutes that permit grandparents (and sometimes other persons, as revealed in *Troxel*) to petition for visitation in certain circumstances.

2. What societal factors explain the expanding legal recognition of grandparents' rights? Professors Andrew Cherlin and Frank Furstenberg point to several factors:

> All of these trends taken together — changes in mortality, fertility, trans-portation, communications, the work day, retirement, Social Security, and standards of living — have transformed grandparenthood from its pre-World War II state. More people are living longer to become grandparents and to enjoy a lengthy period of life as grandparents. They can keep in touch more easily with their grandchildren; they have more time to devote to them; they have more money to spend on them; and they are less likely still to be raising their own children.

Andrew J. Cherlin and Frank Furstenberg, Jr., The Modernization of Grandparenthood, in Arlene S. Skolnick, The Intimate Environment 131 (6th ed. 1989). Custody rights of grandparents take on renewed importance in an era of AIDS, substance abuse, and the feminization of poverty when it is common for biological parents, facing economic or medical difficulties, to ask their own parents for assistance with child care. See generally Karen Czapanskiy, Grandparents, Parents and Grandchildren: Actualizing Interdependency in Law, 26 Conn. L. Rev. 1315 (1994).

3. Four types of grandparent visitation statutes exist: (1) those conditioned on the related parent's rights ("derivative rights theory"), (2) those based on family disruption (for example, death of parent or divorce), (3) those based on best interests theory, and (4) those requiring a "substantial relationship" between grandparent and child. Patricia S. Fernandez, Grandparent Access: A Model Statute, 6 Yale L. & Pol'y Rev.

109, 118-124 (1988). Some triggering situations (for example, death or divorce) reflect more than one theory. What type was the Washington statute at issue in *Troxel*?

4. *Natural parent presumption.* A presumption favors natural parents in custody (as opposed to visitation) disputes involving parents versus nonparents. That is, courts apply a rebuttable presumption that custody should be awarded to a natural parent absent evidence of parental unfitness. In a landmark grandparents' rights case, a state supreme court refused to follow that presumption. In Painter v. Bannister, 140 N.W.2d 152 (Iowa 1966), *cert. denied,* 385 U.S. 949 (1966), a father left his young son with the boy's maternal grandparents when the boy's sister and mother died in an automobile accident. When the father remarried and requested the return of his son, the grandparents refused. The father brought a habeas corpus action. Refusing to apply the parental presumption, the court held that the child's best interests would be served by remaining with the stable, church-going Midwestern grandparents rather than the bohemian writer/father. For a discussion of the influence of *Painter* on law reform, see Gilbert A. Holmes, The Tie That Binds: The Constitutional Rights of Children to Maintain Relationships with Parent-Like Individuals, 53 Md. L. Rev. 358, 384 (1994).

The presumption played a role in another famous grandparents' rights case, Bottoms v. Bottoms, 457 S.E.2d 102 (Va. 1995), involving a maternal grandmother who petitioned for custody of a child over the objections of the child's lesbian mother. The Virginia Supreme Court affirmed the trial court's award of custody to the grandmother, holding that evidence of the mother's unfitness was sufficient to support the trial court's findings that the parental presumption had been rebutted.

5. Do grandparents' visitation statutes unconstitutionally infringe on the right to privacy (that is, parents' constitutional right to make decisions regarding their children)? Prior to *Troxel,* courts were split on that question. How does *Troxel* respond? How influential are Meyer v. Nebraska and Pierce v. Society of Sisters in the United States Supreme Court's analysis? Do the plurality and dissent (Justice Stevens) treat these precedents differently?

The Washington state supreme court had interpreted Meyer v. Nebraska and Pierce v. Society of Sisters (see Chapter I) to stand for the principle that the state may only interfere in parental rights to control the upbringing of their children to prevent harm to a child. In re Smith, 969 P.2d 21, 29 (Wash. 1998). Does this comport with your understanding of these cases?

Why do you suppose that Tommie Granville wanted to limit her daughters' visitation with their deceased father's parents? Should the law be involved in such private dispute resolution? See generally Sandra Day O'Connor, The Supreme Court and the Family, 3 U. Pa. J. Const. L. 573, 577 (2001) (discussing the law's difficulty in the prioritization of interests).

DP

6. In *Troxel*, the plurality held that the Washington statute, as applied to Tommie Granville, violated the Due Process Clause. In what way(s) was the application defective?

7. By holding the statute unconstitutional as applied, the Court avoided a ruling that the statute was facially unconstitutional. The Court also evaded identifying the appropriate standard of review. What standard of review should courts apply to nonparental visitation statutes? Should courts be especially protective of parental interests and apply strict scrutiny (as Justice Thomas reasons in an omitted concurrence)? Rational relationship? The undue burden standard (i.e., whether visitation unduly burdens the parents' constitutional rights)?

The Justices also disagreed on what the state must show to justify interference with a parent's decision about third-party visitation. What should the test be? The best interests of the child (as Justice Stevens and, in an omitted concurrence, Justice Kennedy believe)? Potential harm to the child if visitation is not granted? What are the advantages and disadvantages of applying each test?

8. To what extent does the Constitution protect the rights of a child to retain a relationship with a nonparent? Does *Michael H.* (discussed in Chapter IV) shed any light on the matter? In his dissent, Justice Stevens is alone in urging that the child's interests should be taken into consideration in the balancing of interests among the parents, grandparents, and state. What role should children's interests, wishes, and preferences play in this decision? (See infra section B(4)).

9. In the wake of *Troxel*, state legislatures and courts must determine the constitutionality of their third-party visitation statutes. If you were a legislator or a judge, what factors would be important to consider in the determination so as not to infringe on parental rights? In the balance between family privacy and state intervention, should it matter if the dispute involves an intact family or one disrupted by death or dissolution? How relevant was this factor in *Troxel*?

10. Should grandparents' rights be accorded more deference among cultural groups in which extended families play an important role? See generally Czapanskiy, supra, at 1327 (citing research showing that African-American grandparents are more than twice as likely to have shared a home with a grandchild for a period exceeding three months).

11. Currently, our modern family is characterized by an increasing number of nonparents seeking to continue their relationships with children. How far does the Court go in recognizing the variation in families? How receptive would the Court be, do you think, in allowing third-party visitation by other members of the extended family? Foster parents? Unrelated caregivers? Same-sex partners, such as Alison D.?

12. *Psychological parent.* Alison D. argues that she is a de facto or "psychological parent." The concept derives from the influential book by Joseph Goldstein et al., Beyond the Best Interests of the Child 17-20

(1973). Based on psychoanalytic theory, Goldstein and his co-authors (Anna Freud and Alfred Solnit) point out:

> Whether any adult becomes the psychological parent of a child is based thus on day-to-day interaction, companionship, and shared experiences. The role can be fulfilled either by a biological parent or by an adoptive parent or by any other caring adult — but never by an absent, interactive adult, whatever his biological or legal relationship to the child may be.

Id. at 19. Goldstein, Freud, and Solnit also advocate the importance of continuity of care. Id. at 31. When asked about the importance courts should attach to the "blood tie," Joseph Goldstein responded:

> The blood tie has become a shorthand, detached over time from its underlying function. It is a nice illustration of how a guideline developed as common law come[s] to be misapplied when the underlying reason for it gets lost. Courts mechanically applied the blood tie notion without taking into account . . . that the reason for it was that the natural parent was expected to be the primary source of care on a continuing basis.

Anne Goldstein, An Interview with Joseph Goldstein, 110 Yale L.J. 925, 930 (2001).

13. How should courts accommodate the parental preference rule and the best interests standard in disputes involving "psychological parents"? Was Alison D. a psychological parent? Consider the following:

> "These judges don't understand what it is to be a mother," Ms. G. [Michelle G., a lesbian co-parent appealing a judge's decision that she has no right to see the children she helped rear] said. "To sit there and say with a straight face that someone who has stayed up all night nursing a child, swabbing her chicken pox, taking joy in her every advancement, picking her up every time she's skinned her knee, or singing her to sleep is not a 'mother' is an absurdity."

Cited in David Margolick, Lesbians' Custody Fight Tests Family Law Frontier, N.Y. Times, July 4, 1990, at A1.

14. *Judicial treatment of lesbian co-parents.* As *Alison D.* reveals, courts have not been receptive to recognition of co-parenting rights after dissolution of a lesbian relationship. In *Alison D.*, the court refused to honor the women's previous oral agreement regarding childrearing. Would the court have enforced a prior written agreement? Compare A.C. v. C.B., 829 P.2d 660 (N.M. Ct. App. 1992), with In re Z.J.H., 459 N.W.2d 602 (Wis. Ct. App. 1990), *aff'd*, 471 N.W.2d 202 (Wis. 1991). Additional cases, similarly, have denied a lesbian partner custody or visitation rights. See, e.g., Nancy S. v. Michele G., 279 Cal. Rptr. 212 (Ct. App. 1991); Curiale v. Reagan, 272 Cal. Rptr. 520 (Ct. App. 1990).

Two recent cases may signal a greater willingness on the part of some courts to recognize lesbian parents' rights. In V.C. v. M.J.B., 748 A.2d 539 (N.J. 2000), the New Jersey Supreme Court affirmed a grant of visitation to the lesbian co-parent of twins (but denied joint custody). On the other hand, in R.E.M. v. S.L.V., No. FD-15-748-98N (N.J., Ocean County Super. Ct. Nov. 2, 1998), a New Jersey trial court awarded the non-biological mother both visitation and joint legal custody. See generally Julie Brienza, Lesbian Partner Awarded Joint Custody of Child Following Couple's Breakup, Trial Mag., Jan. 1999, at 98; Robin Wernik, Custody/Visitation Rights for Non-Biological "Parents": Analyzing V.C. v. M.J.B., N.J. Law. Mag., Feb. 2001, at 17; Robyn Cheryl Miller, Child Custody and Visitation Rights Arising from Same-Sex Relationship, 80 A.L.R.5th 1 (2000). Should the law distinguish between parental rights in the custody versus visitation contexts, as the dissent in *Alison D.* suggests?

15. Commentators have criticized the prevailing approach to lesbian co-parents' rights for its reliance on the Uniform Parentage Act's definition of parenthood, formulated to establish fatherhood for "out of wedlock" children. What problems might follow from applying this approach to lesbian co-parents? See Audra Elizabeth Laabs, Note, Lesbian ART, 19 Law & Ineq. 65, 100 (2001) (arguing that the UPA must respond to changes in the American family by creating an intent-based standard to determine parentage of children of assisted reproduction); Lisa M. Pooley, Note, Heterosexism and Children's Best Interests: Conflicting Concepts in *Nancy S. v. Michele G.,* 27 U.S.F. L. Rev. 477 (1993) (criticizing application of UPA).

16. *Stepparents' rights.* The sharp rise in divorce has contributed to an increase in the number of blended families including stepparents. Should stepparents have custody or visitation rights following dissolution? If a former stepparent seeks custody in the face of parental objection, that stepparent must overcome the biological parental preference. See David R. Fine & Mark A. Fine, Learning from Social Sciences: A Model for Reformation of the Laws Affecting Stepfamilies, 97 Dick. L. Rev. 49, 56 (1992) (citing survey finding that 38 states have such presumptions).

Courts have been increasingly willing to grant visitation rights to former stepparents, especially given a long-term relationship with the child. Fine & Fine, supra, at 56. See also Weinand v. Weinand, 616 N.W.2d 1 (Neb. 2000). See generally Margaret M. Mahoney, Stepfamilies and the Law (1994); Stephen Hellman, The Child, the Step Parent and the State: Step Parent Visitation and the Voice of the Child, 16 Touro L. Rev. 45 (1999); Wendy Evans Lehman, Annotation, Award of Custody of Child Where Contest Is Between Natural Parent and Stepparent, 10 A.L.R.4th 767 (1981 & Supp. 1996).

17. *What is a family?* The parental preference doctrine assumes that a child may have only one parent of each gender. *Alison D.* reveals that

some courts have difficulty recognizing custodial or visitation rights in cases in which a child would have more than one mother or father. See also Bodwell v. Brooks, 686 A.2d 1179 (N.H. 1996) (refusing to recognize status of stepfather that would result in "dual paternity"). Should the law recognize more than one mother or father for a child? (Recall Michael H. v. Gerald D., supra, Chapter 4.) On the other hand, might there be risks in an expansive definition of "family"? See Martha L. Minow, Redefining Families: Who's In and Who's Out?, 62 U. Colo. L. Rev. 269 (1991). See also Peggy Cooper Davis, The Good Mother: A New Look at Psychological Parent Theory, 11 N.Y.U. Rev. L. & Soc. Change 347 (1996) (examining research regarding multiple attachments).

The dissent in *Alison D.* addresses the issue of how far courts should extend the right to visitation. Should visitation extend to great-grandparents? See Wis. Stat. Ann. §767.245 (West 1993 & Supp. 2000). Siblings? See Ellen Marrus, "Where Have You Been, Fran?": The Right of Siblings to Seek Court Access to Override Parental Denial of Visitation, 66 Tenn. L. Rev. 977 (1999); Joel V. Williams, Sibling Rights to Visitation: A Relationship Too Valuable to Be Denied, 27 U. Tol. L. Rev. 259 (1995). A parent's boyfriend or girlfriend? Should co-residence with the child be a prerequisite? See, e.g., Youmans v. Ramos, 711 N.E.2d 165 (Mass. 1999) (awarding visitation to maternal aunt with whom child lived for most of her life).

18. *ALI.* In addition to legal parents, the ALI recognizes parents "by estoppel" as well as "de facto" parents. A parent by estoppel is a person who acts as a parent in circumstances that would estop the child's legal parent from denying the claimant's parental status. Parent-by-estoppel status may be created when an individual (1) is obligated for child support, or (2) has lived with the child for at least two years and has a reasonable belief that he is the father, or (3) has had an agreement with the child's legal parent since birth (or for at least two years) to serve as a coparent provided that recognition of parental status would serve the child's best interests. ALI Principles §2.03(1)(b)(2002). In contrast, a de facto parent is a person, other than a legal parent or parent by estoppel, who has regularly performed an equal or greater share of caretaking as the parent with whom the child primarily lived, lived with the child for a significant period (not less than two years), and acted as a parent for non-financial reasons (and with the agreement of a legal parent) or as a result of a complete failure or inability of any legal parent to perform caretaking functions. Id. at §2.03(1)(c). Which was *Alison D.*?

Both legal parents and parents by estoppel are entitled to presumptive allocations of custodial responsibility (§2.09(1)(a)), joint decisionmaking responsibility (§2.10(b)), and presumptive access to educational and medical records (§2.10(4)). However, the Principles' requirements are more strict regarding de facto parents to avoid inappropriate intrusion into the relationship between the legal parent(s) and children. Thus, a de facto parent is precluded from receiving a majority of custodial responsibility for the child if a legal parent or a parent by estoppel is fit and willing to care for the child (§2.18(1)(a)). Similarly, a de facto parent's rights may be limited or denied if the custodial allocation would be impractical in light of the number of other adults to be allocated custodial responsibility (§2.18(1)(b)). How well do these provisions address the problems inherent in recognizing third-party rights?

19. *What is a parent?* The same court that decided *Alison D.* also decided Braschi v. Stahl (see Chapter IV). Recall that *Braschi* adopted a functional definition of the family (recognizing a gay relationship to confer protection under a rent-control ordinance). *Alison D.* refused to apply a functional definition. What explains the different outcomes? Professor William Rubenstein theorizes differences in (1) the nature of the parties (landlord-tenant versus parents), (2) the litigants' contemplated future relationships (none, in the one case, versus a continuing relationship in the other), (3) the interests at stake (property versus human relationships), (4) the presence of third-party interests in one case (the child's), (5) the hierarchy of rights (one case involved a potential restriction on a biological parent's constitutional rights); and (6) the role of stereotypes (the speculative harm perpetrated on children by gay and lesbian parents). See William Rubenstein, We Are Family: A Reflection on the Search for Legal Recognition of Lesbian and Gay Relationships, 8 J.L. & Pol'y 89 (1991).

20. What, if anything, can risk-averse lesbian co-parents do to assure their recognition in the event of death or dissolution? To what extent should a biological connection help — say, one established using the semen from a male relative of the co-parent to conceive the child? See Nancy D. Polikoff, This Child Does Have Two Mothers — Redefining Parenthood to Meet the Needs of Children in Lesbian-Mother and Other Nontraditional Families, 78 Geo. L.J. 459, 535 (1990). On second-parent adoption for lesbian families, see Chapter IX, section D2.

Should courts and legislators adopt a functional (as opposed to formal) approach that would recognize those who act as parents in nontraditional settings? If so, what factors should be relevant in the determination of a functional "psychological parent"? See In re H.S.H.-K., 533 N.W.2d 419 (Wis. 1995) (mentioning such factors as the biological parent's consent and fostering the third-party's relationship with the child; co-residence; parental obligations for care, education, development, and support; and time sufficient to establish a bonded, dependent relationship). See also Ruthann Robson, Making Mothers: Lesbian Legal Theory and the Judicial Construction of Lesbian Mothers, 22 Women's Rts. L. Rep. 15, 23-27 (2000) (contrasting formalist approach in *Alison D.* to functional approach).

■ **NANCY D. POLIKOFF, THIS CHILD DOES
HAVE TWO MOTHERS: REDEFINING
PARENTHOOD TO MEET THE NEEDS OF
CHILDREN IN LESBIAN-MOTHER AND
OTHER NONTRADITIONAL FAMILIES**
*78 Geo. L.J. 459, 474-479, 482 (1990)*

Neither biology nor legal adoption is sufficient to establish who is a parent in a complex world affected by cultural norms, technology, and patterns of sexual behavior. Deviation from the one-mother/one-father prescription for parenthood is common. Communal child rearing, surrogacy, open adoption, stepfamilies, and extramarital births all destroy the myth of family homogeneity.

Some cultures have family structures that incorporate many parental figures. In Polynesia, for example, parenting is a collective task. The relative insignificance of biology is exemplified in the language, which generalizes the words for mother, father, and grandparent to all relatives of equivalent age and gender. Children have several houses that they regard as home; the death of a parent is not as acute a crisis as it is in the United States; life transition rituals involve numerous people; and parental rights are not exclusive of other adults.

Parenting is also a community responsibility in certain regions of the United States. Anthropologist Carol Stack [All Our Kin: Strategies for Survival in a Black Community (1974)] documented the assumption of parental rights and responsibilities in The Flats, the poorest section of a black community in a Midwestern city. She described child rearing, or "child-keeping," by relatives and friends that in many circumstances creates parental rights and obligations recognized by the community, even if not by the courts. These parental rights may be coterminous with the rights of the biological mother. They are acquired as a result of joint child rearing or the common knowledge that "[w]hatever happens to me, Ethel be the person to keep my kids." The rights may extend even to the exclusion of the rights of the biological mother. In one situation, a great-grandfather who raised his great-granddaughter for eight years acquired the "right" to decide who would raise her when he became too old to continue, even though the child's mother wanted her back at that time.

In the community Stack studied, women who assumed the roles of provider, discipliner, trainer, curer, and groomer on a more than temporary basis acquired the rights of motherhood. The intentions of the biological mother were relevant in assessing whether rights had been transferred. Her intentions were measured by what statements she made in public, how frequently she visited, how much she provided for the child, and the extent to which she continued to occupy the social role of parent. Even when a transfer of rights occurred in the eyes of the community and the child, the legal system did not recognize the existence of shared parental responsibility and cooperative child rearing. Stack describes biological mothers who used the courts to regain custody of their children, even though the community discouraged such action.

In addition to transferring parental rights, communal child rearing may intentionally create multiple parental figures. One comparative study of traditional and alternative child-rearing units in the United States examined fifty-four communal living groups with children, including a few three-parent families consisting of either two men and one woman or two women and one man. For the children living in these families, the one-mother/one-father model of parenthood is inaccurate. . . .

The prevalence of stepfamilies further dilutes the one-mother/one-father norm. Although not all stepparents function as parents, clearly some do. These stepparents are denied legal status as parents as long as the child has an existing parent of the same sex. Even a stepparent with primary parental responsibility cannot become a legal parent through adoption unless the parental rights of the noncustodial biological parent are terminated. If a stepparent adoption is completed, the noncustodial biological parent becomes a legal stranger to the child no matter what the actual relationship. If, in that instance, the custodial biological parent dies, the adoptive parent is the only remaining parent for purposes of determining custody. This is so even if the child is grown, the adoption is recent, and the child would rather live with the remaining biological parent. Open adoption, which has come into existence in recent years, attests to the willingness of some adoptive parents to include and even welcome a child's biological parent into the child's life, yet the law does not easily permit a child to have three legal parents.

The most common challenge to the one-mother/one-father model arises from the ability to determine paternity with a degree of certainty approaching that which exists for maternity. A child may have a biological father and a different functional father, usually the man who is married to that child's mother. The respective rights of these two men have been the subject of a substantial amount of litigation, most of it aimed at identifying one father of the child. In such cases, the state's attempt to reduce all families to the one-mother/one-father model is best exemplified by the presumption, sometimes rebuttable, that the husband of a married woman is the father of her child [citing Michael H. v. Gerald D.].

[C]ourts should protect children's interests within the context of nontraditional families, rather than attempt to eradicate such families by adhering to a fictitious homogenous family model. . . .

## Problem

L.M.K.O. is born to Denise and her partner Valerie in Minneapolis. The women chose a known donor, Mark, for medical reasons. Mark signs a donor agreement, waiving parental rights, but later regrets it. So all parties sign an agreement promising him a "significant relationship" with the child. After the birth, Valerie legally adopts the child. At Mark's request, the court grants him parental rights. Simultaneously, the court voids Valerie's adoption on the ground of fraud (asserting she misled the court about the father's existence).

Denise and Valerie separate, and Denise moves with L.M.K.O to Michigan. The court awards visitation rights to both Valerie and Mark. All three have a voice in decisions regarding education, religion, and health. The child visits Valerie and Mark in Minneapolis every other month; they visit her in the off months. When Valerie and Mark complain that the distance is straining their relationship, the court orders Denise to return to Minneapolis as a condition of her retaining sole custody. The three bicker constantly, even about issues such as a flu shot.

Denise now contends that the arrangement is unworkable. "There is neither a legal nor a sociological way to have three parents," she protests. Minn. Stat. §257.022(2)(b) (1998 & Supp. 2001) provides for "reasonable visitation" to persons who have lived in the child's household for two or more years, if the court finds that (1) visitation rights would be in the best interests of the child, (2) the petitioner and child had established emotional ties creating a parent and child relationship, and (3) visitation rights would not interfere with the relationship between the custodial parent and the child. How should the court rule on custody and visitation? See LaChapelle v. Mitten, 607 N.W.2d 151 (Minn. Ct. App. 2000). See generally Fred Bernstein, This Child Does Have Two Mothers . . . and a Sperm Donor with Visitation, 22 N.Y.U. Rev. L. & Soc. Change (1996); Nancy D. Polikoff, Breaking the Link Between Biology and Parental Rights in Planned Lesbian Families: When Semen Donors are Not Fathers, 2 Georgetown J. Gender & L. 57 (2000). For issues of second parent adoptions and sperm donors' rights, see Chapter IX, section E.

## 4. The Role of Special Participants

### a. The Child's Preference

■ **McMILLEN v. McMILLEN**
*602 A.2d 845 (Pa. 1992)*

LARSEN, Justice.

Appellant Vaughn S. McMillen (father) appeals from an order of the Superior Court vacating the July 22, 1988 child custody order in his favor and reinstating the order of July 31, 1987, which continued primary custody in appellee Carolyn F. Shemo, formerly Carolyn F. McMillen (mother). We reverse.

[The] parties were married on May 2, 1975 and . . . their son Emmett was born on September 30, 1977. The parties were subsequently divorced in . . . Wyoming on September 25, 1981. At the time of the divorce, the Wyoming court awarded primary custody of Emmett to the mother, subject only to the reasonable visitation of the father.

In March of 1982, the father instituted an action in the Court of Common Pleas of Indiana County, Pennsylvania, seeking partial custody of Emmett. On April 27, 1982, the court awarded general custody of Emmett to the mother with the right of visitation in the father. The court limited the father's visitation to alternating weekends and holidays, one day every other week and two weeks during the summer.

Over the next six years, the father sought modification of the custody order four times and the mother one time. Each time, the Court of Common Pleas significantly expanded the father's visitation rights. From 1986 on, Emmett repeatedly and steadfastly expressed his preference to live with his father. Finally, on July 22, 1988, the Court of Common Pleas awarded general custody of Emmett to the father. . . .

On appeal, the Superior Court vacated the July 22, 1988 custody order and reinstated the previous order of July 31, 1987. In doing so, the Superior Court determined that: 1) the record failed to present any circumstances warranting a change in custody; and 2) the child's best interests would not be served by changing custody merely because the child wished it. . . .

The father argues that the Superior Court, in determining Emmett's best interests, usurped the function of the trial court by ignoring the trial court's factual findings and also failed to give proper weight to Emmett's steadfast desire to live with his father. [A]n appellate court is empowered to determine whether the trial court's incontrovertible factual findings support its factual conclusions, but it may not interfere with those conclusions unless they are unreasonable in view of the trial court's factual findings; and thus, represent a gross abuse of discretion. Having reviewed the previous custody orders in this case, the trial court concluded that both the home of the mother and that of the father were equally acceptable. The trial court, therefore, was forced to look at other factors in making its decision. The only testimony taken at the most recent custody hearing was that of the child, Emmett, who was then almost 11 years old. Emmett testified that he preferred to live with his father.

Although the express wishes of a child are not controlling in custody decisions, such wishes do constitute an important factor that must be carefully considered in determining the child's best interest. The child's preference must be based on good reasons, and the child's maturity and intelligence must be considered. The weight to be given a child's testimony as to his preference can best be determined by the judge before whom the child appears.

Our review of the record shows that Emmett's preference to live with his father is supported by more than sufficient good reasons. Emmett testified that his stepfather frightens, upsets and threatens him, and his mother does nothing to prevent this mistreatment. He testified that he does not get along with either his mother or his stepfather, and that he gets along well with his stepmother. His testimony also revealed that his mother and stepfather leave him alone after school and that, even though his father and stepmother work, he is never left alone when he is at his father's home for the summer. Emmett also stated that his mother interferes with his sporting and farming activities and refuses even to watch him play ball. Thus, we find that Emmett's steadfast wish to live with his father was properly considered, and we find no abuse of discretion in the amount of weight afforded that preference.

Nor do we find an abuse of discretion in the trial court's conclusion that Emmett's best interests would be served more appropriately by placing him in his father's custody. The record supports the trial court's finding that both households were equally suitable. This being so, Emmett's expressed preference to live with his father could not but tip the evidentiary scale in favor of his father. Thus, the trial court's conclusion that it would be in Emmett's best interest to modify the prior custody order by transferring primary custody from the mother to the father is supported by the record, and we find no gross abuse of discretion by the trial court in awarding primary custody to the father.

## Notes and Questions

1. Is it appropriate to consider a child's custodial preference? If so, when? Most states have statutes that call for consideration of the child's wishes, including (a) those modeled after the Uniform Marriage and Divorce Act, which requires consideration of the child's wishes; (b) those that require consideration of the child's preference after a preliminary finding of maturity; (c) those that require deference to the child's preference for children of a specified age (12 to 14 years); and (d) those that give judges complete discretion as to whether to consider children's wishes. Kathleen Nemechek, Note, Child Preference in Custody Decisions: Where We Have Been, Where We are Now, Where We Should Go, 83 Iowa L. Rev. 437, 445-460 (1998).

2. In general, the older the child, the more likely a court will consider the child's wishes. How old must the child be? A few states establish a fixed age. Nemechek, supra, at 446-450 (citing four states). Others rely on judicial discretion. Compare Thorlaksen v. Thorlaksen, 453 N.W.2d 770 (N.D. 1990) (considering desire of 9- and 11-year-old girls to remain with mother and denying father's motion for modification), with In re Marriage of D.M.B. and R.L.B., 798 S.W.2d 399, 403 (Tex.

App. 1990) (affirming exclusion of testimony of eight-year-old girl absent a preliminary finding of maturity).

3. *Empirical research.* One empirical study reports that judges consider the preference of children aged 14 and older dispositive or extremely important (89 percent of respondents), preferences of children age 10 to 13 extremely important (54 percent), and the preferences of those children 6 to 9 somewhat important or not important (92 percent). Elizabeth S. Scott et al., Children's Preference in Adjudicated Custody Decisions, 22 Ga. L. Rev. 1035, 1050 nn.54-55 (1988). See also Nemechek, supra, at 460-461 (reporting empirical data suggesting that judges place little faith in children's decisionmaking ability). How likely is a court to force a teenager to live with a parent against the child's will? See Abbott v. Abbott, 481 N.W.2d 864 (Minn. Ct. App. 1992) (affirming wishes of 16-year-old girl who moved out of her mother's home after unequivocally stating her desire to live with her father).

4. *ALI.* The ALI recommends that courts should depart from a policy of deference to the primary caretaker to accommodate the preference of those children who have attained a specified age (suggesting 11 to 14 years as possible ages for a uniform rule). More weight should be given to the preferences of older children. ALI Principles §208, cmt. f (2002). See also Nemechek, supra, at 467 (concluding, based on a study of developmental theory, that statutes should require that judges allow children age 12 and older to make custody decisions). What do you think of these recommendations?

5. Should the child's reason influence whether the court considers the child's wishes? For example, should a child's testimony be given *more* weight in cases of suspected substance abuse or physical violence? See, e.g., In re Marriage of Valter, 548 N.E.2d 29 (Ill. 1989). Or if the custodial parent is relocating and the child wants to remain in the area with the noncustodial parent? See, e.g., McDonough v. Murphy, 539 N.W.2d 313 (N.D. 1995). Should the child's testimony be given *less* weight if the court determines that one parent has purposely alienated the child from the other parent? See, e.g., Price v. Price, 611 N.W.2d 425, 434 (S.D. 2000).

6. Children's preferences are more likely to be considered when both parents are fit (as in *McMillen*) or marginally fit. In such cases, the child's preference may serve as a tie-breaker. Children's preferences may be overridden if the court finds the preferred parent unfit. See, e.g., T.C.H. v. K.M.H., 784 S.W.2d 281 (Mo. Ct. App. 1989) (denying lesbian mother custody despite child's wish).

7. *Procedure.* If it is appropriate to take into account a child's preference, who should do so? The judge? The child's representative? A parent's attorney? A mental health professional? By what procedure? Should the child testify in open court? Should other witnesses testify in open court about the child's preference? Should the child discuss the prefer-

ence with the judge *in camera* (in a private interview)? Should these *in camera* conversations be recorded? Should they be limited to a determination of the child's preference or encompass any matter relevant to the custody decision? Are constitutional concerns implicated by broad-based inquiries or *in camera* interviews without opposing counsel present? See Molloy v. Molloy, 2001 WL 1013354 (Mich. Ct. App. 2001) (holding that interview must be restricted to determining preference and noting trend that reflects concern for parents' due process rights).

## Problem

Donny's mother dies two weeks after his birth. His father, Nicholas, gives Donny to his sister-in-law and her husband (the Millers) until Nicholas can care for him. Donny comes to think of the Millers as his parents even though he knows the truth. When Donny is six, Nicholas remarries and wants Donny back. The Millers persuade Nicholas to wait, saying that Donny needs more time. Nicholas subsequently insists. Eight-year-old Donny goes to live with his father, stepmother, and seven siblings. One month later, Donny runs away, calls the Millers, and pleads to return. After they return him to his father, Donny again runs away. He is so upset that he has intestinal distress, including vomiting. The Millers petition for "custody" (technically, guardianship). At the hearing, Donny (now age 9) tells the judge that he wants to live with the Millers, he does not get along well with his siblings, and his stepmother and father pay him little attention. The court-appointed expert testifies that Nicholas is less involved with Donny than the Millers and that, when questioned as to why he wanted Donny's return, Nicholas replied, "If you had a golf club that belonged to you, wouldn't you want it back?" The expert recommends that Donny remain with the Millers. What result under a statute that (a) has a parental presumption that requires parental unfitness before awarding custody to a nonparent, or (b) requires a finding of detriment-plus-best interests? See In re Guardianship of Marino, 106 Cal. Rptr. 655 (Ct. App. 1973).

### b. Representation for the Child

■ **LEARY v. LEARY**
*627 A.2d 30 (Md. Ct. Spec. App. 1993)*

BELL, Judge.
Appellant, Richard J. Leary, III, asks us to resolve several issues raised by his divorce from appellee, Barbara C. Leary. [Mr. Leary contends that the trial court erred in awarding his ex-wife sole legal custody

by failing to instruct the children's counsel as to her duties. He complains that due process requires that the parties know precisely the role of the child's representative, from the time of appointment, in order to properly prepare for, and respond to, the evidence. The court then discusses possible roles of the child's representative.]

### The Attorney as Guardian or Advocate?

When the court appoints an attorney to be a guardian ad litem for a child, the attorney's duty is to make a determination and recommendation after pinpointing what is in the best interests of the child. The attorney who assumes the traditional guardian ad litem role has a responsibility primarily to the court and therefore has absolute immunity for "judicial functions," which include testifying and making reports and recommendations. This more traditional role is defined by the court and the attorney looks to the court for direction and remuneration. . . .

A dichotomy exists between the attorney as guardian and the attorney as advocate, and the lines become very easily blurred. An attorney who has been appointed by the court has to be ever mindful of the Rules of Professional Conduct. In particular, an attorney may run afoul of the dictates of Rule 1.14, which sets forth the guidelines for representation of a client under a disability.[5] The Comment that accompanies Rule 1.14 states in part:

> The normal client-lawyer relationship is based on the assumption that the client, when properly advised and assisted, is capable of making decisions about important matters. When the client is a minor or suffers from a mental disorder or disability, however, maintaining the ordinary client-lawyer relationship may not be possible in all respects. In particular, an incapacitated person may have no power to make legally binding decisions. Nevertheless, a client lacking legal competence often has the ability to understand, deliberate upon, and reach conclusions about matters affecting the client's own well-being. Furthermore, to an increasing extent the law recognizes intermediate degrees of competence. For example, children as young as five or six years of age, and certainly those of ten or twelve, are regarded as having opinions that are entitled to weight in legal proceedings concerning their custody.

Perhaps the best example, for purposes of illustration, is when the child expresses an interest in living with one parent, yet the attorney believes that this would not be in the child's "best interests." Does the at-

---

5. Another Rule that must be considered is Rule 1.2, Scope of Representation, which provides: "(a) A lawyer shall abide by a client's decisions concerning the objectives of representation [and] when appropriate, shall consult with the client as to the means by which they are to be pursued. . . ."

torney vigorously advocate the child's position as required by the Rules, or does the attorney make the decision as to what is best for the child and present that to the court? . . .

There appears to be two schools of thought in answering that question: "One school holds that the child's preference is but one fact to be found, while the other maintains that without full advocacy of the preference there would be little reason to have a child's representative at all." Note, Lawyering for the Child: Principles of Representation in Custody and Visitation Disputes Arising from Divorce, 87 Yale L.J. 1126, 1141 (1978). An intermediate view suggests that there should be a "continuum of roles rather than the extremes of advocate and factfinder." Id. at 1141.

In a study of 18 Connecticut attorneys who had received appointments as counsel for children in divorce-related disputes, the researchers observed that some of the attorneys would characterize their role as either advocate or factfinder, yet they would discuss responsibilities that were inconsistent with the characterization. Those attorneys who stated that they served an advocate's role explained that this meant representing the child the way that they would an adult client. These same "advocates," however, also stated that there were instances in which they felt compelled to serve child-protective functions, which included counselling the parents, attending to the child's emotional needs during the litigation, and, in one extreme instance, making a recommendation that was the direct opposite of what the child/client wanted.

One attorney who was questioned during the study described his role as that of an advocate; however, upon questioning, it was determined that the attorney never discussed or discerned his client's custodial preference. Instead, the attorney stated that he spent his time with the parents trying to concentrate on a resolution "in which the 'losing parent' would not feel 'terribly embittered, vilified.' " [Id. at 1149.] The Yale article concludes that this type of deviation from a pure advocacy role might not be such a bad thing:

> Attorneys who identified themselves as advocates had clear conceptions of that role. An advocate should work to persuade the court to follow the client's preference by making motions, asserting arguments, drawing stipulations, and taking appeals if necessary. An advocate should help the adversary process by freeing parents' lawyers to give their clients undiluted loyalty. In practice, however, these attorneys performed in ways not suggested by their own role conceptions. They ignored, evaluated, or rejected the preference of the child; they worked to gather all available facts and sometimes did not advance a position to the court; they mediated between and counseled parents and tried to help them develop realistic perspectives. By responding to the needs of children in the process as well as in the outcome of adjudications, these attorneys may have advanced the interests of their clients more than would an attorney who limits himself to advocacy.

Id. at 1150.

The Yale authors also examined the role of attorneys who identified their tasks as aiding the court by fact finding. Some of the members of this group stated that their role was to "take on advocacy, counseling, and mediating responsibilities." Id. at 1150. . . . "In sum, attorneys who labeled themselves factfinders frequently described ways in which they evaluated evidence, shaped an argument for the court, decided to curtail an investigation, and negotiated settlements. The one attorney who confined himself to investigation concluded that this failed to protect the interests of the child. For the other attorneys, who went ahead and took on duties other than factfinding, the theoretical role conceptions proved simply irrelevant and were discarded unnoticed as the attorneys responded to their perceptions of the child's interests." Id. at 1153.

Recognizing that there is a growing need to define more clearly an attorney's role in custody disputes, the American Bar Association is looking toward drafting standards. Also the bar associations in various states, such as Connecticut, are in the process of drafting their own individual guidelines. . . .

There has been little discussion in Maryland of the role an attorney should play in custody cases. In [Levitt v. Levitt, 556 A.2d 1162 (Md. Ct. Spec. App. 1989)], we established the importance of child counsel in contested custody matters, sending the trial courts a message on "what child counsel's role should be." We do not retreat from that perspective and encourage trial judges to tell their appointed attorneys what they expect — waiver, pure representation, pure investigation, or a combination. . . .

### COUNSEL FOR THE LEARY CHILDREN

In the instant case, the trial judge did not enter an order stating the purpose for the appointment. While it would have been preferable for him to have done so, we do not conclude that the omission in this case was fatal. . . .

[Mr. Leary] complains that "Ms. Coates [appointed counsel for the children] clearly perceived her role to be that of 'mouthpiece,' not guardian ad litem or investigator"; her purpose, as she perceived it according to him, was "to simply convey to the Court what the desire of the nine and thirteen year-old boys were. . . ." We do not agree.

[Ms. Coates] described two very intelligent young boys who were outgoing, doing well in school, and able to express their preferences. She was not acting strictly as an advocate of their position, but as a conveyer of their preferences, which she concluded were not improperly motivated. In other words, the circumstances forced her to take the middle ground between advocacy and fact finding.

Ms. Coates investigated what the trial judge wanted to know — namely, the children's preferences — but it was the trial judge, not Ms.

Coates, who concluded that joint custody was not to be. In fact, although her recommendations were struck, Ms. Coates concluded that joint custody would be appropriate. We fail to see how the lack of articulated directions by the trial judge, even if preserved, hurt Mr. Leary. . . .

## Notes and Questions

1. The debate over mandatory representation for children in custody and visitation disputes first surfaced in the 1960s and 1970s. The debate was sparked by the rising divorce rate, concerns about the effects of divorce on children, and recognition of the child's right to counsel in the delinquency context (In re Gault, 387 U.S. 1 (1967)). Should counsel for the child in contested disputes be mandatory? Or at the parents' discretion? See Joseph Goldstein et al., Before the Best Interests of the Child 119 (1979) (so arguing). Does the child have a due process right to counsel?

2. Despite considerable support by commentators and practitioners for mandatory counsel, appointment of the child's representative in custody disputes is generally at the court's discretion. Only one state mandates representation in contested cases. See, e.g., Wis. Stat. Ann. §767.045 (West 1993 & Supp. 2000).

3. Some jurisdictions provide for representation in custody cases involving allegations of abuse or neglect. Some courts even have found an abuse of discretion for failure to appoint a guardian ad litem in such cases. See, e.g., G.S. v. T.S., 582 A.2d 467 (Conn. App. Ct. 1990). But cf. Schenk v. Schenk, 564 N.E.2d 973 (Ind. Ct. App. 1991). Why is representation necessary in such proceedings? See generally David Peterson, Comment, Judicial Discretion Is Insufficient: Minors' Due Process Right to Participate with Counsel When Divorce Custody Disputes Involve Allegations of Child Abuse, 25 Golden Gate U. L. Rev. 513 (1995).

4. Is a discretionary standard appropriate for appointment of counsel? What factors might influence judicial discretion? See Linda Elrod, Counsel for the Child in Custody Disputes: The Time Is Now, 26 Fam. L.Q. 53, 56 (1992) (identifying the cost factor and also concerns about guardian ad litem competence and the possible redundancy of representation because the parents are represented). See also La. Rev. Stat. Ann. §9:345 (West 2000) (offering guidelines).

5. *Models of representation.* As *Leary* reveals, considerable debate exists about the appropriate role of the child's representative and the scope of that representation. Although courts and commentators characterize the possible roles differently, several models exist: (1) the court-designated investigator who investigates and makes recommendations to the court, (2) the attorney who represents the child's wishes, (3) the advocate for the "best interests" of the children, (4) the facilitator/mediator, and (5) some combination of the above. Raven C. Lidman & Betsy R. Hollingsworth,

The Guardian Ad Litem in Child Custody Cases: The Contours of Our Judicial System Stretched Beyond Recognition, 6 Geo. Mason L. Rev. 255, 256-257 (1998). See also Dana E. Prescott, The Guardian Ad Litem in Custody and Conflict Cases: Investigator, Champion, and Referee?, 22 U. Ark. Little Rock L. Rev. 529 (2000).

Which roles are most/least invasive of family privacy? See Martin Guggenheim, The Right to Be Represented But Not Heard: Reflections on Legal Representation for Children, 59 N.Y.U. L. Rev. 76, 121-122 (1978); Wallace Mlyniec, The Child Advocate in Private Custody Disputes: A Role in Search of a Standard, 16 J. Fam. L. 1, 16 (1977-1978).

If the representative serves as an advocate, should the representative advocate the child's wishes regardless of what the advocate believes is in the child's best interests? Should the attorney ever advocate an outcome that conflicts with the client's wishes? If the representative ascertains the child's best interests, does this role usurp the authority of the judge? Is it redundant in representing a position already represented?

Does the investigator-neutral factfinder's role conflict with the duty to represent a client zealously (Model Code of Professional Responsibility EC 7-1)? If so, does the child need both a representative and an advocate? See In re Marriage of Rolfe, 699 P.2d 79 (Mont. 1985), aff'd, 766 P.2d 223 (Mont. 1988).

Should the representative's role change based on the type of proceeding (e.g., abuse, delinquency, custody)? Based on the child's age or abilities? See Annette R. Appell, Decontextualizing the Child Client: The Efficacy of the Attorney-Client Model for Very Young Children, 64 Fordham L. Rev. 1955 (1996). Professor Martin Guggenheim proposes a rule that an attorney should advocate the child's wishes if the child is at least seven years old. Guggenheim, supra, at 91. What are the merits of such a proposal? See also Martin Guggenheim, Reconsidering the Need for Counsel for Children in Custody, Visitation and Child Protection Proceedings, 29 Loy. U. Chi. L.J. 299 (1998).

6. Where does the role of "mouthpiece" (Mr. Leary's term) fit in the continuum? What difficulties does it raise?

7. The study, cited in *Leary*, points out that some attorneys who characterize their role as advocate or factfinder then act inconsistently with those characterizations. Possible factors that might influence an attorney's perception of his or her role include (a) how the role is described, if at all, by state law; (b) any instruction given by, or exceptions of, the appointing judge; (c) the training that the guardian ad litem has received as to his or her role; (d) the age of the child and the guardian's ad litem understanding of child development, bonding and attachment, and permanency planning issues. Howard A. Davidson, The Child's Right to Be Heard and Represented in Judicial Proceedings, 18 Pepp. L. Rev. 255, 263 (1991).

8. Few jurisdictions require that the child's representative be an attorney. Lidman & Hollingsworth, supra, at 263. Should a court-

appointed representative be an attorney? Guardians ad litem may come from other professions (for example, social work). What problems ensue from the participation of nonattorney guardians? For example, if the representative is a nonattorney guardian ad litem, then communications between a child and the guardian ad litem are not privileged. Confidentiality problems may exist even if the court appoints an attorney if the court denominates the attorney to serve in the role of guardian ad litem. See Bruce A. Green, Lawyers as Nonlawyers in Child-Custody and Visitation Cases: Questions from the "Legal Ethics" Perspective, 73 Ind. L.J. 665 (1998). See also Emily Buss, "You're My What?" The Problem of Children's Misperceptions of Their Lawyers' Roles, 64 Fordham L. Rev. 1699, 1725-1731 (1996); Roy T. Stuckey, Guardians Ad Litem as Surrogate Parents: Implications for Role Definition and Confidentiality, 64 Fordham L. Rev. 1785 (1996).

9. As *Leary* indicates, several states have promulgated standards for guardians ad litem. See Robert E. Shepherd, Jr. & Sharon S. England, "I Know the Child Is My Client, But Who Am I?," 64 Fordham L. Rev. 1917, 1940 (1996). In addition, the American Academy of Matrimonial Lawyers (AAML) in 1995 adopted standards of practice for attorneys and guardians ad litem in custody or visitation disputes. The standards are premised on the idea that representatives should not be appointed routinely but should be reserved for cases where the parents request appointment or the court finds that appointment is necessary. American Academy of Matrimonial Lawyers, Representing Children: Standards for Attorneys and Guardians Ad Litem in Custody or Visitation Proceedings, Standard 1.1 & Cmt. (1995) (reprinted at 13 J. Am. Acad. Matrimonial Law. 1, 2-4 (1995)). The standards suggest that the court should specify in writing the tasks the representative should perform. Standard 1.3 & Cmt.

Further, the standards also address the attorney's role when the court appoints a lawyer as representative, suggesting that the lawyer-representative should advocate the child's wishes for a child who is "unimpaired" (Standards 2.1-2.2). Children under age 12 are rebuttably presumed to be "impaired" (Standard 2.2). The "impaired/unimpaired" distinction parallels that of the ABA Model Rules of Professional Conduct.

### c. Role of Experts

■ **IN RE REBECCA B.**
*611 N.Y.S.2d 831 (App. Div.), motion for leave to appeal denied, 645 N.E.2d 1217 (N.Y. 1994)*

**MEMORANDUM DECISION**

[In 1986, after Renee B. and Michael B. had been married for five years, Renee filed for divorce and sole custody of their daughter Rebecca. The Family Court granted both motions. In 1992, upon discovering that Michael was sleeping in the same bed as Rebecca, Renee petitioned to eliminate Michael's overnight visitation and to require supervised visitation. Michael cross-petitioned for sole custody. The Family Court denied Michael's cross-petition and affirmed the award of sole custody to the mother. The father appealed.]

[The Family Court] Order, dated May 8, 1992, which, inter alia, denied the motion of appellant father for a transfer of the sole legal custody of his daughter from her mother, to him, [is] unanimously modified on the law and the facts, and in the exercise of discretion, to the extent of granting the transfer of the sole legal custody to appellant, with liberal visitation rights to respondent mother, and otherwise, insofar as consistent with such transfer of sole legal custody to appellant, in all respects [is] otherwise affirmed, without costs or disbursements. It is ordered that any further proceedings in the matter in the Family Court be held before another judge.

The Clinical Director of the Family Court's Mental Health Service was qualified to testify as an expert in clinical psychology. He had met with the child on three occasions for a total of three hours and with her and each parent for about forty minutes. He also had met with each parent separately for about seven hours. He concluded that the child's best interests required the transfer of custody to appellant with liberal visitation for the mother noting that appellant was a much less detrimental influence on the child than was the mother, that he was less likely to cause long-term harm to her than was the mother, that the child perceived him as more loving than her mother, and that she had a more profound bond with him. The child made it clear repeatedly to the Clinical Director that she would prefer to live with her father; the mother's spanking, slapping, and locking of the child in her room was difficult for the child to comprehend.

Another psychiatrist, also recommended a change in custody, for the "main reason" that the mother tried so to exclude appellant from the child's life; he believed that appellant as the custodial parent would give better access to the noncustodial parent. From age seven to eight the child had slept with her father on overnight visits, but there had been no suggestion of any improper action by appellant and the practice had ceased. The psychiatrist had found nothing "intrinsically detrimental" in the arrangement. A supervising social worker employed by the Legal Aid Society, also recommended that custody be transferred to appellant.

A psychiatrist retained by the mother testified that custody should be continued with the mother. However, he had spoken only with the mother and with people to whom he was referred by the mother and not to the child or appellant.

The law guardian, believing that appellant was more likely to foster the non-custodial parent's relationship, concluded that the transfer of custody to him was in the best interest of the child.

The trial court denied appellant's motion to transfer custody to him, terming the testimony of the Clinical Director, the first mentioned psychiatrist and the Social Worker not credible. They were, however, the only experts making a recommendation as to custody who had spoken to all three family members, but the trial court repeatedly described their testimony as "flawed." By discounting the testimony of these three witnesses, the trial court essentially left itself without expert testimony on the child's preferences and the quality of her relationships with her parents. Since the mother's psychiatrist had not interviewed the child or appellant, moreover, little weight should be accorded to his recommendation that custody be awarded to the mother. . . .

A determination had been made by Family Court in 1987 that the mother should have custody. The burden was thus on appellant to demonstrate a substantial change of circumstances to justify a change in custody. He did so in 1991 by showing the preference of the child — then seven years of age — to live with him, by showing the bond which had grown between them, by showing petitioner's rather punitive disciplining of the child, which would over time have a deleterious effect on the child, and especially by his showing of petitioner's efforts to exclude him from the child's life.

We must respect the advantage of the trial judge in observing the witnesses, but the authority of this court in matters of custody is as broad as that of the trial court. It always comes down, however, to the best interests of the child and the ability of the parents "to provide for the child's emotional and intellectual development, the quality of the home environment and the parental guidance provided." The psychiatrist, testifying on behalf of petitioner, said of her: "She is a somewhat temperamental lady who has a temper, and it would be better if she kept her mouth shut more and didn't get into fights with her former husband and her child, but that's normal within the context of this kind of situation." This is not a severe indictment of a person, but it does support other testimony that petitioner tends to be short-tempered and punitive with her daughter and the inference therefrom that the child is being harmed. There has been no showing, on the other hand, that appellant despite his social isolation, tends to be other than helpful, patient, and constructive in his relationship with his daughter.

It has been shown that petitioner attempts to exclude appellant from the child's life. The Clinical Director and the psychiatrist who met with all concerned believe that, if awarded custody, she will continue to do so. Such acts are "so inconsistent with the best interests of the children as to, per se, raise a strong probability that the mother is unfit to act as custodial parent" (Entwistle v. Entwistle, 402 N.Y.S.2d 213, *appeal dismissed,* 44 N.Y.2d 851).

This court finds the testimony of those experts favoring custody of the child to appellant convincing. . . . The trial court's custody award lacked a sound and substantial basis in the record and should not be allowed to stand.

## Notes and Questions

1. Mental health experts play different roles in custody determinations. The court may appoint an expert to make a recommendation. Or a party's attorney may employ an expert to make an independent evaluation, furnish a second opinion, or rebut testimony. See generally Marc J. Ackerman, Clinician's Guide to Child Custody Evaluations 4-7 (1995). Can you identify the various roles of the professionals in *Rebecca B.*?

2. Psychologists, psychiatrists, and social workers are the professionals who most frequently serve in a custody evaluation. How might their different backgrounds and training influence their evaluations? See Melvin G. Goldzband, Custody Cases and Expert Witnesses: A Manual for Attorneys xxi (1980) (noting, for example, that a psychologist, compared to a psychiatrist, "may often depend more upon the tests they perform with the participants than upon clinical or historical criteria"). Should courts limit the number of experts who can participate in a given case? Should there be one court-appointed expert or as many as the parties desire?

3. Professionals in custody determinations must observe professional codes of ethics and standards of practice. For example, psychologists are subject to the American Psychological Association's (APA) Ethical Principles of Psychologists and Code of Conduct (for members of the APA), Specialty Guidelines for Forensic Psychologists, and Guidelines for Child Custody Evaluations in Divorce Proceedings (guidelines applicable to custody evaluators). See American Psychological Association, Ethical Principles of Psychologists and Code of Conduct, 47 Am. Psychol. 1597 (1992); American Psychological Association, Guidelines for Child Custody Evaluations in Divorce Proceedings, 49 Am. Psychol. 677 (1994); Committee on Ethical Guidelines for Forensic Psychologists, Specialty Guidelines for Forensic Psychologists, 15 Law & Hum. Behav. 655 (1991). See also Marion Gindes, Guidelines for Child Custody Evaluations for Psychologists: An Overview and Commentary, 29 Fam. L.Q. 39 (1995).

4. The appellate court in *Rebecca B.* reversed two prior rulings in favor of the mother (and an 8-year-long custody arrangement) on the basis that the trial judge erred by rejecting much of the expert testimony. In a lengthy opinion (Renee B. v. Michael B., No. V5272186 (N.Y. Fam. Ct. May 8, 1992)), trial judge George L. Jurow (who has a Ph.D. in psychology) explained his reasons for finding certain testimony "not credible" and "flawed":

- the father's expert's objectivity was compromised by his employment as the father's psychiatrist for four years (slip op. at 87); the expert engaged in "collusive interactions" by interviewing the daughter without the mother's knowledge or consent (id. at 88); the expert's conclusion that the mother was alienating the daughter and was responsible for communication difficulties was "factually incorrect and contradicted by other credible evidence" (id. at 89-90) (because the father's confrontations with school officials led them to ban him from the premises, and the father taped all conversations with the wife or daughter); the expert applied a gender-biased standard in recommending paternal custody based on the mother's demanding career as a corporate lawyer (id. at 91-92);

- the supervising social worker (who recommended a custody transfer to the father) adopted "uncritically and without reflection" the opinion of the father's expert without conducting a thorough evaluation (id. at 100);
- the court-appointed expert's evaluation had "important inquiry lapses," (regarding the father's lack of work history and plan to withdraw the daughter from school) (id. at 81); conflicted with that expert's own observations that the father was an "individual who is socially isolated, has no friends, is prone to continued confrontations with people, [and] is 'interpersonally retarded,' . . ." (id. at 82); and, failed to recognize that the daughter's desire to live with her father was the "product of paternal pressure or an excessive degree of overbearing influence" (id. at 83).

Do you agree with the appellate court that the trial court's award "lacked a sound and substantial basis" in the record?

5. *Parental Alienation Syndrome.* The father's expert based his opinion, in part, on evidence of the "Parental Alienation Syndrome," a term that he coined to signify a parent's conscious or subconscious attempts to alienate a client from the other parent. See Richard A. Gardner, The Parental Alienation Syndrome: A Guide for Mental Health and Legal Professionals (1992). Don't many divorcing parents exhibit varying degrees of this syndome? Although the theory is admissible in court, it has not gained widespread acceptance by professionals. For a trenchant critique, see Cheri L. Wood, Note, The Parental Alienation Syndrome: A Dangerous Aura of Reliability, 27 Loy. L.A. L. Rev. 1367, 1368 (1994).

6. Are mental health professionals capable of determining custodial arrangements in the best interests of children? Psychologists Lois Weithorn and Thomas Grisso criticize the judicial tendency to allow professionals to play a dispositive role. Arguing that clinical evaluations give a false aura of reliability and convey the impression that psychologists are uniquely qualified to make such decisions, Weithorn and Grisso suggest that expert opinion often results instead from subjective biases and lifestyle preferences. Lois Weithorn & Thomas Grisso, Psychological

Evaluations in Divorce Custody: Problems, Principles, and Procedures, in Psychology and Child Custody Determinations 157, 160 (Lois Weithorn ed., 1987). See also Martha Fineman, Dominant Discourse, Professional Language and Legal Change in Child Custody Decision-making, 101 Harv. L. Rev. 727, 760-774 (1988) (criticizing the abdication of responsibility to mental health professionals and urging a return of responsibility to legal profession).

7. One expert in *Rebecca B.* was the father's treating psychiatrist. This dual role implicates a potential conflict of interest that many professions regard as an ethical violation. Can a mental health expert who is treating one of the parties be objective? One commentator has argued:

> It would be very difficult, if not impossible, in most cases for a clinician to "set aside" the attitudes and feelings that constitute the "therapeutic orientation" that has been developed with a given individual or family in exchange for the more detached, skeptical, and objective stance that is necessary for the forensic evaluator.

Kirk Heilbrun, Child Custody Evaluation: Critically Assessing Mental Health Experts and Psychological Tests, 29 Fam. L.Q. 63, 70-71 (1995). Recall, too, the excerpt, supra, by Andrew Watson describing countertransference (the therapist's identification with the client). See also Michael R. Freedman, Evaluator Countertransference in Child Custody Evaluations, 7 Am. J. Fam. L. 143 (1993). Is the harm mitigated if the party is a *former* patient? See Heilbrun, supra, at 71 (arguing that the concerns still exist).

8. *Epilogue.* The custody battle cost Renee B. approximately $340,000; the stress resulted in her losing her job.[27] She subsequently filed a motion for leave to appeal, which the New York Court of Appeals denied. 645 N.E.2d 1217 (N.Y. 1994). Subsequently, her husband attempted to hold her in contempt for failure to pay child support. Having difficulty complying with service of process, he decided to have the process server accompany Rebecca on her visitation. Twelve-year-old Rebecca read the legal papers and became distraught at the threat of imprisonment of her mother. On her own initiative, Rebecca contacted her court-appointed guardian and refused to return to her father. In subsequent sessions with her social worker, she described her life with her father as verging on parental abuse: her father prohibited her from calling her mother and required her to disclose all correspondence to prevent her from sending letters to her mother.

In July 1995, Rebecca and her guardian petitioned for a change of custody. The trial court appointed a new expert, awarded the mother

[27]. Lisa Genasci, Working Mothers at Risk in Custody Disputes; Divorce: Scholars Say Courts Often Hold Women to Higher Parenting Standards Than Their Ex-Spouses, L.A. Times, Mar. 5, 1995, at A8.

temporary custody, and granted the father supervised visitation. On appeal, the temporary award of custody to Renee B. was upheld. The father subsequently moved out of the area. He has had no further contact with the daughter, not even telephone calls on her birthday. Telephone interview with Bernard H. Clair, Attorney for Renee B., (Clair and Danielle, New York), July 7, 1995 and Aug. 19, 1997.

## 5. Modification

### a. Standard

The paramount concern with child welfare gives courts continuing power to modify custody orders. The standard for modification is higher than for initial awards of custody in order to ensure stability for the child. The emphasis on stability in child placement decisionmaking is a central tenet of the work by Professors Goldstein, Freud, and Solnit, who strongly oppose alteration in child placement based on the child's need for continuity of care. See Joseph Goldstein et al., Beyond the Best Interests of the Child 37 (1973). Cf. John Batt, Child Custody Disputes and the Beyond the Best Interests Paradigm: A Contemporary Assessment of the Goldstein/Freud/Solnit Position and the Group's *Painter v. Bannister* Jurisprudence, 16 Nova L. Rev. 621, 643 (1992) (arguing that change is a factor of life and that children are resilient).

*Different standards.* According to the prevailing standard, the plaintiff has the burden of showing by a preponderance of the evidence that *conditions since the dissolution decree have so materially and substantially changed that the children's best interests require a change of custody.* A few states have adopted a more liberal requirement that modification serve the best interests of the child (regardless of any change in circumstances). Several states have more stringent rules, influenced by UMDA §409(b), 9A U.L.A. 439 (1998), requiring endangerment for nonconsensual changes. Absent serious endangerment, UMDA §409(a) provides for a two-year waiting period following the initial decree.

Do liberal modification standards threaten the constitutionally-based privacy of the postdivorce family unit? See Joan G. Wexler, Rethinking the Modification of Child Custody Decrees, 94 Yale L.J. 757, 803-818 (1985) (so suggesting). Relying on social science evidence that the custodial parent and child require time for postdivorce adjustment, Wexler supports a type of "serious endangerment" standard, under which the noncustodial parent must prove that modification would outweigh any disruption caused by the change. Id. at 783. Further, she argues for a presumption against modification for children under three years of age. Id. at 783.

*Joint custody.* Joint custody awards also may be changed if custody arrangements prove unsuccessful or if circumstances change. Some states

*sole →joint*
*best interests*

ease the traditional rule when sole custody is modified to joint, requir-ing only that the change to joint custody be in the best interests of the child. See, e.g., Alaska Stat. §25.20.110 (Michie 2000); Mont. Code Ann. §40-4-219 (1999). See also In re Marriage of Wall, 868 P.2d 387 (Colo. 1994) (holding that endangerment test is not required in modification from sole to joint custody).

*ALI*
*nonconsensual*

   *ALI.* The ALI recommends modification upon a showing of (1) a substantial change in the circumstances (relating to the child or one or both parents) on which the parenting plan was based that makes modi-fication necessary to the child's welfare or (2) harm to the child. ALI Principles §2.15(1) & (2)(2002). Changed circumstances must be based on facts "that were not known or have arisen since the entry of the prior order and were not anticipated." §2.15(1). Modification based on a more liberal standard is available for consensual changes, changes in the ex-isting arrangements without objection by the parent opposing the mod-

*consensual or minor mods*

ification, minor modifications to the parenting plan, or the attainment of a specified age for a child who expresses a preference for a custodial change. Id., cmt. a. None of the following justifies modification, absent a showing of harm: a parent's loss of income or employment, remarriage or cohabitation, or use of day care. §2.15(3).

### b. Relocation

■ **TROPEA v. TROPEA**
*642 N.Y.S.2d 575 (N.Y. 1996)*

Titone, Judge.

   In each of these appeals, a divorced spouse who was previously granted custody of the couple's minor offspring seeks permission to move away from the area in which the noncustodial spouse resides. . . .

### Matter of Tropea v. Tropea

   The parties in this case were married in 1981 and have two children, one born in 1985 and the other in 1988. They were divorced in 1992 pursuant to a judgment that incorporated their previously executed sep-aration agreement. Under that agreement, petitioner mother, who had previously been the children's primary caregiver, was to have sole cus-tody of the children and respondent father was granted visitation on holidays and "at least three . . . days of each week." Additionally, the par-ties were barred from relocating outside of Onondaga County, where both resided, without prior judicial approval.

   [P]etitioner brought this proceeding seeking changes in the visita-tion arrangements and permission to relocate with the children to the

Schenectady area. Respondent opposed the requested relief and filed a cross petition for a change of custody. At the ensuing hearing, petitioner testified that she wanted to move because of her plans to marry an architect who had an established firm in Schenectady. According to petitioner, she and her fiance had already purchased a home in the Schenectady area for themselves and the Tropea children and were now expecting a child of their own. Petitioner stated that she was willing to cooperate in a liberal visitation schedule that would afford respondent frequent and extended contact and that she was prepared to drive the children to and from their father's Syracuse home, which is about two and a half hours away from Schenectady. Nonetheless, as all parties recognized, the distance between the two homes made midweek visits during the school term impossible.

Respondent took the position that petitioner's "need" to move was really the product of her own life-style choice and that, consequently, he should not be the parent who is "punished" with the loss of proximity and weekday contact. Instead, respondent proposed that he be awarded custody of the children if petitioner chose to relocate. To support this proposal, respondent adduced evidence to show that he had maintained frequent and consistent contact with his children at least until June of 1993, when the instant proceeding was commenced. He had coached the children's football and baseball teams, participated in their religion classes and had become involved with his older son's academic education during the 1992-1993 school year. . . .

[The presiding Judicial Hearing Officer (JHO) denied petitioner's request.] Applying what he characterized as "a more restrictive view of relocation," the JHO opined that whenever a proposed move "unduly disrupts or substantially impairs the [noncustodial parent's] access rights to [the] children," the custodial spouse seeking judicial consent must bear the burden of demonstrating "exceptional circumstances" such as a "concrete economic necessity." Applying this principle to the evidence before him, the JHO found that petitioner's desire to obtain a "fresh start" with a new family was insufficient to justify a move that would "significantly impact upon" the close and consistent relationship with his children that respondent had previously enjoyed. [The Appellate Division reversed; the father appealed].

### MATTER OF BROWNER V. KENWARD

The parties to this proceeding were married in August of 1983 and had a son three years later. After marital discord led the parties to separate, they executed a stipulation of settlement and agreement in January of 1992 which gave petitioner mother physical custody of the couple's child and gave respondent father liberal visitation, including midweek overnight visits and alternating weekends. Under the stipulation, respondent was to remain in the marital residence, which was located in White Plains, New York, and petitioner and the parties' son were to live with petitioner's parents in nearby Purchase. Petitioner was required to seek prior approval of the court if she intended to move more than 35 miles from respondent's residence. The stipulation was incorporated but not merged in the parties' divorce judgment, which was entered in June of 1992.

In October of 1992, petitioner brought the present proceeding for permission to relocate with the couple's child to Pittsfield, Massachusetts, some 130 miles from respondent's Westchester County home. Petitioner requested this relief because her parents were moving to Pittsfield and she wished to go with them. Respondent opposed the application, contending that he was a committed and involved noncustodial parent and that the proposed move would deprive him of meaningful contact with his son. [At the hearing, the evidence revealed that petitioner's parents decided to move about the same time as petitioner lost her job.] Petitioner testified that she had tried to find work in New York but was unable to do so. She further testified that her prospects of finding affordable housing in the Purchase area were bleak. She ultimately located a marketing job in Pittsfield that would give her enough income to rent a home of her own in that area. Petitioner had also investigated the facilities for children in Pittsfield and had found a suitable school and synagogue for her son.

An additional motivating factor for petitioner was the emotional support and child care that she received from her parents and that she expected to receive from her extended family in Pittsfield. According to the evidence, petitioner was somewhat dependent on her parents for financial and moral support, and petitioner's son had become especially close to his grandparents after his own parents had separated. Further, the boy had a long-standing close relationship with his Pittsfield cousins.

Respondent argued that permission for the move should be denied because it would significantly diminish the quantity and quality of his visits with his child. Respondent noted that the move would eliminate the midweek visits that he had previously enjoyed as well as his opportunity to participate in the child's daily school, sports and religious activities. Accordingly, respondent argued, petitioner's proposed relocation to Pittsfield would deprive him of meaningful access to his child.

The Family Court found petitioner's argument that she was unable to secure employment and new housing within the Westchester area to be less than convincing. The court further found that respondent had been "vigilant" in visiting his son and was "sincerely interested in guiding and nurturing [the] child." Nonetheless, the court ruled in petitioner's favor and authorized the proposed move, [noting] that the move would not deprive respondent of meaningful contact with his son and that, in light of the psychological evidence that had been adduced, the move would be in the child's best interests [because] the parents' separation from each other would reduce the bickering that was causing the child difficulty and would enable the child to have healthy peer relationships that he needed. Additionally, the emotional advantages that petitioner would realize from proximity to her parents would ultimately enhance the child's emotional well being. [The Appellate Division affirmed; respondent appealed.]

Relocation cases such as the two before us present some of the knottiest and most disturbing problems that our courts are called upon to resolve. In these cases, the interests of a custodial parent who wishes to move away are pitted against those of a noncustodial parent who has a powerful desire to maintain frequent and regular contact with the child. Moreover, the court must weigh the paramount interests of the child, which may or may not be in irreconcilable conflict with those of one or both of the parents.

Because the resolution of relocation disputes is ordinarily a matter entrusted to the fact-finding and discretionary powers of the lower courts, our Court has not had frequent occasion to address the question. [T]he lower courts have evolved a series of formulae and presumptions to aid them in making their decisions in these difficult relocation cases. The most commonly used formula involves a three-step analysis that looks first to whether the proposed relocation would deprive the noncustodial parent of "regular and meaningful access to the child." Where a disruption of "regular and meaningful access" is not shown, the inquiry is truncated, and the courts generally will not go on to assess the merits and strength of the custodial parents' motive for moving. On the other hand, where such a disruption is established, a presumption that the move is not in the child's best interest is invoked and the custodial parent seeking to relocate must demonstrate "exceptional circumstances" to justify the move. Once that hurdle is overcome, the court will go on to consider the child's best interests.

The premise underlying this formula is that children can derive an abundance of benefits from "the mature guiding hand and love of a second parent" and that, consequently, geographic changes that significantly impair the quantity and quality of parent-child contacts are to be "disfavored." While this premise has much merit as a tenet of human dynamics, the legal formula that it has spawned is problematic and, in many respects, unsatisfactory. . . .

Accordingly, rather than endorsing the three-step meaningful access exceptional-circumstance analysis that some of the lower courts have used in the past, we hold that each relocation request must be considered on its own merits with due consideration of all the relevant facts and circumstances and with predominant emphasis being placed on what outcome is most likely to serve the best interests of the child. While the respective rights of the custodial and noncustodial parents are unquestionably significant factors that must be considered, it is the rights and needs of the children that must be accorded the greatest weight, since they are innocent victims of their parents' decision to divorce and are the least equipped to handle the stresses of the changing family situation. . . .

Like Humpty Dumpty, a family, once broken by divorce, cannot be put back together in precisely the same way. The relationship between the parents and the children is necessarily different after a divorce and, accordingly, it may be unrealistic in some cases to try to preserve the noncustodial parent's accustomed close involvement in the children's everyday life at the expense of the custodial parent's efforts to start a new life or to form a new family unit. In some cases, the child's interests might be better served by fashioning visitation plans that maximize the noncustodial parent's opportunity to maintain a positive nurturing relationship while enabling the custodial parent, who has the primary child-rearing responsibility, to go forward with his or her life. In any event, it serves neither the interests of the children nor the ends of justice to view relocation cases through the prisms of presumptions and threshold tests that artificially skew the analysis in favor of one outcome or another. . . .

Turning finally to the cases before us, we conclude that the orders of the courts below, which approved each of the petitioners' requests to move, should be upheld. In *Tropea*, petitioner sought permission to relocate from Onondaga County to the Schenectady area so that she could settle into a new home with her fiance and raise her sons within a new family unit. The Appellate Division found that the move was in the children's best interest and that the visitation schedule that petitioner proposed would afford respondent frequent and extended visitation. We find no reason derived from the record to upset the Appellate Division's determinations on these points. . . .

Our analysis in Browner v. Kenward is somewhat different. The Appellate Division in *Browner* found that the proposed move did not deprive the noncustodial parent of regular and meaningful access to his child and that it was therefore not necessary to weigh the validity and strength of petitioner's reasons for moving against the significant change in the parent-child relationship that the move would entail. The Court's methodology was thus at variance with the open-ended balancing analysis that the law requires. [The court then determines that there is no need to apply the balancing test here because the Family Court already evaluated the factors in the equation.] [Respondent is not entitled] to an order reversing the outcome below. . . .

## Notes and Questions

1. Geographic mobility is a feature of contemporary life. Data suggest that in the first four years postseparation or divorce, approximately 75 percent of custodial mothers move at least once.[28] Relocation controversies frequently arise in the postdecree period when a parent who has been awarded physical custody decides to relocate for reasons of remarriage (as in *Tropea*), employment or educational opportunities, or (as in *Browner*) the promise of moral or economic support from relatives. Should the judicial response to a relocation request depend on the reason?

2. Relocation disputes may arise because a decree or statute requires a custodial parent to seek permission to leave the jurisdiction. Absent statute or decree, the noncustodial parent may petition to enjoin the move. Alternatively, when faced with an impending move, a noncustodial parent may request a custody modification. Bowermaster, supra, at 796-797.

3. The trend in "move-away" cases favors decreasing the restrictions on relocation. Mandy S. Cohen, Note, A Toss of the Dice . . . The Gamble with Post-Divorce Relocation Laws, 18 Hofstra L. Rev. 127, 137 (1989). The majority of state supreme courts to have considered the issue support the custodial parent's request to relocate, as in *Tropea*. See In re Marriage of Burgess, 913 P.2d 473 (Cal. 1996), amicus brief (submitted by Carol S. Bruch et al.), at 32-61 (reviewing post-1985 case law); Bowermaster, supra, at 795-831. But cf. Pitt v. Olds, 511 S.E.2d 60, 62 (S.C. 1999) (holding that mother's remarriage was not sufficient change of circumstances to warrant modification, nor was the move in the child's best interests).

4. Before *Tropea*, New York was the most restrictive jurisdiction, requiring the custodial parent to establish "exceptional circumstances" to relocate based on the policy of protecting the noncustodial parent's rights.

5. Does the best interests standard, adopted by *Tropea*, provide sufficient guidance for resolution of relocation disputes? How should courts accommodate the dual objectives of private dispute resolution and child protection?

Are fathers' interests being downplayed unfairly in relocation disputes? See Richard A. Warshak, Social Science and Children's Best Interests in Relocation Cases: *Burgess* Revisited, 34 Fam. L.Q. 83, 84-86 (2000) (arguing that *Burgess* case fails to properly recognize social science data that indicate that children do best when they maintain close attachments to both parents).

[28]. Janet M. Bowermaster, Sympathizing with Solomon: Choosing Between Parents in a Mobile Society, 31 J. Fam. L. 791, 796 (1992-1993) (citing Mary Jo Bane & Robert Weiss, Alone Together, The World of Single-Parent Families, 2 Am. Demographics, May 1980, at 11, 12).

Are children's interests being given short shrift in relocation disputes? One author suggests that children's best interests are lost between the competing interests and personal agendas of the parents. See Edwin J. Terry et al., Relocation: Moving Forward or Moving Backward?, 31 Tex. Tech. L. Rev. 983, 1023-1025 (2000). Should courts pay more attention to children's interests? If so, how? Appoint guardians ad litem? Solicit children's preferences about the proposed relocation? What are the advantages and disadvantages of these approaches?

6. Given the disruptive effects of divorce and relocation for children, should courts adopt a presumption against relocation? See Paula M. Raines, Joint Custody and the Right to Travel: Legal and Psychological Implications, 24 J. Fam. L. 625 (1085-1986) (opposing postdivorce relocation, except in rare circumstances, based on social science research). See also Bowermaster, supra, at 861-862 (rebutting Raines's findings and conclusions).

7. In the accommodation of interests, should courts take into account social science research that documents a gradual decrease in father's visitation patterns? Consider the following:

> [Another] source influencing how children adjust to divorce is open to question: the importance of maintaining ties between the children and their noncustodial parents, usually their fathers. Although most observers, ourselves included, have believed that continued contact makes a difference in children's adjustment, the evidence in support of that assertion is mixed at best. [S]ome observational studies have reported that children adjust better when they have continuing contact with their noncustodial fathers. But other observational studies and large surveys have found that, other things being equal, the frequency of contact with fathers was not related to children's adjustment. . . .
>
> These negative findings about the importance of contact with the father have surprised and puzzled experts in the field. Perhaps the negative findings result from the low levels of contact that most divorced fathers maintain. . . . Although we still advocate strengthening ties to fathers, we believe that public policy should place lower priority on this objective than on [principles that emphasize promoting the effective functioning of custodial parents in order to improve their children's adjustment and to decrease children's exposure to parental conflict].

Frank F. Furstenberg, Jr. & Andrew J. Cherlin, Divided Families: What Happens to Children When Parents Part 107 (1991). But cf. Eleanor M. Maccoby & Robert H. Mnookin, Dividing the Child: Social and Legal Dilemmas of Custody 198 (1992) (finding higher maintenance of contact between children and nonresidential parents than prior studies and speculating on the reasons).

8. If ensuring frequent and continuing contact with both parents is important, should courts restrict the noncustodial parent's right to

move as well? In Fortin v. Fortin, 500 N.W.2d 229 (S.D. 1993), the court stated:

> It is further clear that a noncustodial parent is perfectly free to remove himself from this jurisdiction despite the continued residency here of his children in order to seek opportunities for a better or different life style for himself. And if he does choose to do so, the custodial parent could hardly hope to restrain him from leaving this State on the ground that his removal will either deprive the children of their paternal relationship or depreciate its quality. The custodial parent, who bears the essential burden and responsibility for the children, is clearly entitled to the same option.

Id. at 232.

9. Professor Carol Bruch has suggested that many statutory relocation restrictions (for example, California, Montana, South Dakota) derive from language in the New York Field (Civil) Code of 1865 intended to prevent removal of the child in order to maintain the court's exclusive custody jurisdiction. See Amicus Brief, In re Marriage of Burgess, supra, at 10-11. Therefore, she argues, *intra*state relocations should not be subject to restriction. Id. at 14. Further, given that jurisdictional concerns have been ameliorated on the national level by the Uniform Child Custody Jurisdiction Act and the Parental Kidnapping Act (see infra this chapter), and on the international level by the Hague Convention on the Civil Aspects of International Abduction (see infra this chapter), Bruch queries whether removal restrictions "now undercut rather than advance the goals of interstate and international child custody law." Id. at 12-13.

10. *Constitutional concern.* What were the alternatives open to Ms. Tropea if the trial court prohibited her from moving with the children? Is requiring a parent to forgo the move to retain custody an infringement of parental autonomy and family privacy? See, e.g., Taylor v. Taylor, 849 S.W.2d 319, 329-331 (Tenn. 1993). Does a restriction on a custodial parent's relocation violate that parent's right to travel (recognized in Shapiro v. Thompson, 394 U.S. 618 (1969) and reaffirmed in Saenz v. Roe, 526 U.S. 489 (1999))? See Caroline Ritchie Heil, Relocation Cases as Change in Custody Proceedings: "Judicial Blackmail" or Competing Interests Reconciled?, 51 S.C. L. Rev. 885, 890 (2000) (so arguing). Or is the issue instead whether a parent has the right to take her child(ren) with her when she exercises her right to travel? See Kimberly K. Holtz, Comment, Move-Away Custody Disputes: The Implications of a Case-by-Case Analysis and the Need for Legislation, 35 Santa Clara L. Rev. 319, 356 (1995).

11. *Gender bias.* Do restrictions on a custodial parent's right to relocate reflect gender bias? See Bowermaster, supra, at 846. Do the restrictions reinforce traditional marital roles?

[I]t is difficult, when reading the cases, to overlook the images of traditional marriage and the corresponding traditional gender roles that are reflected. . . . The standard role pattern in marriage was for the husband to predominate in decision making, including the decision of where the family would live, and to provide for the family's financial support. In exchange for this support, the wife was to care for the household and children and follow the husband in his choice of domicile. [After divorce,] [n]on-custodial parents pay child support, and in return, custodial parents care for the children and keep them available for visitation. . . .

There are obvious problems with this approach. First, in the large number of cases where custodial mothers have remarried and seek to relocate to accompany their new spouses, this "child support for child care services" approach creates a paradox. Simply stated, the mother cannot provide services to two husbands at the same time. She cannot fulfill her traditional duty to care for the children and keep them available to both an ex-husband and a present husband when the two have chosen geographically distant domiciles. . . .

[Restrictions] only serve to create a type of domiciliary "squatter's rights." The first husband to choose a domicile for the mother is given tremendous leverage . . . to keep the mother caring for his children within his easy access. . . . Yet the custom for the wife to follow her husband in his choice of marital domicile applies as much to the new spouse as it did to the former spouse.

Id. at 843-845.

12. The ALI Principles permit a primary parent to relocate with the child if that parent has been exercising a significant majority of custodial responsibility and has a <u>legitimate reason</u> for moving to a location that is reasonable in light of the purpose. According to the Principles, relocation justifies a change of custody (as a substantial change in circumstances) only when it "significantly impairs" either parent's ability  to exercise responsibilities under a parenting plan. ALI Principles §2.17(1)(2002). In this event, the court will revise the parenting plan to accommodate the relocation while maintaining the same proportion of residential responsibility. See Margaret F. Brinig, Feminism and Child Custody Under Chapter Two of the American Law Institute's Principles of the Law of Family Dissolution, 8 Duke J. Gender L. & Pol'y 301, 312-313 (2001); Mitzi M. Naucler, Relocation of Parents in Modification of Parenting Plans in Oregon, 35 Willamette L. Rev. 585 (1999).

# Problem

Donna and James are the unmarried parents of a daughter Grace. Initially, a trial court awarded them joint custody, with Donna to have physical custody and James to have visitation. The trial court also ordered that Donna not move with Grace from the San Francisco Bay Area. Donna now seeks to move with Grace (now 6 years old) to Florida, contending that she wants to move there to begin a new career as a "parapsychologist." She has no employment prospects there, only a letter from a school stating that it would employ her as instructor of parapsychology at low pay if she could find enough paying students to enroll in the course. Donna has no prior employment history as a parapsychologist; she has been employed as a jeweler in the Bay Area. James opposes the move, arguing that it would prevent his frequent visitation with Grace, especially his midweek overnight visitation. What result? How should a court resolve relocation disputes in the context of joint custody? Cassady v. Signorelli, 56 Cal. Rptr. 2d 545 (Ct. App. 1996).

### 6. Jurisdiction and Enforcement

■ **GILMAN v. GILMAN**
   *2001 WL 688610 (Conn. Super. Ct. 2001)*

ROBAINA, Judge.

This is a memorandum of decision with respect to a motion to dismiss for lack of jurisdiction. The motion is made on the basis of the Uniform Child Custody Jurisdiction and Enforcement Act (hereinafter UCCJEA) which was enacted as Public Act 99-185, and is now codified as Connecticut General Statutes §46b-115 et seq.

The facts in this matter are as follows: the parties were married on October 6, 1997 in Annapolis, Maryland. They are the parents of a minor child named Austin A. Gilman, who was born on August 30, 1997. The child was born in Connecticut. Around September or October of 1998 the parties moved to Maryland. The parties lived in Maryland for the remainder of 1998, all of 1999 and into the year 2000. In June of the year 2000, the parties returned to Connecticut. The child stayed in Connecticut until approximately mid-July of the same year, at which time he went back to Maryland to visit his maternal grandmother. On July 20, 2000 the defendant mother returned to Maryland. It is unclear whether she told the plaintiff that she was returning to Maryland on a permanent basis or whether she told him the reason at all that she was returning. During the time around July 2000, there is conflicting evidence as to what was communicated between the parties. According to the defendant, she never promised to return to Connecticut. According to the plaintiff, the defendant indicated that she was unsure of her feelings and was in Maryland temporarily in order to consider her options. However, the evidence is clear that she did not return to Connecticut. She stayed in Maryland with the child of this marriage, and another child of hers which is in her custody.

The defendant then lived with her mother and the child in Maryland from approximately July 20, 2000 forward. There was contact between the plaintiff and the defendant during this time. The plaintiff traveled to Maryland immediately upon discovering the defendant had moved from this state, and the parties discussed the status of their relationship. The defendant commenced an action in the circuit court for Anne Arundel County, Maryland in July of 2000, but the action was not served on the plaintiff until January 2001. The child came to Connecticut in November of 2000 for a visit with his father. He stayed approximately three weeks until the first week in December, at which time the father returned the child to the State of Maryland. On or about December 30, 2000 the father took the child with the mother's consent from Maryland and brought him to Connecticut for purposes of a visit. The child was never returned to the State of Maryland. Subsequently, this action was filed, and service was made upon the defendant. The defendant has not been allowed to see the child, except under the supervision of the plaintiff, by unilateral rule of the plaintiff.

Section 46b-115 of the Connecticut General Statutes is entitled "The Uniform Child Custody Jurisdiction and Enforcement Act." The act became effective on July 1, 2000 and by its terms repealed the Uniform Child Custody Jurisdiction Act which had been codified in Connecticut General Statutes §46b-90 et seq. The UCCJEA (C.G.S. §46b-115k) allows that a court of this State has jurisdiction to make an initial child custody determination if: (1) this state is the home state of the child on the date of the commencement of the child custody proceeding; (2) this state was the home state of the child within six months of the commencement of the child custody proceeding, the child was absent from the state, and a parent or person acting as a parent continues to reside in this state. Section 46b-115a(7) provides that "home state" means "the state in which a child lived with a parent or person acting as a parent . . . for at least six consecutive months immediately before the commencement of a child custody proceeding. . . . A period of temporary absence of any such person is counted as part of the period."

Section 46b-115k(3) of the new act further states that this state has jurisdiction to make an initial child custody determination if: "a court of another state does not have jurisdiction under subdivisions (1) or (2) of this subsection, the child and at least one parent or person acting as a parent have a significant connection with this state other than mere physical presence, and there is substantial evidence available in this state concerning the child's care, protection, training and personal relationships."

The new act represents a marked difference from what had been Connecticut General Statute §46b-93. Under the former statute, a court of this state could exercise jurisdiction if this state was the home state of the child at the time the proceeding was commenced *or* it was in the best interest of the child that the court exercise jurisdiction because the child and his parents had a significant connection to the state. The UCCJEA alters the analysis of the initial determination of child custody. Specifically, the new act requires that the "home state" determination be made as a condition precedent to an examination as to whether the child and parent have significant connections with this state. The new act also eliminates that analysis on the basis of "the best interest of the child."

In applying the facts of the instant case to C.G.S. §46b-115k(1) the court finds that the minor child has lived in the State of Maryland with a parent for six consecutive months immediately prior to the commencement of this proceeding. That finding is based upon the evidence submitted at the hearing, and further bolstered by the plaintiff's action in having taken the child for a period of three weeks in November and subsequently returning the child to the State of Maryland to live with his mother. The court also considered the fact that the parties did reside in the State of Maryland from approximately the fall or winter of 1998 until June of the year 2000 when they moved to Connecticut. The defendant and the minor child were here for some 30 days prior to the time that the child returned to Maryland and the time that his mother followed him. From July 20, 2000 until December 30, 2000 the child lived in the State of Maryland. The fact that there may have been some ambiguity as to where the defendant planned to reside, or some ambiguity with respect to her intentions vis-a-vis the marriage does not change the condition that the child "lived" with a parent in the State of Maryland.

The court finds that Connecticut does not have jurisdiction over this matter pursuant to the terms of the UCCJEA, and accordingly, the defendant's motion to dismiss is hereby granted. The court grants the motion without prejudice in the event that the appropriate court in the state of Maryland declines jurisdiction.

## ■ CALIFORNIA v. SUPERIOR COURT (SMOLIN)
### *482 U.S. 400 (1987)*

Justice O'CONNOR delivered the opinion of the Court. . . .

Richard and Judith Smolin were divorced in California in 1978. Sole custody of their two children, Jennifer and Jamie, was awarded to Judith Smolin, subject to reasonable visitation rights for Richard. Until November 1979, all the parties remained in San Bernardino County, California, and Richard apparently paid his child support and exercised his visitation rights without serious incident. In August 1979, however, Judith married James Pope, and in November, Mr. Pope's work required that the family relocate to Oregon. When the Popes moved without informing Richard, the battle over the custody of the minor children began in earnest.

. . . Richard alleged, and the California courts later found, that the Popes deliberately attempted to defeat Richard's visitation rights and to preclude him from forming a meaningful relationship with his children in the course of their succeeding relocations from Oregon to Texas to Louisiana. On February 13, 1981, the Popes obtained a decree from a Texas court granting full faith and credit to the original California order awarding sole custody to Judith. Richard was served but did not appear in the Texas proceeding. Before the Texas decree was issued, however, Richard sought and obtained in California Superior Court modification of the underlying California decree, awarding joint custody to Richard and Judith. Though properly served, the Popes did not appear in these California proceedings; and, though served with the modification order, the Popes neither complied with its terms, nor notified the Texas court of its existence. On January 9, 1981, Richard instituted an action in California Superior Court to find Judith in contempt and to again modify the custody decree to give him sole custody. [S]ole custody was granted to Richard by the California court, subject to reasonable visitation rights for Judith.

This order also was ignored by the Popes, apparently acting on the advice of counsel that the California courts no longer had jurisdiction over the matter. Richard did not in fact obtain physical custody for over two years. When he finally located the Popes in Louisiana, they began an adoption proceeding, later described by the California courts as "verging on the fraudulent," to sever Richard's legal tie to Jennifer and Jamie. After securing a California warrant to obtain custody of the children on February 27, 1984, Richard and his father, Gerard Smolin, resorted to self-help. [T]hey picked up Jennifer and Jamie as they were waiting for their school bus in Slidell, Louisiana, and brought them back to California. On April 11, 1984, the Popes submitted to the jurisdiction of the California Superior Court and instituted an action to modify the 1981 order granting Richard sole custody. Those proceedings are apparently still pending before the California courts.

Meanwhile, the Popes raised the stakes by instituting a criminal action against Richard and Gerard Smolin in Louisiana. . . . Judith Pope swore out an affidavit charging Richard and Gerard Smolin with kidnaping Jennifer and Jamie from her custody and asserting that they had acted "without authority to remove children from [her] custody." On the basis of this affidavit, the [Louisiana] Assistant District . . . filed an information charging Richard and Gerard Smolin each with two counts of violating La. Rev. Stat. Ann. §14:45 (West 1986), the Louisiana kidnaping statute. [T]he Governor of Louisiana formally notified the Governor of California that Richard and Gerard Smolin were charged with "simple kidnaping" in Louisiana and demanded that they be delivered up for trial.

In early August 1984, the Smolins petitioned in the California Superior Court for a writ of habeas corpus to block the anticipated extradition warrants. On August 17, 1984, the anticipated warrants issued and on August 24, 1984, the Superior Court orally granted a writ of habeas corpus after taking judicial notice of the various custody orders that had been issued. The court concluded "that the findings in the family law case adequately demonstrate that, in fact, the process initiated by Mrs. Pope in Louisiana and her declarations and affidavits were totally insufficient to establish any basis for rights of either herself personally or for the State . . . of Louisiana." California then sought a writ of mandate in the California Court of Appeal on the ground that the Superior Court had abused its discretion in blocking extradition. The Court of Appeal reluctantly issued the writ. . . . A divided California Supreme Court reversed. . . . Under the full faith and credit provisions of the federal Parental Kidnaping Prevention Act of 1980, 28 U.S.C. §1738A, the majority determined that those decrees conclusively established that Richard Smolin was the lawful custodian of the children at the time that they were taken from Louisiana to California. Finally, the court found that, under Louisiana law, the lawful custodian cannot be guilty of kidnaping children in his custody. We granted certiorari to consider whether the Extradition Clause, Art. IV, §2, cl. 2, and the Extradition Act, 18 U.S.C. §3182, prevent the California Supreme Court from refusing to permit extradition on these grounds.

The Federal Constitution places certain limits on the sovereign powers of the States, limits that are an essential part of the Framers' conception of national identity and Union. One such limit is found in Art. IV, §2, cl. 2, the Extradition Clause:

> A person charged in any State with Treason, Felony, or other Crime, who shall flee from Justice, and be found in another State, shall on Demand of the executive Authority of the State from which he fled, be delivered up, to be removed to the State having Jurisdiction of the Crime. . . .

The Extradition Clause, however, does not specifically establish a procedure by which interstate extradition is to take place, and, accordingly, has never been considered to be self-executing. Early in our history, the lack of an established procedure led to a bitter dispute between the States [and Congress responded by enacting the Extradition Act of 1793, 18 U.S.C. §3182]. This Court has held the Extradition Act of 1793 to be a proper exercise of Congress' powers under the Extradition Clause and Art. IV, §1. . . . By the express terms of federal law, therefore, the asylum State is bound to deliver up to the demanding State's agent a fugitive against whom a properly certified indictment or affidavit charging a crime is lodged.

The language, history, and subsequent construction of the Extradition Act make clear that Congress intended extradition to be a summary procedure. . . . As the Court held in Michigan v. Doran, [439 U.S. 282,

289 (1978)], the Act leaves only four issues open for consideration before the fugitive is delivered up: (a) whether the extradition documents on their face are in order; (b) whether the petitioner has been charged with a crime in the demanding state; (c) whether the petitioner is the person named in the request for extradition; and (d) whether the petitioner is a fugitive.

The parties argue at length about the propriety of the California courts taking judicial notice of their prior child custody decrees in this extradition proceeding. But even if taking judicial notice of the decrees is otherwise proper, the question remains whether the decrees noticed were relevant to one of these four inquiries. The Smolins do not dispute that the extradition documents are in order, that they are the persons named in the documents and that they meet the technical definition of a "fugitive." Their sole contention is that, in light of the earlier California custody decrees and the federal Parental Kidnaping Prevention Act of 1980, 28 U.S.C. §1738A, they have not been properly charged with a violation of Louisiana's kidnaping statute, La. Rev. Stat. Ann. §14:45 (West 1986).

Section 14:45A(4) prohibits the

> intentional taking, enticing or decoying away and removing from the state, by any parent, of his or her child, from the custody of any person to whom custody has been awarded by any court of competent jurisdiction of any state, without the consent of the legal custodian, with intent to defeat the jurisdiction of the said court over the custody of the child.

A properly certified Louisiana information charges the Smolins with violating this statute by kidnaping Jennifer and Jamie Smolin. The information is based on the sworn affidavit of Judith Pope which asserts:

> On March 9, 1984, at approximately 7:20 A.M., Richard Smolin and Gerard Smolin, kidnapped Jennifer Smolin, aged 10, and James C. Smolin, aged 9, from the affiant's custody while said children were at a bus stop in St. Tammany Parish, Louisiana.
>
> The affiant has custody of the said children by virtue of a Texas court order dated February 5, 1981, a copy of said order attached hereto and made part hereof. The information regarding the actual kidnapping was told to the affiant by witnesses Mason Galatas and Cheryl Galatas of 2028 Mallard Street, Slidell, Louisiana, and Jimmie Huessler of 2015 Dridle Street, Slidell, Louisiana. Richard Smolin and Gerard Smolin were without authority to remove children from affiant's custody.

The information is in proper form, and the Smolins do not dispute that the affidavit, and documents incorporated by reference therein, set forth facts that clearly satisfy each element of the crime of kidnaping as it is defined in La. Rev. Stat. Ann. §14:45A(4) (West 1986). If we accept as true every fact alleged, the Smolins are properly charged with kidnaping under Louisiana law. In our view, this ends the inquiry into the issue whether or not a crime is charged for purposes of the Extradition Act.

The Smolins argue, however, that more than a formal charge is required (citing Roberts v. Reilly, 116 U.S. 80 (1885)). . . . The Smolins claim that [*Roberts* allows] the fugitive, upon a petition for writ of habeas corpus in the asylum State's courts, to show that the demanding State's charging instrument is so insufficient that it cannot withstand some generalized version of a motion to dismiss or common-law demurrer. . . .

To the contrary, our cases make clear that no such inquiry is permitted. . . . This proceeding is neither the time nor place for the Smolins' arguments that Judith Pope's affidavit is fraudulent and that the California custody decrees establish Richard as the lawful custodian under the full faith and credit provision of the federal Parental Kidnapping Prevention Act of 1980. There is nothing in the record to suggest that the Smolins are not entirely correct in all of this . . . ; and, that, accordingly, the Smolins did not violate La. Rev. Stat. Ann. §14:45A(4) (West 1986) as is charged. Of course, the Parental Kidnaping Prevention Act of 1980 creates a uniform federal rule governing custody determinations, a rule to which the courts of Louisiana must adhere when they consider the Smolins' case on the merits. We are not informed by the record why it is that the States of California and Louisiana are so eager to force the Smolins halfway across the continent to face criminal charges that, at least to a majority of the California Supreme Court, appear meritless. If the Smolins are correct, they are not only innocent of the charges made against them, but also victims of a possible abuse of the criminal process. But, under the Extradition Act, it is for the Louisiana courts to do justice in this case, not the California courts. . . . The judgment of the California Supreme Court is reversed.

Justice STEVENS, with whom Justice BRENNAN joins, dissenting.

[W]e should today reject the notion that a parent who holds custody as determined by the Parental Kidnaping Prevention Act of 1980, 28 U.S.C. §1738A, must be extradited as a charged kidnaper. Three reasons compel this conclusion. First, when the fleeing parent lacks child custody under federal law, it is proper to subject him or her to extradition in order to face criminal prosecution. But when the parent acts consistently with the federal law that governs interstate custody disputes, he should not be deemed to have fled from the judicial process of the demanding State. By allowing the custodial parent under federal law to be branded as a fugitive, the Court implicitly approves non-adherence to the uniform federal rule governing custody determinations.

Second, requiring the extradition of Richard Smolin is at cross-purposes with Congress' intent to "discourage continuing interstate controversies over child custody" and to "deter interstate abductions and other unilateral removals of children undertaken to obtain custody and visitation awards." See 28 U.S.C. §1738A note. Compelling extradition to face a criminal charge which cannot lead to a conviction, no less than "child snatching," is the coerced transportation of a party to a custodial dispute to another forum in order to serve a private interest. It is anomalous that the Act, which was clearly intended to deter the former type of coercion, should not also be interpreted to discourage the latter.

Third, the Extradition Clause should be construed consistently with the Parental Kidnaping Prevention Act because both are expressions of the constitutional command of full faith and credit that governs relations among the several States. The Extradition Clause "articulated, in mandatory language, the concepts of comity and full faith and credit, found in the immediately preceding clause of Art. IV." Michigan v. Doran, supra, at 287-288. The courts of every State best adhere to this principle, when considering an extradition request for alleged parental kidnapping, by giving full faith and credit to custody judgments rendered by other States as commanded by the Act. It is clear to a court performing this task that the Smolins are not fugitives within the meaning of the extradition request; as the custodial parent under the federal statute, Richard Smolin did not commit while in Louisiana "an act which by the law of the State constitutes a crime." Hogan v. O'Neill, 255 U.S. 52, 56 (1921).

The Court is scrupulously fair in its recital of the facts and frank in its acknowledgement that the criminal process may have been abused in this case. The reasoning the Court follows nevertheless adopts an overly restrictive view of the questions that the habeas courts of a rendering State must pose. The law governing interstate rendition for criminal proceedings does not foreclose a summary inquiry into whether the crime charged is legally impossible. Moreover, in an area in which Congress has seen fit to enact nationwide legislation, I cannot agree that respect for the criminal laws of other States requires the State of California indiscriminately to render as fugitives those citizens who are conclusorily charged with simple kidnaping for their exercise of a right conferred upon them by a valid custody decree issued by a California court. The Court's contrary conclusion will, I fear, produce unnecessary inconvenience and injustice in this case and provide estranged parents with an inappropriate weapon to use against each other as they wage custody disputes throughout this land. . . .

## Notes and Questions

1. *UCCJA*. Prior to the late 1960s, a state could assert jurisdiction over child custody if it had a "substantial interest" in the case. See Leonard Ratner, Child Custody in a Federal System, 62 Mich. L. Rev.

795, 808 (1964). This interest might stem from the marital domicile or the current residence of either parent or the child. Such a vague standard often led to concurrent assertions of jurisdiction. In addition, because of judicial willingness to reopen custody decisions at the behest of a state resident, decrees were freely modifiable in other states. Supreme Court decisions left unclear whether custody decisions were entitled to the protection of the Full Faith and Credit Clause. Id. at 807. The ease with which parents could reopen child custody cases in other states has been described as "a rule of seize-and-run." May v. Anderson, 345 U.S. 528, 542 (1953) ( Jackson, J., dissenting).

The Uniform Child Custody Jurisdiction Act (UCCJA) was drafted in 1968 to reduce jurisdictional competition and confusion, as well as to deter parents from forum shopping to relitigate custody. The act applies both to initial custody decisions as well as modifications. A version of the UCCJA was adopted in every state.

The UCCJA provides four alternate bases for a state to assert jurisdiction:

> (1) th[e] State (i) is the home state of the child at the time of commencement of the proceeding, or (ii) had been the child's home state within six months before commencement of the proceeding and the child is absent from th[e] State because of his removal or retention by a person claiming his custody or for other reasons, and a parent or person acting as parent continues to live in this State; or
>
> (2) it is in the best interest of the child that a court of th[e] State assume jurisdiction because (i) the child and his parents, or the child and at least one contestant, have a significant connection with th[e] State, and (ii) there is available in this State substantial evidence concerning the child's present or future care, protection, training, and personal relationships; or
>
> (3) the child is physically present in th[e] State and (i) the child has been abandoned or (ii) it is necessary in an emergency to protect the child because he has been subjected to or threatened with mistreatment or abuse or is otherwise neglected [or dependent]; or
>
> (4) (i) it appears no other state would have jurisdiction under prerequisites substantially in accordance with paragraphs (1), (2), or (3), or another state has declined to exercise jurisdiction on the ground that th[e] State is the more appropriate forum to determine the custody of the child and (ii) it is in the best interest of the child that this court assume jurisdiction.

UCCJA §3, 9 U.L.A. (pt. I) 307-308 (1999). "Home state" is defined as the state in which the child lived (immediately preceding the time involved) with a parent, parents, or a person acting as a parent, for at least six consecutive months. For an infant younger than six months, the home state is the state in which the child lived from birth with any of the aforementioned persons.

Under UCCJA §8, a court may decline to exercise jurisdiction if the petitioner for an initial decree has wrongfully taken the child from another state or has engaged in similar reprehensible conduct.

Despite the UCCJA's objective to reduce jurisdictional competition, two states might assert jurisdiction over a custody matter. One of the rationale underlying the UCCJA was to "make custody decisions more acceptable to foreign courts by giving jurisdiction to the forum most likely to have access to current and complete information about the child and the family." Anne B. Goldstein, The Tragedy of the Interstate Child: A Critical Reexamination of the Uniform Child Custody Jurisdiction Act and the Parental Kidnapping Prevention Act, 25 U.C. Davis L. Rev. 845, 880 (1992).

Another method by which the UCCJA attempts to prevent competing assertions of jurisdiction is its prohibition against simultaneous proceedings (§6). Despite this provision, however, courts still find methods of addressing custody matters that another state is also considering. "The courts do this in two main ways: by determining that the case is not 'pending' in the other state, and by determining that the other state did not exercise jurisdiction in 'substantial conformity' with the UCCJA." Goldstein, supra, at 888-889.

In addition, under §13, a court shall recognize and enforce a custody decree issued by a court with jurisdiction under the Act, 9 U.L.A. (pt. I) 559 (1999) and under §14, a court cannot modify a custody decree issued by another state that had jurisdiction consistent with the act unless the decree state no longer has jurisdiction *and* the state seeking to modify has jurisdiction.

2. *PKPA.* In 1980, Congress enacted the Parental Kidnapping Prevention Act (PKPA), 28 U.S.C.A. §1738A (West Supp. 2001). Despite its title, the PKPA is also relevant in cases involving jurisdiction over child custody. The PKPA was drafted for several reasons. First, it attempted to provide rules that would apply in all states, even those that might never enact the UCCJA. (By the late 1970s, only about half of the states had enacted the UCCJA.) Second, the UCCJA did not obtain the hoped-for uniformity in the treatment of custody disputes because some state legislatures changed the UCCJA provisions, and some state courts interpreted those provisions in different ways. Russell M. Coombs, Nuts and Bolts of the PKPA, 22 Colo. Law. 2397 (1993).

A principal purpose of the PKPA is to ensure that custody decrees issued by states asserting jurisdiction in conformity with the PKPA receive recognition and enforcement in other states through full faith and credit. The PKPA provides:

### §1738A. Full Faith and Credit Given to Child Custody Determinations

(a) The appropriate authorities of every State shall enforce according to its terms, and shall not modify except as provided in subsection

(f) of this section [omitted], any child custody determination made consistently with the provisions of this section by a court of another State.

(b) As used in this section, the term — . . .

(4) "home State" means the State in which, immediately preceding the time involved, the child lived with his parents, a parent, or a person acting as a parent, for at least six consecutive months, and in the case of a child less than six months old, the State in which the child lived from birth with any of such persons. Periods of temporary absence of any of such persons are counted as part of the six-month or other period; . . .

(c) A child custody determination made by a court of a State is consistent with the provisions of this section only if —

(1) such court has jurisdiction under the law of such State; and

(2) one of the following conditions is met:

(A) such State (i) is the home State of the child on the date of the commencement of the proceeding, or (ii) had been the child's home State within six months before the date of the commencement of the proceeding and the child is absent from such State because of his removal or retention by a contestant or for other reasons, and a contestant continues to live in such State;

(B)(i) it appears that no other State would have jurisdiction under subparagraph (A), and (ii) it is in the best interest of the child that a court of such State assume jurisdiction because (I) the child and his parents, or the child and at least one contestant, have a significant connection with such State other than mere physical presence in such State and (II) there is available in such State substantial evidence concerning the child's present or future care, protection, training, and personal relationships;

(C) the child is physically present in such State and (i) the child has been abandoned, or (ii) it is necessary in an emergency to protect the child because he has been subjected to or threatened with mistreatment or abuse;

(D)(i) it appears that no other State would have jurisdiction under subparagraph (A), (B), (C), or (E), or another State has declined to exercise jurisdiction on the ground that the State whose jurisdiction is in issue is the more appropriate forum to determine the custody of the child, and (ii) it is in the best interest of the child that such court assume jurisdiction; or

(E) the court has continuing jurisdiction pursuant to subsection (d) of this section.

(d) The jurisdiction of a court of a State which has made a child custody determination consistently with the provisions of this section continues as long as the requirement of subsection (c)(1) of this section continues to be met and such State remains the residence of the child or of any contestant. . . .

Section 1738A differs from the UCCJA in two ways. First, although the jurisdictional criteria under the PKPA parallel those of the UCCJA (and both define "home state" similarly), the "significant connection" basis of jurisdiction is only applicable when "no other state would have jurisdiction under" the home state provision. "Thus, the PKPA, unlike the UCCJA, gives the home state explicit priority to make an initial decree." Coombs, supra, at 2398.

This difference is critical in cases of parental abduction. Under the UCCJA, when an abducting parent flees the child's "home state," that parent might attempt to relitigate in a new forum now having "significant connections" and "substantial evidence." The PKPA restricts this "significant connection" and "substantial evidence" jurisdictional basis to those situations in which there is no home state. See §1738A(c)(2)(B).

The PKPA and the UCCJA also differ on jurisdiction to modify custody. To restrict modification of another state's decree, the PKPA goes beyond the UCCJA. The PKPA provides for "exclusive continuing jurisdiction" in the initial decree-granting state so long as the original decree state continues to have jurisdiction under its own state law and remains the residence of a child or any contestant. In cases of conflict between the PKPA and the UCCJA, many state courts have held that the PKPA preempts the UCCJA based on the Supremacy Clause (and thereby have given preference to the PKPA's home state rule). See, e.g., Doucette v. Murray, 1997 WL 381389 (Conn. Super. Ct. 1997), at *3 (citing cases).

3. *UCCJEA.* In 1997, the National Conference of Commissioners on Uniform State Laws revised the Uniform Child Custody Jurisdiction Act (UCCJA) by drafting the Uniform Child Custody Jurisdiction and Enforcement Act (UCCJEA). The new act is intended to harmonize some of the differences between the UCCJA and PKPA. More than half the states now have adopted the UCCJEA.[29]

The UCCJEA differs from its predecessor UCCJA in several ways. Whereas the UCCJA did not prioritize among the four bases of jurisdiction, the UCCJEA follows the PKPA in giving priority to home state jurisdiction. In addition, the UCCJEA goes further than either the PKPA or UCCJA by eliminating the "best interests" language and severely restricting the use of emergency jurisdiction to the issuance of temporary orders. Also, the UCCJEA provides strict requirements for modification: A court cannot exercise modification jurisdiction if another state has exclusive continuing jurisdiction. The state that makes the initial custody determination has continuing exclusive jurisdiction so long as a party to the original custody determination remains in that state. (Continuing exclusive jurisdiction is a feature of the PKPA but not the original UCCJA.)

The UCCJEA adds definitional clarity to custody decisionmaking. It tracks the PKPA definition of "child-custody determination" to encompass all custody and visitation decrees (temporary, permanent, initial,

[29]. Based on data provided at the Uniform Law Commissioners' web site, www.nccusl.org (27 states), visited Jan. 15, 2002.

and modifications). However, in addition, it expands the definition of "child-custody proceedings" (compared to the UCCJA definition) to include those proceedings related to divorce, separation, neglect, abuse, dependency, guardianship, paternity, termination of parental rights, and protection from domestic violence (but not adoptions).

The UCCJEA specifies how and when courts should assert emergency jurisdiction, providing that courts may take temporary jurisdiction even in cases in which a given jurisdiction is not the home state. A court may assert emergency jurisdiction if the child is present in the state and has been abandoned, or is subjected to or threatened with maltreatment or abuse (or if a parent or sibling has been abused).

How do these various UCCJEA changes improve the enforcement of custody decrees? In *Gilman*, the mother petitioned for custody in Maryland and the father in Connecticut. Was the Connecticut court correct in its determination that it should decline jurisdiction in favor of the Maryland court?

For critical commentary on the UCCJEA, see Russell M. Coombs, Child Custody and Visitation by Non-Parents Under the New Uniform Child Custody Jurisdiction and Enforcement Act: A Rerun of Seize-and-Run, 16 J. Am. Acad. Matrimonial Law. 1 (1999) (noting problems of law and policy and arguing that legislatures should move cautiously in adopting the UCCJEA); David H. Levy & Nanette A. McCarthy, A Critique of the Proposed Uniform Child Custody Jurisdiction and Enforcement Act, 10 J. Am. Acad. Matrim. Law. 149, 154 (1998) (arguing that the UCCJEA does not solve all the problems posed by the UCCJA and creates some new ambiguities).

The UCCJEA provisions regarding initial jurisdiction, exclusive continuing jurisdiction, and modification are set forth below:

### §201. Initial Child-Custody Jurisdiction

(a) Except as otherwise provided in Section 204 [dealing with emergency jurisdiction over abandoned or abused/neglected children], a court of this State has jurisdiction to make an initial child-custody determination only if:

(1) this State is the home state of the child on the date of the commencement of the proceeding, or was the home State of the child within six months before the commencement of the proceeding and the child is absent from this State but a parent or person acting as a parent continues to live in this State;

(2) a court of another State does not have jurisdiction under paragraph (1), or a court of the home State of the child has declined to exercise jurisdiction on the ground that this State is the more appropriate forum . . . and:

(A) the child and the child's parents, or the child and at least one parent or a person acting as a parent, have a significant connection with this State other than mere physical presence; and

(B) substantial evidence is available in this State concerning the child's care, protection, training, and personal relationships;

(3) all courts having jurisdiction under paragraph (1) or (2) have declined to exercise jurisdiction on the ground that a court of this State is the more appropriate forum to determine the custody of the child . . . or

(4) no court of any other State would have jurisdiction under the criteria specified in paragraph (1), (2), or (3).

(b) Subsection (a) is the exclusive jurisdictional basis for making a child-custody determination by a court of this State.

(c) Physical presence of, or personal jurisdiction over, a party or a child is not necessary or sufficient to make a child-custody determination.

## §202. Exclusive, Continuing Jurisdiction

(a) Except as otherwise provided in Section 204 [emergency jurisdiction], a court of this State which has made a child-custody determination consistent with Section 201 or 203 has exclusive, continuing jurisdiction over the determination until:

(1) a court of this State determines that neither the child, the child's parents, and any person acting as a parent do not have a significant connection with this State and that substantial evidence is no longer available in this State concerning the child's care, protection, training, and personal relationships; or

(2) a court of this State or a court of another State determines that the child, the child's parents, and any person acting as a parent do not presently reside in this State.

(b) A court of this State which has made a child-custody determination and does not have exclusive, continuing jurisdiction under this section may modify that determination only if it has jurisdiction to make an initial determination under Section 201.

## §203. Jurisdiction to Modify Determination.

Except as otherwise provided in Section 204 [emergency jurisdiction], a court of this State may not modify a child-custody determination made by a court of another State unless a court of this State has jurisdiction to make an initial determination under Section 201(a)(1) or (2) and:

(1) the court of the other State determines it no longer has exclusive, continuing jurisdiction under Section 202 or that a court of this State would be a more convenient forum . . .; or

(2) a court of this State or a court of the other State determines that the child, the child's parents, and any person acting as a parent do not presently reside in the other State.

4. *Parent locator service.* The PKPA also assists parents in locating an abducting parent by making the federal parent locator service available to state agencies and applying the Fugitive Felon Act to all state felony

parental kidnapping cases. The parent locator service was established to assist state welfare departments to locate and force "deadbeat dads" to provide child support. Some proposed to make the service available to private individuals as well as official agencies. However, in the face of resistance by Department of Health and Human Services officials (concerning possible expense and invasions of privacy), the PKPA made the service available only to official agencies. Goldstein, supra, at 918 n.335.

5. What remedies are available to contestants who might be awarded conflicting decrees by two states? May they seek resolution in the federal courts? Before 1988, several federal courts of appeal interpreted the PKPA to imply federal jurisdiction. See, e.g., Meade v. Meade, 812 F.2d 1473 (4th Cir. 1987); Flood v. Braaten, 727 F.2d 303 (3d Cir. 1984).

The Supreme Court finally resolved the issue of federal court jurisdiction in Thompson v. Thompson, 484 U.S. 174 (1988), stating:

> The PKPA does not provide an implied cause of action in federal court to determine which of two conflicting state custody decisions is valid. The context in which the PKPA was enacted — the existence of jurisdictional deadlocks among the States in custody cases and a nationwide problem of interstate parental kidnapping — suggests that Congress' principle aim was to extend the requirements of the Full Faith and Credit Clause to custody determinations and not to create an entirely new cause of action. The language and placement of the Act reinforce this conclusion, in that the Act is an addendum to, and is therefore clearly intended to have the same operative effect as, the federal full faith and credit statute, the Act's heading is "Full faith and credit given to child custody determinations," and, unlike statutes that explicitly confer a right on a specified class of persons, the Act is addressed to States and to state courts. [T]he PKPA's legislative history provides an unusually clear indication that Congress did not intend the federal courts to play the enforcement role.

Id. at 513-514. Is additional federal legislation needed?

6. *Epilogue.* A Louisiana court found Smolin not guilty of all charges and dismissed the case. The children remained with their father in California until they reached majority. Telephone interview, Dennis Riordan, Attorney for Richard Smolin (Riordan and Rosenthal, San Francisco), Sept. 30, 1997.

■ **IN RE MENDEL**
*897 P.2d 68 (Alaska 1995)*

RABINOWITZ, Justice.

This case requires us to review the propriety of contempt citations against Allison E. Mendel, [an attorney, who] was held in contempt of court for her refusal to answer numerous questions at an in-court deposition.

[The court relates the following background.] In Bock v. Bock, 824 P.2d 723 (Alaska 1992), we vacated a superior court's custody award of Laura and George Bock's twin daughters to their mother, Laura. [W]e held that because Kentucky had retained jurisdiction over the custody matter, the Alaska superior court was precluded from exercising jurisdiction by the continuing jurisdiction provisions of the Parental Kidnapping Prevention Act, 28 U.S.C. §1738A (1988). We also ordered the superior court to enforce a Kentucky decree granting custody of the children to their father.

Rather than turning over custody of the children to their father, Laura went into hiding with the two girls. She also brought suit in federal court against George and this court seeking to set aside our order. Mendel represents Laura in this federal litigation.

In May 1992 George commenced Bock v. Felbert, No. 3AN-92-4375 CI (Alaska Super. filed May 19, 1992), [asserting] various claims for custodial interference in violation of AS25.20.140, common law interference with custodial rights, conspiracy to interfere with custodial rights, the tort of outrage, conspiracy to cause intentional infliction of emotional distress, false imprisonment, and punitive damages. George's complaint names Laura and ten other defendants who he alleges assisted Laura in hiding the children. Mendel is not a named defendant in the *Felbert* litigation.[3]

In February 1993, in the *Felbert* litigation, George subpoenaed Mendel for the purpose of taking her deposition. The subpoena also requested Mendel to bring with her numerous documents in connection with her representation of Laura. Mendel moved to quash the subpoena. [T]he superior court rejected Mendel's claims of privilege, relevancy, and that some of the information was protected from disclosure by the First Amendment. Accordingly, the court ordered her to attend the deposition and produce the requested documents. Mendel appeared for the deposition [but] refused to answer certain questions [and] to produce copies of her billing records other than a copy of the billing headings. (The bills Mendel proffered were redacted.) Mendel answered questions regarding when she had last seen Laura in person and on other matters not relevant to this appeal.

George subsequently moved for an order requiring Mendel to show cause why she should not be held in contempt for violating the court's order by refusing to answer questions during the deposition. The superior court entered an order to show cause and a hearing was held. . . . At the show cause-deposition proceeding Mendel answered numerous

---

3. Following oral argument on this case, Laura and the children were located, and the children were placed in George's custody. Thereafter, Mendel filed a motion to dismiss this appeal as moot. This appeal is not moot. George Bock has not dismissed his claims for custodial interference and therefore discovery may continue in this action.

questions.[4] [She] was held in contempt on five separate occasions for her refusal to answer questions and was ordered to produce specific documents. The questions at issue are as follows:

(A) Did you ever receive phone calls from Laura Bock or to Laura Bock in which she gave you authority to proceed on behalf of her in federal court?

Mendel agreed to answer questions as to when she had last spoken to Laura, but refused to answer questions regarding the content of any of their conversations. Through her attorney, Mendel also asserted that the question had no relevance to any issue in the *Felbert* litigation. The superior court held that the attorney-client privilege did not apply to this "limited question" and held Mendel in contempt for refusing to answer.

(B) What words did Carolyn Johnson speak that led you to believe she was Laura Bock's representative?

After being directed by the court to answer this question, Mendel responded "I can't answer it on the basis of the attorney-client privilege." She also objected because the question wasn't material to any issue in the *Felbert* litigation. The superior court then ruled, "Very well. Again, I find you in contempt."

(C) Once you learned that you might have an opportunity to talk to [a Representative of] Street Stories, [a CBS television show,] did you obtain authority from Laura Bock to speak to the news media from New York?

Mendel refused to answer this question. Her counsel argued that it was not relevant to locating the children or any issue in *Felbert,* and that it was protected by the attorney-client privilege. The superior court directed Mendel to answer the question. Mendel replied, "I can't answer the question based on the attorney-client privilege." The superior court then ruled, "Failure to answer is an act of contempt. . . ."

---

4. . . . Mendel testified that, to the best of her recollection, her last telephone communication from Ms. Bock was in approximately September or October, 1992. She reiterated that she had not seen Ms. Bock since early February, 1992, and she had never known where Ms. Bock was or how to contact her. She testified that, in their first meeting, Ms. Bock did not indicate she intended to hide the children from her ex-husband. Ms. Mendel testified that she receives instructions about her representation orally from Ms. Bock when Ms. Bock calls her. . . . Ms. Mendel testified that she considers Carolyn Johnson an agent or representative of Laura Bock, primarily because Ms. Johnson pays the legal bills for Ms. Mendel's representation of Laura Bock. Additionally, Ms. Mendel testified, she has an attorney-client relationship with Ms. Johnson, apart from her status as representative or agent for Ms. Bock. . . .

(D) [S]tate the names of any people reflected on the billing record with whom you've had conversations concerning this matter, excluding Carolyn Johnson and Laura Bock.

Mendel's counsel instructed her not to answer the question based on both the attorney-client privilege and the attorney work product doctrine. The superior court then remarked in part: "I think that this whole matter is probably better served by taking a fairly broad view. [T]he rules of privilege and confidentiality have to be viewed in light of the potential on-going felony and that's going to guide my rulings." The court then required Mendel to answer the question. Mendel refused based on the attorney-client privilege and the work product doctrine. Mendel was found in contempt.

(E) Produce[ ] . . . [your billing records to Laura] in their entirety.

Mendel invited the superior court to review in camera the unredacted billings she had brought to the hearing. The superior court declined to review the billings in camera, stating

> it's one of the vices of in-camera reviews, not being intimately familiar with every twist and turn that this case has or may take . . . it's not automatically clear that, — to me, that I'm going to recognize strict relevance. So I'm going to produce them. [A]re there any use restrictions [or] confidentiality orders you wish to have me place on Mr. Vitale before I give them to him?

Mendel objected to producing her entire billing records on the basis that they contained narrative statements detailing her legal representation of Laura and thus were protected by the attorney-client privilege. Additionally, Mendel objected on the ground that the records contained no information which was relevant to the *Felbert* litigation or locating the children. The superior court ordered Mendel to produce the billing records in their entirety. However, the court stayed the order pending the outcome of this appeal. . . .

## A. Relevancy — Questions (A), (B), and (C)

Mendel argues that the answers to questions (A), (B), and (C), each of which concerned whether Mendel had authorization from Laura to represent her, could not possibly lead to the discovery of the whereabouts of Laura or the children, nor were they relevant to any issue in *Felbert*. If the discovery questions were not relevant then Mendel "should not be subject to indefinite incarceration for her failure to provide irrelevant information."

Because this contempt citation arises out of the failure to comply with a discovery request, our determination as to whether the information sought is relevant is necessarily guided by Alaska Civil Rule 26(b)(1). Civil Rule 26(b)(1) permits discovery of any matter, not privileged, which is relevant to the subject matter involved in the pending action. . . . It is not ground for objection that the information sought will be inadmissible at the trial if the information sought appears reasonably calculated to lead to the discovery of admissible evidence.

Even under this broad view of relevancy, we are convinced by Mendel's argument. The subject of Mendel's authority to represent Laura is simply not relevant to any inquiry George might pursue in relation to the *Felbert* litigation. Nor do these questions appear reasonably calculated to lead to the discovery of admissible evidence. Finally, George provides no explanation as to the nexus between the information sought and his efforts to locate his children. We therefore hold that Mendel's convictions of contempt for her failure to answer questions (A), (B), and (C) must be set aside.

## B. ATTORNEY-CLIENT PRIVILEGE — QUESTIONS (A), (B), AND (C)

[T]he superior court rejected Mendel's claim of attorney-client privilege with respect to questions (A), (B), and (C). . . . Alaska Evidence Rule 503(b) provides in part: A client has a privilege to refuse to disclose and to prevent any other person from disclosing confidential communications made for the purpose of facilitating the rendition of professional legal services to the client, (1) between the client or the client's representative and the client's lawyer or the lawyer's representative. . . .

Evidence Rule 503(b) gives effect to the policy which underlies the attorney-client privilege. As discussed in United Services Automobile Assn. v. Werley, 526 P.2d 28, 31 (Alaska 1974), "[t]he purpose of the attorney-client privilege is to promote the freedom of consultation of legal advisors by clients by removing the apprehension of compelled disclosure by the legal advisors." It is apparent that requiring Mendel to answer questions (A), (B), and (C) would have required disclosure of confidential communications made for the purpose of facilitating the rendition of professional legal services to Laura.

George takes the position that the privilege is vitiated because Mendel's services "were sought, obtained or used to enable or aid anyone to commit or plan to commit what the client knew or reasonably should have known to be a crime or fraud. . . ." In essence, "[t]he attorney-client privilege is not designed to encourage those planning to commit a wrong to obtain legal assistance in their endeavor." [Munn v. Bristol Bay Housing Authority, 777 P.2d 188, 195 (Alaska 1989).]

In the case at bar, review of the record demonstrates that George failed to establish a prima facie case of crime or fraud in the attorney-client relationship which would abrogate the privilege. We therefore hold that the superior court's contempt rulings against Mendel based on her failure to answer questions (A), (B), and (C) should be vacated on the additional ground that the attorney-client privilege is applicable to each question and the privilege was not lost under the crime/fraud exception to the attorney-client privilege.[12]

## C. QUESTIONS (D) AND (E)

We next address the merits of the superior court's order to produce Mendel's billing records in their entirety and its contempt ruling for Mendel's refusal. . . . Mendel argues that this information constitutes attorney work product [and that] the superior court violated Civil Rule 26(b)(3) by compelling production of her attorney work product without adopting measures to assure that protected information was not disclosed. [D]iscovery of an attorney's work product may be had under Rule 26(b)(3), but the court has a mandatory duty to protect against disclosures of the "mental impressions, conclusions, opinions or legal theories" of the litigating attorney. Mendel argues that the names contained in her billing records to Laura and the detailed billings consisting of narrative descriptions would afford George insight into Mendel's handling of Laura's case.

In interpreting the analogous Federal Rule of Civil Procedure, the United States Supreme Court held that work product which reflects an attorney's thought processes should only be disclosed in rare situations, and should not be disclosed simply upon a showing of substantial need and inability to obtain the equivalent without undue hardship. Hickman v. Taylor, 329 U.S. 495, 510-12 (1947). On the other hand, according to Professor Moore, a litigant may generally seek the "identity and location of persons having knowledge of any discoverable matter" without violating the work product doctrine or the attorney-client privilege. 4 James W. Moore et al., Moore's Federal Practice, ¶26.57[2] (2d ed. 1993).

---

12. George cites several similar cases from other jurisdictions in support of his argument that the crime/fraud exception applies, e.g., Bersani v. Bersani, 565 A.2d 1368 (Conn. 1989); Jafarian-Kerman v. Jafarian-Kerman, 424 S.W.2d 333 (Mo. Ct. App. 1967); In re Jacqueline F., 391 N.E.2d 967 (N.Y. Ct. App. 1979); Dike v. Dike, 448 P.2d 490 (Wash. 1968). Although each of these cases also involves a parental or guardian kidnapping, each is distinguishable from the instant case. In each case, the attorney was compelled against his/her will to divulge the address of the client. In the instant case, Mendel has acknowledged that she would have to divulge Laura's location if she knew where Laura was or the name of anyone she knew who knew Laura's location. Mendel stated, "I don't know those things, and I have never wanted to know those things. And I've been very clear with everyone that if they tell me I will tell."

Here, Mendel proposed a compromise which would disclose the names of those individuals who might have knowledge of discoverable matter without revealing Mendel's litigation strategies. Mendel offered her unredacted billing records to the superior court for in camera review. However, the superior court declined this offer and instead ordered production of the billing records.

On this record we hold that the superior court abused its discretion in declining to conduct an in camera review of the unredacted billing records. We therefore hold that the contempt adjudication against Mendel for her failure to answer question (D) and the order to produce the unredacted billing records must be vacated and set aside. . . .

## Notes and Questions

1. *Enforcement remedies generally.* Many remedies exist to enforce custody determinations. Common remedies include civil contempt proceedings and the writ of habeas corpus. Although the latter was originally utilized by prisoners claiming illegal arrest or unlawful detention, it is increasingly being utilized in child custody cases. See generally Paul J. Buser, Habeas Corpus Litigation in Child Custody Matters: An Historical Mine Field, 11 J. Am. Acad. Matrimonial Law. 1 (1993).

Some states also recognize (either by case law or statute) a tort action for custodial interference. According to the Restatement (Second) of Torts §700 (1977), the tort of interference with the parent-child relationship requires that: "One who, with knowledge that the parent does not consent, abducts or otherwise compels or induces a minor child to leave a parent legally entitled to its custody or not to return to the parent after it has been left him, is subject to liability to the parent." Criminal liability also exists for custodial interference. See generally Ann M. Haralambie, Handling Child Custody, Abuse and Adoption Cases §19.18 (1993). What is the purpose of civil versus criminal statutes? Are both necessary?

2. *Mendel* reveals that attorneys who become entangled in clients' self-help efforts potentially face serious consequences. A nonabducting parent generally may resort to two weapons against the abducting parent's attorney in the efforts to recover the children: to request the court to use its power of contempt to force the attorney to disclose the other parents' (and the children's) whereabouts, and/or to sue the attorney for professional malpractice in some cases. Could Mr. Bock have charged Ms. Mendel with malpractice? See Shehade v. Gerson, 500 N.E.2d 510 (Ill. Ct. App. 1986).

3. *Mendel* addresses the lawyer's ethical obligations to disclose a client's whereabouts when a client decides to hide her children from the other parent. To what extent is an attorney prohibited, permitted, or

mandated to disclose information based on the attorney-client privilege? How do the attorney's ethical obligations differ when the client merely is considering an abduction compared to when the client has already abducted the child? What actions did Ms. Mendel take so that she would not run afoul of her ethical obligations? See also In re Marriage of Decker, 606 N.E.2d 1094 (Ill. 1992). See generally S. Shelton Foss, The Attorney's Dilemma Under Model Rules 1.2 and 1.6: Clients Who Do Not Return Children in Custody Cases, 17 J. Legal Prof. 231 (1992).

4. Attorneys' ethical obligations are governed by both the attorney-client privilege and state ethics code rules on confidentiality. Under the former, the privilege applies where legal advice is sought from a legal adviser, for communications made in confidence by the client. Communications are permanently protected from disclosure by the client or the legal adviser unless the privilege is waived. Like all privileges, the attorney-client privilege is not absolute. Should the attorney-client privilege yield to the best interests of the child principle? See Bersani v. Bersani, 565 A.2d 1368 (Conn. Super. Ct. 1989).

5. The attorney also has ethical obligations under state rules of professional responsibility (influenced, in large part, by the ABA's Model Code of Professional Responsibility and the subsequent Model Rules of Professional Conduct). For example, Rule 1.2(d) of the Model Rules of Professional Conduct provides: "A lawyer shall not counsel a client to engage, or assist a client, in conduct that the lawyer knows is criminal or fraudulent." Many of the rules regarding disclosure, generally, pertain to disclosure of a fugitive client's whereabouts. Should such rules be applied to abducting parents?

6. Only a few jurisdictions have considered the issue whether the attorney-client privilege or the ethical duty of confidentiality protect an attorney from disclosure of a client's whereabouts. One commentator, who surveyed the case law, concludes that courts have not mandated disclosure in those domestic relations cases in which disclosure would threaten the client's safety. Cases that mandate disclosure of a client's whereabouts all involve clients who acted in violation of a court order. Shelly K. Hillyer, Comment, The Attorney-Client Privilege, Ethical Rules of Confidentiality, and Other Arguments Bearing on Disclosure of a Fugitive Client's Whereabouts, 68 Temp. L. Rev. 307, 341, 343 (1995).

## Problem

When John and Loree divorce, Loree is awarded temporary physical custody of their daughter Jessica. Loree and Jessica move in with Loree's parents. At the custody hearing, John is awarded permanent physical custody of Jessica. When John attempts to obtain custody of Jessica from Loree, he is denied access by Loree's father, Franklin Rigenhagen. John then obtains a court order and returns to the parents' home. Franklin informs John that Loree and Jessica have left the state. John commences a seven-year search for Jessica. Based on information from the FBI indicating the Rigenhagens might have information about Loree's and Jessica's whereabouts, John files suit against Loree and the Rigenhagens alleging their actions constituted interference with parental custodial rights. John claims damages of over $50,000 in search-related costs, emotional distress, and loss of Jessica's companionship and society. The jurisdiction must decide whether to recognize the tort of custodial interference based on public policy considerations. What result? Larson v. Dunn, 460 N.W.2d 39 (Minn. 1990) (en banc).

## Note: International Child-Abduction

International child-snatching is a serious problem. Estimates suggest that hundreds of children are abducted either to or from the United States annually.[30] Several factors have contributed to the rise in international abductions, including the ease of international transportation and communication, the increasing number of binational marriages, and the decreasing rigor of passport supervision.[31] In response to this social problem, the Hague Conference on Private International Law adopted the Hague Convention on the Civil Aspects of International Child Abduction in 1980. Seventy nations are signatories to this international treaty, including the United States.[32] The United States implemented the Convention by enabling legislation, the International Child Abduction Remedies Act (ICARA), 42 U.S.C. §§11601-11610 (1994 & Supp. 1999).

The goal of the Hague Convention is to secure the return of children who are wrongfully removed from or retained in a signatory state and to return them to the country of their "habitual residence" (which must be another contracting nation) where the merits of the custody dispute can be adjudicated. Article 13 of the Convention specifies three affirmative defenses that may be invoked by an abducting parent to defeat the child's return: (1) if the abducting parent establishes that the child's caretaker was not actually exercising custody rights at the time of removal or retention or had consented to removal or retention; (2) if the

[30]. Nadine Joy Hazell, New Anti-Abduction Rules on Foreign Travel, Plain Dealer (Cleveland), Aug. 27, 2000, at K4 (reporting that the State Department has approximately 1,000 open international abduction cases at any given time).
[31]. Rania Nanos, Note, The Views of a Child: Emerging Interpretation and Significance of the Child's Objection Defense under the Hague Child Abduction Convention, 22 Brook J. Intl. L. 437, 437 (1996).
[32]. See Hague Conference on Private International Law: Status Sheet Convention #28, www.hcch.net/e/status/abdshte.html, visited Jan. 15, 2002.

abducting parent establishes a grave risk that the return would entail physical or psychological harm to the child; and (3) if the court in the forum of the abducting parent finds that the child, who has attained an appropriate age and maturity (based on the court's discretion), objects to the return.[33]

Courts have interpreted various provisions of the Convention, including the meaning of "habitual residence," the extent of protection of visitation (termed "access" rights), and the "grave risk of harm" defense. See, e.g., Harkness v. Harkness, 577 N.W.2d 116, 121, 123 (Mich. Ct. App. 1998) (noting that habitual residence is not to be simply equated with the last place the child lived, but rather is to be determined on a case-by-case analysis); Croll v. Croll, 229 F.3d 133, 135 (2d Cir. 2000) (holding that "rights of access" do not constitute custodial rights even when a custody decree orders the custodial parent not to leave the country of residence with the child); Blondin v. Dubois, 189 F.3d 240, 242 (2d. Cir. 1999) (concluding that the Convention requires a "complete analysis of the full panoply of arrangements" allowing children to be returned to the country from which they have been abducted while still protecting them from grave risk of harm).

Congress has also addressed international child abduction. In 1993 Congress enacted the International Parental Kidnapping Act (IPKA), 18 U.S.C. §1204 (1994). IPKA (unlike the Hague Convention) imposes criminal sanctions, making it a federal felony for a parent wrongfully to remove or retain a child outside the United States. The IPKA's affirmative defenses differ from those in the Hague Convention: if the defendant has been granted custody or visitation by a court acting pursuant to the UCCJA; is fleeing from domestic violence; or had court-ordered custody and failed to return the child because of circumstances beyond the defendant's control, provided that the defendant made reasonable attempts to notify the other parent.

See generally Anna I. Sapone, Note, Children as Pawns in Their Parents' Fight for Control: The Failure of the United States to Protect Against International Child Abduction, 21 Women's Rts. L. Rep. 129 (2000); Symposium, Celebrating Twenty Years: The Past and Promise of the 1980 Hague Convention on the Civil Aspects of International Child Abduction, 33 N.Y.U. J. Int'l L. & Pol. 1 (2000); Jacqueline D. Golub, Note, International Parental Kidnapping Crime Act of 1993: The United States' Attempt to Get Our Children Back — How Is It Working?, 24 Brook. J. Int'l L. 797 (1999).

---

[33]. Convention on the Civil Aspects of International Child Abduction, Oct. 25, 1980, art. 13, para. 1(a)-(b), T.I.A.S. No. 11,670, at 8, 19 I.L.M. at 1502.

## C. WHAT PROCESS SHOULD GOVERN CUSTODY DISPUTES?

### 1. The Adversary System versus Mediation Process

■ **ELIZABETH S. SCOTT & ROBERT EMERY, CHILD CUSTODY DISPUTE RESOLUTION: THE ADVERSARIAL SYSTEM AND DIVORCE MEDIATION**
*in Psychology and Child Custody Determinations: Knowledge, Roles and Expertise 23, 23-27, 39-42, 45-51 (Lois A. Weithorn ed., 1987)*

Observers have commented on the irony of resolving child custody disputes through the adversary system. While the objective of the law is to resolve the custody issue in a manner that will be in the child's best interests, the legal process may have a destructive impact on both child and parents. Many participants regard child custody disputes negatively. Some mental health professionals who are involved as expert consultants are horrified by the acrimonious exchange and the minimal attention given to its effect on the child. Many lawyers and judges also find custody disputes among the most distasteful of legal confrontations. Perhaps even more significant, many parents who have gone through divorce report dissatisfaction with the legal system and describe negative effects on their postdivorce adjustment.

Several aspects of the full-blown custody battle may evoke criticism. Attorneys employed by the parents may focus their energies single-mindedly on winning custody for their clients, regardless of whether such efforts promote the child's welfare. Private investigators may be hired and neighbors, friends, and teachers interviewed to build the case. Divorcing spouses, who before the onset of marital strife would have readily acknowledged that their children had two competent parents, suddenly attempt to prove otherwise. Any behavior, habit, or character trait that reflects positively on one parent or negatively on the other may be raised in the courtroom if it can be remotely linked to parenting skills or the parent-child relationship. Attorneys representing husband and wife may advise their clients not to communicate with each other. . . .

The adversary system has been well established in Anglo-American law for hundreds of years. There are two basic characteristics of this dispute resolution model: the decision maker is a neutral party not involved in the dispute (the judge), and the evidence about the dispute that the judge considers is controlled and developed by the disputing parties themselves. These characteristics have several implications for the process. Each litigant, through an attorney, attempts to present all the evidence

favorable to his or her side of the case and unfavorable to the opponent's.
. . . Adjudication through this process is designed to produce a "winner"
and "a loser." After hearing each side's evidence, the judge announces the
verdict, holding for the plaintiff or the defendant. . . .

Few other legal confrontations involve the emotional intensity of a
custody dispute. In most litigation the adversaries are strangers, business
associates, or acquaintances. The divorcing couple's prior intimate relationship exaggerates from the outset the potential for hostility. Because
of the prior relationship, each parent may know particularly hurtful and
damaging facts about the other. Further, the subject of the dispute, the
custody of their child, may be crucially important to each parent. . . .

The nature of the inquiry in custody disputes further heightens the
tendency to promote hostility. [C]ustody adjudication focuses on the personal qualities of the parent. Each parent's efforts to persuade the judge
that he or she is the better custodian may involve presenting evidence
about the character, habits, lifestyle, and moral fitness of the former
spouse. While in theory only evidence relating to an individual's capacity as a parent is relevant, any character deficiency or behavior that the
judge is likely to view negatively often will be exposed. . . .

### Divorce Mediation

Because of the dissatisfaction with the adversary system, there has
been an increased interest in developing alternative methods of resolving child custody disputes. In the past several years, divorce mediation
has grown dramatically as the major alternative to either litigation or
out-of-court negotiation between attorneys. . . .

In divorce mediation the divorcing parties meet with an impartial
third party (or parties) to identify, discuss, and one hopes, settle the disputes that result from marital dissolution. While it shares features with
some types of marital and family therapy, mediation can be distinguished
from many forms of psychotherapy in that it is short term and problem-
focused. The process also requires that the mediator be knowledgeable
in the legal and economic as well as the social and psychological consequences of divorce. Further, mediation differs from therapy in its objectives, and the exploration of emotional issues is circumscribed by the
goal of negotiating a fair and acceptable agreement. Finally, unlike marital therapy, the goal of mediation is *not* reconciliation.

Divorce mediation embraces a model of dispute resolution considerably different from that characterizing the adversary process. Whereas
in mediation the parties give up some procedural control in that the mediator directs much of the process, decisional control is not handed over
to a third party as it is in adjudication. That the parents retain decisional
control also distinguishes mediation from arbitration. Arbitration, like
mediation, may encompass less formal procedures than does litigation,

but unlike the mediator, the arbitrator is expected to make a decision for the parties if they do not do so themselves. As with an agreement negotiated out of court by their attorneys, the parties themselves retain the authority to accept or reject a mediated agreement. The judiciary technically retains the right to reject any negotiated settlement that does not promote the best interests of the child. As with agreements reached through attorney negotiations, however, most judges will "rubber stamp" a mediated agreement. . . .

Some divorce mediators attempt to settle all four of the major issues that must be decided in a divorce: property division, spousal support, custody and visitation, and child support. Almost all mediators, however, [who] work in public court settings [limit] their practice to the issues of custody and visitation. Mediation may be a particularly appropriate method of dealing with these child-related issues because of the indeterminacy of child custody law and research on the effects of parental conflict on children. [T]he process by which the dispute is settled — the transaction costs — is particularly important in child custody dispute resolution. The process by which decisions are reached and the impact it has on the parents' relationship is critical to the integrative decisions regarding child rearing, since both parents are likely to maintain at least some contact with their children after a divorce. . . .

Proponents have argued that mediation will have benefits in areas that have been termed the "four C's." That is, mediation is said to reduce *conflict,* increase *cooperation,* give people more *control* over important decisions in their lives, and achieve these goals at a reduced public or private *cost.* [Research] has compared the two methods of dispute resolution along these four dimensions. . . .

[Does mediation reduce conflict?] In Los Angeles County, where couples [in court-based programs] who request a custody or visitation hearing are automatically referred to mediation first, 55% of these parents reach an agreement in mediation. In Connecticut's court-based mediation programs, where referrals to the program are based on local practices and judicial discretion, [of 3,272 cases] 64% reached an agreement in mediation. Other small public mediation services similarly have reported reaching mediated agreements with between one-half and three-quarters of all couples. [Thus,] [c]ourt-based mediators are succeeding in negotiating agreements between parents who had planned to litigate their dispute.

[S]ocial psychological research suggests that people are more likely to value and abide by decisions they participate in. . . . Initial data do indicate that divorcing parties are more satisfied with the mediation process than with proceedings associated with litigation. [In three studies], it was found that (1) three times as many people who went through mediation reported that "things had gotten much better" six weeks after the settlement than those who went through litigation; (2) at six- to twelve-month follow-up, parties who mediated divorce settlements, as opposed to members of a litigation contrast group, reported more satisfaction, were more likely to view their settlement as fair, and indicated a higher level of understanding and cooperation with their former spouses; and (3) when interviewed a short time after they reached a settlement, parents undergoing mediation found mediation to be less biased and more suited to the family than parents undergoing traditional court adjudication found adjudication to be.

Whether parents return to court with postdissolution litigation, which occurs in as many as one-third of all divorces that involve children, is another, objective measure of the quality of mediated agreements. It has been found that parents randomly assigned to mediate their visitation disputes were only one-sixth as likely to return to court two years subsequently as were parents who proceeded through the adversary system. . . .

As to whether mediation is effective in terms of reducing public costs, evidence does suggest that a large percentage of cases can be successfully diverted through the more expensive custody hearing to the less expensive mediation session, that agreements are reached more quickly in mediation, and that mediated agreements last longer. . . .

[A] number of questions remain about the mediation alternative. . . . These questions encompass debates on whether attorneys or mental health professionals are better trained to conduct mediation, whether mediation should be conducted by teams including one member of each profession, or whether a new, distinct profession must be created. Also debated is whether all divorce disputes should be negotiated in mediation or whether mediation should be limited to custody and visitation issues. . . .

Another set of questions about mediation concerns who should be included or excluded: whether referrals to court-based mediation programs should be mandatory; whether participation in mediation should be completely voluntary; and whether parents should be referred to mediation at individual judges' discretion. These three options now are variously used in jurisdictions throughout the United States. It has also been asked whether certain cases should automatically be excluded from mediation: for example, cases where there are apparently great discrepancies in the parties' relative bargaining power, as where spouse abuse has occurred, or where independent legal findings on matters such as child abuse or neglect must be made.

A third set of questions pertains to the process of mediation itself. Should children be included in mediation sessions? Should grandparents, stepparents, or other interested relatives have a role? What part should mediators play in deciding the content of the negotiated agreement? Should mediators, for example, work toward negotiating joint custody settlements? Moreover, should mediators refuse to be party to agreements they object to on ethical or psychological grounds? Important as such issues are, they remain largely unresolved, and policies vary among practitioners. Efforts have been made, however, to develop uniform standards of practice for mediators.

Finally, a set of questions has been raised about what is to happen once mediation ends. What role should attorneys play in regard to a mediated settlement? Can a single attorney review the agreement, should it be reviewed by two attorneys who hold an adversarial perspective, or need it be reviewed by an attorney at all? Perhaps the most controversial debate about the termination of mediation, however, concerns the mediator's role in any subsequent court hearing. Some have argued that when a court hearing is held after mediation fails to produce an agreement, the mediator *should* make a recommendation to the court.

Proponents of this perspective point to the fact that the mediator is already familiar with the family and that such a recommendation will avoid the duplication of efforts inherent in beginning a new custody investigation. Others argue that strict confidentiality is essential to the mediation process. . . . Practice and judicial policy remain unresolved in regard to the important issue of confidentiality. . . .

---

The following case wrestles with "the most controversial debate" (according to the above excerpt).

## ■ McLAUGHLIN v. SUPERIOR COURT
*189 Cal. Rptr. 479 (Ct. App. 1983)*

RATTIGAN, Associate Justice.

Civil Code section 4607 requires prehearing mediation of child custody and visitation disputes in marital dissolution proceedings conducted pursuant to the Family Law Act. The statute also provides that, if the parties fail to agree in the mediation proceedings, the mediator "may, consistent with local court rules, render a recommendation to the court as to the custody or visitation of the child or children" involved. Pursuant to this provision, respondent superior court has adopted a "local court rule," or policy, which (1) requires the mediator to make a recommendation to the court if the parties fail to agree in the mediation proceedings, but (2) prohibits cross-examination of the mediator by the parties. We hold in this original proceeding that the policy is constitutionally invalid in significant respects. . . .

Petitioner Thomas J. McLaughlin and real party in interest Linda Lee McLaughlin were married in 1969. They have three children, whose ages range between 6 and 13 years. [In May 1982, the husband petitioned for dissolution and custody. In response, the wife requested joint legal custody as well as physical custody. Husband then applied for temporary custody with visitation to the wife. The court issued an order to show cause in which the questions of temporary custody and visitation were set for hearing on June 30. The wife filed a declaration in which she requested temporary custody with visitation to the father.]

[At the hearing on the order to show cause,] petitioner's counsel recited his understanding that the pending issues of temporary custody and visitation were to be "referred for mediation." Counsel also stated his view that "the mediation procedure[,] insofar as it allows the mediator to make a recommendation for the Court, and bars the introduction of any testimony from the mediator about what the parties tell him or her[,] is unconstitutional as a denial of the right to cross-examine." On that ground, counsel in effect moved for a "protective order" which would permit mediation proceedings, but which would provide that if they did not result in agreement by the parties, on the issues of temporary custody and visitation, the mediator would be prohibited from making a recommendation to the court unless petitioner were guaranteed the right to cross-examine the mediator.

Speaking to the motion, the court pointed out that Civil Code section 4607 "required" that "a contested custody or visitation matter . . . be preceded . . . by a session of mandatory mediation . . . under the new 1980 law." The court also pointed out that the required mediation proceedings were to be conducted "before the court of conciliation" [that is, by personnel of the Family Conciliation Court]. In an exchange with counsel which followed, the court denied the motion on the ground that the "protective order" requested would violate a policy the court had adopted pursuant to Civil Code section 4607, subdivision (e).

The exchange produced clarification of petitioner's motion. It also included the only available description of respondent court's policy, which has apparently not been memorialized in a written rule. For these reasons, we quote pertinent passages of the exchange in the margin.[3]

---

3. "The Court [addressing Mr. Brunwasser, petitioner's counsel]: Some counties, as you probably know, do not permit or require a recommendation from the mediator in the event the parties are unable to agree. Some do. This county [i.e., respondent court] does, and therefore, I'm not prepared to give you the protective order you wish. The court feels that in the event the mediator were free to testify as to any of the matters mediated, that is[,] the substance of the matter as gleaned from the mediation session, . . . certainly you would have the right to cross-examine the mediator.

"However, our instructions as a matter of court policy to the mediators are that they are not to state the basis for their . . . recommendation. . . . In short, the recommendation of the mediator is simply . . . a recommendation to the court without any statement of underlying basis. . . . That's the way we do business here. . . .

"Mr. Brunwasser: . . . I have no objection to mediation. What I have an objection to is a procedure which allows the mediator . . . to communicate with the court and not be subject to defend [sic] his or her opinion by cross-examination.

"The Court: I understand that. I hope you equally understand that it is our policy to require a recommendation if the mediation is unsuccessful. It's a starting point which enables the court . . . [,] in the absence of other evidence, to make an interim order based upon the opinion of the trained counselor, and it's a procedure we opted for when this law was enacted. We're satisfied that the law permits that, and so your motion for a protective order is denied."

After the court had denied the motion, counsel for both parties agreed to a continuance of the hearing on temporary custody and visitation. They also agreed that custody would remain in "status quo" pending further proceedings. On July 6, respondent court filed a formal order in which it directed mediation of the pending issues [and continued the hearing to August]. On July 30, petitioner commenced the present proceeding by petitioning this court for a writ of prohibition restraining respondent court from "taking any further actions to enforce its order filed July 6, 1982 requiring petitioner and real party to submit their temporary custody dispute to mediation" in the absence of a "protective order" to the effect that the mediator could not make a recommendation to the court unless petitioner were permitted to cross-examine the mediator. Petitioner also asked this court to stay the mediation proceedings pending disposition of his petition.

[The court denied the petition and request for a stay. Petitioner appealed to the California Supreme Court, seeking a stay of the August hearing in the absence of a protective order barring the mediator from making a recommendation to the court. The Supreme Court stayed the August hearing and returned the case to the court of appeals for a hearing on the issue of the constitutionality of the practice of mediator recommendations.]

... With leave of this court, the California Chapter of the Association of Family and Conciliation Courts filed a brief amicus curiae. Amicus expressly disclaimed "taking a position in support of either side," but provided us with detailed information showing the practices followed by some superior courts relative to mediation proceedings conducted pursuant to Civil Code section 4607. (See fn. 7, post.). . . .

It may first be mentioned that we did not state reasons in our order summarily denying the petition in the first instance, but that we denied it on the basis of our views that the mediation proceedings should be permitted to run their course; that the petition was essentially premature unless and until it were made to appear that a recommendation by the mediator might be forthcoming because the parties had failed to agree; and that the challenge raised in the petition would be rendered moot if the parties agreed in fact. The Supreme Court obviously disagreed. [W]e disregard any possibility of mootness on the ground that the issue presented is one of broad public interest and is likely to recur.

Civil Code section 4607, subdivision (a), clearly requires prehearing mediation of child custody and visitation disputes in marital dissolution proceedings. Subdivision (e) of the statute is also clear to the effect that the mediator "may, consistent with local court rules," make a recommendation to the court on either issue, or both, if the parties fail to reach agreement in the mediation proceedings. Subdivision (e) does not require or authorize disclosure to the parties of a recommendation made by the mediator to the court, nor of the mediator's reasons; it neither requires nor authorizes cross-examination of the mediator by the parties, which would necessarily require or bring about disclosure of the recommendation and the reasons for it; and the statute's express deference to "local court rules" has the effect of making disclosure and cross-examination matters of local option.

As we have seen, respondent court has exercised this option by adopting a policy which requires that the mediator make a recommendation to the court if the parties have failed to agree on child custody or visitation in the mediation proceedings; requires that the mediator not state his or her reasons for the recommendation; and denies the parties the right to cross-examine the mediator on the ground that the reasons have not been disclosed to the court. Amicus curiae has shown us that one large metropolitan superior court follows an entirely different procedure, and that another has adopted a policy which is essentially similar to respondent court's.[7]

The feature of respondent court's policy which prohibits cross-examination of the mediator is consistent with the provision in subdivision (c) of the statute that the mediation proceedings "shall be confidential." The requirement that the mediator not state to the court his or her reasons for the recommendation is consistent with the provision in subdivision (c) which protects the confidentiality of the parties' "communications" to the mediator by making them "official information within the meaning of Section 1040 of the Evidence Code." The facts remain that the policy permits the court to receive a significant recommendation on contested issues but denies the parties the right to cross-examine its source. This combination cannot constitutionally be enforced. . . .

Respondent court contends that the enforcement of its policy prohibiting cross-examination of a mediator who makes a recommendation to it is constitutionally permissible because only "temporary" child custody and visitation are involved and "due process is not required at every stage of a proceeding." . . . However, the word "temporary" does

---

7. Amicus curiae describes the practice of the Los Angeles County Superior Court . . . : Where prehearing mediation proceedings have been conducted . . . , the court (1) neither receives nor permits a recommendation by the mediator and (2) proceeds to hear and determine the contested issue or issues without referring to the unsuccessful mediation process in any way.

Amicus curiae has filed declarations showing the related practice followed in the Superior Court for the City and County of San Francisco. . . . When the initial hearing is called on the same day [as the mediation session], the parties' attorneys communicate the mediator's recommendation to the court. . . . This (appellate) court interprets the [above declaration] to mean that the mediator's reasons for his or her recommendation are not disclosed to the parties, the attorneys, or the court when the recommendation is made in the first instance. This declaration fairly shows that the court makes the initial order on temporary custody or visitation without permitting cross-examination of the mediator. The declaration does not show whether cross-examination of the mediator is permitted at any later hearing.

not appear in Civil Code section 4607. We are not at liberty to interpolate it, by construction. . . . The constitutional infirmities in respondent court's policy are such that it may not be enforced on the theory that only "temporary" custody or visitation are involved. . . .

. . . Our conclusions are consistent with our duty to harmonize the provisions of subdivisions (a) and (e) of the statute without doing violence to its salutary purposes. In addition, it has been shown in the present proceeding that disparities among "local court rules" adopted pursuant to subdivision (e) have had the effect of guaranteeing due process in some superior courts but not in others. Our conclusions will terminate this effect, which the Legislature obviously did not intend.

[The court concluded that the husband was entitled to a writ of mandate which] directs that the court not receive a recommendation from the mediator, as to any contested issue on which agreement is not reached, unless (1) the court has first made a protective order which guarantees the parties the rights to have the mediator testify and to cross-examine him or her concerning the recommendation or (2) the rights have been waived. . . .

## Notes and Questions

1. Mediation is a form of alternative dispute resolution that respects the parties' autonomy in decisionmaking ("private ordering"). In the adversarial system, the judiciary asserts authority over the financial aspects of dissolution and child custody. Mediation, however, confers broad latitude on the divorcing couple to resolve such matters for themselves. Why do Professors Scott and Emery suggest that mediation is better suited to the resolution of custody disputes? What are the benefits and costs of the adversary system? Of the mediation process?

See generally Ann L. Diamond & Madeleine Simborg, Divorce Mediation's Weaknesses, Cal. Law., July 1983, at 37; Gary J. Friedman & Margaret L. Anderson, Divorce Mediation's Strengths, Cal. Law., July 1983, at 36; Leonard L. Riskin, Mediation and Lawyers, 43 Ohio State L.J. 29, 33 (1982). For an empirical assessment, see Jessica Pearson & Nancy Thoennes, Divorce Mediation Research Results, in Divorce Mediation: Theory and Practice 443 ( Jay Folberg & Ann Milne eds., 1988).

2. How does mediation differ from other forms of alternative dispute resolution (such as arbitration) and from psychotherapy in terms of objectives, process, and the ultimate decisionmaker? See Joan Kelly, Mediation and Psychotherapy: Distinguishing the Differences, 1 Mediation Q. 33 (1983).

3. Mediation has long-standing roots in ancient China, Japan, and Africa. In the United States, mediation flourished in the late 1970s, fueled by acceptance of no-fault divorce and dissatisfaction with traditional

dispute resolution. One of the first programs was established in 1974 by attorney-therapist O. J. Coogler. See also O. J. Coogler, Structured Mediation in Divorce Settlement (1978).

In 1981, California became the first state to require mediation (formerly Cal. Civ. Code §4607, now Cal. Fam. Code §3170 (West 1994 & Supp. 2001)). Mandatory mediation was intended to facilitate parental agreements for joint custody.[34] Before the parties can proceed to a hearing, mediation is required in all cases in which custody and/or visitation was contested. The statute also reformed California's system of Family Conciliation Courts to provide mediation services.

> Court conciliation staffs, particularly in California, were probably the first to offer divorce mediation services as they are now known. California offered court-connected conciliation services as early as 1939. The initial focus of these services was on providing marriage counseling aimed at reconciliation. With the adoption of no-fault divorce and the increase in the divorce rate, the focus of conciliation shifted from reconciliation to divorce counseling and custody mediation. Court mediation services have proliferated in the last few years, with the encouragement (or actual mandate) of legislation. . . .

Jay Folberg, A Mediation Overview: History and Dimensions of Practice, 1 Mediation Q. 3, 6 (1983). Court-ordered mediation services are often limited to a certain number of sessions.

Many statutes now provide for mediation, either by encouraging the parties to mediate (as an educational tool), providing for discretionary referrals by the court (most common),[35] or, as in California, mandating mediation.[36] Most statutes provide for court-connected mediation only of custody (rather than spousal support and property issues). What are the advantages and disadvantages of mandatory, as opposed to voluntary, mediation? See Elliot G. Hicks, Too Much of a Good Thing?, 12 W.V. Law. 4, 14 (1998) (calling mandatory mediation a "serious oxymoron" because it is useful only when parties are willing to work toward settlement); Holly A. Streeter-Schaefer, Note, A Look at Court Mandated Civil Mediation, 49 Drake L. Rev. 367 (2001) (providing a survey of supporting and opposing viewpoints).

On the history of mediation, see Folberg, supra, at 3; Dane A. Gaschen, Note, Mandatory Custody Mediation: The Debate over Its Usefulness Continues, 10 Ohio St. J. on Disp. Resol. 469 (1995); Hugh

[34]. Susan Kuhn, Comment, Mandatory Mediation: California Civil Code Section 4607, 33 Emory L.J. 733, 743 (1984).
[35]. Maggie Vincent, Note, Mandatory Mediation of Custody Disputes: Criticism, Legislation, and Support, 20 Vt. L. Rev. 255, 271 (1995).
[36]. Dane A. Gaschen, Note, Mandatory Custody Mediation: The Debate Over Its Usefulness Continues, 10 Ohio St. J. on Disp. Resol. 469, 472 (1995) (citing eight states, including California, that have mandatory custody mediation).

McIsaac, Mandatory Conciliation Custody/Visitation Matters: California's Bold Stroke, 19 Conciliation Cts. Rev. 73 (1981); Ann Milne, Mediation: A Promising Alternative for Family Courts, 42 Juv. & Fam. Ct. J. 61 (1991); Laura Nader, Controlling Processes in the Practice of Law: Hierarchy and Pacification in the Movement to Re-Form Dispute Ideology, 9 Ohio St. J. Disp. Resol. 1 (1993).

4. *Gender differences.* Some critics focus on the shortcomings of mediation for women:

> Increased use of mediation in the courts has caused women's advocates to question whether mediation is serving the needs of women who are undergoing divorces. The concern is that in mediation, the woman, who has traditionally held the less powerful position in society and marriage, will not have the bargaining strength, and negotiating skills necessary to get what she needs out of the mediation, and that in some instances, particularly when the mediation is mandated, the process is so coercive she may be forced to negotiate bad bargains.

Maggie Vincent, Note, Mandatory Mediation of Custody Disputes: Criticism, Legislation, and Support, 20 Vt. L. Rev. 255, 266 (1995). Does the adversarial system or mediation better serve women's interests? Are mediators more likely than courts to engage in gender bias, as another commentator suggests? See Trina Grillo, The Mediation Alternative: Process Dangers for Women, 100 Yale L.J. 1545 (1991); Madeleine B. Simborg & Joan B. Kelly, Beware of Stereotypes in Mediation, 17 Fam. Advoc. 69 (1994). But cf. Joshua D. Rosenberg, In Defense of Mediation, 33 Ariz. L. Rev. 467, 488 (1991) (judges may disguise bias better; bias has more devastating impact in adjudication context).

Would voluntary, rather than mandatory, mediation better serve women's interests? Compare Grillo, supra, at 1610 (advocating voluntary, rather than mandatory, mediation), with Rosenberg, supra, at 503-506 (advocating reform of mandatory mediation to address these shortcomings). Do you agree that many women need the "vindication" that the adversarial process provides rather than the compromise of mediation? See Grillo, supra, at 1560. To better protect women's interests, should property and support issues be settled by the adversary system but custody by mediation? Or should mediation be extended to all issues?

See generally Penelope E. Bryan, Killing Us Softly: Divorce Mediation and the Politics of Power, 40 Buff. L. Rev. 441 (1992); Grillo, supra; Vincent, supra, at 275-282 (exploring methods of improving mediation to address feminist criticisms). See also Rosenberg, supra (criticizing Grillo's views). For an empirical assessment of feminist criticisms, see Jessica Pearson, The Equity of Divorce Mediation Agreements, 9 Mediation Q. 179 (1991); Vincent, supra, at 275-282 (both refuting evidence that women who undergo mediation do not fare as well as those who litigate).

5. *Mediation and domestic violence.* Commentators suggest that mediation poses dangers, specifically for battered women.[37] In response to these concerns, some states exclude spousal abuse cases from mediation. In states with mandatory mediation, for example, mediation may be waived "for good cause" or "extraordinary cause" or if a party will suffer "severe emotional distress."[38] What problems of proof might this pose? On the other hand, might substantiation requirements introduce delays that destroy the cost-effectiveness of mediation and allow escalation of the conflict, as some commentators suggest? See McEwen et al., supra, at 1338.

Should mediation ever be used in cases of spousal abuse? Of the four states with mandatory mediation, three provide for waivers (Maine, North Carolina, Oregon); the fourth (California) provides for separate mediation sessions in cases of spousal abuse and permits the abused spouse to bring a support person. See Cal. Fam. Code §3181 (West 1994). Which statutory approach better protects the abused spouse?

Some commentators contend that, despite its shortcomings, mediation can be helpful to battered women by enhancing their self-assertion and helping them dissolve their relationships in a cost-effective manner. Kathleen O'Connell Corcoran & James C. Melamed, From Coercion to Empowerment: Spousal Abuse and Mediation, 7 Mediation Q. 303 (1990); Vincent, supra, at 278. Do these benefits outweigh the risks? For an empirical study of the effectiveness of mediation in spousal abuse cases, see Nancy Thoennes et al., Mediation and Domestic Violence: Current Policies and Practices, 33 Fam. & Conciliation Cts. Rev. 6 (1995).

6. *Qualifications.* Mediation may be provided by publicly funded court services or by mediators in private practice. Early in the development of mediation, many states failed to specify minimum qualifications for mediators. Now statutes often provide for qualifications for court-connected mediators. However, mediators in the private sector continue to be largely unregulated. What should be a mediator's qualifications in terms of education, experience, and specialized training?

Similarly, in the early years of mediation, standards of conduct for professional mediators did not exist. To address this shortcoming, the ABA House of Delegates adopted "Standards of Practice for Lawyer Me-

---

[37]. See, e.g., Kerry Loomis, Domestic Violence and Mediation: A Tragic Combination for Victims in California Family Court, 35 Cal. W. L. Rev. 355, 370 (1999); Jennifer P. Maxwell, Mandatory Mediation of Custody in the Face of Domestic Violence: Suggestions for Courts and Mediators, 37 Fam. & Conciliation Courts Rev. 335 (1999). Evidence suggests that spousal abuse may be present in perhaps half of custody and visitation disputes that are referred to court mediation programs. See Nancy Thoennes et al., Mediation and Domestic Violence: Current Policies and Practices, 33 Fam. & Conciliation Cts. Rev. 6, 7 (1995).

[38]. Vincent, supra note [35], at 273. See also Alison E. Gerencser, Family Mediation: Screening for Domestic Abuse, 23 Fla. St. U. L. Rev. 43, 51 n.54 (1995).

diators" in 1984. See Standards of Practice for Family Mediators in Divorce, 17 Fam. L.Q. 455 (1984). Is the increasing professionalization of mediation a positive or negative development? See McEwen, supra, at 1345 (arguing that raising the qualifications increases the cost of mediation without ensuring better representation). See generally Nancy J. Foster & Joan B. Kelly, Divorce Mediation: Who Should Be Certified?, 30 U.S.F. L. Rev. 665 (1996); Ellen A. Waldman, The Challenge of Certification: How to Ensure Mediator Competence While Preserving Diversity, 30 U.S.F. L. Rev. 723 (1996).

7. *Role of the mediator.* Mental health professionals and lawyers constitute the largest percentage of mediators. How might these different orientations affect the role of the mediator and the practice of mediation? One commentator has suggested four conceptual frameworks: (1) the therapeutic framework, with the mediator as healer; (2) the educational framework, with the mediator as teacher; (3) the rational-analytic framework, with the mediator as strategist; and (4) the normative-evaluative framework, with the mediator as judge. See Jane Becker-Haven, Modes of Mediating Child Custody Disputes, Ph.D. Dissertation, Stanford University (1988).

8. *Ethical problems.* Ethical problems arose when mediation first became popular. Some questions focused on the proper role of the attorney/mediator. That is, did a lawyer mediator violate the prohibition on representation of conflicting or potentially differing interests or the prohibition of dual representation (of both husband and wife)? State bar ethics committees ruled that a lawyer-mediator could mediate a dispute for the husband and wife so long as the mediator informs the parties that she or he represents neither and will refrain from representing either if the mediation proves unsuccessful, and advises the parties to seek independent legal counsel to review the agreement. See Linda J. Silberman, Professional Responsibility Problems of Divorce Mediation, 16 Fam. L.Q. 107, 110-119 (1982).

In Lange v. Marshall, 622 S.W.2d 237 (Mo. Ct. App. 1981), a divorcing couple retained an attorney-friend to represent them jointly and negotiate a settlement for them. After he did so, but before the agreement was approved by the court, the wife secured other legal counsel and obtained a more favorable settlement. She then sued the first attorney for malpractice. In his defense, the attorney claimed that he was acting as a mediator, and, as a result, he had no duty to serve as an advocate for either party. Although reasoning that "[w]e need not resolve the exact nature of defendant's status nor the duties which that status imposed upon him," the court of appeals nonetheless determined that the wife failed to establish damages caused by defendant's alleged negligence. Id. at 238.

Suppose lawyers and therapists collaborate on mediation teams. Is the lawyer facilitating the therapist's unauthorized practice of law? On these and other ethical problems, see Marsha B. Freeman, Divorce Mediation: Sweeping Conflicts Under the Rug, Time to Clean House, 78 U. Det. Mercy L. Rev. 67, 74-90 (2000); Diane K. Vescovo et al., Ethical Dilemmas in Mediation, 31 U. Mem. L. Rev. 59 (2000).

9. *Role of attorneys.* Attorneys fill a variety of roles in the mediation process. As discussed above, they may serve as mediators. In addition, they may also be participant-observers, or reviewers of the mediated agreements. Does the presence of lawyers as participant or reviewer serve to make the system more fair and effective or to undermine the mediation process? See McEwen et al., supra.

10. *Limitations.* What limitations should exist on private ordering? Should a mediator draft an agreement that the mediator does not believe is "fair" to one or both parties? Should the mediator defer to the parties' sense of fairness? Mediators differ concerning the extent to which a mediator should intervene in dispute resolution. See generally Joseph P. Folger & Sydney E. Bernard, Divorce Mediation: When Mediators Challenge the Divorcing Parties, 10 Mediation Q. 5, 19 (1985) (approximately 25 percent of mediators adopt a highly interventionist stance to achieve fairness and protect weaker parties).

11. Should children play a role in mediation? What might be the advantages and disadvantages? If children play a role, what should that role consist of? Active participant? Consultant? What factors should influence the nature and extent of children's participation?

See generally Carol S. Bruch, And How Are the Children? The Effects of Ideology and Mediation on Child Custody Law and Children's Well-Being in the United States, 2 Intl. J.L. & Fam. 106 (1988); Karen K. Irvin, Including Children in Mediation: Considerations for the Mediator, in Divorce and Family Mediation 51 ( James C. Hansen ed., 1985); Gary Paquin, Protecting the Interests of Children in Divorce Mediation, 26 J. Fam. L. 279 (1987-1988); W. Patrick Phear, Involving Children Within the Divorce Mediation Process, in Alternative Means of Family Dispute Resolution 205 (Howard Davidson et al. eds., 1982).

12. *Confidentiality.* Confidentiality is central to the mediation process. As *McLaughlin* explains, some locales permit the mediator to make a recommendation to the court if mediation proves unsuccessful. What is the practical effect?

> The power to make a recommendation to the court gives the mediator considerable authority. Although the court is not bound to follow the mediator's recommendation, such a recommendation will probably influence a judge's decision. The mediator has spent more time with parties than the judge, and the mediator has seen the parties interact. The mediator may have interviewed the children and other significant people. The mediator's education and experience adds credibility to his or her assessment of the case. Based on the collective weight of these factors, there is a high likelihood that the judge will "rubber stamp" the mediator's recommendation.

Kuhn, supra, at 770-771.

Many commentators criticize this practice. What constitutional concerns are implicated? Are they similar to those posed by the admission of expert testimony (supra)? See also In re Marriage of Gayden, 280 Cal. Rptr. 862 (Ct. App. 1991) (family counselor's recommendation, received orally by telephone because of her unavailability, violated due process).

The statute at issue in *McLaughlin* requires that "[m]ediation proceedings shall be held in private and shall be confidential, and all communications, verbal or written, from the parties to the mediator . . . shall be [privileged]." Once a mediator makes a recommendation and is subject to cross-examination, the mediator may have to divulge confidential communications that were elicited during mediation. Might warning the parties of this possibility interfere with the creation of trust?

*McLaughlin* requires that the policy of confidentiality yield to due process concerns. Is this an optimum accommodation of these competing interests?

> Permitting the mediator to make a recommendation undermines the neutrality of the mediator's role. The purpose of the mediation is to encourage the parties to create their own agreement. The mediator's opinion should not matter. . . . When the mediator is given the power to choose between the parties, his role is elevated to that of a judge. The best way to guarantee the parties their due process rights and ensure the confidentiality of the mediation sessions is to prohibit the mediator from making a recommendation at all.

Kuhn, supra, at 776. See generally Kent L. Brown, Comment, Confidentiality in Mediation: Status and Implications, 1991 J. Disp. Resol. 307. See also Foxgate Homeowners Ass'n v. Bramalea Cal., Inc., 108 Cal. Rptr. 2d 642 (Cal. 2001) (holding that plaintiff's motions for sanctions and court's consideration of motion and supporting documents, which recited statements made during mediation, violated statutes mandating confidentiality of mediation).

## 2. Coin Flipping

### ■ ROBERT H. MNOOKIN, CHILD-CUSTODY ADJUDICATION: JUDICIAL FUNCTIONS IN THE FACE OF INDETERMINACY
*39 Law & Contemp. Probs. 226, 289-291 (1975)*

#### RANDOM SELECTION

Assuming that an "intimate" acceptable to both parents cannot be found to make an individualized decision, would not a random process of decision be fairer and more efficient than adjudication under a best-interests principle? Individualized adjudication means that the result will often turn on a largely intuitive evaluation based on unspoken values and unproven predictions. We would more frankly acknowledge both our ignorance and the presumed equality of the natural parents were we to flip a coin. Whether one had a separate flip for each child or one flip for all the children, the process would certainly be cheaper and quicker. It would avoid the pain associated with an adversary proceeding that requires an open exploration of the intimate aspects of family life and an ultimate judgment that one parent is preferable to the other. And it might have beneficial effects on private negotiations.

Resolving a custody dispute by state-administered coin-flip would probably be viewed as unacceptable by most in our society. Perhaps this reaction reflects an abiding faith, despite the absence of an empirical basis for it, that letting a judge choose produces better results for the child. Alternatively, flipping a coin might be unacceptable for some because it represents an abdication of the search for wisdom. While judgments about what is best for the child may be currently beyond our capacity in many cases, this need not be true in fifty years. Movement toward better judgments implies, however, that judges and decision-makers as a group learn from the process of decision. In the absence of systematic feedback, this is not likely. Indeed, adopting a coin-flip now means neither that at a time when more were known and a consensus existed an adjudicatory system might not be adopted, nor that efforts to discover an adjudicatory standard would cease.

Deciding a child's future by flipping a coin might be viewed as callous. Is it more callous, however, than drafting for the military by lottery? In the same way that a lottery is a social affirmation of equality among those upon whom the government might impose the risks of war, a coin-flip would be a government affirmation of the equality of the parents. In a custody case, however, a coin-flip also symbolically abdicates government responsibility for the child and symbolically denies the importance of human differences and distinctiveness. Moreover, flipping a coin would deprive the parents of a process and a forum where their anger and aspirations might be expressed. In all, these symbolic and participatory values of adjudication would be lost by a random process.

While forceful arguments can be made in favor of the abandonment of adjudication and the adoption of an openly random process, the repulsion many would probably feel towards this suggestion may reflect an intuitive appreciation of the importance of the educational, participatory, and symbolic values of adjudication as a mode of dispute settlement. Adjudication under the indeterminate best-interests principle may yield something close to a random pattern of outcomes, while at the same time serving these values, affirming parental equality, and expressing a social concern for the child. Insofar as judges as a group may have value preferences that systematically bias the process and make the pattern less than random, these value preferences may reflect widespread values that have not been acknowledged openly in the form of legal rules.

# VIII

# State Regulation of the Parent-Child Relationship

Historically, the law regarded children as the property of their parents, particularly of their father.[1] Today, the law increasingly views children as individuals with their own distinct interests. Yet children often are too immature and vulnerable to advance their own interests or exercise their own rights — limitations the law has recognized.[2] Further, the principle of parental autonomy (the freedom to rear children as parents see fit) has long limited state intrusion into the family. Given these starting points, a challenge emerges: how to allocate authority among the parents, the child, and the state to make important decisions affecting the child. The materials that follow explore these issues.

[1]. See generally Mary Ann Mason, From Father's Property to Children's Rights: The History of Child Custody in America (1994). See also Barbara Bennett Woodhouse,"Who Owns the Child?": *Meyer* and *Pierce* and the Child as Property, 33 Wm. & Mary L. Rev. 995 (1992).

[2]. See, e.g., Bellotti v. Baird, 443 U.S. 622, 633-637 (1979).

**951**

## A. PARENTAL AUTONOMY: FAMILY PRIVACY REVISITED

### 1. Constitutional Doctrine and Limitations

■ **MEYER v. NEBRASKA**
262 U.S. 390 (1923)

Review case, reprinted in Chapter I, at page 18.

■ **PIERCE v. SOCIETY OF SISTERS**
268 U.S. 510 (1925)

Review case, reprinted in Chapter I, at page 20.

■ **PRINCE v. MASSACHUSETTS**
321 U.S. 158 (1944)

Mr. Justice RUTLEDGE delivered the opinion of the Court.

The case brings for review another episode in the conflict between Jehovah's Witnesses and state authority. This time Sarah Prince appeals from convictions for violating Massachusetts' child labor laws, by acts said to be a rightful exercise of her religious convictions. . . .

. . . Mrs. Prince, living in Brockton, is the mother of two young sons. She also has legal custody of Betty Simmons [her niece, age nine] who lives with them. The children too are Jehovah's Witnesses and both Mrs. Prince and Betty testified they were ordained ministers. The former was accustomed to go each week on the streets of Brockton to distribute "Watchtower" and "Consolation," according to the usual plan. She had permitted the children to engage in this activity previously, and had been warned against doing so by the school attendance officer, Mr. Perkins. But, until December 18, 1941, she generally did not take them with her at night.

That evening, as Mrs. Prince was preparing to leave her home, the children asked to go. She at first refused. Childlike, they resorted to tears and, motherlike, she yielded. Arriving downtown, Mrs. Prince permitted the children "to engage in the preaching work with her upon the sidewalks." That is, with specific reference to Betty, she and Mrs. Prince took positions about twenty feet apart near a street intersection. Betty held up in her hand, for passersby to see, copies of "Watch Tower" and "Consolation." From her shoulder hung the usual canvas magazine bag, on which was printed "Watchtower and Consolation 5 cents per copy." No one accepted a copy from Betty that evening and she received no money. Nor did her aunt. But on other occasions, Betty had received funds and given out copies. . . .

[Appellant argues] squarely on freedom of religion under the First Amendment, applied by the Fourteenth to the states. She buttresses this foundation, however, with a claim of parental right as secured by the due process clause of the latter Amendment. Cf. Meyer v. Nebraska, 262 U.S. 390 [(1923)]. . . . Thus, two claimed liberties are at stake. One is the parent's, to bring up the child in the way he should go, which for appellant means to teach him the tenets and the practices of their faith. The other freedom is the child's, to observe these; and among them is "to preach the gospel . . . by public distribution" of "Watchtower" and "Consolation," in conformity with the scripture: "A little child shall lead them." . . .

To make accommodation between these freedoms and an exercise of state authority always is delicate. . . . It is cardinal with us that the custody, care and nurture of the child reside first in the parents, whose primary function and freedom include preparation for obligations the state can neither supply nor hinder [citing *Pierce*]. And it is in recognition of this that these decisions have respected the private realm of family life which the state cannot enter.

But the family itself is not beyond regulation in the public interest, as against a claim of religious liberty. Reynolds v. United States, 98 U.S. 145 [(1878)]; Davis v. Beason, 133 U.S. 333 [(1890)]. And neither rights of religion nor rights of parenthood are beyond limitation. Acting to guard the general interest in youth's well being, the state as parens patriae may restrict the parent's control by requiring school attendance, regulating or prohibiting the child's labor, and in many other ways. Its authority is not nullified merely because the parent grounds his claim to control the child's course of conduct on religion or conscience. . . .

But it is said the state cannot do so here. . . . The child's presence on the street, with her guardian, distributing or offering to distribute the magazines, it is urged, was in no way harmful to her, nor in any event more so than the presence of many other children at the same time and place, engaged in shopping and other activities not prohibited. . . .

[The] state's authority over children's activities is broader than over like actions of adults. This is peculiarly true of public activities and in matters of employment. A democratic society rests, for its continuance, upon the healthy, well-rounded growth of young people into full maturity as citizens, with all that implies. It may secure this against impeding restraints and dangers, within a broad range of selection. Among evils most appropriate for such action are the crippling effects of child employment, more especially in public places, and the possible harms arising from other activities subject to all the diverse influences of the street. . . .

. . . The case reduces itself therefore to the question whether the presence of the child's guardian puts a limit to the state's power. . . . Parents may be free to become martyrs themselves. But it does not follow they are free, in identical circumstances, to make martyrs of their children before they have reached the age of full and legal discretion when they can make that choice for themselves. Massachusetts has determined that an absolute prohibition, though one limited to streets and public places and to the incidental uses proscribed, is necessary to accomplish its legitimate objectives. . . . The judgment is affirmed.

# ■ WISCONSIN v. YODER
*406 U.S. 205 (1972)*

Burger, C.J., delivered the opinion of the Court. . . .

Respondents Jonas Yoder and Wallace Miller are members of the Old Order Amish religion, and respondent Adin Yutzy is a member of the Conservative Amish Mennonite Church. . . . Wisconsin's compulsory school-attendance law required them to cause their children to attend public or private school until reaching age 16 but the respondents declined to send their children, ages 14 and 15, to public school after they completed the eighth grade. The children were not enrolled in any private school, or within any recognized exception to the compulsory-attendance law, and they are conceded to be subject to the Wisconsin statute.

On complaint of the school district administrator for the public schools, respondents were charged, tried, and convicted of violating the compulsory-attendance law in Green County Court and were fined the sum of $5 each. Respondents defended on the ground that the application of the compulsory-attendance law violated their rights under the First and Fourteenth Amendments. . . .

[The Amish] object to the high school, and higher education generally, because the values they teach are in marked variance with Amish values and the Amish way of life; they view secondary school education as an impermissible exposure of their children to a "worldly" influence in conflict with their beliefs. The high school tends to emphasize intellectual and scientific accomplishments, self-distinction, competitiveness, worldly success, and social life with other students. Amish society emphasizes informal learning-through-doing; a life of "goodness," rather than a life of intellect; wisdom, rather than technical knowledge; community welfare, rather than competition; and separation from, rather than integration with, contemporary worldly society.

Formal high school education beyond the eighth grade is contrary to Amish beliefs, not only because it places Amish children in an environment hostile to Amish beliefs with increasing emphasis on competition in class work and sports and with pressure to conform to the styles, manners, and ways of the peer group, but also because it takes them away from their community, physically and emotionally, during the crucial and formative adolescent period of life. [H]igh school attendance with teachers who are not of the Amish faith — and may even be hostile to it — interposes a serious barrier to the integration of the Amish child into the Amish religious community. . . .

The Amish do not object to elementary education through the first eight grades as a general proposition because they agree that their children must have basic skills in the "three R's" in order to read the Bible, to be good farmers and citizens, and to be able to deal with non-Amish people when necessary in the course of daily affairs. [However, expert] Dr. Hostetler testified that compulsory high school attendance could not only result in great psychological harm to Amish children, because of the conflicts it would produce, but would also, in his opinion, ultimately result in the destruction of the Old Order Amish church community as it exists in the United States today. . . .

[The Wisconsin Supreme Court reversed the convictions, based on the Free Exercise Clause of the First Amendment. The Supreme Court affirms.]

There is no doubt as to the power of a State, having a high responsibility for education of its citizens, to impose reasonable regulations for the control and duration of basic education. See, e.g., Pierce v. Society of Sisters, 268 U.S. 510, 534 (1925). Providing public schools ranks at the very apex of the function of a State. Yet even this paramount responsibility was, in *Pierce*, made to yield to the right of parents to provide an equivalent education in a privately operated system. [A] State's interest in universal education, however highly we rank it, is not totally free from a balancing process when it impinges on fundamental rights and interests, such as those specifically protected by the Free Exercise Clause of the First Amendment, and the traditional interest of parents with respect to the religious upbringing of their children so long as they, in the words of *Pierce*, "prepare [them] for additional obligations." 268 U.S., at 535. It follows that in order for Wisconsin to compel school attendance beyond the eighth grade against a claim that such attendance interferes with the practice of a legitimate religious belief, it must appear either that the State does not deny the free exercise of religious belief by its requirement, or that there is a state interest of sufficient magnitude to override the interest claiming protection under the Free Exercise Clause. [The Court determines that the Amish objection to school attendance beyond eighth grade is rooted in religious beliefs, reflected also in the rejection of other worldly practices and conveniences, including telephones, automobiles, radios, and television as well as in their mode of simple dress. These beliefs directly conflict with the compulsory school attendance law.]

. . . The State advances two primary arguments in support of its system of compulsory education. It notes, as Thomas Jefferson pointed out early in our history, that some degree of education is necessary to prepare citizens to participate effectively and intelligently in our open political system if we are to preserve freedom and independence. Further, education prepares individuals to be self-reliant and self-sufficient participants in society. We accept these propositions.

However, the evidence adduced by the Amish in this case is persuasively to the effect that an additional one or two years of formal high school for Amish children in place of their long-established program of informal vocational education would do little to serve those interests. . . . It is one thing to say that compulsory education for a year or two beyond the eighth grade may be necessary when its goal is the preparation of the child for life in modern society as the majority live, but it is quite another if the goal of education be viewed as the preparation of the child for life in the separated agrarian community that is the keystone of the Amish faith.

The State attacks respondents' position as one fostering "ignorance" from which the child must be protected by the State. No one can question the State's duty to protect children from ignorance but this argument does not square with the facts disclosed in the record. Whatever their idiosyncrasies as seen by the majority, this record strongly shows that the Amish community has been a highly successful social unit within our society, even if apart from the conventional "mainstream." Its members are productive and very law-abiding members of society; they reject public welfare in any of its usual modern forms. . . .

The State, however, supports its interest in providing an additional one or two years of compulsory high school education to Amish children because of the possibility that some such children will choose to leave the Amish community, and that if this occurs they will be ill-equipped for life. . . . However, on this record, that argument is highly speculative. There is no specific evidence of the loss of Amish adherents by attrition, nor is there any showing that upon leaving the Amish community Amish children, with their practical agricultural training and habits of industry and self-reliance, would become burdens on society because of educational shortcomings. . . .

The requirement for compulsory education beyond the eighth grade is a relatively recent development in our history. Less than 60 years ago, the educational requirements of almost all of the States were satisfied by completion of the elementary grades, at least where the child was regularly and lawfully employed. . . . We should also note that compulsory education and child labor laws find their historical origin in common humanitarian instincts, and that the age limits of both laws have been coordinated to achieve their related objectives. . . . The requirement of compulsory schooling to age 16 must therefore be viewed as aimed not merely at providing educational opportunities for children, but as an alternative to the equally undesirable consequence of unhealthful child labor displacing adult workers, or, on the other hand, forced idleness. . . .

In these terms, Wisconsin's interest in compelling the school attendance of Amish children to age 16 emerges as somewhat less substantial than requiring such attendance for children generally. . . . There is no intimation that the Amish employment of their children on family farms is in any way deleterious to their health or that Amish parents exploit children at tender years. . . .

Finally, the State, on authority of Prince v. Massachusetts, [321 U.S. 158 (1944),] argues that a decision exempting Amish children from the State's requirement fails to recognize the substantive right of the Amish child to a secondary education, and fails to give due regard to the power of the State as parens patriae to extend the benefit of secondary education to children regardless of the wishes of their parents. Taken at its broadest sweep, the Court's language in *Prince,* might be read to give support to the State's position. However, the Court was not confronted in *Prince* with a situation comparable to that of the Amish as revealed in this record. . . .

Our holding in no way determines the proper resolution of possible competing interests of parents, children, and the State in an appropriate state court proceeding in which the power of the State is asserted on the theory that Amish parents are preventing their minor children from attending high school despite their expressed desires to the contrary. Recognition of the claim of the State in such a proceeding would, of course, call into question traditional concepts of parental control over the religious upbringing and education of their minor children recognized in this Court's past decisions. It is clear that such an intrusion by a State into family decisions in the area of religious training would give rise to grave questions of religious freedom comparable to those raised here and those presented in [*Pierce*]. On this record we neither reach nor decide those issues. . . .

Indeed it seems clear that if the State is empowered, as parens patriae, to "save" a child from himself or his Amish parents by requiring an additional two years of compulsory formal high school education, the State will in large measure influence, if not determine, the religious future of the child. Even more markedly than in *Prince,* therefore, this case involves the fundamental interest of parents, as contrasted with that of the State, to guide the religious future and education of their children. . . .

Mr. Justice DOUGLAS, dissenting in part.

. . . The Court's analysis assumes that the only interests at stake in the case are those of the Amish parents on the one hand, and those of the State on the other. The difficulty with this approach is that, despite the Court's claim, the parents are seeking to vindicate not only their own free exercise claims, but also those of their high-school-age children. [I]t is essential to reach the question to decide the case, not only because the question was squarely raised in the motion to dismiss, but also because no analysis of religious-liberty claims can take place in a vacuum. If the parents in this case are allowed a religious exemption, the inevitable effect is to impose the parents' notions of religious duty upon their children. Where the child is mature enough to express potentially conflicting desires, it would be an invasion of the child's rights to permit such an imposition without canvassing his views. . . . And, if an Amish child desires to attend high school, and is mature enough to have that desire respected, the State may well be able to override the parents' religiously motivated objections. . . .

This issue has never been squarely presented before today. . . . While the parents, absent dissent, normally speak for the entire family, the education of the child is a matter on which the child will often have decided views. He may want to be a pianist or an astronaut or an oceanographer. To do so he will have to break from the Amish tradition.[2]

It is the future of the student, not the future of the parents, that is imperiled by today's decision. If a parent keeps his child out of school beyond the grade school, then the child will be forever barred from entry into the new and amazing world of diversity that we have today. The child may decide that that is the preferred course, or he may rebel. It is the student's judgment, not his parents', that is essential if we are to give full meaning to what we have said about the Bill of Rights and of the right of students to be masters of their own destiny.[3] . . . The views of the two children in question were not canvassed by the Wisconsin courts. [N]ew hearings [should] be held on remand of the case. . . .

■ **TROXEL v. GRANVILLE**
*530 U.S. 57 (2000)*

Review case, reprinted in Chapter VII, at page 863.

2. A significant number of Amish children do leave the Old Order. Professor Hostetler notes that "the loss of members is very limited in some Amish districts and considerable in others." J. Hostetler, Amish Society 226 (1968). In one Pennsylvania church, he observed a defection rate of 30%. Rates up to 50% have been reported by others. Casad, Compulsory High School Attendance and the Old Order Amish: A Commentary on *State v. Garber*, 16 Kan. L. Rev. 423, 434 n.51 (1968).

3. The court below brushed aside the students' interests with the offhand comment that "when a child reaches the age of judgment, he can choose for himself his religion." 182 N.W.2d 539, 543 [(Wis. 1971)]. But there is nothing in this record to indicate that the moral and intellectual judgment demanded of the student by the question in this case is beyond his capacity. Children far younger than the 14- and 15-year-olds involved here are regularly permitted to testify in custody and other proceedings. Indeed, the failure to call the affected child in a custody hearing is often reversible error. Moreover, there is substantial agreement among child psychologists and sociologists that the moral and intellectual maturity of the 14-year-old approaches that of the adult. See, e.g., J. Piaget, The Moral Judgment of the Child (1948); D. Elkind, Children and Adolescents 75-80 (1970). . . .

## Notes and Questions

1. *Meyer* and *Pierce* establish the foundation for the right to privacy. See Chapter I. They include within the protection of liberty in the Due Process Clause parental autonomy, the right to rear a child as the parent sees fit.

2. Although revered as "liberal icons" that protect privacy and promote pluralism, *Meyer* and *Pierce* express a conservative attachment to the patriarchal family and a view of children as property owned by their parents, according to Professor Barbara Bennett Woodhouse in "Who Owns the Child?": *Meyer* and *Pierce* and the Child as Property, 33 Wm. & Mary L. Rev. 995, 996 (1992). After examining the historical context of the cases, she concludes:

> . . . By constitutionalizing a patriarchal notion of parental rights, *Meyer* and *Pierce* interrupted the trend of family law moving toward children's rights and revitalized the notion of rights of possession. . . . Patriarchal notions of ownership do not lend themselves to a child-centered theory of custody or parenthood. The patriarchal tradition assumes that parents' rights exist for the parent and not . . . for the child. . . .
>
> [O]ur legal system fails to respect children. Children are often used as instruments, as in *Meyer* and *Pierce*. The child is denied her own voice and identity and becomes a conduit for the parents' religious expression, cultural identity, and class aspirations. The parents' authority to speak for and through the child is explicit in *Meyer*'s "right of control" and *Pierce*'s "high duty" of the parent to direct his child's destiny. . . .

Id. at 1113-1114. If property ownership provides the wrong legal model for the parent-child relationship, what alternatives might prove more helpful? See, e.g., Janet L. Dolgin, The Fate of Childhood: Legal Models of Children and the Parent-Child Relationship, 61 Alb. L. Rev. 345, 378-382 (1997) (finding in *Meyer* and *Pierce* "traditional model" that justifies strong parental control as best safeguard of child's interests); Elizabeth S. Scott & Robert E. Scott, Parents as Fiduciaries, 81 Va. L. Rev. 2401 (1995).

3. Based on *Meyer* and *Pierce*, how should the Court have decided *Prince*? Is *Prince* a stronger or weaker case for parental autonomy than *Meyer* or *Pierce*, given that Sarah Prince's parental autonomy claim rested more squarely on her asserted freedom of religion and Betty's own beliefs were put in evidence? In light of the outcome in *Prince*, what does the Court mean by "a private realm of family life which the state cannot enter"?

4. *Prince* reveals that the state's interest (as parens patriae) in protecting children from harm limits parental autonomy. What harm threatened nine-year-old Betty? Was she actually harmed or merely exposed to the risk of harm? Should the mere risk of harm justify state intervention

in the family? Who decides what constitutes harm to a child? Does *Prince* identify the scope of state power to restrict parental freedom in the interest of child protection?

To what extent does *Troxel* depart from *Prince*'s harm standard? What do the different Justices say about this standard in *Troxel*? Do the *Troxel* opinions go beyond the context of third-party visitation to open the door for other state incursions on parental autonomy that cannot be justified as necessary to protect a child from harm or potential harm?

5. Do *Meyer* and *Pierce* dictate the outcome in *Yoder*? Or should *Prince* control? Under *Prince*'s test, is there sufficient harm or risk of harm in *Yoder* to justify state intervention? Are the *Yoder* parents making "martyrs" of their children, despite *Prince*'s admonition?

As the Court explains in *Yoder*, compulsory school attendance laws grew out of the same concerns that produced the child-labor restrictions in *Prince*. What distinguishes work on the family farm for Amish children from other child labor? See James G. Dwyer, Parents' Religion and Children's Welfare: Debunking the Doctrine of Parents' Rights, 82 Cal. L. Rev. 1371, 1381-1382 (1994) (explaining *Prince* as reflecting concern with threat to society as a whole, not individual child). What of the risk of harm to the Amish child who later chooses to leave the fold but has never completed high school?

6. *Yoder* claims to use a "balancing process." What level of judicial scrutiny did the Court in fact employ? Compare City of Boerne v. Flores, 521 U.S. 507, 544 (1997) (O'Connor, J., dissenting) (*Yoder* used compelling state interest test), with Immediato v. Rye Neck School Dist., 73 F.3d 454, 461 (2d Cir.) (*Yoder* used rational basis test), *cert. denied*, 519 U.S. 813 (1996). What does the discussion of harm in the *Troxel* opinions signal about the standard of review that applies to state infringements on parental autonomy?

What facts prove determinative to *Yoder*'s outcome? How far can one generalize from the holding? Does *Yoder* protect a parent's choice of home schooling?[3] See, e.g., Clonlara v. Runkel, 722 F. Supp. 1442 (E.D. Mich. 1989); Jon S. Lerner, Comment, Protecting Home Schooling Through the *Casey* Undue Burden Standard, 62 U. Chi. L. Rev. 363 (1995). If *Yoder* protects home schooling, does it undervalue the state's interest in exposing minors to relationships with diverse peers? See Emily Buss, The Adolescent's Stake in the Allocation of Educational Control Between Parent and State, 67 U. Chi. L. Rev. 1233 (2000).

For an argument that *Yoder*'s deference to parental educational choices does not go far enough, see Stephen G. Gilles, On Educating Children: A Parentalist Manifesto, 63 U. Chi. L. Rev. 937 (1996). For

---

[3]. All 50 states permit home schooling. Ralph D. Mawdsley, Home Schools and the Law, 137 Educ. L. Rep. 1 (1999). Most states have specific legal requirements that home school programs must meet. See National Survey of State Laws 201-216 (Richard A. Leiter ed., 3d ed. 1999) (listing 46).

examinations of recent efforts to enact legislation protecting "parental rights," see Barbara Bennett Woodhouse, A Public Role in the Private Family: The Parental Rights and Responsibilities Act and the Politics of Child Protection and Education, 57 Ohio St. L.J. 393 (1996); David Fisher, Note, Parental Rights and the Right to Intimate Association, 48 Hastings L.J. 399, 416-422 (1997); Linda L. Lane, Comment, The Parental Rights Movement, 69 U. Colo. L. Rev. 825 (1998).

7. *The common law doctrine of parental autonomy.* Longstanding common law principles of family privacy and parental authority reinforce the constitutional analysis in *Meyer, Pierce, Yoder,* and *Troxel.* For example, in Roe v. Doe, 272 N.E.2d 567 (N.Y. 1971), the court applied to the parent-child relationship in the intact family the same rule of nonintervention that McGuire v. McGuire (see Chapter III, at page 259) invoked for married couples. Declining to allow judicial interference with a father's decision to withhold support from his daughter unless she lived in a college dormitory instead of an apartment, the court said:

> It is the natural right, as well as the legal duty, of a parent to care for, control and protect his child from potential harm, whatever the source and absent a clear showing of misfeasance, abuse or neglect, courts should not interfere with that delicate responsibility. Here, the daughter, asserting her independence, chose to assume a status inconsistent with that of parental control. . . . The father has the right, in the absence of caprice, misconduct or neglect, to require that the daughter conform to his reasonable demands. Should she disagree, and at her age [20, when the age of majority was 21] that is surely her prerogative, she may elect not to comply; but in so doing, she subjects herself to her father's lawful wrath. Where, as here, she abandons her home, she forfeits her right to support.

Id. at 570. Does the court suggest that it would reach a different result had it deemed the father's demands "unreasonable"? Who decides reasonableness? Does this standard sufficiently protect the family from state intervention? See id. at 571 (Jasen, J., concurring). *Roe* also exemplifies the traditional view treating as reciprocal the parent's duty of support and the child's duty of obedience. See Katharine T. Bartlett, Re-Expressing Parenthood, 98 Yale L.J. 293, 297-298 (1988).

8. *The children's rights? Yoder* avoided deciding whether Amish children have their own right to a secondary education. Can the interests of parents and their children be separated? Compare the majority opinion with that of Justice Douglas. What weight should the social science data in Douglas's footnote 3 receive? If the children have separate interests, can the state speak for the children more effectively than their parents can?

Courts in other schooling controversies, for example, have recognized the child's own interests. See, e.g., Duro v. District Attorney, 712 F.2d 96 (4th Cir. 1983), *cert. denied,* 465 U.S. 1006 (1984); Davis v. Page, 385 F. Supp. 395, 398 (D.N.H. 1974). On the other hand, in Reno v.

Flores, 507 U.S. 292, 302-303 (1993), a majority held that alien juveniles detained under federal immigration policy have no substantive due process right to be released in the absence of an available parent or guardian, reasoning that juveniles "are always in some form of custody" and children's interests are subordinate to parents'.

If the children have independent interests, how should they be considered? If the goal in *Yoder* should be protecting the Amish child's opportunities to make autonomous choices later (whether to stay within the Amish community or to leave), how can that be accomplished? See Dena S. Davis, The Child's Right to an Open Future: *Yoder* and Beyond, 26 Cap. U. L. Rev. 93 (1997). See also Emily Buss, What Does Frieda Yoder Believe?, 2 U. Pa. J. Const. L. 53 (1999) (examining children's interests in free exercise of religion). In an omitted footnote, Justice Douglas suggests canvassing the small number of Amish school children. If an Amish child expressed a preference for secondary school, would he or she continue to live at home? Receive parental support? What other consequences might follow?

Suppose in *Pierce* the child did not want to go to private school? See Stephen L. Carter, Parents, Religion, and Schools: Reflections on *Pierce*, 70 Years Later, 27 Seton Hall L. Rev. 1194, 1220-1223 (1997). What difference should the child's own wishes make in addressing third-party visitation disputes, the issue in *Troxel*? See Chapter VII, at section B4a.

9. Professor Jane Rutherford has made the intriguing suggestion that the "one person, one vote" principle compels extending to children voting rights, to be exercised by parents as proxies. Jane Rutherford, One Child, One Vote: Proxies for Parents, 82 Minn. L. Rev. 1463 (1998). What do you think of this idea?

## Problems

1. The school board in New York City adopts a condom distribution program for high school students. Designed to curb both the increasing rate of adolescent HIV-infection and the rising number of teenage pregnancies, the program allows any high school student who so wishes to obtain condoms without parental notification or consent. Parents challenge the program, claiming it infringes their due process rights to rear their children as they see fit. They assert that the Constitution requires that the program have a parental "opt-out" provision, to honor their freedom to promote the value of sexual abstinence to their children. The school board asserts that such a provision would leave the children of parents who "opt out" vulnerable to HIV and pregnancy, if those children were sexually active without parental knowledge.

What result and why? Compare Alfonso v. Fernandez, 606 N.Y.S.2d 259 (App. Div. 1993), *appeal dismissed,* 637 N.E.2d 279 (N.Y. 1994), with Curtis v. School Comm. of Falmouth, 652 N.E.2d 580 (Mass. 1995), *cert. denied,* 516 U.S. 1067 (1996). See Miranda Perry, Comment, Kids and Condoms: Parental Involvement in School Condom-Distribution Programs, 63 U. Chi. L. Rev. 727 (1996); Pilar S. Ramos, Comment, The Condom Controversy in the Public Schools: Respecting a Minor's Right of Privacy, 145 U. Pa. L. Rev. 149 (1996). Is the dispute one between parents and the school board alone? What interests do the students have at stake? How should such interests be taken into account?

2. Five-year-old Elian Gonzalez used an inner tube to survive a hazardous boat trip from Cuba to Florida, although his mother and others who were attempting to come to the United States perished. In Miami, Elian was placed temporarily in the custody of his great uncle, Lazaro Gonzalez, and his family. Elian's father, who had separated from his mother several years before but had maintained an ongoing relationship with the boy, asked the Miami relatives to return him to Cuba, where Elian could live with his father, his wife, and their child. The Miami relatives decline and now file a petition for asylum on behalf of Elian under a law that provides in part:

> *Any alien* who is physically present in the United States or who arrives in the United States (whether or not at a designated port of arrival and including an alien who is brought to the United States after having been interdicted in international or United States waters), irrespective of such alien's status, *may apply for asylum.* . . . 8 U.S.C. §1158(a)(1) (Supp. 1999) (emphasis added).

Assuming that "any alien" includes a child, who should decide whether Elian applies for asylum or returns to Cuba? His father? The Miami relatives who now have custody? The Immigration and Naturalization Service? A family court? If so, should the decision be made in Miami or Cuba? Of what relevance is the fact that Elian's custodial parent, his mother, had decided to move with him to the United States? Of what relevance are arguments that Elian's father might have asked for the boy's return because of pressure from the Cuban government? See Gonzalez v. Reno, 212 F.3d 1338 (11th Cir.), *cert. denied,* 530 U.S. 1270 (2000). See generally Mark S. Kende, A Misguided Statutory Interpretation Theory: The Elian Gonzalez Cuban Asylum Case, 18 B.U. Int'l L.J. 201 (2000); Marcia M. Reisman, Comment, Where to Decide the "Best Interests" of Elian Gonzalez: The Law of Abduction and International Custody Disputes, 31 U. Miami Inter-Am. L. Rev. 323 (2000).

## 2. Procedural Challenges

■ PARHAM v. J.R.
*442 U.S. 584 (1979)*

BURGER, C.J., delivered the opinion of the Court.

The question presented in this appeal is what process is constitutionally due a minor child whose parents or guardian seek state administered institutional mental health care for the child and specifically whether an adversary proceeding is required prior to or after the commitment.

(a) Appellee J.R., a child being treated in a Georgia state mental hospital, was a plaintiff in this class action based on 42 U.S.C. §1983, in the District Court for the Middle District of Georgia. Appellants are the State's Commissioner of the Department of Human Resources, the Director of the Mental Health Division of the Department of Human Resources, and the Chief Medical Officer at the hospital where appellee was being treated. Appellee sought a declaratory judgment that Georgia's voluntary commitment procedures for children under the age of 18, Ga. Code §§88-503.1, 88-503.2 (1975), violated the Due Process Clause of the Fourteenth Amendment and requested an injunction against their future enforcement. [The three-judge district court below held the statutory schemes violate due process. J.L. v. Parham, 412 F. Supp. 112, 139 (M.D. Ga. 1976).]

[Two other named plaintiffs are J.L., whose mother requested his indefinite commitment at the hospital and whose parents subsequently relinquished their parental rights, and J.R., a neglected child whom the state removed from his parents and placed in seven different foster homes before successfully seeking his admission to the hospital.]

(d) Georgia Code §88-503.1 (1975) provides for the voluntary admission to a state regional hospital of children such as J.L. and J.R. Under that provision, admission begins with an application for hospitalization signed by a "parent or guardian." Upon application, the superintendent of each hospital is given the power to admit temporarily any child for "observation and diagnosis." If, after observation, the superintendent finds "evidence of mental illness" and that the child is "suitable for treatment" in the hospital, then the child may be admitted "for such period and under such conditions as may be authorized by law."

Georgia's mental health statute also provides for the discharge of voluntary patients. Any child who has been hospitalized for more than five days may be discharged at the request of a parent or guardian. §88-503.3(a) (1975). Even without a request for discharge, however, the superintendent of each regional hospital has an affirmative duty to release any child "who has recovered from his mental illness or who has

sufficiently improved that the superintendent determines that hospitalization of the patient is no longer desirable." §88-503.2 (1975). . . .

In holding unconstitutional Georgia's statutory procedure for voluntary commitment of juveniles, the District Court first determined that
commitment to any of the eight regional hospitals constitutes a severe
deprivation of a child's liberty. The court defined this liberty interest in
terms of both freedom from bodily restraint and freedom from the
"emotional and psychic harm" caused by the institutionalization. Having
determined that a liberty interest is implicated by a child's admission to
a mental hospital, the court considered what process is required to protect that interest. It held that the process due "includes at least the right
after notice to be heard before an impartial tribunal."

In requiring the prescribed hearing, the court rejected Georgia's argument that no adversary-type hearing was required since the State was
merely assisting parents who could not afford private care by making
available treatment similar to that offered in private hospitals and by private physicians. The court acknowledged that most parents who seek to
have their children admitted to a state mental hospital do so in good
faith. It, however, relied on one of appellees' witnesses who expressed
an opinion that "some still look upon mental hospitals as a 'dumping
ground.' " No specific evidence of such "dumping," however, can be
found in the record.

The District Court also rejected the argument that review by the su-
perintendents of the hospitals and their staffs was sufficient to protect
the child's liberty interest. The court held that the inexactness of psychiatry, coupled with the possibility that the sources of information used
to make the commitment decision may not always be reliable, made the
superintendent's decision too arbitrary to satisfy due process. . . .

. . . Assuming the existence of a protectible property or liberty interest, the Court has required a balancing of a number of factors. [W]e
must consider first the child's interest in not being committed. Normally,
however, since this interest is inextricably linked with the parents' interest in and obligation for the welfare and health of the child, the private
interest at stake is a combination of the child's and parents' concerns.
Next, we must examine the State's interest in the procedures it has
adopted for commitment and treatment of children. Finally, we must
consider how well Georgia's procedures protect against arbitrariness in
the decision to commit a child to a state mental hospital.

(a) It is not disputed that a child, in common with adults, has a substantial liberty interest in not being confined unnecessarily for medical
treatment and that the state's involvement in the commitment decision
constitutes state action under the Fourteenth Amendment. See Addington v. Texas, 441 U.S. 418, 425 (1979); In re Gault, 387 U.S. 1, 27
(1967); Specht v. Patterson, 386 U.S. 605 (1967). For purposes of this
decision, we assume that a child has a protectible interest not only in

being free of unnecessary bodily restraints but also in not being labeled erroneously by some persons because of an improper decision by the state hospital superintendent.

(b) . . . Appellees argue that the constitutional rights of the child are of such magnitude and the likelihood of parental abuse is so great that the parents' traditional interests in and responsibility for the upbringing of their child must be subordinated at least to the extent of providing a formal adversary hearing prior to a voluntary commitment.

Our jurisprudence historically has reflected Western civilization concepts of the family as a unit with broad parental authority over minor children. . . . Surely, this [authority] includes a "high duty" to recognize symptoms of illness and to seek and follow medical advice. The law's concept of the family rests on a presumption that parents possess what a child lacks in maturity, experience, and capacity for judgment required for making life's difficult decisions. More important, historically it has recognized that natural bonds of affection lead parents to act in the best interests of their children. 1 W. Blackstone, Commentaries *447; 2 J. Kent, Commentaries on American Law *190. . . .

Nonetheless, we have recognized that a state is not without constitutional control over parental discretion in dealing with children when their physical or mental health is jeopardized. [Yet simply] because the decision of a parent is not agreeable to a child or because it involves risks does not automatically transfer the power to make that decision from the parents to some agency or officer of the state. The same characterizations can be made for a tonsillectomy, appendectomy, or other medical procedure. Most children, even in adolescence, simply are not able to make sound judgments concerning many decisions, including their need for medical care or treatment. Parents can and must make those judgments. Here, there is no finding by the District Court of even a single instance of bad faith by any parent of any member of appellees' class. We cannot assume that the result in [Meyer and Pierce] would have been different if the children there had announced a preference to learn only English or a preference to go to a public, rather than a church, school. The fact that a child may balk at hospitalization or complain about a parental refusal to provide cosmetic surgery does not diminish the parents' authority to decide what is best for the child. Neither state officials nor federal courts are equipped to review such parental decisions. . . .

(c) The State obviously has a significant interest in confining the use of its costly mental health facilities to cases of genuine need. . . . The State in performing its voluntarily assumed mission also has a significant interest in not imposing unnecessary procedural obstacles that may discourage the mentally ill or their families from seeking needed psychiatric assistance. The parens patriae interest in helping parents care for the mental health of their children cannot be fulfilled if the parents are unwilling to take advantage of the opportunities because the admission process is too onerous, too embarrassing, or too contentious. It is surely not idle to speculate as to how many parents who believe they are acting in good faith would forgo state-provided hospital care if such care is contingent on participation in an adversary proceeding designed to probe their motives and other private family matters in seeking the voluntary admission. . . .

(d) [T]he risk of error inherent in the parental decision to have a child institutionalized for mental health care is sufficiently great that some kind of inquiry should be made by a "neutral factfinder" to determine whether the statutory requirements for admission are satisfied. . . . Due process has never been thought to require that the neutral and detached trier of fact be law trained or a judicial or administrative officer. Surely, this is the case as to medical decisions, for "neither judges nor administrative hearing officers are better qualified than psychiatrists to render psychiatric judgments." In re Roger S., 19 Cal. 3d 921, 942, 569 P.2d 1286, 1299 (1977) (Clark, J., dissenting). Thus, a staff physician will suffice, so long as he or she is free to evaluate independently the child's mental and emotional condition and need for treatment. . . .

Another problem with requiring a formalized, factfinding hearing lies in the danger it poses for significant intrusion into the parent-child relationship. Pitting the parents and child as adversaries often will be at odds with the presumption that parents act in the best interests of their child. It is one thing to require a neutral physician to make a careful review of the parents' decision in order to make sure it is proper from a medical standpoint; it is a wholly different matter to employ an adversary contest to ascertain whether the parents' motivation is consistent with the child's interests. Moreover, [there is a risk that such a hearing] would exacerbate whatever tensions already exist between the child and the parents. . . .

It has been suggested that a hearing conducted by someone other than the admitting physician is necessary in order to detect instances where parents are "guilty of railroading their children into asylums" or are using "voluntary commitment procedures in order to sanction behavior of which they [disapprove]." Ellis, Volunteering Children: Parental Commitment of Minors to Mental Institutions, 62 Calif. L. Rev. 840, 850-851 (1974). [Yet it] is unrealistic to believe that trained psychiatrists . . . will often be deceived about the family situation surrounding a child's emotional disturbance. Surely a lay, or even law-trained, factfinder would be no more skilled in this process than the professional. . . .

(e) Georgia's statute envisions a careful diagnostic medical inquiry to be conducted by the admitting physician at each regional hospital, [periodic reviews, and an] affirmative statutory duty to discharge any child who is no longer mentally ill or in need of therapy. . . .

[T]he periodic reviews described in the record reduce the risk of error in the initial admission and thus they are necessary. Whether they are sufficient to justify continuing a voluntary commitment is an issue for the District Court on remand. [For wards of the state, who often have no adults who know them well and care about them, the Court suggests that, on remand, the District Court consider the need for more rigorous review procedures, to prevent such children from "getting lost in the shuffle."]

On this record, we are satisfied that Georgia's medical factfinding processes are reasonable and consistent with constitutional guarantees. . . . The judgment is therefore reversed, and the case is remanded to the District Court for further proceedings consistent with this opinion. . . .

■ **PLANNED PARENTHOOD OF SOUTHEASTERN PENNSYLVANIA v. CASEY**
*505 U.S. 833 (1992)*

Review Part D of case, reprinted in Chapter I, at page 81.

## Notes and Questions

1. *Yoder* demonstrates that constitutional law generally gives parents authority to make important decisions for their children. It does not expressly address, however, whether children have a right to fair *procedures* to ensure that parents are acting to promote their welfare. How does *Parham* answer this question?

2. If the children in *Parham* opposed the commitments, why were they nonetheless classified as *voluntary* commitments (rather than involuntary commitments, which are governed by elaborate procedural protections, including judicial determinations)? Would the district court's approach have implications for all medical treatments parents choose for unwilling children? Of what relevance is empirical evidence showing that minors 14 years and older can engage in mature reasoning about medical treatment decisions? See Lois Weithorn, Developmental Factors and Competence to Make Informed Treatment Decisions, in Legal Reforms Affecting Child and Youth Services, 85, 90-94 (Gary B. Melton ed., 1982). See also Frances J. Lexcen & N. Dickon Reppucci, Effects of Psychopathology on Adolescent Medical Decision-Making, 5 U. Chi. L. Sch. Roundtable 63 (1998).

3. Critics contend that *Parham* rests on myths about the family and about mental hospitals. See Gary B. Melton et al., No Place to Go: The Civil Commitment of Minors 127-138 (1998). Do the changing realities of children's lives — evident in today's variety of family structures and a society that expects children to dress and behave like adults — require rethinking *Parham*'s assumptions about family decisionmaking? See Janet

L. Dolgin, The Fate of Childhood: Legal Models of Children and the Parent-Child Relationship, 61 Alb. L. Rev. 345, 347-350 (1997).

Based on assumptions about how commitment decisions are reached, the majority concluded that Georgia's procedures adequately address the risk that parents will erroneously commit healthy children. What of the risk that children with serious emotional and mental problems will be committed even though they could receive adequate treatment in less drastic settings than a state institution? See James W. Ellis, Some Observations on the Juvenile Commitment Cases: Reconceptualizing What the Child Has at Stake, 31 Loy. L.A. L. Rev. 929, 930 (1998). See also Miye A. Goishi, Unlocking the Closet Door: Protecting Children from Involuntary Civil Commitment Because of Their Sexual Orientation, 48 Hastings L.J. 1137 (1997) (lack of clear admission criteria creates risk of commitment for gay youth); Alexander V. Tsesis, Protecting Children Against Unnecessary Institutionalization, 39 S. Tex. L. Rev. 995, 1005 (1998) (citing findings that most juvenile patients today have eating disorders, problems in school, or disagreements with parents).

4. Not all courts have reached *Parham*'s result. In re Roger S., 569 P.2d 1286 (Cal. 1977), held that, for a child's voluntary commitment to a mental institution, both federal and state constitutions require an administrative hearing, an opportunity to present evidence, an opportunity to cross-examine adverse witnesses, and appointment of counsel for minors not greatly disabled nor dangerous. The court also held parents could not institutionalize minors over 13 under the voluntary commitment statute. The court relied on an article arguing due process requires procedural safeguards to protect against parents' unfettered discretion to institutionalize their children. Id. at 1296 n.9. See James W. Ellis, Volunteering Children: Parental Commitment of Minors to Mental Institutions, 62 Cal. L. Rev. 840 (1974).

Which approach, that in *Parham* or that in *Roger S.*, is more sound? See Elyce H. Zenoff & Alan B. Zients, If Civil Commitment Is the Answer for Children, What Are the Questions?, 51 Geo. Wash. L. Rev. 171 (1983). See also Ira C. Lupu, The Separation of Powers and the Protection of Children, 61 U. Chi. L. Rev. 1317, 1364-1365 (1994).

5. Would enhanced procedural safeguards dissuade parents from seeking psychiatric help for their children, as the *Parham* majority fears? In omitted footnote 18 the Court observes that "a state may elect to provide such adversary hearings [when] parents and a child may be at odds, but nothing in the Constitution compels such procedures." When a state requires adversary hearings before a child's commitment, does the state unconstitutionally infringe parental autonomy? See State ex rel. T.B. v. CPC Fairfax Hosp., 918 P.2d 497 (Wash. 1996) (describing Washington's procedures).

6. *Private facilities.* Can parents avoid all issues of "due process" by choosing the more costly option of a private facility? Compare R.J.D. v.

The Vaughan Clinic, 572 So. 2d 1225 (Ala. 1990) (no state action to invoke federal protection of civil rights), with *T.B.*, 918 P.2d 497 (relying on statutory protections).

In the 1980s, empirical data showed significant increases in the admissions of adolescents to such private facilities. One study quoted congressional hearings to find "a four and one-half fold increase in national juvenile admissions to private psychiatric hospitals between 1980 and 1984." Lois Weithorn, Mental Hospitalization of Troublesome Youth: An Analysis of Skyrocketing Admission Rates, 40 Stan. L. Rev. 773, 783 (1988) (citing Emerging Trends in Mental Health Care for Adolescents: Hearings Before the House Select Comm. on Children, Youth, and Families, 99th Cong., 1st Sess. 5 (1985)). Weithorn ventures the following explanation for the increase:

> Increasing rates of divorce and the social and economic circumstances that typically accompany a divorce have led to greater numbers of children and adolescents experiencing adjustment problems and have interfered with the abilities of families to handle these problems within the context of the home. Increasingly, families are reaching out for help to external resources, such as mental health professionals. . . . Many children now hospitalized in mental health facilities probably would have been admitted to juvenile justice facilities prior to recent efforts to deinstitutionalize the juvenile justice system. . . . Mental hospitalization is accessible, affordable, and convenient because of a relative absence of meaningful legal or other scrutiny of the appropriateness of juvenile admissions and because insurance coverage typically permits, if not encourages, overuse of mental health institutions. The convergence of economic factors (including the rise of corporate medicine), a willing mental health establishment, malleable psychiatric diagnostic categories, and social attraction to the medical approach to deviance has facilitated this shift in society's attempts to manage difficult children. . . .

Weithorn, supra, at 774-775. Should a state regard as a "neutral" factfinder a physician who has a proprietary interest in a private facility? See Zenoff & Zients, supra, at 211-212. See also Sara Rimer, Desperate Measures — A Special Report: Embattled Parents Seek Help, at Any Cost, N.Y. Times, Sept. 10, 2001, at A1 (detailing rise of expensive wildness therapy programs and specialized boarding schools for troubled youth).

7. What does *Parham* mean for efforts to subject to judicial review parental decisionmaking in other contexts? Does the analysis in *Parham* help explain why *Troxel* rejected Washington's attempt to let a court decide whether parental denials of third-party visitation frustrate the child's best interests? In *Troxel*, the plurality opinion and Justice Stevens's dissent both cite *Parham* for the principle that the law presumes fit parents

act in their child's best interests. 530 U.S. at 66; id. at 86. See also id. at 77 (Souter, J., concurring).

Why has the Court departed from this approach in abortion cases? Omitted sections of *Parham* compare commitment to a mental institution with abortion. The Court has held that states seeking to compel parental involvement in abortion decisions must provide an alternative allowing a minor to prove she is sufficiently mature to make her own choice or establish that her best interests favor abortion, as *Casey* indicates. In such cases, the Court has relied on procedure to protect the minor's own rights — a court proceeding (called a "judicial bypass") facilitates the necessary exceptions to state rules that parents should make abortion choices for their minor daughters or should receive advance notice.

What distinctions in the two contexts prompted the Court to require judicial review when the state allows a parent to veto a daughter's abortion but to defer to parental autonomy in civil commitments of minors? Note that a physician plays a key role in both contexts. See Dolgin, supra, at 391-392 (*Parham*'s analysis relied on adult authority, not just parental authority).

# Problem

Mother and Father wish to have their 19-year-old mentally retarded Daughter surgically sterilized after her physicians recommend that she live in a supervised group home with other developmentally disabled adults. Without sterilization Mother and Father fear that group living poses the risk of pregnancy, which would cause Daughter physical and emotional problems.

Is the proposed sterilization a "voluntary" procedure, which Mother and Father should be able to arrange for Daughter so long as they can find a willing physician? If the physician insists the parents obtain a judicial order (as a safeguard against a subsequent malpractice action based on absence of the patient's competent consent), how should a court decide? What are Daughter's rights and interests? Who speaks for her?

See, e.g., Stump v. Sparkman, 435 U.S. 349 (1978); Ruby v. Massey, 452 F. Supp. 361 (D. Conn. 1978); Relf v. Mathews, 403 F. Supp. 1235 (D.D.C. 1975), *vacated as moot sub nom.* Relf v. Weinberger, 565 F.2d 722 (D.C. Cir. 1977); In the Matter of C.D.M., 627 P.2d 607 (Alaska 1981); In re Wirsing, 573 N.W.2d 51 (Mich. 1998); In re Grady, 426 A.2d 467 (N.J. 1981). See generally Elizabeth S. Scott, Sterilization of Mentally Retarded Persons: Reproductive Rights and Family Privacy, 1986 Duke L.J. 806; Steven J. Cleveland, Note, Sterilization of the Mentally Disabled: Applying Error Cost Analysis to the "Best Interest" Inquiry, 86 Geo. L.J. 137 (1997).

## B. CHILD ABUSE AND NEGLECT

Despite the principle of parental autonomy, child abuse and neglect provide a compelling reason for state intervention in the family. In fact, states have elaborate child-protection systems to address such situations. This section explores the extent to which the state can intervene in the family in the interest of child protection. In the materials that follow, consider when the state can invoke its authority and, also, how well the child-protection system achieves its goals.

### 1. Introduction

#### a. The Paradox of Privacy

■ JAMES GARBARINO & GWEN GILLIAM,
UNDERSTANDING ABUSIVE FAMILIES
*41, 42, 44-46 (1980)*

To most Americans, the value of privacy is unquestioned.... Although privacy may be valuable, it does not come without costs to the individual and to the community; some are paid by children in the form of abuse and neglect....

... Families have become less and less dominated by kinship and neighborhood relationships, and more and more by individual privacy. ... Americans place a high value on owning a single-family home, on the freedom a car brings, and on being independent of all regulations. It is as if we were trying to make every man (and woman) an island. Opportunities for privacy have increased markedly in recent decades....

[Yet,] [s]ocial connectedness provides access to social and economic resources that can aid the family in times of stress. Such involvement provides personalized observation of the family. It combats family climates that induce depression, anger, helplessness, loss of control, and violence. Without privacy it is unlikely that a pattern of maltreatment can be established and maintained. Abuse or neglect generally will be inhibited or at least identified at an early stage when families are involved in an active exchange network with prosocial friends, neighbors, and relatives....

The allure of privacy is great. It permits individualism to flourish and insulates the family against external meddling by persons who may have their own interests to advance.... Privacy provides the potential for a quiet atmosphere, whereas kinship intrusion is psychologically noisy. Despite this, privacy may be damaging or even lethal for children when combined with the factors that elicit abusive behavior.

Privacy alone is not, of course, sufficient to produce abuse and neglect. [H]owever, there are circumstances in which parent-child relations are placed in special jeopardy by privacy. . . . When families are exposed to loss of income, excessive work schedules (too much or too little), or other conditions that lead to frustration and tension, the probability of maltreatment is markedly increased. These social conditions interact with the parenting style of the child's caregivers. When the parent is deficient in the ability to empathize with the child, the potential for abuse is heightened. . . . For a child in a stable and psychologically healthy family, isolation is a limiting factor on development. For a child in a family plagued by stress and parental instability, isolation is dangerous and can be lethal. . . .

### b. Child Abuse in Historical Perspective

■ **PETER STEVENS & MARIAN EIDE, THE FIRST CHAPTER OF CHILDREN'S RIGHTS**
*41 Am. Heritage 84, 84-91 (1990)*

In the quiet New York courtroom, the little girl began to speak. "My name is Mary Ellen McCormack. I don't know how old I am. . . . I have never had but one pair of shoes, but can't recollect when that was. . . . My bed at night is only a piece of carpet, stretched on the floor underneath a window, and I sleep in my little undergarment, with a quilt over me. I am never allowed to play with any children or have any company whatever. Mamma has been in the habit of whipping and beating me almost every day. She used to whip me with a twisted whip, a raw hide. The whip always left black and blue marks on my body. I have now on my head two black and blue marks which were made by mamma with the whip, and a cut on the left side of my forehead which was made by a pair of scissors in mamma's hand. . . . I have no recollection of ever having been kissed. . . . I have never been taken on my mamma's lap, or caressed or petted. I never dared to speak to anybody, because if I did I would get whipped. . . . Whenever mamma went out I was locked up in the bedroom. . . . I have no recollection of ever being in the street in my life."

At the beginning of 1874 there were no legal means in the United States to save a child from abuse. Mary Ellen's eloquent testimony changed that, changed our legal system's view of the rights of the child. . . .

When Mary Ellen's mother, Frances Connor, immigrated to the United States from England in 1858, she took a job at the St. Nicholas Hotel in New York City as a laundress. There she met an Irishman named Thomas Wilson who worked in the hotel kitchen shucking oysters. They were married in April 1862, shortly after Wilson had been drafted into the 69th New York, a regiment in the famous Irish Brigade.

Early in 1864 she gave birth to their daughter, whom she named Mary after her mother and Ellen after her sister.

The birth of her daughter seems to have heralded the beginning of Frances Wilson's own decline. Her husband was killed that same year in the brutal fighting at Cold Harbor, Virginia, and with a diminished income she found it necessary to look for a job. In May 1864, unable to pay someone to watch the baby while she was at work, she gave Mary Ellen over to the care of a woman named Mary Score for two dollars a week, the whole of her widow's pension. Child farming was a common practice at that time, and many women made a living taking in unwanted children just as others took in laundry. [When Frances Wilson was unable to pay for the upkeep of her child, Mary Score took Mary Ellen to the Department of Charities.] The little girl — whose mother was never to see her again — was sent to Blackwells Island in July 1865. . . .

[A couple named Thomas and Mary McCormack had lost their three children to disease.] [T]he McCormacks went to the Department of Charities. . . . The child they chose as their own was Mary Ellen Wilson. . . . Shortly after bringing the child home, Thomas McCormack died, and his widow married a man named Francis Connolly. Little more than that is known of the early childhood of Mary Ellen. . . .

Late in 1873 Etta Angell Wheeler, a Methodist caseworker serving in the tenements of New York City, received a disturbing report. It came from Margaret Bingham, a landlord in Hell's Kitchen, and told of a terrible case of child abuse. . . . Though social workers often witnessed scenes of cruelty, poverty, and grief, Wheeler found Mary Ellen's plight especially horrifying. She went first to the police; they told her she must be able to furnish proof of assault in order for them to act. Charitable institutions she approached offered to care for the child, but first she must be brought to them through legal means. There were none. Every effort Wheeler made proved fruitless. Though there were laws to protect children — laws, in fact, to prevent assault and battery to any person — there were no means available for intervention in a child's home.

Finally Wheeler's niece had an idea. The child, she said, was a member of the animal kingdom; surely Henry Bergh, the founder of the American Society for the Prevention of Cruelty to Animals, who was famous for his dramatic rescue of mistreated horses in the streets of New York, might be willing to intervene. Within the hour Wheeler had arranged a meeting with Bergh. [On the basis of observations of a detective hired by Bergh and Etta Wheeler's testimony, Bergh's lawyers, Elbridge T. Gerry and Ambrose Monell, presented a petition on behalf of Mary Ellen to the New York Supreme Court.] They showed that Mary Ellen was held illegally by the Connollys, who were neither her natural parents nor her lawful custodians, and went on to describe the physical abuse Mary Ellen endured, the marks and bruises on her body, and the general state of deprivation that characterized her existence. . . . The lawyers requested that a warrant be issued, the child removed from her home and placed in protective custody, and her parents brought to trial. . . .

On the evening of her detention, Mary Ellen was turned over to the temporary custody of the matron of police headquarters. . . . Two indictments were brought against Connolly, the first for her assault on the child with scissors on April 7, the second for the continual assaults inflicted on the child throughout the years 1873 and 1874. After twenty minutes of deliberation the jury returned a verdict of guilty of assault and battery. Connolly was sentenced to one year of hard labor in the city penitentiary, then known as the Tombs. In handing down this sentence, the judge defined it not only as a punishment to Connolly but also as a statement of precedence in child abuse cases. . . .

[Mary Ellen eventually was raised by Etta Wheeler's sister. She married a widower and had two girls (one named after Etta Wheeler), adopted another child, and raised her husband's children from his prior marriage.] [She] was survived by the beginning of a movement to prevent the repetition of tragedies like her own. On December 15, 1874, Henry Bergh, Elbridge Gerry, and James Wright founded the New York Society for the Prevention of Cruelty to Children (SPCC). . . .

---

See also Stephan Lazoritz, What Ever Happened to Mary Ellen, 14 Child Abuse & Neglect 143 (1990). On the history of child maltreatment, see The History of Childhood (Lloyd deMause ed., 1995); Philip Greven, Spare the Child: The Religious Roots of Punishment and the Psychological Impact of Physical Abuse (1992); Murray A. Straus & Denise A. Donnelly, Beating the Devil Out of Them: Corporal Punishment in American Families and Its Effect on Children (2d ed., 2001).

### c. The Abusive Parent and the Abused Child

### ■ BRANDT STEELE, PSYCHODYNAMIC FACTORS IN CHILD ABUSE
*in The Battered Child 81, 81-84, 89-90 (Ray E. Helfer &*
*Ruth S. Kempe eds., 4th ed. 1987)*

The term *child abuse* [covers the] whole spectrum of maltreatment of children. [It] involves children of all ages, from infancy through adolescence, and caretakers of both sexes, all ages, and with various kinds of relationships to the child. . . .

[I]t is common for abusive or neglectful caretakers to give a history of having experienced some significant degree of neglect, with or without accompanying physical abuse. [I]t is quite rare to see an abuser who does not relate this history if questioned appropriately. [Several persons,] during evaluation for maltreatment of their children, stoutly denied having been mistreated themselves as children. Upon further questioning as to who did the disciplining in the family and what disciplinary measures were used, they freely described being whipped or beaten to the point of lacerations or bruising, but in no way did they consider this abuse, because the discipline was "appropriate punishment for misbehavior." Others will, for some time, maintain a denial of having been abused because of a persistent fear that, even though they are now adults, their parents might again attack them if they complain or criticize parental actions. Others hesitate to give a true history, lest the family be brought into some sort of difficulty or be disgraced in the community. More rarely, there is a genuine amnesia for the unpleasant events of childhood as a result of unusually strong repression. . . . There are others who, although they actually remember maltreatment, find it too painful to deal with and comfort themselves by maintaining a fantasy that their parents really were good to them. . . .

Physical abuse is usually not a constant or daily occurrence. There are often many days, weeks, or even months between attacks. To be sure, there may be almost daily emotional abuse in the form of yelling and verbal castigation, belittlement, and criticism, as well as disregard and lack of attention. But it is the physical attacks occurring intermittently in discrete episodes which give us the clearest picture of the abusive phenomenon. There are four conditions which seem necessary for abuse to occur:

1. A caretaker who has the predisposition for abuse related to the psychological residues of neglect or abuse in his or her own early life.
2. A crisis of some sort placing extra stress on the caretaker.
3. Lack of lifelines or sources of help for the caretaker, because either he or she is unable to reach out or the facilities are not available.
4. A child who is perceived as being in some way unsatisfactory.

These four factors interact in a mutually reinforcing way. Abusive parents live in a state of precarious balance between emotional supply and demand. They are more needy because of their low self-esteem, but less able to reach out for pleasure and support, and so turn with increased need to those who are least able to provide full satisfaction, their infants. Any crisis, even a small one . . . becomes unmanageable because of the parent's poor coping techniques and inability or reluctance to seek help. Financial and housing crises are very upsetting, but most devastating are emotional crises related to loss or abandonment by important persons or the emotional desertion of a spouse after marital conflict. It is the infant's disturbing behavior during ordinary caretaking, excessive crying, or his errors during toilet training which are the common stimuli to parental turmoil that culminates in the abusive act. . . .

---

In 1974 Congress enacted the Child Abuse Prevention and Treatment Act (CAPTA), 42 U.S.C. §§5101-5119 (1994 & Supp. V 1999), to provide comprehensive state programs and procedures to address child abuse and neglect. To receive federal funds, states had to comply with federally mandated standards. The act also established the National Center on Child Abuse and Neglect (NCCAN), one of whose purposes was to gather statistical data. NCCAN conducted several National Incidence Studies (NIS). The most recent NIS,[4] based on a sample of 842 child protective agencies, estimates that 1,553,800 children were abused or neglected in 1993.[5] Reported cases of seriously injured or endangered children have quadrupled since 1986, an increase that the NIS suggests "cannot plausibly be explained on the basis of heightened sensitivity."[6] Instead, researchers attribute it to the rise in both illicit drug use and children living in poverty.[7]

## 2. Standards for Intervention in the Family

### a. Defining the Threshold

### ■ IN RE JUVENILE APPEAL (83-CD)
*455 A.2d 1313 (Conn. 1983)*

SPEZIALE, Chief Justice.

This is an appeal by the defendant, mother of five children, from the order of the Superior Court for juvenile matters granting temporary custody of her children to the plaintiff commissioner of the department of children and youth services [DCYS].

---

[4]. Andrea J. Sedlak & Diane D. Broadhurst, U.S. Dept. of Health & Human Servs., Natl. Center on Child Abuse and Neglect, Third National Incidence Study of Child Abuse and Neglect: Final Report (Sept. 1996) [hereafter NIS III]. The first NIS was published in 1981, the second in 1988, and the third in 1996.

[5]. Andrea J. Sedlak & Diane D. Broadhurst, U.S. Dept. of Health & Human Services, Natl. Center on Child Abuse and Neglect, Executive Summary of the Third National Incidence Study of Child Abuse and Neglect 3 (Sept. 1996) [hereafter NIS III Executive Summary].

[6]. Id. at 17.

[7]. Id.

The defendant and her six children lived in a small apartment in New Haven. They had been receiving services from [DCYS] as a protective service family[1] since 1976, and were supported by the Aid to Families with Dependent Children program. Michelle Spicknall, a DCYS caseworker, was assigned to the defendant's case in January 1979. In the next nine months she visited the defendant's home twenty-seven times. She considered the family situation "marginal," but noted that the children were "not abused [or] neglected." It was Spicknall's opinion that the children were very happy and active, and that they had a "very warm" relationship with their mother.

During the night of September 4-5, 1979, the defendant's youngest child, nine-month-old Christopher, died. The child was brought by ambulance to Yale-New Haven Medical Center where resuscitation was unsuccessfully attempted by his pediatrician, Dr. Robert Murphy. No cause of death could be determined at that time, but the pediatrician noticed some unexplained superficial marks on Christopher's body.

Because of Christopher's unexplained death, the plaintiff commissioner of children and youth services seized custody of the defendant's five remaining children on September 5, 1979, under authority of the "96-hour hold" provision of General Statutes §17-38a(e), which permits summary seizure [of the child and "any other children similarly situated"] if the commissioner has probable cause to believe that a child is "suffering from serious physical illness or serious physical injury or is in immediate physical danger from his surroundings, and that immediate removal from such surroundings *is necessary to insure the child's safety.* . . ." (Emphasis added.)

On September 7, 1979, in the Juvenile Court for New Haven, DCYS filed petitions of neglect . . . for each of the defendant's children. Accompanying each petition was an affidavit for orders of temporary custody asking that the court issue temporary ex parte orders to keep the five children in DCYS custody under authority of §46b-129(b)(2).[5] The petitions alleged, in addition to Christopher's unexplained death, that the defendant's apartment was dirty, that numerous roaches could be

---

1. A protective services family is one which has come to the attention of DCYS as having a potential for abuse, neglect, abandonment, or sexual exploitation. DCYS then investigates the family and, where appropriate, provides "support systems to bolster family functioning."

5. General Statutes §46b-129(b) provides: "If it appears from the allegations of the petition . . . , that there is reasonable cause to find that the [child's] condition or the circumstances surrounding his care require that his custody be immediately assumed to safeguard his welfare, the court shall either (1) issue an order to the parents or other person having responsibility for the care of [the child] to show cause at such time as the court may designate why the court shall not vest in some suitable agency or person the [child's] temporary care and custody pending a hearing on the petition, or (2) vest in some suitable agency or person [the child's] temporary care and custody pending a hearing upon the petition which shall be held within ten days from the issuance of such order on the need for such temporary care and custody. . . .

found there, that beer cans were to be found in the apartment, that the defendant had been observed drinking beer, that on one occasion the defendant may have been drunk, that a neighbor reported that the children once had been left alone all night, and that the two older children had occasionally come to school without having eaten breakfast. On the basis of these allegations, on September 7, 1979, the court granted, ex parte, temporary custody to the commissioner pending a noticed hearing on temporary custody set for September 14, 1979, within ten days of the ex parte order as required. . . .

At the September 14 temporary custody hearing, DCYS presented testimony of Spicknall confirming and elaborating on the conditions of the defendant's home and on the defendant's beer drinking. Christopher's pediatrician testified concerning Christopher's treatment and physical appearance when the child was brought to the hospital on September 5. The doctor also testified that, although the pathologist's report on the autopsy was not complete, the external marks on Christopher's body were not a cause of death, that no internal injuries were found, and that the child had had a viral lung infection. He also explained, on cross-examination, the term "sudden infant death syndrome" and its pathology. At the conclusion of the state's case, the court found "probable cause" and ordered temporary custody of the children to remain with the plaintiff commissioner of children and youth services.

The defendant appealed to this court claiming that General Statutes §46b-129(b) violates the due process clause of the fourteenth amendment both because it is an impermissible infringement on her right to family integrity, and because the statute is unconstitutionally vague. . . .

## A. FAMILY INTEGRITY

The Connecticut legislature has declared: "The public policy of this state is: To protect children whose health and welfare may be adversely affected through injury and neglect; to strengthen the family and to make the home safe for children by enhancing the parental capacity for good child care; to provide a temporary or permanent nurturing and safe environment for children when necessary; and for these purposes to require the reporting of suspected child abuse, investigation of such reports by a social agency, and provision of services, where needed, to such child and family." General Statutes §17-38a(a).

In administering this policy, courts and state agencies must keep in mind the constitutional limitations imposed on a state which undertakes any form of coercive intervention in family affairs. The United States Supreme Court has frequently emphasized the constitutional importance of family integrity. "The rights to conceive and to raise one's children have been deemed 'essential,' 'basic civil rights of man,' and '[r]ights far more precious . . . than property rights.' " "It is cardinal with us that the custody, care and nurture of the child reside first in the parents, whose primary function and freedom include preparation for obligations the state can neither supply nor hinder." The integrity of the family unit has found protection in the Due Process Clause of the Fourteenth Amendment, the Equal Protection Clause of the Fourteenth Amendment, and the Ninth Amendment. [The right to family integrity includes "the most essential and basic aspect of familial privacy — the right of the family to remain together without the coercive interference of the awesome power of the state." [Citations omitted.]

### B. Criteria for Coercive Intervention by the State

Where fundamental rights are concerned we have a two-part test: "[1] regulations limiting these rights may be justified only by a 'compelling state interest,' and . . . [2] legislative enactments must be narrowly drawn to express only the legitimate state interests at stake." The state has a substantial interest in protecting minor children [citing Prince v. Massachusetts]; intervention in family matters by the state is justified, however, only when such intervention is actually "in the best interests of the child," a standard long used in this state.

Studies indicate that the best interests of the child are usually served by keeping the child in the home with his or her parents. "Virtually all experts, from many different professional disciplines, agree that children need and benefit from continuous, stable home environments." Institute of Judicial Administration — American Bar Association, Juvenile Justice Standards Project, Standards Relating to Abuse and Neglect, p.45 (Tentative draft, 1977). The love and attention not only of parents, but also of siblings, which is available in the home environment, cannot be provided by the state. Unfortunately, an order of temporary custody often results in the children of one family being separated and scattered to different foster homes with little opportunity to see each other. Even where the parent-child relationship is "marginal," it is usually in the best interests of the child to remain at home and still benefit from a family environment.

The defendants' challenge to the temporary custody statute, §46b-129(b), must be addressed in light of the foregoing considerations. The defendant contends that only when the child is "at risk of harm" does the state's interest become a compelling one, justifying even temporary removal of the child from the home. We agree.

[A]ny criteria used to determine when intervention is permissible must take into account the competing interests involved. The parent has only one interest, that of family integrity; and the state has only one compelling interest, that of protecting minor children. The child, however, has two distinct and often contradictory interests. The first is a basic interest in safety; the second is the important interest, discussed above, in having a stable family environment. Connecticut's child welfare statutes recognize both the conflicting interests and the constitutional limitations involved in any intervention situation. . . .

The language of [summary seizure provision] §17-38a(e) clearly limits the scope of intervention to cases where the state interest is compelling. . . . Intervention is permitted only where "serious physical illness or serious physical injury" is found or where "immediate physical danger" is present. It is at this point that the child's interest no longer coincides with that of the parent, thereby diminishing the magnitude of the parent's right to family integrity; and therefore the state's intervention as parens patriae to protect the child becomes so necessary that it can be considered paramount. A determination that the state interest is compelling does not alone affirm the constitutionality of the statute. More is needed. The second part of the due process analysis . . . requires that statutes affecting fundamental rights be "narrowly drawn to express only the legitimate state interests at stake." General Statutes §17-38a(e) meets this part of the test by requiring, in addition to the compelling need to protect the child, that the assumption of temporary custody by the commissioner be immediately "necessary to insure the child's safety." This phrase requires that various steps short of removal from the home be used when possible in preference to disturbing the integrity of the family. The statute itself mentions supervised in-home custody, but a wide range of other programs short of removal are a part of existing DCYS procedure.

The challenged [temporary custody] statute, §46b-129(b), does not contain the "serious physical illness or serious physical injury" or "immediate physical danger" language of §17-38a(e). We note, however, [that] statutes on a particular subject be "considered as a whole, with a view toward reconciling their separate parts in order to render a reasonable overall interpretation. . . ." This is no less true when the legislature has chosen to place related laws in different parts of the General Statutes. Therefore, the language limiting coercive intervention [in §17-38a] must be read as applying equally to such intervention [in §46b-129]. Because we hold that General Statutes §46b-129(b) may be applied only on the basis of the criteria enunciated in §17-38a, we reject the defendant's claim that §46b-129(b) is unconstitutional.

In the instant case, no substantial showing was made at the temporary custody hearing that the defendant's five children were suffering from either serious physical illness or serious physical injury, or that they would be in immediate physical danger if they were returned to the defendant's home. The DCYS caseworker admitted at trial, as did the state's counsel at argument before this court, that without the unexplained death of Christopher there was no reason for DCYS to have custody of the other children. The medical evidence at the hearing indicated no connection between Christopher's death and either the defendant or the conditions in her home. . . . There was, therefore, no evidence before the court to indicate whether his death was from natural causes or was the result of abuse. Yet with nothing before it but subjective suspicion, the court granted the commissioner custody of the defendant's other children. It was error for the court to grant to the commissioner temporary custody when no immediate risk of danger to the children was shown. . . .

Petitions for neglect and for temporary custody orders, like the petitions to terminate parental rights . . . , "are particularly vulnerable to the risk that judges or social workers will be tempted, consciously or unconsciously, to compare unfavorably the material advantages of the child's natural parents with those of prospective adoptive parents [or foster parents]." [In re Juvenile Appeal (Anonymous), 420 A.2d 875 (1979).]

This case clearly shows that these dangers do exist; it is shocking that the defendant's children have been in "temporary" custody for more than three years. This is a tragic and deplorable situation, and DCYS must bear full responsibility for this unwarranted and inexcusable delay. . . . The failure of DCYS properly to administer §46b-129 does not, however, affect its constitutionality. . . .

## Notes and Questions

1. *Stages of intervention. Juvenile Appeal* reveals that state intervention must be necessary to protect the child from real, immediate physical harm, given the constitutional right to family integrity. Initial intervention may take one of two forms: summary seizure or temporary custody. At the former hearing (which is ex parte), the court determines if an emergency exists, that is, if the child is in such immediate danger that the child's welfare dictates summary removal from the home. A finding of the need for summary seizure results in deferring the temporary custody determination for a short statutorily designated period of time (for example, 96 hours in *Juvenile Appeal*).

At the adversarial hearing on temporary custody, the court determines whether requisite facts exist to find a child within the statutory definition of "abused," "neglected," "dependent," or "in need of care." This proceeding is referred to as a "jurisdictional," "adjudicatory," or "factfinding" hearing. After making such a determination, the court conducts the next "dispositional" phase. The court chooses among various dispositions: conditions on custody, family preservation services, foster care, or termination of parental rights.

For historical background on the juvenile court's assertion of jurisdiction over children, see Murray Levine & Adeline Levine, Helping Children: A Social History 96-142 (1992); Julian W. Mack, The Juvenile Court, 23 Harv. L. Rev. 104 (1909).

2. *Concurrent jurisdiction.* Concurrent civil and criminal jurisdiction sometimes exists. In addition to civil proceedings in a juvenile or family court to declare the child a ward of the court, the state may also initiate criminal proceedings against a parent. Occasionally, the child (or the child's representative) may also initiate a tort claim against the caretaker. What are the consequences for the child, the abuser, and the family based on civil versus criminal processing?

What factors dictate the nature of the processing? One judge, with experience in both juvenile and criminal courts, remarks that many abuse cases reveal the arbitrary nature of state intervention. Judge Leonard P. Edwards, Corporal Punishment and the Legal System, 36 Santa Clara L. Rev. 983, 1006 (1996). Might civil proceedings sometimes be preferable to criminal proceedings? See Commonwealth v. Ogin, 540 A.2d 549, 555 (Pa. Super. Ct. 1988) (stating that juvenile court proceedings may sometimes be preferable to resolve parenting problems and to avoid the harmful effects of criminal intervention on the family) (cited in Edwards, supra, at 1006 n.161). See also Alison B. Vreeland, Note, The Criminalization of Child Welfare in New York City: Sparing the Rod or Spoiling the Family?, 27 Fordham Urb. L.J. 1053 (2000) (arguing that the use of criminal, rather than civil, proceedings fails to protect children's liberty interest in the parent-child relationship).

3. Abused and neglected children come to the attention of state child protective agencies in several ways: (a) mandatory referrals by professionals under state reporting laws (discussed infra this chapter); (b) referrals by friends, relatives, neighbors, and other observers who suspect child abuse; and (c) referrals from criminal justice personnel following a parent's arrest. See Mark I. Soler et al., Representing the Child Client ¶¶4.01, 4.02 (1994).

4. *The policy of minimal intervention.* As *Juvenile Appeal* illustrates, state intervention in the family sometimes is unnecessary and, in fact, harmful. In the late 1970s, mental health professionals Joseph Goldstein, Anna Freud, and Albert J. Solnit propounded a policy of "minimum intervention" and the adoption of a "least detrimental alternative standard" in child welfare decisionmaking. In *Before the Best Interests of the Child,* they contend:

> [W]e believe that a child's need for continuity of care by autonomous parents requires acknowledging that parents should generally be entitled to raise their children as they think best, free of state interference. This conviction finds expression in our preference for *minimum state intervention* and prompts restraint in defining justifications for coercively intruding on family relationships. . . . So long as a child is a member of a functioning family, his paramount interest lies in the preservation of his family. . . .
>
> [C]omplex and vital developments require the privacy of family life under guardianship by parents who are autonomous. The younger the child, the greater is his need for them. When family integrity is broken or weakened by state intrusion, his needs are thwarted and his belief that his

parents are omniscient and all-powerful is shaken prematurely. The effect on the child's developmental progress is invariably detrimental. The child's need for safety within the confines of the family must be met by law through its recognition of family privacy as the barrier to state intrusion upon parental autonomy in child rearing. These rights — parental autonomy, a child's entitlement to autonomous parents, and privacy — are essential ingredients of "family integrity." . . .

Beyond these biological and psychological justifications for protecting parent-child relationships and promoting each child's entitlement to a permanent place in a family of his own, there is a further justification for a policy of minimum state intervention. It is that the law does not have the capacity to supervise the fragile, complex interpersonal bonds between child and parent. As parens patriae the state is too crude an instrument to become an adequate substitute for flesh and blood parents. The legal system has neither the resources nor the sensitivity to respond to a growing child's ever-changing needs and demands. It does not have the capacity to deal on an individual basis with the consequences of its decisions, or to act with the deliberate speed that is required by a child's sense of time. . . .

To recognize how critical are the developmental stages and how essential are autonomous parents for the protection of their children is also to recognize that parents may fail. Not all parents are able or willing to safeguard their child against the succession of risks which bedevil development from dependent infancy to independent adulthood. They may fail to protect their child from unwarranted risk. . . . Yet, to acknowledge that some parents, whether biological, adoptive, or longtime foster, may threaten the well-being of their children is not to suggest that state legislatures, courts, or administrative agencies can always offer such children something better. . . .

Joseph Goldstein et al., Before the Best Interests of the Child 4-5, 9, 11-13 (1979). See also Joseph Goldstein et al., Beyond the Best Interests of the Child (1973); Joseph Goldstein et al., The Best Interests of the Child: The Least Detrimental Alternative, 91-92 (1996).

Goldstein, Freud, and Solnit's views (cited in an omitted footnote in *Juvenile Appeal*) supported efforts to narrow the bases on which courts could assert jurisdiction over abused or neglected children. Very narrow standards were formulated in model legislation; however, the standards were never approved by the ABA nor adopted by state legislators. See IJA-ABA, Juvenile Justice Standards Relating to Abuse and Neglect, Standard 2.1 (Final Draft 1980) (cited in *Juvenile Appeal*). For another (not as extreme) noninterventionist stance, see Michael Wald, State Intervention on Behalf of "Neglected" Children: A Search for Realistic Standards, 27 Stan. L. Rev. 985 (1975); Michael Wald, State Intervention on Behalf of "Neglected" Children: Standards for Removal of Children from Their Homes, Monitoring the Status of Children in Foster Care, and Termination of Parental Rights, 28 Stan. L. Rev. 623 (1976); Michael Wald, Thinking about Public Policy Toward Abuse and Neglect of Children, 78 Mich. L. Rev. 645 (1980) (reviewing *Before the Best Interests of the Child*).

The work of Goldstein, Freud, and Solnit has received its share of criticisms. See Marsha Garrison, Child Welfare Decisionmaking: In Search of the Least Drastic Alternative, 75 Geo. L.J. 1745, 1762-1765 (1987) (criticizing the lack of empirical basis, overoptimism, neglect of social context in which problems emerge and in which proposed standards would be administered, and failure to address parents' voluntary placement of children in state care).

What are the advantages and disadvantages of narrow versus broad definitions of abuse and neglect? On what grounds *should* legislatures permit intervention into the private family? How should statutes balance the interests in family privacy and child protection?

5. *Vagueness.* Broad definitions of abuse and neglect in both summary seizure and temporary custody provisions pose constitutional shortcomings. For example, in an omitted portion of *Juvenile Appeal,* the court declines to decide whether Connecticut's statutory definition of neglect is unconstitutionally vague. That statute defines the terms "dependent," "neglected," and "uncared for" as follows:

> [A] child or youth may be found "dependent" whose home is a suitable one for him, save for the financial inability of his parents, parent, guardian or other person maintaining such home, to provide the specialized care his condition requires.
>
> [A] child or youth may be found "neglected" who (A) has been abandoned or (B) is being denied proper care and attention, physically, educationally, emotionally or morally or (C) is being permitted to live under conditions, circumstances or associations injurious to his well-being or (D) has been abused. . . .
>
> [A] child or youth may be found "uncared for" who is homeless or whose home cannot provide the specialized care which his physical, emotional or mental condition requires. . . .

Conn. Gen. Stat. Ann. §46b-120 (West 1995 & Supp. 2001). Do the terms "dependent," "neglected," "proper care and attention," or "uncared for" provide parents with adequate warning that their acts may lead to state intervention? Despite numerous constitutional challenges on grounds of vagueness, courts have upheld statutes with broad definitions of abuse and neglect. See Scott A. Davidson, When Is Parental Discipline Child Abuse? The Vagueness of Child Abuse Laws, 34 U. Louisville J. Fam. L. 403, 408-410 (1995-1996) (discussing case law). But cf. Roe v. Conn, 417 F. Supp. 769, 779-780 (M.D. Ala. 1979) (holding Alabama's child neglect statute unconstitutional in the case of a "neglected" Caucasian child who was summarily removed from his home, and his mother's parental rights terminated, on the ground that the mother was socializing with Black males and residing in a Black neighborhood).

6. Was the necessary threshold for intervention met in *Juvenile Appeal*? Did the state intervene because of one child's death or the condition of the home? Would either, alone, have proved sufficient? *Juvenile*

*Appeal* also asks whether harm to one child justifies intervention on behalf of other unharmed siblings. On prospective abuse, see page 1024.

### b. Parental Privilege to Discipline

### ■ CHRONISTER v. BRENNEMAN
*742 A.2d 190 (Pa. Super. Ct. 1999)*

Brosky, J.

This is an appeal from the entry of a Protection From Abuse Order. Appellant raises a single issue, does the Protection From Abuse Act, 23 Pa.C.S.A. §6102(a), prohibit a parent from using physical punishment to discipline a child for misconduct? . . .

The relevant facts do not appear to be in dispute. On the morning of May 18, 1998, appellant administered corporal punishment to his sixteen-year-old daughter, Cassandra Morrison, in the form of hitting her four or five times with a folded belt across the buttocks after she admitted lying to appellant. Ms. Morrison testified that the strapping was painful and made her cry. After the incident she went to school and later reported the incident to her guidance counselor who refused to take action. Ms. Morrison then called her older half-sister, Shannon Chronister, appellee here, and told her what had happened. Ms. Chronister then contacted CYS and reported the incident. . . .

Later on the evening of May 18, 1998, and perhaps prompted by the incident that morning, appellant and his girlfriend were having a discussion with Ms. Morrison on the "rules of the house." Shortly thereafter appellant left the kitchen table and retrieved a pistol from a cupboard, looked at the gun, walked by Ms. Morrison and proceeded upstairs. Appellant testified that he had remembered that he left the gun downstairs and retrieved it, checked to make sure it was unloaded, then took it upstairs to a closet where he stores his firearms. Ms. Morrison testified that she had eye contact with appellant as he walked by.

The next day a Petition for Protection From Abuse [PFA] was filed. . . . At the hearing of July 15, 1998, Ms. Morrison testified to the above facts and also to being frightened and intimidated by the incident as well as by appellant's statements that similar punishment would follow if Ms. Morrison continued to break the rules. . . . Appellant asserted that his actions were solely designed to discipline Cassandra and that he felt it was appropriate and necessary given her history of jumping to various caregivers whenever she did not get her way.[1] On October 8, 1998, the court entered the subject PFA order. The present appeal followed. . . .

---

1. Apparently Ms. Morrison had lived in the homes of her mother, paternal grandmother and appellee in addition to appellant's home.

We would state initially that nothing in this Opinion should be construed to be an approval or condoning of appellant's choice of discipline. Undoubtedly, many individuals regarded as authorities in child rearing would certainly cringe at appellant's choice of punishment for his sixteen-year-old daughter. On the other hand, neither should this Opinion be construed as disapproving of, or critical of, appellant's conduct. Undoubtedly, many individuals believe in the old adage "spare the rod and spoil the child." The topic is certainly suitable for a barstool or roundtable debate. However, it is not for us to dictate, as a policy matter, how a parent should choose to discipline his or her child. . . . The fact of relevance is that our law allows a parent to administer corporal punishment. The fact that a father chose to discipline his child through the means of corporal punishment is relevant only to the extent it reflects the motivation for the physical conduct in question. . . .

While appellant's parental judgment and choice of discipline can certainly be called into question, his motivation appears beyond reproach. That is, there appears to be a lack of any evidence to support the conclusion that appellant's acts were intended to be anything other than punishment for a young woman who the trial court admits "has taxed her father's patience to the limit." Thus it appears clear that the strapping of his daughter across the buttocks, in appellant's mind, constituted "punishment." There is no evidence that it was a malevolent infliction of pain or an attempt to terrorize his daughter, nor did the trial court conclude to the contrary.

Nevertheless, this is not to say that appellant's actions, regardless of innocent intent, cannot amount to "abuse" within the contemplation of the Act. But clearly intent is an important element in the equation. If it had been demonstrated that appellant conducted a sadistic reign of terror upon his daughter strapping her on a frequent basis, we would be inclined to affirm the trial court's disposition. After all, good intentions, regardless of how well founded they are, cannot be an excuse for the frequent infliction of physical or mental pain and/or the terrorizing one's children. In the present case, however, such a factual foundation is absent. What remains is the infliction of a painful, yet otherwise relatively harmless, "good, old fashioned whooping" of appellant's daughter. Thus, the question as we see it is whether or not appellant's conduct constitutes abuse within the meaning of the Act.[3]

---

3. The trial court relies upon 23 Pa.C.S.A. §6102(a)(1) in granting the PFA order. This subsection focuses upon causing or intending to cause "bodily injury." The court also interjects commentary regarding appellant's pulling a gun out in front of his daughter, yet did not appear to rely upon subsection (a)(2) in entering its order. 23 Pa.C.S.A. §6102(a)(2) targets a person's placing of another in "reasonable fear of imminent serious bodily injury." Although the trial court does not specifically raise this issue we would be disinclined to find that this subsection was met by appellant's actions in retrieving the gun and relocating it upstairs. The action was unaccompanied by any verbal threat and the circumstances certainly do not suggest that appellant was "threatening to shoot his daughter" if she continued to disobey him or was a threat to do so.

"Abuse," as defined in the Act encompasses, in relevant part, attempting to cause or intentional, knowingly or recklessly causing bodily injury or serious bodily injury. 23 Pa.C.S.A. §6107(a). At 18 Pa.C.S.A. §2301 "bodily injury" is defined as "impairment of physical condition or substantial pain." In the present case, although the strapping of Cassandra, according to her testimony, "was painful and made her cry," there is no indication that it resulted in anything more than a temporary painful condition, which, of course, was its intent. Nor was there any indication that the punishment resulted in any degree of bodily impairment. In fact, Cassandra told Cindy Leik, who works for CYS, that the strapping did not leave any bruises. Consequently, we do not think the conduct in question amounts to "abuse" for purposes of the Act.

We believe the above conclusion is bolstered by 18 Pa.C.S.A. §509 which, although sounding as a justification defense in the criminal law arena, has been characterized as codifying a parental "privilege" to administer corporal punishment. This section allows the use of force upon another under certain circumstances. For our purposes subsection (1) is relevant and provides for the use of force if the actor is a parent and the force is used for the purpose of safeguarding or promoting the welfare of a minor, including the preventing or punishment of his misconduct, where the force is "not designed to cause or known to create a substantial risk of causing death, serious bodily injury, disfigurement, extreme pain, or mental distress or gross degradation." Cases interpreting this provision have stated that parents may use corporal punishment to discipline their children "so long as the force used is not designed or known to create a substantial risk of death, serious bodily injury, disfigurement, extreme pain, or mental distress or gross degradation." Appeal of E.S., 82 Pa.Cmwlth. 168, 474 A.2d 432 (1984). Other cases have referred to the parental "privilege" to administer corporal punishment. See Commonwealth v. Ogin, 373 Pa.Super. 116, 540 A.2d 549 (1988). If the activity found in the present case were viewed as violating the Protection From Abuse Act then a parent could exercise his or her "privilege" only to suffer the rather inconsistently seeming consequence of losing custody of the child or being banished from his or her home. This seems grossly illogical. For the above reason we reverse the order appealed from.[5]

---

5. One certainly gets the impression that, in the present case, the PFA law has been injected where it does not belong. [T]here is no indication that the PFA law was meant to be utilized to question a parent's personal choice of discipline except for in the rarest of circumstances where a child's welfare is truly jeopardized by the conduct in question. We are unwilling to essentially label appellant an "abuser" of his child merely because his viewpoints on parenting might be viewed as "old fashioned" and out of favor with today's parenting "experts." If allowed to stand one must wonder where we will head next, will any parent who spanks his child be ripe for having a PFA slapped upon him/her?

Orie Melvin, J., Dissenting:

An accurate review of the record reveals that appellant beat his daughter with a belt severely enough to cause bruising and handled her so that imprints from his fingers remained on her body. On the same day he administered this form of "discipline" and while discussing with Cassandra the house rules, appellant felt the need to remove his gun while in his daughter's presence. Based on these circumstances and the fact that appellant admitted he would administer the same form of punishment again if he deems it is warranted, the trial court granted Cassandra's protection from abuse petition. I believe the evidence warranted the protection from abuse order. . . .

In the present case the Majority states that there is no indication that Cassandra's punishment resulted in any degree of bodily impairment. The Majority attempts to distinguish this case from [Miller on Behalf of Walker v. Walker, 445 Pa.Super. 537, 665 A.2d 1252 (1995)], by stating that the strapping of Cassandra did not leave any bruises. It relies on testimony from CYS caseworker, Cindy Leik, in which she indicated that Cassandra told her she did not have any bruises. If Ms. Leik's testimony was the only evidence of bodily injury, I would have to agree with the Majority. However, the Majority conveniently fails to consider testimony from Cassandra that she received a bruise on her thigh and that she had handprints on her from being hit by her father. Her father's beating with his belt caused the girl pain and made her cry. The trial court found Cassandra's testimony credible, noting that her testimony was corroborated by her sister who testified that Cassandra had fingerprints on her arm and bruises on her leg. Moreover, in finding a bodily injury occurred the trial court further took into consideration Ms. Leik's testimony that she did see a bruise on Cassandra's arm and that she did not examine the child's leg personally for bruises. The Majority disregards the trial court's factual findings and its credibility determinations, which are clearly supported by the record. Viewing the evidence in the light most favorable to Cassandra, I believe the trial court's conclusion that she suffered a bodily injury is supported by a preponderance of the evidence. . . .

The Majority opines that because there is no indication that Cassandra's punishment resulted in anything more than a temporary painful condition, she is not warranted protection from further beating. Nothing in the statute requires that the pain must be of a continuing nature. The pain must only be "substantial" in nature. 18 Pa.C.S.A. §2301. I believe the Majority should not make light of such pain. I would submit that thrashing a young lady with a belt hard enough to produce bruising and handling her in such a manner as to leave the imprint of a hand on her body would produce a "substantial" amount of pain. The Majority also makes light of appellant's action of retrieving his gun while in his daughter's presence. The trial court was disturbed by the appellant's action and found the appearance that appellant created by pulling out his gun was inappropriate. I believe that when this action is viewed in light of the surrounding circumstances, including the fact that appellant had just recently beat her and at that time was discussing his rules with Cassandra, the trial court's concern cannot be dismissed so easily.

I agree that the Protection From Abuse Act was not designed to prevent a parent from using corporal punishment. . . . In this case the punishment Cassandra received, which left lasting imprints on her body goes beyond mere corporal discipline and rises to the level of abuse within the meaning of the Protection From Abuse Act. While I recognize in this Commonwealth parents have a right to inflict corporal punishment on their children, their right to do so is restricted. The trial court found through the evidence presented that Appellant crossed the line of moderation and reasonableness in correcting his daughter's behavior. His corrective measures went beyond what is reasonable punishment for purposes of behavior modification and instead rose to the level of abuse. The severity of appellant's punishment of Cassandra demonstrates not a concern to correct her behavior but instead appellant's attempt to satisfy his passions as an enraged parent frustrated with his daughter's disobedience. As I believe the Majority's holding is contrary to both this Court's decision in *Miller* and the evidence presented below, I must dissent.

## Notes and Questions

1. *Battered child syndrome.* One of the most common manifestations of child abuse is "the battered child syndrome." Radiologists played a prominent role in recognition of this problem.[8] In a classic article, Dr. C. Henry Kempe (the principal author) coined the term and speculated that some unexplained traumatic injuries to children may have been inflicted intentionally by parents.[9] The term, now widely accepted in medical literature and case law, signifies a child who manifests multiple fractures in different parts of the body that are in various stages of healing; parental explanations are at odds with clinical findings. Many courts, including the Supreme Court, accept battered child syndrome evidence in criminal cases. See Estelle v. McGuire, 502 U.S. 62 (1991).

2. In Chronister v. Brenneman, the victim was 16 years old. The largest category of child maltreatment victims are young children, typi-

---

[8]. See Stephen Pfohl, The Discovery of Child Abuse, 24 Soc. Probs. 310 (1977).

[9]. C. Henry Kempe et al., The Battered Child Syndrome, 181 JAMA 17 (1962). Although Kempe and his colleagues are credited with the discovery of abuse, another pediatric radiologist, John Caffey, first noticed the phenomenon. See John Caffey, Multiple Fractures in the Long Bones of Infants Suffering from Chronic Subdural Hematoma, 56 Am. J. Roentgenology 163 (1946).

cally under age three.[10] How appropriate is corporal punishment of infants or young children? Of teenagers? If appropriate, what form should it take? Among infants and young children, head injuries are especially common, leading to recognition of the "shaken baby syndrome" by which severe, repetitive shaking may result in brain damage, paralysis, eye injury, seizures, developmental delays, and death.[11] The victim in the principal case was female. Why do you suppose that boys are likely to be more severely injured?[12]

3. The abuser in the case was the child's father. Biological parents are the perpetrators of most physical abuse, followed by stepparents and other parent substitutes.[13] Children are more likely to be neglected by female perpetrators but more likely to be abused, even killed, by males.[14] Do such gender-based findings "demonstrate a serious need for rethinking the design of prevention and treatment strategies that now focus primarily on females."[15] If so, how?

4. *Munchausen's Syndrome by Proxy.* Mothers are more likely to be the perpetrators of one particular form of abuse, "Munchausen's Syndrome by Proxy." In the condition, named after the famous storyteller-soldier Baron Von Munchausen, the parent induces illness, often by poison or medication overdose, in a child (the "proxy"). Sometimes, the illness or injury is fabricated. Abuse stems from the *parent's* craving for attention. See generally Marie M. Brady, Munchausen Syndrome by Proxy: How Should We Weigh the Options?, 18 Law & Psychol. Rev. 361 (1994); Michael T. Flannery, Munchausen Syndrome by Proxy: Broadening the Scope of Child Abuse, 28 U. Rich. L. Rev. 1175 (1994).

5. *Physical abuse or discipline?* A threshold issue in many cases is whether the injury resulted from abuse or discipline. As *Meyer* and *Pierce,* supra, established, parents have a constitutionally protected right to raise their children as they see fit, including the privilege to administer *reasonable* discipline. What distinguishes abuse from discipline? Must the

[10]. Approximately 27 percent of the victims of child maltreatment are three years old or younger. Kempe, supra note [9], at 17-18. According to more recent data, 41 percent of child abuse fatality victims are under the age of one. Approximately 10 percent of deaths occur in victims older than four. See U.S. Dept. of Health & Human Services, A Nation's Shame: Fatal Child Abuse and Neglect in the United States 16 (1995) [hereafter, A Nation's Shame].

[11]. A Nation's Shame, supra note [10], at 15 (reporting that shaken baby syndrome results in 10 to 12 percent of deaths).

[12]. See NIS III Executive Summary, supra note [5], at 6 (boys' risk of serious injury was 24 percent higher than girls').

[13]. NIS III, supra note [4], at 6 (birth parents are the perpetrators in 72 percent of the cases of physical abuse, followed by other parent and parent substitutes in 21 percent of the cases).

[14]. Id. at 13 (87 percent of the children were neglected by females versus 43 percent by males; 67 percent of the children were abused by males versus 40 percent by females); A Nation's Shame, supra note [10], at 13 (men inflict more fatal injuries).

[15]. A Nation's Shame, supra note [10], at 14.

punishment result in bodily harm? See In re Welfare of Minor Children of J.B.B., No. CO-00-1606, 2001 WL 243221 (Minn. Ct. App., Mar. 13, 2001).

When does spanking become child abuse? Some jurisdictions exempt spanking from the definition of child abuse in civil or criminal statutes. See Cal. Welf. & Inst. Code §300(a) (West 1998 & Supp. 2001) (exempting from abuse "reasonable and age-appropriate spanking to buttocks where there is no evidence of serious physical injury"); Okla. Stat. Ann. tit. 21, §844 (West 1983) (exempting from criminal liability "spanking, switching or paddling" accompanied by ordinary force). How helpful are such definitions in the determination of excessive discipline? See generally Kandice K. Johnson, Crime or Punishment: The Parental Corporal Punishment Defense — Reasonable and Necessary or Excused Abuse?, 1998 U. Ill. L. Rev. 413 (1998).

6. *Statutory formulations.* According to the Restatement (Second) of Torts §147(1) (1965), the generally accepted standard for the limits of parental discipline is:

> A parent is privileged to apply such reasonable force or to impose such reasonable confinement upon his child as he reasonably believes to be necessary for its proper control training, or education.

Factors in the determination of reasonableness include age, sex, physical and mental condition of the child; nature of child's offense and apparent motive; influence of child's example on other children of the same family or group; whether the force or confinement is reasonably necessary and appropriate to compel obedience to a proper command; and whether it is disproportionate to the offense, unnecessarily degrading, or likely to cause serious or permanent harm. Restatement (Second) of Torts §150 (1965).

Similarly, the ALI Model Penal Code §3.08 defines the parent's use of force as "justifiable" if the force is used to "promot[e] the welfare of the minor, including the prevention or punishment of his misconduct; and, [if] the force . . . is not designed to cause or known to create a substantial risk of causing death, serious bodily harm, disfigurement, extreme pain or mental distress or gross degradation." The privilege to discipline is delegable by the parent, such as to a teacher or to some other person in loco parentis. See Restatement (Second) of Torts §147(2) (1965); ALI Model Penal Code §3.08(2). See also State v. West, 515 N.W.2d 484 (Wis. Ct. App. 1994) (extending privilege to foster parents). But cf. Teresa Mosher Boyd, Corporal Punishment and the Legal System, 11 J. Contemp. Legal Issues 491, 494 (2000) (stating that some states, such as California, prohibit foster parents from using corporal punishment).

7. Might a child's acts be sufficient provocation to render punishment "reasonable"? See State v. Brunner, 1985 WL 8658 (Ohio Ct. App.

1985) (beating five-year-old with belt for foul language that led to threat of eviction was disciplinary and not excessive).

8. Should the law take into account differences in the perception of reasonableness? For example, one commentator points to the controversy about whether spanking constitutes abuse or discipline. "Therapists are more inclined to believe that it is abusive, possibly leading to negative, long-term sequelae for the child, whereas CPS workers [child protective service] are less prone to see it as actionable." Murray Levine & Howard J. Doueck, The Impact of Mandated Reporting on the Therapeutic Process: Picking Up the Pieces 140 (1995).

Similarly, should the law take into account *cultural* differences in evaluating the reasonableness? See In re D.L.W., 589 N.E.2d 970, 972 (Ill. App. Ct. 1992) (terminating father's parental rights and disregarding father's justification for spanking with wooden board and banging son's head against wall).

9. *Intergenerational transmission of abuse.* Evidence suggests that abuse is "transmissible" intergenerationally. That is, maltreated children are likely, as adults, to choose abusive partners and to become abusive or neglectful parents. See generally Joan Kaufman & Edward Zigler, The Intergenerational Transmission of Abuse, in Child Maltreatment: Theory and Research on the Causes and Consequences of Child Abuse and Neglect 129 (Dante Cicchetti & Vicki Carlson eds., 1989). Different studies estimate the rate of intergenerational transmission at 18 to 70 percent. Id. at 132.

Scholars have proposed different explanations for the "violence begets violence" theory. Some support a social learning perspective (children learn the appropriateness of aggression). Others advance a more psychologically based attachment theory (early experiences with abusive parents are repeated when not well-integrated into the personality). See id. at 136-137.

Should the fear of intergenerational transmission support a custody denial to a grandparent following removal of a child from an abusive parent? See N.A. v. J.H., 571 So. 2d 1130, 1133 (Ala. Civ. App. 1990).

10. *Intergenerational transmission of violence.* Childhood maltreatment also increases the possibility that the victim will commit future delinquent and criminal acts. Abused or neglected children are more likely to have subsequent juvenile and adult arrest records, have a first arrest at a young age, to commit several offenses, and to commit more violent acts.[16]

[16]. Office of Juvenile Justice and Delinquency Prevention, Juvenile Offenders and Victims: A National Report 42 (1995). See also Allen Beck et al., U.S. Dept. of Justice Survey of State Prison Inmates, 1991, at 9 (1993) (suggesting that female inmates were three times more likely than males to have suffered physical or sexual abuse); Cathy Spatz Widom, Child Abuse, Neglect, and Adult Behavior: Research Design and Findings on Criminality, Violence, and Child Abuse, 59 Am. J. Orthopsychiatry 355 (1989).

11. *Witnessing abuse.* Sometimes, other children in the family witness a parent's abuse. Should exposure to domestic violence constitute a form of child abuse and neglect? Evidence suggests that exposure to abuse leads to severe physical and psychological effects (i.e., nightmares, bed-wetting, headaches, stomach aches, anxiety, aggression, withdrawal), similar to those experienced by victims of physical abuse. States are beginning to respond to this problem by incorporating "childhood exposure to domestic violence" into their statutory definitions of child abuse and neglect. See, e.g., Alaska Stat. §47.10.011 (2000). See Lois A. Weithorn, Protecting Children from Exposure to Domestic Violence: The Use and Abuse of Child Maltreatment Statutes, 53 Hastings L.J. 1 (2001) (reviewing research, analyzing recent statutory approches, and suggesting reforms). Many Canadian provinces have had such statutory definitions for years, although they are typically not enforced. Id. at 101. What are the difficulties and risks of interpreting existing child abuse and neglect statutes to incorporate childhood exposure to domestic violence? See id. at 26-41. See also Alan J. Tomkins et al., The Plight of Children Who Witness Women Battering: Psychological Knowledge and Policy Implications, 18 Law & Psychol. Rev. 137 (1994). Note that the National Center for Child Abuse and Neglect and its National Incidence Study of Child Abuse and Neglect defines as emotional neglect "chronic or extreme spouse abuse or other domestic violence in the child's presence."[17]

12. *Cross-cultural perspectives.* In 1979 Sweden became the first country to prohibit corporal punishment by parents. The ban on physical punishment or "humiliating treatment" in the Swedish Parenthood and Guardianship Code followed considerable public concern over the rising incidence of abuse. Some prosecutions have occurred under the Swedish criminal code. In X, Y and Z v. Sweden, 5 EHRR 147 (1983), Swedish parents unsuccessfully challenged the ban as a violation of their rights to family privacy and freedom of religion under the European Convention for the Protection of Human Rights and Fundamental Freedoms. More recently, the European Court of Human Rights considered Britain's legitimization of corporal punishment in A. v. The United Kingdom, 27 EHRR 611 (1998). The European Court held that the acquittal of a stepfather for caning his stepson's buttocks and legs violated international human rights law (Article 3 of the Convention on the Rights of the Child). Currently, several nations (including Finland, Norway, Austria, Cyprus, Italy, Denmark, Latvia, and Croatia) ban corporal punishment by parents. See Susan H. Bitensky, Spare the Rod, Embrace Human Rights: International Law's Mandate Against All Corporal Punishment of Children, 21 Whittier L. Rev. 147 (1999).

---

[17]. NIS III, supra note [4], at 2.19.

## Problem

When Mrs. Jones picks up 11-year-old Bobby after school, he hands his mother a detention slip from a teacher. The detention slip is based on an event that happened six months before. Mrs. Jones requests an explanation from the teacher, who indicates that the note attached to the detention slip was missing. That same night, Mr. and Mrs. Jones discover another disciplinary note from a different teacher in Bobby's backpack; that note has been marked over with black magic marker.

Bobby denies stealing the first note and defacing the second. His parents are particularly distressed at his dishonesty, which has been a disciplinary issue for some time. Mr. Jones tells Bobby, "I don't believe you," and hits Bobby twice on the buttocks. The father then leaves, telling Bobby that his mother will mete out the rest of his punishment. Mrs. Jones orders Bobby to his room to think over his misdeeds. When she enters his room to ask if he is ready to "tell the truth," he insists that his teacher is lying. Mrs. Jones then spanks Bobby several times with a belt, telling him, "I'm going to have to make this hurt for a time." A short time later, Bobby confesses.

That night, when the parents are retiring for bed, they notice Bobby trying to make a quantity of toilet paper go down the shower drain. Mrs. Jones previously had disciplined Bobby's sister for placing wads of toilet paper in the shower. Mrs. Jones demands to know who perpetrated the act. When both children deny their role, Mrs. Jones requires them to do exercises — pushups or squats for a certain length of time. If they are "out of form," they are "swatted with a belt to correct that form." Ultimately, Bobby's sister confesses, and Mrs. Jones then spanks her daughter three times with her belt.

The following day, a school official notices bruises, marks, and welts on both children. Bobby's shoulders and back are almost completely covered by bruises, and his legs are bruised to some extent. The school official reports Mrs. Jones to the authorities. Both children are examined by a physician but require no treatment. Mrs. Jones appeals her conviction of several counts of child abuse. What result? See State v. Jones, 747 N.E.2d 891 (Ohio Ct. App. 2000).

### c. Neglect

#### (i) Physical Neglect

### ■ IN RE N.M.W.
*461 N.W.2d 478 (Iowa Ct. App. 1990)*

HABHAB, Judge.

Appellant, B.W., appeals the adjudication of the juvenile court determining N.M.W. to be a child in need of assistance (CINA) and the subsequent dispositional order directing continued foster care of N.M.W. We affirm.

The child in question is a girl born in July 1983. Her parents are not married to each other. She lived with her mother from the date of her birth until 1989.

The family has had involvement with the Department of Human Services since at least 1984. Over the years, the Department has prepared several abuse reports. The primary concern has been extreme filth in the mother's home, although there have also been concerns about inadequate food in the home, inadequate supervision of the child, and refusal of services by the mother.

On April 12, 1989, N.M.W. was found in front of a house a block from B.W.'s residence. When the police were unable to locate her home, they took N.M.W. to the police station. N.M.W. informed the authorities her mother had told her to go outside. B.W. claimed the child had just taken off without her knowledge. From statements made by law enforcement officers concerning the condition of B.W.'s apartment, a child protective worker visited B.W.'s apartment.

When the worker, who was accompanied by a police officer, approached the apartment, the stench of cat feces and urine became noticeable. Inside the apartment, the worker discovered the entire front room to be strewn with a collection of garbage, clothing, and other general clutter. Ashtrays were found filled to overflowing with some knocked over. Windows and screens were missing and garbage materials were embedded in the carpet. A side closet was packed with a mixture of clutter and refuse. A bedroom was filthy with garbage. Additionally, two litters of cats were living under the bed. Apparently a total of eleven to twelve cats lived in the apartment.

The same squalid conditions existed in the kitchen. The floor was filthy and the garbage container was left uncovered. The refrigerator had smeared food on parts of it and was empty of food except for milk, eggs, and ketchup. Dishes were stacked in the sink, on the counter, and on the table. Also, a cat box filled with cat excrement was found in the kitchen. In the bathroom, the cats had defecated along the bathtub and some of N.M.W.'s clothing was stuck to the feline fecal material. Because of the filthy apartment, N.M.W. stayed with a friend of B.W.

On April 14, 1989, the child protective worker returned to B.W.'s apartment. The squalid conditions still existed. Likewise, the conditions had not improved by April 17, 1989, when the worker again returned to the home. The worker returned again on April 20th to find B.W. had made limited improvement. Later visits to B.W.'s home found the unsanitary conditions unabated.

Following hearing on the matter, the juvenile court made a CINA determination as to N.M.W. At the initial hearing, the State presented evidence concerning three prior child abuse reports. The three reports had formed the basis for a prior CINA proceeding in which the juvenile court had dismissed the petition. . . .

Initially, B.W. argues the trial court erred in finding the existence of sufficient evidence to establish N.M.W. as a child in need of assistance. Iowa Code section 232.2(6)(g) defines CINA as an unmarried child:

> Whose parent, guardian, or custodian fails to exercise a minimal degree of care in supplying the child with adequate food, clothing or shelter and refuses other means made available to provide such essentials.

We find clear and convincing record evidence to support the juvenile court's determination that N.M.W. is a child in need of assistance.

The chronic unsanitary conditions of B.W.'s apartment are of sufficient magnitude to form the basis for a CINA adjudication. We take judicial notice of the health hazards of having animal fecal materials scattered throughout one's living quarters. While the record does not disclose any adverse health effects of this environment on N.M.W., the child's well being demands that action be taken to prevent actual harm. . . .

SACKETT, Judge (dissenting).

I dissent. Over twelve months ago N.M.W., a happy, healthy five-year-old child was removed from her biological mother's care and placed in foster care where she remains today. The majority has determined the child must remain in foster care.

The reason for the removal, and the decision the child should remain in foster care, is that the mother is an inadequate housekeeper and does not keep what the majority terms a sanitary house. I agree with the majority that the record clearly supports a finding this mother is an extremely poor housekeeper. I agree with the majority it would be in the child's best interests to live in a cleaner house. However, the house could have been cleaned without taking the child from her mother. I do not, however, feel removal from the parental home was in the child's best interests and feel the matter should be remanded to direct reasonable efforts be utilized to allow the child to return home. Houses can be cleaned, but the trauma a child experiences when he or she is removed from the only parental home he or she has ever known can cause emotional scars that can last a lifetime. . . .

The majority decision also concerns me because it may be interpreted as setting standards for housekeeping that need to be met before we allow parents to keep their children. If I were convinced: (1) only people in clean houses were good parents, (2) for a child to be healthy it is necessary for him or her to be raised in a sanitary house, and (3) a child suffers less by being removed from his or her parents than from growing up in a dirty house, I could agree with the majority. I am not convinced of these things. I consider parents who devote time and attention to their children, who allow their children to have pets and projects in their home, and who welcome their children's friends in their home are contributing substantially to their children's emotional development. Parents who seek to direct their financial and emotional resources in these directions may have few resources left to keep a sanitary house.

If we concentrate too much on sanitary houses, we may take children away from good and adequate parents, and we may use energies and resources that would best be directed to helping families and to identifying children who suffer serious abuse.

*(ii)  Medical Neglect*

## ■  IN RE PHILLIP B.

*156 Cal. Rptr. 48 (Ct. App. 1979)*

CALDECOTT, Presiding Justice.

A petition was filed by the juvenile probation department in the juvenile court, alleging that Phillip B., a minor, came within the provision of [California] Welfare and Institutions Code section 300, subdivision (b), because he was not provided with the "necessities of life."

The petition requested that Phillip be declared a dependent child of the court for the special purpose of ensuring that he receive cardiac surgery for a congenital heart defect. Phillip's parents had refused to consent to the surgery. The juvenile court dismissed the petition. The appeal is from the order.

Phillip is a 12-year-old boy suffering from Down's Syndrome. At birth his parents decided he should live in a residential care facility. Phillip suffers from a congenital heart defect — a ventricular septal defect that results in elevated pulmonary blood pressure. Due to the defect, Phillip's heart must work three times harder than normal to supply blood to his body. When he overexerts, unoxygenated blood travels the wrong way through the septal hole reaching his circulation, rather than the lungs.

If the congenital heart defect is not corrected, damage to the lungs will increase to the point where his lungs will be unable to carry and oxygenate any blood. As a result, death follows. During the deterioration of the lungs, Phillip will suffer from a progressive loss of energy and vitality until he is forced to lead a bed-to-chair existence.

Phillip's heart condition has been known since 1973. At that time Dr. Gathman, a pediatric cardiologist, examined Phillip and recommended cardiac catheterization to further define the anatomy and dynamics of Phillip's condition. Phillip's parents refused.

In 1977, Dr. Gathman again recommended catheterization and this time Phillip's parents consented. The catheterization revealed the extensive nature of Phillip's septal defect, thus it was Dr. Gathman's recommendation that surgery be performed.

Dr. Gathman referred Phillip to a second pediatric cardiologist, Dr. William French of Stanford Medical Center. Dr. French estimates the surgical mortality rate to be five to ten percent, and notes that Down's Syndrome children face a higher than average risk of postoperative complications. Dr. French found that Phillip's pulmonary vessels have already undergone some change from high pulmonary artery pressure. Without the operation, Phillip will begin to function less physically until he will be severely incapacitated. Dr. French agrees with Dr. Gathman that Phillip will enjoy a significant expansion of his life span if his defect is surgically corrected. Without the surgery, Phillip may live at the outside 20 more years. Dr. French's opinion on the advisability of surgery was not asked.

It is fundamental that parental autonomy is constitutionally protected. The United States Supreme Court has articulated the concept of personal liberty found in the Fourteenth Amendment as a right of privacy which extends to certain aspects of a family relationship. "It is cardinal with us that the custody, care and nurture of the child reside first in the parents, whose primary function and freedom include preparation for obligations the state can neither supply nor hinder." (Prince v. Massachusetts (1944) 321 U.S. 158, 166.) . . .

Parental autonomy, however, is not absolute. The state is the guardian of society's basic values. Under the doctrine of parens patriae, the state has a right, indeed, a duty, to protect children. (See, e.g., Prince v. Massachusetts, supra, 321 U.S. 158 at p.166.) State officials may interfere in family matters to safeguard the child's health, educational development and emotional well-being.

One of the most basic values protected by the state is the sanctity of human life. (U.S. Const., 14th Amend., §1.) Where parents fail to provide their children with adequate medical care, the state is justified to intervene. However, since the state should usually defer to the wishes of the parents, it has a serious burden of justification before abridging parental autonomy by substituting its judgment for that of the parents.

Several relevant factors must be taken into consideration before a state insists upon medical treatment rejected by the parents. The state should examine the seriousness of the harm the child is suffering or the substantial likelihood that he will suffer serious harm; the evaluation for the treatment by the medical profession; the risks involved in medically treating the child; and the expressed preferences of the child. Of course, the underlying consideration is the child's welfare and whether his best interests will be served by the medical treatment.

Section 300, subdivision (b), permits a court to adjudge a child under the age of 18 years a dependent of the court if the child is not provided with the "necessities of life."

The trial judge dismissed the petition on the ground that there was "no clear and convincing evidence to sustain this petition." The rule is clear that the power of the appellate court begins and ends with a determination as to whether there is any substantial evidence, contradicted or uncontradicted, which will support the conclusion reached by the trier of fact. . . .

Turning to the facts of this case, one expert witness testified that Phillip's case was more risky than the average for two reasons. One, he has pulmonary vascular changes and statistically this would make the operation more risky in that he would be subject to more complications than if he did not have these changes. Two, children with Down's Syndrome have more problems in the postoperative period. This witness put the mortality rate at five to ten percent, and the morbidity would be somewhat higher. When asked if he knew of a case in which this type of operation had been performed on a Down's Syndrome child, the witness replied that he did, but could not remember a case involving a child who had the degree of pulmonary vascular change that Phillip had. Another expert witness testified that one of the risks of surgery to correct a ventricular septal defect was damage to the nerve that controls the heart beat as the nerve is in the same area as the defect. When this occurs a pacemaker would be required.

The trial judge, in announcing his decision, cited the inconclusiveness of the evidence to support the petition.

On reading the record we can see the trial court's attempt to balance the possible benefits to be gained from the operation against the risks involved. The court had before it a child suffering not only from a ventricular septal defect but also from Down's Syndrome, with its higher than average morbidity, and the presence of pulmonary vascular changes. In light of these facts, we cannot say as a matter of law that there was no substantial evidence to support the decision of the trial court. . . .

## Notes and Questions on Neglect

1. *Epilogue.* Following In re Phillip B., the appellants' petition for a rehearing was denied; the California Supreme Court also denied appellants' petition for a hearing. Professor Martha Minow relates the sequel:

> Two volunteers, a married couple named Heath, befriended Phillip at the institution and started to bring him home for holiday visits, with his parents' consent. The Heaths grew frustrated when the Beckers continued to refuse treatment for Phillip's heart and when they also successfully

defended against a dependency proceeding brought by the state charging them with neglect. [The Beckers' refusal of treatment stemmed from their worry that Phillip might outlive them and be a burden to his brothers.] The Heaths then initiated their own legal proceedings seeking to become Phillip's guardians and seeking authority to approve surgery to repair Phillip's heart. It was an unusual legal strategy, orchestrated by lawyer Jay Spears and law professor Robert Mnookin. The lawyers, on behalf of the Heaths, converted the earlier legal question of whether the parents had fallen so low in their conduct to justify state intrusion in the private family into a contested custody case between two plausible sets of parents or guardians. Not only did this reworking of the case suggest an easier standard to justify governmental intervention, it also offered a real, long-term option for Phillip beyond approval of heart surgery.

After a twelve-day trial, Judge William Fernandez issued an extensive and unusually candid and expressive opinion. He began by asking, "Who speaks for the child?" He considered Phillip's parents, his friends, and his institutional caretakers. The judge compared the conceptions of Phillip held by his parents and by his friends, the Heaths. According to the court, the Beckers held onto the picture of Phillip they acquired when he was born and their physician had advised institutional care. The Beckers viewed Phillip as an unskilled and devalued person, incapable of loving others. The Heaths, in contrast, pictured Phillip as an educable and valuable person, capable of loving others. The judge found the Heaths' conception more persuasive and likely to provide a less detrimental alternative, but the judge also decided that Phillip's own rights had to be explored before resolving the guardianship issue.

Nothing in the law governing guardianship specified rights for a child or incompetent person like Phillip. Nonetheless, Judge Fernandez noted an emerging constitutional right to "habilitation," a right for persons with mental disabilities to acquire and maintain skills to cope and lead more useful and meaningful lives. Similarly, the judge found California law protections against unfair stigma for persons with mental retardation and minors with grave disabilities. From these principles, the judge inferred that fourteen-year-old Phillip had a right to express his preference regarding his placement.

This was an innovation, as the judge acknowledged, and it created a practical difficulty: how could the preference of a mentally disabled teenager be discerned and respected? For Judge Fernandez, Phillip's own views could no more be ignored that they could themselves be determinative. The judge turned to the doctrine of "substituted judgment" which obliges a court to discern "as nearly as possible the incompetent person's 'actual interests and preferences.' " Judge Fernandez then adopted an unusual method to derive this substituted judgment, a "platonic dialogue with the court posing the choices to Phillip and Phillip's preference being ascertain [sic] from the more logical choice." In the dialogue, the judge again focused on the alternate pictures the Beckers and the Heaths held of Phillip, and what those alternatives implied for his future. The court also credited the apparent psychological closeness between Phillip and the Heaths. The judge in conclusion granted guardianship to the Heaths without terminating the Beckers' parental rights. His decision was affirmed a year and a half later by the appellate court.[18]

Martha Minow, Guardianship of Phillip Becker, 74 Tex. L. Rev. 1257, 1257-1258 (1996).

2. Civil and criminal neglect law constitute a constraint on parental rights. Neglect includes the failure to provide adequate food, clothing, shelter, supervision, education, or medical care. See James M. Gaudin, Jr., Effective Intervention with Neglectful Families, 20 Crim. Just. & Behav. 66, 67 (1993) (defining neglect). Definitional problems abound, however. See Ray E. Helfer, The Litany of the Smoldering Neglect of Children, in The Battered Child 301, 301 (Ray E. Helfer & Ruth S. Kempe eds., 1987). Further, broad-based neglect statutes typically confer considerable discretion on the state to intervene. Did the court correctly assert jurisdiction in *N.M.W.*? For other "deficient housekeeping" cases, see Alsager v. District Court of Polk County, 545 F.2d 1137 (8th Cir. 1976); In re R.T., 778 A.2d 670 (Pa. Super. Ct. 2001).

3. When is court intervention appropriate in cases of neglect? When should a court override parental judgments? Note that in *N.M.W.*, the state fails to prove adverse health effects. Nonetheless, the court finds the child in need of assistance because "the child's well being demands that action be taken to prevent actual harm." Is the *risk* of harm sufficient to justify intervention? If so, when?

4. *Incidence of neglect.* Although more attention is devoted to the battered child, neglect is a far more common form of child maltreatment. Based on 1999 data, 58.4 percent of victims of child maltreatment were reported for neglect.[19] Further, the percentage of neglected children is more than double the number of victims of physical abuse [20] and more than five times the number of children who are sexually abused.[21]

5. *Failure to thrive.* One common form of neglect in young children is "failure to thrive" (FTT), a condition of severe developmental delays and malnutrition. No consensus exists about its characterization; FTT is

[18]. Guardianship of Phillip B., 188 Cal. Rptr. 781 (Ct. App. 1983). Phillip's heart surgery was successful. In a subsequent settlement, the Heaths assumed all responsibility for Phillip, while the Beckers ended judicial proceedings and received visitation at least two days per year. When Phillip turned 18, the Heaths adopted him. See Robert H. Mnookin, The Guardianship of Phillip B.: Jay Spears' Achievement, 40 Stan. L. Rev. 841, 853-854 (1988). In 1999, Phillip B. turned 33 years old. He still resides with the Heaths, has a girlfriend, works, attends a program to learn independent living skills, and participates in the Special Olympics. Despite the settlement agreement, his biological parents had no further contact with him after his heart surgery in 1983. Mr. Becker passed away from cancer in 1995. Personal communication with Pat Heath, Nov. 16, 1999.
[19]. U.S. Dept. of Health & Human Servs., Administration on Children, Youth and Families: Child Maltreatment 1999 at 2-3.
[20]. Id.
[21]. Id.

characterized as abuse, neglect, and emotional maltreatment. See Ann Haralambie, Handling Child Custody, Abuse and Adoption Cases 290 (1993) (categorizing it as neglect); Leonard Karp & Cheryl Karp, Domestic Torts 61 (Supp. 1994) (categorizing it as abuse but mentioning that mental health officials often categorize it as neglect). See, e.g., In re Camera "R", 693 N.Y.S.2d 681 (Sup. Ct. 1999); In re Mendez, 986 P.2d 670 (Or. Ct. App. 1999).

The term originated in the post-World War II period to describe children living in institutions where mortality was high. Physicians subsequently reported the condition in children living at home. Ruth S. Kempe & Richard B. Goldbloom, Malnutrition and Growth Retardation ("Failure to Thrive") in the Context of Child Abuse and Neglect, in The Battered Child, supra, at 312, 313. Failure to thrive is difficult to treat. "Although the cause of the malnutrition is lack of adequate calories, the problem usually occurs in a context of a moderately or severely disturbed parent-child relationship and is not readily cured by simple re-education of the parents about better feeding." Id. at 331.

6. Should the child have a voice in determinations of abuse or neglect? See In re Green, 292 A.2d 387 (Pa. 1972) (remanding determination of neglect in case in which Jehovah's Witness parents refused consent to surgery for son with severe curvature of the spine in order to determine child's wishes). See also Keith R. Cruise et al., Definitions of Physical Abuse: A Preliminary Inquiry into Children's Perceptions, 12 Behav. Sci. & L. 35 (1994).

7. Should homelessness constitute per se neglect? See L.G. v. Lawton, 764 S.W.2d 89 (Mo. 1989) (en banc).

8. *Child abandonment.* One extreme form of neglect is child abandonment. What parental acts constitute abandonment? Incarceration? See, e.g., Michael J. v. Arizona Dept. of Econ. Sec., 995 P.2d 682 (Ariz. 2000). Failure to contact children who are in foster care? See N.A. v. J.H., 571 So. 2d 1130, 1133 (Ala. Civ. App. 1990). Failure to pay child support? See In re S.J., 849 S.W.2d 608 (Mo. Ct. App. 1993).

The growing number of newborn abandonments recently prompted legislative action. Many states have enacted legislation to allow mothers who have given birth to surrender their newborn within the first hours of life to a hospital employee, anonymously, and with impunity. See, e.g., Cal. Health & Safety Code §1255.7 (West 2001). Such legislation, addressed primarily to pregnant teenagers who abandon their newborns because of shame or fear, is intended to prevent the discarding of babies in trash bins or other isolated places. Do you think the legislation is an adequate solution to the problem? See generally Karen Vassilian, A Band-Aid or a Solution? Child Abandonment Laws in California, 32 McGeorge L. Rev. 752 (2001).

9. *Cultural defense.* Should courts take into account cultural differences when evaluating whether the lack of traditional medical treatment

constitutes neglect? See In re Jertrude O., 466 A.2d 885 (Md. Ct. Spec. App. 1983) (affirming finding that child was "in need of assistance" based on evidence that scars resulted from "cupping," an African custom in which a cow horn is heated and pressed against the body to withdraw sickness).

10. *Religious beliefs as defense to neglect.* Some parents' refusal to consent to medical treatment for their child is premised on religious beliefs. The ensuing conflict pits the state's interest in child protection against the parent's First Amendment rights. Cases often arise when state officials petition the juvenile or family court to assume jurisdiction (based on neglect) and request the court to order the necessary medical treatment. In re D.R., 20 P.3d 199 (Okla. Civ. App. 2001). If lack of treatment results in death, criminal prosecutions may ensue. See State v. Hays, 964 P.2d 1042 (Or. Ct. App. 1998).

Many statutes exempt faith healing from definitions of child abuse and neglect. See, e.g., Colo. Rev. Stat. Ann. §18-6-401(6) (West 1999 & Supp. 2000); Idaho Code §16-1602(t)(1) (Supp. 2000); 23 Pa. Cons. Stat. Ann. §6303 (West 2000). Only a few states exempt parents from criminal liability for faith healing under homicide statutes. See, e.g., Ark. Code Ann. §5-10-101(a)(9) (Michie 1997); Or. Rev. Stat. §163.115(4) (Supp. 1998).

The federal response to spiritual treatment exemptions has vacillated. Although the Child Abuse Prevention and Treatment Act (CAPTA), 42 U.S.C. §§5101-5105 (1994 & Supp. V 1999), originally did not include spiritual treatment exemptions, regulations of the Department of Health, Education and Welfare (which were promulgated pursuant to the act) required states to include such exemptions. Subsequent Department of Health and Human Services regulations excluded the spiritual treatment exemption. See Elizabeth A. Lingle, Treating Children by Faith: Colliding Constitutional Issues, 17 J. Legal Med. 301, 307 (1996).

Do laws that exempt parents who refuse consent to medical treatment based on religious objections infringe on the *children*'s right to equal protection? See James G. Dwyer, The Children We Abandon: Religious Exemptions to Child Welfare and Education Laws as Denials of Equal Protection to Children of Religious Objectors, 74 N.C. L. Rev. 1321 (1996).

See generally Jennifer Stanfield, Current Public Law and Policy Issues: Faith Healing and Religious Treatment Exemptions to Child-Endangerment Laws: Should Parents Be Allowed to Refuse Necessary Medical Treatment for Their Children Based on Their Religious Beliefs?, 23 Hamline J. Pub. L. & Pol'y 45 (2000); Jennifer L. Hartsell, Comment, Mother May I . . . Live? Parental Refusal of Life-Sustaining Medical Treatment for Children Based on Religious Objections, 66 Tenn. L. Rev. 499 (1999).

## Problem

Tony, the seven-year-old son of Christina and Loyd Hays, is diagnosed with acute lymphocytic leukemia. His parents are members of a religious sect that believes in spiritual healing through prayer. Christina and Loyd treat Tony by rubbing him with oil and by group prayer. Should the juvenile court assume jurisdiction over Tony and order traditional treatment (assuming that the jurisdiction does not contain a spiritual healing exemption to the child abuse and neglect statute)? What if Tony expresses no desire to see a physician. Should his wishes be taken into account? Suppose that Tony dies. An autopsy reveals that he had a curable form of leukemia. Should the Hayses be criminally liable for homicide (assuming that the jurisdiction does not have a spiritual treatment exemption to their criminal homicide statute)? What constitutional defenses might the parents raise? May the parents claim that the child's exercise of a constitutional right of privacy (to refuse medical treatment) discharges their duty to seek treatment? See Commonwealth v. Nixon, 718 A.2d 311 (Pa. 1998). Should state legislators in the Hays' jurisdiction adopt a spiritual treatment exemption to their child abuse and neglect and/or criminal homicide statutes? See Lingle, supra, at 301 (discussing facts of Oregon case).

## Note: "Baby Does," Disabled Newborns, and Medical Neglect

Parents may refuse medical care for their child because the seriousness of the child's condition leads the parents to believe that treatment would be futile or that death may be a more humane outcome than survival. Do such parental acts constitute neglect? Over a decade ago, this question swirled at the heart of a nationwide controversy. Two legal cases, in Indiana and New York (referred to as the "Baby Doe Cases"), precipitated federal legislative efforts addressing the withholding of medical attention from disabled newborns.

Initially, the federal response viewed medical nontreatment of newborns as a form of discrimination against the disabled. Baby Doe was born in 1982 in Indiana with Down's syndrome and suffering from an esophageal obstruction. Surgery could correct the digestive tract ailment. However, the infant's Down's syndrome (a genetic condition that results in mental retardation) could not be remedied. Without surgery, the baby would die from starvation. Because of the baby's Down's syndrome, the parents decided to withhold both their consent to surgery and all food and water. The juvenile court refused the hospital's request to assert jurisdiction. The Indiana Court of Appeals, likewise, refused to order treatment. In re Infant Doe, No. GU 8204-004A (Monroe County Cir. Ct., Apr. 12, 1982). The Indiana Supreme Court rejected a petition for a writ of mandamus. State ex rel. Infant Doe v. Baker, No. 482 S 140 (Ind. May 27, 1982). In Infant Doe v. Bloomington Hospital, 464 U.S. 961 (1983), the Supreme Court denied certiorari. Baby Doe died six days after birth.

Baby Doe's death precipitated the formulation of a new policy by the Department of Health and Human Services (DHHS). DHHS issued a "Notice to Health Care Providers" warning hospitals that the withholding of food and medical care from seriously ill newborns might possibly result in the providers' loss of federal funding under §504 of the Rehabilitation Act of 1973, 29 U.S.C. §794(e) (1994) (prohibiting discrimination against the disabled by federally funded programs). The failure to treat seriously disabled infants would constitute "discrimination against the handicapped" under the act. Discriminating Against the Handicapped by Withholding Treatment of Nourishment; Notice to Health Care Providers, 47 Fed. Reg. 26,027 (1982). DHHS subsequently published an Interim Final Rule specifying that withholding food or medical attention from disabled newborns did, in fact, violate the act and required that hospitals post a notice that such discrimination was a violation of federal law. Nondiscrimination on the Basis of Handicap, 48 Fed. Reg. 9630 (1983) (codified at 45 C.F.R. §84.61 (2000)).

Medical groups challenged the regulations. American Acad. of Pediatrics v. Heckler, 561 F. Supp. 395 (D.D.C. 1983), invalidated the regulations on procedural grounds (that is, the failure to comply with the public comment requirements of the Administrative Procedure Act). In response, DHHS again promulgated regulations, this time complying with the requisite procedures. DHHS's final regulations in 1984 differed only slightly from the interim regulations.

A second Baby Doe was born while the final federal regulations were being formulated. Baby Jane Doe, born in New York State in 1983, suffered from spina bifida, microcephaly, and hydrocephalus. The baby's condition was not as life threatening as Indiana's Baby Doe. However, even with corrective surgery, the baby risked retardation and impaired physical functioning. Without surgery, the baby risked death within two weeks to two years. The baby's parents eventually decided to withhold their consent to surgery, while consenting to antibiotic and palliative treatment.

Thereupon, a private attorney, representing the "right to life" movement, filed an unsuccessful suit to compel the surgery. Weber v. Stony Brook Hosp., 469 N.Y.S.2d 63 (App. Div. 1983) (per curiam). The Baby Jane Doe case prompted DHHS again to act. Eight days after the baby's birth, DHHS received a complaint that the hospital was engaged in discrimination against the disabled. DHHS sought the baby's medical records. The parents and hospital refused. When DHHS sought to compel the release of the records, a district court found no evidence of a §504 violation nor any basis to order such disclosure. The Second Circuit affirmed. United States v. University Hosp., 729 F.2d 144 (2d Cir. 1984).

Ultimately, medical groups (including the American Medical Association and the American Hospital Association) challenged the validity of the DHHS final regulations. In Bowen v. American Hospital Association, 476 U.S. 610 (1986), the Supreme Court held that parental withholding of consent does not constitute discriminatory nontreatment by the hospital, and also that the promulgation of the federal regulations exceeded DHHS's statutory authority.

In response, the federal government adopted a radically different approach: classifying medical nontreatment as a form of child abuse and neglect. The Child Abuse Amendments of 1984, amending CAPTA, 42 U.S.C. §§5101-5107 (1994 & Supp. V 1999), incorporated a new provision stating that the withholding of medically indicated treatment, with certain exceptions, constitutes a form of child neglect.[22] 42 U.S.C. §5106 (1994 & Supp. V 1999). States failing to include this new definition of neglect faced the loss of federal funds. "Although commentators have questioned their impact and effectiveness, the Child Abuse Amendments remain in place today as the legislation most directly affecting medical decisions for newborns with disabilities."[23]

On the history of the Baby Does and the federal response, see Kathleen Knepper, Withholding Medical Treatment from Infants: When Is It Child Neglect?, 33 U. Louisville J. Fam. L. 1, 12-19 (1995); Steven R. Smith, Disabled Newborns and the Federal Child Abuse Amendments: Tenuous Protection, 37 Hastings L.J. 765, 789 (1986).

---

[22]. 42 U.S.C. §5106(g) (1994) defines "withholding of medically indicated treatment" as follows:

> failure to respond to the infant's life-threatening conditions by providing treatment (including appropriate nutrition, hydration and medication) . . . except that the term does not include the failure to provide treatment (other than appropriate nutrition, hydration, or medication) to an infant when, in the treating physician's or physicians' reasonable medical judgment, (A) the infant is chronically and irreversibly comatose; (B) the provision of such treatment would (i) merely prolong dying, (ii) not be effective in ameliorating or correcting all of the infant's life-threatening conditions, or (iii) otherwise be futile in terms of the survival of the infant; or (C) the provision of such treatment would be virtually futile in terms of the survival of the infant and the treatment itself under such circumstances would be inhumane.

[23]. Mary Crossley, Infants with Anencephaly, the ADA, and the Child Abuse Amendments, 11 Issues L. & Med. 379, 383 (1996).

### d. Emotional Abuse and Neglect

■ **IN RE SHANE T.**
*453 N.Y.S.2d 590 (Fam. Ct. 1982)*

LEDDY, Jr., Judge. . . .

Shane is the natural child of the respondents and presently resides with his mother and two sisters. His father is a construction worker who has been separated from his wife for some time, although they continue to see each other. [Shane is 14 years old.]

Over the course of the last several years, Shane has been subjected to an unrelenting torrent of verbal abuse by his father directed at his sexual identity. Specifically, he has been regularly called a "fag," "faggot," and "queer." In desperation, the boy pleaded with his mother to intervene on his behalf and prevail upon his father to cease making these accusations. However, the mother's efforts were abortive, resulting only in a repetition of the taunts by the father with the added assertion that they were true.

Nor were these accusations limited to the home. On one particular occasion, the respondent father humiliated the boy by calling him a "fag" while they were shopping in a store.

[Family Court Act] Section 1012(e)(i) defines an "abused child" as one

> Less than eighteen years of age whose parent or other person legally responsible for his care . . . inflicts or allows to be inflicted upon such child physical injury by other than accidental means which causes or creates a substantial risk of death, or serious or protracted disfigurement, or protracted impairment of physical or emotional health or protracted loss or impairment of the function of any bodily organ. . . .

As defined in the Penal Law [which uses similar wording], "physical injury means impairment of physical condition or *substantial pain*." Penal Law Section 10.00(9) (emphasis supplied). Whether "substantial pain" has been established is ordinarily a question for the trier of fact. . . . In deciding whether Shane has experienced "substantial pain," the Court initially considers the observation of Chief Judge Cooke: "Pain is, by definition, a subjective concept and cannot be quantified or expressed with precision. Knowledge of the circumstances and the description of the sensation accompanying the use of force, however, provide a ready basis for measuring, within one's own experience, the degree of pain felt by another." Matter of Philip A. [,49 N.Y.2d 198,] 202, 424 N.Y.S.2d 418, 400 N.E.2d 358 (Cooke, J. dissenting).

It must be immediately observed that there is no specific requirement of the use of force in the definition of an abused child. Thus, Judge

Cooke's statement relating to "the use of force" is specifically referenced to the assault statute that was under consideration in Matter of Philip A. (supra). In fact, while Section 1012(e)(i) of the Family Court Act is derived from Section 10.00(10) of the Penal Law, there are substantial differences between the statutes. Thus, it is sufficient for a finding of abuse that there be protracted impairment of emotional health or a substantial risk thereof. It is clear, therefore, that it is the actual or potential impact on the child, as opposed to the per se seriousness of the injury, that forms the predicate for abuse. In this regard, the Family Court Act provision differs markedly from the Penal Law definition of "serious physical injury." Furthermore, while section 1012(e)(i) of the Family Court Act makes specific reference to "emotional health," section 10.00(10) of the Penal Law refers merely to "health."

The foregoing is consistent with the fact that Article 10 of the Family Court Act is a civil proceeding "designed to establish procedures to help protect children from injury or mistreatment and to help safeguard their physical, mental and *emotional well-being*." FCA Section 1011 (emphasis supplied). Therefore, this Court concludes that the "physical injury" referred to in Section 1012(e)(i) of the Family Court Act need not be inflicted by physical force. Rather, to constitute abuse, mere words are sufficient provided that their effect on the child falls within the language of the statute. . . .

As he testified, Shane repeatedly tried to forestall tears, but they beseiged (sic) his eyes, nonetheless. He told the Court how he would cry and his stomach would twist when his father called him a "fag." At one point, he was asked whether he was beginning to believe that he was a homosexual. He clenched his hands, sat forward, and cried out "No!". His demeanor strongly suggested, however, that he would like someone, anyone to reassure him.

It should be noted that, in addition to the verbal indignities to which he was subjected, Shane was frequently forced to remove his father's shoes and massage his feet. The boy complied without protest since he was constantly in fear of his father. This fear was well-founded since the father has a history of assaultive behavior in the home. Against this background, it is hardly surprising that Shane is now in therapy. . . .

To fail to acknowledge this boy's plight would be an affront to the clear legislative intent of Article 10 of the Family Court Act; to fail to label the father's actions as child abuse would strip the phrase of all meaning; to fail to warn other parents against this insidious type of abuse would perpetuate the suffering of countless other defenseless children.

The respondent father seeks to justify his verbal abuse of Shane as a form of legitimate parental discipline designed to cure the child of certain unspecified "girlie" behavior. He stated that it would be embarrasing (sic) to him if Shane were "queer." . . . While a parent's right to raise his or her child remains fundamental, it is equally fundamental that children have constitutional rights which must be respected by all, including their parents. In re Gault, 387 U.S. 1, and its progeny leave no doubt that the bill of rights is not for adults alone. Time and again, courts have reiterated the validity of state interference in the parental-child relationship when necessary to protect the child's health and welfare. . . .

The behavior of this respondent father is as serious a form of abuse as if he had plunged a knife into the stomach of this child. In fact, it's probably worse since the agony and heartache suffered by Shane has already assailed him for several years and constitutes a grave and imminent threat to his future psychological development. . . .

Therefore, on the entire record it is ordered that Shane T. be . . . declared to be an abused child by both respondents, [be] remanded to the Commissioner of Social Services, [and] that the Family Court Clinic be . . . directed to perform an immediate psychiatric and psychological evaluation of Shane on an emergency basis.

## Notes and Questions

1. *Scope of the problem.* Emotional maltreatment accounts for the smallest category of reported cases of abuse and neglect. Similarly, emotional neglect accounts for the smallest category of neglected children.[24] Unlike physical abuse, psychological abuse leaves no physical marks. Courts and commentators were slow to recognize emotional maltreatment as child abuse. Early definitions often were limited to serious physical injuries. Barbara J. Nelson, Making an Issue of Child Abuse 4-5 (1984); Marcia A. Kincanon, Comment, The Child Abuse That Doesn't Count: General and Emotional Neglect, 22 U.C. Davis L. Rev. 1039, 1045-1049 (1989).[25] See generally Maria R. Brassard et al., Psychological Maltreatment of Children and Youth (1987); James Garbarino et al., The Psychologically Battered Child (1986); J. Robert Shull, Note, Emotional and Psychological Child Abuse: Notes on Discourse, History, and Change, 51 Stan. L. Rev. 1665 (1999).

---

[24]. NIS III, supra note [4], at 3.6, 3.7 (emotionally abused children constitute 3.0 children per 1,000, compared to 5.7 physically abused children per 1,000, and 3.2 sexually abused children per 1,000). More specifically, emotionally abused children represent 28 percent of all abused children; emotionally neglected children represent 24 percent of all neglected children. In addition, emotionally abused children constitute 13 percent of all victims of child maltreatment (abuse and neglect combined); emotionally neglected children constitute 14 percent of all such victims. Id. at 3.3 (extrapolated from 1993 data in Table 3-1). Boys are more likely to be emotionally neglected than girls. NIS III Executive Summary, supra note [5], at 6 (boys' risk was 18 percent higher than girls').

[25]. Statistics reveal 46,315 reported cases of emotional abuse, constituting 6.1 percent of incidents of child abuse. U.S. Dept. of Commerce, Statistical Abstracts of the United States 217 (116th ed. 1996).

2. What was the definitional problem posed by the statute in *Shane*? Shane's father attempted to justify his behavior as a "legitimate form of discipline." When does "discipline" become emotional abuse? See In re S.M.B., 597 So. 2d 848 (Fla. Dist. Ct. App. 1992). Part of the difficulty of defining emotional abuse stems from the various purposes for which the term is used, that is, research, program eligibility, legal jurisdiction, medical intervention. See Bruce Fisher & Jane Berdie, Adolescent Abuse and Neglect: Issues of Incidence, Intervention and Service Delivery, 2 Child Abuse & Neglect 173, 177 (1978).

The third NIS defines emotional abuse as close confinement (tying, binding, and other inappropriate confinement or physical restriction); verbal or emotional assaults (belittling, denigrating, scapegoating, or other rejecting treatment as well as threats of abandonment, beatings, or sexual assault); other abusive, exploitative or punitive behaviors where physical contact did not occur (for example, intentional withholding of food, shelter, sleep, or other necessities or excessive demands).[26] Emotional neglect is "inadequate nurturance or affection, chronic or extreme domestic violence in the child's presence, knowingly permitting drug or alcohol abuse or other maladaptive behavior, failure (or refusal) to seek needed treatment for an emotional or behavioral problem, and other inattention of the child's developmental or emotional needs."[27] See also Garbarino, supra, at 8 (emotional maltreatment takes the forms of rejecting, isolating, terrorizing, ignoring, and stimulating antisocial behavior). What are the strengths and weaknesses of these various definitions? See Rolene Szur, Emotional Abuse and Neglect in Child Abuse: The Educational Perspective 110-111 (Peter Maher ed., 1987) (criticizing Garbarino's views).

3. What is the rationale of requiring a physical manifestation of psychological abuse, as in *Shane*? Should physical manifestations be a prerequisite for intervention? How might this requirement pose problems for a child who is more "hardy" than Shane? Suppose the emotional abuse has *not yet* resulted in injury or impairment? Do physical manifestations of a child's psychological problems always justify state intervention? Should statutes confer jurisdiction, for example, in the case of an underweight adolescent who has symptoms of an eating disorder such as anorexia nervosa?

4. Should intervention differ for victims of emotional versus physical abuse? Is psychological abuse always present in physical and sexual abuse? What intervention did *Shane* order? Was it appropriate? Can you think of alternatives? Should a tort action lie for infliction of emotional distress?

[26]. NIS III, supra note [4], at 3.6.
[27]. Id. at 3.9.

5. *Failure to protect.* In *Shane,* the child's mother fails to report the allegations to police and child protective services. Considerable controversy exists about the extent of liability if a mother fails to report the allegations or to protect a child from an abuser. Why might a mother fail to act? If she does fail to act, should she be liable for neglect or "passive" abuse? If she is a victim of abuse herself, should she be able to introduce expert testimony on battered woman syndrome? What should be the disposition in such cases? Should her parental rights be terminated? See In re R.A.L., 440 So. 2d 473 (Fla. Dist. Ct. App. 1983) (finding that the mother's inattentiveness to severe abuse by her boyfriend warranted termination of her parental rights). If the child dies as a result of the father's abuse, should the passive mother be charged with murder?

Short of leaving the marriage, what actions can a mother take? Suppose she is financially unable to leave? Are courts likely to find a *father,* in a similar situation, liable for "passive" abuse? On the issue of failure to protect, see Bryan A. Liang and Wendy L. Macfarlane, Murder by Omission: Child Abuse and the Passive Parent, 36 Harv. J. on Legis. 397, 425, 431-443 (1999); Michelle S. Jacobs, Criminal Law: Requiring Battered Women Die: Murder Liability for Mothers Under Failure to Protect Statutes, 88 J. Crim. L. & Criminology 579 (1998); Evan Stark, A Failure to Protect: Unraveling the "Battered Mother's Dilemma," 27 Western State U.L. Rev. 29 (1999-2000); Jeanne A. Fugate, Note, Who's Failing Whom: A Critical Look at Failure-to-Protect Laws, 76 N.Y.U. L. Rev. 272 (2001).

6. *Adolescent abuse.* Should the form of intervention differ according to the age of the victim? Adolescents predominate as victims of psychological abuse.[28] In addition, adolescents also experience higher rates of sexual abuse. Richard P. Barth & David S. Derezotes, Preventing Adolescent Abuse: Effective Strategies and Techniques 1 (1990). Physical abuse of adolescents often tends to be severe, as parents feel that more "routine" punishments (for example, spanking) are less effective with older children. Pamela D. Mayhall & Katherine Eastlack Norgard, Child Abuse and Neglect: Sharing Responsibility 65 (1986). Despite the frequency and severity of adolescent abuse, adolescents often fail to report such abuse. Barth & Derezotes, supra, at 2. See also Murray A. Straus & Denise A. Donnelly, Corporal Punishment of Adolescents by American Parents, 24 Youth & Soc'y 420 (1993).

7. *Consequences of adolescent abuse.* Adolescent abuse contributes to high rates of substance abuse, suicidal attempts, and suicide ideation. Adolescent abuse is also a contributing factor to runaway behavior and adolescent prostitution. Homeless Youth: The Saga of "Pushouts" and

---

[28]. U.S. Dept. of Health & Human Servs., Natl. Center on Child Abuse and Neglect, Study of National Incidence and Prevalence of Child Abuse and Neglect: 1988 at 5.2.1.

"Throwaways" in America, Hearing Before the Senate Comm. on the Judiciary, 96th Cong., 2d Sess. 15 (1980). Adolescent abuse is linked to a higher incidence of AIDS. Renee M. Cunningham et al., The Association of Physical and Sexual Abuse with HIV Risk Behaviors in Adolescence and Young Adulthood: Implications for Public Health, 18 Child Abuse & Neglect 233 (1994). See generally Jane Levine Powers & Barbara Weiss Jaklitsch, Understanding Survivors of Abuse: Stories of Homeless and Runaway Adolescents (1989); D. Kelly Weisberg, Children of the Night: A Study of Adolescent Prostitution (1985).

Should child abuse serve as an affirmative defense to parricide? Some youths who kill their parents were abused as children. See Jennifer R. James, Turning the Tables: Redefining Self-Defense Theory for Children Who Kill Abusive Parents, 18 Law & Psychol. Rev. 393, 395-396 (1994). This criminal defense has elicited considerable public interest in the wake of the trial of Lyle and Erik Menendez for killing their wealthy parents in 1989. For a criticism of this defense, see Alan Dershowitz, Abuse Excuse (1994). See generally Kathleen M. Heide, Why Kids Kill Parents: Child Abuse and Adolescent Homicide (1992); Paul Mones, Battered Child Syndrome: Understanding Parricide, Trial, Feb. 1994, at 24; Jamie Heather Sacks, Comment, A New Age of Understanding: Allowing Self-Defense Claims for Battered Children Who Kill Their Abusers, 10 J. Contemp. Health L. & Poly. 349 (1993); Joelle A. Moreno, Comment, Killing Daddy: Developing a Self-Defense Strategy for the Abused Child, 137 U. Pa. L. Rev. 1281 (1989).

8. *Abuse of gay and lesbian youth.* Gay and lesbian youth, particularly, are victims of emotional abuse. See Elvira R. Arriola, The Penalties for Puppy Love: Institutionalized Violence Against Lesbian, Gay, Bisexual, and Transgendered Youth, 1 J. Gender Race & Just. 429, 439-445 (1998); Sonia Renee Martin, Note, A Child's Right to Be Gay: Addressing the Emotional Maltreatment of Queer Youth, 48 Hastings L.J. 167 (1996). One reason is parents' difficulty accepting youth's sexual orientation. Dennis Anderson, Family and Peer Relations of Gay Adolescents, 14 Adolescent Psychiatry 162, 165 (1987).[29] Such abuse contributes to the disproportionate number of suicide attempts by gay and lesbian youth.[30]

---

[29]. In a study conducted by the National Gay Task Force, 33 percent of gay and lesbian youth reported emotional abuse by family members. Paul Gibson, Gay Male and Lesbian Youth Suicide, in U.S. Dept. of Health & Human Servs. Youth Suicide Report 110, 127 (1989) (citing the National Gay Task Force study).

[30]. These youth are two to three times more likely to attempt suicide than other youth and constitute 30 percent of completed suicides. Id. at 110. Emotional maltreatment by these youth also contributes to substance abuse. Id. at 113. See also Rich Savin-Williams, Verbal and Physical Abuse as Stressors in the Lives of Lesbian, Gay Male, and Bisexual Youths: Associations with Social Problems, Running Away, Substance Abuse, Prostitution, and Suicide, 62 J. Consulting & Clinical Psychol. 261, 263 (1994) (60 percent of gay and lesbian youth are substance abusers, stemming, in part, from feelings of parental rejection).

Ethnic gay and lesbian adolescents who are abused may suffer the most severe psychological consequences. Rich C. Savin-Williams & R. G. Roderiquez, A Developmental, Clinical Perspective on Lesbian, Gay Male, and Bisexual Youths, in Adolescent Sexuality: Advances in Adolescent Development 77, 94 (T. P. Gullotta et al. eds., 1993).

### e. Sexual Abuse

■ **IN RE JACLYN P.**
*578 N.Y.S.2d 252 (App. Div. 1992),* **appeal dismissed,** *650 N.E.2d 1322, aff'd, 658 N.E.2d 1042,* **cert. denied,** *116 S. Ct. 816 (1996)*

Before KUNZEMAN, J.P., and EIBER, MILLER and RITTER, JJ. . . .

Robert P. is the father of Melissa P. and Jaclyn P. In or about July 1990 the petitioner Nassau County Department of Social Services commenced proceedings [in Family Court] against the respondent, alleging that he had sexually abused and neglected both daughters. . . .

At the fact-finding hearing, Melissa's mother testified that she first became aware of a problem in November 1989 when her niece and her daughter Jaclyn both reported, within approximately one week of one another, that Melissa had hurt each of them by placing her fingers inside their vaginas. When confronted, Melissa reported that she had been "playing the doctor game" taught to her by her father, the respondent. The mother testified that Melissa demonstrated this game by "vigorously" placing her fingers between the legs of a doll. Melissa's mother also testified that Melissa reported to her that her father had taught her "the weenie game" in which her father placed his penis in Melissa's mouth. Furthermore, the witness stated that Melissa was exhibiting behavioral problems such as wetting herself and that she was suffering from nightmares. Alarmed, Melissa's mother contacted the police and the New York State Child Protective Services.

CPS caseworker Debra Ross testified that she saw Melissa twice monthly for a total of 25 visits. On one such visit, Melissa reportedly described the "doctor game" to Ms. Ross, demonstrating it by trying to "poke" her fingers between the legs of a stuffed animal. Melissa reportedly told Ms. Ross that the respondent touched her in the same manner. When Ms. Ross tried to inquire further, Melissa ran from the room, carrying the stuffed animal. Melissa reportedly told Ms. Ross that she was afraid to be left alone with her father.

Pursuant to the recommendation of CPS personnel, Melissa was taken to see Yael Layish, a psychiatric social worker who serves on the "family crisis team" of North Shore University Hospital. Ms. Layish . . . testified that she first examined Melissa in December 1989. [Melissa reported] to Ms. Layish, how, after undressing her, the respondent placed his fingers in her rectum and vagina, exposed his penis for Melissa to touch, and how he placed his penis in Melissa's mouth. Melissa told Ms. Layish that she wanted her father to stop playing the doctor game. Ms. Layish recounted other incidents during her therapy sessions with Melissa. . . . Upon consideration of all of the foregoing, Ms. Layish testified that, in her opinion, Melissa was acting in a manner consistent with that of a sexually abused child. She did not believe that Melissa had been "coached" into making these allegations.

Dr. Bruce Bogard, a pediatrician at Schneider's Children's Hospital of Long Island Jewish Medical Center, testified that he examined Melissa on February 9, 1990, for physical signs of sexual abuse. His rectal examination of Melissa disclosed nothing unusual, and her external genital structures were normal, showing no evidence of trauma. Her hymenal opening, however, measured seven millimeters. Dr. Bogard explained that generally, the hymenal opening in a normal prepubertal child is less than five millimeters. . . . Dr. Bogard explained, however, that sexual abuse may occur without resulting in physical findings and that digital penetration could occur without leaving a mark on the hymen. He stated that a finding of a hymenal opening greater than 10 millimeters would be more indicative of abuse, but that an opening of seven millimeters fell within a borderline area.

Dr. Howard Kirschen, a board-certified child psychiatrist, testified that he interviewed and evaluated Melissa, as well as Melissa's mother, father and younger sister Jaclyn. . . . Dr. Kirschen acknowledged that there was a possibility that Melissa had been "coached" into making false allegations against her father. . . . Nevertheless, it was Dr. Kirschen's opinion that Melissa showed signs consistent with being a victim of sexual abuse.

Testifying for the respondent, Dr. Mark Rich, a pediatric urologist, stated that he examined Melissa and found no physical evidence of sexual abuse. Dr. Rich stated that he found Melissa's genitalia to be normal, without any signs of physical abuse or trauma, and that the size of Melissa's hymen "was not particularly out of the norm of what a normal little girl that age would have . . . approximately one finger breadth." Dr. Rich conceded, however, that physical evidence of abuse is "often" not present in victims of abuse and that the absence of such evidence does not rule out a finding of sex abuse. . . .

Florence P., Melissa's paternal grandmother, testified that she supervised Melissa's visitation with her father. . . . The witness stated that Melissa never complained to her of any problems with the respondent.

Dr. Monty Weinstein, a psychologist and family therapist, testified that he observed Melissa and Jaclyn interact with their father on two occasions. He described a "warm, bonding nurturing type of relationship" between father and children. Based upon his observations of the interactions between the children and their father, Dr. Weinstein opined that the allegations of abuse were unfounded, as abused children would not react to the abuser in the warm and loving manner Jaclyn and Melissa exhibited toward the respondent. . . . However, Dr. Weinstein's observations occurred over a period of "a couple of hours," during which he never spoke to the children, nor did he at any time speak to their mother. Rather, Dr. Weinstein's conclusions rested almost exclusively upon his observations of the children interacting with the respondent, the very party paying his expert fee, who was aware that Dr. Weinstein was observing him at the time of his interactions with the children. Dr. Weinstein made no attempts to question the children as to whether or not they had been abused.

The respondent Robert P. denied that he sexually abused his children. Rather, he stated that the only times he ever touched his daughters' genital areas was in connection with cleaning them after changing their diapers or in bathing them. Furthermore, he asserted that the allegations of sexual abuse were fabricated by his wife, who was engaged in an extramarital affair and who was trying to influence future custody determinations.

Dr. Naomi Adler, a psychologist, testified as the court's expert witness. Dr. Adler saw the respondent over several sessions in an attempt to evaluate his psychological condition. She noted that the respondent refused to submit to two of the tests that would have been administered as part of her evaluation, and she found him to be defensive and suffering from a nonspecified personality disorder. The respondent's refusal to cooperate fully prevented Dr. Adler from determining whether he was aroused by deviant sexual stimuli, and Dr. Adler offered no opinion as to whether or not the respondent had in fact abused his children.

In addition to the reports of the various expert witnesses received in evidence, the court conducted an in camera interview of Melissa. Melissa, however, refused to cooperate during this proceeding, and thus revealed nothing about the allegations of abuse.

At the conclusion of the fact-finding hearing, the [Family Court] dismissed the petition, finding that the evidence was "even," and thus the petitioner DSS had failed to prove its case by a preponderance of the evidence. . . . Although the determination of the trier of fact is entitled to appropriate deference, in this case we find that the weight of the evidence is so strongly in favor of a finding of sexual abuse that the petition should be sustained.

To begin with, Melissa's mother recounted the allegations revealed to her by Melissa. Although these allegations arose within the context of a custody dispute, they were corroborated by the validation testimony of Ms. Layish, the independent court-appointed psychiatric social worker. [Ms. Layish's testimony is] highly reliable, since she has had more than ample opportunity to observe and evaluate Melissa's repeated reports of abuse. Indeed, that Melissa told Ms. Layish of her father's abusive actions on several occasions only further serves to underscore Melissa's veracity, since it is unlikely that she could maintain such a consistent series of fabrications. . . .

Other than the respondent's denials, the only evidence tending to support a finding that Melissa had not been abused was provided by the respondent's paid expert, Dr. Weinstein. [W]e find that Dr. Weinstein's limited access to the children and the limited scope of his analysis renders his opinion unpersuasive. The respondent's other expert witnesses similarly do not persuade us that Melissa had not been abused by her father.

On balance, our review of the entire record leads us to conclude that the allegations of abuse were established by a preponderance of the credible evidence. Accordingly, . . . we remit this matter to the Family Court, Nassau County, for a dispositional hearing.

■ **D. KELLY WEISBERG, THE "DISCOVERY" OF SEXUAL ABUSE: EXPERTS' ROLE IN LEGAL POLICY FORMULATION**
*18 U.C. Davis L. Rev. 1, 1-2, 5-8, 18-19, 25-28, 31 (1984)*

Despite evidence of sexual abuse of children throughout history, the labeling of this phenomenon as a pervasive social problem is relatively recent. The phenomenon has received so much attention that it has been labeled several times in the past half century. . . .

Legal policy directed at sexual abuse of children has undergone several successive reformulations in the past half century. In each stage, a new definition of criminal behavior and proscribed sanctions were enacted into law. Different participants were involved in each successive stage of the labeling process. . . .

### I. ERA OF THE SEXUAL PSYCHOPATH: FROM "BADNESS TO SICKNESS"[15]

The first comprehensive legal labeling of child molestation appeared in the 1930's. [P]sychiatrists were the first experts relied upon to define the problem. Their initial reaction was to label such sexual crimes as indicative of an "illness," one they were uniquely qualified to treat. The impetus for the labeling came from several sexually-motivated murders of children in the late 1930's. . . . The incomprehensibility of sexual

---

15. The term was coined by two sociologists in their social historical analysis of the transformation from religious and criminal to medical designations of deviance. See generally P. Conrad & J. Schneider, Deviance and Medicalization: From Badness to Sickness (1980).

crimes involving children spurred the call for experts — qualified to understand and assess the situation, to study the problem, and to make recommendations for its solution.

[P]sychiatrists diagnosed child molestation as a form of mental illness, terming the illness "sexual psychopathy." They suggested a treatment for the patient: the patient should be hospitalized until "well" or normal again. . . . Statutes utilized medical terminology and labeled the offender with psychiatric nomenclature. . . .

[T]he call for these experts came at a time when the public was increasingly aware of the promise of psychiatry. . . . Freud's writings in the early twentieth century stimulated interest in the use of psychiatry to explain the irrational. World War I increased public awareness of psychiatry's value in treating war casualties. The Leopold-Loeb[16] trial revealed that psychiatry could have specific application to criminal law. These factors contributed to the emergence of psychiatrists in legal policymaking. . . .

## II. The First Relabeling: The 1950's

Legislation in the 1950's reflects the reconstruction and relabeling of child molestation. . . . Several states repealed or amended their sexual psychopath statutes and enacted different legislation dealing with sex offenses. [The sexual psychopath became the "mentally disordered sex offender" or "sexually dangerous person."] One trend was evident: [m]edical nomenclature was deemphasized, and criminal terminology became more prominent. . . .

Several factors explain the relabeling of this social problem in the 1950's. [S]ocietal recognition of psychiatry's shortcomings may [provide one explanation]. [L]egislation of the 1950's reflected a more realistic appraisal of the answers psychiatry could and could not supply. . . . The acute shortage of psychiatric personnel in public institutions after World War II frustrated hopes of treatment for sex offenders. . . . Another explanation for the relabeling process may be found in sexual behavior research. An important influence on policymakers was Alfred Kinsey [who] helped dispel certain widespread beliefs about sex offenders [i.e., that sex criminals progressed from minor to major sex crimes, and that sex crimes were increasing].

## III. The Third Label — Policymaking in the 1970's

In the early 1970's child molestation received yet another label: "sexual abuse," or "child sexual abuse." The new label appeared in both

---

16. This trial in 1924 of two middle-class youths for murder was the first time psychiatrists testified as expert witnesses to explain criminal behavior. See Note, The Leopold-Loeb Case, 97 Cent. L.J. 327 (1924).

federal and state legislation. The federal Child Abuse Prevention and Treatment Act, enacted in 1974, required each state to adopt a uniform definition of abuse that included "physical or mental injury, sexual abuse or exploitation, negligent treatment, or maltreatment" in order to qualify for federal monies for the prevention and treatment of abuse. . . .

New experts played a role in the labeling process: psychologists and social workers became preeminent in this period. These experts focused on the familial offender — the father or stepfather molester. Instead of hospitalization or civil commitment for the patient, the recommended treatment was family counseling. The experts viewed the entire family, rather than merely the perpetrator, as the source of the problem. For the first time attention was also focused on the child victim, for whom counseling was also recommended. . . .

## Notes and Questions

1. *Empirical data.* Sexual abuse constitutes the third most common type of child maltreatment (after neglect and then physical abuse).[31] How does sexual abuse by family members differ from molestation by strangers? In contrast to common belief, most offenders are known to the child, as in *Jaclyn P.* A classic study reveals that 27 percent of offenders are parents, stepparents, or mother's boyfriend (including 13 percent natural fathers compared to 14 percent stepfathers or residential paramours). Only 25 percent are strangers (the remainder were nonresidential relatives or acquaintances).[32] Most sexual abuse occurs in the child's own home. Often, the child is subjected to repeated offenses prior to discovery.

Research studies report many negative long-term effects suffered by the victims of sexual abuse, including truancy, delinquency, running away, promiscuity and prostitution, sexual disturbances, depression, suicide, and revictimization. See Joseph H. Beitchman et al., A Review of the Long-Term Effects of Child Sexual Abuse, 16 Child Abuse & Neglect 101 (1992); A. Browne & David Finkelhor, Impact of Sexual Abuse: A Review of the Research, 99 Psychol. Bull. 66 (1986).

[31]. Based on 1999 data, victims of neglect account for 58.4 percent of all child victims of maltreatment, victims of physical abuse for 21.3 percent, and victims of sexual abuse for 11.3 percent. Child Maltreatment 1999, supra note [19], at 2-3.

[32]. Vincent De Francis, Protecting the Child Victim of Sex Crimes Committed by Adults vii, 40-41 (American Humane Assoc., 2d ed. 1981). Researchers who conducted the national incidence studies categorize perpetrator relationships differently than De Francis in his classic study. For example, NIS data for 1994 reveals that more than one-fourth of sexually abused children were abused by a biological parent; 25 percent were sexually abused by "other parents or parent-substitutes, such as step-parents, fathers' girlfriends," and less than one half were abused by someone other than the above perpetrators. NIS III, supra note [5], at 6.5.

Legal responses to familial sexual abuse may encompass civil proceedings, as in *Jaclyn P.*, conferring jurisdiction over the victim by the juvenile court, as well as criminal proceedings against the perpetrator. Some childhood victims when they become adults also initiate tort claims to recover damages from the perpetrator.

2. The girls in *Jaclyn P.* were prepubescent. Although the median age of sexual abuse victims is 11, children as young as infants may be sexually abused. Girls are sexually abused more often than boys.[33] How might the consequences of sexual abuse differ based on the victim's age? Gender?

See generally Ann W. Burgess et al., Sexual Assault of Children and Adolescents (1978); David Finkelhor, Child Sexual Abuse: New Theory and Research (1984); Judith Lewis Herman, Father-Daughter Incest (1981); Karin Meiselman, Incest: A Psychological Study of Causes and Effects with Treatment Recommendations (1978); P. Mrazek & C. Kempe, eds., Sexually Abused Children and Their Families (1981). On the lesser known problem of sexual abuse of boys, see generally Mic Hunter, Abused Boys: The Neglected Victims of Sexual Abuse (1990).

3. Sexual abuse constitutes a continuum, ranging from indecent exposure and fondling, to sodomy and intercourse. Should the legal consequences (civil versus criminal) differ depending on the type of abuse? The extent of coercion? Consider that in 60 percent of cases, the child was coerced by force or threat of harm; in 15 percent by bribes; and in 25 percent, the "lure was more subtle and was based on the child's natural loyalty and affection." Vincent De Francis, Protecting the Child Victim of Sex Crimes Committed by Adults vii (American Humane Assoc., 2d ed., 1981).

4. How was the abuse in *Jaclyn* discovered? Unlike physical abuse, sexual abuse rarely reveals physical manifestations, although pregnancy and venereal disease do occur.[34] More commonly, behavioral indicators are present, such as unusually sophisticated sexual knowledge, infantile behavior, appearing withdrawn, poor peer relationships, unwillingness to participate in physical activities, delinquent acts, or running away. Irving J. Sloan, Protection of Abused Victims 6-7 (1982). This lack of physical manifestations presents evidentiary problems (see pages 1032-1040).

Many sexually abused children first come to attention when they, in turn, abuse other children. Richard Krugman & David P. H. Jones, Incest and Other Forms of Sexual Abuse, in The Battered Child 286, 290 (Ray E. Helfer & Ruth S. Kempe eds., 1987). How should the courts and child protective services deal with sexually abused children such as Jaclyn P., who in turn abuse other children? Suppose the victim in *Jaclyn P.* was an adolescent boy? Data suggest that rapists and child

[33]. De Francis, supra note [32], at vii (ratio is 10:1).
[34]. De Francis reported that 29 of 263 victims became pregnant as a result of the offense. Id. at x.

molesters often have been sexually abused as children. Nicholas Groth, Sexual Trauma in the Life Histories of Rapists and Child Molesters, 4 Victimology 1023 (1979). See generally Nicholas Groth, The Adolescent Sexual Offender and His Prey, 21 Intl. J. Offender Therapy & Comp. Criminology 249 (1977).

5. The father's expert in *Jaclyn P.* testified as to the warm relationship between the father and children. Is a close parent-child relationship inconsistent with the existence of sexual abuse?

6. *Fabricating abuse and suggestibility.* A psychiatric social worker in *Jaclyn* testified that she did not believe the child had been "coached." How likely are children to fabricate sexual abuse? Some researchers conclude that children are unlikely to fabricate sexual abuse. Gail S. Goodman & Alison Clarke-Stewart, Suggestibility in Children's Testimony: Implications for Sexual Abuse Prosecutions, in The Suggestibility of Children's Recollections: Implications for Eyewitness Testimony 92, 98-99 (John Doris ed., 1991). Other research reveals that children can be motivated to lie only when afraid of reprisal or to keep a secret. Douglass P. Peters, Commentary: Response to Goodman, in Suggestibility of Children's Recollections, supra, at 86, 89-90.

Studies of allegations of abuse report very low incidence of untrue allegations. See Mark D. Everson & Barbara W. Boat, False Allegations of Sexual Abuse by Children and Adolescents, 28 J. Am. Acad. Child & Adolescent Psychiatry 230, 231 (1989); Katherine C. Faller, Child Sexual Abuse: An Interdisciplinary Manual for Diagnosis, Case Management, and Treatment 22, 126 (1988); David P. H. Jones & J. Malbourne Mc-Graw, Reliable and Fictitious Accounts of Sexual Abuse in Children, 2 J. Interpersonal Violence 27, 31 (1987).

How susceptible are children to the suggestions of others (for example, caretakers, interviewers, and so forth) that abuse took place? Can these suggestions distort the child's recollection of events? Psychological studies report that children are not more suggestible than adults, although younger children (younger than age four or five) may be more capable of being influenced. Research also reveals that children tend to be more suggestible about peripheral details (that is, time, place of abuse), rather than salient issues (that is, occurrence of abuse, type of touching). See John E. B. Myers, 1 Evidence in Child Abuse and Neglect 230-233 (1992); Lucy S. McGough, Child Witnesses: Fragile Voices in the American Legal System 67-69 (1994) (both citing research). But cf. Stephen J. Ceci & Richard D. Friedman, The Suggestibility of Children: Scientific Research and Legal Implications, 86 Cornell L. Rev. 33 (2000).

Should the presence of suggestive interrogative techniques require a pretrial ("taint") hearing to determine whether the child's statements have been so tainted by interrogation that the statements should be excluded as unreliable? See State v. Michaels, 642 A.2d 1372, 1379, 1384 (N.J. 1994). See generally Lisa Manshel, The Child Witness and the

Presumption of Authenticity after *State v. Michaels*, 26 Seton Hall L. Rev. 685 (1996); John E. B. Myers, Taint Hearings for Child Witnesses? A Step in the Wrong Direction, 46 Baylor L. Rev. 873 (1994).

7. *Abuse allegations in custody proceedings.* Jaclyn's father denied that he sexually abused his daughter, claiming that his wife fabricated the allegations because the couple was having marital problems and she wanted to influence custody decisionmaking. Should courts treat sexual abuse charges made by a divorcing parent as less credible? Alternatively, is the harm of sexual abuse sufficiently grave that courts should automatically award temporary custody to the other parent when allegations surface? See John E. B. Myers, Allegation of Child Sexual Abuse in Custody and Visitation Litigation: Recommendations for Improved Fact Finding and Child Protection, 28 J. Fam. L. 1, 37 (1989-1990). Might this protective policy result in a large number of unsubstantiated claims? Does the rationale of child protection justify this inroad on family privacy? See generally Alan J. Klein, Forensic Issues in Sexual Abuse Allegations in Custody/Visitation Litigation, 18 Law & Psychol. Rev. 247 (1994); Heather J. Rhoades, Note and Comment, *Zamstein v. Marvasti:* Is a Duty Owed to Alleged Child Sexual Abusers?, 30 Conn. L. Rev. 1411, 1412 (1998).

8. *Representation for the abused child in custody proceedings.* Many commentators advocate the appointment of counsel when allegations of abuse are raised in custody disputes.[35] Under CAPTA, 42 U.S.C. §5106a(b)(6) (1994), states were required (to qualify for federal funding) to provide for the appointment of guardians ad litem for every child involved in child abuse or neglect proceedings. Despite the federal requirement, CAPTA did not require that states appoint attorneys as guardians ad litem. Recent years have witnessed increasing demands for guidelines for guardians ad litem and lawyers who represent children. In 1996, the ABA House of Delegates approved guidelines for lawyers representing abused or neglected children. See American Bar Association, Standards of Practice for Lawyers Who Represent Children in Abuse and Neglect Cases (1996). The Standards clarify the role of the lawyer appointed to represent the child, specifically providing that lawyers should serve in the role of advocate (rather than as guardian ad litem or in a dual capacity) irrespective of the child's age. See generally David R. Katner, Coming to Praise, Not to Bury, the New ABA Standards of Practice for Lawyers Who Represent Children in Abuse and Neglect Cases, 14 Geo. J. Legal Ethics 103 (2000).

9. As the expert in *Jaclyn P.* concedes, sexual abuse rarely leaves physical manifestations. Does sexual abuse evoke intervention merely because

[35]. See Keren S. Bischoff, Comment, The Voice of the Child: Independent Legal Representation of Children in Private Custody Disputes When Sexual Abuse Is Alleged, 138 U. Pa. L. Rev. 1383 (1990); David Peterson, Comment, Judicial Discretion is Insufficient: Minors' Due Process Right to Participate with Counsel When Divorce Custody Disputes Involve Allegations of Child Abuse, 25 Golden Gate U. L. Rev. 513 (1995).

of the ensuing emotional harm? Does it, therefore, present an arguably weaker case for intervention? Psychologist James Garbarino responds:

> [R]ather than casting psychological maltreatment as an ancillary issue, subordinate to other forms of abuse and neglect, we should place it as the centerpiece of efforts to understand family functioning and to protect children. In almost all cases, it is the psychological consequences of an act that define that act as abusive. This is true of physical abuse . . . ; it is also true of sexual abuse (since sexual acts have little or no intrinsic meaning apart from their social psychological connotations — as the incredible variety of norms regarding sexual activity in childhood and adolescence across cultures suggests).

James Garbarino et al., The Psychologically Battered Child 7 (1986).

Should the state intervene only when sexual abuse results in "physical harm at the hands of sexually assaulting parents"? See Joseph Goldstein et al., Before the Best Interests of the Child 62 (1979). Short of this criterion, Goldstein, Freud, and Solnit would permit intervention only if a parent had been convicted (or acquitted by reason of insanity) of a sexual offense. They explain this controversial recommendation:

> Sexual relations between parent and child tend to remain well-guarded family secrets. When suspicion is aroused, the harm done by inquiry may be more than that caused by not intruding. The harm already inflicted on the child — and it may be difficult to learn its extent — is aggravated by violations of family integrity, particularly by the investigation that is triggered. Further, since no consensus exists about the proper treatment or about what disposition would be less harmful, there is no justification from the child's point of view for dragging the matter into the open by invoking the child's placement process. For these reasons, justification for separating the child and offending parent seems best left to the criminal law — to its high standard of evidentiary proof and its goal of reinforcing society's moral position. After a conviction or an insanity acquittal, there is no longer any reason for not incurring the risks of disposition, of determining the least detrimental alternative.[21]

> This ground is therefore limited to children whose parents are convicted, or acquitted by reason of insanity, of a sexual offense against them. It acknowledges that we know enough to declare that a child is harmed even by a parent's nonviolent sexual abuse, but not enough to know that state intervention can offer something less detrimental. Thus, the authority to assume the risks of intervention, including the termination of parental rights, arises only after the parent-child relationship has been severed by the criminal process.

---

21. This ground's recognition of the limits of law and knowledge about treatment should not obscure our belief that it is desirable for such parents on their own initiative to seek psychological assistance for themselves and their child. The state should provide such opportunities for those who want help.

Id. at 64-65. Are these views persuasive?

10. *Prospective abuse.* Researchers have noted a pattern of sequential sexual abuse: When one abused child is removed from the home, a younger sibling is likely to become the next victim. See, e.g., Judith Lewis Herman, Father-Daughter Incest 94 (1981). If a child has been removed from home pending investigation of sexual abuse, should siblings also be removed? Compare In re Katherine J., 335 N.Y.S.2d 815, 819 (Fam. Ct. 1972), with People v. Johnny S., 579 N.E.2d 926 (Ill. App. Ct. 1991). Recall also In re Juvenile Appeal, supra.

## Problems

1. At Angela's first visit to Dr. Smith for prenatal care, he orders blood tests that confirm his suspicion that she is using cocaine. Dr. Smith confronts Angela but she refuses to seek drug treatment as he advises. When she again tests positive, Dr. Smith reports his concerns to Child Protective Services (CPS). CPS files a motion to take Angela's 36-week fetus into immediate protective custody pursuant to a statute that requires a showing "that the welfare of the child demands the child's immediate removal from his or her present custody." The motion is supported by an affidavit from Dr. Smith stating his medical opinion that without intervention, Angela's fetus would suffer serious physical harm.

The juvenile court issues an order for summary removal directing that "petitioner's unborn child shall be detained [pursuant to statute] by the sheriff's department and transported to County Memorial Hospital for inpatient treatment and protection. Such detention will by necessity result in the detention of the unborn child's mother." Before the order is executed, Angela appears voluntarily at an inpatient drug treatment facility. The juvenile court then amends its order to provide that detention will be at that facility but if Angela attempts to leave or fails to participate, both she and her fetus are to be detained and transported to County Memorial Hospital. Following issuance of the summary removal order, CPS files another petition under the state Children in Need of Supervision (CHINS) statute that provides that the juvenile court has jurisdiction if the "parent, guardian or legal custodian neglects, refuses or is unable for reasons other than poverty to provide necessary care, food, clothing, medical or dental care or shelter so as to seriously endanger the physical health of the child." For the designation of birth date, the petition states "Due Date 10/4/95" and for the sex of the child, the petition states "Unknown."

Angela seeks a supervisory writ to prohibit the court from continuing to exercise jurisdiction in the CHINS proceeding. She asserts that the relevant statutes do not vest the juvenile court with jurisdiction over her or her fetus. Alternatively, if the statute does grant authority, she claims that it violates procedural and substantive due process and equal protection. What result? See Angela M.W. v. Kruzicki, 561 N.W.2d 729 (Wis. 1997). Cf. Whitner v. South Carolina, 492 S.E.2d 777 (S.C. 1997). Do drug tests on urine samples of maternity patients who are suspected of using cocaine violate the Fourth Amendment? See Ferguson v. City of Charleston, 532 U.S. 67 (2001).

2. Denise Perrigo, a 29-year-old single mother, is breast-feeding her two-year-old daughter, Cherlyn. Curious about whether it is normal to feel sexually aroused while nursing, Denise calls a community volunteer center to find the number for La Leche League, a breast-feeding support group. She is mistakenly referred to the Rape Crisis Center where a volunteer interprets her question as evidence of sexual abuse and reports it to the child abuse hotline. After an investigation, including a five-hour police interrogation, Denise spends the night in jail. Criminal charges are dismissed subsequently, but social workers summarily remove Cherlyn from Denise's custody and petition the local juvenile court to assert jurisdiction over Cherlyn as an abused or neglected child. The juvenile court awards temporary custody to the state social services department and places the child in foster care. Denise appeals. What result? See Lisa Levitt Ryckman, A Simple Question Leads Mom to Jail, Chi. Trib., Feb. 9, 1992, News, at 16.

3. John, the stepfather of a 15-year-old girl, is a nudist who likes to walk around the house nude. He has a habit of walking in on his stepdaughter while she is in the bathtub and asking her sexually explicit questions, such as whether she wants to show him her genitals or whether she would like help learning how to kiss. He tells her that she is free to say no. His stepdaughter feels uncomfortable with her stepfather's nudity, his embarrassing questions, and his violations of her privacy. She says he often says "weird" things to her. John is charged with sexual abuse. He claims that he has never actually touched his stepdaughter in an inappropriate way, and argues that oral conversations, without any evidence of physical or emotional abuse, do not constitute sexual abuse. What result? See John D. v. Dept. of Soc. Servs., 744 N.E.2d 659 (Mass. App. Ct. 2001).

### 3. Procedures

#### a. Reporting Requirements

■ **PEOPLE v. HODGES**
*13 Cal. Rptr. 2d 412 (App. Dept. Super. Ct. 1992)*

Moon, Acting Presiding Judge.

In what appears to be a case of first impression, we are asked to determine whether appellants, a pastor and assistant pastor of the South

Bay United Pentecostal Church, who are also the president and principal of the South Bay Christian Academy, were properly convicted of violating the Child Abuse and Neglect Reporting Act, Penal Code, section
11166, subdivision (a). The statute provides . . . "[A]ny child care custodian . . . who has knowledge of or observes a child in his or her professional capacity or within the scope of his or her employment whom he
or she knows or reasonably suspects has been the victim of child abuse
shall report the known or suspected instance of child abuse to a child protective agency immediately or as soon as practically possible. . . ." . . .

At trial, the victim, 20-year-old Christine G., testified that she had attended South Bay Christian Academy. [W]hen she was 17 years old (in
March 1988) she decided to seek help from appellant Hodges [president
of the school and pastor of the church] by telling him her stepfather, Lyn
M., a minister in the church, had been molesting her for many years.
Christine testified she confided in a classroom teacher who, in turn,
made an appointment with Mr. Hodges during the schoolday. [Mr.
Hodges then informed her stepfather of the allegations.] Christine testified she met with Mr. Hodges the day after he spoke with her stepfather.
He told her that her stepfather confessed to everything and that he
would be handling the situation. Mr. Hodges told Christine not to tell
anyone about what her stepfather had done to her.

A few days later Mr. Hodges called Christine back into his office. He
told her he had sent her stepfather to a retreat. Mr. Hodges handed her
a letter of apology from her stepfather. This was approximately two
weeks after their initial meeting.

Mr. Hodges wanted Christine's mother and stepfather to come into
the office after she read the letter. . . . Christine told Mr. Hodges she did
not want to talk to her parents. He insisted, and they came into the office and spoke with her. Christine pleaded with Mr. Hodges not to make
her go home with them because she was afraid of her stepfather. Mr.
Hodges arranged to have her parents pick her up from school the next
day and bring her home. Instead, Christine ran away. She also told others about the situation even though Mr. Hodges told her not to.

After running away, Christine received instructions to return to see
Mr. Hodges. She went to his office during school hours. Appellant Nobbs
was also there. Mr. Hodges told her unless she returned home she would
not be allowed to return to school and she would not graduate. This
meeting was held approximately a week and a half after Christine was
given the letter. Christine returned home and left immediately after
graduation. . . .

[During a subsequent investigation by a child abuse detective for the
police department, Mr. Hodges was asked why he did not report the information to the police or child protective services or if he knew he was
mandated to report.] Mr. Hodges told the officer he knew of the reporting laws, and he understood he was a mandated reporter. Mr.

Hodges told the officer he wanted to take care of the matter within the church. Mr. Hodges stated he disciplined the stepfather by having him write a letter of apology to the victim and by having the stepfather confess in front of the entire congregation. Additionally, Mr. Hodges took away his ministerial license. [Nobbs had a similar interview with the detective.]

Mr. Hodges testified [that] he did not contact the police because he believed that his role in the matter was a pastoral one, specifically dealing with Christine's inability to forgive her stepfather. He did not believe the incidents described by Christine were "sexual abuse"; he believed they were sins. He stated he had to follow the Scriptures concerning disciplining a Christian.

Mr. Nobbs testified . . . he discussed the situation with Mr. Hodges primarily in the context of his taking over Lyn M.'s ministerial duties. . . . He believed that when he received information concerning what had taken place between Christine and her stepfather, he was acting in a pastoral capacity as assistant pastor.

[The jury found both appellants guilty; they appealed.] Appellants first contend they were not acting as "child care custodians" within the meaning of the statute. According to appellants, Mr. Hodges was counseling Christine, a member of the church with a spiritual problem, as the pastor of the church. Appellants argue most of the meetings were not during school hours. They also argue Mr. Nobbs was not acting as a child custodian, but rather was called to be informed that Christine's stepfather would be relieved of his ministerial duties and Mr. Nobbs would have to assume them.

The jury was instructed on the definition of a child care custodian pursuant to section 11165.7: " '[C]hild care custodian' means a teacher; . . . administrative officer, supervisor of child welfare and attendance . . . of any public or private school." No objection to this instruction was raised by any party.

The record reflects substantial evidence to support the jury's finding that appellants were child care custodians. The school attended by the victim, South Bay Christian Academy, was operated by South Bay United Pentecostal Church. . . . Religious and academic classes were taught. Appellants were involved in running the school as president and principal (as well as holding pastoral positions with the church). Appellant Nobbs took care of the day-to-day management of the school while appellant Hodges had overall responsibility for decisions concerning the school. . . . Christine testified she sought Hodges's help because he was in charge of the school. . . .

Appellants next contend the statute [§11166(a)] violates due process as applied to them, as it fails to give adequate notice of the obligation to report. . . . As respondent notes, the terms "child," "child abuse," and "child protective agency" are all defined in the Reporting Act, as is "child care custodian." The definition of "child care custodian" includes "an administrative officer, supervisor of child welfare and attendance, or certificated pupil personnel employee of any public or private school." The intent of the Reporting Act, as stated by the Legislature, is to protect children from abuse, including neglect, willful cruelty, or unjustifiable punishment and unlawful corporal punishment or injury. The Legislature has been sufficiently definite in drafting the Reporting Act to give the constitutionally required degree of notice to those subject to its requirements.

Appellants also contend the statute as applied in this case is insufficiently specific given its impact on activities potentially subject to First Amendment protection. . . . Appellants argue they were obligated by the dictates of their faith and precepts stemming therefrom not to disclose to the community the contents of pastoral communications with Christine. . . .

The issue becomes whether appellants' failing to report known child abuse as required by the statute and instead choosing to handle the problem within the church, even if motivated by sincere religious beliefs, is protected religious activity under the First Amendment. . . . Here, if appellants are held to be exempt from the mandatory requirements of the Reporting Act, the act's purpose would be severely undermined. There is no indication teachers and administrators of religious schools would voluntarily report known or suspected child abuse. Children in those schools would not be protected. The protection of all children cannot be achieved in any other way. . . .

Appellants argue the Reporting Act constitutes excessive governmental entanglement with religion [in violation of the First Amendment's establishment clause]. . . . The court, in effect, has barred a pastor from religious counseling of suspected child abuse among the members of his or her congregation, thus interfering substantially with the pastoral role of its ministers.

The comprehensive reporting requirement is designed to ensure the health and safety of children and fulfills a vital and appropriate secular purpose. In Prince v. Massachusetts (1944) 321 U.S. 158, the court stated, "The right to practice religion freely does not include liberty to expose the community or the child to communicable diseases or the latter to ill health or death." (Id., at pp.166-167.) . . . The compelling state interest furthered by the act justifies the interference with appellants' religious practices when appellants are acting in the capacity of child care custodians within the meaning of the statute. . . .

## Notes and Questions

1. *Background.* All states currently require certain professionals to report suspected child abuse and neglect. Reporting statutes were enacted

during a period of unprecedented legislative activity in the mid-1960's. Several organizations (for example, the Children's Bureau of the National Center on Child Abuse and Neglect, American Medical Association, and Program of State Governments) proposed model legislation. A central purpose of these statutes was to encourage reporting by physicians who might treat a victim. Subsequent revisions expanded the mandated reporters (to include schoolteachers, social workers, psychologists, nurses, dentists, opthamologists, coroners, psychiatrists, and in some cases, "any" person), and the types of reportable maltreatment (to include sexual and emotional abuse, and eliminating the requirement for "serious" physical injury).

On the history of reporting statutes, see Allan H. McCoid, The Battered Child and Other Assaults Upon the Family: Part One, 50 Minn. L. Rev. 1 (1965-1966); Monrad G. Paulsen, Child Abuse Reporting Laws: The Shape of the Legislation, 67 Colum. L. Rev. 1 (1967); Stephen Pfohl, The Discovery of Child Abuse, 24 Soc. Probs. 310 (1977).

2. Reporting laws have the following purposes: to facilitate identification of abused children, designate agencies to receive and investigate child maltreatment, and provide services to families to prevent re-abuse. Seth C. Kalichman, Mandated Reporting of Suspected Child Abuse: Ethics, Law, & Policy 13 (1993). Does the legislation accomplish its purposes? Does the dramatic increase in cases of abuse and neglect[36] prove that the legislation serves its purposes?

3. Does a mandated reporter have a responsibility to investigate the alleged abuse, as Mr. Hodges did, or merely to report it? How certain must a professional be before making a report? How certain was Mr. Hodges? Does a "reasonable suspicion" suffice? What constitutes "reasonable suspicion"? Does the objective "reasonable suspicion" standard improve enforcement? Ensure overreporting?

4. What problems ensue from the imposition of liability on the following professionals?

(a) *Clergy.* The pastor-defendants in *Hodges* were convicted as child-care providers. Some states mandate reporting by clergy, although many of these jurisdictions have an exception for penitential communications. See Ruth Cornell, Note and Comment, The Church and the Law in the Ninth Circuit Concerning Mandatory Reporting of Child Sexual Abuse: What the Legal Advocate Representing Church or Clergy Needs to Know About Ninth Circuit Child Sexual Abuse Reporting Statutes, 1 J. Legal Advoc. & Prac. 137, 138, 143 (1999).

Does mandatory reporting by clergy violate the First Amendment? See Arthur Grose Schaefer & Darren Levine, No Sanctuary from the

[36]. The incidence of reported cases of child abuse and neglected children increased 14 times from 1963 to 1987. Seth C. Kalichman, Mandated Reporting of Suspected Child Abuse: Ethics, Law, and Policy 13 (1993) (citing Douglas J. Besharov, Recognizing Child Abuse: A Guide for the Concerned (1990)).

Law: Legal Issues Facing the Clergy, 30 Loy. L.A. L. Rev. 177, 178-183 (1996).

(b) *Attorneys.* Some states mandate reporting by attorneys. Does this requirement abrogate the attorney-client privilege? See Alison Beyea, Competing Liabilities: Responding to Evidence of Child Abuse That Surfaces During the Attorney-Client Relationship, 51 Me. L. Rev. 269 (1999).

(c) *Psychotherapists.* Most states require reporting by mental health professionals. How does the police function inherent in the reporting laws comport with the therapeutic role? With ethical standards for confidentiality? See generally Christopher Bollas & David Sundelson, The New Informants: The Betrayal of Confidentiality in Psychoanalysis and Psychotherapy (1995); Ralph Slovenko, Psychotherapy and Confidentiality: Testimonial Privileged Communication, Breach of Confidentiality, and Reporting Duties (1998). Should legislators create an exemption for psychotherapists, similar to that for clergy in some jurisdictions?

On liability of teachers, see Eric A. Hamilton, Note, Kentucky Law Issue: *Commonwealth v. Allen:* An Eye-Opener for Kentucky's Teachers, 27 N. Ky. L. Rev. 447 (2000); Kimberly S.M. v. Bradford Central School, 649 N.Y.S.2d 588 (App. Div. 1996) (holding teacher liable for breach of statutory duty to report).

5. Are laws that were intended to increase reporting of *physical* abuse, primarily by emergency room *physicians*, well-tailored to encourage reporting of other forms of abuse by other professionals? See Kalichman, supra, at 12 (noting that "a single standard that assumed homogeneity in professional training, circumstances of practice, and conditions under which suspicions of maltreatment occur" ignores particular aspects of various professional contexts).

6. *Criminal and civil liability.* Most states impose misdemeanor liability on professionals who fail to report. Are the rehabilitative and deterrent purposes of the criminal law served by the imposition of penal sanctions against abusers?

Some states also impose civil liability. In Landeros v. Flood, 551 P.2d 389 (Cal. 1976), parents brought a child to a hospital for treatment of bruises and broken bones. The emergency room physician failed to diagnose and report the injuries as abuse. Shortly thereafter, the parents took the child to another hospital where the physician did diagnose and report the abuse. In a suit against the initial physician and hospital, the California Supreme Court recognized the possibility of a civil action for either common law negligence (professional malpractice) or negligence per se (based on violation of the criminal reporting statute). But cf. Fischer v. Metcalf, 543 So. 2d 785 (Fla. Dist. Ct. App. 1989) (en banc) (refusing to recognize a private cause of action). See generally Steven J. Singley, Comment, Failure to Report Suspected Child Abuse: Civil Liability of Mandated Reporters, 19 J. Juv. L. 236 (1998). Additional civil sanctions may include suspension or revocation of professional licenses.

On the other hand, all jurisdictions grant immunity to those persons *making* a report that later is determined erroneous. Some states grant absolute immunity; others provide for immunity only for reports made with "reasonable cause" or in good faith. Are there disadvantages to granting immunity? See Diana Kerckhoff March, Over-Extension of Immunity in the Child Abuse and Neglect Reporting Act, 26 Beverly Hills Bar Assoc. J., Winter 1992, at 9 (discussing cases in which immunity protects negligent or malicious reports).

7. *Central register.* Many statutes require that some state agencies maintain a register of all reported cases of suspected abuse and neglect.[37] Originally, registries were designed to ascertain the incidence of abuse and to assist professionals keep track of parents suspected of abuse. Recently, social service agencies and some employers rely on the registries to preclude child abusers from child care employment. Such registries often contain a high number of unsubstantiated reports of abuse.

Do these registries violate the due process rights of alleged abusers? In Valmonte v. Bane, 18 F.3d 992 (2d Cir. 1994), plaintiff was reported by a school official after she slapped her preteen as punishment for stealing. Although the subsequent proceedings were dismissed, plaintiff's name remained in the state register. Plaintiff argued that the procedures violated her due process rights because she would be harmed if she applied for a position in her chosen field of child care. The court found that the procedures implicated plaintiff's liberty interest (because of the mandatory requirement for employer verification) and failed to protect plaintiff's due process rights. But cf. Hodge v. Jones, 31 F.2d 157 (4th Cir. 1994) (agency's refusal to expunge records, after parents cleared of abuse, does not violate due process).

Criticisms of expungement procedures include (1) the ability to request expungement may lapse after a short period; (2) the agency's burden of proof is slight; (3) statutes often are silent on the right to counsel and to cross-examination of witnesses; (4) some statutes prevent disclosure of accusers' identities; and (5) statutes do not require a neutral hearing officer. Michael R. Phillips, Note, The Constitutionality of Employer-Accessible Child Abuse Registries: Due Process Implications of Governmental Occupational Blacklisting, 92 Mich. L. Rev. 139, 143-144 (1993). How might such statutes' shortcomings be addressed? See also Jill D. Moore, Comment, Charging a Course Between Scylla and Charybdis: Child Abuse Registries and Procedural Due Process, 73 N.C. L. Rev. 2063 (1995).

[37]. Approximately 40 states and the District of Columbia maintain child abuse registries. Michael R. Phillips, Note, The Constitutionality of Employer-Accessible Child Abuse Registries: Due Process Implications of Governmental Occupational Blacklisting, 92 Mich. L. Rev. 139 (1993).

8. *Empirical research.* What are the effects of reporting laws? One study reports that more than one-fourth of abusive parent-clients terminated treatment following a report. Murray Levine & Howard J. Doueck, The Impact of Mandated Reporting on the Therapeutic Process: Picking Up the Pieces 133 (1995) (citing K. Steinberg, In the Service of Two Masters: Psychotherapists Struggle with Child Maltreatment Reporting Laws (1994) (unpublished Ph.D. dissertation)). Other possible negative effects include client anger, distrust and sense of betrayal, and increased resistance to treatment. Id. at 133-134. Other research suggests that reporting might have positive effects on the therapeutic relationship, especially if the abuser is not the client. See Seth C. Kalichman, Mandated Reporting of Suspected Child Abuse: Ethics, Law and Policy 53-54 (1993); Levine & Doueck, supra, at 131-133 (noting increased trust and self-disclosure).

9. *Family privacy.* Some commentators criticize reporting laws for their cultural bias, ensuing burden on the social welfare system, negative effects on families, high proportion of false reports, and questionable effectiveness in protecting children. See, e.g., Douglas J. Besharov, Limiting Abuse Reporting Laws: Should Current Reporting Laws Regarding Sexual and Physical Abuse of Children Be Sharply Limited to Discourage Overreporting? Yes., in Debating Children's Lives: Current Controversies on Children and Adolescents 287 (Mary Ann Mason & E. Gambrill eds., 1994); Joseph Goldstein et al., In the Best Interests of the Child (1986); E. D. Hutchinson, Mandatory Reporting Laws: Child Protective Case Finding Gone Awry?, 38 Social Work 56 (1993). Given these criticisms, do reporting laws justify the considerable intrusion on family privacy?

### b. Evidentiary Issues

*(i) Syndrome Evidence*

■ **FRENZEL v. STATE**
*849 P.2d 741(1993),* aff'd, *938 P.2d 867 (Wyo. 1997),*
cert. denied, *522 U.S. 959 (1997)*

CARDINE, Justice. . .
Appellant has fathered children with four separate women. [He] and his second wife produced D-2 (the prosecutrix). . . . In the Fall of 1989, appellant, [his fourth wife, in addition to D-2 who was then 17 years old, and several of his other children] moved into a trailer home six miles outside of [Cody, Wyoming]. Appellant worked periodically cleaning carpets and driving a truck. The prosecutrix (D-2), went to school occasionally and worked at a local fast food restaurant. It was during this

approximate five-month stay in Cody when D-2 claims the sexual abuse occurred. [A]ppellant allegedly committed seven different acts of first degree sexual assault on his daughter. . . . Each assault involved forced penetration either orally or vaginally with the appellant's penis or another object. . . .

Appellant [challenges] the admission of expert testimony from the State's expert. [A]ppellant asserts that the expert should not have been permitted to testify concerning the "Child Sexual Abuse Accommodation Syndrome" (CSAAS). [Appellant's] objections are premised on [Wyoming Rule of Evidence 702] which permits admission of expert testimony only if it will assist the trier of fact. [A]ppellant argues that expert testimony which discusses CSAAS violates W.R.E. 702 because CSAAS is not generally recognized in the field of psychology and thus is not sufficiently reliable to assist the jury.

In order to properly address these issues, it is necessary to understand the content of the expert's testimony. Dr. Ned Tranel was qualified as an expert in child psychology and child sexual psychopathology. The relevant testimony developed as follows:

* * *

[Dr. Tranel]:   There is, when one encounters a condition of child sexual psychology, child sexual abuse accommodation syndrome and a syndrome refers to a pattern of behaviors which are called symptoms, and in order for this syndrome to exist, then we look at the presence of or question whether they are, there is evidence of certain characteristics or symptoms, and there are five of these.

[Prosecutor]:   Could you list those?

[Dr. Tranel]:   [F]irst one is secrecy. . . . The second one is a sense of helplessness, and the reason that's relevant is because there is usually a child involved and usually the perpetrator is an adult. . . . The third characteristic is a pattern of accommodation, . . . which enables the person to survive over a long period of time. . . . The fourth characteristic is delayed reporting. Sometimes disclosure is used instead of reporting, and reporting is delayed and conflicted, and the reason for this, and in this case there is a classic pattern here. . . . The last characteristic we find in this syndrome is retraction or sometimes called recanting or taking back the disclosure of the sexual abuse. . . .

[Prosecutor]:   And could you tell us, you mentioned about the child accommodation syndrome, what patterns of behavior manifested by [the victim] and the testing results indicated whether or not she may fit within that particular syndrome?

[Dr. Tranel]:   Yes. I listed the symptoms there and then I looked at the test data from my evaluation to determine whether those, whether

there was consistency, and as I indicated, there was. There was evidence that this was, I use the term classic pattern, there was, first
of all, the secrecy that I mentioned, and that was re-enforced by the
abortive attempt that she made early on to disclose the pattern of
abuse. She first attempted to report this to her grandmother who
didn't believe her and called her a liar. She made another abortive
attempt to report this to her uncle, . . . who believed her but
then also participated in the abusive pattern, and there were
other abortive attempts during her academic career but none of
them were followed through on with any length of time because,
mainly because of the frequent and sudden moves that characterized her life throughout her academic career. So the secrecy was
sustained until, I have it in my note, I don't recall the exact date,
it was returning from California to Wyoming with the Sheriff
or Deputy [after her arrest on a charge of writing bad checks], and
that finally led to disclosure, which was pursued more diligently.
The second feature I mentioned was the helplessness, and that was
part of the environment in which she lived as well as the relationship between her and the abusers, those including her father, her
grandfather, and her uncle. All of them, of course, older and big-
ger, plus she was experiencing the helplessness associated with a
pattern of extreme poverty and cultural deprivation and academic
failure, and she had no opportunity to overcome that and feel good
about herself.

　. . . Then the third thing was the entrapment or the accommodation where she eventually learned techniques for surviving or living with this continuing pattern, and one of the techniques she used
or typically was to react initially with aggression and fighting and
succumb and adapt and assume a passive stance as things continued
on. [T]he next thing was the delayed disclosure, and I already mentioned the attempts at disclosure which were not fruitful, and the last
one, and I have no evidence of this from anywhere, that there was
ever an occasion of recantation or taking back what she said. That
apparently did not ever occur as far as I know.

[Prosecutor]:　How does the absence of recantation fit into your evaluation of her as it pertains to that syndrome?

[Dr. Tranel]:　That's not surprising in view of her age. Recantation is a
common part of this syndrome among younger children at early
ages, particularly, and I am talking about four to eight years on, recanting is common. Among older adults it's less common. It's not
surprising we don't see recantation here at the level of eighteen or
nineteen years old. . . .

[Prosecutor]:　Can you summarize for us, Dr. Tranel, your opinion as to
whether or not the character and personality type of [the victim],
based upon your testing of her and evaluation, is consistent with the

behavior pattern of other adolescents who have been victims or manifested symptoms of child sexual psychopathology? . . .

*[Dr. Tranel]:* My opinion is that this is a classic pattern of a long history of child sexual abuse. The symptoms evident today are consistent with a pattern of sexual abuse. The behavior is consistent with a pattern of sexual abuse. The cognitive and the academic functioning is also consistent with a pattern of prolonged severe sexual abuse. . . .

### ADMISSIBILITY OF CSAAS EVIDENCE

. . . Appellant argues that CSAAS is not a recognized diagnosis within the field of psychology, and therefore was inappropriately offered to assist the trier of fact. This argument is couched in terms of United States Supreme Court precedent, Frye v. United States, 293 F. 1013 (D.C. Cir. 1923) and Cullin v. State, 565 P.2d 445 (Wyo. 1977), both of which addressed the admissibility of scientific evidence before we adopted the Federal Rules of Evidence. . . .

Previously, we used three criteria in assessing the admissibility of scientific expert witness testimony. First, the subject matter of the expert testimony must be beyond the understanding of laypersons and be distinctly related to some science. Second, the expert must possess sufficient skill, experience, or knowledge within the science to raise the inference that the expert's testimony will assist the trier of fact. Third, the scientific basis of the expert testimony must be in such a state of development so as to permit the expert to make a reasonable opinion.

[T]his court has not yet faced the admissibility of CSAAS evidence. We will here flesh out the basic purpose of CSAAS and examine how other jurisdictions have dealt with it. The purpose of CSAAS is to define a "common language" for clinical psychologists dealing with child sexual abuse and to assist them in providing therapy and treatment. CSAAS is not intended as a means of detecting the existence of abuse. . . . Because CSAAS is not diagnostic, the majority of courts dealing with CSAAS testimony have limited its admissibility. Some jurisdictions require a limiting instruction when CSAAS evidence is offered. Other courts will not admit testimony concerning CSAAS if offered to prove abuse occurred. Several jurisdictions admit CSAAS testimony solely to rehabilitate the victim's credibility. A few jurisdictions never admit CSAAS because it has not attained scientific acceptance [citations omitted].

CSAAS testimony is restricted because it offers no help to the jury of proof that abuse occurred. There is general agreement on the notion that CSAAS is unreliable for determining whether abuse actually occurred. The evidence is unreliable because there is considerable controversy and dispute over the inclusive traits. The list of symptoms associated with child sexual abuse includes behaviors which might also be manifest in a child who was not sexually abused but has been subject to some other childhood stress. . . . When CSAAS evidence is freely admitted without limitation, the danger of misleading the jury becomes significant.

Today, we adopt, generally, the view taken by [several other jurisdictions to admit CSAAS evidence with certain limitations (discussed below)]. We do so because we find that CSAAS evidence has yet to reach the stage of development which would permit an expert to reasonably conclude, on the basis of CSAAS alone, that abuse occurred. Therefore, CSAAS does not assist the trier of fact on the issue of whether abuse actually occurred. Additionally, we believe that admission of CSAAS evidence, without limitation, would run too high a risk of misleading the jury and therefore be more prejudicial than probative under W.R.E. 403. . . .

Qualified experts on child sexual abuse may, therefore, use evidence of CSAAS characteristics of sexually abused children for the sole purpose of explaining a victim's specific behavior which might be incorrectly construed as inconsistent with an abuse victim or to rebut an attack on the victim's credibility. For example, if the facts of a particular case show that the victim delayed reporting the abuse, recanted the allegations, kept the abuse secretive, or was accommodating to the abuse, then testimony about that particular characteristic of CSAAS would be admissible to dispel any myths the jury may hold concerning that behavior. . . . However, expert testimony of CSAAS cannot be used for the purpose of proving whether the victim's claim of abuse is true.

Having determined the general parameters for admitting CSAAS testimony, we must now discern whether Dr. Tranel's testimony, concerning CSAAS, was proper. . . . Throughout Dr. Tranel's testimony, he never directly states that, because D-2 represents a classic case of CSAAS, she was abused. Instead he explains in detail each specific CSAAS characteristic and how it applies in D-2's case. The majority of this testimony appeared to explain D-2's behavior, which included delayed reporting, accommodation, secrecy and helplessness. Therefore, it was appropriate for the State to explain some of these inconsistencies through Dr. Tranel's CSAAS testimony.

Dr. Tranel, however, also described the fifth trait of CSAAS, recantation, which he explained was inapplicable to D-2. Since D-2 never recanted, the explanation of that particular type of behavior was unnecessary, and Dr. Tranel's CSAAS testimony exceeded its admissible purpose. We cannot say, however, that Dr. Tranel's impermissible comments regarding recantation adversely affected the appellant's substantial rights.

Although Dr. Tranel's testimony references CSAAS often, CSAAS is not the sole basis for his ultimate conclusion that D-2's case represents "a classic pattern of a long history of child sexual abuse." Dr. Tranel performed a battery of psychological and intelligence tests when he examined D-2. In fact, as evidenced by the prosecutor's questions, Dr. Tranel's ultimate conclusion appears to be grounded in the totality of his examination not solely on his CSAAS analysis. Therefore, . . . sufficient admissible bases exist to support Dr. Tranel's testimony. . . .

In reaching our decision today, we acknowledge the inherent difficulties of proving sexual abuse. Usually, only two eye witnesses exist, the victim and the accused, thus putting a premium on credibility. It is, therefore, often necessary for the prosecution to enlist the services of an expert to explain the victim's unusual behavior in delayed reporting, accommodation and like aberrations. However, we cannot abrogate time-tested and fundamental tenets of evidence because child sexual abuse is an increasingly prevalent problem. Rule 702, W.R.E. requires that expert evidence assist the trier of fact in order to be relevant and admissible. The determination of whether the evidence assists the trier of fact is premised on the reliability of that evidence. CSAAS evidence has not yet reached the stage of development to make it, alone, a reliable indicator of the existence of sexual abuse. . . .

## Notes and Questions

1. The Supreme Court first addressed the admissibility of syndrome evidence in child abuse cases in Estelle v. McGuire, 502 U.S. 62 (1991). A defendant, who was found guilty of second degree murder of his infant, challenged the admission of evidence of prior injuries revealing that the infant was a victim of "battered child syndrome." The Court held that the admission of such evidence did not violate his due process rights.

2. Child Sexual Abuse Accommodation Syndrome (CSAAS) is a term coined by psychiatrist Dr. Roland Summit to show that certain behavior is characteristic of sexually abused children. See Roland C. Summit, The Child Sexual Abuse Accommodation Syndrome, 7 Child Abuse & Neglect 177 (1983). In judicial proceedings, CSAAS is useful to explain reasons for certain behavior exhibited by sexually abused children (i.e., delay in reporting, half-truths, and recantations) that might lead jurors to question victims' truthfulness. Although many jurisdictions currently admit evidence of the battered child syndrome, admissibility of the child sexual abuse accommodation syndrome (CSAAS) is more controversial. Why?

*Frenzel* reveals that jurisdictions take different approaches to the admissibility of CSAAS evidence. Some courts exclude behavioral science testimony regarding child sexual abuse because such evidence has not attained scientific acceptance. Among the jurisdictions that admit syndrome evidence in child sexual abuse cases, most (like *Frenzel*) limit its admissibility. What was the limitation adopted by the Wyoming Supreme Court in *Frenzel*? See also People v. Peterson, 537 N.W.2d 857, 866-868

(Mich. 1995) (surveying jurisdictions' treatment of syndrome evidence). See generally Dara Loren Steele, Note, Expert Testimony: Seeking an Appropriate Admissibility Standard for Behavioral Science in Child Sexual Abuse Prosecutions, 48 Duke L.J. 932 (1999).

3. Are the limitations imposed by some states adequate? That is, are jurors able to understand that CSAAS testimony is offered only to assist in evaluating credibility rather than to prove abuse? Or is the limitation too restrictive? See Rosemary L. Flint, Note, Child Sexual Abuse Accommodation Syndrome: Admissibility Requirements, 23 Am. J. Crim. L. 171, 173 (1995) (criticizing the rule that forbids introduction of CSAAS unless the defense has expressly raised issues of the victim's credibility because often contradictions are merely implied, with the result that CSAAS testimony is not permitted).

4. The traditional *Frye* test for the admissibility of novel scientific evidence, named after Frye v. United States, 293 F. 1013 (D.C. Cir. 1923), permits admission of novel scientific evidence if it has attained "general acceptance in the particular field in which it belongs." Id. at 1014. In Daubert v. Merrell Dow Pharmaceuticals, 509 U.S. 579 (1993), the Supreme Court held that Federal Rule of Evidence 702 superseded *Frye*. In so doing, the Court liberalized rules for both the admission of expert testimony and scientific evidence from a focus on "general acceptance" to relevance-plus-reliability. The Supreme Court suggested courts consider the factors of falsifiability, peer review and publication, known or potential error rate, as well as general acceptance.

Although *Daubert* applies in federal courts, many state courts continue to follow *Frye*. How should courts decide on the applicability of the *Frye* test and *Daubert* to CSAAS? Compare Irving v. State, 705 So. 2d 1021 (Fla. Ct. App. 1998) (holding that CSAAS evidence would not pass the *Frye* test) with State v. Edelman, 593 N.W.2d 419 (S.D. 1999) (holding that CSAAS evidence was admissible under *Daubert*).

5. *Other syndromes.* CSAAS, like the battered woman syndrome and the rape trauma syndrome, focus on the victim. Should syndrome evidence that focuses on the abuser (for example, the battering parent syndrome, the sex abuser profile) be admissible? Are evidentiary concerns regarding admissibility similar or different? For example, Underwood v. State, 425 S.E.2d 20 (S.C. 1992), admitted evidence of a sex abuser profile as analogous to the battered child syndrome. Is this an apt analogy? On the battering parent syndrome, see Hoosier v. State, 612 So. 2d 1352 (Ala. Crim. App. 1992); Commonwealth v. Day, 569 N.E.2d 397, 399-400 (Mass. 1991).

Should a parent be entitled to admission of expert testimony indicating that he does *not* fit a battering parent profile? See Hoosier v. State, supra, at 1354 (testimony may not be admitted). Alternatively, should evidence that a parent was an abused child be admissible to establish that the parent is *likely* to abuse? Compare Tucker v. Shelby County Dept. of

Pub. Welfare, 578 N.E. 2d 774 (Ind. Ct. App. 1991) (admitting such evidence), with State v. Pulizzano, 456 N.W.2d 325 (Wis. 1990) (rejecting it).

6. *Other evidentiary issues.* (a) *Prior acts by the abuser.* To admit evidence of prior incidents of child abuse, courts usually require that the prior incident be "substantially similar." See, e.g., People v. Wachal, 509 N.E.2d 648 (Ill. App. Ct. 1987); State v. Norlin, 951 P.2d 1131 (Wash. 1998). In a famous case, Dr. Elizabeth Morgan alleged that her ex-husband Dr. Eric Foretich sexually abused their daughter Hilary. Morgan went to jail for contempt rather than reveal the daughter's whereabouts. In an action for damages for the abuse brought by Morgan and Hilary, the court of appeals held that the trial judge erred in excluding evidence of sexual abuse by Foretich of Hilary's half sister. The court stated that the evidence tended to identify Foretich as the perpetrator because he had access to both girls and also that the relevance of such evidence outweighed its possible prejudicial effect. Morgan v. Foretich, 846 F.2d 941, 944-945 (4th Cir. 1988). The Federal Rules of Evidence were amended in 1994 to permit the admission of evidence of similar crimes in criminal prosecutions for molestation. Fed. R. Evid. 414(a).

(b) *Unusually sophisticated sexual knowledge.* In many courts, the extent of young children's sexual knowledge is one method of determining whether a child's allegations of sexual abuse are credible. See, e.g., State v. Pulizzano, supra, at 334-335. Is a child's sexual *knowledge* an appropriate means of testing the child's *experience?* Are there alternative ways that a child may acquire such knowledge?

(c) *Anatomically correct dolls.* Determinations of child sexual abuse increasingly rely on the use of anatomically correct dolls[38] because many victims are young and unable to testify about incidents of abuse.[39] Dolls may be used either to help children communicate better during an interview or to supply a mental health professional with information from which inferences of sexual abuse may be drawn.[40]

Although early cases wrestled with the admissibility of such evidence, a growing number of jurisdictions now admit such evidence either by statute or case law. See, e.g., Ala. Code §15-25-5 (1995); State v. Waddell, 504 S.E.2d 84 (N.C. Ct. App. 1998). Further, the Child Victims' and Child Witnesses' Rights Act, 18 U.S.C.A. §3509(c)-(1) (West Supp. 2000), applicable to the federal courts, allows the use of anatomical dolls to

---

[38]. See Barbara W. Boat & Mark D. Everson, Use of Anatomical Dolls Among Professionals in Sexual Abuse Evaluations, 12 Child Abuse & Neglect 171, 173 (1988) (citing survey revealing that 68 percent of child protection workers, 35 percent of law enforcement officers, 13 percent of physicians, and 28 percent of mental health practitioners use the dolls, with a significant additional number indicating that they would be using them within a year).

[39]. Cathy Mann, Assessment of Sexually Abused Children with Anatomically Detailed Dolls: A Critical Review, 9 Behav. Sci. & L. 43, 43 (1991) (33 percent of sexually abused victims are abused prior to the age of six).

[40]. John E. B. Myers, 1 Evidence in Child Abuse and Neglect 293 (1992).

assist the child in testifying. Despite the trend favoring admissibility, commentators warn that therapists misuse the dolls, their testimony conveys an aura of infallibility, and the dolls themselves elicit sexual play.[41] Empirical research, however, fails to support the last concern. Comparing sexually abused children with a control group reveals that the nonabused children (unlike the abused children) rarely engage in sexual play with the dolls or demonstrate sexual intercourse and show a pervasive lack of interest in the dolls.[42]

*(ii) Privileges*

■ **BALTIMORE CITY DEPARTMENT OF SOCIAL SERVICES v. BOUKNIGHT**
*493 U.S. 549 (1990)*

Justice O'CONNOR delivered the opinion of the Court.

In this action, we must decide whether a mother, the custodian of a child pursuant to a court order, may invoke the Fifth Amendment privilege against self-incrimination to resist an order of the juvenile court to produce the child. We hold that she may not.

Petitioner Maurice M. is an abused child. When he was three months old, he was hospitalized with a fractured left femur, and examination revealed several partially healed bone fractures and other indications of severe physical abuse. In the hospital, respondent Bouknight, Maurice's mother, was observed shaking Maurice, dropping him in his crib despite his spica cast, and otherwise handling him in a manner inconsistent with his recovery and continued health. Hospital personnel notified Baltimore City Department of Social Services (BCDSS) of suspected child abuse. In February 1987, BCDSS secured a court order removing Maurice from Bouknight's control and placing him in shelter care. [Following a subsequent hearing, the juvenile court asserted jurisdiction over Maurice and returned him to Bouknight's custody subject to conditions, such as her completion of a parenting course.]

Eight months later, fearing for Maurice's safety, BCDSS returned to juvenile court. BCDSS caseworkers related that Bouknight would not co-

---

[41]. See Stephen J. Ceci & Maggie Bruck, Jeopardy in the Courtroom: A Scientific Analysis of Children's Testimony 161-186 (1995); Andrea Weinerman, Note, The Use and Misuse of Anatomically Correct Dolls in Child Sexual Abuse Evaluations: Uncovering Fact ... Or Fantasy? 16 Women's Rts. L. Rep. 347 (1995).

[42]. See Danya Glaser & Carole Collins, The Response of Young, Non-Sexually Abused Children to Anatomically Correct Dolls, 30 J. Child Psychol. & Psychiatry 547 (1989); Lois Jampole & M. Kathie Weber, An Assessment of the Behavior of Sexually Abused and Nonsexually Abused Children with Anatomically Correct Dolls, 11 Child Abuse & Neglect 187 (1987); Abigail B. Sivan et al., Interaction of Normal Children with Anatomical Dolls, 12 Child Abuse & Neglect 295 (1988).

operate with them and had in nearly every respect violated the terms of the protective order. BCDSS stated that Maurice's father had recently died in a shooting incident and that Bouknight, in light of the results of a psychological examination and her history of drug use, could not provide adequate care for the child. On April 20, 1988, the court granted BCDSS' petition to remove Maurice from Bouknight's control for placement in foster care. BCDSS officials also petitioned for judicial relief from Bouknight's failure to produce Maurice or reveal where he could be found. [She had failed to reveal his whereabouts to BCDSS officials visiting her home, and relatives had not seen the child recently.] Also on April 20, the juvenile court, upon a hearing on the petition, cited Bouknight for violating the protective custody order and for failing to appear at the hearing. Bouknight had indicated to her attorney that she would appear with the child, but also expressed fear that if she appeared the State would " 'snatch the child.' "

The court issued an order to show cause why Bouknight should not be held in civil contempt for failure to produce the child. Expressing concern that Maurice was endangered or perhaps dead, the court issued a bench warrant for Bouknight's appearance. [Following a contempt citation for failure to produce the child, the] court directed that Bouknight be imprisoned until she "purge[d] herself of contempt by either producing [Maurice] before the court or revealing to the court his exact whereabouts." The juvenile court rejected Bouknight's subsequent claim that the contempt order violated the Fifth Amendment's guarantee against self-incrimination. . . .

The Fifth Amendment provides that "No person . . . shall be compelled in any criminal case to be a witness against himself." The Fifth Amendment's protection "applies only when the accused is compelled to make a testimonial communication that is incriminating." . . . Bouknight claims the benefit of the privilege because the act of production would amount to testimony regarding her control over, and possession of, Maurice [thereby aiding the state in prosecuting her].

The possibility that a production order will compel testimonial assertions that may prove incriminating does not, in all contexts, justify invoking the privilege to resist production. Even assuming that this limited testimonial assertion is sufficiently incriminating and "sufficiently testimonial for purposes of the privilege," [Fisher v. United States, 425 U.S. 391, 411 (1976),] Bouknight may not invoke the privilege to resist the production order because she has assumed custodial duties related to production and because production is required as part of a noncriminal regulatory regime.

The Court has on several occasions recognized that the Fifth Amendment privilege may not be invoked to resist compliance with a regulatory regime constructed to effect the State's public purposes unrelated to the enforcement of its criminal laws. [The Court then discusses Shapiro

v. United States, 335 U.S. 1 (1948) (holding that no Fifth Amendment protection attaches to protection of business records that were required to be available for public inspection) and California v. Byers, 402 U.S. 424 (1971) (holding that the Fifth Amendment was not implicated by the statutory requirement that drivers must give identifying information after accident).]

These principles readily apply to this case. Once Maurice was adjudicated a child in need of assistance, his care and safety became the particular object of the State's regulatory interests. . . . By accepting care of Maurice subject to the custodial order's conditions (including requirements that she cooperate with BCDSS, follow a prescribed training regime, and be subject to further court orders), Bouknight submitted to the routine operation of the regulatory system and agreed to hold Maurice in a manner consonant with the State's regulatory interests and subject to inspection by BCDSS. In assuming the obligations attending custody, Bouknight "has accepted the incident obligation to permit inspection." *Wilson*, 221 U.S. at 382. The State imposes and enforces that obligation as part of a broadly directed, noncriminal regulatory regime governing children cared for pursuant to custodial orders. . . .

. . . Many [custodial] orders will arise in circumstances entirely devoid of criminal conduct. Even when criminal conduct may exist, the court may properly request production and return of the child, and enforce that request through exercise of the contempt power, for reasons related entirely to the child's well-being and through measures unrelated to criminal law enforcement or investigation. This case provides an illustration: concern for the child's safety underlay the efforts to gain access to and then compel production of Maurice. Finally, production in the vast majority of cases will embody no incriminating testimony, even if in particular cases the act of production may incriminate the custodian through an assertion of possession or the existence, or the identity, of the child. . . . In these circumstances, Bouknight cannot invoke the privilege to resist the order to produce Maurice.

We are not called upon to define the precise limitations that may exist upon the State's ability to use the testimonial aspects of Bouknight's act of production in subsequent criminal proceedings. But we note that imposition of such limitations is not foreclosed. . . .

## Notes and Questions

1. *Bouknight* illustrates a conflict between the state's interest in child protection and the individual's constitutional protection against self-incrimination. Does child protection justify this exception to the privilege against self-incrimination? If the Court had recognized Bouknight's Fifth Amendment right, what would be the implication for child protec-

tion? See Lisa J. Jacobs, Comment, *Baltimore City Department of Social Services v. Bouknight:* Limiting a Mother's Right to Invoke the Fifth Amendment, 17 New Eng. J. Crim. & Civ. Confinement 423, 438 (1991) (suggesting that social workers would be more reluctant to return abused children if supervision of a family had proved difficult).

2. *Epilogue.* Following the Supreme Court opinion, the juvenile court held a new hearing at which Ms. Bouknight again refused to answer questions about Maurice's disappearance. She was remanded to the Baltimore City Detention Center to continue her incarceration for contempt. In 1993, Ms. Bouknight's lawyers moved for her release. She then admitted, for the first time, that Maurice was residing with a friend (whom she would not name). In 1995, at another hearing, Bouknight named the friend with whom Maurice allegedly was residing as "Rachael Anderson" of Kinston, North Carolina. Anderson, according to Bouknight, was a friend with whom she had grown up in Kinston. Police detectives checked motor vehicle, school and foster care records but could not verify Anderson's existence.

Court-appointed lawyers for the child continued to believe that Maurice was dead. They stated, in a confidential report to the court, that they believed Ms. Bouknight was capable of fabricating the story based on prior evidence of her deception (that is, her theft in 1988 from her physician employer to purchase a life insurance premium for Maurice).

In 1995 her attorneys once again petitioned for her release, arguing in part that her incarceration no longer served its coercive purpose because it was unlikely that her continued confinement would induce compliance. Ultimately, she was released after serving seven years for civil contempt. See Kate Shatzkin, Bouknight Is Released After Seven Years in Jail, Baltimore Sun, Nov. 1, 1995, at A1. See also Ellen Alderman & Carolyn Kennedy, In Our Defense 169-179 (1991).

3. In *Bouknight,* the Court did not decide whether Bouknight's testimony could be used against her in subsequent criminal proceedings. Should Bouknight have been granted immunity from prosecution?

4. *Bouknight* analogizes a custodian of a child to a custodian of business records, asserting that both are appropriate for governmental regulation requiring incidental self-incrimination. Is the analogy apt?

5. In a strikingly similar case, physician Elizabeth Morgan was cited for contempt for failure to disclose the whereabouts of her young daughter Hilary. Morgan v. Foretich, 546 A.2d 407 (D.C. 1988). Following divorce from dentist Eric Foretich, Morgan was awarded custody of two-year-old Hilary. A court order gave Foretich visitation. Two months later, Morgan refused to permit Foretich visitation on the grounds that he was sexually abusing the girl. The father moved to hold Morgan in contempt. Finding that Morgan had failed to prove sexual abuse by a preponderance of the evidence, the superior court found her in contempt and ordered a resumption of visitation. When Morgan reiterated

her refusal to permit visitation, she was found in contempt once again. The father's visitation resumed on a supervised basis that evolved, based on a court order, into unsupervised visitation.

The father subsequently moved for a change of custody and termination of Morgan's parental rights; the mother moved to suspend visitation or to require that visitation be supervised. While hearings were continuing, the judge entered an order providing for two weeks' extended visitation during the summer. Morgan appealed the visitation order. Simultaneously, she hid the child and subsequently refused to disclose her daughter's whereabouts. The judge held Morgan in contempt. She was incarcerated for two years. Public outcry, especially by feminists, resulted in the District of Columbia Civil Contempt Imprisonment Limitation Act of 1989, D.C. Code Ann. §11-741 (1995), limiting incarceration in the District for civil contempt in a custody proceeding to 12 months. See generally Jonathan Groner, Hilary's Trial: The Elizabeth Morgan Case (1991).

Is contempt an appropriate sanction in *Bouknight* and *Morgan*?

6. What might explain the lengthy confinement for both Morgan and Bouknight? See Melinda L. Mosely, Comment, Civil Contempt and Child Sexual Abuse Allegations: A Modern Solomon's Choice, 40 Emory L.J. 203, 240 n.130 (1991) (suggesting possibility of bias against women who make allegations of abuse during divorce).

### c. Hearsay and the Confrontation Clause

■ **WHITE v. ILLINOIS**
*502 U.S. 346 (1992)*

Chief Justice Rehnquist delivered the opinion of the Court. . . .

Petitioner was convicted by a jury of aggravated criminal sexual assault, residential burglary, and unlawful restraint. The events giving rise to the charges related to the sexual assault of S.G., then four years old. Testimony at the trial established that in the early morning hours of April 16, 1988, S.G.'s babysitter, Tony DeVore, was awakened by S.G.'s scream. DeVore went to S.G.'s bedroom and witnessed petitioner leaving the room and petitioner then left the house. DeVore knew petitioner because petitioner was a friend of S.G.'s mother, Tammy Grigsby. DeVore asked S.G. what had happened. According to DeVore's trial testimony, S.G. stated that petitioner had put his hand over her mouth, choked her, threatened to whip her if she screamed and had "touched her in the wrong places." Asked by DeVore to point to where she had been touched, S.G. identified the vaginal area.

Tammy Grigsby, S.G.'s mother, returned home about 30 minutes later. Grigsby testified that her daughter appeared "scared" and a "little hyper." Grigsby proceeded to question her daughter about what had happened. At trial, Grigsby testified that S.G. repeated her claims that petitioner choked and threatened her. Grigsby also testified that S.G. stated that petitioner "put his mouth on her front part." Grigsby also noticed that S.G. had bruises and red marks on her neck that had not been there previously. Grigsby called the police. [A few minutes later, S.G. repeated her story to Officer Terry Lewis, and within four hours to Cheryl Reents, an emergency room nurse, and to Dr. Michael Meizen.]

S.G. never testified at petitioner's trial. The State attempted on two occasions to call her as a witness but she apparently experienced emotional difficulty on being brought to the courtroom and in each instance left without testifying. The defense made no attempt to call S.G. as a witness and the trial court neither made, nor was it asked to make, a finding that S.G. was unavailable to testify.

Petitioner objected on hearsay grounds to DeVore, Grigsby, Lewis, Reents, and Meinzen being permitted to testify regarding S.G.'s statements describing the assault. The trial court overruled each objection. With respect to DeVore, Grigsby, and Lewis the trial court concluded that the testimony could be permitted pursuant to an Illinois hearsay exception for spontaneous declarations.[1] Petitioner's objections to Reents' and Meinzen's testimony was similarly overruled, based on both the spontaneous declaration exception and an exception for statements made in the course of securing medical treatment.[2] The trial court also denied petitioner's motion for a mistrial based on S.G.'s "presence [and] failure to testify."

Petitioner was found guilty by a jury, and the Illinois Appellate Court affirmed his conviction. [W]e granted certiorari limited to the constitutional question whether permitting the challenged testimony violated petitioner's Sixth Amendment Confrontation Clause right. . . .

We note first that the evidentiary rationale for permitting hearsay testimony regarding spontaneous declarations and statements made in the course of receiving medical care is that such out-of-court declarations are made in contexts that provide substantial guarantees of their

---

1. The spontaneous declaration exception applies to "[a] statement relating to a startling event or condition made while the declarant was under the stress of excitement caused by the event or condition." [People v. White, 555 N.E.2d 1241, 1246 (Ill. App. Ct. 1990).]

2. Illinois Rev. Stat., ch. 38, para. 115-13 (1989), provides:

In a prosecution for violation of Section 12-13, 12-14, 12-15 or 12-16 of the "Criminal Code of 1961," statements made by the victim to medical personnel for purposes of medical diagnosis or treatment including descriptions of the cause of symptom, pain or sensations, or the inception or general character of the cause or external source thereof insofar as reasonably pertinent to diagnosis or treatment shall be admitted as an exception to the hearsay rule.

trustworthiness.[8] But those same factors that contribute to the statements' reliability cannot be recaptured even by later in-court testimony. A statement that has been offered in a moment of excitement — without the opportunity to reflect on the consequences of one's exclamation — may justifiably carry more weight with a trier of fact than a similar statement offered in the relative calm of the courtroom. Similarly, a statement made in the course of procuring medical services, where the declarant knows that a false statement may cause misdiagnosis or mistreatment, carries special guarantees of credibility. . . .

The preference for live testimony [derives from] the importance of cross examination, "the greatest legal engine ever invented for the discovery of truth." *Green*, 399 U.S., at 158. Thus courts have adopted the general rule prohibiting the receipt of hearsay evidence. But where proffered hearsay has sufficient guarantees of reliability to come within a firmly rooted exception to the hearsay rule, the Confrontation Clause is satisfied.

We therefore think it clear that the out-of-court statements admitted in this case had substantial probative value, value that could not be duplicated simply by the declarant later testifying in court. To exclude such probative statements under the strictures of the Confrontation Clause would be the height of wrong-headedness, given that the Confrontation Clause has as a basic purpose the promotion of the " 'integrity of the factfinding process.' " Coy v. Iowa, 487 U.S. 1012, 1020 (1988) (quoting Kentucky v. Stincer, 482 U.S. 730, 736 (1987)). And as we have also noted, a statement that qualifies for admission under a "firmly rooted" hearsay exception is so trustworthy that adversarial testing can be expected to add little to its reliability. Given the evidentiary value of such statements, their reliability, and that establishing a generally applicable unavailability rule would have few practical benefits while imposing pointless litigation costs, we see no reason to treat the out-of-court statements in this case differently from those we found admissible in [prior case law].

As a second line of argument, petitioner presses upon us two recent decisions involving child-testimony in child-sexual-assault cases, Coy v. Iowa, supra, and Maryland v. Craig, 497 U.S. 836 (1990). Both *Coy* and *Craig* required us to consider the constitutionality of courtroom proce-

---

8. Indeed, it is this factor that has led us to conclude that "firmly rooted" exceptions carry sufficient indicia of reliability to satisfy the reliability requirement posed by the Confrontation Clause. See Idaho v. Wright, 497 U.S. 805, 817, 820-821 (1990). There can be no doubt that the two exceptions we consider in this case are "firmly rooted." The exception for spontaneous declarations is at least two centuries old, see 6 J. Wigmore, Evidence, §1747, p.195 ( J. Chadbourn rev. 1976), and may date to the late 17th century. It is currently recognized under the Federal Rules of Evidence, Rule 803(2), and in nearly four-fifths of the States. The exception for statements made for purposes of medical diagnosis or treatment is similarly recognized in the Federal Rules of Evidence, Rule 803(4), and is equally widely accepted among the States.

dures designed to prevent a child witness from having to face across an open courtroom a defendant charged with sexually assaulting the child. In *Coy* we vacated a conviction that resulted from a trial in which a child witness testified from behind a screen, and in which there had been no particularized showing that such a procedure was necessary to avert a risk of harm to the child. In *Craig* we upheld a conviction that resulted from a trial in which a child witness testified via closed circuit television after such a showing of necessity. Petitioner draws from these two cases a general rule that hearsay testimony offered by a child should be permitted only upon a showing of necessity — i.e., in cases where necessary to protect the child's physical and psychological well-being.

Petitioner's reliance is misplaced. *Coy* and *Craig* involved only the question of what in-court procedures are constitutionally required to guarantee a defendant's confrontation right once a witness is testifying. Such a question is quite separate from that of what requirements the Confrontation Clause imposes as a predicate for the introduction of out-of-court declarations. . . . There is thus no basis for importing the "necessity requirement" announced in those cases into the much different context of out-of-court declarations admitted under established exceptions to the hearsay rule. . . .

Affirmed.

## Notes and Questions

1. The Supreme Court previously grappled with the requirements of the Sixth Amendment right of confrontation in the child abuse context. Two cases addressed special trial procedures. Another examined an exception to the hearsay rule that permits a child's prior out-of-court statement to be admitted into evidence.

(a) In Maryland v. Craig, 497 U.S. 836 (1990), a prosecution of a preschool director for child abuse and sexual abuse, the Court held that the right of confrontation does not prohibit a procedure by which a child victim testifies via one-way closed-circuit television. Despite the procedure's preventing the child from seeing the accused, the Court reasoned that the existence of other requisites of confrontation preserved the defendant's rights: establishment of child's competence; testimony under oath; cross-examination; and the witness's visibility to the judge, jury and defendant. The majority also determined that the state's interest in the well-being of abuse victims "may be sufficiently important to outweigh, at least in some cases, a defendant's right to face his or her accusers in court." Id. at 853. The dissent countered that the Sixth Amendment guaranteed a face-to-face encounter.

(b) Coy v. Iowa, 487 U.S. 1012 (1988), also explored the constitutionality of a special testimonial procedure for sexual abuse victims. A defendant was charged with sexually assaulting two 13-year-old neighbor girls. Based on Iowa law permitting testimony either via closed-circuit television or from behind a screen, the trial judge approved use of a screen that blocked the children from the defendant (although he could see them dimly and hear them). Holding that this procedure violated the right to confrontation, the majority emphasized the necessity for a face-to-face encounter to insure the integrity of the fact-finding process. The dissent disagreed, emphasized that the procedure presented only minimal infringement of the defendant's confrontation right and expressed fear that the holding would stifle procedural innovations.

(c) Another case, similar to *White*, concerned the admissibility of a child's pretrial out-of-court statements to a physician. In Idaho v. Wright, 497 U.S. 805 (1990), the defendant was convicted of molestation of his two daughters (ages five and two), based on statements by the youngest to a pediatrician. The Confrontation Clause prohibits the use of such hearsay, subject to certain exceptions. The girl's statements were admitted under Idaho's "residual" (catch-all) exception to the hearsay rule. Resort to this rule was necessary because the child incriminated her father as her *sister*'s abuser (unlike in *White* where the child's statements to medical personnel incriminated her own abuser and hence were admitted under the medical diagnosis or treatment exception).

Reversing the conviction, the Court stated that, before such evidence can be admitted under the residual exception, the prosecution must demonstrate either the witness's unavailability or adequate indicia of the statement's reliability. Such reliability could be satisfied if the statement falls within a "firmly rooted" hearsay exception, or if it has special guarantees of trustworthiness (such as spontaneity and constant repetition, the child's mental state, use of sophisticated sexual terminology in a young child, and lack of motive to fabricate). Id. at 821-822. The Court concluded that Idaho's residual exception was not a firmly rooted hearsay exception, nor was there any special guarantee that the child's statements to the physician were particularly reliable. Id. at 826-827.

2. In *White*, the Supreme Court held the victim's statements were admissible (and proof of the victim's unavailability was not required) because the statements fell within two "firmly rooted" hearsay exceptions (spontaneous declarations and medical diagnosis or treatment). Is *White* consistent with the above precedents? Are the above precedents consistent; for example, did *Craig* overrule *Coy* sub silentio? What are the implications of *White* for the right of confrontation? Did the Court strike the appropriate balance between child protection and protection of a defendant's constitutional rights?

3. The policy of child protection supports use of special procedures (in the event the child testifies) and expansion of exceptions to the hearsay rule (so that the child need not testify). Is it clear that a child will suffer trauma from testifying? Should trauma be presumed? *Coy,*

supra, ruled unconstitutional a statute incorporating a legislatively imposed presumption of trauma, requiring instead individualized findings
to support special testimonial protection. How is a judge to determine
the likelihood of potential trauma? See U.S. v. Rouse, 111 F.3d 561 (8th
Cir. 1997) (holding that court need not rely on expert testimony of
trauma but may make its own observations). To what extent is a court's
reliance on *predictive* evidence justifiable? Related questions concern the
determination of "unavailability" by which the child is relieved from testifying and permitting admission instead of hearsay evidence.

4. *Empirical evidence.* Although case law and commentary theorize
that child victims of sexual abuse are exposed to trauma by testifying,
little research exists to substantiate this belief. To explore this issue, the
National Institute of Justice and the Office of Juvenile Justice and Delinquency Prevention funded several studies comparing child abuse victim-
witnesses with a control group of abused children whose testimony was
not necessary. One study found that testifying may impede the psychological improvement for some children; another study found that testifying has beneficial effects. Based on this research, "it cannot be stated
conclusively that testifying is either harmful or beneficial to sexually
abused children." Debra Whitcomb et al., The Emotional Effects of Testifying on Sexually Abused Children, National Institute of Justice Research in Brief 1 (April 1994). See also Jennifer Marie Batterman-Faunce
& Gail S. Goodman, Effects of Context on the Accuracy and Suggestibility
of Child Witnesses, in Child Victims, Child Witnesses: Understanding
and Improving Testimony 301, 312 (Gail S. Goodman & Bette L. Bottoms eds., 1993).

5. States have not been universally receptive to the Supreme Court's
expansive interpretation of the Confrontation Clause in the child abuse
context. In the decade since *White,* only nine state supreme courts (as
well as military courts) have followed its lead. Dana T. Blackmore, The
Tug of War Between the Confrontation Clause and Hearsay Exceptions
in Child Sexual Abuse Cases: Implications of *White v. Illinois,* 28 S.U. L.
Rev. 93, 99-100 (2001). "[I]t seems that states are reluctant to adopt a
rule that includes hearsay evidence without a showing of unavailability
of the declarant." Id. at 104.

6. *Videotaped testimony.* Is the admission of videotaped evidence constitutional after *Craig* and *Coy?* Many states have enacted statutes that
permit a child's testimony to be videotaped as a substitute for trial testimony.[43] Requirements vary. Some states require that the defendant be
present and cross-examination allowed during the videotaped session,

---

[43]. As of 1994, 37 states allowed videotaped testimony by child abuse victims, and
30 states permitted their testimony via one-way or two-way closed circuit television. Robert
G. Marks, Should We Believe the People Who Believe the Children?: The Need for a New
Sexual Abuse Tender Years Hearsay Exception Statute, 32 Harv. J. on Legis. 207, 220
(1995).

but others permit use of the videotape subject to an opportunity for subsequent courtroom cross-examination.[44] Some courts have upheld the introduction of videotaped testimony at trial. See, e.g., People v. Pesquera, 625 N.W.2d 407 (Mich. Ct. App. 2001); State v. Smith, 730 A.2d 311 (N.J. 1999); State v. Foster, 957 P.2d 712 (Wash. 1998). Other states have been more reluctant, citing Confrontation Clause concerns. See, e.g., State v. Ford, 626 So. 2d 1338 (Fla. 1993); Doe v. State, 992 P.2d 1211 (Idaho Ct. App. 1999).

7. *Closed circuit television.* Many states have statutes authorizing the use of closed circuit television. Some statutes allow testimony via one-way closed circuit television or screens. Other statutes, modeled on federal legislation, require testimony via two-way closed circuit television. See Janet Leach Richards, Protecting the Child Witness in Abuse Cases, 34 Fam. L.Q. 393, 401 (2000). The federal Child Victims' and Child Witnesses' Rights Act (CVCWR), 18 U.S.C. §3509 (Supp. 1999), providing for testimony via two-way closed circuit television, applies to child victims of physical or sexual abuse or child witnesses to a crime committed against another. The Act requires that the court must make case-specific findings that the child is unable to testify in the defendant's presence because of fear, or would suffer trauma (based on expert testimony), suffers a mental or other infirmity, or is unable to continue testifying because of the defendant's conduct. 18 U.S.C. §3509(b) (West Supp. 2000).

8. *Competency.* Because a child is often the only witness against an abuser, prosecution is difficult without the child's testimony. How does a court determine a child's competency to testify? At early common law, children under age 14 were presumed to be incompetent as witnesses.[45] Case law gradually liberalized this rule, holding that capacity is determined not by age, but rather by the ability to differentiate truth from falsehood and an understanding of the duty to tell the truth. See Rex v. Brasier, 168 Eng. Rep. 202 (1770); Wheeler v. United States, 159 U.S. 523 (1895). The Federal Rules of Evidence bolstered the movement to abolish the presumption of incompetence for young children. Eliminating distinctions between child and adult witnesses, Fed. R. Evid. 601, provides that "[e]very person is competent to be a witness except as otherwise provided in these rules." In response to the adoption of the federal rules in 1975, many states liberalized their competency requirements for child witnesses.[46]

---

[44]. See Note, The Testimony of Child Victims in Sexual Abuse Prosecutions: Two Legislative Innovations, 98 Harv. L. Rev. 806 (1985).

[45]. See Lucy S. McGough, Child Witnesses: Fragile Voices in the American Legal System 97, 99-100 (1994); Myers, supra note [40], at 65-66; Belle Kinnan Deaver, The Competency of Children, 4 Cooley L. Rev. 522 (1987).

[46]. Approximately one-third of the states follow the federal rules for child witnesses. Among the remaining jurisdictions, most retain either a requirement that child witnesses must testify under oath, or the requirement that a competency hearing is a prerequisite for children below a certain age in order for them to testify. McGough, supra note [45], at 98.

9. Several states, following the lead of Washington, have enacted special child hearsay statutes or "tender years hearsay exceptions" to permit the admission of statements about sexual abuse by child victims. See Wash. Rev. Code Ann. §9A.44.120 (West 2000). Approximately 34 states have enacted such statutes. See Robert G. Marks, Should We Believe the People Who Believe the Children?: The Need for a New Sexual Abuse Tender Years Hearsay Exception Statute, 32 Harv. J. on Legis. 207, 236-246 (1995). Statutes generally require that the hearsay is not admissible under another hearsay exception, is determined by the court to be reliable, the child either testifies or is unavailable, and corroborating evidence exists. Jean Montoya, Child Hearsay Statutes: At Once Over-Inclusive and Under-Inclusive, 5 Psychol. Pub. Pol'y & L. 304, 305 (1999). Are these statutes constitutional under *White*?

Suppose a victim's sibling witnesses the abuse of the victim and makes a statement about it to a babysitter. Would the statement be admissible under the special statutes? Suppose the child witnesses her father killing her mother and makes a statement about it to a third party. Would that statement be admissible? See Montoya, supra, at 316-320 (criticizing shortcomings of statutes).

## 4. Dispositional Alternatives

### a. Temporary Dispositions: Foster Care

Once the state establishes that grounds exist for intervention, the state must determine a placement for the child. This section explores various dispositional alternatives.

## ■ SMITH v. ORGANIZATION OF FOSTER FAMILIES FOR EQUALITY AND REFORM (OFFER)
*431 U.S. 816 (1977)*

Mr. Justice BRENNAN delivered the opinion of the Court.

Appellees, individual foster parents[1] and an organization of foster parents, brought this civil rights class action pursuant to 42 U.S.C. §1983 . . . on their own behalf and on behalf of children for whom they have

---

1. Appellee Madeleine Smith is the foster parent with whom Eric and Danielle Gandy have been placed since 1970. The Gandy children, who are now 12 and 9 years old respectively, were voluntarily placed in foster care by their natural mother in 1968, and have had no contact with her at least since being placed with Mrs. Smith. The foster-care agency has sought to remove the children from Mrs. Smith's care because her arthritis, in the agency's judgment makes it difficult for her to continue to provide adequate care. . . .

provided homes for a year or more. They sought declaratory and injunctive relief [alleging] that the procedures governing the removal of foster children from foster homes [N.Y. Soc. Serv. Law §§383(2), 400, and 18 N.Y.C.R.R. §450.14] violated the Due Process and Equal Protection Clauses. . . . A group of natural mothers of children in foster care[5] were granted leave to intervene on behalf of themselves and others similarly situated. [The district court determined that the preremoval procedures were an unconstitutional deprivation of due process by denying the foster child a hearing before transfer to another foster home or return to the natural parents. 418 F. Supp. 277, 282 (S.D.N.Y. 1976).]

The expressed central policy of the New York system is that "it is generally desirable for the child to remain with or be returned to the natural parent because the child's need for a normal family life will usually best be met in the natural home, and . . . parents are entitled to bring up their own children unless the best interests of the child would be thereby endangered," Soc. Serv. Law §384-b(1)(a)(ii). But the State has opted for foster care as one response to those situations where the natural parents are unable to provide the "positive, nurturing family relationships" and "normal family life in a permanent home" that offer "the best opportunity for children to develop and thrive." §§384-b(1)(b), (1)(a)(i).

. . . [T]he distinctive features of foster care are, first, "that it is care in a *family*, it is noninstitutional substitute care," and, second, "that it is for a *planned* period — either temporary or extended. This is unlike adoptive placement, which implies a *permanent* substitution of one home for another." [Alfred Kadushin, Child Welfare Services 355 (1967).]

Under the New York scheme children may be placed in foster care either by voluntary placement or by court order. Most foster care placements are voluntary. They occur when physical or mental illness, eco-

---

Appellees Ralph and Christiane Goldberg were the foster parents of Rafael Serrano, now 14. His parents placed him in foster care voluntarily in 1969 after an abuse complaint was filed against them. [The Goldbergs eventually separated, placing Rafael in residential care.]

Appellees Walter and Dorothy Lhotan were foster parents of the four Wallace sisters, who were voluntarily placed in foster care by their mother in 1970. The two older girls were placed with the Lhotans in that year, their two younger sisters in 1972. In June 1974, the Lhotans were informed that the agency had decided to return the two younger girls to their mother and transfer the two older girls to another foster home. The agency apparently felt that the Lhotans were too emotionally involved with the girls and were damaging the agency's efforts to prepare them to return to their mother. [The children eventually were returned to their mother.]

5. Intervenor Naomi Rodriguez, who is blind, placed her newborn son Edwin in foster care in 1973 because of marital difficulties. When Mrs. Rodriguez separated from her husband three months later, she sought return of her child. Her efforts over the next nine months to obtain return of the child were resisted by the agency, apparently because it felt her handicap prevented her from providing adequate care. [She] finally prevailed, three years after she first sought return of the child. . . .

nomic problems, or other family crises make it impossible for natural parents, particularly single parents, to provide a stable home life for their children for some limited period. Resort to such placements is almost compelled when it is not possible in such circumstance to place the child with a relative or friend, or to pay for the services of a homemaker or boarding school. [Under voluntary placements, a written agreement between the parent and agency may provide for the child's return at a specified date, but if not, the child must be returned within 20 days of notice from the parent.]

The agency may maintain the child in an institutional setting, but more commonly acts under its authority to "place out and board out" children in foster homes. Foster parents, who are licensed by the State or an authorized foster-care agency, provide care under a contractual arrangement with the agency, and are compensated for their services. The typical contract expressly reserves the right of the agency to remove the child on request. Conversely, the foster parent may cancel the agreement at will.

The New York system divides parental functions among agency, foster parents, and natural parents, and the definitions of the respective roles are often complex and often unclear. The law transfers "care and custody" to the agency, but day-to-day supervision of the child and his activities, and most of the functions ordinarily associated with legal custody, are the responsibility of the foster parent. Nevertheless, agency supervision of the performance of the foster parents takes forms indicating that the foster parent does not have the full authority of a legal custodian.[18] Moreover, the natural parent's placement of the child with the agency does not surrender legal guardianship; the parent retains authority to act with respect to the child in certain circumstances.[20] The natural parent has not only the right but the obligation to visit the foster child and plan for his future; failure of a parent with capacity to fulfill the obligation for more than a year can result in a court order terminating the parent's rights on the ground of neglect.

---

18. "The agency sets limits and advances directives as to how the foster parents are to behave toward the child — a situation not normally encountered by natural parents. The shared control and responsibility for the child is clearly set forth in the instruction pamphlets issued to foster parents." [Kadushin, supra], at 394. Agencies frequently prohibit corporal punishment; require that children over a certain age be given an allowance; forbid changes in the child's sleeping arrangements or vacations out of State without agency approval; require the foster parent to discuss the child's behavioral problems with the agency. Furthermore, since the cost of supporting the child is borne by the agency, the responsibility, as well as the authority, of the foster parent is shared with the agency.

20. "[A]lthough the agency usually obtains legal custody in foster family care, the child still legally 'belongs' to the parent and the parent retains guardianship. This means that, for some crucial aspects of the child's life, the agency has no authority to act. Only the parent can consent to surgery for the child, or consent to his marriage, or permit his enlistment in the armed forces, or represent him at law." Kadushin, supra, at 355.

Children may also enter foster care by court order. . . . The consequences of foster-care placement by court order do not differ substantially from those for children voluntarily placed, except that the parent is not entitled to return of the child on demand . . . ; termination of foster care must then be consented to by the court.

The provisions of the scheme specifically at issue in this litigation come into play when the agency having legal custody determines to remove the foster child from the foster home, either because it has determined that it would be in the child's best interests to transfer him to some other foster home, or to return the child to his natural parents in accordance with the statute or placement agreement. Most children are removed in order to be transferred to another foster home.[23] The procedures by which foster parents may challenge a removal made for that purpose differ somewhat from those where the removal is made to return the child to his natural parent.

Section 383(2), n.3, supra, provides that the "authorized agency placing out or boarding (a foster) child . . . may in its discretion remove such child from the home where placed or boarded." Administrative regulations implement this provision. The agency is required, except in emergencies, to notify the foster parents in writing 10 days in advance of any removal. The notice advises the foster parents that if they object to the child's removal they may request a "conference" with the Social Services Department. The department schedules requested conferences within 10 days of the receipt of the request. The foster parent may appear with counsel at the conference, where he will "be advised of the reasons (for the removal of the child), and be afforded an opportunity to submit reasons why the child should not be removed." §450.10(a). The official must render a decision in writing within five days after the close of the conference, and send notice of his decision to the foster parents and the agency. The proposed removal is stayed pending the outcome of the conference.

If the child is removed after the conference, the foster parent may appeal to the Department of Social Services for a [full adversary administrative hearing which is subject to judicial review]; however, the removal is not automatically stayed pending the hearing and judicial review.

This statutory and regulatory scheme applies statewide.[28] In addition, regulations [applicable to New York City] provide even greater pro-

23. The record shows that in 1973-1974 approximately 80 percent of the children removed from foster homes in New York State after living in the foster home for one year or more were transferred to another foster placement. Thirteen percent were returned to the biological parents, and 7 percent were adopted.

28. There is some dispute whether the procedures set out in 18 N.Y.C.R.R. §450.10 and Soc. Serv. Law §400 apply in the case of a foster child being removed from his foster home to be returned to his natural parents. [N]othing in either the statute or the regulations limits the availability of these procedures to transfers within the foster-care system. Each refers to the decision to remove a child from the foster family home, and thus on its face each would seem to cover removal for the purpose of returning the child to its parents. . . .

cedural safeguards [in the form of a *preremoval* trial, upon request of the foster parents, if a child is being transferred to another foster home]. One further preremoval procedural safeguard is available. [Soc. Serv. Law §392] provides a mechanism whereby a foster parent may obtain preremoval judicial review of an agency's decision to remove a child who has been in foster care for 18 months or more.

Foster care of children is a sensitive and emotion-laden subject, and foster-care programs consequently stir strong controversy. The New York regulatory scheme is no exception. . . . From the standpoint of natural parents, such as the appellant intervenors here, foster care has been condemned as a class-based intrusion into the family life of the poor. See, e.g., Jenkins, Child Welfare as a Class System, in Children and Decent People 3 (A. Schorr ed. 1974). It is certainly true that the poor resort to foster care more often than other citizens. . . .

The extent to which supposedly "voluntary" placements are in fact voluntary has been questioned on other grounds as well. For example, it has been said that many "voluntary" placements are in fact coerced by threat of neglect proceedings and are not in fact voluntary in the sense of the product of an informed consent. Mnookin, [Foster Care In Whose Best Interests?, 43 Harv. Educ. Rev. 599, 601 (1973)]. Studies also suggest that social workers of middle-class backgrounds, perhaps unconsciously, incline to favor continued placement in foster care with a generally higher-status family rather than return the child to his natural family, thus reflecting a bias that treats the natural parents' poverty and lifestyle as prejudicial to the best interests of the child. This accounts,[36] it has been said, for the hostility of agencies to the efforts of natural parents to obtain the return of their children.

Appellee foster parents as well as natural parents question the accuracy of the idealized picture portrayed by New York. They note that children often stay in "temporary" foster care for much longer than contemplated by the theory of the system. The District Court found as a fact that the median time spent in foster care in New York was over four years. Indeed, many children apparently remain in this "limbo" indefinitely. Mnookin [Child-Custody Adjudication: Judicial Functions in the Face of Indeterminacy, 39 Law & Contemp. Probs. 226, 273 (1975)]. The District Court also found that the longer a child remains in foster care, the more likely it is that he will never leave. . . . It is not surprising then that many children, particularly those that enter foster care at a very early age and have little or no contact with their natural parents

36. Other factors alleged to bias agencies in favor of retention in foster care are the lack of sufficient staff to provide social work services needed by the natural parent to resolve their problems and prepare for return of the child; policies of many agencies to discourage involvement of the natural parent in the care of the child while in foster care; and systems of foster-care funding that encourage agencies to keep the child in foster care. Wald, [State Intervention on Behalf of "Neglected" Children, 28 Stan. L. Rev. 623, 677-679 (1976)]. . . .

during extended stays in foster care, often develop deep emotional ties with their foster parents.[40]

Yet such ties do not seem to be regarded as obstacles to transfer of the child from one foster placement to another. The record in this case indicates that nearly 60% of the children in foster care in New York City have experienced more than one placement, and about 28% have experienced three or more. [E]ven when it is clear that a foster child will not be returned to his natural parents, it is rare that he achieves a stable home life through final termination of parental ties and adoption into a new permanent family.

[W]e present this summary in the view that some understanding of those criticisms is necessary for a full appreciation of the complex and controversial system with which this lawsuit is concerned. [But, our] task is only to determine whether the District Court correctly held that the present procedures preceding the removal from a foster home of children resident there a year or more are constitutionally inadequate. . . .

Our first inquiry is whether appellees have asserted interests within the Fourteenth Amendment's protection of "liberty." . . . The appellees' basic contention is that when a child has lived in a foster home for a year or more, a psychological tie is created between the child and the foster parents which constitutes the foster family the true "psychological family" of the child. That family, they argue, has a "liberty interest" in its survival as a family protected by the Fourteenth Amendment. Upon this premise they conclude that the foster child cannot be removed without a prior hearing satisfying due process. Appointed counsel for the children, . . . however, disagrees, and has consistently argued that the foster parents have no such liberty interest independent of the interests of the foster children, and that the best interests of the children would not be served by procedural protections beyond those already provided by New York law. The intervening natural parents of children in foster care, . . . also oppose the foster parents, arguing that recognition of the procedural right claimed would undercut both the substantive family law of New York, which favors the return of children to their natural parents as expeditiously as possible, and their constitutionally protected right of family privacy, by forcing them to submit to a hearing and defend their rights to their children before the children could be returned to them.

---

40. The development of such ties points up an intrinsic ambiguity of foster care that is central to this case. The warmer and more homelike environment of foster care is intended to be its main advantage over institutional child care, yet because in theory foster care is intended to be only temporary, foster parents are urged not to become too attached to the children in their care. Mnookin, [43 Harv. Educ. Rev.,] at 613. Indeed, the New York courts have upheld removal from a foster home for the very reason that the foster parents had become too emotionally involved with the child. In re Jewish Child Care Assn. (Sanders), 5 N.Y.2d 222, 183 N.Y.S.2d 65, 156 N.E.2d 700 (1959). See also the case of the Lhotans, named appellees in this case. . . .

[We] turn to appellees' assertion that they have a constitutionally protected liberty interest . . . in the integrity of their family unit. This assertion clearly presents difficulties. . . . There does exist a "private realm of family life which the state cannot enter," Prince v. Massachusetts, 321 U.S. 158, 166 (1944), that has been afforded both substantive and procedural protection. But is the relation of foster parent to foster child sufficiently akin to the concept of "family" recognized in our precedents to merit similar protection?[48] [W]e are not without guides to some of the elements that define the concept of "family" and contribute to its place in our society.

First, the usual understanding of "family" implies biological relationships, and most decisions treating the relation between parent and child have stressed this element. Stanley v. Illinois, 405 U.S. 645, 651 (1972), for example, spoke of "(t)he rights to conceive and to raise one's children" as essential rights. . . . A biological relationship is not present in the case of the usual foster family. But biological relationships are not exclusive determination of the existence of a family. [T]he importance of the familial relationship, to the individuals involved and to the society, stems from the emotional attachments that derive from the intimacy of daily association, and from the role it plays in "promot(ing) a way of life" through the instruction of children, Wisconsin v. Yoder, 406 U.S. 205, 231-233 (1972), as well as from the fact of blood relationship. No one would seriously dispute that a deeply loving and interdependent relationship between an adult and a child in his or her care may exist even in the absence of blood relationship. At least where a child has been placed in foster care as an infant, has never known his natural parents, and has remained continuously for several years in the care of the same foster parents, it is natural that the foster family should hold the same place in the emotional life of the foster child, and fulfill the same socializing functions, as a natural family.[52] For this reason, we cannot dismiss the foster family as a mere collection of unrelated individuals.

But there are also important distinctions between the foster family and the natural family. First, unlike the earlier cases recognizing a right to family privacy, the State here seeks to interfere, not with a relationship having its origins entirely apart from the power of the State, but rather

---

48. Of course, recognition of a liberty interest in foster families for purposes of the procedural protections of the Due Process Clause would not necessarily require that foster families be treated as fully equivalent to biological families for purposes of substantive due process review. Cf. Moore v. City of East Cleveland, [431 U.S. 494, 546-547 (1977) (White, J., dissenting)].

52. The briefs dispute at some length the validity of the "psychological parent" theory propounded in J. Goldstein, A. Freud, & A. Solnit, Beyond the Best Interests of the Child (1973). That book, on which appellee foster parents relied to some extent in the District Court, is indeed controversial. But this case turns, not on the disputed validity of any particular psychological theory, but on the legal consequences of the undisputed fact that the emotional ties between foster parent and foster child are in many cases quite close, and undoubtedly in some as close as those existing in biological families.

with a foster family which has its source in state law and contractual arrangements. . . . Here, however, whatever emotional ties may develop between foster parent and foster child have their origins in an arrangement in which the State has been a partner from the outset. . . .

A second consideration related to this is that ordinarily procedural protection may be afforded to a liberty interest of one person without derogating from the substantive liberty of another. Here, however, such a tension is virtually unavoidable. Under New York law, the natural parent of a foster child in voluntary placement has an absolute right to the return of his child in the absence of a court order obtainable only upon compliance with rigorous substantive and procedural standards, which reflect the constitutional protection accorded the natural family. Moreover, the natural parent initially gave up his child to the State only on the express understanding that the child would be returned in those circumstances. These rights are difficult to reconcile with the liberty interest in the foster family relationship claimed by appellees. It is one thing to say that individuals may acquire a liberty interest against arbitrary governmental interference in the family-like associations into which they have freely entered, even in the absence of biological connection or state-law recognition of the relationship. It is quite another to say that one may acquire such an interest in the face of another's constitutionally recognized liberty interest that derives from blood relationship, state-law sanction, and basic human right an interest the foster parent has recognized by contract from the outset. Whatever liberty interest might otherwise exist in the foster family as an institution, that interest must be substantially attenuated where the proposed removal from the foster family is to return the child to his natural parents.

As this discussion suggests, appellees' claim to a constitutionally protected liberty interest raises complex and novel questions. It is unnecessary for us to resolve those questions definitively in this case, however, for like the District Court, we conclude that "narrower grounds exist to support" our reversal. We are persuaded that, even on the assumption that appellees have a protected "liberty interest," the District Court erred in holding that the preremoval procedures presently employed by the State are constitutionally defective.

Where procedural due process must be afforded because a "liberty" or "property" interest is within the Fourteenth Amendment's protection, there must be determined "what process is due" in the particular context. . . . Consideration of the procedures employed by the City and State of New York [in light of the factors in Mathews v. Eldridge, 414 U.S. 319 (1976), i.e., the private interest affected; the risk of an erroneous deprivation of such interest by the procedures; and, the government's interest, including fiscal or administrative burdens, that additional or substitute procedural requirements would entail] requires the conclusion that those procedures satisfy constitutional standards.

Turning first to the procedure applicable in New York City, [SSC Procedure No. 5] provides that before a child is removed from a foster home for transfer to another foster home, the foster parents may request an "independent review." . . . Such a procedure would appear to give a more elaborate trial-type hearing to foster families than this Court has found required in other contexts of administrative determinations. The District Court found the procedure inadequate on four grounds, none of which we find sufficient to justify the holding that the procedure violates due process.

First, the court held that the "independent review" administrative proceeding was insufficient because it was only available on the request of the foster parents. [That is,] the proceeding should be provided as a matter of course, because the interests of the foster parents and those of the child would not necessarily be coextensive, and it could not be assumed that the foster parents would invoke the hearing procedure in every case in which it was in the child's interest to have a hearing. . . . We disagree. As previously noted, the constitutional liberty, if any, sought to be protected by the New York procedures is a right of *family* privacy or autonomy, and the basis for recognition of any such interest in the foster family must be that close emotional ties analogous to those between parent and child are established when a child resides for a lengthy period with a foster family. If this is so, necessarily we should expect that the foster parents will seek to continue the relationship to preserve the stability of the family; if they do not request a hearing, it is difficult to see what right or interest of the foster child is protected by holding a hearing. [C]onsideration of the interest to be protected and the likelihood of erroneous deprivations . . . do not support the District Court's imposition of [automatic hearings]. Moreover, automatic provision of hearings [would impose] a substantial additional administrative burden on the State. . . .

Second, the District Court faulted the city procedure on the ground that participation is limited to the foster parents and the agency and the natural parent and the child are not made parties to the hearing. This is not fatal in light of the nature of the alleged constitutional interests at stake. When the child's transfer from one foster home to another is pending, the interest arguably requiring protection is that of the foster family, not that of the natural parents. Moreover, the natural parent can generally add little to the accuracy of factfinding concerning the wisdom of such a transfer. . . . Much the same can be said in response to the District Court's statement [that it would sometimes be advisable to appoint a representative for the child]. But nothing in the New York City procedure prevents consultation of the child's wishes. . . . Such consultation, however, does not require that the child or an appointed representative must be a party with full adversary powers in all preremoval hearings.

The other two defects in the city procedure found by the District Court must also be rejected. One is that the procedure does not extend to the removal of a child from foster care to be returned to his natural parent. But as we have already held, whatever liberty interest may be argued to exist in the foster family is significantly weaker in the case of removals preceding return to the natural parent, and the balance of due process interests must accordingly be different. . . . Similarly, the District Court pointed out that the New York City procedure coincided with the informal "conference" and postremoval hearings provided as a matter of state law. This overlap in procedures may be unnecessary or even to some degree unwise, but a State does not violate the Due Process Clause by providing alternative or additional procedures beyond what the Constitution requires.

Outside New York City, where only the statewide procedures apply, foster parents are provided not only with the procedures of a preremoval conference and postremoval hearing provided by 18 N.Y.C.R.R. §450.10 and Soc. Serv. Law §400, but also with the preremoval *judicial* hearing available on request to foster parents who have in their care children who have been in foster care for 18 months or more, Soc. Serv. Law §392. [A] foster parent in such case may obtain an order that the child remain in his care.

The District Court found three defects in this full judicial process. First, a §392 proceeding is available only to those foster children who have been in foster care for 18 months or more. . . . We do not think that the 18-month limitation [renders] the New York scheme constitutionally inadequate. The assumed liberty interest to be protected in this case is one rooted in the emotional attachments that develop over time between a child and the adults who care for him. But there is no reason to assume that those attachments ripen at less than 18 months or indeed at any precise point. . . .

The District Court's other two findings of infirmity in the §392 procedure have already been considered and held to be without merit. . . . Finally, the §392 hearing is available to foster parents, both in and outside New York City, even where the removal sought is for the purpose of returning the child to his natural parents. Since this remedy provides a sufficient constitutional preremoval hearing to protect whatever liberty interest might exist in the continued existence of the foster family when the State seeks to transfer the child to another foster home, a fortiori the procedure is adequate to protect the lesser interest of the foster family in remaining together at the expense of the disruption of the natural family.

. . . Since we hold that the procedures provided by New York State in §392 and by New York City's SSC Procedure No. 5 are adequate to protect whatever liberty interest appellees may have, the judgment of the District Court is reversed.

Mr. Justice STEWART, with whom THE CHIEF JUSTICE and Mr. Justice REHNQUIST join, concurring in the judgment.

. . . I cannot understand why the Court thinks itself obliged to decide these cases on the assumption that either foster parents or foster children in New York have some sort of "liberty" interest in the continuation of their relationship. Rather than tiptoeing around this central issue, I would squarely hold that the interests asserted by the appellees are not of a kind that the Due Process Clause of the Fourteenth Amendment protects.

[T]he predicate for invoking the Due Process Clause — the existence of state-created liberty or property — [is] missing here. New York confers no right on foster families to remain intact, defeasible only upon proof of specific acts or circumstances. Similarly, New York law provides no basis for a justifiable expectation on the part of foster families that their relationship will continue indefinitely. . . .

What remains of the appellees' argument is the theory that the relation of the foster parent to the foster child may generate emotional attachments similar to those found in natural families. The Court surmises that foster families who share these attachments might enjoy the same constitutional interest in "family privacy" as natural families. . . .

But under New York's foster-care laws, any case where the foster parents had assumed the emotional role of the child's natural parents would represent not a triumph of the system, to be constitutionally safeguarded from state intrusion, but a failure. The goal of foster care, at least in New York, is not to provide a permanent substitute for the natural or adoptive home, but to prepare the child for his return to his real parents or placement in a permanent adoptive home by giving him temporary shelter in a family setting. Thus, the New York Court of Appeals has recognized that the development of close emotional ties between foster parents and a child may hinder the child's ultimate adjustment in a permanent home, and provide a basis for the *termination* of the foster family relationship. In re Jewish Child Care Assn. (Sanders), [156 N.E. 2d 700 (N.Y. 1959)]. Perhaps it is to be expected that children who spend unduly long stays in what should have been temporary foster care will develop strong emotional ties with their foster parents. But this does not mean, and I cannot believe, that such breakdowns of the New York system must be protected or forever frozen in their existence by the Due Process Clause of the Fourteenth Amendment.

One of the liberties protected by the Due Process Clause, the Court has held, is the freedom to "establish a home and bring up children." Meyer v. Nebraska, supra, 262 U.S., at 399. If a State were to attempt to force the breakup of a natural family, over the objections of the parents and their children, without some showing of unfitness and for the sole reason that to do so was thought to be in the children's best interest, I should have little doubt that the State would have intruded impermissibly on "the private realm of family life which the state cannot enter." Prince v. Massachusetts, 321 U.S. 158, 166. But this constitutional concept is simply not in point when we deal with foster families as New York law has defined them. The family life upon which the State "intrudes" is simply a temporary status which the State itself has created. It is a "family life" defined and controlled by the law of New York, for which New York pays, and the goals of which New York is entitled to and does set for itself.

## Notes and Questions

1. *OFFER* held that the preremoval hearing regulations afforded by New York City and the state accorded sufficient due process protection to foster parents. *Must* such a hearing be provided before removal, or can a social services agency rely on less formal interviews? In other words, how should the Court decide the substantive issue that Justice Stewart accuses the majority of "tiptoeing around"?

In the wake of *OFFER*, most courts refused to recognize the liberty interests of foster parents. David L. Chambers & Michael S. Wald, *Smith v. OFFER*, in In the Interest of Children 67, 116-117 (Robert H. Mnookin ed., 1985). However, some courts have recognized long-term foster relationships and the rights of foster parents in other limited situations. See, e.g., Richard D. v. Rebecca G., 599 N.W.2d 90 (Wis. Ct. App. 1999); In re R.C., 743 So. 2d 843 (La. Ct. App. 1999). But cf. Rodriguez v. McLoughlin, 214 F.3d 328 (2d Cir. 2000) (declining to recognize foster parent's liberty interest in post-removal visitation), *cert. denied*, 121 S. Ct. 2192 (2001). Should foster parents' rights be recognized via guardianship proceedings? See Division of Family Servs. v. Harrison, 741 A.2d 1016 (Del. Super. Ct. 1999) (holding that foster parents have standing to petition for guardianship). Should courts be concerned with the interests of foster *parents* or foster *families* in remaining intact?

2. The foster care system has its roots in a nineteenth-century social movement. Charles Loring Brace (founder of the New York Children's Aid Society in 1853), using the apprenticeship system as a model, sent poor children via "orphan trains" to live and work with farm families instead of to the almshouse or other institutional settings. See Murray Levine & Adeline Levine, Helping Children: A Social History 190-195 (1992). See also Emma Brace, ed., The Life of Charles Loring Brace (1st ed. 1894, 1976) (autobiographical collection of Brace's letters).

3. As *OFFER* explains, often parents, rather than the state, initiate foster placement. What does *OFFER* reveal about the problems posed by such voluntary surrenders? See, e.g., Young v. County of Fulton, 160 F.3d 899 (2d Cir. 1998) (mother who voluntarily placed sons in foster care brought §1983 action against social services department for denying her right to visit sons without prior hearing and conspiring to take sons permanently in violation of her custodial rights).

4. Like the children in *OFFER*, most children in foster care are placed in foster family homes. Group homes are the second most common living arrangement. Presently, an increasing number of children (especially African-American children and children whose parents are crack cocaine addicts) are placed in kinship care with close relatives.[47] What problems might arise for foster children and foster parents in kinship care? See Lipscomb v. Simmons, 962 F.2d 1374 (9th Cir. 1992 (en banc) (provision of foster care benefits to nonrelatives, but not relatives, does not violate equal protection). See generally Kinship Foster Care: Policy, Practice, and Research (Rebecca L. Hegar & Maria Scannapieco eds., 1999); Note, The Policy of Penalty in Kinship Care, 112 Harv. L. Rev. 1047 (1999); Megan O'Laughlin, Note, A Theory of Relativity: Kinship Foster Care May Be the Key to Stopping the Pendulum of Termination v. Reunification, 51 Vand. L. Rev. 1427 (1998).

5. The concept of the "psychological parent" was developed by Joseph Goldstein, Anna Freud and Alfred Solnit in Beyond the Best Interests of the Child (1973). Does *OFFER* adequately protect the "psychological parent-child" relationship? Why protect this relationship? Why not protect it? An omitted section of footnote 40 in *OFFER* makes the point that foster parents sometimes provide inadequate care, even abusing and neglecting foster children (citing Michael S. Wald, State Intervention on Behalf of "Neglected" Children: Standards for Removal of Children from Their Homes, Monitoring the Status of Children in Foster Care, and Termination of Parental Rights, 28 Stan. L. Rev. 623, 645 (1976)). Does this evidence affect your reasoning?

The common law parental immunity doctrine provides protection from liability for torts committed on one's child. In Nichol v. Stass, 735 N.E.2d 582 (Ill. 2000), two-year-old Jonathan Nichol drowned accidentally in his foster parents' toilet. The Illinois supreme court held that the foster parents were entitled to a limited grant of parental immunity. Do you agree that foster parents should be granted parental immunity from negligent acts regarding the foster children in their care? See generally Sarie E. Winner, *Nichol v. Stass:* Ending Predictability for Foster Parents in the Law of Sovereign and Parental Immunity, 32 Loy. U. Chi. L.J. 735 (2001).

6. *Foster care population.* When *OFFER* was decided, the typical parent who put a child in foster care was divorced with financial problems, an unwed mother, or a mother on welfare who might be temporarily unable to care for her child because of illness or economic problems. A leading authority suggests that family disruption, financial difficulties,

[47]. New York data reveal that the number of foster care children placed with relatives increased from 1,000 in 1986 to more than 20,000 in 1990. Eugene M. Lewit, Children in Foster Care, in The Future of Children: Home Visiting 198 (Center for the Future of Children, David & Lucille Packard Fdn., 1993).

and medical reasons were the primary factors for placement.[48] Neglect, abuse, and abandonment also accounted for many children who entered foster care.

Currently, however, the reasons for placement have changed. Beginning in 1986 the numbers of children in foster care began to rise dramatically.[49] A considerable number of children presently are in foster care because their families are homeless or lack adequate housing.[50] Substance abuse also is a contributing factor.[51] Increasing use of crack cocaine leads to more infants being placed in foster care due to their drug toxicity at birth, substance-related abandonment, or postbirth inadequate parenting.[52]

More African-American and Hispanic children also are in foster care, and more sibling groups need to be placed together.[53] Finally, children with HIV or whose parents die of AIDS are a growing proportion of the foster care population.[54] Because of substance abuse and AIDS, many children now entering foster care are children with special needs. See generally Deborah Weimer, Beyond Parens Patriae: Assuring Timely, Informed, Compassionate Decisionmaking for HIV-Positive Children in Foster Care, 46 U. Miami L. Rev. 379 (1991).

7. *Epilogue.* Although the Supreme Court reversed the district court's finding of unconstitutionality in *OFFER*, the case had an impact. First, the Gandy children (see footnote 1 supra) were permitted to remain with their foster mother Mrs. Smith. Eventually, she adopted them. Second, the litigation put on notice those states without any preremoval conferences that their procedures might be constitutionally flawed. Third, the litigation resulted in new procedural protections in New York City regarding the formal hearings prior to intra-foster care transfers. Foster parents (who must request these hearings) may appear with coun-

---

[48]. Alfred Kadushin, Child Welfare Services 366 (1967).

[49]. Lewit, supra note [47]; National Commission on Children, Just the Facts: A Summary of Recent Information on America's Children and Their Families 156 (1993) [hereafter National Commission Factbook]. The years 1987 and 1988 witnessed a 7 percent and 9 percent gain, respectively. Id. Approximately 400,000 were in foster care in 1990. Meryl Schwartz, Reinventing Guardianship: Subsidized Guardianship, Foster Care, and Child Welfare, 22 N.Y.U. Rev. L. & Soc. Change 441, 442 (1996) (citing House Comm. on Ways and Means, 102d Cong., 2d Sess., Overview of Entitlement Programs, 1992 Green Book 903 (Comm. Print 1992)).

[50]. Families with children account currently for 43 percent of the homeless population. Children's Defense Fund, The State of America's Children 37 (1994).

[51]. The numbers of children entering foster care due to parental substance abuse more than doubled between 1984 and 1992. Lewit, supra note [47], at 198 (although based on California data, the author suggests that such findings are illustrative of national trends).

[52]. Id. at 196.

[53]. Schwartz, supra note [49], at 442.

[54]. Children's Defense Fund, supra note [50] at 20. In 1990, approximately 26 percent of children known to be HIV-positive had been placed in foster care. Deborah Weimer, Beyond Parens Patriae: Assuring Timely, Informed, Compassionate Decisionmaking for HIV-Positive Children in Foster Care, 46 U. Miami L. Rev. 379, 380 (1991).

sel; witnesses are sworn and subject to cross-examination; and expert testimony is often taken. Although only a small number of such hearings are held, the reversal rate for these contested decisions is quite high. Unfortunately, the new regulations apply only in New York City (not New York state) and have not spurred similar changes elsewhere. Chambers & Wald, supra, at 114-116.

8. *Foster care reform: Adoption Assistance and Child Welfare Act.* Congress addressed the "limbo" of foster care, illustrated in OFFER, by enacting the Adoption Assistance and Child Welfare Act of 1980 (AACWA), 42 U.S.C. §§620 et seq., 670 et seq. (1994). The AACWA provides federal matching funds to states for administering foster care and adoption services (emphasizing preventive and reunification services), subject to certain requirements. Specifically, to qualify for federal funding, a state must make "reasonable efforts" (id. at §671(a)(15)) to prevent the need to remove a child from the home and to facilitate the child's return as soon as possible. (On the meaning of "reasonable efforts" and whether a private right of action exists to enforce the AACWA to ensure states make "reasonable efforts," see Marisol v. Giuliani, page 1073.)

The AACWA introduced the concept of "permanency planning" to remedy the problem of foster care drift. After a child is placed in foster care, the AACWA mandates that a case file and plan be created that focuses on family reunification. Case files must be reviewed by agencies and courts every 6 months with dispositional hearings held after 18 months.

9. *Adoption and Safe Families Act (ASFA).* In 1997, Congress enacted the Adoption and Safe Families Act as a response to the concerns of legislators and child welfare agencies that the policy of preservation and reunification of families, as mandated by the AACWA, was exposing children to unnecessary risks. In contrast to AACWA's emphasis on family preservation and reunification, ASFA emphasizes speedier termination of parental rights. To obtain federal funding, ASFA requires states to file a termination petition if a child has been in foster care for 15 of the last 22 months. States need not file such petitions if (1) a relative cares for the child, (2) a state agency believes that termination would not be in the best interests of the child, or (3) a state agency has failed to provide the family with reunification services. (For ASFA's exceptions to the AACWA's "reasonable efforts requirement," see Marisol v. Giuliani, page 1073.)

ASFA also shortens the time frame for permanency hearings. In contrast to AACWA's 18-month time frame, ASFA requires permanency hearings to occur within 12 months from the time that the child enters foster care. For a criticism of the ASFA three policy exceptions (above) to the filing requirements, see Elisabeth Bartholet, Nobody's Children: Abuse and Neglect, Foster Drift, and the Adoption Alternative 193-196 (1999). See also Stephanie Jill Gendell, In Search of Permanency: A

Reflection on the First 3 Years of the Adoption and Safe Families Act Implementation, 39 Fam. & Conciliation Courts Rev. 25 (2001); Martin Guggenheim, Somebody's Children: Sustaining the Family's Place in Child Welfare Policy, 113 Harv. L. Rev. 1716 (2000) (book review of Bartholet's *Nobody's Children*).

### b. Liability for Selection of Disposition

### ■ DESHANEY v. WINNEBAGO COUNTY DEPARTMENT OF SOCIAL SERVICES
*489 U.S. 189 (1989)*

Chief Justice REHNQUIST delivered the opinion of the Court. . . .

The facts of this case are undeniably tragic. Petitioner Joshua DeShaney was born in 1979. In 1980, a Wyoming court granted his parents a divorce and awarded custody of Joshua to his father, Randy DeShaney. The father shortly thereafter moved to Neenah, a city located in Winnebago County, Wisconsin, taking the infant Joshua with him. There he entered into a second marriage, which also ended in divorce.

The Winnebago County authorities first learned that Joshua DeShaney might be a victim of child abuse in January 1982, when his father's second wife complained to the police, at the time of their divorce, that he had previously "hit the boy causing marks and [was] a prime case for child abuse." The Winnebago County Department of Social Services (DSS) interviewed the father, but he denied the accusations, and DSS did not pursue them further. In January 1983, Joshua was admitted to a local hospital with multiple bruises and abrasions. The examining physician suspected child abuse and notified DSS, which immediately obtained an order from a Wisconsin juvenile court placing Joshua in the temporary custody of the hospital. Three days later, the county convened an ad hoc "Child Protection Team" — consisting of a pediatrician, a psychologist, a police detective, the county's lawyer, several DSS caseworkers, and various hospital personnel — to consider Joshua's situation. At this meeting, the Team decided that there was insufficient evidence of child abuse to retain Joshua in the custody of the court. The Team did, however, decide to recommend several measures to protect Joshua, including enrolling him in a preschool program, providing his father with certain counselling services, and encouraging his father's girlfriend to move out of the home. Randy DeShaney entered into a voluntary agreement with DSS in which he promised to cooperate with them in accomplishing these goals.

Based on the recommendation of the Child Protection Team, the juvenile court dismissed the child protection case and returned Joshua to the custody of his father. A month later, emergency room personnel called the DSS caseworker handling Joshua's case to report that he had once again been treated for suspicious injuries. The caseworker concluded that there was no basis for action. For the next six months, the caseworker made monthly visits to the DeShaney home, during which she observed a number of suspicious injuries on Joshua's head; she also noticed that he had not been enrolled in school and that the girlfriend had not moved out. The caseworker dutifully recorded these incidents in her files, along with her continuing suspicions that someone in the DeShaney household was physically abusing Joshua, but she did nothing more. In November 1983, the emergency room notified DSS that Joshua had been treated once again for injuries that they believed to be caused by child abuse. On the caseworker's next two visits to the DeShaney home, she was told that Joshua was too ill to see her. Still DSS took no action.

In March 1984, Randy DeShaney beat 4-year-old Joshua so severely that he fell into a life-threatening coma. Emergency brain surgery revealed a series of hemorrhages caused by traumatic injuries to the head inflicted over a long period of time. Joshua did not die, but he suffered brain damage so severe that he is expected to spend the rest of his life confined to an institution for the profoundly retarded. Randy DeShaney was subsequently tried and convicted of child abuse.

[Joshua and his mother brought this action under 42 U.S.C. §1983 alleging that respondents deprived Joshua of his liberty without due process of law by failing to intervene to protect him. The district court granted summary judgment for respondents and the court of appeals affirmed, 812 F.2d 298 (7th Cir. 1987)].

The Due Process Clause of the Fourteenth Amendment provides that "[n]o State shall . . . deprive any person of life, liberty, or property, without due process of law." . . . But nothing in the language of the Due Process Clause itself requires the State to protect the life, liberty, and property of its citizens against invasion by private actors. The Clause is phrased as a limitation on the State's power to act, not as a guarantee of certain minimal levels of safety and security. It forbids the State itself to deprive individuals of life, liberty, or property without "due process of law," but its language cannot fairly be extended to impose an affirmative obligation on the State to ensure that those interests do not come to harm through other means. Nor does history support such an expansive reading of the constitutional text. . . . Its purpose was to protect the people from the State, not to ensure that the State protected them from each other. The Framers were content to leave the extent of governmental obligation in the latter area to the democratic political processes.

. . . Petitioners contend, however, that even if the Due Process Clause imposes no affirmative obligation on the State to provide the general public with adequate protective services, such a duty may arise out of certain "special relationships" created or assumed by the State with respect to particular individuals. Petitioners argue that such a "special relationship" existed here because the State knew that Joshua faced a special danger of abuse at his father's hands, and specifically proclaimed, by word and by deed, its intention to protect him against that danger. Having actually undertaken to protect Joshua from this danger — which petitioners concede the State played no part in creating — the State acquired an affirmative "duty," enforceable through the Due Process Clause, to do so in a reasonably competent fashion. Its failure to discharge that duty, so the argument goes, was an abuse of governmental power that so "shocks the conscience," Rochin v. California, 342 U.S. 165, 172 (1952), as to constitute a substantive due process violation.

We reject this argument. [The Court distinguished the state's affirmative duty to provide medical care for incarcerated prisoners under the Eighth Amendment's prohibition against cruel and unusual punishment, citing Estelle v. Gamble, 429 U.S. 97 (1976).] In Youngberg v. Romeo, 457 U.S. 307 (1982), we extended this analysis beyond the Eighth Amendment setting, holding that the substantive component of the Fourteenth Amendment's Due Process Clause requires the State to provide involuntarily committed mental patients with such services as are necessary to ensure their "reasonable safety" from themselves and others. . . .

But these cases afford petitioners no help. Taken together, they stand only for the proposition that when the State takes a person into its custody and holds him there against his will, the Constitution imposes upon it a corresponding duty to assume some responsibility for his safety and general well-being. The rationale for this principle is simple enough: when the State by the affirmative exercise of its power so restrains an individual's liberty that it renders him unable to care for himself, and at the same time fails to provide for his basic human needs — e.g., food, clothing, shelter, medical care, and reasonable safety — it transgresses the substantive limits on state action set by the Eighth Amendment and the Due Process Clause. The affirmative duty to protect arises not from the State's knowledge of the individual's predicament or from its expressions of intent to help him, but from the limitation which it has imposed on his freedom to act on his own behalf. In the substantive due process analysis, it is the State's affirmative act of restraining the individual's freedom to act on his own behalf — through incarceration, institutionalization, or other similar restraint of personal liberty — which is the "deprivation of liberty" triggering the protections of the Due Process Clause, not its failure to act to protect his liberty interests against harms inflicted by other means.

The *Estelle-Youngberg* analysis simply has no applicability in the present case. Petitioners concede that the harms Joshua suffered did not occur while he was in the State's custody, but while he was in the custody of his natural father, who was in no sense a state actor.[9] While the State may have been aware of the dangers that Joshua faced in the free world, it played no part in their creation, nor did it do anything to render him any more vulnerable to them. That the State once took temporary custody of Joshua does not alter the analysis, for when it returned him to his father's custody, it placed him in no worse position than that in which he would have been had it not acted at all; the State does not become the permanent guarantor of an individual's safety by having once offered him shelter. Under these circumstances, the State had no constitutional duty to protect Joshua. . . .

The most that can be said of the state functionaries in this case is that they stood by and did nothing when suspicious circumstances dictated a more active role for them. In defense of them it must also be said that had they moved too soon to take custody of the son away from the father, they would likely have been met with charges of improperly intruding into the parent-child relationship, charges based on the same Due Process Clause that forms the basis for the present charge of failure to provide adequate protection.

The people of Wisconsin may well prefer a system of liability which would place upon the State and its officials the responsibility for failure to act in situations such as the present one. They may create such a system, if they do not have it already, by changing the tort law of the State in accordance with the regular law-making process. But they should not have it thrust upon them by this Court's expansion of the Due Process Clause of the Fourteenth Amendment.

Justice BRENNAN, with whom Justice MARSHALL and Justice BLACKMUN join, dissenting. . . .

I cannot agree that respondents had no constitutional duty to help Joshua DeShaney. . . . In a constitutional setting that distinguishes sharply between action and inaction, one's characterization of the misconduct alleged under §1983 may effectively decide the case. Thus, by leading off with a discussion (and rejection) of the idea that the Constitution imposes on the States an affirmative duty to take basic care of

---

9. Had the State by the affirmative exercise of its power removed Joshua from free society and placed him in a foster home operated by its agents, we might have a situation sufficiently analogous to incarceration or institutionalization to give rise to an affirmative duty to protect. Indeed, several Courts of Appeals have held, by analogy to *Estelle* and *Youngberg*, that the State may be held liable under the Due Process Clause for failing to protect children in foster homes from mistreatment at the hands of their foster parents. See Doe v. New York City Dept. of Social Services, 649 F.2d 134, 141-142 (CA2 1981), after remand, 709 F.2d 782, *cert. denied sub nom.* Catholic Home Bureau v. Doe, 464 U.S. 864 (1983); Taylor ex rel. Walker v. Ledbetter, 818 F.2d 791, 794-797 (CA11 1987) (en banc), *cert. pending sub nom.* Ledbetter v. Taylor, No. 87-521. We express no view on the validity of this analogy, however, as it is not before us in the present case.

their citizens, the Court foreshadows — perhaps even preordains — its conclusion that no duty existed even on the specific facts before us. This initial discussion establishes the baseline from which the Court assesses the DeShaneys' claim that, when a State has — "by word and by deed," — announced an intention to protect a certain class of citizens and has before it facts that would trigger that protection under the applicable state law, the Constitution imposes upon the State an affirmative duty of protection.

The Court's baseline is the absence of positive rights in the Constitution and a concomitant suspicion of any claim that seems to depend on such rights. From this perspective, the DeShaneys' claim is first and foremost about inaction (the failure, here, of respondents to take steps to protect Joshua), and only tangentially about action (the establishment of a state program specifically designed to help children like Joshua). And from this perspective, holding these Wisconsin officials liable — where the only difference between this case and one involving a general claim to protective services is Wisconsin's establishment and operation of a program to protect children — would seem to punish an effort that we should seek to promote.

I would begin from the opposite direction. I would focus first on the action that Wisconsin has taken with respect to Joshua and children like him, rather than on the actions that the State failed to take. . . .

Because of the Court's initial fixation on the general principle that the Constitution does not establish positive rights, it is unable to appreciate our recognition in *Estelle* and *Youngberg* that this principle does not hold true in all circumstances. . . . In striking down a filing fee as applied to divorce cases brought by indigents, see Boddie v. Connecticut, 401 U.S. 371 (1971) . . . , we have acknowledged that a State's actions — such as the monopolization of a particular path of relief — may impose upon the State certain positive duties. . . .

Wisconsin has established a child-welfare system specifically designed to help children like Joshua. Wisconsin law places upon the local departments of social services such as respondent (DSS or Department) a duty to investigate reported instances of child abuse. While other governmental bodies and private persons are largely responsible for the reporting of possible cases of child abuse, Wisconsin law channels all such reports to the local departments of social services for evaluation and, if necessary, further action. Even when it is the sheriff's office or police department that receives a report of suspected child abuse, that report is referred to local social services departments for action; the only exception to this occurs when the reporter fears for the child's immediate safety. In this way, Wisconsin law invites — indeed, directs — citizens and other governmental entities to depend on local departments of social services such as respondent to protect children from abuse.

The specific facts before us bear out this view of Wisconsin's system of protecting children. Each time someone voiced a suspicion that Joshua was being abused, that information was relayed to the Department for investigation and possible action. . . . Even more telling . . . is the Department's control over the decision whether to take steps to protect a particular child from suspected abuse. While many different people contributed information and advice to this decision, it was up to the people at DSS to make the ultimate decision (subject to the approval of the local government's Corporation Counsel) whether to disturb the family's current arrangements. . . .

In these circumstances, a private citizen, or even a person working in a government agency other than DSS, would doubtless feel that her job was done as soon as she had reported her suspicions of child abuse to DSS. Through its child-welfare program, in other words, the State of Wisconsin has relieved ordinary citizens and governmental bodies other than the Department of any sense of obligation to do anything more than report their suspicions of child abuse to DSS. If DSS ignores or dismisses these suspicions, no one will step in to fill the gap. . . . Conceivably, then, children like Joshua are made worse off by the existence of this program when the persons and entities charged with carrying it out fail to do their jobs.

It simply belies reality, therefore, to contend that the State "stood by and did nothing" with respect to Joshua. Through its child-protection program, the State actively intervened in Joshua's life and, by virtue of this intervention, acquired ever more certain knowledge that Joshua was in grave danger. These circumstances, in my view, plant this case solidly within the tradition of cases like *Youngberg* and *Estelle*. . . .

I would allow Joshua and his mother the opportunity to show that respondents' failure to help him arose, not out of the sound exercise of professional judgement that we recognized in *Youngberg* as sufficient to preclude liability, but from the kind of arbitrariness that we have in the past condemned. . . .

Justice BLACKMUN, dissenting. . . .

Poor Joshua! Victim of repeated attacks by an irresponsible, bullying, cowardly, and intemperate father, and abandoned by respondents who placed him in a dangerous predicament and who knew or learned what was going on, and yet did essentially nothing except, as the Court revealingly observes, "dutifully recorded these incidents in [their] files." It is a sad commentary upon American life, and constitutional principles — so full of late of patriotic fervor and proud proclamations about "liberty and justice for all," that this child, Joshua DeShaney, now is assigned to live out the remainder of his life profoundly retarded. Joshua and his mother, as petitioners here, deserve — but now are denied by this Court — the opportunity to have the facts of their case considered in the light of the constitutional protection that 42 U.S.C. §1983 is meant to provide.

## Notes and Questions

1. What should be the extent of social service workers' liability in child abuse cases? Should they be immune from liability? If so, in all cases? Some? What are the advantages and disadvantages of conferring immunity?

2. The *DeShaney* majority reasons that Joshua was no worse off after return to his father's custody than had the state not acted. Justice Brennan's dissent offers a counterargument, asserting that reporting laws preclude others from providing assistance. Under tort law, shouldn't an attempted rescuer who precludes others from acting be liable for failure to rescue? See Laura Oren, The State's Failure to Protect Children and Substantive Due Process: *DeShaney* in Context, 68 N.C. L. Rev. 659 (1990); Patricia M. Wald, Government Benefits: A New Look at an Old Gifthorse, 65 N.Y.U. L. Rev. 247, 262 (1990); Mark Levine, Comment, The Need for the "Special Relationship" Doctrine in the Child Protection Context, 56 Brook. L. Rev. 329 (1990). Might the state have worsened the boy's condition by permitting the father to feel secure in his use of violence because he knew the state did not take it seriously enough to terminate custody?

3. Can parents sue the state for abuse of their child by state-designated foster parents? Compare Rayburn v. Hogue, 241 F.3d 1341 (11th Cir. 2001) (declining to recognize such suits because foster parents are not "state actors" under *DeShaney*), with Taylor v. Ledbetter, 818 F.2d 791 (11th Cir. 1987) (en banc) (contra). Should it matter if the parents voluntarily place the children in foster care? See generally Michele Miller, Note, Revisiting Poor Joshua: State-Created Danger Theory in the Foster Care Context, 11 Hastings Women's L.J. 243 (2000).

4. The *DeShaney* majority observes that the Due Process Clause invoked by plaintiffs to compel intrusion protects the family from unwarranted intervention. See also Joseph Goldstein et al., Before the Best Interests of the Child 133 (1979) ("Too Early, Too Late, Too Much, or Too Little"). What is the proper constitutional balance between excessive and insufficient state intrusion, according to the majority? The dissent?

5. The majority in *Bouknight* asserted: "Once Maurice was adjudicated a child in need of assistance, his care and safety became the particular object of the State's regulatory interests," even after his custody was returned to his mother. Can you reconcile *DeShaney* with *Bouknight*? Is it determinative that in *DeShaney* the juvenile court never assumed jurisdiction?

6. Does *DeShaney*'s rejection of substantive due process foreclose litigation against state child protective agencies? Marisol v. Giuliani, infra, addresses this question.

## Problem

An infant is taken into custody by the Virginia Department of Social Services after discovery by medical personnel that he and his older siblings are suffering from severe malnutrition. After the mother moves to Pennsylvania, a Virginia court returns custody of the boy to her, subject to supervision of the Philadelphia Department of Social Services. Nearly two years later, the four-year old (who weighs 13 pounds) is found to have suffered irreversible brain damage. The child, through a guardian ad litem, sues the Philadelphia authorities for damages allegedly caused by their failure to protect him from his mother. Did the Virginia agency's actions impose duties on the Philadelphia Department of Social Services that established a "special relationship" between the latter agency and the child? See McComb v. Wambaugh, 934 F.2d 474 (3d Cir. 1991).

### c. Monitoring the Provision of Foster Care

### ■ MARISOL v. GIULIANI
*929 F. Supp. 662 (S.D.N.Y. 1996)*

Robert J. WARD, District Judge. . . .

Plaintiffs are eleven children all of whom have suffered, and some of whom continue to be at risk of, severe abuse and neglect. These children allege that defendants, who are officials with responsibility for the Child Welfare Administration of the City of New York (CWA) now renamed the New York City Administration for Children's Services (ACS), mishandled plaintiffs' cases and, through defendants' actions or inactions, deprived plaintiffs of their [rights under the state and federal constitutions], as well as under numerous federal and state statutes.

The factual allegations of the complaint portray a child welfare program in crisis and collectively suggest systemic deficiencies of gross proportions. . . .

Marisol A. is a five-year old who was born two days after her mother, Ms. A., was arrested on charges of dealing drugs. CWA placed Marisol with Ms. C. during and subsequent to Ms. A.'s incarceration but, in 1994, CWA restored Marisol to her mother's custody despite her criminal history and reports that she was abusing Marisol during visitations. CWA failed to assess properly the appropriateness of this placement and took no steps to supervise or monitor Ms. A.'s home. Upon regaining custody, Ms. A. confined Marisol to a closet for several months, deprived her of sustenance resulting in her eating her own feces and plastic garbage bags to survive, and both physically and sexually abused her to the point of injury. During this period, Ms. A.'s sister and Ms. C. filed multiple reports of abuse with CWA to no avail. . . . Despite Ms. C.'s eagerness to adopt Marisol, CWA has not begun the process of terminating Ms. A.'s parental rights and has not provided Marisol with counseling or support services.

Lawrence B. died on February 18, 1996 of AIDS-related illness at the age of nineteen. Lawrence's mother died of AIDS in or around 1985 leaving him an orphan and he entered the foster care system in 1995, at age seventeen, pursuant to a voluntary agreement signed by his aunt who could no longer care for him. After taking custody, CWA failed to assess Lawrence's medical condition for almost two months and then shuttled him from one inappropriate placement to another. . . .

Thomas C. is a fifteen-year old who has been in foster care since he was seven. In those eight years, Thomas endured numerous placements including a hospital, a diagnostic center, and a residential treatment center (RTC). In 1993, without adequate investigation, CWA approved Thomas' placement with Rev. D., a minister Thomas met at the RTC, who took him to South Carolina. There Rev. D. sexually abused Thomas who subsequently ran away. In 1994, Thomas was returned to the RTC where he now resides. He has since attempted suicide twice and has run away from the RTC only to return after facing hardship and abuse on the streets. CWA has failed to determine the appropriateness of the RTC placement, to pursue the possibility of adoption, or to provide Thomas with counseling. . . .

Ozzie E. is a fourteen-year old who suffers from seizure disorder, brain lesions, and behavioral problems. In 1995, Ozzie's father placed him in foster care after finding himself unable to care for Ozzie. Although Ozzie and his mother, Ms. E., both want to be reunited, he remains in a group home because CWA has failed to provide any family preservation services to enable Ms. E. to care for him. . . .

Brandon H. is a seven-year old who was placed in foster care at birth because his mother was twelve at the time and in foster care herself. In early 1992, CWA placed Brandon with Ms. W. but did not file a petition seeking termination of parental rights until later that year. The court terminated those rights in 1994 but, despite Ms. W.'s willingness to adopt him, CWA still has not even taken steps to transfer Brandon's case to the agency's adoption division. CWA thus allows Brandon to remain in foster care without addressing his need for permanency.

Steven I. is a sixteen-year old who has developed severe psychiatric and emotional problems after spending his entire life in foster care. Steven exhibits violent behavior and, by age twelve, Steven had attempted to rape a nine-year-old girl, had stabbed other children with pencils, and had lit several fires. After CWA ignored a recommendation that Steven receive long-term residential treatment, his behavior deteriorated to the point that, at age fifteen, he was committed to New York Hospital as a "sexual predator." Upon his release, CWA placed him in an inappropriate group home from which he ran away in 1994. He now lives on the streets and CWA has failed to locate him or to provide him with any treatment.

In support of their claims, plaintiffs specifically allege that defendants fail to: (1) appropriately accept reports of abuse and neglect for investigation; (2) investigate those reports in the time and manner required by law; (3) provide mandated preplacement preventive services to enable children to remain at home whenever possible; (4) provide the least restrictive, most family-like placement to meet children's individual needs; (5) provide services to ensure that children do not deteriorate physically, psychologically, educationally, or otherwise while in CWA custody; (6) provide children with disabilities, including HIV/AIDS, with appropriate placements; (7) provide appropriate case management or plans that enable children to return home or be discharged to permanent placements as quickly as possible; (8) provide services to assist children who are appropriate for adoption in getting out of foster care; (9) provide teenagers adequate services to prepare them to live independently once they leave the system; (10) provide the administrative, judicial, or dispositional reviews to which children are entitled; (11) provide caseworkers with training, support, or supervision; and; (12) maintain adequate systems to monitor, track, and plan for children.

[Plaintiffs bring this action pursuant to 42 U.S.C. §1983 seeking injunctive or declaratory relief and alleging violations of the Constitution, the Adoption Assistance and Child Welfare Act, Child Abuse Prevention and Treatment Act (CAPTA), and Americans with Disabilities Act.]

### A. Plaintiffs' Federal Constitutional Claims ...

Initially, the court agrees with defendants that those abused and neglected children not actually in ACS "custody" have no substantive due process right to be protected from harm under *DeShaney*.] The following analysis of plaintiffs' substantive due process claims, therefore, applies only to custodial plaintiffs. The issue facing this Court with respect to custodial plaintiffs [is not] whether they are entitled to protection from harm but, rather, how broad that protection must be. The Supreme Court has held that the right to be free from harm encompasses the right to essentials of care including adequate food, shelter, clothing, and medical attention. [Youngberg v. Romeo, 457 U.S. 307, 324 (1982).] Additionally, the state must provide reasonably safe conditions of confinement. Custodial plaintiffs, however, ask this Court to take an expansive view and recognize a substantive due process right to be free not only from physical harm but also from psychological, emotional, and developmental harm. Defendants, on the other hand, urge this Court to take a narrower approach to custodial plaintiffs' substantive due process claims.

The Court is inclined, at this juncture, to take a broad view of the concept of harm in the context of plaintiffs' substantive due process claims. Clearly, the state is required to protect children in its custody from physical injury. This Court further finds that custodial plaintiffs have a substantive due process right to be free from unreasonable and unnecessary intrusions into their emotional well-being. . . .

As a key element of their substantive due process claims, plaintiffs allege that defendants have violated "their right to be housed in the least restrictive, most appropriate and family-like placement." In support of their motions to dismiss, however, defendants argue that custodial plaintiffs do not have a Fourteenth Amendment due process right to the least restrictive, optimal level of care or placement and, therefore, that children who are kept in foster care longer than necessary or who are denied services to enable them to reunite with their families fail to state a claim.

Courts generally agree that the Fourteenth Amendment does not require the state to provide children in foster care with an optimal level of care or treatment. Thus, to the extent that custodial plaintiffs allege a substantive due process right to a least restrictive, optimal placement, their claims must be dismissed.

Individuals in state custody, however, do have a constitutional right to conditions of confinement which bear a reasonable relationship to the purpose of their custody. Courts have extended this right to the child welfare context. Doe v. New York City Dept. of Social Servs., 670 F. Supp. 1145, 1174 (S.D.N.Y. 1987). The goal of the child welfare system is "to further the best interest of children by helping to create nurturing family environments without infringing on parental rights." Id. Plaintiffs thus are entitled to conditions and duration of foster care which are reasonably related to this goal. . . .

This Court is satisfied that the right to be free from harm encompasses the right alleged by plaintiffs to appropriate conditions and duration of foster care. Indeed, the crux of plaintiffs' latter claim is that defendants' failure to provide safe and appropriate placements has caused them to suffer impermissible harm. Custodial plaintiffs have alleged sufficient facts to support the claim that they have been deprived of even adequate or appropriate conditions of foster care including certain basic necessities which defendants are obligated to provide. Thus, to the extent that custodial plaintiffs can establish that the conditions and duration of foster care are so inadequate as to violate plaintiffs' Fourteenth Amendment due process right to be free from harm, they are entitled to do so and defendants' motions to dismiss are denied.

Another key element of plaintiffs' substantive due process claims is the allegation that defendants have violated "their right not to be deprived of a family relationship absent compelling reasons." . . . The right to family integrity is derived both from the First Amendment's broad right of association and the Fourteenth Amendment's general substantive due process protections. . . . Although the Supreme Court has held the parent-child relationship to be constitutionally protected, courts nevertheless have been loathe to impose a constitutional obligation on the state to ensure a particular type of family life [for example, adoptive placement].

Plaintiffs in the instant case [challenge] defendants' general failure to provide services that function to preserve the family unit. Courts have held, however, that plaintiffs "do not have a constitutional right to rely on an agency to strengthen and reunite their families even if that agency has a statutory duty to do so." Dixey v. Jewish Child Care Assoc., 522 F. Supp. 913, 916 (S.D.N.Y. 1981) (citing Child v. Beame, 412 F. Supp. 593 (S.D.N.Y. 1976)). Thus, plaintiffs cannot argue that defendants have violated their right to family integrity and, to the extent that custodial plaintiffs allege a substantive due process right to associate with their biological family members, their claims must be dismissed.

Nevertheless, plaintiffs do have a constitutional right to protection from harm as noted above. Plaintiffs' family integrity claims are closely related to those pertaining to the duration of foster care and, by extension, fall within the concept of harm for substantive due process purposes. Indeed, plaintiffs suggest that defendants unnecessarily place children in foster care and allow children properly in foster care to languish without taking steps to reunite them with their biological family where appropriate. Once again, this Court is persuaded that plaintiffs have stated facts sufficient to support a claim. . . .

### B. PLAINTIFFS' FEDERAL STATUTORY CLAIMS . . .

[Defendants request dismissal of plaintiffs' causes of action brought pursuant to various provisions of the Adoption Assistance Act, Multiethnic Placement Act, and CAPTA on the ground that these provisions do not provide for a private right of action.]

When deciding whether a private right of action exists to enforce a federal funding statute, courts are bound by any expression of clear intent on the part of Congress to create such a right. Where no unambiguous statement of intent exists, courts must determine if the statute creates enforceable rights, privileges, or immunities. [The Supreme Court has set forth factors for courts to consider: (1) whether the provision in question was intended to benefit plaintiff; (2) whether the provision "reflects merely a 'congressional preference' for a certain kind of conduct rather than a binding obligation on the governmental unit"; and (3) whether the asserted interest is so vague and amorphous as to be beyond the competence of the judiciary to enforce. Wilder v. Virginia Hosp. Assoc., 496 U.S. 498, 509 (1990).] Once these three factors have been met, the burden shifts to the state actor to show Congressional intent to [foreclose such private enforcement].

... Whether a private right exists to enforce provisions of the Adoption Assistance Act has been the subject of recent debate in both the judicial and legislative branches of government. In 1992, the Supreme Court considered whether a private individual could bring a §1983 claim to enforce §671(a)(15) of the Adoption Assistance Act. [In Suter v. Artist M., 503 U.S. 347, 364 (1992)], the Court held that §671(a)(15) [the "reasonable efforts requirement"] was too vague and amorphous to provide a cause of action under §1983 and that Congress did not intend "to create the private remedy sought by plaintiffs." In the following years, several other courts applied *Suter* to find that no private right of action exists to enforce this statute. Defendants rely on this line of cases in support of their motions to dismiss.

In 1994, however, Congress expressed its disapproval of the Supreme Court's decision in *Suter* and amended the [Social Security Act or SSA]. See 42 U.S.C. §§1320a-2 (1994) [hereinafter "Amendment"]. The Amendment states:

> In an action brought to enforce a provision of this chapter, such provision is not to be deemed unenforceable because of its inclusion in a section of this chapter requiring a State plan or specifying the required contents of a State plan. This section is not intended to limit or expand the grounds for determining the availability of private actions to enforce State plan requirements other than by overturning any such grounds applied in Suter v. Artist M., but not applied in prior Supreme Court decisions respecting such enforceability; provided, however, that this section is not intended to alter the holding in Suter v. Artist M. that section 671(a)(15) of this title is not enforceable in a private right of action.

*Id.* Plaintiffs argue that this Amendment is a clear expression of Congress' intent to create a private right of action to enforce provisions of the Adoption Assistance Act other than §671(a)(15). In the alternative, plaintiffs argue that the Amendment shows Congress' intent to reject the Supreme Court's reasoning in *Suter* and to require courts to return to the pre-*Suter* approach when deciding whether to recognize a private right of action to enforce provisions other than §71(a)(15). Defendants, however, stand by their reading of the import of *Suter.* They argue that not only did Congress preclude any private right to enforce §671(a)(15) but also that it left open to judicial construction whether plaintiffs can rely on §1983 to enforce the other provisions of the Adoption Assistance Act. Defendants urge this Court to apply the reasoning in *Suter* to plaintiffs' claims.

This Court does not read the Amendment as a clear expression of Congress' intent to create a private right of enforcement. Rather, this Court is persuaded that Congress has expressed its intent to require courts to apply pre-*Suter* case law to determine the private enforceability of SSA provisions other than §671(a)(15). Courts that recently have considered this issue have adopted this approach. . . . The Court must now apply the factors set forth in *Wilder* to decide whether plaintiffs are entitled to pursue their claims under §1983.

Plaintiffs allege violations of §622(b)(9) and of §627(a) and (b) of subchapter IV-B of the SSA. The Multiethnic Placement Act, §622(b)(9), sets forth as part of the requirements for federal funding that a state plan for child welfare services "provide for the diligent recruitment" of potential foster and adoptive parents who are racially and ethnically diverse. Of the other provisions relied upon by plaintiffs, §627(a) describes the foster care protections that the state must offer in order to gain additional payments and §627(b) outlines the further requirements the state must meet to avoid a reduction of its allotment. With respect to the first *Wilder* factor, both §§622 and 627 are intended to benefit the members of the proposed class of plaintiffs. Further, the language of these provisions is mandatory and sets forth the requirements that the state must meet to be eligible for funding, to gain additional funding, and to avoid a reduction in funding. The second *Wilder* factor thus is met. Finally, determining state compliance with these provisions is well within the abilities of the Court. None of these provisions is so vague or amorphous as to be beyond the competence of the Court to enforce.

[The court then held that plaintiffs alleged sufficient facts to support claims under SSA §671(a), subchapter IV-E, setting forth the requisite elements of a state foster care plan to qualify for federal funding.]

Plaintiffs further allege violations of two provisions of CAPTA which govern federal grants to states for child abuse and neglect prevention and treatment programs. The first, 42 U.S.C. §5106a(b)(2), requires a state, as a condition of federal funding, to initiate a prompt investigation into all reports of abuse or neglect and to take immediate steps to protect children whom the state believes have suffered or are at risk of suffering abuse or neglect. The second, 42 U.S.C. §5106a(b)(3), requires a state to have in effect administrative procedures, personnel, training procedures, facilities, and related programs and services "to ensure that the State will deal effectively with child abuse and neglect cases" in order to be eligible for federal funds.

Defendants again ask this Court to dismiss these claims on the ground that plaintiffs have no private right of action to enforce these statutes. Courts have differed in their interpretation of whether CAPTA creates rights enforceable by private individuals pursuant to §1983. Plaintiffs do not argue, as they did with respect to the Adoption Assistance Act, that there exists a well-established private right to enforce CAPTA. At the same time, defendants do not argue that Congress has expressed its intent to preclude private enforcement of the statute. Rather, the parties expect this Court to undertake a traditional *Wilder* analysis to determine whether plaintiffs are entitled to pursue these claims.

As to the first prong of *Wilder,* there is no dispute that the members of the proposed class of plaintiffs are the intended beneficiaries of the CAPTA provisions at issue. Moving to the second inquiry, [t]he statute sets forth clear conditions which the state must meet to qualify for a federal grant and does so through the use of mandatory and not precatory language. The sole area of contention is whether these CAPTA provisions meet the third *Wilder* prong or whether they are so vague and amorphous as to be beyond the enforcement power of the Court. . . .

Defendants argue that the language in §5106a(b)(2) requiring the state to conduct prompt investigations and to take immediate steps to protect children at risk is too ambiguous and that the Court, therefore, is not qualified to assess compliance. To the contrary, this Court certainly is competent to determine whether the state has made any efforts to comply with this provision. Further, the Court can look to professional standards to determine whether an investigation was properly and promptly initiated and whether the protective steps taken were appropriate. This provision, therefore, is not so vague as to be beyond the enforcement power of the Court. With respect to §5106a(b)(3), defendants do not cite any language from this provision as being too ambiguous to be enforced judicially. Accordingly, §5106a(b)(3) likewise survives the third prong of *Wilder.* Finally, defendants have not argued that Congress has precluded expressly private plaintiffs from pursuing §1983 claims alleging violations of CAPTA. [The court also held that plaintiffs alleged sufficient facts to support claims under the ADA and the Rehabilitation Act.]

## Notes and Questions

1. *Epilogue.* A settlement was eventually reached between the *Marisol* plaintiffs and the state and city. The settlement required (1) the state to establish an advisory panel of child welfare experts to study the Administration for Children's Services operations and provide recommendations for improvement, (2) the Office of Children and Family Services to establish a regional office in New York City to supervise child welfare services and to file all fatality reports in a timely manner, and (3) the State Central Register to review and update policies relating to the screening of calls to their child abuse hotline and to implement a statewide computer system to collect child welfare information. The settlement, similarly, required New York City to seek the assistance of a panel of experts that would recommend reforms and monitor the city's welfare system to determine if it improved its practices. See Marisol A. v. Giuliani, 185 F.R.D. 152 (S.D.N.Y. 1999).

2. After the federal reform effort to enact the AACWA, many states received federal funds but without complying with federal requirements.

Several class action suits were brought by foster children against state and local governments to enforce the act. The Supreme Court brought a temporary halt to this promising avenue of enforcement in Suter v. Artist M., 503 U.S. 347 (1992). Efforts continued, as *Marisol* reveals, to find other theories on which to reform child protective services. See generally Barbara L. Atwell, "A Lost Generation": The Battle for Private Enforcement of the Adoption Assistance and Child Welfare Act of 1980, 60 U. Cin. L. Rev. 593 (1992).

3. Reformers also attempted to remedy the District of Columbia's child welfare system. See LaShawn v. Kelly, 990 F.2d 1319 (D.C. Cir. 1993) (avoiding *Suter* preclusion by permitting suit under local statutes and regulations), *appeal after remand*, 69 F.3d 356 (D.C. Cir. 1995), *judgment vacated and reh'g en banc granted*, 87 F.3d 1389 (D.C. Cir. 1996).

4. In *Marisol*, the plaintiffs also requested that the court order the state child welfare system into receivership. Is this private-sector creditor's remedy appropriate? What problems does it pose?

5. *Marisol* points out that only the "narrow holding" of *Suter* remains (no private action to enforce AACWA "reasonable efforts" requirement). Are other AACWA provisions less "vague and amorphous" so as to permit private enforcement? What is the policy rationale for such enforcement? Against? What conduct on the part of the state should constitute "reasonable efforts" under the AACWA? Does *Marisol* suggest an answer?

6. In *The Lost Children of Wilder: The Epic Struggle to Change Foster Care* (2001), journalist Nina Bernstein explores the shortcomings of the New York City foster care system through the life stories of Shirley Wilder and her son. Wilder was the abused, runaway, teenage plaintiff in a class action suit, initiated in 1973, challenging the constitutionality of the religious matching provision that resulted in preferential foster care placements for Jewish and Catholic children. See Wilder v. Bernstein, 645 F. Supp. 1292 (S.D.N.Y. 1986) (approving consent decree), *aff'd*, 848 F.2d 1338 (2d Cir. 1988). The settlement in Marisol v. Giuliani (the principal case herein) incorporated some of the *Wilder* requirements. The *Wilder* litigation ultimately resulted in a settlement in 1999. On the same day as the *Wilder* settlement and in the same courthouse, another class action suit (Reynolds v. Giuliani, 118 F. Supp. 2d 352 (S.D.N.Y. 2000)) was filed that challenged some of the city's newly implemented welfare practices. Ironically, and unbeknownst to the plaintiff's attorneys, the plaintiff in that suit was Shirley Wilder's grandson.

7. Because some of the *Marisol* plaintiffs were older adolescents, *Marisol* highlights the problems faced by youth who "age out" of foster care. Foster care ends when children reach the age of majority (from 18 to 21 depending on state law). In 1999, Congress focused on the needs of older youth with the passage of the Foster Care Independence Act (FCIA), Pub. L. No. 106-169, 113 Stat. 1824 (codified as amended in scattered sections of 42 U.S.C.) which provides for a continuing claim of

entitlement to foster care until age 21. FCIA improves services for children aging out of foster care with the goal of "independent living." See generally Susan Vivian Mangold, Extending Non-Exclusive Parenting and the Right to Protection for Foster Children: Creating Third Options in Permanency Planning, 48 Buff. L. Rev. 835 (2000).

### d. Permanent Disposition: Termination of Parental Rights

*(i) Standard of Proof*

## ■ SANTOSKY v. KRAMER
*455 U.S. 745 (1982)*

Justice BLACKMUN delivered the opinion of the Court. . . .

Under New York law, the State may terminate, over parental objection, the rights of parents in their natural child upon a finding that the child is "permanently neglected." The New York Family Court Act §622 requires that only a "fair preponderance of the evidence" support that finding. Thus, in New York, the factual certainty required to extinguish the parent-child relationship is no greater than that necessary to award money damages in an ordinary civil action.

Today we hold that the Due Process Clause of the Fourteenth Amendment demands more than this. . . .

New York authorizes its officials to remove a child temporarily from his or her home if the child appears "neglected," within the meaning of Art. 10 of the Family Court Act. Once removed, a child under the age of 18 customarily is placed "in the care of an authorized agency," Soc. Serv. Law §384-b.7.(a), usually a state institution or a foster home. At that point, "the state's first obligation is to help the family with services to [reunite it]." §384-b.1.(a)(iii). But if convinced that "positive, nurturing parent-child relationships no longer exist," §384-b.1.(b), the State may initiate "permanent neglect" proceedings to free the child for adoption. . . .

New York's permanent neglect statute provides natural parents with certain procedural protections. But New York permits its officials to establish "permanent neglect" with less proof than most States require. Thirty-five States, the District of Columbia, and the Virgin Islands currently specify a higher standard of proof, in parental rights termination proceedings, than a "fair preponderance of the evidence." . . . The question here is whether New York's "fair preponderance of the evidence" standard is constitutionally sufficient.

Petitioners John Santosky II and Annie Santosky are the natural parents of Tina and John III. In November 1973, after incidents reflecting parental neglect, respondent Kramer, Commissioner of the Ulster

County Department of Social Services, initiated a neglect proceeding under Fam. Ct. Act §1022 and removed Tina from her natural home. About 10 months later, he removed John III and placed him with foster parents. On the day John was taken, Annie Santosky gave birth to a third child, Jed. When Jed was only three days old, respondent transferred him to a foster home on the ground that immediate removal was necessary to avoid imminent danger to his life or health.

In October 1978, respondent petitioned the Ulster County Family Court to terminate petitioners' parental rights in the three children. [When petitioners challenged the "preponderance" standard,] [t]he Family Court Judge rejected this constitutional challenge, and weighed the evidence under the statutory standard. While acknowledging that the Santoskys had maintained contact with their children, the judge found those visits "at best superficial and devoid of any real emotional content." After deciding that the agency had made " 'diligent efforts' to encourage and strengthen the parental relationship," he concluded that the Santoskys were incapable, even with public assistance, of planning for the future of their children. The judge later held a dispositional hearing and ruled that the best interests of the three children required permanent termination of the Santoskys' custody.[5] [Petitioners unsuccessfully appealed.]

Last Term in Lassiter v. Department of Social Services, 452 U.S. 18 (1981), this Court [held] that the Fourteenth Amendment's Due Process Clause does not require the appointment of counsel for indigent parents in every parental status termination proceeding. The case casts light, however, on the two central questions here — whether process is constitutionally due a natural parent at a State's parental rights termination proceeding, and, if so, what process is due. . . .

The fundamental liberty interest of natural parents in the care, custody, and management of their child does not evaporate simply because they have not been model parents or have lost temporary custody of their child to the State. Even when blood relationships are strained, parents retain a vital interest in preventing the irretrievable destruction of their family life. If anything, persons faced with forced dissolution of their parental rights have a more critical need for procedural protections than do those resisting state intervention into ongoing family affairs. When the State moves to destroy weakened familial bonds, it must provide the parents with fundamentally fair procedures.

In *Lassiter,* the Court and three dissenters agreed that the nature of the process due in parental rights termination proceedings turns on a

---

5. Since respondent Kramer took custody of Tina, John III and Jed, the Santoskys have had two other children, James and Jeremy. The State has taken no action to remove these younger children. At oral argument, counsel for respondents replied affirmatively when asked whether he was asserting that petitioners were "unfit to handle the three older ones but not unfit to handle the two younger ones."

balancing of the "three distinct factors" specified in Mathews v. Eldridge, 424 U.S. 319, 335 (1976): the private interests affected by the proceeding; the risk of error created by the State's chosen procedure; and the countervailing governmental interest supporting use of the challenged procedure. . . . Evaluation of the three *Eldridge* factors compels the conclusion that use of a "fair preponderance of the evidence" standard in [termination] proceedings is inconsistent with due process.

"The extent to which procedural due process must be afforded the recipient is influenced by the extent to which he may be 'condemned to suffer grievous loss.' " Whether the loss threatened by a particular type of proceeding is sufficiently grave to warrant more than average certainty on the part of the factfinder turns on both the nature of the private interest threatened and the permanency of the threatened loss.

*Lassiter* declared it "plain beyond the need for multiple citation" that a natural parent's "desire for and right to 'the companionship, care, custody, and management of his or her children' " is an interest far more precious than any property right. 452 U.S., at 27 quoting Stanley v. Illinois, 405 U.S., at 651. When the State initiates a parental rights termination proceeding, it seeks not merely to infringe that fundamental liberty interest, but to end it. . . . Thus, the first *Eldridge* factor — the private interest affected — weighs heavily against use of the preponderance standard at a state-initiated permanent neglect proceeding. We do not deny that the child and his foster parents are also deeply interested in the outcome of that contest. But at the factfinding stage of the New York proceeding, the focus emphatically is not on them.

The factfinding does not purport — and is not intended — to balance the child's interest in a normal family home against the parents' interest in raising the child. Nor does it purport to determine whether the natural parents or the foster parents would provide the better home. Rather, the factfinding hearing pits the State directly against the parents. The State alleges that the natural parents are at fault. The questions disputed and decided are what the State did — "made diligent efforts," — and what the natural parents did not do — "maintain contact with or plan for the future of the child." The State marshals an array of public resources to prove its case and disprove the parents' case. Victory by the State not only makes termination of parental rights possible; it entails a judicial determination that the parents are unfit to raise their own children.[10]

---

10. The Family Court judge in the present case expressly refused to terminate petitioners' parental rights on a "non-statutory, no-fault basis." Nor is it clear that the State constitutionally could terminate a parent's rights *without* showing parental unfitness. See Quilloin v. Walcott, 434 U.S. 246, 255 (1978) ("We have little doubt that the Due Process Clause would be offended '[i]f a State were to attempt to force the breakup of a natural family, over the objections of the parents and their children, without some showing of unfitness and for the sole reason that to do so was thought to be in the children's best interest,' " quoting Smith v. Organization of Foster Families, 431 U.S. 816, 862-863 (1977) (Stewart, J., concurring in judgment)).

At the factfinding, the State cannot presume that a child and his parents are adversaries. After the State has established parental unfitness at that initial proceeding, the court may assume at the *dispositional* stage that the interests of the child and the natural parents do diverge. See Fam. Ct. Act §631 (judge shall make his order "solely on the basis of the best interests of the child," and thus has no obligation to consider the natural parents' rights in selecting dispositional alternatives). But until the State proves parental unfitness, the child and his parents share a vital interest in preventing erroneous termination of their natural relationship. Thus, at the factfinding, the interests of the child and his natural parents coincide to favor use of error-reducing procedures. . . .

Under Mathews v. Eldridge, we next must consider both the risk of erroneous deprivation of private interests resulting from use of a "fair preponderance" standard and the likelihood that a higher evidentiary standard would reduce that risk. . . .

In New York, the factfinding stage of a state-initiated permanent neglect proceeding bears many of the indicia of a criminal trial. . . . The State, the parents, and the child are all represented by counsel. The State seeks to establish a series of historical facts about the intensity of its agency's efforts to reunite the family, the infrequency and insubstantiality of the parents' contacts with their child, and the parents' inability or unwillingness to formulate a plan for the child's future. The attorneys submit documentary evidence, and call witnesses who are subject to cross-examination. Based on all the evidence, the judge then determines whether the State has proved the statutory elements of permanent neglect by a fair preponderance of the evidence.

At such a proceeding, numerous factors combine to magnify the risk of erroneous factfinding. Permanent neglect proceedings employ imprecise substantive standards that leave determinations unusually open to the subjective values of the judge. [T]he court possesses unusual discretion to underweigh probative facts that might favor the parent. Because parents subject to termination proceedings are often poor, uneducated, or members of minority groups, such proceedings are often vulnerable to judgments based on cultural or class bias.

The State's ability to assemble its case almost inevitably dwarfs the parents' ability to mount a defense. No predetermined limits restrict the sums an agency may spend in prosecuting a given termination proceeding. The State's attorney usually will be expert on the issues contested and the procedures employed at the factfinding hearing, and enjoys full access to all public records concerning the family. The State may call on experts in family relations, psychology, and medicine to bolster its case. Furthermore, the primary witnesses at the hearing will be the agency's own professional caseworkers whom the State has empowered both to investigate the family situation and to testify against the parents. Indeed, because the child is already in agency custody, the State even has the power to shape the historical events that form the basis for termination.[13]

The disparity between the adversaries' litigation resources is matched by a striking asymmetry in their litigation options. Unlike criminal defendants, natural parents have no "double jeopardy" defense against repeated state termination efforts. If the State initially fails to win termination, as New York did here, it always can try once again to cut off the parents' rights after gathering more or better evidence. Yet even when the parents have attained the level of fitness required by the State, they have no similar means by which they can forestall future termination efforts.

Coupled with a "fair preponderance of the evidence" standard, these factors create a significant prospect of erroneous termination. A standard of proof that by its very terms demands consideration of the quantity, rather than the quality, of the evidence may misdirect the factfinder in the marginal case. . . .

Raising the standard of proof would have both practical and symbolic consequences. . . . An elevated standard of proof in a parental rights termination proceeding would alleviate "the possible risk that a factfinder might decide to [deprive] an individual based solely on a few isolated instances of unusual conduct [or] . . . idiosyncratic behavior." Addington v. Texas, 441 U.S., at 427. "Increasing the burden of proof is one way to impress the factfinder with the importance of the decision and thereby perhaps to reduce the chances that inappropriate" terminations will be ordered. Ibid.

The Appellate Division approved New York's preponderance standard on the ground that it properly "balanced rights possessed by the child . . . with those of the natural parents. . . ." 427 N.Y.S.2d, at 320. By so saying, the court suggested that a preponderance standard properly allocates the risk of error *between* the parents and the child. That view is fundamentally mistaken.

The court's theory assumes that termination of the natural parents' rights invariably will benefit the child.[15] Yet we have noted above that the parents and the child share an interest in avoiding erroneous ter-

---

13. In this case, for example, the parents claim that the State sought court orders denying them the right to visit their children, which would have prevented them from maintaining the contact required by Fam. Ct. Act §614.1.(d). The parents further claim that the State cited their rejection of social services they found offensive or superfluous as proof of the agency's "diligent efforts" and their own "failure to plan" for the children's future. . . .

15. This is a hazardous assumption at best. Even when a child's natural home is imperfect, permanent removal from that home will not necessarily improve his welfare. See, e.g., Wald, State Intervention on Behalf of "Neglected" Children: A Search for Realistic Standards, 27 Stan. L. Rev. 985, 993 (1975) ("In fact, under current practice, coercive intervention frequently results in placing a child in a more detrimental situation than he would be in without intervention").

Nor does termination of parental rights necessarily ensure adoption. Even when a child eventually finds an adoptive family, he may spend years moving between state institutions and "temporary" foster placements after his ties to his natural parents have been severed.

mination. Even accepting the court's assumption, we cannot agree with its conclusion that a preponderance standard fairly distributes the risk of error between parent and child. Use of that standard reflects the judgment that society is nearly neutral between erroneous termination of parental rights and erroneous failure to terminate those rights. For the child, the likely consequence of an erroneous failure to terminate is preservation of an uneasy status quo. For the natural parents, however, the consequence of an erroneous termination is the unnecessary destruction of their natural family. A standard that allocates the risk of error nearly equally between those two outcomes does not reflect properly their relative severity.

Two state interests are at stake in parental rights termination proceedings — a parens patriae interest in preserving and promoting the welfare of the child and a fiscal and administrative interest in reducing the cost and burden of such proceedings. A standard of proof more strict than preponderance of the evidence is consistent with both interests.

. . . As parens patriae, the State's goal is to provide the child with a permanent home. Yet while there is still reason to believe that positive, nurturing parent-child relationships exist, the parens patriae interest favors preservation, not severance, of natural familial bonds. . . . We cannot believe that it would burden the State unduly to require that its factfinders have the same factual certainty when terminating the parent-child relationship as they must have to suspend a driver's license. [Without deciding the outcome under a constitutionally proper standard], we vacate the judgment of the Appellate Division and remand the case for further proceedings not inconsistent with this opinion. . . .

Justice REHNQUIST, with whom THE CHIEF JUSTICE, Justice WHITE, and Justice O'CONNOR join, dissenting.

. . . New York has created an exhaustive program to assist parents in regaining the custody of their children and to protect parents from the unfair deprivation of their parental rights. And yet the majority's myopic scrutiny of the standard of proof blinds it to the very considerations and procedures which make the New York scheme "fundamentally fair." . . .

The three children to which this case relates were removed from petitioners' custody in 1973 and 1974, before petitioners' other two children were born. The removals were made pursuant to [New York's procedures] and in response to what can only be described as shockingly abusive treatment.[10]

---

10. Tina Apel, the oldest of petitioners' five children, was removed from their custody by court order in November 1973 when she was two years old. Removal proceedings were commenced in response to complaints by neighbors and reports from a local hospital that Tina had suffered injuries in petitioners' home including a fractured left femur, treated with a home-made splint; bruises on the upper arms, forehead, flank, and spine; and abrasions of the upper leg. The following summer, John Santosky III, petitioners' second oldest child, was also removed from petitioner's custody. John, who was less than one year old at the time,

[P]etitioners received training by a mother's aide, a nutritional aide, and a public health nurse, and counseling at a family planning clinic. In addition, the plan provided psychiatric treatment and vocational training for the father, and counseling at a family service center for the mother. Between early 1976 and the final termination decision in April 1979, the State spent more than $15,000 in these efforts to rehabilitate petitioners as parents.

Petitioners' response to the State's effort was marginal at best. They wholly disregarded some of the available services and participated only sporadically in the others. As a result, and out of growing concern over the length of the children's stay in foster care, the Department petitioned in September 1976 for permanent termination of petitioners' parental rights so that the children could be adopted by other families. Although the Family Court recognized that petitioners' reaction to the State's efforts was generally "non-responsive, even hostile," the fact that they were "at least superficially cooperative" led it to conclude that there was yet hope of further improvement and an eventual reuniting of the family. Accordingly, the petition for permanent termination was dismissed. [In October 1978, the agency again filed a termination proceeding because petitioners had made few efforts to take advantage of social services or to visit their children.]

[T]he State's extraordinary 4-year effort to reunite petitioners' family was not just unsuccessful, it was altogether rebuffed by parents unwilling to improve their circumstances sufficiently to permit a return of their children. At every step of this protracted process petitioners were accorded those procedures and protections which traditionally have been required by due process of law. . . .

It is inconceivable to me that these procedures were "fundamentally unfair" to petitioners. . . . The interests at stake in this case demonstrate that New York has selected a constitutionally permissible standard of proof.

On one side is the interest of parents in a continuation of the family unit and the raising of their own children. The importance of this interest cannot easily be overstated. Few consequences of judicial action are so grave as the severance of natural family ties. . . . On the other side of the termination proceeding are the often countervailing interests of the child. A stable, loving homelife is essential to a child's physical, emotional, and spiritual well-being. . . .

In addition to the child's interest in a normal homelife, "the State has an urgent interest in the welfare of the child." Lassiter v. Depart-

---

was admitted to the hospital suffering malnutrition, bruises on the eye and forehead, cuts on the foot, blisters on the hand, and multiple pin pricks on the back. Jed Santosky, the third oldest of petitioners' children, was removed from his parents' custody when only three days old as a result of the abusive treatment of the two older children.

ment of Social Services, 452 U.S., at 27. Few could doubt that the most valuable resource of a self-governing society is its population of children who will one day become adults and themselves assume the responsibility of self-governance. . . .

When, in the context of a permanent neglect termination proceeding, the interests of the child and the State in a stable, nurturing homelife are balanced against the interests of the parents in the rearing of their child, it cannot be said that either set of interests is so clearly paramount as to require that the risk of error be allocated to one side or the other. Accordingly, a State constitutionally may conclude that the risk of error should be borne in roughly equal fashion by use of the preponderance-of-the-evidence standard of proof. . . .

## Notes and Questions

1. According to *Santosky*, the minimum standard of proof in termination cases is clear and convincing evidence. States may require a higher standard. See generally Linda Lee Reimer Stevenson, Comment, Fair Play or a Stacked Deck?: In Search of a Proper Standard of Proof in Juvenile Dependency Hearings, 26 Pepp. L. Rev. 613 (1999). Should they do so?

2. Does the clear-and-convincing standard adequately protect the rights of abused children? Adequately protect family autonomy? Ensure that children spend lengthy periods in foster care? See Sharon B. Hershkowitz, Due Process and the Termination of Parental Rights, 19 Fam. L.Q. 245, 292-295 (1985).

3. How far does the *Santosky* standard extend? To restrictions on parental rights that fall short of complete termination? See In re R.W., 10 P.3d 1271 (Colo. 2000) (requiring only preponderance standard when parental rights were terminated until child reached 18). To a termination hearing following a parent's voluntary relinquishment of a child? See Coleman v. Smallwood, 800 S.W.2d 353, 356 (Tex. Ct. App. 1990) (requiring clear and convincing evidence).

4. Can a state terminate a parent's rights without first placing the child in foster care? Compare In re Marin, 499 N.W.2d 400, 402 (Mich. Ct. App. 1993) (termination statutes not meant to identify only circumstances under which rights may be terminated), with In re A.D.B. and N.B., 818 P.2d 483 (Okla. 1991) (termination proceedings must take place after parent has opportunity to remedy conditions giving rise to initial adjudication).

5. The Supreme Court examined the parent's right to counsel in termination of parental rights proceeding in Lassiter v. Department of Social Services, 452 U.S. 18 (1981). The Court rejected the argument that procedural due process requires the appointment of counsel for

indigent parents. Applying a case-by-case balancing test, the Court weighed (1) the state's and parent's shared interest in the accuracy of the decision; (2) the cost of providing indigent parents with counsel; (3) the state's interest in informal procedures; (4) the complexity of the issues; (5) the incapacity of the indigent parent; and (6) the risk of error. The Court held that, although petitioner had not made a sufficient showing of these factors, in a case in which the parent's interests were especially high and the state's interests were particularly low, due process might require the appointment of counsel. Is *Santosky* consistent with *Lassiter?* See also M.L.B. v. S.L.J., 519 U.S. 102 (1996) (Mississippi statute requiring party to pay record preparation fees in advance violated mother's equal protection and due process rights in a termination of parental rights case). See generally Jason T. Jacoby, Casenote, *M.L.B. v. S.L.J.:* "Equal Justice" for Indigent Parents, 32 U. Rich. L. Rev. 571 (1998).

6. Child welfare reform in the 1970s revolved around concerns with "foster care drift," that is, children who were removed from their biological parents but who remained in foster care for years.[55] Reformers pointed out that the foster care system was not effective in achieving stability or a sense of permanence in children's lives. Reformers advocated that state agencies adopt "permanency planning" to enable children in foster care to achieve stability with nurturing caregivers. These efforts culminated in 1980 in the AACWA (page 1065) with its twin goals of family reunification or, alternatively, more rapid termination of parental rights to free children for adoption. Recently, however, commentators are raising provocative questions about the wisdom of severance of the parent-child tie.

■ **MARSHA GARRISON, PARENTS' RIGHTS v. CHILDREN'S INTERESTS: THE CASE OF THE FOSTER CHILD**
*22 N.Y.U. Rev. L. & Soc. Change 371, 373-374, 379, 384, 394-395 (1996)*

The perception that parents do make "uniquely valuable contributions" to their child's development has led children's advocates to favor retention of traditional parental prerogatives in most contexts. [In contrast, in the case of foster care], advocates have here argued in favor of faster and easier termination of the parent-child relationship. A com-

[55]. See, e.g., Robert H. Mnookin, Foster Care: In Whose Best Interests?, 43 Harv. Educ. Rev. 599 (1973); Michael S. Wald, State Intervention on Behalf of "Neglected" Children: A Search for Realistic Standards, 27 Stan. L. Rev. 985 (1975); Michael Wald, State Intervention on Behalf of "Neglected" Children: Standards for Removal of Children from their Homes, Monitoring the Status of Children in Foster Care, and Termination of Parental Rights, 28 Stan. L. Rev. 623 (1976).

parison of the divorce and foster care literature illustrates the difference in approach: In divorce, the child's relationship with a noncustodial parent is almost invariably described as a positive factor in her development that should be encouraged and facilitated; termination of the parental relationship is approved only in extreme cases where the parent threatens the child's health or safety. In foster care, however, the noncustodial parent is typically seen as a threat to the child's relationship with her foster parent or her opportunity to obtain adoptive parents; termination of parental rights is urged whenever the child's return home cannot be accomplished quickly.

[F]rom the child's perspective, divorce and long-term foster care placement are not obviously different. In both contexts, the child's relationship with a noncustodial parent is maintained through visitation and sporadic contact rather than a day-to-day relationship. In both contexts, the child has another parent, or parent-figure, who provides day-to-day care and to whom the child is likely to be deeply attached. In both contexts, the day-to-day parent and the noncustodial parent may cooperate or, alternatively, express hostility and compete for the child's love.

Parents whose children enter foster care are less likely to exhibit capable parenting than those who divorce, but the available evidence does not suggest that parental capacity affects the strength of the parent-child relationship. As John Bowlby, one of our foremost developmental psychologists, has put it, "[t]he attachment of children to parents who by all ordinary standards are very bad parents is a never-ceasing source of wonder to those who seek to help them."

[W]hile foster care and divorce are clearly different and we lack research providing direct comparisons, there is much to suggest that, from the perspective of the child, these two situations present more similarities than differences. In each case, a parental attachment must be maintained through visitation rather than day-to-day contact. . . .

[C]urrent psychological research fails to support the claim that custodial parents are the only ones who count. Although a wealth of data, from diverse sources and theoretical schools, has confirmed the importance of the parent-child relationship as a determinant of the child's personality, resilience, and relationships with others, that research has also established that children are capable of maintaining many emotional bonds simultaneously. The strength of a child's attachments is not subject to precise measurement, and a strong attachment with one parent figure does not mean that attachments to other parent figures are weak.

Decades of research have also established that a child's ties to his parents do not lose their importance simply as a result of separation or loss of day-to-day contact. "The parent-child tie . . . can be greatly distorted [but it] is not to be expunged by mere physical separation." Not even the substitution of a parent replacement, for example a stepparent, renders the absent parent unimportant. . . . An absent parent remains important to the child because the parental relationship is a primary source of the child's identity and self-esteem. . . . The parent also represents the child's history and his unique biological inheritance. Even children adopted at birth often wish to learn about their biological parents. . . .

Rather than resolving the child's relationship with a parent from whom the child is separated, loss of contact thus has the potential consequence of making such a resolution far more difficult. Parental absence may enhance the child's tendency toward self-blame or exaggeration; the child may idealize the absent parent, blame herself for disruption in the relationship, or exaggerate the parent's flaws. Such extreme responses impede the child's ability to effectively mourn her loss and maintain her self-esteem. Loss of contact may also inhibit the child's ability to form a realistic assessment of her situation and current, realistic relationships. . . .

Visitation with a noncustodial parent is not, of course, invariably beneficial to children. Foster children placed as infants who have never experienced more than sporadic office visits with their biological parents may not profit significantly from continued contact. Some abusive parents pose real risks to their child's physical safety; some mentally ill parents may be incapable of meaningful interaction. Exposure to serious conflict between parents — in an intact or separated family — has also been found to pose risks to a child's emotional development. But there is no reason to suppose that serious conflict between biological and foster (or adoptive) parent is more likely than between divorced parents. . . .

[Garrison proposes an alternative to traditional adoption: preservation of parental visitation postadoption.] Adoption's powerful symbolism not only obscures the very real benefits that this solution confers on the taxpayer, but it imposes direct costs on the children we intend to help. The positive future symbolized by an adoption order inexorably darkens the past and stigmatizes both the child's former parents and identity. Her acceptance of a new family implies abandonment of her biological family and the death of her old self. . . . Many older foster children cannot face such a loss, and even those who are willing to do so pay a heavy price: The past can be buried, but it cannot be erased. The attempt to wipe away the past may also cause more harm than good. . . . The price of adoption's symbolic benefits is neglect of the child's real emotional needs. . . .

Divorce law today potentially affects all children while child welfare law is reserved for those who are poor. The result is a class-based divide — in advocacy, theory, and law — that assumes real differences in children's pain based essentially on the receipt of public benefits. We have expected poor children, and only poor children, to gratefully sacrifice their past lives in order to obtain the benefits it suits us to provide. In the process, we have further stigmatized the lives of the children for whom foster placement will be inevitable, and subjected many of them to the further impermanence of "revolving door" care.

But the emotional lives of poor children are not different from those of the more fortunate. Their parents are equally significant. Their need for evidence of parental love and for opportunities for reconciliation are just as great. For most, loving foster or adoptive parents will not, any more than stepparents, erase the ties that bind parent and child. . . .

*(ii) Reasonable Efforts Requirements*

■ STATE EX REL. CHILDREN'S SERVICES
DIVISION v. BRADY
*899 P.2d 691 (Or. Ct. App. 1995)*

HASELTON, Judge.

Michelle Brady appeals from a judgment terminating her parental rights to her daughter.[1] We review de novo, and reverse.

The issue here is whether a mentally impaired mother lacks the capacity to care for her special needs child. [Michelle's daughter] was born two months prematurely on April 21, 1993. She weighed only two-and-a-half pounds at birth and suffered from life-threatening medical conditions, including severe heart and lung problems. Because of those conditions, child spent the first 15 weeks of her life in the neonatal intensive care unit. . . .

Mother was 18 when child was born. She was, and is, a person of low average intelligence, who exhibits certain mental and psychological difficulties. . . . She was a runaway in her early teens, dropped out of school in the eleventh grade, and experienced a series of abusive relationships, including, most recently, with father. Mother met father in 1990, when she was homeless, and their relationship was volatile and periodically violent.

Despite the instability in her life, mother visited child at the hospital daily, spending hours with her. Mother met with the nursing staff to discuss child's special needs, and expressed her commitment and determination to learn and to be a good parent. Nonetheless, following an altercation between mother and father, which required the intervention of hospital security, hospital staff became concerned that the parents might be incapable of meeting child's needs and, consequently, contacted [Children's Services Division or CSD].

[W]hen child was six weeks old, a CSD intake investigator contacted mother and father to determine if they could care for child on her release from the hospital. After the initial interview, the investigator recommended that the couple attend psychological evaluations and CSD-sponsored men's and women's domestic violence groups. CSD did

---

1. The judgment also terminated the parental rights of child's father. He does not appeal.

not offer mother any other assistance or training in parenting a special needs child.[3]

At CSD's insistence, Dr. James Ewell conducted a psychological examination of mother. [He] learned that she had sustained substantial head injuries, including a contusion to the front part of her brain, in an automobile collision when she was 14. Immediately after that collision, mother had experienced a seizure in the emergency room and had been hospitalized for 11 days. After being released from the hospital, she had continued to experience seizures and was placed on appropriate medication. Nonetheless, mother had continuing problems with concentration, memory, and vision, and had experienced blackouts and anxiety attacks.

Ewell also administered several diagnostic tests, which indicated that mother had low average intelligence and impaired empathy, problem solving, and psychological sensitivity. Based on those results and the interview, Ewell concluded that mother has an irreversible condition known as organic personality syndrome with passive-aggressive features. . . . Ewell concluded that mother lacked the skills to care for child on her release from the hospital:

> . . . I do not believe [mother's] current psychological condition would allow her to commit to taking adequate care of her daughter. I do not believe she would be able to adequately assess [child's] needs, or respond appropriately in times of emergency. Her learning ability and follow through seem to be impaired. I also doubt that [mother] would be able to adequately manage her anger so that [child] would not be exposed to domestic violence. At the time of this assessment, [mother] had not yet demonstrated an ability to maintain a home setting that would be adequate for her daughter's specialized care.
>
> In many ways, [mother] must be seen as an adolescent who herself is still in need of parenting. Her problem-solving abilities, "common sense," and psychological sensitivities are impaired. She will probably require extended assistance and guidance in establishing herself as an adult. Her ability to parent a "fragile infant, who will require very specialized care" would seem to be severely lacking. I therefore could not recommend that [child] be sent to live with [mother] once the child is released from the hospital.
>
> *Prior to [mother] assuming responsibility for her daughter, I believe she will need to complete anger management classes, parenting classes and additional educational programs designed to increase her skills and abilities. She may also need to live with [child] in a foster home-like setting, wherein an experienced and responsible adult caregiver can provide constant supervision/guidance.* Long-term psychotherapy for [mother] would also be indicated at this time.

---

3. Mother attended the CSD women's violence group between September 1993, and August 1994, but her participation was sporadic.

(Emphasis supplied.)

[Following Ewell's evaluation, CSD petitioned the circuit court to assume jurisdiction. The court did so and placed the child in the care of Erika Hatzel, a foster parent with experience in caring for medically needy infants.] After child was placed in foster care, mother's access and interaction was limited to two one-hour supervised visits per week at CSD's offices. Mother attended all visitations on time, without fail, and made up the ones that were canceled because of child's periodic health problems. While there, mother used all of the available time to play with child, and child appeared to enjoy being with mother.

In October 1993, CSD requested that Margaret Veltman of the BASE program assess the parents' skills and abilities. [Veltman] concluded: "[Mother and father] are young parents who show an obvious interest in parenting their infant, but who, despite their efforts, are currently unable to meet her needs for interaction. The [child] is a medically fragile, premature infant who will require very specialized care if she is expected to thrive and reach normalcy." Veltman did not, however, specifically assess mother's "task solving" ability to discern and respond to child's special needs.

[After] receiving Veltman's report, CSD decided to petition for termination of the parents' rights. At that time, child was eight months old. Once CSD made that decision, it offered neither parent any further assistance or support in acquiring the skills needed to care for their special needs child. In particular, CSD never offered the educational and training assistance identified in Ewell's report. As the CSD caseworker explained, CSD "did not feel the parents were capable with their limitations to parent this child in the foreseeable future and, therefore, we did not offer further services at that point."

. . . Despite CSD's lack of assistance — or perhaps because of it — mother, on her own initiative, undertook a variety of "self-help" efforts to improve her life generally and her capability as a parent, particularly. Mother (1) contacted the Young Parents Program (administered by a local church) and began individual counseling, as well as parenting classes that included infant CPR; (2) took substantial steps to terminate her relationship with father, including obtaining a restraining order against him; (3) pursued a course of study towards attaining a general equivalency diploma; and (4) provided volunteer services at a senior center.

The termination hearing was held in October 1994. At that time, child was 18 months old. Her medical condition had improved, but her coloration, chest, and breathing still needed to be checked three to four times a day. Child walked with difficulty and still did not speak in any identifiable fashion. She continued to be an "extremely fussy" child who woke up several times each night, was uncomfortable with strangers and was extremely sensitive to noise.

[F]ive aspects of the termination hearing are especially pertinent: First, CSD relied almost exclusively on the Ewell and Veltman evaluations to establish mother's present and future incapacity to care for child. Ewell's report had been generated 16 months earlier; Veltman's, 10 months earlier. Although Ewell defended his original diagnosis, Veltman conceded that she was not capable of rendering an informed opinion as to mother's ability to care for child at the time of the hearing or in the foreseeable future.

Second, Robert Carter, [mother's counselor at the Young Parents Program,] disputed Ewell's diagnosis of an organic personality syndrome. . . . In Carter's view, mother's stress disorder was amenable to treatment. Although Carter testified that it would take mother at least two years to overcome her condition, he believed that she had made substantial progress in handling stress, managing her anger, and developing self worth, and that, with continued treatment, the likelihood of overcoming the effects of her stress syndrome would improve "immeasurably."

With particular reference to mother's ability to care for child, Carter acknowledged that mother had poor organizational skills, which could materially impair her ability to care for a child with diverse special needs. However, Carter testified that mother's organizational deficits were related to her post-traumatic stress disorder and that, as the symptoms of that disorder abated through treatment, mother's organizational skills were improving and would continue to improve.

Third, child's pediatrician, Michael Eustis, testified as to her current medical condition. Eustis stated that, although child's heart and lung problems were "by and large resolving," they would still require careful monitoring, which could not be reduced to a "checklist" form. Eustis observed that, although child's medical problems were decreasing, her developmental needs would increase in the future. He was, however, unable to describe those future needs with particularity. . . .

Fourth, mother testified simply, but cogently, about child's special needs and her ability to meet those needs. Under searching cross-examination, her responses were clear, direct, and thoughtful.

Fifth, and finally, CSD did not present any evidence of an imminent, compelling need to terminate mother's rights, rather than maintaining the status quo, including continuing foster care. There was no evidence that child was immediately adoptable, or that her prospects for adoption would be materially prejudiced if mother's rights were not immediately terminated. Indeed, Eustis testified that, on a one to ten scale of adoptability, with ten being highly adoptable, child is a "two." The CSD case worker concurred that she "would have to really do some recruiting" to find a suitable adoptive family. . . .

The trial court granted CSD's petition [basing] termination on a variety of alternative grounds, including not only mother's inability to provide care because of her mental deficiency, but also mother's "lack of effort . . . to make return of the child possible"; mother's failure to provide, or attempt to provide, "care, attention, and love"; mother's failure to pay a reasonable portion of child's medical care and foster care; and mother's "failure to implement a plan designed to lead to the integration of the child into the parent's home."

[W]e disagree. . . . Our disposition rests, ultimately, on the conjunctive character of the state's burden under ORS 419B.504. The state must prove, by clear and convincing evidence, that a parent is presently unable to meet a child's needs, and that "integration of the child into the home of the parent . . . is improbable in the foreseeable future due to conduct or conditions not likely to change."

Here, the question of mother's present ability to meet child's needs is close and difficult. . . . However, regardless of mother's present capabilities, the state failed to prove by clear and convincing evidence that child's integration into mother's home is "improbable in the foreseeable future due to . . . conditions . . . not likely to change." ORS 419B.504.

Mother has never had a meaningful opportunity to develop and demonstrate parenting skills. Child remained in the hospital after birth and was placed directly in foster care. Thereafter, mother's contact with her was limited. . . .

CSD's principal evaluator, Ewell, acknowledged that, with appropriate guidance and training, mother might ultimately assume primary responsibility for child. Nonetheless, except for referring mother to the women's violence group, CSD never provided such assistance. . . . Mother's circumstances are analogous to those in State ex rel. Juv. Dept. v. Chapman, 631 P.2d 831 (1981), which reversed a termination order because, in part, "CSD had offered no services, suggestions, encouragement, training, or any advice of any kind to the parents to enable them to develop skills to care for the child properly." Indeed, mother's position is more compelling than that of the parents in *Chapman*, because here CSD's retained expert, Ewell, recommended that mother be given such assistance, and CSD disregarded that recommendation.

Given those circumstances, mother's commitment to child, and her undeniable determination to be a good parent, we are not " 'independently satisfied that the conduct and conditions of the mother are not likely to change.' " *Pennington*, 799 P.2d 694 (Or. Ct. App. 1990) (quoting State ex rel. Juv. Dept. v. Wyatt, 34 Or. App. 793, 798, 579 P.2d 889, *rev. den.*, 283 Or. 503 (1978)). In both *Pennington* and *Wyatt*, we granted parents "second chances" by reversing termination orders, because the parents had begun to make progress and were "entitled to a chance to show it is permanent." Here, mother has never been given even a first chance. She deserves that opportunity. . . .

*(iii)  The Significance of Emotional Attachment*

■  **IN RE GUARDIANSHIP OF J.C.**
608 A.2d 1312 (N.J. 1992)

HANDLER, J. . . .

A.C., who was born in Colombia and came to this country as a teenager, is the natural mother of three children. Two girls, J.C. and J.M.C., were born in July 1983 and in January 1985, respectively, and J.C., a boy, was born in August 1986. A.C. voluntarily placed her two girls in foster care with the Division of Youth and Family Services (DYFS) in August 1985. The children were returned to her after three months. Almost a year later, in October 1986, A.C. again placed the two girls, along with her new child, J.C., in foster care, where they have remained for the past five and a half years.

A.C. began unsupervised weekend visits with her children soon after their placement in foster care, seeing them regularly twice a month during the following year. Although DYFS had intended to reunite the family, in November 1987 the agency stopped unsupervised visits out of concern that the children were not being properly cared for. DYFS also came to believe that A.C. was addicted to drugs and was being abused by her husband (who, she claims, was not the father of any of the children). However, bi-monthly visits at the DYFS office continued. In April of the following year, A.C. entered drug treatment. By November 1988 the agency concluded that the children could not be returned successfully and that preparation should be initiated for their permanent placement and adoption.

[The agency filed a petition seeking termination of A.C.'s parental rights. The court concluded that termination was in the best interests of the children, even though A.C. had not, as a matter of law, abandoned the children. A.C. appealed.]

[A] trial court should make [specific findings] before it terminates parental rights. The first finding is that the child's health and development have been or will be seriously impaired by the parental relationship. Secondly, the court must conclude that the parents are unable or unwilling to eliminate the harm and that a delay in permanent placement will add to the harm. Third, the court should be convinced that alternatives to terminating parental rights have been thoroughly explored and exhausted, including sufficient efforts made to help the parents cure the problems that led to the placement. Fourth, all of those considerations must inform the determination that termination of parental rights will not do more harm than good. . . .

When the child's biological parents resist the termination of their parental rights, the court's function will ordinarily be to decide whether the parents can raise their children without causing them further harm.

In most cases proofs will focus on past abuse and neglect and on the likelihood of it continuing. However, the cornerstone of the inquiry is not whether the biological parents are fit but whether they can cease causing their child harm. The analysis of harm entails strict standards to protect the statutory and constitutional rights of the natural parents. The burden falls on the State to demonstrate by clear and convincing evidence that the natural parent has not cured the initial cause of harm and will continue to cause serious and lasting harm to the child. . . .

[T]he bulk of the evidence addressed the issue of harm to the children emanating from the prospect of their being removed from their respective foster parents and returned to their mother. Most of the evidence related to the older girl, J.C.

The DYFS social workers and the psychologist who evaluated J.C. concurred that she was a child with serious emotional problems and potentially-significant learning disabilities. Nonetheless, Ms. Rodriguez testified that J.C. "[was] doing very well [in a new home, that of Mr. and Mrs. D., her foster parents] since July of this year. She [was] well adjusted. She has done remarkably well, especially in school where she has been so behind." Referring to the report of Dr. Paul Kennedy, a child psychiatrist, the witness stated, "[J.C.] is able to attach and trust someone again. And she is very bonded to this new caretaker." . . .

John Frederickson, [the guardian ad litem] submitted a report in which he "found that [J.C.] is very attached to Mr. & Mrs. [D.] as well as Nicole [Mr. D.'s daughter by an earlier marriage]." He noted further, "J.C. indicated that she is very happy here and wished Mr. & Mrs. [D.] to be 'her mommy and daddy' and wants very much to live with them and have Nicole as her sister." . . .

After receiving Mr. Frederickson's report, the court requested a "bonding evaluation between the children and their respective foster parents" from a court psychologist, Regina Johnson. With respect to J.C., Ms. Johnson concluded:

> [J.C.] is most definitely bonded with the [D] family. She is expressive and stated, "I love them a lot, I want to stay with them — they are nice to me." [S]eparation from the [D's] would be detrimental to this child's emotional and physical well-being. . . . Further separation will leave permanent scars.

The evidence relating to the younger child, J.M.C., was not as extensive [but it indicated bonding with her foster family as well]. [The court psychologist] recommended expressly that there be a "termination of parental rights." . . .

[On remand,] the parties stipulated to several facts about A.C.'s rehabilitation. With respect to her housing situation, they agreed that she was living in the same apartment in which she had been living since December 1989. Concerning her work, they agreed that she had a steady job, that she had been working there for the previous two years, and that there was on-site after school child care at her workplace. Finally the parties "stipulated" that A.C. asserted that she was drug and alcohol free and that DYFS had no evidence to suggest otherwise. . . .

Dr. Matthew Johnson testified on behalf of A.C. He found a strong and enduring bonded relationship between J.C. and A.C. He believed "erasing" the biological mother from the child's life would cause the child serious emotional harm, particularly regarding the child's identity and development in adolescence. . . . There was much less focus during the second trial on the younger child, J.M.C. Dr. Johnson found that she had significant relationships with both her foster mother and her natural mother. However, he was not able to say conclusively that there was bonding in either case. . . .

The critical question is whether termination of parental rights is justified under the broad statutory standard of section 15(c) and section 20 predicated on the best interests of the child. [W]e are compelled by the record as it currently stands to conclude that there is not clear and convincing evidence to support the findings necessary to terminate parental rights. . . .

As the contrasting opinions of the experts in this case illustrate, there are competing psychological theories of the effects of parental bonding. In large measure, the variances in their recommendations derive from different assumptions concerning the fragility versus resiliency of the child psyche. Those who . . . urge the wider use of psychological parenting theory see children as highly vulnerable and fragile. Their psyches are easily injured by traumatic events and those injuries can adversely shape their subsequent development. See Goldstein, Freud & Solnit, [Beyond the Best Interests of the Child 33 (1973)]. In contrast, others, presumably like Dr. Johnson, posit more flexibility in children, arguing that attachments "support the development of independence." Change under the right circumstances can play a positive role in children's development. Indeed, a good deal of recent literature on the subject argues that psychological parenting theory overestimates the importance of continuity in care in relation to other factors that affect child development, such as the quality of care children receive. See Marsha Garrison, Why Terminate Parental Rights?, 35 Stan. L. Rev. 423, 458-59 (1983). In addition, experts and commentators differ over the importance of ongoing relationships between children and their natural parents. Although natural parents can be a disruptive influence for children who have been adopted, some commentators and psychologists believe that trying to eliminate the natural parents from the children's lives and memory is impossible, and therefore wrong.

Moreover, there are the grave pitfalls that may be encountered in the application of otherwise sound psychological parenting and bonding theories. Scholars and some courts suggest that theories of parental bonding may be relied on too often to keep children in foster care rather than return them to their parents.

In addition, the uncritical use of bonding theory can increase the risk of institutional bias. That risk may be reflected in attitudes that tilt the process in favor of the agency and its social workers and foster parents. The theories of bonding also may be misused to determine only which set of parents is optimum or even "better" in some vague social sense, rather than capable of rearing the child without serious harm.

Further, to keep termination proceedings based on bonding theory focused on whether the children have a reasonable opportunity for stable and continuous development may be difficult. Termination of parental rights does not always result in permanent placement of the child. . . .

The tangles and snares that surround bonding theory are evident in this case. Important testimony was presented by DYFS employees and valuable information by the guardian. They furnished probative evidence establishing empirically the affection and strength of the relationship of the children with their respective foster parents. However, they were not qualified to express opinions concerning psychological bonding and the harmful consequences to the children from its disruption. . . . The primary support for the trial court's decision came from Ms. Regina Johnson. [H]er testimony revealed that she had little or no formal training in conducting bonding evaluations or comprehensive knowledge of the relevant scientific literature. Nor did she have an opportunity to evaluate A.C. or her relationship with the children. . . .

A.C.'s expert, Dr. Johnson was qualified. His testimony in part supported the conclusion that a strong bond existed between the children and their respective adoptive parents. . . . Nevertheless, we are unable to say here that Dr. Johnson's conclusion that there was a strong relationship between the children and their adoptive parents demonstrated that serious harm would ensue if the children were returned to their mother. . . . Weighing the potential harm that terminating J.C.'s relationship with her mother against that which might come from removing her from her foster home is painfully difficult, but it is a decision that necessarily requires expert inquiry specifically directed to the strength of each relationship.

We thus conclude that there is not clear and convincing evidence to support the determination to terminate A.C.'s parental rights. That does not mean, however, that termination may not be an appropriate resolution. [W]e remand to the trial court in order that additional evidence may be adduced directly addressing whether the two children have bonded with their foster parents and if so whether breaking such bonds would cause the children serious psychological or emotional harm. . . . A.C. should be allowed visitation with the children sufficient to enable the experts to consider those relationships. . . .

## Notes and Questions on *Brady* and *J.C.*

1. Many statutes require that, before terminating parental rights, the state first must provide rehabilitation services (including reunification efforts), and, second, the parent must make "reasonable progress" toward the return of the child. Some statutes contained "reasonable efforts requirements" prior to the Adoption Assistance and Child Welfare Act. The AACWA (with its requirement for state agencies to make "reasonable efforts" to prevent removal from the home and to provide family reunification services) triggered widespread adoption of such requirements. David J. Herring, Inclusion of the Reasonable Efforts Requirements in Termination of Parental Rights Statutes: Punishing the Child for the Failure of the State Child Welfare System, 54 U. Pitt. L. Rev. 139, 171 (1992).

Professor Herring identifies the types of statutes with "reasonable efforts" requirements: (1) most states expressly require the agency to prove it has made reasonable efforts to rehabilitate the parent as a condition precedent to termination of parent rights; (2) some states have implied reasonable efforts requirements; and (3) some jurisdictions hold that "reasonable efforts" are a factor to be considered in termination determinations. Herring, supra, at 172-175. Significantly, if a given statute requires rehabilitation services, a parent may interpose a defense against termination that the state failed to fulfill its statutory mandate. Is the "reasonable efforts" requirement constitutionally compelled?

2. What constitutes "reasonable efforts"? Because neither the AACWA nor many state statutes define the term, courts interpret whether the provision of certain services satisfies the requirement. See Christine H. Kim, Note, Putting Reason Back into the Reasonable Efforts Requirements in Child Abuse and Neglect Cases, 1999 U. Ill. L. Rev. 287, 290-299. Cases have held that reasonable efforts have been satisfied by housing assistance; the provision of day care, medical or legal services; treatment for substance abuse or domestic violence; and counseling. See, e.g., Dvorak v. S.H., 624 N.W.2d 678 (N.D. 2001); In re Rysene W., 2001 WL 861923 (Conn. Super. Ct. July 9, 2001).

3. Are "reasonable efforts" required even when they are likely to be futile? In 1997 Congress enacted the Adoption and Safe Families Act (ASFA), which removed the "reasonable efforts" requirements in certain cases. In contrast to the AACWA policy of family reunification, ASFA emphasizes speedier termination of parental rights. ASFA does not require that states make "reasonable efforts" to prevent removal and provide reunification if (1) the child has been the victim of aggravated circumstances, such as torture, abandonment, or sexual abuse; (2) the parent has killed another child or attempted to do so; or (3) the state has terminated the parent's rights with respect to a sibling. 42 U.S.C.A. §§671 (a)(15)(D)(i), (ii), (iii) (West Supp. 1998). See also Mary Ellen C. v. Ari-

zona Dept. of Econ. Sec., 971 P.2d 1046 (Ariz. Ct. App. 1999) (holding that state must undertake only those measures that offer reasonable probability of success).

4. To what extent can states rely on the duration a child has spent in foster care to trigger termination proceedings? Is the child's stay in foster care an appropriate indicator of parental unfitness? In re H.G., 757 N.E.2d 846 (Ill. 2001), the Illinois Supreme Court held that a statutory presumption of parental unfitness based upon a finding that a child had been in foster care for 15 months out of any 22-month period (modeled on the ASFA rule discussed below) was not narrowly tailored to serve the compelling state interest of child protection and, thus, violates substantive due process. See also Cheryl A. DeMichele, Comment, The Illinois Adoption Act: Should a Child's Length of Time in Foster Care Measure Parental Unfitness?, 30 Loy. U. Chi. L.J. 727 (1999); Katherine A. Hort, Note, Is Twenty-Two Months Beyond the Best Interest of the Child?: ASFA's Guidelines for the Termination of Parental Rights, 28 Fordham Urb. L.J. 1879 (2001). Should the time period differ for younger versus older children? See Joseph Goldstein et al., Before the Best Interests of the Child 46 (1979) (arguing for a shorter period for children under age three).

The AACWA, 42 U.S.C. §§671(a)(16), 675(5)(c) (1994 & Supp. V 1999), requires a "case review system" with hearings no later than 18 months after the child's original placement. The Adoption and Safe Families Act of 1997 requires states to seek termination of parental rights for a child who has been in foster care for 15 of the last 22 months. (This "15/22 provision" is subject to three exceptions: if a child is living in kinship foster care, if a state agency has determined that termination would not be in the child's best interests, and if a state agency has failed to provide family reunification services.) The Act also shortens the period triggering permanency hearings to no later than 12 months after the date the child entered foster care (§302, to amend 42 U.S.C. 675(5)(c)).

5. Does termination of parental rights provide the optimum way to achieve permanence for those children in long-term foster care with no immediate prospect of returning to parents? What alternatives ought to be considered to serve the best interests of such children? Do you agree with Professor Marsha Garrison, supra page 1090, that states should allow continued visitation by biological parents? See also Marsha Garrison, Why Terminate Parental Rights?, 35 Stan. L. Rev. 423 (1983).

6. Does inclusion of "reasonable efforts" requirements before termination inflict immeasurable harm on children by creating insurmountable obstacles to termination of parental rights, as some commentators argue? See especially Elizabeth Bartholet, Nobody's Children: Abuse and Neglect, Foster Drift, and the Adoption Alternative (1999) (arguing that the state should be more aggressive in removing children from their biological families and placing them for adoption). But cf. Martin

Guggenheim, Somebody's Children: Sustaining the Family's Place in Child Welfare Policy, 113 Harv. L. Rev. 1716 (1999) (book review rebutting Bartholet's assumptions and conclusions).

ASFA provides that the state need not meet the requirement of filing a termination petition if the state has failed to provide necessary reunification services. Because child welfare agencies often are unable to provide these services for the reason that the agencies are underfunded and overburdened, does this ASFA provision "punish[] children for the sins of the state"? Bartholet, supra, at 195.

7. Can J.C.'s attachment to her foster family justify termination of her parents' rights? Would such a disposition be constitutional? What does *Santosky* suggest? See Louise A. Leduc, Note, No-Fault Termination of Parental Rights in Connecticut: A Substantive Due Process Analysis, 28 Conn. L. Rev. 1195 (1996).

8. As illustrated in *J.C.*, mothers whose babies are born with symptoms of drug addiction may experience difficulty regaining custody, even after they stop using drugs. Why? Does the Adoption and Safe Families Act provide enough help for drug-addicted parents? See Mary O'Flynn, Comment, The Adoption and Safe Families Act of 1997: Changing Child Welfare Policy Without Addressing Parental Substance Abuse, 16 J. Contemp. Health L. & Pol'y 243, 260-261 (1999) (suggesting ASFA should provide funding for drug treatment programs). *Brady* reveals that courts may also be quick to terminate parental rights of the mentally disabled. See also In re D.R.B., 777 So. 2d 508 (La. Ct. App. 2000). But cf. In re T.J., 745 N.E.2d 608 (Ill. App. Ct. 2001). See generally Susan Kerr, The Application of the Americans with Disabilities Act to the Termination of Parental Rights of Individuals with Mental Disabilities, 16 J. Contemp. Health L. & Pol'y 387 (2000).

## Problem

Bobby B. is removed from home and placed in foster care when he is two years old during a crack-cocaine binge of his single mother. Several months later, Bobby's HIV-infected mother decides that she wants his return so that she can spend her remaining time with him. To achieve this goal, she completes parenting classes and a drug rehabilitation program, as ordered by the Juvenile Court. She has not yet found employment, as directed by the court, because she is participating in a job-training program to achieve that goal.

The year is 2020; Congress has repealed the Adoption Assistance and Child Welfare Act, which required states to seek family preservation and reunification when possible and to hold "permanency planning" hearings within 18 months of children's removal. The governing statute merely requires "reasonable efforts" to unite biological families. As a court-appointed guardian ad litem, you have learned that, although Bobby had regular supervised visits with his mother, he has bonded with his foster mother and father and regards them as his psychological parents. The foster parents have asked to adopt Bobby, an outcome supported by the state Department of Family Welfare because of Bobby's mother's prognosis. In deciding how to handle Bobby's case, you must address the following questions posed by the judge: Should a child in a loving foster home be put through a wrenching separation when the parent seeking return is likely to die or become seriously ill? Alternatively, is time with a parent so important to a child's identity that it should override other considerations? What result? See Felicia R. Lee, Difficult Custody Decisions Being Complicated by AIDS, N.Y. Times, Mar. 4, 1995, at 1, 16.

## C. CHILDREN'S AUTONOMY?

The parental autonomy principle entitles parents to speak for children. In child abuse and neglect proceedings, the state as parens patriae asserts its interest on behalf of children. When can children speak for themselves?

### 1. Emancipation

■ **STATE v. C.R. & R.R.**
*797 P.2d 459 (Utah Ct. App. 1990)*

JACKSON, J. . . .
In October 1984, R.R., nearly fifteen, left his parents' home and lived with various relatives. In the spring of 1985, a petition was filed with the juvenile court alleging that R.R. was a dependent child. See Utah Code Ann. §78-3a-16(1)(c) (1987); Utah Code Ann. §78-3a-2(20) (1987). When R.R.'s mother admitted the allegations in July 1985, the juvenile court found R.R. to be dependent within the meaning of the statute and temporarily awarded legal custody of R.R. to the Utah Department of Family Services (DFS). . . . In October 1986, the temporary order terminated and custody of R.R. was awarded to his parents, to be supervised by DFS until June 1987.

The State filed a petition against R.R.'s parents in the fall of 1988 . . . , seeking reimbursement of $1,159.06 in support for R.R. expended by the State during the period of January 1985 through October 10, 1986. Relying on the common law doctrine of emancipation, R.R.'s parents contested the petition and claimed that their duty to support

R.R. was terminated in October 1984 when he voluntarily left their home to live elsewhere and live a lifestyle of which they disapproved. According to the parents' unrefuted testimony, they never ordered R.R. to leave. They were willing to support him in their own home along with his younger siblings if he would agree to abide by their rules. R.R. left to reside elsewhere, they testified, because he refused to accept their condition that he give up his homosexual lifestyle. In response, the State argued that R.R.'s parents had not met their burden of proving emancipation because there was no evidence R.R. was financially independent or that he was able to provide his own residence. The State also argued that R.R. had not left home voluntarily because his parents had forced him to leave the household.

[In this case and another, the juvenile court declined to apply the doctrine of emancipation.] The basic issue presented in these appeals is whether the juvenile court erroneously concluded that the doctrine of emancipation is not a part of the law in Utah. This ruling involves a question of law, which we review for correctness with no deference to the lower court's determination.

In American law, judicial emancipation refers to the nonstatutory termination of certain rights and obligations of the parent-child relationship during the child's minority. Katz, Schroeder & Sidman, Emancipating Our Children — Coming of Legal Age in America, 7 Fam. L.Q. 211, 214 (1973) (hereinafter Katz).

As a result of statutory and common law developments, the American parent is generally held responsible for his child's financial support, health, education, morality, and for instilling in him respect for people and authority. To facilitate the performance of these obligations, the parent is vested with the custody and control of the child, including the requisite disciplinary authority. And, under a heritage of the past, the parent is also entitled to the child's services, and, by derivation, to his or her earnings. When a child is adjudicated a fully emancipated minor, these reciprocal rights and responsibilities are extinguished and are no longer legally enforceable: the emancipated child is thus legally treated as an adult. Although apparently undeveloped at English common law, the doctrine of emancipation has been described as a "basic tenet of family law" in this country, applied by American courts since the early nineteenth century. . . . In several nineteenth century decisions, the fact that a minor voluntarily abandoned the parent's home to pursue a life free from parental control was alone considered sufficient to support a finding of emancipation that terminated the parent's duty of support. As a result, third parties who subsequently furnished necessaries to the minor could not recover from the parent, even in the absence of evidence that the minor was either capable of self-support or had actually supported himself.

As the cases relied upon below by the parties amply demonstrate, the doctrine of emancipation continues to be an accepted part of the common law in this country. [On remand, the trial court should articulate the factors relevant to showing emancipation, determine whether the parents established that their sons were emancipated, and decide whether application of the doctrine would conflict with any Utah law, such as those providing parental support duties.]

## Notes and Questions

1. The doctrine of emancipation ends certain disabilities of minority even before the age of majority. Correlatively, it releases parents from certain obligations to their minor children. Thus it allows minors to free themselves from parental control before adulthood. See generally Sanford N. Katz et al., Emancipating Our Children — Coming of Legal Age in America, 7 Fam. L.Q. 211 (1973).

What factors should a court use to determine emancipation under the common law? Courts often consider financial independence; living away, especially with parental consent; and creation of new relationships inconsistent with a subordinate role in parents' family, such as marriage. See, e.g., In re Pace, 989 P.2d 297 (Kan. Ct. App. 1999); Young v. Young, 654 N.E.2d 880 (Ind. Ct. App. 1995). Cf. Filippone v. Lee, 700 A.2d 384 (N.J. Super. Ct. App. Div. 1997) (motherhood alone does not emancipate). Traditionally, enlistment in the military triggered emancipation. But see Baker v. Baker, 537 P.2d 171 (Kan. 1975). Today, courts hold enrollment in a military service academy meets the test because attendance at such institutions is inconsistent with parental control. See Porath v. McVey, 884 S.W.2d 692 (Mo. Ct. App. 1994); Bishop v. Bishop, 671 A.2d 644 (N.J. Super. Ct. Ch. Div. 1995). Such issues often arise in postdivorce litigation because, absent an agreement or decree to the contrary, emancipation ends child support obligations. See, e.g., Kuper v. Woodward, 684 A.2d 783 (D.C. 1996).

2. Some states have codified the criteria for emancipation. For example, under California's Emancipation of Minors Act, marriage, active duty in the armed forces, or a judicial declaration emancipates a person under 18. Cal. Fam. Code §7002 (West 1994). To obtain a judicial declaration of emancipation, a minor must petition the court, setting forth that:

(1) The minor is at least 14 years of age.
(2) The minor willingly lives separate and apart from the minor's parents or guardian with the consent or acquiescence of the minor's parents or guardian.
(3) The minor is managing his or her own financial affairs. As evidence of this, the minor shall complete and attach a declaration of income and expenses. . . .

(4) The source of the minor's income is not derived from any activity declared to be a crime by the laws of this state or the laws of the United States.

Id. at §7120(b). The Court must grant the petition if it finds the minor has met these requirements "and that emancipation would not be contrary to the minor's best interest." Id. at §7122(a). Why did California specify the age of 14? Cf., e.g., Kan. Stat. Ann. §§38-108 through 38-109 (2000) (no age specified); Va. Code Ann. §16.1-331 (Michie 1999) (16th birthday). For the history of California's legislation, see Carol Sanger & Eleanor Willemsen, Minor Changes: Emancipating Children in Modern Times, 25 U. Mich. J.L. Reform, 239, 250-263 (1992).

3. Emancipation confers adult status on the child for many legal purposes. For example, California's statute, supra, lists the following as consequences of emancipation: adult treatment for purposes of parental support; control over earnings; and the capacity to enter into a binding contract, make a will, establish a residence, and enroll in school. Cal. Fam. Code §7050 (West 1994). See also, e.g., Va. Code Ann. §16.1-334 (Michie 1999) (effects of order of emancipation).

Notwithstanding emancipation, however, some prerogatives (for example, driver's license, voting) come only with the attainment of a certain age. Why? See Franklin Zimring, The Changing Legal World of Adolescence (1982); John H. Garvey, Freedom and Choice in Constitutional Law, 94 Harv. L. Rev. 1756, 1768 (1981); Martha Minow, Rights for the Next Generation: A Feminist Approach to Children's Rights, 9 Harv. Women's L.J. 1, 1-8 (1986).

4. Who must initiate the child's departure from home for emancipation to occur? Some authorities say the parent's intent is determinative. E.g., Randolph v. Randolph, 8 S.W.3d 160, 164 (Mo. Ct. App. 1999); Foxvog v. Foxvog, 578 N.W.2d 916, 919 (Neb. Ct. App. 1998). Yet disobeying parental authority, without good cause, triggers emancipation. Compare Commissioner of Soc. Servs. v. Jones-Gamble, 643 N.Y.S.2d 182 (App. Div. 1996), with Weigert v. Weigert, 699 N.Y.S.2d 597 (App. Div. 1999). Who decides whether parent or child caused the "breakdown"? See also Roe v. Doe, 272 N.E.2d 567 (N.Y. 1971). On remand in *C.R.*, must the court determine whether R.R. or his parents initiated his departure from home? The principal case, in reviewing early precedents, refers to the minor's "voluntarily" leaving the parental home.

California's statute, supra, contemplates "the consent or acquiescence of the minor's parents or legal guardians." Cal. Fam. Code §7120(b)(2) (West 1994). In a study based on interviews with 18 minors in the San Francisco Bay Area, Professors Carol Sanger and Eleanor Willemsen found "an unexpected level of adult participation in almost all aspects of the decision-making process," although the California statute contemplates a child-initiated process. Sanger & Willemsen, supra, at 271. They concluded that, in most cases, adults initiated and influenced the child's decision to become emancipated; the quick and simple process "involves no significant investigation of the minors' living circumstances or best interests"; most minors and their parents experience significant conflict before emancipation; and, for the minors, "[l]ife after emancipation is often precarious and lonely, and the decision to become emancipated is regarded with ambivalence." Id. at 297.

5. Of what relevance to the question of R.R.'s emancipation is the family disagreement about his "homosexual lifestyle"? See Richard H. Cornfield, Emancipation by Eviction: The Problem of Domestic Pushout, 1 Fam. L. Rep. (BNA) 4021 (1975).

The family conflict precipitating R.R.'s departure from home is not uncommon, with empirical studies showing a substantial number of gay youths running away or otherwise becoming homeless. See Gabe Kruks, Gay and Lesbian Homeless/Street Youth: Special Issues and Concerns, 12 J. Adolescent Health 515 (1991); Gary Remafedi, Adolescent Homosexuality: Psychosocial and Medical Implications, 79 Pediatrics 331 (1987). See also Karolyn Ann Hicks, Comment, "Reparative" Therapy: Whether Parental Attempts to Change a Child's Sexual Orientation Can Legally Constitute Child Abuse, 49 Am. U. L. Rev. 505 (1999); Sonia Renee Martin, A Child's Right to be Gay: Addressing the Emotional Maltreatment of Queer Youth, 48 Hastings L.J. 167, 176-177 (1996).

6. The juvenile court found R.R. "dependent" (statutorily defined to include "a minor who is homeless or without proper care through no fault of his parent, guardian, or custodian," Utah Code Ann. §78-3a-103 (Supp. 2001)). Does this designation and the award of temporary custody to the Department of Family Services preclude a finding of emancipation on remand? Suppose R.R. left home but relied on public assistance for support? Does the availability of public assistance undermine parental autonomy by allowing a child to become "emancipated" from parental control without becoming self-supporting?

Parker v. Stage, 371 N.E.2d 513 (N.Y. 1977), held that, after a daughter voluntarily left home to live with her lover, her father could refuse to support her although she was receiving public assistance. By contrast, in Ragan v. Ragan, 931 S.W.2d 888 (Mo. Ct. App. 1996), the court rejected a father's argument that his 17-year-old twin sons had emancipated themselves by running away to live with their aunt, who received welfare payments for their support. The court reasoned that "self-supporting" did not encompass a child dependent on public assistance. See also Oneida County Comm'r of Soc. Servs. v. William S., 659 N.Y.S.2d 606 (App. Div. 1997) (duty of support continues although daughter moved out and received public assistance).

Teenage parents must live with their parents or in other adult-supervised settings to qualify for assistance under the Personal Responsibility and Work Opportunity Reconciliation Act of 1996, 42 U.S.C.

§608(a)(5) (Supp. V 1999). Another provision, designed to deter teen pregnancy, gives the states the option of enforcing support orders against the grandparents of children whose parents are minors receiving welfare; the provision explicitly refers to the "parents of the noncustodial parent." Id. at §666(a)(18). What impact will this requirement have on parental autonomy? On the ability of children to escape parental authority? See generally Lisa Knott Garfinkle, Comment, Two Generations at Risk: The Implications of Welfare Reform for Teen Parents and Their Children, 32 Wake Forest L. Rev. 1233 (1997); April Kaplan, Teen Parents and Welfare Reform Policy, 32 Clearinghouse Rev. 408 (1999).

7. Once achieved, does emancipation last forever? Most authorities have answered in the negative. Thus, for example, if the marriage that emancipated a child is annulled, the emancipation terminates. See, e.g., Eyerman v. Thias, 760 S.W.2d 187 (Mo. Ct. App. 1988). Recently, courts have begun to reject this approach. See Rennie v. Rennie, 718 So. 2d 1091 (Miss. 1998); State ex rel. Dept. of Health & Human Resources v. Farmer, 523 S.E.2d 840 (W.Va. 1999). Why? Note that R.R.'s emancipation was only temporary.

8. Is emancipation "all or nothing"? The maturity deemed necessary for different adult activities may vary. Should the law therefore recognize partial or limited emancipation? See, e.g., Mitchell v. Mitchell, 963 S.W.2d 222 (Ky. Ct. App. 1998) (married emancipated minor cannot settle personal injury claim). Cf. Hillary Rodham, Children Under the Law, 43 Harv. Educ. Rev. 487, 507 (1973) (advocating "abolition of the general status of minority and adoption of an area-by-area approach (as has already been done . . . in the motor vehicle statutes)").

9. *The mature minor rule.* The mature minor rule, followed in many jurisdictions, is a species of limited or partial emancipation. Under this exception to the common law rule requiring parental consent for medical treatment of a minor, a child close to majority can give effective consent if capable of appreciating the nature, extent, and consequences of the treatment. See, e.g., Cardwell v. Bechtol, 724 S.W.2d 739 (Tenn. 1987); Rhonda Gay Hartman, Adolescent Autonomy: Clarifying an Ageless Conundrum, 51 Hastings L.J. 1265 (2000). See generally Christine M. Hanisco, Note & Comment, Acknowledging the Hypocrisy: Granting Minors the Right to Choose Their Medical Treatment, 16 N.Y. L. Sch. J. Hum. Rts. 899 (2000). If the parent nonetheless remains financially responsible for the medical treatment in question, does the rule undermine parental autonomy and control?

Some states statutorily adopted a mature minor rule specifically for medical care related to drug abuse, venereal disease, and pregnancy, excluding abortion. See, e.g., 410 Ill. Comp. Stat. Ann. 210/4 (West 1997); Mo. Rev. Stat. §431.061(4) (2000). Why do such statutes cover these particular situations? Is a lesser degree of maturity necessary for the medical care specified by these statutes than for other treatment? Or do such statutes reflect altogether different concerns? Cf. Planned Parenthood of Southeastern Pa. v. Casey, Chapter I, section C1. What explains the requirement of parental or judicial involvement for abortion and the absence of similar requirements for medical treatment incident to childbirth? See Planned Parenthood of Cent. N.J. v. Farmer, 762 A.2d 620 (N.J. 2000).

Should mature minors be able to refuse life-sustaining treatment? Compare In re E.G., 549 N.E.2d 322 (Ill. 1989), with O.G. v. Baum, 790 S.W.2d 839, 842 (Tex. Ct. App. 1990). See Commonwealth v. Nixon, 761 A.2d 1151 (Pa. 2000), *cert. denied*, 121 S. Ct. 1735 (2001); Melinda T. Derish & Kathleen Vanden Heuvel, Mature Minors Should Have the Right to Refuse Life-Sustaining Treatment, 28 J. L. Med. & Ethics 109 (2000).

## Problem

Assume that Elian Gonzalez arrived in the United States at age 12, not 5. (See problem 2, page 963.) He firmly expressed his desire to stay with his Miami relatives instead of returning to Cuba to live with his father, stepmother, and half brother. Six months after Elian's arrival, his father seeks the assistance of the family court in Miami in returning Elian to his custody; the Department of Children and Family Services asks this court to adjudge Elian a minor in need of supervision and a ward of the state (so that he can remain in the United States); and Elian seeks a declaration of emancipation. What result and why?

(This problem is based on the case of Walter Polovchak, who came to the United States with his parents from the then Ukrainian Soviet Socialist Republic and refused to accompany them when they returned.) See In re Polovchak, 454 N.E.2d 258 (Ill. 1983), *cert. denied*, 465 U.S. 1065 (1984). See also Polovchak v. Meese, 774 F.2d 731 (7th Cir. 1985); Leslie A. Fithian, Note, Forcible Repatriation of Minors: The Competing Rights of Parent and Child, 37 Stan. L. Rev. 187 (1984). Walter tells his own story in Walter Polovchak & Kevin Klose, Freedom's Child (1988).

## 2. When Can Children Sue Their Parents?

### a. A Reasonable Parent Standard?

### ■ HARTMAN v. HARTMAN
*821 S.W.2d 852 (Mo. 1991)*

COVINGTON, Judge. . . .

In the *Hartman* case, Christine and Todd Hartman, by their mother and next friend, Sheila Hartman, filed an action in the Circuit Court of

Jefferson County [alleging] their father and grandfather negligently maintained and operated a propane gas stove and propane tank causing them to explode, thereby injuring the children. [The courts below applied the doctrine of parental immunity to bar tort recovery.]

   ... Prior to 1891 no reported cases in the United States applied the doctrine [of parental immunity]. The first recorded application of the doctrine, a product of judicial policy making without common law basis, was in Mississippi in Hewellette v. George, 68 Miss. 703, 9 So. 885 (Miss. 1891). The *Hewellette* court grounded its decision in the need to preserve family harmony.

A Missouri court first recognized and applied the doctrine [in 1939]. This Court [subsequently decided] Baker v. Baker, 364 Mo. 453, 263 S.W.2d 29 (1953), holding that a fifteen-month-old infant could not sue her father for negligent operation of an automobile. The decision was grounded in the interest in preserving family harmony.

[Over the years, this court declined to apply the immunity to suits by emancipated minors as well as to suits against noncustodial parents and the estates of deceased parents, on the theory that no threat to family harmony is presented in such cases.] In evaluating the decisions since *Baker*, it becomes clear that this Court has engaged in a piecemeal abrogation of the immunity. . . .

Determining whether to abrogate, retain, further modify, or carve yet additional exceptions to the doctrine requires reconsideration of the policy underpinning the immunity, which is an exception to the general rule of tort liability. . . . Re-examination of the significant interest in avoiding disruption of family harmony reveals that the interest exists in tension with the consequences of the sometimes brutal application of the doctrine, which bars an injured party's right to recover for injuries. In certain circumstances family harmony may be jeopardized by disallowing compensation for a child injured by the negligent act of a parent. . . . Taken to its logical conclusion, the doctrine has the effect of causing the parent to owe a greater duty to the general public than to his or her own child. . . . The preferred course is to abrogate the doctrine in its entirety.

What remains of concern, however, is the interest in avoiding subversion of parental care, control, and discipline. In view of this interest, the question becomes whether the need to preserve parental prerogatives regarding child rearing justifies barring all suits for negligence between child and parent. This Court believes not. Parents should not be permitted to exercise parental prerogatives completely without concern for liability. It is uncontrovertible, however, that parents must be able to exercise a great degree of discretion in control over the relationship with their child. . . .

A review of other jurisdictions' efforts is instructive. One approach to parental immunity attempts to ensure that suits between parent and child will never engender familial discord by retaining immunity except to the extent of the parent's insurance. See Ard v. Ard, 414 So. 2d 1066, 1067-70 (Fla. 1982). . . . Formulation of different rules for the insured and uninsured, however, is not justified. . . .

Other jurisdictions have abrogated parental immunity and substituted approaches that they believe adequately protect the family unit without unduly denying unemancipated minors a tort remedy. The first attempt at reform was undertaken by the Supreme Court of Wisconsin in 1963, which held that parental immunity was abrogated except: "(1) where the alleged negligent act involves an exercise of parental authority over the child; and (2) where the alleged negligent act involves an exercise of ordinary parental discretion with respect to the provision of food, clothing, housing, medical and dental services, and other care." Goller v. White, 20 Wis. 2d 402, 122 N.W.2d 193, 198 (1963).

. . . The principal difficulty with the *Goller* approach has been found to be that the exceptions are vague. . . . Arbitrary line-drawing in determining which parental activities involve exercise of discretion or authority has resulted in inconsistent verdicts among courts applying *Goller.* . . .

Perhaps even more troubling than the interpretative difficulties associated with the *Goller* approach is that the exceptions appear to give parents "carte blanche" to act negligently with respect to their children so long as the parents' conduct falls within one of the exceptions. Gibson v. Gibson, 3 Cal. 3d 914, 92 Cal. Rptr. 288, 479 P.2d 652, 653 (1971). There is no sound reason to distinguish among the various parental duties so as to permit unfettered parental discretion with respect to provision of necessities or the administration of discipline.

[T]he Supreme Court of California adopted a "reasonable parent" standard. The reasoning of *Gibson* gives deference to a parent's exercise of broad discretion in performing parental functions yet recognizes that parental prerogatives must be exercised within reasonable limits. . . . The *Gibson* alternative is sufficiently flexible to accommodate disparate child-rearing practices yet protects children from negligent parental excesses. The reasonable parent standard permits an injured child, or a third party plaintiff, to recover only if the parent fails to meet the standard of care required of parents. . . .

The Restatement (Second) of Torts (1979) [in] Section 895(G) provides: "(1) A parent or child is not immune from tort liability to the other solely by reason of that relationship; (2) repudiation of general tort immunity does not establish liability for an act or omission that, because of the parent-child relationship, is otherwise privileged or not tortious." The Restatement recognizes that the reasonable prudent parent is the applicable standard to be applied in suits involving negligent exercises of parental discretion. §895(G), Comment k. . . .

This Court concludes that a reasonable parent standard should be adopted. The primary criticism of the reasonableness standard is the belief that parental judgment regarding the required degree of discipline and supervision of a particular child cannot be subjected to a judicial determination of reasonableness. Use of the reasonable parent standard, however, provides a single test for all aspects of the parent-child relationship. The standard can be managed to ensure that clearly unacceptable conduct giving rise to tort liability may be subjected to scrutiny. . . . Adoption of a reasonable parent standard is particularly appropriate in Missouri in view of the fact that the legislature has adopted the standard in relation to a parent's duty in the context of the juvenile code. A parent is expected "to exercise *reasonable* parental discipline or authority" and may be subject to a judgment of restitution, along with the child, to a victim, a governmental entity, or a third party payor, when the child has inflicted property damage or caused damages resulting in personal injury or death. §211.185.1-2, RSMo. Supp. 1990 (emphasis added). . . .

## Notes and Questions

1. Despite the increasing number of jurisdictions abolishing or limiting parental immunity, some modern courts retain the doctrine. E.g., Spears v. Spears, 3 S.W.3d 691 (Ark. 1999); Renko v. McLean, 697 A.2d 468 (Md. Ct. App. 1997). Courts have recognized immunity for noncustodial parents, Ascuitto v. Farricielli, 711 A.2d 708 (Conn. 1998), and foster parents, Nichol v. Stass, 735 N.E.2d 582 (Ill. 2000). Courts have more readily abrogated immunity for intentional torts. E.g., Herzfeld v. Herzfeld, 781 So. 2d 1070 (Fla. 2001) (sexual abuse); Pavlick v. Pavlick, 491 S.E.2d 602 (Va. 1997) (murder).

2. What explains the continuing vitality of the parental immunity doctrine in some jurisdictions? Consider the analysis of the Connecticut Supreme Court in rejecting an approach that would make insurance coverage determinative:

> We . . . note that the "unseemly discord" engendered by intrafamily lawsuits is not solely financial in origin. "The prospect of greeting an adolescent judgment creditor at the dinner table each day would likely strain the familial relationship even for the most saintly of parents." Dzenutis v. Dzenutis, [512 A.2d 130, 134 (Conn. 1986).] Although we have noted that this discord may be lessened by the presence of insurance, the manner in which an adverse judgment is satisfied is not the sole, or even the primary, threat to family harmony that results when an unemancipated child brings an action against a parent.[9] Additionally, we recognize that attorneys fre-

───────

9. . . . A negligence action for personal injury uniquely implicates the parent's authority to care for his or her child in a way that is not inherently present in a property dispute. A negligence action is, therefore, especially likely to be disruptive of family harmony.

quently advise their clients not to communicate personally with opposing parties. The practical difficulties in maintaining this confidentiality between a parent and child would seem almost insurmountable. . . .

*Ascuitto*, 711 A.2d at 716-717. Compare this reasoning with *Hartman*'s analysis. Which one represents the sounder approach? If parental immunity should be abolished, is the "reasonable parent" standard preferable to the Wisconsin rule in Goller v. White, 122 N.W.2d 193, 198 (Wis. 1963), which abrogates immunity except for actions involving the exercise of parental authority or discretion? What impact does each approach have on parental autonomy? On children's rights and interests?

3. Should special rules govern cases in which the child suffers injuries because of negligent parental supervision, as when the child suffers brain damage because of the parent's negligent supervision at a swimming pool? See, e.g., Ashley v. Bronson, 473 N.W.2d 757 (Mich. Ct. App. 1991) (examining exceptions to abrogation). Why? Compare Foldi v. Jeffries, 461 A.2d 1145, 1152 (N.J. 1983) (retaining parental immunity for simple negligence in supervision but not for "parent's willful or wanton misconduct in supervising his or her child"), with Broadbent v. Broadbent, 907 P.2d 43 (Ariz. 1995) (applying reasonable parent standard to negligent supervision). How should a jurisdiction that has abolished parental immunity apportion liability for the child's injuries between a babysitter who intentionally abuses the child and the parents who negligently fail to detect the signs of danger? See Glomb v. Glomb, 530 A.2d 1362 (Pa. Super. Ct. 1987). See also Rider v. Speaker, 692 N.Y.S.2d 920 (Sup. Ct. 1999) (holding babysitter but not parents liable for negligent supervision).

4. Why is the juvenile code provision, quoted at the end of *Hartman*, relevant to an intrafamily suit? Should the same standard apply both to third-party claims against a parent for the child's misconduct and claims within the family?

Laws holding parents responsible for the crimes of their children have received renewed attention in the wake of school shootings. See, e.g., Linda A. Chapin, Out of Control? The Uses and Abuses of Parental Liability Laws to Control Juvenile Delinquency in the United States, 37 Santa Clara L. Rev. 621 (1997); Paul W. Schmidt, Note, Dangerous Children and the Regulated Family: The Shifting Focus of Parental Responsibility Laws, 73 N.Y.U. L. Rev. 667 (1998). Criminal responsibility for a child's crimes requires a showing that the parent committed a prohibited act or omission with the requisite mens rea; parental status alone does not suffice. See generally John Kip Cornwell, Preventing Kids from Killing, 37 Hous. L. Rev. 21, 54-59 (2000). Similarly, imputing tort liability to parents generally requires establishing foreseeability or knowledge on their part. Deborah A. Nicholas, Note, Parental Liability for Youth Violence: The Contrast Between Moral Responsibilities and Legal

Obligations, 53 Rutgers L. Rev. 215, 227 (2000). Parental liability laws also have been used to prosecute parents for allowing their children to engage in sexual activities. See People v. Maness, 732 N.E.2d 545 (Ill. 2000) (holding unconstitutionally vague prohibition on parent's knowingly permitting sexual abuse of minor); Susan S. Kuo, A Little Privacy, Please: Should We Punish Parents for Teenage Sex?, 89 Ky. L.J. 135 (2000/2001).

Will parental liability laws help curb youth violence and sex? Will they invite intrusion into minors' privacy? See, e.g., Alison S. Aaronson, Notes & Comments, Changing with the Times: Why Rampant School Violence Warrants Legalization of Parental Wiretapping to Monitor Children's Activities, 9 J. L. & Pol'y 785 (2001). Can you square such laws with the growing practice of trying juvenile offenders as adult criminal defendants?

To what extent does the notion of parental responsibility follow from the basic principle of parental autonomy, which lets parents make decisions and speak for their children? Notwithstanding parental autonomy, do parental liability laws assume knowledge, supervision, and control many parents realistically cannot exercise? Consider, for example, the work requirements that the Personal Responsibility and Work Opportunity Reconciliation Act imposes on parents of even young children. 42 U.S.C. §607 (Supp. V 1999). What's a "reasonable parent" to do?

5. *Emotional injuries.* Should courts allow children to recover damages for emotional harm intentionally inflicted by their parents? This question divided the court in Burnette v. Wahl, 588 P.2d 1105 (Or. 1978), a suit by five children in state custody whose mothers abandoned them, depriving them of support and nurture and causing psychological damage. The majority affirmed dismissal of the case, on the theory that such litigation would undermine child welfare laws and the state policy favoring family reunification. One dissent, citing the psychological harm resulting from the separation of mother and child (and its costs to society), would find such harm compensable, with defendants shouldering so much of the financial burden as possible. Id. at 1112-1115 (Lent, J., concurring and dissenting in part). A second dissent would also allow the case to proceed, finding support for this new tort in the state's child protection laws and its criminal prohibitions punishing child abandonment as a felony. Id. at 1115-1119 (Linde, J., dissenting).

Which analysis is most persuasive? Why would the majority conclude civil liability threatens family unity more than criminal liability? Than juvenile court intervention? Why not apply *Hartman*'s reasonable parent standard here to allow recovery at least in cases of willful abandonment?[56]

---

[56]. In suits against third parties, some courts have held compensable a child's loss of parental care, guidance, and nurturance. These courts recognize a child's cause of action for loss of parental consortium. E.g., Giuliani v. Guiler, 951 S.W.2d 318 (Ky. 1997); Ferriter v. Daniel O'Connell's Sons, Inc., 413 N.E.2d 690 (Mass. 1980). But see Borer v.

The scope of the problem explored in *Burnette* is significant. Data compiled by the federal National Incidence Study: Missing, Abducted, Runaway and Thrownaway Children in America classified 127,100 children as "thrownaway," that is, abandoned or kept away from home by parents or caretakers. See Eugene M. Lewit & Linda Schuurmann Baker, Missing Children, in The Future of Children, Summer/Fall 1998, at 141, 145.

6. How far would the dissenters in *Burnette* extend parental liability for emotional harm? Should parents be liable for the emotional harm and resulting costs of therapy caused by the physical abuse a stepparent inflicts on the child's mother while the child watches?[57] See Courtney v. Courtney, 413 S.E.2d 418 (W. Va. 1991) (recognizing the cause of action), *after remand,* 437 S.E.2d 436 (W. Va. 1993) (specifying applicable statute of limitations). By the parents' divorce? See Judith S. Wallerstein et al., The Unexpected Legacy of Divorce: A 25 Year Landmark Study (2000) (finding lifelong emotional scars from parental divorce). Parental pressure to attend law school despite the child's wish to become a musician? See Hansen v. Hansen, 608 P.2d 364 (Colo. Ct. App. 1979) (unsuccessful "parental malpractice" case). Parental refusal to accept their child's homosexuality? Cf. *C.R.,* supra section C1. See generally G. Steven Neeley, The Psychological and Emotional Abuse of Children: Suing Parents in Tort for the Infliction of Emotional Distress, 27 N. Ky. L. Rev. 689 (2000).

## Problem

Lindsay sues her mother for injuries suffered as the result of a car accident caused by her mother when Lindsay was a five-month fetus. Assume that this state has created exceptions to the parental immunity doctrine to permit direct suits for personal injuries from motor torts and also has case law allowing suits against third parties for prenatal and preconception torts. E.g., Renslow v. Mennonite Hospital, 367 N.E.2d 1250 (Ill. 1977).

Should the court submit to the jury the question whether the mother negligently inflicted Lindsay's prenatal injuries? Why? Compare Stallman v. Youngquist, 531 N.E.2d 355 (Ill. 1988), with Bonte v. Bonte, 616 A.2d 464 (N.H. 1992). Should the answer change if Lindsay were suing her mother for prenatal injuries caused by her mother's employment in

---

American Airlines, Inc., 563 P.2d 858 (Cal. 1977). Why is the child's suit against the parent for similar losses different?

How should courts respond to suits by parents for loss of a child's consortium? Compare, e.g., Elgin v. Bartlett, 994 P.2d 411 (Colo. 1999) (rejecting claim), with Frank v. Superior Court, 722 P.2d 955 (Ariz. 1986) (allowing claim).

[57]. Between 3.3 million and 10 million children reportedly observe domestic violence in their homes each year. Howard A. Davidson, Child Abuse and Domestic Violence: Legal Connections and Controversies, 29 Fam. L.Q. 357, 369 (1995).

a hazardous workplace? Cf. International Union, UAW v. Johnson Controls, Inc., 499 U.S. 187 (1991). For fetal alcohol syndrome caused by her mother's drinking during pregnancy or for the effects of her mother's illegal drug use? See Chenault v. Huie, 989 S.W.2d 474 (Tex. App. 1999). See also Barbara Katz Rothman, Recreating Motherhood 109-110 (2000) (fetus is part of woman, who cannot sue herself).

Finally, can Lindsay sue her mother for "wrongful life" for choosing to have Lindsay born with impairments, rather than terminating the pregnancy once she learned of Lindsay's injuries (or a genetic disease)? See Lois Shepherd, Protecting Parents' Freedom to Have Children with Genetic Differences, 1995 U. Ill. L. Rev. 761. Cf. generally Mark Strasser, Wrongful Life, Wrongful Birth, Wrongful Death, and the Right to Refuse Treatment: Can Reasonable Jurisdictions Recognize All But One?, 64 Mo. L. Rev. 29 (1999).

Do such suits call for the development of a "reasonable pregnant woman" standard? What are the implications for parental autonomy? For the right to privacy?

### b. Statutes of Limitations

■  **HEARNDON v. GRAHAM**
*767 So. 2d 1179 (Fla. 2000)*

PER CURIAM.

We have for review a decision [below] passing upon the following certified question of great public importance: [Where a plaintiff in a tort action based on childhood sexual abuse alleges that she suffered from traumatic amnesia caused by the abuse, does the delayed discovery doctrine postpone accrual of the cause of action?] The facts established by the district court and its ruling below are as follows:

> Paula Jean Hearndon [filed a complaint in 1991] against Kenneth Graham, Hearndon's stepfather, for injuries that resulted from sexual abuses he allegedly committed upon her beginning in 1968 when she was 8, and continuing until 1975 when she turned 15 (at which time, according to the complaint, Graham allegedly murdered Hearndon's mother). The complaint was dismissed with prejudice on the sole ground that the alleged cause of action was barred, as a matter of law, by the four-year statute of limitations. . . . Hearndon argued to the trial court that it should apply the doctrine of delayed discovery of an injury to toll the statute of limitations in her case on the basis that, as an adult survivor of childhood sexual abuse, she suffered from so-called "traumatic amnesia," or a related syndrome [until approximately 1988], caused by the abuses allegedly perpetrated by Graham, thereby explaining why earlier commencement of the action had not been possible. The trial court dismissed Hearndon's complaint. . . .

[The district court affirmed, reasoning that the] Legislature provided explicit tolling provisions that did not include delayed discovery due to lack of memory. . . . For the sake of our review, petitioner suffered childhood sexual abuse that caused her to suppress or lose memory of the events for several years; she later recalled the abuse and filed suit. We do not pass on the merits of whether she actually lost and then retrieved her memory of these alleged events, and we do not pass on the reliability of any psychological techniques that may have been employed in arousing her memory.

The district court recognized that there is credible medical support for the proposition that many victims of childhood sexual abuse develop amnesia because of the horrible nature of the abuse so that they completely lose or suppress the memory for years, only to later recall the events as adults. See Jocelyn B. Lamm, Easing Access to the Courts for Incest Victims: Toward an Equitable Application of the Delayed Discovery Rule, 100 Yale L. J. 2189, 2194 (1991). . . . Nevertheless, we recognize that the acceptance of theories supporting memory loss of childhood sexual abuse is a disputed area of psychological study. It is debated whether such memory loss actually occurs or whether plaintiffs are coached into believing that such abuse occurred by suggestions posed by psychologists. For example, one law journal article advocated the application of the delayed discovery doctrine in the case of childhood sexual abuse based on view that:

> The classic psychological responses to incest trauma are numbing, denial, and amnesia. During the assaults the incest victim typically learns to shut off pain by "dissociating," achieving "altered states of consciousness . . . as if looking in on from a distance at the child suffering the abuse." To the extent that this defense mechanism is insufficient, the victim may partially or fully repress her memory of the assaults and the suffering associated with them: "Many, if not most, survivors of child sexual abuse develop amnesia that is so complete that they simply do not remember that they were abused at all; or . . . they minimize or deny the effects of the abuse so completely that they cannot associate it with any later consequences." Many victims of incest abuse exhibit signs of Post-Traumatic Stress Disorder ("PTSD"), a condition characterized by avoidance and denial that is associated with survivors of acute traumatic events such as prisoners of war and concentration camp victims. . . .

Lamm, supra at 2194. On the other hand, another author has stated that

> Without some objective corroboration courts probably ought not to allow delayed recall incest litigation, and thus avoid the . . . task of attempting to sort out "retrieved" recollections of actual events from similarly retrieved fantasies. . . .

Edward Greer, Tales of Sexual Panic In the Litigation Academy: The Assault on Reverse Incest [Suits], 48 Case W. Res. L. Rev. 513, 553-54 & n.158 (1998). Organizations have been founded to counter what is believed by some to be the inappropriate use of psychology to invent "repressed" memories of abuse. . . . Richard A. Leo, The Social and Legal Construction of Repressed Memory, 22 Law & Soc. Inquiry 653, 654 (1997) [(noting that as of 1994 17,000 families had contacted the False Memory Syndrome Foundation reporting false accusations of childhood sexual abuse)].

The "delayed discovery" doctrine generally provides that a cause of action does not accrue until the plaintiff either knows or reasonably should know of the tortious act giving rise to the cause of action. . . . The district court correctly identified a certain amount of confusion regarding this Court's application of the delayed discovery doctrine [in other contexts] — sometimes the Court stated that the doctrine delayed the "accrual" of the cause of action and other times we stated that the doctrine affected the "tolling" of the statute of limitations. . . .

The determination of whether a cause of action is time-barred may involve the separate and distinct issues of when the action accrued and whether the limitation period was tolled. A statute of limitations "runs from the time the cause of action accrues" which, in turn, is generally determined by the date "when the last element constituting the cause of action occurs." §95.031, Fla. Stat. (1987). The "tolling" of a limitation period would interrupt the running thereof subsequent to accrual. To that end, the Legislature enumerated specific grounds for tolling limitation periods, but did not include delayed discovery due to lack of memory. See §95.051(1), Fla. Stat. (1987). [W]hile accrual pertains to the existence of a cause of action which then triggers the running of a statute of limitations, tolling focuses directly on limitation periods and interrupting the running thereof. That both accrual and tolling may be employed to postpone the running of a statute of limitations so that an action would not become time-barred should not cause confusion between these distinct concepts. . . .

In light of the above distinction, we recognize that the Legislature limited the justification for tolling limitation periods to the exclusion of delayed discovery due to loss of memory, but did not likewise limit the circumstances under which accrual may have been delayed. . . .

Numerous courts around the country apply the delayed discovery doctrine to cases alleging childhood sexual abuse followed by a temporary loss of memory. See, e.g., Johnson v. Johnson, 701 F. Supp. 1363, 1370 (N.D. Ill. 1988); Doe v. Roe, 191 Ariz. 313, 955 P.2d 951, 960 (Ariz. 1998); Evans v. Eckelman, 216 Cal. App. 3d 1609, 265 Cal. Rptr. 605, 610 (Ct. App. 1990); Phinney v. Morgan, 39 Mass. App. Ct. 202, 654 N.E.2d 77, 79-80 (Mass. App. Ct. 1995); Jones v. Jones, 242 N.J. Super. 195, 576 A.2d 316, 321 (N.J. Super. Ct. App. Div. 1990); Ault v. Jasko,

70 Ohio St. 3d 114, 637 N.E.2d 870 (Ohio 1994). Application of the doctrine to such cases constitutes both the majority rule and the modern trend in American jurisprudence.

Reasons in favor of application of the doctrine in the case of childhood sexual abuse are as follows. First, it is widely recognized that the shock and confusion resultant from childhood molestation, often coupled with authoritative adult demands and threats for secrecy, may lead a child to deny or suppress such abuse from his or her consciousness. Second, the doctrine is well established when applied, for example, in cases involving breach of implied warranty or medical malpractice; it would seem patently unfair to deny its use to victims of a uniquely sinister form of abuse. Accordingly, application of the delayed discovery doctrine to childhood sexual abuse claims is fair given the nature of the alleged tortious conduct and its effect on victims. . . .

We therefore hold that the delayed discovery doctrine applies to the accrual of the instant cause of action [and we remand the case for proceedings consistent with this opinion]. However, our decision does not pass on the factual development of the issue that will be addressed at trial. . . .

## Notes and Questions

1. How does *Hearndon* justify lengthening the time for adult survivors of childhood to sue? Although the court notes the division in authority about the authenticity of "repressed memory" claims, hasn't the court sided with supporters of the theory? On the controversy, see First Report of the American Psychological Association Working Group on the Investigation of Memories of Childhood Abuse, 4 Psychol. Pub. Pol'y & L. 931-1306 (1998).

One critic of survivors' suits states that "not a single therapeutically de-repressed and recovered memory of abuse has ever been corroborated by objective evidence." Richard A. Leo, The Social and Legal Construction of Repressed Memory, 22 Law & Soc. Inquiry 653, 666 (1997) (citing Mark Pendergrast, Victims of Memory: Incest Accusations and Shattered Lives 516-518 (1995)). Another asserts that, without external corroboration, the truth of any individual claim based on a retrieved memory of childhood incest becomes impossible to determine. Edward Greer, Tales of Sexual Panic in the Legal Academy: The Assault on Reverse Incest Suits, 48 Case W. Res. L. Rev. 513, 538 (1998). But see Lynne Henderson, Suppressing Memory, 22 Law & Soc. Inquiry 695, 730 (1997) ("some memories of abuse are factually and interpretatively accurate, some are not, and many fall in between").

Some jurisdictions have responded to the controversy with corroboration requirements, e.g., eyewitness accounts, a criminal conviction, or circumstantial evidence, and expert testimony to prove both the abuse and the repressed memory. E.g., Moriarty v. Garden Sanctuary Church of God, 534 S.E.2d 672 (S.C. 2000). Do such requirements fairly balance the competing interests, or do they erect an insurmountable hurdle for plaintiffs?

Assuming not all repressed memory claims are true, what role should attorneys play in sorting out false claims? Should they be liable for filing suits based on false claims? See Cynthia Grant Bowman & Elizabeth Mertz, Attorneys as Gatekeepers to the Court: The Potential Liability of Attorneys Bringing Suits Based on Recovered Memories of Childhood Sexual Abuse, 27 Hofstra L. Rev. 223 (1998).

2. *Hearndon* lists many jurisdictions allowing sex abuse claims that might otherwise be time-barred. Nonetheless, a number of courts have ruled otherwise. See, e.g., Dalrymple v. Brown, 701 A.2d 164 (Pa. 1997); Lemmerman v. Fealk, 534 N.W.2d 695 (Mich. 1995); Peterson v. Huso, 552 N.W.2d 83 (N.D. 1996).

3. *Hearndon* distinguishes measures that toll the statute of limitations from measures that delay the accrual of a cause of action. What is the difference? Note that in many states, minority tolls statutes of limitations. Under such rules, the applicable period for initiating suit begins after the plaintiff reaches majority or becomes emancipated, regardless of when the cause of action might have arisen.

The plight of adult survivors of childhood sexual abuse has led a number of legislatures to find ways to extend statutes of limitations on civil actions against the perpetrators. Some jurisdictions toll the statute of limitations until well past the victim's adulthood in such cases. See, e.g., Conn. Gen. Stat. Ann. §52-577d (West 1991) (departing from general limit of three years after tort occurred to allow sexually abused minors to sue within 17 years of reaching age of majority). Do such statutes recognize that, emotionally, some challenges to parental authority may be possible only well after the age of majority? Other legislatures have codified the delayed discovery approach examined in *Hearndon*. See, e.g., Or. Rev. Stat. §12.117 (1995) (three years after injury or causal connection discovered or should have been discovered).

4. Some authorities classify Paula Hearndon's claim, based on memories completely suppressed until just before the lawsuit, as a "type 2" case. See Messina v. Bonner, 813 F. Supp. 346, 348 (E.D. Pa. 1993). Suppose the plaintiff claimed that she had always recalled the abuse, had long experienced emotional problems, but sued only after belatedly realizing, thanks to therapy, that the abuse caused her problems? Is an extended opportunity to sue also justified in such circumstances (sometimes called "type 1" cases)? See id. See also Clay v. Kuhl, 727 N.E.2d 217 (Ill. 2000); McCreary v. Weast, 971 P.2d 974 (Wyo. 1999); Lonnie Brian Richardson, Notes & Comment, Missing Pieces of Memory: A Rejection of "Type" Classifications and a Demand for a More Subjective Approach

Regarding Adult Survivors of Childhood Sexual Abuse, 11 St. Thomas L. Rev. 515 (1999). Does "discovery" occur when plaintiff had the "first flashback of abuse," when she realized the majority of the facts, or when a jury decides that she knows enough to establish a claim? See Doe v. Roe, 955 P.2d 951, 961-962 (Ariz. 1998). If the limitations period depends on the successful completion of psychotherapy, what problems does this approach present for courts? For defendants? See *Messina*, 813 F. Supp. at 349-350.

5. Does extending the period for suit in abuse cases violate constitutional rights of the defendants? See Starnes v. Cayouette, 419 S.E.2d 669 (Va. 1992) (finding due process violation in extending limitation after original period expired).

6. Until recently, therapists and others largely denied the existence of childhood sexual abuse, considering reports of it largely the product of children's "fantasies." See Melissa G. Salten, Note, Statutes of Limitations in Civil Incest Suits: Preserving the Victim's Remedy, 7 Harv. Women's L.J. 189 (1984). The past decade has witnessed some increased acceptance of such claims, in part because of public revelations of abuse and the use of therapeutic techniques designed to elicit repressed memories. See, e.g., Henderson, supra.

Survivors' suits continue to raise questions about the admissibility of evidence. See, e.g., Logerquist v. McVey, 1 P.3d 113 (Ariz. 2000) (holding admissible expert testimony on recovered memory); Ramona v. Superior Ct., 66 Cal. Rptr. 2d 766 (Ct. App. 1997) (ruling memories refreshed by sodium amytal inadmissible); Leo, supra, at 677-680 (urging inadmissibility of testimony about hypnotically refreshed memories).

7. The use of recovered-memory therapy has also produced a backlash. Some scientists challenge the very existence of "recovered memory," demonstrating how therapists can produce "memories" in their patients. See Elizabeth Loftus & Katherine Ketchum, The Myth of Repressed Memory: False Memories and Allegations of Sexual Abuse (1994). Malpractice actions against recovered-memory therapists have followed. In one highly publicized case, a jury awarded a father $500,000 against two therapists he claimed planted false memories of child sexual molestation in his adult daughter's mind. Ramona v. Ramona, No. 61898 (Super. Ct. Napa Cty. Cal.) (cited in Ramona v. Superior Ct., 66 Cal. Rptr. 2d at 770 n.5). But see Trear v. Sills, 82 Cal. Rptr. 2d 281 (Ct. App. 1999) (rejecting liability because therapist owes no duty to patient's parents). Compare Cynthia Grant Bowman & Elizabeth Mertz, A Dangerous Direction: Legal Intervention in Sexual Abuse Survivor Therapy, 109 Harv. L. Rev. 549 (1996) (arguing against therapists' liability to third parties), with Edward Greer, Tales of Sexual Panic in the Legal Academy: The Assault on Reverse Incest Suits, 48 Case W. Res. L. Rev. 513 (1998) (challenging, inter alia, empirical bases for arguments of Bowman and Mertz).

### c. "Divorce" Actions Against Parents

## ■ KINGSLEY v. KINGSLEY
*623 So. 2d 780 (Fla. Dist. Ct. App. 1993)*

DIAMANTIS, Judge.

Rachel Kingsley, the natural mother of Gregory, a minor child, appeals the trial court's final orders terminating her parental rights based upon findings of abandonment and neglect, and granting the petition for adoption filed by Gregory's foster parents, George and Elizabeth Russ. . . .

On June 25, 1992, Gregory, then 11 years of age, filed in the juvenile division of the circuit court a petition for termination of the parental rights of his natural parents. He separately filed, in the civil division of the circuit court, a complaint for declaration of rights and adoption by his foster parents. This adoption was later transferred to the juvenile division by court order. On July 21, 1992, the trial court ruled that Gregory, as a natural person who had knowledge of the facts alleged, had standing to initiate the action for termination of parental rights. In that order, the trial court implicitly accorded Gregory capacity to file the petition although he was an unemancipated minor. Prior to entering this order, the trial court, noting that there was a distinction between the roles of guardian ad litem and attorney ad litem, appointed one of Gregory's attorneys, Jerri A. Blair, as his attorney ad litem. The trial court made no ruling concerning Gregory's standing to file the adoption petition; however, Gregory's foster parents filed a petition for adoption on September 3, 1992, with the written consent of Gregory and Gregory's natural father. [The trial court tried the termination of parental rights and adoption proceedings together, over the biological mother's objection. The court terminated the mother's parental rights and granted the foster parents' adoption petition. The biological mother appeals.]

Rachel contends that the trial court erred in holding that Gregory has the capacity to bring a termination of parental rights proceeding in his own right. Specifically, Rachel argues that the disability of nonage prevents a minor from initiating or maintaining an action for termination of parental rights. We agree.

Capacity to sue means the absence of a legal disability which would deprive a party of the right to come into court. . . . Courts historically have recognized that unemancipated minors do not have the legal capacity to initiate legal proceedings in their own names. This historic concept is incorporated into Florida Rule of Civil Procedure 1.210(b). . . .

The necessity of a guardian ad litem or next friend, the alter ego of a guardian ad litem, to represent a minor is required by the orderly administration of justice and the procedural protection of a minor's welfare and interest by the court and, in this regard, the fact that a minor is represented by counsel, in and of itself, is not sufficient. Unless a child has a guardian or other like fiduciary, a child must sue by his next friend; however, the next friend does not become a party to the suit. Where the next friend brings the suit, the minor is the real party in interest.

This disability of nonage has been described as procedural, rather than jurisdictional, in character because if a minor mistakenly brings an action in his own name such defect can be cured by the subsequent appointment of a next friend or guardian ad litem. . . .

Section 39.461(1), Florida Statutes (Supp. 1992), provides that petitions for termination of parental rights may be initiated

> either by an attorney for [the Department of Health and Rehabilitative Services (HRS)], or by any other person who has knowledge of the facts alleged or is informed of them and believes that they are true.

This court has construed the term "any other person who has knowledge" to mean

> someone who is in a peculiar position so that such knowledge can be reasonably inferred; for example, the judge familiar with the file, the guardian or attorney for the children, neighbors or friends of the parties who, because of their proximity, would be expected to have such knowledge.

This construction contemplates the situation which arose here — that Jerri Blair, an attorney, would file a termination petition on Gregory's behalf. She must do so, however, as his next friend. The next friend may be an attorney, but need not be one. . . .

As a general rule, states "may require a minor to wait until the age of majority before being permitted to exercise legal rights independently." Bellotti v. Baird, 443 U.S. 622, 650 (1979). Objective criteria, such as age limits, although inevitably arbitrary, are not unconstitutional unless they unduly burden the minor's pursuit of a fundamental right. *Bellotti*, 443 U.S. at 640, 643 n.23. Gregory's lack of capacity due to nonage is a procedural, not substantive, impediment which minimally restricts his right to participate as a party in proceedings brought to terminate the parental rights of his natural parents; therefore, we conclude that this procedural requirement does not unduly burden a child's fundamental liberty interest to be "free of physical and emotional violence at the hands of his . . . most trusted caretaker."

Although we conclude that the trial court erred in allowing Gregory to file the petition in his own name because Gregory lacked the requisite legal capacity, this error was rendered harmless by the fact that separate petitions for termination of parental rights were filed on behalf of Gregory by the foster father, the guardian ad litem, HRS, and the foster mother. [It was also harmless error to try the adoption proceeding with the termination but reversible error to enter the adoption order before a written termination order had become final.]

HARRIS, Chief Judge, concurring in part, dissenting in part:

This rather ordinary termination of parental rights case was transformed into a *cause celebre* by artful representation and the glare of klieg lights. It is the judge's obligation, however, to look beyond the images created by light and shadow and concentrate on the real-life drama being played out on center stage. Florida recognizes no cause of action that permits a child to divorce his parents.

I concur with the majority holding that so long as the parents do nothing to forfeit their fundamental liberty interest in the care, custody and management of their child, no one (including the child) can interfere with that interest [citing Prince v. Massachusetts]. While the child has the right not to be abused, neglected or abandoned, there is no right to change parents simply because the child finds substitutes that he or she likes better or who can provide a better standard of living.

Florida does not recognize "no-fault" termination of parental rights. That is why the focus in a termination case is (and must be), at least in the first analysis, on the alleged misconduct of the biological parent or parents which would authorize termination of parental rights. Termination of parental rights requires a two step analysis. First, did the parents do something that the State has determined to be sufficiently egregious to permit forfeiture of their right to continue as parents (abuse, neglect, abandonment, voluntary consent to adoption)? Unless the answer to this first question is affirmative, the second step in the analysis (the best interest of the child) is unnecessary. . . .

[The majority's finding of harmless error] ignores the fact that the "best interest" factors themselves should not have been considered by the court until *after* the court first determined that there was abandonment. . . .

## Notes and Questions

1. "Gregory K.'s" suit to "divorce" his biological mother received extensive publicity. The trial court granted his petition, on the ground that a child has a "constitutional right to terminate his relationship with his biological parents on the basis of their neglect and abuse." See Jerri A. Blair, *Gregory K.* and Emerging Children's Rights, Trial, June 1993, at 22.

Gregory's "divorce" suit is really a petition to terminate his mother's parental rights, as *Kingsley* recognizes on appeal. *Kingsley* holds that Gregory cannot sue on his own behalf because of the procedural disability of nonage. To what extent does this holding undercut the constitutional right recognized by the court below? If the Constitution does give children such rights, who should exercise them if nonage prohibits the child from doing so? See generally George H. Russ, Through the Eyes of a Child, "Gregory K.": A Child's Right to Be Heard, 27 Fam. L.Q. 365 (1995) (attorney, now Gregory's adoptive father, advocates recognition of child's constitutional right). Does the child have a voice in selecting the "next friend" or guardian ad litem? Cf. Emily Buss, "You're My What?" The Problems of Children's Misperceptions of Their Lawyers' Roles, 64 Fordham L. Rev. 1699 (1996).

2. Framing Gregory's claim in constitutional terms recalls an earlier era when the Supreme Court recognized a number of constitutional rights for children, apart from the interests of parents or the state. E.g., In re Gault, 387 U.S. 1 (1967) (procedural due process guarantees juvenile delinquent notice and counsel); Tinker v. Des Moines Indep. Community Sch. Dist., 393 U.S. 503 (1969) (recognizing First Amendment right of student to wear black arm band). Subsequent decisions including *Yoder* and *Parham,* however, reflected greater deference to state authority and parental prerogatives. E.g., McKeiver v. Pennsylvania, 403 U.S. 528 (1971) (procedural due process does not guarantee juvenile delinquent a jury trial); Hazelwood Sch. Dist. v. Kuhlmeier, 484 U.S. 260 (1988) (upholding school control of student newspaper, over First Amendment challenge). What explains the retreat from "children's liberation"? See Martha Minow, What Ever Happened to Children's Rights?, 80 Minn. L. Rev. 267 (1995). See also Lee E. Teitelbaum, Children's Rights and the Problem of Equal Respect, 27 Hofstra L. Rev. 799 (1999) (exploring difficulties of "rights talk" about children).

3. What do cases like Gregory's portend for parental autonomy? For the parent-child relationship? For children's autonomy? According to one analysis, the answers depend on one's perspective:

> [P]arents' rights advocates argued that permitting a child to present such a petition to the court unwisely undermines parental rights and gives too much power to children. In contrast, those who focus on "children's rights" expressed suspicion of allowing either the state or parents to exercise power over children without giving children a voice. . . .

Theresa Glennon & Robert G. Schwartz, Looking Back, Looking Ahead: The Evolution of Children's Rights, 68 Temp. L. Rev. 1557, 1563 (1995).

4. *Kingsley* precipitated a debate about the parameters of family privacy. To what extent does privacy for the family entity require "a right of exit" for children, comparable to spouses' right to divorce? Professor Barbara Bennett Woodhouse observes:

> Most fictive entities recognized by the state, from corporations to marriages, are created through voluntary acts and offer various rights of

participation as well as a right of exit. The caretaking unit, composed . . . by persons who are inherently and essentially in positions of inequality, is uniquely dangerous and more open, rather than less open, to abuse if completely privatized. This is especially true because children have few, if any, exit options. The right of exit was integral to the message of *McGuire* [in Chapter III, at page 259]. Compare the situation of children whose parents fail to live up to their duties. Children have limited exit options, they cannot file for divorce, no matter how badly their parent has treated them.

Barbara Bennett Woodhouse, The Dark Side of Family Privacy, 67 Geo. Wash. L. Rev. 1247, 1253 (1999).

Philosopher Laura M. Purdy proposes a "flexible approach" or middle ground that falls short of full-fledged parental autonomy, children's liberation, or state authority. Under this approach, children should be able to "divorce" their parents only when there is no other way to protect their interests. Purdy also advocates establishing "institutional mechanisms" that support the parent-child relationship, protect both parents' and children's interests, and aim to prevent termination. Laura M. Purdy, Boundaries of Authority: Should Children Be Able to Divorce Their Parents?, in Having and Raising Children: Unconventional Families, Hard Choices, and the Social Good 153, 155 (Uma Narayan & Julia J. Bartkowiak eds., 1999). What sort of "institutional mechanisms" might address Purdy's concerns? Evaluate her suggestion of "divorce" as a last resort.

5. What does "Gregory K.'s" suit say about the state's ability to protect children from abuse and neglect? How might the case affect the child welfare system? See Jamie D. Manasco, Parent-Child Relationships: The Impetus Behind the *Gregory K.* Decision, 17 Law & Psychol. Rev. 243, 244 (1993) (case revealed system's numerous flaws). *Kingsley* may be viewed as a critique of state child welfare programs that allow children to languish in foster care despite the Adoption Assistance and Child Welfare Act's mandates to prevent removals from home and to preserve families. Russ, supra, at 391; Christina Dugger Sommer, Note, Empowering Children: Granting Foster Children the Right to Initiate Parental Rights Termination Proceedings, 79 Cornell L. Rev. 1200 (1994).

The Adoption and Safe Families Act of 1997 requires states receiving federal funds for their adoption and foster care programs to petition for termination of parental rights for any child under state responsibility for 15 of the last 22 months, as well as in cases in which the parent has committed certain violent crimes against the child or another child. The state must also take steps designed to result in the adoption of the child. 42 U.S.C. §675(5) (Supp. V 1999). Will this legislation prevent the problems highlighted by *Kingsley*? For critical views, compare Elizabeth Bartholet, Nobody's Children: Abuse and Neglect, Foster Drift, and the Adoption Alternative 158-159 (1999), with Dorothy Roberts, Shattered Bonds: The Color of Child Welfare 104-133 (2001).

6. Although the state (through social service agencies) always has the power to terminate parental rights, some statutes confer on private parties the right to initiate a petition for termination. Depending on statute, these parties include relatives, the other natural parent, and foster parents. Ann M. Haralambie, Handling Child Custody, Abuse and Adoption Cases §13.04 (1993). *Kingsley* involved the interpretation of a broad-based statute that conferred standing on "any . . . person."

Should children be able to initiate termination petitions as well? See In re Appeal in Pima County Juvenile Severance Action No. S-113432, 872 P.2d 1240 (Ariz. Ct. App. 1993); Haralambie, supra. If children are given standing to initiate terminations, must the court ascertain whether the petitioner is sufficiently mature? See In re Appeal, supra, at 1243 ("Maturity has nothing to do with a child's interest in the substance of [a termination] proceeding"). Cf. Jay C. Laubscher, Note, A Minor of "Sufficient Age and Understanding" Should Have the Right to Petition for the Termination of the Parental Relationship, 40 N.Y.L. Sch. L. Rev. 565 (1996).

7. The same day *Kingsley* was decided, another Florida court held that a minor had standing to petition to terminate parental rights. In Twigg v. Mays, 1993 WL 330624 (Fla. Cir. Ct. Aug. 18, 1993), the Twiggs sought discovery on the issue of paternity of Kimberly Mays. The Twiggs alleged that Kimberly, who was raised by Robert Mays and his wife (now deceased), was actually the Twiggs' daughter who had been switched by the hospital at birth. (The daughter reared by the Twiggs had died of a heart ailment.) After stipulated blood tests corroborated the Twiggs' claim and the Twiggs sued for custody, Kimberly successfully petitioned for termination of their parental rights, with the court recognizing standing for both her and Mays.[58] Can you reconcile this case with *Kingsley*?

8. On children's rights as part of the international human rights movement, see generally Rochelle D. Jackson, The War Over Children's Rights: And Justice for All? Equalizing the Rights of Children, 5 Buff. Hum. Rts. L. Rev. 223 (1999); Jonathan Todres, Emerging Limitations on the Rights of the Child: The U.N. Convention on the Rights of the Child and Its Early Case Law, 30 Colum. Hum. Rts. L. Rev. 159 (1998).

## Problem

Sheila (age 15) goes to court following disagreements with her parents about her conduct, including running away. She relies on a state statute authorizing the juvenile court to order alternative residential placement of a minor for families in conflict. Sheila testifies: "I just feel

---

[58]. Subsequently, Kimberly left Mays, falsely accusing him of child abuse, and began living with the Twiggs. See Kim Mays Happy with Family, St. Petersburg Times, Nov. 15, 1994, at 5B.

that there's a communication gap [in the home]." Based on her testimony and pursuant to the statute, the court orders Sheila placed in a nonsecure licensed facility, with visitation for her parents and a review in six months.

Sheila's parents challenge the statute as an infringement of their constitutional right to direct her upbringing. What are Sheila's interests? How great is the infringement of parental autonomy? How should the court decide? See In re Sumey, 621 P.2d 108 (Wash. 1980). See also In re Snyder, 532 P.2d 278 (Wash. 1975); Bruce C. Hafen, Children's Liberation and the New Egalitarianism: Some Reservations About Abandoning Youth to Their "Rights," 1976 BYU L. Rev. 605; Purdy, supra, at 160-162 (proposing "children's houses" or group living arrangements to allow partial separation of parent and child in cases of abuse, serious conflict, and failed reconciliation attempts).

# IX

# *Adoption and Alternatives to Adoption*

Adoption law traditionally has focused on the placement of children with biologically unrelated adults, with "best interests" as the guiding principle. Recently, however, the focus of adoption law has expanded beyond child welfare. High divorce and remarriage rates as well as the emergence of nontraditional family forms have brought increasing attention to such variations as stepparent adoptions, second-parent adoptions, and adult adoptions. The setting of adoption law also has changed as the number of white infants available for placement shrinks, the number of children with special needs awaiting homes grows, and new medical procedures offer the infertile alternatives to adoption.

This chapter highlights the conflict between the right to privacy and the state's authority to intervene in family decisionmaking in the context of adoption and its alternatives. Interests in reproductive self-determination, family integrity, and confidentiality sometimes clash with the state's interest in the welfare of children (or children-to-be). Consider how the law balances these competing interests and whether it adequately addresses the differing needs of biological parents, adopters, and adoptees.

## A. BACKGROUND

## ■ STEPHEN B. PRESSER, THE HISTORICAL BACKGROUND OF THE AMERICAN LAW OF ADOPTION
*11 J. Fam. L. 443, 446-489 (1971)*

We can document the practice of adoption among the ancient Babylonians, Egyptians, and Hebrews, as well as the Greeks, but the most advanced early law on adoption which we have is from the Romans. In contrast with current adoption law, which has as its purpose the "best interests" of the child, it appears that ancient adoption law, and particularly the Roman example, was clearly designed to benefit the *adopter,* and any benefits to the adoptee were secondary. There were two broad purposes that Roman adoption law served: (1) to avoid extinction of the family, and (2) to perpetuate rites of family religious worship. . . .

[Adoption was not known at common law.] The usual explanation for the absence of a legal recognition of adoption in the English common law is the inordinately high regard for blood lineage of the English. [Another possible reason was xenophobia.]

The purpose of the American adoption statutes passed in the middle of the nineteenth century was to provide for the welfare of dependent children, a purpose quite different from that of the old Roman laws. [On the other hand, in England] there were mechanisms for the care of children, dependent and otherwise, that made adoption for social welfare purposes unnecessary. These mechanisms, which were instituted early and which were very well developed by the seventeenth century, were the institutions of "putting out" and "apprenticeship." In a very real sense these institutions were a form of "adoption," although the purpose was neither inheritance nor the perpetuation of the adopter's family, but the temporary training of the child. [T]he customs of "apprenticeship" and "service" were brought to America by the New England Puritans. . . .

The first comprehensive adoption statute was passed in 1851 in Massachusetts. Among its key provisions were requirements 1) that written consent be given by the natural parents . . . ; 2) that the child himself must consent if he is fourteen years of age or older; 3) that the adopter's [spouse] must join in the petition for adoption; 4) that the probate judge . . . must be satisfied that the petitioner(s) were "of sufficient ability to bring up the child . . . and that it is fit and proper that such adoption should take effect" . . . ; 5) that once the adoption was approved by the probate court, the adopted child would become "to all intents and purposes" the legal child of the petitioner(s); [and] 6) that the natural parents would be deprived by the decree of adoption of all legal rights and obligations respecting the adopted child. . . .

[The purpose of the Massachusetts law and others like it remains unclear. One theory says that an increase in adoptions arranged by foundling societies prompted these statutes.] It is naive to attribute the passage of adoption statutes in so many states solely to the activities of "foundling societies." The activities of these societies *is* demonstrative of a larger movement for child welfare of which the passage of the adoption statutes also represents a part. This movement came about as a result of the economic changes which made the stop-gap institutions of apprenticeship, service, and indenture quite unable to cope with the great numbers of children who had been neglected by their families and also were neglected, until about the middle of the nineteenth century in most cases, by the society and the state. In order to understand better the motives that lay behind the passage of the adoption statutes, it is important to understand some of these other developments in child welfare work. . . .

[F]rom philanthropic motives most probably inspired by the continuing plight of dependent children in the hands of public authorities, private agencies for the care of such children were founded. . . . In the first half of the nineteenth century, at least seventy-seven such agencies were founded. . . . After 1850 the increase in the number of such agencies was even more rapid. . . . Before 1850, the private agencies sought to teach their charges to read and write. . . . Prior to the establishment of the public school systems and compulsory attendance, the agencies felt their primary service should be to give to their children the rudiments of an education before they were placed out in indenture or service.

Around 1850, however, private agencies began to be founded with the avowed purpose of placing younger children in a suitable family atmosphere. The work of some of the "infant's hospitals," "foundling asylums," and "maternity hospitals" in New York and Boston stands out in this regard, as does the work of the Children's Aid Societies started in those cities in 1853 and 1865, respectively. . . . The Children's Aid Societies made efforts to place children in suitable homes, usually homes far from the city, in the expanding states and territories of the West. [T]he Children's Aid Society of New York [ ] placed over twenty thousand children in homes out of New York City in the twenty years after it was founded. . . .

[Many of] the children placed by such agencies as the New York Children's Aid Society found themselves in situations which not only resembled "adoption" as we know it today but which was called by the same name. As the phenomenon of children in adopted homes became more common, there was increased pressure not only to pass laws regulating and insuring the legal relations between adopted children and their natural and adoptive parents, but to guarantee that some benefits of heirship were conferred on the adopted child. This pressure, which originated with the activities of the charitable associations working in child welfare, led to passage of the general adoption statutes in the third quarter of the nineteenth century. . . .

---

On the Massachusetts adoption statute, see Jamil S. Zainaldin, The Emergence of a Modern American Family Law: Child Custody, Adoption, and the Courts, 1796-1851, 73 Nw. U.L. Rev. 1038 (1979). On the history of American adoption generally, see Michael Grossberg, Governing the Hearth: Law and Family in Nineteenth-Century America 271-280 (1985).

## B. PARENTAL CONSENT TO ADOPTION

### 1. *Validity and Revocability*

■ **SCARPETTA v. SPENCE-CHAPIN ADOPTION SERVICE**
*269 N.E.2d 787 (N.Y. 1971)*

JASEN, J.
This appeal involves the return of an out-of-wedlock infant to its natural mother after she had executed a purported surrender of the child to an authorized adoption agency. . . .

The infant child was born on May 18, 1970, to Olga Scarpetta, who was unmarried and 32 years old. She had become pregnant in her native Colombia by a married Colombian in the summer of 1969. Seeking to minimize the shame of an out-of-wedlock child to herself and her family, Miss Scarpetta came to New York for the purpose of having her child. She was well acquainted with this country and its language. She had had her early schooling in New Jersey and her college education in California. Indeed, she had been trained in the social sciences.

Four days after the birth of the child, she placed the infant for boarding care with Spence-Chapin Adoption Service, an agency authorized by statute to receive children for adoption. Ten days later, a surrender document was executed by Miss Scarpetta to the agency, and on June 18, 1970, the baby was placed with a family for adoption. Five days later, on June 23, 1970, the mother repented her actions and requested that the child be returned to her.

After several unsuccessful attempts to regain her child from the agency, the mother commenced this habeas corpus proceeding. Before the surrender, the mother had had a number of interviews with representatives of the adoption agency. On the other hand, shortly before or after the birth of the child, her family in Colombia, well-to-do, and devout in their religion, were shocked that she should put out her child for adoption by strangers. They assured her of their support and backing and urged her to raise her own child. [The courts below ruled in favor of Scarpetta. This court affirms.]

The resolution of the issue of whether or not a mother, who has surrendered her child to an authorized adoption agency, may regain the child's custody, has received various treatment by the legislatures and courts in the United States. At one extreme, several jurisdictions adhere to the rule that the parent has an absolute right to regain custody of her child prior to the final adoption decree. On the other hand, some jurisdictions adhere to the rule that the parent's surrender is final, absent fraud or duress. The majority of the jurisdictions, however, place the parent's right to regain custody within the discretion of the court — the position which, of course, our Legislature has taken. The discretionary rule allows the court leeway to approve a revocation of the surrender when the facts of the individual case warrant it and avoids the obvious dangers posed by the rigidity of the extreme positions.

In New York, a surrender executed by a mother, in which she voluntarily consents to a change of guardianship and custody to an authorized agency for the purpose of adoption, is expressly sanctioned by law. (Social Services Law, §384.) The statute nowhere endows a surrender with irrevocability foreclosing a mother from applying to the court to restore custody of the child to her. In fact, the legislation is clear that, until there has been an actual adoption, or the agency has met the requirements of the Social Services Law [requiring agency or court approval of surrender following notice], the surrender remains under, and subject to, judicial supervision.

Inherent to judicial supervision of surrenders is the recognition that documents of surrender are unilateral, not contracts or deeds, and are almost always executed under circumstances which may cast doubt upon their voluntariness or on understanding of the consequences of their execution. . . . Of necessity, therefore, there is always an issue about the fact of surrender, document or no document. On the other hand, the courts have the strongest obligation not to permit surrenders to be undone except for the weightiest reasons. . . .

Having the power to direct a change of custody from the agency back to the natural parent, notwithstanding the document of surrender, the court should exercise it only when it determines "that the interest of such child will be promoted thereby and that such parent is fit, competent and able to duly maintain, support and educate such child." (Social Services Law, §383, subd. 1.) . . . It has repeatedly been determined, insofar as the best interests of the child are concerned, that "[the] mother or father has a right to the care and custody of a child, superior to that of all others, unless he or she has abandoned that right or is proved unfit to assume the duties and privileges of parenthood." [Citations omitted.]

The primacy of status thus accorded the natural parent is not materially altered or diminished by the mere fact of surrender under the statute, although it is a factor to be considered by the court. To hold, as the agency suggests — that a surrender to an authorized adoption agency constitutes, as a matter of law, an abandonment — would frustrate the policy underlying our legislation, which allows a mother to regain custody of her child, notwithstanding the surrender to the agency, provided, of course, that there is some showing of improvidence in the making of the surrender, that the interest of such child will be promoted and "that such parent is fit, competent and able to duly maintain, support and educate such child." . . . Consequently, to give the fundamental principle meaning and vitality, we have explicitly declared that "[except] where a nonparent has obtained legal and permanent custody of a child by adoption, guardianship or otherwise, he who would take or withhold a child from mother or father must sustain the burden of establishing that the parent is unfit and that the child's welfare compels awarding its custody to the nonparent." (People ex rel. Kropp v. Shepsky, [113 N.E.2d 801 (N.Y. 1953)]. . . .

In no case, however, may a contest between a parent and nonparent resolve itself into a simple factual issue as to which affords the better surroundings, or as to which party is better equipped to raise the child. It may well be that the prospective adoptive parents would afford a child some material advantages over and beyond what the natural mother may be able to furnish, but these advantages, passing and transient as they are, cannot outweigh a mother's tender care and love unless it is clearly established that she is unfit to assume the duties and privileges of parenthood.

We conclude that the record before us supports the finding by the courts below that the surrender was improvident and that the child's best interests — moral and temporal — will be best served by its return to the natural mother.

Within 23 days after the child had been given over to the agency, and only 5 days after the prospective adoptive parents had gained provisional custody of the child, the mother sought its return. If the matter had been resolved at that time, much heartache and distress would have been avoided. However, since the child was not returned, the mother had no alternative but to commence legal proceedings to regain its custody, and this she did without delay. . . .

[The court rejects the prospective adoptive parents' petition to intervene on the ground that intervention would necessarily lead to disclosure of the names of the natural parents and prospective adoptive parents to each other in violation of the policy of secrecy, which relies on the adoption agency to serve as intermediary.] Similarly, we find no merit to the contention that the failure to allow the prospective adoptive parents to intervene in the instant proceeding deprived them of due process of law so as to render the court's determination awarding custody of the child to the mother, constitutionally invalid. The prospective adoptive parents do not have legal custody of the baby. Spence-Chapin, the adoption agency, by virtue of the mother's surrender, was vested with legal custody. The agency, in turn, had placed the baby with the prospective adoptive parents pursuant to an arrangement reached between them, for the purpose of prospective adoption of the child. This arrangement is, of course, subject to our adoption statutes, and in no way conveys any vested rights in the child to the prospective adoptive parents. . . .

## Notes and Questions

1. *Epilogue.* After the court's decision, the adoptive family (the DiMartinos) fled with "Baby Lenore" to Florida. Scarpetta filed a habeas corpus action there, claiming full faith and credit for the New York decision. The DiMartinos successfully argued that they should not be bound by litigation in which they were not permitted to participate. At the ensuing trial, the court focused on the child's best interests. Experts testified on her development with the DiMartinos and the trauma separation would cause. The Florida court ruled the DiMartinos should retain custody. Henry H. Foster, Jr., Adoption and Child Custody: Best Interests of the Child?, 22 Buff. L. Rev. 1, 8 (1972). The U.S. Supreme Court denied certiorari, DiMartino v. Scarpetta, 404 U.S. 805 (1971).

In response to the case, New York amended the statute. It now provides that in contested revocation cases parents who consented "have no right to the custody of the child superior to that of the adoptive parents" and custody "shall be awarded solely on the basis of the best interests of the child," with no presumption favoring any particular disposition. N.Y. Dom. Rel. Law §115-b(6)(d)(v) (McKinney 1999).

2. *Agency placement.* The adoption process often begins, as *Scarpetta* illustrates, when the birth parent voluntarily relinquishes (or "surrenders") the child to a state-licensed or state-operated agency. The agency takes legal custody and selects an adoptive family. After a residential period under the agency's supervision, a court issues an adoption decree. Traditionally, neither the birth parents nor the adopters learn the others' identities. Moreover, if the placement fails during the trial period, the child returns to the agency's care, not to the birth parent whose rights are terminated by the relinquishment. Advocates claim that only agency adoptions serve the birth parents' needs for counseling and support, the child's needs for placement with capable and prepared adopters, and the adopters' needs for a full range of services. See L. Jean Emery,

Agency Versus Independent Adoption: The Case for Agency Adoption, The Future of Children, Spring 1993, at 139, 140-142; Susan A. Munson, Comment, Independent Adoption: In Whose Best Interest?, 26 Seton Hall L. Rev. 803, 804-809 (1996). Today, most agency placements involve older children who spent time in foster care. Ruth-Arlene W. Howe, Adoption Laws and Practices in 2000: Serving Whose Interests?, 33 Fam. L.Q. 677, 681-683 (1999).

3. *Scarpetta* surveys different approaches to revocation: recognizing a parent's absolute right to regain custody before a final adoption decree; treating a surrender as irrevocable, absent fraud or duress; and entrusting the question of revocation to judicial discretion. What competing interests are implicated in these approaches? Which one strikes the best balance?

In balancing the competing interests, what weight should be accorded to the emotional experiences of birth parents in relinquishment? See Holli Ann Askren & Kathaleen C. Bloom, Postadoptive Reactions of the Relinquishing Mother: A Review, JOGNN, July/Aug. 1999, at 395 ("at risk for long-term physical, psychologic, and social repercussions"). Advocates of reform have questioned the traditional postrelinquishment goal of encouraging the birth mother to "reconstitute her life quickly by bolstering the defenses of denial and repression at the cost of other emotional needs." Eva Y. Deykin et al., The Postadoption Experience of Surrendering Parents, 54 Am. J. Orthopsychiatry 271, 272 (1984). See Adam Pertman, Adoption Nation: How the Adoption Revolution Is Transforming America 110-111 (2000).

4. Jurisdictions recognize several bases for revoking consent to adoption:

(a) *Time period.* One approach makes determinative the timing of consent or revocation. For example, under the Uniform Adoption Act (UAA) §§2-408, 2-409, a parent can revoke relinquishment of consent within 192 hours (8 days) of the child's birth. 9 U.L.A. (pt. IA) 60-63 (1999). See also, e.g., In re Adoption of Baby Girls Mandell, 572 N.E.2d 359 (Ill. App. Ct. 1991) (12-month limit). An alternative approach makes voidable consents executed less than a certain number of days after birth. See, e.g., In re Baby Girl T., 21 P.3d 581 (Kan. Ct. App. 2001) (upholding statute's 12-hour period). Finally, some jurisdictions allow withdrawal of consent anytime before the final decree of termination of parental rights or adoption. 25 U.S.C. §1913(c) (1994) (Indian Child Welfare Act). How much time for revocation ought to be allowed? See Catherine Sakach, Note & Comment, Withdrawal of Consent for Adoption: Allocating the Risk, 18 Whittier L. Rev. 879 (1997) (proposing two months).

(b) *Fraud, duress or immaturity.* Some states invalidate consent procured by fraud or coercion. E.g., Ariz. Rev. Stat. Ann. §8-106(D) (West Supp. 2000); Va. Code Ann. §63.1-219.12 (Michie Supp. 2000); Wuertz

v. Craig, 458 So. 2d 1311 (La. 1984). But see T.R. v. Adoption Servs., Inc., 724 So. 2d 1235 (Fla. Dist. Ct. App. 1999) (youth and poverty do not constitute duress). Some allow revocation by a birth parent too immature to understand the consequences of consent. See Adoption of Thomas, 559 N.E.2d 1230 (Mass. 1990); Janet G. v. New York Foundling Hosp., 403 N.Y.S.2d 646 (Fam. Ct. 1978). Some jurisdictions address this problem by requiring the consent of the minor birth parent's parents. See, e.g., Minn. Stat. Ann. §259.24(2) (West Supp. 2001). But see Mo. Rev. Stat. §453.050 (2000) (waiver of consent valid even if parent is under age 18). Can a minor birth parent who subsequently seeks to revoke consent be bound by her own parents' consent?

(c) *Other bases.* Some states make revocation of relinquishment to an agency more difficult than revocation of other types of consent to adoption. See, e.g., N.J. Stat. Ann. §§9:2-14, 9:2-16 (West 1993) (only surrender to approved agency valid and irrevocable); Sees v. Baber, 377 A.2d 628 (N.J. 1977).

5. Can a state constitutionally grant an adoption *without* valid parental consent? Involuntary termination of parental rights comporting with all procedural and substantive requirements dispenses with the need for parental consent. (See Chapter VIII, section B4d.) Can a state replace consent or the usual grounds for termination of parental rights with a showing that adoption serves the child's best interests? See, e.g., Mass. Gen. Laws ch. 210, §3(a)(ii) (Supp. 2001) (so permitting). What considerations should this statute's best interests analysis encompass? See Hickman v. Futty, 489 S.E.2d 232 (Va. Ct. App. 1997) (using Virginia statute). Will a statutory time period in foster care meet the constitutional test? See In re H.G., 757 N.E.2d 864 (Ill. 2001) (statutory presumption fails strict scrutiny).

If the state can dispense with parental consent, can it do so in a way that treats birth fathers and mothers differently? The next case explores this question.

## 2. Unmarried Fathers' Rights

### ■ ADOPTION OF KELSEY S.
*823 P.2d 1216 (Cal. 1992)*

BAXTER, J.
The primary question in this case is whether the father of a child born out of wedlock may properly be denied the right to withhold his consent to his child's adoption by third parties despite his diligent and legal attempts to obtain custody of his child and to rear it himself, and absent any showing of the father's unfitness as a parent....

Kari S. gave birth to Kelsey, a boy, on May 18, 1988. The child's undisputed natural father is petitioner Rickie M. He and Kari S. were not married to one another. At that time, he was married to another woman but was separated from her and apparently was in divorce proceedings. He was aware that Kari planned to place their child for adoption, and he objected to her decision because he wanted to rear the child.

Two days after the child's birth, petitioner filed an action in superior court under Civil Code section 7006 to establish his parental relationship with the child and to obtain custody of the child. [The court awarded petitioner temporary custody, stayed all adoption proceedings, and prohibited contact with the prospective adopters.] On May 24, 1988, Steven and Suzanne A., the prospective adoptive parents, filed an adoption petition under Civil Code section 226 [, alleging] that only the mother's consent to the adoption was required because there was no presumed father under section 7004, subdivision (a). [The court modified its order and awarded the birth mother temporary custody.] The court ordered the mother to live with the child in a shelter for unwed mothers. [T]he trial court prohibited visitation by either the prospective adoptive parents or petitioner. [The prospective adopters then petitioned under §7017 to terminate petitioner's parental rights.] The superior court consolidated that proceeding with the adoption proceeding. The court allowed petitioner to have supervised visitation with the child at the women's shelter where the child was living with his mother. The court also allowed the prospective adoptive parents to have unsupervised visitation at the shelter.

The parties subsequently stipulated that petitioner was the child's natural father. The superior court, however, ruled that he was not a "presumed father" within the meaning of section 7004, subdivision (a)(4). The court held four days of hearings under section 7017, subdivision (d)(2) to determine whether it was in the child's best interest for petitioner to retain his parental rights and whether the adoption should be allowed to proceed. (The attorney appointed by the trial court to represent the child's interests advocated that petitioner should retain his parental rights.) On August 26, 1988, the court found "by a *bare* preponderance" of the evidence that the child's best interest required termination of petitioner's parental rights. (Italics added.)

Petitioner appealed. He contended the superior court erred by: (1) concluding that he was not the child's presumed father; (2) not granting him a parental placement preference; and (3) applying a preponderance-of-the-evidence standard of proof. The Court of Appeal rejected each of his contentions. . . .

Section 7004 states, "A man is presumed to be the natural father of a child . . ." if the man meets any of several conditions set forth in the statute. Whether a biological father is a "presumed father" under section 7004 is critical to his parental rights. If the mother of a child . . . consents to the child's adoption, [t]he child's best interest is the sole criterion where there is no presumed father. As in the present case, the trial court's determination is frequently that the child's interests are better served by a third party adoption than by granting custody to the unwed natural father.

Mothers and presumed fathers have far greater rights. [A] mother or a presumed father must consent to an adoption absent a showing by clear and convincing evidence of that parent's unfitness. . . .

A man becomes a "presumed father" under section 7004, subdivision (a)(4) if "*[h]e receives the child into his home* and openly holds out the child as his natural child." (Italics added.) It is undisputed in this case that petitioner openly held out the child as being his own. Petitioner, however, did not physically receive the child into his home. He was prevented from doing so by the mother, by court order, and allegedly also by the prospective adoptive parents. . . .

There remains . . . the question of whether a natural father's federal constitutional rights are violated if his child's mother is allowed to unilaterally preclude him from obtaining the same legal right as a presumed father to withhold his consent to his child's adoption by third parties. [This question] has not been addressed by the United States Supreme Court. We are guided, however, by a series of high court decisions dealing with the rights of unwed fathers. [The Court then analyzed three Supreme Court precedents: Stanley v. Illinois, 405 U.S. 645 (1972); Quilloin v. Walcott, 434 U.S. 246 (1978); and Caban v. Mohammed, 441 U.S. 380 (1979). These cases are presented in Chapter IV, section D2.]

The high court again considered the rights of biological fathers only four years later in Lehr v. Robertson (1983) 463 U.S. 248. The father and mother lived together before the child's birth, and he visited the child in the hospital when the child was born. He did not, however, live with either the mother or child after its birth, and he did not provide them with any financial support. Nor did he offer to marry the mother. Eight months after the child's birth, the mother married another man. When the child was two years old, the mother and her new husband began adoption proceedings. One month later, the biological father filed an action seeking a determination of his paternity, an order of support, and visitation with the child. Shortly thereafter, the biological father learned of the pending adoption proceeding, and almost immediately he sought to have it stayed pending the determination of his paternity petition. The state court informed him that it had already signed the adoption order earlier that day, and then dismissed his paternity action. . . . The *Lehr* court, held that, "because appellant, like the father in *Quilloin,* has never established a substantial relationship with his daughter . . . the New York statutes at issue in this case did not operate to deny appellant equal protection [in treating him differently from other fathers]."

*[Lehr]* did not purport to decide the legal question in the present case, that is, whether the mother may constitutionally prevent the father from establishing the relationship that gives rise to his right to equal protection. The *Lehr* court, however, recognized the uniqueness of the biological connection between parent and child. "The significance of the biological connection is that it offers the natural father an opportunity that no other male possesses to develop a relationship with his offspring. If he grasps that opportunity and accepts some measure of responsibility for the child's future, he may enjoy the blessings of the parent-child relationship and make uniquely valuable contributions to the child's development." (Id., at p.262.) *Lehr* can fairly be read to mean that a father need only make a reasonable and meaningful attempt to establish a relationship, not that he must be successful against all obstacles.

The most recent relevant high court decision arose in California. (Michael H. v. Gerald D. (1989) 491 U.S. 110.) Michael H. claimed to be the father of a child and sought a declaration of paternity and visitation rights. Blood tests showed a 98.07 percent probability that Michael H. was the father. The mother, however, was married to and living with another man at the time of conception. [T]he high court upheld the denial of Michael H.'s request for a declaration of paternity and visitation rights. [F]our justices agreed that the biological father had a protected liberty interest in his relationship with his child. [E]ven the author of the two-justice lead opinion in *Michael H.* (Scalia, J.) left open the question of whether the result would have been different if the marital parents had not wanted to raise the child as their own. [A] majority of the justices were solicitous of the rights of unwed biological fathers. For them, the determinative factor was whether a biological father has attempted to establish a relationship with his child.

[O]ne unifying and transcendent theme emerges. The biological connection between father and child is unique and worthy of constitutional protection if the father grasps the opportunity to develop that biological connection into a full and enduring relationship. . . .

Petitioner asserts a violation of equal protection and due process under the federal Constitution; more specifically, that he should not be treated differently from his child's mother. . . . Respondents do not adequately explain how an unwed mother's control over a biological father's rights [substantially furthers the state's important] interest in the well-being of the child. The linchpin of their position, however, is clear although largely implicit: Allowing the biological father to have the same rights as the mother would make adoptions more difficult because the consent of both parents is more difficult to obtain than the consent of the mother alone. This reasoning is flawed in several respects.

A. Respondents' view too narrowly assumes that the proper governmental objective is adoption. [T]he constitutionally valid objective is the protection of the child's well-being. . . . If the possible benefit of adoption were by itself sufficient to justify terminating a parent's rights, the state could terminate an unwed mother's parental rights based on nothing more than a showing that her child's best interest would be served by adoption. . . .

B. Nor is there evidence before us that the statutory provisions allowing the mother to determine the father's rights are, in general, substantially related to protecting the child's best interest. [Respondent] assumes an unwed mother's decision to permit an immediate adoption of her newborn is always preferable to custody by the natural father, even when he is a demonstrably fit parent. . . .

C. The lack of any substantial relationship between the state's interest in protecting a child and allowing the mother sole control over its destiny is best demonstrated by the results that can arise when a mother prevents the father from obtaining presumed status under section 7004, subdivision (a). . . . Under the statute, the father has basically two ways in which to achieve that status: he can either marry the mother, or he can receive the child into his home and hold it out as his natural child. Of course, the first alternative is entirely within the mother's control. . . . The system also leads to irrational distinctions between fathers. Based solely on the mother's wishes, a model father can be denied presumed father status, whereas a father of dubious ability and intent can achieve such status by the fortuitous circumstance of the mother allowing him to come into her home, even if only briefly — perhaps a single day. . . .

The system also makes little sense from a child's perspective. A child may have a wholly acceptable father who wants to nurture it, but whose parental rights can be terminated under the best-interest standard because the mother has precluded the father from attaining presumed father status. Conversely, if a presumed father is highly questionable in every respect, he is nevertheless allowed to withhold consent absent proof by clear and convincing evidence that he is unfit. . . .

D. We must not lose sight of the way in which the present case and others like it come before the courts. A mother's decision to place her newborn child for adoption may be excruciating and altogether altruistic. Doing so may reflect the extreme of selflessness and maternal love. As a legal matter, however, the mother seeks to sever all ties with her child. [Yet even if] the mother somehow has a greater connection than the father with their child and thus should have greater rights in the child, the same result need not obtain when she seeks to relinquish custody and to sever her legal ties with the child and the father seeks to assume his legal burdens. . . .

E. In summary, we hold that section 7004, subdivision (a) and the related statutory scheme [unconstitutional]. If an unwed father promptly comes forward and demonstrates a full commitment to his parental responsibilities — emotional, financial, and otherwise — his federal constitutional right to due process prohibits the termination of his parental relationship absent a showing of his unfitness as a parent. Absent such a showing, the child's well-being is presumptively best served by continuation of the father's parental relationship. Similarly, when the father has come forward to grasp his parental responsibilities, his parental rights are entitled to equal protection as those of the mother.

A court should consider all factors relevant to that determination. The father's conduct both before and after the child's birth must be considered. Once he knows or reasonably should know of the pregnancy, he must promptly attempt to assume his parental responsibilities as fully as the mother will allow and his circumstances permit. In particular, the father must demonstrate "a willingness himself to assume full custody of the child — not merely to block adoption by others." [In Matter of Raquel Marie, 559 N.E.2d 418, 428 (N.Y. 1990).] A court should also consider the father's public acknowledgement of paternity, payment of pregnancy and birth expenses commensurate with his ability to do so, and prompt legal action to seek custody of the child. . . .

[I]f (but only if) the trial court finds petitioner demonstrated the necessary commitment to his parental responsibilities, there will arise the further question of whether he can be deprived of the right to withhold his consent to the adoption. . . . For purposes of remand, . . . any finding of petitioner's unfitness must be supported by clear and convincing evidence. Absent such evidence, he shall be permitted to withhold his consent to the adoption.

[If] the trial court concludes that petitioner has a right to withhold consent, that decision will bear only on the question of whether the adoption will proceed. Even if petitioner has a right to withhold his consent (and chooses to prevent the adoption), there will remain the question of the child's custody. That question is not before us, and we express no view on it. . . .

## Notes and Questions

1. *Independent placement.* The independent adoption in *Kelsey S.* contrasts with the agency placement in *Scarpetta.* Generally, in independent adoptions the birth parents select the adopters themselves, often with the assistance of an intermediary such as an attorney, and place the child directly with the adopters, pending the issuance of a final adoption decree. The UAA has several distinct provisions for "direct" and agency placements (for example, §§2-102, 2-103). 9 U.L.A. (pt. IA) 30-33 (1999). Three states (Connecticut, Delaware, and Massachusetts) prohibit independent placements. See id. at 31 (comment to §2-102).

Critics claim independent adoptions primarily help adults seeking a child to adopt, at the expense of child welfare. L. Jean Emery, Agency

Versus Independent Adoption: The Case for Agency Adoption, The Future of Children, Spring 1993, at 139, 143. See also David Ray Papke, Pondering Past Purposes: A Critical History of American Adoption Law, 102 W. Va. L. Rev. 459, 471 (1999) (consumer-driven private placements growing in response to adopters' preferences). Supporters assert: (a) birth parents prefer independent adoption because it allows them to select the adopters; (b) adopters avoid long waiting lists and play an active role in the process; and (c) children avoid the necessity of spending a transitional period in foster care. Mark T. McDermott, Agency Versus Independent Adoption: The Case for Independent Adoption, The Future of Children, Spring 1993, at 146, 147. Because adoptive parents often pay birth parents' expenses in independent placements, some call these "gray market" adoptions. See Melinda Lucas, Adoption: Distinguishing Between Gray Market and Black Market Activities, 34 Fam. L.Q. 553, 556 (2000).

2. *Kelsey S.* considers the rights of a "thwarted father" to veto an infant's adoption planned by the birth mother. In deciding in favor of the father, how accurate is the court's analysis of the Supreme Court's precedents? See Lehr v. Robertson, 463 U.S. 248, 268-269 (1983) (White, J., dissenting). Justice White describes how Lehr and the mother had cohabited, how he had visited her and the infant in the hospital upon birth, and how later he "never ceased his efforts to locate" them (even hiring a detective), despite the mother's efforts to conceal their whereabouts. Lehr also offered financial support. If Justice White's recitation of the facts in *Lehr* is accurate, then the Supreme Court had already rejected the equal protection claims of a father who tried to maintain a relationship with his child but was thwarted by the mother's unilateral actions. Do the two cases warrant different approaches because *Lehr*, unlike *Kelsey S.*, concerned a stepparent adoption in which the birth mother would continue to rear the child?

Are there constitutionally acceptable reasons for giving biological mothers greater authority than fathers to determine placement of a nonmarital child? To what extent did *Kelsey S.* correctly assess Michael H. v. Gerald D. (Chapter IV, section D2) to find a majority of Justices "solicitous of the rights of unwed biological fathers"? See generally Mary L. Shanley, Unwed Fathers' Rights, Adoption, and Sex Equality: Gender-Neutrality and the Preservation of Patriarchy, 95 Colum. L. Rev. 60 (1995).

3. Professor David Meyer identifies two different ways to interpret the Supreme Court precedents. Under the "child centered" view, only an actual parent-child relationship matters, not the efforts of a father whom the mother successfully thwarts. David D. Meyer, Family Ties: Solving the Constitutional Dilemma of the Faultless Father, 41 Ariz. L. Rev. 753, 764 (1999). Under a second reading, "the Supreme Court is concerned not simply with the existence or non-existence of a

meaningful father-child relationship, but ultimately also with the strength of the father's moral claim [, that is,] whether the claimant has acted in a way deserving of protection." Id. Which view do you discern in the Supreme Court cases, including the opinions in *Michael H.* (see Chapter IV, at pages 518-525)? In *Kelsey S.*?

Under the second view, how does a father show he is deserving? See Jeffrey A. Parness, Abortions of the Parental Prerogatives of Unwed Natural Fathers: Deterring Lost Paternity, 53 Okla. L. Rev. 345, 378-380 (2000) (examining possible required affirmative acts). Can the father's prebirth conduct toward the mother be determinative? Compare In re Adoption of Baby E.A.W., 658 So. 2d 961 (Fla. 1995) (father's prebirth "abandonment" of mother suffices to free child for adoption), with Ex Parte C.V., 2001 Ala. LEXIS 141 (Ala. Apr. 27, 2001) (court divides on whether prebirth abandonment satisfies statute). If there are several possible fathers, must they all take affirmative steps before birth to preserve their rights? See In re Adoption of D.M.M., 955 P.2d 618 (Kan. Ct. App. 1997) (yes). If the child is conceived as the result of the father's sexual assault of the mother, must he consent to adoption? An omitted footnote in *Kelsey S.* states that the constitutional protections for unmarried fathers do not apply in such circumstances. 823 P.2d at 1237 n.14. Compare In re Adoption of A.F.M., 15 P.3d 258 (Alaska 2001), with Shepherd v. Clemens, 752 A.2d 533, 539-542 (Del. 2000). See Angela D. Lucchese, Note, *Pena v. Mattox:* The Parental Rights of a Statutory Rapist, 36 Brandeis J. Fam. L. 285 (1997-98).

4. Put Professor Meyer's two different views to the test: Suppose the mother lies, purposely misidentifying the father. Later, she marries the biological father and joins with him to halt adoption proceedings then in progress. Should this mother and the father she "thwarted" regain custody of a child she relinquished? See In the Interest of B.G.C., 496 N.W.2d 239 (Iowa 1992) ("Baby Jessica" case). Will recognition of the biological father's rights raise the "specter of newly named genetic fathers, upsetting adoptions, perhaps years later"? Id. at 247 (Snell, J., dissenting). Should (could) a state require a woman to identify the father correctly or to notify him of her pregnancy as a precondition to adoption? Cf. In re TMK, 617 N.W.2d 925 (Mich. Ct. App. 2000); In re Termination of Parental Rights of Biological Parents of Baby Boy W., 988 P.2d 1270 (Okla. 1999).

Consider the highly publicized "Baby Richard" case, in which the mother falsely told the father the newborn had died. Later they married and joined in seeking the child's return. The court held the father had shown sufficient interest in the child to preclude termination of rights and consideration of the child's best interests. It invalidated Baby Richard's adoption, removing him from the home of adoptive parents with whom he had lived for four years. In re Petition of John Doe, 638 N.E.2d 181 (Ill.), *cert. denied,* 513 U.S. 994 (1994). The birth father then successfully sought a writ of habeas corpus, requiring the child's transfer to his custody. In re Petition of Kirchner, 649 N.E.2d 324 (Ill.), *stay denied sub nom.* O'Connell v. Kirchner, 513 U.S. 1138 (1995). Later the birth parents separated, leaving the child in the birth mother's custody. Dirk Johnson, Father Who Won Custody Case Over Adopted Boy Moves Out, N.Y. Times, Jan. 22, 1997, at A10.

5. *The child's rights.* How should a court balance the rights of biological parents against the asserted due process liberty interests of a child in remaining with a "psychological family"? In Baby Richard's case and similar controversies, courts have declined to allow a child's best interests to trump a thwarted father's rights. See *John Doe,* 638 N.E.2d 181; *B.G.C.,* 496 N.W.2d 239.

If a court makes the child's best interests determinative, should it focus on short-term or long-term interests? What weight should a court accord to alleged trauma from separation from the psychological family? See Marcus T. Boccaccini & Eleanor Willemsen, Contested Adoption and the Liberty Interest of the Child, 10 St. Thomas L. Rev. 211, 291 (1998) (disrupted early attachment jeopardizes future relationships). To evidence that many adoptees later feel a "void" in the absence of their biological parents? See, e.g., Katherine A. Kowal & Karen Maitland Schilling, Adoption Through the Eyes of Adult Adoptees, 55 Am. J. Orthopsychiatry 354, 361 (1985). See also Joan Heifetz Hollinger, The Uniform Adoption Act: Reporter's Ruminations, 30 Fam. L.Q. 345, 356 (1996); Carol Sanger, Separating from Children, 96 Colum. L. Rev. 375, 441-450 (1996) (examining legal regulation of separations of mothers from children in several contexts, including adoption). Media reports claim that Baby Jessica and Baby Richard have fared well despite their traumatic removal from long-term adoptive placements. See Leonard Greene, Heartbreak Kids Enjoy Normal Childhoods, N.Y. Post, Mar. 9, 2001, at 19. But separations later occurred in both children's birth families. Gregory A. Kelson, In the Best Interest of the Child: What Have We Learned from Baby Jessica and Baby Richard?, 33 J. Marshall L. Rev. 353, 362, 370-371 (2000). See also infra pages 1186-1187.

6. *Statutory reforms.* In the wake of high-profile challenges to adoptive placements by the thwarted fathers of Baby Jessica and Baby Richard, several states expanded the grounds for terminating parental rights, broadening definitions of "abandonment" and "unfitness." Most of these laws, however, have not been interpreted to allow "no-fault" terminations. See Meyer, supra, at 770-792.

Several states use "putative father registries," which eliminate the need for adoption notification or consent for a man who failed to take the initiative by registering. See id. at 756-757. The Supreme Court approved reliance on a registry system in Lehr v. Robertson, 463 U.S. 248 (1983). The Uniform Parentage Act, revised in 2000, follows this approach to facilitate and expedite infant adoptions, where "time is of the essence," while requiring notification to fathers of older children and exempting fathers of infants who initiate timely proceedings to establish paternity. 9B U.L.A. 321 (2001) (Prefatory Comment to Article 4). See also id. at 322 (§402 requires registration no later than 30 days after birth or commencement of paternity proceedings before termination of his parental rights). What information must the risk-averse man provide if he registers before he knows of a pregnancy? What problems do you see in this approach? See generally Rebeca Aizpuru, Note, Protecting the Unwed Father's Opportunity to Parent: A Survey of Paternity Registry Statutes, 18 Rev. Litig. 703 (1999).

Another approach requires notifying unidentified fathers by posting or publication. See, e.g., Uniform Putative and Unknown Fathers Act, 9C U.L.A. 63, 67-68 (2001) (§3 allows court to order publication or posting of notice if likely to lead to actual notice of father). How well will these methods achieve actual notification if they exclude the mother's name to protect her privacy? See Jones v. South Carolina Dept. of Soc. Servs., 534 S.E.2d 713 (S.C. Ct. App. 2000); South Carolina Dept. of Soc. Servs. v. Doe, 527 S.E.2d 771 (S.C. Ct. App. 2000).

Finally, the new Uniform Parentage Act eliminates the presumption at issue in *Kelsey S.*, while retaining the presumption of paternity in the context of marriage. There is no longer a presumption that a man who receives a child into his home and holds out the child as his own is the father. Further, voluntary acknowledgment of paternity now establishes paternity, not merely a presumption of paternity. 9B U.L.A. 311-312 (2001) (§204 cmt.). See also American Law Institute, Principles of the Law of Family Dissolution: Analysis and Recommendations §§2.03, 3.03 (2002) (recognizing parents by estoppel).

The UAA, §3-504(c)-(d), provides for termination of the rights of a birth father who has not demonstrated by action or deed an interest in parenting his child unless he can show a "compelling reason" for his failure to do so. 9 U.L.A. (pt. IA) 86-87 (1999). Even if he can make this showing, the court can nevertheless terminate his rights if it finds evidence that failure to terminate will be "detrimental" to the child or granting custody to him would pose a risk of "substantial harm" to the child's physical or psychological well-being. Id. Although the act protects a birth mother's right to remain silent about the birth father, it requires advising her that her choice may delay the adoption or subject it to challenge, that the lack of information about the father's medical and genetic history may be detrimental to the adoptee, and that she faces a civil penalty for knowingly misidentifying the father. UAA §3-404, id. at 79-80. See generally Joel D. Tenenbaum, Introducing the Uniform Adoption Act, 30 Fam. L.Q. 333, 339-340 (1996).

7. *Adoption versus custody. Kelsey S.* explicitly distinguishes adoption from custody, stating that even if the biological father can block the

adoption, custody remains a separate issue. Does the court suggest that the prospective adoptive parents might retain custody even without an adoption decree? Yet if custody might remain with the adopters, why does the court say that to prevail in blocking an adoption a birth father must demonstrate a willingness to assume *full custody?* The UAA §3-506 follows the court's approach, allowing a court that denies an adoption petition to determine the child's legal custody. 9 U.L.A. (pt. IA) 90 (1999). See Meyer, supra, at 792-812 (critiquing Illinois and other laws allowing custody without adoption, in response to Baby Richard case). But see Mark A. v. Elizabeth L. (Adoption of Haley A.), 57 Cal. Rptr. 2d 361, 376-383 (Ct. App. 1996). Professor Meyer proposes instead adoption with visitation rights for biological parents, in other words, "nonconsensual open adoption." Meyer, supra, at 833-845. Evaluate this "solution."

8. In a concurring and dissenting opinion in *Kelsey S.,* Justice Mosk would have reached the same result based on equitable estoppel: the conduct of the biological mother and adoptive parents, thwarting the father's efforts, should equitably estop them from challenging his status as a presumed father. Mosk claims this approach would avoid an unnecessary declaration of unconstitutionality and "needless uncertainty in the application of statutory categories that have been consistently employed for almost 20 years," to the detriment of all parties, "especially the child." 823 P.2d at 1239. Is this approach preferable?

9. *Empirical evidence.* A survey of 125 self-identified birth fathers, drawn from adoption support and advocacy groups, indicates that the surrender of a child for adoption long remains an emotional issue. Eva Y. Deykin et al., Fathers of Adopted Children: A Study of the Impact of Child Surrender on Birthfathers, 58 Am. J. Orthopsychiatry 240, 246-247 (1988). Most had negative views of the surrender and some felt obsessed with finding the child. Id. at 244, 246. Despite such data, many birth mothers, adoptive parents, and adoptees hold negative attitudes about birth fathers, associating them with desertion and failure to take responsibility. Most respondents did not support the release of identifying information on adoptees to birth fathers even when supporting the same for birth mothers. Paul Sachdev, The Birth Father: A Neglected Element in the Adoption Equation, 72 Fam. in Socy.: J. Contemp. Hum. Servs. 131 (1991). Compare Elizabeth S. Cole & Kathryn S. Donley, History, Values, and Placement Policy Issues in Adoption, in The Psychology of Adoption 273, 285 (David M. Brodzinsky & Marshall D. Schecter eds., 1990) (research fails to confirm birth fathers guilty of rape or incest or unconcerned about child's well-being), with Anne B. Brodzinsky, Surrendering an Infant for Adoption: The Birthmother Experience, in The Psychology of Adoption, supra, at 295, 315 ("interested, committed birthfathers remain in the minority").

## Problems

1. Mark (then 20) asks Stephanie (then 15) to marry after a short acquaintance. She declines. A few months later they learn Stephanie is pregnant. They decide on adoption. Stephanie then leaves Arizona to visit California. After meeting John and Margaret there, she chooses them to adopt the baby.

On her return to Arizona, Stephanie's relationship with Mark deteriorates. Stephanie excludes him from birthing classes. Following two violent outbursts, Mark attempts suicide and enters drug rehabilitation therapy. He then informs Stephanie he no longer favors adoption.

Stephanie returns to California, gives birth, places the child with John and Margaret, and consents to their adoption. Mark, when he learns of the birth a week later, immediately consults an attorney, sends out birth announcements, and purchases baby supplies. Thereafter, he consistently expresses his desire to take full parental responsibilities.

John and Margaret seek to terminate Mark's parental rights in California. They claim that *Kelsey S.* gives Mark no veto over the adoption because he failed to demonstrate full commitment to parental responsibilities throughout the pregnancy. Mark also invokes *Kelsey S.,* counter-arguing that he attempted to maintain a relationship with Stephanie during the pregnancy and that since birth he has done everything possible to assume full parental responsibility. He also claims that John and Margaret's interpretation of *Kelsey S.* discriminates by allowing mothers to decide after birth to withhold consent for adoption while requiring fathers to decide early in the pregnancy.

What result and why? What policy issues does each reading of *Kelsey S.* raise? See Adoption of Michael H., 898 P.2d 891 (Cal. 1995); Carol A. Gorenberg, Fathers' Rights vs. Children's Best Interests: Establishing a Predictable Standard for California Adoption Disputes, 31 Fam. L.Q. 169 (1997).

2. In response to highly publicized cases of abandonment and infanticide by teen parents, several states have enacted statutes that provide anonymity and immunity from prosecution for parents who leave their babies at designated safe sites. You are the assistant to a state legislator who is exploring the enactment of a "Baby Moses" law, as these legalized abandonment provisions are often called. Noting that such measures are generally aimed at mothers, the legislator has asked for a memorandum on what the proposal should say, if anything, about how to terminate the rights of fathers of abandoned babies so the babies can be placed for adoption. What would your memorandum say? See generally Michael S. Raum & Jeffrey L. Skaare, Encouraging Abandonment: The Trend Towards Allowing Parents to Drop Off Unwanted Newborns, 76 N.D. L. Rev. 511 (2000).

## C. CHOOSING AN ADOPTIVE FAMILY

### 1. Placement Criteria: "Matching"

■ **IN RE D.L.**
    *479 N.W.2d 408 (Minn. Ct. App. 1991)*

DAVIES, Judge.

D.L.'s foster parents and maternal grandparents both sought to adopt her. The foster parents appeal the trial court's ruling granting the grandparents' petition. We affirm.

D.L., whose birth date is July 12, 1989, was the third child born during the marriage of Debra L. and Jonathan L. D.L. has been in the care of appellants, her foster parents, since a few days after her birth. [D.L.'s parents' rights were terminated on the ground of abandonment.] D.L., Debra, and the respondent grandparents are African-American; the foster parents and the father are not. . . .

Debra's two other daughters have lived with her parents, respondents herein, since 1988. One of the daughters is from the marriage with Jonathan and the other from a prior relationship. Respondents have legal custody of both girls, now six and eight years old. Another child of the marriage, a boy, lived with them for a time. At the request of both the boy and his father, respondents returned the boy to Jonathan.

Respondents live in rural Halifax County, Virginia. They first learned of D.L.'s existence in August of 1989 when Debra called from Minnesota and told them she had a daughter. Debra refused to give her parents any further information or a telephone number where she could be reached.

Debra visited respondents for a few days in late December 1989. They urged her to get the baby and live with them. Debra, however, returned to Minnesota and respondents had no contact with her until February of 1990, when they learned she was in jail in Minneapolis. Respondents called Debra who assured them that D.L. was with good people and she would get her back.

In June 1990, Debra called her mother to say for the first time that if she could not get out of jail, she was going to lose D.L. Promptly thereafter, respondent grandmother came to Minneapolis to look for D.L.; she was able to locate her granddaughter through the placement agency. Within a few weeks respondents notified Hennepin County's adoption unit that they wished to adopt D.L.

[Appellants and then respondents filed petitions to adopt D.L.] [T]he court issued an order limiting the hearing to the issue of whether there was good cause not to approve respondents as D.L.'s adoptive parents under the "relative" preference of the Minority Adoption Act, Minn. Stat. §259.28, subd. 2.

At the seven-day trial, respondents provided a detailed description of their background, marriage, and family life. . . . Sandra Lawson, a Hennepin County social worker, testified pertaining to her favorable study of respondents' home. Lawson's testimony regarding the positive relationship between respondents and their children and grandchildren was confirmed by D.L.'s guardian ad litem, Jane Moore, who also visited respondents in Virginia.

[Appellants] testified they have been married since 1966. Except for a teenage son, appellants' children are married and living away from home. Appellants testified they have a profound love for D.L. and that D.L. is deeply attached to them. A primary issue at trial was the consequences to D.L. of breaking the emotional bond between her and appellants. . . .

[The trial court upheld the constitutionality of the Minority Adoption Act and granted the grandparents' petition based on a finding of D.L.'s best interests. D.L. remained in appellants' home pending appeal.]

The trial court's authority to grant an adoption petition is governed by Minn. Stat. §259.28 (1990). The statute provides that a decree of adoption shall be made if the court finds that it is in "the best interests of the child." Minn. Stat. §259.28, subd. 1(a).

The Minority Adoption Act, codified at Minn. Stat. §259.28, subd. 2, requires the court, in the absence of good cause to the contrary, to follow certain placement preferences in the adoption of a child of "minority racial or minority ethnic heritage." In determining adoptive placement of such children, the court "shall" give preference first to a relative of the child, or, if that would be "detrimental" to the child or a relative is not available, to a family with the same racial or ethnic heritage as the child. If such a placement is not "feasible," the court shall give preference to a family of different racial or ethnic heritage from the child that is "knowledgeable and appreciative" of the child's racial or ethnic heritage.

Appellants [joined by D.L.'s guardian ad litem and the NAACP] contend that Minn. Stat. §259.28, subd. 2, impermissibly classifies adoptive children based upon their race, thereby violating the 14th Amendment's Equal Protection Clause. . . . A core purpose of the 14th Amendment is to do away with all governmentally imposed discrimination based on race. Palmore v. Sidoti, 466 U.S. 429, 432 (1984). To pass constitutional muster, racial classifications are subject to the most exacting scrutiny, that is, they must be justified by compelling governmental interest and must be "necessary . . . to the accomplishment" of their legitimate purpose. McLaughlin v. Florida, 379 U.S. 184, 196 (1964). . . .

On its face, Minn. Stat. §259.28, subd. 2, establishes a racial classification by requiring, in the adoptive placement of a child of minority racial or ethnic heritage, that the trial court follow certain preferences not required for non-minority children. The statute recites a benevolent purpose for the classification, that is, "to ensure that the best interests of children are met by requiring due consideration of the child's minority race or minority ethnic heritage." Id.

The racial classification here fails [under the Equal Protection Clause], however, because it is not necessary to the accomplishment of the legislative purpose. The heritage of minority children can be protected without the classification by making the preferences for relatives applicable to all children, as the legislature has directed in related statutes. See, e.g., Minn. Stat. §259.255 (child placing agency shall give preference to relatives in placing "the child" in adoption placements); Minn. Stat. §260.181, subd. 3 (court shall follow preferences for relatives in transferring legal custody of "any child"). . . .

In view of our decision that the Minority Adoption Act is unconstitutional, respondents are not entitled to a mandatory preference under that statute. There is, however, both longstanding common law which favors providing "custodial preference to near relatives," In re M.M., 452 N.W.2d 236, 238 (Minn. 1990), and a strong legislative policy of awarding "the permanent care and custody" of a child to a relative. Id.; see Minn. Stat. §257.02 (1990). The legislature has emphasized the importance of preserving the biological family, see Minn. Stat. §256F.01 (1990), and, if necessary, transferring legal custody or guardianship to a relative, Minn. Stat. §260.181 (1990). Basically the same language regarding a preference for relatives which appears in Minn. Stat. §260.181, dealing with custody or guardianship, appears in Minn. Stat. §259.255 (1990), which deals with the duties of the child placement agency in an adoption. . . .

Our supreme court has recognized a common law doctrine which, although not as compelling as the right of a parent to custody of a child, accords a custodial preference to other near relatives, as opposed to strangers. In re M.M., 452 N.W.2d at 238. This is based on the common sense notion that those near of kin will be disposed to do more for the welfare of the child and to advance his or her interests than those who lack the prompting of kinship. . . .

[I]ndependent of the preference in Minn. Stat. §259.28, subd. 2, which we find unconstitutional, the appropriate test for a proposed adoptive placement is whether it would serve "the best interests of the child." Minn. Stat. §259.28, subd. 1(a). We are able to affirm the result in this case because the record supports the trial court's separate independent conclusion that D.L.'s adoptive placement with her grandparents is in her best interest.

Appellants urge that the removal of D.L. from their care will permanently harm her because of the disruption of the primary caretaker bond. The experts agreed, and the trial court found, that D.L.'s separation from appellants will cause her severe short-term pain. Based on the testimony of Kenneth Watson, however, the trial court found that the injury will heal well in the loving environment provided by the grandparents. . . .

[T]he record supports the trial court's findings of significant benefits to D.L. from placement with her grandparents. These include the opportunity to grow up with her two siblings and the support of a closely-knit extended family. . . .

■ ELIZABETH BARTHOLET, WHERE DO
BLACK CHILDREN BELONG? THE
POLITICS OF RACE MATCHING IN
ADOPTION
*139 U. Pa. L. Rev. 1163, 1164-1188, 1237 (1991)*

When I first walked into the world of adoption, I was stunned at the dominant role race played. . . . Early in the process of exploring how I might adopt, I discovered that the first order of business for the agencies responsible for matching children waiting for homes with prospective parents is to sort and allocate by race. The public and most of the traditional private adoption agencies would not consider assigning a waiting minority child to me, a white person, except as a last resort, and perhaps not even then. The organizations and individual entrepreneurs that arrange independent adoptions, while more willing to place across racial lines, also sorted children by race. In this part of the adoption world, minority children might actually be easier for the white prospective parent to find than a white child, and they were often available for a lesser fee. . . .

The familiar refrain that there are no children available for adoption is a reflection of the racial policies of many adoption agencies and the racial preferences of many adoptive parents. The reality is that there are very few *white* children by comparison to the large pool of would-be white adopters. But there are many *non-white* children available to this pool, both through independent adoption in this country and through international adoption. And there are many non-white children waiting in foster care who are unavailable solely because of adoption agency insistence that they not be placed transracially.

Racial thinking dominates the world of international adoption as well. [Bartholet, a single mother of one child from an early marriage, adopted two children from Peru.] I discovered during my two adoption trips to Peru something about how children may be rated in racial terms in their own country as well as here. Most of the children available for adoption in Peru are of mixed indian and spanish heritage. But there is tremendous variety in ethnic features and skin color. For my second adoption I was offered by the government adoption agency an unusually white, one-month-old baby. My initial reaction upon meeting him was disappointment that he did not look like my first child from Peru. Christopher's brown-skinned face with its indian features had become the quintessence of what a child — my child — should look like. But I decided that it was foolish to look for another baby-Christopher, as I had decided years earlier that it would be foolish to look in adoption for a clone of my biological son. I took this baby home and named him Michael. Within twenty-four hours I found myself tearing through the streets in a taxi, mopping his feverish body with a wet cloth, and terrified, as I saw his eyes lose contact with mine and begin to stare off into the middle distance, that he would die in my arms before we got to the hospital emergency room. . . . Sometime during that taxi ride, or in the hospital room, I became hopelessly attached.

Several weeks later I sat with a blanketed Michael in my arms in the office of one of Lima's fanciest pediatricians. Michael had recovered from the fever but had been suffering from nausea and diarrhea almost ever since. . . . I had been to three different doctors. . . . I told this new doctor the story of Michael's troubles, trying with my words and tone to convey my sense of desperation — to make him understand that if he didn't help us Michael might die. The doctor sat impassively, interrupting me only when my three-year old Christopher wandered over to the bookshelves. Pointing with apparent disgust, as if some small and dirty animal had invaded his office, the doctor asked, "What is he?" I thought the question truly peculiar and the answer rather obvious, but explained that this was my son (perhaps he thought it was the child of the Peruvian nanny who was with me?). At the end of my story the doctor, who had still made no move to look at Michael, assured himself that the nanny spoke no English, and he then proceeded to tell me that he could get me another child, in a way that would avoid all the troublesome procedures of a Peruvian adoption. Women were giving birth in his hospital all the time who would not keep their babies. He could have the birth certificate for one of these babies made out showing me as the mother and the baby would be mine.

When I finally realized that this hospital baby was being suggested as a substitute for the one on my lap, I said in what I hoped was a polite but firm tone that I planned to keep this child and that I was here because I was afraid the child was seriously ill. I asked if the doctor could please now examine the child. . . . I put Michael on the table and started to undress him, and for the first time the doctor looked at him. . . . It was overwhelmingly clear that Michael's value had been transformed in the doctor's eyes by his whiteness. Whiteness made it comprehensible that someone would want to cure and keep this child rather than discard him. . . .

I learned more about my own feelings about race as I puzzled through the process of creating my adoptive family. Adoption compels this kind of learning. You don't just get at the end of one general child line when you're doing adoption. There are a lot of lines, each identified by the race, disabilities, and age of the children available, together with the length of wait and the difficulty and cost of adoption. In choosing which line to join, I had to think about race, and to think on a level that was new to me. I had to try to confront without distortion the reality of parenting someone of another race — since the child and I would have to live that reality. . . . I had to think about whether it would be racist to look for a same-race child or racist to look for a child of another race. . . .

[O]ne day, when he is three and one-half, Christopher says to me across the kitchen table at dinner, "I wish you looked like me." . . . I am left to puzzle at the meaning of this pain. . . . Is it, as the opponents of transracial adoption would have us believe, a piece of a permanent anguish at the sense that he does not truly belong in the place where he should most surely belong — his family? Or should I simply take it as a signal that living as a part of a multi-racial, multi-ethnic, multi-cultural family will force us to confront the meaning of racial and other differences on a regular basis?

This child is as inside my skin as any child could be. It feels entirely right that he should be there. Yet the powers that be in today's adoption world proclaim with near unanimity that race-mixing in the context of adoption should be avoided if at all possible, at least where black or brown-skinned American children are involved. . . .

[C]urrent racial matching policies represent a coming together of powerful and related ideologies — old fashioned white racism, modern-day black nationalism, and what I will call "biologism" — the idea that what is "natural" in the context of the biological family is what is normal and desirable in the context of adoption. Biological families have same-race parents and children. The laws and policies surrounding adoption in this country have generally structured adoption in imitation of biology, giving the adopted child a new birth certificate as if the child had been born to the adoptive parents, sealing off the birth parents as if they had never existed, and attempting to match adoptive parents and children with respect to looks, intellect and religion. The implicit goal has been to create an adoptive family which will resemble as much as possible "the real thing" — the "natural" or biological family that is not. . . .

But the question is . . . whether today's powerful racial matching policies make sense from the viewpoint of either the minority children involved or the larger society. . . . Minority children are pouring, in increasing numbers, into the already overburdened foster care system, and current policies stand in the way of placing these children with available adoptive families. . . .

The controversy over transracial adoption that has arisen in recent decades has primarily involved the placement of children generally identified as black with white families. . . . Through the middle of this century there were near-absolute barriers to transracial adoption posed by adoption agency practice, by social attitudes, and by the law. As adoption agencies gained increasing power in the late nineteenth and early twentieth centuries to screen prospective parents and to assign waiting children to particular homes, they helped to institutionalize the racial barriers. Agencies adopted a powerful "matching" philosophy. Prospective parents were ideally to be matched with children who were physically and mentally as close a match as possible to the biological children they might have produced. This kind of matching was thought to maximize the chances for a successful bonding and nurturing relationship between parent and child. . . .

The 1960s represented a period of relative openness to transracial adoption. Foreign adoptions helped pave the way. In the aftermath of the Korean War, South Korea made many of its abandoned and orphaned children available for adoption. Large numbers of these were mixed race children who had been fathered by black American soldiers stationed in Korea. . . . The civil rights movement in this country brought increasing attention to the plight of the minority children who had languished in the foster care systems over the years. This movement's integrationist ideology made transracial adoption a sympathetic idea to many adoption workers and prospective parents. Transracial adoption also served the needs of the waiting white parents, for whom there were not enough color-matched children available, as well as the interests of the agencies in putting together adoptive families and reducing the foster care population. And so agencies began to place waiting black children with white parents when there were no black parents apparently available. The reported number of transracial placements rose gradually to 733 in 1968, and it more than tripled in the next three years to reach a peak of 2574 in 1971. . . .

In 1972 this brief era of relative openness to transracial adoption came to an abrupt end. That year an organization called the National Association of Black Social Workers (NABSW) issued a position statement against transracial adoption [calling it a form of "genocide"]. It stated:

> Black children should be placed only with Black families whether in foster care or for adoption. Black children belong, physically, psychologically and culturally in Black families in order that they receive the total sense of themselves and develop a sound projection of their future. Human beings are products of their environment and develop their sense of values, attitudes and self concept within their family structures. Black children in white homes are cut off from the healthy development of themselves as Black people. . . .

Others joined in the attack on transracial adoption, arguing with the NABSW that transracial adoption constituted an attack upon the black community and that it harmed black children by denying them their black heritage and the survival skills needed for life in a racist society.

The attack on transracial adoption appeared to have an immediate and significant impact. The numbers fell from a peak of 2574 in 1971 [to 831 in 1975]. [The Child Welfare League and adoption] agency bureaucrats moved swiftly to accommodate the position taken by the NABSW. . . . A parallel development occurred with respect to the adoptive placement of Native American children. [My own] investigation has made clear to me that race is used as the basis for official decision-making in adoption in a way that is unparalleled in a society that has generally endorsed an anti-discrimination and pro-integration ideology. . . .

This matching scheme confronts a major problem in the fact that the numbers of children falling into the black and the white pools do not "fit," proportionately, with the number of prospective parents falling into their own black and white pools. In 1987, 37.1% of the children in out-of-home placement were black as compared with 46.1% white. Although no good statistics are available, the general understanding is that a very high percentage of the waiting adoptive parent pool is white. . . .

The matching process surfaces, to a degree, in written rules and documented cases. But it is the unwritten and generally invisible rules that are central to understanding the nature of current policies. . . . The rules generally make race not simply "a factor," but an overwhelmingly important factor in the placement process. . . .

[A]doption is not supposed to be about parent or community rights and interests, but rather about serving the best interests of children. Adoption laws throughout this country provide that agencies are to make children's interests paramount in placement decisions. Arguments can be made that black children in general will benefit from efforts to strengthen the black community, and that racial matching policies represent one such effort. The problem is that . . . racial matching policies seem contrary to the immediate and long-term interests of the specific black children waiting for homes. . . .

## Notes and Questions

1. In an omitted dissenting opinion in *D.L.*, Judge Schumacher disagreed with the majority's reliance on a common law preference for placement with near relatives. First, adoption is purely statutory. Second, the preference for custody with relatives should not apply in adoption, which severs all ties with biological relatives and creates a new family relationship. 479 N.W.2d at 416.

The Minnesota Supreme Court affirmed *D.L.*, finding the constitutional issues unnecessary to address. 486 N.W.2d 375 (Minn. 1992). The United States Supreme Court denied certiorari sub nom. Sharp v. Hennepin County Bureau of Social Services, 506 U.S. 1000 (1992). Minnesota then revised the statutes to apply the listed preferences to all. Minn. Stat. Ann. §259.29 (West Supp. 1996). Later it deleted reference to race altogether and enacted an explicit preference for placement with relatives, absent an explicit parental request not to consider placement with relatives. Minn. Stat. Ann. §259.29 (West Supp. 2001).

2. Courts have held unconstitutional absolute prohibitions on transracial adoptions. Compos v. McKeithen, 341 F. Supp. 264 (E.D. La. 1972); In re Adoption of Gomez, 424 S.W.2d 656 (Tex. Ct. App. 1967). See also McLaughlin v. Pernsley, 693 F. Supp. 318 (E.D. Pa. 1988) (longterm foster placement), *aff'd*, 876 F.2d 308 (3d Cir. 1989).

3. In holding the Minority Adoption Act unconstitutional, *D.L.* relied on Palmore v. Sidoti, 466 U.S. 429 (1984), reprinted in Chapter VII, at pages 810-812. Does *Palmore* apply to adoption? What factors differentiate postdivorce custody adjudications from adoptions?

Does *Palmore* forbid *all* consideration of race in adoptive placements? Was Minnesota's first effort to revise its statute (applying to all children a preference for same-race placement) constitutional?

In a dispute with facts similar to *D.L.*, In re Petition of R.M.G., 454 A.2d 776 (D.C. App. 1982), one judge, Judge Ferren, wrote that a statute allowing race to be taken into account as one factor survives strict scrutiny because it advances a compelling interest, the child's best interest. Another, Judge Newman, applying intermediate scrutiny to this "benign" use of race, reached the same result, while making the following observations about racial matching:

> Some of the risks of interracial adoption involve the child's development of identity (including racial and cultural identity), self-esteem, and a sense of belonging in the family — relevant considerations which the majority recognizes as legitimate and important. One problem is the possibility that the child may not perceive herself as black or develop an identity as a black person. . . . Another aspect of the identity problem is the possibility that the child may experience a "conflict of loyalties" as she grows older. . . . In other words, the child may be caught between two cultures and accepted by neither. . . .
>
> In addition to a strong sense of identity, the black child must learn to develop certain survival skills. Regardless of how she is identified by herself or her family, she will be identified as a black person by society and will inevitably experience racism. [And] while *all* adopted children have to cope with the fact that they are adopted, the interracial adoptee may have an even more difficult experience since his status is evident to the world at large. . . .

Id. at 802-803. Judge Mack, in a concurring opinion, cautioned against the use of generalities:

> In a custody or adoption proceeding, we are not concerned with the best interests of children generally; we are concerned, rather, with the best

interests of THE child. While my colleagues are quibbling about [the standard of review,] a little girl is reaching school age under the care of the
only parents she has even known. . . .

Id. at 795. See Nancy D. Polikoff, Context and Common Sense: The
Family Law Jurisprudence of Julia Cooper Mack, 40 How. L.J. 443, 450,
451 (1997). Which view do you find more persuasive, that of Judge
Newman or Professor Bartholet? Whose side does Judge Mack take?

4. Empirical studies support transracial adoption as a "basically positive" alternative to long-term foster care. Rita J. Simon et al., The Case
for Transracial Adoption 74, 115 (1994) (20-year study tracking and interviewing parents, adoptees, and adoptive siblings in 83 families). A review of studies of transracial adoptions of Native American, Korean, and
African-American children concludes that most minority children fare
well and have a sense of identity, though its strength varies. Delayed
placement causes greater harm than transracial placement. Arnold R.
Silverman, Outcomes of Transracial Adoption, The Future of Children,
Spring 1993, at 104. See also Arnold R. Silverman & William Feigelman,
Adjustment in Interracial Adoptees: An Overview, in The Psychology of
Adoption 187, 197-198 (David M. Brodzinsky & Marshall D. Schechter
eds., 1990) (reviewing empirical studies and emphasizing importance for
good outcomes of parents' commitment to child's identification and
racial heritage). In 1991, approximately 108 transracial adoptees, now
young adults, were asked whether they wished they had had a same-race
placement. Seven percent answered affirmatively, 67 percent answered
negatively, 4 percent were not sure, and 22 percent did not reply. Rita
J. Simon & Rhonda M. Roorda, In Their Own Voices: Transracial
Adoptees Tell Their Stories 21, 25 (2000) (including personal perspectives). See also, e.g., Susan R. Harris, Race, Search, and My Baby-Self:
Reflections of a Transracial Adoptee, 9 Yale J.L. & Feminism 5 (1997).

5. Professor Twila Perry agrees with Bartholet that an emphasis on
race can overlook whether a child will remain in an institution or find a
family in which racial identity will be nurtured. Twila L. Perry, Race and
Child Placement: The Best Interests Test and the Cost of Discretion, 29
J. Fam. L. 51, 81-83 (1990-1991). She claims, however, that Bartholet's
perspective ("liberal colorblind individualism") is one-sided and overlooks significant inequities:

> It seems clear that advocates of transracial adoption are not in fact ar-
> guing for a system based on colorblindness, since they envision neither a
> purely random assignment of children and parents regardless of race nor
> a system in which parents and children are matched on a first-come, first-
> served basis, regardless of race. Instead, they affirm a system based on
> racial choice. Under this system, race apparently still can be used to match
> white families with their choice of the valuable commodity of a white baby.
> White families are, of course, also free to select Black children for adop-

tion. The problem, however, is that this principle operates only one way. Choosing across racial lines is reserved for whites. . . . Such a system defends the right of white families to secure the kind of child that is most valued in this society — white infants. It perpetuates the subordination of Black children by reaffirming the idea that they are a less valuable commodity on the market. . . .

. . . The vision of transracially adopted Black children as pioneers in the creation of a future, nonracist society [requires them to] bear a disproportionate burden in changing the society. . . . It is Black children who are placed in environments that are dominated by whites. Leaving aside the question of whether or not this results in actual psychological harm, Black children bear the emotional strains of being the minority "outsider" group in the process of integration.

The willingness to use Black children as agents in the eradication of racism is an interesting twist to the colorblind individualism perspective. In making Black children the creators of a new society, advocates of transracial adoption focus on more than the interests of the individual child. They betray an agenda no less political than the insistence of some Blacks that the interests of the Black community be considered in formulating policies concerning the adoption of Black children. . . .

Twila L. Perry, The Transracial Adoption Controversy: An Analysis of Discourse and Subordination, 21 N.Y.U. Rev. L. & Soc. Change 33, 104-107 (1993-1994). See also Sandra Patton, BirthMarks: Transracial Adoption in Contemporary America 190 (2000) (concluding transracial adoption became popular when white, heterosexual couples could not find white babies to adopt); Dorothy Roberts, Shattered Bonds: The Color of Child Welfare 165-167 (2001). What does the debate about transracial adoption say about mothering, hierarchy, and other themes emphasized in feminist analysis? See Twila L. Perry, Transracial and International Adoption: Mothers, Hierarchy, Race, and Feminist Legal Theory, 10 Yale J.L. & Feminism 101 (1998).

6. Congress has legislated "removal of barriers to interethnic adoption" by providing that no state nor other entity in a state receiving federal funds can "deny to any individual the opportunity to become an adoptive or a foster parent, on the basis of the race, color, or national origin of the individual, or of the child, involved" or "delay or deny" placements on these bases. 42 U.S.C. §1996b (Supp. V 1999). An earlier law, the Multiethnic Placement Act (now repealed), reflected political compromise by allowing consideration of "the cultural, ethnic or racial background of the child and the capacity of the prospective foster or adoptive parents to meet [the child's needs] as one of a number of factors used to determine [the child's] best interests." 42 U.S.C. §5115a (1994). Does the new statute limit only the practices of adoption agencies, or does it bind judges as well? See In re Adoption of Vito, 712 N.E.2d 1188, 1196 (Mass. Ct. App. 1999) (law does not constrain judge in "crafting an order she determines to be in the child's best interests"),

*vacated and remanded,* 728 N.E.2d 292, 305 n.27 (Mass. 2000) (avoiding this issue).

7. If race is a factor in placement, which of the families in *D.L.* provides the better match, given the child's mixed race? See Jane Maslow Cohen, Race-Based Adoption in a Post-*Loving Frame,* 6 B.U. Pub. Int. L.J. 653 (1997); Jennifer L. Rosato, "A Color of Their Own": Multiracial Children and the Family, 36 Brandeis J. Fam. L. 41 (1997-98). Professor Ruth-Arlene W. Howe predicts that eliminating consideration of race will actually increase discrimination:

> Elimination of race from all placement decision-making sets the stage for reinforcing old prejudices and discriminatory practices toward African Americans and for anachronistic recommodification of *young* African American children, without providing any strong assurance that the needs of such children will be met appropriately. Instead, white adults seeking healthy infants now have an opportunity to "garner the market" on the only expanding "crop" of healthy newborns — voluntarily relinquished biracial nonmarital infants (many with one black and one white parent). Prior to Interethnic Adoption Provisions, these babies would be considered black under the customary "one-drop" rule for determining race.

Ruth-Arlene W. Howe, Adoption Laws and Practices in 2000: Serving Whose Interests?, 33 Fam. L.Q. 677, 684-685 (1999). Should Congress go further, restricting states from honoring adoptive parents' race-based preferences? See R. Richard Banks, The Color of Desire: Fulfilling Adoptive Parents' Racial Preferences through Discriminatory State Action, 107 Yale L.J. 875 (1998).

8. *Indian Child Welfare Act.* Federal law makes ethnic background decisive for placement of Native American children under the Indian Child Welfare Act of 1978 (ICWA), 25 U.S.C. §1915(a) (1994). Preference is given (absent good cause) to placement with: (1) a member of the child's extended family, (2) other members of the Indian child's tribe, or (3) other Indian families.

The ICWA stemmed from "rising concern in the mid-1970's over the consequences to Indian children, Indian families, and Indian tribes [and their culture] of abusive child welfare practices that resulted in the separation of large numbers of Indian children from their families and tribes through adoption or foster care placement, usually in non-Indian homes." Mississippi Band of Choctaw Indians v. Holyfield, 490 U.S. 30 (1989). Can the statute's goals be served by applying the law to a child who never has lived with an Indian family? See In re Santos Y., 112 Cal. Rptr. 2d 692, 716 & n.16 (Ct. App. 2001) (noting division among courts on "existing Indian family doctrine"). See also Christine Metteer, The Existing Indian Family Exception: An Impediment to the Trust Responsibility to Preserve Tribal Existence and Culture as Manifested in the Indian Child Welfare Act, 30 Loy. L.A. L. Rev. 647 (1997); Samuel Prim, The Indian Child Welfare Act & the Existing Indian Family Exception: Rerouting the Trail of Tears?, 24 Law & Psychol. Rev. 115 (2000).

Congress's prohibition on the use of race in adoptive and foster care placements exempts applications of the ICWA. 42 U.S.C. §1996b(3) (Supp. V 1999). Why should the law treat adoptions of Indian children differently from adoptions of racial minorities? See Cynthia G. Hawkins-Leon, The Indian Child Welfare Act and the African American Tribe: Facing the Adoption Crisis, 36 Brandeis J. Fam. L. 201 (1997-98). *Santos Y.* said a child whose birth parents had lived in Los Angeles and Oregon and who had been placed just after birth in California with non-Indian foster parents seeking adoption could not be sent to a reservation in Minnesota. The court reasoned that " 'repatriation' to the Reservation of a child of assimilated parents, solely because of the child's one-quarter Minnesota Chippewa Tribe genetic heritage, [is] constitutionally impermissible . . . ." 112 Cal. Rptr. 2d at 726. What constitutional interests are implicated?

9. In *Holyfield,* supra, the Supreme Court applied the common law definition of "domicile" to hold that twins, born to unmarried parents domiciled on a tribal reservation, were themselves domiciled there, even though their mother traveled 200 miles to give birth elsewhere and arrange for placement with a non-Indian family. On this basis, the Court concluded that tribal courts (rather than the Mississippi court that issued adoption decrees to a non-Indian couple) had exclusive jurisdiction over the twins' placement under the ICWA, 25 U.S.C. §1911(a) (1994). Should the policies underlying the ICWA give way to parental autonomy? See Twila L. Perry, Transracial and International Adoption: Mothers, Hierarchy, Race, and Feminist Legal Theory, 10 Yale J.L. & Feminism 101, 150-151 (1998) (feminists must address conflict between parental autonomy and argument for deference to ethnic groups' desires for intra-ethnic placement).

10. *Religion.* Some states honor parental autonomy through statutes allowing birth parents to designate the adopters' religion. E.g., Ark. Code Ann. §9-9-102 (Michie 1998); Mass. Gen. Laws ch. 210, §5B (1998). Other states require the placement of children with adoptive parents of the same religious faith, when practicable. See, e.g., Del. Code Ann. tit. 13, §911 (1999). What constitutional issues do these laws raise? Should they survive constitutional challenge? Compare, e.g., Dickens v. Ernesto, 281 N.E.2d 153 (N.Y. 1972) (no unconstitutional establishment of religion), with Orzechowski v. Perales, 582 N.Y.S.2d 341 (Sup. Ct. 1992) (Establishment Clause claim). See Donald L. Beschle, God Bless the Child?: The Use of Religion as a Factor in Child Custody and Adoption Proceedings, 58 Fordham L. Rev. 383, 404-406 (1989); Note, Religious Matching Statutes and Adoption, 51 N.Y.U. L. Rev. 262 (1976).

In religious matching, how does the state determine an infant's religion? Suppose the biological mother and father have different religions? Can the state constitutionally consider whether the presence or absence of any religion creates an environment likely to serve the child's best interests? See Scott v. Family Ministries, 135 Cal. Rptr. 430 (Ct. App. 1976); In the Matter of Adoption of "E," 279 A.2d 785 (N.J. 1971).

11. Traditionally, adoption agencies sought to imitate nature by trying to match children with adopters and otherwise create a "perfect" family. In attempting to create a successful adoptive placement today, what factors should be considered?

(a) *Age?* At what age is an adoptive parent "too" old? Compare In re Jennifer A., 650 N.Y.S.2d 691 (App. Div. 1996), with In re K.K.J., 984 S.W.2d 548, 552-553 (Mo. Ct. App. 1999). "Too" young? See Middlecoff v. Leofanti, 272 N.E.2d 289 (Ill. App. Ct. 1971). On adoptions of adults, see Chapter IV, section C4e.

(b) *Intelligence?* Should adoption of a child of below average intelligence be denied to very intelligent foster parents? See Crump v. Montgomery, 154 A.2d 802 (Md. 1959).

(c) *Deafness?* See Adoption of Scott James Richardson, 59 Cal. Rptr. 323 (Ct. App. 1967) (denial of adoption by deaf couple violates equal protection and due process).

(d) *Marital status?* Can unmarried adults adopt a child? Compare In re Jason C., 533 A.2d 32 (N.H. 1987), with In re Adoption of Carl, 709 N.Y.S.2d 905 (Fam. Ct. 2000). See also Angela Mae Kupenda, Two Parents Are Better Than None: Whether Two Single African American Adults — Who Are Not in a Traditional Marriage or a Romantic or Sexual Relationship with Each Other — Should Be Allowed to Jointly Adopt and Co-Parent African American Children, 35 U. Louisville J. Fam. L. 703 (1996-97).

(e) *Homosexuality?* A few state statutes expressly restrict adoption and foster care by homosexuals. See Fla. Stat. Ann. §63.042(3) (West 1997) (prohibition); Conn. Gen. Stat. Ann. §45a-726a (West Supp. 2001) (sexual orientation may be considered and nothing shall require placement of a child "with a prospective adoptive or foster parent or parents who are homosexual or bisexual"). But see N.H. Rev. Stat. Ann. §170-B:4 (Supp. 2000) (statute revised to remove prohibition). Cf. Utah Code Ann. §78-30-1 (Supp. 2000) (child cannot be adopted by person cohabiting with another in relationship not a valid marriage). Do such laws violate the Constitution? See Lofton v. Kearney, 157 F. Supp. 2d 1372 (S.D. Fla. 2001) (no violation of fundamental due process rights or equal protection). What impact does Romer v. Evans, 517 U.S. 620 (1996), have? See Chapter I, at page 59. Does the legitimacy of restrictions on adoption by homosexuals depend on empirical evidence about the impact of gay parents on children? Compare Lynn D. Wardle, The Potential Impact of Homosexual Parenting on Children, 1997 U. Ill. L.J. 833 (condeming literature as one-sided and advocating rebuttable presumption that such placements do not serve child's best interests), with Carlos A. Ball & Janice Farrell Pea, Warring with Wardle: Morality, Social Science, and Gay and Lesbian Parents, 1998 U. Ill. L. Rev. 253 (challenging Wardle's proposal on practical, normative, and constitutional grounds). See also Erica Goode, A Rainbow of Differences in Gays' Children, N.Y. Times, July 17, 2001, at F1 (reporting that evidence of greater tolerance, open-mindedness, and flexibility about gender roles and sexuality among children raised by gays and lesbians is often ignored because findings of any differences might present "political dangers"). See also infra section D2 (second-parent adoption).

12. The UAA, §2-104, lists in order of preference factors an *agency* should consider in determining a child's best interests in the selection of adoptive parents: the previous adoption of a sibling, characteristics requested by the minor's birth parent or guardian, custody of the minor for 6 months within the preceding 24 months or half the child's life, and status as relative with whom child has established a positive emotional relationship by one who makes a written adoption request. After considering these possibilities, the agency can consider other individuals. 9 U.L.A. (pt. IA) 33-34 (1999). Alternatively, the child's parent or guardian can select an adoptive family and place the child directly. UAA §2-102, id. at 12. Under the act, most adopters must have a favorable preplacement evaluation. UAA §§2-102, 2-104, 7-101, id. at 30-31, 33-34, 124. All placements require an evaluation before the adoption becomes final. UAA §§3-601 through 3-603, id. at 91-92.

13. Authorities recognize that there is no constitutionally protected right to adopt. See Griffith v. Johnston, 899 F.2d 1427, 1437 (5th Cir. 1990); Howe, supra, at 678-679. Does it follow that state actors can reject adoption applications for *any* reason, except perhaps those resting on a "suspect classification"? Do applicants have a right to a statement of reasons for their rejection? Do long waiting lists of prospective adopters allow agencies to disguise a rejection as a problem of "supply and demand"? Does the absence of a right to adopt imply an absence of rights in the adoption process? See Janet Hopkins Dickson, Comment, The Emerging Rights of Adoptive Parents: Substance or Specter?, 38 UCLA L. Rev. 917 (1991).

## Problems

1. Megan relinquishes her son for adoption. Subsequently, she marries and then two years after the relinquishment and a series of foster home placements for her son, she learns (through media publicity) about

the state agency's placement of her son with a same-sex male couple for prospective adoption. Megan describes this placement as her "worst nightmare." Should the court allow Megan to revoke her consent, now that the same-sex couple is petitioning to adopt? If not, should it allow her and her husband also to petition to adopt the child, enabling the court to consider the two available adoptive placements? See In re Dependency of G.C.B., 870 P.2d 1037 (Wash. Ct. App.), *review denied,* 881 P.2d 254 (Wash. 1994); Shannon E. Phillips, Note, Preventing Bidding Wars in Washington Adoptions: The Need for Statutory Reform After *In re Dependency of G.C.B.,* 70 Wash. L. Rev. 277 (1995).

2. Suppose, instead, that Megan had knowingly relinquished her baby for adoption by a same-sex couple. Under state statutes, the biological parent can select the adoptive parents so long as a court determines the placement serves the child's best interests. During the adoption proceedings, Megan's parents (with whom Megan and the baby lived for four months after the birth) submit a competing petition to adopt the child. They argue that, despite a favorable home study for the placement Megan chose, adoption by homosexuals is not in the child's best interests. They also attack the constitutionality of the adoption statutes, arguing that (a) the Constitution requires a preference for placement with relatives, particularly those who have established a relationship with the child; (b) the absence of a statutory preference for placement with relatives in the adoption statute violates equal protection, given the relative preference in the foster care statute; and (c) the adoption statutes are unconstitutional because they permit the biological parent to select a placement to the exclusion of other biological relatives, to the detriment of the child. Are these arguments persuasive? See In re Adoption of M.J.S., 44 S.W.3d 41 (Tenn. Ct. App. 2000).

3. Scholars have proposed that states screen and license *all* parents, not only those who take children into their homes through adoption and foster care. The argument claims that the state ought to show as much concern about the responsibilities of parenthood as it demonstrates about the responsibilities of using a motor vehicle, which requires a driver's license. See, e.g., Hugh LaFollette, Licensing Parents, 9 Phil. & Pub. Aff. 182 (1980). With the development of Norplant, a long-term contraceptive for women, the means of implementing a parental licensing program exist. Would this program be desirable? Constitutional? If neither, what justifies parental screening and state approval for adoption? For literature supporting the idea, see Roger W. McIntire, Parenthood Training or Mandatory Birth Control: Take Your Choice, Psychology Today, Oct. 1973, at 34; Claudia Pap Mangel, Licensing Parents: How Feasible?, 22 Fam. L.Q. 17 (1988). For a counterargument, see Lawrence E. Frisch, On Licentious Licensing: A Reply to Hugh LaFollette, 11 Phil. & Pub. Aff. 173 (1982).

## 2. The Attorney's Role

■ **IN RE PETRIE**
742 P.2d 796 (Ariz. 1987)

HOLOHAN, J. . . .

The complainants, Gregory and Barbara Pietz, consulted with respondent [an attorney] on July 21, 1981 to express their interest in adopting an infant child. Respondent told the Pietzes that he did not know of any infants available at that time. The Pietzes and respondent agreed that if the Pietzes located a baby for adoption, respondent would represent them in the adoption. The Pietzes paid $30 for this consultation.

[S]hortly before January 26, 1983, the Pietzes received information from a long-time friend, Carolyn Iverson, about a child that would be available for adoption. The Pietzes asked Iverson to make an appointment for respondent to meet with the natural mother, and to inform the respondent specifically that the mother was being referred by the Pietzes. [Iverson did so and also] gave respondent the Pietzes' current address and telephone number in Sierra Vista. She also told him that the Pietzes had become certified by the State of Arizona as acceptable to adopt children. . . .

The evidence indicates that respondent met with the natural mother and her sister, and he advised them that he had a set of adoptive parents in mind. On January 26, 1983, he wrote to the Pietzes, telling them that he had recently interviewed a woman who intended to place a child for adoption and that the Pietzes' names were given when the interview was arranged. Respondent inquired in the letter whether the Pietzes were interested in the adoption. Respondent received a written response on February 3, 1983, in which the Pietzes stated that they were interested in adopting the child, that they were certified by the State to adopt children, and that they were very hopeful concerning the present situation. The Pietzes' letter disclosed knowledge of facts about the natural mother that respondent had not conveyed to them in his original correspondence. Respondent interpreted the Pietzes' letter as "equivocal" because the Pietzes had questions about the adoption and the fees.

Shortly thereafter, respondent received a phone call from another couple, the Buckmasters, who expressed an interest in adopting a second child. In response to respondent's inquiry on February 18, 1983, the natural mother's sister stated that the mother had no obligation to the Pietzes. At respondent's recommendation, the mother agreed to place the baby with the Buckmasters. The Committee found that respondent recommended placement with the Buckmasters because they were more cooperative than the Pietzes and they were locally situated. In addition, respondent was not "excited" about making two appearances in Cochise County, which may have been necessary if the Pietzes were to adopt the child.

When the Pietzes learned from Iverson that the child was going to another couple, Mr. Pietz called respondent, and respondent advised Mr. Pietz for the first time that he had recommended to the natural mother that the child be placed with someone else. Mr. Pietz told respondent that the Pietzes had referred the child to the respondent and consequently they wanted the child placed with them. Respondent refused to do so. Mr. Pietz then initiated this complaint with the State Bar [charging respondent violated Disciplinary Rule 5-105(A) and (B) (requiring that the attorney refuse to accept or continue employment if the interests of another client may impair the independent professional judgment of the lawyer)].

It is common for the parties to an independent adoption to retain an attorney to represent their individual interests. The adoption proceeding itself is unusual because generally the parties to the adoption — the natural parents and the adoptive parents — are not in a true adversary relationship. Usually, both sides in the proceeding have complementary interests and no real negotiating or posturing is necessary; in most cases the natural parents want to find a good home for the baby and need to have the birthing expenses paid, and the adoptive parents want to provide a home for the baby and are willing to pay the expenses. Legal counsel is necessary only to facilitate the exchange and ensure that the legal requirements are met.

Despite the spirit of cooperation often present in an adoption, conflict of interest situations are likely to arise for an attorney involved in the proceedings. First, the interests of potential adoptive parents of the same child are always adverse to one another. . . . An attorney cannot simultaneously represent both sets of adoptive parents without compromising his representation of one of them.

Second, and perhaps less apparent, the interests of the adoptive parents may be adverse to the interests of the natural parents. The decision to give the baby up for adoption is often a difficult one to make. The natural parents' attorney has a duty to provide them with counsel about such matters as paternity issues, economic matters, and the legal effect of signing the consent to adopt. Under our statute, the natural parents' consent to the adoption is not valid unless it is given at least 72 hours after the birth of the child. A.R.S. §8-107(B). The statute protects the right of the natural parents to withhold a decision on whether to keep the baby until after the baby is born. The attorney must counsel the natural parents on the adoption decision right up until the natural parents consent to the adoption. Clearly, the adoptive parents want the natural parents to consent to the adoption rather than to keep the baby. . . .

Notwithstanding the foregoing discussion, in some instances an attorney may be able to represent multiple parties in an adoption proceeding. Disciplinary Rule 5-105(C) provides for an exception to the dictates of DR 5-105(A) and (B). It provides that a lawyer may represent multiple clients "if it is obvious that he can adequately represent the interests of each and if each consents to the representation after full disclosure of the possible effect of such representation on the exercise of his independent professional judgment on behalf of each." DR 5-105(C). . . . This exception has no application to the current case, however, because there is no evidence that respondent complied with its provisions. . . .

. . . If Petrie simultaneously had an attorney-client relationship with more than one of the parties involved in the adoption — the Pietzes, the Buckmasters, or the natural mother — Petrie has violated DR 5-105(A) or (B). An attorney-client relationship does not require the payment of a fee but may be implied from the parties' conduct. The relationship is proved by showing that the party sought and received advice and assistance from the attorney in matters pertinent to the legal profession. The appropriate test is a subjective one. . . . An important factor in evaluating the relationship is whether the client thought an attorney-client relationship existed. The relationship is ongoing and gives rise to a continuing duty to the client unless and until the client clearly understands, or reasonably should understand that the relationship is no longer depended on. . . .

We find that respondent violated DR 5-105. . . . Respondent had a duty to advocate for the Pietzes in the adoption proceeding. The natural mother's indication that she was not committed to the Pietzes did not lessen the respondent's duty of loyalty to them. . . . By accepting employment from the Buckmasters while already representing the Pietzes in the same adoption proceeding without full disclosure and consent, respondent violated DR 5-105(A); by continuing in the simultaneous representation and by ultimately recommending the Buckmasters over the Pietzes, respondent violated DR 5-105(B).

We find that respondent also violated DR 5-105 by representing both the natural mother and the adoptive parents in an adoption proceeding. Respondent claimed that he always represented the natural mother in adoption proceedings. From his testimony, it appears that his usual custom was to maintain a file of potential adoptive parents from which the natural mother who is his client may select the couple best suited to adopt the baby. We do not expressly prohibit this practice. However, the attorney must take special care to avoid violating the ethical rules regarding representation of multiple clients. . . . In independent adoptions an attorney cannot represent multiple parties absent disclosure and consent. See DR 5-105(C). [Respondent also violated DR 7-101(A)(2) by failing to withdraw.]

[I]t is unclear whether respondent was only negligent in determining a conflict of interest existed or whether he actually knew of the conflict. Respondent testified that his only client was the natural mother. . . . If respondent did not think either the Pietzes or the Buckmasters were his clients, he would not have "known" a conflict of interest existed. However, at a minimum, respondent was negligent in failing to recognize that the potential adoptive parents were his clients and that a conflict existed. Accordingly, we agree with the Local Committee that the appropriate sanction due respondent is censure. . . .

## Notes and Questions

1. "Baby Broker" statutes in many states impose tight restrictions on child placement. For example, New York law provides:

> No person, agency, association, corporation, institution, society or other organization except an authorized agency shall place out or board out any child but the provisions of this section shall not restrict or limit the right of a parent, legal guardian or relative within the second degree to place out or board out a child.

N.Y. Soc. Serv. Law §374(2) (McKinney 1992).

> "Place out" means to arrange for the free care of a child in a family other than that of the child's parent, step-parent, grandparent, brother, sister, uncle, or aunt or legal guardian, for the purpose of adoption or for the purpose of providing care. . . .

Id. at §371(12). See also, e.g., Ala. Code §26-10A-33 (1992); Del. Code Ann. tit. 13, §904 (1999); Mass. Gen. Laws ch. 210, §11A (1998). Such laws were enacted to prevent commercial trafficking in babies ("baby selling") and to prevent placement by the untrained. See In re Pre-adoption Certificate Concerning Carballo, 521 N.Y.S.2d 375 (Fam. Ct. 1987). Given the latter goal, what activities do such statutes prohibit? Why do such laws exempt parents and some relatives? To what extent can attorneys or other third parties serve as intermediaries under the New York statute? For what can attorneys receive fees? See also, e.g., Galison v. District of Columbia, 402 A.2d 1263 (D.C. 1979); People v. Schwartz, 356 N.E.2d 8 (Ill. 1976), *cert. denied,* 429 U.S. 1098 (1977).

2. Despite the usual exemption for parents in placement restrictions, of course, even parents cannot "sell" their children. See, e.g., People v. Daniel, 241 Cal. Rptr. 3 (Ct. App. 1987). See also Maryland v. Runkles, 605 A.2d 111 (Md. Ct. App. 1992). On the other hand, payment of the birth mother's medical expenses by the adoptive parents has long been permissible. See, e.g., Or. Rev. Stat. §163.537 (1999); In re Baby Boy P., 700 N.Y.S.2d 792 (Fam. Ct. 1999). What costs can be reimbursed? See In re Baby Girl D., 517 A.2d 925 (Pa. 1986) (no reim-

bursement for counseling, housing, medical expenses not directly beneficial to the child, including Lamaze classes and sonograms); In re Adoption No. 9979, 591 A.2d 468 (Md. Ct. App. 1991) (not maternity clothes).
See generally Opinions of the New Hampshire Probate Court: In re
Adoption of Baby D, 12 Quinnipiac Prob. L.J. 49 (1997) (permitting
adopters to pay birth parents' reasonable legal fees).

The UAA, §7-102, prohibits payments for placement, parental consent, or relinquishment, subject to a civil penalty. 9 U.L.A. (pt. IA) 125
(1999). The UAA, §7-103, permits, however, payment for the services of
an agency, advertising, medical and travel expenses, counseling, living
expenses for the birth mother for a reasonable period, disclosure of the
child's medical and psychological history, legal services and court costs,
evaluations of the adopters, and any other service the court finds reasonably necessary. Such payments cannot be made contingent on placement, relinquishment, or consent to adoption. Id. at 126.

3. When only parents and licensed agencies can place children,
what services can nonagency intermediaries provide to assist a parent in
selecting a placement? According to the Nevada Attorney General, a
lawyer who merely sends video or audio tapes, letters, resumes, or other
information describing prospective adoptive parents to the birth mother
violates a statute prohibiting adoptive placement by a person not licensed to place children. Nev. Rev. Stat. §127.310 (2000) makes it a misdemeanor for any unlicensed person or organization to place, arrange
the placement of, or assist in placing or arranging the placement of any
child for adoption. This statute defines "[a]rrange the placement of a
child" as "to make preparations for or bring about any agreement or understanding concerning the adoption of a child." Id. at §127.220.

How would the sending of tapes, letters, and resumes fare under the
following statute?

> The selection of prospective adoptive parent or parents shall be person-
> ally made by the child's birth parent or parents and may not be delegated
> to an agent. The act of selection by the birth parent or parents shall be
> based upon his, her, or their personal knowledge of the prospective adop-
> tive parent or parents.

Cal. Fam. Code §8801(a) (West 1994). The statute then lists specific information required to satisfy "personal knowledge." Id. at §8801(b). But
see also Cal. Fam. Code §8637 (West Supp. 2002) (attorneys as adoption
facilitators).

4. Even in states allowing independent placements, adoptions present difficulties for attorneys, as Petrie shows. Rule 2.2 of the Model Rules
of Professional Conduct addresses attorneys as intermediaries, requiring
full disclosure of the implications of common representation, client consent thereto, full explanations of each decision to be made, and withdrawal from the matter altogether upon request or dissatisfaction.

Further, the attorney must reasonably believe that the matter can be resolved impartially and consistent with the clients' best interests. Does this
general rule provide appropriate regulation of adoption intermediaries
in particular?

Although the American Bar Association has stated expressly that "a
lawyer may not ethically represent both the adoptive and biological parents in a private adoption proceeding," it recognizes that "some authorities have held otherwise." ABA Comm. on Ethics and Professional
Responsibility, Informal Op. 1523 (1987). See also Restatement (Third)
of the Law Governing Lawyers §130 (2000) (requiring consent for multiple representation in nonlitigated matter if substantial risk of material
and adverse effect on one client's interests). For example, California
statutorily treats as unethical joint representation in independent adoptions in the absence of both parties' written consent. The consent must
include, inter alia, notice to the birth parents of the right to independent counsel with reasonable attorneys' fees assumed by the adoptive
parents, waiver by the birth parents of independent representation, and
an agreement that the attorney for the adoptive parents will represent
the birth parents. Cal. Fam. Code §8800 (West 1994). See also Debra Lyn
Bassett, Three's A Crowd: A Proposal to Abolish Joint Representation,
32 Rutgers L.J. 387 (2001); Pamela K. Strom Amlung, Comment, Conflicts of Interest in Independent Adoptions: Pitfalls for the Unwary, 59
U. Cin. L. Rev. 169 (1990) (how attorney conflicts of interest can compromise the validity of the birth mother's consent).

5. Despite legal restrictions, stories of "black market adoptions" persist. See, e.g., Rick Bragg, Town Secret Is Uncovered in Birth Quest,
N.Y. Times, Aug. 23, 1997, §1, at 1 (babyselling in McCaysville, Georgia
in 1960s); Sarah Lyall, Battle by Two Couples to Adopt U.S. Twins Moves
to Britain, N.Y. Times, Jan. 18, 2001, at A3 (British couple and California couple both paid adoption broker for same infant twins). Indeed, the
modern practice of independent adoption often entails the payment of
money, particularly for white infants. See Adam Pertman, Adoption Nation: How the Adoption Revolution Is Transforming America 185-203
(2000). See also David Ray Papke, Pondering Past Purposes: A Critical
History of American Adoption Law, 102 W. Va. L. Rev. 459, 468-474
(1999) (private adoptions growing "in an era of consumption"); Melinda
Lucas, Adoption: Distinguishing Between Gray Market and Black Market Activities, 34 Fam. L.Q. 553 (2000).

Why not legitimize baby selling, given the existence of a market and
controversy about matching and other placement practices? A provocative article contends that an adopter's willingness to pay insures the child
will be well cared for. Elisabeth M. Landes & Richard A. Posner, The Economics of the Baby Shortage, 7 J. Legal Stud. 323 (1978). The authors
attribute discomfort with the idea to concerns about overreaching, racial
ranking, and the spectre of baby breeding. Nonetheless they continue:

The emphasis placed by critics on the social costs of a free market in babies blurs what would probably be the greatest long-run effect of legalizing the baby market: inducing women who have unintentionally become pregnant to put up the child for adoption rather than raise it themselves or have an abortion. Some of the moral outrage directed against the idea of "trafficking" in babies bespeaks a failure to consider the implications of contemporary moral standards. At a time when illegitimacy was heavily stigmatized and abortion was illegal, to permit the sale of babies would have opened a breach in an otherwise solid wall of social disapproval of procreative activity outside of marriage. At the same time, the stigma of illegitimacy, coupled with the illegality of abortion, assured a reasonable flow of babies to the adoption market. Now that the stigma has diminished and abortion has become a constitutional right, not only has the flow of babies to the (lawful) adoption market contracted but the practical alternatives to selling an unwanted baby have increasingly become either to retain it and raise it as an illegitimate child, ordinarily with no father present, or to have an abortion. What social purposes are served by encouraging these alternatives to baby sale?

Id. at 345-346. See also Richard A. Posner, The Regulation of the Market in Adoptions, 67 B.U. L. Rev. 59 (1987). Is this analysis persuasive?

For critical responses, see Ronald A. Cass, Coping with Life, Law, and Markets: A Comment on Posner and the Law-and-Economics Debate, 67 B.U. L. Rev. 73 (1987); Jane Maslow Cohen, Posnerism, Pluralism, Pessimism, 67 B.U. L. Rev. 105 (1987); Tamar Frankel & Francis H. Miller, The Inapplicability of Market Theory to Adoptions, 67 B.U. L. Rev. 99 (1987). Judge Posner's more recent work advocates removing the "price ceiling" for independent adoptions, given the decreasing supply of available children. Richard A. Posner, Sex and Reason 409-416 (1992).

## Note: Adoption of Children with Special Needs

The rise of state intervention to protect abused and neglected children has resulted in the removal of significant numbers of minors from parental custody. Increased parental substance abuse also has played a role. These developments, together with legal policies favoring permanent placement over long-term foster care, have made many older children available for adoption. In fact, children removed from home as infants may become free for adoption only after a considerable wait, because required "permanency planning" must include efforts to reunite children and their biological parents.

Because many children in foster care have histories of abuse and neglect and ensuing psychological problems, these prospective adoptees are often called "children with special needs" or "hard-to-place children."

These terms also include all children over four years of age, children of color, sibling groups, and children with handicaps, including HIV infection.[1]

To encourage such adoptions, state and federal programs provide financial assistance to those adopting children with special needs.[2] Tax law offers incentives.[3] The UAA, §2-105, requires agencies receiving federal funds to make diligent efforts to recruit adopters for these children. 9 U.L.A. (pt. IA) 35-36 (1999).

Adoptions of children with special needs have risen to constitute almost half of all domestic adoptions by nonrelatives.[4] Although about 75 percent of adopters of children with special needs report satisfaction with these placements, about 10 to 15 percent end before the final decree is issued. Most of these disrupted adoptions involve older children, while placements of younger children with disabilities and serious medical problems produce higher success rates. Like age, emotional and behavioral problems (including a past history of physical and sexual abuse) are predictors of disruption. Adopters' unrealistic expectations and their rigidity in family interactions also tend to correlate with poor outcomes.[5]

Critics claim that existing governmental support is inadequate. Adoptive families complain about the state's failure to disclose the full extent of the problems experienced by some children in subsidized adoption programs, preventing appropriate treatment; they also contend that more services are necessary to make such placements work.[6] Child welfare advocates recommend improved efforts to recruit adopters, the re-

[1]. See Judith K. McKenzie, Adoption of Children with Special Needs, The Future of Children, Spring 1993, at 62, 63. On September 30, 1999, 127,000 children were awaiting adoption. Their median age was 7.7 years. The largest fraction, 42 percent, were classified as "Black Non-Hispanic." During 1999, 251,000 children exited foster care. Only 16 percent left for adoption. U.S. Dept. of Health and Human Servs., Administration for Children and Families, Administration on Child, Youth, and Families, Children's Bureau, The AFCARS Report, Interim FY 1999 Estimates as of June 2001 (6).

[2]. See 42 U.S.C. §673(c) (Supp. V 1999); Griffith v. Johnston, 899 F.2d 1427, 1431 (5th Cir. 1990) (describing Texas program); Amanda T. Perez, Note, Transracial Adoption and the Federal Adoption Subsidy, 17 Yale L. & Pol'y Rev. 201 (1998).

[3]. After 2002, the Code allows those who adopt children with special needs a credit of $10,000 regardless of actual expenses, while allowing adopters of other children a credit for expenses actually incurred, not to exceed $10,000. I.R.C. §23 (West Supp. 2001 & Pamphlet No. 1 (Sept. 2001)). The Code uses this same approach in allowing income exclusions for employees under an employer's adoption assistance plan: After 2002, adopters of children with special needs can exclude $10,000 while other adopters can exclude expenses actually incurred by the employer up to $10,000. Id. at §137. Under a sunset clause, reforms in §§23 and 137 are repealed at the end of 2010, unless reinstated by Congress and the President.

[4]. National Council for Adoption, Adoption Factbook III 27 (1999) (48.5 percent in 1996, up from 26.5 percent in 1986).

[5]. These figures and conclusions are reported in James A. Rosenthal, Outcomes of Adoption of Children with Special Needs, The Future of Children, Spring 1993, at 77, 79-81.

[6]. See Griffith v. Johnston, 899 F.2d 1427 (5th Cir. 1990).

moval of barriers to nontraditional families, acceleration of the process by which children removed from parental custody become available for adoption, and provision of postadoption services.[7] Because children of color are usually included in the definition of children with special needs, the debate about transracial adoption inevitably surfaces in these calls for reform.

The Adoption and Safe Families Act of 1997 attempts to promote the adoption of children with special needs by requiring states to seek terminations of parental rights after a limited period of foster care (42 U.S.C. §675(5) (1994 & Supp. V 1999)); providing financial incentives for states to increase adoptions of children in foster care and those with special needs (id. at §673b); and requiring state plans to provide for health insurance for special needs children covered by adoption assistance agreements (id. at §671(a)). Supporters praise ASFA for recognizing adoption's benefits.[8] Critics condemn the legislation for favoring adoptive homes over birth families[9] and for failing to encourage needed systemic reform.[10]

## 3. Equitable Adoption

### ■ YORK v. MOROFSKY
*571 N.W.2d 524 (Mich. Ct. App. 1997)*

MARKMAN, J. . . .

. . . During divorce proceedings, plaintiff disclaimed defendant's parentage of Joshua, who was born during their marriage on April 17, 1987. Before this disclosure, defendant had always acted as, and believed himself to be, Joshua's father. No paternity testing has been performed to test plaintiff's claim. The trial court entered the divorce judgment excluding Joshua as a child of the marriage. The trial court later determined that defendant was not Joshua's biological or equitable parent and denied defendant's requests for . . . stepparent visitation. . . .

Defendant first argues that the trial court erred in terminating defendant's parental rights and in denying defendant's rights as an equitable parent. As part of its jurisdiction over the divorce proceeding, the

---

[7]. See McKenzie, supra note [1], at 73-75; Rosenthal, supra note [5], at 84-86.

[8]. See Elizabeth Bartholet, Nobody's Children: Abuse and Neglect, Foster Drift, and the Adoption Alternative 188-189 (1999).

[9]. See Dorothy E. Roberts, Poverty, Race, and New Directions in Child Welfare Policy, 1 Wash. U. J.L. & Pol'y 63, 66 (1999).

[10]. Robert M. Gordon, Drifting Through Byzantium: The Promise and Failure of the Adoption and Safe Families Act of 1997, 83 Minn. L. Rev. 637 (1999). See also Bernadine Dohrn, Foster Care & Adoption Reform Legislation: Implementing the Adoption and Safe Families Act of 1997, 14 St. John's J. Legal Comment. 419, 423-424 (2000) (ASFA ignores welfare reform and creates "punishing environment").

trial court had the power to determine the paternity of Joshua. Atkinson v. Atkinson, [408 N.W.2d 516, 518 (Mich. Ct. App. 1987).] The trial court's finding that defendant is not Joshua's biological parent was not against the great weight of the evidence, given defendant's admissions at several hearings that he believed plaintiff's claim that he is not the child's biological father and his waiver of court-ordered blood testing.

The trial court, however, misapplied the test for determining if defendant could be Joshua's equitable parent. . . . The test provides:

> [A] husband who is not the biological father of a child born or conceived during the marriage may be considered the natural father of that child where (1) the husband and the child mutually acknowledge a relationship as father and child, or the mother of the child has cooperated in the development of such a relationship over a period of time prior to the filing of the complaint for divorce, (2) the husband desires to have the rights afforded to a parent, and (3) the husband is willing to take on the responsibility of paying child support. [Id. at 519.]

[D]espite defendant's contention that he was willing to provide child support, the trial court held that defendant failed to satisfy the third prong because his actions during the pendency of the divorce litigation did not demonstrate "an actual, sincere effort" to provide support. [T]he trial court focused only on defendant's actions *after* the filing of the divorce action. The court entirely ignored defendant's role in supporting the child for the first four years of his life. . . .

More fundamentally, the trial court's interpretation of the third prong erroneously suggests that equitable parenthood is a condition that may ebb and flow over time. [E]quitable parenthood is a permanent status once it attaches. Once it is determined that a party is an equitable parent, that party becomes endowed with both the rights and responsibilities of a parent. There is no distinction at that point between the "equitable" parent and any other parent. . . . To be an equitable parent, it is not necessary that a party continually meet the three *Atkinson* criteria any more than it is necessary for a biological or adoptive parent to perpetually meet such criteria in order to retain parental status. . . . If a party satisfies these criteria for a reasonable period at some point, the party is an equitable parent with both the rights and responsibilities of any other parent. A subsequent change regarding any of the criteria, e.g., a subsequent unwillingness to pay child support, would not alter such a party's status any more than it would alter the status of an adoptive parent who developed second thoughts about an adoption. . . .

The view that equitable parenthood is fluid — i.e., a condition that could change over time — rather than a permanent status, is untenable for a number of reasons. First, it would undermine the principle set forth in [Soumis v. Soumis, 553 N.W.2d 619 (Mich. Ct. App. 1996)] that equitable parents stand on equal footing with natural and adoptive parents. If equitable parenthood could ebb and flow over time, it would be a class of parenthood inferior to natural or adoptive parenthood, which are usually permanent statuses. Second, stability in acknowledged parent-child relationships is generally in the child's best interests. In the instant case, for example, for Joshua to suddenly be deprived of the only father that he has ever known might well be emotionally traumatizing. . . . Third, stability and security in familial relationships are also in the parents' best interests. Defendant's — or any other individual's — status as a parent should not be subject to continuing judicial evaluations regarding whether he satisfies the criteria set forth in *Atkinson*. Finally, a view of equitable parenthood as a permanent status would foster legal certainty and predictability in such collateral areas as inheritance, income tax status, and medical care responsibility. . . .

Here, the child in question was born during the parties' marriage. Accordingly, there was a [strong but rebuttable] presumption that he was defendant's child. The evidence indicates that during the marriage defendant and Joshua had a full father-son relationship and that plaintiff cooperated in the development of this relationship. In plaintiff's divorce complaint, she initially listed both her children as children of the marriage. It appears that it was not until March 1992 that plaintiff informed defendant that he was not Joshua's biological father. Joshua was then nearly five years old. This evidence indicates that defendant meets the first *Atkinson* criterion: both parents and the child acknowledge a five-year-long relationship. It is also clear that defendant desired (and continues to desire) to be Joshua's father, thus meeting the second criterion. Finally, it is clear that defendant stated that he was willing to provide support and, in fact, provided considerable support to Joshua during the first four years of his life (before the filing of the divorce complaint), thereby satisfying the third of the *Atkinson* criteria. Accordingly, we conclude that defendant is Joshua's equitable parent and that the trial court erred in determining otherwise. . . .

## Notes and Questions

1. The equitable parent theory represents a modern variation of the doctrine of equitable adoption (sometimes called "virtual adoption") long used in inheritance cases. Courts rely on two theories to establish an equitable adoption: implied contract and equitable estoppel. Under the former, the court enforces an implied promise to adopt. Under the latter, the court considers the child's performance of filial services. See, e.g., Mize v. Sims, 516 S.W.2d 561 (Mo. Ct. App. 1974); Wooley v. Shell Petroleum Corp., 45 P.2d 927 (N.M. 1935); Jones v. Guy, 143 S.W.2d 906 (Tex. 1940); Rebecca C. Bell, Comment, Virtual Adoption: The

Difficulty of Creating an Exception to the Statutory Scheme, 29 Stetson L. Rev. 415 (1999).

Each approach has shortcomings, however. The implied contract theory ignores the child's best interests; equitable estoppel overlooks the need to prove detrimental reliance. As a result, one court has rejected implied contract as "an unnecessary fiction" in favor of an alternative rationale. Wheeling Dollar Savings & Trust Co. v. Singer, 250 S.E.2d 369 (W. Va. 1978). The court explained:

> While formal adoption is the only safe route [to legal recognition], in many instances a child will be raised by persons not his parents from an age of tender years, treated as a natural child, and represented to others as a natural or adopted child. In many instances, the child will believe himself to be the natural or formally "adopted" child of the "adoptive" parents only to be treated as an outcast upon their death. We cannot ascertain any reasonable distinction between a child treated in all regards as an adopted child but who has been led to rely to his detriment upon the existence of formal legal paperwork imagined but never accomplished, and a formally adopted child. Our family centered society presumes that bonds of love and loyalty will prevail in the distribution of family wealth along family lines, and only by affirmative action, i.e., writing a will, may this presumption be overcome. An equitably adopted child in practical terms is as much a family member as a formally adopted child and should not be the subject of discrimination. . . .

Id. at 373. According to *Wheeling*, clear and convincing evidence that the child's *status* is identical to that of a formally adopted child, except for the absence of a formal adoption order, establishes equitable adoption. While most courts rely on equitable adoption to permit inheritance from the adoptive parent, *Wheeling* takes a minority position by using the doctrine to allow inheritance by an equitably adopted child through a parent (under a trust for a niece's "child or children"). For the majority view, see, e.g., In re Estate of Jenkins, 904 P.2d 1316, 1320 (Colo. 1995) (will); Board of Educ. v. Browning, 635 A.2d 373 (Md. Ct. Spec. App. 1994) (intestate succession).

2. What evidence will establish equitable adoption? See *Wheeling*, 250 S.E.2d at 373-374 (evidence includes affection, child's services, surrender of ties by biological parents, companionship and obedience, invalid or ineffectual adoption, reliance by adoptee, and representations of status). See also James R. Robinson, Comment, Untangling the "Loose Threads": Equitable Adoption, Equitable Legitimation, and Inheritance in Extralegal Family Arrangements, 48 Emory L.J. 943 (1999).

Are the criteria the same for proving equitable parenthood? In *York*, how significant was the fact that the party seeking such status was married to the child's mother? In Van v. Zahorik, 597 N.W.2d 15 (Mich. 1999), a divided Michigan Supreme Court refused to apply the doctrine in a custody dispute to a man who met all the functional criteria but had never married the child's mother. The majority explained:

> [I]n light of the policy considerations at issue, it is necessary to stop the expanding application of equitable estoppel and the corresponding decay of the equitable parent doctrine. Such a holding may seem arbitrary, but we feel strongly that such action is necessary to prevent further, improper, judicial intrusion into this legislative policy arena.

Id. at 17-18. Does this holding suggest the equitable parenthood doctrine is just a way of according formal legal recognition to stepparents? But see Margaret M. Mahoney, Stepfamilies and the Law 61 (1994) (stepchildren rarely inherit via equitable adoption). In *York,* suppose Joshua's biological father also sought recognition? Cf. W. v. W., 779 A.2d 716 (Conn. 2001). Suppose Joshua's mother married his biological father following her divorce?

3. What explains the long-standing recognition of equitable adoption in the inheritance context? Why does the state intervene in such cases to treat an arrangement as a legally recognized family despite noncompliance with formal adoption requirements? Why does equity recognize a family here but not in so many other functional family cases? (See Chapter VII, section B3 (*Alison D.*).) Because the dispute concerns "only" money? Because it concerns private parties, one of whom is dead?

Does *York*'s equitable parent doctrine represent a sound extension of equitable adoption outside the inheritance context? See Carolee Kvoriak Lezuch, Comment, Michigan's Doctrine of Equitable Parenthood: A Doctrine Best Forgotten, 45 Wayne L. Rev. 1529, 1554-1557 (1999). Courts remain divided on whether equitable adoption has any place in child support litigation or whether it applies only in inheritance cases. Compare Johnson v. Johnson, 617 N.W.2d 97 (N.D. 2000) (applicable to child support), with Pierce v. Pierce, 645 P.2d 1353 (Mont. 1982) (inapplicable). Some cases have rejected application of the doctrine to custody and visitation disputes as well. E.g., Engel v. Kenner, 926 S.W.2d 472 (Mo. Ct. App. 1996); D.G. v. D.M.K., 557 N.W.2d 235 (S.D. 1996). Others, like *York*, will rely on an equitable parent doctrine to decide such matters. E.g., In re Marriage of Gallagher, 539 N.W.2d 479 (Iowa 1995). See also American Law Institute, Principles of the Law of Family Dissolution: Analysis and Recommendations §§2.03, 3.03 (2002) (recognizing parents by estoppel).

4. In some states, equitable adoption traces back to the era when "orphan trains" brought indigent children from urban centers to families in the west. See *Johnson,* 617 N.W.2d at 101-102. For additional historical background, see Jamil S. Zainaldin, The Emergence of a Modern Family Law: Child Custody, Adoption, and the Courts, 1796-1851, 73 Nw. U. L. Rev. 1038, 1076 (1979) (tracing development of equitable adoption from voluntary parental transfers of custody and emphasis on

the child's interests in custody awards). On equitable adoption generally, see Jan Ellen Rein, Relatives by Blood, Adoption, and Association: Who Should Get What and Why?, 37 Vand. L. Rev. 711, 766-806 (1984); Note, Equitable Adoption: They Took Him Into Their Home and Called Him Fred, 58 Va. L. Rev. 727 (1972).

## Problem

When Jennifer and Stephen marry, both know she is pregnant with a child fathered by another man. After the birth, Stephen treats the child as his own, although he never formally adopts her. During divorce proceedings, Stephen seeks visitation as an equitable parent, and Jennifer objects, claiming he is a legal stranger. How should the court rule? Cf. In re Marriage of Roberts, 649 N.E.2d 1344 (Ill. App. Ct. 1995). Suppose Stephen is Jennifer's lesbian partner, seeking visitation upon dissolution of their relationship? See In re T.L., 1996 WL 393521 (Mo. Cir. Ct., May 7, 1996) (recognizing lesbian partner as equitable parent). Cf. In re Marriage of Halvorsen, 521 N.W.2d 725, 728 (Iowa 1994).

## 4. Jurisdiction

■  **IN RE BABY GIRL CLAUSEN**
   *502 N.W.2d 649 (Mich. 1993)*

PER CURIAM. . . .

[O]n February 8, 1991, Cara Clausen gave birth to a baby girl in Iowa. . . . On February 10, 1991, Clausen signed a release of custody form, relinquishing her parental rights to the child. Clausen, who was unmarried at the time of the birth, had named Scott Seefeldt as the father. On February 14, 1991, he executed a release of custody form.

[On February 25, 1991, petitioners Roberta and Jan DeBoer, Michigan residents, petitioned a juvenile court in Iowa to adopt the child. At a hearing held the same day,] the parental rights of Cara Clausen and Seefeldt were terminated, and petitioners were granted custody of the child during the pendency of the proceeding. The DeBoers returned to Michigan with the child, and she has lived with them in Michigan continuously since then.

However, the prospective adoption never took place. On March 6, 1991, nine days after the filing of the adoption petition, Cara Clausen filed a motion in the Iowa Juvenile Court to revoke her release of custody. In an affidavit accompanying the request, Clausen stated that she had lied when she named Seefeldt as the father of the child, and that the child's father actually was Daniel Schmidt. Schmidt filed an affidavit of paternity on March 12, 1991, and on March 27, 1991, he filed a petition in the Iowa district court, seeking to intervene in the adoption proceeding initiated by the DeBoers. [He and Clausen married in April, 1992.]

[The Iowa district court found that Schmidt was the biological father and that the DeBoers failed to establish either that Schmidt had abandoned the child or that his rights should be terminated. It determined that a best interests of the child analysis becomes appropriate only after a showing of abandonment.] On the basis of these findings, the court concluded that the termination proceeding was void with respect to Schmidt, and that the DeBoers' petition to adopt the child must be denied. Those decisions have been affirmed by the Iowa appellate courts. [In re BGC, 496 N.W.2d 239 (Iowa, 1992). On remand, the Iowa district terminated the DeBoers' rights as temporary guardians and custodians.]

On the same day their rights were terminated in Iowa, the DeBoers filed a petition in Washtenaw Circuit Court [in Michigan], asking the court to assume jurisdiction under the UCCJA. The petition requested that the court enjoin enforcement of the Iowa custody order and find that it was not enforceable, or, in the alternative, to modify it to give custody to the DeBoers. [The Michigan court] entered an ex parte temporary restraining order, which directed that the child remain in the custody of the DeBoers, and ordered Schmidt not to remove the child from Washtenaw County.

[The Michigan court] found that it had jurisdiction to determine the best interests of the child. It denied Schmidt's motion for summary judgment [to dissolve the preliminary injunction and enforce the Iowa judgment], and directed that the child remain with the DeBoers until further order of the court.[9] [The court of appeals reversed, concluding Michigan lacked jurisdiction under the UCCJA and the DeBoers lacked standing. Following a petition for declaratory and injunctive relief by the child's guardian ad litem, the circuit court entered an order temporarily continuing the status quo. This court granted the DeBoers' application to appeal, limited to issues of jurisdiction and standing, and the Schmidts' application to appeal, limited to the question whether the complaint should be dismissed for failure to state a claim.]

Interstate enforcement of child custody orders has long presented vexing problems. This arose principally from uncertainties about the

---

9. [P]roceedings have continued in Iowa. On January 27, 1993, the Iowa district court held the DeBoers in contempt of court, and issued bench warrants for their arrest. The Iowa juvenile court entered an order on February 17, 1993, restoring Cara (Clausen) Schmidt's parental rights.

A best interests of the child determination hearing began in Washtenaw Circuit Court on January 29, 1993, and continued for eight days. In a decision rendered from the bench on February 12, 1993, the Washtenaw Circuit Court found that it was in the best interests of the child for her to remain with the DeBoers. That decision is not at issue in the instant appeal.

applicability of the Full Faith and Credit Clause of the United States Constitution. Because custody decrees were generally regarded as subject to modification, states had traditionally felt free to modify another state's prior order.

The initial attempt to deal with these jurisdictional problems was the drafting of the Uniform Child Custody Jurisdiction Act, promulgated by the National Conference of Commissioners on Uniform State Laws in 1968. That uniform act has now been enacted, in some form, in all fifty states, the District of Columbia, and the U.S. Virgin Islands. The Michigan version of the act is found at M.C.L. §600.651 et seq.; M.S.A. §27A.651 et seq. The act provides standards for determining whether a state may take jurisdiction of a child custody dispute, and sets forth the circumstances in which the courts of other states are prohibited from subsequently taking jurisdiction, are required to enforce custody decisions of the original state, and are permitted to modify such decisions.

. . . In 1980, Congress [enacted] the Parental Kidnapping Prevention Act, 28 U.S.C. §1738A. The PKPA "imposes a duty on the States to enforce a child custody determination entered by a court of a sister State if the determination is consistent with the provisions of the Act." Thompson v. Thompson, 484 U.S. 174, 175-176 (1988). The PKPA includes provisions similar to the UCCJA, and emphatically imposes the requirement that sister-state custody orders be given effect. . . .

In its March 29, 1993, opinion, the Court of Appeals agreed with Daniel Schmidt that the Washtenaw Circuit Court lacked jurisdiction to modify the Iowa custody orders and was instead required to enforce them. [It explained that adoption proceedings are custody proceedings under the UCCJA; that the custody matter was still pending in Iowa, where further proceedings had been scheduled; and that Iowa did not fail to conform to the UCCJA when it did not determine the best interests of the child.]

The congressionally declared purpose of the PKPA is to deal with inconsistent and conflicting laws and practices by which courts determine their jurisdiction to decide disputes between persons claiming rights of custody. Inconsistency in the determination by courts of their jurisdiction to decide custody disputes contributes to "the disregard of court orders, excessive relitigation of cases, [and] obtaining of conflicting orders by the courts of various jurisdictions. . . ." For these reasons, among others, Congress declared that the best interests of the child required the establishment of a uniform system for the assumption of jurisdiction. . . .

The [DeBoers' argument] that in this context the best interests purpose of the PKPA mandates a best interests analysis in Iowa, failing which the Iowa decision is not entitled to full faith and credit, would permit the forum state's view of the merits of the case to govern the assumption of jurisdiction to modify the foreign decree. . . .

It has been aptly noted that the vulnerability of a custody decree to an out-of-state modification presented the greatest need of all for the reform effort of the PKPA. . . . Certainty and stability are given priority under the PKPA, which gives the home state exclusive continuing jurisdiction. Thus, the PKPA expressly provides that if a custody determination is made consistently with its provisions, "the appropriate authorities of every State *shall* enforce [it] according to its terms, and *shall not* modify" that custody decision. 28 U.S.C. §1738A(a) (emphasis added). . . . At the time of commencement of both the termination and adoption proceedings, Iowa unquestionably had jurisdiction under its own laws and Iowa was unquestionably the home state of the child. . . .

Where the custody determination is made consistently with the provisions of the PKPA, the jurisdiction of the court that made the decision is exclusive and continuing as long as that state "remains the residence of the child or of any contestant," and it still has jurisdiction under its own laws. 28 U.S.C. §1738A(d). Unquestionably, Daniel Schmidt continues to reside in Iowa. Furthermore, Iowa law provides for continuing jurisdiction in custody matters. . . . The courts of this state may only modify Iowa's order if Iowa has declined to exercise its jurisdiction to modify it. 28 U.S.C. §1738A(f). Iowa has not declined to exercise its jurisdiction to modify its custody order; it has simply declined to order the relief sought by the DeBoers. . . .

The DeBoers advance a variety of arguments in support of their claim that they have standing to litigate regarding the custody of the child. First, they argue that the UCCJA grants them standing, pointing particularly to two of the jurisdictional provisions in §653(1).[37] . . .

It may be that the Iowa district court's February 25, 1991, order appointing the DeBoers as custodians during the pendency of the Iowa

---

37. Subsection (1)(a) says, in part:

"This state is the home state of the child at the time of commencement of the proceeding or had been the child's home state within 6 months before commencement of the proceeding . . . and a parent *or person acting as parent* continues to live in this state."

M.C.L. §600.653(1)(a); M.S.A. §27A.653(1)(a). (Emphasis added.)

The UCCJA defines "[p]erson acting as parent" as "a person, other than a parent, who *has physical custody* of a child and . . . *claims a right to custody*." M.C.L. §600.652(i); M.S.A. §27A.652(i). (Emphasis added.)

Subsection (1)(b) refers to a "contestant":

"It is in the best interest of the child that a court of this state assume jurisdiction because the child and his parents, or the child and at least 1 *contestant*, have a significant connection with this state. . . ."

M.C.L. §600.653(1)(b); M.S.A. §27A.653(1)(b). (Emphasis added.)

"Contestant," as defined in the UCCJA, means, "a person, including a parent, who *claims a right to custody* or visitation rights with respect to a child." M.C.L. §600.652(a); M.S.A. §27A.652(a). (Emphasis added.)

adoption proceeding was sufficiently analogous to a Michigan guardianship (which would create standing) to have given them standing to prosecute a custody action during the effectiveness of that order. However,
as the Court of Appeals said, when the temporary custody order was re-
scinded, they became third parties to the child and no longer had a basis on which to claim a substantive right of custody. . . .

[T]he next friend for the child argues that we should recognize the
right of a minor child to bring a Child Custody Act action and obtain a
best interests of the child hearing regarding her custody. . . . We do not
believe that the Child Custody Act can be read as authorizing such an
action. The act's consistent distinction between the "parties" and the
"child" makes clear that the act is intended to resolve disputes among
adults seeking custody of the child.

It is true that children, as well as their parents, have a due process
liberty interest in their family life. However, in our view those interests
are not independent of the child's parents. [T]he natural parent's right
to custody is not to be disturbed [absent a showing of unfitness], sometimes despite the preferences of the child. [The court rejected the due
process and equal protection arguments raised on the child's behalf.] In
the Iowa proceedings, a challenge to Daniel Schmidt's fitness was vigorously prosecuted by the DeBoers, and they failed to prove that he was
unfit. . . .

We also disagree with the next friend's assertion that the child's interests were not considered in Iowa. A guardian ad litem was appointed
before Daniel Schmidt moved to intervene in the action. . . . While that
proceeding did not use the "best interests of the child" standard that the
next friend and the DeBoers prefer, there is no basis for requiring use
of that standard.[48] . . .

We direct the Washtenaw Circuit Court to enter an order enforcing
the custody orders entered by the Iowa courts. In consultation with
counsel for the Schmidts and the DeBoers, the circuit court shall
promptly establish a plan for the transfer of custody [within 31 days]. It
is now time for the adults to move beyond saying that their only concern
is the welfare of the child and to put those words into action by assuring that the transfer of custody is accomplished promptly with minimum
disruption of the life of the child.

LEVIN, J. (dissenting).

I would agree with the majority's analysis if the DeBoers had gone
to Iowa, purchased a carload of hay from Cara Clausen, and then found

---

48. Even if we were to conclude that the child has [constitutional] interests that were
not adequately represented in the previous Iowa proceedings, the PKPA would require
that any new action on her behalf be brought in Iowa, which has continuing exclusive
jurisdiction. . . .

themselves in litigation in Iowa with Daniel Schmidt, who also claimed an interest in the hay. It could then properly be said that the DeBoers "must be taken to have known" that, rightly or wrongly, the Iowa courts might rule against them, and they should, as gracefully as possible, accept an adverse decision of the Iowa courts. Michigan would then have had no interest in the outcome, and would routinely enforce a decree of the Iowa courts against the DeBoers. But this is not a lawsuit concerning the ownership, the legal title, to a bale of hay. . . .

The PKPA was enacted to protect the child. . . . Congress enacted the PKPA, not because of an abstract concern about "interstate controversies over child custody," but rather "in the interest of greater stability of home environment and of secure *family relationships* for the child." . . . Congress identified the "home state" of the child as the "state which can best decide the case in the interest of the child." "Home state" is defined as the "State in which, immediately preceding the time involved, the child lived with his parents, a parent, *or a person acting as a parent, for at least six consecutive months,* and in the case of a child less than six months old, the State in which the child lived from birth with any of such persons." (Emphasis added.)

In this case, the child did not "live from birth" with either Cara Clausen or the DeBoers. The child resided for a few days at the hospital where she was born, then for two weeks with caregivers to whom the child had been entrusted, and has lived in Michigan since the end of February 1991, when, within three weeks of birth, physical custody was transferred to the DeBoers pursuant to a court order then entered in Iowa.

Michigan is the child's home state because she has lived in Michigan with the DeBoers, persons "acting as a parent," for at least six consecutive months — actually for over two years. Michigan, the home state, would also qualify as the state having jurisdiction under the PKPA pursuant to the alternative "significant connection" test for a case where no state is the home state. . . . There is more substantial evidence concerning the child's present or future care, protection, training and personal relationships in Michigan than in Iowa. . . . There was no contact between Daniel Schmidt and the child in Iowa, minimum contact between Cara Schmidt and the child in Iowa, and maximum contact between the child and the DeBoers in Michigan. . . . Assuming that the PKPA applies to adoption proceedings, and that is the assumption on which the majority opinion is predicated, the underlying themes of the act must be observed. . . .

Professor Clark wrote that subject matter jurisdiction in adoption should be given to the home state of the child. . . . As Professor Clark explains, the only issues in an adoption proceeding with respect to the natural parents, are "whether the consent is genuine, or whether the alleged abandonment or neglect did occur. These resemble *the issues in the ordinary transitory lawsuit,* and there is thus no need for any requirements of domicile or residence on the part of the natural parents."[53]

But, suggests Professor Clark, "since adoption consists of matching a child with a new parent or set of parents," there is a need for a "thorough opportunity to study the child and his background. To give the court this opportunity, the child must be present and available in the jurisdiction."[54] He concludes . . . that that subject matter jurisdiction in adoption should be where the adoptive parents reside and the child is physically present. . . .

A decree rendered by a state other than the home state is not a determination made "consistent with the provisions" of the PKPA. A decree rendered without consideration of the child's best interests is not a decree that the Congress intended that all other states must enforce. [Michigan law would require a best interests hearing.]

The sympathetic portrayal of the Schmidts in the majority opinion ignores that it was Cara Schmidt's fraud on the Iowa court and on Daniel Schmidt that is at the root of this controversy. . . . To fault the DeBoers is unwarranted. [They left Iowa with the child in good faith.] Why should they have believed that Cara Schmidt was telling the truth when she said she had fraudulently named the other man as the father? The DeBoers discovered that Schmidt had a dismal record as a father. . . . The Iowa courts thought there was sufficient merit in the DeBoers' claims that they maintained custody of the child with the DeBoers until after the Iowa Supreme Court ruled. One [dissenting] justice agreed with the DeBoers. . . .

If the danger confronting this child were physical injury, no one would question her right to invoke judicial process to protect herself against such injury. There is little difference, when viewed from the child's frame of reference, between a physical assault and a psychological assault. . . . It is only because this child cannot speak for herself that adults can avert their eyes from the pain that she will suffer.

## Notes and Questions

1. *Epilogue.* The United States Supreme Court refused to stay the order entered pursuant to the Michigan Supreme Court's opinion. 509 U.S. 1301 (1993). After the transfer, Baby Jessica became Anna Schmidt. In 1999, the Schmidts divorced, with custody of Anna and her younger sister going to the father. Separate Ways; Having Once Fought to Bring Baby Jessica Home, Her Parents Now File for Divorce, People Mag., Oct. 25, 1999, at 138. His later unemployment threatened another custody change, back to Cara Clausen Schmidt. Baby Jessica's Father Again Faces Losing Her, Grand Rapids Press, Mar. 7, 2001, at A6. Although some say

---

53. [2 Clark, Domestic Relations, 2d ed., §21.3] p.595. (Emphasis added.)
54. Id., §21.3, p.596.

Anna has fared well, experts remain divided about the long-term impact of her removal from the DeBoers. See Leonard Greene, Heartbreak Kids Enjoy Normal Childhoods, N.Y. Post, Mar. 9, 2001, at 19. As for the DeBoers, the stress of the adoption battle caused them to end their 17-year marriage, but they later reconciled. Pair Who Fought for Baby Jessica Plan to Remarry, Atlanta J. & Atlanta Const., Feb. 4, 2001, at A6.

2. How sound is the majority's premise that statutes governing multijurisdictional *custody* disputes (the Uniform Child Custody Jurisdiction Act (UCCJA) and the Parental Kidnapping Prevention Act (PKPA)) control in termination and adoption proceedings as well? Several courts have applied these statutes to such cases. See, e.g., In re Adoption of Asente, 734 N.E.2d 1224, 1231 (Ohio 2000) (majority of jurisdictions apply UCCJA and PKPA to adoptions). But see, e.g., In re Johnson, 415 N.E.2d 108 (Ind. Ct. App. 1981) (UCCJA inapplicable to adoptions); Williams v. Knott, 690 S.W.2d 605 (Tex. Ct. App. 1985) (PKPA inapplicable to terminations and adoptions).

Do custody and adoption proceedings differ in ways that call for different jurisdictional rules? See generally Bernadette W. Hartfield, The Uniform Child Custody Jurisdiction Act and the Problem of Interstate Adoption: An Easy Fix?, 43 Okla. L. Rev. 621 (1990); Herma Hill Kay, Adoption in the Conflict of Laws: The UAA, Not the UCCJA, Is the Answer, 84 Cal. L. Rev. 703, 712-728 (1996).

3. Assuming that the UCCJA and the PKPA apply, which analysis is more convincing, the majority's or the dissent's? Did Iowa satisfy the requirements for "home state" or any other jurisdictional basis? Do the statutes require a best interests inquiry? Will the majority's reasoning invite fraudulent identification of a child's father (as the dissent predicts)? Will the dissent's approach encourage prospective adopters to delay returning a child, despite an impediment to adoption in the state where the child was relinquished, in hopes of obtaining in their domicile a more favorable outcome based on a best interests analysis (as the majority fears)?

4. If the UCCJA and the PKPA do not apply, what connections with the forum state confer adoption jurisdiction? Considerable authority uses as an alternative domicile, traditionally that of the child, or according to some modern courts, that of the adoptive parent. Eugene F. Scoles et al., Conflict of Laws §16.5 (3d ed. 2000); see Homer H. Clark, The Law of Domestic Relations in the United States 870-872 (2d ed. 1988); Restatement (Second) of Conflict of Laws §78 (1971). Is domicile preferable to the bases used under the UCCJA and the PKPA? Where is an infant domiciled? See Mississippi Band of Choctaw Indians v. Holyfield, 490 U.S. 30, 47-48 (1989) (common law assigns illegitimate children their mother's domicile; hence, a child's domicile of origin may be a place where child has never been).

Must a court at the child's or adopter's domicile have personal jurisdiction over the child's birth parents, absent a previous termination of parental rights? Cf. Armstrong v. Manzo, 380 U.S. 545 (1965). Would this requirement remain controlling if the UCCJA and the PKPA govern adoptions? See Chapter VII, section B6.

5. The widely enacted Interstate Compact on the Placement of Children also governs multistate adoptions. See, e.g., Mo. Ann. Stat. §210.620 (Vernon 1996 & Supp. 2001) (including list of complementary laws in 50 other jurisdictions). The statute specifies procedural requirements for transferring the custody of a child to adoptive parents from another state but does not establish jurisdiction. *Asente*, 734 N.E.2d at 1230-1231. Courts have cited failure to comply with the ICPC as a reason to allow revocation of parental consent to adoption. See, e.g., In re Adoption of A.M.M., 949 P.2d 1155 (Kan. Ct. App. 1997).

6. Drafted in the wake of the Baby Jessica case, the UAA modifies the UCCJA to account for the distinctive features of adoption proceedings, in which there is often no "home state." Under §3-101,

> (a) Except as otherwise provided . . . , a court of this State has jurisdiction over a proceeding for the adoption of a minor commenced under this [Act] if:
>
> (1) immediately before commencement of the proceeding, the minor lived in this State with a parent, a guardian, a prospective adoptive parent, or another person acting as parent, for at least six consecutive months, excluding periods of temporary absence, or, in the case of a minor under six months of age, lived in this State from soon after birth with any of those individuals and there is available in this State substantial evidence concerning the minor's present or future care;
>
> (2) immediately before commencement of the proceeding, the prospective adoptive parent lived in this State for at least six consecutive months, excluding periods of temporary absence, and there is available in this State substantial evidence concerning the minor's present or future care;
>
> (3) the agency that placed the minor for adoption is located in this State and it is in the best interest of the minor that a court of this State assume jurisdiction because:
>
>> (i) the minor and the minor's parents, or the minor and the prospective adoptive parent, have a significant connection with this State; and
>>
>> (ii) there is available in this State substantial evidence concerning the minor's present or future care;
>
> (4) the minor and the prospective adoptive parent are physically present in this State and the minor has been abandoned or it is necessary in an emergency to protect the minor because the minor has been subjected to or threatened with mistreatment or abuse or is otherwise neglected; or
>
> (5) it appears that no other State would have jurisdiction under prerequisites substantially in accordance with paragraphs (1) through (4), or another State has declined to exercise jurisdiction on the ground that this State is the more appropriate forum to hear a petition for adoption of the minor, and it is in the best interest of the minor that a court of this State assume jurisdiction. . . .

9 U.L.A. (pt. IA) 67-68 (1999). The section goes on to disallow a state from exercising jurisdiction if a proceeding is pending in another state (with jurisdiction under the act) or another state has issued a decree, unless that state no longer has jurisdiction. This legislation would not displace the Interstate Compact, supra; rather, once a court assumes jurisdiction under the UAA, it considers whether the parties complied with the Compact. See Joan Heifetz Hollinger, The Uniform Adoption Act: Reporter's Ruminations, 30 Fam. L.Q. 345, 368 (1996).

How would the UAA apply in Baby Jessica's case? See Joan Heifetz Hollinger, Adoption and Aspiration: The Uniform Adoption Act, the DeBoer-Schmidt Cases, and the American Quest for the Ideal Family, 2 Duke J. Gender L. & Poly. 15 (1995); Kay, supra. Only Vermont has enacted the UAA. See 9 U.L.A. (pt. IA) 2 (Supp. 2001).

To eliminate any confusion, the Uniform Child Custody Jurisdiction and Enforcement Act (UCCJEA), which revises the UCCJA to make it more consistent with the PKPA, explicitly states in §103 that it does not apply to adoption proceedings. The comment explains that the UAA governs adoption jurisdiction. 9 U.L.A. (pt. IA) 660-661 (1999). See, e.g., White v. Adoption of Baby Boy D., 10 P.3d 212 (Okla. 2000).

## Problem

Thomaszine moves from Texas to Washington state four months before giving birth to a son. A few weeks after the birth, Carl and Yvonne, a married couple living in Oregon, meet Thomaszine in Washington to discuss adopting the child. Because Thomaszine is not ready to relinquish him permanently, no agreement results. For the next several months, Thomaszine and her son live in a crisis shelter. When forced to move, she places the child in foster care, and the state (Washington) initiates dependency proceedings.

When her son is seven months old, Thomaszine finally decides to place him for adoption. Her physician contacts Carl and Yvonne, who travel to Washington to pick up the child. Thomaszine signs a consent, stating that Carl and Yvonne "will car[e] for the child during the adoptive process, after which they will become his legal parents." Carl and Yvonne return to Oregon with the child. A week later, the dependency proceedings are dismissed. Two months thereafter, Thomaszine informs Carl and Yvonne she wants her child back and no longer consents to adoption. In Oregon, Carl and Yvonne have just completed a home study and have prepared a petition for adoption.

As attorney for Carl and Yvonne, what would you advise? Should they return the child to Thomaszine? What "compromises" might you explore? Alternatively, if they insist on filing their adoption petition, what problems should they anticipate? Which state has jurisdiction under the UCCJA and PKPA? The UAA? Suppose, instead, the biological father (whom Thomaszine refused to identify) contacts you just before the adoption petition is filed to convey his refusal to consent? See Stubbs v. Weathersby, 892 P.2d 991 (Or. 1995). But see In re Hayes, 979 P.2d 779 (Or. Ct. App. 1999).

## Note: International Adoptions

The shortage of "highly desirable" adoptees, as well as agency restrictions on adopters, have led some Americans to seek children from abroad. International adoptions account for 17.2 percent of all nonrelative domestic adoptions in this country.[11] The highly publicized cases of Baby Richard (supra pages 1146-1147) and Baby Jessica, which returned children to biological parents after lengthy periods with adoptive families, reportedly sparked increased interest in transnational adoptions, believed by many to be less vulnerable to such disruptions.[12]

Several bodies of law apply to international adoptions: federal immigration laws, state adoption standards, and the foreign country's relinquishment requirements. Often a child must be adopted in the country of origin in order to be able to travel to the United States and then again in the state where the adoptive parents live, because decrees from foreign countries are not entitled to full faith and credit.[13]

Some long-standing barriers have begun to change. For example, federal law, which limits entry to foreign adoptees who are "orphans," has been relaxed through an expanded definition. The term now includes not only children whose parents both have died but also those whose parents both have disappeared, abandoned or deserted them, or become separated or lost from them.[14] In 2000, the United States ratified and enacted implementing legislation for the Hague Convention

---

[11]. Adoption Factbook III, supra note [4], at 27 (based on 1996 figures).

[12]. In fact, these cases have led some U.S. mothers to relinquish children in other countries to avoid the need for paternal consent. See Alexandra Maravel, Intercountry Adoption and the Flight from Unwed Fathers' Rights: Whose Right Is It Anyway?, 48 S.C. L. Rev. 497 (1997). International adoptions can also prove vulnerable because of defects in parental consent, however. See Diana Jean Schemo, The Baby Trail: A Special Report; Adoptions in Paraguay: Mothers Cry Theft, N.Y. Times, Mar. 19, 1996, at A1.

[13]. See Elizabeth Bartholet, International Adoption: Current Status and Future Prospects, The Future of Children, Spring 1993, at 89, 93; Jordana P. Simov, Comment, The Effects of Intercountry Adoptions on Biological Parents' Rights, 22 Loy. L.A. Int'l & Comp. L. Rev. 251 (1999).

[14]. 8 U.S.C.A. §1101(b)(1)(F) (West Supp. 2001); 8 C.F.R.§204.3 (2001). See also Michelle Van Leeuwen, Comment, The Politics of Adoptions Across Borders: Whose Interests Are Served? (A Look at the Emerging Market of Infants from China), 8 Pac. Rim L. & Pol'y J. 189, 208 (1999) (noting differences among countries' definitions of terms such as "abandoned child" and "orphan").

on Protection of Children and Cooperation in Respect of Intercountry Adoption.[15] This Convention, which applies only when both countries involved are Convention parties, is designed to regularize international adoptions by requiring a finding that the child is adoptable and a determination that the adoption would serve the child's best interests. The Convention also establishes supervisory Central Authorities to impose minimum norms and procedures and mandate recognition of such adoptions elsewhere.[16]

Some states no longer require a full state proceeding if a foreign adoption has been completed. See, e.g., In re Adoption of W.J., 942 P.2d 37 (Kan. 1997). Finally, federal legislation now provides that, when certain statutory conditions are met, children adopted from abroad by U.S. citizens automatically become U.S. citizens.[17]

Similar questions make transracial and international adoptions controversial: Are privileged Americans satisfying their own need for children by exploiting poor children, separating them from their birth families and cultures?[18] Or do international adoptions provide opportunities for growth, love, and well-being that would otherwise elude these children,[19] while simultaneously demonstrating to all the importance of common humanity?[20]

[15]. See 42 U.S.C.A. §§14901-14954 (West Supp. 2001). The INS has proposed amended regulations to facilitate immigration of children adopted from countries implementing the Hague Convention. 66 Fed. Reg. 25645 (May 14, 2001).

[16]. See 19 Fam. L. Rep. (BNA) 2037 (July 20, 1993) (convention text). Under the federal implementing legislation, the U.S. State Department is the central authority with responsibility for international adoptions, including contracting with nonprofit organizations to accredit and monitor adoption agencies, facilitating individual adoptions under the Convention, making annual reports to Congress, establishing a registry, and issuing certificates for adoptions finalized under the Convention. See House, Senate Clear a Variety of Immigration Measures, 77 No. 40 Interpreter Releases 1476 (Oct. 16, 2000). See generally Lisa K. Gold, Who's Afraid of Big Government? The Federalization of Intercountry Adoption: It's Not as Scary as It Sounds, 34 Tulsa L. J. 109 (1998) (proposing federal requirements before U.S. ratified and implemented Hague Convention); Bridget M. Hubing, International Child Adoptions: Who Should Decide What Is in the Best Interests of the Family, 15 Notre Dame J.L. Ethics & Pub. Pol'y 655 (2001).

[17]. 8 U.S.C.A. §1431(b) (West Supp. 2001). See also 8 U.S.C.A. §1101(b)(1)(G) (West Supp. 2001 & Pamphlet No. 1 Sept. 2001) (immediate relative classification for children so adopted).

[18]. See, e.g., Seth Mydans, U.S. Interrupts Cambodian Adoptions, N.Y. Times, Nov. 5, 2001, at A7 (allegations of trafficking); Alessandra Stanley, Hands Off Our Babies, A Georgian Tells America, N.Y. Times, June 29, 1997, §1, at 1.

[19]. See, e.g., Patrick E. Tyler, In China's Orphanages, a War of Perception, N.Y. Times, Jan. 21, 1996, §2, at 31 (dispute about conditions in orphanages from which Americans often adopt).

[20]. See Bartholet, supra note [13], at 90. See also Anthony D'Amato, Cross-Country Adoption: A Call to Action, 73 Notre Dame L. Rev. 1239 (1998).

## D. CONSEQUENCES OF ADOPTION

### 1. Legal Status of the Child

An adoption decree terminates the legal relationship between the adoptee and all biological relatives and replaces it with new ties to the adoptive family. This principle treats the adoptee as a legitimate blood descendant of the adopter for all purposes.[21] Certain consequences regarding inheritance law follow: Many courts hold that adopted children inherit by intestate succession from their adoptive, but not from their biological, parents. See, e.g., In re Estate of Shehady, 491 P.2d 528 (N.M. 1971). Similarly, some courts have construed the term "issue" in wills or trusts to exclude (from testate succession or as trust beneficiaries) those biological children adopted out of the decedent's family, unless a contrary intent plainly appears. E.g., Crumpton v. Mitchell, 281 S.E.2d 1 (N.C. 1981).

Moreover, modern law largely has replaced the "stranger-to-the-adoption" doctrine (which excludes the adoptee from class-gift language[22] in a will or trust when the testator or settlor was not the adoptive parent) with a presumption that inclusion is intended, unless the document expressly excludes adoptees.[23]

The general rule that adoption creates new relationships in place of biological ties raises questions other than inheritance. For example, does the preference for placing siblings together still apply once one sibling has been adopted? See In re Shanee Carol B., 550 S.E.2d 636 (W. Va. 2001). Should laws barring marriages between close relatives (incest restrictions) apply to relationships by adoption? Compare Israel v. Allen, 577 P.2d 762 (Colo. 1978), with In re MEW, 4 Pa. D.&C.3d 51 (C.P. Allegheny 1977).

Contemporary authorities show increasing flexibility about whether the consequences of adoption must be "all or nothing." The new UAA,

---

[21]. The 1969 version of the UAA was written in these terms. Unif. Adoption Act §14, 9 U.L.A. (pt. IA) 198-199 (1999). The drafters' comment explains:

> The termination of relationship of parent and child between the adopted person and his natural parents and the family of the natural parents follows the trend of modern statutes and is desirable for many reasons. It eases the transition from old family to new family by providing for a clean final "cutoff" of legal relationships with the old family. It also preserves the secrecy of adoption proceedings . . . by reducing the selfish reasons an individual might have to discover his antecedents.

Id. at 199.

[22]. Examples of class-gift language are "children," "issue," and "heirs."

[23]. See Unif. Probate Code §2-611, 8 U.L.A. (pt. I) 434 (1998) (Prior Art. II); In re Estate of Jenkins, 904 P.2d 1316 (Colo. 1995). Cf. In re Estate of Zastrow, 166 N.W.2d 251 (Wis. 1969) (testatrix intended to include as nephew's "children of the body" nephew's biological sons, despite their adoption by another man).

while adhering to the general rule severing legal ties with the biological family, §§1-104, 1-105, provides that adoption does not terminate a former parent's duty to pay arrearages for child support, §1-105. 9 U.L.A. (pt. IA) 23-24 (1999). Similarly, some statutes provide for inheritance by adopted children from their biological parents. See, e.g., Tex. Fam. Code Ann. §161.206 (West 1996).

## 2. Stepparent and Second-Parent Adoptions

### ■ ADOPTION OF TAMMY
*619 N.E.2d 315 (Mass. 1993)*

GREANEY, J.

In this case, two unmarried women, Susan and Helen, filed a joint petition in the Probate and Family Court Department under G.L. c. 210, §1 (1992 ed.) to adopt as their child Tammy, a minor, who is Susan's biological daughter. . . . Based on [a] finding that Helen and Susan "are each functioning, separately and together, as the custodial and psychological parents of [Tammy]," and that "it is the best interest of said [Tammy] that she be adopted by both," the judge entered a decree allowing the adoption. Simultaneously, the [Probate and Family Court] judge reserved and reported to the Appeals Court the evidence and all questions of law, in an effort to "secure [the] decree from any attack in the future on jurisdictional grounds." We transferred the case to this court on our own motion. We conclude that the adoption was properly allowed under G.L. c. 210.

. . . Helen and Susan have lived together in a committed relationship, which they consider to be permanent, for more than ten years. In June, 1983, they jointly purchased a house in Cambridge. Both women are physicians specializing in surgery. At the time the petition was filed, Helen maintained a private practice in general surgery at Mount Auburn Hospital and Susan, a nationally recognized expert in the field of breast cancer, was director of the Faulkner Breast Center and a surgical oncologist at the Dana Farber Cancer Institute. Both women also held positions on the faculty of Harvard Medical School.

For several years prior to the birth of Tammy, Helen and Susan planned to have a child, biologically related to both of them, whom they would jointly parent. Helen first attempted to conceive a child through artificial insemination by Susan's brother. When those efforts failed, Susan successfully conceived a child through artificial insemination by Helen's biological cousin, Francis. The women attended childbirth classes together and Helen was present when Susan gave birth to Tammy on April 30, 1988. Although Tammy's birth certificate reflects Francis as her biological father, she was given a hyphenated surname using Susan and Helen's last names.

Since her birth, Tammy has lived with, and been raised and supported by, Helen and Susan. Tammy views both women as her parents, calling Helen "mama" and Susan "mommy." Tammy has strong emotional and psychological bonds with both Helen and Susan. Together, Helen and Susan have provided Tammy with a comfortable home, and have created a warm and stable environment which is supportive of Tammy's growth and over-all well being. Both women jointly and equally participate in parenting Tammy, and both have a strong financial commitment to her. . . . Francis does not participate in parenting Tammy and does not support her. His intention was to assist Helen and Susan in having a child, and he does not intend to be involved with Tammy, except as a distant relative. Francis signed an adoption surrender and supports the joint adoption by both women.

Helen and Susan, recognizing that the laws of the Commonwealth do not permit them to enter into a legally cognizable marriage, believe that the best interests of Tammy require legal recognition of her identical emotional relationship to both women. Susan expressed her understanding that it may not be in her own long-term interest to permit Helen to adopt Tammy because, in the event that Helen and Susan separate, Helen would have equal rights to primary custody. Susan indicated, however, that she has no reservation about allowing Helen to adopt. Apart from the emotional security and current practical ramifications which legal recognition of the reality of her parental relationships will provide Tammy, Susan indicated that the adoption is important for Tammy in terms of potential inheritance from Helen. Helen and her living issue are the beneficiaries of three irrevocable family trusts. Unless Tammy is adopted, Helen's share of the trusts may pass to others. . . .

Over a dozen witnesses, including mental health professionals, teachers, colleagues, neighbors, blood relatives and a priest and nun, testified to the fact that Helen and Susan participate equally in raising Tammy, that Tammy relates to both women as her parents, and that the three form a healthy, happy, and stable family unit. . . . [Both extended families unreservedly endorsed the adoption. The home study conducted by the Department of Social Services, the psychiatrist appointed as Tammy's guardian ad litem, and the attorney appointed to represent her interests all supported the adoption for her best interests.]

1. The initial question is whether the Probate Court judge had jurisdiction under G.L. c. 210 to enter a judgment on a joint petition for adoption brought by two unmarried cohabitants in the petitioners' circumstances. We answer this question in the affirmative.

There is nothing on the face of the statute which precludes the joint adoption of a child by two unmarried cohabitants such as the petitioners. Chapter 210, §1, provides that "[a] person of full age may petition the probate court in the county where he resides for leave to adopt as his child another person younger than himself, unless such other person is his or her wife or husband, or brother, sister, uncle or aunt, of the whole or half blood." Other than requiring that a spouse join in the petition, if the petitioner is married and the spouse is competent to join therein, the statute does not expressly prohibit or require joinder by any person. [I]t is apparent from the first sentence of G.L. c. 210, §1, that the Legislature considered and defined those combinations of persons which would lead to adoptions in violation of public policy. Clearly absent is any prohibition of adoption by two unmarried individuals like the petitioners. . . .

In this case all requirements in [the statute] are met, and there is no question that the judge's findings demonstrate that the directives [in the statute,] and in case law, have been satisfied. Adoption will not result in any tangible change in Tammy's daily life; it will, however, serve to provide her with a significant legal relationship which may be important in her future. At the most practical level, adoption will entitle Tammy to inherit from Helen's family trusts and from Helen and her family under the law of intestate succession, to receive support from Helen, who will be legally obligated to provide such support, to be eligible for coverage under Helen's health insurance policies, and to be eligible for social security benefits in the event of Helen's disability or death.

Of equal, if not greater significance, adoption will enable Tammy to preserve her unique filial ties to Helen in the event that Helen and Susan separate, or Susan predeceases Helen. As the case law and commentary on the subject illustrate, when the functional parents of children born in circumstances similar to Tammy separate or one dies, the children often remain in legal limbo for years while their future is disputed in the courts. Polikoff, This Child Does Have Two Mothers: Redefining Parenthood to Meet the Needs of Children in Lesbian-Mother and Other Nontraditional Families, 78 Geo. J.L. 459, 508-522 (1990); Comment, Second Parent Adoption for Lesbian-Parented Families: Legal Recognition of the Other Mother, 19 U.C. Davis L. Rev. 729, 741-745 (1986). In some cases, children have been denied the affection of a functional parent who has been with them since birth, even when it is apparent that this outcome is contrary to the children's best interests. [Citations omitted.] The conclusion that the adoption is in the best interests of Tammy is also well warranted.

2. The judge also posed the question whether, pursuant to G.L. c. 210, §6 (1992 ed.), Susan's legal relationship to Tammy must be terminated if Tammy is adopted. Section 6 provides that, on entry of an adoption decree, "all rights, duties and other legal consequences of the natural relation of child and parent shall . . . except as regards marriage, incest or cohabitation, terminate between the child so adopted and his natural parents and kindred." Although G.L. c. 210, §2, clearly permits a child's

natural parent to be an adoptive parent, §6 does not contain any express exceptions to its termination provision. The Legislature obviously did not intend that a natural parent's legal relationship to its child be terminated when the natural parent is a party to the adoption petition.

Section 6 clearly is directed to the more usual circumstances of adoption, where the child is adopted by persons who are not the child's natural parents (either because the natural parents have elected to relinquish the child for adoption or their parental rights have been involuntarily terminated). The purpose of the termination provision is to protect the security of the child's newly-created family unit by eliminating involvement with the child's natural parents. . . . Reading the adoption statute as a whole, we conclude that the termination provision contained in §6 was intended to apply only when the natural parents (or parent) are not parties to the adoption petition. . . .

## Notes and Questions

1. *Stepparent adoptions.* Today, stepparent adoptions are estimated to comprise half of all adoptions. Typically, the adopter is the spouse of one biological parent. See Unif. Adoption Act, 9 U.L.A. (pt. IA) 103-104 (1999) (comment on Art. 4). Under the UAA, §4-103, stepparent adoptions do not affect:

> (1) the relationship between the adoptee and the adoptee's parent who is the adoptive stepparent's spouse or deceased spouse;
>
> (2) an existing order for visitation or communication with a minor adoptee by an individual related to the adoptee through the parent who is the adoptive stepparent's spouse or deceased spouse;
>
> (3) the right of the adoptee or a descendant of the adoptee to inheritance or intestate succession through or from the adoptee's former parent; or
>
> (4) a court order or agreement for visitation or communication with a minor adoptee which is approved by the court. . . .

Id. at 106.

Such statutory protections raise the possibility of dual inheritance, affording adoptees an advantage denied to biological children. The Uniform Probate Code's general rule against dual inheritance (§2-113) does not explicitly prevent an adoptee from inheriting from biological and adoptive relatives. 8 U.L.A. (pt. I) 91 (1998) (Rev. Art. II). Indeed, this Code (§2-114(b)) creates an exception to the general rule in stepparent adoptions, providing that the adoptee and his or her descendants continue to inherit from and through the biological noncustodial parent in cases of intestate succession. Id.

Why permit dual inheritance in these cases? See e.g., Raley v. Spikes, 614 So. 2d 1017 (Ala. 1993). Note that, without such provisions, courts might deny stepparent adoptions because the loss of intestate inheritance from the biological parent would prevent the adoption from serving the child's best interest. See Matter of Gerald G.G., 403 N.Y.S.2d 57 (App. Div. 1978). Cf. In re Estate of Best, 485 N.E.2d 1010 (N.Y. 1985) (holding subsequent statutory exception inapplicable to class gifts from biological kin, unless adoptee specifically named or described in will).

2. *Tammy* contrasts with *Alison D.* (Chapter VII, section B3), in which the court refused to recognize a lesbian co-parent's relationship with her partner's child. The outcome in *Tammy* exemplifies what commentators call second-parent adoption. See, e.g., Jane S. Schacter, Constructing Families in a Democracy: Courts, Legislatures, and Second-Parent Adoption, 75 Chi.-Kent L. Rev. 933 (2000). Would traditional adoption law permit two women to adopt a child? A female to adopt a child without terminating the parental rights of the biological mother? Suppose state law allows second-parent adoption. What is the impact of a co-parent's failure to adopt her partner's child in a subsequent dispute about visitation or inheritance? See Titchenal v. Dexter, 693 A.2d 682 (Vt. 1997). But cf. ALI Principles §§2.03, 3.03 (estoppel).

3. In an omitted dissent, Justice Lynch said the statute does not permit joint adoption by Susan and Helen, but it does allow Helen to adopt Tammy while Susan retains her parental rights. Which presents the more persuasive statutory interpretation in *Tammy,* the majority or the dissent? In general, which of the two approaches (joint adoption versus adoption by a woman without terminating the mother's rights) is preferable? In another case in which a lesbian couple sought to formalize their family relationship, the court allowed the same-sex partner's adoptions to come within a statutory exception for stepparents; under this exception, adoption does not terminate the rights of the biological parent who intends to continue rearing the child. Adoptions of B.L.V.B. & E.L.V.B., 628 A.2d 1271 (Vt. 1993). The legislature later codified this holding. Vt. Stat. Ann., tit. 15A, §1-102(b) (Supp. 2000). The UAA follows this approach, indicating in comments that the provisions on stepparent adoption should apply. 9 U.L.A. (pt. IA) 105 (1999) (comment to §4-102). Will courts necessarily construe "stepparent" to cover someone like Helen in *Tammy?* See Sharon S. v. Superior Ct., 113 Cal. Rptr. 2d 107 (Ct. App. 2001); In re Adoption of Baby Z., 724 A.2d 1035 (Conn. 1999) (both ruling that second-parent adoptions do not meet criteria for any statutorily authorized adoptions, including stepparent adoptions). But see Cal. Fam. Code §9000 (West Supp. 2002); Conn. Gen. Stat. Ann. §45a-724(a)(3) (West Supp. 2001) (both amending prior statutes to permit second-parent adoptions under specific conditions).

4. Beyond questions of statutory construction (which the legislature can always correct), can or should the law recognize two mothers for a

child? Second-parent adoptions are becoming more widely recognized. E.g., In re M.M.D. & B.H.M., 662 A.2d 837 (D.C. 1995); In re Jacob, 660 N.E.2d 397 (N.Y. 1995). But see In re Angel M., 516 N.W.2d 678 (Wis. 1994). In addition to preventing disputes at death or dissolution, second-parent adoptions have important consequences even while the couple's relationship remains intact. For example, such adoptions permit the co-parent to consent to medical treatment for the child, to have access to the child's school records, or to obtain insurance coverage for the child through an employer. See In re Adoption of Evan, 583 N.Y.S.2d 997, 998-999 (Surr. Ct. 1992).

See generally Suzanne Bryant, Second Parent Adoption: A Model Brief, 2 Duke J. Gender L. & Poly. 233 (1995); Julie Shapiro, A Lesbian-Centered Critique of Second-Parent Adoptions, 14 Berkeley Women's L.J. 17 (1999); Mark Strasser, Courts, Legislatures, and Second-Parent Adoptions: On Judicial Deference, Specious Reasoning, and the Best Interests of the Child, 66 Tenn. L. Rev. 1019 (1999).

## 3. Secrecy versus Disclosure

### a. Sealed-Record Laws

Since World War II, secrecy shrouded the adoption process in most states. The reasons included the stigma associated with illegitimate births, the fear that birth parents would intrude in adoptive families, and the belief that adoptive families should imitate biological families. To maintain this secrecy, statutes provide for the issuance of a new birth certificate when a child is adopted, changing the name of the adoptee to that of the adoptive parents. (The original birth certificate is then sealed.)

Courts have rejected adult adoptees' constitutional challenges to sealed-record laws, concluding that the right to privacy does not include a fundamental "right to know" one's biological parents and that adoptees do not constitute a suspect class for equal protection purposes. The laws survive rational basis review as protection for the interests of all parties. See, e.g., In re Roger B., 418 N.E.2d 751 (Ill.), *appeal dismissed sub nom.* Barth v. Finley, 454 U.S. 806 (1981). Would courts reach the same result today? See Naomi Cahn & Jana Singer, Adoption, Identity, and the Constitution: The Case for Opening Closed Records, 2 U. Pa. J. Const. L. 150 (1999).

Most sealed-record statutes permit disclosure on a showing of good cause. E.g., Ga. Code Ann. §19-8-23(a) (Supp. 2001). Courts have been more willing to find good cause for medical (such as for diagnosis of genetic disease) than psychological reasons. See In re Assalone, 512 A.2d 1383 (R.I. 1986); Bradley v. Children's Bureau of S.C., 274 S.E.2d 418 (S.C. 1981). Although courts have declined to treat a psychological "need to know" as good cause, in a concurring opinion in In Application of Maples, 563 S.W.2d 760 (Mo. 1978), Judge Seiler explained the need adoptees have for finding their origins: "All of us need to know our past, not only for a sense of lineage and heritage, but for a fundamental and crucial sense of our very selves: our identity is incomplete and our sense of self retarded without a real personal historical connection. . . ." Id. at 767. Experts in other fields view adoptees' searches as a helpful response to the psychological problems caused by secrecy.[24]

Many states permit access to "nonidentifying information," such as medical histories, while requiring good cause or consent of all parties for identifying information. See, e.g., 23 Pa. Cons. Stat. Ann. §2905 (1991 & Supp. 2001). Some states have special provisions for access to medical information and history. See Del. Code Ann. tit. 13, §924 (1999).

Sealed records can create special problems for adoptive parents of "special needs" children whose medical histories might yield important information about their current problems. Some states now routinely authorize release of the child's medical history (and that of the parents and grandparents) to adoptive parents. See Okla. Stat. Ann. tit. 10, §7504-1.1 (West 1998).

### b. Law Reform

Two states, Alaska and Kansas, have long allowed adult adoptees to view their birth records. Alaska Stat. §18.50.500 (Michie 2000); Kan. Stat. Ann. §65-2423 (Supp. 2000). The modern wave of legislative reform elsewhere includes different approaches. (1) Some states have created voluntary registries that will provide information when both parties, e.g., birth family member and adoptee, have registered. E.g., Ark. Code Ann. §9-9-503 (Supp. 2001). Voluntary matching over the Internet, without state assistance, has made such laws obsolete. Adam Pertman, Adoption Nation: How the Adoption Revolution Is Transforming America 32 (2000). (2) Some states have statutes under which an intermediary will contact one party to obtain consent to release information once the other party has registered. E.g., Ind. Code Ann. §31-19-25-8 (Michie Supp. 2000). (3) Some states have enacted laws honoring a party's request for information in the absence of a veto registered by the other party. E.g., Mich. Comp. Laws Ann. §710.68(7) (Supp. 2001).

---

[24]. See, e.g., Robert S. Andersen, Why Adoptees Search: Motives and More, 67 Child Welfare 15, 18 (1988); Katherine A. Kowal & Karen Maitland Schilling, Adoption Through the Eyes of Adult Adoptees, 55 Am. J. Orthopsychiatry 354, 361 (1985). See also Annette Baran & Reuben Pannor, Open Adoption, in The Psychology of Adoption 316, 318 (David M. Brodzinky & Marshall D. Schechter eds., 1990).

More recently, some states have gone further. Tennessee enacted both a disclosure provision opening adoption records and a "contact veto" to be exercised if one party does not want communication from the other. Tenn. Code Ann. §§36-1-127; 36-1-128 (1996). An initiative in Oregon, Measure 58, gave adult adoptees access to their birth records. See Or. Rev. Stat. §432.240 (1999). These laws have been challenged by birth mothers who relinquished children under promises of confidentiality along with opponents who claim the reforms will encourage abortion and discourage adoption. Both state and federal courts have rejected arguments that these reforms unconstitutionally impair vested rights and the obligation of contracts and violate the rights of reproductive privacy and nondisclosure. See Doe v. Sundquist, 106 F.3d 702 (6th Cir.), *cert. denied,* 522 U.S. 810 (1997); Doe 1 v. State, 993 P.2d 822 (Or. Ct. App. 1999), *rev. denied,* 6 P.3d 1098 (Or.), *stay denied,* 530 U.S. 1228 (2000); Doe v. Sundquist, 2 S.W.3d 919 (Tenn. 1999). See generally Pertman, supra; Cahn & Singer, supra; Elizabeth J. Samuels, The Idea of Adoption: An Inquiry into the History of Adult Adoptee Access to Birth Records, 53 Rutgers L. Rev. 367 (2001).

### c. "Open Adoption"

The movement to open adoption records has focused on adoptees who have reached adulthood. In addition, the asserted "need to know" and the belief that secrecy can result in psychological difficulties for all parties have prompted a new approach, "open adoption," that focuses on young adoptees.[25]

### ■ GROVES v. CLARK
*982 P.2d 446 (Mont. 1999)*

Justice WILLIAM E. HUNT, SR. delivered the Opinion of the Court. . . .

This is the second appeal filed in this case concerning post-adoption visitation between Groves and L.C. A more detailed account of the facts of this case can be found in Groves v. Clark, 920 P.2d 981 [(Mont. 1996)]. To summarize, in January 1994, when L.C. was three years old, Groves signed a document terminating her parental rights to L.C., relinquishing custody of L.C. to Lutheran Social Services (LSS), and consenting to adoption. Groves and the Clarks signed a written visitation agreement

---

[25]. Open adoption was introduced in the literature in 1976 in an article noting the absence of secrecy in adoption in traditional Hawaiian culture. Annette Baran et al., Open Adoption, 21 Soc. Work 97 (1976). See Reuben Pannor & Annette Baran, Open Adoption as Standard Practice, 63 Child Welfare 245 (1984).

which provided the following: Groves would have unrestricted visitation with L.C. so long as she gave the Clarks two days notice; Groves would have unrestricted telephone contact with L.C.; and Groves would have the right to take L.C. out of school in the event she had to "go to Butte for some emergency." This agreement was drafted by the LSS and neither party consulted an attorney before signing it. In February 1994, the District Court entered an order terminating Groves' parental rights to L.C. and awarding custody of L.C. to LSS. In September 1994, the Clarks legally adopted L.C.

Groves and the Clarks abided by the terms of the visitation agreement until June 5, 1995, when Groves notified the Clarks that she wanted to take L.C. to Butte for the weekend and the Clarks refused. The Clarks told Groves that she was welcome to visit L.C. in their home, but could not take L.C. on extended out-of-town trips. [Groves then sought specific performance of the visitation agreement, and the Clarks objected, moving for summary judgment. The District Court denied Groves' petition for specific performance on the ground that the post-adoption visitation agreement was void and unenforceable. Groves appealed to this Court, which reversed, holding:]

> Birth parents and prospective adoptive parents are free to contract for post-adoption visitation and . . . trial courts must give effect to such contracts when continued visitation is in the best interest of the child.

We remanded the case to the District Court for a hearing on whether enforcement of the parties' visitation agreement would be in the best interest of L.C.

Based on the evidence produced at trial, the [District Court] found that a bond existed between Groves and L.C. and that it was highly likely L.C. would suffer from issues of abandonment, identity, and grieving unless appropriate visitation with Groves was granted. Ultimately, the court found that continued visitation between Groves and L.C. was in L.C.'s best interest. . . . Specifically, the court granted Groves unsupervised monthly weekend visitation with L.C. and required the parties to share equally in the transportation costs. Additionally, the court granted Groves telephone contact with L.C. at least once per week. The court recommended that the parties seek adoption counseling and attempt to agree upon future visitation modifications that may be appropriate as L.C. matures.

[On appeal,] the Clarks assert that the adoptive parents' wishes are paramount in deciding whether a post-adoption visitation agreement should be enforced. The Clarks cite several cases from other jurisdictions purportedly holding that adoptive parents have the right to determine whether it is in the best interest of the adopted child to maintain contact with the birth mother. [Citations omitted.] The Clarks also cite cases from other jurisdictions purportedly holding that the mere fact that the adoptive parents oppose visitation provides a sufficient basis for finding that visitation is not in the best interest of the child. [Citations omitted.]

We reject the Clarks' assertions. . . . The law in Montana, which also happens to be the law of this case, is clear: whether a post-adoption visitation agreement is enforceable shall be decided by the District Court pursuant to a "best interests" analysis. The adoptive parents' wishes is but one factor among many to be considered by the District Court.

Next, the Clarks argue that the court did not adequately consider and evaluate the evidence when applying the "best interests" standard. [The Clarks] testified that visitation adversely affected L.C. in that afterward she would evidence insecurity about her adoption status, would be moody and difficult to discipline. On the other hand, the court heard the testimony of the [Groves'] experts including Kathy Gerhke [an adoptive parenting instructor] and Debbie O'Brien [a family counselor] which explained this as a normal occurrence. Based on their testimony, this court finds that it is highly likely L.C. will suffer from issues of abandonment, identity, and grieving unless appropriate visitation is granted. L.C. lived with her mother for over three years. The evidence, including from a visitation facilitator, was that visitation was a happy experience for L.C.

We also reject the Clarks' assertion that the evidence did not support a finding that a bond existed between Groves and L.C. The record demonstrates that L.C. and Groves were together for the first three years of L.C.'s life. The court heard testimony from Debbie O'Brien, . . . who had been counseling Groves since August 1996. . . .

[T]he Clarks assert that visitation with Groves is not in L.C.'s best interests because the Clarks do not know the details of the visitation such as where L.C. will be, what L.C. will be doing, and with whom L.C. will be associating. The Clarks have expressed concern over L.C.'s sleeping arrangements at Groves' residence. The Clarks disapprove of L.C. snowmobiling and riding in a car without wearing a seatbelt. . . . These concerns were not presented to the District Court at trial. . . .

[W]e determine that the court's finding that visitation between Groves and L.C. was in the best interest of L.C. was not clearly erroneous. The finding was supported by substantial evidence, the court did not misapprehend the effect of the evidence, and we do not believe a mistake was committed. . . .

The Clarks argue that the court erred in modifying sua sponte the terms of the original visitation agreement because no statute or other legal authority exists granting the court this power. The Clarks argue that when the court found that visitation was in the best interests of L.C., the court was bound to enforce the parties' visitation agreement as written.

We agree with the District Court that modification of the parties' original visitation agreement was within its discretion in accordance with determining the best interests of L.C. The policy of this state is that "in matters relating to children, the best interests of the children are paramount." [F]ailure to apply this rule to disputes involving post-adoption visitation agreements could potentially lead to absurd results. It would be incongruous for a court to hold that visitation is in the best interest of a child and then enforce a visitation agreement that was not in the best interest of the child. For these reasons, we determine that the District Court did not abuse its discretion in modifying the parties' post-adoption visitation agreement. . . .

## Notes and Questions

1. The rise of open or cooperative adoption emerged from several developments: First, an increasing number of older children, with established bonds to their birth families, have been freed for adoption. Second, because of the decreased availability of the most sought-after infants for adoption following the legalization of abortion, birth parents can demand enhanced conditions in placement, including open-adoption arrangements. Finally, experts claim that an open system avoids the damaging psychological effects of anonymity for adoptees, birth parents and adopters. Annette Ruth Appell, The Move Toward Legally Sanctioned Cooperative Adoption: Can It Survive the Uniform Adoption Act?, 30 Fam. L.Q. 483, 483 (1996); Annette Baron & Reuben Pannor, Perspectives on Open Adoption, The Future of Children, Spring 1993, at 119, 119-121; Judith S. Lee & James A. Twaite, Open Adoption and Adoptive Mothers: Attitudes Toward Birthmothers, Adopted Children, and Parenting, 67 Am. J. Orthopsych. 576 (1997). See also Adam Pertman, Adoption Nation: How the Adoption Revolution Is Transforming America 47 (2000); Marianne Berry, Risks and Benefits of Open Adoption, The Future of Children, Spring 1993, at 125.

With data showing a majority of adoptions by relatives and stepparents and another fifth involving foster children, most adoptions today are not anonymous. Appell, supra, at 488-489.

2. Several states allow voluntary open adoption but permit the adoptive parents to determine whether to abide by such agreements. *Groves* cites cases from Arizona, Colorado, Maryland, and Pennsylvania taking this position. Alternatively, some states authorize judicial approval of such agreements upon a finding of best interests and then enforcement of agreements so approved. See, e.g., Minn. Stat. Ann. §259.58 (West Supp. 2001).

The UAA, §4-113, expressly provides for judicial enforcement of visitation agreements in stepparent adoptions. 9 U.L.A. (pt. IA) 110-112 (1999). Otherwise, however, it permits "mutually agreed-upon communication between birth and adoptive families" without making such agreements enforceable. See id. at 15 (Prefatory Note ¶9). The UAA's failure to dictate enforceability has evoked criticism from proponents of open adoption. See, e.g., Appell, supra. But see Margaret M. Mahoney, Open Adoption in Context: The Wisdom and Enforceability of Visitation Orders for Former Parents Under Uniform Adoption Act §4-113, 51 Fla. L. Rev. 89 (1999) (stepparent adoption as preferred context for openness).

3. Why does *Groves* go beyond all of these approaches, allowing courts to fashion arrangements that the parties have not chosen? Does *Groves* make adoptive parents "second class" parents? Should adoptive parents have the same rights as other parents to determine the extent of their children's visitation, if any, with legal strangers? See Troxel v. Granville, Chapter VII, at page 863. In *Groves*, who should resolve the asserted disputes about snowmobiling and seatbelts? Does open adoption conflict with the very concept of adoption, as some older cases have held? E.g., Hill v. Moorman, 525 So. 2d 681 (La. Ct. App. 1988); Cage v. Harrisonburg Dept. of Soc. Servs., 410 S.E.2d 405 (Va. Ct. App. 1991). Evaluate Professor Meyer's proposal for non-consensual open adoptions to solve the legal problem posed by birth parents' flawed consent in cases such as Baby Jessica and Baby Richard. See David D. Meyer, Family Ties: Solving the Constitutional Dilemma of the Faultless Father, 41 Ariz. L. Rev. 753, 833-846 (1999).

4. Some states have special rules permitting postadoption visitation by grandparents. E.g., Mo. Rev. Stat. §452.402.1(4) (2000); Tex. Fam. Code §161.206(c) (West 1996). Why not rely on the general best interests test for such cases? To what extent does *Troxel* make these laws constitutionally vulnerable? See, e.g., J.S. v. D.W., 2001 Ala. Civ. App. LEXIS 188 (Ala. Civ. App. May 4, 2001).

Case law has reached inconsistent results on postadoption grandparent visitation. Compare Jackson v. Tangreen, 18 P.3d 100 (Ariz. Ct. App. 2000) (no need for "clean break" with biological relatives in stepparent adoptions), with In re Adoption of RDS, 787 P.2d 968 (Wyo. 1990) (despite oral agreement, adoption severs relationship with biological family, so biological grandmother has no standing to seek visitation under grandparent visitation statute).

Are special rules warranted for postadoption visitation by biological siblings? Compare In re Adoption of Anthony, 448 N.Y.S.2d 377 (Fam. Ct. 1982) (ordering visitation in child's best interests), with Degrenier v. Reid, 716 N.E.2d 667 (Mass. Ct. App. 1999) (adoptive parents can bar sibling visitation).

5. *Guardianship.* Open adoption forms part of a larger debate about whether the parent-child relationship must be complete and exclusive or whether the law ought to recognize a child's connections with multiple parental figures. See, e.g., Katharine T. Bartlett, Rethinking Parenthood as an Exclusive Status: The Need for Legal Alternatives When the Premise of the Nuclear Family Has Failed, 70 Va. L. Rev. 879 (1984).

Professor Brigitte Bodenheimer pioneered this approach, suggesting as a "compromise" in contested adoption cases naming a guardian without terminating biological parents' rights. Brigitte M. Bodenheimer, New Trends and Requirements in Adoption Law and Proposals for Legislative Change, 49 S. Cal. L. Rev. 10, 41 (1975).

Traditionally, parents serve as a child's "natural guardians," but courts appoint a guardian for a minor (or incompetent) when parental care is unavailable or inadequate to serve a particular need of the child. See, e.g., Cotton v. Wise, 977 S.W.2d 263 (Mo. 1998). Most courts defer to parental autonomy in the appointment of a minor's guardian even after the parent's death. See, e.g., Bristol v. Brundage, 589 A.2d 1 (Conn. App. Ct. 1991). For illustrations of the use of guardianship law, see In re Guardianship of Kowalski, Chapter IV, section C4; Guardianship of Philip B., Chapter VIII, section B2c(ii).

The HIV/AIDS epidemic has prompted the development of a new type of guardianship, standby guardianship, enabling parents suffering from terminal illness to plan for the future of their children before death or incapacitation. This approach responds to the particular needs of ill single mothers by allowing for a "backup" guardian without requiring the mother to relinquish parental rights. See, e.g., Va. Code Ann. §§16.1-349 to -355 (Michie 1999).

For a review of the basic legal principles and a proposal for concurrent guardianship for children of single parents, see generally Joyce E. McConnell, Securing the Care of Children in Diverse Families: Building on Trends in Guardianship Reform, 10 Yale J.L. & Feminism 29 (1998).

### 4. Adoption Failure

■ **IN RE LISA DIANE G.**
   *537 A.2d 131 (R.I. 1988)*

KELLEHER, J.

The single but significant issue presented by this controversy is whether a Family Court justice can grant relief to the plaintiffs, the adoptive parents of a daughter who was eight years old in 1983 when the decree of adoption was entered in the Family Court. The gist of the parents' complaint is that the adoption decree was procured by the fraudulent conduct or misrepresentations of certain representatives of the Department of Children and Their Families (DCF). The parents contend that DCF never informed them that the staff at Bradley Hospital, an institution noted for its treatment of the emotionally disturbed, had informed DCF that the eight-year-old, because of her behavioral problems, should not be placed for adoption. In the Family Court the parents sought nullification of the adoption decree and compensation for the expenses they incurred in caring for the child.

For the most part, the 1987 hearing in the Family Court consisted of a bit of testimony by the child's adoptive parents and arguments of counsel. The trial justice brought matters to a halt, however, when he expressed doubt that the Family Court had jurisdiction over the relief sought. An order was entered denying the parents' complaint for a lack of jurisdiction. At the trial justice's insistence, counsel for DCF had filed a petition asking that the daughter, who is now a teenager, be declared a dependent child and placed in the custody of the state. This petition was granted. . . .

[W]e have ruled that a natural mother who has consented to have her child placed for adoption but subsequently seeks to vacate the adoption decree must prove her claim to relief by clear and convincing evidence. We believe that the same standard should be satisfied in situations in which, as here, the adopting parents are the ones seeking to invalidate the adoption decree. . . .

The Legislature has seen fit to vest exclusive jurisdiction in the area of adoptions in the Family Court. If the adoptive parents are to prevail on their claim of fraud or misrepresentation that has been perpetrated on them, the fraud or the misrepresentation has also been perpetrated on the Family Court. In these circumstances [of asserted fraud] we are of the belief that the Family Court, because of its exclusive jurisdiction in the subject matter of adoption, has the inherent power to adjudicate the claim now put forth by the adoptive parents.

The issue presently before us appears not to have been encountered with any degree of regularity in most jurisdictions. However, there have been instances where courts have permitted a challenge of adoption decrees by adoptive parents where fraud, misrepresentation, or undue influence has been alleged. County Department of Public Welfare v. Morningstar, 128 Ind. App. 688, 151 N.E.2d 150 (1958); Phyillips v. Chase, 203 Mass. 556, 89 N.E. 1049 (1909); In re Welfare of Alle, 304 Minn. 254, 230 N.W.2d 574 (1975); and Allen v. Allen, 214 Or. 664, 330 P.2d 151 (1958). See also 2 The Law of Domestic Relations in the United States 702 (2d ed. 1983); Annot., 2 A.L.R.2d 887, §§2, 8, 11 (1948). Any determination of the plaintiff's claim in the Family Court will necessarily involve a consideration of the child's best interest. However, this consideration must be balanced against the harm suffered by the adoptive parents as a result of the alleged conduct of DCF.

Accordingly the adoptive parents' appeal is sustained, and the dismissal order is vacated. The case is remanded to the Family Court for a trial and adjudication of the plaintiffs' claim.

---

The following excerpt amplifies the facts of In re Lisa Diane G.

■  **DANIEL GOLDEN, WHEN ADOPTION
    DOESN'T WORK . . .**
    *Boston Globe, June 11, 1989, Magazine Section, at 16.*

For years after Sheila was born in 1968, Bob and Joan Gordon
wanted another child, but the timing never seemed right. Even with two
incomes — he was a mechanic, she a lab technician — they barely scraped
by. They couldn't afford for Joan to take a maternity leave, never mind
paying for day care.

[In 1981,] Joan heard that Rhode Island, like other states, was offering older children for adoption. Here, she thought, was a practical
alternative. She would not have to quit her job, and Sheila's longing for
a younger sister might be fulfilled at last.

The Gordons, whose names have been changed in this story to protect their privacy, were very specific when social workers from the Rhode
Island Department of Children and Their Families visited their suburban home. They wanted a girl between the ages of 6 and 10 who would
be in school while they worked. She could have a physical disability, they
said, but not an emotional one. The Gordons knew their limits: A troubled girl would need more care than they felt ready to give. . . .

When Joan saw blond, blue-eyed Lisa, the hard-headed attitude she
had maintained throughout the adoption process yielded to her heart.
"Something instinctively told me to go with this child," she says. "Her
background was so traumatic. You wanted to just reach out and love this
little girl."

Only 6 years old, Lisa had suffered a lifetime's worth of pain and
separation. She never knew her father, and her mother abused her. Covered with bites and bruises, she was placed in a foster home. She was
adored there, but her stay ended abruptly when her foster father died
of a heart attack. She was removed from her next foster home after the
family accused her of killing its cat and trying to smother a baby. She
was then sent to a state-supervised group home. Along the way, she lost
contact with her older brother and sister, who had been adopted.

Lisa's social worker assured the Gordons that Lisa had emerged
from these upheavals emotionally intact. . . . "We were led to believe that
once she was part of a good, secure home, she would be fine, and her
problems would disappear," Joan says. Assuming they had been told all,
the Gordons never asked to read Lisa's file. . . .

Adoption is supposed to last a lifetime. Like marriage, it is meant to
be an unswerving commitment, for better or for worse. Yet, while adoption has a far higher success rate than marriage, it too is plagued by divorce. Today, an increasing number of adoptive parents are relinquishing
their children to the state, or even going to court to nullify the adoption. Most of these "disruptions," as they are termed, involve adoptions
of older children with physical or emotional problems stemming from

abuse by their natural parents. Infant adoptions are less prone to break up. . . . Beset by lawsuits from disenchanted parents, adoption agencies are reassessing their credo that all children can be adopted. . . .

The main reason for the surge in disruptions is a shift in the type of children being adopted. Until the 1970s, only infants were considered adoptable. Then an increase in abortions, coupled with greater social acceptance of single mothers, reduced the pool of available infants. At the same time, the number of abused and neglected older children was on the rise. Advocacy groups argued that these children, who were often warehoused in institutions or shunted from one foster home to another, needed adoptive homes. In 1980, a federal law enshrined "permanency planning" as a goal for children in state care; the law also expanded subsidies for adoptive parents. Like the deinstitutionalization of mental patients in the same era, this policy was both humanely intended and inexpensive, but it had the consequence of dumping some difficult people into a society that was not equipped to handle them. . . .

Once Lisa Gordon's adoption was finalized in 1983, the Department of Children and Their Families closed her case. Soon afterward, Joan Gordon decided that her daughter needed psychotherapy, and she asked the department to pay for it. . . . Late in 1984, Joan finally obtained medical insurance that covered therapy, and the family began seeing a psychologist. Instead of helping, Joan says, "the therapy was a catalyst for her to get worse." [For example, Lisa, who disliked the chore of fetching wood from the backyard, set fire to the wood pile.]

By 1985, the Gordons' house simmered with antagonism. Sensing the tension, Sheila's friends stopped coming over. . . . Bob's relationship with Lisa was, by turns, more antagonistic and more affectionate than Joan's. Lisa could goad her father into angry outbursts one minute and cuddle up to him the next. So Joan was not surprised one morning in April 1986 when Lisa . . . volunteered to fix the soup that Bob, as was his custom, would take to work. When Lisa gave him the thermos on his way out the door, he opened the lid and smelled something unusual. It was the disinfectant Lysol. . . .

It took one more incident for Joan to make up her mind. [Lisa told the school nurse her father had hit her with a board.] Obeying the law, the nurse reported the allegation to the state. After an investigation, the charges were dropped, and Joan went to the office of the state Department of Children and Their Families, saying she wouldn't leave until Lisa was removed from her house. State officials gave in and arranged for Lisa to be evaluated at Bradley Hospital, a psychiatric facility for children in Rhode Island.

Three members of the hospital's staff listened to Lisa describe the Lysol episode in a passionless monotone. One of them asked, "Did you want to kill him?" She said, simply, "Yes." She was admitted to the hospital immediately. . . .

## Notes and Questions

1. *Epilogue.* On remand, the court revoked the adoption. Lisa was institutionalized. The adoptive parents, who had also sought damages, withdrew that request. Subsequently, they dissolved their marriage, in part because of the stress Lisa had created. Telephone interview with Stephen E. Cicilline, attorney for plaintiffs ( July 23, 1997).

2. Adoption failure occurs either when the child is removed before the adoption is final (disruption) or when a final adoption is abrogated or annulled (dissolution). See Kathy S. Stolley, Statistics on Adoption in the United States, The Future of Children, Spring 1993, at 26, 31. The adoption failure rate is increasing because of the growing number of placements of special needs children (including older children) and children with previous foster care. About 10-14 percent of adoptions of special needs children "disrupt"; children placed between ages 10 and 14 have a disruption rate of 21 percent, with 35 percent for those over 15. Richard P. Barth, Risks and Rates of Adoption Disruption, in National Council for Adoption, Adoption Factbook III 381, 382 (1999).

3. When, if ever, should courts abrogate an adoption? Does abrogation ever serve the child's best interests? See Elizabeth N. Carroll, Abrogation of Adoption by Adoptive Parents, 19 Fam. L.Q. 155 (1985) (questioning arguments that it does). But see In re Adoption of B.J.H., 564 N.W.2d 387, 392-393 (Iowa 1997). Should cases be decided by courts based on equitable discretion or legislative criteria? See, e.g., Cal. Fam. Code §9100 (West 1994) (developmental disability or mental illness arising from conditions prior to adoption); Ky. Rev. Stat. Ann. §199.540(1) (Michie 1999) (different racial heritage). Who may petition for abrogation? What time limits, if any, should control? See, e.g., Mich. Comp. Laws Ann. §710.64(1) (West Supp. 2001) (21 days); Neb. Rev. Stat. §43-116 (1998) (2 years). See generally Anne Harlan Howard, Annulment of Adoption Decrees on Petition of Adoptive Parents, 22 J. Fam. L. 549 (1984). Does abrogation infringe the adoptee's constitutional rights? See In re Adoption of Kay C., 278 Cal. Rptr. 907 (Ct. App. 1991) (no).

4. *Wrongful adoption.* As an alternative to abrogation, some parents have successfully sued adoption agencies for fraud or the tort of "wrongful adoption," based on the defendant's concealment of the child's medical condition. See, e.g., Jackson v. State, 956 P.2d 35 (Mont. 1998); Mallette v. Children's Friend & Serv., 661 A.2d 67 (R.I. 1995).

Does recovery based on negligence violate public policy? One court explains:

> In short, to impose liability in a case such as this would in effect make the adoption agency a guarantor of the infant's future good health. That, of course, would be entirely unreasonable. After all, such a guarantee is

unavailable to natural parents who, when fortunate enough to bring into
the world a healthy child, have no guarantee whatsoever that the child will
continue to enjoy good physical and emotional health.

Richard P. v. Vista Del Mar Child Care Serv., 165 Cal. Rptr. 370, 374 (Ct.
App. 1980). But another concludes that "public policy does not preclude
a negligent misrepresentation action against an adoption agency where
the agency, having undertaken to disclose information about the child's
genetic parents and medical background to the adoptive parents, negligently withholds information in such a way that the adoptive parents
were misled as to the truth." M.H. v. Caritas Fam. Servs., 488 N.W.2d
282, 288 (Minn. 1993).

Must plaintiffs prove they would not have adopted but for the misrepresentation? See McKinney v. State, 950 P.2d 461 (Wash. 1998). Can
they recover for emotional distress? See Juman v. Louise Wise Servs.,
678 N.Y.S.2d 611 (App. Div. 1998). See generally Erica Shultz, Note, Ignoring Distress Signals: Why Courts Should Recognize Emotional Distress Damages in Wrongful Adoption Claims, 52 Fla. L. Rev. 1073 (2000).
Can agencies obtain valid waivers of disclosure? See Ferenc v. World
Child, Inc., 977 F. Supp. 56 (D.D.C. 1997), aff'd, 172 F.3d 919 (D.C. Cir.
1998) (yes). Does the adopted child have a claim? See Dahlin v. Evan-
gelical Child & Fam. Agency, 2001 U.S. Dist. LEXIS 10749 (N.D. Ill. July
24, 2001) (probably not).

5. Several modern statutes require full disclosure to prospective adoptive parents of the child's medical history, e.g., Ariz. Rev.
Stat. Ann. §8-129(A) (West 1999); Cal. Fam. Code §8706 (West Supp.
2001).

The UAA, §2-106, contains a detailed list of background information that must be disclosed to prospective adopters before they accept
physical custody of the child. The list includes current medical and
psychological history (including prenatal care), genetic diseases or
drug addictions by the genetic parent, performance in school, and allegations of parental abuse or neglect. 9 U.L.A. (pt. IA) 36-37 (1999).
How readily can such information be obtained? For exploration of this
question, see Marianne Brower Blair, The Uniform Adoption Act's
Health Disclosure Provisions: A Model That Should Not Be Overlooked, 30 Fam. L.Q. 427 (1996). See generally D. Marianne Brower
Blair, Lifting the Geneological Veil: A Blueprint for Legislative Reform
of the Disclosure of Health-Related Information in Adoption, 70 N.C.
L. Rev. 681 (1992).

6. To what extent do sealed-record laws, supra at pages 1198-1199,
facilitate fraud by adoption agencies? Do biological parents have a duty
of full disclosure in relinquishing their children? Will subsidized adoption of children with special needs reduce the need for fraud?

## Problems

1. Tony and Sam, biological brothers, are adopted by a childless couple. Six years later, the couple persuades a court to annul the adoption of Tony (now 10) because of his failure to bond with them. The couple keeps Sam (now 8) as their son and refuses to let him visit Tony, whom they regard as a bad influence.

Tony approaches a social worker in the orphanage where he now resides and requests a lawyer to help secure him visitation with Sam. The social worker persuades you to take Tony's case. How will you proceed? What strategies will you explore? What result? See Barbara Jones, Note, Do Siblings Possess Constitutional Rights?, 78 Cornell L. Rev. 1187 (1993). See also William Wesley Patton & Sara Latz, Severing Hansel From Gretel: An Analysis of Siblings' Association Rights, 48 U. Miami L. Rev. 745 (1994). Compare In re Adoption of Deborah, 681 So. 2d 22 (La. Ct. App. 1996), with In re Adoption of Anthony, 448 N.Y.S.2d 377 (Fam. Ct. 1982).

2. Barbara gives birth to a child and relinquishes him to the Children's Home Society (CHS), a state-licensed private adoption agency, which places the baby in an adoptive family. As part of the relinquishment process, CHS provides counseling for Barbara. It also obtains detailed health and background information from her. Ten years later Barbara marries and has two children, a daughter and a son. When this son dies in infancy, Barbara learns she carries a genetic defect that afflicts male offspring. Barbara contacts CHS to determine the health of her first son and learns from CHS that he, too, suffers from the genetic disease.

Barbara sues CHS for wrongful death, negligent and intentional infliction of emotional distress, and fraud. In essence, she claims CHS had a duty to inform her of the genetic disease of the son she relinquished, to enable her to make informed choices about future childbearing. What result? See Olson v. Children's Home Soc., 252 Cal. Rptr. 11 (Ct. App. 1988). But cf. Viccaro v. Milunsky, 551 N.E.2d 8 (Mass. 1990).

## E. ALTERNATIVES TO ADOPTION

### 1. Artificial Insemination

Medicine and technology offer alternatives to adoption, enabling childless couples to become parents. Artificial insemination, which has been practiced the longest, is the simplest and most commonly used of these methods of assisted conception.[26]

---

[26]. Well over 100,000 women undergo artificial insemination in the United States each year. In 1987, the number was 172,000. Congress of the United States, Office of Technology Assessment, Artificial Insemination in the United States: Summary of a 1987 Survey — Background Paper 3 (1988). Some authorities now prefer the term "alternative

### a. Creating Traditional Families

■ **IN RE ADOPTION OF ANONYMOUS**
*345 N.Y.S.2d 430 (Surr. Ct. 1973)*

SOBEL, Surrogate. . . .

As a preliminary, there are two types of artificial insemination. Homologous insemination is the process by which the wife is artificially impregnated with the semen of her husband [(AIH).] Heterologous insemination is the artificial insemination of the wife by the semen of a third-party donor [(AID).]

. . . The utilization of AID procedures is bound to increase because of the unavailability — no doubt due to the "pill" and liberalized abortion laws — of adoptive children. Relatively recent too is the practice of AID where the husband's family has a history of hereditary disease or where RH incompatibility has led to repeated stillbirths. . . .

The facts in this proceeding are briefly stated. During the marriage the child was born of consensual AID. The husband was listed as the father on the birth certificate. Later the couple separated and the separation was followed by a divorce. Both the separation agreement and the divorce decree declare the child to be the "daughter" and "child" of the couple. The wife was granted support and the husband visitation rights. He has faithfully visited and performed all the support conditions of the decree. The wife later remarried and her new husband is petitioning to adopt the child. The first husband has refused his consent. Confronted with that legal impediment, the petitioner has suggested that the first husband's consent is not required since he is not the "parent" of the child. . . . If the husband is the "parent" of a child born of consensual AID, in the absence of his consent to the adoption, the petition must be dismissed. . . .

The leading case . . . is People v. Sorensen [, 68 Cal. 2d 680 (1968)]. *Sorensen* was a criminal prosecution on complaint of the welfare authorities against the husband for failure to support a minor child born during the marriage of consensual AID. The California Supreme Court without dissent held: the defendant is the lawful father of a dependent child born of consensual AID; that the term "father" as used in the penal statute is not limited to a biologic or natural father; the determinative factor is whether the legal relationship of father and child exists. The court reasoned that a child conceived through AID does not have a "natural" father; that the anonymous donor is not the "natural" father; that he does have a "lawful" father and the intent of the Legislature was

---

insemination" to "artificial insemination." See Mary Lyndon Shanley, Making Babies, Making Families: What Matters Most in an Age of Reproductive Technologies, Surrogacy, Adoption, and Same-Sex and Unwed Parents 80 (2001).

to include a lawful father in the penal sanctions; further, that "In light of these principles of statutory construction, a reasonable man who, because of his inability to procreate, actively participates and consents to his wife's artificial insemination in the hope that a child will be produced whom they will treat as their own, knows that such behavior carries with it the legal responsibilities of fatherhood and criminal liability for nonsupport. . . ." This is the principle of equitable estoppel found in several other cases.

With respect to AID as constituting adultery of the mother the court added: "In the absence of legislation prohibiting artificial insemination, the offspring of defendant's valid marriage to the child's mother was lawfully begotten and was not the product of an illicit or adulterous relationship." As respects the legitimacy of the child: "Nor are we persuaded that the concept of legitimacy demands that the child be the actual offspring of the husband of the mother and if semen of some other male is utilized the resulting child is illegitimate."

The leading case in New York and the only one which discusses the issue is Gursky v. Gursky [39 Misc. 2d 1083 (1963)]. The court found an implied promise to support the child and equitable estoppel from the consent of the husband to the AID procedures. The basic finding however was that "the child . . . which was indisputably the offspring of artificial insemination by a third-party donor with the consent of the mother's husband, is not the legitimate issue of the husband." . . .

. . . *Gursky* is not persuasive. It is the only published decision which flatly holds that AID children are illegitimate. It has been criticized. (Note, 1968 U. of Ill. L. Forum 203, 208.) The "historical concept" and the statutory definition of "a child born out of wedlock" upon which it relies were developed and enacted long before the advent of the practice of artificial insemination. The birth of AID children was not then contemplated. An AID child is not "begotten" by a father who is not the husband; the donor is anonymous; the wife does not have sexual intercourse or commit adultery with him; if there is any "begetting" it is by the doctor who in this specialty is often a woman. The suggestion that the husband might not regard the child as his own has been dispelled by our gratifying experience with adoptive parents. Since there is consent by the husband, there is no marital infidelity. The child is not born "out of wedlock" but in and during wedlock. And finally legislative inaction is an unsound basis for any inferences favorable or unfavorable. . . .

Basically the problem of the status of AID children vis-à-vis the "father" is one of policy. . . . New York has a strong policy in favor of legitimacy [so] it would seem absurd to hold illegitimate a child born during a valid marriage, of parents desiring but unable to conceive a child, and both consenting and agreeing to the impregnation of the mother by a carefully and medically selected anonymous donor. [O]ur liberal policy is for the protection of the child, not the parents. It serves no purpose whatsoever to stigmatize the AID child; or to compel the parents formally to adopt in order to confer upon the AID child the status and rights of a naturally conceived child.

[A] child born of consensual AID during a valid marriage is a legitimate child entitled to the rights and privileges of a naturally conceived child of the same marriage. The father of such child is therefore the "parent" (Domestic Relations Law, §111) whose consent is required to the adoption of such child by another. . . .

## Notes and Questions

1. Approximately 5.3 million Americans or 9 percent of the population of reproductive age suffer infertility. Of the 80 percent of the cases with a diagnosed cause, about half stem from male factors and half from female factors. Tamar Nordenberg, Overcoming Infertility, U.S. Food and Drug Administration, FDA Consumer, Jan.-Feb. 1997, at 18. Use of AIH as a medical response to male infertility reportedly began in the 1790s and AID in 1884. See Lee M. Silver, Remaking Eden: How Genetic Engineering and Cloning Will Transform the American Family 178-179 (1998).

2. *Statutory responses.* Many jurisdictions now address by statute the issue presented in *Anonymous.* Eighteen have followed the 1973 Uniform Parentage Act, whose §5 recognizes as the father the husband who consents in writing to AID performed by a licensed physician and states that the "donor of semen provided to a licensed physician for artificial insemination of a woman other than the donor's wife is treated in law as if he were not the natural father. . . ." Unif. Parentage Act, 9B U.L.A. 377, 407-408 (2001). The new Uniform Parentage Act (UPA (2000)) reaches the same result in §§702 and 704, while also stating that the husband's failure to consent to assisted reproduction does not preclude his recognition as father. 9B U.L.A. 355-356 (2001). See also ALI Principles §§2.03, 3.03 (estoppel).

3. *The adoption analogy. Anonymous* examines *Gursky,* in which the husband's duty to support an AID child rested on his implied promise and equitable estoppel. Does this approach apply the principle of equitable adoption or equitable parenthood to consensual artificial insemination? See generally Bridget R. Penick, Note, Give the Child a Legal Father: A Plea for Iowa to Adopt a Statute Regulating Artificial Insemination by Anonymous Donor, 83 Iowa L. Rev. 633 (1998).

What other principles from adoption law should apply to artificial insemination cases? Should the husband of a woman who uses AID undertake a stepparent adoption of the child? See Welborn v. Doe, 394 S.E.2d 732 (Va. Ct. App. 1990). If a state recognizes an adoptee's "right to know" information about biological parents, should the same right be-

long to an individual conceived by AID? The 1973 Uniform Parentage
Act (§5) explicitly provided for sealed records. 9B U.L.A. 407 (2001).
But see Lori B. Andrews & Nanette Elster, Adoption, Reproductive
Technologies, and Genetic Information, 8 Health Matrix 125, 135 (1998)
(AID laws in 18 states allow access to records for good cause shown, but
identifying information not necessarily available).

4. The practice of artificial insemination resulted in a famous case
of fraud. In 1992, Dr. Cecil Jacobson was convicted on 52 counts of fraud
and perjury for telling his patients he used semen from anonymous
donors for artificial insemination when in fact he used his own. For federal prosecutors, the case posed unique questions about privacy rights
versus law enforcement: On the one hand, the patients had a right to
know about their physician's alleged fraud, and genetic testing of the
children would be necessary to prove the case. On the other hand, suppose the family members would prefer not to know. How should the
prosecutors proceed? See Sabra Chartrand, Parents Recall Ordeal of
Prosecuting in Artificial-Insemination Fraud Case, N.Y. Times, Mar. 15,
1992, §1, at 16. The DNA tests ultimately revealed that Jacobson had fathered 15 children in the seven families participating in the case until
conclusion. Id. Jacobson was sentenced to five years in prison and ordered to pay fines and restitution exceeding $116,000. See United States
v. Jacobson, 4 F.3d 987, 1993 WL 343172 (4th Cir. 1993) (unpublished
opinion upholding convictions on appeal), cert. denied, 511 U.S. 1069
(1994). In subsequent malpractice litigation, the court of appeals directed the trial judge to consider affording Jacobson's patients the "rare
dispensation" of proceeding as anonymous plaintiffs in recognition of
the "critical" privacy concerns raised. James v. Jacobson, 6 F.3d 233, 238
(4th Cir. 1993).

5. What role should the state play in screening and checking the
medical histories of semen donors? What records should be kept? What
risks follow from inadequate donor screening and record-keeping?

A government study examined donor screening in artificial insemination. Physician practice of artificial insemination results in the birth of
approximately 65,000 babies each year. The study found wide variations
in donor screening, with only about half the physicians screening for genetic diseases and defects or requiring diagnostic tests of donors other
than for fertility and a similar fraction keeping records that would permit donor identification. See Congress of the United States, Office of
Technology Assessment, Artificial Insemination Practice in the United
States: Summary of a 1987 Survey — Background Paper 9-11 (1988).
See also Johnson v. Superior Ct., 95 Cal. Rptr. 2d 864 (Ct. App. 2000)
(plaintiff family can compel anonymous donor's deposition in negligence
action against sperm bank for using semen with family history of kidney
disease). But see N.H. Rev. Stat. Ann. §§168-B:10, 168-B:12 (Supp.
2000) (medical evaluation of sperm donors and recipients required). See

generally Karen M. Ginsberg, Note, FDA Approved? A Critique of the Artificial Insemination Industry in the United States, 30 U. Mich. J.L. Reform 823 (1997); Anita M. Hodgson, Note, The Warranty of Sperm: A Modest Proposal to Increase the Accountability of Sperm Banks and Physicians in the Performance of Artificial Insemination Procedures, 26 Ind. L. Rev. 357 (1993).

6. *AIH. Anonymous* distinguishes AID from AIH, a practice sometimes used when the husband's fertility problems consist of a low sperm count or decreased motility. Families might also use AIH when the husband (or other prospective father) faces a life- or health-threatening situation, such as war or illness. Semen frozen and stored in advance can be used later even after the man's death.

But storing sperm entails risks as well. A New York lawsuit claimed that a woman had received semen other than that her deceased husband had stored before undergoing chemotherapy. She learned of the mix-up when the daughter born from the procedure had African-American characteristics although the mother and her husband were both white. Barbara Kantrowitz et al., Not the Right Father, Newsweek, March 19, 1990, at 50. See also Harnicher v. University of Utah Med. Ctr., 962 P.2d 67 (Utah 1998) (no emotional distress damages in malpractice claims for use of wrong donor semen, preventing couple from presenting children as husband's biological offspring); Marlise Simons, Uproar Over Twins and a Dutch Couple's Anguish, N.Y. Times, June 28, 1995, at A3 (Caucasian husband's semen accidently mixed, resulting in one white and one multi-race twin). See generally Fred Norton, Note, Assisted Reproduction and the Frustration of Genetic Affinity: Interest, Injury, and Damages, 74 N.Y.U. L. Rev. 793 (1999). For consideration of other problems arising from the preservation of genetic material, see infra at pages 1218-1219, 1248-1254.

## Problem

Marcia wants to have children but her husband Eric does not. Marcia decides to pursue AID. Although Eric voices his objection, Marcia proceeds. She later gives birth to a son, whom blood tests show cannot be Eric's biological child. In divorce proceedings that begin before the baby's birth, Marcia seeks child support from Eric. She argues the child has a right to support. In claiming that he has no duty to pay, Eric invokes a state statute like the provision of the 1973 Uniform Parentage Act expressly referring to the husband's consent. What result? See In re Marriage of Witbeck-Wildhagen, 667 N.E.2d 122 (Ill. App. Ct. 1996). See also R.S. v. R.S., 670 P.2d 923 (Kan. Ct. App. 1983); K.S. v. G.S., 440 A.2d 64 (N.J. Super. Ct. Ch. Div. 1981); Lane v. Lane, 912 P.2d 290 (N.M. Ct. App. 1996); 9B U.L.A. 357 (2001) (§705 of new UPA). Who has the burden of proof on the consent issue? See Jackson v.

Jackson, 739 N.E.2d 1203 (Ohio Ct. App. 2000). Can Eric recover in tort from the physician? Cf. Shin v. Kong, 95 Cal. Rptr. 2d 304 (Ct. App. 2000). See generally Karen DeHaan, Note, Whose Child Am I? A Look at How Consent Affects a Husband's Obligation to Support a Child Conceived Through Heterologous Artificial Insemination, 37 Brandeis L.J. 809 (1998-1999).

### b. Creating Nontraditional Families

■ **ALISON D. v. VIRGINIA M.**
*572 N.E.2d 27 (N.Y. 1991)*

Review case, reprinted in Chapter VII, at page 870.

### Notes and Questions

1. When an unmarried woman like Virginia M. (or Susan in *Adoption of Tammy,* supra) uses artificial insemination from a known donor to conceive, does the resulting child have *no* father on the theory that the law does not recognize semen donors as fathers?

Should the answer depend on the donor's wishes? The mother's? See In re R.C., 775 P.2d 27 (Colo. 1989) (en banc). The conduct of the parties? See LaChapelle v. Mitten, 607 N.W.2d 151 (Minn. Ct. App.), *cert. denied,* 531 U.S. 1011 (2000); Thomas S. v. Robin Y., 618 N.Y.S.2d 356 (App. Div. 1994). The participation of a physician? See Jhordan C. v. Mary K., 224 Cal. Rptr. 530 (Ct. App. 1986). See also Alexandria S. v. Pacific Fertility Med. Ctr., 64 Cal. Rptr. 2d 23 (Ct. App. 1997). The best interests of the child? See C.M. v. C.C., 377 A.2d 821 (N.J. Super. Ct. 1977); C.M. v. C.C., 407 A.2d 849 (N.J. Juv. & Dom. Rel. Ct., Cumberland County 1979). The child's place in a two-parent family unit headed by two lesbians? See *Tammy,* supra. The asserted constitutional rights of any of these individuals? See McIntyre v. Crouch, 780 P.2d 239 (Or. Ct. App. 1989), *cert. denied,* 495 U.S. 905 (1990). Note that recognition as father entails not only support obligations but also visitation rights. See also Unif. Parentage Act (2000) §702 & cmt. 9B U.L.A. 355 (2001) (donor not recognized even if woman unmarried); Unif. Putative and Unknown Fathers Act §1, 9C U.L.A. 63 (2001) (excluding from definition of "father" semen donor whose identity is not known to mother or whose circumstances indicate no anticipation of interest in resulting child). See generally Anne R. Schiff, Frustrated Intentions and Binding Biology: Seeking AID in the Law, 44 Duke L.J. 524 (1994).

2. Should states restrict artificial insemination to "conventional families"? Some statutes provide that practitioners can perform artificial insemination "only at the request and with the written consent of the

husband and wife." See Okla. Stat. Ann. tit. 10, §553 (West 1998). Should recipients receive the same screening and state approval (through judicial proceedings) as adoptive parents?

Would restricting AID to married couples withstand the constitutional challenge of an individual denied the opportunity to use AID? In a Michigan case, settled out of court, a single woman sued Wayne State University's artificial insemination clinic, which restricted its services to married women. See Lori B. Andrews, New Conceptions 194-195 (1984). See generally Catherine DeLair, Ethical, Moral, Economic and Legal Barriers to Assisted Reproductive Technologies Employed by Gay Men and Lesbian Women, 4 DePaul J. Health Care L. 147 (2000); Holly J. Harlow, Paternalism Without Paternity: Discrimination Against Single Women Seeking Artificial Insemination by Donor, 6 S. Cal. Rev. L. & Women's Stud. 173 (1996).

Although physicians accept four out of five women requesting artificial insemination, the most common reason for rejection is the woman's unmarried status. Artificial Insemination Practice in the United States, supra, at 27. By contrast, the Sperm Bank of Northern California is committed to accepting any healthy woman or couple regardless of marital status, sexual preference, age, race, or religion. Id. at 65. What rights and responsibilities does the mother's domestic partner have? See, e.g., Dunkin v. Boskey, 98 Cal. Rptr. 2d 44 (Ct. App. 2000) (male partner who was promised parental role can recover economic losses in unjust enrichment for exclusion from child's life); In re M.J. 759 N.E.2d 121 (Ill. App. Ct. 2001) (no responsibility without written agreement).

3. What are the implications of AID for gender roles and the traditional family? Judge Posner observes:

> Artificial insemination, even of the old-fashioned sort, is rich with social implications. We have seen that, as a practical matter, it places lesbian custody of children beyond the reach of governmental regulation. Beyond that, it allows women to escape having to share parental rights with men, since the sperm donor, whether provided through the woman's physician or through a sperm bank, is anonymous. It therefore accelerates the shift of economic power from men to women. . . .

Richard A. Posner, Sex and Reason 421 (1992).

4. *Posthumous insemination.* What "property" rights does a semen donor retain in his sperm? For example, if man who had cryogenically preserved his semen dies, does he have testamentary disposition over this "asset"?

Hecht v. Superior Court, 20 Cal. Rptr. 2d 275 (Ct. App. 1993), addressed this question in a will contest between Deborah Hecht, the girlfriend of decedent William Kane, and Kane's adult children from a prior marriage. Before committing suicide, Kane deposited semen in a sperm bank and willed the semen to Hecht. Kane's children urged destruction of the semen, to prevent the birth of children outside "a traditional family" and to protect existing family members from financial and emotional distress. Id. at 279.

The court concluded that "at the time of his death, decedent had an interest, in the nature of ownership, to the extent that he had decision-making authority as to the use of his sperm for reproduction. Such interest is sufficient to constitute 'property' within the meaning of [the] Probate Code." Id. at 283. According to the court, California case law and statutes fail to support a public policy against insemination of unmarried women, and Kane's children failed to persuade the court initially that it would be better for a posthumously conceived child not to be born, sufficient to overcome the decedent's decision. The court subsequently ordered release of the sperm to Hecht. 59 Cal. Rptr. 2d 222 (Ct. App. 1996). See also Hall v. Fertility Inst. of New Orleans, 647 So. 2d 1348 (La. Ct. App. 1994).

Posthumous reproduction presents challenges for traditional legal rules, for example, a presumption of legitimacy that applies to children born during or within 300 days of the end of a marriage. See, e.g., In re Estate of Kolacy, 753 A.2d 1257 (N.J. Super. Ct. Chan. Div. 2000) (recognizing children born 18 months after father's death as his intestate heirs). In Woodward v. Commissioner of Soc. Sec., 760 N.E.2d 257 (Mass. 2002), the court answered a certified question about the intestacy rights of twins conceived posthumously with the widow's husband's frozen semen. The court held that the right to intestate succession would be recognized for such children when the surviving parent in a timely manner establishes the decedent's genetic relationship and the decedent's affirmative consent to posthumous conception and support. Section 707 of the Uniform Parentage Act of 2000 provides that a spouse who dies before the implantation of eggs, sperm, or embryos is not a parent unless he or she consented in a record to posthumous reproduction. 9B U.L.A. 358 (2001). A predecessor model statute articulated the same rule but used the term "individual" rather than "spouse." §4(b) Unif. Status of Children of Assisted Conception Act, 9C U.L.A. 371 (2001). What explains the change?

See generally Gloria J. Banks, Traditional Concepts and Nontraditional Conceptions: Social Security Survivor's Benefits for Posthumously Conceived Children, 32 Loy. L.A. L. Rev. 251 (1999); Anne Reichman Schiff, Arising from the Dead: Challenges of Posthumous Procreation, 75 N.C. L. Rev. 901 (1997); Michelle L. Brenwald & Kay Redeker, Note, A Primer on Posthumous Conception and Related Issues of Assisted Reproduction, 38 Washburn L.J. 599 (1999).

## Problems

1. SB and DB, husband and wife, actively try to start a family. Tragedy strikes unexpectedly. SB is admitted to a hospital with suspected

meningitis. He becomes unconscious and comatose. At DB's request, physicians take several sperm samples from SB and stores them, just before SB dies.

DB now seeks release of the sperm samples to her for purposes of artificial insemination. The hospital (assume it is a state hospital in the United States) refuses, citing the absence of SB's written consent. On what bases might DB challenge the hospital's decision? Will she succeed? See R. v. Human Fertilisation and Embryology Auth., [1996] 3 C.M.L.R. 921. See also Lori B. Andrews, The Clone Age: Adventures in the New World of Reproductive Technology 222-236 (1999); Carson Strong, Consent to Sperm Retrieval and Insemination After Death or Persistent Vegetative State, 14 J.L. & Health 243 (1999-2000); Laura A. Dwyer, Note, Dead Daddies: Issues in Postmortem Reproduction, 52 Rutgers L. Rev. 881, 886-888 (2000).

2. Ellen and Lynn, two women living in Vermont, enter a civil union under the law enacted in response to Baker v. State (see Chapter II, at pages 181-182). With Lynn's enthusiastic agreement, Ellen conceives through donor insemination (AID) and gives birth to a daughter, Tess. Ellen and Lynn share equally in the childrearing and financial responsibilities for Tess although Lynn never formally adopts the child. When Tess is five, Ellen and Lynn dissolve their civil union. In court, Ellen claims that she alone should have custody as the child's only legal parent. Lynn argues that she too is a legal parent on two bases: the presumption of legitimacy and the rules governing AID that would have applied to her if she had been a man married to Ellen. Invoking *Baker*, Lynn asserts that the civil union legislation must give her the benefit of *all* of the legal consequences of marriage, including the presumption of legitimacy and the rules governing AID for married women. Ellen counterargues that the presumption and the AID rules apply only to the mother's husband and that a female partner in a civil union can never be a husband. What result and why? See Vt. Stat Ann. tit. 15 §1204(f) (Supp. 2000). See also ALI Principles §§2.03, 3.03 (estoppel).

## 2. Surrogacy[27]

When a female factor causes infertility, some couples turn to a "surrogate mother" to bear a child for them. This form of assisted conception may also appeal to couples in which the woman has a genetic or other disease, single men, and gay male couples. Under what legal rubric

---

[27]. The terminology raises legitimate questions. For example, how can a woman who conceives and gestates a child be considered the "surrogate" or substitute mother — rather than simply the mother? Despite this problem, we continue to use the language associated with the famous *Baby M* case although other authorities now have developed different terms. See, e.g., Unif. Parentage Act, 9B U.L.A. 360-361 (2001) (Prefatory Comment to Art. 8, "Gestational Agreement").

should surrogacy cases be approached? Does surrogacy resemble adoption? Or artificial insemination? Or does surrogacy raise unique problems meriting development of special rules?

■ **IN RE BABY M**
*537 A.2d 1227 (N.J. 1988)*

WILENTZ, C.J. . . .

In February 1985, William Stern and Mary Beth Whitehead entered into a surrogacy contract. It recited that Stern's wife, Elizabeth, was infertile, that they wanted a child, and that Mrs. Whitehead was willing to provide that child as the mother with Mr. Stern as the father.

The contract provided that through artificial insemination using Mr. Stern's sperm, Mrs. Whitehead would become pregnant, carry the child to term, bear it, deliver it to the Sterns, and thereafter do whatever was necessary to terminate her maternal rights so that Mrs. Stern could thereafter adopt the child. Mrs. Whitehead's husband, Richard, was also a party to the contract; Mrs. Stern was not. Mr. Whitehead promised to do all acts necessary to rebut the presumption of paternity under the Parentage Act. N.J.S.A. 9:17-43a(1), -44a. Although Mrs. Stern was not a party to the surrogacy agreement, the contract gave her sole custody of the child in the event of Mr. Stern's death. . . .

Mr. Stern, on his part, agreed to attempt the artificial insemination and to pay Mrs. Whitehead $10,000 after the child's birth, on its delivery to him. In a separate contract, Mr. Stern agreed to pay $7,500 to the Infertility Center of New York ("ICNY"). The Center's advertising campaigns solicit surrogate mothers and encourage infertile couples to consider surrogacy. ICNY arranged for the surrogacy contract by bringing the parties together, explaining the process to them, furnishing the contractual form, and providing legal counsel.

The history of the parties' involvement in this arrangement suggests their good faith. William and Elizabeth Stern were married in July 1974, having met at the University of Michigan, where both were Ph.D. candidates. Due to financial considerations and Mrs. Stern's pursuit of a medical degree and residency, they decided to defer starting a family until 1981. . . . Based on the perceived risk [of Mrs. Stern's possible multiple sclerosis,] the Sterns decided to forego having their own children. The decision had special significance for Mr. Stern. Most of his family had been destroyed in the Holocaust. As the family's only survivor, he very much wanted to continue his bloodline.

Initially the Sterns considered adoption, but were discouraged by the substantial delay apparently involved and by the potential problem they saw arising from their age and their differing religious backgrounds. . . .

The paths of Mrs. Whitehead and the Sterns to surrogacy were similar. Both responded to advertising by ICNY. . . . Mrs. Whitehead's response apparently resulted from her sympathy with family members and others who could have no children (she stated that she wanted to give another couple the "gift of life"); she also wanted the $10,000 to help her family. . . . On February 6, 1985, Mr. Stern and Mr. and Mrs. Whitehead executed the surrogate parenting agreement. After several artificial inseminations over a period of months, Mrs. Whitehead became pregnant. The pregnancy was uneventful and on March 27, 1986, Baby M was born. . . .

Mrs. Whitehead realized, almost from the moment of birth, that she could not part with this child. . . . Nonetheless, Mrs. Whitehead was, for the moment, true to her word. Despite powerful inclinations to the contrary, she turned her child over to the Sterns on March 30 at the Whiteheads' home.

The Sterns were thrilled with their new child [whom they named Melissa]. They had planned extensively for its arrival. . . . Later in the evening of March 30, Mrs. Whitehead became deeply disturbed, disconsolate, stricken with unbearable sadness. She had to have her child. . . . The Sterns, concerned that Mrs. Whitehead might indeed commit suicide, not wanting under any circumstances to risk that, and in any event believing that Mrs. Whitehead would keep her word [that she would return her in a week], turned the child over to her. . . .

The struggle over Baby M began when it became apparent that Mrs. Whitehead could not return the child to Mr. Stern. Due to Mrs. Whitehead's refusal to relinquish the baby, Mr. Stern filed a complaint seeking enforcement of the surrogacy contract. . . . After the order [in favor of Stern] was entered, ex parte, the process server, aided by the police, in the presence of the Sterns, entered Mrs. Whitehead's home to execute the order. Mr. Whitehead fled with the child, who had been handed to him through a window while those who came to enforce the order were thrown off balance by a dispute over the child's current name.

The Whiteheads immediately fled to Florida with Baby M. . . . Police in Florida enforced [a court order obtained by Mr. Stern], forcibly removing the child from her grandparents' home. She was soon thereafter brought to New Jersey and turned over to the Sterns. [The ex parte order awarding custody to the Sterns pendente lite was affirmed.] Pending final judgment, Mrs. Whitehead was awarded limited visitation with Baby M. . . .

The trial took thirty-two days over a period of more than two months. [The trial court] held that the surrogacy contract was valid; ordered that Mrs. Whitehead's parental rights be terminated and that sole custody of the child be granted to Mr. Stern; and, after hearing brief testimony from Mrs. Stern, immediately entered an order allowing the adoption of Melissa by Mrs. Stern, all in accordance with the surrogacy contract.

Pending the outcome of the appeal, we granted a continuation of visitation to Mrs. Whitehead, although slightly more limited than the visitation allowed during the trial.

Although clearly expressing its view that the surrogacy contract was valid, the trial court devoted the major portion of its opinion to the question of the baby's best interests. . . . Its rationalization . . . was that while the surrogacy contract was valid, specific performance would not be granted unless that remedy was in the best interests of the child. The factual issues confronted and decided by the trial court were the same as if Mr. Stern and Mrs. Whitehead had had the child out of wedlock, intended or unintended, and then disagreed about custody. . . .

On the question of best interests [in this appeal by Mrs. Whitehead, we] agree substantially with both [the trial court's] analysis and conclusions on the matter of custody. The court's review and analysis of the surrogacy contract, however, is not at all in accord with ours. . . .

### INVALIDITY AND UNENFORCEABILITY OF SURROGACY CONTRACT . . .

#### A. CONFLICT WITH STATUTORY PROVISIONS

The surrogacy contract conflicts with: (1) laws prohibiting the use of money in connection with adoptions; (2) laws requiring proof of parental unfitness or abandonment before termination of parental rights is ordered or an adoption is granted; and (3) laws that make surrender of custody and consent to adoption revocable in private placement adoptions. . . .

(1) . . . Considerable care was taken in this case to structure the surrogacy arrangement so as not to violate [the prohibition on payment in connection with adoption]. The arrangement was structured as follows: the adopting parent, Mrs. Stern, was not a party to the surrogacy contract; the money paid to Mrs. Whitehead was stated to be for her services — not for the adoption; the sole purpose of the contract was stated as being that "of giving a child to William Stern, its natural and biological father"; the money was purported to be "compensation for services and expenses and in no way . . . a fee for termination of parental rights or a payment in exchange for consent to surrender a child for adoption"; the fee to the Infertility Center ($7,500) was stated to be for legal representation, advice, administrative work, and other "services." Nevertheless, it seems clear that the money was paid and accepted in connection with an adoption [in violation of criminal law]. As for the contention that the Sterns are paying only for services and not for an adoption, we need note only that they would pay nothing in the event the child died before the fourth month of pregnancy, and only $1,000 if the child were stillborn, even though the "services" had been fully rendered. . . .

The prohibition of our statute is strong. Violation constitutes a high misdemeanor, N.J.S.A. 9:3-54c, a third-degree crime, N.J.S.A. 2C:43-1b, carrying a penalty of three to five years imprisonment. N.J.S.A. 2C:43-6a(3). The evils inherent in baby-bartering are loathsome for a myriad of reasons. The child is sold without regard for whether the purchasers will be suitable parents. The natural mother does not receive the benefit of counseling and guidance to assist her in making a decision that may affect her for a lifetime. In fact, the monetary incentive to sell her child may, depending on her financial circumstances, make her decision less voluntary. . . . Baby-selling potentially results in the exploitation of all parties involved. . . .

(2) The termination of Mrs. Whitehead's parental rights, called for by the surrogacy contract and actually ordered by the court fails to comply with the stringent requirements of New Jersey law. Our law, recognizing the finality of any termination of parental rights, provides for such termination only where there has been a voluntary surrender of a child to an approved agency or to the Division of Youth and Family Services ("DYFS"), accompanied by a formal document acknowledging termination of parental rights, N.J.S.A. 9:2-16, -17; N.J.S.A. 9:3-41; N.J.S.A. 30:4C-23, or where there has been a showing of parental abandonment or unfitness. A termination may ordinarily take one of three forms: an action by an approved agency, an action by DYFS, or an action in connection with a private placement adoption. . . .

In this case a termination of parental rights was obtained not by proving the statutory prerequisites but by claiming the benefit of contractual provisions. . . . Since the termination was invalid, it follows, as noted above, that adoption of Melissa by Mrs. Stern could not properly be granted.

(3) The provision in the surrogacy contract stating that Mary Beth Whitehead agrees to "surrender custody . . . and terminate all parental rights" contains no clause giving her a right to rescind. It is intended to be an irrevocable consent. . . .

It is clear that the Legislature so carefully circumscribed all aspects of a consent to surrender custody — its form and substance, its manner of execution, and the agency or agencies to which it may be made — in order to provide the basis for irrevocability. . . . There is only one irrevocable consent, and that is the one explicitly provided for by statute: a consent to surrender of custody and a placement with an approved agency or with DYFS. The provision in the surrogacy contract, agreed to before conception, requiring the natural mother to surrender custody of the child without any right of revocation is one more indication of the essential nature of this transaction: the creation of a contractual system of termination and adoption designed to circumvent our statutes.

## B. PUBLIC POLICY CONSIDERATIONS...

The surrogacy contract guarantees permanent separation of the child from one of its natural parents. Our policy, however, has long been that to the extent possible, children should remain with and be brought up by both of their natural parents. . . .

The surrogacy contract violates the policy of this State that the rights of natural parents are equal concerning their child, the father's right no greater than the mother's. . . . The whole purpose and effect of the surrogacy contract was to give the father the exclusive right to the child by destroying the rights of the mother.

The policies expressed in our comprehensive laws governing consent to the surrender of a child . . . stand in stark contrast to the surrogacy contract and what it implies. Here there is no counseling, independent or otherwise, of the natural mother, no evaluation, no warning. . . .

*protect natural mother*

Worst of all, however, is the contract's total disregard of the best interests of the child. There is not the slightest suggestion that any inquiry will be made at any time to determine the fitness of the Sterns as custodial parents, of Mrs. Stern as an adoptive parent, their superiority to Mrs. Whitehead, or the effect on the child of not living with her natural mother.

This is the sale of a child, or, at the very least, the sale of a mother's right to her child, the only mitigating factor being that one of the purchasers is the father. Almost every evil that prompted the prohibition on the payment of money in connection with adoptions exists here. . . .

*baby selling is evil*

The differences between adoption and a surrogacy contract should be noted, since it is asserted that the use of money in connection with surrogacy does not pose the risks found where money buys adoption. First, and perhaps most important, all parties concede that it is unlikely that surrogacy will survive without money. . . . That conclusion contrasts with adoption; for obvious reasons, there remains a steady supply, albeit insufficient, despite the prohibitions against payment. The adoption itself, relieving the natural mother of the financial burden of supporting an infant, is in some sense the equivalent of payment.

Second, the use of money in adoptions does not produce the problem— conception occurs, and usually the birth itself, before illicit funds are offered. With surrogacy, the "problem," if one views it as such, consisting of the purchase of a woman's procreative capacity, at the risk of her life, is caused by and originates with the offer of money.

Third, with the law prohibiting the use of money in connection with adoptions, the built-in financial pressure of the unwanted pregnancy and the consequent support obligation do not lead the mother to the highest paying, ill-suited, adoptive parents. She is just as well-off surrendering the child to an approved agency. In surrogacy, the highest bidders will presumably become the adoptive parents regardless of suitability, so long as payment of money is permitted. . . .

The main difference, that the unwanted pregnancy is unintended while the situation of the surrogate mother is voluntary and intended, is really not significant. [T]he essential evil is the same, taking advantage of a woman's circumstances (the unwanted pregnancy or the need for money) in order to take away her child. . . . Intimated, but disputed, is the assertion that surrogacy will be used for the benefit of the rich at the expense of the poor. . . . The point is made that Mrs. Whitehead agreed to the surrogacy arrangement, supposedly fully understanding the consequences. Putting aside the issue of how compelling her need for money may have been, and how significant her understanding of the consequences, we suggest that her consent is irrelevant. There are, in a civilized society, some things that money cannot buy. . . .

The long-term effects of surrogacy contracts are not known, but feared — the impact on the child who learns her life was bought, that she is the offspring of someone who gave birth to her only to obtain money; the impact on the natural mother as the full weight of her isolation is felt along with the full reality of the sale of her body and her child; the impact on the natural father and adoptive mother once they realize the consequences of their conduct. . . . In New Jersey the surrogate mother's agreement to sell her child is void.

### TERMINATION . . .

Although the question of best interests of the child is dispositive of the custody issue in a dispute between natural parents, it does not govern the question of termination. It has long been decided that the mere fact that a child would be better off with one set of parents than with another is an insufficient basis for terminating the natural parent's rights. . . . There is simply no basis . . . to warrant termination of Mrs. Whitehead's parental rights. . . .

### CONSTITUTIONAL ISSUES . . .

The right to procreate, as protected by the Constitution, has been ruled on directly only once by the United States Supreme Court. See Skinner v. Oklahoma, 316 U.S. 535 (forced sterilization of habitual criminals violates equal protection clause of fourteenth amendment). Although Griswold v. Connecticut, 381 U.S. 479, is obviously of a similar class, strictly speaking it involves the right not to procreate. The right to procreate very simply is the right to have natural children, whether through sexual intercourse or artificial insemination. It is no more than that. Mr. Stern has not been deprived of that right. Through artificial insemination of Mrs. Whitehead, Baby M is his child. . . . To assert that Mr. Stern's right of procreation gives him the right to the custody of Baby M . . . would be to assert that the constitutional right of procreation includes within it a constitutionally protected contractual right to destroy someone else's right of procreation. . . .

Mr. Stern also contends that he has been denied equal protection of the laws by the State's statute granting full parental rights to a husband in relation to the child produced, with his consent, by the union of his wife with a sperm donor. N.J.S.A. 9:17-44. The claim really is that of Mrs. Stern. It is that she is in precisely the same position as the husband in the statute: she is presumably infertile, as is the husband in the statute; her spouse by agreement with a third party procreates with the understanding that the child will be the couple's child. . . .

. . . The State has more than a sufficient basis to distinguish the two situations — even if the only difference is between the time it takes to provide sperm for artificial insemination and the time invested in a nine-month pregnancy — so as to justify automatically divesting the sperm donor of his parental rights without automatically divesting a surrogate mother. Some basis for an equal protection argument might exist if Mary Beth Whitehead had contributed her egg to be implanted, fertilized or otherwise, in Mrs. Stern, resulting in the latter's pregnancy. That is not the case here, however.

Mrs. Whitehead, on the other hand, . . . claims the right to the companionship of her child. This is a fundamental interest, constitutionally protected. Furthermore, it was taken away from her by the action of the court below. . . . Having held the contract invalid and having found no other grounds for the termination of Mrs. Whitehead's parental rights, we find that nothing remains of her constitutional claim. We express no opinion on whether a prolonged suspension of visitation would constitute a termination of parental rights, or whether, assuming it would, a showing of unfitness would be required.

## CUSTODY

. . . With the surrogacy contract disposed of, the legal framework becomes a dispute between two couples over the custody of a child produced by the artificial insemination of one couple's wife by the other's husband. Under the Parentage Act the claims of the natural father and the natural mother are entitled to equal weight, i.e., one is not preferred over the other solely because he or she is the father or the mother.[17] [T]he child's best interests determine custody. . . .

---

17. . . . This does not mean that a mother who has had custody of her child for three, four, or five months does not have a particularly strong claim arising out of the unquestionable bond that exists at that point between the child and its mother; in other words, equality does not mean that all of the considerations underlying the [sex-based] "tender years" doctrine have been abolished.

*best interests* . . . The Whiteheads claim that even if the child's best interests would be served by our awarding custody to the Sterns, we should not do so, since that will encourage surrogacy contracts. . . . We disagree. Our declaration that this surrogacy contract is unenforceable and illegal is sufficient to deter similar agreements. We need not sacrifice the child's interests in order to make that point sharper. . . .

The Whiteheads also contend that the award of custody to the Sterns *pendente lite* was erroneous and that the error should not be allowed to affect the final custody decision. [They argue that] one of the most important factors, whether mentioned or not, in favor of custody in the Sterns is their continuing custody during the litigation, now having lasted for one-and-a-half years. . . . We disagree with the premise, however, that in determining custody a court should decide what the child's best interests would be if some hypothetical state of facts had existed. Rather, we must look to what those best interests are, today, even if some of the facts may have resulted in part from legal error. . . .

[Eleven experts testified on the child's best interests.] Our reading of the record persuades us that the trial court's decision awarding custody to the Sterns (technically to Mr. Stern) should be affirmed. . . .

Our custody conclusion is based on strongly persuasive testimony contrasting both the family life of the Whiteheads and the Sterns and the personalities and characters of the individuals. The stability of the Whitehead family life was doubtful at the time of trial. Their finances were in serious trouble (foreclosure by Mrs. Whitehead's sister on a second mortgage was in process). Mr. Whitehead's employment, though relatively steady, was always at risk because of his alcoholism, a condition that he seems not to have been able to confront effectively. Mrs. Whitehead had not worked for quite some time, her last two employments having been part-time. One of the Whiteheads' positive attributes was their ability to bring up two children, and apparently well, even in so vulnerable a household. Yet substantial question was raised even about that aspect of their home life. The expert testimony contained criticism of Mrs. Whitehead's handling of her son's educational difficulties. Certain of the experts noted that Mrs. Whitehead perceived herself as omnipotent and omniscient concerning her children. . . . Her inconsistent stories about various things engendered grave doubts about her ability to explain honestly and sensitively to Baby M — and at the right time — the nature of her origin. Although faith in professional counseling is not a *sine qua non* of parenting, several experts believed that Mrs. Whitehead's contempt for professional help, especially professional psychological help, coincided with her feelings of omnipotence in a way that could be devastating to a child who most likely will need such help. . . . The prospects for wholesome, independent psychological growth and development would be at serious risk. [Mrs. Whitehead subsequently divorced, became pregnant by another man and remarried, developments that the court said had no effect on its decision.]

The Sterns have no other children, but all indications are that their household and their personalities promise a much more likely foundation for Melissa to grow and thrive. There is a track record of sorts — during the one-and-a-half years of custody Baby M has done very well, and the relationship between both Mr. and Mrs. Stern and the baby has become very strong. The household is stable, and likely to remain so. Their finances are more than adequate, their circle of friends supportive, and their marriage happy. Most important, they are loving, giving, nurturing, and open-minded people. They have demonstrated the wish and ability to nurture and protect Melissa, yet at the same time to encourage her independence. Their lack of experience is more than made up for by a willingness to learn and to listen, a willingness that is enhanced by their professional training, especially Mrs. Stern's experience as a pediatrician. They are honest; they can recognize error, deal with it, and learn from it. They will try to determine rationally the best way to cope with problems in their relationship with Melissa. When the time comes to tell her about her origins, they will probably have found a means of doing so that accords with the best interests of Baby M. All in all, Melissa's future appears solid, happy, and promising with them. Based on all of this we have concluded . . . that Melissa's best interests call for custody in the Sterns [an outcome favored by the expert witnesses].

Some comment is required on the initial *ex parte* order awarding custody *pendente lite* to the Sterns (and the continuation of that order after a plenary hearing). The issue, although irrelevant to our disposition of this case, may recur; and when it does, it can be of crucial importance. When father and mother are separated and disagree, at birth, on custody, only in an extreme, truly rare, case should the child be taken from its mother *pendente lite*. . . . The probable bond between mother and child, and the child's need, not just the mother's, to strengthen that bond, along with the likelihood, in most cases, of a significantly lesser, if any, bond with the father — all counsel against temporary custody in the father [absent the mother's unfitness or danger to the child.]

Even [the mother's] threats to flee should not suffice to warrant any other relief unless her unfitness is clearly shown. At most, it should result in an order enjoining such flight. The erroneous transfer of custody, as we view it, represents a greater risk to the child than removal to a foreign jurisdiction. . . .

### VISITATION

. . . Our reversal of the trial court's order . . . requires delineation of Mrs. Whitehead's rights to visitation. [The experts called by Melissa's court-appointed guardian] were concerned that given Mrs. Whitehead's determination to have custody, visitation might be used to undermine the Sterns' parental authority and thereby jeopardize the stability and security so badly needed by this child. Two of the experts recommended suspension of visitation for five years and the other suspension for an undefined period. [The guardian ad litem] now argues that instead of five years, visitation should be suspended until Melissa reaches majority. . . .

We also note the following for the trial court's consideration: First, this is not a divorce case where visitation is almost invariably granted to the non-custodial spouse. To some extent the facts here resemble cases where the non-custodial spouse has had practically no relationship with the child, but it only "resembles" those cases. In the instant case, Mrs. Whitehead spent the first four months of this child's life as her mother and has regularly visited the child since then. Second, she is not only the natural mother, but also the legal mother, and is not to be penalized one iota because of the surrogacy contract. [A touchstone of visitation is] that it is desirable for the child to have contact with both parents. . . .

We have decided that Mrs. Whitehead is entitled to visitation at some point, and that question is not open to the trial court on this remand. [T]he guardian's recommendation of a five-year delay is most unusual — one might argue that it begins to border on termination. Nevertheless, if the circumstances as further developed by appropriate proofs or as reconsidered on remand clearly call for that suspension under applicable legal principles of visitation, it should be so ordered. . . .

### CONCLUSION

This case affords some insight into a new reproductive arrangement: the artificial insemination of a surrogate mother. The unfortunate events that have unfolded illustrate that its unregulated use can bring suffering to all involved. . . .

We have found that our present laws do not permit the surrogacy contract used in this case. Nowhere, however, do we find any legal prohibition against surrogacy when the surrogate mother volunteers, without any payment, to act as a surrogate and is given the right to change her mind and to assert her parental rights. Moreover, the Legislature remains free to deal with this most sensitive issue as it sees fit, subject only to constitutional constraints. . . .

The judgment is affirmed in part, reversed in part, and remanded for further proceedings consistent with this opinion.

■ **LORI B. ANDREWS, BETWEEN STRANGERS: SURROGATE MOTHERS, EXPECTANT FATHERS AND BRAVE NEW BABIES**
*11-24 (1989)*

. . . Carol Pavek knew exactly why she was different from the people of Amarillo. She was adopted. She came, at least prenatally, from somewhere else. . . . Carol felt no need to seek out her birth parents. She loved the couple who raised her, and felt she could get from them any help and advice she needed. But when she got pregnant with her own child, her link to her biological mother became crucially important. . . .

[After her child's birth, Carol began training as a midwife. She and her husband Rick were disappointed they could not experience the home birth they had planned for their son.] "We felt unfulfilled," says Carol. "We teased each other that we would keep giving birth until we got it right, only we would have to find families to give the children to."

When their son, Chris, was eighteen months old, their joking took a serious turn. That's when they first heard about the possibility of surrogate motherhood on a television show. The guest on the show was Noel Keane, the Dearborn, Michigan, attorney. . . . As Noel Keane and an infertile couple described surrogate motherhood to the television audience, Carol Pavek recognized how she could connect her dream of a home birth with a couple's dream of a baby. . . . "This was a way for Carol to express herself and do something for others," Rick said later. "There was a lot of altruism. . . ." . . .

It took six months' reflection before Carol actually began to fashion a letter to Noel expressing her interest. "It wasn't actually a letter," she says. "It was more like a book." . . . Carol was candid in her portrait of herself, mentioning her receding chin, heavy hips, and nearsightedness. She was equally blunt about what she was looking for in a couple. They would have to agree, of course, to a home birth and the adoptive mother would have to be present. If possible, the father and any other children in the family should be present as well. Carol would breast-feed the baby for three to five days to pass on her immunities.

At the time Carol contacted Noel, in 1980, surrogate mothers were not being paid. It hadn't even occurred to Carol to ask for any money. Her main concern was the quality of the relationship she would have with the couple. . . .

Noel received the letter the same day he received a desperate call from a couple of modest means who lived in a rural section of northern California. Nancy's first husband had died when she was pregnant with their second child. She raised their two daughters alone through childhood, then required a hysterectomy. When she later married Andy, it was clear that she would not be able to bear children. But now, in part because of his attachment to Nancy's two daughters, they were wishing they could have another child [one with Andy's traits].

By sundown, Andy and Nancy had called Carol. Within a week, they had taken the tiresome three-and-a-half-day bus ride to the Texas panhandle to meet Carol and Rick face-to-face. . . . Carol and Rick immediately took to the couple. . . . Their conversations over the next few days were not at all like a business negotiation; they were getting to know each other like new neighbors. Surrogacy is not like a merger of corporations. It is the creation of a relationship — and, as with any intimate relationship, it takes a certain level of compatability to allow the relationship to flower. . . .

The first insemination [at Carol's house] did not result in a pregnancy, so the following month, May of 1980, Carol flew out to their home in the California mountains. They lived out in the country in a cabin with a dog and horses, about four miles from an old mining town. Carol was immediately enchanted by the area as the perfect place to raise a child. [E]very other day for a week, Carol artificially inseminated herself. [She became pregnant.]

Four days before the scheduled due date, Andy, Nancy, and the two teenaged daughters drove down to Amarillo in a motor home. The four of them rushed to Carol's house once her labor began. By this time, Carol had helped with thirty-five successful home births; she hoped her own would be the thirty-sixth. But, again, there was a problem with Carol's delivery and by midnight she was giving birth in a local hospital. . . . Andy and Nancy stayed with Carol through the labor, but once delivery began, they had to leave because no advance arrangements had been made for their presence. Rick was left to coach Carol through and oversee the birth of a ten-pound boy. . . .

The baby was gently lowered onto Carol's abdomen. She slowly opened her eyes, and was relieved to find that she didn't have any feeling of possession. Her only thought was "What a gorgeous baby."

Two hours later, Andy and Nancy wanted to give Carol the baby to breast-feed. A nurse took Nancy aside, saying "Oh you must not let her breast-feed the baby, she will bond."

"I've trusted her this far, I'm going to trust her again," Nancy replied.

Carol fed the baby, then spent a peaceful hour watching Nancy hold her son. Carol thought of how, in traditional adoptions, the hospital staff did everything they could to keep the biological mother and the baby apart. It wasn't right to rip a baby away, Carol thought as she drifted off to sleep; the mother must have a chance to say good-bye.

The next day, back at home, Rick turned to Carol before she fell asleep. "You're already thinking of trying again, aren't you?" he asked.[28]

■ **MARY BETH WHITEHEAD WITH LORETTA SCHWARTZ-NOBEL, A MOTHER'S STORY: THE TRUTH ABOUT THE *BABY M* CASE**
*25-27 (1989)*

Rick [the then husband of Mary Beth Whitehead] tried to comfort me. He tried everything he knew. Nothing worked. . . . You don't comfort somebody who is giving away her child.

[28]. Carol twice subsequently served as a "surrogate."

Everybody said, "You have two other children." It wasn't as if my baby were dead. My child was alive, and I had given her to two strangers. . . .

The Sterns and the Infertility Center had told me I was doing a beautiful thing, but I wasn't. All the way through my pregnancy, I had tried to believe it. I had suppressed the reality; I had denied my feelings. I had not allowed myself to deal with it. But now I couldn't pretend anymore. I just didn't want to be a party to it, no matter how much it was going to disappoint them. I couldn't bear to be a woman who gave away her child. . . .

I began to feel angry and defensive. My body, my soul, my heart, my breathing, my everything had gone into making this baby. What had Bill Stern done? Put some sperm in cup. What had Betsy done? Bought some clothes, a box of diapers, and a case of formula. . . .

. . . I just couldn't stop crying. It just kept coming, and the emptiness that I felt was something I never want to feel again.

Eventually I fell asleep. Suddenly I opened my eyes. The room was dark, and I was lying in a pool of milk. The sheets were full of milk. I knew it was time to feed my baby. I knew she was hungry, but I could not hear her crying. The room was quiet as I sat up in the bed, alone in the darkness, with the milk running down my chest and soaking my nightgown. I held out my empty arms and screamed at the top of my lungs, "Oh, God, what have I done — I want my baby!" . . .

## Notes and Questions

1. In the vast majority of surrogacy arrangements, the parties perform their agreements without resort to judicial intervention. See John A. Robertson, Children of Choice: Freedom and the New Reproductive Technologies 131 (1994). See also Susan Fischer & Irene Gillman, Surrogate Motherhood: Attachment, Attitudes and Social Support, 54 Psychiatry 13, 19 (1991) (describing Whitehead as an "anomaly").

Two primary questions, then, posed by surrogacy are: First, what legal restrictions ought to apply to consensual arrangements in which all parties are willing to perform? For example, *Baby M* holds surrogacy for pay to constitute an illegal sale of a child, regardless of the parties' wishes. Second, what rules ought to govern "failed" surrogacy arrangements such as *Baby M*? Note that failure also can occur when the intended parents repudiate the agreement, as when they reject the child because of birth defects. Cf., e.g., Stiver v. Parker, 975 F.2d 261 (6th Cir. 1992). Both questions ask about the appropriate limits on private ordering in what *Baby M* calls "a new way of bringing children into a family." See also, e.g., R.R. v. M.H., 689 N.E.2d 790 (Mass. 1998).

2. *Surrogacy and adoption.* How does surrogacy resemble adoption? *Baby M* looks to adoption law to rule the contract void. Yet, how can the

court ignore the contract when, without it, this particular child would not exist? For that reason, is not surrogacy distinguishable from adoption?

What are the advantages and disadvantages of surrogacy over adoption? For prospective parents? Birth mothers (surrogates)? Children? Society?

Had the arrangement not failed, adoption by Elizabeth Stern would have followed termination of Mary Beth Whitehead's parental rights. Should the adoption be treated as a stepparent adoption, in which there is typically little screening of adopters, or as an adoption of an unrelated child, in which the state usually intervenes more extensively? See also infra page 1237 (preconception adoption).

3. *Surrogacy and artificial insemination.* Alternatively, does the law of artificial insemination (rather than adoption) provide a more appropriate framework for surrogacy? Are not the two simply the biologically dictated responses to different kinds of infertility that couples experience? Consider the reasoning of Judge Sorkow, the trial judge in *Baby M.* He reasoned that surrogate mothers must be allowed to sell their services and the intended mother must be recognized as a legal parent because these rules apply to AID: "To rule otherwise denies equal protection of the law to the childless couple, the surrogate, whether male or female, and the unborn child." 525 A.2d 1128, 1165 (N.J. Super. Ct. Ch. Div. 1987). See also Carmel Shalev, Birth Power: The Case for Surrogacy 87 (1989) ("surrogacy presents a mirror situation to that of artificial insemination of a married woman with donor sperm").

What is the biological father's legal status with respect to the child if the surrogate conceives while married, as did Whitehead? Isn't he just a sperm donor with no legal status under AID law? See *R.R.*, 689 N.E.2d at 795-796. Then how could the resulting adoption be classified as a stepparent adoption? If it must be treated as an adoption by a nonrelative, why should the state have more opportunities for intervention in, and thus more control over, surrogacy than AID?

4. *"Gender neutrality."* Given his biological limitations, what more could William Stern — or any man — have done to show his interest in his anticipated child? (Recall *Kelsey S.*, supra section B2.) Or do gender-specific contributions to reproduction compel different treatment of mothers and fathers? According to Professor Marjorie Shultz, the *Baby M* court missed an opportunity to treat men and women equally:

> . . . To say that the factual issues are "the same" as if Whitehead and William Stern had simply had a child out of wedlock, ignores the centrally important fact that modern reproductive techniques allow the separation of personal and sexual intimacy from procreation. . . . It ignores that the father here differs in important ways from stereotypical unwed fathers. In particular, it ignores that the child in question exists only because of its

progenitors' individual intentions, their reciprocal decisions, and their behavior and expectations in the wake of such decisions. . . .

. . . Unlike biologically-based variables, the capacity to form and express intentions is gender-neutral. [H]aving rejected any role for intention,
the court fell back on gender stereotypes to resolve the issues. . . . The
court's decision reinforced stereotypes regarding the desirability of segre-
gating women from the market, the unpredictability of women's intentions
and decisions, and the givenness of women's biological destiny. Perhaps
worst of all, it acted to lock in existing gender-based spheres of influence
in our society, refusing to recognize fragile, emergent male efforts to claim
a meaningful role in access to and nurture of children. . . .

Marjorie Maguire Shultz, Reproductive Technology and Intent-Based
Parenthood: An Opportunity for Gender Neutrality, 1990 Wis. L. Rev.
297, 376-379.

5. *Feminism and surrogacy. Baby M* engendered sharp divisions
among feminists. Some submitted briefs supporting Whitehead, others
for the Sterns.[29] Although most feminists support reproductive freedom in the context of abortion, there is no such consensus about the
legal treatment of surrogacy. Some feminists advocate the prohibition
of surrogacy agreements, even those women willingly make.[30] These
scholars condemn surrogacy as a practice that commodifies and exploits women and children.[31] From this point of view, surrogacy reduces women to "baby machines,"[32] subjects them to the patriarchial
control of the medical profession,[33] and resembles slavery[34] and

---

[29]. Lori B. Andrews, Between Strangers: Surrogate Mothers, Expectant Fathers and
Brave New Babies 171-182 (1989).

[30]. See, e.g., Shari O'Brien, Commercial Conceptions: A Breeding Ground for Surrogacy, 65 N.C. L. Rev. 127 (1986); Margaret Jane Radin, Market-Inalienability, 100 Harv.
L. Rev. 1849 (1987); Robin L. West, Taking Preferences Seriously, 64 Tul. L. Rev. 659
(1990).

[31]. See, e.g., Anita L. Allen, Privacy, Surrogacy, and the *Baby M* Case, 76 Geo. L.J.
1759, 1783, 1791 (1988) (rejecting linkage of freedom-of-contract theory and privacy jurisprudence of *Griswold* because of unique harms risked by surrogates); Cass R. Sunstein,
Neutrality in Constitutional Law (With Special Reference to Pornography, Abortion, and
Surrogacy), 92 Colum. L. Rev. 1, 47 (1992) ("[A] world in which female sexual and reproductive services are freely traded on markets would legitimate and reinforce a pervasive form of inequality — one that sees the social role of women as that of breeders, and
that uses that role to create second-class citizenship.").

[32]. See, e.g., Gena Corea, Junk Liberty, in Reconstructing Babylon: Essays on
Women and Technology 142, 153-156 (H. Patricia Hynes ed., 1991). See also Robyn Rowland, Living Laboratories: Women and Reproductive Technologies 198 (1992) (use of
brain-dead "surrogates" as "female incubators").

[33]. See, e.g., Gena Corea, The Mother Machine: Reproductive Technologies from
Artificial Insemination to Artificial Wombs (1985).

[34]. Professor Allen observes that slavery "had the effect of causing black women to
become surrogate mothers on behalf of slave owners." Anita L. Allen, Surrogacy, Slavery
and the Ownership of Life, 13 Harv. J.L. & Pub. Poly. 132, 140 (1990).

prostitution.[35] Surrogacy also reflects racist and eugenic motivations, at the expense of existing children who need homes.[36]

Would banning consensual surrogacy, however, suggest that women need protection from their own decisions? Some feminists thus condemn efforts to outlaw surrogacy as an unwarranted intrusion on reproductive autonomy, reflecting gender stereotypes and paternalism.[37] This position supports legality for surrogacy on the ground that it respects freedom of contract and offers women new employment opportunities.[38]

Still other feminists take an intermediate position, recommending that the law permit surrogacy but allow the birth mother to renounce the contract.[39] Which of these positions is most consistent with the right of privacy? The increasing importance of gender equality in family law? The best interests of children? How do the stories of Carol Pavek and Mary Beth Whitehead influence your answers?

For additional feminist perspectives, see, e.g., Expecting Trouble: Surrogacy, Fetal Abuse, and New Reproductive Technologies 156 (Patricia Boling ed., 1995); Barbara Katz Rothman, Recreating Motherhood (2000); Patricia J. Williams, On Being the Object of Property, 14 Signs 5 (1988). For a review of different feminist legal theorists' views on surrogacy, see generally Applications of Feminist Legal Theory to Women's Lives: Sex, Violence, Work, and Reproduction 1041-1062 (D. Kelly Weisberg ed., 1996).

6. *Failed surrogacy agreements.* When an arrangement fails (because it is illegal or a court refuses enforcement), numerous questions arise. Using *Baby M* as an example, what is the legal status of Elizabeth Stern, who cannot adopt the child? See Nancy D. Polikoff, This Child Does Have Two Mothers: Redefining Parenthood to Meet the Needs of Children in Lesbian-Mother and Other Nontraditional Families, 78 Geo. L.J. 459, 474-477 (1990). Should courts and legislatures formally recognize

---

[35]. E.g., Carole Pateman, The Sexual Contract 209-218 (1988); Margaret Jane Radin, Contested Commodities 131-153 (1996).

[36]. Elizabeth S. Anderson, Is Women's Labor a Commodity?, 19 Phil. & Pub. Affairs 71, 91 (1990).

[37]. See, e.g., Debra Satz, Markets in Women's Reproductive Labor, 21 Phil. & Pub. Affairs 107, 117 (1992) ("dilemma for those who wish to use the mother-fetus bond to condemn [surrogacy] contracts while endorsing [privacy] right to choose abortion"); Carmel Shalev, Birth Power 9-10 (1989) ("[A]mid the serious debate on the morality of [all varieties of] medical reproduction, only surrogacy has been addressed in terms of criminal norms. It occurred to me that the reason for this was the untraditional role that women play in these arrangements."); Marjorie Maguire Shultz, Reproductive Technology and Intent-Based Parenthood: An Opportunity for Gender Neutrality, 1990 Wis. L. Rev. 297.

[38]. See, e.g., Shalev, supra note [37], at 160-166 (reviewing how public-private dichotomy excluded women from market and concluding that "exclusion of domestic reproductive labor from the public economy is the ultimate manifestation of a patriarchal double standard").

[39]. Martha A. Field, Surrogate Motherhood (1988). See also Lawrence O. Gostin, Surrogacy from the Perspectives of Economic and Civil Liberties, 17 J. Contemp. Health L. & Pol'y. 429 (2001).

long-term caregivers, such as Dr. Stern? See Doe v. Doe, 710 A.2d 1297 (Conn. 1998) (declining to recognize intended mother as equitable parent despite rearing of child, but awarding her custody as third party after divorce); ALI Principles §2.03 (recognizing de facto parents only in limited circumstances, i.e., agreement with child's parent or parent's failure to provide care).

Should William Stern and Mary Beth Whitehead share parenting of the child, through joint custody or a custody-visitation arrangement?[40] Even if such arrangements routinely follow divorce or the dissolution of an intimate nonmarital relationship, do they make sense when the parents have only a contractual relationship? What do the best interests of the child dictate in *Baby M*? To what extent does the Constitution permit termination of Mary Beth Whitehead's parental rights altogether on grounds of the child's best interests?

7. *Legislative responses.* Should legislatures regulate surrogacy? If so, how? What policy considerations should they consider? Should participants face criminal penalties? Which participants? Should the law distinguish commercial surrogacy from unpaid arrangements? What rules should govern in the event of breach?

The National Conference of Commissioners on Uniform State Laws, unable to promulgate a single model in 1988, included two alternatives in the Uniform Status of Children of Assisted Conception Act: Alternative A, which regulated surrogacy arrangements through a preconception adoption proceeding, and Alternative B, which made surrogacy agreements void. See 9C U.L.A. 383 (2001). The new Uniform Parentage Act, UPA (2000), replaces USCACA, see 9B U.L.A. 297 (2001) (Prefatory Note to UPA). Like Alternative A of USCACA, UPA (2000) authorizes "gestational agreements," including the payment of consideration (§801); requires a home study of the intended parents and judicial validation of the agreement (§802); and provides for a court order of parentage consistent with the judicially validated agreement upon the child's birth (§807). Id. at 360-370.

About half the states have enacted statutes addressing surrogacy, with some banning the practice. E.g., N.Y. Dom. Rel. Law §§121-123 (McKinney 1999). See Lisa L. Behm, Legal, Moral & International Perspectives on Surrogate Motherhood: The Call for a Uniform Regulatory Scheme in the United States, 2 DePaul J. Health Care L. 557, 582 (1999).

Some states permit the practice but subject it to close regulation. Typical regulations disallow payment and allow the "surrogate" the opportunity to rescind. See, e.g., Fla. Stat. Ann. §63.212(1)(i) (West Supp. 2001) (allowing "preplanned adoption agreement" but not for valuable

---

[40]. On remand, the court granted Mary Beth Whitehead unsupervised visitation for one eight-hour period per week, increasing to two days every other week beginning in September 1988; overnight visits followed after one year as well as a two-week visit in summer, 1989. 14 Fam. L. Rep. (BNA) 1276 (Apr. 12, 1988).

consideration beyond expenses and with opportunity for mother to rescind consent within seven days of birth). Some states require advance
judicial approval, like Alternative A of USCACA, supra. See, e.g., N.H.
Rev. Stat. Ann. §168-B:16 (Supp. 2000) (requiring "judicial preautho-
rization"); Va. Code Ann. §§20-160 & 20-162 (Michie 2000) (prior judicial approval and reformation). Other states take a still more permissive
stance: Arkansas declares that the legal parents of such children are the
intended parents (including the biological father only, if unmarried).
Ark. Code Ann. §9-10-201 (Michie 1998). And Nevada exempts surrogacy agreements from the ban on payment in adoptive placements. Nev.
Rev. Stat. §127.287(5) (2000).

Following some of the recommendations of the famous Warnock
Commission in England, Parliament outlawed commercial surrogacy
agencies. §2 Surrogacy Arrangements Act of 1985, ch. 49. A subsequent
amendment makes surrogacy arrangements unenforceable against a
party unwilling to perform. Id. at §1A (added by §36(1) Human Fertilisation and Embryology Act of 1990, ch. 37). Yet the law also provides for
judicial recognition of the intended parents when certain requirements
are met. §30 Human Fertilisation and Embryology Act of 1990, ch. 37.
See Amy Garrity, Comment, A Comparative Analysis of Surrogacy Law
in the United States and Great Britain — A Proposed Model Statute for
Louisiana, 60 La. L. Rev. 809 (2000). Israel allows but regulates "full"
(gestational) surrogacy (examined infra section E3c). See Ruth Halperin-
Kaddari, Redefining Parenthood, 29 Cal. W. Int'l L.J., 313, 318-321,
329-332 (1999).

8. *Conflict of laws issues.* The varied responses to surrogacy by states
and foreign countries may draw individuals to the most permissive jurisdictions. Such forum shopping will result in legal questions parallel to
those posed at one time or another by out-of-state abortions, "marriage
evasion," migratory divorce, and interstate (and international) child custody battles. See 9B U.L.A. 360-361 (2001) (Prefatory Comment to Art.
8, "Gestational Agreement"). Can residents of states with restrictive laws
evade them elsewhere? How should the restrictive states respond? See
Susan Frelich Appleton, Surrogacy Arrangements and the Conflict of
Laws, 1990 Wis. L. Rev. 399; Anastasia Grammaticaki-Alexiou, Artificial
Reproduction Technologies and Conflict of Laws: An Initial Approach,
60 La. L. Rev. 1113 (2000).

Should the federal government establish uniformity, as in the
Parental Kidnapping Prevention Act, 28 U.S.C.A. §1738A (West Supp.
2001)? Alternatively, does surrogacy call for uniformity through constitutional adjudication, as in Roe v. Wade? Or, is surrogacy a problem
whose solution must emerge from the " 'laboratory' of the States"? See
Cruzan v. Director, Missouri Dept. of Health, 497 U.S. 261, 292 (1990)
(O'Connor, J., concurring). What approach should be taken on international surrogacy arrangements?

9. *The attorney's role.* What role should attorneys play in surrogacy arrangements? What payments are appropriate? See Joan Heifetz Hollinger, Baby M, Lawyers, and Legal Education, 37 Buff. L. Rev. 675 (1988/1989); Andrew W. Vorzimer, The Egg Donor and Surrogacy Controversy: Legal Issues Surrounding Representation of Parties to an Egg Donor and Surrogacy Contract, 21 Whittier L. Rev. 415 (1999). Recall the material on the attorney's role in adoptive placements, supra section C2. Should similar limitations apply? Cf. Stiver v. Parker, 975 F.2d 261 (6th Cir. 1992) (broker and physicians owed affirmative duty of protection to mother, her husband and intended father); Huddleston v. Infertility Ctr. of Am., 700 A.2d 453 (Pa. Super. Ct. 1997) (broker can be liable to surrogate for failing to screen father who fatally abused child).

## Problems

1. Suppose the *Baby M* court awards custody to Mary Beth Whitehead. Should it now order William Stern to pay child support? What precedents would compel this result? Alternatively, what risks would such child support duties create? What should the legislature say on this subject? See Martha A. Field, Surrogate Motherhood 98-101 (1988).

2. Jim and Tom, a gay couple, live in a state that has enacted UPA (2000). They locate a woman willing to serve as a commercial surrogate for them. The court refuses to grant the necessary preconception adoption, however, because the legislation (§801(b)) allows only married couples to be "intended parents." 9B U.L.A. 362 (2001). On what grounds can Jim and Tom challenge this restriction? Will they succeed? See generally Marla J. Hollandsworth, Gay Men Creating Families Through Surro-Gay Arrangements: A Paradigm for Reproductive Freedom, 3 Am. U.J. Gender & L. 183 (1995); Ann MacLean Massie, Restricting Surrogacy to Married Couples: A Constitutional Problem? The Married-Parent Requirement in the Uniform Status of Children of Assisted Conception Act, 18 Hastings Con. L.Q. 487 (1991).

## 3. In Vitro Fertilization

Advances in medicine offer new responses to infertility that go well beyond artificial insemination and surrogacy. Many of these forms of assisted conception use or build on in vitro fertilization (literally, fertilization in glass), first successfully used to produce a human birth in 1978. The law has lagged behind medicine, however, leaving important questions unanswered.

### a. Expanding Reproductive Privacy

■ **LIFCHEZ v. HARTIGAN**
*735 F. Supp. 1361 (N.D. Ill. 1990)*

Williams, Judge.

Dr. Lifchez represents a class of plaintiff physicians who specialize in reproductive endocrinology and fertility counselling. . . . Dr. Lifchez is suing the Illinois Attorney General and the Cook County State's Attorney, seeking a declaratory judgment that [§6(7)] of the Illinois Abortion Law is unconstitutional. . . .

#### Vagueness

Section 6(7) of the Illinois Abortion Law provides as follows:

> No person shall sell or experiment upon a fetus produced by the fertilization of a human ovum by a human sperm unless such experimentation is therapeutic to the fetus thereby produced. Intentional violation of this section is a Class A misdemeanor. Nothing in this subsection (7) is intended to prohibit the performance of in vitro fertilization.

Ill. Rev. Stat., Ch. 38 para. 81-26, §6(7) (1989). Dr. Lifchez claims that the Illinois legislature's failure to define the terms "experimentation" and "therapeutic" renders the statute vague, thus violating his due process rights under the Fourteenth Amendment. . . .

One of the more common procedures performed by reproductive endocrinologists is amniocentesis. Amniocentesis involves withdrawing a portion of the amniotic fluid in order to test it for genetic anomalies. It is performed on women considered to be at risk for bearing children with serious defects. The purpose of the procedure is to provide information about the developing fetus; this information is often used by women in deciding whether or not to have an abortion. Although now routinely performed, amniocentesis could be considered experimental under at least two of Dr. Lifchez' [proposed] definitions: it could be classified as pure research, since there is no benefit to the fetus, the subject being "experimented" on; it could also be experimental . . . if the particular practitioner or clinic were doing it for the first time.

Amniocentesis illustrates well the problem of deciding at what point a procedure graduates from "experimental" to routine. . . . Dr. Lifchez can hardly be expected to know which of his medical activities would be illegal now if he were to look back on the quick evolution of amniocentesis from (very likely) illegal experiment in 1975 to explicitly endorsed "process" in 1985. [B]ecause of the meteoric growth in reproductive endocrinology, any classification of a particular procedure as either "ex-

perimental" or "routine" could easily be out-of-date within six months.
. . . A statute is unconstitutionally vague if the mere passage of time can
transform conduct from being unlawful to lawful. . . .

Many other procedures that Dr. Lifchez performs on his patients
could fall within the ambit of §6(7). Among these are in vitro fertilization and the many techniques spawned through research into in vitro
fertilization. The difficulty posed by these procedures is not just whether
or not they are "experimental," but whether they are "therapeutic to the
fetus." . . . In vitro fertilization itself is explicitly permitted by the statute.
Related reproductive technologies are less certain. Embryo transfer, for
example, involves removal of an embryo from one woman's uterus and
placing it in the uterus of a second woman. The variations on this basic
technique are considerable. A donated egg could be fertilized in vitro
(with a partner's or a donor's sperm), be placed in a second woman's
uterus to gestate for five days, and then be flushed out for implantation
in the woman trying to get pregnant. That this procedure is experimental is undisputed. Whether it is "therapeutic to the fetus" (actually,
embryo . . .) is more complicated. . . . Removing an embryo from one
woman's uterus, where it is gestating, for implantation in another woman,
may be therapeutic for the woman trying to get pregnant, but it is not
necessarily therapeutic for that embryo. . . .

. . . In genetic screening of in vitro embryos, one cell of an eight-cell
embryo is removed for testing, while the rest are frozen. If the genetic
screening on the single cell is negative, the remaining seven cells can be
gestated to produce a child. This experimental procedure is undisput-
edly non-therapeutic to the embryo, and although it could fall within the
statute's in vitro exception, that exception speaks to fertilization, not genetic testing. A failed implantation following in vitro fertilization genetic
screening could subject Dr. Lifchez to criminal liability.

. . . Super-ovulation involves administering various hormones to induce ovulation, resulting in multiple ova [for in vitro fertilization]. However, the hormones that are used for super-ovulation may have two
negative effects on a woman's ability to get pregnant: lower-quality ova
are produced and the uterus becomes less receptive to the embryo being implanted. In order to improve the chances of super-ovulation resulting in a pregnancy, Dr. Lifchez may need to experiment with
particular elements in the procedure to achieve a more receptive uterine lining or better quality embryos. Not all such attempts will be successful, and any particular one might not be therapeutic to the embryos,
thus violating §6(7). . . .

A third class of procedures that Dr. Lifchez performs for his patients
are those that are exclusively for the benefit of the pregnant woman.
[T]reatment for virtually any maternal complaint, whether it be high
blood pressure, diabetes, epilepsy, or headaches, has the potential to affect the fetus. . . .

[The court concluded that the scienter requirement in §6(7) did not save it from being unconstitutionally vague.]

### REPRODUCTIVE PRIVACY

Section 6(7) of the Illinois Abortion Law is also unconstitutional because it impermissibly restricts a woman's fundamental right of privacy, in particular, her right to make reproductive choices free of governmental interference with those choices. Various aspects of this reproductive privacy right have been articulated in a number of landmark Supreme Court cases [citing *Griswold, Eisenstadt,* and *Roe*].

Section 6(7) intrudes upon this "cluster of constitutionally protected choices." Embryo transfer and chorionic villi sampling [a method of prenatal testing for birth defects] are illustrative. Both procedures are "experimental" by most definitions of that term. Both are performed directly, and intentionally, on the fetus. Neither procedure is necessarily therapeutic to the fetus. . . .

Both procedures, however, fall within a woman's zone of privacy as recognized in Roe v. Wade, Carey v. Population Services International, [431 U.S. 678 (1977),] and their progeny. Embryo transfer is a procedure designed to enable an infertile woman to bear her own child. It takes no great leap of logic to see that within the cluster of constitutionally protected choices that includes the right to have access to contraceptives, there must be included within that cluster the right to submit to a medical procedure that may bring about, rather than prevent, pregnancy. Chorionic villi sampling is similarly protected. The cluster of constitutional choices that includes the right to abort a fetus within the first trimester must also include the right to submit to a procedure designed to give information about that fetus which can then lead to a decision to abort. Since there is no compelling state interest sufficient to prevent a woman from terminating her pregnancy during the first trimester, there can be no such interest sufficient to intrude upon these other protected activities during the first trimester. By encroaching upon this protected zone of privacy, §6(7) is unconstitutional. . . .

## Notes and Questions

1. *Lifchez* relies on Roe v. Wade to conclude that the right to privacy protects use of and access to reproductive technologies. The leading proponent of this position, Professor Robertson, has written that "procreative liberty is a deeply held moral and legal value that deserves a strong measure of respect in all reproductive activities [to be] equally honored when reproduction requires technological assistance." John A. Robertson, Children of Choice: Freedom and The New Reproductive Tech-

nologies 4 (1994). Robertson's book goes on to advocate reproductive autonomy for seven major reproductive technologies, including in vitro fertilization (IVF) and forms of collaborative reproduction.

To what extent does the legal status of IVF depend upon the continued vitality of *Roe*? If the Supreme Court overturns *Roe* (or substantially limits it), could states then ban new reproductive technologies? Cf. Webster v. Reproductive Health Servs., 492 U.S. 490, 523 (1989) (O'Connor, J., concurring) (no indication that statute's preamble stating life begins at conception might be applied to prohibit in vitro fertilization). Does the Constitution protect a "right" to use such technologies?

2. Assuming this constitutional right exists, what state interests justify its infringement? Feminist Gena Corea raises moral and ethical objections to IVF, claiming that it exploits women. See Gena Corea, The Mother Machine: Reproductive Technologies from Artificial Insemination to Artificial Wombs 100-134 (1985). The Catholic Church has found IVF morally illicit because it deprives the child "*of being the result and fruit of a conjugal act* in which spouses can become 'cooperators with God for giving life to a new person.' " Congregation for the Doctrine of the Faith, Instruction on Respect for Human Life in its Origin and on the Dignity of Procreation: Replies to Certain Questions of the Day 29-31 (1987). On the other hand, a British commission concluded the practice is ethically acceptable. Department of Health & Social Security, Report of the Committee of Inquiry into Human Fertilisation and Embryology 31-34 (Chairman: Dame Mary Warnock DBE) (Presented to Parliament by Command of Her Majesty, July 1984).

Can moral and ethical objections to IVF support state prohibitions? Cf. Bowers v. Hardwick and Stenberg v. Carhart, Chapter I, sections B1-B2. Of what significance in the constitutional analysis are theological considerations? Cf. *Webster* 492 U.S. at 569 (Stevens, J., dissenting) (positing religious basis of any law that would equate a "freshly fertilized egg" with "a 9-month-gestated, fully sentient fetus on the eve of birth" and raising First Amendment concerns).

3. Can IVF be banned or restricted to protect the health of children or children-to-be? *Lifchez* observes that many reproductive technologies, including prenatal testing, are not beneficial to the embryo or fetus. How does one assess harm to a not-yet-conceived individual who would not exist without the technology? See Philip G. Peters, Jr., Harming Future Persons: Obligations to the Children of Reproductive Technology, 8 S. Cal. Interdisciplinary L.J. 375 (1999). On the other hand, do parents have a right to such tests, to enable them to select the genetic characteristics of their children? Preimplantation testing and selection of embryos together with new information from the Human Genome Project are increasing such choices. See, e.g., Lee M. Silver, Remaking Eden: How Genetic Engineering and Cloning Will Transform the American Family 266-280 (1998) ("the designer child"); Maxwell J. Mehlman, The Law of Above Averages: Leveling the New Genetic Enhancement Play-

ing Field, 85 Iowa L. Rev. 517 (2000). See also Dena S. Davis, Genetic Dilemmas and the Child's Right to an Open Future, 28 Rutgers L.J. 549 (1997); Lois Shepherd, Protecting Parents' Freedom to Have Children with Genetic Differences, 1995 U. Ill. L. Rev. 761.

Prenatal testing, including amniocentesis and chorionic villi sampling, began to flourish after *Roe*'s legalization of abortion. Such testing and the larger practice of genetic counseling became a form of defensive medicine as families successfully sued for "wrongful birth," claiming that professional negligence resulted in the birth of a child with handicaps whom the parents, if properly informed, would have aborted. E.g., Bader v. Johnson, 732 N.E.2d 1212 (Ind. 2000); Berman v. Allan, 404 A.2d 8 (N.J. 1979). Courts have been less hospitable to "wrongful life" claims brought on behalf of the afflicted child. Compare, e.g., Hester v. Dwivedi, 733 N.E.2d 1161 (Ohio 2000), with Procanik v. Cillo, 478 A.2d 755 (N.J. 1984). See also, e.g., Wendy Lovejoy, Note, Ending the Genetic Discrimination Barrier: Regaining Confidence in Preconception, Prenatal, and Neonatal Genetic Testing, 74 S. Cal. L. Rev. 873 (2001).

*Lifchez* treats these technologies as a positive development, enhancing reproductive autonomy. Several feminist scholars, however, have explored the negative consequences for women, including the contradiction posed for pregnant women, who are asked "to accept their pregnancies and their babies . . . and yet be willing to abort the genetically damaged fetus." Barbara Katz Rothman, The Tentative Pregnancy: How Amniocentesis Changes the Experience of Motherhood 6 (1993). See also, e.g., Women and Prenatal Testing: Facing the Challenges of Genetic Technology (Karen H. Rothenberg & Elizabeth J. Thomson eds., 1994).

4. Some feminists condemn IVF. Professor Dorothy Roberts observes that "new reproductive technologies, such as in vitro fertilization and surrogacy, function primarily to fulfill men's desires for genetically related offspring." Dorothy E. Roberts, The Genetic Tie, 62 U. Chi. L. Rev. 209, 239 (1995). Another commentator, contrasting "consumer" and feminist perspectives, writes that "feminists fear that the application of the new reproductive technologies will be manipulated so as to limit women's autonomy, ensuring that [the] female capacities [as 'sex object' and 'child bearer'] will be used in the interest of the male-dominated social order." Norma Juliet Wikler, Society's Response to the New Reproductive Technologies: The Feminist Perspectives, 59 S. Cal. L. Rev. 1043, 1044 (1986). See also Elizabeth Bartholet, Family Bonds: Adoption and the Politics of Parenting 187-229 (1993); Corea, supra; Robyn Rowland, Living Laboratories: Women and Reproductive Technologies (1992).

What legal conclusions for IVF follow from feminist critiques? A ban on these procedures? Government intervention through mandated warnings to ensure "informed" consent, as some states require for abortions? If the state can outlaw surrogacy in part to protect even those women who want to participate, can it not outlaw IVF despite the wishes of otherwise infertile women? Could women bring a successful sex-discrimination challenge to such laws? Or do technologies such as IVF, in contrast to abortion, perpetuate a stereotypical view of women, as Wikler suggests? Suppose some women yearn to contribute to this stereotype?

5. Both women and men react to infertility with strong emotions. But data suggest gender differences:

> Although men considered childlessness as a painful experience, it did not preclude a full and enjoyable life. . . . Wives spoke of enjoying their quality of life, but described something as missing. [For women, infertility] overtook other aspects of life. It was a continuous, biopsychosocial, spiritual struggle; a loss; a feeling of being passed by; and a feeling of incompleteness or emptiness. . . .

Su An Arnn Phipps, A Phenomenological Study of Couples' Infertility: Gender Influence, 7 Holistic Nurse Prac. 44, 46-47 (1993). See also Linda J. Lacey, "O Wind, Remind Him That I Have No Child": Infertility and Feminist Jurisprudence, 5 Mich. J. Gender & L. 163 (1998).

6. Early criticisms focused on the poor success rates for IVF and the inconsistent ways clinics reported results. Now federal law requires assisted reproductive technologies programs to report their pregnancy rates to the Department of Health and Human Services for annual publication and distribution to the public. 42 U.S.C. §§263a-1 to 263a-7 (1994). See U.S. Department of Health and Human Services Centers for Disease Control and Prevention et al., 1998 Assisted Reproductive Technology Success Rates: National Summary and Fertility Clinic Reports (Dec. 2000).

7. Is infertility an "illness" and IVF a "treatment" therefor? The issue arises in determining whether the procedure is covered by medical insurance that reimburses only treatment of illness. See Egert v. Connecticut General Life Ins. Co., 900 F.2d 1032 (7th Cir. 1990). Some successful challenges to restrictive insurance coverage have been brought under the Americans with Disabilities Act. See, e.g., Pacourek v. Inland Steel Co., 858 F. Supp. 1393 (N.D. Ill. 1994); 916 F. Supp. 797 (N.D. Ill. 1996). See also Bragdon v. Abbott, 524 U.S. 624 (1998). But see Krauel v. Iowa Methodist Med. Ctr., 95 F.3d 674 (8th Cir. 1996). See generally, e.g., Peter K. Rydel, Comment, Redefining the Right to Reproduce: Asserting Infertility as a Disability Under the Americans with Disabilities Act, 63 Alb. L. Rev. 593 (1999). Cf. Elizabeth Bartholet, Family Bonds, supra, at 213-214 (criticizing move toward mandated insurance coverage for IVF, because it "would simply stack the deck even more in favor of procreation," rather than adoption).

Should Medicaid provide assistance for poor persons seeking fertility treatments? What consequences follow from the prevailing approach, under which Medicaid benefits do not cover IVF and most private physicians are unwilling to serve Medicaid recipients? See Dorothy Roberts, Killing the Black Body: Race, Reproduction, and the Meaning of Liberty 253 (1997) (most Blacks excluded from access).

8. For an historical examination of infertility in the United States, see Elaine Tyler May, Barren in the Promised Land: Childless Americans in Pursuit of Happiness (1995). Can the law enhance privacy and autonomy by addressing infertility? Recall the debate about family leave and the difficulties of balancing work and family (Chapter III, section B6b) while considering the following:

■ **BARBARA KATZ ROTHMAN,**
  **RECREATING MOTHERHOOD**
  *93-94, 97-98 (2000)*

The treatment of infertility needs to be recognized as an issue of self-determination. It is as important an issue for women as access to contraception and abortion, and freedom from forced sterilization. There is no contradiction in assuring access to both infertility services and abortion services for all women who would choose them. Not only do different women have different needs, but the same women have different needs at different points in their lives. . . . The issue is not getting more women pregnant or fewer: the concern is women having as much control as they can over entry into motherhood.

Of course the issue of individual control is inherently complicated. It raises the basic questions of free will, individual choice in any social structure, and our limitations as embodied beings whose bodies do not always accede to our will.

Feminists have been struggling with all of these questions in one area or another. In regard to motherhood, we have become particularly sensitive to the loss of individual choice in a pro-natalist system. There is no question but that women have been forced into motherhood, and into repeated motherhood, when that is not what they themselves wanted. And it is also true that social systems create our wants as surely as they create the ways in which we meet them. Women have been carefully trained to want motherhood, to experience themselves and their womanhood, their very purpose in life, through motherhood. And that is wrong.

And yet. Wanting children, and wanting our children to want children, is not such an awful thing. I am frankly at a loss as to how I could possibly raise my own children in a way that was not pro-natalist. I love them, I love having them in my life, my children bring me joy — and I share that with them. . . . I love it when someone brings a baby around, and my son is eager for his turn to hold and play with it. . . . I look at him and I think, He's going to be a great father. It's not that I insist on this for them, or insist that they experience children in the same way I do, as a parent, but I want them to have the pleasures life can bring, and to me children are one such pleasure. . . .

Much infertility is avoidable, though no one knows quite how much. . . . But a focus on prevention has its negative side as well, in that it may lead to a "victim-blaming" stance, individuals being held accountable for their own infertility. Consider the attention paid in recent years to the infertility problems of the so-called delayed-childbearing women, the women who "put off" motherhood until their thirties, or sometimes even forties. One reason their infertility gets so much attention is that precisely because they are older, and put off childbearing to develop careers, they are the ones who can now afford the high-tech, high-cost treatments. . . .

[T]his blaming of the women themselves ignores the context in which women have "chosen" to delay childbearing: a lack of maternity leave, of child care, of shared parenting by men, and so on. Shall we blame the woman for putting off childbearing while she became a lawyer, art historian, physician, set designer, or engineer? Or shall we blame the system that makes it so very difficult for young lawyers, art historians, physicians, set designers, and engineers to have children without having wives to care for them? Men did not have to delay entry into parenthood for nearly as many years in the pursuit of their careers as women now do.

It is easier to blame the individual woman than to understand the political and economic context in which she must act, but it does not make for good social policy. If we want to decrease infertility in part by having women concentrate childbearing in their twenties and early thirties, we have to make that possible for them. . . .

## Problem

Melinda's employer, a state university, fires her because she used so many of her available sick leave and vacation days, usually in half-day increments, to undergo (so far unsuccessful) fertility treatments. Melinda sues the university, claiming that her termination violates the Pregnancy Discrimination Act. The university moves to dismiss, arguing the PDA does not apply. What result? Would the Family and Medical Leave Act provide protection for Melinda's job? (For the PDA and FMLA, see Chapter III, at pages 300, 313-316.) See Erickson v. Board of Governors, 911 F. Supp. 316 (N.D. Ill. 1995), *rev'd on other grounds*, 207 F.3d 945 (7th Cir. 2000), *cert. denied sub nom.* United States v. Board of Governors, 531 U.S. 1190 (2001). But see Krauel v. Iowa Methodist Med. Ctr., 95 F.3d 674 (8th Cir. 1996).

### b. Deciding the Fate of Frozen Preembryos

■ **A.Z. v. B.Z.**
*725 N.E.2d 1051 (Mass. 2000)*

COWIN, J. . . .

. . . The husband [A.Z.] and wife [B.Z.] were married in 1977. For the first two years of their marriage they resided in Virginia, where they both served in the armed forces. [They moved to Maryland and later to Massachusetts. They experienced fertility problems, including failure to achieve pregnancy with medical assistance, ectopic pregnancies, and removal of wife's fallopian tubes, before they turned to IVF, using wife's ova and husband's sperm.] They underwent IVF treatment from 1988 through 1991. As a result of the 1991 treatment, the wife conceived and gave birth to twin daughters in 1992. During the 1991 IVF treatment, more preembryos were formed than were necessary for immediate implantation, and two vials of preembryos were frozen for possible future implantation.

In the spring of 1995, before the couple separated, the wife desired more children and had one of the remaining vials of preembryos thawed and one preembryo was implanted. [No pregnancy resulted. The husband first learned of this attempt] when he received a notice from his insurance company regarding the procedure. During this period relations between the husband and wife deteriorated. The wife sought and received a protective order against the husband. . . . Ultimately, they separated and the husband filed for divorce [while] one vial containing four frozen preembryos remained in storage at the clinic. . . .

In order to participate in fertility treatment, including . . . IVF, the clinic required egg and sperm donors (donors) to sign certain consent forms for the relevant procedures. . . . The only forms that both the husband and the wife were required to sign were those entitled "Consent Form for Freezing (Cyropreservation) of Embryos" (consent form), one of which is the form at issue here.

Each consent form explains the general nature of the IVF procedure and outlines the freezing process, including the financial cost and the potential benefits and risks of that process. The consent form also requires the donors to decide the disposition of the frozen preembryos on certain listed contingencies: "wife or donor" reaching normal menopause or age forty-five years; preembryos no longer being healthy; "one of us dying"; "should we become separated"; "should we both die." Under each contingency the consent form provides the following as options for disposition of the preembryos: "donated or destroyed — choose one or both." A blank line beneath these choices permits the donors to write in additional alternatives not listed as options on the form, and the form notifies the donors that they may do so. The consent form also informs the donors that they may change their minds as to any disposition, provided that both donors convey that fact in writing to the clinic. . . .

. . . Every time before eggs were retrieved from the wife and combined with sperm from the husband, they each signed a consent form. The husband was present when the first form was completed by the wife in October, 1988. They both signed that consent form after it was finished. The form, as filled out by the wife, stated, inter alia, that if they "should become separated, [they] both agree[d] to have the embryo(s) . . . return[ed] to [the] wife for implant." The husband and wife thereafter underwent six additional egg retrievals for freezing and signed six additional consent forms. . . .

Each time after signing the first consent form in October, 1988, the husband always signed a blank consent form. . . . Each time, after the husband signed the form, the wife filled in the disposition and other information, and then signed the form herself. . . . In each instance the wife specified in the option for "should we become separated," that the preembryos were to be returned to the wife for implantation. . . .

. . . The probate judge concluded that, while donors are generally ~~PROBATE~~ free to agree as to the ultimate disposition of frozen preembryos, the agreement at issue was unenforceable because of a "change in circumstances" occurring during the four years after the husband and wife signed the last, and governing, consent form in 1991: the birth of the twins as a result of the IVF procedure, the wife's obtaining a protective order against the husband, the husband's filing for a divorce, and the wife's then seeking "to thaw the preembryos for implantation in the hopes of having additional children." . . . In the absence of a binding agreement, the judge determined that the "best solution" was to balance the wife's interest in procreation against the husband's interest in avoiding procreation. Based on his findings, the judge determined that the husband's interest in avoiding procreation outweighed the wife's interest in having additional children and granted the permanent injunction in favor of the husband.

. . . While IVF has been available for over two decades and has been the focus of much academic commentary,[13] there is little law on the

13. See, e.g., Coleman, Procreative Liberty and Contemporaneous Choice: An Inalienable Rights Approach to Frozen Embryo Disputes, 84 Minn. L. Rev. 55 (1999); Note, To Have or Not to Have: Whose Procreative Rights Prevail in Disputes Over Dispositions of Frozen Embryos?, 27 Conn. L. Rev. 1377 (1995); Forster, The Legal and Ethical Debate Surrounding the Storage and Destruction of Frozen Human Embryos: A Reaction to the Mass Disposal in Britain and the Lack of Law in the United States, 76 Wash. U. L.Q. 759 (1998); Robertson, Prior Agreements for Disposition of Frozen Embryos, 51 Ohio St. L.J. 407 (1990); Sheinbach, Examining Disputes Over Ownership Rights to Frozen Embryos: Will Prior Consent Documents Survive if Challenged by State Law and/or Constitutional Principles?, 48 Cath. U. L. Rev. 989 (1999); Note, Divergent Conceptions: Procreational Rights and Disputes Over the Fate of Frozen Embryos, 7 B.U. Pub. Int. L.J. 315 (1998); Walter, His, Hers, or Theirs — Custody, Control, and Contracts: Allocating Decisional Authority Over Frozen Embryos, 29 Seton Hall L. Rev. 937 (1999).

enforceability of agreements concerning the disposition of frozen pre-embryos. Only three States have enacted legislation addressing the issue. See Fla. Stat. Ann. §742.17 (West 1997) (requiring couples to execute written agreement for disposition in event of death, divorce or other un-foreseen circumstances); N.H. Rev. Stat. Ann. §§168-B:13 to 168-B:15, 168-B:18 (1994 & Supp. 1999) (requiring couples to undergo medical examinations and counseling and imposing a fourteen-day limit for maintenance of ex utero prezygotes); La. Rev. Stat. Ann. §§9:121-9:133 (1991) (providing that "prezygote considered 'juridical person' that must be implanted[,]" Kass v. Kass, 696 N.E.2d 174 [1998]). Two State courts of last resort, the Supreme Court of Tennessee and the Court of Appeals of New York, have dealt with the enforceability [after divorce] of agree-ments between donors regarding the disposition of preembryos and have concluded that such agreements should ordinarily be enforced. [I]n Davis v. Davis 842 S.W.2d 588 (Tenn. 1992), *cert. denied sub nom.* Stowe v. Davis, 507 U.S. 911, (1993), [the] wife sought to donate the pre-embryos at issue to another couple for implantation. The court stated that agreements between donors regarding disposition of the preem-bryos "should be presumed valid and should be enforced." 842 S.W.2d at 597. In that case, because there was no agreement between the donors regarding disposition of the preembryos, the court balanced the equi-table interests of the two parties and concluded that the husband's in-terest in avoiding parenthood outweighed the wife's interest in donating the preembryos to another couple for implantation. Id. at 603.

The Court of Appeals of New York, in Kass v. Kass, supra, agreed with the Tennessee court's view that courts should enforce agreements where potential parents provide for the disposition of frozen preem-bryos. . . . The wife sought custody of the preembryos for implantation. According to the New York court, agreements "should generally be pre-sumed valid and binding, and enforced in any dispute between [the donors].". . . Therefore the court enforced the agreement that provided that the frozen preembryos be donated to the IVF clinic.

. . . This is the first reported case involving the disposition of frozen preembryos in which a consent form signed between the donors on the one hand and the clinic on the other provided that, on the donors' sep-aration, the preembryos were to be given to one of the donors for im-plantation. In view of the purpose of the form (drafted by and to give assistance to the clinic) and the circumstances of execution, we are du-bious at best that it represents the intent of the husband and the wife re-garding disposition of the preembryos in the case of a dispute between them. In any event, for several independent reasons, we conclude that the form should not be enforced in the circumstances of this case.

First, the consent form's primary purpose is to explain to the donors the benefits and risks of freezing, and to record the donors' desires for disposition of the frozen preembryos at the time the form is executed in order to provide the clinic with guidance if the donors (as a unit) no longer wish to use the frozen preembryos. The form does not state, and the record does not indicate, that the husband and wife intended the consent form to act as a binding agreement between them should they later disagree as to the disposition. . . .

Second, the consent form does not contain a duration provision. . . . Third, the form uses the term "should we become separated" in referring to the disposition of the frozen preembryos without defining "become separated." Because this dispute arose in the context of a divorce, we cannot conclude that the consent form was intended to govern in these circumstances. Separation and divorce have distinct legal meanings. . . .

The donors' conduct in connection with the execution of the consent forms also creates doubt whether the consent form at issue here represents the clear intentions of both donors. . . . A clinic representative told her that "she could cross out any of the language on the form and fill in her own [language] to fit [the wife's] wishes." Further, although the wife used language in each subsequent form similar to the language used in the first form that she and her husband signed together, the consent form at issue here was signed in blank by the husband, before the wife filled in the language indicating that she would use the preembryos for implantation on separation. . . . Finally, the consent form is not a separation agreement that is binding on the couple in a divorce proceeding pursuant to G. L. c. 208, §34. The consent form does not contain provisions for custody, support, and maintenance, in the event that the wife conceives and gives birth to a child.

With this said, we conclude that, even had the husband and the wife entered into an unambiguous agreement between themselves regarding the disposition of the frozen preembryos, we would not enforce an agreement that would compel one donor to become a parent against his or her will.[22] As a matter of public policy, we conclude that forced procreation is not an area amenable to judicial enforcement. It is well-established that courts will not enforce contracts that violate public policy. . . .

The Legislature has already determined by statute that individuals should not be bound by certain agreements binding them to enter or not enter into familial relationships. [T]he Legislature abolished the cause of action for the breach of a promise to marry [and] provided that no mother may agree to surrender her child "sooner than the fourth calendar day after the date of birth of the child to be adopted" regardless

---

22. . . . We express no view regarding whether an unambiguous agreement between two donors concerning the disposition of frozen preembryos could be enforced over the contemporaneous objection of one of the donors, when such agreement contemplated destruction or donation of the preembryos either for research or implantation in a surrogate. . . .

of any prior agreement. . . . In our decisions, we have also indicated a reluctance to enforce prior agreements that bind individuals to future family relationships. In R. R. v. M. H., 689 N.E.2d 790 (1998), we held that a surrogacy agreement in which the surrogate mother agreed to give up the child on its birth is unenforceable unless the agreement contained, inter alia, a "reasonable" waiting period during which the mother could change her mind. . . .

*option to revoke*

We glean from these statutes and judicial decisions that prior agreements to enter into familial relationships (marriage or parenthood) should not be enforced against individuals who subsequently reconsider their decisions. This enhances the "freedom of personal choice in matters of marriage and family life." Moore v. East Cleveland, 431 U.S. 494, 499 (1977), quoting Cleveland Bd. of Educ. v. LaFleur, 414 U.S. 632, 639-640 (1974). . . .

In this case, we are asked to decide whether the law of the Commonwealth may compel an individual to become a parent over his or her contemporaneous objection. . . . Enforcing the [1991 consent form against the husband] would require him to become a parent over his present objection to such an undertaking. We decline to do so. . . .

## Notes and Questions

1. Before *A.Z.*, most authorities indicated that agreements and consent forms signed by the "progenitors" would determine the disposition of frozen preembryos. *A.Z.* reviews the case law that led many IVF clinics to obtain agreements designed to prevent future disputes about disposition. Why does *A.Z.* decline to follow the statement on the consent form? What changes, if any, in the form or the signing process would have been necessary to create an enforceable agreement? See Ellen A. Waldman, Disputing Over Embryos: Of Contracts and Consents, 32 Ariz. St. L.J. 897 (2000). Or, does the opinion mean that a progenitor can always reconsider? See J.B. v. M.B., 783 A.2d 707 (N.J. 2001); Carl H. Coleman, Procreative Liberty and Contemporaneous Choice: An Inalienable Rights Approach to Frozen Embryo Disputes, 84 Minn. L. Rev. 55 (1999); William A. Sieck, Comment, In Vitro Fertilization and the Right to Procreate: The Right to No, 147 U. Pa. L. Rev. 435 (1998). What are the implications of the court's analysis for the trend toward "private ordering" in family law?

2. Despite the disputes it can produce, cryopreservation of preembryos offers several advantages. It allows a woman to attempt to achieve pregnancy on several successive occasions without repeating surgery to remove ova. This process also allows for the possibility of replacing preembryos during a spontaneous ovulatory cycle and avoids the risk of multiple pregnancy that inheres in the simultaneous use of numerous

preembryos. The Ethics Committee of the American Fertility Society, Ethical Considerations of the New Reproductive Technologies, 53 Fertility and Sterility 58S (Supp. 2 1990). Finally, the process allows for posthumous reproduction by women. See Anne Reichman Schiff, Arising from the Dead: Challenges of Posthumous Procreation, 75 N.C. L. Rev. 901 (1997).

3. How should the law classify frozen preembryos when resolving disputes? See York v. Jones, 717 F. Supp. 421 (E.D. Va. 1989) (property). See also Del Zio v. Columbia Presbyterian Med. Ctr., No. 74-3558 (S.D.N.Y. 1978) (as cited in Davis v. Davis, 842 S.W.2d 588, 602 n.23 (Tenn. 1992)) (unreported case awarding woman $50,000 for emotional distress from deliberate destruction of petri dish containing her egg and husband's sperm). Cf. Moore v. Regents of the Univ. of Cal., 793 P.2d 479 (Cal. 1990), cert. denied, 499 U.S. 936 (1991). Should frozen embryos and frozen sperm be classified the same way? See Hecht v. Superior Court, 20 Cal. Rptr. 2d 275, 283 (Ct. App. 1993) (relying on Davis to conclude that decedent had ownership interest in his frozen sperm at the time of his death sufficient to constitute "property" within Probate Code). See generally Katheleen R. Guzman, Property, Progeny, Body Part: Assisted Reproduction and the Transfer of Wealth, 31 U.C. Davis L. Rev. 193 (1997); Kermit Roosevelt III, The Newest Property: Reproductive Technologies and the Concept of Parenthood, 39 Santa Clara L. Rev. 79 (1998).

Louisiana has a statutory scheme defining the "in vitro fertilized human ovum" as both a "juridical person" until implanted and a "biological human being" and entitling "such ovum to sue or be sued." La. Rev. Stat. Ann. §§9:121-9:124 (West 2000). The law prohibits intentional destruction of "viable" fertilized ova, explaining that "[a]n in vitro fertilized human ovum that fails to develop further over a thirty-six hour period except when the embryo is in a state of cryopreservation, is considered non-viable and is not a juridical person." Id. at §9:129. The statute makes available for "adoptive implantation" those fertilized ova for which the IVF patients have renounced their own parental rights for in utero implantation. Id. at §9:130. The law precludes inheritance rights for an ovum unless live birth occurs. Id. at §9:133. Louisiana applies the "best interest of the in vitro fertilized ovum" test in any disputes. Id. at §9:131. Does this test mean that the party seeking implantation must prevail? The trial court in Davis so ruled. See 842 S.W.2d at 594.

4. Without a controlling agreement, courts have "balanced" the competing interests of progenitors. When such disagreements arise in the abortion context, the Supreme Court has said the woman's decision must prevail. See Planned Parenthood of Southeastern Pa. v. Casey, Chapter I, section C1. On what basis might one argue that a woman's interests in implanting frozen preembryos should trump a man's in

avoiding parenthood? See, e.g., Kass v. Kass, 1995 WL 110368 (N.Y. Sup. Ct. 1995), rev'd, 663 N.Y.S.2d 581 (App. Div. 1997), aff'd, 696 N.E.2d 174 (N.Y. 1998); Judith F. Daar, Assisted Reproductive Technologies and the Pregnancy Process: Developing an Equality Model to Protect Reproductive Liberties, 25 Am. J.L. & Med. 455 (1999); Ruth Colker, Pregnant Men Revisited or Sperm Is Cheap, Eggs Are Not, 47 Hastings L.J. 1063 (1996). See also Jennifer M. Stolier, Comment, Disputing Frozen Embryos: Using International Perspectives to Formulate Uniform U.S. Policy, 9 Tul. J. Int'l. & Comp. L. 459, 471-473 (2001) (describing Nakhmani case in Israel in which woman prevailed). Suppose the woman opposes use of the preembryos, but the man wishes to have a "surrogate" carry them to term? See J.B., 783 A.2d 707. Should the balance take into account other opportunities to become a parent for the party seeking implantation? See id. at 717. See also Davis, 842 S.W.2d at 604. To what extent did Roe v. Wade, Chapter I, at page 25, address the burdens of unwanted genetic parenthood, apart from the burdens of unwanted pregnancy?

5. What legal rules should govern the disposition of the growing number of unused cryopreserved preembryos? British law has a five-year limit, amended to allow additional time if both progenitors consent. See §14 Human Fertilisation and Embryology Act of 1990, ch. 37; Human Fertilisation and Embryology Regulations 1996, SI 1996 No 375, reg 2, Schedule. Six to ten thousand preembryos were destroyed August 1, 1996, pursuant to the law. See Youssef M. Ibrahim, Ethical Furor Erupts in Britain: Should Embryos Be Destroyed?, N.Y. Times, Aug. 1, 1996, at A1. What approach should the United States follow? See, e.g., Lee Kuo, Comment, Lessons Learned from Great Britain's Human Fertilization and Embryology Act: Should the United States Regulate the Fate of Unused Frozen Embryos?, 19 Loy. L.A. Int'l & Comp. L.J. 1027 (1997). In 2001, President George W. Bush denied federal funding for stem cell research that would have destroyed frozen preembryos donated for research, while allowing support on cell lines already established from such sources. See Katharine Q. Seelye with Frank Bruni, The President's Decision: The President; A Long Process That Led Bush to His Decision, N.Y. Times, Aug. 11, 2001, at A1.

### c. IVF's Progeny: Egg Donation, Gestational Surrogacy, and "Embryo Adoption"

## ■ IN RE MARRIAGE OF BUZZANCA
*72 Cal. Rptr. 2d 280 (Ct. App. 1998)*

Sills, P. J.

Jaycee was born because Luanne and John Buzzanca agreed to have an embryo genetically unrelated to either of them implanted in a woman

— a surrogate — who would carry and give birth to the child for them. After the fertilization, implantation and pregnancy, Luanne and John split up, and the question of who are Jaycee's lawful parents came before the trial court.

Luanne claimed that she and her erstwhile husband were the lawful parents, but John disclaimed any responsibility, financial or otherwise. The woman who gave birth also appeared in the case to make it clear that she made no claim to the child.

The trial court then reached an extraordinary conclusion: Jaycee had *no* lawful parents. . . . We disagree. Let us get right to the point: Jaycee never would have been born had not Luanne and John both agreed to have a fertilized egg implanted in a surrogate.

The trial judge erred because he assumed that legal motherhood, under the relevant California statutes, could *only* be established in one of two ways, either by giving birth or by contributing an egg. He failed to consider the substantial and well-settled body of law holding that there are times when *fatherhood* can be established by conduct apart from giving birth or being genetically related to a child. The typical example is when an infertile husband consents to allowing his wife to be artificially inseminated. . . . Just as a husband is deemed to be the lawful father of a child unrelated to him when his wife gives birth after artificial insemination, so should a husband *and* wife be deemed the lawful parents of a child after a surrogate bears a biologically unrelated child on their behalf. In each instance, a child is procreated because a medical procedure was initiated and consented to by intended parents. . . . We therefore must reverse the trial court's judgment and direct that a new judgment be entered, declaring that both Luanne and John are the lawful parents of Jaycee. . . .

Perhaps recognizing the inherent lack of appeal for any result which makes Jaycee a legal orphan, John now contends that the surrogate is Jaycee's legal mother; and further, by virtue of that fact, the surrogate's husband is the legal father. His reasoning goes like this: Under the [1973] Uniform Parentage Act (the Act), and particularly as set forth in section 7610 of Family Code, there are only two ways by which a woman can establish legal motherhood, i.e., giving birth or contributing genetically. Because the genetic contributors are not known to the court, the only candidate left is the surrogate who must therefore be deemed the lawful mother. And, as John's counsel commented at oral argument, if the surrogate and her husband cannot support Jaycee, the burden should fall on the taxpayers.

The law doesn't say what John says it says. . . . Here is the complete text of Family Code section 7610:

> The parent and child relationship may be established as follows:
> (a) Between a child and the natural mother, it may be established by proof of her having given birth to the child, or under this part.

(b) Between a child and the natural father, it may be established under this part.

(c) Between a child and an adoptive parent, it may be established by proof of adoption. . . .

[The California Supreme Court's first surrogacy case, Johnson v. Calvert, 851 P.2d 776 (Cal. 1993), recognized as the mother the woman who had provided the ovum and intended to rear the child, not the recanting "gestational surrogate" whom she and her husband had hired. In] construing the words "under this part" to include genetic testing, the high court in *Johnson* relied on several statutes in the Evidence Code all of which, by their terms, only applied to *paternity*. . . . It was only by a parity of reasoning from statutes which, on their face, referred only to *paternity* that the court in Johnson v. Calvert reached the result it did on the question of *maternity*. . . .

In addition to blood tests there are several other ways the Act allows paternity to be established. Those ways are not necessarily related at all to any biological tie. Thus, under the Act, paternity may be established by [marrying the child's mother]. A man may also be deemed a father under the Act in the case of artificial insemination of his wife, as provided by section 7613 of the Family Code. . . .

As noted in *Johnson*, "courts must construe statutes in factual settings not contemplated by the enacting legislature." [851 P.2d at 779.] So it is, of course, true that application of the artificial insemination statute to a gestational surrogacy case where the genetic donors are unknown to the court may not have been contemplated by the Legislature. Even so, the two kinds of artificial reproduction are *exactly* analogous in this crucial respect: Both contemplate the procreation of a child by the consent to a medical procedure of someone who intends to raise the child but who otherwise does not have any biological tie.

If a husband who consents to artificial insemination under Family Code section 7613 is "treated in law" as the father of the child by virtue of his consent, there is no reason the result should be any different in the case of a married couple who consent to in vitro fertilization by unknown donors and subsequent implantation into a woman who is, as a surrogate, willing to carry the embryo to term for them. The statute is, after all, the clearest expression of past legislative intent when the Legislature did contemplate a situation where a person who caused a child to come into being had no biological relationship to the child. . . .

. . . While the Johnson v. Calvert court was able to predicate its decision on the Act rather than making up the result out of whole cloth, it is also true that California courts, prior to the enactment of the Act, had based certain decisions establishing paternity merely on the common law doctrine of estoppel. . . . The estoppel concept, after all, is *already* inherent in the artificial insemination statute. . . . John argues that the artificial insemination statute should not be applied because, after all, his wife did not give birth. But for purposes of the statute with its core idea of estoppel, the fact that Luanne did not give birth is irrelevant. . . .

In the present case Luanne is situated like a husband in an artificial insemination case whose consent triggers a medical procedure which results in a pregnancy and eventual birth of a child. Her motherhood may therefore be established "under this part," by virtue of that consent. In light of our conclusion, John's argument that the surrogate should be declared the lawful mother disintegrates. The case is now postured like the Johnson v. Calvert case, where motherhood could have been "established" in either of two women under the Act, and the tie broken by noting the intent to parent as expressed in the surrogacy contract. . . .

We should also add that neither could the woman whose egg was used in the fertilization or implantation make any claim to motherhood, even if she were to come forward at this late date. Again, as between two women who would both be able to establish motherhood under the Act, the *Johnson* decision would mandate that the tie be broken in favor of the intended parent, in this case, Luanne. . . .

Our decision in In re Marriage of Moschetta, [30 Cal. Rptr. 2d 893 (Ct. App. 1994),] relied on by John, is inapposite and distinguishable. In *Moschetta*, this court held that a contract giving rise to a "traditional" surrogacy arrangement where a surrogate was simply inseminated with the husband's sperm could not be *enforced* against the surrogate by the intended father. In order for the surrogate not to be the lawful mother she would have to give the child up for adoption. . . . There is a difference between a court's *enforcing* a surrogacy agreement and making a legal determination based on the intent *expressed in* a surrogacy agreement. . . . In the case before us, we are not concerned, as John would have us believe, with a question of the enforceability of the oral and written surrogacy contracts into which he entered with Luanne. This case is not about "transferring" parenthood pursuant to those agreements. . . .

The legal paradigm adopted by the trial court, and now urged upon us by John, is one where all forms of artificial reproduction in which intended parents have no biological relationship with the child result in legal parentlessness. It means that, absent adoption, such children will be dependents of the state. One might describe this paradigm as the "adoption default" model: The idea is that by not specifically addressing some permutation of artificial reproduction, the Legislature has, in effect, set the default switch on adoption. The underlying theory seems to be that when intended parents resort to artificial reproduction without biological tie the Legislature wanted them to be *screened* first through the adoption system. (Thus John, in his brief, argues that a surrogacy contract must be "subject to state oversight.")

The "adoption default" model is, however, inconsistent with both statutory law and the Supreme Court's *Johnson* decision. As to the statutory law, the Legislature has already made it perfectly clear that public policy (and, we might add, common sense) favors, whenever possible, the establishment of legal parenthood with the concomitant responsibility. . . .

The same reasons which impel us to conclude that Luanne is Jaycee's lawful mother also require that John be declared Jaycee's lawful father. [I]t is still accurate to say, as we did the first time this case came before us, that for all practical purposes John caused Jaycee's conception every bit as much as if things had been done the old-fashioned way. (Jaycee B. v. Superior Court, [49 Cal. Rptr. 2d 694 (Ct. App. 1996)].)

When pressed at oral argument to make an offer of proof as to the "best facts" which John might be able to show if this case were tried, John's attorney raised the point that Luanne had (allegedly, we must add) promised to assume all responsibility for the child and would not hold him responsible for the child's upbringing. [This fact] could make no difference as to John's lawful paternity. It is well established that parents cannot, by agreement, limit or abrogate a child's right to support. . . .

Even though neither Luanne nor John are biologically related to Jaycee, they are still her lawful parents given their initiating role as the intended parents in her conception and birth. . . . Fortunately, as the *Johnson* court also noted, intent to parent " 'correlate[s] significantly' " with a child's best interests. [851 P.2d at 783, quoting Shultz, Reproductive Technology and Intent-Based Parenthood: An Opportunity for Gender Neutrality, 1990 Wis. L. Rev. 297, 397.]

Again we must call on the Legislature to sort out the parental rights and responsibilities of those involved in artificial reproduction. No matter what one thinks of artificial insemination, traditional and gestational surrogacy (in all its permutations), and — as now appears in the not-too-distant future, cloning and even gene splicing — courts are still going to be faced with the problem of determining lawful parentage. A child cannot be ignored. Even if all means of artificial reproduction were outlawed with draconian criminal penalties visited on the doctors and parties involved, courts will still be called upon to decide who the lawful parents really are and who — other than the taxpayers — is obligated to provide maintenance and support for the child. These cases will not go away. . . .

## Notes and Questions

1. In vitro fertilization makes possible new forms of "collaborative reproduction." An intended mother can gestate a fetus conceived with a donor's egg and her husband's sperm. Or the intended parents can hire a gestational surrogate after creating a preembryo with their own genetic material. Or a lesbian couple can decide that one of them will serve

as gestational mother and the other as genetic mother. Ryiah Lilith, The G.I.F.T. of Two Biological and Legal Mothers, 9 Am. U.J. Gender Soc. Pol'y & L. 201 (2001). In *Buzzanca,* the commissioning couple purchased unrelated genetic material and the services of a gestational surrogate — illustrating one version of what some commentators call "technological adoptions" or "embryo adoptions." See Elizabeth Bartholet, Family Bonds: Adoption and the Politics of Parenting 219 (1993); Paul C. Redman II & Lauren Fielder Redman, Seeking a Better Solution for the Disposition of Frozen Embryos: Is Embryo Adoption the Answer?, 35 Tulsa L.J. 583 (2000).

2. *Buzzanca* relies on Johnson v. Calvert, in which the California Supreme Court recognized as parents the commissioning couple who provided the genetic material and intended to rear the child, rather than the gestational surrogate who decided during pregnancy that she did not wish to relinquish the child. Given the conflicting indicia of maternity, the court used the parties' intent and causation to resolve the uncertainty — factors that *Buzzanca* also makes determinative. What are the advantages and disadvantages of this approach? To what extent is this approach similar to recognizing parents by estoppel? Cf. ALI Principles §§2.03, 3.03. Consider the alternatives to intent-based parenthood:

(a) The 1973 version of the Uniform Parentage Act, which California enacted, indicates that genetic parentage establishes legal parentage (§11). 9B U.L.A. 445 (2001) (blood tests). See also Culliton v. Beth Israel Med. Ctr., 756 N.E.2d 1133 (Mass. 2001); A.H.W. v. G.H.B., 772 A.2d 948 (N.J. Super. Ct. Ch. Div. 2000). But see Barbara Katz Rothman, Recreating Motherhood 20 (2000) (criticizing patriarchy's central "seed" concept extended to women). As applied in an egg-donation case, however, this principle would require issuance of a birth certificate identifying the genetic mother as the legal mother and a subsequent adoption by the intended mother. Given the legal treatment of AID, does this approach violate equal protection? See Soos v. Superior Ct., 897 P.2d 1356 (Ariz. Ct. App. 1994). As a practical matter, would the state require genetic testing of each child at birth to determine parentage?

(b) UPA (2000) generally treats egg donors as sperm donors, with no legal status (§702), and makes the intended mother the legal mother without government intervention. 9B U.L.A. 355 (2001). More broadly, this model always recognizes as the legal mother the woman giving birth (§201(a)), with her husband as the presumed father. Id. at 309. See also, e.g., McDonald v. McDonald, 608 N.Y.S.2d 477 (App. Div. 1994) (recognizing gestational, intended mother). The Act includes an exception to this rule for judicially approved "gestational agreements" (§807). 9B U.L.A. 368. If a court has, in advance, approved a gestational surrogacy arrangement through procedures tantamount to an adoption (including a home study), then the intended parents are the legal parents (§803). Id. at 364.

(c) Professor Marsha Garrison proposes an "interpretive approach" that would apply to children conceived with technological assistance the same legal principles that govern parentage of other children. Marsha Garrison, Law Making for Baby Making: An Interpretive Approach to the Determination of Legal Parentage, 113 Harv. L. Rev. 835 (2000). Under this approach, which relies on analogy and "fairness," the court properly classified *Baby M*, see page 1221, as an adoption case because one woman intended to rear the child of another. Id. at 882, 898. This approach also leads Garrison to conclude that the law should treat semen donors as fathers when unmarried women use AID (because, outside this context, the law always recognizes two parents). Id. at 903-912. Considering the closest analogies, she goes on to recommend that the law treat egg donors as semen donors, recognize the genetic mother in gestational surrogacy cases, and require adoption proceedings in cases like *Buzzanca*. Id. at 897-898, 912-920. Is this the "adoption default" model that *Buzzanca* rejects?

3. The drafters of UPA (2000) indicate that, in response to *Baby M*, the assisted reproductive community strongly disfavors having one surrogate provide both the eggs and gestation. 9B U.L.A. 361 (2001) (Prefatory Comment to Art. 8). Hence, *Buzzanca*'s facts or arrangements using the husband's sperm, donor eggs, and a gestational surrogate are becoming more common. The legal consequences are significant: In California, the woman giving birth is the mother in a traditional surrogacy arrangement like *Baby M*. But when indicia of maternity conflict, as in *Johnson* or *Buzzanca*, intent resolves the uncertainty. What are the implications? Will these different rules offer the benefits of intent-based parenthood only to those able to purchase the most expensive and "high-tech" responses to infertility?

4. These cases highlight issues of race and class in collaborative reproduction. In *Johnson*, the gestational surrogate was part African-American; the genetic, intended mother was Filipina; and the genetic, intended father was white. Janet L. Dolgin, Just a Gene: Judicial Assumptions About Parenthood, 40 UCLA L. Rev. 637, 687 (1993). To what extent did the race of the parties influence the determination of parentage? See April L. Cherry, Nurturing in the Service of White Culture: Racial Subordination, Gestational Surrogacy, and the Ideology of Motherhood, 10 Tex. J. Women & L. 83 (2001). Will gestational surrogacy produce a new class of poor and minority women who provide care for the children of wealthy whites — prenatally? See, e.g., Dorothy E. Roberts, Spiritual and Menial Housework, 9 Yale J.L. & Feminism 51 (1997); Angie Godwin McEwen, Note, So You're Having Another Woman's Baby: Economics and Exploitation in Gestational Surrogacy, 32 Vand. J. Transnat'l L. 271 (1999).

What limits would you recommend on payment for egg donation? Many college newspapers publish advertisements for young, white donors, with high SAT scores. See Kenneth Baum, Golden Eggs: Towards the Rational Regulation of Oocyte Donation, 2001 B.Y.U. L. Rev. 107; Julia D. Mahoney, The Market for Human Tissue, 86 Va. L. Rev. 163 (2000). Some fertility clinics have oocyte sharing programs, allowing patients to receive treatment for reduced fees in exchange for donating some of their eggs to other patients. What is the proper way to balance autonomy, protection from exploitation, and fair compensation for hormonal therapy and surgery that entail some risks? See The Ethics Committee of the American Society for Reproductive Medicine, Financial Incentives in Recruitment of Oocyte Donors, 74 Fertility & Sterility 216 (2000) (more than $5,000 requires justification, more than $10,000 is inappropriate, and sharing programs need clear and fair policies).

5. A few states have legislation governing egg donation. See, e.g., Fla. Stat. Ann. §742.14 (West 1997) (donor relinquishes parental rights and can get only reasonable compensation). Texas has adopted UPA (2000). Tex. Fam. Code Ann. Ch. 160 (Vernon Supp. 2002). See Anne Reichman Schiff, Solomonic Decisions in Egg Donation: Unscrambling the Conundrum of Legal Maternity, 80 Iowa L. Rev. 265 (1995) (urging legislation respecting parties' intent).

6. When assisted reproductive technologies make "embryo adoption" possible, what is the impact on our understanding of adoption? If adoption traditionally served the goal of child welfare, can the same be said of "embryo adoption"? Should the law attempt to encourage or discourage such advances? What effect would Professor Garrison's adoption analogy have? See, Garrison, supra, at 917-920. Would additional restrictions prompt more adoptions of already born children awaiting placements? But see John A. Robertson, Children of Choice: Freedom and the New Reproductive Technologies 277 (1993) (critics "never state why infertile couples alone and not all persons who reproduce have the obligation to adopt kids in need of parents"). To what extent does a preference for white babies explain why couples might choose "embryo adoption" over conventional adoption? Alternatively, does use of the term "adoption" in this new context reinforce the stigma of adoption by suggesting "there is something deeply suspect" about parenting someone else's child? See Bartholet, supra, at 69.

7. Should the state screen intended parents who resort to these technologies, as adoption law requires? In response to pregnancies achieved by postmenopausal women using donor eggs, France enacted legislation restricting infertility procedures to living heterosexual couples of childbearing age. Sherri A. Jayson, Comment, "Loving Infertile Couple Seeks Woman Age 18-31 to Help Have Baby. $6,500 Plus Expenses and a Gift": Should We Regulate the Use of Assisted Reproductive Technologies by Older Women?, 11 Alb. L.J. Sci. & Tech. 287, 325-327 (2001). Would similar legislation in the United States survive constitutional challenge? Does "old" parenthood pose harm to children?

Parents? Society? Should similar restrictions apply to artificial insemination to deter old fatherhood? Such questions followed reports of the birth of a daughter to a 63-year-old California woman, who used a donor egg. See Gina Kolata, Childbirth at 63 Says What About Life?, N.Y. Times, Apr. 27, 1997, §1, at 20.

## Problems

1. Frozen preembryos stored at the University of California at Irvine were implanted in some of the fertility clinic's patients without the progenitors' or the recipients' consent — resulting in the birth of approximately 15 children. Jane and John underwent fertility treatments that failed to produce a child — or so they thought. They learn that they are the genetic parents of twins born to another couple, because of the clinic's misappropriation of some of their preembryos. Assess the likelihood that a court would declare Jane and John parents of the twins, over the objection of the woman who gave birth and her husband. Can intent resolve this conflict? Suppose Jane and John want only to establish a relationship with the twins, including some opportunity for visitation? See Alice M. Noble-Allgire, Switched at the Fertility Clinic: Determining Maternal Rights When a Child Is Born from Stolen or Misdelivered Genetic Material, 64 Mo. L. Rev. 517 (1999). On what legal basis should Jane and John sue the clinic? See Judith D. Fischer, Misappropriation of Human Eggs and Embryos and the Tort of Conversion: A Relational View, 32 Loy. L.A. L. Rev. 381 (1999).

2. Ruth and Rob have discovered that he is infertile. They wish to have a child, but they find abhorrent the thought of using a third party's genetic material, as AID would require. They are interested in the possibilities presented by cloning, which would allow them to have a child genetically related only to one of them. Their state, however, is one of several banning human cloning. E.g., Cal. Health & Safety Code §24185 (West Supp. 2001); R.I. Gen. Laws §23-16.4-2 (Supp. 2000). What constitutional challenges can they raise against the state ban? Do their reasons for pursuing cloning matter? Will their challenge succeed? See, e.g., Lori B. Andrews, The Clone Age: Adventures in the New World of Reproductive Technology 237-260 (1999); John A. Robertson, Why Human Reproductive Cloning Should Not in All Cases Be Prohibited, 4 NYU J. Legis. & Pub. Pol'y 35, 37-38 (2000-2001); Cass R. Sunstein, The Constitution and the Clone, in Clones and Clones: Facts and Fantasies About Human Cloning 207-220 (Martha C. Nussbaum & Cass R. Sunstein eds., 1998) (two possible Supreme Court opinions in hypothetical case). Note that one variant on cloning techniques can allow the creation of a child with two genetic mothers — an option that might hold particular interest for lesbian couples. See Lee M. Silver, Remaking Eden:

How Genetic Engineering and Cloning Will Transform the American Family 206-222 (1998). Would a lesbian couple have a stronger or weaker constitutional case against the cloning ban than Ruth and Rob?

3. Martha and Charles from San Francisco hired Helen from England to serve as a gestational surrogate. Martha and Charles wanted only one baby, so the detailed agreement signed by the parties in California expressly said that Helen would use a procedure called "selective reduction" if she became pregnant with more than one fetus. Three ova from an anonymous donor were fertilized with Charles's semen and transferred to Helen's uterus. As a result, Helen became pregnant with twins.

Helen refused to undergo the reduction procedure (which would kill one fetus but not the other) because Martha and Charles did not make timely arrangements and she considered 13 weeks gestation too late for an abortion, for medical and moral reasons. Helen cannot afford to rear the twins, and Martha and Charles will refuse to accept them although they will pay Helen even if she terminates the entire pregnancy. The parties now cannot agree who will have the right to select adoptive parents for the twins and how much such candidates, if selected, must reimburse Martha and Charles for their costs. See Chris Taylor & Helen Gibson, One Baby Too Many: With Twins on the Way a Surrogate Mom Says She Has Been Abandoned by the Would-be Parents, Time, Aug. 27, 2001, at 55. If they go to court, what result and why? (For subsequent developments, see Greg Moran, Surrogate Mother Has Twin Girls; Woman in Disputed Case Has Moved Back to England, San Diego Union-Tribune, Nov. 22, 2001, at B-2:6.)

# Table of Cases

**1265**

# Index

**1281**